CASES AND MATERIALS ON

EC LAW

Fifth Edition

Stephen Weatherill

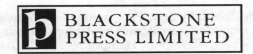

BLACKSTONE PRESS LIMITED

Published by
Blackstone Press Limited
Aldine Place
London W12 8AA
United Kingdom

Sales enquiries and orders
Telephone +44-(0)-20-8740-2277
Facsimile +44-(0)-20-8743-2292
e-mail:sales@blackstone.demon.co.uk
website: www.blackstonepress.com

ISBN 1-84174-012-8
© Stephen Weatherill, 2000
First published 1992
Reprinted 1993
Second edition 1994
Reprinted 1995
Third edition 1996
Reprinted 1997
Fourth edition 1998
Reprinted 1999
Fifth edition 2000
Reprinted 2001

British Library Cataloguing in Publication Data
A catalogue record for this book is available from the British Library

Typeset in 10/11pt Plantin by Style Photosetting Ltd, Mayfield, East Sussex
Printed and bound in Great Britain by Ashford Colour Press Ltd,
Gosport, Hampshire

CONTENTS

Part Two: Community Trade Law and Policy

Part Three: Enforcement of Community Law

PREFACE

It may seem perverse to write a Preface explaining what a book is *not* about, but in the case of Community law I think it is justified. The subject has grown at such a pace over recent years that it is no longer possible to aspire to write a book which is truly comprehensive. The best that one can do is to select areas for examination which seem particularly important and then to use those areas as illustrations to draw out the themes and principles on which the law is based. In this way, one can encourage the student to develop a *communautaire* approach which will permit him or her to tackle substantive areas beyond the scope of this book. So, although it is easy to explain away a failure to cover the full extent of Community law simply by pointing out how much there is of it, I hope that this book has adopted a coherent principle in deciding what to include and what to exclude.

The book is *not* about English law and its reaction to the Community. There is no deep exploration of Parliamentary Sovereignty or the European Communities Act 1972. This is a Community law book. Nevertheless, the development of the Community legal order has not occurred in isolation and is in part dependent on action and reaction at national level. In depicting this process, I have tended to draw on the example of the British experience of the impact of Community membership. However, the *Cohn Bendit* decision (p. 111) will provide an example of practice in another Member State and the student should always be prepared to look beyond domestic law. Most of all, the attitudes of German courts cannot be ignored, and I have included the *Brunner* decision relating to ratification of the Maastricht Treaty.

I have touched little on the external competence of the Community. There is, for example, passing reference only to the Common Customs Tariff, the Common Commercial Policy and Treaty-making competence generally. Anti-dumping law is examined more for what it tells us about judicial review than for its substantive importance. I have adopted this primarily internal focus with regret, aware that it smacks of an unappealing 'Fortress Europe' attitude. But I think that my choice is in this respect in accordance with most British University degree courses in Community law.

This Fifth Edition has been written now that the Treaty of Amsterdam has entered into force; it did so on 1 May 1999. I have provided an overview of the Treaty in the *Introduction* and the reader might quickly look at p. 29 to learn of the Treaty's most dramatically trivial impact, the re-numbering of the Treaties. The table of equivalence between Treaty provisions is set out at p. l and the Community judicature's approach to citation of Treaty articles is found at p. lxi. Naturally the place of the new Treaty is discussed where appropriate throughout the book. It is worth mentioning explicitly that I have embedded treatment of the new provisions on the free movement of persons into Chapter 5, as well as Chapters 9 and 10, in order to emphasise the widening and deepening of the Community's economic and political ambitions. Much else apart from Amsterdam receives attention, including the Commission's strategies for managing the post-1992 internal market and its scrutiny of competition policy. Case law and legislation have been up-dated. Where appropriate I have included pointers to the likely impact of enlargement to the east and of the current and future intergovernmental conferences.

However, I have in the main once again followed the pattern of the previous editions. I hope this meets with the approval of those who have grown familiar with the book. Apart from necessary updating, I have deliberately tended to leave material untouched rather than fiddle with it.

As in the previous editions, my concern remains to depict the dynamic process of evolution in the Community (and, to some extent, in the Union, although my unwillingness to abandon 'Community' for 'Union' is explained in the *Introduction*). I have maintained the range of material used in the previous editions — I use lawyers, practising and academic, but also economists, political scientists and journalists. My aim remains to encourage the student to appreciate how the legal order has been developed (and is still in the process of being developed) in response to sometimes conflicting economic, social and political pressures.

I continue to owe countless debts of gratitude. Thank you to everyone who has helped. To those who filled in the Blackstone 'Questionnaires', I assure you that these are read and digested — I remain eager to receive consumer views on this book. I thank Blackstone Press, whose enthusiasm and attention to detail is unsurpassed in my experience. But above all I thank Catherine Redgwell, without whom this book would have been written in a much less happy frame of mind.

Stephen Weatherill
June 2000

ACKNOWLEDGEMENTS

The permission of the following authors and publishers, who have kindly agreed to allow the use of material in this book, is gratefully acknowledged:

Extracts from the following articles published in the *European Law Review* (Sweet and Maxwell Ltd):

R. Greaves, '*Locus Standi* under Article 173 EEC when seeking Annulment of a Regulation', (1986) 11 EL Rev 119.

J. Usher, 'The Influence of National Concepts on Decisions of the European Court', (1976) 1 EL Rev 359.

R. White and A. Dashwood, 'Enforcement Actions under Articles 169 and 170 EEC', (1989) 14 EL Rev 388.

Extracts from the following articles published in the *Common Market Law Review* (© Kluwer Academic Publishers):

O. Brouwer, 'Free movement of foodstuffs and quality requirements: has the Commission got it wrong?', (1988) 25 CML Rev 237.

C. Closa, 'The Concept of Citizenship in the Treaty on European Union' (1992) 29 CML Rev 1137.

F. Mancini, 'The Making of a Constitution for Europe', (1989) 26 CML Rev 595.

D. Waelbroeck and D. Fosselard, 'Annotation of Case C–309/89 *Codorniu SA* v *Council*', (1995) 32 CML Rev 257.

Extracts from the following article published in the *Journal of Consumer Policy* (Kluwer Academic Publishers): N. Reich, 'Protection of Diffuse Interests in the EEC and the Perspective of Progressively Establishing an Internal Market', (1988) 11 JCP 395.

Extracts from the following article published in the *Journal of Common Market Studies* (Basil Blackwell, Oxford): J. Pelkmans, 'The New Approach to Technical Harmonization and Standardization', (1986–87) JCMS 249.

Extract from the following article published in the *Notre Dame Law Review* (© Matthew Bender Inc., reprinted with permission from the original source,

1983 Fordham Corporate Law Institute, Antitrust and Trade Policies of the EEC): E. Fox, 'Monopolization and Dominance in the US and the EC: Efficiency, Opportunity and Fairness' (1986) 61 Notre Dame Law Rev 981.

Extracts from the following article published in the *American Journal of Comparative Law* (American Association for Comparative Study of Law Inc.): J. Peeters, 'The Rule of Reason Revisited: Prohibition on Restraints of Competition in the Sherman Act and the EEC Treaty', (1989) AJCL 521.

Extracts from the following article published in *Legal Issues of European Integration* (Kluwer Academic Publishers): R. Dehousse, '1992 and Beyond: the Institutional Dimension of the Internal Market Programme', [1989/1] LIEI 109.

Extract from the following articles published in the *Northern Ireland Legal Quarterly* (SLS Legal Publications): G. Howells, 'Implications of the Implementation and Non-Implementation of the EC Products Liability Directive', (1990) 41 NILQ 22 and R. Harmsen, 'A European Union of Variable Geometry: Problems and Perspectives' (1994) 45 NILQ 109.

Extract from the following article published in the *Modern Law Review* (Blackwell Publishers, Oxford): F. Snyder, 'The Effectiveness of European Community Law: Institutions, Processes, Tools and Techniques', (1993) 56 MLR 19.

Extract from the following article published in the *Oxford Review of Economic Policy* (Oxford: Oxford University Press): H. Siebert and M.J. Koop, 'Institutional Competition versus Centralization: Quo Vadis Europe?' 9/1 Oxford Rev Ec Pol 15. By permission of Oxford University Press.

Extract from the *Common Market Law Reports* (reproduced with the permission of Sweet and Maxwell Ltd): *Minister of the Interior* v *Cohn Bendit* [1980] 1 CMLR 543.

Extracts from the *Weekly Law Reports* (reproduced with the permission of the Incorporated Council of Law Reporting for England and Wales):

> *Duke* v *GEC Reliance* [1988] 2 WLR 359
> *Garden Cottage Foods* v *Milk Marketing Board* [1983] 3 WLR 143
> *Webb* v *EMO Air Cargo* [1993] 1 WLR 49.

Extracts from *Economics of the European Community*, ed. A. M. El-Agraa (1998). Extracts reprinted with the permission of Philip Allan Publishers/ Harvester Wheatsheaf.

Extracts from *1992: One European Market?*, eds R. Bieber, R. Dehousse, J. Pinder and J. Weiler (1988, Nomos Verlagsgesellschaft, Baden Baden).

Extracts from P. Cecchini, *The European Challenge: 1992, the Benefits of a Single Market* (1988, Wildwood House/Gower Publishing). Permission of the EC Commission is also gratefully acknowledged.

Extracts from R. Dudley, *1992: Strategies for the Single Market*, (1990, Kogan Page, London).

Extracts from *The European Community and the Challenge of the Future*, ed. J. Lodge (1990 and 2nd ed., 1993, Pinter Publishers Ltd, London). All rights reserved.

Extracts from J. Pinder, *European Community: The Building of a Union* (3rd ed., 1998, Oxford University Press). Copyright J. Pinder.

Extract from J. Harrop, *The Political Economy of Integration in the EC* (2nd ed., 1992, Gower/Edward Elgar).

Extracts from R. Merkin, *A Guide to the Consumer Protection Act 1987* (1987, Financial Training Publications Ltd, London).

Extracts from M. Wilke and H. Wallace, *Subsidiarity: Approaches to Power-Sharing in the European Community* (1990, Royal Institute of International Affairs, London). Published as RIIA Discussion Paper 27.

Extract from Allen and Overy (Solicitors), *The EC Inspector at the Door* (2000, London).

Extract from *The Guardian* of 13 March 1987.

Extract from *The Independent* of 24 November 1989.

For the use of material from the *European Court Reports*, the Court of Justice of the European Communities.

For the use of Community source material, the Commission of the European Communities.

Extracts from E. Noel, *Working Together: the Institutions of the European Community* (1993, Office for Official Publications of the European Communities).

Extract from *The Court of Justice after Maastricht* in D. O'Keeffe and P. Twomey (eds.), *Legal Issues of the Maastricht Treaty* (Chancery, 1994); permission granted by the author, William Robinson, *Cabinet* of Judge Edward, Court of Justice of the European Communities.

Extract from the following article published in the *European Law Journal* (Blackwell Publishers, Oxford): J. Habermas, 'Remarks on Dieter Grimm's "Does Europe Need a Constitution?"' (1995) 1 ELJ 303.

Extract from *Société Stenuit* v *France* Series A no. 232-A (European Commission on Human Rights), the Council of Europe.

Extract from the following article published in the *Cambridge Law Journal*: R. Caranta, 'Government Liability after Francovich' (1993) 52 CLJ 272, permission kindly granted by both journal and author.

Extracts from the following articles published in *Aussenwirtschaft* (published by Verlag Rüegger AG/ The Swiss Institute for Research into International Economic Relations, Economic Structures and Regional Science at St Gallen): H. Hauser and A. Müller, 'Legitimacy: the Missing Link for Explaining EU-Institution Building' (1995) 50 *Aussenwirtschaft* 17 and D. Curtin, 'The Shaping of a European Constitution and the 1996 IGC' (1995) 50 *Aussenwirtschaft* 237.

Extracts from H.U. Jessurun D'Oliveira, 'Union Citizenship: Pie in the Sky?' in A. Rosas and E. Antola (eds), *A Citizens' Europe* (1995), Sage Publications, London).

Extract from the following article published in the *Maastricht Journal of European and Comparative Law*: M. Den Boer, 'Justice and Home Affairs Cooperation in the Treaty on European Union: More Complexity Despite Communautarization' (1997) 4 MJ 310.

Extract from Occasional Paper No. 3 published by the Centre for European Legal Studies in the University of Cambridge: G. Edwards and E. Philippart, *Flexibility and the Treaty of Amsterdam: Europe's New Byzantium?* (1997).

Extract from Harvard Jean Monnet Chair Working Paper Series 2/98, published by Harvard Law School: M. Petite, *The Treaty of Amsterdam* (1998).

Extract from D. Dinan, *Ever Closer Union: An Introduction to European Integration* (Macmillan Press, Basingstoke, 1999).

Extract from S. Bulmer and K. Armstrong, *The Governance of the Single European Market* (Manchester University Press, 1998).

Extract from V. Heiskaner and K. Kulovesi, *Function and Future of European Law* (Publications of the Faculty of Law, University of Helsinki).

TABLE OF CASES

Court of Justice of the European Communities

Cases have been arranged in chronological order by case number and year. See page xxv for an alphabetical list of cases. Cases reported in full are shown in heavy type. The page at which the report is printed is shown in heavy type.

Table of Cases xxi

Court of Justice of the European Communities

TABLE OF LEGISLATION

For the EC Treaty 1957 below, articles are listed as per the numbering system introduced by the Treaty of Amsterdam in 1999, with the pre-Amsterdam numbering in parentheses. Where no pre-Amsterdam number is given, article numbers should be taken to be post-Amsterdam. Please note that although article numbers below are post-Amsterdam, their references may still appear in the text of extracts throughout the book as pre-Amsterdam numbers. (For further information on the renumbering of the Treaty, see p. 29, as well as the Table of Equivalence on pp. l–lx.)

AMSTERDAM TREATY TABLE OF EQUIVALENCE

The function of this Table of Equivalence, which is annexed to the Amsterdam Treaty, is explained fully at pp. 29–31 below.

Previous numbering	New numbering
Part One	Part One
Article 1	Article 1
Article 2	Article 2
Article 3	Article 3
Article 3a	Article 4
Article 3b	Article 5
Article 3c(*)	Article 6
Article 4	Article 7
Article 4a	Article 8
Article 4b	Article 9
Article 5	Article 10
Article 5a(*)	Article 11
Article 6	Article 12
Article 6a	Article 13
Article 7 (repealed)	—
Article 7a	Article 14
Article 7b (repealed)	—
Article 7c	Article 15
Article 7d(*)	Article 16
Part Two	Part Two
Article 8	Article 17
Article 8a	Article 18
Article 8b	Article 19
Article 8c	Article 20
Article 8d	Article 21
Article 8e	Article 22

Previous numbering	New numbering
Part Three Title I Article 9 Article 10 Article 11 (repealed)	Part Three Title I Article 23 Article 24 –
Chapter 1 Section 1 (deleted) Article 12 Article 13 (repealed) Article 14 (repealed) Article 15 (repealed) Article 16 (repealed Article 17 (repealed) Section 2 (deleted) Article 18 (repealed) Article 19 (repealed) Article 20 (repealed) Article 21 (repealed) Article 22 (repealed) Article 23 (repealed) Article 24 (repealed) Article 25 (repealed) Article 26 (repealed) Article 27 (repealed) Article 28 Article 29	Chapter 1 – Article 25 – – – – – – – – – – – – – – – – Article 26 Article 27
Chapter 2 Article 30 Article 31 (repealed) Article 32 (repealed) Article 33 (repealed) Article 34 Article 35 (repealed) Article 36 Article 37	Chapter 2 Article 28 – – – Article 29 – Article 30 Article 31
Title II Article 38 Article 39 Article 40 Article 41 Article 42 Article 43 Article 44 (repealed)	Title II Article 32 Article 33 Article 34 Article 35 Article 36 Article 37 –

Previous numbering	New numbering
Title II *continued*	Title II *continued*
Article 45 (repealed)	–
Article 46	Article 38
Article 47 (repealed)	–
Title III	Title III
Chapter 1	Chapter 1
Article 48	Article 39
Article 49	Article 40
Article 50	Article 41
Article 51	Article 42
Chapter 2	Chapter 2
Article 52	Article 43
Article 53 (repealed)	–
Article 54	Article 44
Article 55	Article 45
Article 56	Article 46
Article 57	Article 47
Article 58	Article 48
Chapter 3	Chapter 3
Article 59	Article 49
Article 60	Article 50
Article 61	Article 51
Article 62 (repealed)	–
Article 63	Article 52
Article 64	Article 53
Article 65	Article 54
Article 66	Article 55
Article 67 (repealed)	–
Article 68 (repealed)	–
Article 69 (repealed)	–
Article 70 (repealed)	–
Article 71 (repealed)	–
Article 72 (repealed)	–
Article 73 (repealed)	–
Article 73a (repealed)	–
Article 73b	Article 56
Article 73c	Article 57
Article 73d	Article 58
Article 73e (repealed)	–
Article 73f	Article 59
Article 73g	Article 60
Article 73h (repealed)	–

Previous numbering	New numbering
Title IIIa(★★)	Title IV
Article 73i(★)	Article 61
Article 73j(★)	Article 62
Article 73k(★)	Article 63
Article 73l(★)	Article 64
Article 73m(★)	Article 65
Article 73n(★)	Article 66
Article 73o(★)	Article 67
Article 73p(★)	Article 68
Article 73q(★)	Article 69
Title IV	Title V
Article 74	Article 70
Article 75	Article 71
Article 76	Article 72
Article 77	Article 73
Article 78	Article 74
Article 79	Article 75
Article 80	Article 76
Article 81	Article 77
Article 82	Article 78
Article 83	Article 79
Article 84	Article 80
Title V Chapter 1	Title VI Chapter 1
Article 85	Article 81
Article 86	Article 82
Article 87	Article 83
Article 88	Article 84
Article 89	Article 85
Article 90	Article 86
Section 2 (deleted)	–
Article 91 (repealed)	–
Section 3	Section 2
Article 92	Article 87
Article 93	Article 88
Article 94	Article 89
Chapter 2	Chapter 2
Article 95	Article 90
Article 96	Article 91
Article 97 (repealed)	–
Article 98	Article 92
Article 99	Article 93

Previous numbering	New numbering
Chapter 3	Chapter 3
Article 100	Article 94
Article 100a	Article 95
Article 100b (repealed)	–
Article 100c (repealed)	–
Article 100d (repealed)	–
Article 101	Article 96
Article 102	Article 97
Title VI	Title VII
Chapter 1	Chapter 1
Article 102a	Article 98
Article 103	Article 99
Article 103a	Article 100
Article 104	Article 101
Article 104a	Article 102
Article 104b	Article 103
Article 104c	Article 104
Chapter 2	Chapter 2
Article 105	Article 105
Article 105a	Article 106
Article 106	Article 107
Article 107	Article 108
Article 108	Article 109
Article 108a	Article 110
Article 109	Article 111
Chapter 3	Chapter 3
Article 109a	Article 112
Article 109b	Article 113
Article 109c	Article 114
Article 109d	Article 115
Chapter 4	Chapter 4
Article 109e	Article 116
Article 109f	Article 117
Article 109g	Article 118
Article 109h	Article 119
Article 109i	Article 120
Article 109j	Article 121
Article 109k	Article 122
Article 109l	Article 123
Article 109m	Article 124
Title VIa(★★)	Title VIII
Article 109n(★)	Article 125
Article 109o(★)	Article 126

Previous numbering	New numbering
Title VIa *continued*	Title VIII *continued*
Article 109p(*)	Article 127
Article 109q(*)	Article 128
Article 109r(*)	Article 129
Article 109s(*)	Article 130
Title VII	Title IX
Article 110	Article 131
Article I11 (repealed)	–
Article 112	Article 132
Article 113	Article 133
Article 114 (repealed)	–
Article 115	Article 134
	Title X
Title VIIa(**)	
Article 116(*)	Article 135
Title VIII	Title XI
Chapter 1(***)	Chapter 1
Article 117	Article 136
Article 118	Article 137
Article 118a	Article 138
Article 118b	Article 139
Article 118c	Article 140
Article 119	Article 141
Article 119a	Article 142
Article 120	Article 143
Article 121	Article 144
Article 122	Article 145
Chapter 2	Chapter 2
Article 123	Article 146
Article 124	Article 147
Article 125	Article 148
Chapter 3	Chapter 3
Article 126	Article 149
Article 127	Article 150
Title IX	Title XII
Article 128	Article 151
Title X	Title XIII
Article 129	Article 152
Title XI	Title XIV
Article 129a	Article 153

Previous numbering	New numbering
Title XII	Title XV
Article 129b	Article 154
Article 129c	Article 155
Article 129d	Article 156
Title XII	Title XVI
Article 130	Article 157
Title XIV	Title XVII
Article 130a	Article 158
Article 130b	Article 159
Article 130c	Article 160
Article 130d	Article 161
Article 130e	Article 162
Title XV	Title XVIII
Article 130f	Article 163
Article 130g	Article 164
Article 130h	Article 165
Article 130i	Article 166
Article 130j	Article 167
Article 130k	Article 168
Article 130l	Article 169
Article 130m	Article 170
Article 130n	Article 171
Article 130o	Article 172
Article 130p	Article 173
Article 130q (repealed)	–
Title XVI	Title XIX
Article 130r	Article 174
Article 130s	Article 175
Article 130t	Article 176
Title XVII	Title XX
Article 130u	Article 177
Article 130v	Article 178
Article 130w	Article 179
Article 130x	Article 180
Article 130y	Article 181
Part Four	Part Four
Article 131	Article 182
Article 132	Article 183
Article 133	Article 184
Article 134	Article 185
Article 135	Article 186
Article 136	Article 187

Previous numbering	New numbering
Part Four *continued*	Part Four *continued*
Article 136a	Article 188
Part Five	Part Five
Title I	Title I
Chapter 1	Chapter 1
Section 1	Section 1
Article 137	Article 189
Article 138	Article 190
Article 138a	Article 191
Article 138b	Article 192
Article 138c	Article 193
Article 138d	Article 194
Article 138e	Article 195
Article 139	Article 196
Article 140	Article 197
Article 141	Article 198
Article 142	Article 199
Article 143	Article 200
Article 144	Article 201
Section 2	Section 2
Article 145	Article 202
Article 146	Article 203
Article 147	Article 204
Article 148	Article 205
Article 149 (repealed)	–
Article 150	Article 206
Article 151	Article 207
Article 152	Article 208
Article 153	Article 209
Article 154	Article 210
Section 3	Section 3
Article 155	Article 211
Article 156	Article 212
Article 157	Article 213
Article 158	Article 214
Article 159	Article 215
Article 160	Article 216
Article 161	Article 217
Article 162	Article 218
Article 163	Article 219
Section 4	Section 4
Article 164	Article 220
Article 165	Article 221
Article 166	Article 222

Previous numbering	New numbering
Section 4 *continued*	Section 4 *continued*
Article 167	Article 223
Article 168	Article 224
Article 168 a	Article 225
Article 169	Article 226
Article 170	Article 227
Article 171	Article 228
Article 172	Article 229
Article 173	Article 230
Article 174	Article 231
Article 175	Article 232
Article 176	Article 233
Article 177	Article 234
Article 178	Article 235
Article 179	Article 236
Article 180	Article 237
Article 181	Article 238
Article 182	Article 239
Article 183	Article 240
Article 184	Article 241
Article 185	Article 242
Article 186	Article 243
Article 187	Article 244
Article 188	Article 245
Section 5	Section 5
Article 188a	Article 246
Article 188b	Article 247
Article 188c	Article 248
Chapter 2	Chapter 2
Article 189	Article 249
Article 189a	Article 250
Article 189b	Article 251
Article 189c	Article 252
Article 190	Article 253
Article 191	Article 254
Article 191a(*)	Article 255
Article 192	Article 256
Chapter 3	Chapter 3
Article 193	Article 257
Article 194	Article 258
Article 195	Article 259
Article 196	Article 260
Article 197	Article 261

Previous numbering	New numbering
Chapter 3 *continued*	Chapter 3 *continued*
Article 198	Article 262
Article 198a	Article 263
Article 198b	Article 264
Article 198c	Article 265
Chapter 5	Chapter
Article 198d	Article 266
Article 198e	Article 267
Title II	Title II
Article 199	Article 268
Article 200 (repealed)	–
Article 201	Article 269
Article 201a	Article 270
Article 202	Article 271
Article 203	Article 272
Article 204	Article 273
Article 205	Article 274
Article 205a	Article 275
Article 206	Article 276
Article 206a (repealed)	–
Article 207	Article 277
Article 208	Article 278
Article 209	Article 279
Article 209a	Article 280
Part Six	Part Six
Article 210	Article 281
Article 211	Article 282
Article 212(*)	Article 283
Article 213	Article 284
Article 213a(*)	Article 285
Article 213b(*)	Article 286
Article 214	Article 287
Article 215	Article 288
Article 216	Article 289
Article 217	Article 290
Article 218(*)	Article 291
Article 219	Article 292
Article 220	Article 293
Article 221	Article 294
Article 222	Article 295
Article 223	Article 296
Article 224	Article 297

Previous numbering	New numbering
Part Six *continued*	Part Six *continued*
Article 2215	Article 298
Article 226 (repealed)	–
Article 227	Article 299
Article 228	Article 300
Article 228a	Article 301
Article 229	Article 302
Article 230	Article 303
Article 231	Article 304
Article 232	Article 305
Article 233	Article 306
Article 234	Article 307
Article 235	Article 308
Article 236(*)	Article 309
Article 237 (repealed)	–
Article 238	Article 310
Article 239	Article 311
Article 240	Article 312
Article 241 (repealed)	–
Article 242 (repealed)	–
Article 243 (repealed)	–
Article 244 (repealed)	–
Article 245 (repealed)	–
Article 246 (repealed)	–
Final Provisions	Final Provisions
Article 247	Article 313
Article 248	Article 314

(*)   New Article introduced by the Treaty of Amsterdam.
(**)   New Title introduced by the Treaty of Amsterdam.
(***) Chapter 1 restructured by the Treaty of Amsterdam.

NOTE ON THE CITATION OF ARTICLES OF THE TREATIES IN COURT PUBLICATIONS

Pursuant to the renumbering of the articles of the Treaty on European Union (EU) and of the Treaty establishing the European Community (EC) brought about by the Treaty of Amsterdam, the Court of Justice and the Court of First Instance have introduced, with effect from 1 May 1999, a new method of citation of the articles of the EU, EC, ECSC and Euratom Treaties.

The new method is primarily designed to avoid all risk of confusion between the version of an article as it stood prior to 1 May 1999 and the version applying after that date. The principles on which that method operates are as follows:

— Where reference is made to an article of a Treaty *as it stands after* 1 May 1999, the number of the article is immediately followed by two letters indicating the Treaty concerned:

   — EU for the Treaty on European Union
   — EC for the EC Treaty
   — CS for the ECSC Treaty
   — EA for the Euratom Treaty.

   Thus, 'Article 234 *EC*' denotes the article of that Treaty as it stands *after* 1 May 1999.

— Where, on the other hand, reference is made to an article of a Treaty *as it stood before* 1 May 1999, the number of the article is followed by the words 'of the Treaty on European Union', 'of the EC (or EEC) Treaty', 'of the ECSC Treaty' or 'of the EAEC Treaty', as the case may be.

   Thus, 'Article 85 *of the EC Treaty*' refers to Article 85 of that Treaty *before* 1 May 1999.

— In addition, as regards the EC Treaty and the Treaty on European Union, again where reference is made to an article of a Treaty *as it stood before* 1 May 1999, the initial citation of the article in a text is followed by a reference in brackets to the corresponding provision of the same Treaty as it stands *after* 1 May 1999, as follows:

— '*Article 85 of the EC Treaty (now Article 81 EC)*', where the article has not been amended by the Treaty of Amsterdam;
— '*Article 51 of the EC Treaty (now, after amendment, Article 42 EC)*', where the article has been amended by the Treaty of Amsterdam;
— '*Article 53 of the EC Treaty (repealed by the Treaty of Amsterdam)*', where the article has been repealed by the Treaty of Amsterdam.

— By way of exception to the latter rule, the initial citation of (the former) Articles 117 to 120 of the EC Treaty, which have been replaced *en bloc* by the Treaty of Amsterdam, is followed by the following wording in brackets: '*(Articles 117 to 120 of the EC Treaty have been replaced by Articles 136 EC to 143 EC)*'.
    For example:

— '*Article 119 of the EC Treaty (Articles 117 to 120 of the EC Treaty have been replaced by Articles 136 EC to 143 EC)*'.

The same applies to Articles J to J.11 and K to K.9 of the Treaty on European Union.
    For example:

— '*Article J.2 of the Treaty on European Union (Articles J to J.11 of the Treaty on European Union have been replaced by Articles 11 EU to 28 EU)*';
— '*Article K.2 of the Treaty on European Union (Articles K to K.9 of the Treaty on European Union have been replaced by Articles 29 EU to 42 EU)*'.

ABBREVIATIONS

AC	Appeal Cases
AJCL	American Journal of Comparative Law
All ER	All England (Law) Reports
CA	Court of Appeal (England)
CDE	Cahiers de Droit Européen
CEE	Charges having equivalent effect (Art. 12)
Ch	Chancery Reports
CLJ	Cambridge Law Journal
CMLR	Common Market Law Reports
CML Rev	Common Market Law Review
Cmnd.	Command Paper
Crim LR	Criminal Law Review
EC	(ECs) European Community (-ies)
ECB	European Central Bank
ECLJ	European Consumer Law Journal
ECLR	European Competition Law Review
ECR	European Court Reports
ECSC	European Coal and Steel Community
EEC	European Economic Community
EEIG	European Economic Interest Grouping
EIPR	European Intellectual Property Review
EJIL	European Journal of International Law
EL Rev	European Law Review
EU	European Union
ERPL	European Review of Private Law
EuR	Europarecht
EURATOM	European Atomic Energy Community
GATT	General Agreement on Tariffs and Trade
HL	House of Lords (UK)
IBL	International Business Lawyer
ICLQ	International and Comparative Law Quarterly
ILJ	Industrial Law Journal
IRLR	Industrial Relations Law Reports
JBL	Journal of Business Law
JCMS	Journal of Common Market Studies
JCP	Journal of Consumer Policy
JEL	Journal of Environmental Law
JEPP	Journal of European Public Policy
JSWFL	Journal of Social Welfare and Family Law

J Law and Econ	Journal of Law and Economics	OJ	Official Journal (of the ECs)
LIEI	Legal Issues of European Integration	OJLS	Oxford Journal of Legal Studies
LQR	Law Quarterly Review	QB	Queen's Bench
MEQR	Measures having equivalent effect to a quantitative restriction (Article 28)	RTDE	Revue Trimistrelle de Droit Européen
		SEA	Single European Act
		SI	Statutory Instrument
MJ	Maastricht Journal of European & Comparative Law	TEU	Treaty on European Union
		WLR	Weekly Law Reports
MLR	Modern Law Review	WTO	World Trade Organisation
NILQ	Northern Ireland Legal Quarterly	YEL	Yearbook of European Law

PART ONE:
THE CONSTITUTIONAL
LAW OF THE EC

INTRODUCTION

For students in British law schools, EC law (or Community law) has long held a well-deserved reputation for being extremely difficult to come to grips with. Yet at the end of the course most students tend to look back on Community law as a subject which they have found more interesting than most of the others which they have studied. There are good reasons for this apparent paradox. Community law *is* initially difficult, because it represents an adventure into a new legal system. When a student starts the study of a new English or Scots law subject, he or she comes to it with an accumulated fund of knowledge and expectation about the basic principles of the legal order. It is possible immediately to approach the substance of the subject. Not so with Community law. Indeed, nothing could be worse than to try to leap into the study of Community law equipped with domestic preconceptions about what judges do and about how law should be interpreted and applied. Community law is simply different, and it is necessary to learn to walk before one can run. For the law student who had thought that he or she had already picked up a spanking pace in legal education, this return to basic constitutional law can be a dispiriting experience. However, once the essentials of the subject are mastered, Community law is likely to prove a rewarding race to have run. It is a subject which enjoys internal coherence. Its themes and principles are consistent and can be understood and applied relatively easily. There are themes in the substantive law, such as the objective of market integration and the establishment of a common market, and there are principles in the constitutional law, such as the supremacy and direct effect of Community law. The approach of the judges of the European Court may initially seem odd, but it too displays a certain thematic consistency which can quickly be appreciated. There is even consistency in the difficulties and tensions which beset the development of Community law. The problems of integrating the features of the Community legal order with the traditions of domestic legal systems will be observed on many occasions.

As an academic lawyer with a particular interest in Community law, I hope that it will one day be possible to abandon these cautionary notes. Most Law Schools are aware of the need to integrate the key elements of the study of Community law into their degree programmes from the earliest possible stage, so that Community law does not present to the student this initially forbidding prospect. Those who teach substantive Community law courses remain aware that this task is by no means complete.

Part One of this book deals with the constitutional law of the EC. This covers the sources of Community law in Chapter 1, and then examines in Chapters 2 to 4 the fundamental ground rules of the Community legal order. These are the doctrines of supremacy and of direct effect, and the preliminary reference procedure.

However, given the comments above, is it right to start with Chapter 1? I have already mentioned that the early weeks of study of Community law are difficult, even intimidating. True, in examining a legal system, there is an obvious logic in beginning with its sources. But there is an equally strong argument for starting by acquiring a knowledge of the purpose of the system. This broader perspective can help the subject to come alive more quickly. Chapter 5, in Part Two, therefore deserves the student's examination at an early stage. So too does Chapter 15, which considers the Community's policy-making capacity and which will help to illustrate what the Community actually does. Equally, once the student has grasped the substantive law of the Community it would be helpful then to refer back once again to the earlier Constitutional law chapters. They will make more sense in the broader context.

It would be ill-advised to approach study of EC law as a purely legal undertaking. Narrowness of focus is damaging in any branch of the law, but perhaps especially so in Community law, where economic, political and social objectives are close to the surface and exert a profound formative influence on the law. From this perspective, then, the student about to read Part One of this book, might be well advised to equip him- or herself in advance with a basic understanding of modern European history and the post-war maelstrom out of which the Community emerged. So, too, an understanding of the basic nature and purpose of the Community's four major institutions – the Council, Commission, Parliament and Court – would be an advantage. Such introductory material may be found in the opening chapter or chapters of the major textbooks listed in the Selected Bibliography. Other more general sources of information, which do not offer a specifically legal focus, are also mentioned there and deserve the student's attention.

However, the following extracts provide a short but valuable introductory overview of some of the elements of the Community's past, present and future, which will be glimpsed, but not studied directly, in the course of this book. The opportunity is also taken to clarify terminology – a Community or a Union?

J. Pinder, *The Building of the European Union*
(1998, 3rd ed.), pp. 3–8
[Reproduced by permission of Oxford University Press]

(Footnotes omitted.)

1 Creating the Community and the Union: Nation-State and Federal Idea

The European Community, which remains the central element in the European Union, is a remarkable innovation in relations among states. Its institutions are more powerful than those of conventional international organisations, and offer more scope for development. Much of their specific character was determined in a few weeks in the summer of 1950, when representatives of the six founder members, France, the German Federal Republic, Italy, Belgium, the Netherlands, and Luxembourg, agreed on the outline of the Treaty to establish the European Coal and Steel Community. The initiative had been taken by Robert Schuman, the French foreign minister, who explained the gist of his proposal with these words:

> . . . the French Government proposes to take action immediately on one limited but decisive point . . . to place Franco-German production of coal and steel under a common High Authority, within the framework of an organisation open to the participation of the other countries of Europe . . . The solidarity in production thus established will make it plain that any war between France and Germany becomes not merely unthinkable, but materially impossible . . . this proposal will build the first concrete foundation of a European federation which is indispensable to the preservation of peace . . .

World War II, national sovereignty, the federal idea
World War II was a catastrophe that discredited the previous international order and, for many Europeans, the basic element in that order: the absolutely sovereign nation-state. In the Europe of such states, France and Germany had been at war three times in less than a century, twice at the centre of terrible world wars. Autarky and protection, fragmenting Europe's economy, had caused economic malaise and political antagonism. Fascist glorification of the nation-state had been revealed as a monstrosity; and many felt that insistence on its sovereignty, even without fascist excess, distorted and ossified the political perspective.

This critique pointed towards the limitation of national sovereignty. It was accepted by many people of the anti-fascist resistance, in Germany and Italy as well as the occupied countries. While the idea of limiting sovereignty in a united Europe was widespread, some influential figures were more precise. They envisaged a federal constitution for Europe, giving powers over trade, money, security, and related taxation, to a federal parliament, government, and court, leaving all other powers to be exercised by the institutions of the member states.

Such ideas evoked a ready echo from those Europeans who asked themselves why the war had occurred and what could be done to ensure a better future; and they were encouraged by Winston Churchill who, in a speech in Zurich in September 1946, suggested that France should lead Germany into a United States of Europe. Not everybody noticed that he was reticent about the part that Britain should play in such a union; and many, impressed by the magnanimous vision of the wartime leader with his immense prestige, did not realise how hard it would be to accomplish. For despite the popularity of the federal idea in Continental countries, the structures of the states were gathering strength again and were to prove resistant to radical federal reform.

Some of this resistance stemmed from the principle of national sovereignty as a basic political value. General de Gaulle was to be the most powerful and eloquent exponent of this view; and Mrs Thatcher was a subsequent protagonist. But most of the resisters were more pragmatic. Many bureaucrats, central bankers, and politicians would allow that sovereignty could in principle be shared on the right terms and at the right time: but the right terms were not on offer and the right time would be later.

Two main strategies were devised to overcome the reluctance of governments. One, promoted by the Italian federalist leader, Altiero Spinelli, was to mobilise popular support for a constituent assembly, in which the people's representatives would draw up a European constitution. But this idea bore little fruit until, with the direct elections to the European Parliament in 1979, Spinelli persuaded the people's newly elected representatives to design and approve a Draft Treaty to constitute a European Union. The other strategy, devised by Jean Monnet, was to identify a 'limited but decisive point', as Schuman's declaration put it, on which governments could be persuaded to agree and which, without going the whole way, would mark a significant step towards federation. With this idea, Monnet was to secure an early and spectacular success.

Founding the Community: the ECSC

Monnet's 'limited but decisive point' was the need for a new structure to contain the resurgent heavy industries of the Ruhr, the traditional economic basis for Germany's military might, which had been laid low as a result of the war. It was clear by 1950 that industry in West Germany must develop if Germans were to pay their way in the world and help the West in its rivalry with the Soviet Union, and that this required the revival of German steel production. Of the western Allies then responsible for West Germany, the United States and Britain were increasingly insistent on this. France, through history and geography more sensitive to the potential danger of German power, insisted that the Ruhr's heavy industries should be kept under control. But France lacked the means to restrain the Americans and British; and there were Frenchmen in key positions who realised that the perpetuation of an international Ruhr authority such as had been set up in 1948 to exert control over the Germans, apart from being unacceptable to the two Allies, would be an unstable arrangement, apt to be overturned by Germany at the first opportunity. Hence the idea of a common structure to govern the coal and steel industries, not only of the Ruhr but also of France and other European countries.

This idea was not the invention of Monnet alone. Officials in the French foreign ministry were also working on it. But they would surely have created a conventional international organisation, governed by committees of ministers, whereas Monnet was determined that the new institutions should have a political life independent of the existing governments: that they should be 'the first concrete foundation of a European federation'.

It is the theme of this book that the concept of European institutions which go beyond a conventional system of intergovernmental co-operation, however imperfectly realised so far, has given the Community, and now the Union, its special character: its stability, capacity for achievement, and promise for the future. It is of course possible to argue that the Community is, on the contrary, essentially an intergovernmental organisation to secure free trade and economic co-operation, and that the rest is frills and rhetoric. This book sets out a case for seeing it as more than that.

Monnet, from his vantage point as head of the French *Commissariat du Plan*, persuaded Schuman to adopt the more radical project; and he did it at the moment when the French government was most apt to accept, because a solution to the problem of German steel could no longer be delayed. Monnet's solution had the merit of meeting not only the French national interest in the control of German steel but also a wider interest in the development of European political institutions. The proposal was immediately welcomed by the governments of West Germany, Italy, Belgium, the Netherlands, and Luxembourg; and it was enthusiastically received by the wide sectors of opinion in those countries and in France that could be called broadly federalist, in the sense of supporting steps towards a federal end, even if not all would be precise in defining this. The project also received strong and steady support from the United States.

Support for the federal idea had mushroomed in Britain too in 1939 and the first half of 1940, culminating with the Churchill government's proposal for union with France. But after the fall of France in June 1940, with Nazi domination of the Continent, British interest in European union ebbed. For more than a decade after the war, British governments wanted to confine their relationship with the Continent to no more than a loose association. They were not ready to accept the federal implications of Monnet's proposal. So the six founder members negotiated the Treaty establishing the European Coal and Steel Community (ECSC) without Britain or the other West European countries that took the same view.

As chairman of the intergovernmental conference that drew up the ECSC Treaty, Monnet was well placed to ensure that his basic idea was followed through. The High Authority was to be the executive responsible for policy relating to the coal and steel industries in the member countries, and its decisions were to apply directly to the economic agents in each country, without requiring the approval of its government. The policies envisaged in the Treaty bore the mark of French planning ideas. Investment in the two industries was to be influenced by the High Authority, though not subject to much control. Prices and production could be regulated, but only if there were crises of shortage or over-production. Policies for training, housing, and redeployment were to cater for workers' needs. Competition was at the same time to be stimulated by rules on price transparency, as well as by anti-trust laws on American lines.

Monnet insisted on the principle of the High Authority's independence from the member states' governments because his experience as an international civil servant had convinced him that it would be hamstrung if they controlled it too directly. But that raised the question of the High Authority's accountability. Monnet, in his inaugural speech as the first President of the High Authority in August 1952, was to explain the Treaty's answer like this. The High Authority was responsible to an Assembly (now called the European Parliament), which would eventually be directly elected, and which had the power to dismiss it. There was recourse to the European Court of Justice in cases that concerned the High Authority's acts. In short, the powers defined by the Treaty would be exercised by institutions with federal characteristics, sovereign within the limits of their competences. The policy of the High Authority and those of the member states would be 'harmonised' by a Council of ministers, voting by majority 'save in exceptional cases'. Monnet ensured that the federal elements in the Community would be clearly explained by employing Spinelli's help in drafting the speech.

Monnet's idea was that the European federation would be built over the years on this 'first concrete foundation' as new sectors of activity were brought within the scope of the pre-federal institutions; and the establishment of the European Economic Community and Euratom in 1958 lent remarkable support to this view. But he does not appear to have foreseen how much the Council would come to dominate the politics of the Community, as the political structures of member states came to assert themselves against the realisation of the federal idea. This reaction led to a long-drawn-out conflict within the Community, which began with a major assault by General de Gaulle as President of France and continued up to the 1990s, with Britain succeeding de Gaulle as champion of national sovereignty. . . .

Note
The Treaties of Rome, signed in 1957 and creating the EEC and EURATOM in 1958, led to a deepening of the process. The EEC envisaged the creation of a common market and was not limited to particular sectors of the economy. Its institutions followed the pattern of the ECSC. The EEC had a Commission, where the ECSC has a High Authority. (Since 1967 the two have functioned as one under the title 'Commission'.) The EEC also had three other institutions – Council, Parliament and Court. The next extract explains in outline the Community's institutional structure.

E. Noel, *Working Together: the Institutions of the European Community* (1993), pp. 5–8

(Footnotes omitted.)

The institutional system of the European Communities is difficult to classify. The Community is much more than an intergovernmental organisation: it has its own special legal status and extensive powers of its own. But the Community is not a true federation to which national parliaments and governments are subordinate in important matters. Our best course may be to leave it to future historians to find an appropriate label and simply describe it as a 'Community' system.

The task of achieving the aims of the three Communities – the European Coal and Steel Community (ECSC) (established in 1952), the European Economic Community (EEC) (1958) and the European Atomic Energy Community (Euratom) (1958) – rests with five institutions: the European Parliament, the Council, the Commission, the Court of Justice and the Court of Auditors, with the support of the Economic and Social Committee and the Committee of the Regions.

A European System of Central Banks and a European Central Bank are to be added (if possible in 1997, but in any event no later than 1999) as a result of the establishment of economic and monetary union. From the beginning of 1994 their activities are to be prepared by a European Monetary Institute, whose functions will pass to the European Central Bank as soon as it is set up. [See further Chapter 5.]

Until July 1967 the three Communities had separate Councils and executive Commissions (known as the 'High Authority' in the ECSC). But since then there has been a single Commission and a single Council, which exercise all the powers and responsibilities rested in their respective predecessors by the three Community

Treaties. By contrast, the European Parliament and the Court of Justice have been common to the three Communities since 1958.

The merger of the institutions was seen as the first step towards setting up a single European Community to be governed by a single Treaty, replacing the Paris Treaty (establishing the ECSC) and the Rome Treaty (establishing the EEC and Euratom).

But this idea was not followed through at the time; nor was it taken up again in the negotiations on the Single Act in 1985 or on the Treaty on European Union in 1991.

What this last Treaty did, however, was to provide that the European Economic Community was henceforth to be called simply the European Community; this underscores its general role. The ECSC Treaty was originally concluded for 50 years and will expire in 2002; in all likelihood those of its functions which are preserved will then be taken over by the European Community.

The successive enlargements of the Communities – with the accession of the United Kingdom, Ireland and Denmark on 1 January 1973, Greece on 1 January 1981, and most recently Spain and Portugal on 1 January 1986 – have not affected the basic structure or responsibilities of the Community institutions although their composition has altered. [The same is true of the accessions of Austria, Finland and Sweden on 1 January 1995.]

With the unification of Germany on 3 October 1990, the Community was enlarged to include the territory of the former German Democratic Republic (GDR), and Community legislation is now applicable there, subject to a number of temporary exceptions (some of them valid for a considerable number of years). Germany's representation in the various Community institutions remains unchanged, though the membership of Parliament is to be adjusted (see below).

The Single European Act (which was signed in February 1986 and entered into force on 1 July 1987) has extended the Community's field of competence and brought about significant changes in relations between the institutions and in their operating rules. It also gave formal legal status to European political cooperation, which has been operating since 1970 simply on the basis of intergovernmental agreements.

The Treaty on European Union (the Maastricht Treaty), which was signed at Maastricht on 7 February 1992 and entered into force on 1 November 1993, makes far-reaching changes. It establishes a European Union founded on the European Communities and embracing all the forms of cooperation that have built up with them, including political cooperation (already mentioned) and cooperation on justice and home affairs. Before the decade is out the Community is to establish an economic and monetary union leading to the introduction of a single currency. Major institutional changes have also been made, chiefly to enhance the powers of Parliament and the Court of Auditors (now raised to full institution status) and to set up a new Committee of the Regions.

The **European Parliament** has been directly elected since 1979. The Edinburgh European Council (December 1992) decided to alter its membership to take account of, among other things, the unification of Germany. The decision is now up for ratification by the Member States and should be in operation in time for the next elections in June 1994 [it was]. Its membership will then be 567, the breakdown of seats being as follows: Belgium 25: Denmark 16; France 87; Germany 99; Greece 25; Ireland 15; Italy 87; Luxembourg 6; Netherlands 31; Portugal 25; Spain 64; United Kingdom 87. [Now 626 members: Austria 21; Finland 16; Sweden 22.]

The **Council** is made up of representatives of the governments of the 12 [now 15] Member States. Each government normally sends one of its ministers. Its membership thus varies with the subjects down for discussion. The Foreign Minister is regarded as his country's 'main' representative in the Council, but Ministers for Agriculture, Transport, Economic and Financial Affairs, Social Affairs, Industry, the Environment and so on also meet frequently for specialised Council meetings.

The Maastricht Treaty also made the Council responsible for intergovernmental cooperation in the European Union (common foreign and security policy, justice and home affairs).

At their December 1974 Summit, the Heads of State (for France) or Government agreed to meet regularly together with the President of the Commission as the 'European Council', accompanied by their Foreign Ministers and a Member of the Commission.

The first formal provision for the European Council was made in the Single European Act; the Maastricht Treaty followed it up by confirming its central role of providing the European Union (the Community and political cooperation combined) with the necessary impetus for its development and defining its general guidelines. Since 1986 the European Council has generally met every six months, but additional meetings may be held where circumstances so require.

The Presidency of the Council and of the European Council rotates between the member governments at six-monthly intervals. When decisions are taken in the Council by majority vote, France, Germany, Italy and the United Kingdom have 10 votes each, Spain has eight, Belgium, Greece, The Netherlands and Portugal five each, Denmark and Ireland three each and Luxembourg two. A qualified majority means 54 votes out of a total of 76. [Now 62 out of 87; Austria and Sweden have four votes, Finland three.]

The Council is assisted by a **Permanent Representatives Committee** which comprises the Permanent Representatives (ambassadors) of the Member States to the Communities. Its main task is to prepare the ground for Council meetings. A large number of working parties operate under its authority.

The **European Commission** consists of 17 [now 20] Members, appointed by agreement between the member governments. There are two nationals each from France, Germany, Italy, Spain and the United Kingdom and one from each of the other seven [now ten] Member States. Throughout their four-year term of office Members must remain independent of the governments and of the Council. The Council cannot remove any Member from office. Parliament, however, can pass a motion of censure compelling the Commission to resign as a body (in which case, it would continue to handle everyday business until its replacement). The Maastricht Treaty substantially altered the procedure for appointing the Commission with effect from 1995. . . . [The resignation of the Commission headed by President Santer in March 1999 did not of itself involve formal constitutional change, but created a climate within which greater attention has been paid to the need for reform of the Commission under its new President, Romano Prodi. See D. Spence, 'Plus ça change, plus C'est las même chose? Attempting to reform the European Commission' (2000) 7 JEPP 1.]

The **Court of Justice**, composed of 13 [now 15] judges appointed for six years by agreement among the governments, ensures that implementation of the Treaties is in accordance with the rule of law. The judges are assisted by six [now nine] advocates-general. An additional **Court of First Instance** was set up in 1989. It consists of 10 [now 15] judges, also appointed for six years by agreement among the governments.

The **Court of Auditors** has 12 [now 15] members appointed by unanimous decision of the Council after consulting Parliament. It began operating in October 1977. It audits the accounts of the Community and of Community bodies, examines whether revenue and expenditure have been properly and lawfully received and incurred, checks that financial management has been sound, and reports back to the Community institutions. It is also required to provide Parliament and the Council with a statement of assurance as to the reliability of the accounts and the legality and regularity of the underlying transactions.

In EEC and Euratom matters, the Council and the Commission are assisted by the **Economic and Social Committee**. This consists of 189 [now 222] members, representing various sectors of economic and social life. It must be consulted before decisions are taken on a large number of subjects, and is also free to issue opinions on its own initiative.

In ECSC matters, the Commission is assisted by a Consultative Committee, which has 96 members representing producers, workers, consumers and dealers in the coal and steel industries. It too must be consulted before decisions are taken on a large number of subjects and it can also issue opinions on its own initiative.

Through the Economic and Social Committee and the Consultative Committee, the various interest groups concerned are actively involved in the development of the Community.

The Maastricht Treaty further established a **Committee of the Regions** to assist the Commission and the Council. It is composed of 189 [now 222] members (plus the same number of alternates) representing regional and local bodies. It must be consulted prior to the adoption of any decision affecting regional interests. It may also issue opinions of its own motion.

The **European Investment Bank** contributes, by raising funds on the capital markets, to financing investment projects that will promote the development of the common market, particularly in the less-developed regions and in conjunction with the Structural Funds.

At the Edinburgh European Council in December 1992, the governments of the Member States finally came to a decision, awaited for 40 years, on the headquarters of the Community institutions, which hitherto only had provisional places of work. The decision broadly confirmed the status quo. The Commission's headquarters are in Brussels, but some departments operate in Luxembourg. The Council also has its headquarters in Brussels, but meets in Luxembourg for three months each year. Luxembourg is the headquarters of the Court of Justice, the Court of First Instance, the Court of Auditors and the European Investment Bank, while the Economic and Social Committee and the Committee of the Regions are based in Brussels. The real change, which made the final compromise possible, concerns Parliament, whose headquarters are in Strasbourg, where it holds its plenary sessions, while its secretariat remains in Luxembourg and its committees meet in Brussels. The novel element is that it may now hold shorter 'additional' plenary sessions in Brussels.

E. Noel, writing in 1993, goes on to provide a brief survey of the Community's development (pp. 56–8):

The EEC and Euratom have been in existence for 35 years now; the ECSC even longer. After several crises and the accession of six [now nine] new Member States, it can be said that the Community system has proved its durability.

Through its institutions the Community has succeeded in attaining most of the Treaties' objectives, and in many areas it has progressed even further. But integration remains incomplete, and worse still, unbalanced. Substantial progress must still be made, otherwise ground will be lost.

The 1969 Hague Summit of the six Heads of State or Government gave birth to two major plans: economic and monetary union and greater political solidarity.

At the prompting of Pierre Werner, the Luxembourg Prime Minister, an ambitious project for economic union was presented to the national governments, but progress towards it was slowed and eventually halted by the economic crisis of the 1970s.

Then, in the autumn of 1977, the President of the Commission relaunched the idea of monetary union. Following initiatives by a number of governments and by the Commission itself, and thanks to the active efforts of the European Council, the European Monetary System came into effect on 13 March 1979, with eight of the nine Member States as full participants (at the time the United Kingdom opted to remain outside the exchange rate mechanism). In the following years the EMS weathered several storms. A hard core of participating countries kept it on an even keel. It strengthened monetary cooperation remarkably: exchange rates have become a matter of mutual interest and changes (both devaluations and revaluations) are discussed and agreed on at special meetings of Finance Ministers. This has also engendered tighter economic discipline and a gradual alignment of the Members' economic policies.

Some Member States have at times responded to economic difficulties (and currency speculation) by withdrawing from the exchange rate mechanism. However, full participation in the EMS leading to economic and monetary union remains the publicly stated objective of most of the Twelve [now 15].

In today's world, economic solidarity is inseparable from political solidarity. In this respect, the conclusions of the Hague Summit did have a tangible impact: a system of political cooperation was brought into operation by the governments of the Member States. This has been gradually extended to almost every area of foreign policy, including the political and economic aspects of security, and was made legally binding by the Single European Act. It operates on a consensual basis. Although it has its own structures, it has functioned in increasingly close harmony with the Community institutions. Its President reports regularly to Parliament and the Commission is involved in all meetings.

In the autumn of 1972, when the United Kingdom, Denmark and Ireland were about to join the Community, the Heads of State or Government set themselves the ambitious goal of transforming relations between the Member States into a European Union by the end of the decade. However, that date was to mark the beginning of a long and painful crisis for the Community. Yet it led to a political leap forward which bears witness to the deep-seated trend towards European integration—the adoption of the draft Treaty on European Union (the Spinelli draft) by the European Parliament in February 1984, and the opening in June 1985 of negotiations which culminated in the Single European Act (which came into force on 1 July 1987). This gave the Community the means to complete the internal market by the end of 1992 while at the same time making significant improvements in its internal operations.

The signing of the Maastricht Treaty and its entry into force represent completion of a major new stage in the Community's march towards the goals it fixed in 1969 and 1972.

We have described the major institutional changes this entails. A detailed programme has been drawn up to bring about economic and monetary union before the end of the century while a single operating structure has been set up for intergovernmental cooperation (foreign affairs, internal affairs and justice). The Member States (subject to derogations for Denmark) have undertaken to establish a common external and security policy (which could lead in time to a common defence policy). Intergovernmental cooperation will be administered by the Council with the assistance of the Commission and in consultation with Parliament. It is regrettable that involvement of the institutions was not accompanied by the adoption of Community rules for the administration of these areas, but it is a significant step forward all the same.

Implementation of the Maastricht Treaty was linked to further enlargement of the Community to include four new members—Austria, Finland, Norway and Sweden [Norway subsequently chose not to join]. Following the collapse of the communist system, countries in Central and Eastern Europe and several Mediterranean countries have expressed their wish to join the Community as soon as possible. Further enlargement will entail the need for a radical review of the Community system . . .

Note
Questions about political accountability and institutional development demand the attention of any student with an interest in the Community. If the Community is to develop autonomous policy-making competence, it is necessary to provide the appropriate democratic safeguards. The future of the Community is likely to be characterised by controversial debates about how best to subject the institutions to political and legal control. It is impossible for this book to explore these issues in detail. The next extract covers some specific points which will not yet be familiar, but the themes which it introduces are already valuable.

R. Dehousse, '1992 and Beyond: the Institutional Dimension of the Internal Market Programme' [1989/1] LIEI 109, at pp. 133–136

(Footnotes omitted.)

The evolution of the Community in the last few years teaches us a series of lessons on what might be called the politics of institutional reform. The first conclusion to be drawn from this experience is that institutional reform is easier to arrive at when it is not pursued for its own sake, but emerges as a logical implication of other political choices. Once the general idea of completing the internal market by 1992 had been accepted, it proved possible to convince even the most reluctant Member States that a shift towards more majority voting was necessary. Had the objective itself not met with consensus, the change would not have been possible. The same logic is apparent in the Single Act's provisions on economic and social cohesion, on research and technological development or on the environment. In all these sectors, unanimous agreement is needed in order to define the objectives to be pursued at Community level; it is only at a second stage that resort to majority voting can be envisaged. The rationale of all these provisions is the same: when a decision of principle is to be taken, Member States must be able to preserve what they regard as their essential interests but, precisely because they have been given this guarantee, no vital interest to be harmed at the implementation stage; the 'Community interest' – and in particular the necessity of an efficient decision-making system – can therefore be given precedence.

Thus, most of the developments which have taken place in these years find their origin in the Commission's capacity to capitalise on the political pressures exerted by the Parliament and to define a 'new frontier' which would be acceptable to all Member States. But the way in which the institutional reform was accomplished also deserves attention. The main feature of the process was certainly its piecemeal character, which is often the case with compromises achieved in decentralised systems. As is known, the Single European Act was not the result of an inspired exercise in constitution-making, but the product of strenuous international negotiation. This cumbersome process had a direct incidence on the final result, which reflects the various aspirations and fears of more or less all Member States. In a typical *quid pro quo* exercise, France and Germany secured the adoption of provisions on political cooperation, and the backward countries a general commitment in favour of the reinforcement of economic and social cohesion within the Community, while several countries managed to limit the Community's capacity to act autonomously as far as the environment is concerned. Several of the institutional problems mentioned above are linked to the complexity of the structure which eventually emerged. The lengthy discussions on the subject of legal basis offer good examples of difficulties connected with the ambiguity of the compromises made at the time of drafting the Single Act.

With the White Paper on the internal market, questions which were previously considered as essentially technical gained the status of major political objectives. This change was paralleled by an evolution in the decision-making process: the creation of an internal market Council, with its induced effects at national level, has made it easier to coordinate national and Community action in this sphere. The introduction of majority voting has had a similar effect. Even if it is not systematically used, the possibility of a vote reinforces the weight of political decision-makers over that of specialised departments, which are to a large extent deprived of the veto right they had in the past.

These changes account for the relatively positive results reached so far. The Commission has now presented most of the proposals envisaged in the White Paper; approximately one third of them have been adopted so far, which certainly represents no meagre achievement. However, these figures should not generate an excessive optimism, for the most delicate matters – tax harmonisation, the free movement of persons, and the social dimension of the internal market – remain to be dealt with. It is therefore not unreasonable to think that the pace of implementation of the White Paper programme will slow down in coming months. Much will certainly depend on the Commission's capacity to forge the coalitions which are needed for the adoption of its proposals, and to transpose into operational terms the choices made in the White Paper. It is one thing to make a conceptual distinction between what is essential and what is not, and quite another to draw a clear line between the two in different sectors.

In spite of all the difficulties which can be foreseen, it is clear that the Community has now embarked on an era of dynamism which few expected a couple of years ago. Part of this dynamism finds its origin in external factors like the economic growth experienced in recent years; but it is equally clear that the momentum generated by the White Paper would not have been possible without its healthy institutional pragmatism. Not only did this approach make possible advances generally regarded as beyond reach not so long ago; but it might lead to even further-reaching results. For whether it is achieved by 1992 or only later, completion of the internal market could well generate its own dynamic. It has, for instance, often been argued that the liberalisation of capital movements in a Community with stable exchange rates will make it more difficult for Member States to pursue autonomous macro-economic policies. If at some stage two thirds of the economic and social legislation will have to be adopted at the Community level, as President Delors recently hinted, Community citizens and interest groups might press for a stronger voice in the decision-making process. At the same time, Member States might also realise that more systematic resort to voting, or a stronger involvement of Parliament in the legislative process, do not necessarily mean unbearable threats to their national interests. . . .

Note
Even before the deadline for the completion of the internal market, the end of 1992, both the dynamism and the taste for ambiguous compromises noted

by Dehousse in this extract were redeployed. In December 1991 agreement was reached at Maastricht on the next step forward – the Treaty on European Union. The Treaty was signed at Maastricht on 7 February 1992. However, only on 1 November 1993 did the Treaty finally come into force following hard-fought campaigns surrounding the ratification process in several Member States. The Danish people voted narrowly against ratification in a referendum in 1992 before voting in favour by a slightly larger margin in a second referendum in 1993. The British government chose not to hold a referendum, but John Major's government secured Parliamentary approval only by a slim majority amid turbulent Parliamentary scenes in summer 1993. Germany was the last of the 12 Member States to ratify and could do so only after its Constitutional Court had ruled in October 1993 that ratification was not incompatible with the German Constitution ([1994] 1 CMLR 57).

The basic structure instituted by the Maastricht Treaty on European Union is best presented in diagrammatic form.

Article A of the Treaty on European Union declares that 'The Union shall be founded on the European Communities'. Be that as it may, the Union structure fashioned at Maastricht is built on three pillars and the European Communities are only one of those three pillars. Two of the pillars, those relating to a Common Foreign and Security Policy (Title V TEU) and Cooperation in the Fields of Justice and Home Affairs (Title VI TEU), exist outside the traditional, developed EC structure and are essentially intergovernmental in nature. Meanwhile, the three European Communities remain in existence as components of what is commonly termed the European Community pillar. In fact, the most important of three Communities, the EEC, was formally renamed the EC. It was also amended in a number of more substantial respects, such as the inclusion of new Titles enhancing the Community's competences, the creation of the status of Citizenship of the Union and adjustments to the legislative procedure which enhance the position of the Parliament. Perhaps the centrepiece of the Treaty is the insertion into the EC Treaty of detailed provisions designed to lead to Economic and Monetary Union. These provisions carry immense constitutional significance, but could also be viewed as an important but natural consequence of the increasing stability of the Exchange Rate Mechanism of the European Monetary System, referred to above in positive terms in the extract from E. Noel's *Working Together* (p. 10). The Treaty timetable has been adhered to and the third stage of economic and monetary union was launched on 1 January 1999, when 11 Member States (all save Denmark, Greece, Sweden and the UK) adopted the euro as their common currency (although euro banknotes will circulate validly only from 1 January 2002). EMU is discussed further at p. 211 below.

There is a disjointed facade to the European Union. The nature of each of the three pillars is different. The Council seems to be the only institution which is in any significant sense an institution of the whole Union. In November 1993, it accordingly chose to rename itself the Council of the European Union. The Commission, Parliament and Court remain institutions whose principal role is within the European Community pillar. The impression of a disjointed structure is heightened when one appreciates that even within the EC there are emerging tendencies towards fragmentation. Denmark and the United Kingdom, most prominently, were permitted certain 'opt-outs' from EC policies (see p. 621 below on Social Policy). Curtin expressed concern about the growth of a 'Europe of Bits and Pieces' ((1993) 30 CML Rev 17). The picture was complicated yet further by the coming into existence of the European Economic Area at the start of 1994, which extended a mass of EC rules relevant to free trade into the wider area of the majority of the European Free Trade Association States, Austria, Finland, Iceland, Norway and Sweden (but not Switzerland or Liechtenstein). The EEA structure established further institutions: the EEA Council, Joint Committee, Joint Parliamentary Committee and Consultative Committee. The accession of Austria, Finland and Sweden to the Union at the start of 1995 greatly reduced the practical importance of the EEA.

It has been astutely commented that 'the success of the internal market programme lay in its apparent lack of ambition' (Dehousse, Joerges, Majone, Snyder (eds), 'Europe after 1992: New Regulatory Strategies', EUI Working Paper Law 92/31, Florence). In sharp contrast, as the European Union project unfolds, what is apparent is the breadth of the ambition. How this will affect the prospects for success dominates the European agenda.

Further reading on the Maastricht Treaty on European Union
Curtin, D., 'The Constitutional Structure of the Union: a Europe of Bits and Pieces' (1993) 30 CML Rev 17.
Dehousse, R. (ed.), *Europe After Maastricht* (Law Books, 1994), which contains nine separate essays.
O'Keeffe, D., and Twomey P., (eds), *Legal Issues of the Maastricht Treaty* (Chancery Law Publishing, 1994), which contains 23 separate essays.
Wincott, D., 'Is the Treaty of Maastricht an Adequate Constitution for the European Union?' (1994) 72 *Public Administration* 573.

Question
'Since EU matters will be dealt with by the same people, sitting in the same rooms . . . as EC matters, it is hard to imagine a sufficient justification for

creating the charade of constitutional obscurity which is EU . . . . It would have been perfectly possible to devise exceptional but constitutionally coherent Title V and Title VI systems within the EC system itself.' (P. Allott, Written Evidence to the House of Lords Scrutiny of the Intergovernmental Pillars of the European Union (1992-93) HL 124.)

Discuss.

Note

There is much discussion about the nature of the entity into which the Community/Union is evolving. Although not itself a State, the Community (and, to a lesser extent, the Union) possesses an institutional and constitutional sophistication which marks it out from normal intergovernmental associations. Moreover, the creature has developed not only through the formal process of periodic Treaty revision, but also (as will be traced in this book) through wide-ranging legislative action and through the remarkable activism of its Court. So the Community/Union may not be a State, but it displays some State-like features and it affects the nature of the States that are members of it.

It was mentioned above (at p. 13) that Germany was the last State to ratify the Mastricht Treaty and that it did so only after its Constitutional Court (*Bundesverfassungsgericht*) approved ratification. The German Court rejected an individual's constitutional complaint, but the ruling is remarkable for observations about the Treaty-defined limits of Community competence and the inapplicability of acts of the Community's institutions which trespass on areas of exclusive national competence. In the following extract the German Federal Constitutional Court considers its perception of the nature of the European Union, both generally and in the light of Germany's 'Basic Law':

Ruling of the Federal Constitutional Court, Second Division, 12 October 1993, 2 BvR 2134/92, 2 BvR 2159/92 (*Brunner* v *European Union Treaty*)

. . . b 1) The European Union is, in accordance with its understanding of itself as a union of the peoples of Europe (Art. A para. 2 Union Treaty), a confederation of allied democratic states whose objectives include dynamic development (see, e.g., Arts. B para. 1 last indent and C para. 1, Union Treaty). If the Union carries out its sovereign duties and thereby exercises sovereign powers, it is in the first place the nationals of the Member States through their national parliaments who have to legitimise this democratically.

At the same time, with the development of the functions and powers of the Community it becomes increasingly necessary to allow the democratic legitimation and influence provided by way of national parliaments to be accompanied by a representation of the nationals of a Member State through a European Parliament as the source of a supplementary democratic support for the policies of the European Union. With the establishment of union citizenship by the Maastricht Treaty, a lasting legal tie is knotted between the nationals of the individual Member States which, though not as strong as the common nationality of a single state, provides a legally binding expression of the degree of *de facto* community already in existence (see especially Art. 8b paras. 1 and 2, EC Treaty). The influence extending from the citizens of the Union can eventually become a part of the democratic legitimation of the European institutions, to the extent that the peoples of the European Union fulfill the necessary preconditions for such.

Democracy, if it is not to remain as merely a formal principle of accountability, is dependent on the existence of certain pre-legal conditions, such as a continuous free debate between opposing social forces, interests, and ideas, in which political goals become clarified and change course (see 5 BVerfGE 85 at 135, 198 and 205; 69 BVerfGE 315 at 344 *et seq.*) and out of which a public opinion emerges which starts to shape a political will. This also means that the decision-making processes of the organs exercising sovereign powers and the various political objectives pursued can be generally perceived and understood, and therefore that citizens entitled to vote can communicate, in their own language, with the sovereign authority to which they are subject.

Such factual conditions, to the extent that they do not yet exist, can develop in the course of time within the institutional framework of the European Union. Such development to no small extent is dependent on a process for imparting the objectives of the Community institutions and the effects of their decisions to the member nations. Parties, associations, the press and the broadcasting services are as much a medium as a factor of this process, out of which a European public opinion may come into being (see Art. 138a, EC Treaty). The European Council is also eager for more openness and transparency in the European decision-making process (see Birmingham Declaration: A Community close to its citizens nos, 2, 3, BullBReg. No. 115 of 23 Oct. 1992, p. 1058; Final Conclusions of the European Council Presidency in Edinburgh, 11/12 Dec. 1992, part A, sect. 7, and annex 3 BullBReg. No. 140 of 28 Dec. 1992, pp. 1278, 1284 *et seq.*

b 2) In the confederation of allied states formed by the European Union, therefore, democratic legitimation necessarily comes about through the feed-back of the actions of the European institutions into the parliaments of the Member States; within the institutional structure of the Union there is the additional factor (which increases as European nations grow closer together) of the provision of democratic legitimation by means of the European Parliament which is elected by the citizens of the Member States. Already at the present stage of development the legitimation of the European Parliament has a supporting function, which could become stronger were it to be elected by uniform voting rules in all the Member States in accordance with Art. 138 para. 3 of the EC Treaty and if its influence on the policies and legislation of the European Community were to increase. What is decisive is that the democratic bases of the European Union are built up in step with integration, and that as integration proceeds a thriving democracy is also maintained in the Member States. Excessive functions and powers within the sphere of responsibility of the European confederation of states would effectively weaken democracy at the national level, so that the parliaments of the Member States could no longer adequately provide the legitimation for the sovereign power exercised by the Union.

If, as at present, the peoples of the individual states provide democratic legitimation through their national parliaments, limits to the extension of the European Communities' functions and powers are then set by virtue of the democratic principle. Each of the peoples of the individual states is the starting point for the public authority relating to that people. The states need sufficiently important spheres of activity of their own in which the peoples of each can develop and articulate in a process of political will – formation which it legitimates and controls, in order to give legal expression to what – relatively homogeneously – binds the people spiritually, socially, and politically together (see H. Heller, *Politische Demokratie and soziale Homogenität, Gesammelte Schriften*, Vol. 2 (1971), p. 421 at 427 *et seq.*).

From all that it follows that functions and powers of substantial importance must remain for the German *Bundestag*.

c) The exercise of sovereign power through a confederation of allied states such as the European Union is based on authorisations from states which remain sovereign and which in international matters generally act through their governments and thereby control the integration process. It is therefore primarily governmentally determined. If such a community power is to rest on the political will-formation which is supplied by the people of each individual state, and is to that extent democratic, it presupposes that the power is exercised by an entity made up of representatives sent by Member States' governments, which in turn are subject to democratic control. The issue of European legal regulations may – without prejudice to the need for democratic control of the government – as well lie with an institution composed of representatives of Member States' governments, i.e., an executive organ, to a greater extent than would be constitutionally acceptable at national level.

3. As the German voter essentially exercises his right to participate in the democratic legitimation of the institutions and agencies entrusted with sovereign powers by means of the elections for the German *Bundestag*, the *Bundestag* must also decide on German membership in the European Union and on its continuation and development.

Article 38 of the Basic Law is accordingly breached if a law that opens up the German legal system to the direct validity and application of the law of the – supranational – European Communities does not establish with adequate certainty what powers are transferred and the intended program of integration (see 58 BVerfGE 1 at 37). When it is unclear to what extent and degree the German legislature has assented to the transfer of the exercise of sovereign powers, then the European Communities may possibly claim functions and powers that were not specified. That would be equivalent to a general authorisation, and therefore would be a relinquishment of powers, against which Art. 38 of the Basic Law provides protection.

In view of the fact that the text of an international treaty must be negotiated by the treaty parties, the certainty and tightness of the treaty provisions cannot be set in the same way as for a law under parliamentary jurisdiction (see 77 BVerfGE 170 at 231 *et seq.*). What is decisive is that Germany's membership and the pendant rights and duties – especially the immediately binding legal effect of the Communities' actions within the national sphere – have been defined in the Treaty so as to be predictable for the legislature and are enacted by it in the Law on Accession with sufficient certainty (see 58 BVerfGE 1 at 37; 68 BVerfGE 1 at 98 *et seq.*). At the same time that means that subsequent important changes to the integration program set up in the Union Treaty and to the Union's powers of action are no longer covered by the Law on Accession to the present Treaty (see *ibid*; Mosler in *Handbuch des Staatsrechts*, Vol. VII, 1992, sec. 175, n. 60). Thus, if European institutions or agencies were to treat or develop the Union Treaty in a way that was no longer covered by the Treaty in the form that is the basis for the Law on Accession, the resulting legislative instruments would not be legally binding within the sphere of German sovereignty. The German state organs would be prevented, for constitutional reasons, from applying them in Germany. Accordingly, the Federal Constitutional Court reviews legal instruments of European institutions and organs to see whether they remain within the limits of the sovereign rights conferred on them or whether they transgress those limits (see 58 BVerfGE 1 at 30 *et seq*; 75 BVerfGE 223 at 235, 242). . . .

The German Court concluded that the Union Treaty measured up to these standards, thereby clearing the way for German ratification. However, in the later stages of the ruling it reaffirmed its sensitivity to the location of the outer limits of Community competence:

. . . Inasmuch as the Treaties establishing the European Communities on the one hand in limited circumstances confer sovereign rights, and on the other hand regulate Treaty amendments – through a normal and also in a simplified procedure – does this distinction take on meaning for the future treatment of the individual powers. Whereas a dynamic extension of the existing Treaties has been supported so far on the basis of a broad treatment of Art. 235 of the EEC Treaty [now Art. 308 EC] in the sense of a 'lacuna-filling competence' (*Vertragsabrundungskompetenz*) and on the basis of considerations relating to the implied powers of the Communities and of Treaty interpretation as allowing maximum exploitation of Community powers of 'effect utile' (see Zuleeg in: von der Groeben/Thiesing/Ehlermann, *EWG-Vertrag*, 4th ed. 1991, Art. 2, note 3), in future the interpretation of enabling provisions by institutions and agencies of the Community will have to consider that the Union Treaty basically distinguishes between the exercise of a conferred limited sovereign power and the amendment of the Treaty, thus the interpretation will not result in an extension of the Treaty: such an interpretation of enabling provisions would not have a binding effect for Germany. . . .

The *Bundesverfassungsgericht's* parting shot was:

The Maastricht Treaty – especially by the extension of EC competences and the inclusion of monetary policy – confers further essential functions and powers on European organs – which at Treaty level are not yet supported by a corresponding strengthening and extension of the democratic bases. It sets up a new stage of European unification, which according to the stated intentions of the Contracting Parties is to enhance further the democratic and efficient functioning of the institutions (fifth considérant of the Preamble). Democracy and efficiency are here not to be separated; it is also expected that the strengthening of the democratic principle will improve work at the Community level in all its organs. At the same time, in accordance with Art. F para. 1 of the Union Treaty [now Art. 6 TEU], the Union will respect the national identities of its Member States, the governmental systems of which are based on democratic principles. To that extent the Union preserves the democratic bases already existing in the Member States and builds on them.

Any further development of the European Union cannot evade the conceptual framework set out above. The constitution-amending legislature had in connection with this Treaty taken that into account when they inserted Art. 23 into the Basic Law, as there the development of the European Union is expressly mentioned, subject to the principles of democracy and the rule of law, social and federal principles, and the subsidiarity principle. It is decisive, therefore, from the point of view of both the Treaties and of constitutional law, that the democratic bases of the Union will be built in step with integration, and also as integration progresses a living democracy will be maintained in the Member States.

Note
It is hard to read these observations other than as warnings for the future. Note that they are addressed to *all* the Community/Union institutions.

H. Hauser and A. Muller summarise the Court's view in the following terms ((1995) 50 *Aussenwirtschaft* 17, 30):

> EU institutions provide no primary source for democratic legitimisation. The democratic systems of the Member States are the primary source for democratic legitimisation of EU legislation. Because citizen participation is only guaranteed on the national and not on the European level, democratic legitimisation needs clearly defined restrictions on the transfer of sovereignty. National constitutional courts should have the ultimate interpretation whether EU legislation corresponds to the principle of specific delegation of power.

It is important to realise that the German Court is, in effect, threatening to deprive the European Court of exclusive competence to determine the limits of EC competence, but that it is doing so out of a declared perception based on the need to secure effective democratic control of political decision-making. Nevertheless, there is much to be said for the view that the *Bundesverfassungsgericht's* concerns are not prompted by the pattern of the Maastricht Treaty itself, but rather by a belated recognition of expansionist trends in the evolution of Community law and policy through legislative and judicial activism over an extended period (the subject matter of this book!). J. Weiler suggests that for the *Bundesverfassungsgericht* 'the only way out was to legitimate the past by . . . weak notions of Member State democratic mediation, and put the polity on notice that German constitutionalism will not be caught napping again.' ('Does Europe need a Constitution? Reflections on Demos, Telos, and the German Maastricht Decision') (1995) 1 *European Law Journal* 219, 237). It will be suggested at several points in this book that a new post-Maastricht sensitivity affects the Community institutions when they are invited to act at the outer limits of Community competence; and that this is in part attributable to an awareness that the Community system, built on willing and active cooperation between Community and national bodies, can survive only if negative reactions at national level are absorbed and answered at Community level.

The following two extracts build beyond the 'Maastricht ruling' of the *Bundesverfassungsgericht* to discuss the present and future shaping of the Union.

H. Hauser and A. Müller, 'Legitimacy: The Missing Link for Explaining EU-Institution Building' (1995) 50 *Aussenwirtschaft* 17, 18–22

(Footnotes omitted, small linguistic alterations made with the copyright holder's permission.)

1.1. FROM INTERGOVERNMENTAL TO SUPRANATIONAL

The EU is an institution 'sui generis' with no historical precedent. Accordingly, it is difficult to describe the institution in traditional terms. . . . The institutional structure goes far beyond an international agreement between sovereign states, even beyond a confederation between sovereign states with unlimited veto power. On the other hand, the EU clearly lacks main features of a federal state. Until now the European Union was qualified as a supranational co-operation, but this organisation never achieved the quality of a state. The Preamble speaks about the growing union of the peoples of Europe. It is difficult to qualify the nature of the European Union, e.g. the German Constitutional Court in the judgment of Maastricht talks about a 'parent organisation' . . . and other new qualifications. Similarly, when the German Constitutional Court talks about the future of Europe, it explains itself very carefully, 'state-connection' . . . and 'growing union of the peoples of Europe' . . . are expressions which reveal its fear of becoming more concrete. The Court describes the European Union not as no state, not even a 'federal' one . . ., but as a process of integration of its own nature as an 'interstate establishment'. . . . The complex structure of supranational and intergovernmental elements in institutions and decision making processes must be at the core of a theoretical discussion of EU institutional development.

The Treaty incorporates two intergovernmental pillars, whereas the EC pillar contains intergovernmental as well as supranational elements. A mix of intergovernmental and supranational can also be observed in procedural questions. The most striking examples for this complex set of supranational and intergovernmental elements are the following:

(a) The EC as economic pillar of the EU has strong supranational elements whereas CFSP and WEU as well as the cooperation in the field of justice and Home Affairs have intergovernmental structures. Besides the competences of the Union which are exercised on a supranational level, the intergovernmental competences also have to be regarded. The CFSP is an example of unfinished integration, it is still an intergovernmental co-operation. The Member States remain responsible in this area even if the competences have been brought nearer to the European Union. But even if operations are organised in common (Art. J.3 and Art. K. 3 2 EU), the decisions can only be made unanimously.

(b) Revisions of the supranational EU treaty are prepared by intergovernmental conferences and not by a constitutional assembly. The intergovernmental orientation of constitutional amendments is also exemplified by the fact that they need unanimous approval by all member states. Article N EU Treaty says: '*The amendments shall enter into force after being ratified by all Member States in accordance with their respective constitutional requirements.*'

(c) In the exercise of competences, the mix between intergovernmental and supranational aspects is also obvious. Competences of the EU must be based on specific delegation of power by the Treaty. The union can only legislate in areas which are directly mentioned in the Treaty of Maastricht. As a general rule. 'exclusive competences' . . . of the European Union have to be the exception and are only accepted under restrictive conditions. If the European Union is not explicitly entitled to act, competences remain with the Member States. Nevertheless, this principle does not have the intended limiting effect, because the European Court of Justice developed the theory of implied powers, which justifies further regulations if it is in the logic of the goals of integration. Even if a regulation has no basis in the Treaty, it can be enacted by the Union due to this principle. The teleological interpretation of EU competences by the European Court of Justice and the former frequent use of Art. 235 of the EC Treaty have opened the door for expanding EU competences and have reduced the binding effect of the principle of specific delegation.

(d) The legislative power of the EU is further strengthened by the priority of European law over national law and by the judgments of the European Court of

Justice, which have 'prejudicial effects' on judgments of the national courts. The recent Karlsruhe decision of the German Constitutional Court [on the Maastricht Treaty, above] highlights a fundamental ambiguity: Should the European Court of Justice or should national constitutional courts of member countries decide in the event of disagreement on the separation of power between the EU and its Member States? Presently, we have no case in question, but the potential for future conflicts exists. Jurisprudence of the Court of Justice clearly states that a decision about the distribution of competences is only decided by the European Court of Justice, whereas the ruling of Karlsruhe places the final decision about the distribution of competences in the hands of national self-determination.

(e)   It is difficult to decide whether decision making in the EU is supranational or intergovernmental. The important role of the Commission, co-decision rights of the Parliament and majority voting in the Council are clearly supranational elements. The fact that legislative power is vested primarily with the Council, which is composed of delegate ministers of member states, the fact that important decisions, particularly in fiscal issues, still require unanimity, and the decision procedures for defining fiscal guidelines are closer to intergovernmental structures. Intergovernmental is also the distribution of voting rights, which give smaller Member States a more than proportional representation in decision-making. By the Treaty of Maastricht, the Parliament acquires co-decision, but this does not give Parliament the final say in the legislative procedure. All legislation must still be approved by the Council, so the democratic deficit problem remains. Nevertheless, a veto by the Parliament ends the legislative process. The co-decision procedure has only led to a modest increase in the Parliament's participation.

(f)   The evolution toward a supranational organisation is also reflected in the ambition to create a 'European Law' having primacy over the national legislatures. EU primary law, within the limitations of direct applicability as defined by the European Court of Justice, and regulations as part of secondary law is clearly supranational law. Directives must be translated into national law by the national legislature, but the increasing specificity of directives and the ruling of the European Court of Justice that directives can develop direct applicability under certain conditions bring them also very close to supranational law. EU institutions can create directly applicable supranational law within a broad range of competences with unclear boundaries. At least in the field of economic regulation, there seem to be no effective constitutional restrictions for EU institutions to take over responsibility. According to the European Court of Justice, the European Treaty is seen as a Constitution and has priority over national constitutions. Since the Treaty of Maastricht, the ruling of the Court has even more importance under the new Article 171 [now Art. 228 EC]: '*If the Member State concerned fails to take the necessary measures to comply with the Court's judgment within the time-limit laid down by the Commission, the latter may bring the case before the Court of Justice. In so doing it shall specify the amount of the lump or penalty payment to be paid by the Member State concerned which it considered appropriate in the circumstances. If the Court of Justice finds that the Member State concerned has not complied with its judgment it may impose a lump sum or penalty payment on it.*' This possibility of the European Court of Justice to force Member States to transform EU ruling into national legislation points out the strong supranational power of the EU.

To summarise: Institutional tensions in the EU can best be explained by the weak correspondence between the distribution of power to regulate and the institutional structure of decision making. With regard to the separation of power in the field of economic regulation, the EU comes very close to a federation: within the broad competences of the Maastricht Treaty, EU institutions decide on the separation of power (with the restriction of unanimity vote in some areas), the European Court of Justice has the right for authoritative interpretation, in areas of majority voting Member States have lost control over future regulation. Institutional structures do not follow these developments. The separation of power within the EU does not correspond to requirements of a democratic state: EU legislation is in the hands of members of the executive of Member States, the executive function in the EU is a shared responsibility of the Commission and the Council, the exclusive right to initiatives gives the Commission an important role in the legislative process, members of the Commission and of the European Court of Justice are delegated by national governments and not appointed by the legislator.

The tension between the regulative power of a federation and the weak institutional structure which does not meet basic requirements of a democratic state is at the heart of most critical voices in the academic and political debate. They should also be a primary focus of the intergovernmental conference on institutional reforms of 1996. Complaints about democratic deficits, weak accountability of EU institutions, inefficient decision procedures, or over-centralisation are the symptoms. Reforms to either better restrict EU competences or to develop democratic EU institutions are proposals to ease the underlying tensions. . . .

J. Habermas, 'Remarks on Dieter Grimm's "Does Europe Need a Constitution?"' (1995) 1 *European Law Journal* 303–307

The Diagnosis
From a constitutional perspective, one may discern a contradiction in the European Union's present situation. On the one hand, the EU is a supranational organisation established by international treaties and without a constitution of its own. In this respect it is not a state (in the modern sense of a constitutional state characterised by a monopoly on violence and a domestically and internationally recognised sovereignty). On the other hand, Community institutions create European law that binds the Member States – thus the EU exercises a supreme authority previously claimed only by individual states. From this results the oft-bemoaned democratic deficit. Commission and Council pronouncements, as well as decisions by the European Court, are intervening ever more profoundly into the Member States' internal affairs. Within the framework of the rights conferred upon the Union, the European Executive may enforce its pronouncements over and against the opposition of the national governments. At the same time, as long as the European Parliament is equipped with only weak competences, these pronouncements and enactments lack direct democratic legitimation. The executive institutions of the community derive their legitimacy from that of the member governments. They are not institutions of a state that is itself constituted by the act of will on the part of the united citizens of Europe. The European passport is not as yet associated with rights constitutive for democratic citizenship.

Political Conclusion
In contrast with the Federalists, who recommend a democratic pattern for the EU, Grimm warns [in an article to be found in the ṣame issue of the *European Law Journal*] against any further European-law-induced eroding of national competences. The democratic deficit would not be effectively filled by a 'statist shortcut' to the problem, but rather deepened. New political institutions such as a European Parliament with

the usual powers, a government formed out of the Commission, a Second Chamber replacing the Council, and a European Court of Justice with expanded competences, as such offer no solutions. If they are not filled with life, they will instead accelerate tendencies already apparent within the national frameworks, tendencies towards autonomisation of bureaucratised politics. The real prerequisites for a European-wide integration of citizen will-formation have been absent up to now. Constitutional Euroscepticism thus amounts to the empirically-based argument that runs as such: as long as there is not a European people which is sufficiently 'homogenous' to form a democratic will, there should be no constitution.

The Discussion
My reflections are directed against (a) the insufficient account of alternative courses and (b) the not entirely unambiguous normative underpinnings of the functional requirements for democratic will-formation.

(a) Grimm sets before us the undesired consequences that would result from the transition of the European Community to a democratically-constituted, federal state should the new institutions not take root. So long as a European-networked civil society, a European-wide political public sphere and a common political culture are lacking, the supranational decision processes would become increasingly independent of the still nationally organised opinion- and will-formation processes. This dangerous prognosis is plausible as far as I am concerned. However what is the alternative? Grimm's option seems to suggest that the constitutional status quo can at least freeze the extant democratic deficit. Completely independent of constitutional innovations however this deficit expands day by day because the economic and social dynamics even within the existing institutional framework perpetuate the erosion of national powers through European law. As Grimm himself acknowledges: 'The democratic principle is valid for the Member States whose own decision capabilities are however diminishing: decisional capability is accruing to the European Community where the democracy principle is developing only weakly.' But if the gap is steadily widening between the European authorities' expanding scope and the inadequate legitimation of the proliferating European regulations, then decisively adhering to an exclusively nation-state mode of legitimation does not necessarily mean opting for the lesser evil. The Federalists at least face the foreseeable - and perhaps avoidable - risk of the autonomisation of supranational organisations as a challenge. The Eurosceptics have, from the start, acquiesced in the supposedly irresistible erosion of democratic substance so that they do not have to leave what appears as the reliable shelter of the nation-state.

In fact the shelter is becoming increasingly less comfortable. The debates on national economic competitiveness and the international division of labour in which we are engaged make us aware of quite another gap – a gap between the nation state's increasingly limited maneuverability, and the imperatives of modes of production interwoven worldwide. Modern revenue-states profit from their respective economies only so long as there are 'national economies' that can still be influenced by political means. With the denationalisation of the economy, especially of the financial markets and of industrial production itself, national governments today are increasingly compelled to accept permanently high unemployment and the marginalisation of a growing minority for the sake of international competitiveness. If there is to be at least some substantive maintaining of the welfare state and some avoiding the further segmentation of an underclass, then institutions capable of acting supranationally must be formed. Only regionally comprehensive regimes like the European Community can still affect the global system in line with a coordinated world domestic policy.

In Grimm's account, the EU appears as an institution to be *put up with*, and with whose abstractions we must live. The reasons why we should *want* it politically are not presented. I would submit that the greater danger is posed by the autonomisation of globalised networks and markets which simultaneously contribute to the fragmentation of public consciousness. If these systemic pressures are not met by politically capable institutions then the crippling fatalism of the Old Empires will grow again in the midst of a highly mobile economic modernity. The decisive elements of this future scenario would be the postindustrial misery of the 'surplus' population produced by the surplus society – the Third world within the First – and an accompanying moral erosion of community. *This* future-present would in retrospect view itself as the future of a past illusion – the democratic illusion according to which societies could still determine their own destinies through political will and consciousness.

(b)   *Apropos* the second problem. Naturally any assessment of the chances for a European-wide democracy depends in the first place upon empirically grounded arguments. But we first have to determine the functional requirements; and for that the normative perspective in which the former are supposed to fit is crucial.

Grimm rejects a European constitution 'because there is as yet no European people'. This would on first glance seem founded upon the same premise that informed the tenor of the German Constitutional Court's Maastricht judgment: namely, the view that the basis of the state's democratic legitimation requires a certain homogeneity of the state-constituting people. However Grimm immediately distances himself from a Schmittian kind of definition of *völkischen* homogeneity: 'The presuppositions for democracy are developed here not of the people, but from the society that wants to constitute itself as a political unit. But this presumes a collective identity, if it wants to settle its conflicts without violence, accept majority rule and practice solidarity.' This formulation leaves open the question of how the called-for collective identity is to be understood. I see the nub of republicanism in the fact that the forms and procedures of the constitutional state together with the democratic mode of legitimation simultaneously forge a new level of social integration. Democratic citizenship establishes an abstract, legally mediated solidarity among strangers. This form of social integration which first emerges with the nation-state is realised in the form of a politically socialising *communicative context*. Indeed this is dependent upon the satisfaction of certain important functional requirements that cannot be fulfilled by administrative means. To these belong conditions in which an ethical political self-understanding of citizens can communicatively develop and likewise be reproduced – but in no way a collective identity that is *independent of the democratic process itself* and as such existing prior to that process. What unites a nation of citizens as opposed to a *Volksnation* is not some primordial substrate but rather an intersubjectively shared context of possible understanding.

It is therefore crucial in this context whether one uses the term 'people' in the juristically neutral sense of 'state-constituting people', or whether one associates the term with notions of identity of some other kind. In Grimm's view the identity of a nation of citizens 'need not' be 'rooted in ethnic origin, but may also have other bases'. I think on the contrary that it *must* have another basis if the democratic process is to finally guarantee the social integration of a differentiated – and today increasingly differentiating – society. This burden must not be shifted from the levels of political will-formation to pre-political, pre-supposed substrates because the constitutional state guarantees that it will foster necessary social integration in the legally abstract form of political participation and that it will actually secure the status of citizenship in democratic ways. The examples of culturally and ideologically pluralistic societies only serve to emphasise this normative point. The multicultural self-understanding of the nations of citizens formed in classical countries of immigration like the USA is more instructive in this respect than that derived from the assimilationist French model. If in the same democratic political community various cultural, religious and ethnic forms of life are to exist among and with each other then the majority culture must be sufficiently detached from its traditional fusion with the *political* culture shared by all citizens.

To be sure, a politically constituted context of solidarity among citizens who despite remaining strangers to one another are supposed to stand up for each other is a communicative context *rich in prerequisites*. In this point there is no dissent. The core is formed by a political public sphere which enables citizens to take positions at the same time on the same topics of the same relevance. This public sphere must be deformed neither through external nor internal coercion. It must be embedded in the context of a freedom-valuing political culture and be supported by a liberal associational structure of a civil society. Socially relevant experience from still-intact private spheres must flow into such a civil society so that they may be processed there for public treatment. The political parties – not state-dependent – must remain rooted in this complex so as to mediate between the spheres of informal public communication, on the one hand, and the institutionalised deliberation and decision processes, on the other. Accordingly, from a normative perspective, there can be no European Federal state worthy of the name of a democratic Europe unless a European-wide, integrated public sphere develops in the ambit of a common political culture: a civil society with interest associations; non-governmental organisations; citizens' movements etc.; and naturally a party system appropriate to a European arena. In short, this entails public communication that transcends the boundaries of the until now limited national public spheres.

Certainly, the ambitious functional requirements of democratic will-formation can scarcely be fulfilled in the nation-state framework; this is all the more true for Europe. What concerns me, however, is the perspective from which these functional prerequisites are normatively justified; for this, as it were, prejudices the empirical evaluation of the present difficulties. These must, for the time being, seem insuperable if a pre-political collective identity is regarded as necessary, that is an independent cultural substrate which is *articulated only* in the fulfilment of the said functional requirements. But a communications-theoretical understanding of democracy, one that Grimm also seems to favour, can no longer rest upon such a concretistic understanding of 'the people'. This notion falsely pretends homogeneity, where in fact something still quite heterogeneous is met.

The ethical-political self-understanding of citizens in a democratic community must not be taken as an historical-cultural *a priori* that makes democratic will-formation possible, but rather as the flowing contents of a circulatory process that is generated through the legal institutionalisation of citizens' communication. This is precisely how national identities were formed in modern Europe. Therefore it is to be expected that the political institutions to be created by a European constitution would have an inducing effect. Europe has been integrating economically, socially and administratively for some time and in addition can base itself on a common cultural background and the shared historical experience of having happily overcome nationalism. Given the political will, there is no *a priori* reason why it cannot subsequently create the politically necessary communicative context as soon as it is constitutionally *prepared* to do so. Even the requirement of a common language – English as a second first language – ought not be an insurmountable obstacle with the existing level of formal schooling. European identity can in any case mean nothing other than unity in national diversity. And perhaps German Federalism, as it developed after Prussia was shattered and the confessional division overcome, might not be the worst model.

Question
How can democratic participation best be secured within the EU? Insofar as the EU is a response to the inadequacies of a system based on the nation state, is it helpful to look to the national level as a model for the future institutional and constitutional development of the EU?

Further reading on the constitutional debate
Special Issue on Sovereignty, Citizenship and the European Constitution, (1995) 1/3 *European Law Journal.*
Special Issue on Legal Theory in the European Union, (1998) 4/4 *European Law Journal.*
Special Issue on Constructing Legal Systems: '"European Union" in Legal Theory', (1997) 16/4 *Law and Philosophy.*
Special Issue on The European Union and a Changing European Order, (1996) 34/1 *Journal of Common Market Studies.*
Boom, S. J., 'The European Union after the Maastricht Decision: Will Germany be the 'Virginia of Europe'?' (1995) XLIII Amer J Comp Law 177.
Craig, P., 'Democracy and Rule-Making within the EC: an Empirical and Normative Assessment' (1997) 3 ELJ 105.
Joerges, C., 'Taking the Law Seriously: On Political Science and the Role of Law in the Process of European Integration' (1996) 2 ELJ 195.
MacCormick, N., 'Beyond the Sovereign State' (1993) 56 MLR 1.
Marks, G., Hooghe, L., and Blank, K., 'European Integration from the 1980s' (1996) 34 JCMS 341.
Petersmann, E.-U., 'Proposals for a New Constitution for the European Union: Building Blocks for a Constitutional Theory and Constitutional Law of the EU' (1995) 32 CML Rev 1123.
Piris, J.-C., 'After Maastricht, are the Community Insitutions more Efficacious, more Democratic and more Transparent?' (1994) 19 El Rev 449.
Stone Sweet, A., and Sandholtz, W., 'European integration and supranational governance' (1997) 4 JEPP 297.
Zuleeg, M., 'The European Constitution under Constitutional Constraints: The German Scenario' (1997) 22 EL Rev 19.

Note
The *Bundesverfassungsgericht's* apparent refusal to accept that the European Court has exclusive jurisdiction to decide on the validity of Community law may imperil the uniform application of EC law, but words, if not deeds, emanating from other supreme courts in the Member States have also begun to display attitudes which do not correspond to the European Court's own approach to the nature of EC law (which is examined in this book, see Chapters 2 to 4, and 16 in particular). It is, of course, in the interest of the

European Court to maintain the loyal support of national courts, for the evolution of the EC legal system and its practical enforcement depend heavily on the inter-penetration of Community law and national law. Coercive measures are not available to the European Court, so it must seek to persuade. This is an intriguing process given the depth of the constitutional issues at stake, mapped in the previous pages. See A.-M. Slaughter, A. Stone Sweet and J. Weiler (eds), *The European Courts and National Courts: Doctrine and Jurisprudence* (Hart Publishing, 1997); M. Kumm, 'Who is the final arbiter of constitutionality in Europe?' (1999) 36 CMLRev 351, to which C. Schmid responds at (1999) 36 CMLRev 509; and, reviewing the case law concerning the regulation of banana markets which has generated incidents that have veered closest to taking this constitutional conflict from the realms of the possible to the actual, see S. Peers, 'Banana split: WTO law and preferential agreements in the EC legal order' (1999) 4 *European Foreign Affairs Review* 195. You should also read P. Kirchhof, 'The Balance of Powers between National and European institutions' (1999) 5 ELJ 225; the author is a member of the *Bundesverfassungsgericht* and widely supposed to have exerted significant influence over the drafting of its 'Maastricht' judgment. It is of interest that his discussion includes explicit reference to judicial anxieties expressed in other Member States (pp. 240–41). In the chapters that follow examination of judicial attitudes to the shaping of EC law will need to be undertaken with awareness of the underlying depth of the constitutional issues. These are debates of persisting importance.

Question

. . . [S]tates in the European Union are being melded gently into a multilevel polity by their leaders and by the actions of numerous subnational and supranational actors. State-centric theorists are right when they argue that states are extremely powerful institutions that are capable of crushing direct threats to their existence. The organizational form of the state emerged because it proved a particularly effective means of systematically wielding violence, and it is difficult to imagine any generalized challenge along these lines. But this is not the only, nor even the most important, issue facing the institution of the state. One does not have to argue that states are on the verge of political extinction to believe that their control of those living in their territories has significantly weakened. (L. Hooghe and G. Marks, 'Contending Models of Governance in the European Union', in A. Cafruny and C. Lankowski, *Europe's Ambiguous Unity: Conflict and Consensus in the Post-Maastricht era* (1997), Ch. 1, p. 38.)

Assess the contribution of the European Union to the weakening of state power.

Note
The process of Treaty revision continues. As advertised by Hauser and Müller (above, p. 22), an intergovernmental conference opened in Turin in March 1996 and was concluded at Amsterdam in June 1997, where the Treaty of

Amsterdam was agreed. It was formally signed in October 1999. The Treaty of Amsterdam secured ratification according to domestic constitutional procedures in the 15 Member States while attracting noticeably less opposition than the Maastricht Treaty and it duly entered into force on 1 May 1999. Its principal features are explained below. It will be immediately apparent that there was no attempt at Amsterdam to address the grand issues of legitimacy exposed in the preceding pages of this book. The Amsterdam changes are incremental.

Already post-Maastricht, the legal structure of the Union, understood in formal terms, was not one-dimensional. There is EC law, which is part of EU law. There is also 'non-EC EU law', emerging from the other two pillars of the Union. What emerges from the traditional architecture of the EC – from the EC Treaty itself, and from the activity of the Council, Commission and Parliament, all of which is supervised by the Courts – is called EC law in this book, despite the case for replacing that term with 'EU law'. As yet, it is submitted that completely to replace the label 'EC law' with 'EU law' is to misrepresent the divided and peculiar reality of the three-pillar EU. However, such scrupulousness may eventually have to be set aside. As the practice of the EU evolved post-Maastricht it was increasingly possible to make a case in favour of fusion based on legal analysis and on observation of practice. The Amsterdam Treaty adds velocity to this trend (see A. Von Bogdandy, 'The legal case for unity: the EU as a single organisation with a single legal system' (1999) 36 CMLRev 887; B. De Witte, 'The Pillar Structure and the Nature of the European Union: Greek Temple or French Gothic Cathedral?' in T. Heukels, N. Blokker and M. Brus, *The European Union after Amsterdam* (Kluwer Law International, 1998)). In principle, the EU after Amsterdam maintains the three-pillar structure of the Union presented in diagramatic form at p. 13 above. However, it moves material between the pillars (especially in favour of the first pillar, the EC, at the expense of the third, formerly dealing with Justice and Home Affairs but now re-styled Provisions on Police and Judicial Co-operation in Criminal Matters). Crucially, as part of the package deal according to which these apparent additions to the scope of *communautaire* method were made, aspects of 'non-EC EU' method are now absorbed into the EC pillar, while, conversely, the third pillar is itself endowed with characteristics of a type more familiar to the EC pillar (for example, a much enhanced role for the European Court, largely shut out of the third pillar by the Maastricht Treaty). So there are clear signs of a move towards a unified 'EU legal order' involving a rapprochement between the EC and the non-EC EU, which for Advocate General Fennelly, writing in his personal capacity, represents 'the most positive general aspect of the Amsterdam Treaty' ('Preserving the Legal Coherence within the new Treaty' (1998) 5 MJ 185). But this process of rapprochement is not yet complete. And, in fact, there are counter trends towards fragmentation, because, as will be seen in this book, legal sub-systems of an increasingly distinct nature govern matters such as the law of persons (p. 192), economic and monetary union (p. 211) and, broader still, the Amsterdam innovation of 'closer cooperation' involving enhanced activity in common agreed by most but not all Member States (p. 635).

Try not to confuse EC law 'pre-Amsterdam' and EC law 'post-Amsterdam'; although there is a disturbing source of confusion created by the Amsterdam Treaty's most immediately visible feature, the re-numbering from start to finish of the whole EC Treaty and of the EU Treaty (Article 12 of the Treaty of Amsterdam). Both Treaties now run from Article 1 upwards (to Article 314 in the case of the EC Treaty; Article 53 in the EU Treaty). This cleans out the unwieldy insertions made by the Single European Act and the Maastricht Treaty that littered the EC Treaty with Articles denoted as numbers-plus-letters (e.g. Articles 3b, 100a); and it eliminates entirely the lettering system used in the TEU (which in turn makes it now vital to be clear whether one is referring to the EC Treaty or to the TEU since both use numbers). The obvious disadvantage of this spring-clean lies in the need to become accustomed to the replacement of familiar numbers for Articles of the Treaty with new numbers. Article 30 became Article 28; Article 177, Article 234, and so on. This change will always have to be borne in mind when reading pre-Amsterdam texts, including legislation and Court judgments, and in fact the EC lawyer will need to become adept at this form of 'currency conversion'. Page 1 of this book contains the table of equivalence between the previous and the new numbering which is annexed to the Amsterdam Treaty, and the reader will find frequent resort to that table invaluable while he or she is making the necessary mental adjustments. Moreover (see Preface, p. ix above), references to the numerical changes are made in introducing key Treaty provisions throughout the book. The Court's own approach to the citation of Treaty articles is set out at p. lxi above, and this will be adhered to in this book.

The Treaty of Amsterdam amends the Treaty on European Union, the Treaties establishing the European Communities and certain related acts. It achieves this according to the following structure:

Part One of the Treaty of Amsterdam, entitled 'Substantive Amendments', comprises Articles 1–5.

Article 1 of the Treaty of Amsterdam amends the Treaty on European Union. Prominent features include:

- The 'second pillar' (p. 13 above), dealing with common foreign and security policy, is substantially re-worked.
- Provision is made for the suspension of a Member State guilty of serious and persistent breach of the principles concerning fundamental rights mentioned in Article 7 EU (p. 73 below).
- The 'third pillar', concerning justice and home affairs, is re-worked and is now entitled 'Provisions on police and judicial co-operation in criminal matters'. Notable features include a modest enhancement of the role of the European Court in this area (Article 35 EU); and provisions envisaging closer cooperation between some, but not all, Member States in pursuit of accelerated development towards an area of freedom, security and justice (Article 40 EU, and see p. 636 below). Of greatest significance, however, is the transfer of material relevant to the free movement of

people within the Union from the third pillar to the first pillar, the EC; see diagram at p. 13 above and more fully p. 192 below.

Article 2 of the Treaty of Amsterdam amends the EC Treaty. There is a mass of detailed adjustments, many of which are mentioned throughout this book, but prominent features include:

- A new provision envisaging closer cooperation between some, but not all, Member States (Article 11 EC, see p. 635 below).
- A new provision creating a power to legislate by unanimous vote in Council in order to combat discrimination based on sex, racial or ethnic origin, religion or belief, disability, age or sexual orientation (Article 13 EC).
- A new Title on 'Visas, asylum, immigration and other policies related to free movement of persons' which is dedicated to the progressive establishment of 'an area of freedom, security and justice'. This is Title IV and comprises Articles 61–69 EC. The Title is built around a five-year timetable for dismantling internal borders, although special provision is made in Protocols to the Treaty for Denmark, the United Kingdom and Ireland; see further p. 192 below. This Title in the EC Treaty is home to modified versions of material allocated to the 'third pillar', on justice and home affairs, by the Maastricht Treaty on European Union. This suggests that Amsterdam saw a triumph of EC institutional and constitutional method over the species of intergovernmentalism found in the non-EC EU, although that perspective should be tempered by awareness that the new Title, although part of the EC Treaty, is marked by some aspects which are alien to the EC system, notably with regard to the role of the Court (p. 196 below).
- A new Title on Employment. This is Title VIII and comprises Articles 125–130 EC.
- The former Articles 117–120 dealing with social policy are replaced by a new set of provisions, Articles 136–143 EC; (p. 622 below). These have as their core mission the abandonment of the Maastricht arrangements, which caused a rupture in the uniform application of EC social policy by providing that all the Member States except the UK would be enabled to deepen their rule-making via the Social Policy Protocol-plus-Agreement. The deepening now occurs within the context of the Treaty 'proper' and binds all the Member States; the Protocol is repealed by Article 2 of the Amsterdam Treaty.
- The so-called 'co-decision' procedure, involving both Council and Parliament as the Community legislator, has been streamlined and is more widely applicable. This is Article 251 EC.

Article 3 of the Treaty of Amsterdam amends the European Coal and Steel Community Treaty; *Article 4* amends the European Atomic Energy Community Treaty; *Article 5* amends the Act concerning the election of the representatives of the European Parliament by direct universal suffrage annexed to the Council Decision of 20 September 1976.

Part Two of the Treaty of Amsterdam, entitled 'Simplification', comprises Articles 6–11. Of most significance to this book is *Article 6 of the Treaty*, which makes 81 separate amendments to the EC Treaty and, in addition, further amendments to the annexes and protocols. These alterations are designed to delete lapsed provisions and to adapt other provisions in consequence. *Articles 7 and 8* 'simplify' the ECSC and the EURATOM Treaties respectively.

Part Three of the Treaty of Amsterdam, 'General and Final Provisions', comprises Articles 12–15, and the Treaty then concludes with a string of Protocols, 51 Declarations adopted by the Conference and 8 further Declarations of which the Conference took note.

Further reading on the Amsterdam Treaty

Special Issue, 'The European Union and the Treaty of Amsterdam', (1999) 22 *Fordham International Law Journal*.

Favret, B., 'Le Traité d'Amsterdam: une revision à minima de la Charte constitutionnelle de l'Union européenne' (1997) 33 CDE 555.

Heukels, T., Blokker, N. and Brus, M., *The European Union after Amsterdam* (Kluwer Law International, Dordrecht, 1998).

Moravscik, A., and Nicolaides, K., 'Explaining the Treaty of Amsterdam' (1999) 37 JCMS 59.

O'Keeffe, D. and Twomey, P., 'Legal Issues of the Amsterdam Treaty' (Hart Publishing, Oxford, 1999 – a collection of 23 essays).

Pernice, I., 'Multilevel Constitutionalism and the Treaty of Amsterdam: European Constitution-Making Revisited?' (1999) 36 CML Rev 703.

Piris, J.-C., 'Does the European Union have a Constitution? Does it need one?' (1999)24 EL Rev 557.

For good or ill (*cf* p. 14 above), the Amsterdam Treaty seems bereft of any 'big idea'. Even the quest for institutional reform to render the EU ready for enlargement was in part fruitless; decisions on, for example, reducing the number of Commissioners were left for future resolution. For J. Weiler, finding 'no shared agenda and no mobilising force behind the exercise', this was 'an Intergovernmental Conference which should never have started'; and in the light of the complexity of the unresolved issues, 'it was, too, an Intergovernmental Conference which should never have ended'. The product was 'an inconclusive Treaty leaving all hard issues for tomorrow' ((1997) 3 ELJ, Editorial, 309, 310). The following extract reflects the sense of unfinished business.

Michel Petite, *The Treaty of Amsterdam*

(1998), published as a Harvard Jean Monnet Chair Working Paper, 2/98 available at http://www.law.harvard.edu/Programs/JeanMonnet

CONCLUSION

Predicting the future role of the Treaty is a hazardous business. The Single Act, adopted in a climate of indifference, proved a powerful tool for federalisation. The

Maastricht Treaty, on the other hand, was ratified with the greatest of difficulty but probably did not radically transform existing practice, with the exception of the single currency, yet still managed to divide opinion into pro- and anti-Maastricht camps and coin a whole new vocabulary to go with it.

The issues and content of the Amsterdam Treaty were partly overshadowed at the Amsterdam Summit by the simultaneous debate on the Stability Pact to accompany EMU. It was greeted with scepticism for failing to reach agreement on some of the aspects exposed to the most intense media coverage because they supposedly pitted the large states against the smaller ones.
. . .

The Amsterdam Treaty is by no means the last word on European integration. Like its predecessors it marks a further stage in the process. However one views it, it probably represents the most that the Member States were prepared to agree among themselves at a given moment. And like any treaty, everything will depend on what is made of it in practice.

It does, however, have some potential strengths (the role of the European Parliament; the change in the status of justice and home affairs; perhaps a new landmark in the creation of a European foreign policy; the chapter on employment) and several likely weaknesses (institutional questions, particularly the retention of the unanimity requirement for too many decisions). These will certainly give rise to further conferences, some of which have already been scheduled.

Commentators who were hoping for some great institutional overhaul before enlargement have been disappointed and have consequently written Amsterdam off as a fiasco or farce. But it has to be said that after two years of reflection the great institutional debate has proved to be curiously vacuous and misguided.

If the debate boils down to the measures proposed but not agreed in Amsterdam, these hardly amounted to the major reform for which such rash claims were sometimes made:

– the reweighting of votes in the Council, which was justified to some extent to offset the impact of enlargement, was couched in political terms and thus became a political problem. But if we look more closely at the issue and add up the numbers involved, a reweighting of the majority according to any of the formulas envisaged in Amsterdam would have produced no change whatever in any of the decisions adopted by the Council over the past three years;

– the question of the number of Commissioners is more fundamental, and the case for slimming down the Commission is a strong one. But if it is simply a matter of whether there should be 20 or 26 Commissioners it is hard to see this as the tremendous reform that would transform the workings of the Union.

Two simple remarks suggest cause for both humility and perseverance:

– firstly, all of the delegations asserted their commitment to maintaining the institutional balance (yet this balance is constantly shifting, as exemplified by the increased role of the European Parliament); this commitment means that everyone wants to build on the foundations of the achievements of forty years of European integration – and will continue to do so for the foreseeable future. There will be no *tabula rasa* on which radically new institutional formulas will be rebuilt;

– secondly, there is no magic formula that can confound the mathematics: the organisation will inevitably be more difficult for a group of 21, 26 or 30 than one of 6 or even 15. Enlargement has certain inherent consequences.

What this amounts to is that the reforms to be undertaken in response to the demands of enlargement cannot be achieved by new constitutional formulas so much as by a less headline-grabbing series of changes to the way our institutions operate. Most of these reforms are a question of fine-tuning, and many rightfully belong in the internal rules of procedure rather than in the Treaty itself.

The Commission, for example, is currently reexamining the way its departments operate and experimenting with working methods involving groups of Commissioners. [Note p. 8 above and reform of the Commission in the wake of the 'mass resignation' in 1999.] The most urgent measures should probably relate to the Council, as the institution most affected by the increase in its membership. Problems with conducting meetings and discussions and administering implementing measures all increase exponentially as the number of members grows. Written procedures need to be invented, authority has to be delegated more systematically, and a rationalisation of the General Affairs Council is essential. None of these points requires an amendment to the Treaty. The same cannot be said of a reweighting of votes in the Council, but freed of the political baggage with which it has been encumbered it can join the ranks of those adjustments that should not be insurmountable.

Apart from these much needed operational improvements, does this mean there is no such thing as a single, important, easily identifiable institutional reform which would enable us to look ahead to enlargement without apprehension?

Not exactly. In fact we have known for some time that what is required is an end to unanimous decision-making and the general use of qualified majority voting. It is on this score that the Treaty still has far to go: in the short term for justice and home affairs, progressively for foreign policy decisions, and ultimately, when everyone is mentally ready for it, for amending the Treaty itself.

Note

As Petite mentions, some institutional and constitutional questions, relating most of all to Council voting and the composition of the Commission, were left unresolved by the Amsterdam Treaty. These need to be settled in order to re-shape the Union's institutional architecture in anticipation of the pressures imposed by enlargement into central and eastern Europe, which presents itself as the next great challenge for the European Union. Accession negotiations are under way with a number of applicant States, and in the meantime a new intergovernmental conference opened in February 2000. Its progress may be followed via the 'europa' web site, http://europa.eu.int. The target was the end of 2000 for completion of the conference so that a further amending Treaty may enter into force sufficiently rapidly to perform surgery designed to improve the efficiency of the EU's institutions without delaying enlargement.

More generally the Amsterdam Treaty did not – could not and, probably, should not – bring to an end the lively debate about the proper shaping of the Union and its relationship with its Member States which was not begun by but which was supplied with great impetus by the 'Maastricht' ruling of the *Bundesverfassungsgericht* (p. 15). Petite identifies the Treaty as 'a further stage in the process'. The diminished capacity of the nation-State to provide a 'reliable shelter', to which Habermas refers at p. 23 above, continues to attract differing views on what could and should be put in its place, or at least what could and should supplement it. This is central to imagining what we want 'Europe' to deliver more than half a century after the end of the Second World War.

J. Weiler, 'The Function and Future of European Law' in V. Heiskanen and K. Kulovesi (eds), *Function and Future of European Law* (1999), pp. 12–16

There are, it seems to me, two basic human strategies of dealing with the alien and these two strategies have played a decisive role in Western civilisation. One strategy is to remove the boundaries. It is the spirit of 'come, be one of us'. It is noble since it involves, of course, elimination of prejudice, of the notion that there are boundaries that cannot be eradicated. But the 'be one of us,' however well intentioned, is often an invitation to the alien to be one of us, by being us. Vis-à-vis the alien, it risks robbing him of his identity. Vis-à-vis one's self, it may be a subtle manifestation of intolerance. If I cannot tolerate the alien, one way of resolving the dilemma is to make him like me, no longer an alien. This is, of course, infinitely, better than the physical annihilation. But it is still a form of dangerous internal and external intolerance.

The alternative strategy is to acknowledge the validity of certain forms of bounded identity but simultaneously to reach across boundaries. We acknowledge and respect difference (and what is special and unique about ourselves as individuals and groups) and yet we reach across differences in recognition of our essential humanity. I never tire of referring to Hermann Cohen (1842–1918), the great neo-Kantian philosopher of religion, in an exquisite modern interpretation of the Mosaic law on this subject which captures its deep meaning in a way which retains its vitality even in today's ever closer union. It can be summarised as follows: The law of shielding the alien from all wrong is of vital significance. The alien was to be protected, not because he was a member of one's family, clan, religious community or people; but because he was a human being. In the alien, therefore, man discovered the idea of humanity. What is significant in this are the two elements I have mentioned. On the one hand, the identity of the alien, as such, is maintained. One is not invited to go out and, for example, 'save him' by inviting him to be one of you. One is not invited to recast the boundary. On the other hand, despite the boundaries which are maintained, and constitute the I and the Alien, one is commanded to reach over the boundary and love him, in his alienship, as oneself. The alien is accorded human dignity. The soul of the I is tended to not by eliminating the temptation to oppress but by maintaining it and overcoming it.

Europe represents this alternative, civilising strategy of dealing with the 'other'. This is, more than peace and prosperity, Europe's true soul. The constitutional expression of this strategy is the principle of Constitutional Tolerance and it is encapsulated in that most basic articulation of its meta-political objective in the Preamble of the EC Treaty:

Determined to lay the foundations of an ever closer union among the peoples of Europe.

No matter how close the Union, it is to remain among distinct peoples. An ever closer union could be achieved by an amalgam of distinct peoples into one nation – which is both the ideal and/or the de facto experience of most federal and non federal states. The rejection by Europe of that one nation ideal, or destiny, is usually understood as intended to preserve the rich diversity – cultural and other – of the distinct European peoples as well as to respect their political self-determination. But 'the European choice' has an even deeper spiritual meaning.

An ever closer union is altogether more easy if differences among the components are eliminated, if they come to resemble each other, if they aspire to become one. The more identical the 'Other's' identity is to my own, the easier it is for me to identify with him and accept him. It demands less of me to accept another if he is very much like me. It is altogether more difficult to attain an ever closer Union if the components of that Union preserve their distinct identities, if they retain their 'otherness' vis-à-vis each other, if they do not become 'one flesh,' politically speaking.

Herein resides the principle of Constitutional Tolerance. Inevitably I define my distinct identity by a boundary which differentiates me from those who are unlike me. My continued existence as a distinct identity depends, ontologically, on that boundary and, psychologically and sociologically, on preserving that sentiment of otherness. The call to bond with those very others in an ever closer union demands an internalisation (individual and societal) of a very high degree of toleration. The Leviticus imperative to love thy neighbour as oneself is so difficult and hence civilising because that neighbour is not like myself. Living the Kantian categorical imperative is most meaningful when it is extended to those who are unlike me.

It is in legal terms that the principle of Constitutional Tolerance finds its deepest and most remarkable expression. The European *Courts* of Justice – in Luxembourg and the various Member States – have enjoined us to accept European law as the supreme law of the land. This, despite the fact that at face value this law defies the normal premise of democracy. Normally in democracy, we demand democratic discipline, i.e. accepting the authority of the majority over the minority only within a polity which understands itself as being constituted of one people, however defined. A majority demanding obedience from a minority which does not regard itself as belonging to the same people is usually regarded as subjugation. And yet, in the Community, through the doctrines of direct effect and supremacy we subject the European peoples to the discipline of democracy even though the European polity is composed of distinct peoples. It is a remarkable instance of Constitutional Tolerance to accept to be bound by a decision not by 'my people' but by a majority among peoples which are precisely not mine – a people, if you wish, of 'others'. I compromise my self-determination in this fashion as an expression of this kind of internal (towards myself) and external (towards others) Constitutional Tolerance.

However – and there is a big 'however' at this point. This, the Union's most fundamental principle, that of Constitutional Tolerance, becomes a travesty if the norms I follow, if the democratic discipline I obey is not adopted by others, my fellow European citizens, with whom I do not share the bonds of peoplehood but instead the bonds of a community of values and a new civic and political culture of transnational tolerance, but by a technocratic bureaucracy over which I have little control – presided over in the unreachable supranational Olympus of the European Council (and even European Parliament) and within the infranational netherworld of comitology. A non-democratic Europe extinguishes the principle of Constitutional Tolerance just as a statal or a one nation Europe would.

And that exactly is the weakness of the European Court of Justice ('ECJ') and some of its national counterparts. Their scant regard for, and weak sensibility to, the democratic processes by which the norms of which they demand supreme loyalty are enacted. It was evident in the Court's historic decisions such as *Van Gend en Loos* [see Chapter 3] where the Court said:

The objective of the EEC Treaty, which is to establish a Common Market, the functioning of which is of direct concern to interested parties in the Community, implies that this Treaty is more than an agreement which merely creates mutual obligations between the contracting states. This view is confirmed by the preamble to the Treaty which refers not only to governments but to peoples. It is also confirmed more specifically by the establishment of institutions endowed with sovereign rights, the exercise of which affects Member States and also their citizens. *Furthermore, it must be noted that the nationals of the states brought together in the Community are called upon to cooperate in the functioning of this Community through the intermediary of the European Parliament and the Economic and Social Committee.'* (Recital 10, emphasis added)

There is something deeply unsettling to present the European Parliament and the Economic and Social Committee as a chamber that can be said to express a meaningful democratic notion of citizen cooperation in governance and justify rendering laws coming out of the Community process an obligatory nature binding upon States and individuals:

Independently of the legislation of Member States. (Recital 12)

This original sin of the Court and its acceptance by national jurisdictions may have been justified at the time when the international legal nature of the Community was strong and ratification of the EC Treaty in national parliaments could have been considered as an effective means for democratic legitimacy. But in today's incredibly complex and wide ranging Community when national ratification after each Inter-Governmental Conference ('IGC') is an impossible take-it-or-leave-it pact, reminiscent of the worst plebiscites in authoritarian regimes and nothing more than a formal act rather than a civic exercise of democracy, the continued indifference of the Court to the weak democratic basis of many of the norms which it upholds – notably in those coming out of the comitology process is more than unsettling – it is an act of Constitutional abdication.[4]

The late Judge Mancini was right: The Court assumes that – respectable democracy – which is not there.[5]

---

[4] For the debate about Comitology, democracy and the courts see, e.g. the various essays in C. Joerges and E. Voss, *EU Committees: Social Regulation, Law and Politics* (Hart Publishing, Oxford 1999).

[5] See Mancini v Weiler, *Europe — The Case for Statehood . . . and the Case Against: An Exchange.* Harvard Jean Monnet Working Paper No. 6/98, available at http://law.harvard.edu/programs/Jean/Monnet (also Vol. 4 ELJ (1998)). [This is a particularly vivid and vigorous exchange — SW].

1 THE SOURCES OF COMMUNITY LAW

The three major sources of Community law are examined in this chapter. Part (A) discusses the founding Treaties; Part (B) explains the nature and method of adoption of Community legislation; Part (C) examines the general legal principles which have been shaped by the Court of Justice of the European Communities. Another basis for making this three-fold classification is to view Part (A), the Treaties, as the product of the Member States, Part (B), legislation, as the product of the Community's own autonomous political institutions acting as a legislature and Part (C), general principles, as the contribution of the Community's judicial institution.

In *A Guide to European Community Law* Professor Mathijsen declares that 'the Community legal order grew and developed mainly at the hands of the Community judges' (p. 54). The Court's creativity will be introduced in Part (C) of this chapter, but it also exerts an important influence over the sources in Parts (A) and (B) by virtue of its interpretative function. The activism of the judges will be observed throughout this book in many aspects of the Community's constitutional and institutional law. Two questions in particular will be addressed. First, to what extent is such judicial activism appropriate? This raises the general jurisprudential issue of the respective roles of courts and legislators. The second, more modern, more specifically European, question is the extent to which such judicial initiative is still forthcoming. Some observers have identified a more cautious, 'minimalist' approach by the European Court; see T. Koopmans (then a judge of the Court) (1986) 35 ICLQ 925 and *Further reading* at the end of this chapter.

(A) THE TREATIES

The Community has three founding Treaties. The Treaty of Paris came into force in 1952 and established the European Coal and Steel Community (ECSC). The two Treaties of Rome came into force in 1958 and established

EURATOM, The European Atomic Energy Community, and the EEC, the European Economic Community. The six original parties were France, Germany, Luxembourg, Belgium, The Netherlands and Italy. Since the Merger Treaty 1965, the three Communities are administered on a day-to-day basis as one – hence the 'European Community'.

The first major formal Treaty revision which the original Treaties underwent was the Single European Act 1986 (SEA). This adjusted several aspects of the Community structure and brought about a modest extension in its competence. The SEA was chiefly motivated by the plan to complete the internal market of the Community by the end of 1992.

The Treaties share common principles. The two Treaties of Rome are closely analogous in their specific provisions. The Treaty of Paris contains certain distinct features. The primary focus of this book is on the most important of the Communities, the EC. The EC enjoys the broadest field of activity.

As of 1 November 1993, the structure was affected by the Treaty on European Union. That Treaty left in place the original three Treaties under the European Union umbrella. It retitled the EEC the 'EC' and amended that Treaty significantly, most notably to insert detailed provisions for the establishment of Economic and Monetary Union. The fact that what was referred to as the 'EEC' is now properly referred to as the 'EC' must be carefully remembered when reading this book (see also p. 13 above).

The Amsterdam Treaty, which entered into force on 1 May 1999 (p. 28 above), retains the overall three-pillar structure of the Union, though it moves some matters from the Third Pillar into the First Pillar (the EC). It also amends a substantial number of provisions of the EC Treaty.

All the Treaties share the broad objective of market integration. The EC covers the integration of the economy generally, whereas the ECSC and EURATOM are specific to particular sectors. The creation of an integrated economy which transcends national frontiers is the most obvious of the Community's tasks. The substantive legal provisions which are examined in this book are primarily concerned to eliminate barriers to trade between Member States and to establish a common market. The constitutional principles too are shaped in accordance with this central objective. However, it is important to appreciate that the Community is about more than economics. This is plain even from a superficial understanding of the tensions in post-war Europe from which the Communities emerged. It is wise to begin by reading the Preambles to the Treaties in order to appreciate that the Communities are based on a vision rather less tangible, but, to many, more inspiring, than Gross Domestic Product.

Treaty of Paris Establishing the European Coal and Steel Community 1951, Preamble

The President of the Federal Republic of Germany, His Royal Highness The Prince Royal of Belgium, the President of the French Republic, the President of the Italian

Republic, Her Royal Highness the Grand Duchess of Luxembourg, Her Majesty The Queen of the Netherlands,

Considering that world peace can be safeguarded only by creative efforts commensurate with the dangers that threaten it,

Convinced that the contribution which an organised and vital Europe can make to civilisation is indispensable to the maintenance of peaceful relations,

Recognising that Europe can be built only through practical achievements which will first of all create real solidarity, and through the establishment of common bases for economic development,

Anxious to help, by expanding their basic production, to raise the standard of living and further the works of peace,

Resolved to substitute for age-old rivalries the merging of their essential interests; to create, by establishing an economic community, the basis for a broader and deeper community among peoples long divided by bloody conflicts; and to lay the foundations for institutions which will give direction to a destiny henceforward shared,

Have decided to create a European Coal and Steel Community. . . .

Treaty of Rome Establishing the European Economic Community 1957, Preamble

His Majesty The King of the Belgians, the President of the Federal Republic of Germany, the President of the French Republic, the President of the Italian Republic, Her Royal Highness the Grand Duchess of Luxembourg, Her Majesty The Queen of the Netherlands,

Determined to lay the foundations of an ever closer union among the peoples of Europe,

Resolved to ensure the economic and social progress of their countries by common action to eliminate the barriers which divide Europe,

Affirming as the essential objective of their efforts the constant improvement of the living and working conditions of their peoples,

Recognising that the removal of existing obstacles calls for concerted action in order to guarantee steady expansion, balanced trade and fair competition,

Anxious to strengthen the unity of their economies and to ensure their harmonious development by reducing the differences existing between the various regions and the backwardness of the less favoured regions,

Desiring to contribute, by means of a common commercial policy, to the progressive abolition of restrictions on international trade,

Intending to confirm the solidarity which binds Europe and the overseas countries and desiring to ensure the development of their prosperity, in accordance with the principles of the Charter of the United Nations,

Resolved by thus pooling their resources to preserve and strengthen peace and liberty, and calling upon the other peoples of Europe who share their ideal to join in their efforts,

Have decided to create a European Economic Community. . . .

Note
These sentiments must be taken to influence the more specific provisions of the Treaty which are examined in the course of this book.

(B) LEGISLATION

(i) Community legislation

The Treaties are *traite cadre*: frameworks which set out an overall design, but which require more specific amplification. That task belongs to the institutions of the Community. The creative role of the Court of Justice of the European Communities (the Court) is considered below, but it is the other three principal EC institutions, the Council, the Commission and the Parliament, which are responsible for the adoption of legislation. The available measures are set out in Article 249 EC:

Article 249 EC

Article 249

In order to carry out their task and in accordance with the provisions of this Treaty, the European Parliament acting jointly with the Council, the Council and the Commission shall make regulations and issue directives, take decisions, make recommendations or deliver opinions.

A regulation shall have general application. It shall be binding in its entirety and directly applicable in all Member States.

A directive shall be binding, as to the result to be achieved, upon each Member State to which it is addressed, but shall leave to the national authorities the choice of form and methods.

A decision shall be binding in its entirety upon those to whom it is addressed.

Recommendations and opinions shall have no binding force.

Note

Article 249 EC was Article 189 pre-Amsterdam (p. 29 above), but the text is unaltered.

The Court has insisted that the different acts available under Article 249 are distinguishable on the basis of their nature, not their form. A label is not conclusive. In *International Fruit Company* v *Commission* (Cases 41–44/70) [1971] ECR 411, a measure was labelled a Regulation. The applicant company argued that in reality it was a set of Decisions. The Court's examination of the substance of the measure led it to agree with the applicant:

International Fruit Company v *Commission (Cases 41–44/70)*
[1971] ECR 411
Court of Justice of the European Communities

[21]   Consequently, Article 1 of Regulation No 983/70 is not a provision of general application within the meaning of the second paragraph of Article 189 of the Treaty, but must be regarded as a conglomeration of individual decisions taken by the Commission under the guise of a regulation pursuant to Article 2(2) of Regulation No 459/70, each of which decisions affects the legal position of each author of an application for a licence.

Note
The primary significance which flows from classifying a measure under one Article 249 pigeonhole rather than another, relates to the individual's opportunity to challenge its validity. Showing a measure to be a Decision, rather than a Regulation, greatly increases the likelihood that an applicant can persuade the Court to hold the legislation invalid. Judicial review of Community legislation will be examined in more depth in Chapter 16.

To return to the task of identifying the types of Community legislation which exist, the Court held in the next case that the list of measures in Article 249 is not exhaustive. Community institutions are capable of adopting other acts of legal significance.

Commission v Council (Case 22/70)
[1971] ECR 263
Court of Justice of the European Communities

The Member States acting together in Council had adopted a Resolution on 20 March 1970, in which they agreed to coordinate their approaches in negotiations for the conclusion of a European Road Transport Agreement (ERTA/AETR). The question of the Resolution's legal status arose when the Commission brought proceedings under Article 173 of the EC Treaty (now, after amendment, Article 230 EC), which provides for judicial review of Community acts. Was the Resolution an act? The Council observed that it did not fit into any of the categories in Article 189 of the EC Treaty (now Article 249 EC). The Court, however, was more concerned to identify whether the Resolution had legal effects. That possibility could not be excluded simply because the resolution was not within the Article 189 list.

[44]   In the course of the meeting on 20 March 1970, the Council, after an exchange of views between its members and the representative of the Commission, reached a number of 'conclusions' on the attitude to be taken by the Governments of the Member States in the decisive negotiations on the AETR.

[45]   These proceedings were concerned partly with the objective of the negotiations and partly with negotiating procedure.

[46]   As regards the objective to be pursued, the Council settled on a negotiating position aimed at having the AETR adapted to the provisions of the Community system, apart from the concession of certain derogations from that system which would have to be accepted by the Community.

[47]   Having regard to the objective thus established, the Council invited the Commission to put forward, at the appropriate time and in accordance with the provisions of Article 75 of the Treaty, the necessary proposals with a view to amending Regulation No 543/69.

[48]   As regards negotiating, the Council decided, in accordance with the course of action decided upon at its previous meetings, that the negotiations should be carried

on and concluded by the six Member States, which would become contracting parties to the AETR.

[49]   Throughout the negotiations and at the conclusion of the agreement, the States would act in common and would constantly coordinate their positions according to the usual procedure in close association with the Community institutions, the delegation of the Member State currently occupying the Presidency of the Council acting as spokesman.

[50]   It does not appear from the minutes that the Commission raised any objections to the definition by the Council of the objective of the negotiations.

[51]   On the other hand, it did lodge an express reservation regarding the negotiating procedure, declaring that it considered that the position adopted by the Council was not in accordance with the Treaty, and more particularly with Article 228.

[52]   It follows from the foregoing that the Council's proceedings dealt with a matter falling within the power of the Community, and that the Member States could not therefore act outside the framework of the common institutions.

[53]   It thus seems that in so far as they concerned the objective of the negotiations as defined by the Council, the proceedings of 20 March 1970 could not have been simply the expression or the recognition of a voluntary coordination, but were designed to lay down a course of action binding on both the institutions and the Member States, and destined ultimately to be reflected in the tenor of the regulation.

[54]   In the part of its conclusions relating to the negotiating procedure, the Council adopted provisions which were capable of derogating in certain circumstances from the procedure laid down by the Treaty regarding negotiations with third countries and the conclusion of agreements.

[55]   Hence, the proceedings of 20 March 1970 had definite legal effects both on relations between the Community and the Member States and on the relationship between institutions.

Notes
1.   The significance of finding that the Council's act, although not mentioned in Article 189 of the EC Treaty (now Article 249 EC), nevertheless had legal effects, was that its validity could be challenged by the Commission before the Court. As in the *International Fruit Company* case, above, the task of identifying a legal act occurred in the context of a challenge to it. *Commission* v *Council* (Case 22/70) will be considered again in Chapter 16 which examines challenges to Community acts.
2.   Community law is becoming increasingly multi-dimensional. An increasingly wide range of acts may carry direct or indirect legal implications. Read Case C-322/88 *Grimaldi* v *Fonds des Malaises Professionelles* [1989] ECR 4407 and J. Klabbers, 'Informal Instruments before the European Court of Justice' (1994) 31 CML Rev 997.

(ii) The legislative process
The Community has neither a general legislative competence nor a single uniform legislative procedure. This is reflected in Article 249 EC (p. 40

above), which insists that legislation be made 'in accordance with the provisions of this Treaty'. Legal challenge to Community legislation is accordingly possible. The next case concerns a dispute about legislative competence.

Germany v Commission (Case 281/85)
[1987] ECR 3203
Court of Justice of the European Communities

The case arose out of the Commission's attempts to develop a policy at Community level relating to immigration into the Community from third countries. Five Member States applied to the European Court to have Commission Decision 85/381 annulled. (See the definition of a Decision in Article 249, at p. 40 above.) The applicant States argued, *inter alia*, that the Commission had exceeded its legal competence in adopting the Decision and that it had unlawfully trespassed on Member State territory.

[2]   Decision 85/381/EEC sets up a prior communication and consultation procedure on migration policies in relation to non-member countries. Under Article 1 the Member States are to inform the Commission and the other Member States of their draft measures and draft agreements with regard to workers from non-member States and members of their families relating to the following areas: entry, residence and employment, including illegal entry, residence and employment; the achievement of equal treatment in living and working conditions, wages and economic rights; the promotion of integration into the workforce, society and cultural life; and the voluntary return of such persons to their countries of origin. Under Article 2 that notification procedure may be followed by consultation between the Member States and the Commission, arranged by the Commission. The consultation procedure may be initiated by a Member State or by the Commission. Under Article 3 the objectives of the consultation procedure are, *inter alia*, to facilitate the mutual exchange of information and the identification of problems of common interest and, as a result, the adoption of a common position by the Member States; to ensure that the agreements and measures are in conformity with Community policies and actions; and to examine the desirability of measures, aimed, in particular, at achieving progress towards the harmonization of national legislation on foreigners and the inclusion of a maximum of common provisions in bilateral agreements.

In addressing the problem of competence the Court had to undertake a close examination of the allocation of functions between Community and Member States. The Treaty is simply not explicit enough to yield a definite, predictable answer in difficult cases such as this:

The competence of the Commission
[9]   The applicant Member States maintain that neither Article 118 nor any other Treaty provision empowers the Commission to adopt a binding decision in a field which, moreover, falls within their exclusive jurisdiction. The French Republic maintains that matters relating to the conditions of entry, residence and employment of nationals of non-member countries affect the Member States' security and go substantially beyond the social field referred to in Article 118.

[10]   In that connection it should be borne in mind that the first paragraph of Article 118 of the EEC Treaty confers on the Commission 'the task of promoting close cooperation between Member States in the social field'. Its second paragraph provides that, to that end, the Commission is to act in close contact with the Member States by making studies, delivering opinions and arranging consultations.

[11]   The first submission raises two separate questions, that is to say whether collaboration between Member States in the social field, as provided for in the first paragraph of Article 118, extends to migration policies in relation to non-member countries, and secondly whether the arrangement of consultations, a task conferred on the Commission by the second paragraph of Article 118, empowers the latter to issue binding measures. Those two questions should be considered in turn.

[12]   The first paragraph of Article 117 of the EEC Treaty, which appears in Chapter 1, 'Social provisions', of Title III, 'Social policy', makes it the duty of the Member States to promote improved working conditions and an improved standard of living for workers, so as to make possible their harmonization while the improvement is being maintained. Under the second paragraph of Article 117 such a development is to ensue not only from the functioning of the common market, which is to favour the harmonization of social systems, but also from the procedures provided for by the Treaty and from the approximation of national legislation.

[13]   It is with that approximation in mind that Article 118 gives the Commission the task of promoting close cooperation between Member States in the social field, particularly in matters relating to employment and working conditions.

[14]   Consequently, whilst Article 118 of the EEC Treaty does not encroach upon the Member States' powers in the social field so far as the latter is not covered by other provisions of the Treaty, such as, for example, the provisions on the free movement of workers, the common agricultural policy or the common transport policy, it nevertheless provides that those powers must be exercised in the framework of cooperation between Member States, which is to be organized by the Commission.

[15]   The essence of the arguments put forward by the applicant Member States is that migration policy in relation to non-member countries is not part of the social field envisaged by Article 118 or, alternatively, that it falls only partly within that field.

[16]   As regards the applicants' main argument it must be observed that the employment situation and, more generally, the improvement of living and working conditions within the Community are liable to be affected by the policy pursued by the Member States with regard to workers from non-member countries. In the preamble to Decision 85/381/EEC the Commission rightly considers that it is important to ensure that the migration policies of Member States in relation to non-member countries take into account both common policies and the actions taken at Community level, in particular within the framework of Community labour market policy, in order not to jeopardize the results.

[17]   As early as 1974, in its resolution of 21 January 1974 concerning a social action programme (Official Journal 1974, C 13, p. 1), the Council recognized that the migration policies pursued by the Member States affect the Community's social policy, in particular in view of their influence on the Community employment market and on Community workers' employment conditions. In that resolution it acknowledged the need, and expressed the political resolve, to promote consultation on immigration policies *vis-à-vis* non-member countries. It reiterated that view in its

resolution of 9 February 1976 on an action programme for migrant workers and members of their families (Official Journal 1976, C 34, p. 2) and in its resolution of 27 June 1980 on guidelines for the Community labour-market policy (Official Journal 1980, C 168, p. 1), which is referred to in the Commission's decision. The decision also refers to the resolution on guidelines for a Community policy on migration already approved by the Council, which was to be formally adopted on 16 July 1985 (Official Journal 1985, C 186, p. 3).

[18]   It must therefore be held that the argument that migration policy in relation to non-member States falls entirely outside the social field, in respect of which Article 118 provides for cooperation between the Member States, cannot be accepted.

[19]   The merits of the applicant Member States' alternative argument to the effect that the contested decision covers matters falling outside the social field within the meaning of Article 118 now falls to be considered. The Member States argue that Decision 85/381/EEC aims to introduce a consultation procedure in the cultural field in so far as it refers, in particular, to the 'integration into . . . cultural life' of workers from non-member countries.

[20]   That objection refers to Article 1 of the contested decision, which includes in the communication and consultation procedure the 'promotion of integration into the workforce, society and cultural life' of migrant workers from non-member countries and members of their families.

[21]   The promotion of the integration into the workforce of workers from non-member countries must be held to be within the social field within the meaning of Article 118, in so far as it is closely linked to employment. This also applies to their integration into society, having regard to the objectives pursued by the contested decision, inasmuch as the draft measures in question are those connected with problems relating to employment and working conditions, and there is no reason to consider that the decision intended to give a different meaning to that concept.

[22]   As regards the cultural integration of immigrant communities from non-member countries, whilst this may be linked, to an extent, with the effects of migration policy, it is aimed at immigrant communities in general without distinction between migrant workers and other foreigners, and its link with problems relating to employment and working conditions is therefore extremely tenuous.

[23]   Moreover, migration policy is capable of falling within the social field within the meaning of Article 118 only to the extent to which it concerns the situation of workers from non-member countries as regards their impact on the Community employment market and on working conditions.

[24]   As a result, in so far as Decision 85/381/EEC includes the promotion of cultural integration as a whole among the subjects for consultation it goes beyond the social field in which, under Article 118, the Commission has the task of promoting cooperation between Member States.

[25]   The French Republic's argument that the whole area of policy on foreign nationals falls outside the social field inasmuch as it involves questions of public security for which the Member States alone are responsible cannot be accepted. Whilst it is true that pursuant to their rules governing foreign nationals Member States may take measures with regard to workers who are nationals of non-member countries – either by adopting national rules or by negotiating international instruments – which

are based on considerations of public policy, public security and public health and which are, as such, their sole responsibility, this does not mean that the whole field of migration policy in relation to non-member countries falls necessarily within the scope of public security.

[26] The argument raised by the French Republic and the Federal Republic of Germany to the effect that the duty of notification is liable to jeopardize the requirements of secrecy and confidentiality, particularly in negotiations with non-member countries, must likewise be rejected since there is no imperative requirement for the drafts to be notified until such time as they are published. Moreover, under Article 4 of the decision the Member States are required to take all necessary steps to safeguard the confidential nature of the information exchanged, which must cover information communicated voluntarily before publication.

[27] Since the contested decision falls only partly outside the social field covered by Article 118, it must be considered whether the second paragraph of Article 118, which provides that the Commission is to act, *inter alia*, by arranging consultations, gives it the power to adopt a binding decision with a view to the arrangement of such consultations.

[28] In that connection it must be emphasized that where an article of the EEC Treaty – in this case Article 118 – confers a specific task on the Commission it must be accepted, if that provision is not to be rendered wholly ineffective, that it confers on the Commission necessarily and *per se* the powers which are indispensable in order to carry out that task. Accordingly, the second paragraph of Article 118 must be interpreted as conferring on the Commission all the powers which are necessary in order to arrange the consultations. In order to perform that task of arranging consultations the Commission must necessarily be able to require the Member States to notify essential information, in the first place in order to identify the problems and in the second place in order to pinpoint the possible guidelines for any future joint action on the part of the Member States; likewise it must be able to require them to take part in consultations.

[29] Indeed, the collaboration between Member States required by Article 118 is only possible within the framework of organized consultations. In the absence of any action to initiate it that collaboration might remain a dead letter, even though provision is made for it in the Treaty. Since the Commission was specifically given the task of promoting such collaboration and arranging it, it is entitled to initiate consultation procedures within the social field referred to in Article 118.

[30] It must be borne in mind that that power of the Commission must be confined to arranging a procedure for the notification of information and consultation and that in the present stage of development of Community law the subject-matter of the notification and consultation falls within the competence of the Member States. It must also be pointed out that the power which the Commission seeks to exercise under Article 118 is simply a procedural one to set up the notification and consultation machinery which is to result in the adoption of a common position on the part of the Member States.

[31] Consequently, since Article 118 provides a specific basis for the Commission's decision there is no need to consider whether the outcome sought by the decision in question might have been achieved through other general provisions of the Treaty or other procedures necessitating action on the part of other institutions.

[32] Now that it has been established that the Commission is empowered under Article 118 to adopt a binding decision *vis-à-vis* the Member States establishing a communication and consultation procedure, it must be considered whether the contested decision does not go beyond the limits of such a procedure, as the applicant Member States claim.

[33] The Member States maintain that the decision does not merely arrange a consultation procedure, but, by assigning an aim to that consultation, seeks to determine its outcome and hence exceeds the Commission's powers, which are of a procedural nature. The second indent of Article 3 of the contested decision provides, in fact, that the purpose of the consultation procedure is to ensure that the agreements and measures communicated are in conformity with Community policies in the fields covered by the decision, including policy on development aid.

[34] Since the Commission has a power of a purely procedural nature to initiate a consultation procedure it cannot determine the result to be achieved in that consultation and cannot prevent the Member States from implementing drafts, agreements and measures which it might consider not to be in conformity with Community policies and actions.

[35] As a result, in so far as the second indent of Article 3 lays down a precise obligation on the Member States and is intended to debar them from adopting national measures or concluding agreements that the Commission considers not to be in conformity with Community policies and actions, it must be regarded, as the applicant Member States rightly argue, as exceeding the scope of the Commission's powers under Article 118.

[36] As a result of the foregoing the applicant Member States are entitled to succeed in their request that the contested decision be declared void in so far as the Commission lacked competence

(a) to extend, by means of Article 1, the scope of the consultation procedure to cover matters relating to the cultural integration of workers from non-member States and members of their families; and
(b) to provide, in the second indent of Article 3, that the objective of the consultation is to ensure that the national draft measures and agreements are in conformity with Community policies and actions.

Note
Although the nature of the Court's process of reasoning retains general significance, the subject matter of this case is affected by the changes made by the Maastricht Treaty and further adjusted by the new patterns introduced by the Treaty of Amsterdam, p. 192 below. See H. Staples, *The Legal Status of Third Country Nationals Resident in the European Union* (Kluwer, 1999); S. Peers, 'Building Fortress Europe: The Development of EU Migration Law' (1998) 35 CML Rev 1235.

The challenge was brought under Article 173 of the EC Treaty (now, after amendment, Article 230 EC). The same judicial review procedure was used in both the cases examined earlier in this chapter. Many of the principles of Community law emerge from applications to the Court to annul Community acts. The Court has been able to use the procedure as a means of developing the Community legal order. Article 230 is examined in more depth in Chapter 16.

The broadest statement of Community legislative competence in the Treaty is found in Article 308:

Article 308 EC

Article 308

If action by the Community should prove necessary to attain, in the course of the operation of the common market, one of the objectives of the Community and this Treaty has not provided the necessary powers, the Council shall, acting unanimously on a proposal from the Commission and after consulting the European Parliament, take the appropriate measures.

Notes

1. Article 308 was Article 235 pre-Amsterdam (see p. 29 above), though the text is unaltered.

2. The judgment in *Germany* v *Commission* (Case 281/85) above reveals careful attention to legal base. The correct Treaty base for proposed legislation must be identified, because different Treaty provisions dealing with different subject matter demand different procedures. The Community's legislative procedure, loosely described, used to involve a Commission proposal, with Parliament's right to be consulted in some circumstances, but it was the Council which adopted the final legislation. However, there are a number of variations on that pattern – variations which exist for reasons which seem to defy rational explanation.

3. So under some provisions in the Treaty Title on Economic and Monetary Policy, the Parliament can require the adoption of the 'cooperation procedure', which gives it an enhanced role; if the matter falls instead under other provisions, its role is greatly diminished. Article 251 EC, introduced by the Maastricht Treaty (and then numbered 189b), gives the Parliament for the first time the power to veto legislative proposals – but only in the areas to which Article 251 applies. The Council's role also varies depending on the applicable legal base. For example, if the matter concerns social provisions in fields covered by Article 137(1) EC, which include health and safety at work, a dissentient State in Council can be outvoted because adoption by qualified majority is possible under the applicable legislative procedure, which is Article 251 EC. But if the matter concerns other rights of employed persons falling within Article 137(3) EC or outside the scope of the Treaty's Social Policy Title altogether, each State holds a veto. Article 95 EC does not permit qualified majority in this field. Article 308, above, it will be noted, requires unanimity.

4. The Single European Act 1987 effected a shift towards more adoption by majority in order to accelerate the legislative process in the approach to 1992 (see C. Ehlermann, 'The Internal Market following the Single European Act' (1987) 24 CML Rev 361); this shift was maintained in the Maastricht Treaty and the Treaty of Amsterdam confirms the trend and widens the sphere of application of the Article 251 EC procedure.

5. The technical differences between different Treaty bases for legislative action may induce tactical manoeuvring by the political institutions, concerned to maximise their influence at the expense of other institutions. In case of dispute, the European Court is forced to decide which is the correct Treaty base for legislative action. It insists that the correct base is as a matter of law identifiable, not a matter of discretion.

Commission v Council (Case 45/86)
[1987] ECR 1493
Court of Justice of the European Communities

A Council Regulation dealing with external trade policy contained no explicit statement of its legal base. The Council, challenged by the Commission under Article 173 of the EC Treaty (now, after amendment, Article 230 EC), informed the European Court that the base was Articles 113 and 235 of the EC Treaty (now, after amendment, Articles 133 and 308 EC). The Court observed:

[11]   It must be observed that in the context of the organization of the powers of the Community the choice of the legal basis for a measure may not depend simply on an institution's conviction as to the objective pursued but must be based on objective factors which are amenable to judicial review.

Different rules governed Articles 113 and 235 – the former allowed qualified majority voting, whereas the latter insisted on unanimity. (The same is true of the post-Amsterdam versions.) The Court observed of Article 235 of the EC Treaty (now Article 308 EC), set out at p. 48 above, that:

[13]   It follows from the very wording of Article 235 that its use as the legal basis for a measure is justified only where no other provision of the Treaty gives the Community institutions the necessary power to adopt the measure in question.

[14]   It must therefore be considered whether in this case the Council had the power to adopt the contested regulations pursuant to Article 113 of the Treaty alone, as the Commission maintains.

The Court held that the measures were adoptable under Article 113; that accordingly adoption under Article 235 was unjustified; and held them void.

Note
The next case also arose out of the need to select the correct legal base. In *Commission v Council* (Case C-300/89) [1991] ECR I-2867, the Commission, supported by the Parliament, sought the annulment of Directive 89/428. The Directive approximated national programmes for reducing and eventually eliminating pollution caused by waste in the production of titanium dioxide. The Council had based it on Article 130s of the EC Treaty (environmental protection: now, after amendment, Article 175 EC). The application asserted

that the correct legal base was Article 100a of the EC Treaty (internal market: now, after amendment, Article 95 EC). The Court confirmed that choice of legal base is a matter of law. It agreed that the Directive had two objectives, but in the following extract it held that the combined use of both Article 100a and Article 130s would be unacceptable because of the detrimental impact on the role of the Parliament (para. 20). It proceeded to choose Article 100a of the EC Treaty (now, after amendment, Article 95 EC) as the correct base.

Commission v Council (Case C-300/89)
[1991] ECR I-2867
Court of Justice of the European Communities

[16]   . . . in view of its aim and content, the directive at issue displays the features both of action relating to the environment with which Article 130s of the Treaty is concerned and of a harmonizing measure which has as its object the establishment and functioning of the internal market, within the meaning of Article 100a of the Treaty.

[17]   As the Court held in Case 165/87 *Commission v Council* [1988] ECR 5545, paragraph 11, where an institution's power is based on two provisions of the Treaty, it is bound to adopt the relevant measures on the basis of the two relevant provisions. However, that ruling is not applicable to the present case.

[18]   One of the enabling provisions at issue, Article 100a, requires recourse to the cooperation procedure provided for in Article 149(2) of the Treaty, whereas the other, Article 130s, requires the Council to act unanimously after merely consulting the European Parliament. As a result, use of both provisions as a joint legal basis would divest the cooperation procedure of its very substance.

[19]   Under the cooperation procedure, the Council acts by a qualified majority where it intends accepting the amendments to its common position proposed by the Parliament and included by the Commission in its re-examined proposal, whereas it must secure unanimity if it intends taking a decision after its common position has been rejected by the Parliament or if it intends modifying the Commission's re-examined proposal. That essential element of the cooperation procedure would be undermined if, as a result of simultaneous reference to Articles 100a and 130s, the Council were required, in any event, to act unanimously.

[20]   The very purpose of the cooperation procedure, which is to increase the involvement of the European Parliament in the legislative process of the Community, would thus be jeopardized. As the Court stated in its judgments in Case 138/79 *Roquette Frères v Council* [1980] ECR 3333 and Case 139/79 *Maizena v Council* [1980] ECR 3393, paragraph 34, that participation reflects a fundamental democratic principle that the peoples should take part in the exercise of power through the intermediary of a representative assembly.

[21]   It follows that in the present case recourse to the dual legal basis of Articles 100a and 130s is excluded and that it is necessary to determine which of those two provisions is the appropriate legal basis.

[22]   It must be observed in the first place that, pursuant to the second sentence of Article 130r(2) of the Treaty, 'environmental protection requirements shall be a

component of the Community's other policies'. That principle implies that a Community measure cannot be covered by Article 130s merely because it also pursues objectives of environmental protection.

[23]   Secondly, as the Court held in its judgments in Cases 91/79 and 92/79 *Commission* v *Italy* [1980] ECR 1099 (paragraph 8) and 1115 (paragraph 8), provisions which are made necessary by considerations relating to the environment and health may be a burden upon the undertakings to which they apply and, if there is no harmonization of national provisions on the matter, competition may be appreciably distorted. It follows that action intended to approximate national rules concerning production conditions in a given industrial sector with the aim of eliminating distortions of competition in that sector is conducive to the attainment of the internal market and thus falls within the scope of Article 100a, a provision which is particularly appropriate to the attainment of the internal market.

[24]   Finally, it must be observed that Article 100a(3) requires the Commission, in its proposals for measures for the approximation of the laws of the Member States which have as their object the establishment and functioning of the internal market, to take as a base a high level of protection in matters of environmental protection. That provision thus expressly indicates that the objectives of environmental protection referred to in Article 130r may be effectively pursued by means of harmonizing measures adopted on the basis of Article 100a.

[25]   In view of all the foregoing considerations, the contested measure should have been based on Article 100a of the EEC Treaty and must therefore be annulled.

Note
This decision seemed to give a priority to Article 100a over Article 130s of the EC Treaty (now, after amendment, Articles 95 and 175 EC respectively), thereby undermining the utility of the latter which had been inserted into the Treaty by the Single European Act. However, in Case C-155/91 *Commission* v *Council* [1993] ECR I-939, which concerned a challenge to the validity of Directive 91/156, the Waste Framework Directive which obliges Member States to prevent or reduce waste and to set up treatment facilities, the Court decided that the appropriate legal base was Article 130s not Article 100a and the challenge failed. The Court ruled that the measure's main object was waste management as part of environmental protection. The contribution to the development of the internal market was ancillary only. This led the Court to a different result from that reached in 'Titanium Dioxide'.

Plainly these are complex issues, yet they are important ones in determining the institutional balance of power in the Community. They have arisen in recent years in many other areas apart from internal market *versus* environmental protection; see, for example, Case C-295/90, *Parliament* v *Council*, [1992] ECR I-4193, p. 374 below; and Case C-269/97, *Commission* v *Council* judgment of 4 April 2000. The amendments to the Treaty effected by the Maastricht Treaty both increased the variety of available legislative procedures and also added new competences which are not easy to demarcate from existing competences. Happily, the Amsterdam Treaty's expansion of the scope of application of the Article 251 co-decision procedure has reduced the practical importance of the awkward task of demarcating legal bases in the Treaty. Case C-300/89, the 'Titanium Dioxide' case, and the subsequent decision in Case C-155/91 ('Waste Framework'), discussed above, were both decided against the background of the Treaty as it stood before the entry into force of the Maastricht Treaty. Both remain significant in showing how to fix the line between an internal market measure (now, post-Amsterdam, based on Article 95 EC) and an environmental protection measure (Article 175 EC). The main object of the measure must be identified. But the *practical consequences* of making that choice are altered by successive Treaty revisions, and the gulf between the two has narrowed, though it has not been eliminated entirely. Both Articles 95 and 175 now employ the Article 251 co-decision procedure. However, note the exceptional cases reserved to a distinct legislative procedure by Article 175(2); and also the more generous leeway allowed to Member States in areas occupied by Community legislation by Article 176 when contrasted to Article 95(4)–(9). Consider also, in the field of public health, Article 95/ Article 152 EC. Pay special attention to the limit imposed on the latter by Article 152(4)(c), which supplies a temptation to prefer the former as the base for measures setting common standards of health policy. But, as the Court insists, the choice must be made on the basis of objective factors amenable to judicial review, and the validity of Directive 98/43 (OJ 1998 L213/9) on tobacco advertising has been attacked before the Court for allegedly improper use of the internal market legal base (then Article 100a, now, post-Amsterdam, Article 95) for a measure dealing with public health – see Case C-376/98 *Germany* v *Council and Parliament*, pending before the Court.

The divide between rules concerning health and safety at work, for which the Treaty stipulates qualified majority voting in Council, and other rules governing the rights of employed persons which require a unanimous vote was mentioned at p. 48 above. The UK's attempt in the post-Maastricht, pre-Amsterdam era to preserve a veto in Council prompted it to seek to persuade the Court that Directive 93/104 concerning the organisation of Working Time had been wrongly treated by the Council as capable of adoption under Article 118a of the EC Treaty (Articles 117 to 120 of the EC Treaty have been replaced by Articles 136 EC to 143 EC). The UK, unsuccessful in Council in a political argument about the desirable intensity of EC social regulation (*cf* generally Chapter 15), was also unable to persuade the Court of the legal merits of its application. The Court found the Directive validly adopted under Article 118a.

United Kingdom v Council (Case C-84/94)
[1996] ECR I-5755
Court of Justice of the European Communities

[15]   There is nothing in the wording of Article 118a to indicate that the concepts of 'working environment', 'safety' and 'health' as used in that provision should, in the absence of other indications, be interpreted restrictively, and not as embracing all

factors, physical or otherwise, capable of affecting the health and safety of the worker in his working environment, including in particular certain aspects of the organization of working time. On the contrary, the words 'especially in the working environment' militate in favour of a broad interpretation of the which Article 118a confers upon the Council for the protection of the health and safety of workers. Moreover, such an interpretation of the words 'safety' and 'health' derives support in particular from the preamble to the Constitution of the World Health Organization to which all the Member States belong. Health is there defined as a state of complete physical, mental and social well-being that does not consist only in the absence of illness or infirmity.

The Court, having explained the nature and purpose of Article 118a, repeated its view that the choice of legal basis must be based on objective factors amenable to judicial review. It then proceeded to examine Directive 93/104 on Working Time.

[26]   As regards the aim of the directive, the applicant argues that it represents a continuation of the Community's earlier thinking and of a series of earlier initiatives at Community level concerned with the organization of working time in the interests of job creation and reduced unemployment. It is in reality a measure concerned with the overall improvement of the living and working conditions of employees and with their general protection, and is so broad in its scope and coverage as to be capable of classification as a social policy measure, for the adoption of which other legal bases exist.

[27]   It is to be noted in that respect that, according to the sixth recital in its preamble, the directive constitutes a practical contribution towards creating the social dimension of the internal market. However, it does not follow from the fact that the directive falls within the scope of Community social policy that it cannot properly be based on Article 118a, so long as it contributes to encouraging improvements as regards the health and safety of workers. Indeed, Article 118a forms part of Chapter 1, headed 'Social Provisions', of Title VIII of the Treaty, which deals in particular with 'Social Policy'. This led the Court to conclude that that provision conferred on the Community internal legislative competence in the area of social policy (Opinion 2/91, cited above, [[1993] ECR I-1061] paragraph 17).

[28]   Furthermore, as the Advocate General has demonstrated in points 85 to 90 of his Opinion, the organization of working time is not necessarily conceived as an instrument of employment policy. In this case, the fifth recital in the preamble to the directive states that the improvement of workers' safety, hygiene and health at work is an objective which should not be subordinated to 'purely economic considerations'. Were the organization of working time to be viewed as a means of combating unemployment, a number of economic factors would have to be taken into account, such as, for example, its impact on the productivity of undertakings and on workers' salaries.

[29]   The approach taken by the directive, viewing the organization of working time essentially in terms of the favourable impact it may have on the health and safety of workers, is apparent from several recitals in its preamble. Thus, for example, the eighth recital states that, in order to ensure the safety and health of Community workers, they must be granted minimum rest periods and adequate breaks and that it is also necessary in that context to place a maximum limit on weekly working hours.

In addition, the eleventh recital states that 'research has shown that . . . long periods of night work can be detrimental to the health of workers and can endanger safety at the workplace', while the fifteenth recital states that specific working conditions may have detrimental effects on the safety and health of workers and that the organization of work according to a certain pattern must take account of the general principle of adapting work to the worker.

[30]   While, in the light of those considerations, it cannot be excluded that the directive may affect employment, that is clearly not its essential objective.

[31]   As regards the content of the directive, the applicant argues that the connection between the measures it lays down, on the one hand, and health and safety, on the other, is too tenuous for the directive to be based on Article 118a of the Treaty.

[32]   In that respect, it argues that no adequate scientific evidence exists to justify the imposition of a general requirement to provide for breaks where the working day is longer than six hours (Article 4), a general requirement to provide for a minimum uninterrupted weekly rest period of twenty-four hours in addition to the usual eleven hours' daily rest (Article 5, first sentence), a requirement that the minimum rest period must, in principle, include Sunday (Article 5, second sentence), a general requirement to ensure that the average working time for each seven-day period, including overtime, does not exceed forty-eight hours (Article 6(2)), and a general requirement that every worker is to have a minimum of four weeks' paid annual leave (Article 7).

[33]   The applicant points out in that connection that Directive 89/391 provides for employers to carry out assessments to evaluate specific risks to the health and safety of workers, taking into account the nature of the activities of the undertaking. The risk assessment procedure laid down by Directive 89/391 could not apply to the restrictions on working time contained in Section II of the contested directive (and is applicable only to a very limited extent in Section III), the provisions in question being quite simply mandatory and leaving no scope for such an assessment in order to determine whether they are to apply.

[34]   The applicant maintains, moreover, that unlike other provisions based on Article 118a of the Treaty, the contested measures were not referred to the Advisory Committee on Safety, Hygiene and Health Protection at Work for an opinion (on the role of such committees, it cites Case C-212/91 *Angelopharm* [1994] ECR I-171, paragraphs 31 and 32). Although consultation of that committee is not expressly provided for in cases such as this, the fact that the Council did not call on the Commission to undertake such consultation casts further doubt on the link between the directive and the health and safety of workers.

[35]   Finally, in the applicant's view, contrary to the requirements of Article 118a(2), the provisions of the directive do not constitute 'minimum requirements for gradual implementation, having regard to the conditions and technical rules obtaining in each of the Member States' and do not take account of their effects on the creation and development of small and medium-sized undertakings'.

[36]   In order to deal with those arguments, a distinction must be drawn between the second sentence of Article 5 of the directive and its other provisions.

[37]   As to the second sentence of Article 5, whilst the question whether to include Sunday in the weekly rest period is ultimately left to the assessment of Member States, having regard, in particular, to the diversity of cultural ethnic and religious factors in

those States (second sentence of Article 5, read in conjunction with the tenth recital), the fact remains that the Council has failed to explain why Sunday, as a weekly rest day, is more closely connected with the health and safety of workers than any other day of the week. In those circumstances, the applicant's alternative claim must be upheld and the second sentence of Article 5, which is severable from the other provisions of the directive, must be annulled.

[38] The other measures laid down by the directive, which refer to minimum rest periods, length of work, night work, shift work and the pattern of work, relate to the 'working environment' and reflect concern for the protection of 'the health and safety of workers'. The scope of those terms has been explained in paragraph 15 of this judgment. Moreover, as the Belgian Government has pointed out, the evolution of social legislation at both national and international level confirms the existence of a link between measures relating to working time and the health and safety of workers.

[39] Legislative action by the Community, particularly in the field of social policy, cannot be limited exclusively to circumstances where the justification for such action is scientifically demonstrated (see points 165 to 167 of the Advocate General's Opinion).

[40] Similarly, the applicant's argument that the directive precludes any assessment of the risks involved for certain workers or for those working in a particular sector cannot be regarded as well founded. The Community legislature did take certain special situations into account, as is demonstrated by Article 1 of the directive, which excludes certain sectors or activities from its scope; by Article 14, which excludes occupations and occupational activities where more specific Community provisions apply; and by Article 17(1) and (2) which allow derogations from Articles 3, 4, 5, 6 and 8 in respect of certain groups of workers or certain sectors of activity (see points 114 to 117 of the Advocate General's Opinion).

[41] It is true that the Council did not consult the Advisory Committee on Safety, Hygiene and Health Protection at Work established by Council Decision 74/325/EEC of 27 June 1974 (OJ 1974 L 185, p. 15) with regard to the measures envisaged by the directive. However, under Article 2(1) of that decision, such consultation is intended only '[to assist] the Commission in the preparation and implementation of activities in the fields of safety, hygiene and health protection at work', and does not therefore constitute a condition precedent for action by the Council. In those circumstances, failure to consult that committee cannot be relied on to cast doubt on the link between the measures laid down by the directive and the protection of the health and safety of workers.

[42] Furthermore, the provisions of the directive are 'minimum requirements' within the meaning of Article 118a of the Treaty. Whilst ensuring a certain level of protection for workers, the directive authorizes Member States in Article 15 to apply, or facilitate the application of, measures which are more favourable to the protection of the health and safety of workers, thereby guaranteeing them a more stringent level of protection, in accordance with Article 118a(3). Similarly, Article 18(3) of the directive states that, whilst Member States may provide for different measures in the field of working time, subject to compliance with the requirements it lays down, implementation of the directive does not constitute valid grounds for reducing the general level of protection afforded to workers.

[43] The measures laid down by the directive are also, in accordance with Article 118a, 'for gradual implementation, having regard to the conditions and technical rules

obtaining in each of the Member States'. In the first place, it is not in dispute that legislation in all the Member States includes measures on the organization of working time. Furthermore, Article 18 of the directive authorizes Member States, subject to certain conditions, not to apply, after the expiry of the time-limit for implementing the directive (23 November 1996), the provisions of Article 6 on weekly working time or, for a three-year transitional period, the provisions of Article 7 on paid annual leave, which may during that period be limited to three weeks.

[44] Finally, the directive has taken account of the effects which the organization of working time for which it provides may have on small and medium-sized undertakings. Thus, the second recital in the preamble to the directive refers to the overriding requirement not to hold back the development of such undertakings. Moreover, as the Court held in its judgment in Case C-189/91 *Kirsammer-Hack* v *Sidal* [1993] ECR I-6185, paragraph 34, by providing that directives adopted in the field of health and safety of workers are to avoid imposing administrative, financial and legal constraints such as to hold back the creation and development of small and medium-sized undertakings, the second sentence of Article 118a(2) indicates that such undertakings may be the subject of special economic measures. Contrary to the view taken by the applicant, however, that provision does not prevent those undertakings from being subject to binding measures.

[45] Since it is clear from the above considerations that, in terms of its aim and content, the directive has as its principal objective the protection of the health and safety of workers by the imposition of minimum requirements for gradual implementation, neither Article 100 nor Article 100a could have constituted the appropriate legal basis for its adoption.

[46] The applicant further maintains that the Community legislature neither fully considered nor adequately demonstrated whether there were transnational aspects which could not be satisfactorily regulated by national measures, whether such measures would conflict with the requirements of the EC Treaty or significantly damage the interests of Member States or, finally, whether action at Community level would provide clear benefits compared with action at national level. In its submission, Article 118a should be interpreted in the light of the principle of subsidiarity, which does not allow adoption of a directive in such wide and prescriptive terms as the contested directive, given that the extent and the nature of legislative regulation of working time vary very widely between Member States. The applicant explains in this context, however, that it does not rely upon infringement of the principle of subsidiarity as a separate plea.

[47] In that respect, it should be noted that it is the responsibility of the Council, under Article 118a, to adopt minimum requirements so as to contribute, through harmonization, to achieving the objective of raising the level of health and safety protection of workers which, in terms of Article 118a(1), is primarily the responsibility of the Member States. Once the Council has found that it is necessary to improve the existing level of protection as regards the health and safety of workers and to harmonize the conditions in this area while maintaining the improvements made, achievement of that objective through the imposition of requirements necessarily presupposes Community-wide action, which otherwise, as in this case, leaves the enactment of the detailed implementing provisions required largely to the Member States. The argument that the Council could not properly adopt measures as general and mandatory as those forming the subject-matter of the directive will be examined below in the context of the plea alleging infringement of the principle of proportionality.

[48]   Finally, as regards Article 235 of the Treaty, it is sufficient to point to the Court's case-law, which holds that that article may be used as the legal basis for a measure only where no other Treaty provision confers on the Community institutions the necessary power to adopt it (see, in particular, *Parliament* v *Council*, cited above, paragraph 13).

[49]   It must therefore be held that the directive was properly adopted on the basis of Article 118a, save for the second sentence of Article 5, which must accordingly be annulled.

. . .

The Court, having allowed the UK only an insignificant shred of success (paras 37, 49), then concluded its judgment by rejecting pleas of breach of the proportionality principle (p. 65 below) and of infringement of essential procedural requirements.

Note
The background to this litigation lies in the hostility of the UK government at the time to an enhanced EC competence in the social field. This generated the so-called UK opt-out from the extra commitments undertaken in the field by all the other Member States in the Maastricht Treaty (see Chapter 15), although that mechanism was not directly at issue in this case. The election of a Labour government in the UK in 1997 cleared the way for the deletion by the Amsterdam Treaty of these special arrangements for the UK, and the EC Treaty's coverage of social policy is now found in renovated form, applying to all 15 Member States, in Articles 136–145 EC, which replace Articles 117–120. The Court's ruling in Case C-84/94 retains significance in principle in fixing the post-Amsterdam demarcation between Articles 95 and 308, on the one hand, and the renovated Articles 136–145 EC on social policy on the other, but the Court's firm embrace of the wide interpretation of health and safety preferred by the majority of Member States, combined with the electoral elimination of the UK grit in the EU oyster, reduces the incentives to pursue litigation on this particular point. Nonetheless, as a general observation, the Treaty of Amsterdam reduces, but does not eliminate, these complex choices between legal bases demanding distinct legislative procedures, and one may expect the Court to be further taxed in future in this fertile field for litigation.

Question
What reforms would you advocate for the Community's legislative procedure in order to improve:

(i)   the efficacy of judicial control; and
(ii)   democratic accountability?

Further reading on the issue of legal base

Pre-Amsterdam
Barents, R., 'The Internal Market Unlimited: Some Observations on the Legal Basis of Community Legislation' (1993) 30 CML Rev 85.

Emiliou, N., 'Opening Pandora's Box: The Legal Basis of Community Measures before the Court of Justice' (1994) 19 EL Rev 488.

Lenaerts, K., 'Constitutionalism and the Many Faces of Federalism' (1990) 30 AJCL 205.

Post-Amsterdam

Cullen, H. and Charlesworth, C., 'Diplomacy by other means' (1999) 36 CML Rev 1243.

Dashwood, A., 'Community Decision-making after Amsterdam' (1998) 1 *Cambridge Yearbook of European Legal Studies* 25.

See also Craig, P., 'The Nature of the Community: Integration, Democracy, and Legitimacy' and De Búrca, G., 'The Institutional Development of the EU: a Constitutional Analysis' in Craig, P., and De Búrca, G., *The Evolution of EU Law* (Oxford, OUP. 1999).

(iii) Reasoning

Article 253 declares that Community administrative and legislative acts must be reasoned.

Article 253 EC

Article 253

Regulations, directives and decisions adopted jointly by the European Parliament and the Council, and such acts adopted by the Council or the Commission shall state the reasons on which they are based and shall refer to any proposals or opinions which were required to be obtained pursuant to this Treaty.

Notes

1.   Article 253 was Article 190 pre-Amsterdam, though the text is unaltered.

2.   In an early decision, the Court explained the objective and scope of the requirement to give reasons in the following terms:

Germany v *Commission (Case 24/62)*
[1963] ECR 63
Court of Justice of the European Communities

In imposing upon the Commission the obligation to state reasons for its decisions, Article 190 is not taking mere formal considerations into account but seeks to give an opportunity to the parties of defending their rights, to the Court of exercising its supervisory functions and to Member States and to all interested nationals of ascertaining the circumstances in which the Commission has applied the Treaty. To attain these objectives, it is sufficient for the Decision to set out, in a concise but clear and relevant manner, the principal issues of law and of fact upon which it is based and which are necessary in order that the reasoning which has led the Commission to its Decision may be understood. . . .

Applying this test, the Court proceeded to consider whether the Commission had supplied sufficient information to support a Decision which granted Germany a wine tariff quota far below that for which it had submitted a request:

. . . [T]he Commission has been content to rely upon 'the information collected', without specifying any of it, in order to reach a conclusion 'that the production of the wines in question is amply sufficient'.

This elliptical reasoning is all the more objectionable because the Commission gave no indication, as it did belatedly before the Court, of the evolution and size of the surpluses, but only repeated, without expanding the reasons for it, the same statement 'that there was no indication that the existing market situation within the Community did not allow these branches of the industry in the German Federal Republic a supply which is adequate in quantity and in quality'. On the other hand, although it maintained that the production of the Community was sufficient, the Commission restricted itself to 'deducing from this' that 'the grant of a tariff quota of the volume requested might therefore lead to serious disturbances of the market in the products in question', but these disturbances were not specified. Thus it neither described the risk involved in this case, nor did it disclose what it considered to be the necessary and sufficient connexion in the present case between the two concepts which it links one with the other by a simple deduction. However, by granting a restricted quota notwithstanding its description of production as 'amply sufficient', and thereby admitting that Article 25(3) applied, the Commission thus conceded that this factor was not enough to make it possible 'to deduce from it' the risk of serious disturbance.

Thus the statement of reasons expressed appears on this point to be contradictory, since in spite of its statement with regard to an adequate supply and of the automatic conclusion to be drawn therefrom the Commission grants a quota and thereby implies that it would not cause any serious disturbance. Moreover, several, of the recitals in the German text, which is authentic, lack the necessary clarity.

It follows from these factors that the inadequacy, the vagueness and the inconsistency of the statement of reasons for the Decision, both in respect of the refusal of the quota requested and of the concession of the quota, granted, do not satisfy the requirements of Article 190.

Those parts of the Decision which have been submitted to the Court must therefore be annulled.

Note

The extent of the detail which must be provided in support of a measure will vary according to the circumstances.

Schwarze v *Einfuhr- und Vorratsstelle Getreide (Case 16/65)*
[1965] ECR 877
Court of Justice of the European Communities

The challenged Decision fixed prices for cereals. It referred back to an earlier Decision without explicitly setting out the reasons contained therein. The Court accepted that given the manner in which one measure built on the other in the administration of the policy, it was permissible for the Commission simply to refer back in this way. But were the reasons in the original Decision, thus incorporated, themselves sufficient?

The degree of precision of the statement of reasons for such a decision must be weighed against practical realities and the time and technical facilities available for making such a decision. A specific statement of reasons for each individual decision fixing a free-at-frontier price as envisaged by the Finanzgericht would mean the publication and technical evaluation of all the facts submitted by the exporting Member State or gathered by the Commission's staff for several hundreds of prices requiring to be fixed. In view, first, of the time available for the issue of the decisions and, secondly, of the number of prices to be fixed, the requirement of such a specific statement of reasons would be incompatible with the proper functioning of the machinery provided for in Regulation No 19 of the Council and Regulation No 89 of the Commission. The preparation and drafting of this kind of statement of reasons would take up so much time that the determination of prices would run the risk of being, to some extent, out of date by the time it was issued.

Moreover a comparison of the free-at-frontier prices as fixed with the general criteria published is sufficient to inform persons with a legitimate interest of the character of the data on the basis of which the decision was taken and of the conclusions to be drawn therefrom. The need to protect the parties to whom the decision is addressed and nationals of Member States affected by the decision, as also the need for proper judicial review, is sufficiently met as long as the Commission, as here, puts at the disposal of the parties the technical data used by it in fixing the free-at-frontier prices whenever the decision is challenged before a court having the appropriate jurisdiction.

For these reasons it must be concluded that the Commission was entitled to confine itself to setting out in a general form the essential factors to and the procedure which formed the background to its evaluation of the facts without its being necessary to specify the facts themselves.

Notes
1.   The Court is concerned with balance between protecting the rights of the individual and imposing unreasonable burdens on administrative authorities in complicated, rapidly moving areas of market regulation.
2.   *Commission* v *Council* (Case 45/86) was examined above (p. 49). The Court held that the measures were adopted on the wrong legal basis. It also found them flawed for inadequate reasoning on this point:

Commission v *Council (Case 45/86)*
[1987] ECR 1493
Court of Justice of the European Communities

[5]   Article 190 of the Treaty provides that: 'Regulations, directives and decisions of the Council and of the Commission shall state the reasons on which they are based'. According to the case-law of the Court (in particular the judgment of 7 July 1981 in Case 158/80 *REWE-Handelsgesellschaft Nord GmbH* v *Hauptzollamt Kiel* [1981] ECR 1805), in order to satisfy that requirement to state reasons, Community measures must include a statement of the facts and law which led the institution in question to adopt them, so as to make possible review by the Court and so that the Member States and the nationals concerned may have knowledge of the conditions under which the Community institutions have applied the Treaty.

[6]   It is therefore necessary to consider whether the contested regulations satisfy those requirements.

[7]   In that connection the Council contends that, although the indication of the legal basis is not precise, the recitals in the preambles to the regulations, taken as a whole,

provide sufficient alternative information as to the aims pursued by the Council, that is to say both commercial aims and aims of development-aid policy.

[8]   However, those indications are not sufficient to identify the legal basis by virtue of which the Council acted. Although the recitals in the preambles to the regulations do refer to improving access for developing countries to the markets of the prefer-ence-giving countries, they merely state that adaptations to the Community system of generalized preferences have proved to be necessary in the light of experience in the first 15 years. Moreover, according to information given the Court by the Council itself, the wording 'Having regard to the Treaty' was adopted as a result of differences of opinion about the choice of the appropriate legal basis. Consequently, the wording chosen was designed precisely to leave the legal basis of the regulations in question vague.

[9]   Admittedly, failure to refer to a precise provision of the Treaty need not necessarily constitute an infringement of essential procedural requirements when the legal basis for the measure may be determined from other parts of the measure. However, such explicit reference is indispensable where, in its absence, the parties concerned and the Court are left uncertain as to the precise legal basis.

(C) GENERAL PRINCIPLES OF COMMUNITY LAW

The substance of Community law concerns market integration, market regulation and the establishment of a common market. These provisions are examined in Part Two of this book. Because these rules of law, which permit regulation of the economy, directly affect individuals, the procedures must respect the position of the individual. Community law accordingly contains important principles protecting the individual. The legislative and adminis-trative tasks performed by the Community institutions are subject to review on the basis of these principles.

The Treaty contains some explicit principles which protect the individual. Article 12, for example, imposes a requirement that there shall be no discrimination on grounds of nationality within the scope of application of the Treaty. However, the Court has proved vigorous in developing a substantial body of principles independently of explicit Treaty support. These principles are important in themselves. More generally, the Court's influence in this area reveals its concern to develop a broadly based Community legal system. Some of these principles are considered below. For an extended analysis see J. Schwarze, *European Administrative Law*; T. Tridimas, *The General Principles of EC Law*.

(i) Proportionality

The following case arose before English courts. It reached the European Court via the Article 234 preliminary reference procedure which allows national courts to cooperate with the Community Court and is discussed in Chapter 4. It allows the European Court to answer questions about Commu-nity law referred to it by a national court. The European Court took the opportunity in this case to insist that Community legislation must conform to the principle of proportionality.

R v Intervention Board, ex parte Man (Sugar) Ltd (Case 181/84)
[1985] ECR 2889
Court of Justice of the European Communities

The case involved the sugar market, which is regulated by Community legislation administered at national level. Man, a British sugar trader, submitted to the Intervention Board, the regulatory agency, tenders for the export of sugar to States outside the Community. It lodged securities with a bank. Under relevant Community legislation, Man ought to have applied for export licences by noon on 2 August 1983. It was nearly four hours late, because of its own internal staff difficulties. The Board, acting pursuant to Community Regulation 1880/83, declared the security forfeit. This amounted to £1,670,370 lost by Man. Man claimed that this penalty was disproportionate; a small error resulted in a severe sanction. It accordingly instituted judicial review proceedings before the English courts in respect of the Board's action and argued that the authorising Community legislation was invalid because of its disproportionate effect. The matter was referred to the European Court under the preliminary reference procedure. Man's submission was explained by the Court as follows:

[16] . . . Man Sugar maintains that, even if it is accepted that the obligation to apply for an export licence is justifiable, the forfeiture of the entire security for failure to comply with that obligation infringes the principle of proportionality, in particular for the following reasons: the contested regulation unlawfully imposes the same penalty for failure to comply with a secondary obligation – namely, the obligation to apply for an export licence – as for failure to comply with the primary obligation to export the sugar. The obligation to apply for an export licence could be enforced by other, less drastic means than the forfeiture of the entire security and therefore the burden imposed is not necessary for the achievement of the aims of the legislation. The severity of the penalty bears no relation to the nature of the default, which may, as in the present case, be only minimal and purely technical.

The Court held:

[20] It should be noted that, as the Court held in its judgments of 20 February 1979 (Case 122/78, *Buitoni* v *FORMA*, [1979] ECR 677) and of 23 February 1983 (Case 66/82, *Fromançais SA* v *FORMA*, [1983] ECR 395), in order to establish whether a provision of Community law is in conformity with the principle of proportionality it is necessary to ascertain whether the means which it employs are appropriate and necessary to attain the objective sought. Where Community legislation makes a distinction between a primary obligation, compliance with which is necessary in order to attain the objective sought, and a secondary obligation, essentially of an administrative nature, it cannot, without breaching the principle of proportionality, penalize failure to comply with the secondary obligation as severely as failure to comply with the primary obligation.

[21] It is clear from the wording of the abovementioned Council and Commission regulations concerning standing invitations to tender for exports of white sugar, from an analysis of the preambles thereto and from the statements made by the Commission in the proceedings before the Court that the system of securities is intended above all to ensure that the undertaking, voluntarily entered into by the trader, to export the

quantities of sugar in respect of which tenders have been accepted is fulfilled. The trader's obligation to export is therefore undoubtedly a primary obligation, compliance with which is ensured by the initial lodging of a security of 9 ECU per 100 kilograms of sugar.

[22] The Commission considers, however, that the obligation to apply for an export licence within a short period, and to comply with that time-limit strictly, is also a primary obligation and as such is comparable to the obligation to export; indeed, it is that obligation alone which guarantees the proper management of the sugar market. In consequence, according to the Commission, failure to comply with that obligation, and in particular failure to comply with the time-limit, even where that failure is minimal and unintentional, justifies the forfeiture of the entire security, just as much as the total failure to comply with the primary obligation to export justifies such a penalty.

[23] In that respect the Commission contended, both during the written procedure and in the oral argument presented before the Court, that export licences fulfil four separate and important functions:

(i) They make it possible to control the release onto the market of sugar.
(ii) They serve to prevent speculation.
(iii) They provide information for the relevant Commission departments.
(iv) They establish the system of monetary compensatory amounts chosen by the exporter.

[24] As regards the use of export licences to control the release onto the world market of exported sugar, it must be noted that the traders concerned have a period of five months within which to export the sugar and no Community provision requires them to export it at regular, staggered intervals. They may therefore release all their sugar onto the market over a very short period. In those circumstances export licences cannot be said to have the controlling effect postulated by the Commission. That effect is guaranteed, though only in part, simply by staggering the invitations to tender.

[25] The Commission considers, secondly, that the forfeiture of the entire security for failure to comply with the time-limit for applying for an export licence makes it possible to prevent traders from engaging in speculation with regard to fluctuations in the price of sugar and in exchange rates and accordingly delaying the submission of their applications for export licences.

[26] Even if it is assumed that there is a real risk of such speculation, it must be noted that Article 12(c) of Regulation No 1880/83 requires the successful tenderer to pay the additional security provided for in Article 13(3) of the same regulation. The Commission itself recognized at the hearing that that additional security removes any risk of speculation by traders. It is true that at the hearing the Commission expressed doubts about the applicability of Article 13(3) before export licences have been issued. However, even if those doubts are well founded, the fact remains that a simple amendment of the rules regarding the payment of an additional security, requiring for example that, in an appropriate case, the additional security should be paid during the tendering procedure, in other words, even before the export licence has been issued, would make it possible to attain the objective sought by means which would be much less drastic for the traders concerned. The argument that the fight against speculation justifies the contested provision of Regulation No 1880/83 cannot therefore be accepted.

[27]   With regard to the last two functions attributed by the Commission to export licences, it is true that those licences make it possible for the Commission to monitor accurately exports of Community sugar to non-member countries, although they do not provide it with important new information not contained in the tenders and do not, in themselves, guarantee that the export will actually take place. It is also true that the export licence makes it possible for the exporter to state whether he wishes the monetary compensatory amounts to be fixed in advance.

[28]   However, although it is clear from the foregoing that the obligation to obtain export licences performs a useful administrative function from the Commission's point of view, it cannot be accepted that that obligation is as important as the obligation to export, which remains the essential aim of the Community legislation in question.

[29]   It follows that the automatic forfeiture of the entire security, in the event of an infringement significantly less serious than the failure to fulfil the primary obligation, which the security itself is intended to guarantee, must be considered too drastic a penalty in relation to the export licence's function of ensuring the sound management of the market in question.

[30]   Although the Commission was entitled, in the interests of sound administration, to impose a time-limit for the submission of applications for export licences, the penalty imposed for failure to comply with that time-limit should have been significantly less severe for the traders concerned than forfeiture of the entire security and it should have been more consonant with the practical effects of such a failure.

[31]   The reply to the question submitted must therefore be that Article 6(3) of Regulation No 1880/83 is invalid inasmuch as it prescribes forfeiture of the entire security as the penalty for failure to comply with the time-limit imposed for the submission of applications for export licences.

Note
A key element in the practical expression of the principle of proportionality is the need to show a link between the nature and scope of the measures taken and the object in view. The next extract is taken from a case in which a firm sought to show that a measure affected it disproportionately and that it was accordingly invalid. The issue arose in the coal and steel sector, and therefore the provisions in question were found in the ECSC Treaty. However, the Court explained the nature of the principle of proportionality in terms of general application.

Valsabbia v *Commission (Case 154/78)*
[1980] ECR 907
Court of Justice of the European Communities

[117]   It is now necessary to examine whether in view of the omissions established the obligations imposed upon the undertakings cast disproportionate burdens upon the applicants which would constitute an infringement of the principle of proportionality. In reply to the applicants' allegations on this matter, the Commission states that the validity of a general decision cannot depend on the existence or absence of other formally independent decisions.

[118]   That argument is not relevant in this case and the Court must inquire whether the defects established imposed disproportionate burdens upon the applicants, having regard to the objectives laid down by Decision No 962/77. But the Court has already recognized in its judgment of 24 October 1973 in Case 5/73, *Balkan-Import-Export* v *Hauptzollamt Berlin-Packhof* [1973] ECR 1091, that 'In exercising their powers, the Institutions must ensure that the amounts which commercial operators are charged are no greater than is required to achieve the aim which the authorities are to accomplish; however, it does not necessarily follow that that obligation must be measured in relation to the individual situation of any one particular group of operators'.

[119]   It appears that, on the whole, the system established by Decision No 962/77 worked despite the omissions disclosed and in the end attained the objectives pursued by that decision. Although it is true that the burden of the sacrifices required of the applicants may have been aggravated by the omissions in the system, that does not alter the fact that that decision did not constitute a disproportionate and intolerable measure with regard to the aim pursued.

[120]   In those circumstances, and taking into consideration the fact that the objective laid down by Decision No 962/77 is in accordance with the Commission's duty to act in the common interest, and that a necessary consequence of the very nature of Article 61 of the ECSC Treaty is that certain undertakings must, by virtue of European solidarity, accept greater sacrifices than others, the Commission cannot be accused of having imposed disproportionate burdens upon the applicants.

Note
The nature of the Court's scrutiny is influenced by the type of act subject to challenge. It was mentioned above (p. 57) that the UK's submission that Directive 93/104 on Working Time violated the principle of proportionality was rejected. The Court explained its role in the following terms.

United Kingdom v *Council (Case C-84/94)*
[1996] ECR I-5755
Court of Justice of the European Communities

[57]   As regards the principle of proportionality, the Court has held that, in order to establish whether a provision of Community law complies with that principle, it must be ascertained whether the means which it employs are suitable for the purpose of achieving the desired objective and whether they do not go beyond what is necessary to achieve it (see, in particular, Case C-426/93 *Germany* v *Council* [1995] ECR I-3723, paragraph 42).

[58]   As to judicial review of those conditions, however, the Council must be allowed a wide discretion in an area which, as here, involves the legislature in making social policy choices and requires it to carry out complex assessments. Judicial review of the exercise of that discretion must therefore be limited to examining whether it has been vitiated by manifest error or misuse of powers, or whether the institution concerned has manifestly exceeded the limits of its discretion.

There were no such flaws and consequently the plea failed.

Note
The principle of proportionality applies not only to Community legislation, but also arises in the application of substantive Treaty provisions. It will be examined further in several of the chapters in Part Two of this book.

(ii) Fundamental rights
The absence of explicit fundamental rights protection in the Treaty of Rome was in part due to the impossibility of predicting in 1957 how deeply the Community legal order would intrude into the social sphere and the field of individual rights. However, once that development had occurred it would have been unacceptable for the Community to fail to show respect for the protection of fundamental rights. It has been for the Court to fill the gaps.

It made a hesitant start; a terse start. The preliminary reference to the European Court by a German court in *Stauder* v *Ulm* (Case 29/69) arose out of concern that a provision of Community legislation infringed fundamental rights.

Stauder v Ulm (Case 29/69)
[1969] ECR 419
Court of Justice of the European Communities

[7]   . . . the provision at issue contains nothing capable of prejudicing the fundamental human rights enshrined in the general principles of Community law and protected by the Court.

Note
The next case constituted a much more serious judicial commitment to the protection of fundamental rights as part of the Community legal order.

Nold v Commission (Case 4/73)
[1974] ECR 491
Court of Justice of the European Communities

Nold, a wholesale coal and construction materials dealer, sought annulment of a Commission Decision. The Decision had authorised Nold's supplier, Ruhrkohle AG, to sell coal only subject to onerous conditions which Nold could not fulfil. Nold therefore suffered damage to its business due to the Decision, because it could no longer buy direct from its supplier. The Court first considered Nold's submissions relating to discrimination and inadequate reasoning:

[9]   In the reasoning given in its Decision the Commission emphasized that it was aware that the introduction of the new terms of business would mean that a number of dealers would lose their entitlement to buy direct from the producer, due to their inability to undertake the obligations specified above.

It justifies this measure by the need for Ruhrkohle AG, in view of the major decline in coal sales, to rationalize its marketing system in such a way as to limit direct business association to dealers operating on a sufficient scale.

The requirement that dealers contract for an annual minimum quantity is in fact intended to ensure that the collieries can market their products on a regular basis and in quantities suited to their production capacity.

[10]   It emerges from the explanations given by the Commission and the interveners that the imposition of the criteria indicated above can be justified on the grounds not only of the technical conditions appertaining to coal mining but also of the particular economic difficulties created by the recession in coal production.

It therefore appears that these criteria, established by an administrative act of general application, cannot be considered discriminatory and, for the purposes of law, were sufficiently well-reasoned in the Decision of 21 December 1972.

As regards the application of these criteria, it is not alleged that the applicant is treated differently from other undertakings which, having failed to meet the requirements laid down under the new rules, have likewise lost the advantage of their entitlement to purchase direct from the producer.

[11]   These submissions must therefore be dismissed.

The Court then examined the status of fundamental rights:

[12]   The applicant asserts finally that certain of its fundamental rights have been violated, in that the restrictions introduced by the new trading rules authorized by the Commission have the effect, by depriving it of direct supplies, of jeopardizing both the profitability of the undertaking and the free development of its business activity, to the point of endangering its very existence.

In this way, the Decision is said to violate, in respect of the applicant, a right akin to a proprietary right, as well as its right to the free pursuit of business activity, as protected by the Grundgesetz of the Federal Republic of Germany and by the Constitutions of other Member States and various international treaties, including in particular the Convention for the Protection of Human Rights and Fundamental Freedoms of 4 November 1950 and the Protocol to that Convention of 20 March 1952.

[13]   As the Court has already stated, fundamental rights form an integral part of the general principles of law, the observance of which it ensures.

In safeguarding these rights, the Court is bound to draw inspiration from constitutional traditions common to the Member States, and it cannot therefore uphold measures which are incompatible with fundamental rights recognized and protected by the Constitutions of those States.

Similarly, international treaties for the protection of human rights on which the Member States have collaborated or of which they are signatories, can supply guidelines which should be followed within the framework of Community law.

The submissions of the applicant must be examined in the light of these principles.

[14]   If rights of ownership are protected by the constitutional laws of all the Member States and if similar guarantees are given in respect of their right freely to choose and practice their trade or profession, the rights thereby guaranteed, far from constituting unfettered prerogatives, must be viewed in the light of the social function of the property and activities protected thereunder.

For this reason, rights of this nature are protected by law subject always to limitations laid down in accordance with the public interest.

Within the Community legal order it likewise seems legitimate that these rights should, if necessary, be subject to certain limits justified by the overall objectives pursued by the Community, on condition that the substance of these rights is left untouched.

As regards the guarantees accorded to a particular undertaking, they can in no respect be extended to protect mere commercial interests or opportunities, the uncertainties of which are part of the very essence of economic activity.

[15]   The disadvantages claimed by the applicant are in fact the result of economic change and not of the contested Decision.

It was for the applicant, confronted by the economic changes brought about by the recession in coal production, to acknowledge the situation and itself carry out the necessary adaptations.

[16]   This submission must be dismissed for all the reasons outlined above.

Notes
1.   This is a 'give and take' judgment. Nold fails on the facts; its rights must yield. However, of more importance in the long-term development of the law, the Court explicitly acknowledges the importance of fundamental rights within the Community legal order.
2.   In *Hoechst* v *Commission* (Case 46/87) [1989] ECR 2859, [1991] 4 CMLR 410, the Court insisted that the exercise of the Commission's powers of investigation under the Treaty competition law regime must respect fundamental rights. This case is considered in its substantive context at p. 507, but in its constitutional aspects it belongs here as a demonstration of the link between constitutional principles and the substantive law of Community market integration and regulation.
3.   The Court knows that it will earn (and deserve) the confidence of national constitutional courts only if it demonstrates that the Community observes fundamental rights. Without such a guarantee one could expect that national courts would deny the legitimacy and autonomy of Community law by testing it against national fundamental constitutional principles. This prospect seems to motivate the Court's observations in the next case.

Hauer v Rheinland-Pfalz (Case 44/79)
[1979] ECR 3727
Court of Justice of the European Communities

The case was a preliminary reference from a German court and concerned the validity of a Regulation. The first paragraph set out below details the anxiety of the national court. The *Grundgesetz* is the Federal Republic's Basic Law, established immediately after the war, and understandably much cherished. The Court responds by delicately but firmly re-writing the question.

[13]   In its order making the reference, the Verwaltungsgericht states that if Regulation No 1162/76 must be interpreted as meaning that it lays down a prohibition of general application, so as to include even land appropriate for wine growing, that provision might have to be considered inapplicable in the Federal Republic of Germany owing to doubts existing with regard to its compatibility with the fundamental rights guaranteed by Articles 14 and 12 of the Grundgesetz concerning, respectively, the right to property and the right freely to pursue trade and professional activities.

[14]   As the Court declared in its judgment of 17 December 1970, *Internationale Handelsgesellschaft* [1970] ECR 1125, the question of a possible infringement of fundamental rights by a measure of the Community institutions can only be judged in the light of Community law itself. The introduction of special criteria for assessment stemming from the legislation or constitutional law of a particular Member State would, by damaging the substantive unity and efficacy of Community law, lead inevitably to the destruction of the unity of the Common Market and the jeopardizing of the cohesion of the Community.

[15]   The Court also emphasized in the judgment cited, and later in the judgment of 14 May 1974, *Nold* [1974] ECR 491, that fundamental rights form an integral part of the general principles of the law, the observance of which it ensures; that in safeguarding those rights, the Court is bound to draw inspiration from constitutional traditions common to the Member States, so that measures which are incompatible with the fundamental rights recognized by the constitutions of those States are unacceptable in the Community; and that, similarly, international treaties for the protection of human rights on which the Member States have collaborated or of which they are signatories, can supply guidelines which should be followed within the framework of Community law. That conception was later recognized by the joint declaration of the European Parliament, the Council and the Commission of 5 April 1977, which, after recalling the case-law of the Court, refers on the one hand to the rights guaranteed by the constitutions of the Member States and on the other hand to the European Convention for the Protection of Human Rights and Fundamental Freedoms of 4 November 1950 (Official Journal C 103, 1977, p. 1).

[16]   In these circumstances, the doubts evinced by the Verwaltungsgericht as to the compatibility of the provisions of Regulation No 1162/76 with the rules concerning the protection of fundamental rights must be understood as questioning the validity of the regulation in the light of Community law. In this regard, it is necessary to distinguish between, on the one hand, a possible infringement of the right to property and, on the other hand, a possible limitation upon the freedom to pursue a trade or profession.

The Court then proceeded to examine the nature of the right to property:

[17]   The right to property is guaranteed in the Community legal order in accordance with the ideas common to the constitutions of the Member States, which are also reflected in the first Protocol to the European Convention for the Protection of Human Rights.

[18]   Article 1 of the Protocol provides as follows:

'Every natural or legal person is entitled to the peaceful enjoyment of his possessions. No one shall be deprived of his possessions except in the public interest and subject to the conditions provided for by law and by the general principles of international law.

The preceding provisions shall not, however, in any way impair the right of a State to enforce such laws as it deems necessary to control the use of property in accordance with the general interest or to secure the payment of taxes or other contributions or penalties.'

[19]   Having declared that persons are entitled to the peaceful enjoyment of their property, that provision envisages two ways in which the rights of a property owner may be impaired, according as the impairment is intended to deprive the owner of his

right or to restrict the exercise thereof. In this case it is incontestable that the prohibition on new planting cannot be considered to be an act depriving the owner of his property, since he remains free to dispose of it or to put it to other uses which are not prohibited. On the other hand, there is no doubt that that prohibition restricts the use of the property. In this regard, the second paragraph of Article 1 of the Protocol provides an important indication in so far as it recognizes the right of a State 'to enforce such laws as it deems necessary to control the use of property in accordance with the general interest'. Thus the Protocol accepts in principle the legality of restrictions upon the use of property, whilst at the same time limiting those restrictions to the extent to which they are deemed 'necessary' by a State for the protection of the 'general interest'. However, that provision does not enable a sufficiently precise answer to be given to the question submitted by the Verwaltungsgericht.

[20]   Therefore, in order to be able to answer that question, it is necessary to consider also the indications provided by the constitutional rules and practices of the nine Member States. One of the first points to emerge in this regard is that those rules and practices permit the legislature to control the use of private property in accordance with the general interest. Thus some constitutions refer to the obligations arising out of the ownership of property (German Grundgesetz, Article 14(2), first sentence), to its social function (Italian constitution, Article 42(2)), to the subordination of its use to the requirements of the common good (German Grundgesetz, Article 14(2), second sentence, and the Irish constitution, Article 43.2.2°), or of social justice (Irish constitution, Article 43.2.1°). In all the Member States, numerous legislative measures have given concrete expression to that social function of the right to property. Thus in all the Member States there is legislation on agriculture and forestry, the water supply, the protection of the environment and town and country planning, which imposes restrictions, sometimes appreciable, on the use of real property.

[21]   More particularly, all the wine-producing countries of the Community have restrictive legislation, albeit of differing severity, concerning the planting of vines, the selection of varieties and the methods of cultivation. In none of the countries concerned are those provisions considered to be incompatible in principle with the regard due to the right to property.

[22]   Thus it may be stated, taking into account the constitutional precepts common to the Member States and consistent legislative practices, in widely varying spheres, that the fact that Regulation No 1162/76 imposed restrictions on the new planting of vines cannot be challenged in principle. It is a type of restriction which is known and accepted as lawful, in identical or similar forms, in the constitutional structure of all the Member States.

[23]   However, that finding does not deal completely with the problem raised by the Verwaltungsgericht. Even if it is not possible to dispute in principle the Community's ability to restrict the exercise of the right to property in the context of a common organization of the market and for the purposes of a structural policy, it is still necessary to examine whether the restrictions introduced by the provisions in dispute in fact correspond to objectives of general interest pursued by the Community or whether, with regard to the aim pursued, they constitute a disproportionate and intolerable interference with the rights of the owner, impinging upon the very substance of the right to property. Such in fact is the plea submitted by the plaintiff in the main action, who considers that only the pursuit of a qualitative policy would permit the legislature to restrict the use of wine-growing property, with the result that she possesses an unassailable right from the moment that it is recognized that her land

is suitable for wine growing. It is therefore necessary to identify the aim pursued by the disputed regulation and to determine whether there exists a reasonable relationship between the measures provided for by the regulation and the aim pursued by the Community in this case.

[24] The provisions of Regulation No 1162/76 must be considered in the context of the common organization of the market in wine which is closely linked to the structural policy envisaged by the Community in the area in question. The aims of that policy are stated in Regulation (EEC) No 816/70 of 28 April 1970 laying down additional provisions for the common organization of the market in wine (Official Journal, English Special Edition 1970 (1), p. 234), which provides the basis for the disputed regulation, and in Regulation No 337/79 of 5 February 1979 on the common organization of the market in wine (Official Journal L 54, p. 1), which codifies all the provisions governing the common organization of the market. Title III of that regulation, laying down 'rules concerning production and for controlling planting', now forms the legal framework in that sphere. Another factor which makes it possible to perceive the Community policy pursued in that field is the Council Resolution of 21 April 1975 concerning new guidelines to balance the market in table wines (Official Journal C 90, p. 1).

[25] Taken as a whole, those measures show that the policy initiated and partially implemented by the Community consists of a common organization of the market in conjunction with a structural improvement in the wine-producing sector. Within the framework of the guidelines laid down by Article 39 of the EEC Treaty that action seeks to achieve a double objective, namely, on the one hand, to establish a lasting balance on the wine market at a price level which is profitable for producers and fair to consumers and, secondly, to obtain an improvement in the quality of wines marketed. In order to attain that double objective of quantitative balance and qualitative improvement, the Community rules relating to the market in wine provide for an extensive range of measures which apply both at the production stage and at the marketing stage for wine.

[26] In this regard, it is necessary to refer in particular to the provisions of Article 17 of Regulation No 816/70, re-enacted in an extended form by Article 31 of Regulation No 337/79, which provide for the establishment by the Member States of forecasts of planting and production, co-ordinated within the framework of a compulsory Community plan. For the purpose of implementing that plan measures may be adopted concerning the planting, re-planting, grubbing-up or cessation of cultivation of vineyards.

[27] It is in this context that Regulation No 1162/76 was adopted. It is apparent from the preamble to that regulation and from the economic circumstances in which it was adopted, a feature of which was the formation as from the 1974 harvest of permanent production surpluses, that that regulation fulfils a double function: on the one hand, it must enable an immediate brake to be put on the continued increase in the surpluses; on the other hand, it must win for the Community institutions the time necessary for the implementation of a structural policy designed to encourage high-quality production, whilst respecting the individual characteristics and needs of the different wine-producing regions of the Community, through the selection of land for grape growing and the selection of grape varieties, and through the regulation of production methods.

[28] It was in order to fulfil that twofold purpose that the Council introduced by Regulation No 1162/76 a general prohibition on new plantings, without making any

distinction, apart from certain narrowly defined exceptions, according to the quality of the land. It should be noted that, as regards its sweeping scope, the measure introduced by the Council is of a temporary nature. It is designed to deal immediately with a conjunctural situation characterized by surpluses, whilst at the same time preparing permanent structural measures.

[29] Seen in this light, the measure criticized does not entail any undue limitation upon the exercise of the right to property. Indeed, the cultivation of new vineyards in a situation of continuous over-production would not have any effect, from the economic point of view, apart from increasing the volume of the surpluses; further, such an extension at that stage would entail the risk of making more difficult the implementation of a structural policy at the Community level in the event of such a policy resting on the application of criteria more stringent than the current provisions of national legislation concerning the selection of land accepted for wine-growing.

[30] Therefore it is necessary to conclude that the restriction imposed upon the use of property by the prohibition on the new planting of vines introduced for a limited period by Regulation No 1162/76 is justified by the objectives of general interest pursued by the Community and does not infringe the substance of the right to property in the form in which it is recognized and protected in the Community legal order.

Note

Citing *Nold* (Case 4/73), the Court also concluded that there was no breach of the freedom to pursue a trade or profession. For a more recent decision, comparable in both its reasoning and result, see Cases C–248/95 & C–249/95 *SAM Schiffahrt* [1997] ECR I-4475.

In *Wunsche Handelsgesellschaft* [1987] 3 CMLR 225, the German Federal Constitutional Court, the *Bundesverfassungsgericht*, declared it would not test Community legislation against the requirements of the German Constitution, because it was satisfied that the Community legal order offered adequate protection against violation of fundamental rights. The Community legal order has thus been shaped in the context of litigation at national level and in response to national constitutional concerns. (These issues have already been aired at pp. 19 and 27 above and will be examined further in Chapter 2, for they impinge on the doctrine of the supremacy of Community law.)

Questions

1. The European Court is the only Community institution not susceptible to legal challenge. Would it be desirable to establish a control over the European Court by putting it in turn under the supervision of the European Court of Human Rights?

In Opinion 2/94 on Accession by the Community to the European Convention for the Protection of Human Rights and Fundamental Freedoms [1996] ECR I-1759, the Court stated that 'as Community law now stands, the Community has no competence to accede to the Convention'. A Treaty amendment would be required. One was not forthcoming at Amsterdam.

2. According to Article 6(2) EU, 'the Union shall respect fundamental rights, as guaranteed by the European Convention for the Protection of Human Rights and Fundamental Freedoms signed in Rome on 4 November 1950 and as they result from the constitutional traditions common to the

Member States, as general principles of Community law.' Bearing in mind the three-pillar structure of the European Union described at p. 13 above, how can this respect be ensured throughout the whole field of the Union's activity?
3. As mentioned at p. 29 above, Article 7 EU makes provision for the suspension of a Member State guilty of serious and persistent breach of the principles concerning fundamental rights mentioned in that article. Is it surprising that after a period in which so much attention was paid to the possibility of sharpening supervision of the Community and/or the Union as an actor in the field of human fields, it proved to be control of Member States which formed the most innovative aspect of the Amsterdam amendments in this area? See J. L. Duvigneau, 'From Advisory Opinion 2/94 to the Amsterdam Treaty: Human Rights Protection in the EU' [1998/2] LIEI 61; D. McGoldrick, 'The European Union after Amsterdam: An Organisation with general Human Rights Competence?', in D. O'Keeffe and P. Twomey, *Legal Issues of the Amsterdam Treaty* (Hart Publishing, 1999), Ch. 15; P. Alston (ed.), *The EU and Human Rights* (Oxford, 1999 – a collection of 28 essays).
4. The Helsinki European Council in December 1999 took the opportunity to issue a 'millennium declaration' which asserts that the European Union is based on democracy and the rule of law and that its citizens are joined by common values such as freedom, tolerance, equality, solidarity and cultural diversity. The European Council in Cologne in June 1999, the month after the entry into force of the Amsterdam Treaty, had already decided to pursue the drawing up of an EU Charter of Fundamental Rights in order, *inter alia*, to make more visible such rights to the Union's citizens. This is now under preparation. What rights should be included in such document? What legal form might such a Charter take? Remember the Preambles to the Treaties of Paris and Rome, extracted at pp. 38 and 39 above. How much has changed?

(iii) Technique
The Court's technique in realising the elaboration of the principles of Community law is of more general interest beyond the content of those principles. Article 288 of the EC Treaty, examined in Chapter 16, requires the Court to construct a principle of non-contractual liability, 'in accordance with the general principles common to the laws of the Member States'. It has become increasingly apparent that Article 288 is a statement of a broader principle of Community legal technique. The Court develops Community law by building from the foundations of national law. As the fundamental rights case law shows, this is an incremental process. The comparative tradition in the Court is often most visible in the Opinions of its Advocate-General.

Transocean Marine Paint v *Commission (Case 17/74)*
[1974] ECR 1063
Court of Justice of the European Communities

Advocate-General Warner was concerned to establish the nature of the principle of a fair hearing to which a party under investigation by the

Commission is entitled. It is the method of his inquiry, rather than the substance, which is particularly interesting in this context. After explaining the problem of identifying the scope of the Commission's obligation to offer a hearing, he continued:

ADVOCATE-GENERAL WARNER: There is a rule embedded in the law of some of our countries that an administrative authority, before wielding a statutory power to the detriment of a particular person, must in general hear what that person has to say about the matter, even if the statute does not expressly require it. '*Audi alteram partem*' or, as it is sometimes expressed, '*audiatur et altera pars*'. I say that the rule applies 'in general' because it is subject to exceptions, as are most legal principles.

In the law of England the rule is centuries old, firmly established and of daily application. It is considered to be a 'rule of natural justice', a somewhat flamboyant and sometimes criticized phrase embodying a concept akin to what is, in French-speaking countries, more soberly and, I think, more accurately, referred to as 'les principes généraux du droit'. The late Professor de Smith, in his book 'Judicial Review of Administrative Action' (3rd Ed. at p. 134 et seq.), traced its origins and development. I will not take up your Lordships' time with an account of them. The most often cited expression of the rule is in the judgment of Byles J. in *Cooper* v *Wandsworth Board of Works* (1863) 14 CBNS 180, where he said that 'although there are no positive words in a statute requiring that the party shall be heard, yet the justice of the common law will supply the omission of the legislature'. In England today there is no scope for controversy about the existence of the rule, but only about the circumstances in which it may be held inapplicable and about the manner in which it is to be applied in particular instances – consider the judgments in the House of Lords in *Ridge* v *Baldwin* [1964] AC 40. I know, my Lords, of no exception to the rule, acknowledged in English law, which could have deprived the Applicants in the circumstances of the present case of the right to be heard before being subjected to an obligation such as that contained in Article 3(1)(d) of the Commission's Decision.

There can be no doubt that the rule forms part also of the law of Scotland (consider *Malloch* v *Aberdeen Corporation* 1971 SLT 245; [1971] 1 WLR 1578) and of the laws of Denmark (see Andersen, 'Dansk Forvaltningsret', at p. 337 et seq.), of Germany (see Forsthoff, 'Lehrbuch des Verwaltungsrechts', 10th Ed., at p. 235 et seq.) and of Ireland (see Kelly, 'Fundamental Rights in the Irish Law and Constitutions', at pp. 313–314).

It has been said by Professor Vedel that the rule '*audi alteram partem*' does not exist in French administrative law (see, for instance, his 'Cours de Droit Administratif', p. 536). Professor Waline, on the other hand, in an article on the rule ('Livre Jubilaire' du Conseil d'État du Grand-Duché de Luxembourg, 1957, pp. 495–506) suggests on the contrary that it does. In my opinion, it matters little whether the applicable rule is subsumed under the title '*audi alteram partem*' or, as Professor Vedel would prefer, under the concept of the 'droits de la défense'. What is undoubted is that French administrative law does acknowledge the existence of those 'principes généraux du droit' which I have mentioned and which are applicable even in the absence of any specific legislative provision. The relevant decisions of the Conseil d'État are collected by Professor Waline in his article, and I need not rehearse them. It appears that the principle here in question is of fairly recent origin in French law, and that its scope is not yet settled. The decisions of the Conseil d'État evince three different approaches: the narrowest being to apply it only when the decision of the administrative authority concerned is in the nature of a sanction; a slightly wider approach which would apply it in any case where the decision of that authority is based on the character or on the behaviour of the person to be affected; and a third approach which is virtually as wide as that of the English common law. I should perhaps add that Professor Vedel refers to French law as being in this respect 'plutôt retardataire' and 'en voie d'évolution' (see 'Cours de Droit Administratif', p. 534, and 'Droit Administratif' 5th Ed., p. 279); and this is echoed by Professor Waline who refers to the principle '*audi alteram partem*' as 'un principe en voie de développement' (p. 496).

The position in Belgium and in Luxembourg is similar, though the Conseils d'État of those countries seem to have been less hesitant in developing the principle than that of France (see as to Belgium an article by Professor L. P. Suetens in Tijdschrift voor Bestuurswetensschappen en Publiek Recht, 1970, et p. 388, and as to Luxembourg the decisions of the Conseil d'État of 13 April 1961 in *Lorse* v *Ministre des Transports* (Aff. No 5811), of 5th August 1966 in *Roth* v *Ministres de l'Intérieur, de la Santé Publique et des Travaux Publics* (Aff. No 5968) and of 9th July 1971 in *Colot* v *Ministre du Trésor* (Aff. No 6136)).

In Italy the Consiglio di Stato has held that there is no general principle of law requiring an administrative authority to inform those concerned of its proposals so as to enable them to comment (Sez. IV, 15 May 1970, n. 345, Rass. Cons. di Stato 1970, I, p. 828, at p. 834). And it seems that the law of the Netherlands is similar, in this respect, to that of Italy.

My Lords, that review, which I have sought to keep short, of the laws of the Member States, must, I think, on balance, lead to the conclusion that the right to be heard forms part of those rights which 'the law' referred to in Article 164 of the Treaty upholds, and of which, accordingly, it is the duty of this Court to ensure the observance.

I would therefore reject the contention of the Commission that it was under no duty to inform the Applicants of what it had in mind before imposing on them the obligation contained in Article 3(1)(d) of its Decision.

Note
Chapter 13 examines in greater depth the procedures involved in Community competition law. *AM & S* v *Commission* (Case 155/79) provides a similar example of legal technique, in connection with legal professional privilege; see p. 513.

The next extract comments on the approach taken in the *Transocean Marine Paint* case. As footnote 84 indicates, it is rather well-informed!

J. Usher, 'The Influence of National Concepts on Decisions of the European Court'
(1976) 1 EL Rev 359

A case-study: the Transocean case[78]
A study may now be made of the techniques involved in applying national concepts in a case before the Court.

In 1967 the Commission had granted an exemption under Article 85(3) EEC [now 81(3) EC] with regard to the agreement between the undertakings forming the Transocean Marine Paint Association, subject to a condition obliging the Association

---
[78] Case 17/74, *Transocean Marine Paint Association* v *Commission* [1974] ECR 1063, [1974] 2 CMLR 459.

to keep the Commission informed, *inter alia*, of any change in the composition of its membership.[79] In December 1973[80] this exemption was renewed subject to certain new conditions, including Article 3(1)(*d*) which required members of the Association to inform the Commission without delay of 'any links by way of common directors or managers between a member of the Association and any other company or firm in the paints sector or any financial participation by a member of the Association in such outside companies or vice versa including all changes in such links or participations already in existence.'

The applicants brought an action to annul this provision of the decision, on the basis that, since it had neither been mentioned in the Commission's 'Notice of Objections' nor raised at the hearing before the Commission, the Commission had infringed the rules of procedure laid down in Regulation 99/63,[81] in particular Articles 2 and 4 thereof.

The Commission had in fact indicated that it was willing to renew the exemption for five years, subject to certain fresh conditions and obligations. One of these was that the Association should, according to the literal English translation, 'notify any change in the participatory relationships of the members,' which could be interpreted, amongst other things, as requiring merely that the information which had already had to be supplied under the 1967 decision be supplemented by the notification of any links which might exist between the undertakings which were members of the association.

On the question of Regulation 99/63, Advocate-General Warner suggested in his Opinion,[82] and the Court in fact decided,[83] that Articles 2 and 4 of Regulation 99/63 concern the objections which would either bring an agreement within Article 85(1) or prevent it being granted an exemption under Article 85(3) and do not deal with conditions which may be imposed upon a grant of an exemption.

However, the Court is not dependent solely upon the arguments which the parties choose to put before it. Its purpose is to ensure as far as possible the uniform application of Community law and to a certain degree it has its own staff which it can use to enable it to do this. There exists a 'Library and Research Division,'[84] the members of which when requested by members of the Court provide research notes on points of law. In this particular case, as Advocate-General Warner was of the opinion that, at any rate in English law, this would be a situation where *audi alteram partem* could be invoked, he requested a comparative study of the laws of the other Member States to see whether this was a principle generally accepted in other Member States.

It should hardly be necessary in this *Review* to cite the well-known English cases on the question,[85] although in fact the *dictum* which is perhaps most appropriate to the facts of that particular case was pronounced in an extra-judicial capacity by Lord Morris of Borth-y-Gest when he said that 'if someone has a right to be heard he must be entitled to know what he needs to be heard about. He must know what is the case against him. He must know what he has to meet.'[86]

---

[79] Decision of June 27, 1967, JO 1967, 163/10, [1967] CMLR D9.
[80] Decision of December 21, 1973, OJ 1974, L19/18, [1974] CMLR D11.
[81] Commission Reg. 99/63 of July 25, 1963, JO 1963, 2268.
[82] [1974] ECR 1063, 1087.
[83] *Ibid.* p. 1079.
[84] Of which the present writer was a member at the time.
[85] e.g. *Cooper* v *Wandsworth Board of Works* (1863) 14 CB (NS) 180; *Ridge* v *Baldwin* [1964] AC 40.
[86] *Current Legal Problems*, 1973, p. 11.

Turning then to the various national legal systems, and looking first at French law, it is interesting to note that an English text book on French administrative law[87] states that the French concept, *droit de la défense*, is much wider than the English concept of *audi alteram partem*; on the other hand, a French writer, Professor Vedel,[88] is of the opinion that the rule *audi alteram partem* is much wider than the principle of *droit de la défense* in French law, largely because he is of the opinion that the doctrine of *droit de la défense* only applies where the administrative measure in question has been taken by reason of the character or personal conduct of the person concerned. However, other writers take a somewhat wider view, notably Professor Waline, in a contribution to a publication celebrating the centenary of the Luxembourg Conseil d'État,[89] where he deduces from the many specific statutory instances, as well as the case-law, that the principle is in the course of development.

In the case of the Federal Republic, it is interesting to note that Article 103 of the Basic Law provides only that the right to be heard applies before the ordinary civil law courts. There is no specific provision for it in administrative law. However, commentators seem to agree that the principle applies despite the absence of any legislative necessity for it. In fact one text book[90] manages to quote 14 pre-Federal Republic decisions supporting the general idea that the right to a hearing (*das rechtliche Gehör*) is an essential element of correct procedure not by virtue of principles of written law but by principles of unwritten law, i.e. as a general principle of law.[91] This principle has been taken up by the Federal German courts and a clear illustration is a decision of the Verwaltungsgerichtshof of Kassel in 1956[92] concerned with an administrative decision to change what might be termed a 'milk-catchment area' (*Milcheinzugsgebiet*). It was stated there that even without any express provision of a statute the administration must, as a requirement of the rule of law, hear the persons affected before taking a decision imposing any burden on them.

Similar formulations can be found, for example, in the case-law of the Luxembourg Conseil d'État, which has held that in the case of administrative decisions which might affect proprietary interests, the administration must hear those affected, even if the actual legislation in question is silent upon the point.[93]

The same would appear to be true in Ireland,[94] Scotland[95] and Denmark.[96] As far as Belgian law is concerned, there do not appear to be any decisions directly in point though academic opinion is in favour of giving a person affected by an administrative decision the right to be heard.[97] It appears, however, that there is no general right to

---

[87] Brown and Garner, *French Administrative Law* 2nd ed., p. 124–125, citing *Trompier-Gravier* (Conseil d'État, May 5, 1944, *Sirey* 1945, 3, 14) and *SA Co-opérative d'HBM de Vichy-Cusset-Bellerive* (Conseil d'État, April 24, 1964, *Recueil*, p. 244).

[88] *Droit Administratif*, p. 281; *Cours de Droit Administratif*, p. 536.

[89] *Livre Jubilaire*, 1957, pp. 495–506; see also his *Droit Administratif*, 9th ed., at pp. 460, 552, 586 and 606 for specific examples.

[90] Forsthoff, *Lehrbuch des Verwaltungsrechts*, 10th ed., p. 235 *et seq.*

[91] See e.g. Decision of administrative court of Saxony (Sächs OVG), October 24, 1908, *Jahrbuch* t. 13 p. 97.

[92] May 18, 1956, *Neue juristische Wochenschrift*, 1956, p. 1940.

[93] August 5, 1966, Aff. No. 5968, *Roth* v *Ministres de l'Intérieur, de la Santé Publique et des Travaux Publics* – the number of Ministers involved was the result of the subject-matter of the action, a refusal of an authorisation to work a quarry so as to protect underground water supplies.

[94] Kelly, *Fundamental Rights in the Irish Law and Constitution*, pp. 313–314.

[95] *Malloch* v *Aberdeen Corporation* [1971] 1 WLR 1578.

[96] Andersen, *Dansk Forvaltningsret*, at pp. 337 and 339.

[97] See e.g. Dembour, *Droit Administratif*, p. 266.

be heard in Dutch administrative law, and the problem is complicated by the fact that there is no general right of appeal against administrative decisions, in the absence of a special statutory provision. However, a law of June 20, 1963, provides for appeals against the administrative acts of the central government authorities.[98]

Finally, in Italy, it has been held that the right to be heard is not protected by the Constitution in administrative proceedings[99] and that there is no general principle of administrative law requiring the Administration to communicate preparatory acts to those liable to be affected to enable them to put their view.[100]

Mr Warner reviewed the position under the various national legal systems in his Opinion and concluded that the right to be heard forms part of those rights which 'the law' referred to in Article 164 EEC [now 220 EC] upholds and of which accordingly it is the duty of the Court to ensure the observance.[101]

The way the Court introduced this general principle into its judgment was to state that notwithstanding the cases specifically dealt with in Articles 2 and 4 of Regulation 99/63, the Regulation is an application of 'the general rule that a person whose interests are perceptibly affected by a decision taken by a public authority, must be given the opportunity to make his point of view known.'[102] Under the Court's formulation it was stated that the rule requires that an undertaking be clearly informed in good time of the essence of conditions to which the Commission intends to subject an exemption and it must have the opportunity to submit its observations to the Commission. 'This is especially so in the case of conditions which, as in this case, impose considerable obligations having far-reaching effects.'

The Court deduced from this that breach of the rule would be regarded as a breach of an essential procedural requirement under Article 173 of the Treaty, and that this was the case with regard to Article 3(1)(d) of the Decision. Since this condition was severable, it alone was annulled, and the rest of the decision was allowed to stand whilst the Commission was given the opportunity to reach a fresh decision on the point after hearing the observations or suggestions of the members of the association.[103]

Conclusion

It is hoped that this article will have shown the importance of concepts derived from national sources in the case-law of the European Court, subject always to the proviso that once adopted by the Court, they are applicable as principles of Community law, not as rules of national law.

From the point of view of English readers, it will be evident from the account of the *Transocean* case that English concepts are beginning to make their presence felt. However, it will also have been noticed that certain of the most important principles applied by the Court can be regarded as derived from German sources or at least as having become principles of Community law in a formulation closely resembling that current in the Federal Republic, a point which may not be totally unconnected with the fact that of the 353 cases referred to the Court by national courts up to the end of 1975, no fewer than 167 were referred by courts in the Federal Republic. In the nature of things, judges tend to regard as common principles those which they hear cited before them day-in, day-out; perhaps there is something of a moral here for English (and Scottish) courts and lawyers.

---

[98] See Van Wijk, Netherlands Report, *8 International Congress of Comparative Law* 1970, pp. 303 *et seq.*
[99] Cons. di Stato, Sez. IV, 9 nov. 1971, n. 959, Rass. Cons. di Stato 1971, I, p. 2076.
[100] Cons. di Stato, Sez. IV, 15 mai 1970, n. 345, Rass. Cons. di Stato 1970, I, p. 828 (834).
[101] [1974] ECR 1063, 1089.
[102] [1974] ECR 1063, 1080.
[103] The new Decision was in fact taken on October 23, 1975, OJ 1975 L286/24.

Notes

1. National law spills over into Community law and *vice versa*. The Community legal order is broadened and replenished by the comparative approach. In 'European Public Law: Reality and Prospects' [1991] *Public Law* 53, at p. 58, T. Koopmans, a former judge of the Court, refers to general principles 'defined and developed at the Community level . . . [which] tend to extend their influence to the application of purely national law. They are discovered, by the Court of Justice, on the basis of the existing national legal systems, but they then "travel back" to these same systems with a kind of added force'. Our examination of fundamental rights shows that sources such as the European Convention on Human Rights are also influential, even though formally independent of the Community structure.

2. It is notable that these principles are developed both in Article 230 judicial review actions and in Article 234 preliminary reference procedures. There is more than one context in which the European Court is offered the opportunity to develop the Community's legal order.

In *The Community Legal Order*, J.-V. Louis points out that the Court, in shaping the principles of Community law, must 'determine the solution that appears most appropriate having regard to the requirements of the Community legal order'. However, he warns that 'it may not . . . usurp the role of the Community legislator if the deficiency could be filled by legislation. . . . In applying the general principles common to the laws of the Member States it must exercise self-restraint' (pp. 98–99). Has it? The most notable proponent of the view that the Court lacks such due inhibition is H. Rasmussen. In *On Law and Policy in the ECJ*, he comments (at p. 508) that

> The Court of Justice's lawmaking activities, defiant of much European tradition in that respect, were regularly preceded by deep involvements in making choices between competing public policies for which the available sources of law did not offer the Court judicially applicable guidelines.

Rasmussen's more recent views may be explored in *European Court of Justice* (Copenhagen: Gadjura, 1998), although this is explicitly *not* designed as a 2nd edition of *On Law and Policy in the ECJ* (p. 36).

3. There will be much more discussion of this issue later in the book, but do not expect the European Court to follow the methods of an English court. As Advocate-General Warner observed in the extract at p. 75 above, Article 164 of the EC Treaty (now Article 220 EC) declares that, 'The Court of Justice shall ensure that in the interpretation and application of this Treaty the law is observed.' Yet many of the Treaty obligations are loosely worded, which has given the Court great latitude in developing the shape of the law. It is expected to be creative in pursuit of broad general objectives in an overt manner unfamiliar to the English judiciary.

4. Community law may begin to seem like a Constitution. The European Court contends that the 'Treaty, albeit concluded in the form of an international agreement, nonetheless constitutes the constitutional charter of a

Community based on the rule of law' (Opinion 1/91 [1991] ECR I-6079).
Beyond Treaty sources and secondary legislation, there are general principles
which permeate the fabric of the law. The Community offers both a
Constitution for economic integration and a Constitution for the protection
of the individual. This twin purpose of Community law will be observed in
many manifestations throughout this book.

Nevertheless, the Court's 'constitutionalisation' of the EC Treaty has
attracted increasing attention as one part of a broader inquiry into the nature
of the Union and its impact on the constitutional structures of the Member
States, considered at pp. 13–36 above. The ruling of the *Bundesverfassungsgericht,* at p. 15 above, may be taken as a warning to the Court (although
not just to the Court) that an over-ambitious development of the law may not
attract support at national level. One should not neglect the perception that
successful constitutionalisation of the Community legal order is dependent on
the active support of national judiciaries. Absent such support, the system is
likely to fragment. Neither the European Court nor the other EC institutions
are able to use physical coercion to secure respect for their rulings. (See, e.g.,
J. Weiler, 'Journey to an Unknown Destination: A Restrospective and
Prospective of the European Court of Justice in the Arena of Political
Integration' (1993) 31 JCMS 417.) The reader is accordingly invited to
apply the questions about the shaping of the Union that were raised at
pp. 13–36 above to the particular case of the role of the European Court
in supervising the complex relationships between individuals, States and
Community institutions.

Further reading
De Burca, G., 'Proportionality and *Wednesbury* Unreasonableness: The Influ-
    ence of European Legal Concepts on UK Law' (1997) 3 *Euro Public Law*
    561.
Dehousse, R., *The European Court of Justice* (Basingstoke, Macmillan Press,
    1998).
Ellis, E. (ed), *The Principle of Proportionality in the Laws of Europe* (Oxford,
    Hart Publishing, 1999).
Hartkamp, A. S., et al. (eds), *Towards a European Civil Code* (2nd ed., The
    Hague, Kluwer, 1998).
Jacobs, F., 'Is the Court of Justice of the European Communities a Constitu-
    tional Court?' in Curtin, D. and O'Keeffe, D. (eds), *Constitutional Adjudi-
    cation in European Community and National Law* (1992).
Markesinis, B., (ed), *The Gradual Convergence* (Oxford, OUP, 1994).
Mestmäcker, E.-J., 'On the Legitimacy of European Law' (1994) 58 *Rabels
    Z* 615.
Shapiro, M., 'The European Court of Justice' in Craig, P. and de Burca, G.,
    The Evolution of EU Law (Oxford, OUP, 1999).
Slaughter, A.-M., Stone Sweet, A., and Weiler, J., (eds), *The European Courts
    and National Courts: Doctrine and Jurisprudence* (Oxford, Hart Publishing,
    1997), especially Ch. 8, Alter, L., 'Explaining National Court Acceptance

of European Court Jurisprudence: a Critical evaluation of Theories of Legal Integration' and Ch. 11, Stone Sweet, A., 'Constitutional Dialogues in the European Community'.

Weiler, J., 'The Transformation of Europe' (1991) 100 Yale LJ 2403.

Wilhelmsson, T., 'Jack-in-the-box theory of European Community Law', in Krämer, L., et al. (eds), *Law and Diffuse Interests in the European Legal Order* (Baden-Baden, Nomos, 1997), p. 177.

2 THE NATURE OF COMMUNITY LAW: SUPREMACY

The Court's development of the key notions of *supremacy* and of *direct effect* represents a classic exercise of the teleological interpretative function favoured by the Court. Nowhere in the Treaty is it possible to find an explicit commitment to the idea that Community law shall be supreme, nor to the notion that it shall be directly effective. Yet the Court has deduced the existence of both these fundamental principles from the *object* of the Treaty. It would be impossible to create the structure envisaged by the Treaties *unless* the law is supreme and directly effective. So, reasoned the Court, the Treaty impliedly contains the principles of supremacy and direct effect. This chapter examines supremacy and its consequences; the next chapter studies direct effect.

(A) SUPREMACY

The case of *Costa* v *ENEL* (Case 6/64) provided the Court with one of its earliest opportunities to explain the nature of the Community legal order. (Naturally, the references to Treaty Articles use the 'old', i.e. pre-Amsterdam, numbering — see p. 29 above.)

Costa v *ENEL (Case 6/64)*
[1964] ECR 585
Court of Justice of the European Communities

By contrast with ordinary international treaties, the EEC Treaty has created its own legal system which, on the entry into force of the Treaty, became an integral part of the legal systems of the Member States and which their courts are bound to apply.

By creating a Community of unlimited duration, having its own institutions, its own personality, its own legal capacity and capacity of representation on the international plane and, more particularly, real powers stemming from a limitation of sovereignty or a transfer of powers from the States to the Community, the Member States have limited their sovereign rights, albeit within limited fields, and have thus created a body of law which binds both their nationals and themselves.

The integration into the laws of each Member State of provisions which derive from the Community, and more generally the terms and the spirit of the Treaty, make it impossible for the States, as a corollary, to accord precedence to a unilateral and subsequent measure over a legal system accepted by them on a basis of reciprocity. Such a measure cannot therefore be inconsistent with that legal system. The executive force of Community law cannot vary from one State to another in deference to subsequent domestic laws, without jeopardizing the attainment of the objectives of the Treaty set out in Article 5(2) and giving rise to the discrimination prohibited by Article 7.

The obligations undertaken under the Treaty establishing the Community would not be unconditional, but merely contingent, if they could be called in question by subsequent legislative acts of the signatories. Wherever the Treaty grants the States the right to act unilaterally, it does this by clear and precise provisions (for example, Articles 15, 93(3), 223, 224 and 225). Applications, by Member States for authority to derogate from the Treaty are subject to a special authorization procedure (for example, Articles 8(4), 17(4), 25, 26, 73, the third subparagraph of Article 93(2), and 226) which would lose their purpose if the Member States could renounce their obligations by means of an ordinary law.

The precedence of Community law is confirmed by Article 189, whereby a regulation 'shall be binding' and 'directly applicable in all Member States'. This provision, which is subject to no reservation, would be quite meaningless if a State could unilaterally nullify its effects by means of a legislative measure which could prevail over Community law.

It follows from all these observations that the law stemming from the Treaty, an independent source of law, could not, because of its special and original nature, be overridden by domestic legal provisions, however framed, without being deprived of its character as Community law and without the legal basis of the Community itself being called into question.

The transfer by the States from their domestic legal system to the Community legal system of the rights and obligations arising under the Treaty carries with it a permanent limitation of their sovereign rights, against which a subsequent unilateral act incompatible with the concept of the Community cannot prevail. . . .

Note

In the next case the Court made plain its view of the implications of Community law before national courts asked to rule on a conflict between Community law and domestic law.

Amministrazione delle Finanze v *Simmenthal (Case 106/77)*
[1978] ECR 629
Court of Justice of the European Communities

[14] . . . [R]ules of Community law must be fully and uniformly applied in all the Member States from the date of their entry into force and for so long as they continue in force.

[15] These provisions are therefore a direct source of rights and duties for all those affected thereby, whether Member States or individuals, who are parties to legal relationships under Community law.

[16]   This consequence also concerns any national court whose task it is as an organ of a Member State to protect, in a case within its jurisdiction, the rights conferred upon individuals by Community law.

[17]   Furthermore, in accordance with the principle of the precedence of Community law, the relationship between provisions of the Treaty and directly applicable measures of the institutions on the one hand and the national law of the Member States on the other is such that those provisions and measures not only by their entry into force render automatically inapplicable any conflicting provision of current national law but – in so far as they are an integral part of, and take precedence in, the legal order applicable in the territory of each of the Member States – also preclude the valid adoption of new national legislative measures to the extent to which they would be incompatible with Community provisions.

[18]   Indeed any recognition that national legislative measures which encroach upon the field within which the Community exercises its legislative power or which are otherwise incompatible with the provisions of Community law had any legal effect would amount to a corresponding denial of the effectiveness of obligations undertaken unconditionally and irrevocably by Member States pursuant to the Treaty and would thus imperil the very foundations of the Community.

[19]   The same conclusion emerges from the structure of Article 177 of the Treaty which provides that any court or tribunal of a Member State is entitled to make a reference to the Court whenever it considers that a preliminary ruling on a question of interpretation or validity relating to Community law is necessary to enable it to give judgment.

[20]   The effectiveness of that provision would be impaired if the national court were prevented from forthwith applying Community law in accordance with the decision or the case-law of the Court.

[21]   It follows from the foregoing that every national court must, in a case within its jurisdiction, apply Community law in its entirety and protect rights which the latter confers on individuals and must accordingly set aside any provision of national law which may conflict with it, whether prior or subsequent to the Community rule.

[22]   Accordingly any provision of a national legal system and any legislative, administrative or judicial practice which might impair the effectiveness of Community law by withholding from the national court having jurisdiction to apply such law the power to do everything necessary at the moment of its application to set aside national legislative provisions which might prevent Community rules from having full force and effect are incompatible with those requirements which are the very essence of Community law.

[23]   This would be the case in the event of a conflict between a provision of Community law and a subsequent national law if the solution of the conflict were to be reserved for an authority with a discretion of its own, other than the court called upon to apply Community law, even if such an impediment to the full effectiveness of Community law were only temporary.

[24]   The first question should therefore be answered to the effect that a national court which is called upon, within the limits of its jurisdiction, to apply provisions of Community law is under a duty to give full effect to those provisions, if necessary refusing of its own motion to apply any conflicting provision of national legislation,

even if adopted subsequently, and it is not necessary for the court to request or await the prior setting aside of such provision by legislative or other constitutional means.

[25]   The essential point of the *second question* is whether – assuming it to be accepted that the protection of rights conferred by provisions of Community law can be suspended until any national provisions which might conflict with them have been in fact set aside by the competent national authorities – such setting aside must in every case have unrestricted retroactive effect so as to prevent the rights in question from being in any way adversely affected.

[26]   It follows from the answer to the first question that national courts must protect rights conferred by provisions of the Community legal order and that it is not necessary for such courts to request or await the actual setting aside by the national authorities empowered so to act of any national measures which might impede the direct and immediate application of Community rules.

[27]   The second question therefore appears to have no purpose.

The Court's ruling in response to the questions referred was:

A national court which is called upon, within the limits of its jurisdiction, to apply provisions of Community law is under a duty to give full effect to those provisions, if necessary refusing of its own motion to apply any conflicting provision of national legislation, even if adopted subsequently, and it is not necessary for the court to request or await the prior setting aside of such provisions by legislative or other constitutional means.

Note

The cases dealing with fundamental rights in Chapter 1 should be recalled. It was precisely Community law's aspiration to supremacy that led to concern at national level about respect for fundamental rights. That in turn motivated the Court to develop the content of Community law to meet such concerns. So was built the Community legal order. It remains a developing project.

The next case examines the scope of the obligation on Member States to ensure that the influence of Community law, which is supreme, is not obstructed. (Once again, it should be borne in mind that the vintage of the case means that pre-Amsterdam Treaty numbering is used.)

Commission v *France (Case 167/73)*
[1974] ECR 359
Court of Justice of the European Communities

The French *Code du Travail Maritime* required the crew of merchant ships to comprise at least three French for every non-French sailor. This is in principle unlawful discrimination on grounds of nationality, forbidden by Community law. However, the French authorities were prepared in practice to allow nationals of other Member States to count as French for these purposes. It was argued that because it was proper to focus on the application of the law in practice, not its terms in the abstract, France had not violated Community law.

[41]   . . . [A]lthough the objective legal position is clear, namely, that Article 48 and Regulation No 1612/68 are directly applicable in the territory of the French Republic, nevertheless the maintenance in these circumstances of the wording of the Code du Travail Maritime gives rise to an ambiguous state of affairs by maintaining, as regards those subject to the law who are concerned, a state of uncertainty as to the possibilities available to them of relying on Community law.

[42]   This uncertainty can only be reinforced by the internal and verbal character of the purely administrative directions to waive the application of the national law.

[43]   The free movement of persons, and in particular workers, constitutes, as appears both from Article 3(c) of the Treaty and from the place of Articles 48 to 51 in Part Two of the Treaty, one of the foundations of the Community.

[44]   According to Article 48(2) it entails the abolition of any discrimination based on nationality, whatever be its nature or extent, between workers of the Member States as regards employment, remuneration and other conditions of work and employment.

[45]   The absolute nature of this prohibition, moreover, has the effect of not only allowing in each State equal access to employment to the nationals of other Member States, but also, in accordance with the aim of Article 177 of the Treaty, of guaranteeing to the State's own nationals that they shall not suffer the unfavourable consequences which could result from the offer or acceptance by nationals of other Member States of conditions of employment or remuneration less advantageous than those obtaining under national law, since such acceptance is prohibited.

[46]   It thus follows from the general character of the prohibition on discrimination in Article 48 and the objective pursued by the abolition of discrimination that discrimination is prohibited even if it constitutes only an obstacle of secondary importance as regards the equality of access to employment and other conditions of work and employment.

[47]   The uncertainty created by the maintenance unamended of the wording of Article 3 of the Code du Travail Maritime constitutes such an obstacle.

[48]   It follows that in maintaining unamended, in these circumstances, the provisions of Article 3(2) of the Code du Travail Maritime as regards the nationals of other Member States, the French Republic has failed to fulfil its obligations under Article 48 of the Treaty and Article 4 of Regulation No 1612/68 of the Council of 15 October 1968.

(B) DIRECT APPLICABILITY

The attribute of *direct applicability*, referred to in *Simmenthal* (Case 106/77) at p. 83 above, is linked to the doctrine of supremacy. Article 249 EC declares Regulations to be directly applicable in the national legal order. This means that they are automatically law in all the Member States when made under the Community legislative procedure. In principle it is not open to Member States to interfere with the direct application of the Regulation in the national legal order. Only exceptionally will a Regulation require implementation at national level.

Variola v *Amministrazione delle Finanze (Case 34/73)*
[1973] ECR 981
Court of Justice of the European Communities

[9]   In the fourth and fifth questions, the Court is, in effect, asked to determine whether the disputed provisions of the Regulations can be introduced into the legal order of Member States by internal measures reproducing the contents of Community provisions in such a way that the subject-matter is brought under national law, and the jurisdiction of the Court is thereby affected.

[10]   The direct application of a Regulation means that its entry unto force and its application in favour of or against those subject to it are independent of any measure of reception into national law.
   By virtue of the obligations arising from the Treaty and assumed on ratification, Member States are under a duty not to obstruct the direct applicability inherent in Regulations and other rules of Community law.
   Strict compliance with this obligation is an indispensable condition of simultaneous and uniform application of Community Regulations throughout the Community.

[11]   More particularly, Member States are under an obligation not to introduce any measure which might affect the jurisdiction of the Court to pronounce on any question involving the interpretation of Community law or the validity of an act of the institutions of the Community, which means that no procedure is permissible whereby the Community nature of a legal rule is concealed from those subject to it.
   Under Article 177 of the Treaty in particular, the jurisdiction of the Court is unaffected by any provisions of national legislation which purport to convert a rule of Community law into national law.

. . .

[15]   A legislative provision of internal law could not be set up against the direct effect, in the legal order of Member States, of Regulations of the Community and other provisions of Community law, including the prohibition, under Articles 9 *et seq.* of the Treaty, of charges having equivalent effect to customs duties, without compromising the essential character of Community rules as such and the fundamental principle that the Community legal system is supreme.
   This is particularly true as regards the date from which the Community rule becomes operative and creates rights in favour of private parties.
   The freedom of each Member State to vary, in relation to itself and without express authority, the date on which a Community rule comes into force is excluded by reason of the need to ensure uniform and simultaneous application of Community law throughout the Community.

(C) PRE-EMPTION

A further aspect of the nature of the Community legal order is that in some fields the competence of the Community is exclusive. In order to maintain integrity and uniformity in the Community's legal order, Member States are held to have lost the power to act independently in particular areas.
   Commission v *Council* (Case 22/70) was examined in Chapter 1 as an instance of an act, a Council Resolution, falling outside the list in Article 189

of the EC Treaty (now Article 249 EC), which was held nevertheless to have legal effects. Of interest here is exactly what that act related to – its substance.

Commission v *Council (Case 22/70)*
[1971] ECR 263
Court of Justice of the European Communities

The Resolution adopted by the States relating to negotiation of the European Road Transport Agreement was based on the assumption that it was for the Member States to participate independently in the conclusion of the Agreement. The ostensible purpose of the Commission's challenge was to show that it was for the Community to participate, and that it had replaced the Member States as the competent actor in the field. The Court embarked on a close examination of the Treaty in order to determine the correct allocation of competence.

[12]   In the absence of specific provisions of the Treaty relating to the negotiation and conclusion of international agreements in the sphere of transport policy – a category into which, essentially, the AETR falls – one must turn to the general system of Community law in the sphere of relations with third countries.

[13]   Article 210 provides that 'The Community shall have legal personality'.

[14]   This provision, placed at the head of Part Six of the Treaty, devoted to 'General and Final Provisions', means that in its external relations the Community enjoys the capacity to establish contractual links with third countries over the whole field of objectives defined in Part One of the Treaty, which Part Six supplements.

[15]   To determine in a particular case the Community's authority to enter into international agreements, regard must be had to the whole scheme of the Treaty no less than to its substantive provisions.

[16]   Such authority arises not only from an express conferment by the Treaty – as is the case with Articles 113 and 114 for tariff and trade agreements and with Article 238 for association agreements – but may equally flow from other provisions of the Treaty and from measures adopted, within the framework of those provisions, by the Community institutions.

[17]   In particular, each time the Community, with a view to implementing a common policy envisaged by the Treaty, adopts provisions laying down common rules, whatever form these may take, the Member States no longer have the right, acting individually or even collectively, to undertake obligations with third countries which affect those rules.

[18]   As and when such common rules come into being, the Community alone is in a position to assume and carry out contractual obligations towards third countries affecting the whole sphere of application of the Community legal system.

[19]   With regard to the implementation of the provisions of the Treaty the system of internal Community measures may not therefore be separated from that of external relations.

[20]   Under Article 3(e), the adoption of a common policy in the sphere of transport is specially mentioned amongst the objectives of the Community.

[21]   Under Article 5, the Member States are required on the one hand to take all appropriate measures to ensure fulfilment of the obligations arising out of the Treaty or resulting from action taken by the institutions and, on the other hand, to abstain from any measure which might jeopardize the attainment of the objectives of the Treaty.

[22]   If these two provisions are read in conjunction, it follows that to the extent to which Community rules are promulgated for the attainment of the objectives of the Treaty, the Member States cannot, outside the framework of the Community institutions, assume obligations which might affect those rules or alter their scope.

[23]   According to Article 74, the objectives of the Treaty in matters of transport are to be pursued within the framework of a common policy.

[24]   With this in view, Article 75(1) directs the Council to lay down common rules and, in addition, 'any other appropriate provisions'.

[25]   By the terms of subparagraph (a) of the same provision, those common rules are applicable 'to international transport to or from the territory of a Member State or passing across the territory of one or more Member States'.

[26]   This provision is equally concerned with transport from or to third countries, as regards that part of the journey which takes place on Community territory.

[27]   It thus assumes that the powers of the Community extend to relationships arising from international law, and hence involve the need in the sphere in question for agreements with the third countries concerned.

[28]   Although it is true that Articles 74 and 75 do not expressly confer on the Community authority to enter into international agreements, nevertheless the bringing into force, on 25 March 1969, of Regulation No 543/69 of the Council on the harmonization of certain social legislation relating to road transport (OJ L 77, p. 49) necessarily vested in the Community power to enter into any agreements with third countries relating to the subject-matter governed by that regulation.

[29]   This grant of power is moreover expressly recognized by Article 3 of the said regulation which prescribes that: 'The Community shall enter into any negotiations with third countries which may prove necessary for the purpose of implementing this regulation'.

[30]   Since the subject-matter of the AETR falls within the scope of Regulation No 543/69, the Community has been empowered to negotiate and conclude the agreement in question since the entry into force of the said regulation.

[31]   These Community powers exclude the possibility of concurrent powers on the part of Member States, since any steps taken outside the framework of the Community institutions would be incompatible with the unity of the Common Market and the uniform application of Community law.

Notes

1.   It is clearly apparent from the final paragraph of this extract that the ruling is based on the nature of the Community legal order. However, despite this ruling in principle in favour of the Community at the expense of the Member States acting independently, the Commission's application was

rejected on the facts. Given the long history of negotiations on the Agreement, the Community had not yet fully assumed competence in this particular matter. The resolution was not invalid.

2.   See also *Kramer* (Case 3/76) [1976] ECR 1279, in which the Court was still firmer in its insistence on pre-emption. Some of these issues have already been explored in part in Chapter 1. The Court's most significant recent ruling on the allocation of competences between Community and Member States in external relations is Opinion 1/94, [1994] ECR I-5267. It found that some aspects of the World Trade Organization Agreement fell within the EC's exclusive competence, while others fell outside the scope of exclusive competence.

3.   Similar issues arise in the Community's internal legal order. So where the Community legislates, for example, in the area of health inspections for animals, Member States may be precluded from adopting different legislation in that area. This is examined in Chapter 7 in relation to the free movement of goods in the Community under Articles 28–30. Broader questions relating to the respective competences of the Community and the Member States are addressed in Chapter 15.

3 THE NATURE OF COMMUNITY LAW: DIRECT EFFECT

(A) THE NATURE AND PURPOSE OF DIRECT EFFECT

No decision in Community law is more important than the following:

Van Gend en Loos v *Nederlandse Administratie der Belastingen*
(Case 26/62)
[1963] ECR 1
Court of Justice of the European Communities

Van Gend en Loos had imported ureaformaldehyde from Germany into The Netherlands. It had been charged a customs duty. This violated the principle of the free movement of goods between Member States – specifically Article 12 of the Treaty of Rome (which is now Article 25 post-Amsterdam, Chapter 6). Van Gend en Loos claimed reimbursement of the sum before the Dutch courts. The Dutch court made a preliminary reference to the European Court under Article 177 (which is now Article 234 post-Amsterdam) in order to discover whether Article 12 of the Treaty could assist a private litigant before a national court.

The first question of the Tariefcommissie is whether Article 12 of the Treaty has direct application in national law in the sense that nationals of Member States may on the basis of this Article lay claim to rights which the national court must protect.

To ascertain whether the provisions of an international treaty extend so far in their effects it is necessary to consider the spirit, the general scheme and the wording of those provisions.

The objective of the EEC Treaty, which is to establish a Common Market, the functioning of which is of direct concern to interested parties in the Community, implies that this Treaty is more than an agreement which merely creates mutual obligations between the contracting states. This view is confirmed by the preamble to the Treaty which refers not only to governments but to peoples. It is also confirmed more specifically by the establishment of institutions endowed with sovereign rights, the exercise of which affects Member States and also their citizens. Furthermore, it must be noted that the nationals of the states brought together in the Community are called upon to cooperate in the functioning of this Community through the intermediary of the European Parliament and the Economic and Social Committee.

In addition the task assigned to the Court of Justice under Article 177, the object of which is to secure uniform interpretation of the Treaty by national courts and tribunals, confirms that the states have acknowledged that Community law has an authority which can be invoked by their nationals before those courts and tribunals.

The conclusion to be drawn from this is that the Community constitutes a new legal order of international law for the benefit of which the states have limited their sovereign rights, albeit within limited fields, and the subjects of which comprise not only Member States but also their nationals. Independently of the legislation of Member States, Community law therefore not only imposes obligations on individuals but is also intended to confer upon them rights which become part of their legal heritage. These rights arise not only where they are expressly granted by the Treaty, but also by reason of obligations which the Treaty imposes in a clearly defined way upon individuals as well as upon the Member States and upon the institutions of the Community.

Having established this point of principle, the Court then considered Article 12 of the Treaty itself (now, remember, Article 25 EC post-Amsterdam). Community law *can* be directly effective before a national court; but is Article 12?

The wording of Article 12 contains a clear and unconditional prohibition which is not a positive but a negative obligation. This obligation, moreover, is not qualified by any reservation on the part of states which would make its implementation conditional upon a positive legislative measure enacted under national law. The very nature of this prohibition makes it ideally adapted to produce direct effects in the legal relationship between Member States and their subjects.

The implementation of Article 12 does not require any legislative intervention on the part of the states. The fact that under this Article it is the Member States who are made the subject of the negative obligation does not imply that their nationals cannot benefit from this obligation.

In addition the argument based on Articles 169 and 170 of the Treaty put forward by the three Governments which have submitted observations to the Court in their statements of case is misconceived. The fact that these Articles of the Treaty enable the Commission and the Member States to bring before the Court a State which has not fulfilled its obligations does not mean that individuals cannot plead these obligations, should the occasion arise, before a national court, any more than the fact that the Treaty places at the disposal of the Commission ways of ensuring that obligations imposed upon those subject to the Treaty are observed, precludes the possibility, in actions between individuals before a national court, of pleading infringements of these obligations.

A restriction of the guarantees against an infringement of Article 12 by Member States to the procedures under Article 169 and 170 would remove all direct legal protection of the individual rights of their nationals. There is the risk that recourse to the procedure under these Articles would be ineffective if it were to occur after the implementation of a national decision taken contrary to the provisions of the Treaty.

The vigilance of individuals concerned to protect their rights amounts to an effective supervision in addition to the supervision entrusted by Articles 169 and 170 to the diligence of the Commission and of the Member States.

It follows from the foregoing considerations that, according to the spirit, the general scheme and the wording of the Treaty, Article 12 must be interpreted as producing direct effects and creating individual rights which national courts must protect.

Note

The Court shows itself in this judgment determined carefully to justify its discovery of the key principle of direct effect from the point of view of the purpose of Community law. The inclusion of individuals as those capable of benefiting from and being subject to Community law immeasurably deepens the impact of Community law. It also makes it more likely to be observed. Breach of directly effective Community law may be challenged at Community level (principally by the Commission using what was Article 169 and is now Article 226) and also at national level by individuals. This is the key notion of 'dual vigilance' to which the Court refers in the *Van Gend en Loos* judgment.

In the next two cases the Court repeats its views of the nature and purpose of the direct effect doctrine. It also explains further the conditions which must be satisfied before a provision will be held directly effective. The test is one which will more readily be fulfilled than might initially have been expected. Direct effect, it seems, is the rule rather than the exception.

Van Duyn v Home Office (Case 41/74)
[1974] ECR 1337
Court of Justice of the European Communities

Van Duyn, a Dutch woman, had been refused leave to enter the UK, where she wished to take up employment with the Church of Scientology. Her action against the Home Office was based on Community law guaranteeing the free movement of workers. This is contained in Article 48 of the EC Treaty (now, after amendment, Article 39 EC) and amplified in other measures, including Directive 64/221. Chapter 9 of this book examines these provisions. There is a basic right to travel from Member State A to Member State B to take up work, subject to exceptions based on, *inter alia*, public policy. The UK sought to exclude Van Duyn on the basis of the exceptions, claiming the Church to be socially undesirable. The High Court made a preliminary reference to the European Court to seek clarification of the issues involved. The first two questions concerned the enforceability of Community law provisions before national courts – direct effect.

[4]   By the first question, the Court is asked to say whether Article 48 of the EEC Treaty is directly applicable so as to confer on individuals rights enforceable by them in the courts of a Member State.

[5]   It is provided, in Article 48(1) and (2), that freedom of movement for workers shall be secured by the end of the transitional period and that such freedom shall entail

'the abolition of any discrimination based on nationality between workers of Member States as regards employment, remuneration and other conditions of work and employment.'

[6]   These provisions impose on Member States a precise obligation which does not require the adoption of any further measure on the part either of the Community institutions or of the Member States and which leaves them, in relation to its implementation, no discretionary power.

[7]   Paragraph 3, which defines the rights implied by the principle of freedom of movement for workers, subjects them to limitations justified on grounds of public policy, public security or public health. The application of these limitations is, however, subject to judicial control, so that a Member State's right to invoke the limitations does not prevent the provisions of Article 48, which enshrine the principle of freedom of movement for workers, from conferring on individuals rights which are enforceable by them and which the national courts must protect.

[8]   The reply to the first question must therefore be in the affirmative.

Second question

[9]   The second question asks the Court to say whether Council Directive No 64/221 of 25 February 1964 on the co-ordination of special measures concerning the movement and residence of foreign nationals which are justified on grounds of public policy, public security or public health is directly applicable so as to confer on individuals rights enforceable by them in the courts of a Member State.

[10]   It emerges from the order making the reference that the only provision of the Directive which is relevant is that contained in Article 3(1) which provides that 'measures taken on grounds of public policy or public security shall be based exclusively on the personal conduct of the individual concerned.'

[11]   The United Kingdom observes that, since Article 189 of the Treaty distinguishes between the effects ascribed to regulations, directives and decisions, it must therefore be presumed that the Council, in issuing a directive rather than making a regulation, must have intended that the directive should have an effect other than that of a regulation and accordingly that the former should not be directly applicable.

[12]   If, however, by virtue of the provisions of Article 189 regulations are directly applicable and, consequently, may by their very nature have direct effects, it does not follow from this that other categories of acts mentioned in that Article can never have similar effects. It would be incompatible with the binding effect attributed to a directive by Article 189 to exclude, in principle, the possibility that the obligation which it imposes may be invoked by those concerned. In particular, where the Community authorities have, by directive, imposed on Member States the obligation to pursue a particular course of conduct, the useful effect of such an act would be weakened if individuals were prevented from relying on it before their national courts and if the latter were prevented from taking it into consideration as an element of Community law. Article 177, which empowers national courts to refer to the Court questions concerning the validity and interpretation of all acts of the Community institutions, without distinction, implies furthermore that these acts may be invoked by individuals in the national courts. It is necessary to examine, in every case, whether the nature, general scheme and wording of the provision in question are capable of having direct effects on the relations between Member States and individuals.

[13]   By providing that measures taken on grounds of public policy shall be based exclusively on the personal conduct of the individual concerned, Article 3(1) of Directive No 64/221 is intended to limit the discretionary power which national laws generally confer on the authorities responsible for the entry and expulsion of foreign nationals. First, the provision lays down an obligation which is not subject to any exception or condition and which, by its very nature, does not require the intervention of any act on the part either of the institutions of the Community or of Member States. Secondly, because Member States are thereby obliged, in implementing a clause which derogates from one of the fundamental principles of the Treaty in favour of individuals, not to take account of factors extraneous to personal conduct, legal certainty for the persons concerned requires that they should be able to rely on this obligation even though it has been laid down in a legislative act which has no automatic direct effect in its entirety.

[14]   If the meaning and exact scope of the provision raise questions of interpretation, these questions can be resolved by the courts, taking into account also the procedure under Article 177 of the Treaty.

[15]   Accordingly, in reply to the second question, Article 3(1) of Council Directive No 64/221 of 25 February 1964 confers on individuals rights which are enforceable by them in the courts of a Member State and which the national courts must protect.

Defrenne v SABENA (Case 43/75)
[1976] ECR 455
Court of Justice of the European Communities

This was a preliminary reference from a Brussels court. It concerned Article 119, which contained the principle of equal pay for equal work. The post-Amsterdam version is found in Article 141 EC, though, as explained in Chapter 15, the Amsterdam Treaty made significant alterations to the Treaty provisions on social policy. It is the Treaty's major provision in the field of sex discrimination. Defrenne, an air hostess, was seeking compensation from SABENA, her employer, for low pay she had received in comparison with male workers. But could she rely on the Treaty provision before a national court?

[16]   Under the terms of the first paragraph of Article 119, the Member States are bound to ensure and maintain 'the application of the principle that men and women should receive equal pay for equal work'.

[17]   The second and third paragraphs of the same article add a certain number of details concerning the concepts of pay and work referred to in the first paragraph.

[18]   For the purposes of the implementation of these provisions a distinction must be drawn within the whole area of application of Article 119 between, first, direct and overt discrimination which may be identified solely with the aid of the criteria based on equal work and equal pay referred to by the article in question and, secondly, indirect and disguised discrimination which can only be identified by reference to more explicit implementing provisions of a Community or national character.

[19]   It is impossible not to recognize that the complete implementation of the aim pursued by Article 119, by means of the elimination of all discrimination, direct or

indirect, between men and women workers, not only as regards individual undertakings but also entire branches of industry and even of the economic system as a whole, may in certain cases involve the elaboration of criteria whose implementation necessitates the taking of appropriate measures at Community and national level.

[20] This view is all the more essential in the light of the fact that the Community measures on this question, to which reference will be made in answer to the second question, implement Article 119 from the point of view of extending the narrow criterion of 'equal work', in accordance in particular with the provisions of Convention No 100 on equal pay concluded by the International Labour Organization in 1951, Article 2 of which establishes the principle of equal pay for work 'of equal value'.

[21] Among the forms of direct discrimination which may be identified solely by reference to the criteria laid down by Article 119 must be included in particular those which have their origin in legislative provisions or in collective labour agreements and which may be detected on the basis of a purely legal analysis of the situation.

[22] This applies even more in cases where men and women receive unequal pay for equal work carried out in the same establishment or service, whether public or private.

[23] As is shown by the very findings of the judgment making the reference, in such a situation the court is in a position to establish all the facts which enable it to decide whether a woman worker is receiving lower pay than a male worker performing the same tasks.

[24] In such situation, at least, Article 119 is directly applicable and may thus give rise to individual rights which the courts must protect.

[25] Furthermore, as regards equal work, as a general rule, the national legislative provisions adopted for the implementation of the principle of equal pay as a rule merely reproduce the substance of the terms of Article 119 as regards the direct forms of discrimination.

[26] Belgian legislation provides a particularly apposite illustration of this point, since Article 14 of Royal Decree No 40 of 24 October 1967 on the employment of women merely sets out the right of any female worker to institute proceedings before the relevant court for the application of the principle of equal pay set out in Article 119 and simply refers to that article.

[27] The terms of Article 119 cannot be relied on to invalidate this conclusion.

[28] First of all, it is impossible to put forward an argument against its direct effect based on the use in this article of the word 'principle', since, in the language of the Treaty, this term is specifically used in order to indicate the fundamental nature of certain provisions, as is shown, for example, by the heading of the first part of the Treaty which is devoted to 'Principles' and by Article 113, according to which the commercial policy of the Community is to be based on 'uniform principles'.

[29] If this concept were to be attenuated to the point of reducing it to the level of a vague declaration, the very foundations of the Community and the coherence of its external relations would be indirectly affected.

[30] It is also impossible to put forward arguments based on the fact that Article 119 only refers expressly to 'Member States'.

[31]   Indeed, as the Court has already found in other contexts, the fact that certain provisions of the Treaty are formally addressed to the Member States does not prevent rights from being conferred at the same time on any individual who has an interest in the performance of the duties thus laid down.

[32]   The very wording of Article 119 shows that it imposes on States a duty to bring about a specific result to be mandatorily achieved within a fixed period.

[33]   The effectiveness of this provision cannot be affected by the fact that the duty imposed by the Treaty has not been discharged by certain Member States and that the joint institutions have not reacted sufficiently energetically against this failure to act.

[34]   To accept the contrary view would be to risk raising the violation of the right to the status of a principle of interpretation, a position the adoption of which would not be consistent with the task assigned to the Court by Article 164 of the Treaty.

[35]   Finally, in its reference to 'Member States', Article 119 is alluding to those States in the exercise of all those of their functions which may usefully contribute to the implementation of the principle of equal pay.

[36]   Thus, contrary to the statements made in the course of the proceedings this provision is far from merely referring the matter to the powers of the national legislative authorities.

[37]   Therefore, the reference to 'Member States' in Article 119 cannot be interpreted as excluding the intervention of the courts in direct application of the Treaty.

[38]   Furthermore it is not possible to sustain any objection that the application by national courts of the principle of equal pay would amount to modifying independent agreements concluded privately or in the sphere of industrial relations such as individual contracts and collective labour agreements.

[39]   In fact, since Article 119 is mandatory in nature, the prohibition on discrimination between men and women applies not only to the action of public authorities, but also extends to all agreements which are intended to regulate paid labour collectively, as well as to contracts between individuals.

[40]   The reply to the first question must therefore be that the principle of equal pay contained in Article 119 may be relied upon before the national courts and that these courts have a duty to ensure the protection of the rights which this provision vests in individuals, in particular as regards those types of discrimination arising directly from legislative provisions or collective labour agreements, as well as in cases in which men and women receive unequal pay for equal work which is carried out in the same establishment or service, whether private or public.

Notes
1.   In *Van Duyn* v *Home Office* (Case 41/74), the Court found the provisions directly effective despite the existence of derogations available to Member States; in *Defrenne* v *SABENA* (Case 43/75), direct effect was upheld despite the very broad, underdeveloped terms of the provision in question.
2.   Two particular aspects of *Defrenne* v *SABENA* (Case 43/75) should not be overlooked. First, the Treaty provision was held directly effective against a private party, the employer (para. 39 above). Community law, then, is capable of binding not only the State, as in *Van Gend en Loos* and *Van Duyn*

(so-called vertical direct effect), but also private parties (horizontal direct effect). The second aspect worthy of attention is that the Court decided to restrict the implications of its ruling:

Defrenne v SABENA (Case 43/75)
[1976] ECR 455
Court of Justice of the European Communities

[69]   The Governments of Ireland and the United Kingdom have drawn the Court's attention to the possible economic consequences of attributing direct effect to the provisions of Article 119, on the ground that such a decision might, in many branches of economic life, result in the introduction of claims dating back to the time at which such effect came into existence.

[70]   In view of the large number of people concerned such claims, which undertakings could not have foreseen, might seriously affect the financial situation of such undertakings and even drive some of them to bankruptcy.

[71]   Although the practical consequences of any judicial decision must be carefully taken into account, it would be impossible to go so far as to diminish the objectivity of the law and compromise its future application on the ground of the possible repercussions which might result, as regards the past, from such a judicial decision.

[72]   However, in the light of the conduct of several of the Member States and the views adopted by the Commission and repeatedly brought to the notice of the circles concerned, it is appropriate to take exceptionally into account the fact that, over a prolonged period, the parties concerned have been led to continue with practices which were contrary to Article 119, although not yet prohibited under their national law.

[73]   The fact that, in spite of the warnings given, the Commission did not initiate proceedings under Article 169 against the Member States concerned on grounds of failure to fulfil an obligation was likely to consolidate the incorrect impression as to the effects of Article 119.

[74]   In these circumstances, it is appropriate to determine that, as the general level at which pay would have been fixed cannot be known, important considerations of legal certainty affecting all the interests involved, both public and private, make it impossible in principle to reopen the question as regards the past.

[75]   Therefore, the direct effect of Article 119 cannot be relied on in order to support claims concerning pay periods prior to the date of this judgment, except as regards those workers who have already brought legal proceedings or made an equivalent claim.

Note

The Court has subsequently insisted that it alone can declare that a directly effective provision may not be relied on retrospectively. This power does not belong to a national court; see *Blaizot v University of Liège* (Case 24/86) [1988] ECR 379; *Barra v Belgium* (Case 309/85) [1988] ECR 355; and *Evangelischer Krankenhausverein Wien* (Case C-437/97) judgment of 9 March 2000.

(B) DIRECT EFFECT AS A POLICY CHOICE

The Court has made a conscious policy choice in asserting the central significance of direct effect in the Community legal order. Most of the key substantive provisions of Community law studied in Part Two of this book are directly effective and therefore susceptible to enforcement by private individuals before national courts.

Read particularly P. Pescatore, 'The Doctrine of Direct Effect: an infant disease of Community law' (1983) 8 EL Rev 155. At p. 157 he observes that, 'the reasoning of the Court shows that the judges had "une certaine idee de l'Europe" of their own and that it is this idea which has been decisive and not arguments based on the legal technicalities of the matter'.

Read also R. Lecourt, *L'Europe des Juges*. At p. 248 he explains that:

En effet, ou bien la Communauté est, pour les particuliers, une séduisante mais lointaine abstraction intéressant seulement les gouvernements qui leur en appliquent discrétionnairement les règles; ou bien elle est pour eux une réalité effective et par conséquence créatrice de droits.

The following extract provides an elegantly written overview of the course pursued by the Court in shaping the constitutional principles of the Community legal order. The author is not impartial. He was a judge of the Court from 1988 until his death in 1999.

F. Mancini, 'The Making of a Constitution for Europe' (1989) 26 CML Rev 595
[Reproduced by permission of Kluwer Academic Publishers]

(Some footnotes omitted.)

1. For educated observers of European affairs, whether friends or foes of a strong Community, the magnitude of the contribution made by the Court of Justice to the integration of Europe has almost become a by-word. It is unnecessary to quote the friends, which in any event, since they tend to be enthusiastic, would be somewhat embarrassing for a member of the Court. Far more interesting are the enemies or the less than lukewarm supporters of a united Europe. In England politicians who openly criticise judges are frowned upon; Mrs Thatcher, a barrister, is aware of this rule and cannot therefore be quoted, though her private reactions to judgments encroaching on British sovereign rights and interests are easy to visualise. But that old, unredeemed Gaullist, the former Prime Minister Michel Debré, is eminently quotable: 'J'accuse la Cour de Justice' – he said as late as 1979 – 'de mégalomanie maladive', by which, of course, he meant insufficient deference to the sovereign rights and interests of France.

If one were asked to synthetise the direction in which the case-law produced in Luxembourg has moved since 1957, one would have to say that it coincides with the making of a constitution for Europe. Unlike the United States, the EC was born as a peculiar form of international organisation. Its peculiarity resided in the unique institutional structure and the unprecedented law-making and judicial powers it was given. But these features – admittedly reminiscent of a federal State – should not overshadow two essential facts. First: while the American Declaration of Independence spoke of '*one people*' dissolving the bonds which connected them with '*another people*', the preamble of the Rome Treaty recites that the contracting parties are 'determined to lay the foundations of an ever closer union among the *peoples* of Europe'. Second and more important: the instrument giving rise to the Community was a traditional multilateral *treaty*.

Treaties are basically different from constitutions. In many countries (and 'many' includes even some of the founding States of the EC) they do not enjoy the status of higher law. The interpretation of treaties is subject to canons unlike all others (such as, for example, the presumption that States do not lose their sovereignty). As a rule, treaties devise systems of checks and balances whose main function is to keep under control the powers of the organisation which they set up. In the case of the Rome Treaty these differences are emphasised by two highly significant characteristics. The Treaty does not safeguard the fundamental rights of the individuals affected by its application, nor does it recognise, even in an embryonic form, a constitutional right to European citizenship. Europe cannot confer citizenship; this remains the prerogative of the Member States. By the same token, individual citizens of a Member State are entitled to move from their State to another Member State exclusively by virtue of their being workers, self-employed persons or providers of services, that is *qua* units of a production factor.

The main endeavour of the Court of Justice has precisely been to remove or reduce the differences just mentioned. In other words, the Court has sought to 'constitutionalise' the Treaty, that is to fashion a constitutional framework for a federal-type structure in Europe. Whether this effort was always inspired by a clear and consistent philosophy is arguable, but that is not really important. What really matters are its achievements – and they are patent to all.

To be sure, the Court has been helped by favourable circumstances. The combination of being, as it were, out of sight and out of mind by virtue of its location in the fairy-tale Grand Duchy of Luxembourg and the benign neglect of the media has certainly contributed to its ability to create a sense of belonging on the part of its independent-minded members and, where necessary, to convert them into confirmed Europeans. Furthermore, the judges and advocates general have usually been middle-aged and at least half of them have been academics. As a group, therefore, they have never met the three conditions of Lord Diplock's famous verdict: 'by training, temperament and age judges are too averse to change to be entrusted with the development of rules of conduct for a brave new world'.

Nevertheless, these circumstances do not explain the whole story. The Court would have been far less successful had it not been assisted by two mighty allies: the national courts and the Commission. The institutional position of the former will be clarified below. It is sufficient to mention here that by referring to Luxembourg sensitive questions of interpretation of Community law they have been indirectly responsible for the boldest judgments the Court has made. Moreover, by adhering to these judgments in deciding the cases before them, and therefore by lending them the credibility which national judges usually enjoy in their own countries, they have rendered the case-law of the Court both effective and respected throughout the Community.

As to the Commission, the founding fathers and especially Jean Monnet conceived it as a sort of 'Platonic embodiment of Communitarian spirit, with Gallic élan, self-confidence and expertise'. As the executive-political branch of the Community, the Commission may not have always lived up to those expectations, but as 'watchdog of the Treaty', that is both as the prosecutor of Member State infractions and as an *amicus curiae* in cases referred by the national courts, it has undoubtedly played a positive rôle. In other words, the Commission has led the Court – particularly by assuaging the concern some of the judges may have felt regarding the acceptability of their rulings – on the path toward further integration and increased Community power.

On the other hand, the Parliament and the Council are not natural allies of the Court. The Parliament evinced great sympathy for the Court in the 1960s and the 1970s, but then its function was simply that of a debating forum. More recently, however, the Parliament has been involved in a permanent trial of strength with the Council: the stake is a new allocation of power in the budgetary and legislative areas. The Court is a victim of this (in itself entirely legitimate) turbulence. The reason is obvious. Luxembourg is more and more encumbered by increasingly political and emotion-loaded intra-Community controversies: hence a visibility and an exposure to scrutiny by the media that are in sharp contrast with the conditions under which progress was made in the past.

The Council, the Community legislative body, is bound not to be an ally of the Court. Although formally an institution with supranational characteristics like the others, it was drawn by its very composition – a gathering of national Ministers – into resembling an intergovernmental round table often characterised by all the warmth of a love match in a snake-pit. In other words, its members regularly speak, and no doubt think, in terms of negotiating with their partners much as they would do in any other international context. The observation that 'decisionally, the Community is closer to the United Nations than it is to the United States' is therefore particularly telling.

This situation is heightened by the weight acquired in the area of law-making by COREPER (the Committee of Permanent Representatives of the Member States) and its many subcommittees. The permanent representatives are ambassadors and the subcommittees are composed of national officials. While a minister may occasionally be expected to deal with a given problem in a supranational spirit, it would be naïve to expect an ambassador or a national bureaucrat, whatever his leanings, to assist willfully in the process of the wasting away of Member State power, thereby blighting his own career.

2. It was noted above that, unlike federal constitutions, the treaties creating international organisations do not usually enjoy higher-law status with regard to the laws of the contracting powers. Article VI of the American Constitution reads: 'the laws of the United States . . . shall be the supreme law of the land; and the judges in every state shall be bound thereby; any thing in the constitution or laws of any state to the contrary notwithstanding'. In the same vein section 109 of the Australian Constitution provides that 'When a law of a State is inconsistent with the law of the Commonwealth the latter shall prevail and the former shall be . . . invalid', and the German Fundamental Law stipulates just as clearly that *Bundesrecht bricht Landesrecht*. On the contrary, the Rome Treaty, while including some hortatory provisions to the same effect (Article 5), fails to state squarely whether Community law is pre-eminent *vis-à-vis* prior and subsequent Member State law.

The now undisputed existence of a supremacy clause in the Community framework is therefore a product of judicial creativeness. In *Costa* v *Enel*, a case which arose in the early 1960s before a *giudice conciliatore* (local magistrate) in Milan, a shareholder of a nationalised power company challenged as being contrary to the Treaty the Italian law nationalising the electric industry. The Italian Government claimed before the Court of Justice that the Court had no business to deal with the matter: the magistrate, it said, should apply the nationalisation law as the most current indication of parliamentary intention and could not avail of the reference procedure provided for by the Treaty. But the Court ruled that 'by creating a Community of unlimited duration, having its own institutions, its own personality . . . and, more particularly, real powers stemming from a limitation of sovereignty or a transfer of powers from the States to the Community, the Member States have limited their sovereign rights . . . and have thus created a body of law which binds both their nationals and themselves'.

Is this line of reasoning entirely cogent? Some legal writers doubt it and a few have regarded *Costa* v *Enel* as an example of judicial activism 'running wild'.[10] Yet, the Court's supremacy doctrine was accepted by the judiciaries and the administrations of both the original and the new Member States, with the exception of some grumblings by the French *Conseil d'État*, the Italian *Corte costituzionale* and a couple of English law lords. Lord Denning, a majestic but irritable elderly gentleman, was caught intimating that 'once a bill is passed by Parliament, that will dispose of all this discussion about the Treaty'.[11] A few years later, however, Lord Diplock admitted that even subsequent acts of Parliament must be interpreted in line with Community law, no matter how far-fetched the interpretation.[12] Lord Diplock, and many other national judges before him, obviously realised that the alternative to the supremacy clause would have been a rapid erosion of the Community; and this was a possibility that nobody really envisaged, not even the most intransigent custodians of national sovereignty. Actually, the 'or else' argument, though not fully spelled out, was used by the Court, and it was this argument, much more than the one I have quoted, that led to a ready reception of the doctrine in *Costa* v *Enel*.

But the recognition of Community pre-eminence was not only an indispensable development, it was also a logical development. It is self-evident that in a federal or quasi-federal context the issue of supremacy will arise only if federal norms are to apply directly, that is to bear upon the federation's citizens without any need of intervention by the Member States. Article 189 of the Rome Treaty identifies a category of Community norms that do not require national implementing measures but are binding on the States and their citizens as soon as they enter into force: the founding fathers called them 'regulations' and provided them principally for those areas where the Treaty itself merely defines the thrust of Community policy and leaves its elaboration to later decisions of the Council and the Commission. One year before *Costa* v *Enel*, however, the Court had enormously extended the Community power to deal directly with the public by ruling in *Van Gend en Loos* that even Treaty provisions may be relied upon by private individuals if they expressly grant them rights and impose on the Member States an obligation so precise and unconditional that it can be fulfilled without the necessity of further measures.

Note

The observations made in the penultimate paragraph of this extract are particularly pertinent in the light of the anxieties about the patterns of development of the EC legal order that have emerged among national judges in the decade since Mancini wrote these words. These are traced at pp. 15–27 above and some of the suggested reading material listed at the end of Chapter 1 (p. 80 above) deserves re-consideration in the light of

---

[10] Rasmussen, *On Law and Policy in the European Court of Justice: A Comparative Study in Judicial Policymaking* (Dordrecht-Boston-Lancaster: Martinus Nijhoff, 1986). [*Cf* p. 79 above.]
[11] *Felixstowe Dock and Ry Co.* v *British Transport Docks Board*, [1976] 2 CMLR 655.
[12] *Garland* v *British Rail Engineering*, [1982] 2 All ER 402.

Mancini's portrayal here of the needs of the EC legal order. Assess the weight of his "or else' argument' (set out in the final sentence of the penultimate paragraph of this extract).

(C) THE DIRECT EFFECT OF DIRECTIVES

(i) Establishing the principle
The most difficult area relating to 'direct effect' arises in the application of the notion to EC *Directives*. Although the rest of this chapter concentrates on this area, it is important not to develop an inflated notion of the importance of the problem of the direct effect of Directives. Directives are after all only one source of Community law. However, the issue deserves examination in some depth, because Directives are a rather peculiar type of act – Community law but implemented at national level through national legal procedures. An examination of this area, then, should reveal much about the general problem of the interrelation of national law with the Community legal order.

The starting point is Article 249 EC, formerly Article 189, set out at p. 40. This suggests that a Directive, in contrast to a Regulation, would *not* be directly effective. Regulations are directly applicable, and if they meet the *Van Gend en Loos* (Case 26/62) test for direct effect they are directly effective too. They are law in the Member States (direct applicability) and they may confer legally enforceable rights on individuals (direct effect). Directives, in marked contrast, are clearly dependent on implementation by each State, according to Article 249. When made by the Community, they are not designed to be law in that form at national level. Nor are they designed directly to affect the individual. Yet in *Van Duyn* (Case 41/74), at p. 93 above, the Court held that a Directive might be relied on by an individual before a national court. In the next case, *Pubblico Ministero* v *Ratti* (Case 148/78), the European Court explains how, when and why Directives can produce direct effects (or, at least, effects analogous thereto) at national level.

Pubblico Ministero v *Ratti (Case 148/78)*
[1979] ECR 1629; [1980] 1 CMLR 96
Court of Justice of the European Communities

Directive 73/173 required Member States to introduce into their domestic legal orders rules governing the packaging and labelling of solvents. This had to be done by December 1974. Italy had failed to implement the Directive and maintained in force a different national regime. Ratti produced his solvents in accordance with the Directive, not the Italian law. In 1978 he found himself the subject of criminal proceedings in Milan for non-compliance with Italian law. Could he rely on the Directive which Italy had left unimplemented?

[18]   This question raises the general problem of the legal nature of the provisions of a directive adopted under Article 189 of the Treaty.

[19] In this regard the settled case-law of the Court, last reaffirmed by the judgment of 1 February 1977 in Case 51/76 *Nederlandse Ondernemingen* [1977] 1 ECR 126, lays down that, whilst under Article 189 regulations are directly applicable and, consequently, by their nature capable of producing direct effects, that does not mean that other categories of acts covered by that article can never produce similar effects.

[20] It would be incompatible with the binding effect which Article 189 ascribes to directives to exclude on principle the possibility of the obligations imposed by them being relied on by persons concerned.

[21] Particularly in cases in which the Community authorities have, by means of directive, placed Member States under a duty to adopt a certain course of action, the effectiveness of such an act would be weakened if persons were prevented from relying on it in legal proceedings and national courts prevented from taking it into consideration as an element of Community law.

[22] Consequently a Member State which has not adopted the implementing measures required by the directive in the prescribed periods may not rely, as against individuals, on its own failure to perform the obligations which the directive entails.

[23] It follows that a national court requested by a person who has complied with the provisions of a directive not to apply a national provision incompatible with the directive not incorporated into the internal legal order of a defaulting Member State, must uphold that request if the obligation in question is unconditional and sufficiently precise.

[24] Therefore the answer to the first question must be that after the expiration of the period fixed for the implementation of a directive a Member State may not apply its internal law – even if it is provided with penal sanctions – which has not yet been adapted in compliance with the directive, to a person who has complied with the requirements of the directive.

Note

Directive 77/728 applied a similar regime to varnishes. But here Ratti had jumped the gun. The deadline for implementation was November 1979. Yet in 1978 his varnishes were already being made according to the Directive, not Italian law. In the criminal prosecution for breach of Italian law he sought to rely on this Directive too. He argued that he had a legitimate expectation that compliance with the Directive prior to its deadline for implementation would be permissible:

Pubblico Ministero v *Ratti (Case 148/78)*
[1979] ECR 1629; [1980] 1 CMLR 96
Court of Justice of the European Communities

[43] It follows that, for the reasons expounded in the grounds of the answer to the national court's first question, it is only at the end of the prescribed period and in the event of the Member State's default that the directive – and in particular Article 9 thereof – will be able to have the effects described in the answer to the first question.

[44] Until that date is reached the Member States remain free in that field.

[45]   If one Member State has incorporated the provisions of a directive into its internal legal order before the end of the period prescribed therein, that fact cannot produce any effect with regard to other Member States.

[46]   In conclusion, since a directive by its nature imposes obligations only on Member States, it is not possible for an individual to plead the principle of 'legitimate expectation' before the expiry of the period prescribed for its implementation.

[47]   Therefore the answer to the fifth question must be that Directive No 77/728 of the Council of the European Communities of 7 November 1977, in particular Article 9 thereof, cannot bring about with respect to any individual who has complied with the provisions of the said directive before the expiration of the adaptation period prescribed for the Member State any effect capable of being taken into consideration by national courts.

Note

A small indentation into the Court's insistence that the expiry of the period prescribed for a Directive's implementation is the vital trigger for its relevance in law before national courts was made in Case C-129/96 *Inter-Environnement Wallonie ASBL* v *Région Wallone* [1997] ECR I-7411. In advance of the deadline, Member States are obliged 'to refrain . . . from adopting measures liable seriously to compromise the result prescribed' by the Directive. In normal circumstances, however, it is the expiry of the prescribed deadline which converts an unimplemented (and sufficiently unconditional) Directive into a provision on which an individual may rely before a national court.

Question

Why did the European Court decide to uphold Ratti's ability to rely on the unimplemented 1973 solvents Directive in the face of the apparently conflicting wording of the Treaty (Article 189, now 249)? One may return to Judge Mancini for one explanation:

F. Mancini, 'The Making of a Constitution for Europe' (1989) 26 CML Rev 595

(Footnotes omitted.)

   3.   *Costa* v *Enel* may be therefore regarded as a sequel of *Van Gend en Loos*. It is not the only sequel, however. Eleven years after *Van Gend en Loos*, the Court took in *Van Duyn* v *Home Office* a further step forward by attributing direct effect to provisions of Directives not transposed into the laws of the Member States within the prescribed time limit, so long as they met the conditions laid down in *Van Gend en Loos*. In order to appreciate fully the scope of this development it should be borne in mind that while the principal subjects governed by Regulations are agriculture, transport, customs and the social security of migrant workers, Community authorities resort to Directives when they intend to harmonise national laws on such matters as taxes, banking, equality of the sexes, protection of the environment, employment contracts and organisation of companies. Plain cooking and haute cuisine, in other words. The hope of seeing Europe grow institutionally, in matters of social relationships and in terms

of quality of life rests to a large extent on the adoption and the implementation of Directives.

Making Directives immediately enforceable poses, however, a formidable problem. Unlike Regulations and the Treaty provisions dealt with by *Van Gend en Loos*, Directives resemble international treaties, in so far as they are binding *only* on the States and *only* as to the result to be achieved. It is understandable therefore that, whereas the *Van Gend en Loos* doctrine established itself within a relatively short time, its extension to Directives met with bitter opposition in many quarters. For example, the French *Conseil d'État* and the German *Bundesfinanzhof* bluntly refused to abide by it and Professor Rasmussen, in a most un-Danish fit of temper, went so far as to condemn it as a case of 'revolting judicial behaviour'.

Understandable criticism is not necessarily justifiable. It is mistaken to believe that in attributing direct effect to Directives not yet complied with by the Member States, the Court was only guided by political considerations, such as the intention of by-passing the States in a strategic area of law-making. Non-compliance with Directives is the most typical and most frequent form of Member State infraction; moreover, the Community authorities often turn a blind eye to it and, even when the Commission institutes proceedings against the defaulting State under Article 169 of the Treaty, the Court cannot impose any penalty on that State. [See now Article 228 EC, a Maastricht innovation.] This gives the Directives a dangerously elastic quality: Italy, Greece or Belgium may agree to accept the enactment of a Directive with which it is uncomfortable knowing that the price to pay for possible failure to transpose it is non-existent or minimal.

Given these circumstances, it is sometimes submitted that the *Van Duyn* doctrine was essentially concerned with assuring respect for the rule of law. The Court's main purpose, in other words, was 'to ensure that neither level of government can rely upon its malfeasance – the Member State's failure to comply, the Community's failure or even inability to enforce compliance', with a view to frustrating the legitimate expectation of the Community citizens on whom the Directive confers rights. Indeed, 'if a Court is forced to condone wholesale violation of a norm, that norm can no longer be termed law'; nobody will deny that 'Directives are intended to have the force of law under the Treaty'.

Doubtless, in arriving at its judgment in *Van Duyn*, the Court may also have considered that by reducing the advantages Member States derived from non-compliance, its judgment would have strengthened the 'federal' reach of the Community power to legislate and it may even have welcomed such a consequence. But does that warrant the revolt staged by the *Conseil d'État* or the *Bundesfinanzhof*? The present author doubts it; and so did the German Constitutional Court, which sharply scolded the *Bundesfinanzhof* for its rejection of the *Van Duyn* doctrine. This went a long way towards restoring whatever legitimacy the Court of Justice had lost in the eyes of some observers following *Van Duyn*. The wound, one might say, is healed and the scars it has left are scarcely visible.

Question

Do you agree with Mancini that the Court's work in this area is 'essentially concerned with assuring respect for the rule of law'? See also N. Green, 'Directives, Equity and the Protection of Individual Rights' (1984) 9 EL Rev 295.

Note

Difficult constitutional questions arise at Community level and at national level in relation to the direct effect of Directives. You will quickly notice that many of the issues have arisen in the context of cases about sex discrimination. This has happened because equality between the sexes constitutes an area of Community competence which is given shape by a string of important Directives, often inadequately implemented at national level (see further Chapter 15).

(ii) Curtailing the principle
The next case allowed the Court to refine its approach to the direct effect of Directives.

Marshall v *Southampton Area Health Authority (Case 152/84)*
[1986] ECR 723; [1986] 1 CMLR 688
Court of Justice of the European Communities

Ms Marshall was dismissed by her employers, the Health Authority, when she reached the age of 62. A man would not have been dismissed at that age. This was discrimination on grounds of sex. But was there a remedy in law? Apparently not under the UK's Sex Discrimination Act 1975, because of a provision excluding discrimination arising out of treatment in relation to retirement. Directive 76/207, requiring equal treatment between the sexes, *did* appear to envisage a legal remedy for such discrimination, but that Directive had not been implemented in the UK, even though the deadline was past. So could Ms Marshall base a claim on the unimplemented Community Directive before an English court? The European Court was asked this question in a preliminary reference by the Court of Appeal.

The European Court first held that Ms Marshall's situation was an instance of discrimination on grounds of sex contrary to the Directive. It continued:

[39] Since the first question has been answered in the affirmative, it is necessary to consider whether Article 5(1) of Directive No 76/207 may be relied upon by an individual before national courts and tribunals.

[40] The appellant and the Commission consider that that question must be answered in the affirmative. They contend in particular, with regard to Articles 2(1) and 5(1) of Directive No 76/207, that those provisions are sufficiently clear to enable national courts to apply them without legislative intervention by the Member States, at least so far as overt discrimination is concerned.

[41] In support of that view, the appellant points out that directives are capable of conferring rights on individuals which may be relied upon directly before the courts of the Member States; national courts are obliged by virtue of the binding nature of a directive, in conjunction with Article 5 of the EEC Treaty, to give effect to the provisions of directives where possible, in particular when construing or applying relevant provisions of national law (judgment of 10 April 1984 in Case 14/83 *von Colson and Kamann* v *Land Nordrhein-Westfalen* [1984] ECR 1891). Where there is any inconsistency between national law and Community law which cannot be removed by

means of such a construction, the appellant submits that a national court is obliged to declare that the provision of national law which is inconsistent with the directive is inapplicable.

[42]   The Commission is of the opinion that the provisions of Article 5(1) of Directive No 76/207 are sufficiently clear and unconditional to be relied upon before a national court. They may therefore be set up against section 6(4) of the Sex Discrimination Act, which, according to the decisions of the Court of Appeal, has been extended to the question of compulsory retirement and has therefore become ineffective to prevent dismissals based upon the difference in retirement ages for men and for women.

[43]   The respondent and the United Kingdom propose, conversely, that the second question should be answered in the negative. They admit that a directive may, in certain specific circumstances, have direct effect as against a Member State in so far as the latter may not rely on its failure to perform its obligations under the directive. However, they maintain that a directive can never impose obligations directly on individuals and that it can only have direct effect against a Member State *qua* public authority and not against a Member State *qua* employer. As an employer a State is no different from a private employer. It would not therefore be proper to put persons employed by the State in a better position than those who are employed by a private employer.

[44]   With regard to the legal position of the respondent's employees the United Kingdom states that they are in the same position as the employees of a private employer. Although according to United Kingdom constitutional law the health authorities, created by the National Health Service Act 1977, as amended by the Health Services Act 1980 and other legislation, are Crown bodies and their employees are Crown servants, nevertheless the administration of the National Health Service by the health authorities is regarded as being separate from the Government's central administration and its employees are not regarded as civil servants.

[45]   Finally, both the respondent and the United Kingdom take the view that the provisions of Directive No 76/207 are neither unconditional nor sufficiently clear and precise to give rise to direct effect. The directive provides for a number of possible exceptions, the details of which are to be laid down by the Member States. Furthermore, the wording of Article 5 is quite imprecise and requires the adoption of measures for its implementation.

[46]   It is necessary to recall that, according to a long line of decisions of the Court (in particular its judgment of 19 January 1982 in Case 8/81 *Becker* v *Finanzamt Münster-Innenstadt* [1982] ECR 53), wherever the provisions of a directive appear, as far as their subject-matter is concerned, to be unconditional and sufficiently precise, those provisions may be relied upon by an individual against the State where that State fails to implement the directive in national law by the end of the period prescribed or where it fails to implement the directive correctly.

[47]   That view is based on the consideration that it would be incompatible with the binding nature which Article 189 confers on the directive to hold as a matter of principle that the obligation imposed thereby cannot be relied on by those concerned. From that the Court deduced that a Member State which has not adopted the implementing measures required by the directive within the prescribed period may not plead, as against individuals, its own failure to perform the obligations which the directive entails.

[48]   With regard to the argument that a directive may not be relied upon against an individual, it must be emphasized that according to Article 189 of the EEC Treaty the binding nature of a directive, which constitutes the basis for the possibility of relying on the directive before a national court, exists only in relation to 'each Member State to which it is addressed'. It follows that a directive may not of itself impose obligations on an individual and that a provision of a directive may not be relied upon as such against such a person. It must therefore be examined whether, in this case, the respondent must be regarded as having acted as an individual.

[49]   In that respect it must be pointed out that where a person involved in legal proceedings is able to rely on a directive as against the State he may do so regardless of the capacity in which the latter is acting, whether employer or public authority. In either case it is necessary to prevent the State from taking advantage of its own failure to comply with Community law.

[50]   It is for the national court to apply those considerations to the circumstances of each case; the Court of Appeal has, however, stated in the order for reference that the respondent, Southampton and South West Hampshire Area Health Authority (Teaching), is a public authority.

[51]   The argument submitted by the United Kingdom that the possibility of relying on provisions of the directive against the respondent *qua* organ of the State would give rise to an arbitrary and unfair distinction between the rights of State employees and those of private employees does not justify any other conclusion. Such a distinction may easily be avoided if the Member State concerned has correctly implemented the directive in national law.

[52]   Finally, with regard to the question whether the provision contained in Article 5(1) of Directive No 76/207, which implements the principle of equality of treatment set out in Article 2(1) of the directive, may be considered, as far as its contents are concerned, to be unconditional and sufficiently precise to be relied upon by an individual as against the State, it must be stated that the provision, taken by itself, prohibits any discrimination on grounds of sex with regard to working conditions, including the conditions governing dismissal, in a general manner and in unequivocal terms. The provision is therefore sufficiently precise to be relied on by an individual and to be applied by the national courts.

[53]   It is necessary to consider next whether the prohibition of discrimination laid down by the directive may be regarded as unconditional, in the light of the exceptions contained therein and of the fact that according to Article 5(2) thereof the Member States are to take the measures necessary to ensure the application of the principle of equality of treatment in the context of national law.

[54]   With regard, in the first place, to the reservation contained in Article 1(2) of Directive No 76/207 concerning the application of the principle of equality of treatment in matters of social security, it must be observed that, although the reservation limits the scope of the directive *ratione materiae*, it does not lay down any condition on the application of that principle in its field of operation and in particular in relation to Article 5 of the directive. Similarly, the exceptions to Directive No 76/207 provided for in Article 2 thereof are not relevant to this case.

[55]   It follows that Article 5 of the Directive No 76/207 does not confer on the Member States the right to limit the application of the principle of equality of treatment in its field of operation or to subject it to conditions and that that provision

is sufficiently precise and unconditional to be capable of being relied upon by an individual before a national court in order to avoid the application of any national provision which does not conform to Article 5(1).

[56]   Consequently, the answer to the second question must be that Article 5(1) of Council Directive No 76/207 of 9 February 1976, which prohibits any discrimination on grounds of sex with regard to working conditions, including the conditions governing dismissal, may be relied upon as against a State authority acting in its capacity as employer, in order to avoid the application of any national provision which does not conform to Article 5(1).

Notes
1.   Ms Marshall was able to rely on the Directive because she was employed by the State. Her subsequent quest for compensation took her back to the European Court, where it was made clear that national limits on compensatory awards should not be applied in so far as they impede an effective remedy (Case C-271/91 [1993] ECR I-4367). However, had she been employed by a private firm she would have been unable to rely on the direct effect of the Directive. So, as far as direct effect is concerned, there are requirements which always apply – those explained above in *Van Gend en Loos* (Case 26/62) (pp. 91–93). But for Directives there are extra requirements: first, that the implementation date has passed; and, second, that the State is the party against which enforcement is claimed. Directives may be vertically directly effective, but not horizontally directly effective.
2.   In rejecting the horizontal direct effect of Directives, the Court in fact made a choice between competing rationales for the direct effect of Directives. In its early decisions the Court laid emphasis on the need to extend direct effect in this area in order to secure the 'useful effect' of measures left unimplemented by defaulting States. Consider para. 12 of *Van Duyn* (Case 41/74) (p. 93 above); and, for example, in *Nederlandse Ondernemingen* (Case 51/76) [1977] ECR 113, the Court observed (at para. 23) that:

> where the Community authorities have, by Directive, imposed on Member States the obligation to pursue a particular course of conduct, the useful effect of such an act would be weakened if individuals were prevented from relying on it before their national courts and if the latter were prevented from taking it into consideration as an element of Community law.

This dictum came in the context of a case against the State, but this logic would lead a bold court to hold an unimplemented Directive enforceable against a private party too, in order to improve its useful effect. However, in *Ratti* (Case 148/78) (p. 103 above) and in *Marshall* (Case 152/84) (p. 107 above), the Court appears to switch its stance away from the idea of 'useful effect' to 'estoppel' as the legal rationale for holding Directives capable of direct effect. See para. 49 of the judgment in *Marshall* (Case 152/84).
3.   The Court's curtailment of the impact of Directives before national courts may also be seen as a manifestation of judicial minimalism, mentioned

at p. 37 above. The realist would examine the awareness of the Court that in this area it risks assaulting national sensitivities if it insists on deepening the impact of Community law in the national legal order. The next case was mentioned in passing by Judge Mancini (p. 106 above), but the decision deserves further attention.

Minister of the Interior v *Cohn Bendit*
[1980] 1 CMLR 543
Conseil d'État

The matter concerned the exclusion from France of Cohn Bendit, a noted political radical (who subsequently became a Member of the European Parliament!). He relied on Community rules governing free movement to challenge the exclusion. The Conseil d'État, the highest court in France dealing with administrative law, addressed itself to the utility of a Directive in Cohn Bendit's action before the French courts.

According to Article 56 of the Treaty instituting the European Economic Community of 25 March 1957, no requirement of which empowers an organ of the European Communities to issue, in matters of *ordre public*, regulations which are directly applicable in the member-States, the co-ordination of statute and of subordinate legislation (*dispositions législatives et réglementaires*) 'providing for special treatment for foreign nationals on grounds of public policy (*ordre public*), public security or public health' shall be the subject of Council directives, enacted on a proposal from the Commission and after consultation with the European Assembly. It follows clearly from Article 189 of the Treaty of 25 March 1957 that while these directives bind the member-States 'as to the result to be achieved' and while, to attain the aims set out in them, the national authorities are required to adapt the statute law and subordinate legislation and administrative practice of the member-States to the directives which are addressed to them, those authorities alone retain the power to decide on the form to be given to the implementation of the directives and to fix themselves, under the control of the national courts, the means appropriate to cause them to produce effect in national law. Thus, whatever the detail that they contain for the eyes of the member-States, directives may not be invoked by the nationals of such States in support of an action brought against an individual administrative act. It follows that M. Cohn-Bendit could not effectively maintain, in requesting the Tribunal Administratif of Paris to annul the decision of the Minister of the Interior of 2 February 1976, that that decision infringed the provisions of the directive enacted on 25 February 1964 by the Council of the European Communities with a view to coordinating, in the circumstances laid down in Article 56 of the EEC Treaty, special measures concerning the movement and residence of foreign nationals which are justified on grounds of public policy, public security or public health. Therefore, in the absence of any dispute on the legality of the administrative measures taken by the French Government to comply with the directives enacted by the Council of the European Communities, the solution to be given to the action brought by M. Cohn-Bendit may not in any case be made subject to the interpretation of the directive of 25 February 1964. Consequently, without it being necessary to examine the grounds of the appeal, the Minister of the Interior substantiates his argument that the Tribunal Administratif of Paris was wrong when in its judgment under appeal of 21 December 1977 it referred to the Court of Justice of the European Communities questions relating to the interpretation of that directive and stayed proceedings until the decision of the European Court.

In the circumstances the case should be referred back to the Tribunal Administratif of Paris to decide as may be the action of M. Cohn-Bendit.

Note
See, similarly, the *Bundesfinanzhof* (German federal tax court) in *VAT Directives* [1982] 1 CMLR 527.

As D. Anderson observed in the wake of the Court's rejection in *Marshall* (Case 152/84) of the enforceability of unimplemented Directives against private parties, '[t]he present concern of the Court is to consolidate the advances of the 1970s rather than face the legal complexities and political risks of attempting to extend the doctrine [of direct effect] further' (*Boston College International & Comparative Law Review* (1988) XI 91, 100). This implies that the Court might be expected to return to the matter. This proved correct. In 1993 and 1994 three Advocates-General pressed the Court to reconsider its rejection of the horizontal direct effect of Directives: Van Gerven in '*Marshall 2*'(Case C–271/91) [1993] ECR I-4367; Jacobs in *Vaneetveld* v *SA Le Foyer* (Case C–316/93) [1994] ECR I–763 and Lenz in *Paola Faccini Dori* v *Recreb Srl* (Case C–91/92) [1994] ECR I–3325. Advocate-General Lenz insisted that the Citizen of the Union was entitled to expect equality before the law throughout the territory of the Union and observed that, in the absence of horizontal direct effect, such equality was compromised by State failure to implement Directives. Advocate-General Jacobs thought that the effectiveness principle militated against drawing distinctions based on the status of a defendant. All three believed that the pursuit of coherence in the Community legal order dictated acceptance of the horizontal direct effect of Directives. Only in the third of these cases, *Faccini Dori* v *Recreb*, was the European Court unable to avoid addressing the issue directly.

Paola Faccini Dori v *Recreb Srl (Case C–91/92)*
[1994] ECR I–3325
Court of Justice of the European Communities

Ms Dori had concluded a contract at Milan Railway Station to buy an English language correspondence course. By virtue of Directive 85/577, which harmonises laws governing the protection of consumers in respect of contracts negotiated away from business premises, the so-called 'Doorstep Selling Directive', she ought to have been entitled to a 'cooling-off' period of at least seven days within which she could exercise a right to withdraw from the contract. However, she found herself unable to exercise that right under Italian law because Italy had not implemented the Directive. She therefore sought to rely on the Directive to defeat the claim brought against her by the private party with which she had contracted. The ruling in *Marshall* (Case 152/84) appeared to preclude reliance on the Directive and the Court, despite the promptings of Advocate-General Lenz, *refused* to overrule *Marshall*. It maintained that Directives are incapable of horizontal direct effect.

[23]   It would be unacceptable if a State, when required by the Community legislature to adopt certain rules intended to govern the State's relations – or those of State entities – with individuals and to confer certain rights on individuals, were able to rely on its own failure to discharge its obligations so as to deprive individuals of the benefits of those rights. Thus the Court has recognised that certain provisions of directives on conclusion of public works contracts and of directives on harmonisation of turnover taxes may be relied on against the State (or State entities) (see the judgment in Case 103/88 *Fratelli Costanzo* v *Comune di Milano* [1989] ECR 1839 and the judgment in Case 8/81 *Becker* v *Finanzamt Münster-Innenstadt* [1982] ECR 53).

[24]   The effect of extending that case-law to the sphere of relations between individuals would be to recognise a power in the Community to enact obligations for individuals with immediate effect, whereas it has competence to do so only where it is empowered to adopt regulations.

[25]   It follows that, in the absence of measures transposing the directive within the prescribed time-limit, consumers cannot derive from the directive itself a right of cancellation as against traders with whom they have concluded a contract or enforce such a right in a national court.

Note
Paragraph 48 of the ruling in *Marshall* expresses comparable sentiments to those expressed in para. 24 of the *Dori* ruling, but the emphasis in the latter on the limits of Community competence (specifically under Article 189 EC) is noticeably firmer. Although the Court did not consider that Ms Dori was wholly barred from relying on the Directive (see p. 122 below on 'indirect' effect and p. 130 on a claim against the defaulting State), it nevertheless refused to allow a Directive to exert direct effect in relations between private individuals. In rulings subsequent to *Dori*, the Court has repeated its rejection of the horizontal direct effect of Directives: e.g., Case C-192/94 *El Corte Inglés* v *Cristina Blasquez Rivero* [1996] ECR I-1281; Case C-97/96 *Verband Deutscher Daihatsu Händler eV* v *Daihatsu Deutschland GmbH* [1997] ECR I-6843. (For discussion of an unusual sub-set of cases, see K. Lackhoff and H. Nyssens, 'Direct Effect of Directives in Triangular Situations' (1998) 23 EL Rev 397.) The reader is invited to consider whether, just as the Conseil d'Etat's ruling in *Cohn Bendit* (p. 111 above) may have prompted the European Court's caution in *Marshall*, so too the *Bundesverfassungsgericht's* anxiety about Treaty amendment in the guise of judicial interpretation (p. 15 above) may have prompted the European Court in *Dori*, less than a year later, to emblazon its fidelity to the text of the EC Treaty by declining to extend Community legislative competence to include the enactment of obligations for individuals with immediate effect.

(iii) The scope of the principle: the State
Whatever one's view of the Court's motivations in ruling against the horizontal direct effect of Directives in *Marshall* (Case 152/84), confirmed in *Dori*

(Case C-91/92) and subsequently, the decision left many questions unanswered. First, what is the 'State'? The more widely this is interpreted, the more impact the unimplemented Directive will have.

Foster v British Gas (Case C-188/89)
[1990] ECR I-3133
Court of Justice of the European Communities

The applicant wished to rely on the Equal Treatment Directive 76/207 against her employer before English courts. She and other applicants had been compulsorily retired at an age earlier than male employees. This raised the familiar issue of the enforceability of Directives before national courts where national law is inadequate. The Court examined the nature of the defendant (the British Gas Corporation: BGC).

[3]   By virtue of the Gas Act 1972, which governed the BGC at the material time, the BGC was a statutory corporation responsible for developing and maintaining a system of gas supply in Great Britain, and had a monopoly of the supply of gas.

[4]   The members of the BGC were appointed by the competent Secretary of State. He also had the power to give the BGC directions of a general character in relation to matters affecting the national interest and instructions concerning its management.

[5]   The BGC was obliged to submit to the Secretary of State periodic reports on the exercise of its functions, its management and its programmes. Those reports were then laid before both Houses of Parliament. Under the Gas Act 1972 the BGC also had the right, with the consent of the Secretary of State, to submit proposed legislation to Parliament.

[6]   The BGC was required to run a balanced budget over two successive financial years. The Secretary of State could order it to pay certain funds over to him or to allocate funds to specified purposes.

It then proceeded to explain the legal approach to defining the 'State' for these purposes:

[13]   Before considering the question referred by the House of Lords, it must first be observed as a preliminary point that the United Kingdom has submitted that it is not a matter for the Court of Justice but for the national courts to determine, in the context of the national legal system, whether the provisions of a directive may be relied upon against a body such as the BGC.

[14]   The question what effects measures adopted by Community institutions have and in particular whether those measures may be relied on against certain categories of persons necessarily involves interpretation of the articles of the Treaty concerning measures adopted by the institutions and the Community measure in issue.

[15]   It follows that the Court of Justice has jurisdiction in proceedings for a preliminary ruling to determine the categories of persons against whom the provisions of a directive may be relied on. It is for the national courts, on the other hand, to decide whether a party to proceedings before them falls within one of the categories so defined.

The Court then disposed of the question referred:

[16]   As the Court has consistently held (see the judgment of 19 January 1982 in Case 8/81, *Becker* v *Hauptzollamt Münster-Innenstadt*, [1982] ECR 53 at paragraphs 23 to 25), where the Community authorities have, by means of a directive, placed Member States under a duty to adopt a certain course of action, the effectiveness of such a measure would be diminished if persons were prevented from relying upon it in proceedings before a court and national courts were prevented from taking it into consideration as an element of Community law. Consequently, a Member State which has not adopted the implementing measures required by the directive within the prescribed period may not plead, as against individuals, its own failure to perform the obligations which the directive entails. Thus, wherever the provisions of a directive appear, as far as their subject-matter is concerned, to be unconditional and sufficiently precise, those provisions may, in the absence of implementing measures adopted within the prescribed period, be relied upon as against any national provision which is incompatible with the directive or in so far as the provisions define rights which individuals are able to assert against the State.

[17]   The Court further held in its judgment of 26 February 1986 in Case 152/84 (*Marshall*, at paragraph 49) that where a person is able to rely on a directive as against the State he may do so regardless of the capacity in which the latter is acting, whether as employer or as public authority. In either case it is necessary to prevent the State from taking advantage of its own failure to comply with Community law.

[18]   On the basis of those considerations, the Court has held in a series of cases that unconditional and sufficiently precise provisions of a directive could be relied on against organizations or bodies which were subject to the authority or control of the State or had special powers beyond those which result from the normal rules applicable to relations between individuals.

[19]   The Court has accordingly held that provisions of a directive could be relied on against tax authorities (the judgments of 19 January 1982 in Case 8/81, *Becker*, cited above, and of 22 February 1990 in Case C-221/88, *ECSC* v *Acciaierie e Ferriere Busseni (in liquidation)*), local or regional authorities (judgment of 22 June 1989 in Case 103/88, *Fratelli Costanzo* v *Comune di Milano*), constitutionally independent authorities responsible for the maintenance of public order and safety (judgment of 15 May 1986 in Case 222/84, *Johnston* v *Chief Constable of the Royal Ulster Constabulary*, [1986] ECR 1651), and public authorities providing public health services (judgment of 26 February 1986 in Case 152/84, *Marshall*, cited above).

[20]   It follows from the foregoing that a body, whatever its legal form, which has been made responsible, pursuant to a measure adopted by the State, for providing a public service under the control of the State and has for that purpose special powers beyond those which result from the normal rules applicable in relations between individuals is included in any event among the bodies against which the provisions of a directive capable of having direct effect may be relied upon.

[21]   With regard to Article 5(1) of Directive 76/207 it should be observed that in the judgment of 26 February 1986 in Case 152/84 (*Marshall*, cited above, at paragraph 52), the Court held that that provision was unconditional and sufficiently precise to be relied on by an individual and to be applied by the national courts.

[22]   The answer to the question referred by the House of Lords must therefore be that Article 5(1) of Council Directive 76/207/EEC of 9 February 1976 may be relied

upon in a claim for damages against a body, whatever its legal form, which has been made responsible, pursuant to a measure adopted by the State, for providing a public service under the control of the State and has for that purpose special powers beyond those which result from the normal rules applicable in relations between individuals.

Note
The case has been widely commented upon; see e.g. N. Grief, (1991) 16 EL Rev 136; E. Szyszczak, (1990) 27 CML Rev 859. For a full examination of the policy issues, see D. Curtin, 'The Province of Government', (1990) 15 EL Rev 195.

Question
The case arose before British Gas was 'privatised' under the Gas Act 1986 (sold to the private sector). What difference would this sale make to the application of the Court's test?

Note
The notion of the 'State' embraces local authorities.

Fratelli Costanzo v *Milano (Case 103/88)*
[1989] ECR 1839
Court of Justice of the European Communities

The case arose out of the alleged failure of the municipal authorities in Milan to respect, *inter alia*, a Community Directive in awarding contracts for the construction of a football stadium for the 1990 World Cup. Could a disappointed contractor rely on the unimplemented Directive before Italian courts against the municipal authorities? The matter reached the European Court by way of a preliminary reference.

[28]   In the fourth question the national court asks whether administrative authorities, including municipal authorities, are under the same obligation as a national court to apply the provisions of Article 29(5) of Council Directive 71/305 and to refrain from applying provisions of national law which conflict with them.

[29]   In its judgments of 19 January 1982 in Case 8/81 *Becker* v *Finanzamt Münster-Innenstadt* [1982] ECR 53, at p. 71 and 26 February 1986 in Case 152/84 *Marshall* v *Southampton and South-West Hampshire Area Health Authority* [1986] ECR 723, at p. 748, the Court held that wherever the provisions of a directive appear, as far as their subject-matter is concerned, to be unconditional and sufficiently precise, those provisions may be relied upon by an individual against the State where that State has failed to implement the directive in national law by the end of the period prescribed or where it has failed to implement the Directive correctly.

[30]   It is important to note that the reason for which an individual may, in the circumstances described above, rely on the provisions of a directive in proceedings before the national courts is that the obligations arising under those provisions are binding upon all the authorities of the Member States.

[31]   It would, moreover, be contradictory to rule that an individual may rely upon the provisions of a directive which fulfil the conditions defined above in proceedings before the national courts seeking an order against the administrative authorities, and yet to hold that those authorities are under no obligation to apply the provisions of the directive and refrain from applying provisions of national law which conflict with them. It follows that when the conditions under which the Court has held that individuals may rely on the provisions of a directive before the national courts are met, all organs of the administration, including decentralized authorities such as municipalities, are obliged to apply those provisions.

[32]   With specific regard to Article 29(5) of Directive 71/305, it is apparent from the discussion of the first question that it is unconditional and sufficiently precise to be relied upon by an individual against the State. An individual may therefore plead that provision before the national courts and, as is clear from the foregoing, all organs of the administration, including decentralized authorities such as municipalities, are obliged to apply it.

Note
It should be appreciated that this action could be pursued at national level by virtue of the combined effect of the principles of direct effect and supremacy, and the preliminary reference procedure. However, Community law did not dictate the remedy to be made available at national level for violation of Community law rights. Enforcement of Community law through the national legal order is explored more fully in Chapter 17.

(iv) The principle of indirect effect
A more fundamental problem than defining the State arises out of the *Marshall* (Case 152/84) decision. This relates to the anomaly in the scope of the direct effect of Directives. Consider the sex discrimination Directives. If a State has failed to implement a Directive properly, then, provided that the standard *Van Gend en Loos* (Case 26/62) 'test' for direct effect is met by the provision in question, a State employee can rely on the direct effect of the Directive (vertical direct effect). A private employee cannot (horizontal direct effect). So, in the UK, where Directive 76/207 on Equal Treatment of the Sexes was not properly implemented in time, Ms Marshall (above), a State employee, succeeded in relying on Community law, whereas Ms Duke (*Duke v GEC Reliance* [1988] 2 WLR 359, [1988] 1 All ER 626), who was making the same complaint, failed, for she happened to be a private sector employee.

The UK had made this point in *Marshall* (Case 152/84) as a reason for *withholding* direct effect, but its objections were swept aside by the Court in para. 51 of the judgment (p. 109 above). Yet the anomaly is real, even if the Court's refusal to permit a recalcitrant State to benefit from pointing it out is understandable. Submissions in *Dori* (Case C-91/92, p. 112 above) urged the Court to eliminate the anomaly by *extending* direct effect, but these were not successful.

The European Court's contribution to the resolution of this anomaly is found in *Von Colson and Kamann* v *Land Nordrhein-Westfalen* (Case 14/83) and *Harz* v *Deutsche Tradax* (Case 79/83). Mention is made of Case 14/83 in para. 41 of the judgment in *Marshall* at p. 107 above, but the Court's approach in the case deserves careful separate attention.

Von Colson and Kamann v *Land Nordrhein-Westfalen (Case 14/83)*
[1984] ECR 1891; [1986] 2 CMLR 430
Court of Justice of the European Communities

The case was a preliminary reference from Germany, and concerned that fertile source of litigation, the Equal Treatment Directive 76/207. The issue was described by the Court as follows:

[2]   Those questions were raised in the course of proceedings between two qualified social workers, Sabine von Colson and Elisabeth Kamann, and the Land Nordrhein-Westfalen. It appears from the grounds of the order for reference that Werl prison, which caters exclusively for male prisoners and which is administered by the Land Nordrhein-Westfalen, refused to engage the plaintiffs in the main proceedings for reasons relating to their sex. The officials responsible for recruitment justified their refusal to engage the plaintiffs by citing the problems and risks connected with the appointment of female candidates and for those reasons appointed instead male candidates who were however less well-qualified.

[3]   The Arbeitsgericht Hamm held that there had been discrimination and took the view that under German law the only sanction for discrimination in recruitment is compensation for 'Vertrauensschaden', namely the loss incurred by candidates who are victims of discrimination as a result of their belief that there would be no discrimination in the establishment of the employment relationship. Such compensation is provided for under Paragraph 611a(2) of the Bürgerliches Gesetzbuch.

[4]   Under that provision, in the event of discrimination regarding access to employment, the employer is liable for 'damages in respect of the loss incurred by the worker as a result of his reliance on the expectation that the establishment of the employment relationship would not be precluded by such a breach [of the principle of equal treatment]'. That provision purports to implement Council Directive No 76/207.

[5]   Consequently the Arbeitsgericht found that, under German law, it could order the reimbursement only of the travel expenses incurred by the plaintiff von Colson in pursuing her application for the post (DM 7.20) and that it could not allow the plaintiffs' other claims.

Von Colson's objection centred on Article 6 of the Directive:

[18]   Article 6 requires Member States to introduce into their national legal systems such measures as are necessary to enable all persons who consider themselves wronged by discrimination 'to pursue their claims by judicial process'. It follows from the provision that Member States are required to adopt measures which are sufficiently effective to achieve the objective of the directive and to ensure that those measures may in fact be relied on before the national courts by the persons concerned. Such measures may include, for example, provisions requiring the employer to offer a post to the candidate discriminated against or giving the candidate adequate financial compensation, backed up where necessary by a system of fines. However the directive

does not prescribe a specific sanction; it leaves Member States free to choose between the different solutions suitable for achieving its objective.

Was this adhered to in the German legal order? The Court's approach was markedly different from standard 'direct effect' analysis:

[22] It is impossible to establish real equality of opportunity without an appropriate system of sanctions. That follows not only from the actual purpose of the directive but more specifically from Article 6 thereof which, by granting applicants for a post who have been discriminated against recourse to the courts, acknowledges that those candidates have rights of which they may avail themselves before the courts.

[23] Although, as has been stated in the reply to Question 1, full implementation of the directive does not require any specific form of sanction for unlawful discrimination, it does entail that that sanction be such as to guarantee real and effective judicial protection. Moreover it must also have a real deterrent effect on the employer. It follows that where a Member State chooses to penalize the breach of the prohibition of discrimination by the award of compensation, that compensation must in any event be adequate in relation to the damage sustained.

[24] In consequence it appears that national provisions limiting the right to compensation of persons who have been discriminated against as regards access to employment to a purely nominal amount, such as, for example, the reimbursement of expenses incurred by them in submitting their application, would not satisfy the requirements of an effective transposition of the directive.

[25] The nature of the sanctions provided for in the Federal Republic of Germany in respect of discrimination regarding access to employment and in particular the question whether the rule in Paragraph 611a (2) of the Bürgerliches Gesetzbuch excludes the possibility of compensation on the basis of the general rules of law were the subject of lengthy discussion before the Court. The German Government maintained in the oral procedure that that provision did not necessarily exclude the application of the general rules of law regarding compensation. It is for the national court alone to rule on that question concerning the interpretation of its national law.

[26] However, the Member States' obligation arising from a directive to achieve the result envisaged by the directive and their duty under Article 5 of the Treaty to take all appropriate measures, whether general or particular, to ensure the fulfilment of that obligation, is binding on all the authorities of Member States including, for matters within their jurisdiction, the courts. It follows that, in applying the national law and in particular the provisions of a national law specifically introduced in order to implement Directive No 76/207, national courts are required to interpret their national law in the light of the wording and the purpose of the directive in order to achieve the result referred to in the third paragraph of Article 189.

[27] On the other hand, as the above considerations show, the directive does not include any unconditional and sufficiently precise obligation as regards sanctions for discrimination which, in the absence of implementing measures adopted in good time may be relied on by individuals in order to obtain specific compensation under the directive, where that is not provided for or permitted under national law.

[28] It should, however, be pointed out to the national court that although Directive No 75/207/EEC, for the purpose of imposing a sanction for the breach of the prohibition of discrimination, leaves the Member States free to choose between the

different solutions suitable for achieving its objective, it nevertheless requires that if a Member State chooses to penalize breaches of that prohibition by the award of compensation, then in order to ensure that it is effective and that it has a deterrent effect, that compensation must in any event be adequate in relation to the damage sustained and must therefore amount to more than purely nominal compensation such as, for example, the reimbursement only of the expenses incurred in connection with the application. It is for the national court to interpret and apply the legislation adopted for the implementation of the directive in conformity with the requirements of Community law, in so far as it is given discretion to do so under national law.

Note
J. Steiner, (1985) 101 LQR 491, has observed that the decision marks 'a subtle but significant change of direction' in the European Court's approach to the enforceability of EEC Directives before national courts'. P. Morris, (1989) JBL 233, at p. 241, suggested that 'if national judiciaries respond positively to this exhortation [in *Von Colson*] something approaching horizontal direct effect may be achieved by a circuitous route'. B. Fitzpatrick, (1989) 9 OJLS 336, at p. 346, refers to *Von Colson* having established a principle of 'indirect effect' and suggests that 'it may effectively bridge the gap between vertical and horizontal direct effect'.

Question
To what extent do you think the *Von Colson* approach succeeds in resolving the anomalies of the horizontal/vertical direct effect distinction which emerges from the Court's ruling in *Marshall* (Case 152/84)?

Note
B. Fitzpatrick commented that 'what is crucial now is for the scope of the indirect effect principle to be clarified by the European Court of Justice' ((1989) 9 OJLS 336, at p. 355). In the *Von Colson* (Case 14/83) judgment itself, one can pick out important contradictions in respect of the national court's task; compare the second sentence of para. 26 with the more qualified statement in the concluding sentence of the Court's ruling in answer to the questions referred above). The next two cases are both worthy of examination from the perspective of clarifying the ambit of *Von Colson* (Case 14/83).

Officier van Justitie v *Kolpinghuis Nijmegen (Case 80/86)*
[1987] ECR 3969
Court of Justice of the European Communities

A criminal prosecution was brought against a cafe owner for stocking mineral water which was in fact simply fizzy tap water. The Dutch authorities sought to supplement the basis of the prosecution by relying on definitions of mineral water detrimental to the defendant which were contained in a Directive which had not been implemented in The Netherlands. A preliminary reference was made to the European Court.

The Court ruled that 'a national authority may not rely, as against an individual, upon a provision of a Directive whose necessary implementation in national law has not yet taken place'. It then turned to the third question referred to it:

[11]   The third question is designed to ascertain how far the national court may or must take account of a directive as an aid to the interpretation of a rule of national law.

[12]   As the Court stated in its judgment of 10 April 1984 in Case 14/83 *Von Colson and Kamann* v *Land Nordrhein-Westfalen* [1984] ECR 1891, the Member States' obligation arising from a directive to achieve the result envisaged by the directive and their duty under Article 5 of the Treaty to take all appropriate measures, whether general or particular, to ensure the fulfilment of that obligation, is binding on all the authorities of Member States including, for matters within their jurisdiction, the courts. It follows that, in applying the national law and in particular the provisions of a national law specifically introduced in order to implement the directive, national courts are required to interpret their national law in the light of the wording and the purpose of the directive in order to achieve the result referred to in the third paragraph of Article 189 of the Treaty.

[13]   However, that obligation on the national court to refer to the content of the directive when interpreting the relevant rules of its national law is limited by the general principles of law which form part of Community law and in particular the principles of legal certainty and non-retroactivity. Thus the Court ruled in its judgment of 11 June 1987 in Case 14/86 *Pretore di Salò* v *X* [1987] ECR 2545 that a directive cannot, of itself and independently of a national law adopted by a Member State for its implementation, have the effect of determining or aggravating the liability in criminal law of persons who act in contravention of the provisions of that directive.

[14]   The answer to the third question should therefore be that in applying its national legislation a court of a Member State is required to interpret that legislation in the light of the wording and the purpose of the directive in order to achieve the result referred to in the third paragraph of Article 189 of the Treaty, but a directive cannot, of itself and independently of a law adopted for its implementation, have the effect of determining or aggravating the liability in criminal law of persons who act in contravention of the provisions of that directive.

Note
The Court is anxious to emphasise the importance of preserving legal certainty and protecting reasonable expectations. See also Case C-168/95 *Luciano Arcaro* [1996] ECR I-4705.

Marleasing SA v *La Comercial Internacional de Alimentacion SA* *(Case C-106/89)*
[1990] ECR I-4135
Court of Justice of the European Communities

The case arose out of a conflict between the Spanish Civil Code and Community Company Law Directive (68/151) which was unimplemented in Spain. The litigation was between private parties, which, following

Marshall (Case 152/84), ruled out the direct effect of the Directive. The European Court explained the national court's duty of interpretation in the following terms:

[8]   . . .[T]he Member States' obligation arising from a directive to achieve the result envisaged by the directive and their duty under Article 5 of the Treaty to take all appropriate measures, whether general or particular, to ensure the fulfilment of that obligation, is binding on all the authorities of Member States including, for matters within their jurisdiction, the courts. It follows that, in applying national law, whether the provisions in question were adopted before or after the directive, the national court called upon to interpret it is required to do so, as far as possible, in the light of the wording and the purpose of the directive in order to achieve the result pursued by the latter and thereby comply with the third paragraph of Article 189 of the Treaty.

Note
The obligation imposed on national courts in *Marleasing* (Case C-108/89) has a firmer feel than that in *Von Colson* (Case 14/83, p. 118 above). See J. Stuyck and P. Wytinck, (1991) 28 CML Rev 205.

The Court also confirmed the obligation of sympathetic interpretation that is cast on national courts by virtue of what was Article 5 and is now Article 10 EC post-Amsterdam in its ruling in *Paola Faccini Dori* (Case C–91/92). Even though Ms Dori was not able to rely directly on the unimplemented Directive in proceedings involving another private party (p. 112 above), she was entitled to expect that the national court would not simply ignore the Directive in applying national law.

Paola Faccini Dori v Recreb Srl (Case C–91/92)
[1994] ECR I–3325
Court of Justice of the European Communities

[26]   It must also be borne in mind that, as the Court has consistently held since its judgment in Case 14/83 *Von Colson and Kamann* v *Land Nordrhein-Westfalen* [1984] ECR 1891, paragraph 26, the Member States' obligation arising from a directive to achieve the result envisaged by the directive and their duty under Article 5 of the Treaty to take all appropriate measures, whether general or particular, is binding on all the authorities of Member States, including, for matters within their jurisdiction, the courts. The judgments of the Court in Case C-106/89 *Marleasing* v *La Comercial Internacional de Alimentación* [1990] ECR I-4135, paragraph 8, and Case C-334/92 *Wagner Miret* v *Fondo de Garantia Salarial* [1993] ECR I-6911, paragraph 20, make it clear that, when applying national law, whether adopted before or after the directive, the national court that has to interpret that law must do so, as far as possible, in the light of the wording and the purpose of the directive so as to achieve the result it has in view and thereby comply with the third paragraph of Article 189 of the Treaty.

Note
Marleasing seems clearly to require interpretation of pre-existing national legislation in the light of a subsequent Directive and this is confirmed in *Dori*. This is by no means uncontroversial. Lord Slynn, who served as both

Advocate-General and judge in Luxembourg before assuming the role of a Law Lord, has observed extra-judicially that:

> I find it difficult to say that a statute of 1870 must be interpreted in the light of a 1991 directive. If the former is in conflict with the latter, it is not for judges to strain language but for Governments to introduce new legislation. (*Introducing a European Legal Order*, Stevens/Sweet and Maxwell, 1992, p. 124; see also 'Looking at European Community Texts' (1993) 14/1 Statute L Rev 12)

Question
Do you think the European Court is improperly asking national courts to perform tasks which belong with national legislatures?

(v) Indirect effect in the courts of the UK
Even assuming a readiness to interpret national law in the light of Directives whether the national law pre-dates or post-dates the Directive, there remains scope for debate about what is meant by 'interpretation' – a notoriously imprecise science in any legal system. In fact the notion of 'indirect effect' through interpretation casts a heavy burden on national courts. It is a burden derived from Community law; ultimately from Article 10 EC. Ideally, one ought to study the approach taken by courts in all the Member States, but this is not feasible here. How have courts in the UK reacted to this task?

The most recent major decision of the House of Lords demonstrates a willingness to interpret national law in the light of Community law combined with a perception that there are limits to the capacity of a court to give (indirect) effect to Community law when confronted by national law that is incapable of being read in such a way as to conform with the Community text.

Webb v EMO Air Cargo (UK) Ltd
[1993] 1 WLR 49
House of Lords

Ms Webb had been hired to cover for the maternity leave of another employee, although she was to carry on in employment after the return of that other employee. Webb became pregnant and was dismissed. There was relevant domestic legislation in the field (Sex Discrimination Act 1975) in addition to the EC Equal Treatment Directive, Directive 76/207 (the same Directive that was at stake in *Marshall* (Case 152/84)), which had been the subject of relevant European Court rulings. The litigation was between employer and employee, both private parties. Lord Keith explained:

. . . The Directive (76/207/EEC) does not have direct effect upon the relationship between a worker and an employer who is not the state or an emanation of the state, but nevertheless it is for a United Kingdom court to construe domestic legislation in any field covered by a Community Directive so as to accord with the interpretation of the Directive as laid down by the European Court of Justice, if that can be done without distorting the meaning of the domestic legislation: *Duke* v *GEC Reliance Systems Ltd* [1988] AC 618, 639–640, *per* Lord Templeman. This is so whether the domestic legislation came after or, as in this case, preceded the Directive: *Marleasing SA* v *La Comercial Internacional de Alimentación SA* (Case 106/89) [1990] ECR I–4135. That was a case where a Spanish company had been founded with the alleged purpose of defrauding the creditors of one of its founders. A provision of the Spanish Civil Code on the validity of contracts laid down that contracts lacking cause or whose cause was unlawful should have no legal effect. A creditor of the company relied upon this provision in order to obtain a declaration that the instrument incorporating the company was invalid. The company relied in its defence upon article 11 of Council Directive (68/151 EEC), which contained an exhaustive list of the cases in which the nullity of a company might be declared. The list did not include lack of lawful cause. The article had not been implemented in Spanish national law. The European Court of Justice held that the Spanish courts must not interpret the relevant provision of the Civil Code in such a manner that the nullity of a public limited company might be ordered on grounds other than those listed in article 11 of the Directive. The question being whether or not that might be done, the European Court of Justice said in its judgment, at p. I–4159:

> [8]   In order to reply to that question, it should be observed that, as the court pointed out in its judgment in case 14/83, *von Colson* v *[Land] Nordrhein-Westfalen* [1984] ECR 1891; [1986] 2 CMLR 430, para. [26], the member states' obligation arising from a Directive to achieve the result envisaged by the Directive and their duty under article 5 of the Treaty to take all appropriate measures, whether general or particular, to ensure the fulfilment of that obligation, is binding on all the authorities of member states including, for matters within their jurisdiction, the courts. It follows that, in applying national law, whether the provisions in question were adopted before or after the directive, the national court called upon to interpret it is required to do so, so far as possible, in the light of the wording and the purpose of the Directive in order to achieve the result pursued by the latter and thereby comply with the third paragraph of article 189 of the Treaty. [9]   It follows that the requirement that national law must be interpreted in conformity with article 11 of Directive (68/151/EEC) precludes the interpretation of provisions of national law relating to public limited companies in such a manner that the nullity of a public limited company may be ordered on grounds other than those exhaustively listed in article 11 of the Directive in question.

It is to be observed that the provision of Spanish law in issue in that case was of a general character capable of being construed either widely or narrowly. It did not refer specifically to the grounds upon which the nullity of a public limited company might be ordered. If it had done so, and had included among such grounds the case where the company had been formed with the purpose of defrauding creditors of one of the corporators, the Spanish court would have been entitled and bound to give effect to it notwithstanding the terms of the Directive. As the European Court of Justice said, a national court must construe a domestic law to accord with the terms of a Directive in the same field only if it is possible to do so. That means that the domestic law must be open to an interpretation consistent with the Directive whether or not it is also open to an interpretation inconsistent with it. . . .

Note

The European Court was asked whether it would be contrary to Directive 76/207 for an employer to dismiss an employee who, because of pregnancy, would be unable to carry out the job at the particular time. It decided in *Carole Louise Webb* v *EMO Air Cargo (UK) Ltd* (Case C–32/93) [1994] ECR I–3567 that the dismissal of a pregnant woman recruited for an indefinite period cannot be justified on grounds that she was temporarily prevented from performing the work (thus leaving open the possibility that a woman *recruited on a fixed-term contract* might be vulnerable to a lawful dismissal if she became pregnant). The House of Lords applied the ruling in *Webb* v *EMO Air Cargo (UK) Ltd* [1995] 4 All ER 577. (For the sake of completeness: the field is now affected by Directive 92/85 OJ 1992 L348/1, which puts in place protection for pregnant workers.)

In the above extract from *Webb*, Lord Keith refers to dicta of Lord Templeman in *Duke* v *GEC Reliance*. This decision was mentioned at p. 117 above; it is a case with a fact pattern that resembles that in *Marshall* (Case 152/84), but with the critical distinguishing feature that the employer in *Duke* was a private party and therefore Duke, unlike Marshall who was employed by the 'State', was unable to rely on the direct effect of the Equal Treatment Directive. The House of Lords in *Duke* was unreceptive to an exhortation to interpret national law in the light of the Directive.

Duke v *GEC Reliance*
[1988] 2 WLR 359, [1988] 1 ALL ER 626
House of Lords

Lord Templeman cited the European Court's judgment in *Von Colson* (Case 14/83, p. 118 above) and continued:

. . . In the *von Colson* case the German court which submitted the case for a ruling asked whether it was acceptable that a woman who applied for a job and was refused because she was a woman, contrary to the intent of the Equal Treatment Directive, was only entitled under the German domestic law prohibiting such discrimination to the recovery of her expenses (if any) of her application. The German Government in making representations to the European Court expressed the view that under German law compensation for discrimination could include general damages for the loss of the job or of the opportunity to take up the job. The ruling of the European Court of Justice did not constrain the national court to construe German law in accordance with Community law but ruled that if under German law the German court possessed the power to award damages which were adequate and which fulfilled the objective of the Equal Treatment Directive then it was the duty of the German court to act accordingly.

The *von Colson* case is no authority for the proposition that the German court was bound to invent a German law of adequate compensation if no such law existed and no authority for the proposition that a court of a member state must distort the meaning of a domestic statute so as to conform with Community law which is not directly applicable. If, following the *von Colson* case, the German court adhered to the view that under German law it possessed no discretion to award adequate compensation, it would have been the duty of the German Government in fulfilment of its obligations under the Treaty of Rome to introduce legislation or evolve some other method which would enable adequate compensation to be obtained, just as the United Kingdom Government became bound to introduce legislation to amend the Equal Pay

Act 1970 and the Sex Discrimination Act 1975 in the light of *Marshall's* case. Mrs. Advocate-General Rozes in her opinion, delivered on 31 January 1984 in the *von Colson* case, said, at p. 1919:

> 'In proceedings under article 177 it is not for me to express a view on questions which fall exclusively within the jurisdiction of the national courts inasmuch as they concern the application of national law.'

The EEC Treaty does not interfere and the European Court of Justice in the *von Colson* case did not assert power to interfere with the method or result of the interpretation of national legislation by national courts.

It would be most unfair to the respondent to distort the construction of the 1975 Sex Discrimination Act in order to accommodate the 1976 Equal Treatment Directive as construed by the European Court of Justice in the 1986 *Marshall* case. As between the appellant and the respondent the Equal Treatment Directive did not have direct effect and the respondent could not reasonably be expected to reduce to precision the opaque language which constitutes both the strength and the difficulty of some Community legislation. The respondent could not reasonably be expected to appreciate the logic of Community legislators in permitting differential retirement pension ages but prohibiting differential retirement ages. The respondent is not liable to the appellant under Community law. I decline to hold that liability under British law attaches to the respondent or any other private employer to pay damages based on wages which women over 60 and under 65 did not earn before the amending Sex Discrimination Act 1986 for the first time and without retrospective effect introduced the statutory tort of operating differential retirement ages. I would dismiss this appeal.

Notes

1.   Notice that the House of Lords is not denying that the UK has acted wrongly in failing to implement the Directive, but it indicates that the appropriate enforcement mechanism is action by the Commission under Article 169, now Article 226 post-Amsterdam (Chapter 17). It rules out an action by an individual before national courts relying on the unimplemented Directive directly or indirectly against another individual.

2.   The UK finally remedied its failure to implement the rules at issue in *Marshall* (Case 152/84) and *Duke* in the Sex Discrimination Act 1986. So the issue of direct effect of Directives will not recur in that particular factual context. But the general problem is bound to persist while Directives remain unimplemented after their deadlines in at least some States. Such tardiness is common.

Questions

1.   Is there any *material* distinction between the situation in *Marshall* (Case 152/84) and that in *Duke* which would justify the different results in the two cases?

2.   'To have held that the UK courts had to give effect to the directive in the *Duke* case by interpreting s. 6(4) of the 1975 Act in a way which was manifestly contrary to the intentions of Parliament would have been to allow the notion that directives are capable of horizontal direct effect in by the back

door at the same time as *Marshall* closed the front door upon it.'
C. Greenwood (1988) All ER Annual Rev 122, at p. 126. Discuss.

The European Court's insistence in *Marleasing* that the obligation of interpretation extends to national law adopted before or after the Directive
post-dates the House of Lords' decision in *Duke*, but is absorbed by Lord
Keith in *Webb* (p. 124 above). However, the margin between permissible
'interpretation' and what Lord Templeman in *Duke* regards as impermissible
'distortion' of national texts is hard to locate (see E. Szyszczak, 'Sovereignty:
Crisis, Compliance, Confusion, Complacency?' (1990) 15 EL Rev 480; P.
Craig, 'Indirect Effect of Directives in the Application of National Legislation', in M. Andenas and F. Jacobs (eds), *EC Law in the English Courts*
(Oxford, 1998)). In cases other than *Duke*, their Lordships have been
prepared to interpret national law to conform with an inadequately implemented Directive in the field even in litigation involving private parties;
e.g., *Pickstone* v *Freemans plc* [1989] AC 66, where their Lordships inspected
Hansard to satisfy themselves that Parliament intended domestic law to
comply with Community obligations, and *Litster* v *Forth Dry Dock* [1989]
2 WLR 634, [1989] 1 All ER 1134, where Lord Oliver observed that
'the greater flexibility available to the Court in applying a purposive
construction to legislation designed to give effect to the United Kingdom's
Treaty obligations to the Community enables the court, where necessary, to supply by implication words appropriate to comply with those
obligations'.

When one recalls that the severe difficulties in defining the proper scope of
the obligation of judicial interpretation in this context are in effect multiplied
by 15, since courts in all the Member States are forced to grapple with the
issue, one may doubt whether the notion of 'indirect effect' underpinned by
Article 10 EC is a fully satisfactory method of securing the application at
national level of unimplemented Community Directives. The Court has now
deployed Article 10 EC to construct a system for penalising the defaulting
State in cases of non-implementation.

(vi)   Penalising the defaulting State
Even if the national court is willing and able to carry out the interpretative
function, there remains a persisting concern about this ingenious application
of the notion of 'useful effect' or 'effectiveness'. Where national courts
actively interpret national law in the light of unimplemented Community
Directives, interference with the legitimate expectations of private parties may
result. Private parties may find themselves bound by obligations drawn by
interpretation from Directives of which they are quite unaware. That concern
seems to motivate the Court's reluctance to sanction indirect effect in
Kolpinghuis Nijmegen (Case 80/86 above) where the State would be the
beneficiary. Before English courts, one may identify comparable anxieties
expressed by Lord Templeman in *Duke*, which involved purely private parties
(p. 125 above). However, in *Marleasing* (Case C-106/89) the Court appears

ready to enhance indirect effect despite the possible impact on private parties. It might be possible to contend that this is justified as a means of protecting the expectations of the intended beneficiary of rights under an unimplemented Directive. In that sense, the issue is a choice between two deserving private parties, one of which must ultimately be prejudiced. Yet at bottom the problem is that this route fails to impose a burden on the party responsible for the gap in legal protection – the *Member State* which has failed to implement the Directive. There is a strong case for holding that the primary target for the individual who has suffered loss through non-implementation of a Directive should be the public authorities. This was a point astutely made by commentators (N. Green, (1984) 9 EL Rev 295, at pp. 321–4; J. Usher, (1989) 10 Statute Law Rev 95, at p. 102; D. Curtin, (1990) 27 CML Rev 709, at p. 729) and the Court had the chance to develop its jurisprudence in the direction of State liability in Cases C-6/90 and C-9/90 *Francovich and Others* v *Italian State* [1991] ECR I-5357.

Directive 80/987 required Member States to set up guarantee funds to compensate workers in the event of employer insolvency. Italy failed to implement the Directive. That Treaty violation had already been recorded in a Court ruling – Case 22/87, *Commission* v *Italy* [1989] ECR 143. Italian workers, among them Andrea Francovich, believed themselves denied the protection envisaged by the Directive but not transposed into Italian law. Proceedings before the Italian courts yielded a preliminary reference to the European Court.

The Court determined that the workers could claim no directly effective rights, for the relevant provisions of the Directive lacked sufficient unconditionality. The provider of the guarantee could not be identified. The Court then turned to the question of the liability of the State to make good loss suffered by individuals as a result of the failure to implement. The Court considered that this was an issue which fell to be considered in the light of the general system of the Treaty and its fundamental principles:

Francovich and Others v Italian State (Cases C-6/90 and C-9/90)
[1991] ECR I-5357
Court of Justice of the European Communities

(a)   *The existence of State liability as a matter of principle*

[31]   It should be borne in mind at the outset that the EEC Treaty has created its own legal system, which is integrated into the legal systems of the Member States and which their courts are bound to apply. The subjects of that legal system are not only the Member States but also their nationals. Just as it imposes burdens on individuals, Community law is also intended to give rise to rights which become part of their legal patrimony. Those rights arise not only where they are expressly granted by the Treaty but also by virtue of obligations which the Treaty imposes in a clearly defined manner both on individuals and on the Member States and the Community institutions (see the judgments in Case 26/62 *Van Gend en Loos* [1963] ECR 1 and Case 6/64 *Costa* v *ENEL* [1964] ECR 585).

[32] Furthermore, it has been consistently held that the national courts whose task it is to apply the provisions of Community law in areas within their jurisdiction must ensure that those rules take full effect and must protect the rights which they confer on individuals (see in particular the judgments in Case 106/77 *Amministrazione delle Finanze dello Stato* v *Simmenthal* [1978] ECR 629, paragraph 16, and Case C-213/89 *Factortame* [1990] ECR I-2433, paragraph 19).

[33] The full effectiveness of Community rules would be impaired and the protection of the rights which they grant would be weakened if individuals were unable to obtain redress when their rights are infringed by a breach of Community law for which a Member State can be held responsible.

[34] The possibility of obtaining redress from the Member State is particularly indispensable where, as in this case, the full effectiveness of Community rules is subject to prior action on the part of the State and where, consequently, in the absence of such action, individuals cannot enforce before the national courts the rights conferred upon them by Community law.

[35] It follows that the principle whereby a State must be liable for loss and damage caused to individuals as a result of breaches of Community law for which the State can be held responsible is inherent in the system of the Treaty.

[36] A further basis for the obligation of Member States to make good such loss and damage is to be found in Article 5 of the Treaty, under which the Member States are required to take all appropriate measures, whether general or particular, to ensure fulfilment of their obligations under Community law. Among these is the obligation to nullify the unlawful consequences of a breach of Community law (see, in relation to the analogous provision of Article 86 of the ECSC Treaty, the judgment in Case 6/60 *Humblet* v *Belgium* [1960] ECR 559).

[37] It follows from all the foregoing that it is a principle of Community law that the Member States are obliged to make good loss and damage caused to individuals by breaches of Community law for which they can be held responsible.

(b) *The conditions for State liability*

[38] Although State liability is thus required by Community law, the conditions under which that liability gives rise to a right to reparation depend on the nature of the breach of Community law giving rise to the loss and damage.

[39] Where, as in this case, a Member State fails to fulfil its obligation under the third paragraph of Article 189 of the Treaty to take all the measures necessary to achieve the result prescribed by a directive, the full effectiveness of that rule of Community law requires that there should be a right to reparation provided that three conditions are fulfilled.

[40] The first of those conditions is that the result prescribed by the directive should ntail the grant of rights to individuals. The second condition is that it should be possible to identify the content of those rights on the basis of the provisions of the directive. Finally, the third condition is the existence of a causal link between the breach of the State's obligation and the loss and damage suffered by the injured parties.

[41] Those conditions are sufficient to give rise to a right on the part of individuals to obtain reparation, a right founded directly on Community law.

[42]   Subject to that reservation, it is on the basis of the rules of national law on liability that the State must make reparation for the consequences of the loss and damage caused. In the absence of Community legislation, it is for the internal legal order of each Member State to designate the competent courts and lay down the detailed procedural rules for legal proceedings intended fully to safeguard the rights which individuals derive from Community law (see the judgments in Case 60/75 *Russo v AIMA* [1976] ECR 45, Case 33/76 *Rewe v Landwirtschaftskammer Saarland* [1976] ECR 1989 and Case 158/80 *Rewe v Hauptzollamt Kiel* [1981] ECR 1805).

[43]   Further, the substantive and procedural conditions for reparation of loss and damage laid down by the national law of the Member States must not be less favourable than those relating to similar domestic claims and must not be so framed as to make it virtually impossible or excessively difficult to obtain reparation (see, in relation to the analogous issue of the repayment of taxes levied in breach of Community law, *inter alia* the judgment in Case 199/82 *Amministrazione delle Finanze dello Stato v San Giorgio* [1983] ECR 3595).

[44]   In this case, the breach of Community law by a Member State by virtue of its failure to transpose Directive 80/987 within the prescribed period has been confirmed by a judgment of the Court. The result required by that directive entails the grant to employees of a right to a guarantee of payment of their unpaid wage claims. As is clear from the examination of the first part of the first question, the content of that right can be identified on the basis of the provisions of the directive.

[45]   Consequently, the national court must, in accordance with the national rules on liability, uphold the right of employees to obtain reparation of loss and damage caused to them as a result of failure to transpose the directive.

[46]   The answer to be given to the national court must therefore be that a Member State is required to make good loss and damage caused to individuals by failure to transpose Directive 80/987.

Note

It should be appreciated that this ruling, like that in *Marleasing* (Case C–106/89), makes an important contribution to the vigour of Community law at national level *even in circumstances where direct effect is lacking*.

The Court repeated its formulation in *Dori* (Case C–91/92). Having denied Ms Dori the possibility of relying on the Directive as such to defeat the claim against her by a private supplier (p. 112 above), the Court proceeded to rule that the Italian court was subject to the obligation of interpretation drawn from Article 5, now Article 10 EC post-Amsterdam ('indirect effect', p. 122 above). It then directed Dori to a different target – the defaulting State.

Paola Faccini Dori v Recreb Srl (Case C–91/92)
[1994] ECR I-3325
Court of Justice of the European Communities

[27]   If the result prescribed by the directive cannot be achieved by way of interpretation, it should also be borne in mind that, in terms of the judgment in Joined Cases C–6/90 and C–9/90 *Francovich and Others v Italy* [1991] ECR I–5357, paragraph 39,

Community law requires the Member States to make good damage caused to individuals through failure to transpose a directive, provided that three conditions are fulfilled. First, the purpose of the directive must be to grant rights to individuals. Second, it must be possible to identify the content of those rights on the basis of the provisions of the directive. Finally, there must be a causal link between the breach of the State's obligation and the damage suffered.

[28] ·The directive on contracts negotiated away from business premises is undeniably intended to confer rights on individuals and it is equally certain that the minimum content of those rights can be identified by reference to the provisions of the directive alone (see paragraph 17 above).

[29]   Where damage has been suffered and that damage is due to a breach by the State of its obligation, it is for the national court to uphold the right of aggrieved consumers to obtain reparation in accordance with national law on liability.

Question

To what extent do the techniques of 'indirect effect' and State liability under *Francovich* provide an adequate protection for the individual deprived of rights against a private party that are envisaged under an unimplemented Directive? (See, in particular, the Opinion of Advocate-General Jacobs in *Vaneetveld* v *SA Le Foyer* (Case C–316/93) [1994] ECR I-763.) Has the Court repaired the damage done to individual protection by its refusal in *Marshall* and *Dori* to accept that Directives are capable of horizontal direct effect?

Note

The *Francovich* focus on State liability appears to be acquiring an increasing priority within the Community system governing effective judicial protection at national level, at the expense of other devices for addressing the consequences of State failures to implement Directives in accordance with Articles 10 and 249 EC. The implications of this tendency were interrogated in part in the question above. A further aspect concerns time limits in national proceedings brought to secure repayment of charges levied, or payment of sums not made, in breach of a Directive that has not been properly implemented. The European Court has accepted that restrictions on back-dating claims may be imposed under national law; and that reasonable <u>time limits</u> may be applied in the interests of legal certainty. These procedural rules may be permissible even though they may serve to shelter the State from the full consequences of its unlawful failure to implement (Case C-338/91 *Steenhorst-Neerings* [1993] ECR I-5475; Case C-90/94 *Haahr Petroleum* [1997] ECR I-4142; Case C-188/95 *Fantask* [1997] ECR I-6783) unless, exceptionally, the Member State has made the exercise of rights excessively difficult (Case 45/76 *Comet* v *Produktschap voor Siergewassen* [1976] ECR 2043 on which see p. 726 below; Case C-208/90 *Emmott* v *Minister of Social Welfare* [1991] ECR I-4269; Case C-246/96 *Magorrian and Cunningham* v *Eastern Health and Social Services Board and Department of Health and Social Services* [1997] ECR I-7153.) The Court also insists on a rule of non-discrimination between Community law claims and similar claims under domestic law (Case C-228/96 *Aprile Srl* v *Amministrazione delle Finanze dello Stato* [1998] ECR I-7141).

Advocate General Jacobs in *Fantask* (Case C-188/95) argued strongly in favour of the contribution to legal security made by the application of time limits even in cases involving unimplemented Directives and suggested that a *Francovich* claim was the appropriate method of protecting an individual suffering loss in such circumstances. This approach to the protection of the individual would place great emphasis on the significance of the defaulting State's culpability as an element in the criteria governing *Francovich* liability (pp. 136 and 747 below).

More broadly still, H. Schermers has argued that in the wake of rulings such as *Francovich* and *Faccini Dori* 'we do not need direct effect for directives any more. When Member States do not fulfil their obligations under a directive, the affected individuals will be able to claim damages' ('No Direct Effect for Directives' (1997) 3 *Euro Public Law* 527, 539). He observes that the abandonment of the capacity of Directives to exert direct effect in favour of emphasis on *Francovich* claims against the defaulting State would expel from the Community legal order the current imbalance, which lends direct effect to Directives only in *some* circumstances (individual versus State). Does this provocative suggestion appeal to you?

It is, however, important to appreciate that the increasing tendency of *Francovich* to take centre stage in the pattern of individual protection developed by the European Court has not been universally welcomed. C. Harlow ('Francovich and the Problem of the Disobedient State' (1996) 2 ELJ 199), for example, finds the theoretical underpinnings for State liability in the EC to be weak, and fears that the intermingling of Community law with national liability systems may corrupt both. One may certainly question the *practical* feasibility of pursuing a *Francovich* claim other than in instances involving very wealthy applicants; yet Community law is supposed to confer rights on a wider range of interest groups than large commercial concerns.

The judgment in *Francovich* counts as one of the European Court's most remarkable. It has created a remedy defined by criteria under Community law which must be absorbed into the national legal order. *Francovich* represents a statement of the European Court's readiness to employ Article 5, now Article 10 EC post-Amsterdam, as a basis for establishing a system of judicial remedies that will further the cause of effective protection of Community law rights. But, at a more general level, the Court is presiding over the development of a Community 'common law'. The next extract traces the Court's development of the notion of effective judicial protection (at national level), before concluding with observations in this wider context.

R. Caranta, 'Government Liability after Francovich' (1993) 52 *Cambridge Law Journal* 272, 279–82

. . . The ground upon which the *Francovich* case was decided is the principle of effective protection of individuals.

The case law concerning this principle has evolved remarkably during the past ten years, the court having moved from an initial position which amounted to almost complete indifference to the remedial aspect of the rights conferred on individuals by Community law, to an ever greater involvement in questions concerning the conditions under which the protection of such rights is ensured by the judiciary of the Member States.

The initial position was the result of a widespread belief that Community law in general was only interested in substantive aspects of law, the procedural aspects having been left to the competence of the Member States. In the *Rewe*[42] and *Comet*[43] cases, for example, the court ruled that it was for each national legal system to determine the procedural aspects of actions claiming the protection of individual rights provided by Community law. There were two qualifications, namely that the domestic remedies had to be no less favourable than those established for comparable national rights, and that in any case the remedies conferred had to be effective, but the actual incidence of Community law on procedure was virtually non-existent.

The *Francovich* decision does maintain the traditional rule whereby procedures to ensure the execution of Community law are left to national legal systems, but with a small, and not so innocent, change; the competence of Member States ceases to be the governing principle, and becomes the rule only in the absence of relevant Community provisions.[44]

These qualifications of the principle of the competence of Member States in procedural matters acquired relevance long before *Francovich*. In the *Simmenthal* case, notably, the principle of the effectiveness of judicial protection ceased to be a mere obiter dictum and began to bite. In that case another Italian judge of first instance, the *Pretore* of Susa, had asked the Court of Justice whether it was consistent with Community law for a national system of judicial review of legislation to make it the duty of every judge, before excluding the operation of a national legal provision in conflict with Community law, to request a preliminary ruling by the country's Constitutional Court. The European Court, as is well known, held that:[45]

> any provision of a national legal system and any legislative, administrative or judicial practice which might impair the effectiveness of Community law by withholding from the national court having jurisdiction to apply such law the power to do everything necessary at the moment of its application to set aside national legal provisions which might prevent Community rules from having full force and effect are incompatible with those requirements which are the very essence of Community law.

On this ground the Court held that a system of centralised judicial review such as the one existing in Italy which delayed the final decision by requiring the matter to be referred to the Constitutional Court was not compatible with the principle of the effective protection of individual rights which was based upon Community law, and for this reason had to be set aside by every judge in the Member State.

Even in *Simmenthal*, however, it could be thought that the real issue was not just the effective protection of individuals; what was actually at stake in that case was which court was to have the last word when national law conflicted with Community

---

[42] Case 33/76, [1976], ECR 1997, cons. 5.
[43] Case 45/76, [1976] ECR 2053, cons. 12-17.
[44] But for a traditional reading of the rule *see* G. de Burca, 'Giving Effect to European Community Directives' (1992) 55 MLR 215, at p. 238.
[45] Case 106/77, [1978] ECR 629, para. 22.

law. If every national judge had to make a reference to the Constitutional Court, it would be that Court which determined the consistency of the national law with Community law, without even consulting the Court of Justice, because the Italian Constitutional Court in practice never made a reference under article 177 of the EEC Treaty. On the other hand, if every judge was left free to decide the conflict between national and Community law on his own, he would probably resort to the European Court to have Community law interpreted and the question of compatibiity assessed. It was a contest for power, the Court of Justice against the Italian Constitutional Court, and the latter finally bowed to the supremacy of Community law and of its court.[46]

More relevant to the protection of individuals were the decisions concerning the repayment of wrongly paid taxes. On references by some Italian courts, the Court of Justice in the *San Giorgio* case[47] held it to be inconsistent with Community law for a national provision to subject the right to restitution of sums paid pursuant to a national tax law contrary to Community law to proof that the charge had not been transferred to the final consumer of the goods; the court thought it contrary to the principle of effective judicial protection to impose on citizens invoking their Community law rights an onus of proof which it was almost impossible to discharge.

There can be no doubt that *Factortame*[48] is the most important decision so far concerning the consequences of the principle of the effectiveness of judicial protection of individuals; its impact upon the respective roles of the Community and Member States in the creation of remedies for infringements of Community law rights seriously undermines the position according to which procedure is a matter to be left to Member States.

The facts which constitute the background to, and the legal questions involved in, the *Factortame* decision are widely known on the Continent as well as in Britain.[49] It is sufficient to recall that some Spanish owners of fishing vessels had challenged the conformity with Community law of a British statute and regulations designed to ensure that ships flying the Union Jack were owned and operated by British citizens or corporations.

Fearing that irrecoverable damage could accrue pending the judgment, the plaintiffs had asked for an interim injunction, but this was refused by the Court of Appeal[50] which held that courts had no authority under the law to suspend the application of a legal provision which had not yet been judicially determined to be in conflict with Community law. The House of Lords,[51] having come to the same conclusion on the

---

[46] Corte cost, 8 giugno 1984 n. 170, in *Giurisprudenza costituzionale* 1984, I, 1098: for a commentary see J-V. Louis, 'Droit communautaire et loi postérieure: un revirement de la Cour constitutionelle italienne', in *Cah. dr. europ*, 1986, 194.

[47] Case 199/82, [1983] ECR 3595.

[48] *R v Secretary of State for Transport, ex parte Factortame Ltd No. 2.* [1991] 1 AC 603; see the commentaries by D. Oliver, 'Fishing on the Incoming Tide' (1991) 54 MLR 442, and A.G. Toth (1990) 27 CML Rev 574; see also H.W.R.Wade, 'What has Happened to the Sovereignty of Parliament?' (1991) 107 LQR 1; *Id.*, 'Injunctive Relief against the Crown and Ministers' *ibidem*, 4; N.P. Gravells, 'Disapplying an Act of Parliament Pending Ruling: Constitutional Enormity or Community Law Right?' [1989] PL 568; A. Barav, 'Enforcement of Community Rights in the National Courts: The Case for Jurisdiction to Grant an Interim Relief' (1989) 26 CML Rev 369 ff.

[49] See R.R. Churchill,'"Quota hopping": The Common Fisheries Policy Wrongfooted?' (1990) 27 CML Rev 209, and the commentary by the same author in (1992) 29 CML Rev 415.

[50] [1989] 2 CMLR 353.

[51] [1990] 2 AC 85.

point of English law as the Court of Appeal, thought it necessary to ask the Court of Justice for a preliminary ruling under article 177 whether, in relation to the grant of interim protection in the circumstances of the case, Community law overrode English law.[52] The Court of Justice, following the learned conclusions of Advocate General Tesauro, held that:[53]

> Community law must be interpreted as meaning that a national court which, in a case before it concerning Community law, considers that the sole obstacle which precludes it from granting interim relief is a rule of national law must set aside that rule.

Decisive to the outcome of the *Factortame* case was, according to the Court of Justice which laid great emphasis on its previous decision in the *Simmenthal* case,[54] the consideration that:[55]

> the full effectiveness of Community law would be . . . much impaired if a rule of national law could prevent a court seised of a dispute governed by Community law from granting interim relief in order to ensure the full effectiveness of the judgment to be given on the existence of the rights claimed under Community law.

Just as in *Factortame* it was from the principle of the effectiveness of Community law that the Court of Justice deduced the necessity for interim protection, so in *Francovich* it distilled the necessity for an entitlement to damages when Community law is infringed.

These decisions, it is submitted, mark the definitive departure by the Court of Justice from the model, recalled above, according to which Community law was confined to the substantive aspects of law, to the definition of rights and duties, while the rules governing the actual enforcement of such rights and duties depended entirely on the possibly different legal rules in force in the various Member States.

The new approach is not limited to the case law. It is sufficient to mention two EEC directives, namely directive 89/665[56] and the more recent 92/13,[57] both designed to promote uniformity of national remedies for violation of Community rules applicable to public works and procurement contracts.[58]

From a comparative point of view it is clear that, under the mounting pressure exerted by the case law of the Court of Justice and also by the legislator, Community law has increasingly begun to 'fasten upon remedies', in this way introducing at a continental level a style of legal thinking which was characteristic of common law rather than civil law systems.

The author concludes his examination in the following terms (pp. 296–7):

. . . The *Francovich* decision has a relevance which goes beyond the field of governmental liability. It marks the birth of a 'jus commune', of a law common to all

---

[52] [1990] 2 AC 85 at 152, *per* Lord Bridge of Harwich, with whom all the other Law Lords concurred.
[53] [1991] 1 AC 603, 644.
[54] [1991] 1 AC 603, 643-4.
[55] [1991] 1 AC 603, 644.
[56] OJEC 1989, No. L. 395/34.
[57] OJEC 1992, No. L. 76/14.
[58] See M. Bronckers, 'Private Enforcement of 1992: Do Trade and Industry Stand a Chance against Member States?' (1989) 26 CML Rev 528.

the Member States and to the Community itself, in the field of the judicial protection of individuals against public powers.[107]

In *Factortame* and to a larger degree in *Zuckerfabrik Süderdithmarschen*[108] the Court of Justice laid down the rules to be applied by domestic courts when granting interim relief in Community law cases. The rules were the same as those applied by the European Court itself in proceedings under articles 185 and 186 of the EEC Treaty, the first of which was explicitly referred to by the court.[109]

In *Francovich* the the Court of Justice applied to actions of the Member States inconsistent with Community law the same rules which had been elaborated by the court itself in relation to non-contractual liability for invalid acts of Community organs—but with a qualification: it forgot that in Community law the breach has to be 'sufficiently serious'. But qualifications are inconsistent with a 'jus commune'; they destroy its inherent condition, namely, to be common. . . .

Note

It is apparent from this extract that the issue of effective protection extends far beyond the question of the application of Directives alone and beyond questions of a remedy in damages alone. *Francovich* is part of a wider phenomenon. The European Court is building a notion of effective protection as a general principle of the Community legal order. This was already plain from the *Factortame* saga, mentioned by Caranta. This involved violation of primary Treaty provisions. It is explored in the general context of 'Enforcement of Community law against Member States' in Chapter 17, where it will be seen that EC law exerts a deepening influence over the remedies which must be available at national level for the vindication of Community law rights. The reader should also reconsider the discussion at p. 79 above relating to the convergence of national legal systems via the medium of Community law.

The one sure consequence of *Francovich* was that the Court would be invited to clarify the scope of liability. For example, as Caranta suggests in the final paragraph of the above extract, the Court neglected to elaborate in *Francovich* on requirements of culpability as a precondition to State liability. The Court's rulings in March 1996, including a further episode in the *Factortame* saga, '*Factortame III*' (Case C–48/93), are now crucial. These are relevant beyond the specific issue of unimplemented Directives and, alongside other key 'post *Francovich* rulings, they are examined in Chapter 17, p. 737 below.

Further reading

Barav, A., 'Omnipotent Courts' in Curtin, D. and Heukels, T. (eds), *Institutional Dynamics of European Integration* (Dordrecht, Martinus Nijhoff, 1994).

---

[107] See more generally J. Schwarze, 'Tendencies towards a Common Administrative Law in Europe' (1991) 16 EL Rev 3; J. Rivero, 'Vers un droit commun européen: nouvelles perspectives en droit administratif', in *Pages de doctrine* (Paris 1980), p. 489 *et. seq.*; M.P. Chiti, 'I signori del diritto comunitario: la Corte di giustizia e lo sviluppo del diritto amministrativo europeo', in *Rivista trimestrale di diritto pubblico* 1991, 796.

[108] Joint Cases C–143/88 and C–92/89, [1991] 1 ECR 415; the decision was considered by Lord Goff of Chieveley in *Kirklees Metropolitan Borough Council* v *Wickes Building Supplies Ltd* [1992] 3 WLR 170, 187.

[109] See cons. 27.

Boch, C., 'The Iroquois at the Kirchberg: or some naive remarks on the status and relevance of direct effect' in J. Usher (ed.), *The State of the European Union* (Longman, Harlow, 2000).

Caranta, R., 'Judicial Protection against Member States: a new jus commune takes shape' (1995) 32 CML Rev 703.

Curtin, D. and Mortelmans, K., 'Application and Enforcement of Community Law by the Member States: Actors in Search of a Third Generation Script' in Curtin, D. and Heukels, T. (eds) *Institutional Dynamics of European Integration* (Dordrecht, Martinus Nijhoff, 1994).

De Witte, B., 'Direct effect, supremacy and the Nature of the Legal Order', in Craig, P., and de Burca, G. (eds), *The Evolution of EU Law* (OUP, Oxford, 1999), Ch. 5.

Hilson, C. and Downes, T., 'Making Sense of Rights: Community Rights in EC Law' (1999) 24 EL Rev 121.

Maher, I., 'National Courts as European Community Courts' (1994) 14 *Legal Studies* 226.

Mastroianni, R., 'On the distinction between vertical and horizontal direct effect of Directives: what role for the principle of equality?' (1999) 5 *Euro Public Law* 417.

Plaza Martin, C., 'Furthering the Effectiveness of EC Directives and the Judicial Protection of Individual Rights Thereunder' (1994) 43 ICLQ 26.

Szyszczak, E., 'Making Europe more relevant to its Citizens' (1996) 21 EL Rev 351.

Tesauro, G., 'The Effectiveness of Judicial Protection and Co-operation between the Court of Justice and the National Courts' (1993) 13 YEL 1.

Timmermans, C., 'Community Directives Revisited' (1997) 17 YEL 1.

Van Gerven, W., 'The Horizontal Effect of Directive Provisions Revisited: the Reality of Catchwords' in Curtin, D. and Heukels, T. (eds), *Institutional Dynamics of European Integration* (Dordrecht, Martinus Nijhoff, 1994).

Van Gerven, W., 'Bridging the gap between Community and national laws' (1995) 32 CML Rev 679.

Questions

1. (Imaginary) Directive 1/97 provides that from January 2000, all workers shall be entitled to bring a claim that they have been unfairly dismissed before a national tribunal, provided they have been employed for at least one year prior to dismissal. A UK Statutory Instrument made in 1985 provides that the relevant qualifying period for an unfair dismissal claim in the UK is two years. The UK has not implemented the Directive. It ought to have done so by 1 July 1998, but the Government has been unable to introduce implementing measures because of protests by the opposition parties and some of its own backbench MPs. At the start of 1999, Alice took up a post with British Stodge plc, a firm which supplies catering services to National Health Service hospitals. It is June 2000 and she has just been dismissed. Advise Alice of any assistance she may derive from EC law.

2. How might the Community legal order rid itself of the complexities engendered by the extension of the notion of direct effect to Directives?

4 ARTICLE 234: THE PRELIMINARY REFERENCE PROCEDURE

Article 234 EC

Article 234
The Court of Justice shall have jurisdiction to give preliminary rulings concerning:

(a)   the interpretation of this Treaty;
(b)   the validity and interpretation of acts of the institutions of the Community and of the ECB;
(c)   the interpretation of the statutes of bodies established by an act of the Council, where those statutes so provide.

Where such a question is raised before any court or tribunal of a Member State, that court or tribunal may, if it considers that a decision on the question is necessary to enable it to give judgment, request the Court of Justice to give a ruling thereon.

Where any such question is raised in a case pending before a court or tribunal of a Member State, against whose decisions there is no judicial remedy under national law, that court or tribunal shall bring the matter before the Court of Justice.

Note
The text was untouched by the Treaty of Amsterdam, but Article 234 was formerly numbered Article 177 (see p. 29 above). Clearly this must be borne in mind when reading pre-Amsterdam documents, including judgments of the Court.

(A) THE PURPOSE OF ARTICLE 234

The purpose of Article 234 can be traced directly to the need to secure uniformity in the Community legal order throughout the Member States. The introduction delivered by Advocate-General Lagrange 30 years ago in his Opinion in *Bosch* v *de Geus* (Case 13/61), can hardly be bettered:

Bosch v de Geus (Case 13/61)
[1962] ECR 45
Court of Justice of the European Communities

ADVOCATE-GENERAL LAGRANGE: *Mr President, Members of the Court,*
This case – the first submitted to you under the provisions of Article 177 of the Treaty establishing the European Economic Community – is of importance under that head alone, since it involves the working of a procedure for the submission of preliminary questions which is apparently designed to play a central part in the application of the Treaty. The progressive integration of the Treaty into the legal, social and economic life of the Member States must involve more and more frequently the application and, when the occasion arises, the interpretation of the Treaty in municipal litigation, whether public or private, and not only the provisions of the Treaty itself but also those of the Regulations adopted for its implementation will give rise to questions of interpretation and indeed of legality. Applied judiciously – one is tempted to say loyally – the provisions of Article 177 must lead to a real and fruitful collaboration between the municipal courts and the Court of Justice of the Communities with mutual regard for their respective jurisdictions. It is in this spirit that each side must solve the sometimes delicate problems which may arise in all systems of preliminary procedure, and which are necessarily made more difficult in this case by the differences in the legal systems of the Member States as regards this type of procedure.

Rheinmühlen-Düsseldorf v Einfuhr-und Vorratsstelle für Getreide und Futtermittel (No. 1) (Case 166/73)
[1974] ECR 33
Court of Justice of the European Communities

Article 177 is essential for the preservation of the Community character of the law established by the Treaty and has the object of ensuring that in all circumstances the law is the same in all States of the Community.

Note
Stauder v *Ulm* (Case 29/69) was examined at p. 66 above in connection with the protection of fundamental rights. The case was also illuminating for its use of the preliminary reference procedure to secure uniform interpretation of Community texts:

Stauder v Ulm (Case 29/69)
[1969] ECR 419
Court of Justice of the European Communities

[2] . . . Article 4 of Decision No 69/71 stipulates in two of its versions, one being the German version, that the States must take all necessary measures to ensure that beneficiaries can only purchase the product in question on presentation of a 'coupon indicating their names', whilst in the other versions, however, it is only stated that a 'coupon referring to the person concerned' must be shown, thus making it possible to employ other methods of checking in addition to naming the beneficiary. It is

therefore necessary in the first place to ascertain exactly what methods the provision at issue prescribes.

[3]   When a single decision is addressed to all the Member States the necessity for uniform application and accordingly for uniform interpretation makes it impossible to consider one version of the text in isolation but requires that it be interpreted on the basis of both the real intention of its author and the aim he seeks to achieve, in the light in particular of the versions in all four languages.

Notes
1.   It will be recalled from p. 66, above, that the Court's interpretation led it to reject the contention that the rules infringed fundamental rights.
2.   The preliminary reference procedure's role in securing authoritative interpretation of Community law places it alongside the principles of supremacy and direct effect and the notion of effective judicial protection (which, as illustrated in *Francovich*, extends beyond direct effect) as one of the pillars of the Community legal order.

(B) THE SEPARATION OF FUNCTIONS

The preliminary reference procedure under Article 234 EC – which was Article 177 pre-Amsterdam – is based on a separation of function. It does not elevate the European Court to an appellate status. The Court may not rule on the validity of national law. This was made clear in *Van Gend en Loos* (Case 26/62), which was examined at p. 91 above for its explanation of the nature of direct effect. It will be recalled that the substance of the case concerned the compatibility of a Dutch levy with the Treaty.

Van Gend en Loos v *Nederlandse Administratie der Belastingen* (Case 26/62)
[1963] ECR 1
Court of Justice of the European Communities

According to the observations of the Belgian and Netherlands Governments, the wording of this question appears to require, before it can be answered, an examination by the Court of the tariff classification of ureaformaldehyde imported into the Netherlands, a classification on which Van Gend & Loos and the Inspector of Customs and Excise at Zaandam hold different opinions with regard to the 'Tariefbesluit' of 1947. The question clearly does not call for an interpretation of the Treaty but concerns the application of Netherlands customs legislation to the classification of aminoplasts, which is outside the jurisdiction conferred upon the Court of Justice of the European Communities by subparagraph (a) of the first paragraph of Article 177.

The Court has therefore no jurisdiction to consider the reference made by the Tariefcommissie.

However, the real meaning of the question put by the Tariefcommissie is whether, in law, an effective increase in customs duties charged on a given product as a result not of an increase in the rate but of a new classification of the product arising from a change of its tariff description contravenes the prohibition in Article 12 of the Treaty.

Viewed in this way the question put is concerned with an interpretation of this provision of the Treaty and more particularly of the meaning which should be given to the concept of duties applied before the Treaty entered into force.

Therefore the Court has jurisdiction to give a ruling on this question.

As to whether the facts of the case disclosed a violation of Article 12, which is Article 25 post-Amsterdam, the Court concluded:

The Court has no jurisdiction to check the validity of the conflicting views on this subject which have been submitted to it during the proceedings but must leave them to be determined by the national courts.

Note

The same approach may be observed in *Costa* v *ENEL* (Case 6/64), examined above at p. 82 in relation to the doctrine of the supremacy of Community law.

Costa v *ENEL* *(Case 6/64)*
[1964] ECR 585
Court of Justice of the European Communities

The complaint is made that the intention behind the question posed was to obtain, by means of Article 177, a ruling on the compatibility of a national law with the Treaty.

By the terms of this Article, however, national courts against whose decisions, as in the present case, there is no judicial remedy, must refer the matter to the Court of Justice so that a preliminary ruling may be given upon the 'interpretation of the Treaty' whenever a question of interpretation is raised before them. This provision gives the Court no jurisdiction either to apply the Treaty to a specific case or to decide upon the validity of a provision of domestic law in relation to the Treaty, as it would be possible for it to do under Article 169.

Nevertheless, the Court has power to extract from a question imperfectly formulated by the national court those questions which alone pertain to the interpretation of the Treaty. Consequently a decision should be given by the Court not upon the validity of an Italian law in relation to the Treaty, but only upon the interpretation of the abovementioned Articles in the context of the points of law stated by the Giudice Conciliatore.

Note

However, the Court's inability to rule on the validity of national law may not be as absolute as it first seems. In *Walter Rau* v *de Smedt* (Case 261/81), the Court was asked to interpret Article 30 of the EC Treaty (now, after amendment, Article 28; see Chapter 7). The case concerned a challenge to Belgian rules requiring the packaging of margarine in cubes. The Court's response was rather more full and direct than mere interpretation of Community law.

Walter Rau v *de Smedt* *(Case 261/81)*
[1982] ECR 3961
Court of Justice of the European Communities

The application in one Member State to margarine imported from another Member State and lawfully produced and marketed in that State of legislation prohibiting the marketing of margarine or edible fats where each block or its external packaging does not have a particular shape, for example the shape of a cube, in circumstances in which the consumer may be protected and informed by means which hinder the free movement of goods to a lesser degree constitutes a measure having an effect equivalent to a quantitative restriction within the meaning of Article 30 of the Treaty.

Notes
1.   Look out for other examples of the Court adopting an approach beyond mere interpretation in its answers to questions referred.
2.   In fact, it would be rather unrealistic to expect the Court to adhere to the abstract in its answers. It also typically expands its answers when it is eager to ensure that an important principle is fully understood; *Van Gend en Loos* (Case 26/62) (p. 91 above) stands as a classic example of this.
3.   Since the European Court's formal role under the Article 234 procedure relates to Community law only, it should not question the national court's decision in the case before it to make a reference. Whether it is necessary to obtain a decision on a question is a matter for the national court. This stems from the separation of functions between national courts and the European Court.

Van Gend en Loos v *Nederlandse Administratie der Belastingen (Case 26/62)*
[1963] ECR 1
Court of Justice of the European Communities

The Belgian Government further argues that the Court has no jurisdiction on the ground that no answer which the Court could give to the first question of the Tariefcommissie would have any bearing on the result of the proceedings brought in that court.

However, in order to confer jurisdiction on the Court in the present case it is necessary only that the question raised should clearly be concerned with the interpretation of the Treaty. The considerations which may have led a national court or tribunal to its choice of questions as well as the relevance which it attributes to such questions in the context of a case before it are excluded from review by the Court of Justice.

It appears from the wording of the questions referred that they relate to the interpretation of the Treaty. The Court therefore has the jurisdiction to answer them.

Costa v *ENEL (Case 6/64)*
[1964] ECR 585
Court of Justice of the European Communities

The complaint is made that the Milan court has requested an interpretation of the Treaty which was not necessary for the solution of the dispute before it.

Since, however, Article 177 is based upon a clear separation of functions between national courts and the Court of Justice, it cannot empower the latter either to investigate the facts of the case or to criticize the grounds and purpose of the request for interpretation.

Irish Creamery Milk Suppliers v *Government of Ireland (Case 36/80)*
[1981] ECR 735
Court of Justice of the European Communities

[4]   The first question raised by the High Court of Ireland is worded as follows:

'Was the decision by the High Court, at this stage of the hearing, to refer to the European Court under Article 177 of the Treaty the question set out in paragraph 2 below a correct exercise on the part of the High Court of its discretion pursuant to the said article?'.

[5]   Before an answer is given to that question it should be recalled that Article 177 of the Treaty establishes a framework for close co-operation between the national courts and the Court of Justice based on the assignment to each of different functions. The second paragraph of that article makes it clear that it is for the national court to decide at what stage in the proceedings it is appropriate for that court to refer a question to the Court of Justice for a preliminary ruling.

[6]   The need to provide an interpretation of Community law which will be of use to the national court makes it essential, as the Court has already stated in its judgment of 12 July 1979 (Union Laitière Normande, Case 244/78 [1979] ECR 2663) to define the legal context in which the interpretation requested should be placed. From that aspect it might be convenient, if circumstances permit, for the facts in the case to be established and for questions of purely national law to be settled at the time the reference is made to the Court of Justice so as to enable the latter to take cognizance of all the features of fact and of law which may be relevant to the interpretation of Community law which it is called upon to give.

[7]   However, those considerations do not in any way restrict the discretion of the national court, which alone has a direct knowledge of the facts of the case and of the arguments of the parties, which will have to take responsibility for giving judgment in the case and which is therefore in the best position to appreciate at what stage in the proceedings it requires a preliminary ruling from the Court of Justice.

[8]   Hence it is clear that the national court's decision when to make a reference under Article 177 must be dictated by considerations of procedural organization and efficiency to be weighed by that court.

[9]   The reply to the first question which has been raised should therefore be that under Article 177 the decision at what stage in proceedings before it a national court should refer a question to the Court of Justice for a preliminary ruling is a matter for the discretion of the national court.

Notes
1.   It is perfectly permissible to refer in interim proceedings, although this will not be normal; *Hoffman la Roche* v *Centrafarm* (Case 107/76) [1977] ECR 957.
2.   An outstanding exception to the receptiveness of the Court to references made by national courts is found in the two *Foglia* v *Novello* cases (Cases 104/79 and 244/80).

Foglia v *Novello (No. 1) (Case 104/79)*
[1980] ECR 745
Court of Justice of the European Communities

Foglia, an Italian wine dealer, dispatched goods to Novello in France. The contract stipulated that Novello would not be liable for any charges levied by the French or Italian authorities which were incompatible with Community law. A tax then levied by the French authorities formed the basis of the litigation. Novello refused to bear the cost. Foglia sued Novello before the Italian courts; Novello's defence was based on the incompatibility of the charge with Community law (Article 95 of the EC Treaty (now Article 90 EC)). A reference was made by the Italian judge, the *Pretura di Bra*.

[8]   The parties to the main action submitted a certain number of documents to the Pretura which enabled it to investigate the French legislation concerning the taxation of liqueur wines and other comparable products. The court concluded from its investigation that such legislation created a 'serious discrimination' against Italian liqueur wines and natural wines having a high degree of alcoholic strength by means of special arrangements made for French liqueur wines termed 'natural sweet wines' and preferential tax treatment accorded certain French natural wines with a high degree of alcoholic strength and bearing a designation of origin. On the basis of that conclusion the court formulated the questions which it has submitted to the Court of Justice.

[9]   In their written observations submitted to the Court of Justice the two parties to the main action have provided an essentially identical description of the tax discrimination which is a feature of the French legislation concerning the taxation of liqueur wines; the two parties consider that that legislation is incompatible with Community law. In the course of the oral procedure before the Court Foglia stated that he was participating in the procedure before the Court in view of the interest of his undertaking as such and as an undertaking belonging to a certain category of Italian traders in the outcome of the legal issues involved in the dispute.

[10]   It thus appears that the parties to the main action are concerned to obtain a ruling that the French tax system is invalid for liqueur wines by the expedient of proceedings before an Italian court between two private individuals who are in agreement as to the result to be attained and who have inserted a clause in their contract in order to induce the Italian court to give a ruling on the point. The artificial nature of this expedient is underlined by the fact that Danzas [the carrier] did not exercise its rights under French law to institute proceedings over the consumption tax although it undoubtedly had an interest in doing so in view of the clause in the contract by which it was also bound and moreover of the fact that Foglia paid without protest that undertaking's bill which included a sum paid in respect of that tax.

[11]   The duty of the Court of Justice under Article 177 of the EEC Treaty is to supply all courts in the Community with the information on the interpretation of Community law which is necessary to enable them to settle genuine disputes which are brought before them. A situation in which the Court was obliged by the expedient of arrangements like those described above to give rulings would jeopardize the whole

system of legal remedies available to private individuals to enable them to protect themselves against tax provisions which are contrary to the Treaty.

[12] This means that the questions asked by the national court, having regard to the circumstances of this case, do not fall within the framework of the duties of the Court of Justice under Article 177 of the Treaty.

[13] The Court of Justice accordingly has no jurisdiction to give a ruling on the questions asked by the national court.

Note
The judge was evidently perplexed that the Court seemed to have abandoned its policy of non-interference with the decision of the referring judge, and referred further questions in the second *Foglia* v *Novello* case.

Foglia v *Novello (No. 2) (Case 244/80)*
[1981] ECR 3045
Court of Justice of the European Communities

[17] In order that the Court of Justice may perform its task in accordance with the Treaty it is essential for national courts to explain, when the reasons do not emerge beyond any doubt from the file, why they consider that a reply to their questions is necessary to enable them to give judgment.

[18] It must in fact be emphasized that the duty assigned to the Court by Article 177 is not that of delivering advisory opinions on general or hypothetical questions but of assisting in the administration of justice in the Member States. It accordingly does not have jurisdiction to reply to questions of interpretation which are submitted to it within the framework of procedural devices arranged by the parties in order to induce the Court to give its views on certain problems of Community law which do not correspond to an objective requirement inherent in the resolution of a dispute. A declaration by the Court that it has no jurisdiction in such circumstances does not in any way trespass upon the prerogatives of the national court but makes it possible to prevent the application of the procedure under Article 177 for purposes other than those appropriate for it.

[19] Furthermore, it should be pointed out that, whilst the Court of Justice must be able to place as much reliance as possible upon the assessment by the national court of the extent to which the questions submitted are essential, it must be in position to make any assessment inherent in the performance of its own duties in particular in order to check, as all courts must, whether it has jurisdiction. Thus the Court, taking into account the repercussions of its decisions in this matter, must have regard, in exercising the jurisdiction conferred upon it by Article 177, not only to the interests of the parties to the proceedings but also to those of the Community and of the Member States. Accordingly it cannot, without disregarding the duties assigned to it, remain indifferent to the assessments made by the courts of the Member States in the exceptional cases in which such assessments may affect the proper working of the procedure laid down by Article 177.

[20] Whilst the spirit of co-operation which must govern the performance of the duties assigned by Article 177 to the national courts on the one hand and the Court of Justice on the other requires the latter to have regard to the national court's proper

responsibilities, it implies at the same time that the national court, in the use which it makes of the facilities provided by Article 177, should have regard to the proper function of the Court of Justice in this field.

[21]   The reply to the first question must accordingly be that whilst, according to the intended role of Article 177, an assessment of the need to obtain an answer to the questions of interpretation raised, regard being had to the circumstances of fact and of law involved in the main action, is a matter for the national court it is nevertheless for the Court of Justice, in order to confirm its own jurisdiction, to examine, where necessary, the conditions in which the case has been referred to it by the national court.

The Court then observed:

[25]   The reply to the fourth question must accordingly be that in the case of preliminary questions intended to permit the national court to determine whether provisions laid down by law or regulation in another Member State are in accordance with Community law the degree of legal protection may not differ according to whether such questions are raised in proceedings between individuals or in an action to which the State whose legislation is called in question is a party, but that in the first case the Court of Justice must take special care to ensure that the procedure under Article 177 is not employed for purposes which were not intended by the Treaty.

Notes
1.   In the result, the Court did not significantly modify the stance which it had taken in the first *Foglia* v *Novello* case (Case 104/79).
2.   There are sound arguments both for and against the Court's stance. See, e.g., discussion by A. Barav (1980) 5 EL Rev 443; D. Wyatt (1982) 7 EL Rev 186; and G. Bebr (1982) 19 CML Rev 421. However, contrary to the impression left by these two judgments, subsequent case law suggests that the Court has *not* embarked on a new policy of inquiry into the national court's decision to refer. It is striking that in the main the Court has routinely declined subsequent invitations to repeat the *Foglia* v *Novello* approach. In *Walter Rau* (Case 261/81), mentioned above at p. 141, the Court was curt when presented with objections to its jurisdiction:

Walter Rau v de Smedt (Case 261/81)
[1982] ECR 3961
Court of Justice of the European Communities

[8]   The Belgian Government points out that the importation of margarine into Belgium by the defendant in the main action is already the subject of criminal proceedings in Belgium and that the Court should therefore inquire whether the dispute which gave rise to the request for a preliminary ruling is a genuine dispute. In this regard the Belgian Government recalls the judgment of the Court of 16 December 1981 in Case 244/80 *Foglia* [1981] ECR 3045.

[9]   In this instance there is nothing in the file on the case which provides grounds for doubting that the dispute is genuine. Therefore there is no reason for concluding that the Court has no jurisdiction.

Note
In *Parfumerie-Fabrik* v *Provide* (Case C-150/88), the Court confirmed that it will not lightly infer an absence of a genuine dispute.

Parfumerie-Fabrik v *Provide (Case C-150/88)*
[1989] ECR 3891
Court of Justice of the European Communities

[11]　The Italian Government notes that the preliminary questions arose in the context of a dispute between individuals, the genuineness of which is open to doubt, and that they are intended to permit a court in one Member State to determine whether the rules of another Member State are compatible with Community law. Referring to the Court's judgment of 16 December 1981 in Case 244/80 *Foglia* v *Novello* [1981] ECR 3045, the Italian Government therefore expresses its doubts as to the propriety of the request for a preliminary ruling. It further maintains that the Court has no jurisdiction under Article 177 to rule on the compatibility of national legislation with Community law.

[12]　Those objections must be dismissed. First, the documents before the Court do not allow any doubt as to the genuineness of the dispute in the main proceedings or, therefore, the propriety of the request for a preliminary ruling. Secondly, the Court has consistently held (see, in particular, its judgment of 9 October 1984 in Joined Cases 91 and 127/83 *Heineken Brouwerijen BV* v *Inspecteurs der Vennootschapsbelasting, Amsterdam and Utrecht* [1984] ECR 3435) that, when ruling on questions intended to permit the national court to determine whether national provisions are in accordance with Community law, the Court may provide the criteria for the interpretation of Community law which will enable the national court to solve the legal problem with which it is faced. The same is true when it is to be determined whether the provisions of a Member State other than that of the court requesting the ruling are compatible with Community law.

Note
In *Wienand Meilicke* v *ADV/ORGA FA Meyer AG* (Case C-83/91) [1992] ECR I-4871, the Court declined to answer questions referred to it by a German court. The Court considered it was being asked to rule on a purely hypothetical general problem. It had not had made available to it information necessary to enable it to provide a useful reply. In *Telemarsicabruzzo* v *Circostel* (Cases C-320-322/90) [1993] ECR I-393, the Court refused to give a ruling where it had been supplied with inadequate background information. It seems that these rejections are exceptional and it does not appear that the Court is proposing to embark on a new restrictive policy, although the rulings may be taken in part as an encouragement to a referring court to take more care in the preparation of relevant documentation (see *Further reading* at the end of this Chapter). It is pertinent to recall that the fact that the parties to litigation may be in agreement about the desired result does not necessarily eliminate the existence of a real dispute calling for a ruling by the European Court (e.g. Case C–412/93 *Société d'Importation Édouard Leclerc-Siplec* v *TFI Publicité SA & M6 Publicité SA* [1995] ECR I-179). In the absence of

exceptional circumstances, the European Court's readiness to answer questions of interpretation of Community law which a national court chooses to refer seems likely to continue. In *Landesgrundverkehrsreferent der Tiroler Landesregierung* v *Beck, Bergdorf Wohnbau* (Case C-355/97), judgment of 7 September 1999, for example, questions posed by an Austrian court were answered despite submissions by the Austrian government and the Commission that answers could be of no value whatsoever in resolving the dispute. The 'presumption of relevance' attaching to questions referred was not rebutted on the facts. In *Wiener* (Case C-338/95) [1997] ECR I-6495, the Court coolly ignored Advocate General Jacobs' plea for more self-restraint by both national courts and the European Court. That does not rule out the possibility that national courts may refer fewer cases to Luxembourg as they gain confidence in their ability to handle Community law materials. However, in recent years the number of referrals has remained fairly constant. The figures are 251 in 1995, 256 in 1996, 239 in 1997 and 264 in 1998. From 1994 to 1997 Italy produced the highest number of referrals (46, 58, 70 and 50 in 1994, 1995, 1996 and 1997 respectively), with Germany the next highest in each of the four years. In 1998 Spain led the way (55 referrals), followed by Germany (49) and Italy (39). Courts in the UK made 21 references to Luxembourg in 1996, 18 in 1997 and 24 in 1998 (*source:* 16th Annual Report on the Application of Community Law, COM (99) 301, OJ 1999 C354). It seems probable that the weight of preliminary references transmitted to the Court will increase, under pressures caused by *inter alia* enlargement of the Union and the enhanced jurisdiction conferred on the Court by the Amsterdam Treaty (even outside the EC pillar of the Union, in a modified version of the preliminary reference procedure found in Article 35 EU). On anxieties about the ability of the Court to meet this burden and possible reform, see section (H) of this chapter, p. 162 below.

Question
F. Mancini has compared the structure of the preliminary reference procedure with 'a fully fledged dual system of federal courts as can be found in the US,' and found it 'legally frailer, but politically more faithful to the federal ethos' ((1989) 26 CML Rev 595, at p. 605; see also D. Edward (also a judge at the Court) (1995) 20 EL Rev 539, 546–7). Discuss. What alterations to the Article 234 division of function might improve the procedure?

(C) THE EFFECT OF AN ARTICLE 234 RULING

ICC v *Amministrazione delle Finanze (Case 66/80)*
[1981] ECR 1191
Court of Justice of the European Communities

[9]   Article 177 of the Treaty provides that the Court shall have jurisdiction to give preliminary rulings on the interpretation of the Treaty and on the validity and interpretation of acts of the institutions of the Community, including regulations of both the Council and the Commission. The second and third paragraphs of that

provision go on to state that national courts may or must, as the case may be, bring such matters before the Court where they need a decision on that issue in order to give their judgment.

[10]   The scope of judgments given under this head should be viewed in the light of the aims of Article 177 and the place it occupies in the entire system of judicial protection established by the Treaties.

[11]   The main purpose of the powers accorded to the Court by Article 177 is to ensure that Community law is applied uniformly by national courts. Uniform application of Community law is imperative not only when a national court is faced with a rule of Community law the meaning and scope of which need to be defined; it is just as imperative when the Court is confronted by a dispute as to the validity of an act of the institutions.

[12]   When the Court is moved under Article 177 to declare an act of one of the institutions to be void there are particularly imperative requirements concerning legal certainty in addition to those concerning the uniform application of Community law. It follows from the very nature of such a declaration that a national court may not apply the act declared to be void without once more creating serious uncertainty as to the Community law applicable.

[13]   It follows therefrom that although a judgment of the Court given under Article 177 of the Treaty declaring an act of an institution, in particular a Council or Commission regulation, to be void is directly addressed only to the national court which brought the matter before the Court, it is sufficient reason for any other national court to regard that act as void for the purposes of a judgment which it has to give.

[14]   That assertion does not however mean that national courts are deprived of the power given to them by Article 177 of the Treaty and it rests with those courts to decide whether there is a need to raise once again a question which has already been settled by the Court where the Court has previously declared an act of a Community institution to be void. There may be such a need in particular if questions arise as to the grounds, the scope and possibly the consequences of the invalidity established earlier.

[15]   If that is not the case national courts are entirely justified in determining the effect on the cases brought before them of a judgment declaring an act void given by the Court in an action between other parties.

Notes
1.   Case 66/80 concerned a reference relating to the validity of Community legislation. A comparable approach should be taken in relation to the effect of preliminary rulings on the interpretation of Community law. Read A. Toth, 'The authority of judgments of the European Court of Justice: binding force and legal effects' (1984) 4 YEL 1.
2.   The Court has the competence to restrict the temporal effects of its rulings; see, e.g., in relation to a ruling on interpretation (*Defrenne* (Case 43/75)) and the other cases mentioned at p. 98 above; and read W. Alexander (1988) 8 YEL 11.
3.   These issues will be re-addressed in Chapter 16. The Court is determined to construct a comprehensive Community system of remedies which is coherent. It accordingly draws inspiration in interpreting Article 234 from

other Treaty provisions, notably Article 234 (e.g. *Société Produits de Maïs* v *Administration des Douanes* (Case 112/83), at p. 709 below).

(D) BODIES COMPETENT TO REFER

Broeckmeulen v *Huisarts Registratie Commissie (Case 246/80)*
[1981] ECR 2311
Court of Justice of the European Communities

Broeckmeulen was refused registration as (the equivalent of) a General Practitioner in the Netherlands by the defendant *Commissie*. He held a Belgian medical qualification and sought to rely on Community rules relating to the free movement of professionals between Member States. The first issue for the European Court to consider was whether the Appeals Committee was competent to refer questions relating to Community law under Article 177 – now, remember, Article 234 post-Amsterdam – which refers only to a 'court or tribunal of a Member State'.

[10]   According to the internal rules of the Society, the Appeals Committee, appointed for a period of five years, is composed of three members appointed by the Netherlands medical faculties, three members appointed by the Board of the Society and three members, including the chairman (preferably a high-ranking judge), who are appointed by the ministers responsible for higher education and health respectively. It may therefore be seen that the composition of the Appeals Committee entails a significant degree of involvement on the part of the Netherlands public authorities.

[11]   Pursuant to those rules, the Appeals Committee determines disputes on the adversarial principle, that is to say having heard the Registration Committee and the doctor concerned, as well as his adviser or lawyer, if necessary.

[12]   The Netherlands Government stated that, in its opinion, the Appeals Committee cannot be considered a court or tribunal under Netherlands law. However, it pointed out that that fact is not decisive for the interpretation of Article 177 of the Treaty and suggested that the question whether a body such as the Appeals Committee is entitled to refer a case to the Court under that provision should be determined in the light of the function performed by that body within the system of remedies available to those who consider that their rights under Community law have been infringed.

[13]   In this regard, the order for reference mentions a Royal Decree of 1966, the decree concerning benefits ('Verstreckingenbesluit'), adopted under the Sickness Fund Law; for the purposes of that decree the term 'general practitioner' refers exclusively to a doctor enrolled on the register of general practitioners maintained by the Society. The practice of a doctor who is not enrolled on the register would thus not be recognized by the sickness insurance schemes. Under those circumstances a doctor who is not enrolled on the register is unable to treat, as a general practitioner, patients covered by the social security system. In fact, private practice is likewise made impossible by the fact that private insurers also define the term 'general practitioner' in their policies in the same way as the provisions of the decree concerning benefits.

[14]   A study of the Netherlands legislation and of the statutes and internal rules of the Society shows that a doctor who intends to establish himself in the Netherlands

may not in fact practise either as a specialist, or as an expert in social medicine, or as a general practitioner, without being recognized and registered by the organs of the Society. In the same way it may be seen that the system thus established is the result of close cooperation between doctors who are members of the Society, the medical faculties and the departments of State responsible for higher education and health.

[15]   It is thus clear that both in the sector covered by the social security system and in the field of private medicine the Netherlands system of public health operates on the basis of the status accorded to doctors by the Society and that registration as a general practitioner is essential to every doctor wishing to establish himself in the Netherlands as a general practitioner.

[16]   Therefore a general practitioner who avails himself of the right of establishment and the freedom to provide services conferred upon him by Community law is faced with the necessity of applying to the Registration Committee established by the Society, and, in the event of his application's being refused, must appeal to the Appeals Committee. The Netherlands Government expressed the opinion that a doctor who is not a member of the Society would have the right to appeal against such a refusal to the ordinary courts, but stated that the point had never been decided by the Netherlands courts. Indeed all doctors, whether members of the Society or not, whose application to be registered as a general practitioner is refused, appeal to the Appeals Committee, whose decisions to the knowledge of the Netherlands Government, have never been challenged in the ordinary courts.

[17]   In order to deal with the question of the applicability in the present case of Article 177 of the Treaty, it should be noted that it is incumbent upon Member States to take the necessary steps to ensure that within their own territory the provisions adopted by the Community institutions are implemented in their entirety. If, under the legal system of a Member State, the task of implementing such provisions is assigned to a professional body acting under a degree of governmental supervision, and if that body, in conjunction with the public authorities concerned, creates appeal procedures which may affect the exercise of rights granted by Community law, it is imperative, in order to ensure the proper functioning of Community law, that the Court should have an opportunity of ruling on issues of interpretation and validity arising out of such proceedings.

[18]   As a result of all the foregoing considerations and in the absence, in practice, of any right of appeal to the ordinary courts, the Appeals Committee, which operates with the consent of the public authorities and with their cooperation, and which, after an adversarial procedure, delivers decisions which are in fact recognized as final, must, in a matter involving the application of Community law, be considered as a court or tribunal of a Member State within the meaning of Article 177 of the Treaty. Therefore, the Court has jurisdiction to reply to the question asked.

Note
The Court thus felt itself able to proceed to examine the substance of the case.

Nordsee v Reederei Mond (Case 102/81)
[1982] ECR 1095
Court of Justice of the European Communities

This was a reference by an arbitrator in a dispute between three German firms.

[7]   Since the arbitration tribunal which referred the matter to the Court for a preliminary ruling was established pursuant to a contract between private individuals the question arises whether it may be considered as a court or tribunal of one of the Member States within the meaning of Article 177 of the Treaty.

[8]   The first question put by the arbitrator concerns that problem. It is worded as follows:

'Is a German arbitration court, which must decide not according to equity but according to law, and whose decision has the same effects as regards the parties as a definitive judgment of a court of law (Article 1040 of the Zivilprozeßordnung [rules of civil procedure]) authorized to make a reference to the Court of Justice of the European Communities for a preliminary ruling pursuant to the second paragraph of Article 177 of the EEC Treaty?'

[9]   It must be noted that, as the question indicates, the jurisdiction of the Court to rule on questions referred to it depends on the nature of the arbitration in question.

[10]   It is true, as the arbitrator noted in his question, that there are certain similarities between the activities of the arbitration tribunal in question and those of an ordinary court or tribunal inasmuch as the arbitration is provided for within the framework of the law, the arbitrator must decide according to law and his award has, as between the parties, the force of *res judicata*, and may be enforceable if leave to issue execution is obtained. However, those characteristics are not sufficient to give the arbitrator the status of a 'court or tribunal of a Member State' within the meaning of Article 177 of the Treaty.

[11]   The first important point to note is that when the contract was entered into in 1973 the parties were free to leave their disputes to be resolved by the ordinary courts or to opt for arbitration by inserting a clause to that effect in the contract. From the facts of the case it appears that the parties were under no obligation, whether in law or in fact, to refer their disputes to arbitration.

[12]   The second point to be noted is that the German public authorities are not involved in the decision to opt for arbitration nor are they called upon to intervene automatically in the proceedings before the arbitrator. The Federal Republic of Germany, as a Member State of the Community responsible for the performance of obligations arising from Community law within its territory pursuant to Article 5 and Articles 169 to 171 of the Treaty, has not entrusted or left to private individuals the duty of ensuring that such obligations are complied with in the sphere in question in this case.

[13]   It follows from these considerations that the link between the arbitration procedure in this instance and the organization of legal remedies through the courts in the Member State in question is not sufficiently close for the arbitrator to be considered as a 'court or tribunal of a Member State' within the meaning of Article 177.

Note

Read W. Alexander and E. Grabandt (1982) 19 CML Rev 413. See further on the determination of whether a referring body is a court or tribunal for these purposes, a matter which the European Court treats as governed by Community law alone, C-54/96 *Dorsch Consult* [1997] ECR I-4961 (referral

admissible); Cases C-69/96 to C-79/96 *Maria Antonella Garofalo* [1997] ECR
I-5603 (referral admissible); Cases C-74/95 and C-129/95 *X* [1996] ECR
I-6609 (referral by Italian public prosecutor inadmissible); Case C-111/94
Job Centre Coop. arl, [1995] ECR I-3361 (referral by administrative body
performing a non-judicial function inadmissible, though an appeal to a court
against the decision of the administrative body prompted an admissible
reference in Case C-55/96 *Job Centre Coop. arl* [1997] ECR I-7119; Case
C-134/97 *Victoria Film A/S* [1998] ECR I-7023 (referral by body within
Swedish tax administration inadmissible)).

(E) THE DOCTRINE OF *ACTE CLAIR*

Article 234 makes a distinction in paras 2 and 3 between courts which can
refer and those which must. The latter category covers highest courts. Its
function was explained by the Court as follows:

Hoffman la Roche v *Centrafarm (Case 107/76)*
[1977] ECR 957
Court of Justice of the European Communities

[5]   In the context of Article 177, whose purpose is to ensure that Community law
is interpreted and applied in a uniform manner in all the Member States, the
particular objective of the third paragraph is to prevent a body of national case-law not
in accord with the rules of Community law from coming into existence in any Member
State . . .

Note
Even highest courts need not refer if the doctrine of *acte clair* applies. The
European Court carefully explained the nature of this doctrine in the
following case.

CILFIT (Case 283/81)
[1982] ECR 3415
Court of Justice of the European Communities

[1]   By order of 27 March 1981, which was received at the Court on 31 October
1981, the Corte Suprema di Cassazione [Supreme Court of Cassation] referred to the
Court of Justice for a preliminary ruling under Article 177 of the EEC Treaty a
question on the interpretation of the third paragraph of Article 177 of the EEC Treaty.

[2]   That question was raised in connection with a dispute between wool importers
and the Italian Ministry of Health concerning the payment of a fixed health inspection
levy in respect of wool imported from outside the Community. The firms concerned
relied on Regulation (EEC) No 827/68 of 28 June 1968 on the common organization
of the market in certain products listed in Annex II to the Treaty (Official Journal,
English Special Edition 1968 (I) p. 209). Article 2(2) of that regulation prohibits
Member States from levying any charge having an effect equivalent to a customs duty
on imported 'animal products', not specified or included elsewhere, classified under

heading 05.15 of the Common Customs Tariff. Against that argument the Ministry for Health contended that wool is not included in Annex II to the Treaty and is therefore not subject to a common organization of agricultural markets.

[3]   The Ministry of Health infers from those circumstances that the answer to the question concerning the interpretation of the measure adopted by the Community institutions is so obvious as to rule out the possibility of there being any interpretative doubt and thus obviates the need to refer the matter to the Court of Justice for a preliminary ruling. However, the companies concerned maintain that since a question concerning the interpretation of a regulation has been raised before the Corte Suprema di Cassazione, against whose decisions there is no judicial remedy under national law, that court cannot, according to the terms of the third paragraph of Article 177, escape the obligation to bring the matter before the Court of Justice.

[4]   Faced with those conflicting arguments, the Corte Suprema di Cassazione referred to the Court the following question for a preliminary ruling:

'Does the third paragraph of Article 177 of the EEC Treaty, which provides that where any question of the same kind as those listed in the first paragraph of that article is raised in a case pending before a national court or tribunal against whose decisions there is no judicial remedy under national law that court or tribunal must bring the matter before the Court of Justice, lay down an obligation so to submit the case which precludes the national court from determining whether the question raised is justified or does it, and if so within what limits, make that obligation conditional on the prior finding of a reasonable interpretative doubt?'

[5]   In order to answer that question it is necessary to take account of the system established by Article 177, which confers jurisdiction on the Court of Justice to give preliminary rulings on, *inter alia*, the interpretation of the Treaty and the measures adopted by the institutions of the Community.

[6]   The second paragraph of that article provides that any court or tribunal of a Member State *may*, if it considers that a decision on a question of interpretation is necessary to enable it to give judgment, request the Court of Justice to give a ruling thereon. The third paragraph of that article provides that, where a question of interpretation is raised in a case pending before a court or tribunal of a Member State against whose decisions there is no judicial remedy under national law, that court or tribunal *shall* bring the matter before the Court of Justice.

[7]   That obligation to refer a matter to the Court of Justice is based on cooperation, established with a view to ensuring the proper application and uniform interpretation of Community law in all the Member States, between national courts, in their capacity as courts responsible for the application of Community law, and the Court of Justice. More particularly, the third paragraph of Article 177 seeks to prevent the occurrence within the Community of divergences in judicial decisions on questions of Community law. The scope of that obligation must therefore be assessed, in view of those objectives, by reference to the powers of the national courts, on the one hand, and those of the Court of Justice, on the other, where such a question of interpretation is raised within the meaning of Article 177.

[8]   In this connection, it is necessary to define the meaning for the purposes of Community law of the expression 'where any such question is raised' in order to determine the circumstances in which a national court or tribunal against whose decisions there is no judicial remedy under national law is obliged to bring a matter before the Court of Justice.

[9]   In this regard, it must in the first place be pointed out that Article 177 does not constitute a means of redress available to the parties to a case pending before a national court or tribunal. Therefore the mere fact that a party contends that the dispute gives rise to a question concerning the interpretation of Community law does not mean that the court or tribunal concerned is compelled to consider that a question has been raised within the meaning of Article 177. On the other hand, a national court or tribunal may, in an appropriate case, refer a matter to the Court of Justice of its own motion.

[10]   Secondly, it follows from the relationship between the second and third paragraphs of Article 177 that the courts or tribunals referred to in the third paragraph have the same discretion as any other national court or tribunal to ascertain whether a decision on a question of Community law is necessary to enable them to give judgment. Accordingly, those courts or tribunals are not obliged to refer to the Court of Justice a question concerning the interpretation of Community law raised before them if that question is not relevant, that is to say, if the answer to that question, regardless of what it may be, can in no way affect the outcome of the case.

[11]   If, however, those courts or tribunals consider that recourse to Community law is necessary to enable them to decide a case, Article 177 imposes an obligation on them to refer to the Court of Justice any question of interpretation which may arise.

[12]   The question submitted by the Corte di Cassazione seeks to ascertain whether, in certain circumstances, the obligation laid down by the third paragraph of Article 177 might none the less be subject to certain restrictions.

[13]   It must be remembered in this connection that in its judgment of 27 March 1963 in Joined Cases 28 to 30/62 (*Da Costa* v *Nederlandse Belastingadministratie* [1963] ECR 31) the Court ruled that: 'Although the third paragraph of Article 177 unreservedly requires courts or tribunals of a Member State against whose decisions there is no judicial remedy under national law . . . to refer to the Court every question of interpretation raised before them, the authority of an interpretation under Article 177 already given by the Court may deprive the obligation of its purpose and thus empty it of its substance. Such is the case especially when the question raised is materially identical with a question which has already been the subject of a preliminary ruling in a similar case.'

[14]   The same effect, as regards the limits set to the obligation laid down by the third paragraph of Article 177, may be produced where previous decisions of the Court have already dealt with the point of law in question, irrespective of the nature of the proceedings which led to those decisions, even though the questions at issue are not strictly identical.

[15]   However, it must not be forgotten that in all such circumstances national courts and tribunals, including those referred to in the third paragraph of Article 177, remain entirely at liberty to bring a matter before the Court of Justice if they consider it appropriate to do so.

[16]   Finally, the correct application of Community law may be so obvious as to leave no scope for any reasonable doubt as to the manner in which the question raised is to be resolved. Before it comes to the conclusion that such is the case, the national court or tribunal must be convinced that the matter is equally obvious to the courts of the other Member States and to the Court of Justice. Only if those conditions are satisfied, may the national court or tribunal refrain from submitting the question to the Court of Justice and take upon itself the responsibility for resolving it.

[17]   However, the existence of such a possibility must be assessed on the basis of the characteristic features of Community law and the particular difficulties to which its interpretation gives rise.

[18]   To begin with, it must be borne in mind that Community legislation is drafted in several languages and that the different language versions are all equally authentic. An interpretation of a provision of Community law thus involves a comparison of the different language versions.

[19]   It must also be borne in mind, even where the different language versions are entirely in accord with one another, that Community law uses terminology which is peculiar to it. Furthermore, it must be emphasized that legal concepts do not necessarily have the same meaning in Community law and in the law of the various Member States.

[20]   Finally, every provision of Community law must be placed in its context and interpreted in the light of the provisions of Community law as a whole, regard being had to the objectives thereof and to its state of evolution at the date on which the provision in question is to be applied.

[21]   In the light of all those considerations, the answer to the question submitted by the Corte Suprema di Cassazione must be that the third paragraph of Article 177 of the EEC Treaty is to be interpreted as meaning that a court or tribunal against whose decisions there is no judicial remedy under national law is required, where a question of Community law is raised before it, to comply with its obligation to bring the matter before the Court of Justice, unless it has established that the question raised is irrelevant or that the Community provision in question has already been interpreted by the Court or that the correct application of Community law is so obvious as to leave no scope for any reasonable doubt. The existence of such a possibility must be assessed in the light of the specific characteristics of Community law, the particular difficulties to which its interpretation gives rise and the risk of divergences in judicial decisions within the Community.

Question

'The real strategy of *CILFIT* is not to incorporate an *acte clair* concept into Community law. It is to call the national judiciaries to circumspection when they are faced with problems of interpretation and application of Community law' (H. Rasmussen (1984) 9 EL Rev 242). Discuss.

Note

The Court explored these realms in the unusual context of the Benelux Court in Case C-337/95 *Parfums Christian Dior SA and Parfums Christian Dior BV* v *Evora BV* [1997] ECR I-6013, a reference made by the Dutch Hoge Raad (Supreme Court). The Benelux Court was established by a 1965 Treaty between Belgium, Luxembourg and The Netherlands. Given that the Benelux Court interprets Community rules in the performance of its functions, it was treated by the European Court in *Dior* as capable of making preliminary references in order to ensure the uniform interpretation of Community law. The Court, citing *CILFIT*, then added that in so far as no appeal lies against its decisions, the Benelux Court may be *obliged* to make a reference. However, the authority of an interpretation provided by the Court under the procedure may deprive that obligation of its purpose and thus empty it of its substance. In the Benelux context, this may arise where, prior to making a reference to the Benelux Court, a national court has already made use of its power to submit the question raised to Luxembourg. The obligation imposed by the third paragraph of Article 234 loses its purpose when the question raised is 'substantially the same' as a question already the subject of a preliminary ruling in the same national proceedings.

(F) THE POWER TO REFER

When should a lower court exercise its Article 234(2) discretion to make a reference?

Notes
1.   The European Court's approach is distinctly flexible. In acknowledging 'considerations of procedural organization and efficiency to be weighed by [the national] court', the ruling in *Irish Creamery Milk Suppliers* (Case 36/80, at p. 143 above) shows an openness on the part of the European Court and a concern not to raise technical obstacles to referral. Remember also how in *CILFIT* (Case 283/81) the Court pointed out the perils of non-referral (p. 156 above).
2.   In the English courts, the notoriously mechanistic attitude expounded by Lord Denning MR in *Bulmer* v *Bollinger SA* [1974] 3 WLR 202 has been superseded by a more flexible, *communautaire* approach. In *Customs and Excise Commissioners* v *Samex* [1983] 1 All ER 1042, Bingham J made a reference to Luxembourg after conceding

> the advantages enjoyed by the Court of Justice. It has a panoramic view of the Community and its institutions, a detailed knowledge of the treaties and of much subordinate legislation made under them, and an intimate familiarity with the functioning of the Community market which no national judge denied the collective experience of the Court of Justice could hope to achieve.

For discussion see A. Arnull, 'References to the European Court' (1990) 15 EL Rev 375, especially pp. 380–87.
3.   In one respect, however, the European Court has decided to abandon its flexible approach to the power to refer. In the next case it takes to itself an important jurisdiction, thus insisting on referral.

Firma Foto Frost v *HZA Lubeck Ost (Case 314/85)*
[1987] ECR 4199
Court of Justice of the European Communities

Foto Frost instituted proceedings before the German courts in order to secure the annulment of a demand by the customs authorities for payment of duties on imported binoculars. The basis for the customs authorities' demand was a Commission Decision addressed to Germany. The basis of

Foto Frost's application was that the Commission Decision was invalid. The referring court (*Finanzgericht*) addresses in its first question the important jurisdictional point.

[11]   In its first question the Finanzgericht asks whether it itself is competent to declare invalid a Commission decision such as the decision of 6 May 1983. It casts doubt on the validity of that decision on the ground that all the requirements laid down by Article 5(2) of Regulation No 1697/79 for taking no action for the post-clearance recovery of duty seem to be fulfilled in this case. However, it considers that in view of the division of jurisdiction between the Court of Justice and the national courts set out in Article 177 of the EEC Treaty only the Court of Justice is competent to declare invalid acts of the Community institutions.

[12]   Article 177 confers on the Court jurisdiction to give preliminary rulings on the interpretation of the Treaty and of acts of the Community institutions and on the validity of such acts. The second paragraph of that article provides that national courts may refer such questions to the Court and the third paragraph of that article puts them under an obligation to do so where there is no judicial remedy under national law against their decisions.

[13]   In enabling national courts, against those decisions where there is a judicial remedy under national law, to refer to the Court for a preliminary ruling questions on interpretation or validity, Article 177 did not settle the question whether those courts themselves may declare that acts of Community institutions are invalid.

[14]   Those courts may consider the validity of a Community act and, if they consider that the grounds put forward before them by the parties in support of invalidity are unfounded, they may reject them, concluding that the measure is completely valid. By taking that action they are not calling into question the existence of the Community measure.

[15]   On the other hand, those courts do not have the power to declare acts of the Community institutions invalid. As the Court emphasized in the judgment of 13 May 1981 in Case 66/80 *International Chemical Corporation* v *Amministrazione delle Finanze* [1981] ECR 1191, the main purpose of the powers accorded to the Court by Article 177 is to ensure that Community law is applied uniformly by national courts. That requirement of uniformity is particularly imperative when the validity of a Community act is in question. Divergences between courts in the Member States as to the validity of Community acts would be liable to place in jeopardy the very unity of the Community legal order and detract from the fundamental requirement of legal certainty.

[16]   The same conclusion is dictated by consideration of the necessary coherence of the system of judicial protection established by the Treaty. In that regard it must be observed that requests for preliminary rulings, like actions for annulment, constitute means for reviewing the legality of acts of the Community institutions. As the Court pointed out in its judgment of 23 April 1986 in Case 294/83 *Parti écologiste 'les Verts'* v *European Parliament* [1986] ECR 1339), 'in Articles 173 and 184, on the one hand, and in Article 177, on the other, the Treaty established a complete system of legal remedies and procedures designed to permit the Court of Justice to review the legality of measures adopted by the institutions'.

[17]   Since Article 173 [now 230: see Chapter 16] gives the Court exclusive jurisdiction to declare void an act of a Community institution, the coherence of the system requires that where the validity of a Community act is challenged before a national court the power to declare the act invalid must also be reserved to the Court of Justice.

[18]   It must also be emphasized that the Court of Justice is in the best position to decide on the validity of Community acts. Under Article 20 of the Protocol on the Statute of the Court of Justice of the EEC, Community institutions whose acts are challenged are entitled to participate in the proceedings in order to defend the validity of the acts in question. Furthermore, under the second paragraph of Article 21 of that Protocol the Court may require the Member States and institutions which are not participating in the proceedings to supply all information which it considers necessary for the purposes of the case before it.

[19]   It should be added that the rule that national courts may not themselves declare Community acts invalid may have to be qualified in certain circumstances in the case of proceedings relating to an application for interim measures; however, that case is not referred to in the national court's question.

[20]   The answer to the first question must therefore be that the national courts have no jurisdiction themselves to declare that acts of Community institutions are invalid.

The Court proceeded to hold the contested Commission Decision invalid.

Questions
1.   Why did the Court deny national courts competence to declare Community acts invalid?
   Read G. Bebr (1988) 25 CML Rev 667.
2.   To what extent is the approach taken by the Court to its own exclusive jurisdiction in *Foto Frost* (Case 314/85) equally applicable to cases where Community acts are challenged on the basis of their alleged interference with areas of exclusive national competence? Is the European Court's stance on jurisdiction in *Foto Frost* capable of reconciliation with the views of the *Bundesverfassungsgericht* in its Maastricht ruling (p. 15 above)?

Note
Foto Frost (Case 314/85) involved a challenge to the validity of a Community provision before a national court. Chapter 16 examines in more depth the ways in which Article 234 can be used as a device to support such an indirect challenge to the legality of Community legislation. The matter is also touched on in the next subsection.

(G) THE COURT'S NOTES FOR GUIDANCE

In 1996 the Court issued guidelines on the use of what was then Article 177 EC, now Article 234 EC post-Amsterdam (p. 29 above). These serve as a useful distillation of the principles of law and the practice explained in the course of this chapter.

Note for guidance on references by national courts for preliminary rulings issued by the European Court of Justice

The development of the Community legal order is largely the result of cooperation between the Court of Justice of the European Communities and national courts and tribunals through the preliminary ruling procedure under Article 177 of the EC Treaty and the corresponding provisions of the ECSC and Euratom Treaties.[1]

In order to make this cooperation more effective, and so enable the Court of Justice better to meet the requirements of national courts by providing helpful answers to preliminary questions, this Note for Guidance is addressed to all interested parties, in particular to all national courts and tribunals.

It must be emphasised that the Note is for guidance only and has no binding or interpretative effect in relation to the provisions governing the preliminary ruling procedure. It merely contains practical information which, in the light of experience in applying the preliminary ruling procedure, may help to prevent the kind of difficulties which the Court has sometimes encountered.

1. Any court or tribunal of a Member State may ask the Court of Justice to interpret a rule of Community law, whether contained in the Treaties or in acts of secondary law, if it considers that this is necessary for it to give judgment in a case pending before it.

Courts or tribunals against whose decisions there is no judicial remedy under national law must refer questions of interpretation arising before them to the Court of Justice, unless the Court has already ruled on the point or unless the correct application of the rule of Community law is obvious.[2]

2. The Court of Justice has jurisdiction to rule on the validity of acts of the Community institutions. National courts or tribunals may reject a plea challenging the validity of such an act. But where a national court (even one whose decision is still subject to appeal) intends to question the validity of a Community act, it must refer that question to the Court of Justice.[3]

Where, however, a national court or tribunal has serious doubts about the validity of a Community act on which a national measure is based, it may, in exceptional cases, temporarily suspend application of the latter measure or grant other interim relief with respect to it. It must then refer the question of validity to the Court of Justice, stating the reasons for which it considers that the Community act is not valid.[4]

3. Questions referred for a preliminary ruling must be limited to the interpretation or validity of a provision of Community law, since the Court of Justice does not have jurisdiction to interpret national law or assess its validity. It is for the referring court or tribunal to apply the relevant rule of Community law in the specific case pending before it.

4. The order of the national court or tribunal referring a question to the Court of Justice for a preliminary ruling may be in any form allowed by national procedural law. Reference of a question or questions to the Court of Justice generally involves

---

[1] A preliminary ruling procedure is also provided for by protocols to several conventions concluded by the Member States, in particular the Brussels Convention on Jurisdiction and the Enforcement of Judgments in Civil and Commercial Matters.

[2] Judgment in Case 283/81 *CILFIT* v *Ministry of Health* [1982] ECR 3415.

[3] Judgment in Case 314/85 *Foto-Frost* v *Hauptzollamt Lübeck-Ost* [1987] ECR 4199.

[4] Judgments in Joined Cases C-143/88 and C-92/89 *Zuckerfabrik Süderdithmarschen and Zuckerfabrik Soest* [1991] ECR I-415 and in Case C-465/93 *Atlanta Fruchthandelsgesselschaft* [1995] ECR I-3761.

stay of the national proceedings until the Court has given its ruling, but the decision to stay proceedings is one which it is for the national court alone to take in accordance with its own national law.

5. The order for reference containing the question or questions referred to the Court will have to be translated by the Court's translators into the other official languages of the Community. Questions concerning the interpretation or validity of Community law are frequently of general interest and the Member States and Community institutions are entitled to submit observations. It is therefore desirable that the reference should be drafted as clearly and precisely as possible.

6. The order for reference should contain a statement of reasons which is succinct but sufficiently complete to give the Court, and those to whom it must be notified (the Member States, the Commission and in certain cases the Council and the European Parliament), a clear understanding of the factual and legal context of the main proceedings.[5]

In particular, it should include:

– a statement of the facts which are essential to a full understanding of the legal significance of the main proceedings;
– an exposition of the national law which may be applicable;
– a statement of the reasons which have prompted the national court to refer the question or questions to the Court of Justice; and
– where appropriate, a summary of the arguments of the parties.

The aim should be to put the Court of Justice in a position to give the national court an answer which will be of assistance to it.

The order for reference should also be accompanied by copies of any documents needed for a proper understanding of the case, especially the text of the applicable national provisions. However, as the case-file or documents annexed to the order for reference are not always translated in full into the other official languages of the Community, the national court should ensure that the order for reference itself includes all the relevant information.

7. A national court or tribunal may refer a question to the Court of Justice as soon as it finds that a ruling on the point or points of interpretation or validity is necessary to enable it to give judgment. It must be stressed, however, that it is not for the Court of Justice to decide issues of fact or to resolve disputes as to the interpretation or application of rules of national law. It is therefore desirable that a decision to refer should not be taken until the national proceedings have reached a stage where the national court is able to define, if only as a working hypothesis, the factual and legal context of the question; on any view, the administration of justice is likely to be best served if the reference is not made until both sides have been heard.[6]

8. The order for reference and the relevant documents should be sent by the national court directly to the Court of Justice, by registered post, addressed to:

The Registry
Court of Justice of the European Communities
L-2925 Luxembourg
Telephone (352) 43031

---

[5] Judgment in Joined Cases C-320/90, C-321/90 and C-322/90 *Telemarsicabruzzo* [1993] ECR I-393.
[6] Judgment in Case 70/77 *Simmenthal* v *Amministrazione delle Finanze dello Stato* [1978] ECR 1453.

The Court Registry will remain in contact with the national court until judgment is given, and will send copies of the various documents (written observations, Report for the Hearing, Opinion of the Advocate General). The Court will also send its judgment to the national court. The Court would appreciate being informed about the application of its judgment in the national proceedings and being sent a copy of the national court's final decision.

9. Proceedings for a preliminary ruling before the Court of Justice are free of charge. The Court does not rule on costs.

(H) REFORMING THE COURT SYSTEM

Institutional reform is the *leitmotif* of the intergovernmental conference that commenced in 2000 (p. 33 above), and the structure of the Court is on the agenda. The preliminary reference procedure was one of the main points for consideration in the Report of the Working Party on the Future of the European Communities' Court System established by the Commission under the Chairmanship of Ole Due, former President of the European Court, which was published in January 2000. On this report is based the Commission's contribution to the intergovernmental conference on reform of the Community courts. The success of the preliminary reference procedure is trumpeted, but adjustment is proposed.

Reform of the Community Courts (additional Commission contribution to the Intergovernmental Conference on institutional reform), COM (2000) 109, 1 March 2000

a. Preliminary rulings

(i) Jurisdiction of the Court of Justice

The preliminary ruling procedure is undoubtedly the keystone of the Community's legal order. Forty years' experience have shown that it is the most effective means of securing the uniform application of Community law throughout the Union and that it is an exceptional factor for integration owing to the simple, direct dialogue which it establishes with national courts. The Commission considers that this regulating function, which is essential to the Community legal order, must therefore in principle be the exclusive responsibility of the Court of Justice.

The Working Party shares this opinion. But it proposes that the last sentence of Article 225(1) of the EC Treaty be deleted to give the CFI exceptional jurisdiction to give preliminary rulings in very specialised areas of Community law.[5] The Working Party considers that special categories of case, including preliminary questions in such areas, should be entrusted as a whole to the CFI and that the Court of Justice, as the supreme court of the Union, should become involved where appropriate only in appeals on points of law lodged by the Commission.[6]

This proposal will have to be examined in connection with any specific changes to jurisdiction that will have to be provided for in certain categories of special case, such as intellectual property proceedings.

---

[5] E.g. intellectual property (trade marks, patents and industrial designs, etc.).
[6] As provided by, for instance, Article 68(3) of the Treaty.

(ii) Clarification of the roles of the Court of Justice and the national courts

To preserve the effectiveness of the preliminary ruling procedure, it is essential that the Court of Justice should be able to concentrate on genuinely new questions and give its judgments considerably sooner. To this end, the Commission believes it is necessary to amend Article 234 (ex Article 177) of the Treaty in order to clarify the distribution of jurisdiction between the Court of Justice and national courts.

1. The first amendment proposed seeks to give national courts greater responsibility as courts of ordinary law in Community matters. At present, this function is not expressly laid down in the Treaty. It can only be inferred from reading Articles 234 and 240 together. It is therefore essential to correct this omission by spelling out the introductory provision in Article 234, clearly stating that it is for the national courts in the first place to apply Community law to the cases before them and that they may consult the Court of Justice when faced with a specific problem of interpretation.

2. In similar vein, it could be worthwhile amending the second paragraph of Article 234, so as to invite national courts other than those of final instance to specify why they have doubts as to the meaning of the rule of Community law applicable in the case before them and why they feel the need to put a question to the Court of Justice. This provision could be accompanied by the requisite corollary changes to the Rules of Procedure.

3. As part of this clarification exercise, it is necessary, lastly, to insert in Article 234 the rule established in case-law whereby, **in cases of doubt as to the validity of a Community act**, whereby all national courts must consult the Court of Justice since the latter has the monopoly of the review of Community legality.

The Commission does not feel it would be right to give flexibility to the obligation on courts of final instance to refer preliminary questions, currently laid down in the third paragraph of Article 234, requiring them to consult the Court of Justice only if the question were sufficiently important for Community law and if, after examination by the lower courts, there were still reasonable doubts as to the reply. The Commission considers that the advantages of such flexibility as far as the Court's workload is concerned are very slight and that there are real dangers for the uniform application of Community law, especially with enlargement on the horizon. It therefore thinks it is essential to stick with the current wording of the third paragraph of Article 234. Naturally, the flexibility introduced by case-law would continue to apply.

The Commission further wonders whether it might be worth harmonising the procedure for preliminary rulings in matters of free movement of persons (Title IV) with the ordinary procedure.

. . .

Proposed new wording

ARTICLE 234

1. Subject to the provisions of this Article, the courts and tribunals of the Member States shall rule on the questions of Community law which they encounter in exercise of their national jurisdiction.

2. The Court of Justice shall have jurisdiction to give preliminary rulings concerning:

    (a) the interpretation of this Treaty,

(b) the validity and interpretation of acts of the institutions of the Community and of the ECB;

(c) the interpretation of the statutes of bodies established by an act of the Council, where those statutes so provide.

3.   Where such a question is raised before any national court or tribunal, that court or tribunal may, if it considers that a decision on the question is necessary to enable it to give a judgement, request the Court of Justice to give a ruling thereon. **In that event, it shall specify why the validity or interpretation of the rule of Community law raises difficulties in the case before it.**

4.   Where any such question is raised in a case pending before a national court or tribunal against whose decisions there is no judicial remedy under national law, that court or tribunal shall bring the matter before the Court of Justice.

5.   **A national court or tribunal must consult the Court of Justice where it proposes not to apply an act of Community law on the grounds that the latter is invalid.**

Questions

1.   Read the following decisions. Comment critically on their application of Article 177 of the EC Treaty (now Article 234 EC). What do the decisions tell you about the strengths and weaknesses of the preliminary reference procedure? Would the proposals extracted in section (H) above, if adopted, make any difference to the way in which such cases would be dealt with by national courts?

R v *Henn and Darby*; contrast the Court of Appeal [1978] 1 WLR 1031 with the House of Lords [1981] AC 850, [1980] 2 WLR 597;

Minister of the Interior v *Cohn Bendit* [1980] 1 CMLR 543 (p. 111 above);

Procurator Fiscal, Stranraer v *Marshall* [1988] 1 CMLR 657 (this case eventually reached the Court as Case 370/88 via the High Court in Edinburgh, and the Court's decision is reported at [1990] ECR I-4071);

R v *International Stock Exchange, ex parte Else Ltd* [1993] 1 All ER 420.

2.   'Two somewhat contradictory principles – the effectiveness of Community law and the procedural autonomy of the State – must be reconciled. The result is that the direct effect of Community law is to some extent restricted while national autonomy must sometimes yield to the requirements of Community law.' (R. Kovar, *Thirty Years of Community Law*, p. 146). Discuss.

Further reading

Anderson, D., 'The admissibility of Preliminary References' (1994) 14 YEL 179.

Arnull, A., 'The Evolution of the Court's Jurisdiction under Article 177 EEC' (1993) 18 EL Rev 129.

Barnard, C., and Sharpston, E., 'The Changing Face of Article 177 References' (1997) 34 CML Rev 1113.

De La Mare, T., 'Article 177 in Social and Political Context', in Craig, P., and de Búrca, G., *The Evolution of EU Law* (OUP, Oxford, 1999), Ch. 6.

Lenaerts, K., 'Form and Substance of the Preliminary Rulings Procedure' in Curtin, D. and Heukels, T., *Institutional Dynamics of European Integration* (Dordrecht; Martinus Nijhoff, 1994).

Mancini, F., and Keeling, D., 'From *CILFIT* to *ERT*: the Constitutional Challenge Facing the European Court' (1991) 11 YEL 1.

O'Keeffe, D., 'Is the spirit of Article 177 under attack?' (1998) 23 EL Rev 509.

Voss, R., 'The National Perception of the Court of First Instance and the European Court of Justice' (1993) 30 CML Rev 1119.

PART TWO:
COMMUNITY TRADE LAW
AND POLICY

INTRODUCTION

This Part of the book examines the major provisions of Community substantive law. These are the provisions which are designed to eliminate barriers to trade between Member States and to suppress distortions in the competitive structure of the market. These provisions are the instruments for transforming the territory of the Community into a common market.

Chapter 5 provides an introduction to the subject. It explains basic economic theory. It shows why a common market is economically advantageous and discusses the shortcomings of the Community hitherto. It also examines the project which has in the last decade catapulted the Community into the forefront of national and international affairs – the completion of the single (or internal) market by the end of 1992. It shows how this is a dynamic process, reverberating long after the 1992 deadline has passed. Chapter 5 also examines the Amsterdam Treaty's impact on the law relating to the free movement of persons. It concludes with an introduction to the Community's objective of Economic and Monetary Union which was elaborated in the (Maastricht) Treaty on European Union and the development of which is set fair to be the most momentous internal challenge for the Community over the next decade.

Thereafter Part Two is sub-divided. Chapters 6 to 10 examine the legal provisions which permit the opening up of the market; Chapters 11 to 15 examine the regulation of the market. That sub-division might broadly be regarded as the split between negative and positive Community law. Opening up the market is initially achieved by prohibiting States from imposing barriers to the free movement of the factors of production (goods, persons, services, capital) between Member States. Chapters 6 to 8 examine the legal instruments for securing the free movement of goods; Chapters 9 and 10 examine the free movement of persons and services. These provisions are negative in the sense that they involve prohibitions on State action. On the positive side, the Community possesses a range of rules which regulate the market from which State barriers to trade have been eliminated. Chapters 11 to 14 examine the Treaty competition rules, which serve to ensure free and fair competition in the common market; Chapter 15 provides a broader framework for consideration of the Community's policy-making competence. These provisions are termed positive, in the sense that they involve the establishment of regulation at Community level and, in some cases, administrative capacity at Community level. Admittedly, the neat sub-division between negative and positive is on closer examination rather glib. For example, aspects of the competition rules may be seen as instruments for the suppression of market partitioning, which aligns them with the rules on free movement. Nonetheless, it is helpful to realise that substantive Community law has a broad sweep and that Community law is about a great deal more than merely forbidding Member States from keeping out imports from other Member States. Above all, the status of citizenship of the Union and the pursuit of economic and monetary union confirm the depth of constitutional ambition which is at stake in the process of integration through law. The Amsterdam Treaty's identification of 'an area of freedom, security and justice' as a Community goal (Article 61, p. 192 below) operates at a much grander and constitutionally demanding level than the pursuit of market integration.

5 LAW AND THE ECONOMIC
OBJECTIVES OF THE COMMUNITY

(A) THE COMMON MARKET

Article 2 EC

The Community shall have as its task, by establishing a common market and an economic and monetary union and by implementing common policies or activities referred to in Articles 3 and 4, to promote throughout the Community a harmonious, balanced and sustainable development of economic activities, a high level of employment and of social protection, equality between men and women, sustainable and non-inflationary growth, a high degree of competitiveness and convergence of economic performance, a high level of protection and improvement of the quality of the environment, the raising of the standard of living and quality of life, and economic and social cohesion and solidarity among Member States.

Note
It may first be observed that the Community has chosen to place emphasis on the establishment of a *common market*. What distinguishes the common market from other types of economic integration?

A. M. El-Agraa (ed.), *The European Union: History, Institutions, Economics and Policies* (5th ed., 1998), pp. 1–3

'International economic integration' (hereafter, simply economic integration) is one aspect of 'international economics' which has been growing in importance for well over four decades. The term itself has a rather short history; indeed, Machlup [*A History of Thought on Economic Integration* (Macmillan, 1977)] was unable to find a single instance of its use prior to 1942. Since then the term has been used at various times to refer to practically any area of international economic relations. By 1950, however, the term had been given a specific definition by economists specializing in international trade to denote a state of affairs or a process which involves the amalgamation of separate economies into larger free trading regions. It is in this more limited sense that the term is used today. However, one should hasten to add that economists not familiar with this branch of international economics have for quite a while been using the term to mean simply increasing economic interdependence between nations.

More specifically, economic integration is concerned with the discriminatory removal of all trade impediments between at least two participating nations and with the establishment of certain elements of cooperation and coordination between them. The latter depends entirely on the actual form that integration takes. Different forms of economic integration can be envisaged and many have actually been implemented (see Table 1.1 for schematic presentation):

1. *Free trade areas*, where the member nations remove all trade impediments among themselves but retain their freedom with regard to the determination of their own policies *vis-à-vis* the outside world (the non-participant – for example, the European Free Trade Association (EFTA) and the demised Latin American Free Trade Area (LAFTA)).

2. *Customs unions*, which are very similar to free trade areas except that member nations must conduct and pursue common external commercial relations – for instance, they must adopt common external tariffs (CETs) on imports from the non-participants as is the case in, *inter alia*, the European Union (EU, which is in this particular sense a customs union, but, as we shall presently see, it is more than that), the Central American Common Market (CACM) and the Caribbean Community and Common Market (CARICOM).

3. *Common markets*, which are custom unions that allow also for free factor mobility across national member frontiers, i.e. capital, labour, technology and enterprises should move unhindered between the participating countries – for example, the EU (but again it is more complex).

4. *Complete economic unions*, which are common markets that ask for complete unification of monetary and fiscal policies, i.e. the participants must introduce a central authority to exercise control over these matters so that member nations effectively become regions of the same nation – the EU is heading in this direction.

5. *Complete political unions*, where the participating countries become literally one nation, i.e. the central authority needed in complete economic unions should be paralleled by a common parliament and other necessary institutions needed to guarantee the sovereignty of one state – an example of this is the unification of the two Germanies in 1990.

Table 1.1 • Schematic presentation of economic integration schemes

Scheme	Free intrascheme trade	Common commercial policy	Free factor mobility	Common monetary and fiscal policy	One Government
Free trade area	Yes	No	No	No	No
Customs union	Yes	Yes	No	No	No
Common market	Yes	Yes	Yes	No	No
Economic union	Yes	Yes	Yes	Yes	No
Political union	Yes	Yes	Yes	Yes	Yes

However, one should hasten to add that political integration need not be, and in the majority of cases will never be, part of this list. Nevertheless, it can of course be introduced as a form of unity and for no economic reason whatsoever, as was the case with the two Germanies and as is the case with the pursuit of the unification of the Korean Peninsula, although one should naturally be interested in its economic consequences (see below). More generally, one should indeed stress that each of these forms of economic integration can be introduced in its own right; hence they should not be confused with *stages* in a *process* which eventually leads to either complete economic or political union.

It should also be noted that there may be *sectoral* integration, as distinct from general across-the-board integration, in particular areas of the economy as was the case with the European Coal and Steel Community (ECSC), created in 1950, but sectoral integration is a form of cooperation not only because it is inconsistent with the accepted definition of economic integration but also because it may contravene the rules of the General Agreement on Tariffs and Trade (GATT), now called the World Trade Organization (WTO) – see below. Sectoral integration may also occur within any of the mentioned schemes, as is the case with the EU's Common Agricultural Policy (CAP), but then it is nothing more than a 'policy'.

One should further point out that it has been claimed that economic integration can be *negative* or *positive*. The term negative integration was coined by Tinbergen (*International Economic Integration* (Elsevier, 1954)) to refer to the removal of impediments on trade between the participating nations or to the elimination of any restrictions on the process of trade liberalization. The term positive integration relates to the modification of existing instruments and institutions and, more importantly, to the creation of new ones so as to enable the market of the integrated area to function properly and effectively and also to promote other broader policy aims of the scheme. Hence, at the risk of oversimplification, according to this classification, it can be stated that sectoral integration and free trade areas are forms of economic integration which require only negative integration, while the remaining types require positive integration, since, as a minimum, they need the positive act of adopting common relations. However, in reality this distinction is oversimplistic not only because practically all existing types of economic integration have found it essential to introduce some elements of positive integration, but also because theoretical considerations clearly indicate that no scheme of economic integration is viable without certain elements of positive integration . . . .

Question

What are the economic advantages of integration in general and a common market in particular?

A. M. El-Agraa (ed.), *The European Union: History, Institutions, Economics and Policies* (5th edn, 1998), pp. 14–15

At the customs union (CU) and free trade area (FTA) levels, the possible sources of economic gain from economic integration can be attributed to:

1. enhanced efficiency in production made possible by increased specialization in accordance with the law of comparative advantage, due to the liberalized market of the participating nations;

2. increased production levels due to better exploitation of economies of scale made possible by the increased size of the market;

3. an improved international bargaining position, made possible by the larger size, leading to better terms of trade (cheaper imports from the outside world and higher prices for exports to them);

4. enforced changes in efficiency brought about by intensified competition between firms;

5. changes affecting both the amount and quality of the factors of production due to technological advances, themselves encouraged by (4).

If the level of economic integration is to go beyond the free trade area and customs union levels, then further sources of economic gain also become possible:

6. factor mobility across the borders of the member nations will materialize only if there is a net economic incentive for them, thus leading to higher national incomes;

7. the coordination of monetary and fiscal policies may result in cost reductions since the pooling of efforts may enable the achievement of economies of scale;

8. the unification of efforts to achieve better employment levels, lower inflation rates, balanced trade, higher rates of economic growth and better income distribution may make it cheaper to attain these targets.

It should be apparent that some of these possible gains relate to static resource reallocation effects while the rest relate to long-term or dynamic effects. It should also be emphasized that these are *possible* economic gains, i.e. there is no guarantee that they can ever be achieved; everything would depend on the nature of the particular scheme and the type of competitive behaviour prevailing prior to integration. Indeed, it is quite feasible that in the absence of 'appropriate' competitive behaviour, economic integration may worsen the situation. Thus the possible attainment of these benefits must be considered with great caution:

Membership of an economic grouping cannot of itself guarantee to a member state or the group a satisfactory economic performance, or even a better performance than in the past. The static gains from integration, although significant, can be – and often are – swamped by the influence of factors of domestic or international origin that have nothing to do with integration. The more fundamental factors influencing a country's economic performance (the dynamic factors) are unlikely to be affected by integration except in the long run. It is clearly not a necessary condition for economic success that a country should be a member of an economic community as the experience of several small countries confirms, although such countries might have done better as members of a suitable group. Equally, a large integrated market is in itself no guarantee of performance, as the experience of India suggests. However, although integration is dearly no panacea for all economic ills, nor indispensable to success, there are many convincing reasons for supposing that significant economic benefits may be derived from properly conceived arrangements for economic integration. (Robson, *The Economics of International Integration* Allen & Unwin, 1985).

However, in the case of the EU, one should always keep in mind that the 'founding fathers' had the formation of a United States of Western (hopefully all) Europe as the ultimate goal and that economic integration became the immediate objective so as to facilitate the attainment of political unity via the back door. . . . Those who fail to appreciate this will always undermine the EU's serious attempts at the achievement of economic and monetary union via the Maastricht Treaty . . . .

Note

The Community is a response to the post-war devastation of the continent of Europe, and grew in part because of the perceived failure of the nation State as an international actor. The final paragraph of the preceding extract makes the particularly important point that the Community encompasses aspirations beyond economics. This should already have become clear from your reading of the Introduction to Part One of this book (pp. 1–36).

What, then, is the role of law in achieving these goals?

Article 3 EC

Article 3

1. For the purposes set out in Article 2, the activities of the Community shall include, as provided in this Treaty and in accordance with the timetable set out therein:

(a)   the prohibition, as between Member States, of customs duties and quantitative restrictions on the import and export of goods, and of all other measures having equivalent effect;

(b)   a common commercial policy;

(c)   an internal market characterised by the abolition, as between Member States, of obstacles to the free movement of goods, persons, services and capital;

(d)   measures concerning the entry and movement of persons as provided for in Title IV;

(e)   a common policy in the sphere of agriculture and fisheries;

(f)   a common policy in the sphere of transport;

(g)   a system ensuring that competition in the internal market is not distorted;

(h)   the approximation of the laws of Member States to the extent requited for the functioning of the common market;

(i)   the promotion of coordination between employment policies of the Member States with a view to enhancing their effectiveness by developing a coordinated strategy for employment;

(j)   a policy in the social sphere comprising a European Social Fund;

(k)   the strengthening of economic and social cohesion;

(l)   a policy in the sphere of the environment;

(m)   the strengthening of the competitiveness of Community industry;

(n)   the promotion of research and technological development;

(o)   encouragement for the establishment and development of trans-European networks;

(p)   a contribution to the attainment of a high level of health protection;

(q)   a contribution to education and training of quality and to the flowering of the cultures of the Member States;

(r)   a policy in the sphere of development cooperation;

(s)   the association of the overseas countries and territories in order to increase trade and promote jointly economic and social development;

(t)   a contribution to the strengthening of consumer protection;

(u) measures in the spheres of energy, civil protection and tourism.
2. In all the activities referred to in this Article, the Community shall aim to eliminate inequalities, and to promote equality, between men and women.

Notes
1. Article 3 sets out the 'four fundamental freedoms' in Community trade law: the free movement of goods, persons, services, and capital. In addition, it refers to the need for common policy-making in several areas. The Maastricht Treaty on European Union and the Amsterdam Treaty both added significantly to the list of such areas (one consequence of which is the increased profile of cases involving choice of 'legal base' for EC legislation, p. 48 above).
2. There are, then, both negative and positive aspects to Community law. The law is negative in the sense that it is designed to eliminate national laws which act as obstacles to trade within the wider Community market. It is positive in the sense that it implies regulation of that wider market through Community legislation. Sometimes positive Community policy-making may be seen as a means of breaking down remaining barriers to trade which are lawful under Community law. On other occasions Community policies may be designed more to cope with the consequences of free movement rather than simply to bring it about. From this perspective Community social policy has taken shape. The matter is discussed more fully in Chapter 15.
3. The substantive provisions of Community law which are studied in the following 10 chapters are essentially the provisions alluded to in Article 3, which are designed to achieve the common market broadly conceived.

Question
To what extent are the *substantive* rules alluded to in Article 3 EC achievable only through the development of the *constitutional* principles examined in Chapters 1–4? Could a common market be achieved without a legal system which is supreme and directly effective; or without a procedure under which authoritative uniform interpretation of the law can be supplied?

(B) THE INTERNAL MARKET: 1992

(i) The background
Why does the common market referred to in Article 2 not exist? Economic barriers to trade proved enduring in the early years. Moreover the institutional and legislative apparatus of the Community also proved inadequate to secure the advancement of the Community. There was a marked weakening in political will. Difficult decisions were stifled by the effect of the requirement in practice of unanimity in voting in Council. Violation of Community law became more common. The Community was in a state of stagnation by the early-1980s. Loss of confidence in its prospects reduced cross-border investment.

Leon Brittan, EC Commissioner,
Annual General Meeting of *JUSTICE*
London, 7 July 1989

. . . [W]hy [was] the 1992 process . . . necessary in the first place. Really, in a way, it was necessary because of the recognition that the prescriptions of the Treaty of Rome had not been fully fulfilled. The idea of a single European market in which there would be freedom of goods and services had manifestly not been created by the early 1980s, and although there was freedom of physical goods, the unseen barriers to trade were so substantial that you could not say that we had created a single Common Market. That perception was allied with the further perception that in order to achieve that progress towards a genuine single market, it was necessary for there to be constitutional change in the Community, because as long as all decisions had to be taken by unanimity, in practice, if not in strict theory, it was impossible to remove the non-tariff barriers, whether in public procurement, whether through the abuse of standards, whatever their nature, towards the creation of a genuine single market. And so, alongside the programmes of 1992, went the Single European Act and the constitutional changes, giving greater power to the European Parliament, and the ability for decisions to be taken in many, if not all, areas by qualified majority vote. It was that that provided the impetus to 1992.

Note

For a collection of essays, see D. Swann (ed.), *The Single European Market and Beyond* (Routledge, 1992).

Thus, the 1992 project is properly seen as an attempt to secure the reinvigoration of the Community. It is the New Impetus, without which the Community would at best have remained marginalised and at worst have collapsed.

The blueprint for the 1992 programme was provided by COM (85) 310 – the Commission White Paper on Completing the Internal Market. This declared that 'A well developed free trade area offers significant advantages . . . but it would fail and fail dismally to release the energies of the people of Europe; it would fail to deploy Europe's immense economic resources to the maximum advantage; and it would fail to satisfy the aspirations of the people of Europe' (para. 220). The White Paper provided a policy agenda of some 300 measures which needed to be adopted by the end of 1992 in order to make the internal market a reality. The legal propulsion to give the plan the might to succeed was provided by the Single European Act, which came into force on 1 July 1987. That Treaty amended the Treaty of Rome in certain important respects; most notably for present purposes it shifted voting procedures in relation to 1992 measures towards qualified majority voting, instead of unanimous voting (contrast Article 100a, introduced by the SEA, with the original Treaty's Article 100 – becoming Articles 95 and 94 respectively post-Amsterdam). More generally, the Member States had committed themselves to a new wave of European integration through an explicit political act.

H. Schmitt von Sydow, 'Basic Strategies of the Commission's White Paper', in R. Bieber, R. Dehousse, J. Pinder, J. Weiler (eds), *1992: One European Market?* (1988), pp. 79, 86–92

(Footnotes omitted.)

The idea

A successful politician does not always need to have brilliant ideas, but he must be aware of existing problems and possible solutions and, most of all, he needs a sense of good timing, knowing when an ambitious idea is ripe to be pushed with vigour.

When the Delors Commission took office in January 1985, the Commissioners – 14 out of 17 were newcomers – looked for a motto, for a major goal to be achieved during the next four or eight years, the lifetime of one or two Commissions.

There were about five topics to choose from. Two concerned the reform of the agricultural policy and of the budget. These were significant tasks and, no doubt, they had to be fulfilled. But were they sufficient to give a positive trade mark to the Commission? Repairing the errors of the past was important, but a quantum leap forward was even more so.

Institutional reform and progress towards political union were overdue, but would they be sufficient to reach the citizens of Europe? The man on the street would not be convinced of the usefulness of Community institutions as long as, crossing the borders between Member States, he met the same old customs officials and had to take along the same whole set of different currencies in order to pay the local taxi driver. Commissioners were influenced by the disappointing results of the 1984 election to the European Parliament where the campaigns had focused on national policies and where voters had snubbed the polling stations not only because the Parliament was lacking powers, but also because the whole Community did not seem able to solve citizens' problems.

These problems concern employment and economic prosperity, and they need a regenerative impetus of which the European countries are intrinsically capable if they overcome the fragmentation of their economies and their markets. The instruments for this kind of integration are Economic and Monetary Union and the Internal Market.

Economic and Monetary Union was certainly an attractive goal, especially to the five Commissioners who previously had been Ministers of Finance in their national governments; and there was no doubt that it should be pursued vigourously. But Member States' fears regarding its political and financial impact made it difficult to draft a realistic timetable.

So the choice became the Internal Market. Indeed this file was ripe for a decisive breakthrough.

First of all, since 1983, a new momentum in the right direction had been taking shape, which just needed a determined push and a precise perspective. Never before had there been such a promising basis for removing all visible and most of the invisible barriers to free movement inside the Community.

Second, there was a clear political will. Since the early 1980s, Heads of State and Government, as well as Parliament and Commission, had repeatedly committed themselves to achieve the goals – already enshrined in the Treaty – of the internal market. Even down in the Council's expert groups, there was no fundamental opposition, neither from economic, regional nor sectoral interests, to the completion of the internal market. Delays were mainly due to procedural difficulties such as quarrels about legal base, reluctance to delegate powers of implementation, conflicting priorities, and lack of flexibility fostered by the practice of unanimity. These difficulties within the institutions were supposed to vanish once the global vision of the immense economic advantages of an integrated market became consolidated by a binding overall programme.

Third, the completion of the internal market required no additional spending from national or Community budgets. On the contrary, it would set free gains several times superior to the Community budget. The European Parliament had just given widespread publicity to the calculations of Messrs. Albert and Ball demonstrating that money lost by the fragmentation of public markets and by the delays encountered by barriers at intra-Community borders was equal to two years' Community budgets. And these were only two items on the costs of Non-Europe bill; if one added the expenses for the infrastructure of intra-Community borders and the potential prosperity resulting, directly and indirectly, from the increased competitivenes of industry in a home market of continental dimensions, then it became increasingly surprising that Heads of State and Government had personally, for years and years, wasted time and energy on trying to adjust percentages of national contributions to the Community budget, neglecting the internal market with its much greater, intrinsic benefits. As was stated in the House of Lords, the cost of just one single barrier to trade, namely the discriminatory element of tax levied from 1978 to 1981 on Scotch Whisky, was four times as much as the British annual net contribution to the Community budget.

The formulation

The Commission lost no time. Only one week after he took office, President Delors went to the Parliament and announced the new Commission's intention to ask the European Council to pledge itself to completion of a fully unified internal market by 1992, to be achieved with the help of a programme comprising a realistic and binding timetable. This intention was repeated in the overall 'Programme of the Commission for 1985'.

The members of the Parliament and the Heads of State and Government could not help but approve the target and the procedure. In its meeting of 29 and 30 March, the European Council identified as its first priority 'action to achieve a single large market by 1992 thereby creating a more favourable environment for stimulating enterprise, competition and trade'; it called upon the Commission to draw up a detailed programme with a specific timetable before its next meeting.

The Commission's White Paper in response to this invitation was rapid, bold and radical. The document was written in seven weeks. It covered a vast series of topics and left no stone unturned. Seldom before had a single paper required such detailed inter-service discussions with so many Commission departments necessitating the redefinition of so many policies. It took seventeen drafts before Lord Cockfield, the Vice-President responsible for internal market, could present the Paper to the public on Saturday, 15 June 1985. He was aware that the strategy proposed in the White Paper implied a profound change in the habits and traditional ways of thinking; but he also knew the pledge of the Heads of State and Government to the target of 1992. 'They asked for it', he calmly said, 'they have got it'.

The contents

The White Paper does not propose the target of 1992, nor does it rehearse the arguments in favour of that target. Instead the Commission, given the European Council's clear commitment to the target, just spells out the logical consequences of the commitment, together with an action programme for achieving the objective.

Consequently, the fields of action proposed by the White Paper have not been chosen because of their feasibility, but because of their necessity. The question to be answered was not: 'What can be realistically done by 1992?', but: 'What must be done in order to achieve the internal market and how could one squeeze it into the 1992 timetable?' Paradoxically, this 'unrealistic' approach has largely contributed to the Paper's credibility, since the global vision of what has to be done – with no jack-in-the-box-barriers hidden – helps to make the overall efforts measurable and to scale the 'unfeasible' actions down to their real political and economic proportions. During the drafting of the White Paper, all Commission departments had been warned that afterwards they would not be allowed to raise additional problems, and they responded to the challenge as if they – and not national administrations – were personally responsible for the emergence of new barriers to the free movement.

Identifying all problems without exception, the White Paper did not hesitate to tackle sensitive areas where no realistic immediate solution was at hand, e.g. commercial policy vis-à-vis third countries, nor to deal with policies for which no clear Community competence could be established, e.g. the right of asylum or the fight against terrorism. Whatever the underlying reason giving rise to a physical or technical barrier is, the White Paper spells it out and examines how justified interests can be taken care of without disturbing free movement inside the Community.

On the other hand, there are numerous other policies, such as regional, social, environmental, consumer, transport, research, competition, economic and monetary policies, which are closely linked to the internal market and the integration of economies; but they are touched by the White Paper only where they have a direct bearing on the abolition of physical and technical barriers. While progress on these policies becomes even more important because of the completion of the internal market, and indeed has been positively enhanced by the verve of the White Paper and the perspective of the great 'rendez-vous' of 1992, they must not constitute a precondition to completing the internal market. The White Paper mentions them only for the record refraining from offering any recipe.

Similarly, institutional reforms are not explicitly called for in the White Paper. Its main merit is not to have presented detailed solutions, but to have identified the problems. Of course, where problems had been tackled for a long time and where formal Commission proposals were already on the table, the White Paper refers, in many cases, to those proposals. But in cases where the problems had not been tackled at Community level before or where rapid but realistic solutions were difficult to define, such as asylum or commercial policy, the White Paper just sketches the responsibilities and possible ways of solution, maintaining nevertheless the pressure stemming from the time schedule.

Comprehensive as the White Paper's strategy is, its fields of action form a single entity. One cannot extract individual files which seem to have a higher priority or to be easier, and postpone the decision on other files, without jeopardising the objective of complete abolition of all border controls.

This objective has been confirmed by the Single European Act which defines the internal market as 'an area without internal frontiers in which the free movement of goods, persons, services and capital is ensured'. A Europe without internal frontiers – not a Europe with fewer or simpler controls, but one with no such divisive frontier controls at all.

The structure
In line with this comprehensive character, the chapters of the White Paper do not follow the legal categories of the Treaty (goods, persons, services, capital) but the types

of barriers which are met in practice; hence the division of the Paper in three parts dealing with physical, technical and fiscal barriers.

The physical barriers at the customs posts are the most obvious and glaring manifestation of the continued fragmentation of the Community; they must be removed for both economic and political reasons. It should be noted that the White Paper understands the notion of 'border' not in a geographical, but in a practical sense. Physical barriers are to be abolished not only where they are carried out at the very frontier of Member States, but also where they are carried out, thanks for example to the Community Transit Procedure, inside the Member States' territory at the premises of consignors and consignees of goods. In this sense, physical barriers are those barriers which are triggered by the fact of crossing a border; which are discriminatory insofar as they are opposed only to goods, persons, services and capital coming from abroad and are not identical to, and an integrated part of, internal controls.

The technical barriers result from national legislation which, in practice, hampers free movement even if, from a legal point of view, it does not refer to border crossings, and which is indistinctly applied to foreign and indigenous goods, persons, services and capital. Again, the White Paper's definition goes beyond the traditional notion of technical barriers: It is not limited to goods but intentionally includes services, capital movements, public procurement, industrial property and other national policies insofar as they risk to obstruct free movement and to annihilate the benefits of the removal of physical barriers.

The fiscal barriers appear in both forms, as physical and as technical barriers. The White Paper devotes a special chapter to them because they are the most important single group of impediments; their abolition had fallen a long way behind the advances made in other fields of integration, and they required a particularly radical change of strategy.

The Annex to the White Paper contains a detailed timetable for approximately 300 Commission proposals and Council decisions in order to implement the Commission's proposed programme. . . .

R. Bieber, R. Dehousse, J. Pinder, J. Weiler,
'Back to the Future: Policy, Strategy and Tactics of the White Paper
on the Creation of a Single European Market',
in R. Bieber et al. (eds), *1992: One European Market*
(1988), pp. 13–16

(Footnotes omitted.)

The Aim and Method

If you want to attract support for a big political project, you do well to explain in half a dozen words what it is all about. The Cockfield White Paper selected the words 'action to achieve a single market by 1992'. At a time when the EC member governments disagreed about most major issues, it was possible to focus their minds and secure their agreement on making a priority of this apparently simple aim. . . .

Yet the apparent simplicity of the aim and the definition conceal the enormous complexity of the undertaking. . . . it involves the most intricate adjustment of regulations, taxes and laws. Completing a single market among advanced industrial economies is an exercise not of laissez-faire but of *Ordnungspolitik*; and *Ordnungspolitik* has become immensely more complicated since the idea of the social market economy was developed nearly half a century ago. In the terms of integration theory, negative integration, or the removal of barriers to transactions across the frontiers of different states, implies also the more exacting effort to achieve positive integration, or common policies with aims going beyond the straightforward removal of discrimination, when the barriers are not just tariffs and quotas, but differing regulations, taxes or laws. The White Paper gives rise, indeed, to some large and complex political, social and even ideological problems. . . .

Virtues and Limits of an Inductive Method:
What we have learnt in the intervening thirty years is a healthy disrespect of programmes which are not linked to specific executory commitments and to adequate institutional arrangements.

The White Paper presents a striking difference from other ambitious attempts to reform the Community in depth. Unlike the Draft Treaty Establishing the European Union adopted by the European Parliament which invited theological debates about the nature of Community governance, the White Paper is essentially inductive. It spells out in detail over 300 specific measures which will have to be adopted to complete the internal market; it even sets a proximate goal which, while it may fall short of a fully-formed single market, is at least unambiguous: to do away with frontier controls in their entirety by the end of 1992.

. . .

(ii)   The internal market defined

What exactly *was* the 1992 project? What constitutes the completion of the internal market?

Article 8a was inserted into the original Treaty of Rome by the Single European Act; it was renumbered as Article 7a by the Treaty on European Union. But post-Amsterdam it reads as follows:

Article 14
1.   The Community shall adopt measures with the aim of progressively establishing the internal market over a period expiring on 31 December 1992, in accordance with the provisions of this Article and of Articles 15, 26, 47(2), 49, 80, 93 and 95 and without prejudice to the other provisions of this Treaty.
2.   The internal market shall comprise an area without internal frontiers in which the free movement of goods, persons, services and capital is ensured in accordance with the provisions of this Treaty.
3.   The Council, acting by a qualified majority on a proposal from the Commission, shall determine the guidelines and conditions necessary to ensure balanced progress in all the sectors concerned.

Note
Lord Cockfield was the Commissioner responsible from 1985–1989 for the development of the 1992 strategy. Speaking in London on 22 February 1988, he confirmed the uncompromising nature of the objective: '[it is] *not* an area where frontier controls have merely been simplified or are retained for this reason or that: but an area *without* internal frontiers.' (Lord Cockfield reflects on the project in *The European Union* (Wiley Chancery Law, 1994.)

Question
To what extent does the pursuit of the internal market remain less ambitious
than a common market?

(iii)   The anticipated benefits of the completion of the internal market
Much of the comment above about the economic advantages of a *common*
market applies to the aspiration to create an *internal* market. The Commission
supported its campaign to set the Community the medium-term objective of
completing the internal market by funding an extensive survey of the 'The
Costs of Non-Europe' – the Cecchini Report.

An immensely optimistic picture is painted by the following summary of
the survey's conclusions:

P. Cecchini, *The European Challenge:*
1992, the Benefits of a Single Market
(1988), pp. xvii–xxi

(Endnotes omitted.)

The research
The outlook emerges from an unprecedented research programme, launched in 1986
by EC Commission vice-president Lord Cockfield. Its purpose was to provide a solid
body of scientifically-assembled evidence as a means of judging the extent of the
market fragmentation confronting European business and Community policy-makers
alike. In the process, the research has thrown up a vivid illustration and rigorous
analysis of the costs imposed on Europeans by the mosaic of non-tariff barriers which
– 30 years after the Community's birth – continue to mock the term 'common
market'. The findings of this research into the 'costs of non-Europe', are outlined in
their essential detail in the pages of this book.

The research is unprecedented for various reasons – first for the sheer size of its scope,
but also because of the novelty of the subject-matter and the methodological difficulties
that were encountered in making the analysis and calculations based on it. A further
problem was the unevenness of the empirical data on European market fragmentation.
Yet despite these fragilities, the results that emerge tell an unmistakable story.

They estimate the size of the costs and thus a potential for gains exceeding Ecu 200
billions. This basic benefit, which could be magnified by modestly positive economic
policies, is the reward for removing the barriers targetted by the 1992 legislative
programme set out in the EC's 1985 White Paper *Completing the Internal Market*. Thus
when EC political decisions are taken and the business community has fully adjusted
to the new competitive environment, gains of this order of magnitude would be
acquired once and for all, meaning that the European economy would be lifted onto
a higher plane of overall performance.

The barriers – like border controls and customs red-tape, divergent standards and
technical regulations, conflicting business laws and protectionist procurement practice
– are well enough known by name. But not until now has their impact, and that of
their removal, been charted and costed. These results, the product of the extensive
field-work and subsequent analysis, are outlined in Part I, together with illustrations
of the workings of non-Europe in a broad range of industries and services.

Likewise, the White Paper's legislative programme for removing market barriers,
reinforced since mid-1987 by the Single European Act, is also well known. But what

has not been estimated until now is the value of the ultimate prize which Community governments could, by enacting it in full, deliver to Europe's citizens, its companies – and to themselves. Detailed estimates of these overall gains, and the mechanisms by which they are to be realized, are made by two separate but complementary approaches – respectively a micro-economic and a macro-economic analysis – and are presented in simplified form in Part II.

The shock and the prospect

For all the complexities, the essential mechanism is simple. The starting point of the whole process of economic gain is the removal of non-tariff barriers.

The release of these constraints will trigger a supply-side shock to the Community economy as a whole. The name of the shock is European market integration. Costs will come down. Prices will follow as business, under the pressure of new rivals on previously protected markets, is forced to develop fresh responses to a novel and permanently changing situation. Ever-present competition will ensure the completion of a self-sustaining virtuous circle. The downward pressure on prices will in turn stimulate demand, giving companies the opportunity to increase output, to exploit resources better and to scale them up for European, and global, competition.

However, the effect of the shock is to be gauged not just in terms of the market, and of the companies and consumers who buy and sell there. Its waves will ripple out into the economy at large. By its very size, the shock will have reverberations on general economic management. Over time, creation of a European home market will unbind the macro-economic constraints which have chronically fettered the prospects of sustained growth in Europe for the best part of twenty years.

Public deficits will be eased, under the dual impact of open public procurement and the economy's regeneration. Inflation, traditionally growth's ugly sister, will be cooled down by the drop in prices provoked by open markets. The jolt so imparted to Europe's competitivity should ensure that growth is achieved without damage to the Community's external trade position.

But, perhaps most important of all, is the medium-term impact of market integration on employment. With its injection of inflation-free growth, coupled with a loosening of the constraints on public exchequers in the Community's member states, the European home market of the 1990s raises the prospect, for the first time since the early 1970s, of very substantial job creation. The added financial elbow-room given to governments should, in addition, enable any unevenness in the rewards distributed by market integration to be compensated.

This medium-term prospect of substantial growth is not just a boon for Europe. The world economy of the late 1980s and early 1990s, overshadowed by American deficits, a fickle dollar and the spectre of a US recession, needs to take confidence where it can. The expectation may be that a dynamic European market, trading with the world on a footing of revamped competitivity, will provide a much-needed shot in the arm for other markets and economies in less buoyant shape.

In return, EC governments will have the right to expect appropriate responses from the Community's economic partners abroad, notably the US and Japan. If the fruits of the European home market are to be shared internationally, there must also be a fair share-out of the burdens of global economic responsibility, with market opening measures extended internationally on a firm basis of clear reciprocity.

The actors and the opportunity

The European home market will not materialize at the wave of a wand. 1992 will not come by whispering words of mysterious Eurospeak into a receding future, or the future will return the compliment by staying conveniently out of reach. For business and government, the two main actors, the road to market integration will be paved with tough adjustments and the need for new strategies.

For business, removing protective barriers creates a permanent opportunity, but signals a definitive end to national soft options. Cost reductions will be good news, but market opening means also the permanent threat, actual or potential, of competition. This is also good news for the company which is gearing up to capitalize on the enlarged market's enhanced opportunities for innovation and economies of scale. But profits which derive from cashing in on monopoly or protected positions will tend to be squeezed. The situation will be one of constant competitive renewal.

Managing change will mean changing management – or rather the focus of its business strategy. There is already widespread evidence that this is happening, as companies – ahead of 1992 and often way ahead of the politicians – are adjusting both their management goals and business structures in readiness for new patterns of competition. But opportunities must continue to be seized – merely to neglect them will create a threat. One thing is certain. Firms from outside the EC, who are already positioning themselves in Community markets in anticipation of the White Paper programme's success, will not miss opportunities overlooked by their indigenous rivals.

Governments, already being watched closely by business, will be expected to give clear signs of their commitment to the 1992 goal. The credibility of the European market as an operational environment for business depends in the first instance on the legislator persuading companies of the seriousness of its intentions. There is only one way of doing this. EC governments must enact the White Paper programme fully and on schedule. In so doing, they will release the costs, outlined in this book, which presently inhibit Europe's market and economic expansion.

This means a further role for companies. Business cannot afford to sit passively by, idly expecting governments to keep to long-term legislative commitments, unaided. There is a need of more active political involvement, in the sense of constructive input to policy, orchestrated at Community level but targetted above all at the seats of national political power.

But governments must do more than achieve the European home market. They must maintain it – and, once again, give companies tangible proof that they are committed to doing so.

No great insight is needed to see that maintaining market integration will in turn pose the Community with some ineluctable choices. The business managers of the European market of the 1990s cannot be indefinitely divorced from the political managers of the Community economy.

Attempting to sustain this unserviceable dichotomy would be to invite disaster. Market integration, for example, particularly in its early stages, is likely to accentuate pressures on exchange rates and thus the need for firm currency management and for a stronger European monetary system. Without an institutional framework to deal effectively with these and other problems inherent in the success of the 1992 programme, the European home market will soon be put in jeopardy. The tensions that will be created will not be susceptible of management in an institutional vacuum. In short, for Europe to meet its market challenge, it must also, sooner rather than later, review the overall structure of its economic organisation.

Note

The following extract is rather more restrained:

A. M. El-Agraa (ed.), *The European Union: History, Institutions, Economics and Policies* (5th edn, 1998), pp. 158–62

7.3 The expected benefits

7.3.1 The Cecchini estimates

According to the Cecchini Report, which summarises in sixteen volumes the findings of a study carried out on behalf of the EC Commission . . . the completion of the internal market will regenerate both the goods and services sectors of the EC. The study estimates the total potential gain for the EC as a whole to be in the region of 200 billion ECU, at constant 1988 prices. This would increase EC gross domestic product (GDP) by 5% or more. The gains will come not only from the elimination of the costs of barriers to intra-EC trade, but also from the exploitation of economies of scale which are expected to lower costs by about 2% of EC GDP. The medium-term impact of this on employment will be to increase it by about 2 million jobs. These estimates are considered to be minimal since the study points out that, if the governments of the member nations of the EC pursue macroeconomic policies that recognise this potential for faster economic growth, the total gains could reach 7% of EC GDP and increase employment by about 5 million jobs. If these predictions become a reality, the EC will gain a very substantial competitive edge over non-participating nations.

The summary of the Cecchini Report . . . is written for the general public. The definitive technical work is that by Emerson *et al.* (1988); Emerson is a leading economist who then worked for the Directorate-General for Economic and Financial Affairs, and in this capacity his (and his collaborators') work presents the official Commission analysis; hence the interested reader is advised to consult this work. Here it should be asked why the elimination of the various barriers mentioned above should lead to economic benefits for the EC. To answer this question meaningfully, one needs to specify the barriers, which are all of the non-tariff type, slightly differently, and in a more general context.

1. Differences in the technical regulations adopted in the various member nations which tend to increase the cost of intra-EC trade transactions.
2. Delays in the customs procedures at border-crossing points and related extra administrative tasks on both private firms and public organisations which further increase the costs of intra-EC trade transactions.
3. Public procurement procedures which effectively limit if not completely eliminate competition for public purchases to own member nation suppliers, a procedure often claimed to raise the price of such purchases.
4. Curtailment of one's ability either to transact freely in certain services, especially finance and transport, where barriers to entry are supposedly great, or to get established in them in another EC member nation.

No claim has been made to suggest that the cost of eliminating each of these barrier categories is substantial, but Emerson *et al.* (1988) have argued that the combination of these barriers, in an EC dominated by oligopolistic market structures, amounts to 'a considerable degree of non-competitive segmentation of the market', with the implication that the cost of eliminating all the barrier categories then becomes considerable. Since the emphasis is on costs (the Cecchini Report stresses them as the 'cost of non-Europe'), it follows that the elimination of these barriers will reduce the costs, i.e. increase the benefits; these are two sides of the same coin. . . .

These benefits can also be expressed forthrightly. The elimination of the costs of non-Europe is tantamount to the removal of constraints which 'today prevent enterprises from being as efficient as they could be and from employing their resources to the full' (Emerson *et al.*, 1988 p. 2). They go on to argue that since these are constraints, their removal will 'establish a more competitive environment which will incite [the enterprises] to exploit new opportunities (p. 2). They then claim that the combination of the elimination of the constraints and the creation of a more competitive situation will have four major types of effect;

1.   A significant reduction in costs due to a better exploitation of several kinds of economies of scale associated with the size of production units and enterprises.
2.   An improved efficiency in enterprises, a rationalisation of industrial structures and a setting of prices closer to costs of production, all resulting from more competitive markets.
3.   Adjustments between industries on the basis of a fuller play of comparative advantages in an integrated market.
4.   A flow of innovations, new processes and new products, stimulated by the dynamics of the internal market.

They were quick to add that these processes free resources for alternative productive uses, and when they are so utilised, the total sustainable level of consumption and investment in the EC economy will be increased. They stressed that this was their fundamental criterion of economic gain.

Given the definitive nature of the Emerson *et al.* (1988) book, it may be useful, at the risk of duplication, to quote the estimates of the gains as presented by them. To make sense of their calculations and, of course, of the overall results given above, it has to be recalled that all the calculations relate to 1985 when the total EC GDP was 3,300 billion ECU for the twelve member nations. However, the actual calculations were made for the seven largest EC member countries (accounting for 88% of EC GDP for the twelve) with a total GDP of 2,900 billion ECU.

They claim that the overall estimates range from 70 billion ECU (2.5% of EC GDP) for 'a rather narrow conception of the benefits' of eliminating the remaining barriers to the single market, to about 125 – 190 billion ECUs (4.5 – 6.5% of EC GDP) in the case of a more competitive and integrated market. Applying the same percentages to the 1988 GDP data, the gains were estimated to be between 175 and 255 billion ECUs. These gains are expected to increase the EC's annual growth rate by about 1 percentage point for the years until 1992. Also, 'there would be good prospects that longer-run dynamic effects could sustain a buoyant growth rate further into the 1990s' (p. 5).

These gains were obtained on the understanding that it might take five or more years for the upper limits to be achieved and that policies at both the microeconomic and macroeconomic level would ensure that the resources (basically labour) released by the savings in costs would be fully and effectively utilised elsewhere in the EC. These assumptions were made to simplify the analysis. However, in order to make the calculations look more professional, they used the estimates to generate macro-economic simulations from macrodynamic models. For this purpose, the effects of the single market were classified into four groups according to their type of macro-economic impact:

1.   The elimination of customs delays and costs.

2. The exposing of public markets to competition.

3. The liberalisation and integration of financial markets.

4. Broader supply-side effects, 'reflecting changes in the strategic behaviour of enterprises in a new competitive environment' (p. 5).

The results of the simulations are then presented according to whether or not passive macroeconomic policies are pursued.

In the case of passive macroeconomic policies, the overall impact of the measures is felt most sharply in the earlier years in reduced prices and costs; but after a modest time lag output begins to increase. It is reported that the major impact is felt in the medium term (five to six years) when a cumulative impact of 4.5% increase in GDP and a 6% reduction in the price level may be expected. The effect on employment is slightly negative at the beginning, but increases by 2 million jobs (almost 2% of the initial level of employment) by the medium term. Moreover, there is a marked improvement in the budget balance and a significant improvement in the current account.

In the case of more active macroeconomic policies, it is argued that since the main indicators of monetary and financial equilibrium would then be improved, it would be perfectly in order to 'consider adjusting medium-term macroeconomic strategy onto a somewhat more expansionary trajectory' (p. 6). Obviously, the extent of adjustment rests upon which constraint (inflation, budget or balance of payments deficit) is considered crucial. In the text, a number of variants is illustrated. For example, in the middle of the range there is a case in which the level of GDP is 2.5% higher after the medium term. Since this is additional to the 4.5% boost obtained with passive macroeconomic policies, the total effect is therefore 7%. It is pointed out that in this instance, inflation would still be below its projected value in the absence of the Single Market, the budget balance would also be improved and the balance of payments might be worsened by a 'moderate but sustainable amount'.

Before going further, it is important to be explicit about certain assumptions behind these estimates:

> It is implicit, in order to attain the highest sustainable level of consumption and investment, that productivity and employment be also of a high order. In particular, where rationalisation efforts cause labour to be made redundant, this resource has to be successfully re-employed. Also implicit is a high rate of growth in the economy. The sustainability condition, moreover, requires that the major macro-economic equilibrium constraints are respected, notably as regards price stability, balance of payments and budget balances. It further implies a positive performance in terms of world-wide competitivity. (Emerson *et al.*, 1988, p. 2)

Although these estimates depend largely on a number of crucial qualifications, Emerson *et al.* state that irrespective of these qualifications, the upper limits to the gains are unlikely to be overestimates of the potential benefits of a fully integrated EC market. This is because:

> the figures exclude some important categories of dynamic impact on economic performance. Three examples may be mentioned. Firstly, there is increasing evidence that the trend rate of technological innovation in the economy depends upon the presence of competition; only an integrated market can offer the benefits both of scale of operation and competition. Secondly, there is evidence in fastgrow-ing high technology industries of dynamic or learning economies of scale, whereby

costs decline as the total accumulated production of certain goods and services increase[s]; market segmentation greatly limits the scope of these benefits and damages performance in key high-growth industries of the future. Thirdly, the business strategies of European enterprises are likely to be greatly affected in the event of a rapid and extensive implementation of the internal market programme, a full integration of the internal market will foster the emergence of truly European companies, with structures and strategies that are better suited to securing a strong place in world market competition. (Emerson *et al*, 1988, pp. 6–7)

Note
The study referred to in this extract is M. Emerson *et al.*, *The Economics of 1992: the EC Commission's assessment of the economic effects of completing the internal market* (Oxford: OUP, 1988).

A. M. El-Agraa (ed.), *The European Union: History, Institutions, Economics and Policies* (5th edn, 1998), pp. 166–7

. . . There are two reservations to consider. The first is advanced by Pelkmans and Robson (1987). It is that the categorisation by the EC of these three types of barrier is somewhat arbitrary. Physical barriers are concerned with frontier controls on the movement of goods and persons. Fiscal barriers consist of all impediments and substantial distortions among member states that emanate from differences in the commodity base as well as in the rates of VAT and the duties on excises. . . . All remaining impediments fall into the category of technical barriers. Therefore, this category comprises not only barriers arising from absence of technical harmonisation and public procurement procedures, but also institutional impediments on the free movement of people, capital and financial services, including transport and data transmission. It also comprises a miscellaneous collection of obstacles to the business environment which take the form of an inadequately harmonised company law, the lack of an EC patent and of an EC trademark, together with issues of corporate taxation and several diverse problems concerned with the national application of EC law. However, even though this categorisation may make analysis more cumbersome, the approach adopted in this book shows that this is not a serious reservation.

The second reservation is more serious. It is that the estimates given in the Cecchini Report should not be taken at face value. First, in spite of the endorsement of the SEA by all the member nations, there does not seem to be a philosophy common to all of them to underpin the internal market. Second, these estimates do not take into consideration the costs to be incurred by firms, regions and governments in achieving them. Third, the internal market aims at the elimination of internal barriers to promote the efficient restructuring of supply, but it remains silent on the question of demand; thus the internal market seems to be directed mainly at the production side. Fourth, putting too much emphasis on economies of scale, when their very existence has to be proved, will encourage concentration rather than competition, and there is no evidence to support the proposition that there is a positive correlation between increased firm size and competitive success. Finally, the estimates are for the EC as a whole; thus it is likely that each member nation will strive to get the maximum gain for itself with detrimental consequences for all, i.e. this is like the classical oligopoly problem where the best solution for profit-maximisation purposes is for oligopolists to behave as joint monopolists, but if each oligopolist firm tries to maximise its own share of the joint profit, the outcome may be losses all round.

. . . In the previous edition of this book, I added that here 'it is sufficient to state that such potential benefits may prove rather elusive since the creation of the appropriate environment does not guarantee the expected outcomes. However, this does not mean that the EC should not be congratulated for its genuine attempts to create the necessary competitive atmosphere, only that one should not put too much emphasis on estimates which can easily be frustrated by the realities of everyday EC economic life. However, some of the quotations given above clearly show that the experts are aware of these problems'. The part of that statement relating to the benefits expected from the internal market remains true at the time of writing.

Notes
1.   The study referred to is J. Pelkmans and P. Robson, 'The Aspirations of the White Paper', (1987) 25 JCMS 181.
2.   It should be apparent from this analysis that these issues have not suddenly dropped from view after the end of 1992. Market integration is a continuing process. Building and maintaining an internal market demands a long-term agenda.

(iv)   Measuring the impact of '1992'
Roughly a decade after providing the impetus needed to pilot the Community on a course to complete the internal market by the end of 1992, the Commission sponsored a research programme designed to discover what economic benefits had actually accrued. The fruits were published in a set of 38 sector-specific volumes, divided into six sub-sets: impact on manufacturing; impact on services; dismantling of barriers; impact on trade and investment; impact on competition and scale effects; and aggregate and regional impact. These volumes were co-published in 1997 by the Commission and Kogan Page. Naturally, the inquiry is not straightforward, for, sector by sector, it is difficult to demarcate advantages accruing from the '1992' initiative and those that would have occurred in any event or which are attributable to other factors such as global trade liberalisation. Moreover, the essence of the internal market programme is that benefits will be felt not only in the shortterm, but also in the longterm, and accordingly measurement cannot yet be decisive. However, the Commission, presenting a Communication to the Parliament and Council on 30 October 1996, summarised the results of its research in the following broadly positive terms.

Summary – The Impact and Effectiveness of the Single Market
(available via http://europa.eu.int/comm/dg15/en/update/impact/
smsumen.htm)

1   Jobs and sustainable growth are at the top of the Union's agenda. The Commission's Confidence Pact, 'Action for Employment in Europe', identified the Single Market as the launching pad for attaining higher levels of job creation and sustainable growth. The Commission now has solid evidence of the positive effects of the Single Market, based on a first exhaustive survey of its economic impact and effectiveness conducted over the past two years.

2.   In terms of economic impact the news is encouraging. It is still too early for many Single Market measures to have taken full effect but there are clear signs of significant change in the European economy. We now have evidence of the following positive, albeit preliminary effects of the Single Market in triggering the expected reinforcement of integration, competition, economic performance and benefits for consumers:

- growing competition between companies in both manufacturing and services;
- an accelerated pace of industrial restructuring, with the resultant benefits in terms of greater competitiveness;
- a wider range of products and services available to public sector, industrial and domestic consumers at lower prices, particularly in newly liberalised service sectors such as transport, financial services, telecommunications and broadcasting;
- faster and cheaper cross-frontier deliveries resulting from the absence of border controls on goods;
- greater mobility between Member States for both workers and those not economically active (including students and retired people).

3.   Calculations of the overall economic effects of these changes suggest that the SMP has resulted in:

- between 300,000 and 900,000 more jobs than would have existed in the absence of the Single Market;
- an extra increase in EU income of 1.1–1.5% over the period 1987–93;
- inflation rates which are 1.0–1.5% lower than they would be in the absence of the SMP;
- economic convergence and cohesion between different EU regions.

4.   These benefits have been gained without any reduction in safety standards for consumers or workers. In many areas standards of protection for the citizen have in fact increased. Citizens of the Union also enjoy more personal freedom and have more choice than ever before. The Commission's survey confirms that Community legislation in the Single Market area has, taken as a whole, created the basic conditions for free movement and economic efficiency. The situation in today's Single Market is in sharp contrast to that of the mid-1980s when:

- all goods were stopped and subject to checks at frontiers;
- most products had to comply with different laws in each Member State;
- services such as transport, telecommunications, banking and broadcasting were not subject to competition; and
- citizens who were not employed could be subject to restrictions on residence and risk losing social security rights in another Member State.

5.   It is up to economic operators to make the most of the Single Market. The role of public authorities at national and Community level is confined to creating appropriate economic and institutional conditions. In the context of a more favourable economic climate, operators will be better placed to exploit to the full the opportunities that are now available. This report shows that where these opportunities are taken the benefits are significant.

6.   The Commission's analysis suggests that these opportunities would have been even greater if Member States had been more diligent in putting in place the Single Market measures already agreed and applying the principles of the Community law on which they are based. Delays in applying and enforcing Single Market rules at

national level continue to limit the Single Market's positive contribution to growth, competitiveness and more employment.

7. The Community must build on its successes and iron out the remaining political and practical difficulties which inhibit the Single Market's full potential from being achieved. The Commission is putting forward clear policy recommendations for action at two levels:

- first and foremost, *at the national level*, where the main responsibility for applying Single Market rules lies. The Commission is urging that enforcement of Single Market legislation and Treaty rules be stepped up. In addition, the Commission calls for vigorous action to be taken to reduce excessive regulation at national level which inhibits both competition and competitiveness;
- at the *Community level*, where further efforts must be made to complete the 1985 agenda in a few key areas (such as abolition of border controls on persons, taxation and company law), where further means have to be devoted to the control of implementation and to updating the legislation and where Community policies in related areas such as competition, consumer policy, information and the environment may need to be developed further in order to ensure the most effective use and development of the Single Market.

The introduction of a single currency in 1999 will also make the Single Market more effective, by eliminating the constraints which now result from exchange risks and by generally increasing transparency and competition.

8. In its conclusions to this report, the Commission calls for action to deliver a properly working Single Market. It spells out what is required in terms of a renewed commitment to the Single Market, not only at the highest political level – the European Council in Dublin – but also from all those who must contribute to making the Single Market a success – national authorities, the European Institutions and, above all, economic operators themselves.

(v) The business response

The assumption must be that the opportunities presented by the completion of the internal market will be seized by business. As the Commission insists in the above extract, it is essentially private commercial interests, not governments, that will make 1992 a visible reality. Business, then, must plan ahead. More: it must *keep* planning!

R. Dudley, *1992: Strategies for the Single Market*
(1990), pp. 74–75
[reproduced by permission of Kogan Page]

The effects of competition on industry structures

The intensification of business activity triggered by the creation of the Single Market will have a number of effects on the shaping of industry structures across the community. The main elements will be:

- the exit of a number of firms due to competitive intensity;
- the relocation of production by companies needing to produce more competitive products in recognised centres of excellence or needing to find lower-cost production centres;

- the acquisition by predatory companies of firms located within Community markets to provide or strengthen their marketing and manufacturing dispositions in target markets or to acquire essential technology;
- acquisition of smaller companies which may in themselves be at a competitive disadvantage but are attractive enough for them to successfully offer themselves to larger firms;
- acquisitions by external Community firms as a means of creating an indigenous presence;
- acquisition and mergers for vertical integration reasons to control upstream and downstream elements of their industry's value system; and
- mergers and joint ventures to reinforce the strength and position of companies in the face of the need to scale up activities, collaborate on distribution, meet R & D needs etc.

It is these potential changes to industry structures which will affect the competitive conditions under which both suppliers and customers will have to operate. It is vital, therefore, that managers look more closely at the risks of change and the impact they will bring to their individual firms.

Industry structures in which companies compete are transaction points within an overall industry value system. The relationship between, say, a finished product manufacturer and its channels of distribution are just as much affected by the costs the manufacturer pays for its raw materials as the competition the company faces itself in supplying the distribution channels. Restructuring is not confined to the larger countries in the European Community. Despite the much publicised takeovers by BSN (the French food conglomerate in France, Italy and the UK) or the acquisitions of strategic companies such as Rowntree in the UK by Nestlé, the small countries – Belgium, Holland, Greece and Portugal – are selling domestic firms to multinationals from both within and outside the European Community. Belgium, for example, has seen between one-quarter and one-third of its national businesses acquired in the last five years. A number of major names in Greece have also been acquired, such as Inco Pharmaceuticals by Akzo-Shell, Loumidis by Nestlé, Pavlides by Jacob Suchard and Metaxa by Grand Metropolitan.

Whilst many of the examples of restructuring through merger and acquisition are food companies, other industries including automotive (Ford-Jaguar), pharmaceutical (Beecham-Smith Kline), financial services (Morgan Grenfell in the UK, Kosmos Insurance Services in Greece) are undergoing a similar experience.

The effect of restructuring is to change the nature of competition, customers and suppliers. Yet it can provide a major threat to those firms who remain independent. Why? – because not only do multinationals bring in a depth to management quality, they offer wider global markets for the products made by the acquired firm. They may or may not introduce more capital and financial resources but what they do bring to the party is management and markets. The effect of this is to sharpen the acquired company's competitive edge in terms of cost and strategies. Remaining independent companies suddenly find themselves facing tougher opponents who can bring more to the market than they can.

Similarly, firms which have traditionally exported to markets using distributors or agents may also find that increased competition in local markets from multinationals will beg them to reconsider their methods of operation. The issue will obviously be one of deciding how to organise against competition, ie set up a local company, acquire, merge or create some sort of joint venture. A more competitive environment will demand that companies become much more market responsive, yet at the same time they will be competing against multinational businesses which have both scale and resource advantages.

Note

The effect of the completion of the single market varies according to the sector of the economy under review, but no sector escapes unaffected. A firm planning its internal market strategy must consider a range of factors touching, for example, its production, marketing and distribution strategies, opportunities for structural growth through takeovers and research and development policy.

In addition to decisions about responding to the nature of the market, business must become accustomed to dealing with the Community regulatory authorities.

R. Dudley, *1992: Strategies for the Single Market* (1990), pp. 60–61

(Footnote omitted.)

With such an amount of change being brought about by the SEA [Single European Act] a new feature of company strategy development will be the need to become adept at the political level. The European Community recognises the need for companies to become involved in the development of a number of legal areas. It encourages their participation in the processes of eliminating discriminatory anti-competitive activity. It provides forums for the views of industry to be heard. It provides the machinery for firms to involve themselves with product standards and so on.

. . .

Companies need, therefore, to put a political strategy somewhere towards the top of their agenda. They will need to understand the political motivations of the different member states within the Community and the workings of the Community's executive and legislative. Competition is no longer a mere market phenomenon, it is exercised at the political level. Companies, therefore, not having their views and interests represented will have to accept what is handed out to them whether or not it is in their interests.

Companies will need to assess what interests they need to preserve and seek a route to political access. This is not as difficult as it may seem. On-line data is available through agencies such as Spearhead to provide information on the progress of legislation. This will enable managers to watch for developments. Trade associations mindful of their members' interests are also researching members' attitudes and providing a system for alerting members to developments. The ways of gaining political access to decision-making are also less formidable than might be perceived. The following list gives some of the routes open to companies.

- Sponsoring executives to sit on the various Commission's committees.
- Participating in trade association lobbies and national standards authorities' initiatives.
- Contacts through national members of parliament.
- Contacts through members of the European Parliament.
- Contacting the SME Task Force.
- Accessing the European Social and Economic Committee.
- Employing political consultants.

The importance of a political strategy cannot be over-emphasised. Even where trade associations are becoming involved it is imperative that companies clearly make their own interests known and pursue them either individually or collectively. It is vital too that companies ensure that their rights of free and fair competition are upheld. It will, therefore, be incumbent on companies and their legal advisors to keep abreast of legal developments in the Community and to file protests and complaints where abuse is detected.

Questions
1.   This extract insists on the need for a 'political strategy'. To what extent is the increasing *power* of the Community authorities matched by increased *responsibility* (e.g., to electors)? How, if at all, would you like to see the institutional framework of the Community adjusted in order to improve democratic accountability for the decisions which are presently being taken in relation to the advancement of the Community?
2.   The Community is firmly on the national political agenda in a way which would have seemed scarcely credible 20 years ago. As an advertising campaign slogan, '1992' proved a remarkable success.

As a mobilising theme, as an impulse for innovation and restructuring, as a justification and sometimes as an alibi for unpopular decisions, the myth of 1992 has had a deep influence which we have every reason to be satisfied with and must congratulate those who conceived it. (Mertens de Wilmars [1989/1] LIEI 1 (Editorial))

Who do you think make up the 'we' who have every reason to be satisfied?

(C) FREE MOVEMENT OF PERSONS WITHIN AN AREA OF FREEDOM, SECURITY AND JUSTICE

Article 14 EC's insistence on the removal of internal frontiers within the Community at the end of 1992 suggested that date as a 'Big Bang' in the historical evolution of the Community. For consumers, there was certainly a very specific advantage to be enjoyed at the turn of the year 1992. It became possible to buy goods for private consumption in another Member State and to return home with those goods without the need to pay any duties to the home State. However, frontier controls did not vanish at the end of 1992. '1992' – Article 14 EC – is not legally unambiguous.

In December 1992, the European Council meeting in Edinburgh concluded that:

The European Council has had to take note of the fact that free movement of persons within the Community, in accordance with Article 8a of the Treaty of Rome [converted with amendment at Amsterdam into Article 14 EC], cannot be completely assured on 1 January 1993. The work necessary to achieve this result without creating dangers for public security and compromising the fight against illegal immigration, although having progressed, is still under way. Further progress is needed in particular to complete the ratification process of the Dublin Asylum Convention, to conclude the External Frontiers Convention and to complete negotiations on a Convention on the European Information System.

The view of the European Council is constitutionally not the final word within the EC system. The authoritative source of interpretation of EC law is the European Court. In 1999, the European Court finally had the opportunity to rule on the point. In Case C-378/97 *Florius Ariel Wijsenbeek*, judgment of 21 September 1999, decided in the light of the law of the post-Maastricht, pre-Amsterdam period, the Court accepted that a Member State was entitled to require a person crossing an internal EU frontier to establish his or her nationality. The expiry of the 1992 deadline had not altered this. Article 14 EC has no automatic effect. The Court referred to the need for, and absence of, common rules governing, in particular, the crossing of the external frontiers of the EU as a precondition to elimination of internal frontiers. The Treaty provisions on European Citizenship (Article 18 EC, p. 343 below) were also considered insufficient to deprive the Member States of the legal right to perform border checks.

The 'flanking measures', the adoption of which the European Council in 1992 regarded as necessary preconditions for securing the free movement of persons in accordance with what is now Article 14, were not envisaged as creatures of the EC legal order. They were primarily the province of cooperation between the Member States in Justice in Home Affairs, the 'third pillar' of the EU created at Maastricht (p. 13 above). However, negligible progress was made in agreeing flanking measures outwith the EC structure.

The Treaty of Amsterdam alters the structure by substantially re-working the provisions governing the free movement of persons, in particular by modifying relevant material from the 'third pillar' created at Maastricht (Justice and Home Affairs, p. 13 above) and transferring it to the first, EC, pillar. The EC Treaty post-Amsterdam contains a Title on 'Visas, asylum, immigration and other policies related to free movement of persons' which is dedicated to the progressive establishment of 'an area of freedom, security and justice'. This is Title IV, and comprises Articles 61–69 EC. As already suggested at p. 30 above, this 'communitiarization' suggests that Amsterdam saw a triumph of EC institutional and constitutional method over the species of intergovernmentalism found in the non-EC EU, although the validity of that observation must be judged after an inspection of the relevant provisions, which display some characteristics which are, at least, unorthodox in EC practice. The following is the text of the Title, which deserves careful reading.

Title IV
Visas, Asylum, Immigration and Other Policies Related to Free Movement of Persons

Article 61
In order to establish progressively an area of freedom, security and justice, the Council shall adopt:

(a)   within a period of five years after the entry into force of the Treaty of Amsterdam, measures aimed at ensuring the free movement of persons in accordance with Article 14, in conjunction with directly related flanking measures with respect to external border controls, asylum and immigration, in accordance with the provisions of Article 62(2) and (3) and Article 63(1)(a) and (2)(a), and measures to prevent and combat crime in accordance with the provisions of Article 31(e) of the Treaty on European Union;

(b)   other measures in the fields of asylum, immigration and safeguarding the rights of nationals of third countries, in accordance with the provisions of Article 63;

(c)   measures in the field of judicial cooperation in civil matters as provided for in Article 65;

(d)   appropriate measures to encourage and strengthen administrative cooperation, as provided for in Article 66;

(e)   measures in the field of police and judicial cooperation in criminal matters aimed at a high level of security by preventing and combating crime within the Union in accordance with the provisions of the Treaty on European Union.

Article 62

The Council, acting in accordance with the procedure referred to in Article 67, shall, within a period of five years after the entry into force of the Treaty of Amsterdam, adopt:

(1)   measures with a view to ensuring, in compliance with Article 14, the absence of any controls on persons, be they citizens of the Union or nationals of third countries, when crossing internal borders;

(2)   measures on the crossing of the external borders of the Member States which shall establish:

(a)   standards and procedures to be followed by Member States in carrying out checks on persons at such borders;

(b)   rules on visas for intended stays of no more than three months, including:

(i)   the list of third countries whose nationals must be in possession of visas when crossing the external borders and those whose nationals are exempt from that requirement;

(ii)   the procedures and conditions for issuing visas by Member States;

(iii)   a uniform format for visas;

(iv)   rules on a uniform visa;

(3)   measures setting out the conditions under which nationals of third countries shall have the freedom to travel within the territory of the Member States during a period of no more than three months.

Article 63

The Council, acting in accordance with the procedure referred to in Article 67, shall, within a period of five years after the entry into force of the Treaty of Amsterdam, adopt:

(1)   measures on asylum, in accordance with the Geneva Convention of 28 July 1951 and the Protocol of 31 January 1967 relating to the status of refugees and other relevant treaties, within the following areas:

(a)   criteria and mechanisms for determining which Member State is responsible for considering an application for asylum submitted by a national of a third country in one of the Member States,

(b)   minimum standards on the reception of asylum seekers in Member States,

(c)   minimum standards with respect to the qualification of nationals of third countries as refugees,

(d)   minimum standards on procedures in Member States for granting or withdrawing refugee status;

(2)   measures on refugees and displaced persons within the following areas:

(a)   minimum standards for giving temporary protection to displaced persons from third countries who cannot return to their country of origin and for persons who otherwise need international protection,

(b)   promoting a balance of effort between Member States in receiving and bearing the consequences of receiving refugees and displaced persons;

(3)   measures on immigration policy within the following areas:

(a)   conditions of entry and residence, and standards on procedures for the issue by Member States of long term visas and residence permits, including those for the purpose of family reunion,

(b)   illegal immigration and illegal residence, including repatriation of illegal residents;

(4)   measures defining the rights and conditions under which nationals of third countries who are legally resident in a Member State may reside in other Member States. Measures adopted by the Council pursuant to points 3 and 4 shall not prevent any Member State from maintaining or introducing in the areas concerned national provisions which are compatible with this Treaty and with international agreements.

Measures to be adopted pursuant to points 2(b), 3(a) and 4 shall not be subject to the five year period referred to above.

Article 64

1.   This Title shall not affect the exercise of the responsibilities incumbent upon Member States with regard to the maintenance of law and order and the safeguarding of internal security.

2.   In the event of one or more Member States being confronted with an emergency situation characterised by a sudden inflow of nationals of third countries and without prejudice to paragraph 1, the Council may, acting by qualified majority on a proposal from the Commission, adopt provisional measures of a duration not exceeding six months for the benefit of the Member States concerned.

Article 65

Measures in the field of judicial cooperation in civil matters having cross-border implications, to be taken in accordance with Article 67 and insofar as necessary for the proper functioning of the internal market, shall include:

(a)   improving and simplifying:
- the system for cross-border service of judicial and extrajudicial documents;
- cooperation in the taking of evidence;
- the recognition and enforcement of decisions in civil and commercial cases, including decisions in extrajudicial cases;

(b)   promoting the compatibility of the rules applicable in the Member States concerning the conflict of laws and of jurisdiction;

(c)   eliminating obstacles to the good functioning of civil proceedings, if necessary by promoting the compatibility of the rules on civil procedure applicable in the Member States.

Article 66

The Council, acting in accordance with the procedure referred to in Article 67, shall take measures to ensure cooperation between the relevant departments of the administrations of the Member States in the areas covered by this Title, as well as between those departments and the Commission.

Article 67

1.   During a transitional period of five years following the entry into force of the Treaty of Amsterdam, the Council shall act unanimously on a proposal from the Commission or on the initiative of a Member State and after consulting the European Parliament.

2.   After this period of five years:
   - the Council shall act on proposals from the Commission; the Commission shall examine any request made by a Member State that it submit a proposal to the Council;
   - the Council, acting unanimously after consulting the European Parliament, shall take a decision with a view to providing for all or parts of the areas covered by this Title to be governed by the procedure referred to in Article 251 and adapting the provisions relating to the powers of the Court of Justice.

3.   By derogation from paragraphs 1 and 2:
   - measures referred to in Article 62(2)(b) (i) and (iii) shall, from the entry into force of the Treaty of Amsterdam, be adopted by the Council acting by a qualified majority on a proposal from the Commission and after consulting the European Parliament;
   - measures referred to in Article 62(2)(b) (ii) and (iv) shall, after a period of five years following the entry into force of the Treaty of Amsterdam, be adopted by the Council acting in accordance with the procedure referred to in Article 251.

Article 68

1.   Article 234 [see Chapter 4 of this book] shall apply to this Title under the following circumstances and conditions: where a question on the interpretation of this Title or on the validity or interpretation of acts of the institutions of the Community based on this Title is raised in a case pending before a court or a tribunal of a Member State against whose decisions there is no judicial remedy under national law, that court or tribunal shall, if it considers that a decision on the question is necessary to enable it to give judgment, request the Court of Justice to give a ruling thereon.

2.   In any event, the Court of Justice shall not have jurisdiction to rule on any measure or decision taken pursuant to Article 62(1) relating to the maintenance of law and order and the safeguarding of internal security.

3.   The Council, the Commission or a Member State may request the Court of Justice to give a ruling on a question of interpretation of this Title or of acts of the institutions of the Community based on this Title. The ruling given by the Court of Justice in response to such a request shall not apply to judgments of courts or tribunals of the Member States which have become res judicata.

Article 69

The application of this Title shall be subject to the provisions of the Protocol on the position of the United Kingdom and Ireland and to the Protocol on the Position of Denmark and without Prejudice to the Protocol on the application of certain aspects of Article 14 of the Treaty establishing the European Community to the United Kingdom and to Ireland.

Question

Assess the competing weight of the *advantages* of these provisions in moving beyond the Mastricht Treaty by establishing a fuller and time-limited framework within the EC 'pillar' for achieving the free movement of persons within an area of freedom, security and justice, and their *disadvantages* in the shape of what may be regarded as regression from standard EC method in, e.g., Articles 67(2) and 68. Are these prices worth paying for (imperfect) commu-nitiarization?

Article 68 EC deserves your close attention, in particular its second paragraph. If the Court of Justice is denied jurisdiction over such Council acts, how *is* supervision to be achieved? Is Article 68(2) EC consistent with the rule of law?

Aspects of this debate will also be encountered in Chapters 9 and 10 of this book, which deal with the wider sweep of the law relating to persons, but you may be assisted by the insights offered by the following extract, written before the Amsterdam Treaty entered into force. It also serves to elucidate the nature of the Protocols mentioned in Article 69 EC, which, in different ways, exclude the UK, Ireland and Denmark from the full impact of this new Title. Here is a form of 'flexible' integration (see further p. 625); here is a further price to be paid for the progress towards open borders achieved at Amster-dam via communtiarization of 'third pillar' and Schengen material.

Monica den Boer, 'Justice and Home Affairs Cooperation in the Treaty on European Union: More Complexity Despite Communautarization' (1997) 4 *Maastricht Journal of European and Comparative Law* 310, pp. 311–15

1. A New Title: 'Free Movement of Persons, Asylum and Immigration'

. . . Even if the Member States succeed in the progressive establishment of the Free Movement of Persons Area [according to the 5-year deadline envisaged by Article 62, which falls on 1 May 2004], free movement will not apply integrally to the whole EU. Exceptions to the abolition of internal border controls are made for the United Kingdom and Ireland. By means of Protocol Y, the UK and Ireland have not only secured the maintenance of their border controls, but also the unscathed continuation of their 'Common Travel Area'. This solution is also seen as beneficial for Spain, because a solution to the dispute concerning the status of Gibraltar does not need to be found immediately. A special protocol for Denmark has been designed to overcome (expected) domestic constitutional difficulties, which are anticipated following the rejection of the Maastricht Treaty in the first referendum. This protocol stipulates Denmark's position regarding the free movement of persons and non-participation in the drawing up and implementation of decisions with defence implications (but without preventing cooperation by other Member States in this field). According to chief negotiator Patijn, this is a 'special' position, with a sort of 'legal opt-out' and a 'political opt-in'. . . .

Furthermore, there is a protocol on the external relations of the Member States with regard to the crossing of external borders. The Member States can negotiate or conclude agreements with third countries as long as they respect Community Law and other relevant international agreements. Deeper, or more intensive cooperation, between Member States and third states can thus be pursued. One might wonder whether the protocol should be seen as a pretext for a different set of security standards and arrangements at the external border of the EU.

The new Title reveals a much clearer emphasis on flanking measures. This becomes apparent from an amendment to Article [62] (see also Article [61(a)]), which rules that the free movement of persons is to be assured in conjunction with appropriate measures with respect to external border controls, immigration, asylum and the prevention and combating of crime. This 'twin-arrangement' has led to the creation of one Title, which comprises both the measures that should encourage free movement of persons as well as the flanking measures that should guarantee the security of citizens who live in Europe. Hence, this area is entitled 'An Area of Freedom, Security and Justice'. The emphasis on security becomes more than obvious from the French insistence on a declaration that the level of security within the New Area should remain the same as in Schengen, which implies that Member States who fear that their internal security is at stake, can reintroduce internal border controls (Article 2A Schengen Implementing Agreement), similar to what France has done with its northern borders with Belgium and Luxembourg. The Amsterdam Treaty does not explicitly state the criteria for what constitutes a real threat to the internal security of Member States. In this regard, Article [64] of the new Title reasserts the sovereignty of the individual Member States in the maintenance of law and order and the safeguarding of internal security. The Council can decide by qualified majority (on a proposal from the Commission) to 'adopt provisional measures of a duration not exceeding six months for the benefit of the Member States concerned.' Such a rule would become operational in the event of an emergency situation characterized by a sudden inflow of third country nationals (old Article 100C (2)).

Germany, with its major intake of asylum seekers, won a case by insisting that the unanimity rule will not automatically change into a qualified majority decision-making process once the five years have passed (Article [67]). The application of qualified majority voting will not only be subject to an evaluation but also to a unanimous decision of the Council whether or not to actually introduce this new method. The much heralded extension of Community competence therefore only seems to be 'apparent'. However, the right of initiative, which during the initial five years will be shared between the Member States and the Commission, will be exclusively for the Commission.

The protocol on asylum for nationals of EU Member States is a blow in the face of human rights organizations across Europe. Spain had wanted a total suppression of that right, following the refusal by Belgium to extradite suspected ETA terrorists. To a certain extent the Spanish wish has been diluted because the final protocol lists certain conditions under which an application made by a national of a Member State may be taken into consideration or declared admissible. The protocol starts from the presumption that all EU Member States are safe countries. Apparently, the Dutch Presidency proposed amending a passage and adding a declaration which stipulates that the Protocol would be interpreted in accordance with the provisions of the 1951 Geneva Convention and the 1967 New York protocol. The latest draft reveals that only Belgium has made a declaration to this extent. Other EU Member States should follow this example.

The communautarization of immigration, asylum, external borders and legal cooperation in civil matters enhances the role of the institutions more generally. The European Parliament has to be consulted prior to the taking of initiatives. The role of the Court of Justice is expanded (Article [68]): if there is no remedy under national law, the Court may be requested to give a ruling, but it can only be asked to do so by the highest judicial authorities in the Member States. Its position is strengthened as the Commission is enabled to question certain practices.

2. The Incorporation of Schengen into the New Treaty

The Protocol which integrates the Schengen *Acquis* into the framework of the European Union requires that not only the two Schengen Conventions (1985 and 1990), but also all the decisions of the Executive Committee (about 200 mostly unpublished decisions), should be incorporated into the New Treaty. The Schengen Implementing Convention states that all rules should be compatible with Community law, which calls into question whether all the decisions by the Executive Committee are also in line with Community law.

The consequence of the incorporation of Schengen is that the *Acquis* will be separated between the already existing *acquis communautaire*, the new Title (see above) and the remaining Third Pillar. Some parts of Schengen had already been encapsulated by Community directives (firearms, money laundering). Rules and regulations that relate to visa, immigration and asylum will be moved to the new Title, while provisions providing for cross-border police competencies and mutual legal assistance in criminal matters will be moved to the Third Pillar.

The Summit invited the Council to take appropriate measures as quickly as possible to ensure, as soon as the Treaty enters into force, 'the adoption of certain implementing measures relating to the protocol incorporating the Schengen *Acquis* into the Treaty and the integration of the Schengen Secretariat into the Council's General Secretariat.' The Dutch Presidency was determined to guarantee more institutional coherence.

Protocols are apparently again the price to pay for progress. The UK, Ireland and Denmark negotiated special protocols. The first two countries are allowed to opt into certain Schengen clauses, which, as already has been said, is a form of differentiated integration (Article C of the Schengen Protocol allows the UK and Ireland to request 'at any time' participation in some or all of the provisions of the Schengen *Acquis*). This creates a situation in which the UK can maintain its border controls and deny citizens the freedom to travel, and at the same time take part in compensatory security arrangements, such as the Schengen Information System. The balance between the two constituents seems to have got lost in the negotiation process.

The positive side of the integration of Schengen into the TEU is that we get rid of a complex multi-tiered integration. While we lose this kind of flexibility, we will have it back in another form however. There may also be considerable confusion at implementation level. Another risk is the (indirect) contamination effect Schengen rules have on Community legislation, as they are mostly negotiated behind closed doors can with little or no participation of the EC institutions. This contamination effect may be countered by the formal adoption rules that apply to the Schengen provisions before they they are transformed into Community rules.

3. The New Third Pillar: Provisions on Police and Judicial Co-operation

The new Article K [which, on re-numbering, has become Title VI TEU comprising Articles 29–45 TEU (see p. 29 above)] comprises fewer matters of common interest than its predecessor, but its provisions should be interpreted as a prelude to intensified cooperation between police forces, customs authorities and other competent authorities (Article [29]). The latter, rather open-ended, formulation possibly opens the door to wider participation of the Secret Intelligence Services which may imply less transparency. The deepening of police cooperation finds its basis in a number of new provisions, the most spectacular of which are the possibility for operational cooperation between competent authorities (Article [30(1)]; the executive cross-border police competencies from the Schengen Implementing Agreement will most likely be inserted into this Article), and the assignment of operative powers to Europol and joint task forces (respectively Article [30(2)(a) and (b)]). Apparently, the negotiations on the strengthening of Europol's powers were quite arduous. Although politicians have often said that they absolutely do not want executive powers to be assigned to Europol liaison officers, the door has been set ajar for a truly executive European police agency. This gives rise to concern, certainly when read in conjunction with the protocol that assigns immunity to Europol liaison officers. The liaison officers will be subject to fifteen different regimes given the fact that they and their activities will be under the judicial review of the competent national authorities only. Even if these liaison officers have no operational competencies, their role in international intelligence-gathering can be decisive for court cases against criminal organizations.

The Third Pillar also introduces two new legal instruments, namely decisions and framework decisions, both of which have a binding character (Article [34(2)(b) and (c)]). Although this implies more distancing from the legal instruments that were originally introduced under the umbrella of European Political Cooperation, considerable vagueness remains about what is to happen to the old battery of 'grey' legal instruments (conclusions, recommendations, resolutions and declarations), and about how the Third Pillar *Acquis* is to be transferred to the new Title.

The revamped Third Pillar assigns a larger role to the European Parliament and the Court of Justice. The European Parliament (Article [39 EU]) will now be consulted by the Council before the adoption of a new legal instrument (with the exception of common positions). The EP has to deliver an opinion within three months or less if so laid down by the Council. It is also significant that the EP will have more to say about the Third Pillar budget in its competence as budget control authority (administrative and in most cases also operational expenditure will be charged to the budget of the EC; Article [41]). The competence of the European Court of Justice (Article [35]) has been widened to more legal instruments, as it can now also give preliminary rulings on the validity and interpretation of decisions and framework decisions (and, of course, Third Pillar conventions). The whole matter will be arranged by means of opt-in declarations (Article [35(3): declarations made by Member States pursuant to Article 35 EU at the date of entry into force of the Amsterdam Treaty, 1 May 1999, are recorded at OJ 1999 C120/24]), which has become practice with the Europol Convention. There is a considerable danger that this condition has an in-built capacity to excavate any competence that the Court may exercise. With regard to some of its other competencies it is important to note an exemption applies, namely that the Court will not be allowed to review the validity or proportionality of operations carried out by the police or other law enforcement agencies (Article [35(5)]). Hence, official judgments on international policing activities will remain a matter for the national courts and the European Court of Human Rights.

Progress under the Third Pillar has been rather slow as a consequence of the unanimous voting system and the arduous ratification procedures in the Member States. The only Convention – which actually predates Maastricht – which is ready for entry into force per 1 September 1997, is the Dublin Asylum Convention. The IGC has come up with a trick to accelerate the implementation of Conventions. Article [34(2)(d)] allows entry into force of a convention once it has been adopted by at least half of the Member States unless conventions provide otherwise: 'rolling ratification'. Interestingly though, the Dutch and the English version of the Treaty differ on the question whether or not ratification by half of the Member States implies that the Convention enters into force in all Member States.

And then there is Article [40], which authorizes Member States to make use of institutions, procedures and mechanisms of the Community if they want to establish closer cooperation [see p. 635 below]. Article [40] . . . is interspersed with all kinds of 'ifs' and 'buts'. The Justice and Home Affairs Council may, for instance, refer authorisation to the General Council if one Member State opposes the closer cooperation on the basis of a qualified majority vote. What scenario did the negotiators have in mind when they inserted this condition into the text? . . .

Note
The possibility that the UK might seek to join parts of the cooperation from which the Protocol to the Amsterdam Treaty allows it to stand aside is mentioned in this extract by den Boer. This has been the subject of subsequent negotiation and seems likely to occur. For discussion of the implications, see the Report of the House of Lords Select Committee on the European Union, HL 34, 1999–2000.

Further reading
Peers, S., 'Who's judging the watchmen? The judicial system of the area of freedom, security and justice' (1998) 18 YEL 337.
Wagner, E., 'The Integration of Schengen into the Framework of the EU' [1998/2] LIEI 1.
See also essays by O'Keeffe, D., Hedemann-Robinson, M., den Boer, M., Hervey, T. and Twomey P., in O'Keeffe, D. and Twomey, P., *Legal Issues of the Amsterdam Treaty* (Hart Publishing, 1999).

(D) MANAGING THE INTERNAL MARKET

The end of 1992 plainly had major significance for the Commission, but it signified a shift in its internal market strategy rather than a termination of it. It was true that most of the major measures had been prepared by the Commission and agreed by the Member States by the end of 1992 (although some matters remained outstanding, not least those concerning persons), but there then arose questions of monitoring compliance. The summary at p. 187 above highlights the central role of proper application of the rules of the internal market in ensuring full realisation of its economic advantages. The Commission produces an annual report on the monitoring of the application of Community law, which provides information on, *inter alia*, the progress of implementation of Directives. These reports have typically told of an accelerating pace of implementation by the Member States up to and beyond the '1992' deadline (e.g., COM (98) 317, COM (99) 301), but there remain many gaps between Community law on paper and Community law in practice.

The reports contain 'league tables' which reveal in percentage terms the success of each Member State in complying with its obligation to notify its transposition measures to the Commission. In order to sharpen this statistical spur to the Member States to respond to the obligations agreed in Directives, the Commission established a 'Single Market Scoreboard' in 1997. This is available, and is regularly up-dated, on the website of the Directorate-General which deals with internal market matters. Enter via http://europa.eu.int; the site also carries a great deal of up-to-date information on broader policy direction. The first published scoreboard revealed that on 1 November 1997, over 25% of internal market Directives were not implemented in all Member States. Particular problem areas were the transport and public procurement sectors, where over 50% of Directives were unimplemented in one or more States. The data available in November 1999, set out below, suggest steady improvement.

Single Market Scoreboard

. . . Progress in implementation of Internal Market Directives, 1997–99 Percentage of Directives overdue at 15 November 1999

	B	DK	D	EL	E	F	IRL	I	L	NL	A	P	FIN	S	UK	EU
Nov. 1999	3.5	1.3	2.9	6.2	2.2	5.6	4.4	3.9	5.7	2.8	3.7	4.9	1.7	2.1	2.8	12.6
Nov. 1998	5.2	1.5	2.7	5.2	2.7	5.5	5.8	5.7	6.2	3.8	4.2	5.6	0.9	1.5	2.1	14.9
Nov. 1997	8.5	3.2	8.5	7.5	4.7	7.4	5.4	7.6	6.5	4.6	10.1	5.9	4.3	6.2	3.5	26.7

Some 40% of Directives whose deadline for implementation expired in 1997 have still not been fully implemented by all Member States. For 1998 the figure rises to 78% and for those due for implementation before 15 November 1999, it is 95.7%. The slow implementation of recent legislation remains a source of concern because it fragments the Internal Market and delays economic reform. Measures adjusting rules to take account of technological developments and new provisions to improve consumer protection or protect the environment cannot take full effect if not implemented in all Member States.

Note

The dynamic nature of the process of market-building and market-management, which makes enduring demands of the Commission's capacities, is captured in the next extract, taken from a major survey of the evolving political and legal implications of a 'post-1992' Community.

K. Armstrong and S. Bulmer, *The Governance of the Single European Market* (1998), pp. 307–308

In procedural terms there are serious concerns about the 'holy trinity' of transposition, enforcement and redress. Although the Commission report states that the transposition rate for the White Paper measures was on average 90 per cent for the EU-15, it notes that 'fifty-six per cent . . . have been transposed in *every* Member State' ([COM (96) 520]). That yields a rather different picture and one which is arguably more pertinent to those firms conducting business across the SEM. The comparability of enabling legislation also remains a concern. Enforcement is more complex still because the relevant agencies may be national, regional or local, thus making it extremely difficult to monitor the impact of the SEM 'on the ground' to ensure equivalence across the EU. The Commission's resources simply do not permit sufficient oversight of this dimension . . . . Finally, the ability of private parties to secure redress through the courts is complex and variable because of differences in national legal systems.

A final issue worthy of mention here concerns over-zealous regulation: where national transposition introduces costs over and above those necessitated by the relevant EC Directive. This phenomenon, known in the UK as 'gold-plating', lies behind the recent emphasis in SEM policy on reducing the regulatory burden . . .

Despite the legislation to open up public procurement in the utilities . . ., the results in this area of activity have been much more limited. Although a major area of economic activity – 11.5 per cent of EU GDP in 1994 – the achievements have been limited, with only 10 per cent import penetration of import markets. A major explanation for this situation is 'the substantial delay in incorporating the 11 procurement Directives into national legislation and enforcing them effectively' ([COM (96) 520]). The 1996 Florence European Council underlined the importance of accelerating national transposition in this area. Finally, it is worth mentioning that the general impact of the single market upon small and medium-sized enterprises has been rather limited.

The Commission is aware that it requires a more sophisticated strategy than mere publication of figures and establishment of timetables. In order to foster a 'compliance culture' among the Member States, it has placed increasing emphasis on administrative cooperation as a basis for managing the internal market. The following extract places vigilance in securing application of existing rules alongside administrative cooperation as devices for ensuring the internal market includes credible methods for practical problem-solving.

The Commission's Twelfth Annual Report on Monitoring the Application of Community Law, 1994
(1995) OJ C254, COM (95) 500, pp. 10–11

. . . the Commission prepared a report for the Council meeting on 8 December 1994 that gives an indication of the state of play of national transposition of the [1985] White Paper measures and other legislation that is critical for the functioning of the internal market. . . .

A large proportion of infringements are the result of failure to incorporate Community directives into national law within the time limits set. Procedural problems related to the national decision-making process or the technical complexity of the texts are often the reason for the delays. To remedy this situation the Commission carries out systematic examination of the application of the directives which have entered into force. It will continue to assess the national legislation notified to it, as far as its resources allow, and will vigorously pursue infringements both through consultation with Member States concerned and, when necessary, informal infringement proceedings.

The Sutherland report [1992] and the Strategic Programme ['Making the Most of the Internal Market', 1993] identified administrative cooperation as a key factor in the operation of the single market. The removal of barriers between Member States gives rise to a new situation in which Community law, and the way in which it is applied in other Member States, takes on greater importance for individuals and business in the Union. They need to feel confident that administration of the law is as reliable and effective as it is for their own national regulations. So it is essential that the authorities responsible for enforcing internal market measures maintain a high degree of cooperation and that they keep each other informed. Administrative cooperation is already working well in many areas (such as veterinary and plant health controls, pharmaceuticals, foodstuffs, customs and indirect taxation), but completion of the internal market requires a thorough study of the way it works in all areas.

With this in mind, in 1993 the Commission initiated a programme to promote administrative cooperation. In February 1994 it sent the Council and Parliament a communication setting out a framework for this exercise. The Council, in response, adopted a resolution in June calling on the Commission to continue its programme of discussions with representatives of the Member States to identify needs in different areas and sectors. The resolution also called on the Member States to notify to the Commission contact points for mutual assistance on enforcement matters by the end of 1994. This subject has been regularly discussed in the Advisory Committee for Coordination in the Internal Market Field.

The existing schemes for exchanges of officials between Member States, such as the Karolus programme and the Matthaeus programme for customs officials, are a way of helping national officials become accustomed to the procedures and ways of thinking of other Member States. They form part of the support measures provided by the Commission for administrative cooperation. These programmes will continue to be applied to help create confidence between the administrations of Member States.

Note

It is plain from this extract that the evolution of the internal market is properly regarded as a process which is continuing long after the end of 1992. The Commission, energised by Mario Monti, the Commissioner who held responsibility for the internal market until 1999, prepared an *Action Plan for the Single Market*, which was published in June 1997. It was submitted to the European Council in Amsterdam in that month, where it was firmly endorsed as a basis for renewed effort to eliminate remaining obstacles to realisation of the full benefits of the single market programme. The *Action Plan* picked out four priority areas ripe for action designed to improve the functioning of the internal market.

Action Plan for the Single Market
Communication of the Commission to the European Council, CSE(97)1, final, 4 June 1997

Why an Action Plan now?

The European Single Market is the world's largest domestic market. It has contributed significantly to growth, competitiveness and employment. It has been responsible for an increase in EU income of between 1.1% and 1.5% and for the creation of between 300.000 and 900.000 jobs. But its full potential has not yet been realised. Barriers still remain. Europe needs a better Single Market for more growth, more innovation and more jobs; a market that works for everyone – citizens, consumers, small companies and larger business; a market that contributes to a balanced development of the economy in all regions of the EU and the European Economic Area; a dynamic, knowledge-based market, socially responsible and sensitive to the concerns of everyone affected by it. A properly functioning Single Market will help to ensure a transition to the single currency in the most favourable conditions and will contribute to a successful enlargement. The Commission's 1996 Report on the Impact and Effectiveness of the Single Market has received a very wide degree of support from Member States. The political will is evident. This needs to be translated into targeted action.

The Single Market is not simply an economic structure. At its heart are 370 million people seeking better employment opportunities, improved living and working conditions, and a wider choice of quality products and services – including access for everyone to services of general interest – at lower prices. The Single Market is working in their interests. Much has already been achieved. Individuals already enjoy the right to move and work throughout the Union. The Single Market sets basic standards of health and safety, equal opportunities and labour law. However, more needs to be done to enforce these rights effectively. In addition, social policy must help smooth the process of change, promoting a new interplay between flexibility and security, for example through appropriate information and consultation and an increased contribution from the social partners. The European employment strategy, agreed at the Dublin European Council, underpinned by the Commission's Confidence Pact for Employment, will help to give people the opportunity to upgrade and improve their skills. Similarly, the Commission will work with Member States to help modernise social protection systems and make them more employment-friendly. The Single Market must also continue to contribute to greater convergence and cohesion in favour of Member States on the Community's periphery, backed up by continuous monitoring and, where necessary, by appropriate Community support. Further efforts need to be made to ensure coherence between Single Market and other policies.

The Single Market stands or falls on confidence: confidence that all the key rules are in place; that they are fully and fairly applied; that problems will be addressed quickly; that the ground-rules for fair competition are fully respected; confidence for consumers in the reliability of goods and services and of information; confidence for smaller companies, the employment generators, that the market can work for them; confidence that each and every government is committed to making it work. Doing business, moving, living or working in the Union's 'area without internal frontiers' should become as easy as within any Member State.

The Action Plan announced in the conclusions of the Dublin European Council has the clear objective of improving the performance of the Single Market in the years ahead. The third stage of EMU represents a critical juncture. The Single Market will provide underlying economic support for Monetary Union and the euro will provide added value and efficiency to the Single Market. The actions proposed are ambitious. It will take considerable political will to carry them through. Time is short. But if we succeed, Europe will have a Single Market capable of generating more growth and more jobs, while safeguarding and developing the European social model.

The Commission will regularly publish and draw to the attention of each Internal Market Council and European Council a 'Single Market Scoreboard' containing detailed indicators of the state of the Single Market and of Member States' level of commitment to implementing the Action Plan.

Four Strategic Targets
The Action Plan follows the Commission's report on the Impact and Effectiveness of the Single Market. It sets priorities to give a clear and strategic vision of what is now needed. Four *Strategic Targets* have been set. They are of equal importance and must be pursued in parallel:

1. **Making the rules more effective:** The Single Market is based on confidence. Proper enforcement of common rules is the only way to achieve this goal. Simplification of rules at Community and national level is also essential to reduce the burden on business and create more jobs.

2. **Dealing with key market distortions:** There is general agreement that tax barriers and anti-competitive behaviour constitute distortions that need to be tackled.

3. **Removing sectoral obstacles to market integration:** The Single Market will only deliver its full potential if barriers that remain – and, of course, any new ones that emerge – are removed. This may require legislative action to fill gaps in the Single Market framework, but it also calls for a significant change in national administrations' attitudes towards the Single Market.

4. **Delivering a Single Market for the benefit of all citizens:** The Single Market generates employment, increases personal freedom and benefits consumers, while ensuring high levels of both health and safety and environmental protection. But further steps are needed, including steps to enhance the social dimension of the Single Market. And to enjoy their Single Market rights to the full, citizens must be aware of them and be able to obtain speedy redress.

. . .

Within the first Strategic Target, 'Making the Rules More Effective', the Commision offers the following observations on the need to establish a framework for enforcement and problem-solving:

The primary responsibility for enforcing Single Market rules rests with the Member States. The Single Market will not operate effectively unless they ensure that the rules are fully respected by all concerned. Those who breach the rules should be subject to penalties under national law that are effective and proportionate and that act as a deterrent. Problems also need to be sorted out quickly in today's Single Market to avoid undermining the confidence of business and consumers. The informal arrangements for cooperation on enforcement and problem solving between Member States, and between them and the Commission, have proved only partly successful and now need to be upgraded. The Commission will therefore press each Member State to designate a coordination centre within its administration responsible for ensuring that problems raised by other Member States or the Commission are solved by the national or regional authorities directly concerned within strict deadlines. Easily identifiable contact points must also be designated in national administrations to which citizens and businesses can address any Single Market problems. These coordination centres and contact points will be key components in a simple but effective framework for enforcement cooperation and problem solving. It will provide for more transparency about enforcement structures and peer review or mutual audit of national enforcement. Telematic links between enforcement authorities will be further developed under the second IDA programme. If necessary, the Commission will submit serious cases of non-application to the Internal Market Council to allow strong commitment and involvement in problem solving to be demonstrated at political level. The Commission will accelerate the investigation of complaints from business and individuals and the treatment of infringement proceedings. For their part, Member States must respect strictly the procedures laid down for infringement proceedings and ensure, expeditiously, operational results. In cases of serious breach of Community law which gravely affect the functioning of the Single Market, the Commission should be able to take urgent action against Member States which fail in these obligations, using sanctions where necessary. Strengthening of the Commission's enforcement powers would contribute to this end and to the reduction of delays in problem solving.

Note
Lists of the 'contact points' referred to in the final paragraph of this extract as methods for facilitating problem-solving may now be accessed via the website of the Directorate-General for the internal market (enter via http://europa.eu.int). Contact Points are available for both citizens and business. The website also contains many other relevant documents. In February 1999 the Commission expressed satisfaction about the *Action Plan's* success, although realisation of all its aspirations plainly lies in the future. In November 1999 the Commission published its *Strategy for Europe's Internal Market*, designed to cover the next five years. The scope of the programme is mapped in the next extract:

European Commission, *Strategy for Europe's Internal Market* (1999), pp. 1–3

INTRODUCTION

On 5 October 1999, the Commission adopted a consultative Communication[1] in which it set out its thinking on a strategy for the Internal Market over the next five years. The Communication launched a short but highly-focused debate in the Council, Parliament and the Economic and Social Committee and among interested parties.

The response was positive. There is clearly broadly-based support for combining longer-term strategic objectives with short-term, annually reviewed, target actions. An exchange of views on the consultative communication took place at the Internal Market Council of 28 October 1999. Ministers gave a broad welcome to the proposed approach. In its resolution of 4 November[2] Parliament welcomed the proposed structure and underlined the need for a unified approach in achieving a coherent and consistent framework for legislation and non-legislative measures, while ensuring the proper involvement of the Parliament. The Single Market Observatory, a study group operating under the auspices of the Industry section of the Economic and Social Committee, considered the Communication at their meetings of 8 October and 8 November. The Commission organised a hearing on 29 October which was well-attended by representatives of industry trade unions, other non-governmental organisations and of the candidate countries.[3]

This Communication provides the Commission's strategy for the Internal Market over the next five years. It sets out four strategic objectives; the operational objectives; that flow from them and, for the first time, the (annually reviewed) target actions the Commission recommends to deliver these objectives. The target actions reflect the Commission's priorities, guided and informed by the views expressed by interested

---

[1] COM (1999) 464 final.
[2] B5-0204/1999.
[3] A full report of the hearing can be found on the Commissions website at http://europa.eu.int/comm/dg15/en/update/strategy. Other comments were received by e-mail and letter.

parties and in particular by the European Parliament and by Member States – including the current and incoming Presidents of the Council of Ministers.

The Commission invites the European Parliament, the Council, the Economic and Social Committee and all interested parties to support the proposed overall approach and in particular the four strategic objectives. The Parliament and the Council are further invited to support the implementation of the target actions and to ensure rapid adoption of the key legislative measures.

THE STRATEGY

This strategy for the Internal Market provides a coherent framework for policy development for the years 2000–2004. It sets out a longer-term strategic vision which should direct the identification of more immediate priorities for action. The overarching aim is constantly to improve the performance of the Internal Market in the years ahead for the benefit of citizens and business alike. The Commission recognises that the credibility of the Internal Market will depend on its delivering and being seen to deliver these benefits. The strategy has been conceived to reflect the characteristics of a more mature internal Market:

- the need to enhance the competitiveness of the European economy as well as to improve the quality of life of European citizens. Where the interests of business and the consumer diverge, they must be equitably reconciled. Community policies on the environment, economic and social cohesion, health and safety and consumer rights need not only to be co-ordinated with Internal Market policies but integrated into them, as required by the Treaty.
- the need to involve all stakeholders in the continuing development of the Internal Market, be they citizens or business and whatever their location and circumstances. The continuing development of the Internal Market should be at the heart of bringing the EU closer to its citizens through its impact on their daily lives, as employees, employers, consumers, pensioners, students, borrowers, savers, investors and taxpayers.
- the need to remove all unjustified barriers to the free movement of goods, services, persons and capital. The new legal framework, created by integrating national markets must function optimally, in order to maximise the benefits to consumers, citizens and business. A proper balance will be sought between legislative and non-legislative activity and between harmonisation and mutual recognition. Wherever appropriate, the Commission will support self-regulation and ensure that if achieves results in an open and transparent way.
- the need to promote comprehensive structural reform and modernisation through the microeconomic strand of the process of multilateral economic surveillance, as established by the Cardiff European Council.
- the need to monitor and review the effects of existing Internal Market measures by using and developing instruments such as the Scoreboard and the Cardiff report.[4] The Dialogue with Citizens and Business should make full use of the opportunities created by information technology to enhance inclusive and interactive policy-shaping.
- the need to provide an adequate framework to unleash the great potential for the development of the Internal Market for information and communication technologies, including e-commerce.

---

[4] The Single Market Scoreboard has proved to be a valuable monitor of legal and administrative progress. The Cardiff report provides an annual assessment of the functioning of product and capital markets.

- the need to prepare for the next enlargement of the Union. The accession of ten or more countries represents a major challenge to both current and future Member States. The operation of the existing rules needs to be improved and the candidate countries associated as soon as possible in their practical application.
- the need to look beyond the borders of the Union, The internet and e-commerce offer even the smallest of companies the opportunity to trade globally. The Union's experience in creating its Internal Market provides extensive experience on which discussions with its main trading partners can be based.

Finally, reference should be made to the separate but related Union objective of creating the area of Freedom, Security and Justice. The Treaty of Amsterdam offers new possibilities to ensure that the freedoms derived, from the Internal Market can be enjoyed in conditions of security and justice accessible to all. The European Council in Tampere highlighted the importance of the link between this objective and the concerns of citizens in their daily lives. It is clear that progress towards creating the area of Freedom, Security and Justice (for example, in relation to legal aid) will be an important element in the wider background against which this strategy is developed.

STRATEGIC OBJECTIVES

Four *strategic objectives* have been identified. They are:

- to improve the quality of life of citizens
- enhance the efficiency of Community product and capital markets
- to improve the business environment
- to exploit the achievements of the Internal Market in a changing world

These strategic objectives provide a frame of reference for policy development. They are not mutually exclusive but overlap and are complementary. Progress in achieving them must be assessed. The Commission will identify quantitative and qualitative indicators. Sectoral policy frameworks (some, such as public procurement and the Financial Services Action Plan[5] are already in place) are part of this wider policy picture.

OPERATIONAL OBJECTIVES

A series of *operational objectives* has also been defined. Each covers a particular policy dimension that contributes to the achievement of one or more strategic objectives. The operational objectives will provide the benchmark against which progress can be judged.

TARGET ACTIONS

Within the strategic and operational objectives, short-term priorities are identified as *target actions*. These have been precisely described in order to provide a measurable outcome. They encompass initiatives and actions both at Community and national level. In order to ensure continuity from one year to another target actions have been established with an 18-month horizon. Some will not be achieved by the first review in the May 2000 Internal Market Council, but identifying such targets will enable crucial preparatory work to begin by the successive Presidencies of the Council and by the Commission itself thereby optimising the possibility of achieving them in the

---

[5] See COM (1999) 232, 'Financial Services: implementing the framework for financial markets Action Plan', 11.05.1999.

course of the next year. However neither the selection of the target actions nor the accompanying deadlines prejudges the political priority to be attached to any individual action.

THE ANNUAL CYCLE

The present annual Internal Market cycle incorporates the twice-yearly Scoreboard and the report on the functioning of product and capital markets (the Cardiff report). In addition, the Commission will present an annual review and update of target actions for discussion by the European Parliament and at the second Internal Market Council of each year. This review will examine progress and consider how well the present rolling programme meets longer-term goals. The Commission will come forward with a comprehensive set of indicators which will enable us to gauge the effectiveness of our policies and to assess how far they have contributed to the attainment of the broader objectives.

The annual adjustments to Internal Market target actions will be consistent with the priorities for structural reform identified in the Broad Economic Policy Guidelines, which play a central role in the co-ordination of economic policies between the Member States. The various elements of the Internal Market Strategy, including the results of the Internal Market Councils discussion of the Cardiff report and the views expressed by the European Parliament, will provide an input to both the Commission's proposals for the review of target actions and the Commission's recommendations for the Broad Economic Policy Guidelines. The onus will be on the Commission, initially and later on Member States to maintain a coherent approach.

Note

For commerce too, as well as for the institutions of the Community, it should be apparent from much of the material in this chapter that the significance of the 'legal deadline' of 31 December 1992 in Article 14 EC should not be accorded undue weight. Important though the end of 1992 was, the development of the internal market is commercially an evolving process. The Cecchini Report (p. 180 above) is based on the perception that the benefits of integration persist over time – they are not obtained once and for all. Equally, the debate about how extensive the benefits of the internal market will really prove to be, presented through the foregoing extracts, continues as integration evolves. For commerce, the process involves questions about how best to restructure operations which will persist for many years yet.

Integration also poses questions about the patterns of supporting legal regulation. This issue was visible in 1988 as the internal market programme began to take shape.

R. Bieber, R. Dehousse, J. Pinder, J. Weiler,
1992: One European Market?
(1988), pp. 30–31

Despite the beguiling simplicity of the ideas of completing the single market and abolishing the frontier controls, it is not hard to see that the project outlined by the White Paper is a complex one: a vast exercise in harmonising laws, regulations and practices, presenting a tough challenge to the Community's political and institutional capacity. That is hardly contestable. More open to judgment, but nevertheless plausible, are the propositions that the process of completion carries with it pressures for related policies in fields such as the environment, competition, industry, cohesion, monetary integration and macro economic management. These in turn would not only require the creation of new common policy instruments, but also imply the strengthening of Community institutions, in matters such as majority voting in the Council, codecision with the Parliament, and enhancing the Community's juridical capacity and the Commission's role. All this would not only develop the Community internally, but would also strengthen its international position and bargaining power, not only in trade policy but also in the fields of money and of technological development.

In so far as this is accepted, the White Paper should be viewed not in the minimalist perspective of a Community which emphasises free trade at the expense of other values, but as a bold initiative to impel the Community forward where agreement among all the member governments was possible, which, if it succeeds, will imply also a major effort of policy integration in related fields and development of the Community institutions.

(E) ECONOMIC AND MONETARY UNION

The questions raised in the concluding extract of the preceding subsection remain high on the agenda. They may be assessed in the light of the impact of the Maastricht Treaty on European Union. The most specific next step of policy integration envisaged by that Treaty was the process of Economic and Monetary Union. Cecchini (p. 180 above) identified the single currency as a potential major element in the integrative process and the Commission's 1996 Communication (p. 187) also stands in the shadow of this major project.

Article 4 EC provides an outline for the plan.

Article 4 EC

Article 4

1. For the purposes set out in Article 2, the activities of the Member States and the Community shall include, as provided in this Treaty and in accordance with the timetable set out therein, the adoption of an economic policy which is based on the close coordination of Member States' economic policies, on the internal market and on the definition of common objectives, and conducted in accordance with the principle of an open market economy with free competition.

2. Concurrently with the foregoing, and as provided in this Treaty and in accordance with the timetable and the procedures set out therein, these activities shall include the irrevocable fixing of exchange rates leading to the introduction of a single currency, the ecu, and the definition and conduct of a single monetary policy and exchange-rate policy the primary objective of both of which shall be to maintain price stability and, without prejudice to this objective, to support the general economic policies in the Community, in accordance with the principle of an open market economy with free competition.

3. These activities of the Member States and the Community shall entail compliance with the following guiding principles: stable prices, sound public finances and monetary conditions and a sustainable balance of payments.

Note
Title VII of the EC Treaty, 'Economic and Monetary Policy', which occupies
Articles 112–124 EC, provides elaboration of the plan. The economic
convergence criteria on which the entry into being of the single currency is
predicated are found in Article 121:

- the achievement of a high degree of price stability; this will be apparent
  from a rate of inflation which is close to that of, at most, the three best
  performing Member States in terms of price stability;
- the sustainability of the government financial position; this will be
  apparent from having achieved a government budgetary position without
  a deficit that is excessive as determined in accordance with Article
  104(6);
- the observance of the normal fluctuation margins provided for by the
  exchange-rate mechanism of the European Monetary System, for at least
  two years, without devaluing against the currency of any other Member
  State;
- the durability of convergence achieved by the Member State and of its
  participation in the exchange-rate mechanism of the European Monetary
  System being reflected in the long-term interest-rate levels.

After conformity with these criteria was (in some instances, controversially)
confirmed in accordance with Article 121 EC (see Decision 98/317, OJ 1998
L139/30), the third stage of economic and monetary union began on 1
January 1999, with 11 participants: Belgium, Germany, Spain, France,
Ireland, Italy, Luxembourg, the Netherlands, Austria, Portugal and Finland.
The exchange rates between these States' currencies are fixed. In effect, the
national currencies have become simply representations of the euro. The UK
has an opt-out from the third stage, secured at the time of the Maastricht
negotiations, and its currency remains outside 'euroland' and therefore
continues to fluctuate against the euro. Coins and banknotes of the euro –
which according to Regulation 1103/97 is the term that should be used in
preference to the Treaty term 'ecu' – will be physically available from 1
January 2002, and it is currently intended that national currencies will be
withdrawn by mid-2002 at the latest. The next extract offers a broader
perspective on the prospects for Economic and Monetary Union.

H. Siebert and M. Koop, *Institutional Competition versus*
Centralization: Quo Vadis Europe?
(1993) 9 *Oxford Review of Economic Policy* 15, 25–27

VII. HARMONIZING MONEY
The Maastricht Treaty has put macroeconomics back on the EC's agenda and it has
done so by applying the *ex-ante* harmonization approach. The most exposed single
issue is the creation of the European Monetary Union (EMU), the design of a single
currency for twelve different nations with twelve heterogeneous sets of preferences

regarding price level stability, twelve distinct histories of monetary policies, twelve track records on inflation, and twelve systems of administering monetary policy.

The risk of creating a weak European currency partly derives from the possibility of merging countries with different attitudes towards monetary stability and different levels of economic development. Therefore, participation in EMU was made dependent on the fulfilment of various convergence criteria: total government debt must be less than 60 per cent of GDP and annual budget deficits must be smaller than 3 per cent of GDP. The inflation rate may only be 1.5 percentage points above the average inflation rate of the three lowest inflation rates in the EC. Finally, the exchange rate may not have been devalued two years before entering EMU and long-term interest rates must broadly be in line with comparable rates in the low inflation countries.

By setting quantitative criteria in advance, the Maastricht Treaty seeks to mitigate the risk of a weak Euro-currency. However, two objections must be raised. First, the quality of some indicators is uncertain. For obvious reasons, the requirement of a low budget deficit in the year before entering EMU should have been extended for a number of consecutive years and it should include stealth budgets. The criterion on indebtedness conveys limited information. It reflects a long history of running up debts and it does not take into account whether the funds were used for consumption or investment. Therefore, the number 60 seems to be chosen arbitrarily. On the other hand, the interest rate and inflation criteria are useful measures because they comprise an element of competition. If, for example, a low-inflation country reduces its inflation rate it simultaneously forces high-inflation countries to follow suit – a competition for stable money. To enhance this competition, the European Council and the Commission will be constantly assessing the stabilization efforts (and success) of the member countries. In the second half of the decade they will even be allowed to enforce this goal by withholding EC benefits – another safeguard clause for achieving economic stability.

Second, a serious question will be to what extent the criteria will be interpreted in a politically soft way in order to bring countries into EMU that would normally not qualify for membership. For instance, the wish of the EC-founding countries, Belgium and Italy, also to co-found EMU may generate pressures to soften the interpretation of the convergence criteria. In that case monetary stability would be at risk because a European monetary policy that aims for stable money needs accommodation by sound national fiscal policies.

The main problem for the EMU will be to transfer credibility from the national central banks to their European successor. One important aspect is that the national central banks are independent before a European currency would start. A period of independence of at least two years in which national central banks could build up a reputation of pursuing an independent monetary policy would be helpful. The political decision of some countries to make the central bank independent just the second before the starting signal of monetary union, calls into question the independence of the European Central Bank (ECB) and undermines its credibility even before it is founded.

Even if the ECB is legally independent, it may not be in practice. National ECB governors who seek reappointment after serving a relatively short term may choose to please their national governments by voting for a less stringent monetary policy. The most decisive issue, however, is whether a European monetary policy can be insulated from the moral-hazard problem of political pressure. A European monetary policy affects each region of Europe in a uniform way – the same interest rate will be effective from Aberdeen to Heraklion; but the policy-making process remains at the national level. This represents a systematic source of conflict, and it is hard to say to what extent a European monetary policy can withstand this conflict. A European Central Bank needs extremely strong safeguards in such a context and it is open to question whether institutional arrangements with respect to fiscal policy can provide sufficiently strong ones.

Leaving aside such intricate issues as the ECB's independence, the level of transfers needed in a currency union without exchange rates, and the willingness of countries to pay the price of transfers in favour of European integration, the central question is whether the EC is an optimum currency area. As Eichengreen (1991) shows, the EC does not fulfil the requirements for an optimum currency area too well, i.e. high factor mobility and no region-specific shocks and disturbances. Possibly, the Internal Market leads to more specialization of regions, owing to the fact that firms are increasingly able to exploit economies of scale. This would make European economies even more diverse – not less. As German unification has proved, asymmetric shocks cannot be ruled out. Then, flexible nominal exchange rates are more important than before to adjust to real shocks. The foreign exchange turmoil of mid-September 1992 has lent additional support to this view. Two devaluations and suspension of two currencies from the European Exchange Rate Mechanism (ERM) have shown that the degree of economic convergence is lower than expected.

Although the ERM has, by and large, functioned properly, its recent shake-up made it obvious that the system is in need of repair. A solution may consist in allowing competition between the national central banks and the institutional rules defining their behaviour such as operating procedures, monetary policy instruments, money targets, and the space to manoeuvre in open-market operations. Those banks and currencies that have similar institutional arrangements (reflecting similar preferences on stable money) and low inflation rates, and that represent economies that have converged close enough to make exchange rates unnecessary for internal adjustments, could merge of their own free will. This leaves open how many currencies join and when they do. The 'new' central bank could start with the credibility it inherits from its national predecessors that must be truly independent beforehand. Imagine the Netherlands, Germany, and Austria forming a currency union, institutionalizing the policies they have pursued for years. The other countries would be left with an adjustment mechanism to absorb real shocks that hit their economies, and the central banks would face an incentive to build up their own credibility. This solution, however, calls for a more flexible approach to EC membership than the current 'all or none'.

Notes
1. The reference to Eichengreen is to 'Is Europe an Optimum Currency Area?', NBER Working Paper, 3579, Cambridge MA, National Bureau of Economic Research. For further reading from a legal perspective, try P. Beaumont and N. Walker, *The Legal Framework of the Single European Currency* (Hart Publishing, 1999).
2. Economic, political and legal perspectives converge in acknowledging that the significance of Economic and Monetary Union is profound. One rather central question asks: will it prove a success?

D. Dinan, *Ever Closer Union: an Introduction to European Integration* (1999), pp. 477–9

WILL EMU WORK?

The short answer to the question 'Will EMU work?' is yes, it *will* work because a majority of Europeans have decided that it *must* work. During the transition stages, member states displayed a determination to make it happen; new and existing administrative bodies demonstrated the necessary expertise to bring it about; and public opinion showed surprising compliance with it. Having concluded during the transition stages not only that EMU was feasible but also that the political and economic costs of failure were greater than the costs of success, politicians, technocrats, and ordinary Europeans alike were bound to conclude after the launch of Stage III that the costs of maintaining the single currency are considerably less than the costs of its collapse.

Nevertheless, the challenges of managing the single currency and generating public support for it are considerable. At one level, acceptance of the single currency will most likely prove surprisingly easy. Few people will mourn their national currencies. As long as the new currency is a strong one that is not eroded by inflation, the public will quickly come to terms with it.

The strength of the currency, in turn, will depend on prevailing international circumstances and on the judgment and credibility of the ECB, whose board consists of highly reputable and experienced former national bankers. Governments may try to pressure individual members, but the likely loss of credibility resulting from public knowledge of a board member's surrender to such pressure serves as a strong deterrent. There is no guarantee that board members will not succumb privately to national pressure, although obvious nationalistic behaviour is unlikely to escape their colleagues' notice and opprobrium.

The fate of the ECB depends not only on its integrity and independence but also on its effectiveness and legitimacy. The euro's value is a prime determinant of the ECB's credibility. But managing the single currency, like preparing for it, imposes costs that are unevenly spread among member states and that vary over time. Given the diversity of national economic and financial systems, a euro-zone-wide monetary policy cannot fit each member state equally well. Monetary tightening affects member states in different ways and at different times. An economic shock in one member state may prompt a monetary response that disadvantages another member state; alternatively, the ECB's refusal to respond to a regional economic shock could undermine support for the ECB in that part of euroland. Without financial transfers to compensate those parts of euroland in recession and with little cross-border labour mobility and strong constraints on the use of national fiscal instruments, the ECB's response to asymmetrical shocks assumes even greater importance.

Those who are disadvantaged by prevailing monetary policy will direct their anger at 'Brussels' and 'Frankfurt'. Inevitably, the ECB's legitimacy will be called into question. This problem relates to a wider, longstanding one of democratic accountability and representation in the EU. Nevertheless, the legitimacy of the ECB is especially troublesome because of the necessity to maintain its political independence and also because its decisions will have a profound impact on economic activity throughout euroland.

Public doubts about the bank's legitimacy make it imperative for ECB board members to give frequent speeches, interviews, and press conferences about the bank's policy goals and instruments, within the bounds of confidentiality The EP is the ECB's obvious official interlocutor at the European level. Regular meetings with the EP's Committee on Economic and Monetary Affairs may help to personalize the ECB and build public support for its actions. Yet it will be difficult to build the legitimacy of the ECB on that of the EP, which, despite being directly elected, is neither well liked nor well understood in the EU.

EMU will most likely work at least in the narrow sense of the euro's survival. Beyond that, EMU has the potential to succeed by prompting economic restructuring, boosting employment, and propelling growth. As Commission president Jacques Santer commented during the selection of the eleven euro countries in early 1998, the euro is 'not an end in itself but an instrument to spur and sustain economic growth into the next century'. A small degree of economic growth is likely to follow in the wake of EMU because of the abolition of currency conversions between participating countries and because of greater price transparency, although proponents of EMU have exaggerated the cost of currency conversions and the prospect that their abolition will spur cross-border trade. Nevertheless, the eradication of bank charges and commissions, as well as of personnel and other costs relating to currency management and hedging, will save exporters money. Similarly, the removal of currency barriers will stimulate some additional cross-border trade. A rise in business and consumer spending may also follow a fall in prices in some member states due to price transparency across borders. Yet prices are unlikely to converge in the euro zone because of vastly different tax rates among member states.

Whether EMU spurs greater economic growth and makes a serious dent in unemployment depends not only on the global economic situation but also on whether EMU results in major economic and financial restructuring. EMU will generate momentum for such restructuring, but individual national responses will depend on political and cultural considerations. The follow-on debate about a possible overhaul of taxation, subsidies, and labour market policies touches a raw nerve in France, especially because of the implication that EMU is incompatible with the much-vaunted European model of society and is a stalking horse for the despised Anglo-Saxon model. Stereotypically, the European model, based on a fusion of capitalism and socialism, values solidarity and cohesion; the Anglo-Saxon model, based on naked capitalism, thrives on individualism and greed.

Even without EMU, the European model as idealized in France and elsewhere is unsustainable. Domestically, welfare costs impose a huge economic burden; internationally, liberalized trade and free capital movements are irreconcilable with overregulation of the workforce and market place. The high cost of hiring and firing workers accounts in large part for double-digit unemployment in parts of Europe, yet calls for welfare and labour market reform evoke a defensive, ideological response not only in France but also in Germany following the Social Democrats' September 1998 election victory.

A more realistic version of the European model exists in the Netherlands, which has enjoyed high employment and low inflation since the mid-1990s. The ingredients of the Dutch model are social partnership, wage moderation, budget discipline, and gradual welfare reform. The German model is traditionally closer to the Dutch than to the French model, but the high costs of unification and weak domestic leadership made it impossible in the late 1990s for the Christian Democratic government to emulate the Dutch entirely. By contrast, Germany's Social Democratic government may be unable to resist the temptation to try to cut unemployment through government spending rather than through taxation, labour market, and other reforms, despite the constraints of the stability pact. If so, EMU may succeed in a narrow sense, but will not achieve its full potential.

Note

Analysis now turns over the following chapters contained in Part Two of this book to the substantive legal rules which serve to eliminate national rules which act as impediments to trade between Member States. The concern, then, is initially with the negative aspect of the creation of the internal/common market. Chapters 6 to 8 and Chapters 9 to 10 examine 'Opening up the Market', first in relation to the free movement of goods, then in relation to the free movement of persons and services.

As the maintenance of border controls declines, in part as a result of legal prohibition but also because of the irrelevance of border controls to supervision of technologically advanced economic activity, so the question for negative Community law becomes more one of coping with regulatory diversity between the Member States rather than physical frontiers or discriminatory practices. In many fields it is the simple fact of differences between non-discriminatory regulatory standards State-by-State that impedes traders from constructing an integrated strategy for the territory of the whole Community. Where States tax products at different rates, the trader in a low-taxing state will face a demand for extra payment when he or she tries to sell the product in the high-taxing state. Where States make different demands with regard to the composition of, say, foodstuffs, the trader in a State which allows use of ingredient *alpha* will be unable to gain access to the market of a State which forbids use of *alpha*. And where States apply different standards of professional qualification, a lawyer trained in State X may be refused the opportunity of working, establishing him- or herself or providing services in State Y simply because State Y has a different training regime.

Were these cases based on overt discrimination against out-of-State providers, then they would be rather easy to resolve in favour of free trade. But there is no discrimination in such cases; all products are highly taxed irrespective of origin in the first example, all products are denied use of ingredient *alpha* in the second example, and all lawyers must meet the host State's requirements in the third. The rules are different, but this tends to lead to protection of home State producers who naturally comply with their own State's rules. The rules restrict cross-border trade. The validity of such rules comes into sharper focus as the integrative process evolves and such less-than-obvious technical barriers to trade are revealed. In the EC, the three examples given above would be considered under different Treaty provisions – Article 90 (tax, Chapter 6), Article 28 (goods, Chapters 7 and 8) and Articles 39, 42 and 49 (persons, Chapter 10) respectively. They would not be dealt with in precisely the same way; but they raise the same policy issue – the compatibility with EC trade law of regulatory diversity between the States in so far as that diversity acts as an impediment to integration.

The European Court has developed principles for judging the acceptable limits of regulatory diversity where trade restriction is caused. The roots of this case law pre-date '1992' by over a decade (*Cassis de Dijon*, p. 290 below), which emphasises once again that 1992 was a dynamic process, constructed on already well-established principles that are of continuing significance; but the management of regulatory diversity is a quintessentially post-1992, post-border control issue.

Reinhard Gebhard v *Consiglio dell'Ordine degli Avvocati e Procuratori di Milano (Case C-55/94)*
[1995] ECR I-4165, [1996] 1 CMLR 603
Court of Justice of the European Communities

Gebhard, a German national and a member of the Bar of Stuttgart, was resident in Italy. He had worked as a lawyer in Milan, but found himself the subject of disciplinary proceedings by the Milan Bar Council on the ground that he had infringed Italian law by pursuing a professional activity in Italy on a permanent basis using the title *avvocato*. The Court rejected the view of the Milan Bar Council that Gebhard could not be regarded for the purposes of the Treaty as 'established' in Italy unless he belonged to the professional body, or at least pursued his activity in collaboration or in association with persons belonging to that body. The Court conceded that the pursuit of certain self-employed activities may be conditional on complying with certain provisions justified by 'the general good', such as rules relating to organisation, qualification, professional ethics, supervision and liability. It added that where the pursuit of a specific activity is subject to such conditions in the host State, a national of another Member State intending to pursue that activity must in principle comply with them. This concedes regulatory diversity, and the Court referred to the role of secondary Community legislation governing recognition of professional qualifications (especially Directive 89/48, p. 394 below). It then stated:

[37]   It follows, however, from the Court's case-law that national measures liable to hinder or make less attractive the exercise of fundamental freedoms guaranteed by the Treaty must fulfil four conditions: they must be applied in a non-discriminatory manner; they must be justified by imperative requirements in the general interest; they must be suitable for securing the attainment of the objective which they pursue; and they must not go beyond what is necessary in order to attain it. . . .

Note

The *Gebhard* case concerned the free movement of persons, but the principle stated is capable of application in the context of Article 28, which deals with the free movement of goods (though not, it would seem, to Article 90 where the Court's control of non-discriminatory regulatory diversity is less assertive, Chapter 6 below). This is part of an emerging, though (as will be seen) not entirely consistent, pattern of EC trade law applicable to all national rules that impede the exercise of economic freedoms. The principles expressed by the Court in this ruling will be traced through the chapters on negative trade law that follow.

It is plain that the Court envisages that States may justify rules against standards recognised under Community law (e.g, environmental and consumer protection) even where there is a restrictive effect on cross-border trade. How, then, can integration be achieved? As already suggested above in connection with *Gebhard*, the classic Community answer is to move beyond negative law to positive law – to harmonise the diverse national laws so that a common Community rule is put in place. The Community measure governs the interests that underpinned national intervention but achieves protection of those interests at Community level. Traders may then plan integrated strategies according to this common rule which applies throughout the common market territory.

Areas in which a positive contribution from Community law is required may be observed on several occasions, and accordingly the themes set out in this chapter will be seen to underlie the substantive rules. This becomes more explicit in the remaining chapters of Part Two of this book which examine 'Regulating the Market'. Chapters 11 to 14 concern the competition rules. Chapter 15 examines positive Community policy-making generally, where several of the themes introduced in the present chapter are reassessed in the light of the substantive law examined in Chapters 6–14. It will be seen that the beguiling notion of common rules for a common market is under strain. In part this is attributable to the geographic and functional expansion of the EC which renders agreement increasingly hard to achieve. The range of interests at stake in the EC cannot readily be reduced to a single agreed norm. More fundamentally, there is an increasingly voiced case against harmonisation. Better, it is said by some sources, to allow traders access to the markets of all Member States subject only to compliance with the rules of their home State. The host State could retain a regulatory regime different from other States, but could not use those regulatory differences as a basis for denying access to an out-of-State trader. This would be a system of mutual recognition of national rules. Firms could then choose where to locate in order to supply the whole market, and their choice would be informed by prevailing regulatory strategies. Firms – the market – would select which regulatory regime suited them best. It can readily be appreciated that this approach not only downplays the need for harmonisation and a level playing field, it also portrays harmonisation as an undesirable suppression of a market in which regulators compete for customers. The debate is not only directed at the internal aspects of EC policy; it is also argued that externally the EC will lose its competitive position if it locks itself into a single standard.

This is an inevitably superficial summary of a key philosophical debate about the Community's future. This preference for 'competition between regulators' over the 'level playing field' is most closely associated with the now ousted Thatcher/Major administrations in the UK, although it is a debate with global resonances. The debate is being conducted in many sectors, although Social Policy was the most high-profile example at Maastricht. The United Kingdom fought against provisions permitting a deepening of regulation; unable to win that argument, it then successfully argued that it should be insulated from the regulations that other Member States wished to introduce. The United Kingdom thus competed in social policy standards against the other 11, then 14, in the area covered by the Protocol-plus-Agreement. This is examined more fully in Chapter 15 (p. 621) although, via the Amsterdam Treaty, the UK's exclusion was brought to an end by the Labour government which took office in May 1997. At a more general level, the reader should consider whether the EC is adjusting to new patterns of growth to which all members need not necessarily subscribe, or whether these patterns of fragmentation are fatal to its survival. This is variable geometry – and it challenges many of the assumptions about the role of positive law beyond negative law. It is nothing new. Variable geometry has already been touched on in this chapter (and see the final sentence of the extract from Siebert and Koop above (p. 214)), but, as the EC pursues its

path of geographic and functional expansion marked by periodic intergovernmental conferences, the debate about how far to move beyond deregulation
and market liberalisation towards patterns of substantive and institutional
re-regulation (in common or not) is becoming increasingly acute. The Treaty
provisions on 'closer cooperation' envisaged by the Treaty of Amsterdam
constitute the latest manifestation. The matter will be re-addressed in the
concluding subsection of Chapter 15 (p. 625 below), by which time the
reader will be more fully informed about the relevant patterns of substantive
EC law.

6 FISCAL BARRIERS TO TRADE: ARTICLES 25 AND 90

Note

Article 23 of the Treaty commits the Community to the creation of a customs union.

Article 23 EC

The Community shall be based upon a customs union which shall cover all trade in goods and which shall involve the prohibition between Member States of customs duties on imports and exports and of all charges having equivalent effect, and the adoption of a common customs tariff in their relations with third countries.

Note

Article 26 EC empowers the Council acting by qualified majority on a proposal from the Commission to fix common customs tariff duties. It is the internal aspects of the customs union which form the focus of this chapter.

Article 25 EC

Customs duties on imports and exports and charges having equivalent effect shall be prohibited between Member States. This prohibition shall also apply to customs duties of a fiscal nature.

Note

The elimination of customs duties on trade between Member States is essential as part of the process of market integration, but it is not enough on its own to secure origin neutrality in fiscal law. Consequently the provisions which prohibit customs duties are supplemented by provisions directed at the internal taxation systems of the Member States. Article 90 forbids discrimination against imported goods in the State's internal system of taxation.

Article 90 EC

No Member State shall impose, directly or indirectly, on the products of other Member States any internal taxation of any kind in excess of that imposed directly or indirectly on similar domestic products.

Furthermore, no Member State shall impose on the products of other Member States any internal taxation of such a nature as to afford indirect protection to other products.

Notes
1.   These are fundamentally important provisions. Both plainly connect with Article 14, examined in the previous chapter. The wording, though not the substance, of both provisions was adjusted by the Amsterdam Treaty. That Treaty also adjusted the numbering (p. 29 above). Article 25 was formerly Article 12; Article 90 was Article 95. This must be kept in mind when reading pre-Amsterdam case law.
2.   It has become axiomatic in Community law that Article 25 and Article 90 are *complementary but mutually exclusive*. Both are directed at the abolition of fiscal barriers to trade; but a charge is controlled by one or the other, not both. There is no overlap. (See *Commission* v *Italy* (Case 24/68), p. 224 below.)
3.   The nature of the control exercised over domestic competence to levy tax is distinct. Article 25 forbids customs duties and charges having equivalent effect. Article 90 does not forbid internal taxation; it merely forbids discrimination according to nationality. States remain otherwise free to levy taxation as they see fit.

(A) ARTICLE 25

The Court has used the prohibition on customs duties and charges having equivalent effect to challenge a range of levies imposed on goods which cross a frontier. The Court is concerned with the restrictive *effect* on trade, not the purpose of the charge. The following cases, both infringement proceedings against Italy (see Chapter 17), illustrate the Court's application of the Article 25 prohibition (which, at the time the cases were decided, was contained in Article 12).

Commission v *Italy (Case 7/68)*
[1968] ECR 423
Court of Justice of the European Communities

The case concerned an Italian tax on the export of artistic, historical and archaeological articles.

1. *The scope of the disputed tax*

By basing its action on Article 16 of the Treaty, the Commission considers that articles of an artistic, historic, archaeological or ethnographic nature, which are the subject of the Italian Law of 1 June 1939, No 1089, fall under the provisions relating to the customs union. This point of view is disputed by the defendant, which considers that the articles in question cannot be assimilated to 'consumer goods or articles of general use' and are not therefore subject to the provisions of the Treaty which apply to 'ordinary merchandise'; for that reason they are excluded from the application of Article 16 of the Treaty.

Under Article 9 of the Treaty the Community is based on a customs union 'which shall cover all trade in goods'. By goods, within the meaning of that provision, there must be understood products which can be valued in money and which are capable, as such, of forming the subject of commercial transactions.

The articles covered by the Italian Law, whatever may be the characteristics which distinguish them from other types of merchandise, nevertheless resemble the latter, inasmuch as they can be valued in money and so be the subject of commercial transactions. That view corresponds with the scheme of the Italian Law itself, which fixes the tax in question in proportion to the value of the articles concerned.

It follows from the above that the rules of the Common Market apply to these goods subject only to the exceptions expressly provided by the Treaty.

2. *The classification of the disputed tax having regard to Article 16 of the Treaty*

In the opinion of the Commission the tax in dispute constitutes a tax having an effect equivalent to a customs duty on exports and therefore the tax should have been abolished, under Article 16 of the Treaty, no later than the end of the first stage of the common market, that is to say, from 1 January 1962. The defendant argues that the disputed tax does not come within the category, as it has its own particular purpose which is to ensure the protection and safety of the artistic, historic and archaeological heritage which exists in the national territory. Consequently, the tax does not in any respect have a fiscal nature, and its contribution to the budget is insignificant.

Article 16 of the Treaty prohibits the collection in dealings between Member States of any customs duty on exports and of any charge having an equivalent effect, that is to say, any charge which, by altering the price of an article exported, has the same restrictive effect on the free circulation of that article as a customs duty. This provision makes no distinction based on the purpose of the duties and charges the abolition of which it requires.

It is not necessary to analyse the concept of the nature of fiscal systems on which the defendant bases its argument upon this point, for the provisions of the section of the Treaty concerning the elimination of customs duties between the Member States exclude the retention of customs duties and charges having equivalent effect without distinguishing in that respect between those which are and those which are not of a fiscal nature.

The disputed tax falls within Article 16 by reason of the fact that export trade in the goods in question is hindered by the pecuniary burden which it imposes on the price of the exported articles.

Note

The Court went on to reject Italian arguments of justification based on Article 30 (formerly 36). Article 30 is available only in respect of physical and technical barriers to trade caught by Article 28, and is unavailable in the field of fiscal barriers to trade. Chapter 7 examines Articles 28–30.

Commission v Italy (Case 24/68)
[1969] ECR 193; [1971] CMLR 611
Court of Justice of the European Communities

Italy collected a levy on goods exported to other Member States in order to fund the compilation of statistical data relating to trade patterns. The Court began by examining the nature of the Article 25 (then Article 12) prohibition before proceeding to find the charge incompatible with the Treaty.

[6] . . . the purpose of the abolition of customs barriers is not merely to eliminate their protective nature, as the Treaty sought on the contrary to give general scope and effect to the rule on the elimination of customs duties and charges having equivalent effect, in order to ensure the free movement of goods.

[7] It follows from the system as a whole and from the general and absolute nature of the prohibition of any customs duty applicable to goods moving between Member States that customs duties are prohibited independently of any consideration of the purpose for which they were introduced and the destination of the revenue obtained therefrom.

The justification for this prohibition is based on the fact that any pecuniary charge, however small, imposed on goods by reason of the fact that they cross a frontier constitutes an obstacle to the movement of such goods.

[8] The extension of the prohibition of customs duties to charges having equivalent effect is intended to supplement the prohibition against obstacles to trade created by such duties by increasing its efficiency.

The use of these two complementary concepts thus tends, in trade between Member States, to avoid the imposition of any pecuniary charge on goods circulating within the Community by virtue of the fact that they cross a national frontier.

[9] Thus, in order to ascribe to a charge an effect equivalent to a customs duty, it is important to consider this effect in the light of the objectives of the Treaty, in the Parts, Titles and Chapters in which Articles 9, 12, 13 and 16 are to be found, particularly in relation to the free movement of goods.

Consequently, any pecuniary charge, however small and whatever its designation and mode of application, which is imposed unilaterally on domestic or foreign goods by reason of the fact that they cross a frontier, and which is not a customs duty in the strict sense, constitutes a charge having equivalent effect within the meaning of Articles 9, 12, 13 and 16 of the Treaty, even if it is not imposed for the benefit of the State, is not discriminatory or protective in effect and if the product on which the charge is imposed is not in competition with any domestic product.

[10] It follows from all the provisions referred to and from their relationship with the other provisions of the Treaty that the prohibition of new customs duties or charges having equivalent effect, linked to the principle of the free movement of goods, constitutes a fundamental rule which, without prejudice to the other provisions of the Treaty, does not permit of any exceptions.

. . .

[15] The Italian Government further maintains that the disputed charge constitutes the consideration for a service rendered and as such cannot be designated as a charge having equivalent effect.

According to the Italian Government the object of the statistics in question is to determine precisely the actual movements of goods and, consequently, changes the state of the market. It claims that the exactness of the information thus supplied affords importers a better competitive position in the Italian market whilst exporters enjoy a similar advantage abroad and that the special advantages which dealers obtain from the survey justifies their paying for this public service and moreover demonstrates that the disputed charge is in the nature of a *quid pro quo*.

[16]   The statistical information in question is beneficial to the economy as a whole and *inter alia* to the relevant administrative authorities.

Even if the competitive position of importers and exporters were to be particularly improved as a result, the statistics still constitute an advantage so general, and so difficult to assess, that the disputed charge cannot be regarded as the consideration for a specific benefit actually conferred.

[17]   It appears from the abovementioned considerations that in so far as the disputed charge is levied on exports it is contrary to Article 16 of the Treaty.

Notes

1.   Paragraph 9 of the judgment constitutes the Court's definition of the scope of the prohibition; a formula which has proved enduring through subsequent case law.

2.   See also, on the Court's approach, e.g., *Sociaal Fonds voor de Diamantarbeiders* v *Brachfeld* (Cases 2 & 3/69) [1969] ECR 211, [1969] CMLR 335.

3.   The Court accepts that a State is permitted to levy a fee for services provided to an importer. Such a charge is demanded as part of a commercial transaction, not because of the passage of the goods across a frontier. The charge is accordingly not caught by Article 25. However, the risk that States may use this approach as a device for imposing charges on importers for unwanted services which impede free trade has led the Court to scrutinise with great care arguments of this nature. In paras 15 and 16 of its judgment in *Commission* v *Italy* (Case 24/68) above, the Court rejected submissions along these lines by the Italian government. It took a similar approach in *Bresciani* v *Amministrazione Italiana delle Finanze* (Case 87/75).

Bresciani v *Amministrazione Italiana delle Finanze (Case 87/75)*
[1976] ECR 129; [1976] 2 CMLR 62
Court of Justice of the European Communities

The case involved the imposition of a charge for compulsory veterinary and public health inspections carried out on the importation of raw cowhides. The Court was asked by a court in Genoa to consider whether such a levy constitutes a charge having equivalent effect to a customs duty on imports.

[9]   . . . [A]ny pecuniary charge, whatever its designation and mode of application, which is unilaterally imposed on goods imported from another Member State by reason of the fact that they cross a frontier, constitutes a charge having an effect equivalent to a customs duty. In appraising a duty of the type at issue it is. . . of no importance that it is proportionate to the quantity of the imported goods and not to their value.

[10]   Nor, in determining the effects of the duty on the free movement of goods, is it of any importance that a duty of the type at issue is proportionate to the costs of a compulsory public health inspection carried out on entry of the goods. The activity of the administration of the State intended to maintain a public health inspection system imposed in the general interest cannot be regarded as a service rendered to the importer such as to justify the imposition of a pecuniary charge. If, accordingly, public health inspections are still justified at the end of the transitional period, the costs which they occasion must be met by the general public which, as a whole, benefits from the free movement of Community goods.

[11]   The fact that the domestic production is, through other charges, subjected to a similar burden matters little unless those charges and the duty in question are applied according to the same criteria and at the same stage of production, thus making it possible for them to be regarded as falling within a general system of internal taxation applying systematically and in the same way to domestic and imported products.

Note
Arguments of fee-for-service also failed in, e.g., *Cadsky* v *ICE* (Case 63/74) [1975] ECR 281, [1975] 2 CMLR 246. See *Commission* v *Belgium* (Case 132/82) [1983] ECR 1649, [1983] 3 CMLR 600 for discussion of circum-stances in which a fee might legitimately be demanded; the case was nonetheless still decided against the charging State.

However, where the inspection is carried out under mandatory provisions of Community law, then a charge may be lawful.

Commission v *Germany (Case 18/87)*
[1988] ECR 5427
Court of Justice of the European Communities

German *Länder* (regions) charged fees on the importation of live animals to cover costs of inspections undertaken under Directive 81/389. The Court adopted a step-by-step approach in ruling on the compatibility of the system with Community law.

[5]   It should be observed in the first place that, as the Court has held on a number of occasions, the justification for the prohibition of customs duties and any charges having an equivalent effect lies in the fact that any pecuniary charge, however small, imposed on goods by reason of the fact that they cross a frontier, constitutes an obstacle to the movement of goods which is aggravated by the resulting administrative formalities. It follows that any pecuniary charge, whatever its designation and mode of application, which is imposed unilaterally on goods by reason of the fact that they cross a frontier and is not a customs duty in the strict sense constitutes a charge having an equivalent effect to a customs duty within the meaning of Articles 9, 12, 13 and 16 of the Treaty.

[6]   However, the Court has held that such a charge escapes that classification if it relates to a general system of internal dues applied systematically and in accordance with the same criteria to domestic products and imported products alike (judgment of 31 May 1979 in Case 132/78 *Denkavit* v *France* [1979] ECR 1923), if it constitutes payment for a service in fact rendered to the economic operator of a sum in proportion

to the service (judgment of 9 November 1983 in Case 158/82 *Commission* v *Denmark* [1983] ECR 3573), or again, subject to certain conditions, if it attaches to inspections carried out to fulfil obligations imposed by Community law (judgment of 25 January 1977 in Case 46/76 *Bauhuis* v *Netherlands* [1977] ECR 5).

[7]   The contested fee, which is payable on importation and transit, cannot be regarded as relating to a general system of internal dues. Nor does it constitute payment for a service rendered to the operator, because this condition is satisfied only if the operator in question obtains a definite specific benefit (see judgment of 1 July 1969 in Case 24/68 *Commission* v *Italy* [1969] ECR 193), which is not the case if the inspection serves to guarantee, in the public interest, the health and life of animals in international transport (see judgment of 20 March 1984 in Case 314/82 *Commission* v *Belgium* [1984] ECR 1543).

[8]   Since the contested fee was charged in connection with inspections carried out pursuant to a Community provision, it should be noted that according to the case-law of the Court (judgment of 25 January 1977 in *Bauhuis*, cited above; judgment of 12 July 1977 *Commission* v *Netherlands* [1977] ECR 1355; judgment of 31 January 1984 in Case 1/83 *IFG* v *Freistaat Bayern* [1984] ECR 349) such fees may not be classified as charges having an effect equivalent to a customs duty if the following conditions are satisfied:

(a)   they do not exceed the actual costs of the inspections in connection with which they are charged;

(b)   the inspections in question are obligatory and uniform for all the products concerned in the Community;

(c)   they are prescribed by Community law in the general interest of the Community;

(d)   they promote the free movement of goods, in particular by neutralizing obstacles which could arise from unilateral measures of inspection adopted in accordance with Article 36 of the Treaty.

[9]   In this instance these conditions are satisfied by the contested fee. In the first place it has not been contested that it does not exceed the real cost of the inspections in connection with which it is charged.

[10]   Moreover, all the Member States of transit and destination are required, under, *inter alia*, Article 2 (1) of Directive 81/389/EEC, cited above, to carry out the veterinary inspections in question when the animals are brought into their territories, and therefore the inspections are obligatory and uniform for all the animals concerned in the Community.

[11]   Those inspections are prescribed by Directive 81/389/EEC, which establishes the measures necessary for the implementation of Council Directive 77/489/EEC of 18 July 1977 on the protection of animals during international transport, with a view to the protection of live animals, an objective which is pursued in the general interest of the Community and not a specific interest of individual States.

[12]   Finally, it appears from the preambles to the two abovementioned directives that they are intended to harmonize the laws of the Member States regarding the protection of animals in international transport in order to eliminate technical barriers resulting from disparities in the national laws (see third, fourth and fifth recitals in the preamble to Directive 77/489/EEC and third recital in the preamble to Directive 81/389/EEC). In addition, failing such harmonization, each Member State was entitled to maintain or introduce, under the conditions laid down in Article 36 of the

Treaty, measures restricting trade which were justified on grounds of the protection of the health and life of animals. It follows that the standardization of the inspections in question is such as to promote the free movement of goods.

[13]   The Commission has claimed, however, that the contested fee is to be regarded as a charge having equivalent effect to a customs duty because, in so far as fees of this type have not been harmonized, such harmonization, moreover, being unattainable in practice – their negative effect on the free movement of goods could not be compensated or, consequently, justified by the positive effects of the Community standardization of inspections.

[14]   In this respect, it should be noted that since the fee in question is intended solely as the financially and economically justified compensation for an obligation imposed in equal measure on all the Member States by Community law, it cannot be regarded as equivalent to a customs duty; nor, consequently, can it fall within the ambit of the prohibition laid down in Articles 9 and 12 of the Treaty.

[15]   The negative effects which such a fee may have on the free movement of goods in the Community can be eliminated only by virtue of Community provisions providing for the harmonization of fees, or imposing the obligation on the Member States to bear the costs entailed in the inspections or, finally, establishing that the costs in question are to be paid out of the Community budget.

[16]   It follows from the foregoing that the Commission's application must be dismissed.

Note
The Court appears prepared to accept in such a case that the Community as a whole obtains a benefit from the facilitation of free trade secured through a harmonised system of health inspections, and that accordingly the State is permitted to pass on the costs to individual traders. It has adopted the same view in respect of inspections mandatory under international conventions to which all Member States are party; *Commission* v *Netherlands* (Case 89/76) [1977] ECR 1355.

It should however be noted that that where Community law does no more than permit the inspection, any fee levied to cover costs is incompatible with Article 25; *Commission* v *Belgium* (Case 314/82) [1984] ECR 1543.

Question
Are these anomalies in the allocation of costs defensible? How might they be resolved more satisfactorily (see para. 15 of the judgment in *Commission* v *Germany* (Case 18/87), above)?

(B) ARTICLE 90

Note
A charge may fall to be considered in the light of Article 90 (text at p. 222 above) where it is imposed not on an importer as such, but instead on all traders irrespective of origin. If the State can show that the charge 'relates to a general system of internal dues applied systematically and in accordance

with the same criteria to domestic products and imported products alike' (para. 6 of *Commission* v *Germany* (Case 18/87 at p. 226 above), then the charge is lawful, provided only that the non-discrimination requirements of Article 90 are complied with.

The next case shows the application of Article 90 to an internal system of taxation which was held to favour the domestic trader over the importer. Remember that pre-Amsterdam Article 90 was numbered Article 95.

Schottle v *Finanzamt Freudenstadt (Case 20/76)*
[1977] ECR 247, [1977] 2 CMLR 98
Court of Justice of the European Communities

The case arose out of German taxation of carriage of goods by road. Long-distance road transport was taxed as part of a policy to encourage use of rail and waterways instead, but no tax was imposed on short-distance road transport. The definition of 'short distance' included special arrangements for importers. The net result was that a short journey might be exempt if purely internal to Germany, but subject to tax if it crossed a border.

[20]   The first paragraph of Article 95 is infringed where the taxation on the imported product and that on the similar domestic product are calculated in a different manner on the basis of different criteria which lead, if only in certain cases, to higher taxation being imposed on the imported product.

[21]   Higher taxation of the imported product exists when the conditions under which the carrier is subject to tax are different with regard to international transport and purely domestic transport so that in comparable situations the product moving within the Member State is not subject to the tax to which an imported product is subject. Indeed in order to compare the tax on goods moving within the national territory with that on the imported product for the purposes of the application of Article 95, account must be taken of both the basis of assessment of the tax and the advantages or exemptions which each tax carries with it. For the taxation of the imported product to be higher it is sufficient that in certain circumstances the national product may be transported without being subject to tax for the same distance within the Member State while the imported product is subject to the tax solely because the border was crossed. In this respect it is for the national judge to compare in specific cases the situations which may arise.

[22]   The information supplied by the national court shows that a real obstacle to free movement of goods may sometimes result from the application of different conditions for the imposition of taxation with regard to both international transport and domestic transport. The minor and incidental nature of the obstacle created by a national tax and the fact that it could only have been avoided in practice by abolishing the tax are not sufficient to prevent Article 95 from being applicable. Title IV of Part Two of the Treaty concerning the common transport policy enables Member States to resolve problems of competition between means of transport without however adversely affecting the free movement of goods. However the lack of such a policy is no justification for a derogation from Article 95 of the Treaty.

Note
The tax system lacked origin neutrality. However, States are commonly more devious. It is possible to avoid direct discrimination on grounds of nationality (the problem in *Schottle*), but to achieve a similar result by instead basing a taxation system on criteria which indirectly prejudice the imported product. In the following case the Court decided that such indirect discrimination on grounds of nationality is also capable of falling foul of Article 90).

Humblot v Directeur des Services Fiscaux (Case 112/84)
[1985] ECR 1367; [1986] 2 CMLR 338
Court of Justice of the European Communities

France imposed two different types of annual car tax. The key threshold between the two was 16 CV, a power rating. Below that level the tax increased gradually in proportion to the car's power, up to a maximum of 1,100 francs. Above 16 CV a flat rate of 5,000 francs was imposed. No French car was rated above 16 CV, so only imported vehicles were burdened by the high flat rate. M. Humblot, charged 5,000 francs tax on his 36 CV imported car, claimed the tax violated what was then Article 95, now Article 90, and sought a refund. The French court in Belfort referred questions under Article 177 (Article 234 post-Amsterdam).

[12]   It is appropriate in the first place to stress that as Community law stands at present the Member States are at liberty to subject products such as cars to a system of road tax which increases progressively in amount depending on an objective criterion, such as the power rating for tax purposes, which may be determined in various ways.

[13]   Such a system of domestic taxation is, however, compatible with Article 95 only in so far as it is free from any discriminatory or protective effect.

[14]   That is not true of a system like the one at issue in the main proceedings. Under that system there are two distinct taxes: a differential tax which increases progressively and is charged on cars not exceeding a given power rating for tax purposes and a fixed tax on cars exceeding that rating which is almost five times as high as the highest rate of the differential tax. Although the system embodies no formal distinction based on the origin of products it manifestly exhibits discriminatory or protective features contrary to Article 95, since the power rating determining liability to the special tax has been fixed at a level such that only imported cars, in particular from other Member States, are subject to the special tax whereas all cars of domestic manufacture are liable to the distinctly more advantageous differential tax.

[15]   In the absence of considerations relating to the amount of the special tax, consumers seeking comparable cars as regards such matters as size, comfort, actual power, maintenance costs, durability, fuel consumption and price would naturally choose from among cars above and below the critical power rating laid down by French law. However, liability to the special tax entails a much larger increase in taxation than passing from one category of car to another in a system of progressive taxation embodying balanced differentials like the system on which the differential tax is based. The resultant additional taxation is liable to cancel out the advantages which certain cars imported from other Member States might have in consumers' eyes over

comparable cars of domestic manufacture, particularly since the special tax continues to be payable for several years. In that respect the special tax reduces the amount of competition to which cars of domestic manufacture are subject and hence is contrary to the principle of neutrality with which domestic taxation must comply.

[16]   In the light of the foregoing considerations the question raised by the national court for a preliminary ruling should be answered as follows: Article 95 of the EEC Treaty prohibits the charging on cars exceeding a given power rating for tax purposes of a special fixed tax the amount of which is several times the highest amount of the progressive tax payable on cars of less than the said power rating for tax purposes, where the only cars subject to the special tax are imported, in particular from other Member States.

Notes
1.   An amended French car tax system was also found incompatible with Article 95 (now Article 90) in *Feldain* (Case 433/85) [1987] ECR 3536. In Case C-284/96 *Didier Tabouillot* [1997] ECR I-7471, the Court was able to avoid answering questions about the French system since the vehicle had been imported directly into France from the USA, a situation falling outside the scope of this Article of the Treaty.
2.   However, the establishment of a taxation system based on a criterion which indirectly affects imported goods more severely than domestic products is not automatically unlawful. It is open to the State to show that there is an objective justification for the use of that criterion which is not connected with nationality. The tax may then be accepted as compatible with Article 90.

Chemial Farmaceutici v *DAF (Case 140/79)*
[1981] ECR 1
Court of Justice of the European Communities

Italian taxation of denatured synthetic ethyl alcohol was higher than taxation of denatured ethyl alcohol obtained by fermentation, although the products were interchangeable in use. Italy produced little of the more heavily taxed synthetic version of the product. The Court explained that the facts and the result were distinguishable from *Humblot* (Case 112/84).

[13]   . . . the different taxation of synthetic alcohol and of alcohol produced by fermentation in Italy is the result of an economic policy decision to favour the manufacture of alcohol from agricultural products and, correspondingly, to restrain the processing into alcohol of ethylene, a derivative of petroleum, in order to reserve that raw material for other more important economic uses. It accordingly constitutes a legitimate choice of economic policy to which effect is given by fiscal means. The implementation of that policy does not lead to any discrimination since although it results in discouraging imports of synthetic alcohol into Italy, it also has the consequence of hampering the development in Italy itself of production of alcohol from ethylene, that production being technically perfectly possible.

[14]   As the Court has stated on many occasions, particularly in the judgments cited by the Italian Government, in its present stage of development Community law does not restrict the freedom of each Member State to lay down tax arrangements which

differentiate between certain products on the basis of objective criteria, such as the nature of the raw materials used or the production processes employed. Such differentiation is compatible with Community law if it pursues economic policy objectives which are themselves compatible with the requirements of the Treaty and its secondary law and if the detailed rules are such as to avoid any form of discrimination, direct or indirect, in regard to imports from other Member States or any form of protection of competing domestic products.

[15]   Differential taxation such as that which exists in Italy for denatured synthetic alcohol on the one hand and denatured alcohol obtained by fermentation on the other satisfies these requirements. It appears in fact that that system of taxation pursues an objective of legitimate industrial policy in that it is such as to promote the distillation of agricultural products as against the manufacture of alcohol from petroleum derivatives. That choice does not conflict with the rules of Community law or the requirements of a policy decided within the framework of the Community.

[16]   The detailed provisions of the legislation at issue before the national court cannot be considered as discriminatory since, on the one hand, it is not disputed that imports from other Member States of alcohol obtained by fermentation qualify for the same tax treatment as Italian alcohol produced by fermentation and, on the other hand, although the rate of tax prescribed for synthetic alcohol results in restraining the importation of synthetic alcohol originating in other Member States, it has an equivalent economic effect in the national territory in that it also hampers the establishment of profitable production of the same product by Italian industry.

Note
Notice that it is only indirect discrimination on grounds of nationality which may be justified in this way; never direct discrimination. Concessions must be made available to all products meeting the criteria, even if in practice few imports conform. See, e.g., *Commission* v *Italy* (Case 21/79) [1980] ECR 1.

Question
Advise a State which has several regions which suffer from abnormally high rainfall and which wishes to introduce a tax which favours production of goods typical of high-rainfall areas in order to confer economic support on the farmers of such areas.
   See *Commission* v *France* (Case 196/85) [1987] ECR 1597, [1988] 2 CMLR 851.

Notes
1.   The second paragraph of Article 90 (p. 222 above) broadens the scope of the provisions beyond tax equality for similar products to equality for competing products. This involves an economic assessment of the relationship of products in order to reveal whether the State is engaged in conferring protection on its domestic producers by imposing undue burdens on competing imports.
2.   The Court explained the nature of the control exercised by the first and second paragraphs of what was then Article 95, now Article 90, in the 'Spirits' cases, a series of cases concerned to challenge taxation laws relating to alcohol alleged to favour domestic products.

Commission v France (Case 168/78)
[1980] ECR 347; [1981] 2 CMLR 631
Court of Justice of the European Communities

[4]   [Article 95 supplements] within the system of the Treaty, the provisions on the abolition of customs duties and charges having equivalent effect. Their aim is to ensure free movement of goods between the Member States in normal conditions of competition by the elimination of all forms of protection which result from the application of internal taxation which discriminates against products from other Member States. As the Commission has correctly stated, Article 95 must guarantee the complete neutrality of internal taxation as regards competition between domestic products and imported products.

[5]   The first paragraph of Article 95, which is based on a comparison of the tax burdens imposed on domestic products and on imported products which may be classified as 'similar', is the basic rule in this respect. This provision, as the Court has had occasion to emphasize in its judgment of 10 October 1978 in Case 148/77, *H. Hansen jun. & O.C. Balle GmbH & Co.* v *Hauptzollamt Flensburg* [1978] ECR 1787, must be interpreted widely so as to cover all taxation procedures which conflict with the principle of the equality of treatment of domestic products and imported products; it is therefore necessary to interpret the concept of 'similar products' with sufficient flexibility. The Court specified in the judgment of 17 February 1976 in the *REWE* case (Case 45/75 [1976] ECR 181) that it is necessary to consider as similar products which 'have similar characteristics and meet the same needs from the point of view of consumers'. It is therefore necessary to determine the scope of the first paragraph of Article 95 on the basis not of the criterion of the strictly identical nature of the products but on that of their similar and comparable use.

[6]   The function of the second paragraph of Article 95 is to cover, in addition, all forms of indirect tax protection in the case of products which, without being similar within the meaning of the first paragraph, are nevertheless in competition, even partial, indirect or potential, with certain products of the importing country. The Court has already emphasized certain aspects of that provision in its judgment of 4 April 1978 in Case 27/77, *Firma Fink-Frucht GmbH* v *Hauptzollamt München-Landsbergerstrasse* [1978] ECR 223, in which it stated that for the purposes of the application of the first paragraph of Article 95 it is sufficient for the imported product to be in competition with the protected domestic production by reason of one or several economic uses to which it may be put, even though the condition of similarity for the purposes of the first paragraph of Article 95 is not fulfilled.

[7]   Whilst the criterion indicated in the first paragraph of Article 95 consists in the comparison of tax burdens, whether in terms of the rate, the mode of assessment or other detailed rules for the application thereof, in view of the difficulty of making sufficiently precise comparisons between the products in question, the second paragraph of that article is based upon a more general criterion, in other words the protective nature of the system of internal taxation.

Note
Most of the 'Spirits' cases, including *Commission* v *France* (Case 168/78), were decided on the basis that the Treaty prohibition was plainly infringed, and without detailed examination of the two paragraphs separately. This was

not possible in the most difficult of the cases, *Commission* v *UK* (Case 170/78), which involved tax differentials between wine and beer. These products are not similar within Article 90(1), and therefore argument centred on the possible application of Article 90(2) (then, of course, Article 95(2)). So complex were the economic calculations that the Court declined to give final judgment at the same time as it upheld the Commission's complaints in the other 'Spirits' cases ([1980] ECR 417). Eventually, however, after deeper investigation had been presented to the Court, the UK was held in breach of the Treaty.

Commission v *UK (Case 170/78)*
[1983] ECR 2263; [1983] 3 CMLR 512
Court of Justice of the European Communities

The Court first explored the nature of the competitive relationship between wine and beer, and built on its initial findings three years earlier.

[8] As regards the question of competition between wine and beer, the Court considered that, to a certain extent at least, the two beverages in question were capable of meeting identical needs, so that it had to be acknowledged that there was a degree of substitution for one another. It pointed out that, for the purpose of measuring the possible degree of substitution, attention should not be confined to consumer habits in a Member State or in a given region. Those habits, which were essentially variable in time and space, could not be considered to be immutable; the tax policy of a Member State must not therefore crystallize given consumer habits so as to consolidate an advantage acquired by national industries concerned to respond to them.

[9] The Court nonetheless recognized that, in view of the substantial differences between wine and beer, it was difficult to compare the manufacturing processes and the natural properties of those beverages, as the Government of the United Kingdom had rightly observed. For that reason, the Court requested the parties to provide additional information with a view to dispelling the doubts which existed concerning the nature of the competitive relationship between the two products.

. . .

[11] The Italian Government contended in that connection that it was inappropriate to compare beer with wines of average alcoholic strength or, *a fortiori*, with wines of greater alcoholic strength. In its opinion, it was the lightest wines with an alcoholic strength in the region of 9°, that is to say the most popular and cheapest wines, which were genuinely in competition with beer. It therefore took the view that those wines should be chosen for purposes of comparison where it was a question of measuring the incidence of taxation on the basis of either alcoholic strength or the price of the products.

[12] The Court considers that observation by the Italian Government to be pertinent. In view of the substantial differences in the quality and, therefore, in the price of wines, the decisive competitive relationship between beer, a popular and widely consumed beverage, and wine must be established by reference to those wines which are the most accessible to the public at large, that is to say, generally speaking, the lightest and cheapest varieties. Accordingly, that is the appropriate basis for making fiscal comparisons by reference to the alcoholic strength or to the price of the two beverages in question.

Having established a competitive relationship between the products, the Court then examined the effect of the taxation system:

[26]   After considering the information provided by the parties, the Court has come to the conclusion that, if a comparison is made on the basis of those wines which are cheaper than the types of wine selected by the United Kingdom and of which several varieties are sold in significant quantities on the United Kingdom market, it becomes apparent that precisely those wines which, in view of their price, are most directly in competition with domestic beer production are subject to a considerably higher tax burden.

[27]   It is clear, therefore, following the detailed inquiry conducted by the Court – whatever criterion for comparison is used, there being no need to express a preference for one or the other – that the United Kingdom's tax system has the effect of subjecting wine imported from other Member States to an additional tax burden so as to afford protection to domestic beer production, inasmuch as beer production constitutes the most relevant reference criterion from the point of view of competition. Since such protection is most marked in the case of the most popular wines, the effect of the United Kingdom tax system is to stamp wine with the hallmarks of a luxury product which, in view of the tax burden which it bears, can scarcely constitute in the eyes of the consumer a genuine alternative to the typical domestically produced beverage.

Notes
1.   For analysis of the Court's approach see A. J. Easson (1984) 6 EL Rev 57.
2.   A product which is available entirely or mainly only as an import can be subject to taxation, provided the tax on that product falls within the general scheme of internal taxation. A State which wishes to tax, for example, an exotic fruit or a raw material of which it has no supplies of its own, will have to demonstrate that the tax is simply an aspect of its broader tax regime for fruit or raw materials of that general type. If it cannot do so – if the tax is a special charge introduced for that import alone – then the charge is covered by Article 25. Even if the charge is part of the internal system, it must nevertheless be shown to be compatible with Article 90 – it must be neither discriminatory nor protective.

See *Commission* v *Denmark* (Case 158/82) [1983] ECR 3573, [1984] 2 CMLR 658 for an example of violation of Article 25; *Cooperativa Cofrutta* v *Amministrazione delle Finanze dello Stato* (Case 193/85) [1987] ECR 2085, *Commission* v *Italy* (Case 184/85) [1987] ECR 2013, Cases C-367/93-C-377/ 93 *F. G. Roders BV e.a.* v *Inspecteur der Invoerrechten en Accijnzen* [1995] ECR I-2229 on the application of Article 90.

Further reading
Danusso, M., and Denton, R., 'Does the European Court of Justice look for a Protectionist Motive under Article 95?' [1990/1] LIEI 67.
Hedemann-Robinson, M., 'Indirect Discrimination: Article 95 EC Back to Front and Inside Out?' (1995) 1 *European Public Law* 439.

(C) FISCAL HARMONISATION

The prohibition on discriminatory internal taxation is insufficient to achieve unrestricted free movement of goods in accordance with Article 14 EC, p. 179 above, as the following extract from COM (85) 310, the '1992 blueprint', the 'White Paper' on the Completion of the Internal Market, explains.

COM (85) 310, 'Completing the Internal Market' White Paper from the Commission to the European Council, 14 June 1985

160.   Fiscal checks feature prominently among the functions carried out at the Community's internal frontiers. Consequently, the removal of frontier controls is bound to have inescapable implications for the Member States as far as indirect taxes are concerned. The adjustments that will be needed to solve these practical problems are also very much in line with the terms of the commitment undertaken by those who signed the Treaties and with historical developments since then.

161.   When the Customs Union was achieved in 1968, it was already apparent that the mere removal of tariffs would not enable a true common internal market to be created; and that differences in turnover taxes in particular were the source of serious distortion and hence a serious obstacle to the completion of the Internal Market. That such a situation might arise was foreseen in the Treaty itself. Article 99 specifically provided that the Commission should make proposals for the approximation of indirect taxation when this was needed for the completion of the internal market; and Article 100 provided the legal means for so doing.

162.   Accordingly, in 1967, the Member States decided that the existing turnover taxes must be replaced by a Value Added Tax levied on a common basis. It was recognized from the outset that the imposition of such a tax on a common basis would raise many difficulties for Member States and would have to be phased in over a period of years. But it is clear from both the First and the Second VAT Directives which gave effect to this decision that a common basis was not only intended but was regarded as essential.

163.   The adoption of a harmonized VAT was given further impetus by the Council Decision in 1970 that the Community should be financed through 'own resources'. A significant element in this new 'own resources' regime was the allocation to the Community of the yield of part (not to exceed a rate of 1 per cent) of the harmonized VAT. It is clear from the Directives that what was in mind was not a notional calculation but the allocation of a specific share of an actual harmonized tax. The following year (1971) saw the adoption of a Council Resolution confirming its intention to create an area within which goods, services and capital could circulate freely and without distortions of competition. Not only was a common tax base regarded as essential to achieve this end, but common tax rates as well were contemplated. In the words of the Resolution: 'Before the end of the first stage, the Council will deliberate on the studies undertaken, and on the proposals made, by the Commission concerning the approximation of rates of value added tax and of excise duties.'

164.   The broad principles of the harmonized common tax base for VAT were laid down in outline in the Second VAT Directive dated 11 April 1967. This was followed after a period of intensive consideration and discussion, by the Sixth VAT Directive, adopted in 1977 which set out in great detail the provisions of the common base. Because of the problems involved in reaching agreement on a number of difficult and

contentious issues, the Sixth Directive contains a number of lacunae as well as special schemes, derogations and transitional provisions. At the same time, Article 35 of the Directive specifically provided that these derogations and special arrangements should ultimately be brought to an end. Nowhere is the general philosophy set out more succinctly than in the preamble to the Directive. This declares:

'Whereas account should be taken of the objective of abolishing the imposition of tax on the importation and the remission of tax on exportation in trade between Member States; whereas it should be ensured that the common system of turnover taxes is non-discriminatory as regards the origin of goods and services, so that a common market permitting fair competition and resembling a real internal market may ultimately be achieved.'

Since 1977 a number of supplementary Directives have been adopted and a number await the Council's decision.

165.   Soon after the first steps were taken to harmonize turnover taxes, the Community turned its attention to excise duties. As a first step the Commission identified tobacco, alcoholic drinks and hydrocarbon oils as the products on which excises should be levied – a choice which coincides with the coverage adopted by most Member States.

166.   In the case of tobacco, a limited degree of harmonization has already been achieved. The basic directive adopted in 1972 defined the structures of excise duty on cigarettes; provided for harmonization in successive stages; and defined a range of relationships between the specific duty and the total duty. In the case of alcoholic drinks and hydrocarbon oils, little progress has been made despite the presentation by the Commission of a whole range of directives. At the same time, however, a limited degree of progress has been made as a result of judgements by the European Court which have compelled Member States to abandon tax arrangements which benefited domestic producers to the detriment of producers in other Member States.

167.   It is clear from what has been said above that the harmonization of indirect taxation has always been regarded as an essential and integral part of achieving a true common market. Momentum has been lost in recent years but this was due essentially to the impact of the recession on the economic policies of Member States and preoccupation with other problems. But progress is being resumed and now we must proceed vigorously if we are to achieve the target date of 1992 for the completion of the Internal Market.

168.   If goods and services and people are to move freely from one member State to another in just the same way as they can move within a member State, it is essential that frontier controls be abolished. Since these are primarily designed to ensure that each member State can collect the revenue in the form of indirect taxation to which it feels entitled, there are clear implications for the indirect taxation policies of individual Member States. Let us be quite clear that we are talking here not in terms of frontier facilitation, i.e. simplifying frontier procedures in the way that the Directive on the Harmonization of Frontier Procedures and the Single Administrative Document aim to do, but in terms of removing the frontiers altogether as only in this way is it possible to achieve the stated objective of free movement of goods and of people.

Note
As this extract suggests, harmonisation of taxation is extremely complex. A major obstacle is the political symbolism of the power to levy tax. Yet progress is being made, although this is an area which continues to demand delicate negotiation beyond the end of 1992, the deadline for the completion of the internal market.

As is well known, the pattern chosen for the internal market after the end of 1992 is based on a sharp distinction between private consumers and commercial traders. Private consumers are free to shop in a State other than their own and to take goods back home without having to pay sums representing the difference between the taxes levied in the State of purchase and their home State. The popularity of day-trips from England to France to buy alcohol is, to the dismay of British brewers, a direct result of this EC initiative; in the area of private consumption there is a 'competition between regulators' in fixing VAT and excise duties (p. 219 above). A high-taxing State unwilling to accept the shortfall in tax revenues may choose to raise rates, but this risks provoking even higher levels of cross-border shopping. The alternative is a reduction in rates to competitive levels in order to remove the incentive to shop elsewhere. See McKelvey, M., 'Cheap Beer or Economic Harmony' (1995) XVIII *Boston College International and Comp Law Rev* 457. However, in commercial trade the tax differentials which persist between the Member States have led to the introduction of a scheme which requires collection of taxes, although not at physical borders. The scheme is found in Directives 92/12 (OJ 1992 L76/1) and 92/108 (OJ 1992 L390/124).

The technical nature of the subject of tax harmonisation precludes exhaustive treatment in this book. However, issues of tax harmonisation remain high profile, even though legislative progress has been relatively slow. The method chosen has typically been 'minimum harmonisation'. States may not set rates lower than the Community minimum, though they may set higher rates. This reflects the political complexity of the subject – States are not prepared to allow their competence to set tax rates to be totally preempted by the Community and, illuminatingly, unanimous voting in Council remains the rule in the area of taxation. Minimum harmonisation yields both a degree of harmonisation and, above the minimum rate, a competition between regulators. This is to be observed in relation to value added tax and excise duties. On the latter, some progress was made in a package of Directives adopted in October 1992. Directives 92/79 and 92/80 (OJ 1992 L316/8, 10) set minimum rates for cigarettes and other tobacco products respectively; Directives 92/81 and 92/82 (OJ 1992 L316/12, 19) set minimum rates for petroleum products; Directives 92/83 and 92/84 (OJ 1992 L316/21, 29) cover the harmonisation of the structure and of the rates respectively of excise duties on alcoholic beverages. Minimum rates are set for beer, wine and other defined categories of alcoholic beverage. The text below reveals the rather remarkable choice made of the minimum figure for excise rates levied on still and sparkling wine.

Council Directive 92/84/EEC (1992) OJ L316/29 on the approximation of the rates of excise duty on alcohol and alcoholic beverages
(1992) OJ L316/29

Article 1
Not later than 1 January 1993, Member States shall apply minimum rates of excise duty in accordance with the rules laid down in this Directive.

. . .

Article 5
As from 1 January 1993, the minimum rate of excise duty on wine shall be fixed:
— for still wine at ECU 0, and
— for sparkling wine at ECU 0
per hectolitre of product.

Question
· Is minimum harmonisation of this type worthwhile? What alternatives are available to the EC in developing a tax policy for the internal market?

Note
At a much broader level, in December 1997 the Finance Ministers of the Member States in Council agreed to a package of measures designed to counter 'Harmful Tax Competition'. This was the result of a vigorous Commission initiative (COM (96) 546, COM (97) 564). Binding legislation within the meaning of Article 249 EC is not involved. A code of conduct on company taxation has been agreed, which includes a review process, and a commitment is made to consider new legislation on a minimum tax on savings income. Naturally, the title chosen for this initiative begs the delicate question of what is truly 'harmful' competition and what are merely different choices about tax rates and policies. This is closely related to the intriguing issue of reconciling a 'competition between regulators' with the pursuit of a level playing field, introduced at p. 219 above and further examined in Chapter 15. Furthermore, in order to site this new package in its wider legal context, it should be appreciated that tax concessions may in some circumstances fall foul of Article 87 EC governing State aids (p. 442 below).

Further reading
Easson, A., *Taxation in the European Community* (London, Athlone Press, 1993).
Farmer, P. and Lyal, R., *EC Tax Law* (Oxford, Clarendon Press, 1994).
Vanistendael, F., 'The limits to the new Community tax order' (1994) 31 CML Rev 293.

See also for some consideration of the association of economic and monetary union with fiscal harmonisation, D. McKay, 'Policy Legitimacy and Institutional Design' (2000) 38 JCMS 25.

7 PHYSICAL AND TECHNICAL BARRIERS TO TRADE: ARTICLES 28–30

(A) THE DEVELOPMENT OF ARTICLE 28

The brevity of Article 28 is out of all proportion to its immense significance as an instrument for the creation of a market in which the free circulation of goods is ensured.

Article 28 EC

Article 28
Quantitative restrictions on imports and all measures having equivalent effect shall be prohibited between Member States.

Article 29 applies a similarly worded prohibition to restrictions on exports.

Article 30 permits Member States to advance justifications for obstacles to trade contrary to Articles 28 and 30. Such purported justifications will be closely scrutinised, for they imply lawful trade barriers which handicap the pursuit of a common market.

Here, more than in most areas, it is vital to remember that pre-Amsterdam material contains pre-Amsterdam Treaty numbering (p. 29 above). Articles 28 and 29 were Articles 30 and 34 respectively, while, in the most unfortunate of all the Amsterdam re-numberings, what is now Article 30 was previously Article 36. Remember this when reading the texts in this chapter and the next.

Articles 28 and 29 on the one hand and Article 30 on the other, are provisions which seek to strike a balance between the impetus towards free trade and the acceptance that Member States retain a strictly defined competence lawfully to restrict free trade in order to protect certain important domestic interests. The interpretation and location of this balance by the judges is itself an interesting exercise in judicial assessment of competing interests. The chapters which follow will frequently refer to the Court's role as an arbiter in this field. Eventually, however, restrictive national rules which remain justifiable may be replaced by Community rules which set common standards for the Community. This is the process of harmonisation. It is designed to secure protection of important interests (as is Article 30), but (unlike Article 30) that protection is achieved within the framework of a Community, not a national, structure, which will permit and stimulate free cross-border trade.

The Court defined the 'quantitative restriction' in *Geddo* v *Ente* (Case 2/73) [1973] ECR 865, [1974] 1 CMLR 13, as 'measures which amount to a total or partial restraint of, according to the circumstances, imports, exports or goods in transit'. But what of the measure 'having equivalent effect' to the quantitative restriction which, according to Article 28, also falls within the scope of the prohibition?

In *Geddo* v *Ente*, (Case 2/73), the Court followed its definition of the quantitative restriction given above by stating briefly that 'measures having equivalent effect not only take the form of restraint described: whatever the description or technique employed, they can also consist of encumbrances having the same effect'.

Further elucidation of the notion may be found in Directive 70/50. Directive 70/50 was formally only of application to the transitional period of the Community's development, which has long since expired, and the relevant Treaty provisions in this area were repealed by the Treaty of Amsterdam. Yet its influence as an indication of the Commission's view of the scope of this Article of the EC Treaty has persisted and the Court continues to refer to it on occasion. The Directive is, then, a useful source of guidance on the nature of the practices which fall foul of the prohibition on 'MEQRs' (measures having equivalent effect to a quantitative restriction).

Directive 70/50 EEC on the Abolition of Measures which have an effect equivalent to the Quantitative Restrictions on Imports and are not covered by other provisions adopted in pursuance of the EEC Treaty
(1970) OJ (Special Edition) (I), p. 17

Article 1
The purpose of this Directive is to abolish the measures referred to in Articles 2 and 3, which were operative at the date of entry into force of the EEC Treaty.

Article 2
1. This Directive covers measures, other than those applicable equally to domestic or imported products, which hinder imports which could otherwise take place, including measures which make importation more difficult or costly than the disposal of domestic production.

2. In particular, it covers measures which make imports or the disposal, at any marketing stage, of imported products subject to a condition – other than a formality – which is required in respect of imported products only, or a condition differing from

that required for domestic products and more difficult to satisfy. Equally, it covers, in particular, measures which favour domestic products or grant them a preference, other than an aid, to which conditions may or may not be attached.

3.   The measures referred to must be taken to include those measures which:

(a)   lay down, for imported products only, minimum or maximum prices below or above which imports are prohibited, reduced or made subject to conditions liable to hinder importation;

(b)   lay down less favourable prices for imported products than for domestic products;

(c)   fix profit margins or any other price components for imported products only or fix these differently for domestic products and for imported products, to the detriment of the latter;

(d)   preclude any increase in the price of the imported product corresponding to the supplementary costs and charges inherent in importation;

(e)   fix the prices of products solely on the basis of the cost price or the quality of domestic products at such a level as to create a hindrance to importation;

(f)   lower the value of an imported product, in particular by causing a reduction in its intrinsic value, or increase its costs;

(g)   make access of imported products to the domestic market conditional upon having an agent or representative in the territory of the importing Member State;

(h)   lay down conditions of payment in respect of imported products only, or subject imported products to conditions which are different from those laid down for domestic products and more difficult to satisfy;

(i)   require, for imports only, the giving of guarantees or making of payments on account;

(j)   subject imported products only to conditions, in respect, in particular of shape, size, weight, composition, presentation, identification or putting up, or subject imported products to conditions which are different from those for domestic products and more difficult to satisfy;

(k)   hinder the purchase by private individuals of imported products only, or encourage, require or give preference to the purchase of domestic products only;

(l)   totally or partially preclude the use of national facilities or equipment in respect of imported products only, or totally or partially confine the use of such facilities or equipment to domestic products only;

(m)   prohibit or limit publicity in respect of imported products only, or totally or partially confine publicity to domestic products only;

(n)   prohibit, limit or require stocking in respect of imported products only; totally or partially confine the use of stocking facilities to domestic products only, or make the stocking of imported products subject to conditions which are different from those required for domestic products and more difficult to satisfy;

(o)   make importation subject to the granting of reciprocity by one or more Member States;

(p)   prescribe that imported products are to conform, totally or partially, to rules other than those of the importing country;

(q)   specify time limits for imported products which are insufficient or excessive in relation to the normal course of the various transactions to which these time limits apply;

(r)   subject imported products to controls, other than those inherent in the customs clearance procedure, to which domestic products are not subject or which are stricter in respect of imported products than they are in respect of domestic products, without this being necessary in order to ensure equivalent protection;

(s) confine names which are not indicative of origin or source to domestic products only.

Article 3

This Directive also covers measures governing the marketing of products which deal, in particular, with shape, size, weight, composition, presentation, identification or putting up and which are equally applicable to domestic and imported products, where the restrictive effect of such measures on the free movement of goods exceeds the effects intrinsic to trade rules.

This is the case, in particular, where:
— the restrictive effects on the free movement of goods are out of proportion to their purpose;
— the same objective can be attained by other means which are less of a hindrance to trade.

Notes

1. The Directive, then, discloses two types of 'MEQR' (measure having equivalent effect to a quantitative restriction), divided according to their application. Article 2 covers national rules which discriminate against imports, which are taken to infringe Article 28; Article 3 covers national rules which apply equally to all goods, which are taken normally to conform to the demands of Article 28.

2. The vigorous work of the Court has transformed Article 28 into a fundamentally important means of dismantling national barriers to the free movement of goods. The Court was naturally little confined by the explicit terms of the Treaty Article in building its approach, for the provision is of such brevity as to yield almost any interpretation. In its celebrated decision in *Dassonville* (Case 8/74) (below), the Court selected an interpretation of Article 28 which is firmly orientated towards market integration through the abolition of obstructive national rules.

The Court declared that Article 28 (then 30) prohibits as MEQRs 'all trading rules enacted by Member States which are capable of hindering, directly or indirectly, actually or potentially, intra-Community trade'. Article 28 has, according to Lord Cockfield, the Commissioner formerly responsible for internal market policy, a 'magnificent sweep'.

On its literal terms, the *Dassonville* formula could even be taken to catch any national measure which circumscribes commercial freedom, even if neither discriminatory against imports nor protective of home production. The Court chose in *Keck and Mithouard* (Joined Cases C-267 and C-268/91) [1993] ECR I-6097, [1995] 1 CMLR 101, to refine the *Dassonville* formula in order to make it clear that Article 28 cannot be invoked where the rule in question impedes trade in imported goods no more than it impedes trade in domestic goods. The Court stated that 'the application to products from other Member States of national provisions restricting or prohibiting certain selling arrangements is not such as to hinder, directly or indirectly, actually or potentially, trade between Member States, provided that the provisions apply to all affected traders operating within the national territory and provided that they affect in the same manner, in law and in fact, the marketing of domestic products and those from other Member States'. The implications of the cautious *Keck* ruling, and its requirement of legal or factual inequality as a threshold to the application of Article 28, are examined more fully at p. 316 below.

At the heart of the Court's declaration in *Dassonville* is the perception that the application of the Article 28 prohibition is dependent on the *effects* of the measure. Article 28 bites where a national rule is shown to have an effect prejudicial to the integration of the markets of the Member States.

3.   The Court's emphasis differs from that in Directive 70/50. Discrimination is *not* the key. Unequal treatment of domestic and imported goods is likely to violate Article 28 because of the consequential restrictive effect on cross-border trade, but such discrimination is plainly not a pre-condition for the application of Article 28. The essential element is *the restrictive effect on inter-State trade*.

Procureur du Roi v *Dassonville (Case 8/74)*
[1974] ECR 837; [1974] 2 CMLR 436
Court of Justice of the European Communities

The Court indicated that a Belgian requirement that importers of Scotch whisky possess a British certificate of authentication was incompatible with Article 30 of the EC Treaty (now, after amendment, Article 28 EC). The rule favoured direct importers over traders importing Scotch whisky into Belgium from other Member States in which the goods were already in free circulation. The rule 'channelled' trade and distorted the market.

[1] By Judgment of 11 January 1974, received at the Registry of the Court on 8 February 1974, the Tribunal de Première Instance of Brussels referred, under Article 177 of the EEC Treaty, two questions on the interpretation of Articles 30, 31, 32, 33, 36 and 85 of the EEC Treaty, relating to the requirement of an official document issued by the government of the exporting country for products bearing a designation of origin.

[2] By the first question it is asked whether a national provision prohibiting the import of goods bearing a designation of origin where such goods are not accompanied by an official document issued by the government of the exporting country certifying their right to such designation constitutes a measure having an effect equivalent to a quantitative restriction within the meaning of Article 30 of the Treaty.

[3] This question was raised within the context of criminal proceedings instituted in Belgium against traders who duly acquired a consignment of Scotch whisky in free circulation in France and imported it into Belgium without being in possession of a certificate of origin from the British customs authorities, thereby infringing Belgian rules.

[4] It emerges from the file and from the oral proceedings that a trader, wishing to import into Belgium Scotch whisky which is already in free circulation in France, can obtain such a certificate only with great difficulty, unlike the importer who imports directly from the producer country.

[5]   All trading rules enacted by Member States which are capable of hindering, directly or indirectly, actually or potentially, intra-Community trade are to be considered as measures having an effect equivalent to quantitative restrictions.

[6]   In the absence of a Community system guaranteeing for consumers the authenticity of a product's designation of origin, if a Member State takes measures to prevent unfair practices in this connexion, it is however subject to the condition that these measures should be reasonable and that the means of proof required should not act as a hindrance to trade between Member States and should, in consequence, be accessible to all Community nationals.

[7]   Even without having to examine whether or not such measures are covered by Article 36, they must not, in any case, by virtue of the principle expressed in the second sentence of that Article, constitute a means of arbitrary discrimination or a disguised restriction on trade between Member States.

[8]   That may be the case with formalities, required by a Member State for the purpose of proving the origin of a product, which only direct importers are really in a position to satisfy without facing serious difficulties.

[9]   Consequently, the requirement by a Member State of a certificate of authenticity which is less easily obtainable by importers of an authentic product which has been put into free circulation in a regular manner in another Member State than by importers of the same product coming directly from the country of origin constitutes a measure having an effect equivalent to a quantitative restriction as prohibited by the Treaty.

Question
What is meant by the Court's suggestion in para. 6 that 'reasonable' measures would not infringe Article 28 (then Article 30)? Could the Belgian authorities have devised an authentication system compatible with Article 28? (The issue of locating the limit to the scope of Article 28 as a means of challenging trade restrictions will be readdressed in the next chapter.)

Note
The fundamental aim of Article 28 is to preclude the isolation of national markets and thereby to induce efficient competition irrespective of the existence of national frontiers. A policy of domestic preference violates that objective. The following case provides a good example of the Court's insistence that competition shall proceed on the basis of quality, not nationality.

Commission v Ireland (Case 45/87)
[1988] ECR 4929; [1989] 1 CMLR 225
Court of Justice of the European Communities

[1]   By application lodged at the Court Registry on 13 February 1987, the Commission of the European Communities brought an action under Article 169 of the EEC Treaty for a declaration that by allowing the inclusion in the contract specification for the Dundalk Water Supply Augmentation Scheme – Contract No 4 of a clause providing that the asbestos cement pressure pipes should be certified as complying with Irish Standard 188: 1975 in accordance with the Irish Standard Mark Licensing

Scheme of the Institute for Industrial Research and Standards (IIRS) and consequently refusing to consider (or rejecting without adequate justification) a tender providing for the use of asbestos cement pipes manufactured to an alternative standard providing equivalent guarantees of safety, performance and reliability, Ireland has failed to fulfil its obligations under Article 30 of the EEC Treaty and Article 10 of Council Directive 71/305/EEC of 26 July 1971 concerning the coordination of procedures for the award of public works contracts (Official Journal, English Special Edition 1971 (II), p. 682).

[2]   Dundalk Urban District Council is the promoter of a scheme for the augmentation of Dundalk's drinking water supply. Contract No 4 of that scheme is for the construction of a water-main to transport water from the River Fane source to a treatment plant at Cavan Hill and thence into the existing town supply system. The invitation to tender for that contract by open procedure was published in the *Supplement of the Official Journal of the European Communities* on 13 March 1986 (Official Journal S 50, p. 13).

[3]   Clause 4.29 of the specification relating to Contract No 4, which formed part of the contract specification, included the following paragraph:

'Asbestos cement pressure pipes shall be certified as complying with Irish Standard Specification 188: 1975 in accordance with the Irish Standard Mark Licensing Scheme of the Institute for Industrial Research and Standards. All asbestos cement watermains are to have a bituminous coating internally and externally. Such coatings shall be applied at the factory by dipping.'

[4]   The dispute stems from complaints made to the Commission by an Irish undertaking and a Spanish undertaking. In response to the invitation to tender for Contract No 4, the Irish undertaking had submitted three tenders, one of which provided for the use of pipes manufactured by the Spanish undertaking. In the Irish undertaking's view, that tender, which was the lowest of the three submitted by it, gave it the best chance of obtaining the contract. The consulting engineers to the project wrote a letter to the Irish undertaking concerning that contract stating that there would be no point in its coming to the pre-adjudication interview if proof could not be provided that the firm supplying the pipes was approved by the IIRS as a supplier of products complying with Irish Standard 188: 1975 ('IS 188'). It is common ground that the Spanish undertaking in question had not been certified by the IIRS but that its pipes complied with international standards, and in particular with ISO 160: 1980 of the International Organization for Standardization.

[5]   Reference is made to the Report for the Hearing for a fuller account of the relevant provisions, the background to the case and the submissions and arguments of the parties and of the intervener, which are mentioned or discussed hereinafter only in so far as is necessary for the reasoning of the Court.

[6]   In the Commission's view, this action raises *inter alia* the question of the compatibility with Community law, in particular Article 30 of the EEC Treaty and Article 10 of Directive 71/305, of the inclusion in a contract specification of clauses like the disputed Clause 4.29. It further argues that the Irish authorities' rejection, without any examination, of a tender providing for the use of Spanish-made pipes not complying with Irish standards also infringed those provisions of Community law. It is appropriate to examine first the issues raised by Clause 4.29.

The Court found no breach of Directive 71/305, even though the Directive contains anti-discrimination provisions, because the Directive excluded from its scope services for the distribution of water. The Court continued:

Article 30 [now 28] of the Treaty

[12]   It must be observed at the outset that the Commission maintains that Dundalk Urban District Council is a public body for whose acts the Irish Government is responsible. Moreover, before accepting a tender, Dundalk Council has to obtain the authorization of the Irish Department of the Environment. Those facts have not been challenged by the Irish Government.

[13]   It must also be noted that according to the Irish Government the requirement of compliance with Irish standards is the usual practice followed in relation to public works contracts in Ireland.

[14]   The Irish Government points out that the contract at issue relates not to the sale of goods but to the performance of work, and the clauses relating to the materials to be used are completely subsidiary. Contracts concerned with the performance of work fall under the Treaty provisions relating to the free supply of services, without prejudice to any harmonization measures which might be taken under Article 100. Consequently, Article 30 cannot apply to a contract for works.

[15]   In that connection, the Irish Government cites the case-law of the Court and, in particular, the judgment of 22 March 1977 in Case *74/76 (Iannelli & Volpi v Meroni* [1977] ECR 557), according to which the field of application of Article 30 does not include obstacles to trade covered by other specific provisions of the Treaty.

[16]   That argument cannot be accepted. Article 30 envisages the elimination of all measures of the Member States which impede imports in intra-Community trade, whether the measures bear directly on the movement of imported goods or have the effect of indirectly impeding the marketing of goods from other Member States. The fact that some of those barriers must be considered in the light of specific provisions of the Treaty, such as the provisions of Article 95 relating to fiscal discrimination, in no way detracts from the general character of the prohibitions laid down by Article 30.

[17]   The provisions on the freedom to supply services invoked by the Irish Government, on the other hand, are not concerned with the movement of goods but the freedom to perform activities and have them carried out; they do not lay down any specific rule relating to particular barriers to the free movement of goods. Consequently, the fact that a public works contract relates to the provision of services cannot remove a clause in an invitation to tender restricting the materials that may be used from the scope of the prohibitions set out in Article 30.

[18]   Consequently, it must be considered whether the inclusion of Clause 4.29 in the invitation to tender and in the tender specifications was liable to impede imports of pipes into Ireland.

[19]   In that connection, it must first be pointed out that the inclusion of such a clause in an invitation to tender may cause economic operators who produce or utilize pipes equivalent to pipes certified as complying with Irish standards to refrain from tendering.

[20]   It further appears from the documents in the case that only one undertaking has been certified by the IIRS to IS 188: 1975 to apply the Irish Standard Mark to pipes of the type required for the purposes of the public works contract at issue. That undertaking is located in Ireland. Consequently, the inclusion of Clause 4.29 had the effect of restricting the supply of the pipes needed for the Dundalk scheme to Irish manufacturers alone.

[21]   The Irish Government maintains that it is necessary to specify the standards to which materials must be manufactured, particularly in a case such as this where the pipes utilized must suit the existing network. Compliance with another standard, even an international standard such as ISO 160: 1980, would not suffice to eliminate certain technical difficulties.

[22]   That technical argument cannot be accepted. The Commission's complaint does not relate to compliance with technical requirements but to the refusal of the Irish authorities to verify whether those requirements are satisfied where the manufacturer of the materials has not been certified by the IIRS to IS 188. By incorporating in the notice in question the words 'or equivalent' after the reference to the Irish standard, as provided for by Directive 71/305 where it is applicable, the Irish authorities could have verified compliance with the technical conditions without from the outset restricting the contract only to tenderers proposing to utilize Irish materials.

[23]   The Irish Government further objects that in any event the pipes manufactured by the Spanish undertaking in question whose use was provided for in the rejected tender did not meet the technical requirements, but that argument, too, is irrelevant as regards the compatibility with the Treaty of the inclusion of a clause like Clause 4.29 in an invitation to tender.

[24]   The Irish Government further maintains that protection of public health justifies the requirement of compliance with the Irish standard in so far as that standard guarantees that there is no contact between the water and the asbestos fibres in the cement pipes, which would adversely affect the quality of the drinking water.

[25]   That argument must be rejected. As the Commission has rightly pointed out, the coating of the pipes, both internally and externally, was the subject of a separate requirement in the invitation to tender. The Irish Government has not shown why compliance with that requirement would not be such as to ensure that there is no contact between the water and the asbestos fibres, which it considers to be essential for reasons of public health.

[26]   The Irish Government has not put forward any other argument to refute the conclusions of the Commission and the Spanish Government and those conclusions must consequently be upheld.

[27]   It must therefore be held that by allowing the inclusion in the contract specification for tender for a public works contract of a clause stipulating that the asbestos cement pressure pipes must be certified as complying with Irish Standard 188: 1975 in accordance with the Irish Standard Mark Licensing Scheme of the Institute for Industrial Research and Standards, Ireland has failed to fulfil its obligations under Article 30 of the EEC Treaty.

Notes

1.   The application of Article 28 stimulates competition. Competition yields consumer choice, lower prices and higher quality. In this way the benefits of a common market are realised. The economic advantages were discussed more generally in Chapter 5.

2.   It is not misleading to view the Court's activism in this area as judicial lawmaking. This integrationist jurisprudence finds little explicit basis in the Treaty or in secondary legislation. Yet implied support exists. The Court has moulded its conception of Article 28 in accordance with the objects of the Treaty. The objective of market integration and, eventually, the establishment of a common market, provide the inspiration for the development of appropriate substantive rules of law. Just as Part One of this book showed how the Court was not constrained by the absence of explicit instruction in the Treaty from eliciting the constitutional doctrines of supremacy and direct effect as the pillars of the Community's legal order in order to achieve the objectives of the Treaty, so too in the area of substantive law the Court is prepared to construct a body of interpretation which is loosely derived from Article 28, but which, more significantly, is justified as a method of bringing to fruition the Treaty objective of market integration.

3.   This approach is certainly distinct from that of the English judges. The traditional English technique is to follow rules laid down with more precision than is the style of the Treaty of Rome. Judicial development of codified law is less readily acknowledged as either familiar or appropriate in the UK.

R v Secretary of State, ex parte Bomore
[1986] 1 CMLR 228
Court of Appeal

MAY LJ: [The European] Court adopts an approach substantially different from that familiar to lawyers in this country . . . the Court of Justice in its decisions on Article 30 has sought both to flesh it out and at the same time to limit its apparent generality so as to produce, by a process of judge-made legislation, a developing code of law, founded upon Article 30.

Questions
1.   Should English judges adopt a more purposive or, perhaps, creative approach (i) in interpreting Community law, (ii) in interpreting domestic law? (Remember the discussion of the implications of *Von Colson* (Case 14/83) and *Marleasing* (Case C-106/89) in Chapter 3.)

You might read Chapter 8 on 'Judicial Creativity' in J. Griffith's *The Politics of the Judiciary* (1997), and consider how the debate there presented might be applied to the development of Community law.

2.   Can you think of any examples from any area of Community law where the European Court has adopted an unduly activist, creative stance which has failed to command respect? Are there cases which demonstrate caution about the perils of judicial overeagerness? Read generally H. Rasmussen, *On Law and Policy in the ECJ* (1986) and reconsider some of the material in Part One of this book.

(B) THE APPLICATION OF ARTICLE 28

Examples of the application of Article 28 follow. The consistent theme is the breadth of Article 28 as a prohibition on national measures which have an effect which is restrictive of trade between Member States. In reading these cases, remember that prior to the re-numbering effected by the Amsterdam Treaty, what is now Article 28 EC was, with minor amendment, Article 30; and what is now Article 30 EC was Article 36.

Schloh v Auto Controle Technique (Case 50/85)
[1986] ECR 1855
Court of Justice of the European Communities

Mr Schloh bought a Ford Granada estate car in Germany. He obtained from a Ford dealer in Belgium a certificate of conformity with vehicle types approved in Belgium. In Belgium he was required to submit his car to two roadworthiness tests, for which fees were charged. He challenged the tests on the basis of Article 30 (now 28), the fees on the basis of Article 13 (now deleted). (See Chapter 6 on fiscal charges.) The matter reached the European Court by way of a preliminary reference from a Belgian court (see Chapter 4). The Court summed up the questions referred as follows:

[9]   It is apparent from the terms of those questions that the Court is being asked in substance:
   (a)   first, whether it is in accordance with Article 30 of the Treaty for a car imported from another Member State and carrying a certificate of conformity to the vehicle types approved in the importing Member State to be subject to a roadworthiness test for the purposes of registration in the latter State;
   (b)   secondly, whether it is in accordance with Article 30 of the Treaty for the same car to be subject to a second roadworthiness test carried out a few days after the first test;
   (c)   thirdly, whether it is in accordance with Article 13 of the Treaty for a fee to be levied at the time of each roadworthiness test.

The first roadworthiness test
[10]   The Danish Government and the Commission take the view that national measures whereby a new imported vehicle carrying a certificate of conformity to the safety standards of the importing Member State is subject to a roadworthiness test constitute measures having an effect equivalent to quantitative restrictions contrary to Article 30 of the Treaty; moreover, they are not justified by any of the imperative requirements referred to in the judgments of the Court or any of the reasons enumerated in Article 36 of the Treaty. However, the Danish Government states that where the vehicle is imported in a used condition a roadworthiness test may be justified by the need to check at least its state of repair.

[11]   It should be noted first of all that, although Council Directive 77/143/EEC of 29 December 1976 (Official Journal 1977, L 47, p. 47) laid down a number of measures for the harmonization of roadworthiness tests for motor vehicles, the terms of Annex I to the directive make it inapplicable to vehicles in the category to which the plaintiff's vehicle belongs. At this stage in the development of Community law it is therefore for the Member States – provided that they comply with the provisions of the Treaty – to lay down rules for the roadworthiness testing of vehicles in that category in order to ensure road safety.

[12]   Under the terms of Article 30 of the Treaty, quantitative restrictions on imports and all measures having equivalent effect are prohibited between Member States.

Roadworthiness testing is a formality which makes the registration of imported vehicles more difficult and more onerous and consequently is in the nature of a measure having an effect equivalent to a quantitative restriction.

[13]   Nevertheless, Article 36 may justify such a formality on grounds of the protection of human health and life, provided that it is established, first, that the test at issue is necessary for the attainment of that objective and, secondly, that it does not constitute a means of arbitrary discrimination or a disguised restriction on trade between Member States.

[14]   As far as the first condition is concerned, it must be acknowledged that roadworthiness testing required prior to the registration of an imported vehicle may, even though the vehicle carries a certificate of conformity to the vehicle types approved in the importing Member State, be regarded as necessary for the protection of human health and life where the vehicle in question has already been put on the road. In such cases roadworthiness testing performs a useful function inasmuch as it makes it possible to check that the vehicle has not been damaged and is in a good state of repair. However, such testing cannot be justified on those grounds where it relates to an imported vehicle carrying a certificate of conformity which has not been placed on the road before being registered in the importing Member State.

[15]   As far as the second condition is concerned, it must be stated that the roadworthiness testing of imported vehicles cannot, however, be justified under the second sentence of Article 36 of the Treaty if it is established that such testing is not required in the case of vehicles of national origin presented for registration in the same circumstances. If that were the case it would become apparent that the measure in question was not in fact inspired by a concern for the protection of human health and life but in reality constituted a means of arbitrary discrimination in trade between Member States. It is for the national court to verify that such non-discriminatory treatment is in fact ensured.

[16]   It must therefore be stated in reply to the juge de paix of Schaerbeek that Article 30 of the Treaty must be interpreted as meaning that a national measure which requires a roadworthiness test for the purpose of registering an imported vehicle carrying a certificate of its conformity to the vehicle types approved in the importing Member State constitutes a measure having an effect equivalent to a quantitative restriction on imports. Nevertheless, such a measure is justified under Article 36 of the Treaty in so far as it relates to vehicles put on the road before such registration and applies without distinction to vehicles of national origin and imported vehicles.

The second roadworthiness test
[17]   The Commission, which was alone in presenting observations on this point, takes the view that the second test, being imposed for the purpose of exempting the vehicle from regular annual testing for the first four years, constitutes a measure having equivalent effect contrary to Article 30 of the Treaty and not justified by Article 36. In that connection the Commission notes that an exemption from regular annual tests could have been obtained simply by means of a declaration concerning the use of the vehicle made on the occasion of the first roadworthiness test.

[18]   It should be pointed out that, as the Court has consistently held, national rules cannot benefit from an exception provided for by Article 36 of the Treaty if the objective pursued by that exception can be as effectively realized by measures which do not restrict intra-Community trade so much.

[19] It must consequently be accepted that Article 36 does not provide justification for roadworthiness testing whose purpose is to obtain from the owner of the imported vehicle a written declaration certifying that the use of the vehicle qualifies it for exemption from annual testing. That purpose may be achieved simply by requiring the owner to supply that written declaration, without its being necessary for the vehicle to be presented to an approved vehicle testing agency.

[20] It must therefore be stated in reply to the question put by the juge de paix of Schaerbeek that Articles 30 and 36 of the Treaty must be interpreted as meaning that, where the roadworthiness testing of an imported vehicle has the purpose of obtaining a written declaration from the owner of the vehicle, it constitutes a measure having an effect equivalent to a quantitative restriction on imports contrary to the Treaty.

The Court held the fees unlawful where the test itself violated Article 30 (now 28), but capable of accommodation within a general system of taxation compatible with Article 95 (now 90) where the inspection itself was lawful under Article 36 (now 30).

Notes
1. Notice how (para. 11) the Court observes that the matter is untouched by the Community's harmonisation programme and that therefore the Treaty alone supplies the basis for judging the permissibility of Member State action. The legal assessment would be different if (as is increasingly common in many sectors) the field had been entered by Community secondary legislation; pp. 285 below.
2. See also Case C-55/93 *Criminal Proceedings against Johannis Gerrit Cornelis van Schaik* [1994] ECR I-4837, in which the Court held that neither primary Treaty provisions including Article 28 nor Directive 77/143 preclude legislation of a Member State which does not permit test certificates in respect of cars registered in that State to be issued by garages established in another Member State.

International Fruit Company v *Produktschap voor Groenten en Fruit (No. 2) (Cases 51–54/71)*
[1971] ECR 1107
Court of Justice of the European Communities

The Court was asked to consider whether Article 30 of the EC Treaty (now, after amendment, Article 28 EC) applies to 'national legislative provisions prohibiting imports and exports without a licence but which in fact are not applied because exemptions are granted from the prohibition and, where this is not so, because the licence is always issued on request'.

[6] The question put refers both to the system of quantitative restrictions on intra-Community trade and the system of such restrictions on trade with third countries.

[7] It is however clear from the scheme of the Treaty that those two systems must be distinguished.

[8]   Under Articles 30 and 34(1) of the Treaty quantitative restrictions and measures having equivalent effect are prohibited between Member States both with regard to imports and exports.

[9]   Consequently, apart from the exceptions for which provision is made by Community law itself those provisions preclude the application to intra-Community trade of a national provision which requires, even purely as a formality, import or export licences or any other similar procedure.

Note

The Court concluded its judgment by taking a more permissive view of the lawfulness of controls over trade with third countries outside the Community.

In *Commission* v *Italy* (Case 159/78) the Court accepted the opportunity to declare its view of the application of Article 30 of the EC Treaty (now, after amendment, Article 28 EC) to customs formalities at frontiers which impede intra-Community trade.

Commission v *Italy (Case 159/78)*
[1979] ECR 3247; [1980] 3 CMLR 446
Court of Justice of the European Communities

[7]   As regards intra-Community trade, since all customs duties on imports and exports and all charges having equivalent effect and all quantitative restrictions on imports and exports and measures having equivalent effect had to be abolished, pursuant to Title I of the Treaty, by the end of the transitional period at the latest, it should be emphasized that customs controls properly so-called have lost their *raison d'être* as regards such trade. Frontier controls remain justified only in so far as they are necessary either for the implementation of the exceptions to free movement referred to in Article 36 of the Treaty; or for the levying of internal taxation within the meaning of Article 95 of the Treaty when the crossing of the frontier may legitimately be assimilated to the situation which, in the case of domestic goods, gives rise to the levying of the tax; or for transit controls; or finally when they are essential in order to obtain reasonably complete and accurate information on movement of goods within the Community. These residuary controls must nevertheless be reduced as far as possible so that trade between Member States can take place in conditions as close as possible to those prevalent on a domestic market.

Note

The final sentence is to some extent a statement of the Community's overall objective.

The completion of, initially, an internal market and, subsequently, a common market (Chapter 5) requires the creation of common Community rules to deal with problems of this nature without the need to impose impediments to cross-frontier trade. The realisation of Article 14's 'area without internal frontiers' demands a deeper intrusion into national compet-ence than is envisaged in the above extract. Community legislation of this nature will be discussed further below.

Most of the cases considered so far involve controls imposed at frontiers. Such barriers are by definition applicable only to imports and therefore discriminatory. However, there is a further large category of discriminatory measures also caught by Article 28. These are measures which involve discrimination against imports once they have reached the market of the State of destination. The discrimination may apply at a different stage in the marketing chain, but the restrictive effect on inter-State trade is equally apparent.

Commission v Ireland (Case 113/80)
[1981] ECR 1625; [1982] 1 CMLR 706
Court of Justice of the European Communities

[1]   By an application lodged at the Court Registry on 28 April 1980, the Commission instituted proceedings under Article 169 of the EEC Treaty, for a declaration that Ireland had failed to fulfil its obligations under Article 30 of the EEC Treaty by requiring that the imported goods falling within the scope of the Merchandise Marks (Restriction on Sale of Imported Jewellery) Order 1971 (SI No 306, Iris Oifigiúil of 21 November 1971) and the Merchandise Marks (Restriction on Importation of Jewellery) Order 1971 (SI No 307, Iris Oifigiúil of 21 November 1971) bear an indication of origin or the word 'foreign'.

[2]   According to the explanatory notes thereto, Statutory Instrument No 306 (hereinafter referred to as 'the Sale Order') prohibits the sale or exposure for sale of imported articles of jewellery depicting motifs or possessing characteristics which suggest that they are souvenirs of Ireland, for example an Irish character, event or scene, wolfhound, round tower, shamrock etc. and Statutory Instrument No 307 (hereinafter referred to as 'the Importation Order') prohibits the importation of such articles unless, in either case, they bear an indication of their country of origin or the word 'foreign'.

[3]   The articles concerned are listed in a schedule to each order. However, in order to come within the scope of the orders the article must be made of precious metal or rolled precious metal or of base metal, including polished or plated articles suitable for setting.

[4]   In the Commission's opinion, the restrictions on the free movement of the goods covered by the two orders constitute measures having an effect equivalent to quantitative restrictions on imports, contrary to the provisions of Article 30 of the EEC Treaty; it also observes that according to Article 2 (3) (f) of Directive 70/50/EEC of 22 December 1969, based on the provisions of Article 33(7) of the Treaty, on the abolition of measures which have an effect equivalent to quantitative restrictions on imports and are not covered by other provisions adopted in pursuance of the EEC Treaty (Official Journal, English Special Edition 1970 (I), p. 17) 'measures which lower the value of an imported product, in particular by causing a reduction in its intrinsic value, or increase its costs' must be regarded as measures having an effect equivalent to quantitative restrictions, contrary to Article 30 of the EEC Treaty.

[5]   The Irish Government does not dispute the restrictive effects of these orders on the free movement of goods. However, it contends that the disputed measures are justified in the interests of consumer protection and of fairness in commercial transactions between producers. In this regard, it relies upon Article 36 of the Treaty which provides that Articles 30 to 34 shall not preclude prohibitions or restrictions on

imports justified on grounds of public policy or the protection of industrial and commercial property.

[6]   The defendant is, however, mistaken in placing reliance on Article 36 of the Treaty as the legal basis for its contention.

[7]   In fact, since the Court stated in its judgment of 25 January 1977 in Case 46/76 *Bauhuis* [1977] ECR 5 that Article 36 of the Treaty 'constitutes a derogation from the basic rule that all obstacles to the free movement of goods between Member States shall be eliminated and must be interpreted strictly', the exceptions listed therein cannot be extended to cases other than those specifically laid down.

[8]   In view of the fact that neither the protection of consumers nor the fairness of commercial transactions is included amongst the exceptions set out in Article 36, those grounds cannot be relied upon as such in connexion with that article.

[9]   However, since the Irish Government describes its recourse to these concepts as 'the central issue in the case', it is necessary to study this argument in connexion with Article 30 and to consider whether it is possible, in reliance on those concepts, to say that the Irish orders are not measures having an effect equivalent to quantitative restrictions on imports within the meaning of that article, bearing in mind that, according to the established case-law of the Court, such measures include 'all trading rules enacted by Member States which are capable of hindering, directly or indirectly, actually or potentially, intra-Community trade' (judgment of 11 July 1974 in Case 8/74 *Dassonville* [1974] ECR 837).

[10]   In this respect, the Court has repeatedly affirmed (in the judgments of 20 February 1979 in Case 120/78 *REWE* [1979] ECR 649, 26 June 1980 in Case 788/79 *Gilli and Andres* [1980] ECR 2071, 19 February 1981 in Case 130/80 *Kelderman* [1981] ECR) that 'in the absence of common rules relating to the production and marketing of the product in question it is for Member States to regulate all matters relating to its production, distribution and consumption on their own territory subject, however, to the condition that those rules do not present an obstacle . . . to intra-Community trade' and that 'it is only where national rules, which apply without discrimination to both domestic and imported products, may be justified as being necessary in order to satisfy imperative requirements relating in particular to . . . the fairness of commercial transactions and the defence of the consumer that they may constitute an exception to the requirements arising under Article 30'.

[11]   The orders concerned in the present case are not measures which are applicable to domestic products and to imported products without distinction but rather a set of rules which apply only to imported products and are therefore discriminatory in nature, with the result that the measures in issue are not covered by the decisions cited above which relate exclusively to provisions that regulate in a uniform manner the marketing of domestic products and imported products.

[12]   The Irish Government recognizes that the contested measures apply solely to imported articles and render their importation and sale more difficult than the sale of domestic products. However, it maintains that this difference in the treatment awarded to home-produced articles and to imported articles does not constitute discrimination on the ground that the articles referred to in the contested orders consist mainly of souvenirs; the appeal of such articles lies essentially in the fact of their being manufactured in the place where they are purchased and they bear in themselves an implied indication of their Irish origin, with the result that the purchaser

would be misled if the souvenir bought in Ireland was manufactured elsewhere. Consequently, the requirement that all imported 'souvenirs' covered by the two orders must bear an indication of origin is justified and in no way constitutes discrimination because the articles concerned are different on account of the differences between their essential characteristics.

[13] The Commission rejects this reasoning. In reliance on the judgment of 20 February 1975 in Case 12/74 *Commission* v *Federal Republic of Germany* [1975] ECR 191, it submits that it is unnecessary for a purchaser to know whether or not a product is of a particular origin, unless such origin implies a certain quality, basic materials or process of manufacture or a particular place in the folklore or tradition of the region in question; since none of the articles referred to in the orders display these features, the measures in question cannot be justified and are therefore 'overtly discriminatory'.

[14] It is therefore necessary to consider whether the contested measures are indeed discriminatory or whether they constitute discrimination in appearance only.

[15] The souvenirs referred to in the Sale Order and in the Importation Order are generally articles of ornamentation of little commercial value representing or incorporating a motif or emblem which is reminiscent of an Irish place, object, character or historical event or suggestive of an Irish symbol and their value stems from the fact that the purchaser, more often than not a tourist, buys them on the spot. The essential characteristic of the souvenirs in question is that they constitute a pictorial reminder of the place visited which does not by itself mean that a souvenir, as defined in the orders, must necessarily be manufactured in the country of origin.

[16] Furthermore, leaving aside the point argued by the Commission – with regard to the articles covered by the contested orders – that it would not be enough to require a statement of origin to be affixed to domestic products also, it is important to note that the interests of consumers and fair trading would be adequately safeguarded if it were left to domestic manufacturers to take appropriate steps such as affixing, if they so wished, their mark of origin to their own products or packaging.

[17] Thus by granting souvenirs imported from other Member States access to the domestic market solely on condition that they bear a statement of origin, whilst no such statement is required in the case of domestic products, the provisions contained in the Sale Order and the Importation Order indisputably constitute a discriminatory measure.

[18] The conclusion to be drawn therefore is that by requiring all souvenirs and articles of jewellery imported from other Member States which are covered by the Sale Order and the Importation Order to bear an indication of origin or the word 'foreign', the Irish rules constitute a measure having equivalent effect within the meaning of Article 30 of the EEC Treaty. Ireland has consequently failed to fulfil its obligations under the article.

Commission v *UK (Case 207/83)*
[1985] ECR 1202; [1985] 2 CMLR 259
Court of Justice of the European Communities

[1] By an application lodged at the Court Registry on 15 September 1983 the Commission of the European Communities brought an action before the Court under Article 169 of the EEC Treaty for a declaration that, by prohibiting the retail sale of

certain goods imported from other Member States unless they are marked with or accompanied by an indication of origin, the United Kingdom has failed to fulfil an obligation incumbent on it under Article 30 of the EEC Treaty.

[2]   The national legislation challenged by the Commission is the Trade Descriptions (Origin Marking) (Miscellaneous Goods) Order 1981 (Statutory Instrument 1981 No 121) which entered into force on 1 January 1982.

[3]   Article 2 of that Order provides that no person may supply or offer to supply by retail the goods listed in the Schedule to the Order, other than second-hand goods and goods supplied in certain special circumstances, unless the goods are marked with or accompanied by an indication of origin. In a case in which the goods are exposed for supply and the indication of origin would not be conveyed until after delivery, such an indication must also be displayed near the goods. The indication of origin must be clear and legible; it must not in any way be hidden or obscured or reduced in conspicuousness by any other matter, whether pictorial or not.

[4]   According to Article 1 of the Order, the 'origin' of goods means 'the country in which the goods were manufactured or produced'.

[5]   The Schedule to the Order lists the goods to which the Order applies. Those goods are divided into four categories: clothing and textile goods, domestic electrical appliances, footwear and cutlery.

. . .

[13]   The United Kingdom's defence is in substance limited to developing the two arguments which it has already put forward during the procedure prior to the application to the Court. First, it contends that the Order is a national measure which applies to imported and national products alike and the effect of which on trade between Member States is uncertain, if not non-existent. Secondly, it maintains that, in the case of the goods to which the Order applies, the requirements relating to indications of origin meet the requirements of consumer protection since consumers regard the origin of the goods which they buy as an indicator of their quality or true value.

[14]   Those two arguments must be examined in turn.

[15]   As regards the possible effect of the contested Order on trade, the United Kingdom points out that the requirements laid down in Article 2 of the Order concern the retail sale of all the goods covered by the Order, whether imported or not. Some of those goods, for example woollen knitwear and cutlery, are produced in the United Kingdom in substantial quantities.

[16]   It should first be observed, with regard to that argument, that in order to escape the obligations imposed on him by the legislation in question the retailer will tend, as the Commission has rightly pointed out, to ask his wholesalers to supply him with goods which are already origin-marked. That tendency has been confirmed by complaints received by the Commission. Thus, it emerges from the documents before the Court that the Groupement des industries françaises des appareils d'équipement ménager [French Domestic Appliance Manufacturers' Association] informed the Commission that French manufacturers of domestic appliances who wish to sell their products on the United Kingdom market have had to mark such products systematically in response to pressure brought to bear on them by their distributors. The effects of the contested provisions are therefore liable to spread to the wholesale trade and even to manufacturers.

[17] Secondly, it has to be recognized that the purpose of indications of origin or origin-marking is to enable consumers to distinguish between domestic and imported products and that this enables them to assert any prejudices which they may have against foreign products. As the Court has had occasion to emphasize in various contexts, the Treaty, by establishing a common market and progressively approximating the economic policies of the Member States seeks to unite national markets in a single market having the characteristics of a domestic market. Within such a market, the origin-marking requirement not only makes the marketing in a Member State of goods produced in other Member States in the sectors in question more difficult; it also has the effect of slowing down economic interpenetration in the Community by handicapping the sale of goods produced as the result of a division of labour between Member States.

[18] It follows from those considerations that the United Kingdom provisions in question are liable to have the effect of increasing the production costs of imported goods and making it more difficult to sell them on the United Kingdom market.

[19] The second argument advanced by the United Kingdom is in effect that the contested legislation, applicable without distinction to domestic and imported products, is necessary in order to satisfy imperative requirements relating to consumer protection. It states that a survey carried out amongst United Kingdom consumers has shown that they associate the quality of certain goods with the countries in which they are made. They like to know, for example, whether leather shoes have been made in Italy, woollen knitwear in the United Kingdom, fashion-wear in France and domestic electrical appliances in Germany.

[20] That argument must be rejected. The requirements relating to the indication of origin of goods are applicable without distinction to domestic and imported products only in form because, by their very nature, they are intended to enable the consumer to distinguish between those two categories of products, which may thus prompt him to give his preference to national products.

[21] It must also be observed that the fact that United Kingdom consumers associate a product's quality with its national origin does not appear to have been a consideration which prompted the United Kingdom Government when it suggested to the Commission that, as far as the Member States of the Community were concerned, it was prepared to accept the indication 'Made in the European Community'. Besides, if the national origin of goods brings certain qualities to the minds of consumers, it is in manufacturers' interests to indicate it themselves on the goods or on their packaging and it is not necessary to compel them to do so. In that case, the protection of consumers is sufficiently guaranteed by rules which enable the use of false indications of origin to be prohibited. Such rules are not called in question by the EEC Treaty.

[22] Those considerations lead to the conclusion that Article 2 of the Order constitutes a measure which makes the marketing of goods imported from other Member States more difficult than the marketing of domestically-produced goods and for which Community law does not recognize any ground of justification. That provision therefore falls within the prohibition laid down in Article 30 of the EEC Treaty.

[23] It must therefore be declared that, by prohibiting the retail sale of certain goods imported from other Member States unless they are marked with or accompanied by

an indication of origin, the United Kingdom has failed to fulfil an obligation incumbent on it under Article 30 of the EEC Treaty.

Note
Notice that para. 17 of the judgment in this case envisages a rather extended notion of discrimination.

In *Commission* v *UK* (Case 207/83), the UK had at an earlier stage in its negotiations with the Commission suggested that it would be prepared to amend its law in order to allow a choice between indicating national origin or marking the item 'Made in the European Community'. The Commission was not dissuaded by this suggestion from bringing the matter before the Court. Paragraph 21 of the Court's judgment shows that this concession ultimately weakened the UK's case.

Question
Could a Member State require all products marketed in its territory to carry a 'Made in the EC' label?

Commission v France (Case 21/84)
[1985] ECR 1356
Court of Justice of the European Communities

The Commission alleged that France had violated Article 30 of the EC Treaty (now, after amendment, Article 28 EC) by refusing to approve postal franking machines from other Member States. The action arose out of a complaint to the Commission by a British manufacturer which, despite repeated applications, had failed to secure the approval of the French authorities, even after France had eliminated an earlier law which explicitly envisaged a preference for domestic machines.

[11]   The fact that a law or regulation such as that requiring prior approval for the marketing of postal franking machines conforms in formal terms to Article 30 of the EEC Treaty is not sufficient to discharge a Member State of its obligations under that provision. Under the cloak of a general provision permitting the approval of machines imported from other Member States, the administration might very well adopt a systematically unfavourable attitude towards imported machines, either by allowing considerable delay in replying to applications for approval or in carrying out the examination procedure, or by refusing approval on the grounds of various alleged technical faults for which no detailed explanations are given or which prove to be inaccurate.

[12]   The prohibition on measures having an effect equivalent to quantitative restrictions would lose much of its useful effect if it did not cover protectionist or discriminatory practices of that type.

[13]   It must however be noted that for an administrative practice to constitute a measure prohibited under Article 30 that practice must show a certain degree of consistency and generality. That generality must be assessed differently according to whether the market concerned is one on which there are numerous traders or whether

it is a market, such as that in postal franking machines, on which only a few undertakings are active. In the latter case, a national administration's treatment of a single undertaking may constitute a measure incompatible with Article 30.

[14]   In the light of those principles it is clear from the facts of the case that the conduct of the French postal administration constitutes an impediment to imports contrary to Article 30 of the EEC Treaty.

[15]   It must therefore be concluded that by refusing without proper justification to approve postal franking machines from another Member State, the French Republic has failed to fulfil its obligations under Article 30 of the EEC Treaty.

Note
Read a casenote by L. Gormley (1985) 10 EL Rev 449.

Questions
1.   What is a measure, what is a mere isolated act, for the purposes of the application of Article 28? Why did the Court consider the structure of the market relevant in the case of the refusal to authorise postal franking machines (para. 13)?
2.   Consider whether the following are capable of falling within Article 28:

(a)   The determined policy adopted by an official at Dover as a result of personal prejudice to obstruct wherever possible the importation of goods originating in Greece. Would it make any difference if the officer's superiors turned a blind eye to these practices?
(b)   A party political broadcast on behalf of the Government declaring an intent 'to protect British interests by stopping importers of foodstuffs thinking they can enjoy a free-for-all on the UK marketplace'.

Note
In the next case, the Court is astute to maintain a broad approach in defining the 'measure' susceptible to control under Article 28. The dispute related to the alleged passive approach of the French authorities in the face of actions such as the interception of lorries transporting imported fruit and vegetables in France and the destruction of their loads, violence against lorry drivers and threats against French supermarkets selling imported agricultural products.

Commission v France (Case C-265/95)
[1997] ECR I-6959
Court of Justice of the European Communities

[24]   In order to determine whether the Commission's action is well founded, it should be stressed from the outset that the free movement of goods is one of the fundamental principles of the Treaty.

[25]   Article 3(c) of the EC Treaty provides that, for the purposes set out in Article 2, the activities of the Community are to include an internal market characterized by the abolition, as between Member States, of, *inter alia*, obstacles to the free movement of goods.

[26] Pursuant to the second paragraph of Article 7a of the EC Treaty, the internal market is to comprise an area without internal frontiers in which the free movement of goods is ensured in accordance with the provisions of the Treaty.

[27] That fundamental principle is implemented by Article 30 et seq. of the Treaty.

[28] In particular, Article 30 provides that quantitative restrictions on imports and all measures having equivalent effect are prohibited between Member States.

[29] That provision, taken in its context, must be understood as being intended to eliminate all barriers, whether direct or indirect, actual or potential, to flows of imports in intra-Community trade.

[30] As an indispensable instrument for the realization of a market without internal frontiers, Article 30 therefore does not prohibit solely measures emanating from the State which, in themselves, create restrictions on trade between Member States. It also applies where a Member State abstains from adopting the measures required in order to deal with obstacles to the free movement of goods which are not caused by the State.

[31] The fact that a Member State abstains from taking action or, as the case may be, fails to adopt adequate measures to prevent obstacles to the free movement of goods that are created, in particular, by actions by private individuals on its territory aimed at products originating in other Member States is just as likely to obstruct intra-Community trade as is a positive act.

[32] Article 30 therefore requires the Member States not merely themselves to abstain from adopting measures or engaging in conduct liable to constitute an obstacle to trade but also, when read with Article 5 of the Treaty, to take all necessary and appropriate measures to ensure that that fundamental freedom is respected on their territory.

[33] In the latter context, the Member States, which retain exclusive competence as regards the maintenance of public order and the safeguarding of internal security, unquestionably enjoy a margin of discretion in determining what measures are most appropriate to eliminate barriers to the importation of products in a given situation.

[34] It is therefore not for the Community institutions to act in place of the Member States and to prescribe for them the measures which they must adopt and effectively apply in order to safeguard the free movement of goods on their territories.

[35] However, it falls to the Court, taking due account of the discretion referred to above, to verify, in cases brought before it, whether the Member State concerned has adopted appropriate measures for ensuring the free movement of goods.

The Court proceeded from this statement of legal principle to determine that the violent acts had created obstacles to intra-Community trade; and that France has failed to meet its legal obligations to respond. In reaching this conclusion, the Court referred to:

- the duration of the incidents (which had been occurring regularly for more than 10 years);
- failure of the French police to attend, despite the fact that in certain cases the competent authorities had been warned of the imminence of demonstrations by farmers, or, even if present, to intervene, even where they far outnumbered the perpetrators;

- the fact that although a number of acts of attacks by identifiable individuals were filmed by television cameras, a very small number of persons had been identified and prosecuted.

[52]   In the light of all the foregoing factors, the Court, while not discounting the difficulties faced by the competent authorities in dealing with situations of the type in question in this case, cannot but find that, having regard to the frequency and seriousness of the incidents cited by the Commission, the measures adopted by the French Government were manifestly inadequate to ensure freedom of intra-Community trade in agricultural products on its territory by preventing and effectively dissuading the perpetrators of the offences in question from committing and repeating them.

[53]   That finding is all the more compelling since the damage and threats to which the Commission refers not only affect the importation into or transit in France of the products directly affected by the violent acts, but are also such as to create a climate of insecurity which has a deterrent effect on trade flows as a whole.

[54]   The above finding is in no way affected by the French Government's argument that the situation of French farmers was so difficult that there were reasonable grounds for fearing that more determined action by the competent authorities might provoke violent reactions by those concerned, which would lead to still more serious breaches of public order or even to social conflict.

[55]   Apprehension of internal difficulties cannot justify a failure by a Member State to apply Community law correctly (see, to that effect, Case C-52/95 *Commission* v *France* [1995] ECR I-4443, paragraph 38).

[56]   It is for the Member State concerned, unless it can show that action on its part would have consequences for public order with which it could not cope by using the means at its disposal, to adopt all appropriate measures to guarantee the full scope and effect of Community law so as to ensure its proper implementation in the interests of all economic operators.

[57]   In the present case the French Government has adduced no concrete evidence proving the existence of a danger to public order with which it could not cope.

[58]   Moreover, although it is not impossible that the threat of serious disruption to public order may, in appropriate cases, justify non-intervention by the police, that argument can, on any view, be put forward only with respect to a specific incident and not, as in this case, in a general way covering all the incidents cited by the Commission.

The Court concluded by declaring that 'by failing to adopt all necessary and proportionate measures in order to prevent the free movement of fruit and vegetables from being obstructed by actions by private individuals, the French Republic has failed to fulfil its obligations under Article 30 of the EC Treaty, in conjunction with Article 5 of that Treaty, and under the common organizations of the markets in agricultural products.'

Notes
1.   The Court's ruling in this case provided a stimulus to the adoption of Regulation 2679/98 on the functioning of the internal market in relation to the free movement of goods (OJ 1998 L337/8). The Commission is equipped

with special powers to act in cases of serious obstacles to free movement, and the Regulation expressly includes inaction by public authorities, not simply action, within its scope for these purposes.

2.   The next case also raises the question of what constitutes a measure for the purposes of defining the MEQR caught by Article 28. The decision confirms that even a State's course of conduct which is merely designed to induce discriminatory practices among private individuals can be held in violation of Article 28. Neither the absence of binding character nor the absence of sanctions for refusal to comply with the State's policy necessarily deprive the act of the required quality. The Court avoids a formalistic assessment of the legal status of the act and concentrates instead on its purpose and effect. However, in addition to its interpretation of the concept of a measure, the 'Buy Irish' case has much to commend it as a broader illustration of the scope of Article 30 of the EC Treaty (now, after amendment, Article 28 EC).

Commission v Ireland (Case 249/81)
[1982] ECR 4005; [1983] 2 CMLR 104
Court of Justice of the European Communities

[1]   By an application lodged at the Court Registry on 15 September 1981 the Commission of the European Communities brought an action before the Court under Article 169 of the EEC Treaty for a declaration that by organizing a campaign to promote the sale and purchase of Irish products in its territory Ireland has failed to fulfil its obligations under the Treaty.

I – The subject-matter of the application
[2]   In a reasoned opinion addressed to Ireland on 25 February 1981 concerning the 'Buy Irish' campaign, the Commission noted that in January 1978 the Irish Government had introduced a three-year programme to help to promote Irish products. The campaign was launched on 18 January 1978 in a speech delivered by the Irish Minister for Industry, Commerce and Energy. The Minister declared on that occasion that the aim of the campaign was to achieve 'a switch from imports to Irish products equivalent to 3% of total consumer spending' and that the campaign was 'a carefully thought out set of initiatives that add up to an integrated programme for promoting Irish goods, with specific proposals to involve the producer, distributor and consumer'.

[3]   The Irish Government, it was said, had taken and was continuing to take a series of measures designed to promote Irish products in accordance with the terms of that speech. The reasoned opinion cited the following measures:

   (a)   The organization of a free information service for consumers wishing to know which products in a particular category of goods are made in Ireland and where they may be obtained (the Shoplink Service);
   (b)   The provision of exhibition facilities, exclusively for exhibiting Irish products, in a large exhibition centre in Dublin run by the Irish Goods Council, which is, it is claimed, a public authority;
   (c)   The encouragement of the use of the 'Guaranteed Irish' symbol for products made in Ireland together with the organization by the Irish Goods Council of a special system for investigating complaints about products bearing that symbol;

(d)   The organization of a big publicity campaign by the Irish Goods Council in favour of Irish products, involving in particular the publication and distribution by that institution of literature encouraging consumers to buy only domestic products.

[4]   The Commission notes in the application that the activities connected with the Shoplink Service and the exhibition facilities in Dublin have now been abandoned by the Irish Government. However, the other two activities have continued, even after the expiry of the three-year period for which the campaign was to last. Moreover, the publicity campaign has been gradually extended, in particular by means of widespread advertising in favour of Irish products in the press and on television.

[5]   The Irish Government admits that there was a three-year programme in favour of buying Irish products in Ireland. It says that since the Shoplink Service and the exhibition facilities in Dublin were abandoned at the request of the Commission the programme consists merely of an advertising campaign, by means of the press and television, the publication of posters and pamphlets and the use of the 'Guaranteed Irish' symbol, designed to make Irish consumers better acquainted with products made in Ireland and to stimulate awareness in the Irish public of the link between the marketing of such products in Ireland and the unemployment problem in that country.

[6]   As far as the advertising campaign is concerned, the Irish Government confirms that it forms part of the activities of the Irish Goods Council. However, that institution cannot be regarded as a public authority; it is merely an arrangement whereby the various industries in Ireland may cooperate for their common good. The activities of the Irish Goods Council are not based on any official enactment and the involvement of the Government consists exclusively of financial aid and moral support.

[7]   The Commission maintains that the actions of the Irish Goods Council are unquestionably attributable to the Irish Government. It points out, in particular, that the members of the Management Committee of the Council are appointed, under the Articles of Association of that body, by the Minister for Industry, Commerce and Energy.

[8]   The Commission is of the opinion that the campaign to promote the sale and purchase of Irish products in Ireland must be regarded as a measure having an effect equivalent to a quantitative restriction on imports. Ireland contends, first, that the Irish Government has never adopted 'measures' within the meaning of Article 30 of the Treaty and, secondly, that the financial aid given to the Irish Goods Council must be judged in the light of Articles 92 and 93 of the Treaty, and not Article 30.

[9]   Before asssessing the merits of those arguments the position of the Irish Goods Council must be considered.

II – The Irish Goods Council

[10]   The Irish Goods Council was created on 25 August 1978, a few months after the disputed campaign was launched, in the form of a company limited by guarantee and not having a share capital; it was registered in accordance with Irish company law (Companies Act 1963). The Council is in fact the result of the amalgamation of two bodies, the National Development Council, a company limited by guarantee and registered under the Companies Act, and the Working Group on the Promotion and Sale of Irish Goods.

[11]   The Irish Government maintains that the Irish Goods Council was created under the sponsorship of the government in order to encourage Irish industry to overcome its own difficulties. The Council was established for the purpose of creating a framework within which the various industries could come together in order to cooperate for their common good.

[12]   The Management Committee of the Irish Goods Council consists, according to the Articles of Association of that institution, of 10 persons appointed in their individual capacities by the Minister for Industry, Commerce and Energy; the same Minister appoints the chairman from among the members of the Management Committee. The members and the chairman are appointed for a period of three years, and their appointments may be renewed. In practice, the members of the Management Committee are selected by the Minister in such a manner as to represent the appropriate sectors of the Irish economy.

[13]   It appears from the information supplied by the Irish Government at the request of the Court that the activities of the Irish Goods Council are financed by subsidies paid by the Irish Government and by private industry. The subsidies from the State and from the private sector amounted, respectively to IRL 1 005 000 and IRL 175 000 for the period between August 1978 and December 1979; IRL 940 000 and IRL 194 000 for 1980; and IRL 922 000 and IRL 238 000 for 1981.

[14]   The Irish Government has not denied that the activities of the Irish Goods Council consist in particular, after the abandonment of the Shoplink Service and the exhibition facilities offered to Irish manufacturers in Dublin, in the organization of an advertising campaign in favour of the sale and purchase of Irish products, and in promoting the use of the 'Guaranteed Irish' symbol.

[15]   It is thus apparent that the Irish Government appoints the members of the Management Committee of the Irish Goods Council, grants it public subsidies which cover the greater part of its expenses and, finally, defines the aims and the broad outline of the campaign conducted by that institution to promote the sale and purchase of Irish products. In the circumstances the Irish Government cannot rely on the fact that the campaign was conducted by a private company in order to escape any liability it may have under the provisions of the Treaty.

III – The applicability of Articles 92 and 93 of the Treaty
[16]   The Irish Government maintains that, even if the purpose or the effect of the campaign was to discourage imports from other Member States, it must be judged on the basis of Articles 92 and 93 of the Treaty, which deal with State aids. The applicability of those provisions excludes the applicability of Article 30 of the Treaty, upon which the Commission has based its case.

[17]   The Irish Government states that the campaign has in fact been conducted by the Irish Goods Council and that the role of the government has been restricted to moral support and financial assistance. If, as the Commission maintains, the campaign was liable to hinder the free movement of goods within the Community by promoting domestic products at the expense of imported ones that circumstance is attributable solely to a single government decision, namely the decision to subsidize the Irish Goods Council.

[18]   It must be observed, however, that the fact that a substantial part of the campaign is financed by the Irish Government, and that Articles 92 and 93 of the

Treaty may be applicable to financing of that kind, does not mean that the campaign itself may escape the prohibitions laid down in Article 30.

[19]   In any case, if the Irish Government considered that such financing amounted to aid within the meaning of Articles 92 and 93 it ought to have notified the aid to the Commission in accordance with Article 93 (3).

IV – The application of Article 30 of the Treaty
[20]   The Commission maintains that the 'Buy Irish' campaign and the measures taken to prosecute the campaign must be regarded, as a whole, as measures encouraging the purchase of domestic products only. Such measures are said to be contrary to the obligations imposed on the Member States by Article 30. The Commission refers to Article 2 (3) (k) of Commission Directive No 70/50/EEC of 22 December 1969, based on the provisions of Article 33 (7), on the abolition of measures which have an effect equivalent to quantitative restrictions on imports and are not covered by other provisions adopted in pursuance of the EEC Treaty (Official Journal, English Special Edition 1970 (I), p. 17). According to Article 2 (3) (k), measures which encourage the purchase of domestic products only must be regarded as contrary to the prohibitions contained in the Treaty.

[21]   The Irish Government maintains that the prohibition against measures having an effect equivalent to quantitative restrictions in Article 30 is concerned only with 'measures', that is to say, binding provisions emanating from a public authority. However, no such provision has been adopted by the Irish Government, which has confined itself to giving moral support and financial aid to the activities pursued by the Irish industries.

[22]   The Irish Government goes on to emphasize that the campaign has had no restrictive effect on imports since the proportion of Irish goods to all goods sold on the Irish market fell from 49.2% in 1977 to 43.4% in 1980.

[23]   The first observation to be made is that the campaign cannot be likened to advertising by private or public undertakings, or by a group of undertakings, to encourage people to buy goods produced by those undertakings. Regardless of the means used to implement it, the campaign is a reflection of the Irish Government's considered intention to substitute domestic products for imported products on the Irish market and thereby to check the flow of imports from other Member States.

[24]   It must be remembered here that a representative of the Irish Government stated when the campaign was launched that it was a carefully thought-out set of initiatives constituting an integrated programme for promoting domestic products; that the Irish Goods Council was set up at the initiative of the Irish Government a few months later; and that the task of implementing the integrated programme as it was envisaged by the government was entrusted, or left, to that Council.

[25]   Whilst it may be true that the two elements of the programme which have continued in effect, namely the advertising campaign and the use of the 'Guaranteed Irish' symbol, have not had any significant success in winning over the Irish market to domestic products, it is not possible to overlook the fact that, regardless of their efficacity, those two activities form part of a government programme which is designed to achieve the substitution of domestic products for imported products and is liable to affect the volume of trade between Member States.

[26]   The advertising campaign to encourage the sale and purchase of Irish products cannot be divorced from its origin as part of the government programme, or from its

connection with the introduction of the 'Guaranteed Irish' symbol and with the organization of a special system for investigating complaints about products bearing that symbol. The establishment of the system for investigating complaints about Irish products provides adequate confirmation of the degree of organization surrounding the 'Buy Irish' campaign and of the discriminatory nature of the campaign.

[27]   In the circumstances the two activities in question amount to the establishment of a national practice, introduced by the Irish Government and prosecuted with its assistance, the potential effect of which on imports from other Member States is comparable to that resulting from government measures of a binding nature.

[28]   Such a practice cannot escape the prohibition laid down by Article 30 of the Treaty solely because it is not based on decisions which are binding upon undertakings. Even measures adopted by the government of a Member State which do not have binding effect may be capable of influencing the conduct of traders and consumers in that State and thus of frustrating the aims of the Community as set out in Article 2 and enlarged upon in Article 3 of the Treaty.

[29]   That is the case where, as in this instance, such a restrictive practice represents the implementation of a programme defined by the government which affects the national economy as a whole and which is intended to check the flow of trade between Member States by encouraging the purchase of domestic products, by means of an advertising campaign on a national scale and the organization of special procedures applicable solely to domestic products, and where those activities are attributable as a whole to the government and are pursued in an organized fashion throughout the national territory.

[30]   Ireland has therefore failed to fulfil its obligations under the Treaty by organizing a campaign to promote the sale and purchase of Irish goods within its territory.

Note
A delicate but important distinction from the 'Buy Irish' case was made in *Apple and Pear Development Council* v *Lewis* (Case 222/82). The case involved the submission that the fruit promotions undertaken by the Council, a body set up in the UK under statutory instrument, infringed, *inter alia*, Article 30 of the EC Treaty (now, after amendment, Article 28 EC) in so far as they concerned the promotion of varieties typical of English and Welsh production.

Apple and Pear Development Council v Lewis (Case 222/82)
[1983] ECR 4083; [1984] 3 CMLR 733
Court of Justice of the European Communities

[17]   As the Court held in its judgment of 24 November 1982 in Case 249/81 (*Commission* v *Ireland* [1982] ECR 4005), a publicity campaign to promote the sale and purchase of domestic products may, in certain circumstances, fall within the prohibition contained in Article 30 of the Treaty, if the campaign is supported by the public authorities. In fact, a body such as the Development Council, which is set up by the government of a Member State and is financed by a charge imposed on growers, cannot under Community law enjoy the same freedom as regards the methods of advertising used as that enjoyed by producers themselves or producers' associations of a voluntary character.

[18]   In particular, such a body is under a duty not to engage in any advertising intended to discourage the purchase of products of other Member States or to disparage those products in the eyes of consumers. Nor must it advise consumers to purchase domestic products solely by reason of their national origin.

[19]   On the other hand, Article 30 does not prevent such a body from drawing attention, in its publicity, to the specific qualities of fruit grown in the Member State in question or from organizing campaigns to promote the sale of certain varieties, mentioning their particular properties, even if those varieties are typical of national production.

[20]   In the observations which it submitted to the Court, the Commission stated that campaigns to promote certain varieties might result in the exclusion of other varieties from the market and make it necessary, either in the Member State in question or in other Member States which export the latter varieties, to apply the intervention measures provided for in the common organization of the market in relation to those varieties.

[21]   Although it is true that such a distortion of the conditions of competition, which would be incompatible with the proper functioning of the common organization of the markets, might occur in a market where the publicity measures related exclusively or essentially to certain varieties to the exclusion of the others, that consideration cannot justify the prohibition of all publicity campaigns whereby an organization such as the Development Council draws attention to the properties of certain varieties and indicates the uses for which those varieties are specifically suitable.

Notes
1.   For subsequent litigation in this area before English courts, see *Meat and Livestock Commission* v *Manchester Wholesale Meat and Poultry Market Ltd* [1997] 2 CMLR 361.
2.   The Commission attempted to extract some general principles from these judgments in order to foster predictable application of the law to such practices in the future. It issued the following guidelines.

Commission Guidelines for Member States' Involvement in Promotion of Agricultural and Fisheries Products – Article 30 Aspects (1986) OJ C 272/3

1.   Introduction
It is clear from the Jurisprudence of the Court of Justice notably in cases 249/81 ('buy Irish') and 222/82 (Apple and Pear Development Council) that direct or indirect involvement of Member States if promotional campaigns for agricultural products on their national markets may in certain criteria are not respected involve a breach of Article 30 of the EEC Treaty. The Commission is aware that many such campaigns presently exist within the Community and considers it appropriate to issue the following guidelines to the Member States.

In the interpretation of these guidelines the intention or implied intention of promotional material is to be judged by the 'message' put over by that material through both words and visual images.

2. Guidelines

2.1 *Promotional actions which are clearly not open to objection under Article 30*

2.1.1. Export promotional campaigns organized directly or indirectly by one Member State on the market of another Member State.

2.1.2 Promotional campaigns organized on the home market of a Member State which advertise the product in a purely generic manner making no reference whatsoever to its national origin.

2.1.3 Campaigns on the home market promoting specific qualities or varieties of products even though they are typical of national production. (These are campaigns which make no specific references to the national origin of the product other than which may be evident from the references made to the qualities or varieties concerned or to the normal designation of the product.)

2.2 *Promotional actions which clearly infringe Article 30*

2.2.1 Promotional campaigns which advise consumers to buy national products solely because of their national origin.

2.2.2 Promotional campaigns intended to discourage the purchase of products from other Member States or disparage those products in the eyes of consumers (negative promotion).

Positive statements about a Member State's product should not be phrased in such a way to imply that other Member State's products are necessarily inferior.

2.3 *Promotional campaigns on a Member State's home market which, because of the references made to the national origin of the products may, unless certain restraints are observed, be open to objection under Article 30*

2.3.1 Promotional campaigns drawing attention to the varieties or qualities of products produced within a Member State are not in practice limited to national or regional specialities and frequently draw attention to the particular qualities of products produced within a Member State and the national origin of the products, even though those products and their qualities are similar to those of products produced elsewhere.

If undue emphasis is placed on the national origin of the product in such promotional campaigns there is a danger of breach of Article 30. The Commission therefore requests Member States to ensure particularly that the following guideline is strictly respected.

Identification of the producing country by word or symbol may be made providing that a reasonable balance between references, on the one hand to the qualities and varieties of the product and, on the other hand, its national origin is kept. The references to national origin should be subsidiary to the main message put over to consumers by the campaign and not constitute the principal reason why consumers are being advised to buy the product.

2.3.2. Qualities of the products which it is permissible to mention include taste, aroma, freshness, maturity, value for money, nutritional value, varieties available, usefulness (recipes, etc.). To be avoided are superlatives such as 'the best', 'the tastiest', 'the finest' and expressions such as 'the real thing' or promotional campaigns which, because of the mention of the national origin, result in the product promoted being compared with the products of other Member States. References to quality control should only be made where the product is subjected to a genuine and objective system of control of its qualities.

2.3.3. Certain promotional campaigns mentioning the national origin of agricultural products may, even though they respect the abovementioned criteria, nevertheless infringe Article 30 of the EEC Treaty if they reflect a considered intention of a Member State to substitute domestic products for products imported from other Member States (see case No 249/81 *Commission* v *Ireland* (1982) ECR p. 4005 and following particularly p. 4022 ground No 23). Such an intention may for example be presumed from the massive nature of a particular promotional campaign.

Note
Wherever possible, the Commission wisely has an eye to developing broadly-based interpretation of the law by building on the accidents of litigation. By expanding understanding of the reach of Community law, it hopes to improve observance through education. However, in Case C-57/95 *France* v *Commission* [1997] ECR I-1627, the Court was alert to the risk that the Commission might seek in this way improperly to impose new obligations on Member States and annulled a communication on pension funds as a binding act in respect of which the Commission lacked the necessary competence. Accordingly, communications and guidelines must be limited to clarification. Moreover the Commission has developed a practice of organising bilateral meetings with national authorities at which non-contentious solutions to instances of infringement are sought (see, e.g., the Twelfth Annual Report on monitoring the application of Community law, (1995) OJ C254/1, pp. 7–8). Reactive, *ad hoc* litigation can be only one component of supervision. Pursuit of administrative cooperation as a basis for management of the internal market is a prominent feature of the *Action Plan for the Single Market* prepared by the Commission in 1997 (p. 204 above) and of the *Strategy for Europe's Internal Market*, published in November 1999 (p. 207 above).

Questions
1. Could a campaign which involved the use of a national flag as a campaign logo fall on the lawful side of the line?
2. In both the 'Buy Irish' and the *Apple and Pear Council* cases (Cases 249/81 and 222/82), the Court dismissed arguments that the acts complained of were those of a private body insufficiently closely aligned to the State to fall within the scope of Article 30 of the EC Treaty (now, after amendment, Article 28 EC). What factors persuaded the Court that the State was sufficiently involved in the practices of the Irish Goods Council and the Apple and Pear Development Council?
3. Would discrimination by a private body on grounds of nationality fall foul of Community law? Consider, for example, a policy decision by a UK supermarket chain to stock only British-made goods; or only French-made goods. You should make reference to the scope of Article 12; and Articles 81 and 82. Consider also the issue of obligatory compliance with national standards. The Commission expressed its view in Written Question 835/82 (1983) OJ C93/1; Written Question 862/83 (1983) OJ C315/15.
4. What other areas of Community law demand close attention to the extent of State involvement? (see p. 114 on the direct effect of Directives). Are the

tests used identical? If not, why not? Read D. Curtin, 'The Province of Government', (1990) 15 EL Rev 195.

Note

Interventionist governments are fond of price-fixing schemes. As a matter of Community law, such schemes must give the importer an opportunity to benefit from any competitive advantage the imported goods may possess (by setting a lower price than the competing domestic product), or to take account of any disadvantage they may possess (by setting a higher price). Schemes which exclude the importer's ability to achieve such flexibility are capable of violating Article 28. These are simply instances of the application of Article 28 to discriminatory practices, but here the discrimination lies in treating imported goods in the *same* way as domestic goods where such equal treatment is not objectively justified, rather than in treating goods differently when in objective terms they should be treated in the same way.

Criminal proceedings against Riccardo Tasca (Case 65/75)
[1976] ECR 291; [1977] 2 CMLR 183
Court of Justice of the European Communities

[12]   The second question asks whether Article 30 of the EEC Treaty and Article 35 of Regulation No 1009/67, especially the prohibition against the application in intra-Community trade of measures having an effect equivalent to quantitative restrictions, prohibit the fixing of maximum prices valid only for the territory of a single Member State.

[13]   Article 30 of the Treaty prohibits in trade between Member States all measures having an effect equivalent to quantitative restrictions and this prohibition is repeated in Article 35 of Regulation No 1009/67 as regards the market in sugar. For the purposes of this prohibition it is sufficient that the measures in question are likely to constitute an obstacle, directly or indirectly, actually or potentially, to imports between Member States. Although a maximum price applicable without distinction to domestic and imported products does not in itself constitute a measure having an effect equivalent to a quantitative restriction, it may have such an effect, however, when it is fixed at a level such that the sale of imported products becomes, if not impossible, more difficult than that of domestic products. A maximum price, in any event in so far as it applies to imported products, constitutes therefore a measure having an effect equivalent to a quantitative restriction, especially when it is fixed at such a low level that, having regard to the general situation of imported products compared to that of domestic products, dealers wishing to import the product in question into the Member State concerned can do so only at a loss.

[14]   It is for the national court to decide whether this is so in the present case.

Openbaar Ministerie v Van Tiggele (Case 82/77)
[1978] ECR 25; [1978] 2 CMLR 528
Court of Justice of the European Communities

[16]   First a national provision which prohibits without distinction the retail sale of domestic products and imported products at prices below the purchase price paid by

the retailer cannot produce effects detrimental to the marketing of imported products alone and consequently cannot constitute a measure having an effect equivalent to a quantitative restriction on imports.

[17]   Furthermore the fixing of the minimum profit margin at a specific amount, and not as a percentage of the cost price, applicable without distinction to domestic products and imported products is likewise incapable of producing an adverse effect on imported products which may be cheaper, as in the present case where the amount of the profit margin constitutes a relatively insignificant part of the final retail price.

[18]   On the other hand this is not so in the case of a minimum price fixed at a specific amount which, although applicable without distinction to domestic products and imported products, is capable of having an adverse effect on the marketing of the latter in so far as it prevents their lower cost price from being reflected in the retail selling price.

[19]   This is the conclusion which must be drawn even though the competent authority is empowered to grant exemptions from the fixed minimum price and though this power is freely applied to imported products, since the requirement that importers and traders must comply with the administrative formalities inherent in such a system may in itself constitute a measure having an effect equivalent to a quantitative restriction.

[20]   The temporary nature of the application of the fixed minimum prices is not a factor capable of justifying such a measure since it is incompatible on other grounds with Article 30 of the Treaty.

[21]   The answer to the first question must therefore be that Article 30 of the EEC Treaty must be interpreted to mean that the establishment by a national authority of a minimum retail price fixed at a specific amount and applicable without distinction to domestic products and imported products constitutes, in conditions such as those laid down in the regulation made by the Produktschap voor Gedistilleerde Dranken on 17 December 1975, a measure having an effect equivalent to a quantitative restriction on imports which is prohibited under the said Article 30.

(C) ARTICLE 30

Article 30 EC

Article 30
The provisions of Articles 28 and 29 shall not preclude prohibitions or restrictions on imports, exports or goods in transit justified on grounds of public morality, public policy or public security; the protection of health and life of humans, animals or plants; the protection of national treasures possessing artistic, historic or archaeological value; or the protection of industrial and commercial property. Such prohibitions or restrictions shall not, however, constitute a means of arbitrary discrimination or a disguised restriction on trade between Member States.

It is an unfortunate coincidence that the Amsterdam re-numbering of the EC Treaty (p. 29 above) converted what was Article 36 into what is now Article 30. It will be recalled that what was Article 30 is now Article 28.

As a general principle of Community trade law, any derogation from freedom of movement is to be construed strictly, because it is hostile to the aim of achieving a common market. This principle can be seen in concrete form in Article 30. In its first sentence, an exhaustive list of possible grounds of derogation is set out. In its second sentence, a caution is issued that reliance on any derogation must be objectively justifiable, not a ruse to protect domestic industry. Moreover, the invocation of Article 30 should be read in the light of Article 14's commitment to an area without internal frontiers (p. 179 above).

The Court, in assessing purported justification under Article 30, consistently requires Member States to show not simply a protectable interest, but also that the means chosen are proportionate to the end in view and the least restrictive of trade available which are necessary to meet that objective.

(i) *Public morality*

R v Henn and Darby (Case 34/79)
[1979] ECR 3795; [1980] 1 CMLR 246
Court of Justice of the European Communities

The defendants were convicted of being 'knowingly concerned in the fraudulent evasion of the prohibition of the importation of indecent or obscene articles' contrary to the Customs Consolidation Act 1876, s. 42, and the Customs and Excise Act 1952, s. 304. They had shipped pornography into Felixstowe from Rotterdam. Their appeal against conviction was based on the submission that the legal control of pornography restricted the free circulation of goods in the Community contrary to Article 30 of the EC Treaty (now, after amendment, Article 28 EC). The matter reached the House of Lords which referred questions of interpretation under Article 177 (now Article 234, Chapter 4) to the European Court. The Court first accepts the applicability of Article 30 (now 28) before proceeding to discuss Article 36 (now 30).

[11] The first question asks whether a law of a Member State which prohibits the import into that State of pornographic articles is a measure having equivalent effect to a quantitative restriction on imports within the meaning of Article 30 of the Treaty.

[12] That Article provides that 'quantitative restrictions on imports and all measures having equivalent effect' shall be prohibited between Member States. It is clear that this provision includes a prohibition on imports inasmuch as this is the most extreme form of restriction. The expression used in Article 30 must therefore be understood as being the equivalent of the expression 'prohibitions or restrictions on imports' occurring in Article 36.

[13] The answer to the first question is therefore that a law such as that referred to in this case constitutes a quantitative restriction on imports within the meaning of Article 30 of the Treaty.

Second and third questions
[14] The second and third questions are framed in the following terms:

'2. If the answer to Question 1 is in the affirmative, does the first sentence of Article 36 upon its true construction mean that a Member State may lawfully impose prohibitions on the importation of goods from another Member State which are of an indecent or obscene character as understood by the laws of that Member State?

3. In particular:

(i) is the member State entitled to maintain such prohibitions in order to prevent, to guard against or to reduce the likelihood of breaches of the domestic law of all constituent parts of the customs territory of the State?

(ii) is the Member State entitled to maintain such prohibitions having regard to the national standards and characteristics of that State as demonstrated by the domestic laws of the constituent parts of the customs territory of that State including the law imposing the prohibition, notwithstanding variations between the laws of the constituent parts?'

It is convenient to consider these questions together.

[15]   Under the terms of Article 36 of the Treaty the provisions relating to the free movement of goods within the Community are not to preclude prohibitions on imports which are justified *inter alia* 'on grounds of public morality'. In principle, it is for each Member State to determine in accordance with its own scale of values and in the form selected by it the requirements of public morality in its territory. In any event, it cannot be disputed that the statutory provisions applied by the United Kingdom in regard to the importation of articles having an indecent or obscene character come within the powers reserved to the Member States by the first sentence of Article 36.

[16]   Each Member State is entitled to impose prohibitions on imports justified on grounds of public morality for the whole of its territory, as defined in Article 227 of the Treaty, whatever the structure of its constitution may be and however the powers of legislating in regard to the subject in question may be distributed. The fact that certain differences exist between the laws enforced in the different constituent parts of a Member State does not thereby prevent that State from applying a unitary concept in regard to prohibitions on imports imposed, on grounds of public morality, on trade with other Member States.

[17]   The answer to the second and third questions must therefore be that the first sentence of Article 36 upon its true construction means that a Member State may, in principle, lawfully impose prohibitions on the importation from any other Member State of articles which are of an indecent or obscene character as understood by its domestic laws and that such prohibitions may lawfully be applied to the whole of its national territory even if, in regard to the field in question, variations exist between the laws in force in the different constituent parts of the Member State concerned.

Fourth, fifth and sixth questions

[18]   The fourth, fifth and sixth questions are framed in the following terms:

'4. If a prohibition on the importation of goods is justifiable on grounds of public morality or public policy, and imposed with that purpose, can that prohibition nevertheless amount to a means of arbitrary discrimination or a disguised restriction on trade contrary to Article 36?

5. If the answer to Question 4 is in the affirmative, does the fact that the prohibition imposed on the importation of such goods is different in scope from that imposed by the criminal law upon the possession and publication of such goods within the Member State or any part of it necessarily constitute a means of arbitrary

discrimination or a disguised restriction on trade between Member States so as to conflict with the requirements of the second sentence of Article 36?
6. If it be the fact that the prohibition imposed upon importation is, and a prohibition such as is imposed upon possession and publication is not, capable as a matter of administration of being applied by customs officials responsible for examining goods at the point of importation, would that fact have any bearing upon the answer to Question 5?'

[19] In these questions the House of Lords takes account of the appellants' submissions based upon certain differences between, on the one hand, the prohibition on importing the goods in question, which is absolute, and, on the other, the laws in force in the various constituent parts of the United Kingdom, which appear to be less strict in the sense that the mere possession of obscene articles for non-commercial purposes does not constitute a criminal offence anywhere in the United Kingdom and that, even if it is generally forbidden, trade in such articles is subject to certain exceptions, notably those in favour of articles having scientific, literary, artistic or educational interest. Having regard to those differences the question has been raised whether the prohibition on imports might not come within the second sentence of Article 36.

[20] According to the second sentence of Article 36 the restrictions on imports referred to in the first sentence may not 'constitute a means of arbitrary discrimination or a disguised restriction on trade between Member States'.

[21] In order to answer the questions which have been referred to the Court it is appropriate to have regard to the function of this provision, which is designed to prevent restrictions on trade based on the grounds mentioned in the first sentence of Article 36 from being diverted from their proper purpose and used in such a way as either to create discrimination in respect of goods originating in other Member States or indirectly to protect certain national products. That is not the purport of a prohibition, such as that in force in the United Kingdom, on the importation of articles which are of an indecent or obscene character. Whatever may be the differences between the laws on this subject in force in the different constituent parts of the United Kingdom, and notwithstanding the fact that they contain certain exceptions of limited scope, these laws, taken as a whole, have as their purpose the prohibition, or at least, the restraining, of the manufacture and marketing of publications or articles of an indecent or obscene character. In these circumstances it is permissible to conclude, on a comprehensive view, that there is no lawful trade in such goods in the United Kingdom. A prohibition on imports which may in certain respects be more strict than some of the laws applied within the United Kingdom cannot therefore be regarded as amounting to a measure designed to give indirect protection to some national product or aimed at creating arbitrary discrimination between goods of this type depending on whether they are produced within the national territory or another Member State.

[22] The answer to the fourth question must therefore be that if a prohibition on the importation of goods is justifiable on grounds of public morality and if it is imposed with that purpose the enforcement of that prohibition cannot, in the absence within the Member State concerned of a lawful trade in the same goods, constitute a means of arbitrary discrimination or a disguised restriction on trade contrary to Article 36.

[23] In these circumstances it is not necessary to answer the fifth and sixth questions.

Note

Both Articles 30 and 36 of the EC Treaty (now, after amendment, Articles 28 and 30 EC) applied. The convictions were accordingly upheld.

The course of the litigation prior to the Court's decision deserves attention. The decision of the Court of Appeal is an instructive misapplication of Article 30 (now 28): [1978] 1 WLR 1031. The House of Lords' approach to Article 177 (now 234, Chapter 4) is an instructive explanation of the function of that provision: [1980] 2 WLR 597.

Conegate v *Customs and Excise Commissioners (Case 121/85)*
[1986] ECR 1007, [1986] 1 CMLR 739
Court of Justice of the European Communities

This case also involved the seizure of pornography. Similar arguments were advanced in relation to the lawfulness of the seizure under EC law. There was, however, a different background under the (non-existent, but for these purposes deemed) 'law of the UK'.

[13]   The Court would observe that the first question raises, in the first place, the general problem of whether a prohibition on the importation of certain goods may be justified on grounds of public morality where the legislation of the Member State concerned contains no prohibition on the manufacture or marketing of the same products within the national territory.

[14]   So far as that problem is concerned, it must be borne in mind that according to Article 36 of the EEC Treaty the provisions relating to the free movement of goods within the Community do not preclude prohibitions on imports justified 'on grounds of public morality'. As the Court held in its judgment of 14 December 1979, cited above [*Henn*] in principle it is for each Member State to determine in accordance with its own scale of values and in the form selected by it the requirements of public morality in its territory.

[15]   However, although Community law leaves the Member States free to make their own assessments of the indecent or obscene character of certain articles, it must be pointed out that the fact that goods cause offence cannot be regarded as sufficiently serious to justify restrictions on the free movement of goods where the Member State concerned does not adopt, with respect to the same goods manufactured or marketed within its territory, penal measures or other serious and effective measures intended to prevent the distribution of such goods in its territory.

[16]   It follows that a Member State may not rely on grounds of public morality in order to prohibit the importation of goods from other Member States when its legislation contains no prohibition on the manufacture or marketing of the same goods on its territory.

[17]   It is not for the Court, within the framework of the powers conferred upon it by Article 177 of the EEC Treaty, to consider whether, and to what extent, the United Kingdom legislation contains such a prohibition. However, the question whether or not such a prohibition exists in a State comprised of different constituent parts which have their own internal legislation, can be resolved only by taking into consideration

all the relevant legislation. Although it is not necessary, for the purposes of the application of the above-mentioned rule, that the manufacture and marketing of the products whose importation has been prohibited should be prohibited in the territory of all the constituent parts, it must at least be possible to conclude from the applicable rules, taken as a whole, that their purpose is, in substance, to prohibit the manufacture and marketing of those products.

[18]   In this instance, in the actual wording of its first question the High Court took care to define the substance of the national legislation the compatibility of which with Community law is a question which it proposes to determine. Thus it refers to rules in the importing Member State under which the goods in question may be manufactured freely and marketed subject only to certain restrictions, which it sets out explicitly, namely an absolute prohibition on the transmission of such goods by post, a restriction on their public display and, in certain areas of the Member State concerned, a system of licensing of premises for the sale of those goods to customers aged 18 years and over. Such restrictions cannot however be regarded as equivalent in substance to a prohibition on manufacture and marketing.

[19]   At the hearing, the United Kingdom again stressed the fact that at present no articles comparable to those imported by Conegate are manufactured on United Kingdom territory, but that fact, which does not exclude the possibility of manufacturing such articles and which, moreover, was not referred to by the High Court, is not such as to lead to a different assessment of the situation.

[20]   In reply to the first question it must therefore be stated that a Member State may not rely on grounds of public morality within the meaning of Article 36 of the Treaty in order to prohibit the importation of certain goods on the grounds that they are indecent or obscene, where the same goods may be manufactured freely on its territory and marketed on its territory subject only to an absolute prohibition on their transmission by post, a restriction on their public display and, in certain regions, a system of licensing of premises for the sale of those goods to customers aged 18 and over.

[21]   That conclusion does not preclude the authorities of the Member State concerned from applying to those goods, once imported, the same restrictions on marketing which are applied to similar products manufactured and marketed within the country.

Questions
1.   What is presented as the key distinction between these two cases? Explain how the concept of the prohibition on 'arbitrary discrimination' found in the second sentence of Article 30 is reflected in the decisions.
2.   T. Van Rijn (1988) 25 CML Rev 593, at pp. 608–9 argues as follows:

the test in *Conegate* depends on whether the purpose of the internal legislation was, in substance, to prohibit the manufacture and marketing of those products. One may wonder, however, whether that criterion is satisfactory in so far as it refers to prohibitions on marketing. The operation of importation takes place on the same level as the operation of manufacture. Imported products are marketed in the Member State after their importation and are then subject to the same rules as products manufactured in that Member State, as the Court rightly underlined. Control of the marketing of imported indecent products should therefore not take place on the basis of legislation on imports (such as the Customs Consolidation Act), but on the basis of the legislation governing the marketing of nationally manufactured products.

Do you agree?

Might it be open to the UK to argue that importation and manufacture are objectively distinct and may therefore be treated differently? The special position of the UK as an island may more readily yield justification for controls at the border, on the basis that control there is the most efficient location. Land borders may lose their economic relevance as market integration accelerates; the same may not be true of division by sea. Can such an argument survive the establishment of an internal market in accordance with Article 14?

3.   Chapter 10 examines EC trade law's application to the services sector, but the reader should ponder here how Article 30's recognition of permissible variation in standards of morality can be translated into laws capable of effective enforcement in a world of cable and satellite broadcasting and the 'Internet'.

4.   Could the UK government have argued that since the morality laws in question were enforced by criminal sanctions, the area fell within the scope of public policy, which is also a protectable interest under Article 30? See *Criminal proceedings against Karl Prantl* (Case 16/83) [1984] ECR 1299, [1985] 2 CMLR 238.

Consider also the Court's refusal to interpret Article 30's reference to public policy in such a way as to include the protection of the economic interests of the consumer in *Commission* v *Ireland* (Case 113/80) [1981] ECR 1625, [1982] 1 CMLR 706, p. 254 above and *Kohl* v *Ringelhan* (Case 177/83) [1984] ECR 3651, [1985] 3 CMLR 340.

5.   One of the issues in both *Henn and Darby* (Case 34/79) and *Conegate* (Case 121/85) was the absence of uniformity in the law of the constituent elements of the UK. How did the Court resolve the problem of applying Article 28 in such circumstances? Is its approach satisfactory? If the sale of an object is banned or severely restricted in Scotland but not in England, what measures could be taken to restrict its importation? Would it matter if importation was into Aberdeen or into Hull? Would it matter if the law was in practice rarely enforced anyway?

(ii) The protection of health and life of humans, animals and plants

Commission v UK (Case 40/82)
[1982] ECR 2793; [1982] 3 CMLR 497
Court of Justice of the European Communities

The UK adopted what amounted in practice to an import ban on poultrymeat and eggs from all other Member States except Denmark and

Ireland. The stated purpose of the system was to prevent the spread of Newcastle disease, a contagious disease affecting poultry. The Commission considered that the measures adopted went beyond the scope of action permissible under the Treaty, whereas the UK defended them as necessary to protect public health. The Court first explained the factual background:

[22] First, there is agreement among the parties that imports of poultrymeat and poultry products into the United Kingdom from other Member States showed a remarkable rise in the years preceding the introduction of the 1981 measures. This increase concerned in particular imports of slaughtered whole turkeys; in 1980 imports of whole turkeys from France showed a steep rise as compared with those in 1979.

[23] It is also agreed that by mid-1981 the United Kingdom Government and British producers were gravely concerned by the continuing increase in the importation of turkeys from France, and that British poultry producers made it known that they were troubled about government subsidies which, they asserted, had been made available to French producers. In these circumstances, a certain pressure was put on the United Kingdom Government, by articles in the press and in other ways, to take action in order to reduce imports of poultry products from France.

[24] Secondly, the United Kingdom does not deny that the date chosen for the introduction of the 1981 measures was such as to prevent imports of Christmas turkeys from France into Great Britain for the 1981 season, and that these imports had constituted a very substantial part of the total imports of turkeys in the preceding years.

[25] It is also an established fact that France tried to retain its poultry outlets on the British market by introducing, in September 1981, a policy on Newcastle disease which was broadly similar to the one recently adopted by the United Kingdom. As from 16 September 1981, it prohibited the use of vaccine and instituted a policy of compulsory slaughter in the event of an outbreak of disease. The British authorities refused, however, to admit French poultry products to their territory on the ground that France had not restricted poultry imports from non-member countries, notably from Spain and from some East European countries, where vaccine was still in use. The French Government maintains that it had previously been able to come to arrangements with Switzerland when outbreaks of the disease occurred in France but not in Switzerland, in such a way that French imports into that country could continue, although health controls at the frontier were substantially reinforced.

It then proceeded to examine whether the UK was entitled to act in this manner:

[36] As the Court has already observed in its judgment of 14 December 1979 in Case 34/79 *Henn and Darby* [1979] ECR 3795, the second sentence of Article 36 is designed to prevent restrictions on trade mentioned in the first sentence of that article from being diverted from their proper purpose and used in such a way as either to create discrimination in respect of goods originating in other Member States or indirectly to protect certain national products.

[37] Certain established facts suggest that the real aim of the 1981 measures was to block, for commercial and economic reasons, imports of poultry products from other

Member States, in particular from France. The United Kingdom Government had been subject to pressure from British poultry producers to block these imports. It hurriedly introduced its new policy with the result that French Christmas turkeys were excluded from the British market for the 1981 season. It did not inform the Commission and the Member States concerned in good time, as the letter in which the Commission was informed of the new measures – which took effect on 1 September 1981 – was dated 27 August 1981. It did not find it necessary to discuss the effects of the new measures on imports with the Community institutions, with the Standing Veterinary Committee or with the Member States concerned.

[38]   It should be noted, in this context, that when the United Kingdom abandoned, in 1964, the policy of non-vaccination and compulsory slaughter conducted till then in Great Britain, in order to adopt a policy of control of Newcastle disease by vaccination, this change of policy was thoroughly prepared by an elaborate report of a committee of experts, by various studies and by prolonged discussions among veterinary experts. The evidence available in the present case does not suggest that any comparable effort was made before the Government decided, in 1981, to reintroduce the policy which it had applied before 1964. The deduction must be made that the 1981 measures did not form part of a seriously considered health policy.

[39]   This conclusion is reinforced by the way in which the United Kingdom dealt with French demands that French poultry products should be readmitted to Great Britain after the French Republic had fulfilled the three conditions laid down by the United Kingdom Government, namely that the exporting country should be totally free from outbreaks of Newcastle disease, should prohibit vaccination and should apply a policy of compulsory slaughter in the event of any future outbreak of the disease. By refusing French imports on the ground that France had not closed its frontiers to poultry imports from non-member countries where vaccine was still in use, the United Kingdom added in fact a fourth condition to the three which it had previously stated in its letter to the Commission of 27 August 1981, and which it still states in its defence in the present case as the only applicable conditions.

[40]   Taken together, these facts are sufficient to establish that the 1981 measures constitute a disguised restriction on imports of poultry products from other Member States, in particular from France, unless it can be shown that, for reasons of animal health, the only possibility open to the United Kingdom was to apply the strict measures which are at issue in this case and that, therefore, the methods prescribed by the 1981 measures for obtaining the high standards of animal health which the United Kingdom Government had in mind when it changed its policy with regard to Newcastle disease, were not more restrictive than was necessary for the protection of the health of poultry flocks in Great Britain.

[41]   It follows from the information given to the Court during the proceedings that there are less stringent measures for attaining the same result. Thus, the manner in which the Danish authorities deal with imports of poultry products from other Member States – even from those where recent outbreaks of Newcastle disease have been recorded – suggests that it is possible to preserve the highest standard of freedom from Newcastle disease without completely blocking imports from countries where vaccine is still in use.

The UK was accordingly found in breach of Article 30 of the EC Treaty (now, after amendment, Article 28 EC).

Note

The case reflects the Court's determination to scrutinise closely purported reliance on Article 30. The Court must be satisfied, first, that a genuine threat to one of the interests specified in Article 30 has been established. Then, the Member State must show that the measures taken are apt to achieve protection from the perceived threat and that they are proportionate to the end in view. As an aspect of this rigorous approach to derogation, the State will fail if the Court considers that it was open to the State to achieve protection of a recognised interest through means which are less restrictive of trade.

At the heart of this approach is the key idea expressed in the second sentence of Article 30 that national measures shall not constitute 'arbitrary discrimination'.

See also, e.g., *Commission* v *France* (Case 42/82) [1983] ECR 1013, [1984] 1 CMLR 160; *Commission* v *Italy* (Case C-128/89) [1990] ECR I-3239; *Commission* v *Germany* (Case C-131/93) [1994] ECR I-3303. *Cf.* the extract from Case C-265/95 *Commission* v *France*, p. 260 above.

Question

If the UK had instituted a fully considered genuine control of the spread of Newcastle disease, including effective domestic regulation, what type of controls over imports could have been introduced in conformity with Article 30 (and Article 14)?

Note

The health risks of many artificial substances are the subject of debate. A Member State may be able to impose controls on products even in the absence of *conclusive* proof of their harmful properties, provided that there is some *objective* reason for doubting the safety of the product. As ever, the State must avoid *arbitrary* discrimination.

Officier van Justitie v *Sandoz BV (Case 174/82)*
[1983] ECR 2445; [1984] 3 CMLR 43
Court of Justice of the European Communities

Sandoz wished to sell in the Netherlands muesli bars to which vitamins had been added. These bars were freely marketable in Belgium and Germany. Authorisation to sell was refused by the Dutch authorities on the basis that the vitamins were dangerous to public health. Questions relating to the applicability of Articles 30 and 36 of the EC Treaty (now, after amendment, Articles 28 and 30 EC) were referred to Luxembourg. The Court had no doubt that a breach of Article 30 (now 28) was established. It proceeded to examine the relevance of Article 36 (now 30).

[11] It appears from the file that vitamins are not in themselves harmful substances but on the contrary are recognized by modern science as necessary for the human

organism. Nevertheless excessive consumption of them over a prolonged period may have harmful effects, the extent of which varies according to the type of vitamin: there is generally a greater risk with vitamins soluble in fat than with those soluble in water. According to the observations submitted to the Court, however, scientific research does not appear to be sufficiently advanced to be able to determine with certainty the critical quantities and the precise effects.

[12]   It is not disputed by the parties who have submitted observations that the concentration of vitamins contained in the foodstuffs of the kind in issue is far from attaining the critical threshold of harmfulness so that even excessive consumption thereof cannot in itself involve a risk to public health. Nevertheless such a risk cannot be excluded in so far as the consumer absorbs with other foods further quantities of vitamins which it is impossible to monitor or foresee.

[13]   The addition of vitamins is thus subject to the general policy in relation to food additives, which are already to a limited extent the subject of Community harmonization. Thus in particular the Council Directive of 23 October 1962 on the approximation of the rules of the Member States concerning the colouring matters authorized for use in foodstuffs intended for human consumption (Official Journal, English Special Edition 1959–62, p. 279) and Council Directive No 64/54/EEC of 5 November 1963 on the approximation of the laws of the Member States concerning the preservatives authorized for use in foodstuffs intended for human consumption (Official Journal, English Special Edition 1963–64, p. 99), as amended, require the Member States to authorize only the colouring matters and preservatives set out in the list annexed but leave the Member States free to restrict, in certain circumstances, the use even of the substances listed.

[14]   As regards foodstuffs intended for particular nutritional uses there has been some degree of harmonization in Council Directive No 77/94/EEC of 21 December 1976 on the approximation of the laws of the Member States relating to foodstuffs for particular nutritional uses (Official Journal 1977, L 26, p. 55). Article 7 thereof requires the Member States to adopt all the measures necessary to ensure that trade in the said products cannot be impeded by the application of non-harmonized national provisions governing the composition, manufacturing specifications, packaging or labelling of foodstuffs, subject nevertheless to provisions justified on grounds, *inter alia*, of protection of public health.

[15]   The abovementioned Community measures clearly show that the Community legislature accepts the principle that it is necessary to restrict the use of food additives to the substances specified, whilst leaving the Member States a certain discretion to adopt stricter rules. The measures thus testify to great prudence regarding the potential harmfulness of additives, the extent of which is still uncertain in respect of each of the various substances, and leave a wide discretion to the Member States in relation to such additives.

[16]   As the Court found in its judgment of 17 December 1981 in Case 272/80 (*Frans-Nederlandse Maatschappij voor Biologische Producten* [1981] ECR 3277), in so far as there are uncertainties at the present state of scientific research it is for the Member States, in the absence of harmonization, to decide what degree of protection of the health and life of humans they intend to assure, having regard however for the requirements of the free movement of goods within the Community.

[17]   Those principles also apply to substances such as vitamins which are not as a general rule harmful in themselves but may have special harmful effects solely if taken

to excess as part of the general nutrition, the composition of which is unforeseeable and cannot be monitored. In view of the uncertainties inherent in the scientific assessment, national rules prohibiting, without prior authorization, the marketing of foodstuffs to which vitamins have been added are justified on principle within the meaning of Article 36 of the Treaty on grounds of the protection of human health.

[18]   Nevertheless the principle of proportionality which underlies the last sentence of Article 36 of the Treaty requires that the power of the Member States to prohibit imports of the products in question from other Member States should be restricted to what is necessary to attain the legitimate aim of protecting health. Accordingly, national rules providing for such a prohibition are justified only if authorizations to market are granted when they are compatible with the need to protect health.

[19]   Such an assessment is, however, difficult to make in relation to additives such as vitamins the abovementioned characteristics of which exclude the possibility of foreseeing or monitoring the quantities consumed as part of the general nutrition and the degree of harmfulness of which cannot be determined with sufficient certainty. Nevertheless, although in view of the present stage of harmonization of national laws at the Community level a wide discretion must be left to the Member States, they must, in order to observe the principle of proportionality, authorize marketing when the addition of vitamins to foodstuffs meets a real need, especially a technical or nutritional one.

[20]   The first question must therefore be answered to the effect that Community law permits national rules prohibiting without prior authorization the marketing of foodstuffs lawfully marketed in another Member State to which vitamins have been added, provided that the marketing is authorized when the addition of vitamins meets a real need, especially a technical or nutritional one.

Second question
[21]   In the second question the national court asks in essence whether Community law precludes national rules such as those referred to by the national court where the authorization to market is subject to proof by the importer that the product in question is not harmful to health.

[22]   Inasmuch as the question arises as to where the onus of proof lies when there is a request for authorization, in view of the answer to the first question, it must be remembered that Article 36 of the Treaty creates an exception, which must be strictly interpreted, to the rule of free movement of goods within the Community which is one of the fundamental principles of the common market. It is therefore for the national authorities who rely on that provision in order to adopt a measure restricting intra-Community trade to check in each instance that the measure contemplated satisfies the criteria of that provision.

[23]   Accordingly, although the national authorities may, in so far as they do not have it themselves, ask the importer to produce the information in his possession relating to the composition of the product and the technical or nutritional reasons for adding vitamins, they must themselves assess, in the light of all the relevant information, whether authorization must be granted pursuant to Community law.

[24]   The second question must therefore be answered to the effect that Community law does not permit national rules which subject authorization to market to proof by the importer that the product in question is not harmful to health, without prejudice to the right of the national authorities to ask the importer to submit all the information in his possession needed to assess the facts.

Note
The circumstances in which a State may impose a health check on products which have already been subjected to a check in the State of origin are closely circumscribed. The key, once again, is the elimination of trade restriction which constitutes 'arbitrary discrimination'.

Frans-Nederlandse Maatschappij voor Biologische Producten (Case 272/80)
[1981] ECR 3277; [1982] 2 CMLR 497
Court of Justice of the European Communities

The case concerned Dutch checks on plant protection products imported from France where the products had been approved and lawfully marketed.

[13]. . . [I]t is not disputed that the national rules in question are intended to protect public health and that they therefore come within the exception provided for by Article 36. The measures of control applied by the Netherlands authorities, in particular as regards the approval of the product, may not therefore be challenged in principle. However, that leaves open the question whether the detailed procedures governing approvals, as indicated by the national court, may possibly constitute a disguised restriction, within the meaning of the last sentence of Article 36, on trade between Member States, in view, on the one hand, of the dangerous nature of the product and, on the other hand, of the fact that it has been the subject of a procedure for approval in the Member State where it has been lawfully marketed.

[14]   Whilst a Member State is free to require a product of the type in question, which has already received approval in another Member State, to undergo a fresh procedure of examination and approval, the authorities of the Member States are nevertheless required to assist in bringing about a relaxation of the controls existing in intra-Community trade. It follows that they are not entitled unnecessarily to require technical or chemical analyses or laboratory tests where those analyses and tests have already been carried out in another Member State and their results are available to those authorities, or may at their request be placed at their disposal.

[15]   For the same reasons, a Member State operating an approvals procedure must ensure that no unnecessary control expenses are incurred if the practical effects of the control carried out in the Member State of origin satisfy the requirements of the protection of public health in the importing Member State. On the other hand, the mere fact that those expenses weigh more heavily on a trader marketing small quantities of an approved product than on his competitor who markets much greater quantities, does not justify the conclusion that such expenses constitute arbitrary discrimination or a disguised restriction within the meaning of Article 36.

[16]   The reply to be given to the question submitted to the Court must therefore be that it follows from Article 30 in conjunction with Article 36 of the Treaty that a Member State is not prohibited from requiring plant protection products to be subject to prior approval, even if those products have already been approved in another Member State. The authorities of the importing State are however not entitled unnecessarily to require technical or chemical analyses or laboratory tests when the same analyses and tests have already been carried out in another Member State and

their results are available to those authorities or may at their request be placed at their disposal.

[17]   It is for the national court to examine, in the light of the foregoing considerations, whether, and if so to what extent, the procedures governing approvals laid down by the national legislation are justified under Article 36.

Note

The judgment in *Sandoz* (Case 174/82) (p. 281 above) indicates that unilateral Member State action in derogation from the basic principle of free movement may be robbed of its legal justification by the introduction of Community legislation which secures the protection of the particular interest in issue. Community legislation was not yet sufficiently comprehensive in that case (para. 19). This is the 'dual function' of harmonisation legislation: a common Community rule which *facilitates* free trade but on terms which *protect* the interests which might previously have justified national rules. The Community's work has been particularly intense in the field of health controls. It has sought to establish a system of controls and checks which will allow the dismantling of the existing obstructions of differing rules in each State, because, as recognised in *Biologische Producten* (Case 272/80), it remains lawful to impose 'double checks' in exceptional circumstances where the legitimate concerns of the State of importation are not met by the exporting State.

   This has given rise to some difficulty in law in ascertaining the scope of permissible Member State action in areas subject to Community legislative intervention.

Rewe-Zentralfinanz Gmbh v *Landwirtschaftskammer (Case 4/75)*
[1975] ECR 843; [1975] 1 CMLR 599
Court of Justice of the European Communities

The case concerned checks of imported apples by the German authorities. This constituted a clear breach of Article 30 of the EC Treaty (now, after amendment, Article 28 EC). Were the checks justifiable? Reliance on Article 36 of the EC Treaty (now, after amendment, Article 30 EC) was complicated by the existence of Community legislation governing the type of controls at issue.

[5] . . . [P]hytosanitary inspections at the frontier which plant products, such as apples, coming from another Member State are required to undergo, constitute measures having an effect equivalent to quantitative restrictions within the meaning of Article 30 of the Treaty, and are prohibited under that provision subject to the exceptions laid down by Community law.

[6]   Under the first sentence of Article 36 of the Treaty, the provisions of Articles 30 to 34 are not to preclude restrictions on imports and, therefore, measures having equivalent effect, which are justified for reasons of protection of the health of plants.
   Council Directive No 69/466/EEC of 8 December 1969 (OJ 1969, L 323, p. 5) on the control of San José Scale, lays down a series of provisions which are common to all the Member States of the Community.

The purpose of this Directive is to introduce certain minimum measures common to all the Member States by which certain harmful organisms may be controlled 'simultaneously and methodically' throughout the Community and prevented from spreading.

At the same time the Directive, which was adopted under Articles 43 and 100 of the Treaty, forms part of the measures intended to remove obstacles to the free movement of agricultural products within the Common Market.

[7] Its fourth recital shows, however, that the measures laid down are intended to supplement and not to replace the protective measures taken against the introduction of harmful organisms into each Member State.

By authorizing those States to adopt such additional or stricter provisions as may be required to control San José Scale or to prevent it from spreading, Article 11 reserves to them the power to maintain such measures in force to the extent necessary.

In the light of the current Community rules in this matter, a phytosanitary inspection carried out by a Member State on the importation of plant products constitutes, in principle, one of the restrictions on imports which are justified under the first sentence of Article 36 of the Treaty.

[8] However, the restrictions on imports referred to in the first sentence of Article 36 cannot be accepted under the second sentence of that article if they constitute a means of arbitrary discrimination.

The fact that plant products imported from another Member State are subject to a phytosanitary inspection although domestic products are not subject to an equivalent examination when they are despatched within the Member State might constitute arbitrary discrimination within the meaning of the abovementioned provision.

Therefore, the phytosanitary inspection of imported products which are shown to originate in areas other than those referred to in Article 3 of Council Directive No 69/466/EEC may constitute an additional or stricter measure which is not justified by Article 11 of that directive and should be regarded as a means of arbitrary discrimination within the meaning of the second sentence of Article 36 of the Treaty.

The different treatment of imported and domestic products, based on the need to prevent the spread of the harmful organism could not, however, be regarded as arbitrary discrimination if effective measures are taken in order to prevent the distribution of contaminated domestic products and if there is reason to believe, in particular on the basis of previous experience, that there is a risk of the harmful organism's spreading if no inspection is held on importation.

[9] The reply to the questions put must therefore be that a requirement to submit imports of plant products, such as apples, from another Member State to a phytosanitary inspection at the frontier in order to establish whether such products are carriers of certain organisms harmful to plants constitutes a measure having an effect equivalent to quantitative restrictions within the meaning of Article 30 of the Treaty and is prohibited under that provision, subject to the exceptions laid down in Article 36 of the Treaty.

The additional or stricter provisions which may be required under Article 11 of Council Directive No 69/466/EEC of 8 December 1969 in order to control San José Scale and prevent it from spreading entitle the Member States to make phytosanitary inspections of imported products if effective measures are taken in order to prevent the distribution of contaminated domestic products and if there is reason to believe, in particular on the basis of previous experience, that there is a risk of the harmful organism's spreading if no inspection is held on importation.

Oberkreisdirektor v *Moormann (Case 190/87)*
[1988] ECR 4689; [1990] 1 CMLR 656
Court of Justice of the European Communities

[10]   The Court has consistently held that where, in application of Article 100 of the Treaty, Community directives provide for the harmonization of the measures necessary to ensure *inter alia* the protection of animal and human health and establish Community procedures to check that they are observed, recourse to Article 36 is no longer justified and the appropriate checks must be carried out and protective measures adopted within the framework outlined by the harmonizing directive (judgments of 5 October 1977 in 5/77, *Tedeschi* v *Denkavit* ((1977)) ECR 155; 5 April 1979 in Case 148/78, *Ratti* ((1979)) ECR 1629; and 8 November 1979 in Case 251/78, *Denkavit* ((1979)) ECR 3369).

[11]   As the Court has already held in its judgment of 6 October 1983 in Joined Cases 2 to 4/82 (*Delhaize* ((1982)) ECR 2973), Council Directive 71/188/EEC of 15 February 1971 on health problems affecting trade in fresh poultrymeat (Official Journal, English Special Edition 1971 (I), p. 106) introduced a harmonized system of health inspections. This system of health inspections, harmonized at Community level and based on full inspection of the goods in the exporting State, replaces inspection in the State of destination and is intended to allow the free movement of the goods concerned under the same conditions as those of an internal market.

[12]   Consequently, with regard to trade in fresh poultrymeat, health inspection carried out systematically on goods when they cross the frontier can no longer be justified on grounds of the protection of health under Article 36 of the Treaty.

[13]   Only occasional health inspections carried out by the State of destination are permissible, provided that they are not increased to such an extent as to constitute a disguised restriction on trade between the Member States (see judgment of 6 October 1983, *Delhaize*, cited above).

Note

Establishing a balance between the responsibility of the Community authorities and those at the national level is perhaps the paramount problem confronting the shapers of the internal market. It is not a problem which miraculously vanished on the last day of 1992! It is deceptively simple to declare that in principle the passage of Community harmonisation legislation precludes an individual State's reliance on Article 30; and that the interest can be protected in a Community measure which also facilitates free trade. The reality is that in a heterogenous Community of 15 Member States a single Community rule cannot encompass all the diffuse interests at work in the structure. So in practice national derogations and differing standards may be judged necessary. Both the two cases just considered illustrate this. The Community has a responsibility to develop a framework in which the objective of free trade will be pursued in accompaniment with the protection of and respect for national diversity and social traditions – see Article 2 EC, p. 168 above. This implies a careful mix between responsibility at Community level and responsibility at national level. In addition, the administration of the law must be allocated to the appropriate level in the structure.

Further discussion of these issues is found below at p. 333 and in Chapter 15.

(iii) The protection of industrial and commercial property
This matter raises issues which overlap with the application of the Treaty competition rules. See Chapter 14.

(D) ELIMINATING REMAINING BARRIERS TO TRADE

It has been observed that *Sandoz* (Case 174/82) (at p. 281 above) is a decision which allows national rules to restrict trade pending Community harmonisation in the pursuit of the protection of public health; *Campus Oil Ltd* v *Minister for Industry and Energy* (Case 72/83) [1984] ECR 2727 provides a parallel example of trade restrictions to protect domestic energy production, permissible in the interest of public security given the inadequacy of existing Community rules guaranteeing energy supplies; *Moormann* (Case 190/87) (at p. 287 above) demonstrates the interaction of Community rules and national competence, again in the area of health protection.

Are all the heads of justification under Article 30 susceptible to harmonisation, or do they perform different functions calling for different solutions? How could a Community approach to public morality or protection of national treasures be achieved which yields free trade? How will the Community develop? To what extent is a balance between the exclusive competence of the Community and the legitimate concerns of the diverse Member States feasible? This is the very essence of the Community's task.

It falls to be considered how these questions have been addressed in the context of the completion of the internal market in accordance with Article 14. As already suggested (in Chapter 5 and subsequently), the problems persist beyond the target date of the end of 1992. However, Articles 100a and 100b were inserted into the Treaty by the Single European Act with a view to resolving some of these issues. In practice, much internal market legislation has been based on Article 100a. The Amsterdam Treaty repealed Article 100b, which proved superfluous, but it amended and re-numbered Article 100a. It is now Article 95 and it is set out at p. 569 in Chapter 15, where harmonisation policy is discussed in its wider context.

Questions
Discuss the impact of Community law in the following cases:

1. The French authorities uncover a scandal involving the use of anti-freeze by wine producers. The adulterated wine has already caused several deaths in France.

The UK immediately introduces a system whereby all French wine must be inspected and granted a licence before it may be imported. The procedure at the ports can result in the detention of goods for up to one month.

A flat rate fee of £1 per case is imposed on all French wine subject to this procedure.

How would your answer differ if the French authorities, in an effort to minimise the detrimental effect of the scandal on their wine export trade, had already introduced a similar system of checks on all wine exported from France?

2.   Franco exports dairy products from France to Germany. He has always sold his milk in Germany in cartons bearing the French flag. He believes that this is a valuable marketing technique. However, he learns that a new German law prohibits the use of national flags in product promotion. This law is part of a programme introduced by the German government to make its population more aware of European integration and less likely to exercise national prejudice.

8 BEYOND DISCRIMINATION: ARTICLE 28

(A) INDISTINCTLY APPLICABLE RULES: THE *CASSIS DE DIJON* FORMULA

The previous chapter examined a range of rules which discriminated against imports. However, even in the absence of discrimination against imported goods, national trading rules are capable of impeding the free circulation of goods in the Community. Article 28 may apply even to national legislation which makes no distinction between domestic and imported goods. The scope and application of Community law in this area is primarily the consequence of the Court's activism, and therefore it is appropriate to allow the leading case to provide the introductory means of explanation. Remember that Article 30, referred to in the judgment, was re-numbered by the Treaty of Amsterdam and is now, with minor amendment, Article 28.

Rewe-Zentrale AG v *Bundesmonopolverwaltung für Branntwein (Case 120/78)*
[1979] ECR 649; [1979] 3 CMLR 494
Court of Justice of the European Communities

[1]   By order of 28 April 1978, which was received at the Court on 22 May, the Hessisches Finanzgericht referred two questions to the Court under Article 177 of the EEC Treaty for a preliminary ruling on the interpretation of Articles 30 and 37 of the EEC Treaty, for the purpose of assessing the compatibility with Community law of a provision of the German rules relating to the marketing of alcoholic beverages fixing a minimum alcoholic strength for various categories of alcoholic products.

[2]   It appears from the order making the reference that the plaintiff in the main action intends to import a consignment of 'Cassis de Dijon' originating in France for the purpose of marketing it in the Federal Republic of Germany.

The plaintiff applied to the Bundesmonopolverwaltung (Federal Monopoly Administration for Spirits) for authorization to import the product in question and the monopoly administration informed it that because of its insufficient alcoholic strength the said product does not have the characteristics required in order to be marketed within the Federal Republic of Germany.

[3]   The monopoly administration's attitude is based on Article 100 of the Branntweinmonopolgesetz and on the rules drawn up by the monopoly administration pursuant to that provision, the effect of which is to fix the minimum alcohol content of specified categories of liqueurs and the potable spirits (Verordnung über den Mindestweingeistgehalt von Trinkbranntweinen of 28 February 1958, Bundesanzeiger No 48 of 11 March 1958).

Those provisions lay down that the marketing of fruit liqueurs, such as 'Cassis de Dijon', is conditional upon a minimum alcohol content of 25%, whereas the alcohol content of the product in question, which is freely marketed as such in France, is between 15 and 20%.

[4]   The plaintiff takes the view that the fixing by the German rules of a minimum alcohol content leads to the result that well-known spirits products from other Member States of the Community cannot be sold in the Federal Republic of Germany and that the said provision therefore constitutes a restriction on the free movement of goods between Member States which exceeds the bounds of the trade rules reserved to the latter.

In its view it is a measure having an effect equivalent to a quantitative restriction on imports contrary to Article 30 of the EEC Treaty.

Since, furthermore, it is a measure adopted within the context of the management of the spirits monopoly, the plaintiff considers that there is also an infringement of Article 37, according to which the Member States shall progressively adjust any State monopolies of a commercial character so as to ensure that when the transitional period has ended no discrimination regarding the conditions under which goods are procured or marketed exists between nationals of Member States.

[5]   In order to reach a decision on this dispute the Hessisches Finanzgericht has referred two questions to the Court, worded as follows:

1.   Must the concept of measures having an effect equivalent to quantitative restrictions on imports contained in Article 30 of the EEC Treaty be understood as meaning that the fixing of a minimum wine-spirit content for potable spirits laid down in the German Branntweinmonopolgesetz, the result of which is that traditional products of other Member States whose wine-spirit content is below the fixed limit cannot be put into circulation in the Federal Republic of Germany, also comes within this concept?

2.   May the fixing of such a minimum wine-spirit content come within the concept of 'discrimination regarding the conditions under which goods are procured and marketed . . . between nationals of Member States' contained in Article 37 of the EEC Treaty?

[6]   The national court is thereby asking for assistance in the matter of interpretation in order to enable it to assess whether the requirement of a minimum alcohol content may be covered either by the prohibition on all measures having an effect equivalent to quantitative restrictions in trade between Member States contained in Article 30 of the Treaty or by the prohibition on all discrimination regarding the conditions under which goods are procured and marketed between nationals of Member States within the meaning of Article 37.

[7]   It should be noted in this connexion that Article 37 relates specifically to State monopolies of a commercial character.

That provision is therefore irrelevant with regard to national provisions which do not concern the exercise by a public monopoly of its specific function – namely, its exclusive right – but apply in a general manner to the production and marketing of alcoholic beverages, whether or not the latter are covered by the monopoly in question.

That being the case, the effect on intra-Community trade of the measure referred to by the national court must be examined solely in relation to the requirements under Article 30, as referred to by the first question.

[8]   In the absence of common rules relating to the production and marketing of alcohol – a proposal for a regulation submitted to the Council by the Commission on 7 December 1976 (Official Journal C 309, p. 2) not yet having received the Council's approval – it is for the Member States to regulate all matters relating to the production and marketing of alcohol and alcoholic beverages on their own territory.

Obstacles to movement within the Community resulting from disparities between the national laws relating to the marketing of the products in question must be accepted in so far as those provisions may be recognized as being necessary in order to satisfy mandatory requirements relating in particular to the effectiveness of fiscal supervision, the protection of public health, the fairness of commercial transactions and the defence of the consumer.

[9]   The Government of the Federal Republic of Germany, intervening in the proceedings, put forward various arguments which, in its view, justify the application of provisions relating to the minimum alcohol content of alcoholic beverages, adducing considerations relating on the one hand to the protection of public health and on the other to the protection of the consumer against unfair commercial practices.

[10]   As regards the protection of public health the German Government states that the purpose of the fixing of minimum alcohol contents by national legislation is to avoid the proliferation of alcoholic beverages on the national market, in particular alcoholic beverages with a low alcohol content, since, in its view, such products may more easily induce a tolerance towards alcohol than more highly alcoholic beverages.

[11]   Such considerations are not decisive since the consumer can obtain on the market an extremely wide range of weakly or moderately alcoholic products and furthermore a large proportion of alcoholic beverages with a high alcohol content freely sold on the German market is generally consumed in a diluted form.

[12]   The German Government also claims that the fixing of a lower limit for the alcohol content of certain liqueurs is designed to protect the consumer against unfair practices on the part of producers and distributors of alcoholic beverages.

This argument is based on the consideration that the lowering of the alcohol content secures a competitive advantage in relation to beverages with a higher alcohol content, since alcohol constitutes by far the most expensive constituent of beverages by reason of the high rate of tax to which it is subject.

Furthermore, according to the German Government, to allow alcoholic products into free circulation wherever, as regards their alcohol content, they comply with the rules laid down in the country of production would have the effect of imposing as a common standard within the Community the lowest alcohol content permitted in any of the Member States, and even of rendering any requirements in this field inoperative since a lower limit of this nature is foreign to the rules of several Member States.

[13]   As the Commission rightly observed, the fixing of limits in relation to the alcohol content of beverages may lead to the standardization of products placed on the market and of their designations, in the interests of a greater transparency of commercial transactions and offers for sale to the public.

However, this line of argument cannot be taken so far as to regard the mandatory fixing of minimum alcohol contents as being an essential guarantee of the fairness of commercial transactions, since it is a simple matter to ensure that suitable information is conveyed to the purchaser by requiring the display of an indication of origin and of the alcohol content on the packaging of products.

[14]   It is clear from the foregoing that the requirements relating to the minimum alcohol content of alcoholic beverages do not serve a purpose which is in the general interest and such as to take precedence over the requirements of the free movement of goods, which constitutes one of the fundamental rules of the Community.

In practice, the principal effect of requirements of this nature is to promote alcoholic beverages having a high alcohol content by excluding from the national market products of other Member States which do not answer that description.

It therefore appears that the unilateral requirement imposed by the rules of a Member State of a minimum alcohol content for the purposes of the sale of alcoholic beverages constitutes an obstacle to trade which is incompatible with the provisions of Article 30 of the Treaty.

There is therefore no valid reason why, provided that they have been lawfully produced and marketed in one of the Member States, alcoholic beverages should not be introduced into any other Member State; the sale of such products may not be subject to a legal prohibition on the marketing of beverages with an alcohol content lower than the limit set by the national rules.

[15]   Consequently, the first question should be answered to the effect that the concept of 'measures having an effect equivalent to quantitative restrictions on imports' contained in Article 30 of the Treaty is to be understood to mean that the fixing of a minimum alcohol content for alcoholic beverages intended for human consumption by the legislation of a Member State also falls within the prohibition laid down in that provision where the importation of alcoholic beverages lawfully produced and marketed in another Member State is concerned.

Note

Notice that such trade restrictions arise simply because national laws are different within the Community. Typical French products were excluded from the German market by a rule which on its face made no reference whatsoever to national origin. The result was the isolation of the German market and the protection of the German producer from competition. Such market partitioning subverts the concept of a common market.

**P. Cecchini, *The European Challenge: 1992, the Benefits of a Single Market*
(1988), pp. 24–27**

Divergences in technical regulations and standards – costs difficult to quantify but impossible to ignore
Rated by companies themselves as one of most acute problems they face in their European operations . . . , disparities between national technical regulations and

standards are a complex and, to the outside observer, an arcane subject. Yet their adverse impact on industry seeking to exploit the full dimension of the EC market, a priority matter for the Community policy-maker as for the businessman, is now widely accepted.

It is not difficult to see why. In an increasing number of sectors, firms will be obliged to survive by selling in quantities much larger than are likely to be absorbed by their share of a single, narrow national market. To compete, they need to produce on a larger scale. To amortize this investment in new plant, and also their spiralling expenditure on research and innovation, they need the larger, European market.

National product regulations and standards, however, impose an entirely contrary logic. They tend, by their differences, to force companies to do what their business strategy tells them is wrong: produce for the national market, innovate for the national market. Manufacturers are thus often constrained either to limit themselves to a sub-optimal market, or to attack new markets via a range of sub-optimal plants and narrowly relevant technology. Either option implies extensive costs – the costs of non-Europe.

Adverse effects are thus not limited to restrictions on cross-border trade. They impact on the core functions of business – production and technology. And the costs they incur are often compounded by their use in combination with other obstacles to market entry, notably restrictive public procurement, e.g. telecommunications equipment . . . . Among the worst affected by these and related barriers are high tech sectors which are precisely those where market fragmentation has a proven track record in putting Europe at a competitive disadvantage with the US and Japan.

Barriers in this field result from differences between EC countries for three types of arrangement: technical regulations, standards, testing and certification procedures.

Technical regulations lay down legal requirements, enacted by the national legislator mainly in the interests of health, safety and the environment; often these requirements refer to standards.

Standards are not legally binding in themselves, since they are written by private national standardisation bodies like DIN (in Germany), BSI (in Britain) and AFNOR (in France). However, although standards are only voluntary codifications for products and product processes, they often assume a quasi-legal status because of their use as a reference in technical regulations and, for example, in insurance and product liability claims, as well as in calls for tender for public procurement.

Testing and certification procedures are used to check that a product or process complies either with voluntary standards or with statutory regulations. If successfully passed, they result in the issuance of certificates of conformity. However, a typical problem is non-recognition by one EC country of another's certification process, meaning at best additional testing and at worst an absolute market entry barrier.

Costs: multi-sector impact

The costs . . . imposed by these barriers hit manufacturing industries right across the board. But they do so in a manner which is so sector-specific and which, even then, is often inextricably combined with the impact of other barriers, as to make a quantified extrapolation at the general level impossible to undertake. But on an individual industry basis, the story is clear. It is illustrated by the investigations carried out by the research into certain selected industries . . . . Their results are in turn corroborated and amplified by company executives themselves in the general survey of manufacturing business conducted for the research.

Telecom equipment, automobiles, foodstuffs, pharmaceuticals and the building products sector are . . . five major EC industries where standards and technical regulations, alone or in combination with other obstacles, inject heavy doses of inefficiency into business operations.

This is most spectacularly the case in the telecom sector. Here the industry's regulators – usually the national PTTs – have traditionally sustained their restrictive procurement practices by demanding observance of narrowly relevant standards reinforced by discriminating certification procedures. The overall cost of these mutually supportive barriers is estimated as high as Ecu 4.8 billion. The experience of telecom equipment, moreover, is to an extent indicative of the massive losses imposed by divergent standards on other high technology sectors, where burgeoning R&D expenditure can only be recouped by manufacturing products to widely marketable standards.

At the other end of industry's product range, foodstuffs and building products have their own experiences to tell. Thus of the total estimated costs of up to Ecu 1 billion attributable to market barriers in the foodstuffs sector, content and ingredient regulations on just four items (chocolates, beer, ice-cream and pasta) contribute over 80% . . . . In the building products sector, research shows unequivocally that divergent standards and lengthy certification (whose procedures can last years rather than months) are the primary causes of non-Europe costs estimated in total at around Ecu 2.5 billion. Pharmaceutical companies, meanwhile, face serious problems and significant costs in getting new products authorized and admitted to the market.

Motor manufacturing enjoys a paradoxical but costly situation. It is both the sector where the removal of technical barriers is judged as most necessary by business itself . . . and yet the one where the Community has had most apparent success in harmonizing technical regulations. As many as 41 EC harmonization directives, dealing with specifications for various parts of the automobile, have been adopted over the years. But the key problem is that there remain three further directives which need to be adopted before full EC type approval can be achieved. In the absence of Community type approval (which is being held up on political rather than technical grounds), and thus of a European certification procedure, EC-wide manufacturers are generally being forced into costly duplications.

Note
The ruling in '*Cassis de Dijon*' (Case 120/78) is one of the main pillars of EC trade law. As already discussed in Chapter 5 (p. 217 above), the Court has constructed a strategy for judging the permissibility of regulatory diversity between the States in an integrating market. The principles set out by the Court in its ruling in *Gebhard* (Case C-55/94, p. 217 above), have their roots in the fertile soil of the '*Cassis de Dijon*' ruling.

A further simple example of market partitioning caused by national laws which in effect enshrine a preference for typical national produce is provided by the following case.

Ministère Public v *Deserbais (Case 286/86)*
[1988] ECR 4907
Court of Justice of the European Communities

French legislation restricted the use of the name 'Edam' to cheese with a minimum fat content of 40%. M. Deserbais imported cheese from

Germany where it was lawfully produced with a fat content of only 34.3%. When he marketed the cheese in France as 'Edam', he was prosecuted for unlawful use of a trade name. M. Deserbais argued that Article 30 of the EC Treaty (now, after amendment, Article 28 EC) provided him with a complete defence to the charge. The matter was referred to the Court under the Article 177 preliminary reference procedure, found in Article 234 post-Amsterdam (Chapter 4).

[10] [T]he national court starts from the premise that the cheese in question, containing 34% fat, has been lawfully and traditionally produced in the Federal Republic of Germany under the name 'Edam' in accordance with the laws and regulations applicable to it there, and that consumers' attention is adequately drawn to that fact by the labelling.

[11] It must also be stated that at the present stage of development of Community law there are no common rules governing the names of the various types of cheeses in the Community. Accordingly, it cannot be stated in principle that a Member State may not lay down rules making the use by national producers of a name for a cheese subject to the observance of a traditional minimum fat content.

[12] However, it would be incompatible with Article 30 of the Treaty and the objectives of a common market to apply such rules to imported cheeses of the same type where those cheeses have been lawfully produced and marketed in another Member State under the same generic name but with a different minimum fat content. The Member State into which they are imported cannot prevent the importation and marketing of such cheeses where adequate information for the consumer is ensured.

[13] The question may arise whether the same rule must be applied where a product presented under a particular name is so different, as regards its composition or production, from the products generally known by that name in the Community that it cannot be regarded as falling within the same category. However, no situation of that kind arises in the circumstances described by the national court in this case.

The Court's reply to the question referred was accordingly:

Article 30 *et seq.* of the Treaty must be interpreted as precluding a Member State from applying national legislation making the right to use the trade name of a type of cheese subject to the observance of a minimum fat content to products of the same type imported from another Member State when those products have been lawfully manufactured and marketed under that name in that Member State and consumers are provided with proper information.

Note

There is every reason to insist that Article 28 is capable of applying to such national rules because of the clear restrictive *effect* on intra-Community trade. The *'Cassis de Dijon'* (Case 120/78) approach has this emphasis on effect in common with the *Dassonville* (Case 8/74) formula (p. 244 above). This interpretation of Article 28 is crucial to the attack on national protectionism and market division. According to P. Verloren van Themaat (1982) 18 CDE 123, at p. 135:

La crise économique actuelle augmente sans doute la tentation pour les
Etats membres de prendre des mesures qui sont susceptibles d'entraver

directement ou indirectement, actuellement ou potentiellement, le commerce intracommunautaire . . . .

The Court's application of Article 28 constitutes an important corrective to that persisting temptation.

Question
To what extent has the Court adopted a more vigorous pro-free trade stance than that envisaged by Article 3 of Directive 70/50 (p. 241 above)?

Notes
1. The result of the Court's approach is that goods produced to a standard which entitles access to the market of the Member State of production should be recognised as a sufficient standard to deserve access to the market of any other Member State. It is assumed that all Member States have a broadly equivalent approach to basic standards of health and safety, and that they should recognise this in dealing with imports from other Member States. The approach taken in '*Cassis de Dijon*' (Case 120/78) is an important impetus towards market integration. A State can no longer present an importer with a rule book full of technical standards and demand that the importer's goods conform to those standards of manufacture or designation.
2. Only in exceptional circumstances can a State stand on its technical rules to prevent the import of a product from another Member State – when it can show that the rules are necessary to satisfy a mandatory requirement. There is, then, a strong presumption in favour of free trade inherent in the Court's approach.

Commission v *Germany (Case 178/84)*
[1987] ECR 1227; [1988] 1 CMLR 780
Court of Justice of the European Communities

This was an infringement procedure against Germany (see Chapter 17) alleging breach of Article 30 of the EC Treaty (now, after amendment, Article 28 EC). Germany prohibited the marketing on its territory of beer lawfully produced and marketed in other Member States if the beer failed to comply with the provisions of the *Biersteuergesetz* of 1952. The law applied equally to all beer produced in Germany itself, so there was no question of discrimination against imports. There were two limbs to the *Biersteuergesetz* which the Commission was concerned to challenge. In the first place, the name 'Bier' could be used only for products brewed using malted barley, hops, yeast and water alone. The use of other ingredients such as maize did not preclude the marketing of the finished product, but it could not be sold as 'Bier'.

[25] [T]he Commission concedes that as long as harmonization has not been achieved at Community level the Member States have the power in principle to lay

down rules governing the manufacture, the composition and the marketing of beverages. It stresses, however, that rules which, like Article 10 of the Biersteuergesetz, prohibit the use of a generic designation for the marketing of products manufactured partly from raw materials, such as rice and maize, other than those whose use is prescribed in the national territory are contrary to Community law. In any event, such rules go beyond what is necessary in order to protect the German consumer, since that could be done simply by means of labelling or notices. Those rules therefore constitute an impediment to trade contrary to Article 30 of the EEC Treaty.

[26]   The German Government has first sought to justify its rules on public-health grounds. It maintains that the use of raw materials other than those permitted by Article 9 of the Biersteuergesetz would inevitably entail the use of additives. However, at the hearing the German Government conceded that Article 10 of the Biersteuergesetz, which is merely a rule on designation, was exclusively intended to protect consumers. In its view, consumers associate the designation 'Bier' with a beverage manufactured from only the raw materials listed in Article 9 of the Biersteuergesetz. Consequently, it is necessary to prevent them from being misled as to the nature of the product by being led to believe that a beverage called 'Bier' complies with the Reinheitsgebot when that is not the case. The German Government maintains that its rules are not protectionist in aim. It stresses in that regard that the raw materials whose use is specified in Article 9(1) and (2) of the Biersteuergesetz are not necessarily of national origin. Any trader marketing products satisfying the prescribed rules is free to use the designation 'Bier' and those rules can readily be complied with outside the Federal Republic of Germany.

[27]   According to a consistent line of decisions of the Court (above all, the judgment of 11 July 1974 in Case 8/74 *Procureur du Roi* v *Dassonville* [1974] ECR 837) the prohibition of measures having an effect equivalent to quantitative restrictions under Article 30 of the EEC Treaty covers 'all trading rules enacted by Member States which are capable of hindering, directly or indirectly, actually or potentially, intra-Community trade'.

[28]   The Court has also consistently held (in particular in the judgment of 20 February 1979 in Case 120/78 *REWE-Zentrale AG* v *Bundesmonopolverwaltung* [1979] ECR 649, and the judgment of 10 November 1982 in Case 261/81 *Walter Rau Lebensmittelwerke* v *De Smedt* [1982] ECR 3961) that 'in the absence of common rules relating to the marketing of the products concerned, obstacles to free movement within the Community resulting from disparities between the national laws must be accepted in so far as such rules, applicable to domestic and to imported products without distinction, may be recognized as being necessary in order to satisfy mandatory requirements relating *inter alia* to consumer protection. It is also necessary for such rules to be proportionate to the aim in view. If a Member State has a choice between various measures to attain the same objective it should choose the means which least restricts the free movement of goods'.

[29]   It is not contested that the application of Article 10 of the Biersteuergesetz to beers from other Member States in whose manufacture raw materials other than malted barley have been lawfully used, in particular rice and maize, is liable to constitute an obstacle to their importation into the Federal Republic of Germany.

[30]   Accordingly, it must be established whether the application of that provision may be justified by imperative requirements relating to consumer protection.

[31]   The German Government's argument that Article 10 of the Biersteuergesetz is essential in order to protect German consumers because, in their minds, the designation 'Bier' is inseparably linked to the beverage manufactured solely from the ingredients laid down in Article 9 of the Biersteuergesetz must be rejected.

[32]   Firstly, consumers' conceptions which vary from one Member State to the other are also likely to evolve in the course of time within a Member State. The establishment of the common market is, it should be added, one of the factors that may play a major contributory role in that development. Whereas rules protecting consumers against misleading practices enable such a development to be taken into account, legislation of the kind contained in Article 10 of the Biersteuergesetz prevents it from taking place. As the Court has already held in another context (judgment of 27 February 1980 in Case 170/78 *Commission* v *United Kingdom* [1980] ECR 417), the legislation of a Member State must not 'crystallize given consumer habits so as to consolidate an advantage acquired by national industries concerned to comply with them'.

[33]   Secondly, in the other Member States of the Community the designations corresponding to the German designation 'Bier' are generic designations for a fermented beverage manufactured from malted barley, whether malted barley on its own or with the addition of rice or maize. The same approach is taken in Community law as can be seen from heading No 22.03 of the Common Customs Tariff. The German legislature itself utilizes the designation 'Bier' in that way in Article 9(7) and (8) of the Biersteuergesetz in order to refer to beverages not complying with the manufacturing rules laid down in Article 9(1) and (2).

[34]   The German designation 'Bier' and its equivalents in the languages of the other Member States of the Community may therefore not be restricted to beers manufactured in accordance with the rules in force in the Federal Republic of Germany.

[35]   It is admittedly legitimate to seek to enable consumers who attribute specific qualities to beers manufactured from particular raw materials to make their choice in the light of that consideration. However, as the Court has already emphasized (judgment of 9 December 1981 in Case 193/80 *Commission* v *Italy* [1981] ECR 3019), that possibility may be ensured by means which do not prevent the importation of products which have been lawfully manufactured and marketed in other Member States and, in particular, 'by the compulsory affixing of suitable labels giving the nature of the product sold'. By indicating the raw materials utilized in the manufacture of beer 'such a course would enable the consumer to make his choice in full knowledge of the facts and would guarantee transparency in trading and in offers to the public'. It must be added that such a system of mandatory consumer information must not entail negative assessments for beers not complying with the requirements of Article 9 of the Biersteuergesetz.

[36]   Contrary to the German Government's view, such a system of consumer information may operate perfectly well even in the case of a product which, like beer, is not necessarily supplied to consumers in bottles or in cans capable of bearing the appropriate details. That is borne out, once again, by the German legislation itself.

Article 26(1) and (2) of the aforementioned regulation implementing the Biersteuergesetz provides for a system of consumer information in respect of certain beers, even where those beers are sold on draught, when the requisite information must appear on the casks or the beer taps.

[37]   It follows from the foregoing that by applying the rules on designation in Article 10 of the Biersteuergesetz to beers imported from other Member States which were manufactured and marketed lawfully in those States the Federal Republic of Germany has failed to fulfil its obligations under Article 30 of the EEC Treaty.

Note

The second limb of the rules involved an absolute ban on the marketing of beers containing additives. This rule also applied to all beers wherever produced; it was not origin specific. Arguments relating to the protection of public health which were rather more powerful than those advanced in relation to the first limb of the *Biersteuergesetz* were advanced.

Commission v Germany (Case 178/84)
[1987] ECR 1227; [1988] 1 CMLR 780
Court of Justice of the European Communities

[38]   In the Commission's opinion the absolute ban on the marketing of beers containing additives cannot be justified on public-health grounds. It maintains that the other Member States control very strictly the utilization of additives in foodstuffs and do not authorize the use of any given additive until thorough tests have established that it is harmless. In the Commission's view, there should be a presumption that beers manufactured in other Member States which contain additives authorized there represent no danger to public health. The Commission argues that if the Federal Republic of Germany wishes to oppose the importation of such beers then it bears the onus of proving that such beers are a danger to public health. The Commission considers that in this case that burden of proof has not been discharged. In any event, the rules on additives applying to beer in the Federal Republic of Germany are disproportionate in so far as they completely preclude the use of additives whereas the rules for other beverages, such as soft drinks, are much more flexible.

[39]   For its part, the German Government considers that in view of the dangers resulting from the utilization of additives whose long-term effects are not yet known and in particular of the risks resulting from the accumulation of additives in the organism and their interaction with other substances, such as alcohol, it is necessary to minimize the quantity of additives ingested. Since beer is a foodstuff of which large quantities are consumed in Germany, the German Government considers that it is particularly desirable to prohibit the use of any additive in its manufacture, especially in so far as the use of additives is not technologically necessary and can be avoided if only the ingredients laid down in the Biersteuergesetz are used. In those circumstances, the German rules on additives in beer are fully justified by the need to safeguard public health and do not infringe the principle of proportionality.

[40]   It is not contested that the prohibition on the marketing of beers containing additives constitutes a barrier to the importation from other Member States of beers containing additives authorized in those States, and is to that extent covered by Article 30 of the EEC Treaty. However, it must be ascertained whether it is possible to justify that prohibition under Article 36 of the Treaty on grounds of the protection of human health.

[41]   The Court has consistently held (in particular in the judgment of 14 July 1983 in Case 174/82 *Sandoz BV* [1983] ECR 2445) that 'in so far as there are uncertainties at the present state of scientific research it is for the Member States, in the absence

of harmonization, to decide what degree of protection of the health and life of humans they intend to assure, having regard however to the requirements of the free movement of goods within the Community'.

[42]   As may also be seen from the decisions of the Court (and especially the judgment of 14 July 1983 in the *Sandoz* case, cited above, the judgment of 10 December 1985 in Case 247/84 *Motte* [1985] ECR 3887, and the judgment of 6 May 1986 in Case 304/84 *Ministère public* v *Muller and Others* [1986] ECR 1511), in such circumstances Community law does not preclude the adoption by the Member States of legislation whereby the use of additives is subjected to prior authorization granted by a measure of general application for specific additives, in respect of all products, for certain products only or for certain uses. Such legislation meets a genuine need of health policy, namely that of restricting the uncontrolled consumption of food additives.

[43]   However, the application to imported products of prohibitions on marketing products containing additives which are authorized in the Member State of production but prohibited in the Member State of importation is permissible only in so far as it complies with the requirements of Article 36 of the Treaty as it has been interpreted by the Court.

[44]   It must be borne in mind, in the first place, that in its judgments in the *Sandoz*, *Motte* and *Muller* cases, cited above, the Court inferred from the principle of proportionality underlying the last sentence of Article 36 of the Treaty that prohibitions on the marketing of products containing additives authorized in the Member State of production but prohibited in the Member State of importation must be restricted to what is actually necessary to secure the protection of public health. The Court also concluded that the use of a specific additive which is authorized in another Member State must be authorized in the case of a product imported from that Member State where, in view, on the one hand, of the findings of international scientific research, and in particular of the work of the Community's Scientific Committee for Food, the Codex Alimentarius Committee of the Food and Agriculture Organization of the United Nations (FAO) and the World Health Organization, and, on the other hand, of the eating habits prevailing in the importing Member State, the additive in question does not present a risk to public health and meets a real need, especially a technical one.

[45]   Secondly, it should be remembered that, as the Court held in its judgment of 6 May 1986 in the *Muller* case, cited above, by virtue of the principle of proportionality, traders must also be able to apply, under a procedure which is easily accessible to them and can be concluded within a reasonable time, for the use of specific additives to be authorized by a measure of general application.

[46]   It should be pointed out that it must be open to traders to challenge before the courts an unjustified failure to grant authorization. Without prejudice to the right of the competent national authorities of the importing Member State to ask traders to produce the information in their possession which may be useful for the purpose of assessing the facts, it is for those authorities to demonstrate, as the Court held in its judgment of 6 May 1986 in the *Muller* case, cited above, that the prohibition is justified on grounds relating to the protection of the health of its population.

[47]   It must be observed that the German rules on additives applicable to beer result in the exclusion of all the additives authorized in the other Member States and not the exclusion of just some of them for which there is concrete justification by reason of the risks which they involve in view of the eating habits of the German population;

moreover those rules do not lay down any procedure whereby traders can obtain authorization for the use of a specific additive in the manufacture of beer by means of a measure of general application.

[48]   As regards more specifically the harmfulness of additives, the German Government, citing experts' reports, has referred to the risks inherent in the ingestion of additives in general. It maintains that it is important, for reasons of general preventive health protection, to minimize the quantity of additives ingested, and that it is particularly advisable to prohibit altogether their use in the manufacture of beer, a foodstuff consumed in considerable quantities by the German population.

[49]   However, it appears from the tables of additives authorized for use in various foodstuffs submitted by the German Government itself that some of the additives authorized in other Member States for use in the manufacture of beer are also authorized under the German rules, in particular the Regulation on Additives, for use in the manufacture of all, or virtually all, beverages. Mere reference to the potential risks of the ingestion of additives in general and to the fact that beer is a foodstuff consumed in large quantities does not suffice to justify the imposition of stricter rules in the case of beer.

[50]   As regards the need, and in particular the technological need, for additives, the German Government argues that there is no need for additives if beer is manufactured in accordance with the requirements of Article 9 of the Biersteuergesetz.

[51]   It must be emphasized that mere reference to the fact that beer can be manufactured without additives if it is made from only the raw materials prescribed in the Federal Republic of Germany does not suffice to preclude the possibility that some additives may meet a technological need. Such an interpretation of the concept of technological need, which results in favouring national production methods, constitutes a disguised means of restricting trade between Member States.

[52]   The concept of technological need must be assessed in the light of the raw materials utilized and bearing in mind the assessment made by the authorities of the Member State where the product was lawfully manufactured and marketed. Account must also be taken of the findings of international scientific research and in particular the work of the Community's Scientific Committee for Food, the Codex Alimentarius Committee of the FAO and the World Health Organization.

[53]   Consequently, in so far as the German rules on additives in beer entail a general ban on additives, their application to beers imported from other Member States is contrary to the requirements of Community law as laid down in the case-law of the Court, since that prohibition is contrary to the principle of proportionality and is therefore not covered by the exception provided for in Article 36 of the EEC Treaty.

[54]   In view of the foregoing considerations it must be held that by prohibiting the marketing of beers lawfully manufactured and marketed in another Member State if they do not comply with Articles 9 and 10 of the Biersteuergesetz, the Federal Republic of Germany has failed to fulfil its obligations under Article 30 of the EEC Treaty.

Questions
1. Is the beer market so important? Why did the Commission deploy scarce resources pursuing an infringement action in this sector? (The fact that the

cutting reproduced below appeared on the front page of the newspaper may assist you in finding an answer.)

2. How is the German brewer likely to react to this judgment (consider p. 170 above on the nature and purpose of a common market)? What factors might the German brewer choose to emphasise in launching a campaign in order to maintain customer loyalty now that the protectionist isolation of the domestic beer market has been broken?

3. How is the German consumer likely to react to this judgment?

The following item appeared on p. 1 of *The Guardian* of 13 March 1987, shortly after the judgment.

'Parts British beers will still not reach', by Anna Tomforde
The Guardian, 13 March 1987

To a chorus of 'Deutschesbier Allein' (German beer only) regulars at Bonn's Haehnchen pub (The Cock) raised their glasses yesterday and vowed to remain true to domestic brews. This is despite a European Court ruling in favour of the import of foreign beers, regarded as impure under Germany's ancient rules.

'The verdict is the best possible advertisement for German beer,' said Detlef Haberland, a 40-year-old doctor enjoying a few pints on his afternoon off. 'It will enhance solidarity among German beer drinkers and stir the German national conscience.'

More than 99 per cent of the 94 million hecto litres of beer drunk each year by Europe's thirstiest country, originates in the country's 1,200 breweries. This, according to the top clientele, will not change.

Judging by comments in the pub, the British Brewers' Society's view that there will now be a 'Willkommen' for the British pint amongst the discerning German beer drinkers, is premature and unduly optimistic.

'I drink an English ale once in a while but I miss the froth. I find it tasteless and without charm,' said Mr Hans Pfotenhauer, a vegetable market worker. 'The German beer drinker wants quality.'

This quality, pub-goers believe, is best guaranteed by a 16th century purity law, the 'Reinheitsgebot,' which states that German beer must consist only of water, hops, malt and yeast. 'After the Austrian wine scandal and general anxiety over chemicals in our food, at least we know our beer is pure,' Dr Harberland said. His friends agreed, ordering another round.

The Luxembourg ruling, given by the court president, Lord Mackenzie Stuart, means that West Germany can no longer exclude foreign beers which do not meet the 471-year-old German beer law, and which contain different ingredients and additives.

'The laws of a member country must not serve to foster consumer habits in the interests of the national industry,' the ruling says in a key sentence that marked the end of a five-year legal battle. The case was brought by a French exporter.

The West German Brewers' Association, which stressed yesterday that it would make sure that additives and ingredients of foreign beers are clearly marked on the labels, said it would mount a £415,000 advertising campaign in all West German newspapers this weekend to reassure consumers that Germany's 4,000 domestic brews will continue to be produced according to the purity rules, promulgated by Duke Wilhelm of Bavaria in 1516.

A publicity campaign is also being planned by French and Dutch brewers, as well as the British, in an attempt to penetrate the German market. Behind the outwardly defiant German reaction there is great anxiety that poor Germans will be tempted by cheaper imported beer on supermarket shelves.

'I can well imagine that broad sections of the public will buy the cheaper beer, and that small, family-run pubs and restaurants will be forced to sell it,' said the barman at The Cock.

Question

How is the German government likely to react to the judgment? Could it introduce labelling requirements relating to ingredients for beers marketed in Germany (see para. 35 of the judgment)?

Fietje (Case 27/80)
[1980] ECR 3839
Court of Justice of the European Communities

[10]   Although the extension to imported products of an obligation to use a certain name on the label does not wholly preclude the importation into the Member State concerned of products originating in other Member States or in free circulation in those States it may none the less make their marketing more difficult, especially in the case of parallel imports. As the Netherlands Government itself admits in its observations, such an extension of that obligation is thus capable of impeding, at least indirectly, trade between Member States. It is therefore necessary to consider whether it may be justified on the ground of the public interest in consumer protection, which, according to the observations of the Netherlands Government and according to the 'Warenwet', underlies the rules in question.

[11]   If national rules relating to a given product include the obligation to use a description that is sufficiently precise to inform the purchaser of the nature of the product and to enable it to be distinguished from products with which it might be confused, it may well be necessary, in order to give consumers effective protection, to extend this obligation to imported products also, even in such a way as to make necessary the alteration of the original labels of some of these products. At the level of Community legislation, this possibility is recognized in several directives on the approximation of the laws of the Member States relating to certain foodstuffs as well as by Council Directive 79/112/EEC of 18 December 1978 on the approximation of the laws of the Member States relating to the labelling, presentation and advertising of foodstuffs for sale to the ultimate consumer (Official Journal 1979, L 33, p. 1).

[12]   However, there is no longer any need for such protection if the details given on the original label of the imported product have as their content information on the nature of the product and that content includes at least the same information, and is just as capable of being understood by consumers in the importing State, as the description prescribed by the rules of that State. In the context of Article 177 of the EEC Treaty, the making of the findings of fact necessary in order to establish whether there is such equivalence is a matter for the national court.

Note

In *Piageme* v *BVBA Peeters* (Case C-369/89) [1991] ECR I-2971, the Court ruled that 'Article 30 of the EEC Treaty and Article 14 of Directive 79/112 preclude a national law from requiring the exclusive use of a specific language for the labelling of foodstuffs, without allowing for the possibility of using another language easily understood by purchasers or of ensuring that the purchaser is informed by other measures'. (See also Case C-85/94 between the same parties, [1995] ECR I-2955; and Case C-385/96 *Hermann Josef Goerres* [1998] ECR I-4431.) In November 1993, the Commission published a communication concerning the use of languages in the marketing of foodstuffs in the light of Case C-369/89 – COM (93) 532. This is a further example of the Commission's penchant for issuing interpretation of specific Court rulings (*cf*. p. 268 above). The communication observes that 'The grounds of consumer protection which may justify the imposition of the official language(s) of a Member State no longer apply when foreign terms and expressions appearing on product labelling are easily understood and therefore fulfil their informative function'. (On review of *Community* rules specifying use of particular languages against the requirements of the Treaty rules governing free movement of goods, see *Meyhui NV* v *Schott Zwiesel Glaswerke AG* (Case C-51/93) [1994] ECR I-3879.)

Questions
1. To what extent is the linguistic competence of consumers relevant to the compatibility of labelling requirements with Community law?
2. Is the German government obliged to abolish the mandatory purity laws for domestic producers too?

Nederlandse Bakkerij v *Edah (Cases 80 & 159/85)*
[1986] ECR 3359; [1988] 2 CMLR 113
Court of Justice of the European Communities

[18]   It is also impossible to accept Edah BV's argument that such provisions are contrary to Article 30 of the EEC Treaty because they enable imported bread to be sold below the minimum selling price applicable to domestically produced bread when the purchase price is sufficiently low. The purpose of that article is to eliminate obstacles to the importation of goods and not to ensure equal treatment in all cases for goods of national origin and imported goods. Unequal treatment which does not have the effect of hindering imports or making the sale of imported goods more difficult but instead favours them does not fall within the prohibition laid down by that article.

(B) JUSTIFYING INDISTINCTLY APPLICABLE RULES

In '*Cassis de Dijon*' (Case 120/78), the Court indicated that measures 'necessary to satisfy mandatory requirements' are capable of being held compatible with Article 28 despite their restrictive effect on trade.

In that case the Court was clearly not satisfied that the German rules on alcohol strength were necessary to satisfy mandatory requirements. In *Commission* v *Germany* (Case 178/84) arguments of justification were similarly dismissed. In both cases no compelling reasons for impeding trade were shown to exist.

It is, however, notable that arguments based on the protection of the economic interests of the consumer were considered available in principle, if rejected on the merits of the case. It will be remembered from the preceding chapter that this had induced both the Irish and the British governments to defend their origin marking rules as measures of consumer protection (pp. 254 and 256 above). In both instances the Court held the argument misplaced because both States had established a *discriminatory* system. The element of discrimination against imported goods precluded reliance on the 'mandatory requirements' encompassing, for example, the protection of the economic interests of the consumer. The insistence on the elimination of discrimination is also plain in *Gebhard* (Case C-55/94, pp. 217 and 295 above).

Even though the Court ruled against the invocation of the mandatory requirements on the facts of the cases considered above ('Cassis', beer purity, etc.), the availability of 'defences' not found in Article 30 indicates a greater willingness to respect national competence to regulate in a manner incompatible with free trade, provided discrimination does not contaminate the system.

The following case demonstrates the Court's attempt to balance the interests of national protection and free trade in the context of its own 'mandatory requirements' formula.

Commission v *Denmark (Case 302/86)*
[1988] ECR 4607; [1989] 1 CMLR 619
Court of Justice of the European Communities

The case concerned the compatibility with Article 30 of the EC Treaty (now, after amendment, Article 28 EC) of national laws designed to protect the environment, where such laws may impede imports.

[1]   By an application lodged at the Court Registry on 1 December 1986, the Commission of the European Communities brought an action under Article 169 of the EEC Treaty for a declaration that by introducing and applying by Order No 397 of 2 July 1981 a system under which all containers for beer and soft drinks must be returnable, the Kingdom of Denmark had failed to fulfil its obligations under Article 30 of the EEC Treaty.

[2]   The main feature of the system which the Commission challenges as incompatible with Community law is that manufacturers must market beer and soft drinks only in re-usable containers. The containers must be approved by the National Agency for the Protection of the Environment, which may refuse approval of new kinds of container, especially if it considers that a container is not technically suitable for a system for returning containers or that the return system envisaged does not ensure that a sufficient proportion of containers are actually re-used or if a container of equal capacity, which is both available and suitable for the same use, has already been approved.

[3]   Order No 95 of 16 March 1984 amended the aforementioned rules in such a way that, provided that a deposit-and-return system is established, non-approved containers, except for any form of metal container, may be used for quantities not exceeding 3,000 hectolitres a year per producer and for drinks which are sold by foreign producers in order to test the market.

[4]   By order of 8 May 1987 the United Kingdom was granted leave to intervene in the case in support of the Commission's conclusions.

[5]   Reference is made to the Report for the Hearing for a fuller account of the facts of the case, the course of the procedure and the submissions and arguments of the parties, which are mentioned or discussed hereinafter only in so far as is necessary for the reasoning of the Court.

[6]   The first point which must be made in resolving this dispute is that, according to an established body of case-law of the Court (judgment of 20 February 1979 in Case 120/78 *Rewe-Zentral AG* v *Bundesmonopolverwaltung für Branntwein* [1979] ECR 649; judgment of 10 November 1982 in Case 261/81 *Walter Rau Lebensmittelwerke* v *De Smedt PvbA* [1982] ECR 3961), in the absence of common rules relating to the marketing of the products in question, obstacles to free movement within the Community resulting from disparities between the national laws must be accepted in so far as such rules, applicable to domestic and imported products without distinction, may be recognized as being necessary in order to satisfy mandatory requirements recognized by Community law. Such rules must also be proportionate to the aim in view. If a Member State has a choice between various measures for achieving the same aim, it should choose the means which least restricts the free movement of goods.

[7]   In the present case the Danish Government contends that the mandatory collection system for containers of beer and soft drinks applied in Denmark is justified by a mandatory requirement related to the protection of the environment.

[8]   The Court has already held in its judgment of 7 February 1985 in Case 240/83 *Procureur de la République* v *Association de défense des brûleurs d'huiles usagées* [1985] ECR 531 that the protection of the environment is 'one of the Community's essential objectives', which may as such justify certain limitations of the principle of the free movement of goods. That view is moreover confirmed by the Single European Act.

[9]   In view of the foregoing, it must therefore be stated that the protection of the environment is a mandatory requirement which may limit the application of Article 30 of the Treaty.

[10]   The Commission submits that the Danish rules are contrary to the principle of proportionality in so far as the aim of the protection of the environment may be achieved by means less restrictive of intra-Community trade.

[11]   In that regard, it must be pointed out that in its aforementioned judgment of 7 February 1985 the Court stated that measures adopted to protect the environment must not 'go beyond the inevitable restrictions which are justified by the pursuit of the objective of environmental protection'.

[12]   It is therefore necessary to examine whether all the restrictions which the contested rules impose on the free movement of goods are necessary to achieve the objectives pursued by those rules.

[13]   First of all, as regards the obligation to establish a deposit-and-return system for empty containers, it must be observed that this requirement is an indispensable element of a system intended to ensure the re-use of containers and therefore appears necessary to achieve the aims pursued by the contested rules. That being so, the restrictions which it imposes on the free movement of goods cannot be regarded as disproportionate.

[14]   Next, it is necessary to consider the requirement that producers and importers must use only containers approved by the National Agency for the Protection of the Environment.

[15]   The Danish Government stated in the proceedings before the Court that the present deposit-and-return system would not work if the number of approved containers were to exceed 30 or so, since the retailers taking part in the system would not be prepared to accept too many types of bottles owing to the higher handling costs and the need for more storage space. For that reason the Agency has hitherto followed the practice of ensuring that fresh approvals are normally accompanied by the withdrawal of existing approvals.

[16]   Even though there is some force in that argument, it must nevertheless be observed that under the system at present in force in Denmark the Danish authorities may refuse approval to a foreign producer even if he is prepared to ensure that returned containers are re-used.

[17]   In those circumstances, a foreign producer who still wished to sell his products in Denmark would be obliged to manufacture or purchase containers of a type already approved, which would involve substantial additional costs for that producer and therefore make the importation of his products into Denmark very difficult.

[18]   To overcome that obstacle the Danish Government altered its rules by the aforementioned Order No 95 of 16 March 1984, which allows a producer to market up to 3 000 hectolitres of beer and soft drinks a year in non-approved containers, provided that a deposit-and-return system is established.

[19]   The provision in Order No 95 restricting the quantity of beer and soft drinks which may be marketed by a producer in non-approved containers to 3 000 hectolitres a year is challenged by the Commission on the ground that it is unnecessary to achieve the objectives pursued by the system.

[20]   It is undoubtedly true that the existing system for returning approved containers ensures a maximum rate of re-use and therefore a very considerable degree of protection of the environment since empty containers can be returned to any retailer of beverages. Non-approved containers, on the other hand, can be returned only to the retailer who sold the beverages, since it is impossible to set up such a comprehensive system for those containers as well.

[21]   Nevertheless, the system for returning non-approved containers is capable of protecting the environment and, as far as imports are concerned, affects only limited quantities of beverages compared with the quantity of beverages consumed in Denmark owing to the restrictive effect which the requirement that containers should be returnable has on imports. In those circumstances, a restriction of the quantity of products which may be marketed by importers is disproportionate to the objective pursued.

[22]   It must therefore be held that by restricting, by Order No 95 of 16 March 1984, the quantity of beer and soft drinks which may be marketed by a single producer in non-approved containers to 3,000 hectolitres a year, the Kingdom of Denmark has failed, as regards imports of those products from other Member States, to fulfil its obligations under Article 30 of the EEC Treaty.

[23]   The remainder of the application must be dismissed.

Note
The Court was forced to revisit the difficult area of making assessments about the validity of national environmental protection strategies which impede inter-State trade in *Commission* v *Belgium* (Case C-2/90) [1992] ECR I-4431, [1993] 1 CMLR 365.

Wallonia (a region of Belgium) prohibited the storage, tipping or dumping of waste from other Member States or from elsewhere in Belgium. The measure was aimed at protecting Wallonia from becoming the target for waste from areas with tighter regulatory regimes. The Commission challenged the rule as a violation of Article 30 of the EC Treaty (now, after amendment, Article 28 EC), but the application was rejected by the Court. This was a restriction on the importation of goods of commercial value, but the Court found it justified as a measure of environmental protection. The Court observed that '[t]he accumulation of waste . . . constitutes a threat to the environment because of the limited capacity of each region or locality for receiving it'. The oddity in the ruling is that the regime appeared, unlike that in the Danish Bottles case (Case 302/86), to be discriminatory – Walloon waste was treated in Wallonia, waste from outside could not be. It is explained at p. 306 above that discriminatory measures are not justifiable with reference to 'the mandatory requirements' which include environmental protection. The Court expressly confirmed this principle in Case C-2/90, but evaded the problem by finding the Walloon measures to be indistinctly applicable and therefore capable of justification as measures of environmental protection. It drew on the principle expressed in Article 130r(2) of the EC Treaty (now, after amendment Article 174(2) EC) that 'environmental damage should as a priority be rectified at source', which dictates a need to minimise transport of waste. Accordingly the Court commented that it 'follows that, having regard to the differences between waste produced in one place and that in another and its connection with the place where it is produced, the contested measures cannot be considered to be discriminatory'.

The ruling attracted divergent comment on its implications (Hancher and Sevenster (1993) 30 CML Rev 351; Von Wilmowsky, *ibid.*, 541; Geradin (1993) 18 EL Rev 144). The Court's reasoning that the measure was *not* discriminatory is not especially convincing and is contradicted by Advocate-General Jacobs's Opinion in the case. However, the Court's reasoning enabled it to achieve a result in conformity with general Treaty principles on environmental protection. It may be as well not to overestimate the ruling's importance, given that this area is increasingly occupied by legislative initiatives which replace the need to test national initiatives against Articles 28–30. Indeed, in Case C-2/90 the Court had also examined Belgian compliance with relevant Directives. At the very least, the decision further demonstrates the sensitivity of Article 28 litigation which raises the potential collision between national environmental protection and market integration. (See further L. Kramer, 'Environmental Protection and Article 30 EEC Treaty' (1993) 30 CML Rev 111; D. Geradin, 'Trade and Environmental Protection:

Community Harmonization and National Environmental Standards' (1993) 13 YEL 151.)

A similar balancing act has to be performed in the context of national laws forbidding unfair competition which impede trade. The Court is driven to a determination of whether the national characterisation of marketing practices as 'unfair' possesses a sufficiently compelling basis to prevail over the interests of integration which would be served by eliminating such local choices. Cases in which trade-restrictive national rules were judged unjustified include *Verband Sozialer Wettbewerb eV* v *Clinique Laboratories SNC* (Case C-315/92) [1994] ECR I-317; and *Mars* (Case C-470/93, p. 327 below). In such instances, the Court's application of Article 28 generates deregulation within the territory of the Member State in question. However, the Court does not insist on a 'lowest common denominator' of regulatory protection within the EC (see S. Weatherill, *EC Consumer Law and Policy* (1997), Ch. 2). As is plain in the environmental sphere (Case 302/86 above) and in cases concerning scientific uncertainty about the safety of products (Case 174/82, p. 281 above), the application of Article 28 is not inevitably destructive of national choices. Laws curtailing practices perceived to be 'unfair' were found compatible with Article 30 in *Diensten Groep* v *Beele* (Case 6/81) [1982] ECR 707 and *Buet* (Case 382/87, p. 321 below); and see also, in connection with similar issues arising in the services sector under Article 49 EC, *Alpine Investments* (Case C-384/93, p. 383 below). An unusual example, in which rules purportedly designed to preserve press diversity in Austria were tested against the Treaty rules governing free movement of goods, is provided by Case C-368/95 *Vereinigte Familiapress Zeitungsverlags- und vertriebs GmbH* v *Heinrich Bauer Verlag* [1997] ECR I-3689, in which the Court's ruling is conspicuous in its readiness to leave the national court room in which to weigh the balance of the competing interests at stake. For recent surveys, see S. Weatherill, 'Recent case law concerning the free movement of goods: mapping the frontiers of market deregulation' (1999) 36 CML Rev 51; M. Poiares Maduro, 'The Saga of Article 30 EC Treaty: to be continued' (1998) 5 MJ 298.

Notice how in '*Cassis de Dijon*' (Case 120/78) and in subsequent cases a key precondition to the application of Article 28 is the absence of common Community rules in the area. Article 28 operates pending Community intervention in the field. How might environmental laws be framed in this area in order to remove the barriers to trade caused by divergent national legislation? At what level should the rules be administered and enforced – Community, national or a combination of both? And it remains to be seen what will be the significance for the relationship between trade and the environment of the provision inserted by the Treaty of Amsterdam as the new Article 6 EC: 'Environmental protection requirements must be integrated into the definition and implementation of the Community policies and activities referred to in Article 3, in particular with a view to promoting sustainable development.'

These are difficult questions about potential collisions between distinct elements within the Community's overall objectives; yet they are exactly the types of question which need to be confronted in many areas in the period of adjustment consequent on the completion of the internal market of the Community. (See, more generally, Chapter 15.)

Questions
1. Consider the necessity to satisfy mandatory requirements in '*Cassis de Dijon*' (Case 120/78) and the rule of reason in *Dassonville* (Case 8/74) (p. 245 above). Do these concepts serve the same *function*; and are they identical in substance?
      Consider also Article 81 (p. 428).
2. Joe imports alcoholic drink from the Republic of Ireland into England. However, he has recently become increasingly frustrated due to a variety of British regulations which impede his business. He seeks your advice about the impact of Community law on the following problems he has encountered with his latest consignment:

(a) British legislation forbids the marketing of whisky above a specified maximum alcohol strength. Joe is therefore unable to sell his 'Super de Luxe Special Irish Whiskey' because it is too strong.
(b) Joe is unable to sell his beers which are marketed in blue glass bottles, because British legislation reserves the use of blue bottles for medicines.

(C) LOCATING THE OUTER LIMIT OF ARTICLE 28

The key to '*Cassis de Dijon*' (Case 120/78) rules is that although they impose burdens on all products irrespective of origin, imported goods feel an extra burden because they have *already* been subject to the technical rules or traditions of the State of origin. In this manner, the '*Cassis de Dijon*' rules protect the domestic economy by subjecting imported goods to *different* technical standards from those to which they have already been exposed in their State of origin. The Court has also been obliged to consider rules which *restrict* trade but which do not *protect* the home market.

For almost a decade the Court was prepared to allow the invocation of Article 30 of the EC Treaty (now, after amendment, Article 28 EC) even where both the application of the rules *and* the consequential burden was felt equally by all goods. However, in its November 1993 ruling in *Keck and Mithouard* (Cases C-267 and 268/91) it changed its mind and set an outer limit to the application of this Article of the Treaty. In order to appreciate the background to the *Keck* ruling, it is appropriate to look first at the notorious 'Sunday trading' litigation.

Torfaen BC v B & Q plc (Case 145/88)
[1989] ECR 765
Court of Justice of the European Communities

[1] By order of 25 April 1988, which was received at the Court on 24 May 1988, Cwmbran Magistrates' Court, United Kingdom, referred to the Court for

a preliminary ruling under Article 177 of the EEC Treaty three questions on the interpretation of Articles 30 and 36 of the EEC Treaty in order to assess the compatibility with those provisions of national rules prohibiting trading on Sunday.

[2] The questions were raised in proceedings between Torfaen Borough Council (hereinafter referred to as 'the Council') and B&Q PLC, formerly B&Q (Retail) Limited (hereinafter referred to as 'B&Q'), which operates do-it-yourself centres and garden centres.

[3] The Council alleges that B&Q contravened sections 47 and 59 of the United Kingdom Shops Act 1950 by causing its retail shop premises to be open for the serving of customers on Sunday other than for the transactions mentioned in the Fifth Schedule to that Act. B&Q is therefore liable to a maximum fine of £1,000.

[4] The Fifth Schedule to the Shops Act lists the items which, by way of exception, may be sold in shops on Sundays. Those items include intoxicating liquors, certain foodstuffs, tobacco, newspapers and other products of everyday consumption.

[5] Before the national court B&Q submitted that section 47 of the Shops Act was a measure having an effect equivalent to a quantitative restriction on imports within the meaning of Article 30 of the EEC Treaty and that it was not justified under Article 36 of the EEC Treaty or by virtue of any 'mandatory requirement'.

[6] The Council denied that the ban on Sunday trading constituted a measure having an effect equivalent to a quantitative restriction on the ground that it applied to domestic and imported products alike and did not put imported products at any disadvantage.

[7] The national court found that in the instant case the ban on Sunday trading had the effect of reducing B&Q's total sales, that approximately 10% of the goods sold by B&Q came from other Member States and that a corresponding reduction of imports from other Member States would therefore ensue.

[8] Having reached those findings the national court took the view that the case raised questions concerning the interpretation of Community law. It therefore requested the Court to give a preliminary ruling on the following questions:

'1. Where a Member State prohibits retail premises from being open on Sunday for the sale of goods to customers, save in respect of certain specified items, sales of which are permitted, and where the effect of the prohibition is to reduce in absolute terms the sales of goods in those premises, including goods manufactured in other Member States, and correspondingly to reduce the volume of imports of goods from other Member States, is such a prohibition a measure having equivalent effect to a quantitative restriction on imports within the meaning of Article 30 of the Treaty?

2. If the answer to Question 1 is in the affirmative, does such a measure benefit from any of the exceptions to Article 30 contained in Article 36, or from any other exception recognized by Community law?

3. Is the answer to Question 1 or Question 2 above affected by any factor so as to render the measure in question a means of arbitrary discrimination or a disguised restriction on trade between Member States or a measure lacking in proportionality or otherwise unjustified?'

[9] Reference is made to the Report for the Hearing for a fuller account of the legal background to, and the facts of, the main proceedings, the course of the procedure

and the written observations submitted to the Court, which are mentioned or discussed hereinafter only in so far as is necessary for the reasoning of the Court.

The first question

[10] By its first question the national court seeks to establish whether the concept of measures having an effect equivalent to quantitative restrictions within the meaning of Article 30 of the Treaty also covers provisions prohibiting retailers from opening their premises on Sunday if the effect of the prohibition is to reduce in absolute terms the sales of goods in those premises, including goods imported from other Member States.

[11] The first point which must be made is that national rules prohibiting retailers from opening their premises on Sunday apply to imported and domestic products alike. In principle, the marketing of products imported from other Member States is not therefore made more difficult than the marketing of domestic products.

[12] Next, it must be recalled that in its judgment of 11 July 1985 in Joined Cases 60 and 61/84 (*Cinéthèque SA and Others* v *Fédération Nationale des Cinémas Françaises* ([1985]) ECR 2618) the Court held, with regard to a prohibition of the hiring of video-cassettes applicable to domestic and imported products alike, that such a prohibition was not compatible with the principle of the free movement of goods provided for in the Treaty unless any obstacle to Community trade thereby created did not exceed what was necessary in order to ensure the attainment of the objective in view and unless that objective was justified with regard to Community law.

[13] In those circumstances it is therefore necessary in a case such as this to consider first of all whether rules such as those at issue pursue an aim which is justified with regard to Community law. As far as that question is concerned, the Court has already stated in its judgment of 14 July 1981 in Case 155/80 (*Oebel* [1981] ECR 1993) that national rules governing the hours of work, delivery and sale in the bread and confectionery industry constitute a legitimate part of economic and social policy, consistent with the objectives of public interest pursued by the Treaty.

[14] The same consideration must apply as regards national rules governing the opening hours of retail premises. Such rules reflect certain political and economic choices in so far as their purpose is to ensure that working and non-working hours are so arranged as to accord with national or regional socio-cultural characteristics, and that, in the present state of Community law, is a matter for the Member States. Furthermore, such rules are not designed to govern the patterns of trade between Member States.

[15] Secondly, it is necessary to ascertain whether the effects of such national rules exceed what is necessary to achieve the aim in view. As is indicated in Article 3 of Commission Directive 70/50/EEC of 22 December 1969 (Official Journal, English Special Edition 1970 (I), p. 17), the prohibition laid down in Article 30 covers national measures governing the marketing of products where the restrictive effect of such measures on the free movement of goods exceeds the effects intrinsic to trade rules.

[16] The question whether the effects of specific national rules do in fact remain within that limit is a question of fact to be determined by the national court.

[17] The reply to the first question must therefore be that Article 30 of the Treaty must be interpreted as meaning that the prohibition which it lays down does not apply to national rules prohibiting retailers from opening their premises on Sunday where the restrictive effects on Community trade which may result therefrom do not exceed the effects intrinsic to rules of that kind.

Questions
1. Why does the Court choose to refer to Directive 70/50 but not to
Dassonville (Case 8/74)?
2. Did the Council or the company 'win' the case in Luxembourg?

'Rivals claim victory after EC ruling on Sunday trade',
by Patricia Wynn Davies
The Independent, 24 November 1989

A European Court of Justice ruling on whether Britain's Sunday trading ban breaks
EC rules was hailed as a victory yesterday by supporters and opponents of the law.

The DIY chain B&Q had claimed that the 1950 Shops Act was an unlawful
restraint on cross-border trade within the European Community, breaching article 30
of the Treaty of Rome.

The Luxembourg court said the article would not apply to the Act if its restrictive
effects did not exceed the socio-cultural aims of the Sunday trading ban. The
magistrates' court which referred the case had to decide whether the Act fell within
that limit.

Sunday traders still face prosecution, but this could change once the Luxembourg
decision is tested here. A higher court ruling will probably be needed to resolve the
uncertainty.

The confusing upshot of the court challenge brought enthusiastic responses from
pro-Sunday groups and reform campaigners.

B&Q said the ruling was a victory for consumers, two-thirds of whom support
liberalising Sunday shopping laws. It means the 1950 Act would breach article 30 if
the effects on intra-community trade were found by UK courts to be excessively
restrictive.

But Lord Brentford, chairman of the Keep Sunday Special Campaign, a pressure
group of retailers and trade associations, said: 'Sunday is a key part of the shared
European cultural tradition and we are very grateful that the court has upheld this
vital part of our heritage.'

Bill Connor, deputy general secretary of the Union of Shop, Distributive and Allied
Workers, which opposes Sunday opening, said: 'We now want to see every retailer who
breaks the law taken to court and fined.'

Roger Boaden, director of the Shopping Hours Reform Council, said: 'The
judgment contains a clear message for the UK Government. It is quite simply to sort
out the mess of your own making.' He said about 60,000 shops in Britain were now
trading on a Sunday, of which only 600 were DIY stores.

B&Q was taken to court by Torfaen Borough Council, South Wales, for opening its
branch in Cwmbran, Gwent, on a Sunday. Cwmbran magistrates referred the case to
Luxembourg when B&Q invoked EC law in its defence.

Bill Whiting, the company's marketing director, said there was now a possibility of
having different interpretations of the law in different parts of the country.

Research by the Sunday Shopping Hours Reform Council shows the law is strictly
enforced in Norwich, Coventry, the London Borough of Bromley, and Welling-
borough, Northamptonshire. Swansea, Blackpool, Birmingham, Bradford, and Cambridge also take a strong enforcement line. But many councils tend to prosecute only
as a result of a direct complaint, mainly because of the cost.

The Consumers' Association said Parliament must 'grit its teeth' and take action
on the 'appalling muddle'.

The law, passed in 1936, bans most goods from being sold on a Sunday but contains a curious amalgam of past lobbying. Meals may be sold, unless they happen to be fish and chips. Newly-cooked provisions and cooked or partly-cooked tripe are allowed. Milk and cream, including clotted cream, may be sold, but dried or tinned milk is banned. Tinned fruit and vegetables are off-limits, but fodder for horses, mules, ponies and donkeys may be purchased at any farm, stables, hotel or inn. Buying DIY goods is prohibited, but if you need to repair a jumbo jet the necessary supplies can be obtained, along with motor and cycle accessories. You can buy a bible, but only at a railway station or airport – where you can also buy pornography.

Question

What does the Court's judgment and this divided response tell you about the division of function between national and Community court under the Article 234 preliminary reference procedure? (See Chapter 4.)

Note

This ruling created confusion at national level, where different English and Welsh courts adopted different views of the compatibility of the Sunday trading laws with the Treaty. (See A. Arnull (1991) 16 EL Rev 112.)

In May 1991, a further preliminary reference was made by the House of Lords. This was motivated in part by the European Court rulings of February 1991 in *Marchandise* (Case C-332/89) [1991] ECR I-1027 and *UDS v Conforama* (Case C-312/89) [1991] ECR I-997. These cases, though factually comparable to *Torfaen*, had revealed the European Court much readier explicitly to rule national measures compatible with Article 30 of the EC Treaty (now, after amendment, Article 28 EC). The second reference yielded a much clearer response from the European Court in December 1992:

Stoke-on-Trent and Norwich City Councils v *B & Q (Cases C-169/91)*
[1992] ECR I-6457, [1993] 1 CMLR 426
Court of Justice of the European Communities

[15] Appraising the proportionality of national rules which pursue a legitimate aim under Community law involves weighing the national interest in attaining that aim against the Community interest in ensuring the free movement of goods. In that regard, in order to verify that the restrictive effects on intra-Community trade of the rules at issue do not exceed what is necessary to achieve the aim in view, it must be considered whether those effects are direct, indirect or purely speculative and whether those effects do not impede the marketing of imported products more than the marketing of national products.

[16] It was on the basis of those considerations that in its judgments in the *Conforama* and *Marchandise* cases the court ruled that the restrictive effects on trade of national rules prohibiting the employment of workers on Sundays in certain retailing activities were not excessive in relation to the aim pursued. For the same reasons, the court must make the same finding with regard to national rules prohibiting shops from opening on Sundays.

[17] It must therefore be stated in reply to the first question that Article 30 of the Treaty is to be interpreted as meaning that the prohibition which it lays down does not apply to national legislation prohibiting retailers from opening their premises on Sundays.

Note
For comment, see R. Rawlings (1993) 20 *Journal of Law and Society* 309; A.
Arnull (1993) 18 EL Rev 314. Eventually, the law in England and Wales was
amended, and made more coherent, by the Sunday Trading Act 1994.

Question
What does *this* ruling tell you about the division of function between national
and Community court under Article 234?

Note
Lurking beneath this litigation was the point made in para. [6] of the ruling
in Case 145/88 (p. 312 above). The Sunday trading rules did not put
imported goods at a disadvantage in comparison with domestic goods. All
goods were equally affected. Had EC free movement law been pushed beyond
its proper scope by the ingenuity of the Sunday traders' lawyers? Many
commentators took this view and tried to develop a test which would allow a
reorientation towards rules which partitioned national markets rather than
general trading rules unconnected with the process of market integration.
Such thoughtful efforts include:

Chalmers, D., 'Free Movement of Goods within the European Community:
an Unhealthy Addiction to Scotch Whisky?' (1993) 42 ICLQ 269.
Mortelmans, K., 'Article 30 of the EEC Treaty and Legislation Relating to
Market Circumstances: time to consider a new definition?' (1991) 28 CML
Rev 115.
Wils, W., 'The search for the rule in Article 30 EEC: much ado about
nothing?' (1993) 18 EL Rev 475.

In the period between the two Sunday trading rulings there had already been
indications that the European Court was ready to rethink its approach in this
area. In *Quietlynn Ltd* v *Southend on Sea BC* (Case C-23/89) [1990] ECR
I-3059 and in *Sheptonhurst* v *Newham BC* (Case C-350/89) [1991] ECR
I-2387, the Court found no effect on inter-State trade adequate to permit the
invocation of Article 30 of the EC Treaty (now, after amendment, Article 28
EC). Accordingly, questions of justification of national rules simply did not
arise, in contrast to the Sunday trading cases. The Court had the chance to
provide a bolder formula in *Keck and Mithouard*.

Bernard Keck and Daniel Mithouard (Cases C-267 & C-268/91)
[1993] ECR I-6097, [1995] 1 CMLR 101
Court of Justice of the European Communities

MM. Keck and Mithouard had resold goods at a loss. This violated a
French law forbidding such practices. Keck and Mithouard submitted that
the law restricted the volume of sales of imported goods by depriving them
of a method of sales promotion and that it was therefore incompatible with

Article 30 of the EC Treaty (now, after amendment, Article 28 EC). Any restrictive effect on trade plainly affected *all* goods, not just imports.

[14]   In view of the increasing tendency of traders to invoke Article 30 of the Treaty as a means of challenging any rules whose effect is to limit their commercial freedom even where such rules are not aimed at products from other Member States, the Court considers it necessary to re-examine and clarify its case-law on this matter.

[15]   In 'Cassis de Dijon' (Case 120/78 *Rewe-Zentral* v *Bundesmonopolverwaltung für Branntwein* [1979] ECR 649) it was held that, in the absence of harmonisation of legislation, measures of equivalent effect prohibited by Article 30 include obstacles to the free movement of goods where they are the consequence of applying rules that lay down requirements to be met by such goods (such as requirements as to designation, form, size, weight, composition, presentation, labelling, packaging) to goods from other Member States where they are lawfully manufactured and marketed, even if those rules apply without distinction to all products unless their application can be justified by a public-interest objective taking precedence over the free movement of goods.

[16]   However, contrary to what has previously been decided, the application to products from other Member States of national provisions restricting or prohibiting certain selling arrangements is not such as to hinder directly or indirectly, actually or potentially, trade between Member States within the meaning of the *Dassonville* judgment (Case 8/74 [1974] ECR 837), provided that those provisions apply to all affected traders operating within the national territory and provided that they affect in the same manner, in law and in fact, the marketing of domestic products and of those from other Member States.

[17]   Where those conditions are fulfilled, the application of such rules to the sale of products from another Member State meeting the requirements laid down by that State is not by nature such as to prevent their access to the market or to impede access any more than it impedes the access of domestic products. Such rules therefore fall outside the scope of Article 30 of the Treaty.

[18]   Accordingly, the reply to be given to the national court is that Article 30 of the EEC Treaty is to be interpreted as not applying to legislation of a Member State imposing a general prohibition on resale at a loss.

Question
In 1989, E. White proposed that Article 30 should be interpreted as catching 'the application by a Member State to products legally produced and marketed in another Member State of its national rules relating to the characteristics required of such products on its territory (which therefore prevents this product from benefitting in the importing Member State from the advantages arising out of its production in the different legal and economic environment prevailing in the other Member State' ('In Search of the Limits to Article 30 of the EEC Treaty' (1989) 26 CML Rev 235). Does this proposal conform to the Court's policy in *Keck*?

Note
The Commission declared that in *Keck* 'the Court has completed its case law' (OJ 1993 C353/6). It is doubtless the case that in future traders will find it

more difficult to employ the Treaty provisions governing free movement of goods to require Member States to justify rules which inhibit commercial freedom. This is well illustrated by the next case, decided by the Court less than seven months after *Keck*, in which a challenge to Dutch rules relating to the compulsory closing of shops at stipulated times was curtly rejected.

Tankstation 't Heukste vof and J.B.E. Boermans
(Cases C–401 & C–402/92)
[1994] ECR I–2199
Court of Justice of the European Communities

[12] . . . the application to products from other Member States of national provisions restricting or prohibiting certain selling arrangements is not such as to hinder, directly or indirectly, actually or potentially, trade between Member States within the meaning of the *Dassonville* judgment . . . provided that those provisions apply to all relevant traders operating within the national territory and provided that they affect in the same manner, in law and in fact, the marketing of domestic products and of those from other Member States. Where those conditions are fulfilled, the application of such rules to the sale of products from another Member State meeting the requirements laid down by that State is not by nature such as to prevent their access to the market or to impede access any more than it impedes the access of domestic products. Such rules therefore fall outside the scope of Article 30 of the Treaty (see the judgment in Joined Cases C–267/91 and C–268/91 *Keck and Mithouard* [1993] ECR I–6097, paragraphs 16 and 17).

[13] The conditions laid down in the judgment last cited are fulfilled in the case of rules such as those at issue in the main proceedings.

[14] The rules in question relate to the times and places at which the goods in question may be sold to consumers. However, they apply to all relevant traders without distinguishing between the origin of the products in question and do not affect the marketing of products from other Member States in a manner different from that in which they affect domestic products.

[15] Consequently, the reply to be given to the Gerechtshof is that Article 30 of the Treaty is to be interpreted as not applying to national rules concerning the closing of shops which apply to all traders operating within the national territory and which affect in the same manner, in law and in fact, the marketing of domestic products and of products from other Member States.

Note
It was suggested above (at p. 295) that the '*Cassis de Dijon*' case law represents the Court's strategy for judging the permissibility of regulatory diversity between the States in an integrating market; *Keck* reflects the Court's concern to establish where regulatory diversity does not affect the integrative process for the purposes of application of Article 28 and where, accordingly, States remain free to make their own regulatory choices unhindered by the demands of EC trade law. Nevertheless, the precise impact of *Keck* requires elaboration. It is instructive to consider cases decided prior to *Keck* in order to determine whether it would now be considered that a

sufficient adverse effect on imported products had been shown such as to permit the invocation of Article 28. Consider from this perspective the extracts in *Commission v UK* (Case 207/83) at p. 256 above; *Tasca* (Case 65/75) and *Van Tiggele* (Case 82/77) at p. 271 above.

The decision in *Cinéthèque* (Cases 60 & 61/84) was mentioned at para. [12] in the *Torfaen* ruling (Case 145/88, p. 313 above) as a basis for the need to embark on consideration of justification of the Sunday trading rules. In the ruling in *Cinéthèque* there was a divergence of approach between the Court and its Advocate-General, although both agreed in the result that the French rules were compatible with the Treaty.

Cinéthèque SA v *Fédération Nationale des Cinémas Français* (Cases 60 & 61/84)
[1985] ECR 2605; [1986] 1 CMLR 365
Court of Justice of the European Communities

French legislation prohibited the selling or hiring of video cassettes of films within the first year of the film receiving its performance certificate. The objective was to encourage attendance at cinemas. Yet the legislation eliminated the market for videos during that year's grace allowed to the cinema. Imported videos could not be sold in France. But neither could French-made videos. A distributor of videos used Article 30 of the EC Treaty (now, after amendment, Article 28 EC) before French courts to challenge the law as a trade barrier.

[21]   . . . [I]t must be observed that such a system, if it applies without distinction to both video-cassettes manufactured in the national territory and to imported video-cassettes, does not have the purpose of regulating trade patterns; its effect is not to favour national production as against the production of other Member States, but to encourage cinematographic production as such.

[22]   Nevertheless, the application of such a system may create barriers to intra-Community trade in video-cassettes because of the disparities between the systems operated in the different Member States and between the conditions for the release of cinematographic works in the cinemas of those States. In those circumstances a prohibition of exploitation laid down by such a system is not compatible with the principle of the free movement of goods provided for in the Treaty unless any obstacle to intra-Community trade thereby created does not exceed that which is necessary in order to ensure the attainment of the objective in view and unless that objective is justified with regard to Community law.

[23]   It must be conceded that a national system which, in order to encourage the creation of cinematographic works irrespective of their origin, gives priority, for a limited initial period, to the distribution of such works through the cinema, is so justified.

[24]   The reply to the questions referred to the Court is therefore that Article 30 of the EEC Treaty must be interpreted as meaning that it does not apply to national legislation which regulates the distribution of cinematographic works by imposing an

interval between one mode of distributing such works and another by prohibiting their simultaneous exploitation in cinemas and in video-cassette form for a limited period, provided that the prohibition applies to domestically produced and imported cassettes alike and any barriers to intra-Community trade to which its implementation may give rise do not exceed what is necessary for ensuring that the exploitation in cinemas of cinematographic works of all origins retains priority over other means of distribution.

Cinéthèque SA v *Fédération Nationale des Cinémas Français* *(Cases 60 & 61/84)*
[1985] ECR 2605; [1986] 1 CMLR 365
Court of Justice of the European Communities

ADVOCATE-GENERAL SLYNN: It seems to me in summary that a measure is in breach of Article 30 (a) if it forbids imports or restricts imports quantitatively; (b) if it discriminates against imports by e.g. imposing more stringent standards on importers than on domestic producers so that in practice importation may be made more difficult and thereby imports may be restricted; (c) if, although not directed to importation as such but covering both national goods and imports, it requires a producer or distributor to take steps additional to those which he would normally and lawfully take in the marketing of his goods, which thereby render importation more difficult, so that imports may be restricted and national producers be given protection in practice. The last category, (c) will not be in breach of Article 30 if it can be shown that the measure is justified by mandatory requirements of the kind contemplated in *Cassis de Dijon*.

On the other hand, in an area in which there are no common Community standards or rules, where a national measure is not specifically directed at imports, does not discriminate against imports, does not make it any more difficult for an importer to sell his products than it is for a domestic producer, and gives no protection to domestic producers, then in my view, *prima facie*, the measure does not fall within Article 30 even if it does in fact lead to a restriction or reduction of imports.

In the present case the law does not discriminate against imports. The importer can in fact import. He is then on exactly the same footing as the domestic trader. The latter gets no extra benefit over the importer, the former suffers no extra detriment over the French trader as a result of the ban on the exploitation of video-cassettes. The factor which would lead a trader in France not to buy from a French video distributor (inability to sell or hire) is the same as that which would lead him not to buy from a distributor in another Member State. In this respect both distributors are subject to the same conditions of trade. They are effectively operating in the same market. Article 30 cannot have been intended in this respect to give the distributor in another Member State better conditions than the domestic distributor. It may be that if it was patently unreasonable to put imports on the same footing as domestic products that the measure could be bad for that reason. That however is not the position here and in my view this law does not fall within Article 30.

Question
In *Tankstation 't Heukste vof and J. B. E. Boermans* (Cases C-401/92 & C-402/92, p. 318 above), Advocate-General Van Gerven commented that the legislation challenged in *Cinéthèque* 'would in any event fulfil the second condition introduced by "provided that" in the judgment in *Keck and Mithouard*'. Do you agree with his view that the law would escape the scope of application of Article 28? Would this be a desirable outcome?

Ministère Public v Buet (Case 382/87)
[1989] ECR 1235
Court of Justice of the European Communities

A trader was convicted under French law forbidding canvassing at private dwellings for the purpose of selling educational material. It was submitted that the law was incompatible with Article 30 of the EC Treaty (now, after amendment, Article 28 EC). The Court found an obstacle to the free movement of goods:

[7]   As the Court held in its judgment of 15 December 1982 in Case 286/81 *Oosthoek* [1982] ECR 4575, the possibility cannot be ruled out that to compel a trader either to adopt advertising or sales promotion schemes which differ from one Member State to another or to discontinue a scheme which he considers to be particularly effective may constitute an obstacle to imports even if the legislation in question applies to domestic and imported products without distinction.

[8]   That finding applies *a fortiori* when the rules in question deprive the trader concerned of the possibility of using not a means of advertising but a method of marketing whereby he realizes almost all his sales.

[9]   Application of a prohibition on canvassing in order to sell foreign-language teaching material from another Member State must therefore be regarded as constituting an obstacle to imports.

The Court then concluded that the French rule was compatible with the Treaty, notwithstanding the obstacle to trade, in view of its contribution to the protection of the consumer.

Question
Would the ruling in *Keck* make any difference in such circumstances?

Note
It seems likely that cases involving restrictions on marketing methods will provide the sternest challenges to the Court's attempt in *Keck* to realign its case law in order to introduce a coherent basis for locating the outer limit of Article 28. The next case features distinct approaches taken by the Court and its Advocate-General when confronted by this issue.

Société d'Importation Edouard Leclerc-Siplec v TF1 Publicité SA and M6 Publicité SA (Case C-412/93)
[1995] ECR I-179
Court of Justice of the European Communities

TF1 and M6 refused to broadcast an advertisement concerning distribution of fuel in Leclerc supermarkets. The refusal was based on French rules excluding the distribution sector from televised advertising. It was submitted that the rules impeded sales opportunities for imported fuel and that they were therefore susceptible to challenge under Article 30 of the EC Treaty (now, after amendment, Article 28 EC). The *Tribunal de Commerce de Paris* made a preliminary reference to the Court in search of an authoritative interpretation.

[18]   It has been consistently held that all rules enacted by Member States which are capable of hindering, directly or indirectly, actually or potentially, intra-Community trade are to be considered as measures having an effect equivalent to quantitative restrictions (judgment in Case 8/74 *Procureur du Roi* v *Dassonville* [1974] ECR 837, paragraph 5).

[19]   A law or regulation such as that at issue in the main proceedings, which prohibits televised advertising in the distribution sector, is not designed to regulate trade in goods between Member States. Moreover, such a prohibition does not prevent distributors from using other forms of advertising.

[20]   Such a prohibition may, admittedly, restrict the volume of sales, and hence the volume of sales of products from other Member States, in so far as it deprives distributors of a particular form of advertising their goods. But the question remains whether such a possibility is sufficient to characterise the prohibition in question as a measure having equivalent effect to a quantitative restriction on imports within the meaning of Article 30 of the Treaty.

[21]   The application to products from other Member States of national provisions restricting or prohibiting certain selling arrangements it not such as to hinder directly or indirectly, actually or potentially, trade between Member States within the meaning of the *Dassonville* judgment, cited above, so long as those provisions apply to all relevant traders operating within the national territory and so long as they affect in the same manner, in law and in fact, the marketing of domestic products and of those from other Member States. Provided that those conditions are fulfilled, the application of such rules to the sale of products from another Member State meeting the requirements laid down by that State is not by nature such as to prevent their access to the market or to impede access any more than it impedes the access of domestic products. Such rules therefore fall outside the scope of Article 30 of the Treaty (see the judgment in Joined Cases C–267/91 and 268/91 *Keck and Mithouard* [1993] ECR I–6097, paragraphs 16 and 17, and Case C–292/92 *Hünermund and Others* [1993] ECR I-6787, paragraph 21).

[22]   A provision such as that at issue in the main proceedings concerns selling arrangements since it prohibits a particular form of promotion (televised advertising) of a particular method of marketing products (distribution).

[23]   Furthermore, those provisions, which apply regardless of the type of product to all traders in the distribution sector, even if they are both producers and distributors, affect the marketing of products from other Member States and that of domestic products in the same manner.

[24]   The reply should accordingly be that on a proper construction Article 30 of the Treaty does not apply where a Member State, by statute or by regulation, prohibits the broadcasting of televised advertisements for the distribution sector.

In his Opinion in the case Advocate-General Jacobs embarked on a careful examination of *Keck*. Although his views were not reflected in the Court's ruling, they deserve attention for the light they shed on some of the complexities generated by the Court's refinement of the law in *Keck*. Advocate-General Jacobs stated that he found the Court's reasoning in *Keck* unsatisfactory, although he agreed with the result. He continued (remember that Article 30, to which he refers, was re-numbered Article 28 by the Amsterdam Treaty):

[41]   The question then is what test should be applied in order to determine whether a measure falls within the scope of Article 30. There is one guiding principle which seems to provide an appropriate test: that principle is that all undertakings which engage in a legitimate economic activity in a Member State should have unfettered access to the whole of the Community market, unless there is a valid reason for denying them full access to a part of that market. In spite of occasional inconsistencies in the reasoning of certain judgments, that seems to be the underlying principle which has inspired the Court's approach from *Dassonville* through 'Cassis de Dijon' to *Keck*. Virtually all of the cases are, in their result, consistent with the principle, even though some of them appear to be based on different reasoning.

[42]   If the principle is that all undertakings should have unfettered access to the whole of the Community market, then the appropriate test in my view is whether there is a substantial restriction on that access. That would of course amount to introducing a *de minimis* test into Article 30. Once it is recognised that there is a need to limit the scope of Article 30 in order to prevent excessive interference in the regulatory powers of the Member States, a test based on the extent to which a measure hinders trade between Member States by restricting market access seems the most obvious solution. Indeed it is perhaps surprising that, in view of the avowed aim of preventing excessive recourse to Article 30, the Court did not opt for such a solution in *Keck*. The reason may be that the Court was concerned lest a *de minimis* test, if applied to all measures affecting trade in goods, might induce national courts, who have primary responsibility for applying Article 30, to exclude too many measures from the scope of the prohibition laid down by that provision. Caution must therefore be exercised and if a *de minimis* test is to be introduced it will be necessary to define carefully the circumstances in which it should apply.

[43]   Clearly it would not be appropriate to apply a *de minimis* test to measures which overtly discriminate against goods from other Member States. Such measures are prohibited by Article 30 (unless justified under Article 36) even if their effect on inter-State trade is slight: there is a *per se* prohibition of overtly discriminatory measures.

[44]   Only in relation to measures which are applicable without distinction to domestic goods and goods from other Member States would it be necessary to introduce a requirement that the restriction, actual or potential, on access to the market must be substantial. The impact on access to the market of measures applicable without distinction may vary greatly, depending on the nature of the measure in issue. Where such a measure prohibits the sale of goods lawfully placed on the market in another Member State (as in 'Cassis de Dijon'), it may be presumed to have a substantial impact on access to the market, since the goods are either denied access altogether or can gain access only after being modified in some way; the need to modify goods is itself a substantial barrier to market access.

[45]   Where, on the other hand, a measure applicable without distinction simply restricts certain selling arrangements, by stipulating when, where, how, by whom or

at what price goods may be sold, its impact will depend on a number of factors, such as whether it applies to certain goods (as in *Blesgen*, *Buet* or *Quietlynn*), or to most goods (as in *Torfaen*), or to all goods (as in *Keck*), on the extent to which other selling arrangements remain available, and on whether the effect of the measure is direct or indirect, immediate or remote, or purely speculative[36] and uncertain.[37] Accordingly, the magnitude of the barrier to market access may vary enormously: it may range from the insignificant to a quasi-prohibition. Clearly, this is where a *de minimis* test could perform a useful function. The distinction recognised in *Keck* between a prohibition of the kind in issue in 'Cassis de Dijon' and a mere restriction on certain selling arrangements is therefore valuable: the former inevitably creates a substantial barrier to trade between Member States, whereas the latter may create such a barrier. But it cannot be maintained that the latter type of measure is not capable of hindering trade contrary to Article 30 in the absence of discrimination. It should therefore be recognised that such measures, unless overtly discriminatory, are not automatically caught by Article 30, as are measures of the type at issue in 'Cassis de Dijon', but may be caught if the restriction which they cause on access to the market is substantial.

Advocate-General Jacobs concluded that 'Article 30 should be regarded as applying to non-discriminatory measures which are liable substantially to restrict access to the market'. Applying this test to the French measures, he continued:

[55] . . . The restriction affects only one form of advertising, although the most effective as far as mass consumer goods are concerned; and advertisement of the goods themselves is not affected other than indirectly. As in the case of legislation restricting the opening hours of shops . . . the measure may result in a slight reduction in the total volume of sales of goods, including imports. But it cannot be said to have a substantial impact on access to the market. It therefore falls in my view outside the scope of Article 30.

Questions
1. Is the approach advocated by Advocate-General Jacobs likely to breed consistency in the application of (what is now) Article 28 by national courts? Is it more or less likely to achieve this objective than the Court's own test laid down in *Keck* and repeated in *Société d'Importation Edouard Leclerc-Siplec* v *TF1 Publicité SA and M6 Publicité SA* (Case C–412/93)?
2. M. Ross identifies 'patchwork pragmatism' and an avoidance of long-term commitment to principle in the Court's recent approach in this area ((1995) 20 EL Rev 507, 512). He finds this 'disappointing, since the central question to be addressed is simple enough to formulate: what does the notion of a single market require and permit?'. Discuss.

Note
The Court continues to be fed a steady diet of cases involving challenge to national rules which limit commercial freedom. *Keck* notwithstanding, there

---

[36] As in paragraph 15 of the judgment in *Stoke-on-Trent Council* v *B&Q*. . . .
[37] As in Case C–69/88 *Krantz* [1990] ECR I-583, paragraph 11 of the judgment.

remains scope for argument about the nature of the impediment to market access that must be shown for Article 28 to come into play where national rules deprive traders of the use of particular practices or require them to adopt practices which they do not favour.

Konsummentombudsmannen v *De Agostini Forlag AB and TV-Shop i Sverige AB*
(Joined Cases C-34/95, C-35/95 & C-36/95)
[1997] ECR I-3843
Court of Justice of the European Communities

The background to this case is provided by satellite broadcasting of television programmes, an activity particularly apt for cross-border commerce. The questions referred were prompted by action taken by the Swedish consumer *ombud* to restrain forms of television advertising, *inter alia* on the ground that contrary to Swedish law they were targeted at children less than 12 years of age. The Court ruled that Directive 89/552 harmonising laws governing television broadcasting did not preclude a Member State from taking action to protect consumers in respect of advertisements broadcast from another Member State, provided that this did not prevent retransmission as such. As regards Article 30 of the EC Treaty (now, after amendment, Article 28 EC):

[39]   In paragraph 22 of its judgment in *Leclerc-Siplec*, cited above [Case C-412/93], the Court held that legislation which prohibits television advertising in a particular sector concerns selling arrangements for products belonging to that sector in that it prohibits a particular form of promotion of a particular method of marketing products.

[40]   In Joined Cases C-267/91 and C-268/91 *Keck and Mithouard* [1993] ECR I-6097, at paragraph 16, the Court held that national measures restricting or prohibiting certain selling arrangements are not covered by Article 30 of the Treaty, so long as they apply to all traders operating within the national territory and so long as they affect in the same manner, in law and in fact, the marketing of domestic products and of those from other Member States.

[41]   The first condition is clearly fulfilled in the cases before the national court.

[42]   As regards the second condition, it cannot be excluded that an outright ban, applying in one Member State, of a type of promotion for a product which is lawfully sold there might have a greater impact on products from other Member States.

[43]   Although the efficacy of the various types of promotion is a question of fact to be determined in principle by the referring court, it is to be noted that in its observations De Agostini stated that television advertising was the only effective form of promotion enabling it to penetrate the Swedish market since it had no other advertising methods for reaching children and their parents.

[44]   Consequently, an outright ban on advertising aimed at children less than 12 years of age and of misleading advertising, as provided for by the Swedish legislation, is not covered by Article 30 of the Treaty, unless it is shown that the ban does not

affect in the same way, in fact and in law, the marketing of national products and of products from other Member States.

[45]   In the latter case, it is for the national court to determine whether the ban is necessary to satisfy overriding requirements of general public importance or one of the aims listed in Article 36 of the EC Treaty if it is proportionate to that purpose and if those aims or requirements could not have been attained or fulfilled by measures less restrictive of intra-Community trade.

Note
The Court proceeded to take a rather different line in response to questions about the impact of Article 59 of the EC Treaty (now, after amendment, Article 49 EC), which concerns the free movement of services (see p. 384 below).

Question
Would a law forbidding retail outlets for widgets from being opened within 10 kilometres of each other be susceptible to challenge under Community law? What about a law forbidding advertising of widgets other than in retail outlets? Or a law forbidding advertising of widgets entirely?

Further reading
The following articles examine the implications of the *Keck* ruling:

Chalmers, D., 'Repackaging the Internal market – the Ramifications of the *Keck* judgment' (1994) 19 EL Rev 385.
Friedbacher, T., 'Motive Unmasked: The European Court of Justice, the Free Movement of Goods and the Search for Legitimacy' (1996) 2 ELJ 226.
Greaves, R., 'Advertising Restrictions and the Free Movement of Goods and Services' (1998) 23 EL Rev 305.
Oliver, P., 'Some Further Reflections on the Scope of Articles 28–30 (ex 30–36) EC' (1999) 36 CML Rev 783.
Poiares Maduro, M., 'Reforming the Market or the State? Article 30 and the European Constitution: Economic Freedom and Political Rights' (1997) 3 ELJ 55.
Reich, N., 'The November revolution of the European Court of Justice: *Keck*, *Meng* and *Audi* revisited' (1994) 31 CML Rev 459.
Snell, J., and Andenas, M., 'Exploring the Outer Limits – Restrictions on the Free Movement of Gods and Services' (1999) 10 Euro Bus Law Rev 252.
Weatherill, S., 'After *Keck*: Some Thoughts on how to Clarify the Clarification' (1996) 33 CML Rev 885.

Note
However the *Keck* ruling may be shaped in future as a method for sheltering national regulatory choices from challenge based on Article 28, it is appropriate to conclude by emphasising that the Court has not lost its determination to use the '*Cassis de Dijon*' principle to root out measures that segregate

national markets and deny consumers choice between goods of different origins.

Verein gegen Unwesen in Handel und Gewerbe Köln v *Mars GmbH*
(Case C–470/93)
[1995] ECR I-1923
Court of Justice of the European Communities

Mars ice-creams were presented in wrappers marked ' + 10%'. This was part of a Europe-wide publicity campaign during which the quantity of the product was increased by 10%. Proceedings were initiated before a German court to restrain this practice as incompatible with German rules forbidding unfair competition. The question of the impact of Article 30 of the EC Treaty (now, after amendment, Article 28 EC) on such intervention in the market was referred to the European Court under the preliminary reference procedure. The European Court observed:

[11]   The first question to be examined is whether a prohibition of the marketing of goods bearing on their packaging a publicity marking such as that in question in the main proceedings constitutes a measure having an effect equivalent to a quantitative restriction within the meaning of Article 30 of the Treaty.

[12]   According to the case-law of the Court, Article 30 is designed to prohibit any trading rules of Member States which are capable of hindering, directly or indirectly, actually or potentially, intra-Community trade (see the judgment in Case 8/74 *Procureur du Roi* v *Dassonville* [1974] ECR 837, paragraph 5). The Court has held that, in the absence of harmonisation of legislation, obstacles to the free movement of goods that are the consequence of applying, to goods coming from other Member States where they are lawfully manufactured and marketed, rules that lay down requirements to be met by such goods, such as those relating, for example, to their presentation, labelling and packaging, are prohibited by Article 30, even if those rules apply without distinction to national products and to imported products (judgment in Joined Cases C–267/91 and C–268/91 *Keck and Mithouard* [1993] ECR I–6097, paragraph 15).

[13]   Although it applies to all products without distinction, a prohibition such as that in question in the main proceedings, which relates to the marketing in a Member State of products bearing the same publicity markings as those lawfully used in other Member States, is by nature such to hinder intra-Community trade. It may compel the importer to adjust the presentation of his products according to the place where they are to be marketed and consequently to incur additional packaging and advertising costs.

[14]   Such a prohibition therefore falls within the scope of Article 30 of the Treaty.

Critical to the *Keck* formula is the point that once a law is shown to apply equally in law and in fact, the State is *not* required to justify its law against standards recognised by Community law. By contrast, in this case, the threshold for invocation of Article 28 was crossed and therefore the State *was* required to show justification for its rules. It was unable to do this to the Court's satisfaction:

The consumer's expectation that the price previously charged is being maintained

[17]   It is argued that the '+ 10%' marking may lead the consumer to think that the 'new' product is being offered at a price identical to that at which the 'old' product was sold.

[18]   As the Advocate-General points out in Paragraphs 39 to 42 of his Opinion, on the assumption that the consumer expects the price to remain the same, the referring court considers that the consumer could be the victim of deception within the meaning of Paragraph 3 of the UWG and that if the price did not increase the offer would meet the consumer's expectation but then a question would arise concerning the application of Paragraph 15 of the GWB, which prohibits manufacturers from imposing prices on retailers.

[19]   As regards the first possibility, it must be observed first of all that Mars has not actually profited from the promotional campaign in order to increase its sale prices and that there is no evidence that retailers have themselves increased their prices. In any case, the mere possibility that importers and retailers might increase the price of the goods and that consequently consumers may be deceived is not sufficient to justify a general prohibition which may hinder intra-Community trade. That fact does not prevent the Member States from taking action, by appropriate measures, against duly proved actions which have the effect of misleading consumers.

[20]   As regards the second possibility, the principle of freedom of retail trade in the matter of the fixing of prices, provided for by a system of national law, and intended in particular to guarantee the consumer genuine price competition, may not justify an obstacle to intra-Community trade such as that in question in the main proceedings. The constraint imposed on the retailer not to increase his prices is in fact favourable to the consumer. It does not arise from any contractual stipulation and has the effect of protecting the consumer from being misled in any way. It does not prevent retailers from continuing to charge different prices and applies only during the short duration of the publicity campaign in question.

The visual presentation of the '+ 10%' marking and its alleged misleading effect

[21]   It is accepted by all the parties that the '+ 10%' marking is accurate in itself.

[22]   However, it is contended that the measure in question is justified because a not insignificant number of consumers will be induced into believing, by the band bearing the '+ 10%' marking, which occupies more than 10% of the total surface area of the wrapping, that the increase is larger than that represented.

[23]   Such a justification cannot be accepted.

[24]   Reasonably circumspect consumers are supposed to know that there is not necessarily a link between the size of publicity markings relating to an increase in a product's quantity and the size of that increase.

[25]   The reply to the preliminary question must therefore be that Article 30 of the Treaty is to be interpreted as precluding a national measure from prohibiting the importation and marketing of a product lawfully marketed in another Member State, the quantity of which was increased during a short publicity campaign and the wrapping of which bears the marking '+ 10%',

    (a)   on the ground that the presentation may induce the consumer into thinking that the price of the goods offered is the same as that at which the goods had previously been sold in their old presentation,

(b) on the ground that the new presentation gives the impression to the consumer that the volume and weight of the product have been considerably increased.

(D) THE COMMISSION'S INTERPRETATION OF THE JUDGMENT IN *CASSIS DE DIJON*

The Court's decision in '*Cassis de Dijon*' (Case 120/78) was seized on with enthusiasm by the Commission as a means of advancing the attack on national rules which partition the market.

Commission Communication
(1980) OJ C256/2, 3 October 1980

The following is the text of a letter which has been sent to the member-States; the European Parliament and the Council have also been notified of it.

In the Commission's Communication of 6 November 1978 on 'Safeguarding free trade within the Community', it was emphasised that the free movement of goods is being affected by a growing number of restrictive measures.

The judgment delivered by the Court of Justice on 20 February 1979 in Case 120/78 (the '*Cassis de Dijon*' case), and recently reaffirmed in the judgment of 26 June 1980 in Case 788/79, has given the Commission some interpretative guidance enabling it to monitor more strictly the application of the Treaty rules on the free movement of goods, particularly Articles 30 to 36 of the EEC Treaty.

The Court gives a very general definition of the barriers to free trade which are prohibited by the provisions of Article 30 *et seq.* of the EEC Treaty. These are taken to include 'any national measure capable of hindering, directly or indirectly, actually or potentially, intra-Community trade'.

In its judgment of 20 February 1979 the Court indicates the scope of this definition as it applies to technical and commercial rules.

Any product lawfully produced and marketed in one member-State must, in principle, be admitted to the market of any other member-State.

Technical and commercial rules, even those equally applicable to national and imported products, may create barriers to trade only where those rules are necessary to satisfy mandatory requirements and to serve a purpose which is in the general interest and for which they are an essential guarantee. This purpose must be such as to take precedence over the requirements of the free movement of goods, which constitutes one of the fundamental rules of the Community.

The conclusions in terms of policy which the Commission draws from this new guidance are set out below.

— Whereas member-States may, with respect to domestic products and in the absence of relevant Community provisions, regulate the terms on which such products are marketed, the case is different for products imported from other member-States. Any product imported from another member-State must in principle be admitted to the territory of the importing member-State if it has been lawfully produced, that is, conforms to rules and processes of manufacture that are customarily and traditionally accepted in the exporting country, and is marketed in the territory of the latter.

This principle implies that member-States, when drawing up commercial or technical rules liable to affect the free movement of goods, may not take an exclusively national viewpoint and take account only of requirements confined to domestic products. The proper functioning of the common market demands that each member-State also give consideration to the legitimate requirements of the other member-States.

Only under very strict conditions does the Court accept exceptions to this principle; barriers to trade resulting from differences between commercial and technical rules are only admissible:

— if the rules are necessary, that is appropriate and not excessive, in order to satisfy mandatory requirements (public health, protection of consumers or the environment, the fairness of commercial transactions, etc.);

— if the rules serve a purpose in the general interest which is compelling enough to justify an exception to a fundamental rule of the Treaty such as the free movement of goods;

— if the rules are essential for such a purpose to be attained, *i.e.* are the means which are the most appropriate and at the same time least hinder trade.

The Court's interpretation has induced the Commission to set out a number of guidelines

— The principles deduced by the Court imply that a member-State may not in principle prohibit the sale in its territory of a product lawfully produced and marketed in another member-State even if the product is produced according to technical or quality requirements which differ from those imposed on its domestic products. Where a product 'suitably and satisfactorily' fulfils the legitimate objective of a member-State's own rules (public safety, protection of the consumer or the environment, etc.), the importing country cannot justify prohibiting its sale in its territory by claiming that the way it fulfils the objective is different from that imposed on domestic products.

In such a case, an absolute prohibition of sale could not be considered 'necessary' to satisfy a 'mandatory requirement' because it would not be an 'essential guarantee' in the sense defined in the Court's judgment.

The Commission will therefore have to tackle a whole body of commercial rules which lay down that products manufactured and marketed in one member-State must fulfil technical or qualitative conditions in order to be admitted to the market of another and specifically in all cases where the trade barriers occasioned by such rules are inadmissible according to the very strict criteria set out by the Court.

The Commission is referring in particular to rules covering the composition, designation, presentation and packaging of products as well as rules requiring compliance with certain technical standards.

— The Commission's work of harmonisation will henceforth have to be directed mainly at national laws having an impact on the functioning of the common market where barriers to trade to be removed arise from national provisions which are admissible under the criteria set by the Court.

The Commission will be concentrating on sectors deserving priority because of their economic relevance to the creation of a single internal market.

To forestall later difficulties, the Commission will be informing member-States of potential objections, under the terms of Community law, to provisions they may be considering introducing which come to the attention of the Commission.

It will be producing suggestions soon on the procedures to be followed in such cases.

The Commission is confident that this approach will secure greater freedom of trade for the Community's manufacturers, so strengthening the industrial base of the Community, while meeting the expectations of consumers.

Note
The Commission thus believes that the extension of Article 30 of the EC Treaty (now, after amendment, Article 28 EC) to cover '*Cassis de Dijon*' (Case 120/78) type rules has reduced the need for harmonisation.

Question
What would have been the consequence for national diversity and tradition if harmonisation at Community level had been required to remove the trade distortive effect of rules governing the content of fruit liqueurs, the fat levels of Edam cheese and the designation of beers?

Note
In the 1985 White Paper (p. 174 above), the Commission located the '*Cassis de Dijon*' (Case 120/78) interpretation of the law governing free movement of goods firmly within the framework of the rules designed to complete the internal market by the end of 1992. The fact that market integration did not stop at the end of 1992, but, as is made plain in Chapter 5, continues to evolve, means that this analysis remains true for the future, subject to the refinements brought about by the ruling in *Keck* (Cases C-267 & C-268/91, p. 316 above).

COM (85) 310, Completing the Internal Market
White Paper from the Commission to the European Council, 14 June 1985

PART TWO: THE REMOVAL OF TECHNICAL BARRIERS

57.   The elimination of border controls, important as it is, does not of itself create a genuine common market. Goods and people moving within the Community should not find obstacles inside the different Member States as opposed to meeting them at the border.

58.   This does not mean that there should be the same rules everywhere, but that goods as well as citizens and companies should be able to move freely within the Community. Subject to certain important constraints (see paragraph 65 below), the general principle should be approved that, if a product is lawfully manufactured and marketed in one Member State, there is no reason why it should not be sold freely throughout the Community. Indeed, the objectives of national legislation, such as the protection of human health and life and of the environment, are more often than not identical. It follows that the rules and controls developed to achieve those objectives, although they may take different forms, essentially come down to the same thing, and so should normally be accorded recognition in all Member States, not forgetting the possibilities of cooperation between national authorities. What is true for goods, is also true for services and for people. If a Community citizen or a company meets the requirements for its activity in one member State, there should be no valid reason why those citizens or companies should not exercise their economic activities also in other parts of the Community.

59.   The Commission is fully aware that this strategy implies a change in habits and in traditional ways of thinking. What is needed is a radical change of attitude which would lead to new and innovative solutions for problems – real or apparent – which may appear when border controls no longer exist.

I. Free movement of goods

60. Whilst the physical barriers dealt with in Part One impede trade flows and add unacceptable administrative costs (ultimately paid by the consumer), barriers created by different national product regulations and standards have a double-edged effect: they not only add extra costs, but they also distort production patterns; increase unit costs; increase stock holding costs; discourage business cooperation, and fundamentally frustrate the creation of a common market for industrial products. Until such barriers are removed, Community manufacturers are forced to focus on national rather than continental markets and are unable to benefit from the economies of scale which a truly unified internal market offers. Failure to achieve a genuine industrial common market becomes increasingly serious since the research, development and commercialisation costs of the new technologies, in order to have a realistic prospect of being internationally competitive, require the background of a home market of continental proportions.

The need for a new strategy

61. The harmonization approach has been the cornerstone of Community action in the first 25 years and has produced unprecedented progress in the creation of common rules on a Community-wide basis. However, over the years, a number of shortcomings have been identified . . .

63. In principle, therefore, given the Council's recognition (Conclusions on Standardization, 16 July 1984) of the essential equivalence of the objectives of national legislation, mutual recognition could be an effective strategy for bringing about a common market in a trading sense. This strategy is supported in particular by Articles 30 to 36 of the EEC Treaty, which prohibit national measures which would have excessively and unjustifiably restrictive effects on free movement.

64. But while a strategy based purely on mutual recognition would remove barriers to trade and lead to the creation of a genuine common trading market, it might well prove inadequate for the purposes of the building up of an expanding market based on the competitiveness which a continental-scale uniform market can generate. On the other hand experience has shown that the alternative of relying on a strategy based totally on harmonization would be over-regulatory, would take a long time to implement, would be inflexible and could stifle innovation. What is needed is a strategy that combines the best of both approaches but, above all, allows for progress to be made more quickly than in the past.

The chosen strategy

65. The Commission takes into account the underlying reasons for the existence of barriers to trade, and recognises the essential equivalence of Member States' legislative objectives in the protection of health and safety, and of the environment. Its harmonization approach is based on the following principles:

— a clear distinction needs to be drawn in future internal market initiatives between what it is essential to harmonize, and what may be left to mutual recognition of national regulations and standards; this implies that, on the occasion of each harmonisation initiative, the Commission will determine whether national regulations are excessive in relation to the mandatory requirements pursued and, thus, constitute unjustified barriers to trade according to Article 30 to 36 of the EEC Treaty;

— legislative harmonisation (Council Directives based on Article 100) will in future be restricted to laying down essential health and safety requirements which will be obligatory in all Member States. Conformity with this will entitle a product to free movement;

— harmonisation of industrial standards by the elaboration of European standards will be promoted to the maximum extent, but the absence of European Standards should not be allowed to be used as a barrier to free movement. During the waiting period while European Standards are being developed, the mutual acceptance of national standards, with agreed procedures, should be the guiding principle.

Notes
1. *Cf.* p. 241 above on the present standing of Directive 70/50.
2. The reaction to the Commission's strategy has been mixed.

R. Dehousse, 'Completing the Internal Market: Institutional Constraints and Challenges' in R. Bieber, R. Dehousse, J. Pinder and J. Weiler (eds), *1992: One European Market?* (1988), pp. 311, 324–329

(Footnotes omitted.)

The success of a programme as ambitious as the White Paper depends not only on changes in rules governing decision-making alone but also on the proposed programme itself and the way in which it takes account of the institutional context. The connection between the decision-making procedure and the decisions which eventually emerge is not purely a one-way system. Just as the way in which a decision is taken can largely determine its content, so the way that the decision-making procedure operates can be modified by altering the final product that is expected to emerge. To some extent the means used for a given end condition the feasibility of the undertaking. To give a specific example: basically it would appear simpler to persuade the Twelve to refrain from introducing new provisions that might harm intra-Community trade, rather than to get them to agree on a definition of the technical specifications which a given product must satisfy. Equally it is possible – without tampering with the existing decision-making structures at all - to reduce the degree of consensus needed by cutting down the number of participants involved: all that has to be done is to circumscribe the problem in such a way that only a few Member States are directly concerned. Another possibility is to reduce the bargaining costs by proposing no more than a general agreement which leaves each Member State some room for manoeuvre, either by allowing relative freedom of implementation or by means of exemptions or safeguard clauses. These are some simple ways of getting round the joint-decision trap referred to earlier. Viewed from this angle, a number of recent developments catch the eye.

The broad interpretation given to the notion of 'measures having equivalent effect to quantitative restrictions' in the *Dassonville* and *Cassis de Dijon* cases unquestionably opened up new avenues for the Commission. The Court has stated that a Member State may not in principle prohibit the sale in its territory of a product lawfully produced and marketed in another Member State even if this product is produced according to technical or quality requirements which differ from those imposed on its domestic products. In the absence of Community provisions, only measures covered by article 36 or 'necessary in order to satisfy mandatory requirements' like the effectiveness of fiscal supervision, the protection of public health and of the environment, the fairness of commercial transactions and the defence of the consumer, can take precedence over the requirements of the free movements of goods. By extending the scope of article 30, the Court has rendered possible an emphasis on the removal of technical barriers to trade in areas where it was generally thought that only harmonization of national measures was possible.

The new strategy outlined in the White Paper rests on the implicit premise of this case law, namely the essential equivalence of national legislative objectives concerning the protection of human health and safety, and of the environment. In its conclusions on standardization of July 1984, the Council has explicitly recognized that

'the objectives being pursued by the Member States to protect the safety and health of their people as well as the consumer are equally valid in principle, even if different techniques are used to achieve them.'

The White Paper takes this new situation to a logical conclusion and proposes a theoretical distinction between matters where harmonization is essential and those where it is sufficient for there to be mutual recognition of the equivalence of the various basic requirements laid down under national law. The concept of mutual recognition also appears in several other places in the White Paper: it is referred to in connection with health controls, frontier checks, University degrees and vocational training, and even in such a sensitive matter as financial services.

This approach has many advantages in view of the cumbersome nature of the decision-making process. Unlike harmonization, mutual recognition does not involve the transfer of powers to the Community but, at the very worst, somewhat restricts the freedom of action of the Member States. Furthermore, this emphasis on mutual recognition avoids all the difficulties linked to the necessity of drafting directives so as to suit the substantive concerns of twelve different actors or the specific requirements of their legal system. Thus the lengthy bargaining which tends to accompany harmonization can be reduced to a minimum, with greater reliance being placed on the (politically more neutral) supervision of the Court to ensure that the continued existence of national rules does not constitute a barrier to trade. Both from a political and from a legalistic viewpoint, this new direction should be easier to follow.
. . .

The reliance on mutual recognition is nothing more than the rediscovery of a principle which is fairly common in structures of a federal type – and to which the draft Treaty on European Union gave a prominent place: the principle of subsidiarity. The essence of this principle is very simple: the higher level of government should only intervene when it can provide public goods that lower levels cannot supply. In the Community context, this would imply that Community action should be limited to fields where it is absolutely necessary for market integration, or where it can reach better results than the Member States. As is so often the case, the espousal of this principle seems dictated by a combination of theoretical considerations as to the level at which certain powers would be most fruitfully exercised and more practical considerations of how best to simplify the decision-making process. In this particular case, it is perfectly in line with the Treaty inclination towards negative integration.

The rediscovery of this principle is not confined to the definition of the conditions in which harmonization must take place. In its present state, Community law possesses a wide range of techniques to provide some measure of flexibility. There is, for example, nothing to prevent the objectives from being defined at Community level, while leaving it to national or Community experts to resolve the technical problems, or giving Member States a range of options in the form of minimum rules or various alternative regulations to choose from. This can sometimes reduce the degree of consensus needed very considerably. The Commission made a first attempt in that direction with the so-called 'Low Voltage Directive' [73/23], which only established minimal safety requirements and left it to international or national bodies to formulate the technical specifications to which goods should conform. Council Resolution of 7 May 1985 tries to generalize this new approach by providing that harmonization should henceforth be restricted to the definition of the essential requirements justified by health and safety concerns or for the protection of the environment.

Like the White Paper's emphasis on mutual recognition, this new approach, which contrasts sharply with the Commission's previous attitude, seems inspired by the conviction that Community action should concentrate on the main obstacle to market integration – the existence of trade barriers arising from the existence of different national provisions – leaving to the States their ultimate responsibility for health, safety, etc. This division of tasks, which combines a harmonization of some essential requirements at Community level with a certain flexibility as regards the means used to pursue these ends at national level, better corresponds to a truly federal model than did the traditional approach to harmonization issues. . . .

. . . Because of its emphasis on negative integration, it will require stricter monitoring by the Commission, but also greater transparency as regards the activities of the Member States. Conversely, mutual recognition should also reduce bottlenecks in implementing Community law at national level, since harmonization directives would be fewer and less detailed – hence reduced compliance problems.

Accordingly, instead of placing the stress on punitive action – a role which it openly admits is beyond its resources – the Commission seems to have paid increasing attention in recent years to prevention. Council Directive 83/189/EEC – the 'Mutual Information' directive [now consolidated in Directive 98/34, see the following note] – lays down for technical regulations and standards a system somewhat reminiscent of that applying to state aids, by imposing on Member States the obligation to notify their plans to amend technical regulations or to introduce new ones. This way, a close watch can be kept on any new national rule: the Commission or any of the other Member States can contest the legality of a planned measure, following which a standstill of up to one year may be imposed. The aim of the system is to prevent the spread both of 'neo-protectionist' measures of the kind that have flourished in recent years and of unintentional infringements of the Treaty. Where appropriate, the problem can be solved by means of harmonization before the adoption of new rules further complicates the situation. The originality of this procedure lies in this relatively new type of 'horizontal transparency', which gives each Member State an interest in seeing that the system works properly. The Commission has also announced its intention to play a guiding role in this transparency process by publishing notices setting out the legal situation in various sectors of the economy or concerning various types of barriers to trade.

Note

Some of these issues have already been touched on in Chapter 5. Some, especially those connected with harmonisation policy, will be readdressed in Chapter 15. It bears repetition that these are general issues for the evolution of the Community market. They were not suddenly solved at the end of 1992.

The Commission is striving to develop strategies for managing the internal market that are more comprehensive and sophisticated than *ex post facto* litigation. Directive 83/189 (OJ 1983 L109/8), mentioned in the final paragraph of the above extract, was designed to enhance transparency and to facilitate *a priori* supervision of national measures liable to thwart integration. Directive 83/189 was twice amended to expand its scope and has been consolidated in Directive 98/34 (OJ 1998 L204/37, itself amended by Directive 98/48 OJ 1998 L217/18), and its impact was deepened by the Court's ruling in Case C-194/94 *CIA Security International SA* v *Signalson SA and Securitel SPRL* [1996] ECR I-2201, that national technical regulations left unnotified in breach of the Directive are unenforceable against third parties before national courts (see Slot, P.-J., 'Annotation' (1996) 33 CML Rev 1035; Weatherill, S., 'Compulsory notification of draft technical regulations: the contribution of Directive 83/189 to the management of the internal market' (1996) 16 YEL 129; Jans, J., 'National Legislative Autonomy? The Procedural Constraints of European Law' [1998/1] LIEI 25). This structure forms an important procedural complement to the principle of mutual recognition developed by the Court in relation to Article 28 EC.

(E) SOME CONSEQUENCES FOR CONSUMER PROTECTION

Many commentators have expressed enthusiasm for the '*Cassis de Dijon*' (Case 120/78) decision as a means of improving the consumer's position. Spurious national rules of consumer protection which were in truth rules of producer protection are exposed as unlawful trade barriers. This opens up the market to competition, which, as far as the consumer is concerned, ought to mean increased choice, lower prices and higher quality.

Bureau Européen des Unions de Consommateurs, *Discussion Document 237/84 on Protectionism and Consumer Protection* (1985), p. 3

. . . [T]he case law of the European Court of Justice . . . serves as a model of how to expose false consumer protection arguments and identify consumers' real interests.

N. Reich, in Bourgoignie (ed.), 'European Consumer Law', *Community Consumer Law* (1982), p. 223

The Court does not denounce consumer policy in general but criticizes *false consumer policy*. In studying consumer law in the EC Member States on a comparative basis, I have come to the conviction that many regulations which carry the label of consumer protection do not really serve the consumer but instead hinder unwanted competition.

Question
Which cases might be cited in support of (or in opposition to) these views?

Note
Nevertheless, concern has been expressed about the consequences of the '*Cassis de Dijon*' (Case 120/78) judgment, and particularly the legislative and

administrative policy which has developed in its wake. The fears lie essentially in the perception that the judgment is heavily biased towards establishing free trade. Member States wishing to uphold national protection bear a heavy burden of proof that the rules are necessary to satisfy mandatory require- ments. The Commission's expressed relief at the reduction in the need for Community regulation implies a *negative* rather than a *positive* approach to regulating the Community market. This is capable of depriving the trader of certainty about the terms of inter-State trade, and the consumer of confi- dence about the safety of products originating in other Member States.

Several of the following extracts, which are selected with the aim of stimulating rather than offering comprehensive coverage, contain discussion of policy matters which impinge on the development of the Community generally, not just Article 28.

N. Reich, 'Protection of Diffuse Interests in the EEC and the Perspective of Progressively Establishing an Internal Market' (1988) 11 JCP 395

(References omitted.)

'Negative Integration'
The concept of 'integration' defines the central political object of the Community since its coming into existence. Integration looks at Member States' regulations which have an effect on the free circulation of goods, services, persons, and capital transfers as restrictions, whatever their political and legal justifications. The thrust of primary and secondary Community law is directed *against* member-State regulations. The Community integrates by eliminating member-State law which is in opposition to its functioning. The term 'negative integration' . . . helps to explain this activity of the Community. Pelkmans . . . therefore defines the Community as a free trade zone which has been enlarged by a customs union. Theories of free trade ideas harmonise well with classical liberal and neo-liberal economic thought, which has always been popular in Germany, because it recognises the de-regulatory spirit of Community law. Oppermann . . . has therefore defined as the basic rule of Community law 'European market freedom.'

Importance of Diffuse Interests
The second point of this complex triangular relation can be defined by employing the theory of *diffuse interests* . . .. It aims at an explanation of the economic and social paradoxes of aggregating and integrating diffuse interests into consumer, environmen- tal, and equal rights protection. From its very beginning the Community did not intend to protect diffuse interests in the quality of life, even though article 2 of the EEC Treaty might be read and has been read in this sense. The Community had primarily allocated right to business, viz., a far-reaching right of market access in the entire common market, in order to achieve economic integration as previously defined. It has only recently tried to develop rights protecting diffuse interests, beginning with article 119 of the EEC Treaty concerning equal treatment of men and women in working conditions [see now Article 148 EC]. The social reform movement which had also reached the Community through the Paris declaration of 1972 of the Heads of States and Governments has added separate Community policies in

environmental . . . , consumer . . . , health . . ., and workplace protection without formally amending the Treaty. Secondary EEC law, based on broad powers of discretion for the EEC institutions, has been responsive in developing social policies of the EEC to protect diffuse interests. This might be called 'positive integration'. . .. The Community is trying to develop its own standards common to all member states and therefore applying to all citizens, and allowing a certain common level in the protection of diffuse interests.

. . . One could conclude from these remarks that the process of positive integration will neither harmonise protective standards nor promote integration. The EEC citizen who has suffered damage from defective products will have to look for his basic right to safety and health where he has left it, more precisely, where it has been violated. An enterprise wanting to compete in a single market via harmonised conditions of liability at uniform insurance rates is subjected to subtle fragmentations, which make impossible a uniform marketing strategy and an EEC-wide product monitoring. Private international law rules, though being viewed somewhat suspiciously by the EEC institutions, still continue to be applied. Does this mean that positive integration will not work?

A solution is only possible if one neither overstrains laws or protective policies nor looks at integration in a somewhat reduced fashion. Harmonisation does not mean uniformity. The EEC is not really an autonomous political entity but must be brought to life, be accepted, and legitimised for action by the member states. Community law should therefore be regarded as running *parallel* to member state law . . . and not, in the words of the Court, as '*limit(ing) their sovereign rights*.' Therefore, the doctrine of supremacy and preemption of Community law should be regarded with a certain scepticism. This doctrine, to take a recent example, will in the eyes of the Court prevent Denmark from setting more protective standards in the trade of hazardous chemicals by obliging importers to notify certain risks to the Danish authorities. The notion of total harmonisation on the basis of which the Court disapproved of the Danish regulation is used as a petrified legal argument to create the illusion that Community law may really regulate all the possible hazards arising in intra-community trade. The principle of market access without restrictions (except those allowed by Community law) does not go along with the previously mentioned balancing test. It also makes it impossible for Denmark and other countries to fulfil obligations which they have under their constitution and under international law in the protection of their own and foreign citizens.

. . . There is an inherent conflict between market integration, protection of diffuse interests, and the rule of law within the Community. Some trends have turned into a genuine 'acquis communautaire'. Others have been taken up by the Single Act but may not have led to the clear solutions which lawyers are always looking for. The role of law itself becomes a main concern within the Community. It is interesting to note that the autonomy and function of law has been reduced and not increased by the Single Act, quite in contrast to 'post-modern legal theory' which insists on the need for autonomy and reformalisation ('autopoiesis') . . . of law.

The main dilemma of EEC law in the future will be whether the objectives of integration, protection, and rule-of-law can really be balanced and harmonised to an equal extent. Mainstream political and legal thinking in the EEC still has as its starting point a basic right to market access for which law is a mere instrument. Protection enters only through a sort of hidden door, or it is regarded as a restriction to free trade. It is quite revealing to read article 8A in this light [see now Article 14 EC]: It comes as no surprise that the free circulation of *goods* is mentioned *before* the free circulation of *persons*! . . .

R. Dehousse, 'Completing the Internal Market:
Institutional Constraints and Challenges' in R. Bieber et al. (eds),
1992: One European Market?
(1988), pp. 334–336

(Footnotes omitted.)

As much as one may approve the White Paper's emphasis on negative integration and the removal of borders, it is clear that market unity will not be possible without a measure of positive integration, even if only in a limited way, for example for the setting up of minimal health and safety requirements or the organization of the cooperation among national customs administrations, which is necessary in order to achieve a real elimination of physical borders. It is likely that the difficulties that traditionally beset Community decision-making will surface again at that level. The Single Act has tried to ease somewhat the taking of decision with a mixture of majority voting and differentiation. The two are closely linked; in a Community of twelve, renewed progress would not be possible without a simplification of decision-making procedures but, at the same time, the latter would have been unthinkable without a measure of flexibility. In substantive terms, additional flexibility is also rendered necessary by the sometimes wide differences which exist between Member States' economies and societal choices. To a certain extent, the impact of these new mechanisms will probably depend on the Commission's ability to maintain a certain degree of momentum in its White Paper programme. At least it will benefit in its quest for an enhanced room for manoeuvre for, as we have seen, the combination of majority voting and derogatory provisions should reinforce the strategic importance of its proposals.

At some point, however, a major challenge will have to be faced, for the objective of market integration itself remains unacceptable, politically speaking, for some Member States if it is not accompanied by a specific effort to improve the social and economic cohesion within the Community. It is worth recalling in this respect that economically weaker countries have been reluctant to accept majority voting, precisely because they are those who might suffer most in the short term from the creation of a single market. Of the many problems linked to the completion of the internal market, this one is perhaps the most difficult: unlike the concerns for a high level of protection for health, consumer safety or the environment, this kind of fear cannot be allayed by derogatory measures alone. A parallel in the Community's allocative and redistributive policies has been strongly advocated by recent studies, both from a theoretical and from a practical viewpoint. The Single Act pledges the Community to reinforce its action in favour of backward areas; it even explicitly states that the completion of the internal market should be pursued taking into account the existence of different levels of development within the Community [see now Article 158]. However, it fails to give the Community additional means to reach that end. The crucial point is that, at a given stage, progress towards the single European market might be conditioned by the capacity to tackle the problem of structural imbalances: if the Community does not find a way to offer some compensation to those countries which feel they have more to lose, market integration could be severely hampered. More than institutional pragmatism will be needed in order to cut this Gordian knot.

Note

The issues discussed are illustrative of some of the most fundamental which confront the Community. How are the differing demands of national interest groups to be accommodated in a broader structure committed to free trade? The Community's harmonisation programme must satisfy many often competing interests. No one doubts that the Community must regulate certain matters in order to achieve genuine integration. Much doubt remains about the nature and scope of that regulation. The rival notions of the 'level playing field' and 'competition between regulators' were introduced at p. 219 above. The future shape of the Community will be governed by the nature of choices about the allocation of responsibility for different functions to different levels of government in the Community – European, national, regional, local. Lately this complex issue has come to be denoted by a single word – 'subsidiarity'. (See, generally, Chapter 15.)

N. Reich, *Internal Market and Diffuse Interests*
(1990), pp. 18–19

On the one hand, the Internal Market may lead to standards which abide to the lowest common denominator. This would be true if there are highly divergent standards, for instance relating to product safety, to environmental quality, or to the contents of contracts in the service areas, and if the EC will simply open up the borders by allowing for a free movement of goods or services without control by the receiving state. Therefore, tendencies in new EC legislation, namely to impose a standard-of-origin principle as a Community-wide rule for marketing, must be viewed with scepticism . . . .

On the other hand, where high Community standards already exist and where they are implemented responsibly by the Member States, one cannot simply forecast a 'dumping' of consumer and environmental standards. One must have regard to a certain 'acquis communautaire'. This is true, e.g., for medicinal products. Protective consumer legislation at the EC level and in the Member States has practically offset the principle of the free circulation of goods, with the exception of so-called arbitrage as parallel imports, and has tightly segregated markets. This shows that a wide variety of options in the area of standard-setting for trade practices must be taken into account. Any simplistic solution will therefore not help political and legal analysis.

. . . As the integration process within the EC develops and as the Internal Market is completed, more powers will be transferred to Community institutions, thus making *federal solutions* in Community law-making and law application more realistic, as far as the protection of diffuse interests is concerned. This means that the future will be characterized by different options, ranging, on the one hand, from a complete deregulation to, on the other hand, a remaining of market segregation by different standards. The first model is true in areas where price/quality relations are concerned, legitimately allowing for consumers' free choice, the second in areas where either health and safety aspects are concerned, or where 'highly sensitive areas' of consumer policy like insurance or job placement services are to be considered . . . . If we take the imperatives of the federal model seriously, Community law will develop a set of rules allowing for a coordination of different areas of law-making and law-implementation. This will explain the paradox, why independent Member State policies protecting diffuse interests will become ever more important if the process of Community integration continues. We therefore reject, as we have mentioned above, any hierarchical model of Community law and will suggest federal solutions for existing or coming conflicts.

Notes

1. For a recent collection of essays grouped around the notion of *diffuse interests*, see Krämer, L., *et al.* (eds), 'Law and diffuse interests in the European Legal Order: Liber Amicorum Norbert Reich' (1997). See also the collection of articles grouped around the theme 'Governance in the Internal Market' in (1997) 4 JEPP, issue 4 (Special Issue).

2. These are inevitably matters of intense political debate. Yet they are vital for the lawyer too, because the legal rules and institutional structures which emerge and which form the lawyer's working materials will be the product of that political debate.

Pelkmans, J., 'A Grand Design by the Piece? An Appraisal of the Internal Market Strategy' in R. Bieber et al. (eds), *1992: One European Market?* (1988), p. 371

Finally whether one likes it or not, an Internal Market cutting so deep into the regulatory environment of consumers, traders and producers and limiting even more severely the Member States in their policy instruments *can no longer pretend to be a-political*. In completing the Internal Market by the piece, it becomes more and more artificial to expect conservatives, liberals, progressives, radicals, christian-democrats and socialists to agree, for the mere sake of 'Europe'. The verbal emphasis in the White Paper is, rightly, on fully free and unhindered mutual market access. But it is not very helpful to postulate that the *'positive integration' needed for that, will come forward and be solved, for the good purpose*. As more and more positive integration reduces the national policy autonomy needed to accentuate different positions in domestic politics, the greater the sensitivity to the Community's implicit or explicit political bias. As one begins to touch upon the most deeply entrenched forms of protection and the most cherished state instruments the process of positive integration will become more politicized. Perhaps wisely, the White Paper does not talk about this. . . . Whatever the present Commission's view, it will become more and more difficult to get an Internal Market of European scope with a political system at the national level. This problem may induce blockages causing the Internal Market to be incomplete in 1993.

Note

Such problems have indeed continued to beset the Community since the end of 1992 – and they have been deepened by the 'ambiguous compromises' (p. 12 above) of the Maastricht and Amsterdam Treaties. The process continues. Even before the entry into force of the Maastricht Treaty, Curtin was looking ahead to the intergovernmental conference scheduled to begin in 1996:

D. Curtin, 'The Constitutional Structure of the Union: A Europe of Bits and Pieces' (1993) 30 CML Rev 17, 69

But what will really matter if the Union Treaty does enter into force [as it subsequently did on 1 November 1993] is the nature of the 1996 *rendez-vous*. The risk is a consolidation of the 'Europe of bits and pieces' with some further diplomatic tinkering and no genuine participation by the European Parliament in the process, or effective pre-emptive accountability of individual governments to their own national parliaments. Surely what must instead be contemplated is a genuine constitutional blueprint for the Union facing into the twenty-first century with some new members, strengthened by a basic constituent text expressed in terms comprehensible to the European 'citizen' and constructed upon the idea of limited government under the rule of law? The Constitution would be amendable only by a pre-determined procedure requiring a very broad consensus.

Note

These debates continue. Amid a maelstrom of competing visions, it was hardly likely that the IGC that began in 1996 would resolve these fundamental questions about the shape of the Union. And the Treaty of Amsterdam, which emerged in 1997 (and entered into force in 1999, p. 28 above) did not do so. The prospect of enlargement, to which Curtin refers, is even more imminent and the challenges for Europe and for the Union ever more pressing.

9 THE FREE MOVEMENT OF WORKERS: ARTICLE 39

Since the entry into force of the Maastricht Treaty on European Union on 1 November 1993, any examination of the impact of EC law on people must begin and end with the notion of Citizenship of the European Union. These two chapters follow that pattern. Yet the notion of citizenship remains obscure despite the Maastricht Treaty's innovations, so the meat of these two chapters remains the long-standing structure of Community law which requires economic activity as a prerequisite to the conferral of rights. Chapter 10 concludes this exposition by asking how far the new notion of citizenship has transcended the focus on the economy (p. 398 below).

The Maastricht Treaty introduced into the EC Treaty a new Part Two, 'Citizenship of the Union'. This comprised Articles 8–8e EC.

The most striking adjustments to the law relating to persons made by the Treaty of Amsterdam are located in the new Title IV on 'Visas, asylum, immigration and other policies related to free movement of persons' (pp. 30, 192). However, the Amsterdam Treaty also adjusts the provisions on citizenship, albeit in rather minor ways. Articles 8–8e EC have become Articles 17–22 EC on re-numbering.

PART TWO
CITIZENSHIP OF THE UNION

Article 17
1. Citizenship of the Union is hereby established. Every person holding the nationality of a Member State shall be a citizen of the Union. Citizenship of the Union shall complement and not replace national citizenship.
2. Citizens of the Union shall enjoy the rights conferred by this Treaty and shall be subject to the duties imposed thereby.

Article 18
1. Every citizen of the Union shall have the right to move and reside freely within the territory of the Member States, subject to the limitations and conditions laid down in this Treaty and by the measures adopted to give it effect.

2.   The Council may adopt provisions with a view to facilitating the exercise of the rights referred to in paragraph 1; save as otherwise provided in this Treaty, the Council shall act in accordance with the procedure referred to in Article 251. The Council shall act unanimously throughout this procedure.

Article 19

1.   Every citizen of the Union residing in a Member State of which he is not a national shall have the right to vote and to stand as a candidate at municipal elections in the Member State in which he resides, under the same conditions as nationals of that State. This right shall be exercised subject to detailed arrangements adopted by the Council, acting unanimously on a proposal from the Commission and after consulting the European Parliament; these arrangements may provide for derogations where warranted by problems specific to a Member State.

2.   Without prejudice to Article 190(4) and to the provisions adopted for its implementation, every citizen of the Union residing in a Member State of which he is not a national shall have the right to vote and to stand as a candidate in elections to the European Parliament in the Member State in which he resides, under the same conditions as nationals of that State. This right shall be exercised subject to detailed arrangements adopted by the Council, acting unanimously on a proposal from the Commission and after consulting the European Parliament; these arrangements may provide for derogations where warranted by problems specific to a Member State.

Article 20

Every citizen of the Union shall, in the territory of a third country in which the Member State of which he is a national is not represented, be entitled to protection by the diplomatic or consular authorities of any Member State, on the same conditions as the nationals of that State. Member States shall establish the necessary rules among themselves and start the international negotiations required to secure this protection.

Article 21

Every citizen of the Union shall have the right to petition the European Parliament in accordance with Article 194.

Every citizen of the Union may apply to the Ombudsman established in accordance with Article 195.

Every citizen of the Union may write to any of the institutions or bodies referred to in this Article or in Article 7 in one of the languages mentioned in Article 314 and have an answer in the same language.

Article 22

The Commission shall report to the European Parliament, to the Council and to the Economic and Social Committee every three years on the application of the provisions of this Part. This report shall take account of the development of the Union.

On this basis, and without prejudice to the other provisions of this Treaty, the Council, acting unanimously on a proposal from the Commission and after consulting the European Parliament, may adopt provisions to strengthen or to add to the rights laid down in this Part, which it shall recommend to the Member States for adoption in accordance with their respective constitutional requirements.

Note

A close reading of these provisions suggests that, until such time as legislative amplification is achieved, the content of citizenship of the Union is in several respects dependent on existing law under the Treaty. Consideration therefore begins with Article 39 and the rights of workers.

Article 39, EC

Article 39

1. Freedom of movement for workers shall be secured within the Community.

2. Such freedom of movement shall entail the abolition of any discrimination based on nationality between workers of the Member States as regards employment, remuneration and other conditions of work and employment.

3. It shall entail the right, subject to limitations justified on grounds of public policy, public security or public health:

    (a)   to accept offers of employment actually made;

    (b)   to move freely within the territory of Member States for this purpose;

    (c)   to stay in a Member State for the purpose of employment in accordance with the provisions governing the employment of nationals of that State laid down by law, regulation or administrative action;

    (d)   to remain in the territory of a Member State after having been employed in that State, subject to conditions which shall be embodied in implementing regulations to be drawn up by the Commission.

4. The provisions of this Article shall not apply to employment in the public service.

Note

The Treaty of Amsterdam merely deleted the words 'by the end of the transitional period at the latest' from the first paragraph, and altered to Article 39 the number of this Article, which was previously 48.

At one level, the Treaty secures the free movement of workers simply as an adjunct to the other freedoms, such as the free movement of goods (Article 28), and services (Article 49). These freedoms all contribute to the realisation of mobility within a common market. But the free movement of persons has implications beyond the economics of market integration. It concerns human beings. It identifies people as the beneficiaries of the Treaty rules in a more direct sense than any other area of Community law.

Article 39 concerns both labour mobility and the rights of the individual. Both the Court and the legislature have developed the scope of the rights conferred upon the migrant worker. These developments mean that, independently of the Maastricht-created notion of citizenship, an individual has an extensive range of rights, first, to move freely between Member States to take up employment and, second, to enjoy non-discriminatory access to social protection once installed in the host Member State. This chapter explores the scope of the worker's right to free movement.

(A) WHO IS A WORKER?

Levin v Staatssecretaris van Justitie (Case 53/81)
[1982] ECR 1035; [1982] 2 CMLR 454
Court of Justice of the European Communities

Mrs Levin was a British national married to a South African national. She was refused a residence permit by the Dutch authorities because she was not in gainful employment. She challenged the refusal before the Dutch courts. Questions were referred to the European Court. The Court was asked to explain the notion of a 'worker' for Community law purposes. The Dutch court was particularly concerned to elucidate the scope of Article 48 of the EC Treaty (now, after amendment, Article 39 EC) where an individual earns an income less than the minimum required for subsistence as defined under national law. The Court observed that no authoritative definition of 'worker' is to be found in the Treaty or secondary legislation. It then claimed for itself the job of carrying out that interpretative task.

[11] . . . [T]he terms 'worker' and 'activity as an employed person' may not be defined by reference to the national laws of the Member States but have a Community meaning. If that were not the case, the Community rules on freedom of movement for workers would be frustrated, as the meaning of those terms could be fixed and modified unilaterally, without any control by the Community institutions, by national laws which would thus be able to exclude at will certain categories of persons from the benefit of the Treaty.

[12] Such would, in particular, be the case if the enjoyment of the rights conferred by the principle of freedom of movement for workers could be made subject to the criterion of what the legislation of the host State declares to be a minimum wage, so that the field of application *ratione personae* of the Community rules on this subject might vary from one Member State to another. The meaning and the scope of the terms 'worker' and 'activity as an employed person' should thus be clarified in the light of the principles of the legal order of the Community.

[13] In this respect it must be stressed that these concepts define the field of application of one of the fundamental freedoms guaranteed by the Treaty and, as such, may not be interpreted restrictively.

[14] In conformity with this view the recitals in the preamble to Regulation (EEC) No 1612/68 contain a general affirmation of the right of all workers in the Member States to pursue the activity of their choice within the Community, irrespective of whether they are permanent, seasonal or frontier workers or workers who pursue their activities for the purpose of providing services. Furthermore, although Article 4 of Directive 68/360/EEC grants the right of residence to workers upon the mere production of the document on the basis of which they entered the territory and of a confirmation of engagement from the employer or a certificate of employment, it does not subject this right to any condition relating to the kind of employment or to the amount of income derived from it.

[15] An interpretation which reflects the full scope of these concepts is also in conformity with the objectives of the Treaty which include, according to Articles 2 and 3, the abolition, as between Member States, of obstacles to freedom of movement for persons, with the purpose *inter alia* of promoting throughout the Community a harmonious development of economic activities and a raising of the standard of living. Since part-time employment, although it may provide an income lower than what is considered to be the minimum required for subsistence, constitutes for a large number of persons an effective means of improving their living conditions, the effectiveness of Community law would be impaired and the achievement of the objectives of the Treaty would be jeopardized if the enjoyment of rights conferred by the principle of

freedom of movement for workers were reserved solely to persons engaged in full-time employment and earning, as a result, a wage at least equivalent to the guaranteed minimum wage in the sector under consideration.

[16]   It follows that the concepts of 'worker' and 'activity as an employed person' must be interpreted as meaning that the rules relating to freedom of movement for workers also concern persons who pursue or wish to pursue an activity as an employed person on a part-time basis only and who, by virtue of that fact obtain or would obtain only remuneration lower than the minimum guaranteed remuneration in the sector under consideration. In this regard no distinction may be made between those who wish to make do with their income from such an activity and those who supplement that income with other income, whether the latter is derived from property or from the employment of a member of their family who accompanies them.

[17]   It should however be stated that whilst part-time employment is not excluded from the field of application of the rules on freedom of movement for workers, those rules cover only the pursuit of effective and genuine activities, to the exclusion of activities on such a small scale as to be regarded as purely marginal and ancillary. It follows both from the statement of the principle of freedom of movement for workers and from the place occupied by the rules relating to that principle in the system of the Treaty as a whole that those rules guarantee only the free movement of persons who pursue or are desirous of pursuing an economic activity.

[18]   The answer to be given to the first and second questions must therefore be that the provisions of Community law relating to freedom of movement for workers also cover a national of a Member State who pursues, within the territory of another Member State, an activity as an employed person which yields an income lower than that which, in the latter State, is considered as the minimum required for subsistence, whether that person supplements the income from his activity as an employed person with other income so as to arrive at that minimum or is satisfied with means of support lower than the said minimum, provided that he pursues an activity as an employed person which is effective and genuine.

[19]   The third question essentially seeks to ascertain whether the right to enter and reside in the territory of a Member State may be denied to a worker whose main objectives, pursued by means of his entry and residence, are different from that of the pursuit of an activity as an employed person as defined in the answer to the first and second questions.

[20]   Under Article 48 (3) of the Treaty the right to move freely within the territory of the Member States is conferred upon workers for the 'purpose' of accepting offers of employment actually made. By virtue of the same provision workers enjoy the right to stay in one of the Member States 'for the purpose' of employment there. Moreover, it is stated in the preamble to Regulation (EEC) No 1612/68 that freedom of movement for workers entails the right of workers to move freely within the Community 'in order to' pursue activities as employed persons, whilst Article 2 of Directive 68/360/EEC requires the Member States to grant workers the right to leave their territory 'in order to' take up activities as employed persons or to pursue them in the territory of another Member State.

[21]   However, these formulations merely give expression to the requirement, which is inherent in the very principle of freedom of movement for workers, that the advantages which Community law confers in the name of that freedom may be relied

upon only by persons who actually pursue or seriously wish to pursue activities as employed persons. They do not, however, mean that the enjoyment of this freedom may be made to depend upon the aims pursued by a national of a Member State in applying for entry upon and residence in the territory of another Member State, provided that he there pursues or wishes to pursue an activity which meets the criteria specified above, that is to say, an effective and genuine activity as an employed person.

[22]   Once this condition is satisfied, the motives which may have prompted the worker to seek employment in the Member State concerned are of no account and must not be taken into consideration.

[23]   The answer to be given to the third question put to the Court by the Raad van State must therefore be that the motives which may have prompted a worker of a Member State to seek employment in another Member State are of no account as regards his right to enter and reside in the territory of the latter State provided that he there pursues or wishes to pursue an effective and genuine activity.

Kempf v *Staatssecretaris van Justitie (Case 139/85)*
[1986] ECR 1741; [1987] 1 CMLR 764
Court of Justice of the European Communities

The Court took the opportunity in this case to refine further its definition.

[11]   As regards, first, the criterion of effective and genuine work as opposed to marginal and ancillary activities not covered by the relevant Community rules, the Netherlands Government expressed doubts at the hearing as to whether the work of a teacher who gives 12 lessons a week may be regarded as constituting in itself effective and genuine work within the terms of the judgment in *Levin*.

[12]   There is, however, no need to consider that question since the Raad van State, in the grounds of the judgment making the reference, expressly found that Mr Kempf's work was not on such a small scale as to be purely a marginal and ancillary activity. According to the division of jurisdiction between national courts and the Court of Justice in connection with references for a preliminary ruling, it is for national courts to establish and to evaluate the facts of the case. The question submitted for a preliminary ruling must therefore be examined in the light of the assessment made by the Raad van State.

[13]   The Court has consistently held that freedom of movement for workers forms one of the foundations of the Community. The provisions laying down that fundamental freedom and, more particularly, the terms 'worker' and 'activity as an employed person' defining the sphere of application of those freedoms must be given a broad interpretation in that regard, whereas exceptions to and derogations from the principle of freedom of movement for workers must be interpreted strictly.

[14]   It follows that the rules on this topic must be interpreted as meaning that a person in effective and genuine part-time employment cannot be excluded from their sphere of application merely because the remuneration he derives from it is below the level of the minimum means of subsistence and he seeks to supplement it by other lawful means of subsistence. In that regard it is irrelevant whether those supplementary means of subsistence are derived from property or from the employment of a member of his family, as was the case in *Levin*, or whether, as in this instance, they

are obtained from financial assistance drawn from the public funds of the Member State in which he resides, provided that the effective and genuine nature of his work is established.

Note
The Court is plainly concerned in these decisions to establish a broad definition of the worker entitled to Community law rights (see also *Lawrie-Blum* v *Land Baden-Württemberg* (Case 66/85) [1986] ECR 2121, [1987] 3 CMLR 389; but note some caution in *Bettray* v *Staatssecretaris van Justitie* (Case 344/87) [1989] ECR 1621). Notice that the notion of worker is held to be a concept of Community, not national, law in order to preclude the destruction of the integrity of Community law through differing national approaches.

It had long been a matter of doubt whether this provision of the Treaty protects an individual who migrates in order to seek work, rather than to take up a job already offered. The Court decided in *R* v *IAT, ex parte Antonissen* (Case C-292/89) that a jobseeker may be a worker, but not indefinitely.

R v *IAT, ex parte Antonissen (Case C-292/89)*
[1991] ECR 1-745, [1991] 2 CMLR 373
Court of Justice of the European Communities

Antonissen, a Belgian, sought to rely on Article 48 of the EC Treaty (now, after amendment, Article 39 EC) to defeat a UK deportation order against him. He had been seeking employment in the UK for more than six months and the Tribunal's view was that he had no Community law rights. *Held* by the European Court:

It is not contrary to the provisions of Community law governing the free movement of workers for the legislation of a Member State to provide that a national of another Member State who entered the first State in order to seek employment may be required to leave the territory of that State (subject to appeal) if he has not found employment there after six months, unless the person concerned provides evidence that he is continuing to seek employment and that he has genuine chances of being engaged.

The equation of genuine jobseeker and 'worker' under Article 39 was confirmed by the Court in *María Martinez Sala* v *Freistaat Bayern* (Case C-85/96) [1998] ECR I-2691.

Notes
1.   The rights conferred by Article 39 apply only to nationals of a Member State, not to non-EC nationals; and only to workers who have actually left their own home State.
2.   In *Morson* v *State of the Netherlands* (Cases 35 & 36/82) [1982] ECR 3723, [1983] 2 CMLR 720, the Court held that Dutch nationals working in The Netherlands had no rights under Article 48 of the EC Treaty (now, after

amendment, Article 39 EC) and therefore could not rely on the Community secondary legislation discussed below to protect their Surinamese mothers who wished to join them. By contrast, in *R v IAT and Singh, ex parte Secretary of State* (Case C-370/90) [1992] ECR I-4265, [1992] 3 CMLR 358, a British national was able to rely on Community law to protect an Indian spouse when returning to the UK after working in Germany.

What if an individual left his or her home State to take up part-time work in another State, but primarily as a ruse to obtain protection for a family member who is a non-EC national? Might 'motive' be relevant to deciding whether or not that individual has any rights under Article 39? The Court is eager to remove motive from the definition in order to provide an objective test which is capable of uniform application. A broad interpretation of 'worker' is envisaged. But has the Court excluded a subjective element from the definition? Contrast para. 17 in *Levin* (Case 53/81) with para. 21. See also *Lair* (Case 39/86), *Brown* (Case 197/86) and other cases mentioned at p. 373 below.

3. It is tempting to suppose that these definitional issues are swept away by the broader notion of citizenship of the Union introduced by the Maastricht Treaty (p. 343 above). However, Articles 17(2) and 18(1), in particular, indicate that this is not so. Moreover, in Cases C-64/96 and C-65/96 *Land Nordrhein-Westfalen* v *Uecker, Jacquet* [1997] ECR I-3171, the Court ruled that the insertion of these provisions is not intended to extend the material scope of the Treaty to internal situations with no link to Community law.

(B) TO WHAT ADVANTAGES IS THE WORKER ENTITLED?

Directive 68/360 sets out more fully than Article 39 the right of entry and residence, and amplifies several procedural aspects of the right of free movement.

Council Directive 68/360/EEC on the Abolition of Restrictions on Movement and Residence within the Community for Workers of Member States and their Families, Articles 1-10 (1968) OJ (Special Edition) (II) 485

Article 1
Member States shall, acting as provided in this Directive, abolish restrictions on the movement and residence of nationals of the said States and of members of their families to whom Regulation (EEC) No 1612/68 applies.

Article 2
1. Member States shall grant the nationals referred to in Article 1 the right to leave their territory in order to take up activities as employed persons and to pursue such activities in the territory of another Member State. Such right shall be exercised simply on production of a valid identity card or passport. Members of the family shall enjoy the same right as the national on whom they are dependent.

2. Member States shall, acting in accordance with their laws, issue to such nationals, or renew, an identity card or passport, which shall state in particular the holder's nationality.

3. The passport must be valid at least for all Member States and for countries through which the holder must pass when travelling between Member States. Where a passport is the only document on which the holder may lawfully leave the country, its period of validity shall be not less than five years.

4. Member States may not demand from the nationals referred to in Article 1 any exit visa or any equivalent document.

Article 3

1. Member States shall allow the persons referred to in Article 1 to enter their territory simply on production of a valid identity card or passport.

2. No entry visa or equivalent document may be demanded save from members of the family who are not nationals of a Member State. Member States shall accord to such persons every facility for obtaining any necessary visas.

Article 4

1. Member States shall grant the right of residence in their territory to the persons referred to in Article 1 who are able to produce the documents listed in paragraph 3.

2. As proof of the right of residence, a document entitled 'Residence Permit for a National of a Member State of the EEC' shall be issued. This document must include a statement that it has been issued pursuant to Regulation (EEC) No 1612/68 and to the measures taken by the Member States for the implementation of the present Directive. The text of such statement is given in the Annex to this Directive.

3. For the issue of a Residence Permit for a National of a Member State of the EEC, Member States may require only the production of the following documents;
   —by the worker:
   (a)   the document with which he entered their territory;
   (b)   a confirmation of engagement from the employer or a certificate of employment;
   —by the members of the worker's family:
   (c)   the document with which they entered the territory;
   (d)   a document issued by the competent authority of the State of origin or the State whence they came, proving their relationship;
   (e)   in the cases referred to in Article 10(1) and (2) of Regulation (EEC) No 1612/68, a document issued by the competent authority of the State of origin or the State whence they came, testifying that they are dependent on the worker or that they live under his roof in such country.

4. A member of the family who is not a national of a Member State shall be issued with a residence document which shall have the same validity as that issued to the worker on whom he is dependent.

Article 5

Completion of the formalities for obtaining a residence permit shall not hinder the immediate beginning of employment under a contract concluded by the applicants.

Article 6

1. The residence permit:
   (a)   must be valid throughout the territory of the Member State which issued it;
   (b)   must be valid for at least five years from the date of issue and be automatically renewable.

2. Breaks in residence not exceeding six consecutive months and absence on military service shall not affect the validity of a residence permit.

3.   Where a worker is employed for a period exceeding three months but not exceeding a year in the service of an employer in the host State or in the employ of a person providing services, the host Member State shall issue him a temporary residence permit, the validity of which may be limited to the expected period of the employment.

Subject to the provisions of Article 8(1)(c), a temporary residence permit shall be issued also to a seasonal worker employed for a period of more than three months. The period of employment must be shown in the documents referred to in paragraph 4(3)(b).

Article 7

1.   A valid residence permit may not be withdrawn from a worker solely on the grounds that he is no longer in employment, either because he is temporarily incapable of work as a result of illness or accident, or because he is involuntarily unemployed, this being duly confirmed by the competent employment office.

2.   When the residence permit is renewed for the first time, the period of residence may be restricted, but not to less than twelve months, where the worker has been involuntarily unemployed in the Member State for more than twelve consecutive months.

Article 8

1.   Member States shall, without issuing a residence permit, recognise the right of residence in their territory of:

(a)   a worker pursuing an activity as an employed person, where the activity is not expected to last for more than three months. The document with which the person concerned entered the territory and a statement by the employer on the expected duration of the employment shall be sufficient to cover his stay; a statement by the employer shall not, however, be required in the case of workers coming within the provisions of the Council Directive of 25 February 1964 on the attainment of freedom of establishment and freedom to provide services in respect of the activities of intermediaries in commerce, industry and small craft industries.

(b)   a worker who, while having his residence in the territory of a Member State to which he returns as a rule, each day or at least once a week, is employed in the territory of another Member State. The competent authority of the State where he is employed may issue such worker with a special permit valid for five years and automatically renewable;

(c)   a seasonal worker who holds a contract of employment stamped by the competent authority of the Member State on whose territory he has come to pursue his activity.

2.   In all cases referred to in paragraph 1, the competent authorities of the host Member State may require the worker to report his presence in the territory.

Article 9

1.   The residence documents granted to nationals of a Member State of the EEC referred to in this Directive shall be issued and renewed free of charge or on payment of an amount not exceeding the dues and taxes charged for the issue of identity cards to nationals.

2.   The visa referred to in Article 3(2) and the stamp referred to in Article 8(1)(c) shall be free of charge.

3.   Member States shall take the necessary steps to simplify as much as possible the formalities and procedure for obtaining the documents mentioned in paragraph 1.

Article 10
Member States shall not derogate from the provisions of this Directive save on grounds of public policy, public security or public health.

Note
Some confusion has arisen as a result of the reference to a residence permit (Article 4). The Court has been obliged to explain that documents may be required of migrant workers; but that they are evidence of rights, not their source. Any penalties for failure to acquire a permit must accordingly respect the principle of proportionality.

R v Pieck (Case 157/79)
[1980] ECR 2171; [1980] 3 CMLR 220
Court of Justice of the European Communities

Pieck, a Dutch national working in Wales, was charged with overstaying his six-month limited leave to remain in the UK. He held no residence permit. The Pontypridd magistrates' court made a preliminary reference in respect of the implications of EC law. The Court dealt with the grant of limited leave by reference to existing case law.

[13] The Court has already stated in its judgment of 14 July 1977 in Case 8/77 *Sagulo, Brenca and Bakhouche* [1977] ECR 1495 that the issue of a special residence document provided for in Article 4 above-mentioned has only a declaratory effect and that, for aliens to whom Article 48 of the Treaty or parallel provisions give rights, it cannot be assimilated to a residence permit such as is prescribed for aliens in general, in connexion with the issue of which the national authorities have a discretion. The Court went on to say that a Member State may not therefore require from a person enjoying the protection of Community law that he should possess a general residence permit instead of the document provided for in Article 4 of Directive No 68/360.

On penalties for non-conformity with formalities:

[18] Among the penalties attaching to a failure to comply with the formalities required as proof of the right of residence of a worker enjoying the protection of Community law, deportation is certainly incompatible with the provisions of the Treaty since, as the Court has already confirmed in other cases, such a measure negates the very right conferred and guaranteed by the Treaty.

[19] As regards other penalties such as fines and imprisonment, whilst the national authorities are entitled to impose penalties in respect of failure to comply with the terms of provisions relating to residence permits which are comparable to those attaching to minor offences by nationals, they are not justified in imposing a penalty so disproportionate to the gravity of the infringement that it becomes an obstacle to the free movement of persons. This would be especially so if that penalty included imprisonment.

[20] It follows that the failure on the part of a national of a Member State of the Community, to whom the rules on freedom of movement for workers apply, to obtain the special residence permit prescribed in Article 4 of Directive No 68/360 may not be punished by a recommendation for deportation or by measures which go as far as imprisonment.

Note
See also *Messner* (Case C-265/88) [1989] ECR 4209, [1991] 2 CMLR 545;
Commission v *Netherlands* (Case C-68/89) [1991] ECR I-2637; and Case
C-378/97 *Florius Ariel Wijsenbeck*, judgment of 21 September 1999 (in which
the effect of what is now Article 18 EC was considered).

Regulation 1612/68 ensures that the migrant worker, once settled in the
host State, shall enjoy non-discriminatory treatment in relation to access to
employment and provision of employment-related benefits. Family members
are also covered. These provisions are wide-ranging on their face, but have
been taken still further by the Court.

**Council Regulation 1612/68 on Freedom of Movement for Workers
within the Community, Articles 1-12**
(1968) OJ (Special Edition) (II) 475

TITLE I   ELIGIBILITY FOR EMPLOYMENT

Article 1
1.   Any national of a Member State, shall, irrespective of his place of residence,
have the right to take up an activity as an employed person, and to pursue such
activity, within the territory of another Member State in accordance with the
provisions laid down by law, regulation or administrative action governing the
employment of nationals of that State.
2.   He shall, in particular, have the right to take up available employment in the
territory of another Member State with the same priority as nationals of the State.

Article 2
Any national of a Member State and any employer pursuing an activity in the territory
of a Member State may exchange their applications for and offers of employment, and
may conclude and perform contracts of employment in accordance with the provisions
in force laid down by law, regulation or administrative action, without any discrimination resulting therefrom.

Article 3
1.   Under this Regulation, provisions laid down by law, regulation or administrative action or administrative practices of a Member State shall not apply:
—   where they limit application for and offers of employment, or the right of
foreign nationals to take up and pursue employment or subject these to conditions not
applicable in respect of their own nationals; or
—   where, though applicable irrespective of nationality, their exclusive or principal
aim or effect is to keep nationals of other Member States away from the employment
offered.
This provision shall not apply to conditions relating to linguistic knowledge required
by reason of the nature of the post to be filled.
2.   There shall be included in particular among the provisions or practices of a
Member State referred to in the first subparagraph of paragraph 1 those which:
(a)   prescribe a special recruitment procedure for foreign nationals;
(b)   limit or restrict the advertising of vacancies in the press or through any other
medium or subject it to conditions other than those applicable in respect of employers
pursuing their activities in the territory of that Member State;

(c)   subject eligibility for employment to conditions of registration with employment offices or impede recruitment of individual workers, where persons who do not
reside in the territory of that State are concerned.

Article 4

1.   Provisions laid down by law, regulation or administrative action of the Member
States which restrict by number or percentage the employment of foreign nationals in
any undertaking, branch of activity or region, or at a national level, shall not apply to
nationals of the other Member States.

2.   When in a Member State the granting of any benefit to undertakings is subject
to a minimum percentage of national workers being employed, nationals of the other
Member States shall be counted as national workers, subject to the provisions of the
Council Directive of 15 October 1963.

Article 5

A national of a Member State who seeks employment in the territory of another
Member State shall receive the same assistance there as that afforded by the
employment offices in that State to their own nationals seeking employment.

Article 6

1.   The engagement and recruitment of a national of one Member State for a post
in another Member State shall not depend on medical, vocational or other criteria
which are discriminatory on grounds of nationality by comparison with those applied
to nationals of the other Member State who wish to pursue the same activity.

2.   Nevertheless, a national who holds an offer in his name from an employer in a
Member State other than that of which he is a national may have to undergo a vocational
test, if the employer expressly requests this when making his offer of employment.

TITLE II   EMPLOYMENT AND EQUALITY OF TREATMENT

Article 7

1.   A worker who is a national of a Member State may not, in the territory of another
Member State, be treated differently from national workers by reason of his nationality in
respect of any conditions of employment and work, in particular as regards remuneration, dismissal, and should he become unemployed, reinstatement or re-employment;

2.   He shall enjoy the same social and tax advantages as national workers.

3.   He shall also, by virtue of the same right and under the same conditions as
national workers, have access to training in vocational schools and retraining centres.

4.   Any clause of a collective or individual agreement or of any other collective
regulation concerning eligibility for employment, employment, remuneration and
other conditions of work or dismissal shall be null and void in so far as it lays down
or authorises discriminatory conditions in respect of workers who are nationals of the
other Member States.

Article 8

1.   A worker who is a national of a Member State and who is employed in the
territory of another Member State shall enjoy equality of treatment as regards
membership of trade unions and the exercise of rights attaching thereto, including the
right to vote and to be eligible for the administration or management posts of a trade
union; he may be excluded from taking part in the management of bodies governed
by public law and from holding an office governed by public law. Furthermore, he
shall have the right of eligibility for workers' representative bodies in the undertaking.
The provisions of this Article shall not affect laws or regulations in certain Member

States which grant more extensive rights to workers coming from the other Member States.

2.   This Article shall be reviewed by the Council on the basis of a proposal from the Commission which shall be submitted within not more than two years.

Article 9
1.   A worker who is a national of a Member State and who is employed in the territory of another Member State shall enjoy all the rights and benefits accorded to national workers in matters of housing, including ownership of the housing he needs.

2.   Such worker may, with the same right as nationals, put his name down on the housing lists in the region in which he is employed, where such lists exist; he shall enjoy the resultant benefits and priorities.

If his family has remained in the country whence he came, they shall be considered for this purpose as residing in the said region, where national workers benefit from a similar presumption.

TITLE III   WORKERS' FAMILIES

Article 10
1.   The following shall, irrespective of their nationality, have the right to install themselves with a worker who is a national of one Member State and who is employed in the territory of another Member State:

(a)   his spouse and their descendants who are under the age of 21 years or are dependants;

(b)   dependent relatives in the ascending line of the worker and his spouse.

2.   Member States shall facilitate the admission of any member of the family not coming within the provisions of paragraph 1 if dependent on the worker referred to above or living under his roof in the country whence he comes.

3.   For the purposes of paragraphs 1 and 2, the worker must have available for his family housing considered as normal for national workers in the region where he is employed; this provision, however must not give rise to discrimination between national workers and workers from the other Member States.

Article 11
Where a national of a Member State is pursuing an activity as an employed or self-employed person in the territory of another Member State, his spouse and those of the children who are under the age of 21 years or dependent on him shall have the right to take up any activity as an employed person throughout the territory of that same State, even if they are not nationals of any Member State.

Article 12
The children of a national of a Member State who is or has been employed in the territory of another Member State shall be admitted to that State's general education-al, apprenticeship and vocational training courses under the same conditions as the nationals of that State, if such children are residing in its territory.

Member States shall encourage all efforts to enable such children to attend these courses under the best possible conditions.

Note
Article 7(2) of the Regulation provides a striking example of a provision which has been developed by the Court in a perhaps unexpectedly broad manner.

Cristini v SNCF (Case 32/75)
[1975] ECR 1085; [1975] 1 CMLR 573
Court of Justice of the European Communities

SNCF, the French railway company, offered a fare reduction for large families. Cristini, an Italian national resident in France and the widow of an Italian national who had worked in France, was refused the reduction card on the basis of nationality. SNCF argued that Article 7(2) of Regulation 1612/68 covered only advantages connected with the contract of employment. The Court did not agree.

[12]   . . . [T]he reference to 'social advantages' in Article 7(2) cannot be interpreted restrictively.

[13]   It therefore follows that, in view of the equality of treatment which the provision seeks to achieve, the substantive area of application must be delineated so as to include all social and tax advantages, whether or not attached to the contract of employment, such as reductions in fares for large families.

[14]   It then becomes necessary to examine whether such an advantage must be granted to the widow and children after the death of the migrant worker when the national law provides that, at the request of the head of the family, each member of the family shall be issued with an identity card entitling him or her to the reduction.

[15]   If the widow and infant children of a national of the Member State in question are entitled to such cards provided that the request had been made by the father before his death, the same must apply where the deceased father was a migrant worker and a national of another Member State.

[16]   It would be contrary to the purpose and the spirit of the Community rules on freedom of movement for workers to deprive the survivors of such a benefit following the death of the worker whilst granting the same benefit to the survivors of a national.

[17]   In this respect it is important to note the provisions of Regulation (EEC) No 1251/70 of the Commission on the right of workers to remain in the territory of a Member State after having been employed in that State.

[18]   Article 3(1) of that regulation provides that if a worker has acquired the right to remain in the territory of a Member State, the members of his family who are residing with him shall be entitled to remain there after his death, whilst Article 7 provides that: 'The right to equality of treatment, established by Council Regulation (EEC) No 1612/68, shall apply also to persons coming under the provisions of this regulation'.

[19]   Accordingly the answer to the question should be that Article 7(2) of Regulation (EEC) No 1612/68 of the Council must be interpreted as meaning that the social advantages referred to by that provision include fares reduction cards issued by a national railway authority to large families and that this applies, even if the said advantage is only sought after the worker's death, to the benefit of his family remaining in the same Member State.

Note

Regulation 1251/70 ((1970) OJ (Special Edition) (II) 402), referred to in the judgment, confers rights on the worker to remain in the host State after retirement.

There is a dual focus to the Court's broad interpretation of Article 7(2) of Regulation 1612/68. On one level, the Court's actions may be seen as intruding on a State's social welfare system, by guaranteeing the individual 'social and tax advantages' which operate beyond the employment relationship and which affect on the wider sphere of life as a citizen. Yet at another level the conferral of such benefits may be presented as an instrument of market integration. Without the lure of extended equal treatment, labour mobility would in practice prove an illusion. This is a controversial debate both in its substance – *should* the Community touch on welfare laws? – and in its institutional aspects – is this the job of the Court or the legislature? This theme is readdressed more generally in Chapter 15.

Article 7(2) of Regulation 1612/68 ensures non-discrimination. It does not confer an absolute right to a rail concession; it confers a right to such provision on terms which do not discriminate according to nationality. So in principle the migrant worker cannot enjoy rights above the ceiling of national provision. If further rights are to be made available, Community legislation must be passed. This re-opens the controversial debate about the proper scope of Community social legislation.

The point made at p. 350 above bears repetition. The notion of Citizenship of the Union is as yet inadequately developed to resolve these issues. However, the Commission has expressed an intention to pursue the recasting of secondary legislation in this area in order to reflect and advance the process of removal of internal frontiers and the creation of Citizenship. This was first aired in COM (93) 545. Subsequently, the High Level Group on the Free Movement of Persons, chaired by Simone Veil, which reported to the Commission in March 1997, concluded that the essential legislation was in place but advocated, *inter alia*, better cooperation between Member States in securing the effective application of the rules and improved dissemination of information about individual rights. Consolidation of relevant legislation was supported as a means of realising these objectives. The Commission's *Action Plan for the Single Market*, submitted to and endorsed by the European Council in Amsterdam in July 1997 (p. 204 above), confirms a commitment to proposing up-dating of legislation in this area. Concern to improve awareness of these legal rules is also visible in the *Strategy for Europe's Internal Market*, published by the Commission in November 1999 (p. 207 above). The Commission continues to accompany presentation of its thinking in these realms with the rhetoric of Union Citizenship (on which see further p. 398 below), and it places great emphasis on increasing publicity for the pattern of Community rules applicable to individual migrants (see http://citizens.eu.int).

The Community also has legislation on social security provision. These measures are based on perceptions similar to those underlying Regulation

1612/68. They are, however, measures of extraordinary complexity, and are best left for discussion in specialist works.

(C) EXCEPTIONS

Article 39(3) and (4) (p. 345 above) contain derogations from the basic principle of free movement. In common with all provisions which are hostile to free movement, these clauses are to be interpreted narrowly. This approach is confirmed by Directive 64/221 which elaborates the substance and procedure of derogation under the third paragraph.

Council Directive 64/221/EEC on the Coordination of Special Measures concerning the Movement and Residence of Foreign Nationals which are Justified on Grounds of Public Policy, Public Security or Public Health, Articles 1-10
(1963-64) OJ (Special Edition) 117

Article 1
1. The provisions of this Directive shall apply to any national of a Member State who resides in or travels to another Member State of the Community, either in order to pursue an activity as an employed or self-employed person, or as a recipient of services.
2. These provisions shall apply also to the spouse and to members of the family who come within the provisions of the regulations and directives adopted in this field in pursuance of the Treaty.

Article 2
1. This Directive relates to all measures concerning entry into their territory, issue or renewal of residence permits, or expulsion from their territory, taken by Member States on grounds of public policy, public security or public health.
2. Such grounds shall not be invoked to service economic ends.

Article 3
1. Measures taken on grounds of public policy or of public security shall be based exclusively on the personal conduct of the individual concerned.
2. Previous criminal convictions shall not in themselves constitute grounds for the taking of such measures.
3. Expiry of the identity card or passport used by the person concerned to enter the host country and to obtain a residence permit shall not justify expulsion from the territory.
4. The State which issued the identity card or passport shall allow the holder of such document to re-enter its territory without any formality even if the document is no longer valid or the nationality of the holder is in dispute.

Article 4
1. The only diseases or disabilities justifying refusal of entry into a territory or refusal to issue a first residence permit shall be those listed in the Annex to this Directive.
2. Diseases or disabilities occurring after a first residence permit has been issued shall not justify refusal to renew the residence permit or expulsion from the territory.

3. Member States shall not introduce new provisions or practices which are more restrictive than those in force at the date of notification of this Directive.

Article 5

1. A decision to grant or to refuse a first residence permit shall be taken as soon as possible and in any event not later than six months from the date of application for the permit.

The person concerned shall be allowed to remain temporarily in the territory pending a decision either to grant or to refuse a residence permit.

2. The host country may, in cases where this is considered essential, request the Member State of origin of the applicant, and if need be other Member States, to provide information concerning any previous police record. Such enquiries shall not be made as a matter of routine. The Member State consulted shall give its reply within two months.

Article 6

The person concerned shall be informed of the grounds of public policy, public security, or public health upon which the decision taken in his case is based, unless this is contrary to the interests of the security of the State involved.

Article 7

The person concerned shall be officially notified of any decision to refuse the issue or renewal of a residence permit or to expel him from the territory. The period allowed for leaving the territory shall be stated in this notification. Save in cases of urgency, this period shall be not less than fifteen days if the person concerned has not yet been granted a residence permit and not less than one month in all other cases.

Article 8

The person concerned shall have the same legal remedies in respect of any decision concerning entry, or refusing the issue or renewal of a residence permit, or ordering expulsion from the territory, as are available to nationals of the State concerned in respect of acts of the administration.

Article 9

1. Where there is no right of appeal to a court of law, or where such appeal may be only in respect the legal validity of the decision, or where the appeal cannot have suspensory effect, a decision refusing renewal of a residence permit or ordering the expulsion of the holder of a residence permit from the territory shall not be taken by the administrative authority, save in cases of urgency, until an opinion has been obtained from a competent authority of the host country before which the person concerned enjoys such rights of defence and of assistance or representation as the domestic law of that country provides for.

This authority shall not be the same as that empowered to take the decision refusing renewal of the residence permit or ordering expulsion.

2. Any decision refusing the issue of a first residence permit or ordering expulsion of the person concerned before the issue of the permit shall, where that person so requests, be referred for consideration to the authority whose prior opinion is required under paragraph I. The person concerned shall then be entitled to submit his defence in person, except where this would be contrary to the interests of national security.

Article 10

1. Member States shall within six months of notification of this Directive put into force the measures necessary to comply with its provisions and shall forthwith inform the Commission thereof.

2.   Member States shall ensure that the texts of the main provisions of national law which they adopt in the field governed by this Directive are communicated to the Commission.

Note
The following case was one of the earliest involving the UK to reach the Court after accession.

Van Duyn v Home Office (Case 41/74)
[1974] ECR 1337; [1975] 1 CMLR 1
Court of Justice of the European Communities

Ms Van Duyn, a Dutch national, was refused leave to enter the UK to work for the Church of Scientology because the UK Government considered the Church's activities to be socially harmful. Ms Van Duyn's reliance on Community law led to a preliminary reference by the High Court. The European Court first held Article 48 of the EC Treaty (now, after amendment, Article 39 EC) and Article 3(1) of Directive 64/221 (above) directly effective and accordingly enforceable before national courts by private individuals. The Court then turned to the substance of the case.

[17]   It is necessary, first, to consider whether association with a body or an organization can in itself constitute personal conduct within the meaning of Article 3 of Directive No 64/221. Although a person's past association cannot in general, justify a decision refusing him the right to move freely within the Community, it is nevertheless the case that present association, which reflects participation in the activities of the body or of the organization as well as identification with its aims and its designs, may be considered a voluntary act of the person concerned and, consequently, as part of his personal conduct within the meaning of the provision cited.

[18]   This third question further raises the problem of what importance must be attributed to the fact that the activities of the organization in question, which are considered by the Member State as contrary to the public good are not however prohibited by national law. It should be emphasized that the concept of public policy in the context of the Community and where, in particular, it is used as a justification for derogating from the fundamental principle of freedom of movement for workers, must be interpreted strictly, so that its scope cannot be determined unilaterally by each Member State without being subject to control by the institutions of the Community. Nevertheless the particular circumstances justifying recourse to the concept of public policy may vary from one country to another and from one period to another, and it is therefore necessary in this matter to allow the competent national authorities an area of discretion within the limits imposed by the Treaty.

[19]   It follows from the above that where the competent authorities of a Member State have clearly defined their standpoint as regards the activities of a particular organization and where, considering it to be socially harmful, they have taken administrative measures to counteract these activities, the Member State cannot be required, before it can rely on the concept of public policy, to make such activities unlawful, if recourse to such a measure is not thought appropriate in the circumstances.

[20]   The question raises finally the problem of whether a Member State is entitled, on grounds of public policy, to prevent a national of another Member State from taking gainful employment within its territory with a body or organization, it being the case that no similar restriction is placed upon its own nationals.

[21]   In this connexion, the Treaty, while enshrining the principle of freedom of movement for workers without any discrimination on grounds of nationality, admits, in Article 48 (3), limitations justified on grounds of public policy, public security or public health to the rights deriving from this principle. Under the terms of the provision cited above, the right to accept offers of employment actually made, the right to move freely within the territory of Member States for this purpose, and the right to stay in a Member State for the purpose of employment are, among others, all subject to such limitations. Consequently, the effect of such limitations, when they apply, is that leave to enter the territory of a Member State and the right to reside there may be refused to a national of another Member State.

[22]   Furthermore, it is a principle of international law, which the EEC Treaty cannot be assumed to disregard in the relations between Member States, that a State is precluded from refusing its own nationals the right of entry or residence.

[23]   It follows that a Member State, for reasons of public policy, can, where it deems necessary, refuse a national of another Member State the benefit of the principle of freedom of movement for workers in a case where such a national proposes to take up a particular offer of employment even though the Member State does not place a similar restriction upon its own nationals.

[24]   Accordingly, the reply to the third question must be that Article 48 of the EEC Treaty and Article 3(1) of Directive No 64/221 are to be interpreted as meaning that a Member State, in imposing restrictions justified on grounds of public policy, is entitled to take into account, as a matter of personal conduct of the individual concerned, the fact that the individual is associated with some body or organization the activities of which the Member State considers socially harmful but which are not unlawful in that State, despite the fact that no restriction is placed upon nationals of the said Member State who wish to take similar employment with these same bodies or organizations.

Note

In both the following decisions, the Court adopted a narrow interpretation of the legitimate scope of Member State action against individual workers.

R v Bouchereau (Case 30/77)
[1977] ECR 1999; [1977] 2 CMLR 800
Court of Justice of the European Communities

Bouchereau, a French national working in England, was convicted of unlawful possession of drugs. He fought proposed deportation using Community law. Could the UK authorities show that his case fell within the exception then located in Article 48(3), now Article 39(3)? The matter reached the Court by way of a preliminary reference. The Court examined the relevance of previous criminal convictions.

[27]   The terms of Article 3(2) of the directive, which states that 'previous criminal convictions shall not in themselves constitute grounds for the taking of such measures' must be understood as requiring the national authorities to carry out a specific appraisal from the point of view of the interests inherent in protecting the requirements of public policy, which does not necessarily coincide with the appraisals which formed the basis of the criminal conviction.

[28]   The existence of a previous criminal conviction can, therefore, only be taken into account in so far as the circumstances which gave rise to that conviction are evidence of personal conduct constituting a present threat to the requirements of public policy.

[29]   Although, in general, a finding that such a threat exists implies the existence in the individual concerned of a propensity to act in the same way in the future, it is possible that past conduct alone may constitute such a threat to the requirements of public policy.

The Court then proceeded to consider the notion of 'public policy' mentioned in Article 48(3) of the EC Treaty (now, after amendment, Article 39(3) EC).

[33]   In its judgment of 4 December 1974 (Case 41/74, *Van Duyn* v *Home Office*, [1974] ECR 1337, at p. 1350) the Court emphasized that the concept of public policy in the context of the Community and where, in particular, it is used as a justification for derogating from the fundamental principle of freedom of movement for workers, must be interpreted strictly, so that its scope cannot be determined unilaterally by each Member State without being subject to control by the institutions of the Community.

[34]   Nevertheless, it is stated in the same judgment that the particular circumstances justifying recourse to the concept of public policy may vary from one country to another and from one period to another and it is therefore necessary in this matter to allow the competent national authorities an area of discretion within the limits imposed by the Treaty and the provisions adopted for its implementation.

[35]   In so far as it may justify certain restrictions on the free movement of persons subject to Community law, recourse by a national authority to the concept of public policy presupposes, in any event, the existence, in addition to the perturbation of the social order which any infringement of the law involves, of a genuine and sufficiently serious threat to the requirements of public policy affecting one of the fundamental interests of society.

Adoui and Cornuaille v *Belgian State (Cases 115 & 116/81)*
[1982] ECR 1665; [1982] 3 CMLR 631
Court of Justice of the European Communities

The applicants were French nationals refused permission to reside in Belgium on public policy grounds. The Court delicately described them as waitresses in a Liège bar which was considered 'suspect from the point of view of morals'. It was more direct in the body of the judgment.

[6]   Those questions are motivated by the fact that prostitution as such is not prohibited by Belgian legislation, although the Law does prohibit certain incidental

activities, which are particularly harmful from the social point of view, such as the exploitation of prostitution by third parties and various forms of incitement to debauchery.

[7]   The reservations contained in Articles 48 and 56 of the EEC Treaty permit Member States to adopt, with respect to the nationals of other Member States and on the grounds specified in those provisions, in particular grounds justified by the requirements of public policy, measures which they cannot apply to their own nationals, inasmuch as they have no authority to expel the latter from the national territory or to deny them access thereto. Although that difference of treatment, which bears upon the nature of the measures available, must therefore be allowed, it must nevertheless be stressed that, in a Member State, the authority empowered to adopt such measures must not base the exercise of its powers on assessments of certain conduct which would have the effect of applying an arbitrary distinction to the detriment of nationals of other Member States.

[8]   It should be noted in that regard that reliance by a national authority upon the concept of public policy presupposes, as the Court held in its judgment of 27 October 1977 in Case 30/77 *Bouchereau* [1977] ECR 1999, the existence of 'a genuine and sufficiently serious threat affecting one of the fundamental interests of society'. Although Community law does not impose upon the Member States a uniform scale of values as regards the assessment of conduct which may be considered as contrary to public policy, it should nevertheless be stated that conduct may not be considered as being of a sufficiently serious nature to justify restrictions on the admission to or residence within the territory of a Member State of a national of another Member State in a case where the former Member State does not adopt, with respect to the same conduct on the part of its own nationals repressive measures or other genuine and effective measures intended to combat such conduct.

[9]   The answer to Questions 1 to 9, 11 and 12 should therefore be that a Member State may not, by virtue of the reservation relating to public policy contained in Articles 48 and 56 of the Treaty, expel a national of another Member State from its territory or refuse him access to its territory by reason of conduct which, when attributable to the former State's own nationals, does not give rise to repressive measures or other genuine and effective measures intended to combat such conduct.

[10]   In the tenth question, the national court asks whether the action taken by a Member State which, 'anxious to remove from its territory prostitutes from a given country because they could promote criminal activities, does so systematically, declaring that their business of prostitution endangers the requirements of public policy and not taking the trouble to consider whether the persons concerned may or may not be suspected of contact with the "underworld", constitutes a measure of a general preventive nature within the meaning of Article 3 of Directive No 64/221.

[11]   It should be noted that Article 3(1) of the directive provides that measures taken on grounds of public policy or of public security are to be based exclusively on the personal conduct of the individual concerned. In that regard it is sufficient to refer to the judgment of 26 February 1975 in Case 67/74 *Bonsignore* [1975] ECR 297, in which the Court held that 'measures adopted on grounds of public policy and for the maintenance of public security against the nationals of Member States of the Community cannot be justified on grounds extraneous to the individual case, as is shown in particular by the requirements set out in paragraph (1) that 'only' the 'personal conduct' of those affected by the measures is to be regarded as determinative'.

Question
There are two aspects of *Van Duyn* (Case 41/74) (p. 361 above) which are of particular interest in the present context: (i) its discussion of the nature of 'personal conduct', mentioned in Article 3(1) of Directive 64/221; (ii) its approach to the competence of Member States to control that conduct, taking account of how nationals behaving in a similar fashion would be treated. Explain how the Court has developed a more rigorous stance since *Van Duyn*.

Notes
1. These rights are frequently invoked at relatively low levels within national legal systems. Several decisions of the Immigration Appeal Tribunal in the UK demonstrate a healthy appreciation of the implications of Community law. In *Monteil* v *Secretary of State* [1984] 1 CMLR 264, the Tribunal ruled against the deportation of a French national who had been convicted of criminal offences and had spent time in gaol. It was shown that he had been cured of the illness which had led to his crimes, and that accordingly he posed no sufficient present threat to society.
2. It remains to be seen how the Article 39(3) derogations can be applied in practice in the light of the Article 14 commitment to an area without internal frontiers. The intimate relationship between the EC rules on free movement and action in common under the EU's 'third pillar' (p. 13 above) in, *inter alia*, asylum policy, immigration policy and police cooperation was acknowledged at Maastricht by the 'transfer' procedure between what were then Article K.9 TEU and Article 100c EC. This remained unused. Partly in consequence of dissatisfaction with the progress made under structures fashioned at Maastricht, the Member States agreed at Amsterdam to adjust the legal framework in favour of increased 'communitiarization' of the material relevant to securing the free movement of persons. The EC Treaty post-Amsterdam contains a Title on 'Visas, asylum, immigration and other policies related to free movement of persons' which is dedicated to the progressive establishment of 'an area of freedom, security and justice'. This is Title IV and comprises Articles 61–69 EC. It is set out and discussed in Chapter 5, p. 192 above. This arrangement casts further doubt on the role in practice of Article 39(3).

Question
Ken, a British national, travels to Belgium with his aged grandmother. He takes up part-time work in a cafe, where he earns below the national minimum wage. He takes part in an anti-racist march organised by a group which, while not illegal in Belgium, is nonetheless one on which the authorities have determined to keep a close watch.

The Belgian authorities serve a deportation order on Ken, stating that his wage is too low for him to obtain any rights under Community law. The Belgian authorities contend that in any event Ken's presence in the country is contrary to the public good on the grounds that:

(a)   he is linked to an organisation of which the State disapproves;
(b)   he may be forced to turn to crime to support his relative; and
(c)   it is contrary to public policy to permit undermining of standard wage
rates.

Discuss the relevant principles of Community law.

Note
Article 39(4), the 'public service' exception, has been subjected by the Court
to a parallel narrow interpretation.

Commission v Belgium (Case 149/79)
[1980] ECR 3881; [1981] 2 CMLR 413
Court of Justice of the European Communities

The case involved the restriction to Belgians alone of several posts on
Belgian railways, including trainee drivers, shunters and signallers, and also
posts with the City of Brussels for, *inter alia*, hospital nurses, plumbers and
electricians. The Court's statements of principle included the following,
directed at Article 48(4) of the EC Treaty (now, after amendment, Article
39(4) EC):

[10]   That provision removes from the ambit of Article 48(1) to (3) a series of posts
which involve direct or indirect participation in the exercise of powers conferred by
public law and duties designed to safeguard the general interests of the State or of
other public authorities. Such posts in fact presume on the part of those occupying
them the existence of a special relationship of allegiance to the State and reciprocity
of rights and duties which form the foundation of the bond of nationality.

[11]   The scope of the derogation made by Article 48(4) to the principles of freedom
of movement and equality of treatment laid down in the first three paragraphs of the
article should therefore be determined on the basis of the aim pursued by that article.
However, determining the sphere of application of Article 48(4) raises special
difficulties since in the various Member States authorities acting under powers
conferred by public law have assumed responsibilities of an economic and social
nature or are involved in activities which are not identifiable with the functions which
are typical of the public service yet which by their nature still come under the sphere
of application of the Treaty. In these circumstances the effect of extending the
exception contained in Article 48(4) to posts which, whilst coming under the State or
other organizations governed by public law, still do not involve any association with
tasks belonging to the public service properly so called, would be to remove a
considerable number of posts from the ambit of the principles set out in the Treaty
and to create inequalities between Member States according to the different ways in
which the State and certain sectors of economic life are organized.

[12]   Consequently it is appropriate to examine whether the posts covered by the
action may be associated with the concept of public service within the meaning of
Article 48(4), which requires uniform interpretation and application throughout the
Community. It must be acknowledged that the application of the distinguishing

criteria indicated above gives rise to problems of appraisal and demarcation in specific cases. It follows from the foregoing that such a classification depends on whether or not the posts in question are typical of the specific activities of the public service in so far as the exercise of powers conferred by public law and responsibility for safeguarding the general interests of the State are vested in it.

Note
The Court felt it had insufficient information to rule in the case itself; the follow-up judgment appears at [1982] ECR 1845.

10 FREEDOM OF ESTABLISHMENT AND THE FREE MOVEMENT OF SERVICES: ARTICLES 43 AND 49

(A) THE RIGHTS

Articles 43 and 49 extend the rights of free movement beyond 'workers' to include free movement of individuals who are self-employed and wish to establish themselves in another Member State, or to provide services there. These rights are granted not just to the natural person who wishes to migrate, but also to the legal person – i.e. the company.

Articles 43 and 49 EC

Article 43
Within the framework of the provisions set out below, restrictions on the freedom of establishment of nationals of a Member State in the territory of another Member State shall be prohibited. Such prohibition shall also apply to restrictions on the setting up of agencies, branches or subsidiaries by nationals of any Member State established in the territory of any Member State.

Freedom of establishment shall include the right to take up and pursue activities as self-employed persons and to set up and manage undertakings, in particular companies or firms within the meaning of the second paragraph of Article 48, under the conditions laid down for its own nationals by the law of the country where such establishment is effected, subject to the provisions of the Chapter relating to capital.

Article 49
Within the framework of the provisions set out below, restrictions on freedom to provide services within the Community shall be prohibited in respect of nationals of Member States who are established in a State of the Community other than that of the person for whom the services are intended.

The Council may, acting by a qualified majority on a proposal from the Commission, extend the provisions of the Chapter to nationals of a third country who provide services and who are established within the Community.

Notes
1. The Treaty of Amsterdam effected merely cosmetic changes to these provisions by removing references to the transitional period. On re-numbering (p. 29 above), what are now Articles 43 and 49 replaced what were previously Articles 52 and 59. These numerical games must be borne in mind in reading the pre-Amsterdam material in this chapter.

The distinction between Article 43, the right of establishment, and Article 49, the right to provide services, is rather artificial. The former envisages a more permanent presence in the host Member State than the latter, but at the margin it may be difficult to select the correct classification. Broadly, however, the problem is unlikely to arise in an acute form, because the Court has wisely recognised the common purpose of the provisions and has shown itself prepared to interpret them in parallel fashion. Article 39 too joins in this shared purpose; see, e.g., *Procureur du Roi* v *Royer* (Case 48/75) [1976] ECR 497; *Walrave* v *Association Union Cycliste Internationale* (Case 36/74) [1974] ECR 1405; *Roux* v *Belgian State*, (Case C–363/89) [1991] ECR I-273.

The rights of the migrating individual to non-discriminatory treatment according to nationality are amplified by Directive 73/148 on the Abolition of Restrictions on Movement and Residence within the Community for Nationals of Member States with regard to Establishment and the Provision of Services, Articles 1-8 (1973) OJ L172/14. This measure is analogous to Directive 68/360 applicable to workers (p. 350 above).

2. Directive 75/34 ((1975) (OJ L14/10) confers rights to remain in the host State. It is analogous to Regulation 1251/70, mentioned at p. 358 above. These two Directives are reproduced in Foster's *EC Legislation* (Blackstone Press).

Derogation from the rights is possible in a fashion comparable to Article 39 (p. 359 above); see Articles 45, 46 and 55.

(B) NON-DISCRIMINATION

The following case illustrates the application of the principle of non-discrimination.

Thieffry v *Conseil de l'Ordre des Avocats à la Cour de Paris*
(Case 71/76)
[1977] ECR 765; [1977] 2 CMLR 373
Court of Justice of the European Communities

Thieffry, a Belgian advocate, held a Belgian diploma of Doctor of Laws, recognised by a French university as equivalent to the French licenciate's degree in law. Despite this recognition of equivalence, he was refused entry to the Paris Bar because he held no French diploma of the required level. Thieffry's challenge reached the Court via the preliminary reference procedure (Chapter 4). The Court cited the General Programme for the abolition of restrictions on freedom of establishment, adopted in 1961, and continued:

[15] . . . [F]reedom of establishment, subject to observance of professional rules justified by the general good, is one of the objectives of the Treaty.

[16] In so far as Community law makes no special provision, these objectives may be attained by measures enacted by the Member States, which under Article 5 of the Treaty are bound to take 'all appropriate measures, whether general or particular, to ensure fulfilment of the obligations arising out of this Treaty or resulting from action taken by the institutions of the Community', and to abstain 'from any measure which could jeopardize the attainment of the objectives of this Treaty'.

[17] Consequently, if the freedom of establishment provided for by Article 52 can be ensured in a Member State either under the provisions of the laws and regulations in force, or by virtue of the practices of the public service or of professional bodies, a person subject to Community law cannot be denied the practical benefit of that freedom solely by virtue of the fact that, for a particular profession, the directives provided for by Article 57 of the Treaty have not yet been adopted.

[18] Since the practical enjoyment of freedom of establishment can thus in certain circumstances depend upon national practice or legislation, it is incumbent upon the competent public authorities – including legally recognized professional bodies – to ensure that such practice or legislation is applied in accordance with the objective defined by the provisions of the Treaty relating to freedom of establishment.

[19] In particular, there is an unjustified restriction on that freedom where, in a Member State, admission to a particular profession is refused to a person covered by the Treaty who holds a diploma which has been recognized as an equivalent qualification by the competent authority of the country of establishment and who furthermore has fulfilled the specific conditions regarding professional training in force in that country, solely by reason of the fact that the person concerned does not possess the national diploma corresponding to the diploma which he holds and which has been recognized as an equivalent qualification.

The Court was accordingly able to conclude, in terms obviously favourable to Thieffry:

[27] In these circumstances, the answer to the question referred to the Court should be that when a national of one Member State desirous of exercising a professional activity such as the profession of advocate in another Member State has obtained a diploma in his country of origin which has been recognized as an equivalent qualification by the competent authority under the legislation of the country of establishment and which has thus enabled him to sit and pass the special qualifying examination for the profession in question, the act of demanding the national diploma prescribed by the legislation of the country of establishment constitutes, even in the absence of the directives provided for in Article 57, a restriction incompatible with the freedom of establishment guaranteed by Article 52 of the Treaty.

Notes
1.　A similar approach had been taken in *Reyners v Belgian State* (Case 2/74) [1974] ECR 631, [1974] 2 CMLR 305, where the Court insisted that the

principle of non-discrimination had direct effect even in the absence of implementing Directives.

2. The Court has extended the scope of these Treaty Articles in order to accommodate tourists. Tourists are neither self-employed nor providers of services, but they are recipients of services and thus fall within the scope of Article 49.

Cowan v Le Trésor Public (Case 186/87)
[1986] ECR 195
Court of Justice of the European Communities

Mr Cowan, a British national, was attacked and robbed while visiting Paris as a tourist. He was refused criminal injuries compensation by the French authorities because of his nationality. He challenged this refusal using Community law. The matter reached the Court as a preliminary reference. The Court placed great emphasis on the principle of non-discrimination on grounds of nationality under (what was then) Article 7 EEC. It should be noted that this became Article 6 EC after the entry into force of the Maastricht Treaty on European Union and post-Amsterdam it is Article 12 EC.

[14]   Under Article 7 of the Treaty the prohibition of discrimination applies 'within the scope of application of this Treaty' and 'without prejudice to any special provisions contained therein'. This latter expression refers particularly to other provisions of the Treaty in which the application of the general principle set out in that article is given concrete form in respect of specific situations. Examples of that are the provisions concerning free movement of workers, the right of establishment and the freedom to provide services.

[15]   On that last point, in its judgment of 31 January 1984 in Joined Cases 286/82 and 26/83 *Luisi and Carbone* v *Ministero del Tesoro* [1984] ECR 377, the Court held that the freedom to provide services includes the freedom for the recipients of services to go to another Member State in order to receive a service there, without being obstructed by restrictions, and that tourists, among others, must be regarded as recipients of services.

[16]   At the hearing the French Government submitted that as Community law now stands a recipient of services may not rely on the prohibition of discrimination to the extent that the national law at issue does not create any barrier to freedom of movement. A provision such as that at issue in the main proceedings, it says, imposes no restrictions in that respect. Furthermore, it concerns a right which is a manifestation of the principle of national solidarity. Such a right presupposes a closer bond with the State than that of a recipient of services, and for that reason it may be restricted to persons who are either nationals of that State or foreign nationals resident on the territory of that State.

[17]   That reasoning cannot be accepted. When Community law guarantees a natural person the freedom to go to another Member State the protection of that person from harm in the Member State in question, on the same basis as that of

nationals and persons residing there, is a corollary of that freedom of movement. It follows that the prohibition of discrimination is applicable to recipients of services within the meaning of the Treaty as regards protection against the risk of assault and the right to obtain financial compensation provided for by national law when that risk materializes. The fact that the compensation at issue is financed by the Public Treasury cannot alter the rules regarding the protection of the rights guaranteed by the Treaty.

[18] The French Government also submitted that compensation such as that at issue in the main proceedings is not subject to the prohibition of discrimination because it falls within the law of criminal procedure, which is not included within the scope of the Treaty.

[19] Although in principle criminal legislation and the rules of criminal procedure, among which the national provision in issue is to be found, are matters for which the Member States are responsible, the Court has consistently held (see *inter alia* the judgment of 11 November 1981 in Case 203/80 *Casati* [1981] ECR 2595) that Community law sets certain limits to their power. Such legislative provisions may not discriminate against persons to whom Community law gives the right to equal treatment or restrict the fundamental freedoms guaranteed by Community law.

[20] In the light of all the foregoing the answer to the question submitted must be that the prohibition of discrimination laid down in particular in Article 7 of the EEC Treaty must be interpreted as meaning that in respect of persons whose freedom to travel to a Member State, in particular as recipients of services, is guaranteed by Community law that State may not make the award of State compensation for harm caused in that State to the victim of an assault resulting in physical injury subject to the condition that he hold a residence permit or be a national of a country which has entered into a reciprocal agreement with that Member State.

Note

Greeting *Cowan* (Case 186/87), F. Mancini has congratulated the Court on 'one of its shrewdest judgments'((1989) 26 CML Rev 595); see also S. Weatherill (1989) 26 CML Rev 563 and (pre-*Cowan*) M. van der Woude and P. Mead (1988) 25 CML Rev 117.

The scope of the principle of non-discrimination, which as *Cowan* (Case 186/87) indicates derives fundamentally from Article 12 EC post-Amsterdam, remains unclear. There is no right to equality in all matters. It seems that the right is tied to the cross-border aspect of the situation. The tourist would not be able to use Article 12 EC in so extensive a manner as the worker is able to rely on Article 7(2) of Regulation 1612/68 (see cases at p. 357 above and consider whether a tourist could claim such rights). The worker is better protected. The Court, then, is able to adapt the material scope of the principle of non-discrimination to reflect varying degrees of social advantage conferred on migrants. This gradation seems unaffected directly by the new status of citizenship of the Union.

In *Gravier v Liège* (Case 293/83) [1985] ECR 593, the Court held that a student wishing to pursue vocational training was covered by Community law by virtue of (what is now, in amended form) Article 150 EC. This then allowed reliance on (what is now) Article 12, which was held to yield the right to non-discriminatory access to the training. In *Brown* (Case 197/86) [1988] ECR 3205, [1988] 3 CMLR 403, an individual working as preparation for university education was held to be entitled to non-discriminatory access to education. But such a person could not rely on Article 7(2) of Regulation 1612/68 in order to claim a maintenance grant to cover the period of study on the same terms as a national of the host State. In *Lair* (Case 39/86) [1988] ECR 3161, [1989] 3 CMLR 545, by contrast, the Court held that a worker whose previous employment was unconnected with a subsequent decision to enrol for university could be entitled to such a grant by virtue of Article 7(2).

The broader competence conferred on the Community by the Maastricht and Amsterdam Treaties in the sphere of education causes a corresponding extension of the impact of Article 12 EC; see K. Lenaerts 'Education in EC Law after Maastricht' (1994) 31 CML Rev 7, also H. Cullen, 'From Migrants to Citizens? EC Policy on Intercultural Education' (1996) 45 ICLQ 109, J. Shaw, 'From the Margins to the Centre: Education and Training Law and Policy' in P. Craig and G. De Búrca, *The Evolution of EU Law* (1999).

Consider also, in the light of the Court's case-by-case approach to acquisition of rights by individuals wishing to migrate, *Centre Public d'Aide Sociale de Courcelles* v *Lebon* (Case 316/85) [1987] ECR 2811; *Commission* v *Italy* (Case 63/86) [1988] ECR 29, [1989] 2 CMLR 601; *Commission* v *Greece* (Case 305/87) [1989] ECR 1461.

Questions
1.   In its case law, the Court is trying to strike a balance between, on the one hand, applying and extending the principle of non-discrimination already set out in both the Treaty and secondary legislation, and, on the other, acknowledging that some areas are dependent on legislative action to extend the law. Has it gone beyond the scope of due judicial restraint?
2.   What is the legal basis of the Commission's action publicised in this Press Release of 14 July 1989:

The Commission scored a success following a complaint by an Irish citizen, resident in Ireland, who was refused admission to pilot training courses organized by British Aerospace because he was not a British citizen. After an approach to British Airways by the Commission, an assurance was received that the company would not discriminate on grounds of nationality or residence against Community citizens wishing to enrol on vocational training courses such as those mentioned or to become British Airways pilots. (Commission Press Release IP (89) 575.)

How might the would-be pilot have sought to protect himself had the Commission refused to assist him?

On horizontal direct effect see *Walrave* v *UCI* (Case 36/74) [1974] ECR 1405 and *URBSFA* v *Bosman* (Case C-415/93) [1995] ECR I-4921.

Note

In 1990 three Directives were adopted which were designed to extend the protection of Community law. These Directives provide a General Right of Residence (Directive 90/364 (1990) OJ L180/26); a Right of Residence for employees and self-employed persons who have ceased their occupational activity (Directive 90/365 (1990) OJ L180/28) and a Right of Residence for Students (Directive 90/366 (1990) OJ L180/30; this Directive was annulled by the Court for choice of incorrect legal base in *Parliament* v *Council* (Case C-295/90) [1992] ECR I-4193, p. 51 above, although the Court ordered that its provisions should remain in force pending the making of a new measure on the correct base which occurred in Directive 93/96 (1993) OJ L317/59). The advances made by these Directives were severely limited by the requirement in each that, according to the Preambles, the 'beneficiaries of the right of residence must not become an unreasonable burden on the public finances of the host Member State'. This considerable limitation is reflected in the specific provisions of each measure. The Commission has issued a report on the implementation of these Directives: COM (99) 127.

(C) BEYOND DISCRIMINATION

The limits of the non-discrimination approach to market integration are significant. Consider *Thieffry* (Case 71/76) (p. 369 above). The key to the application of the principle of non-discrimination was the recognition of Thieffry's Belgian degree as sufficient for French purposes. Without recognition, he could have been excluded from the French lawyer's market. There would have been no nationality discrimination; no one could act as *avocat* without a French degree, irrespective of nationality. (See, e.g., *Procureur de la République* v *Bouchoucha* (Case C-61/89) [1990] ECR I-3551.)

This problem is serious for the professional person, who is faced by the need to meet the professional qualification requirements of the host State; in the absence of cross-recognition as in *Thieffry* (Case 71/76), home State qualifications are unlikely to suffice. Similarly, a company may face serious problems in offering services across borders, because it may find that certain regulations are imposed on all firms supplying services in the host State, but with which it, a non-national firm, does not comply. Articles 43(2) and 50(3) declare that the host State may continue to apply its rules equally to all those active on its market.

It should be immediately apparent that there are potentially close connections with the '*Cassis de Dijon*' case law under Article 28 (Chapter 8). The problem here too arises in relation to national measures which are not discriminatory, but which hinder the exercise of free movement rights. The principles according to which the permissibility of such national measures shall be judged appear to be the same under both Article 28 and Article 49, in so far as both enshrine fundamental Treaty freedoms (*cf* Case C-55/94 *Gebhard*, p. 218 above). However, the Court's scrutiny of regulatory diversity between the Member States in the context of Article 49 has until recently been couched in similar but not identical language to that which occurs under Article 28.

Commission v Germany (Case 205/84)
[1986] ECR 3755; [1987] 2 CMLR 69
Court of Justice of the European Communities

The case involved German law regulating the provision of insurance services on German territory. *All* insurers had to have a permanent establishment in Germany. *All* insurers had to be authorised by the German State. Plainly, insurers from other States wishing to offer services in Germany were impeded by these requirements. The Commission argued that the rules violated Articles 59 and 60 of the EC Treaty (now, after amendment, Articles 49 and 50 EC). The matter reached the Court under Article 169 of the EC Treaty (now Article 226 EC: see Chapter 17)). The first extract sets out the Court's approach.

[25]   According to the well-established case-law of the Court, Articles 59 and 60 of the EEC Treaty became directly applicable on the expiry of the transitional period, and their applicability was not conditional on the harmonization or the coordination of the laws of the Member States. Those articles require the removal not only of all discrimination against a provider of a service on the grounds of his nationality but also all restrictions on his freedom to provide services imposed by reason of the fact that he is established in a Member State other than that in which the service is to be provided.

[26]   Since the German Government and certain other of the governments intervening in its support have referred to the third paragraph of Article 60 as a basis for their contention that the State of the person insured can also apply its supervisory legislation to insurers established in another Member State, it should be added, as the Court made clear in particular in its judgment of 17 December 1981 (Case 279/80 *Webb* [1981] ECR 3305), that the principal aim of that paragraph is to enable the provider of the service to pursue his activities in the Member State where the service is given without suffering discrimination in favour of the nationals of the State. However, it does not follow from that paragraph that all national legislation applicable to nationals of that State and usually applied to the permanent activities of undertakings established therein may be similarly applied in its entirety to the temporary activities of undertakings which are established in other Member States.

[27]   The Court has nevertheless accepted, in particular in its judgments of 18 January 1979 (Joined Cases 110 and 111/78 *Ministère public and Another v van Wesemael and Others* [1979] ECR 35) and 17 December 1981 (Case 279/80 *Webb*, cited above), that regard being had to the particular nature of certain services, specific requirements imposed on the provider of the services cannot be considered to be incompatible with the Treaty where they have as their purpose the application of rules governing such activities. However, the freedom to provide services, as one of the fundamental principles of the Treaty, may be restricted only by provisions which are justified by the general good and which are applied to all persons or undertakings operating within the territory of the State in which the service is provided in so far as that interest is not safeguarded by the provisions to which the provider of a service is

subject in the Member State of his establishment. In addition, such requirements must be objectively justified by the need to ensure that professional rules of conduct are complied with and that the interests which such rules are designed to safeguard are protected.

[28] It must be stated that the requirements in question in these proceedings, namely that an insurer who is established in another Member State, authorized by the supervisory authority of that State and subject to the supervision of that authority, must have a permanent establishment within the territory of the State in which the service is provided and that he must obtain a separate authorization from the supervisory authority of that State, constitute restrictions on the freedom to provide services inasmuch as they increase the cost of such services in the State in which they are provided, in particular where the insurer conducts business in that State only occasionally.

[29] It follows that those requirements may be regarded as compatible with Articles 59 and 60 of the EEC Treaty only if it is established that in the field of activity concerned there are imperative reasons relating to the public interest which justify restrictions on the freedom to provide services, that the public interest is not already protected by the rules of the State of establishment and that the same result cannot be obtained by less restrictive rules.

The Court then proceeded to accept the existence of a protectable interest in this area:

[30] As the German Government and the parties intervening in its support have maintained, without being contradicted by the Commission or the United Kingdom and Netherlands Governments, the insurance sector is a particularly sensitive area from the point of view of the protection of the consumer both as a policy-holder and as an insured person. This is so in particular because of the specific nature of the service provided by the insurer, which is linked to future events, the occurrence of which, or at least the timing of which, is uncertain at the time when the contract is concluded. An insured person who does not obtain payment under a policy following an event giving rise to a claim may find himself in a very precarious position. Similarly, it is as a rule very difficult for a person seeking insurance to judge whether the likely future development of the insurer's financial position and the terms of the contract, usually imposed by the insurer, offer him sufficient guarantees that he will receive payment under the policy if a claimable event occurs.

[31] It must also be borne in mind, as the German Government has pointed out, that in certain fields insurance has become a mass phenomenon. Contracts are concluded by such enormous numbers of policy-holders that the protection of the interests of insured persons and injured third parties affects virtually the whole population.

[32] Those special characteristics, which are peculiar to the insurance sector, have led all the Member States to introduce legislation making insurance undertakings subject to mandatory rules both as regards their financial position and the conditions of insurance which they apply, and to permanent supervision to ensure that those rules are complied with.

[33] It therefore appears that in the field in question there are imperative reasons relating to the public interest which may justify restrictions on the freedom to provide

services, provided, however, that the rules of the State of establishment are not adequate in order to achieve the necessary level of protection and that the requirements of the State in which the service is provided do not exceed what is necessary in that respect.

Note
After due examination, the Court concluded that the public interest was *not* adequately protected by the rules of the State of establishment. In the abstract, then, Germany could lawfully restrict trade in order to serve the public interest. It then fell to be determined whether the actual rules enacted could satisfy Community law. The Court refused to accept that a blanket requirement of establishment in Germany was compatible with Community law. However, it took a rather different view of the necessity to undergo an authorisation procedure.

Commission v Germany (Case 205/84)
[1986] ECR 3755; [1987] 2 CMLR 69
Court of Justice of the European Communities

[42]   The Commission does not dispute that the State in which the service is provided is entitled to exercise a certain control over insurance undertakings which provide services within its territory. At the hearing it even accepted that it was permissible to provide for certain measures of supervision of the undertaking concerned to be applied prior to its conducting any business in the context of the provision of services. It nevertheless maintained that such supervision should take a form less restrictive than that of authorization. It did not however explain how such a system might work.

[43]   The German Government and the governments intervening in its support maintain that the necessary supervision can be carried out only by means of an authorization procedure which makes it possible to investigate the undertaking before it commences its activities, to monitor those activities continuously and to withdraw the authorization in the event of serious and repeated infringements.

[44]   In that respect it should be noted that in all the Member States the supervision of insurance undertakings is organized in the form of an authorization procedure and that the necessity of such a procedure is recognized in the two first coordination directives as regards the activities to which they refer. In each of those directives Article 6 thereof provides that each Member State must make the taking-up of the business of insurance in its territory subject to an official authorization. An undertaking which sets up branches and agencies in Member States other than that in which its head office is situated must therefore obtain an authorization from the supervisory authority of each of those States.

[45]   It must also be observed that the proposal for a second directive provides for the retention of that system. The undertaking must obtain an official authorization from each Member State in which it wishes to conduct business in the context of the provision of services. Although, according to that proposal, the authorization must be obtained from the supervisory authority of the State of establishment, that authority must first consult the authority of the State in which the service is to be provided and

send it all the relevant papers. The proposal also envisages permanent cooperation between the two supervisory authorities, thus making it possible, in particular, for the authority of the State of establishment to take all appropriate measures, which may extend to withdrawal of the authorization, to put an end to the infringements which have been notified to it by the supervisory authority of the State in which the service is provided.

[46] In those circumstances the German Government's argument to the effect that only the requirement of an authorization can provide an effective means of ensuring the supervision which, having regard to the foregoing considerations, is justified on grounds relating to the protection of the consumer both as a policy-holder and as an insured person, must be accepted. Since a system such as that proposed in the draft for a second directive, which entrusts the operation of the authorization procedure to the Member State in which the undertaking is established, working in close cooperation with the State in which the service is provided, can be set up only by legislation, it must also be acknowledged that, in the present state of Community law, it is for the State in which the service is provided to grant and withdraw that authorization.

[47] It should however be emphasized that the authorization must be granted on request to any undertaking established in another Member State which meets the conditions laid down by the legislation of the State in which the service is provided, that those conditions may not duplicate equivalent statutory conditions which have already been satisfied in the State in which the undertaking is established and that the supervisory authority of the State in which the service is provided must take into account supervision and verifications which have already been carried out in the Member State of establishment. According to the German Government, which has not been contradicted on that point by the Commission, the German authorization procedure conforms fully to those requirements.

[48] It is still necessary to consider whether the requirement of authorization which, under the Insurance Supervision Law, applies to any insurance business other than transport insurance, is justified in all its applications. In that respect it has been pointed out, in particular by the United Kingdom Government, that the free movement of services is of importance principally for commercial insurance and that with regard to that particular type of insurance the grounds relating to the protection of policy-holders relied on by the German Government and the governments intervening in its support do not apply.

[49] It follows from the foregoing that the requirement of authorization may be maintained only in so far as it is justified on the grounds relating to the protection of policy-holders and insured persons relied upon by the German Government. It must also be recognized that those grounds are not equally important in every sector of insurance and that there may be cases where, because of the nature of the risk insured and of the party seeking insurance, there is no need to protect the latter by the application of the mandatory rules of his national law.

[50] However, although it is true that the proposal for a second directive takes account of those considerations by excluding *inter alia* commercial insurance, which is defined in detail, from the scope of the mandatory rules of the State in which the service is provided, it must also be observed that, in the light of the legal and factual arguments which have been presented before it, the Court is not in a position to make such a general distinction and to lay down the limits of that distinction with sufficient precision to determine the individual cases in which the needs of protection, which

are characteristic of insurance business in general, do not justify the requirement of an authorization.

[51]   It follows from the foregoing that the Commission's first head of claim must be rejected in so far as it is directed against the requirement of authorization.

Notes
1.   See comment by D. Edward (1987) 12 EL Rev 231; R. Hodgin (1987) 24 CML Rev 273; J. Steenbergen (1987) CDE 526; D. Lasok (1988) 51 MLR 706.
2.   Insurance regulation is increasingly subject to Community legislation (see R. Merkin, *EC Insurance Law* (Longman, 1997) and generally J. Usher, *The Law of Money and Financial Services in the EC* (Oxford, 2000)). The Commission has published an interpretative communication relevant to the sector at (2000) OJ C43/5 (*cf*. pp. 270 and 305 above on the role of such communications). However, the principle that non-discriminatory national rules which have the effect of protecting domestic industry can be challenged under Article 49 applies across the services sector. Increasingly the market for services has been liberalised through the application of the primary Treaty provisions without the need to resort to harmonisation. As suggested above at p. 374, there are clear parallels with the Court's approach in *Cassis de Dijon* (Case 120/78, p. 290 above); see, e.g., the language of para. 29 of the above judgment in Case 205/84. The issue is similar. One State demands compliance with its rules. *All* firms must adhere, but importers/migrants suffer because they too are subjected to controls in their home State. The next case provides an example. The Commission considered France was in violation of Article 59 of the EC Treaty (now, after amendment, Article 49 EC) by making the provision of services by tourist guides accompanying groups of tourists from another Member State subject to the possession of a licence, itself dependent on possession of a particular qualification. The Court agreed with the Commission.

Commission v France (Case C-154/89)
[1991] ECR I-659
Court of Justice of the European Communities

[12]   It should further be pointed out that Articles 59 and 60 of the Treaty require not only the abolition of any discrimination against a person providing services on account of his nationality but also the abolition of any restriction on the freedom to provide services imposed on the ground that the person providing a service is established in a Member State other than the one in which the service is provided. In particular, the Member State cannot make the performance of the services in its territory subject to observance of all the conditions required for establishment; were it to do so the provisions securing freedom to provide services would be deprived of all practical effect.

[13]   The requirement imposed by the abovementioned provisions of French legislation amount to such a restriction. By making the provision of services by tourist guides

accompanying a group of tourists from another Member State subject to possession of a specific qualification, that legislation prevents both tour companies from providing that service with their own staff and self-employed tourist guides from offering their services to those companies for organized tours. It also prevents tourists taking part in such organized tours from availing themselves at will of the services in question.

[14]   However, in view of the specific requirements in relation to certain services, the fact that a Member State makes the provision thereof subject to conditions as to the qualifications of the person providing them, pursuant to rules governing such activities within its jurisdiction, cannot be considered incompatible with Articles 59 and 60 of the Treaty. Nevertheless, as one of the fundamental principles of the Treaty the freedom to provide services may be restricted only by rules which are justified in the general interest and are applied to all persons and undertakings operating in the territory of the State where the service is provided, in so far as that interest is not safeguarded by the rules to which the provider of such a service is subject in the Member State where he is established. In addition, such requirements must be objectively justified by the need to ensure that professional rules of conduct are complied with and that the interests which such rules are designed to safeguard are protected (see *inter alia* the judgment in Case 205/84 *Commission* v *Germany* [1986] ECR 3755, at paragraph 27).

[15]   Accordingly, those requirements can be regarded as compatible with Articles 59 and 60 of the Treaty only if it is established that with regard to the activity in question there are overriding reasons relating to the public interest which justify restrictions on the freedom to provide services, that the public interest is not already protected by the rules of the State of establishment and that the same result cannot be obtained by less restrictive rules.

[16]   The French Government contends that the French legislation in question seeks to ensure the protection of general interests relating to the proper appreciation of places and things of historical interest and the widest possible dissemination of knowledge of the artistic and cultural heritage of the country. According to the French Government, those interests are not adequately safeguarded by the rules to which the provider of the services, in this case the tour company, is subject in the Member State in which it is established. Several States require no occupational qualifications for tourist guides or demand no special knowledge of the historical and cultural heritage of other countries. In the absence of harmonization on that point the French legislation is not, therefore, incompatible with Article 59 of the EEC Treaty.

[17]   The general interest in the proper appreciation of places and things of historical interest and the widest possible dissemination of knowledge of the artistic and cultural heritage of a country can constitute an overriding reason justifying a restriction on the freedom to provide services. However, the requirement in question contained in the French legislation goes beyond what is necessary to ensure the safeguarding of that interest inasmuch as it makes the activities of a tourist guide accompanying groups of tourists from another Member State subject to possession of a licence.

[18]   The service of accompanying tourists is performed under quite specific conditions. The independent or employed tourist guide travels with the tourists and accompanies them in a closed group; in that group they move temporarily from the Member State of establishment to the Member State to be visited.

[19]   In those circumstances a licence requirement imposed by the Member State of destination has the effect of reducing the number of tourist guides qualified to accompany tourists in a closed group, which may lead a tour operator to have recourse instead to local guides employed or established in the Member State in which the service is to be performed. However, that consequence may have the drawback that tourists who are the recipients of the services in question do not have a guide who is familiar with their language, their interests and their specific expectations.

[20]   Moreover, the profitable operation of such group tours depends on the commercial reputation of the operator, who faces competitive pressure from other tour companies; the need to maintain that reputation and the competitive pressure themselves compel companies to be selective in employing tourist guides and exercise some control over the quality of their services. Depending on the specific expectations of the groups of tourists in question, that factor is likely to contribute to the proper appreciation of places and things of historical interest and to the widest possible dissemination of knowledge relating to the artistic and cultural heritage, in the case of conducted tours of places other than museums or historical monuments which may be visited only with a professional guide.

[21]   It follows that in view of the scale of the restrictions it imposes, the legislation in issue is disproportionate in relation to the objective pursued, namely to ensure the proper appreciation of places and things of historical interest and the widest dissemination of knowledge of the artistic and cultural heritage of the Member State in which the tour is conducted.

Note

The ability of a migrant to invoke Community law to challenge restrictive national rules was given important practical support in *Vlassopoulou v Ministerium für Justiz, Bundes- und Europaangelegenheiten Baden-Wurttemberg* (below). Vlassopoulou was a Greek national and a member of the Athens Bar. She wished to work as a lawyer in Germany. The case was decided in the context of Article 52, which has become Article 43 post-Amsterdam and which sets out the right of establishment, but appears to enshrine a general principle of Community trade law.

Vlassopoulou v Ministerium für Justiz, Bundes- und Europaangelegenheiten Baden-Wurttemberg (Case C-340/89)
[1991] ECR I-2357
Court of Justice of the European Communities

[14]   [I]t is also clear from the judgment in Case 71/76 *Thieffry* v *Conseil de l'Ordre des Avocats à la Cour de Paris* [1977] ECR 765, at paragraph 16, that, in so far as Community law makes no special provision, the objectives of the Treaty, and in particular freedom of establishment, may be achieved by measures enacted by the Member States, which, under Article 5 of the Treaty, must take 'all appropriate measures, whether general or particular, to ensure fulfilment of the obligations arising out of this Treaty or resulting from action taken by the institutions of the Community' and abstain from 'any measure which could jeopardize the attainment of the objectives of this Treaty'.

[15] It must be stated in this regard that, even if applied without any discrimination on the basis of nationality, national requirements concerning qualifications may have the effect of hindering nationals of other Member States in the exercise of their right of establishment guaranteed to them by Article 52 of the EEC Treaty. That could be the case if the national rules in question took no account of the knowledge and qualifications already acquired by the person concerned in another Member State.

[16] Consequently, a Member State which receives a request to admit a person to a profession to which access, under national law, depends upon the possession of a diploma or a professional qualification must take into consideration the diplomas, certificates and other evidence of qualifications which the person concerned has acquired in order to exercise the same profession in another Member State by making a comparison between the specialized knowledge and abilities certified by those diplomas and the knowledge and qualifications required by the national rules.

[17] That examination procedure must enable the authorities of the host Member State to assure themselves, on an objective basis, that the foreign diploma certifies that its holder has knowledge and qualifications which are, if not identical, at least equivalent to those certified by the national diploma. That assessment of the equivalence of the foreign diploma must be carried out exclusively in the light of the level of knowledge and qualifications which its holder can be assumed to possess in the light of that diploma, having regard to the nature and duration of the studies and practical training to which the diploma relates (see the judgment in Case 222/86 *Unectef* v *Heylens*, [1987] ECR 4097, paragraph 13).

[18] In the course of that examination, a Member State may, however, take into consideration objective differences relating to both the legal framework of the profession in question in the Member State of origin and to its field of activity. In the case of the profession of lawyer, a Member State may therefore carry out a comparative examination of diplomas, taking account of the differences identified between the national legal systems concerned.

The Court concluded:

[23] Consequently, the answer to the question submitted by the Bundesgerichtshof must be that Article 52 of the EEC Treaty must be interpreted as requiring the national authorities of a Member State to which an application for admission to the profession of lawyer is made by a Community subject who is already admitted to practise as a lawyer in his country of origin and who practises as a legal adviser in the first-mentioned Member State to examine to what extent the knowledge and qualifications attested by the diploma obtained by the person concerned in his country of origin correspond to those required by the rules of the host State; if those diplomas correspond only partially, the national authorities in question are entitled to require the person concerned to prove that he has acquired the knowledge and qualifications which are lacking.

Note

This approach was confirmed by the Court in *Gebhard* (Case C-55/94, p. 218 above) where explicit reference was made to paras 15 and 16 of the ruling in *Vlassopoulou*. See also *Teresa Fernández de Bobadilla* (Case C-234/97) judgment of 8 July 1999. In its Twelfth Annual Report on monitoring the application of Community law, the Commission notes that the Dutch *Raad van State* has applied the principle illustrated by ruling in *Vlassopoulou*, although the court's conclusion was that the relevant Dutch minister had acted properly in withholding recognition of an East German qualification after making comparisons between that qualification and Dutch requirements ((1995) OJ C254/166–7).

Consider also *Stichting Collectieve Antennevoorziening Gouda* v *Commissariaat voor de Media* (Case C-288/89) [1991] ECR I-4007 (which examines the extent to which cultural policy may constitute a requirement in the general interest justifying a restriction on the freedom to provide services); *Säger* v *Dennemeyer & Co. Ltd* (Case C-76/90) [1991] ECR I-4221; *Customs and Excise Commissioners* v *Schindler and Schindler* (Case C-275/92) [1994] ECR I-1039 (in which UK controls over lotteries were ruled capable of justification based on social and cultural considerations – prior to the National Lottery Act 1993!); *Markku Juhani Läärä, Cotswold Microsystems Ltd, Oy Transatlantic Software Ltd* (Case C-124/97), judgment of 21 September 1999 (which concerns Finnish rules reserving to a public body the right to run the operation of slot machines). For an overview see G. Marenco, 'The Notion of Restriction on the Freedom of Establishment and Provision of Services in the Case Law of the Court' (1991) 11 YEL 111; S. O'Leary, 'The Free Movement of Persons and Services', in P. Craig and G. de Búrca, *The Evolution of EU Law* (1999); V. Hatzopoulous, 'Recent developments of the case law of the ECJ in the field of services' (2000) 37 CML Rev 43. The Commission itself published an interpretative communication on this area of law at (1993) OJ C334/3 (*cf.* pp. 270 and 305 above on the role of such communications).

Although there is a strong, deregulatory impulse in this case law, the Court insists that 'the fact that one Member State imposes less strict rules than another Member State does not mean that the latter's rules are disproportionate and hence incompatible with Community law' (e.g., Case C-3/95 *Reiseburo Broede* v *Gerd Sanker* [1996] ECR I-6511; Case C-124/97, mentioned in the previous paragraph). This conforms to the pattern under Articles 28–30, (pp. 281 and 310 above). Respect for national regulatory choices is also visible in the next case, in which the Court found itself asked to deal with the question of the permissibility of national measures of market regulation which impede cross-border provision of services in a rather different context.

Alpine Investments BV v *Minister van Financiën (Case C–384/93)*
[1995] ECR I–1141
Court of Justice of the European Communities

Alpine Investments, a provider of financial services, was prevented by Dutch rules from contacting potential customers by telephone without their prior written consent. This ban on 'cold calling' extended to offers made to individuals both inside and outside The Netherlands. The Court ruled that the matter fell within Article 59 of the EC Treaty (now, after amendment, Article 49 EC) by observing that the restriction impeded offers made by a provider in one Member State to a potential recipient established outside that State. But the restriction applied to all Dutch providers, irrespective of the location of their target clients. The UK and Dutch governments argued by analogy with *Keck* (Cases C–267 and 268/91, p. 316 above) that the rule should be regarded as falling outside the scope of the Treaty rules governing free movement. The Court commented that the ban 'deprives the operators concerned of a rapid and direct technique for marketing and for contacting potential clients in other Member States'. It then stated of the challenged Dutch rules that:

[36] Such a prohibition is not analogous to the legislation concerning selling arrangements held in *Keck and Mithouard* to fall outside the scope of Article 30 of the Treaty.

[37] According to that judgment, the application to products from other Member States of national provisions restricting or prohibiting, within the Member State of importation, certain selling arrangements is not such as to hinder trade between Member States so long as, first, those provisions apply to all relevant traders operating within the national territory and, secondly, they affect in the same manner, in law and in fact, the marketing of domestic products and of those from other Member States. The reason is that the application of such provisions is not such as to prevent access by the latter to the market of the Member State of importation or to impede such access more than it impedes access by domestic products.

[38] A prohibition such as that at issue is imposed by the Member State in which the provider of services is established and affects not only offers made by him to addressees who are established in that State or move there in order to receive services but also offers made to potential recipients in another Member State. It therefore directly affects access to the market in services in the other Member States and is thus capable of hindering intra-Community trade in services.

Note

The reader should consider whether this finding sheds any light on the unclear limits to the scope of EC trade law discussed in connection with *Keck* at p. 321 above. Is this approach peculiar to cases involving 'export'? (See M. Ross (1995) 20 EL Rev 507, N. Bernard (1996) 45 ICLQ 82, S. Weatherill (1996) 33 CML Rev 885, 901, P. Oliver (1999) 36 CML Rev 783, 799.) The Court's treatment of Swedish restrictions on advertising in *Konsumentombud-smannen* v *De Agostini and TV Shop* (Joined Cases C-34/95, C-35/95 and C-36/95) was considered in the light of Article 28 at p. 325 above. For the purposes of Article 49, the Court observed that a restriction on freedom to provide services was imposed where an undertaking established in the broadcasting State was impeded in broadcasting advertisements directed at the public in the receiving State on behalf of advertisers established in that State. It was for the national court to determine whether such trade restrictions were justified (against standards plainly inspired by *Cassis de Dijon*). Articles 28 and 49 appear to have been handled differently by the Court in this decision, although it is notable that the Court focused on the position of the advertiser in its discussion of Article 28, but on that of the broadcaster in approaching Article 49 (for comment see J. Stuyck (1997) 34 CML Rev 1445).

The finding that the measure hindered intra-Community trade such as to trigger the application of Article 59 of the EC Treaty (now, after amendment, Article 49 EC) then required the Court in *Alpine Investments* to examine the justifications advanced in support of the Dutch intervention in the market. The Court was invited to assess various methods of available regulatory techniques in determining whether the Dutch choice was permissible under Community law.

Alpine Investments BV v *Minister van Financiën (Case C–384/93)*
[1995] ECR I–1141
Court of Justice of the European Communities

[40]   The national court's third question asks whether imperative reasons of public interest justify the prohibition of cold calling and whether that prohibition must be considered to be objectively necessary and proportionate to the objective pursued.

[41]   The Netherlands Government argues that the prohibition of cold calling in off-market commodities futures trading seeks both to safeguard the reputation of the Netherlands financial markets and to protect the investing public.

[42]   Financial markets play an important role in the financing of economic operators and, given the speculative nature and the complexity of commodities futures contracts, the smooth operation of financial markets is largely contingent on the confidence they inspire in investors. That confidence depends in particular on the existence of professional regulations serving to ensure the competence and trustworthiness of the financial intermediaries on whom investors are particularly reliant.

[43]   Although the protection of consumers in the other Member States is not, as such, a matter for the Netherlands authorities, the nature and extent of that protection does none the less have a direct effect on the good reputation of Netherlands financial services.

[44]   Maintaining the good reputation of the national financial sector may therefore constitute an imperative reason of public interest capable of justifying restrictions on the freedom to provide financial services.

[45]   As for the proportionality of the restriction at issue, it is settled case-law that requirements imposed on the providers of services must be appropriate to ensure achievement of the intended aim and must not go beyond that which is necessary in order to achieve that objective (see Case C–288/89 *Collectieve Antennevoorziening Gouda and Others* v *Commissariat voor de Media* [1991] ECR I–4007, paragraph 15).

[46]   As the Netherlands Government has justifiably submitted, in the case of cold calling the individual, generally caught unawares, is in a position neither to ascertain the risks inherent in the type of transactions offered to him nor to compare the quality and price of the caller's services with competitors' offers. Since the commodities futures market is highly speculative and barely comprehensible for non-expert investors, it was necessary to protect them from the most aggressive selling techniques.

[47] Alpine Investments argues however that the Netherlands Government's prohibition of cold calling is not necessary because the Member State of the provider of services should rely on the controls imposed by the Member State of the recipient.

[48] That argument must be rejected. The Member State from which the telephone call is made is best placed to regulate cold calling. Even if the receiving State wishes to prohibit cold calling or to make it subject to certain conditions, it is not in a position to prevent or control telephone calls from another Member State without the cooperation of the competent authorities of that State.

[49] Consequently, the prohibition of cold calling by the Member State from which the telephone call is made, with a view to protecting investor confidence in the financial markets of that State, cannot be considered to be inappropriate to achieve the objective of securing the integrity of those markets.

[50] Alpine Investments also argues that a general prohibition of telephone canvassing of potential clients is not necessary for the achievement of the objectives pursued by the Netherlands authorities. Requiring broking firms to tape-record unsolicited telephone calls made by them would suffice to protect consumers effectively. Such rules have moreover been adopted in the United Kingdom by the Securities and Futures Authority.

[51] That point of view cannot be accepted. As the Advocate-General correctly states in point 88 of his Opinion, the fact that one Member State imposes less strict rules than another Member State does not mean that the latter's rules are disproportionate and hence incompatible with Community law.

[52] Alpine Investments argues finally that, since it is of a general nature, the prohibition of cold calling does not take into account the conduct of individual undertakings and accordingly imposes an unnecessary burden on undertakings which have never been the subject of complaints by consumers.

[53] That argument must also be rejected. Limiting the prohibition of cold calling to certain undertakings because of their past conduct might not be sufficient to achieve the objective of restoring and maintaining investor confidence in the national securities markets in general.

[54] In any event, the rules at issue are limited in scope. First, they prohibit only the contacting of potential clients by telephone or in person without their prior agreement in writing, while other techniques for making contact are still permitted. Next, the measure affects relations with potential clients but not with existing clients who may still give their written agreement to further calls. Finally, the prohibition of unsolicited telephone calls is limited to the sector in which abuses have been found, namely the commodities futures market.

[55] In the light of the above, the prohibition of cold calling does not appear disproportionate to the objective which it pursues.

[56] The answer to the third question is therefore that Article 59 does not preclude national rules which, in order to protect investor confidence in national financial markets, prohibit the practice of making unsolicited telephone calls to potential clients resident in other Member States to offer them services linked to investment in commodities futures.

Note
Telephone selling reflects and advances market integration; it is a medium which renders physical borders irrelevant. At paras 47–49 in its ruling in *Alpine Investments*, the Court shows a shrewd awareness of the limits placed on 'destination State control' in such circumstances. Compare the discussion of problems of enforcing laws that differ from those of other Member States which emerge in an integrating market at p. 278 above.

Questions
1. Is there an irreconcilability between the Court's acceptance at para. 48 that home State control of technologically advanced marketing practices is more effective than destination State control and its comment at para. 43 that protection of consumers in other States is not as such a matter for the Dutch authorities? Do you agree that The Netherlands should not be able to export its high standards of consumer protection other than indirectly, as part of a method for securing the high reputation of its own financial services sector (paras 43, 44)?
2. How can the Dutch consumer 'cold-called' from outside The Netherlands be protected? Does this case suggest a need for Community-wide harmonisation, or does it display an acceptable level of regulatory diversity within the common market?

Note
Several of the cases in this chapter display the determination of commercial operators to exploit the freedoms found in Articles 43 and 49 of the EC Treaty to establish themselves or to provide services in another State. Typically such parties are anxious to rely on EC law to preclude the host State insisting on conformity with part or all of its regulatory requirements as a pre-condition of market access. Reducing costs by relying on EC law to evade those burdens is commercially attractive and should intensify consumer-friendly competition. As seen above, the Court has developed a formula, inspired by *Cassis de Dijon*, designed to weigh the balance between trade integration and local regulatory concerns. This theme is prominent in the next case. It involves a company formed in accordance with the law of one Member State wishing to open a branch in another Member State. This is covered by the right granted by Article 43 EC. But the company was not commercially active in the State in which it was formed. It planned to be active in the State in which its branch was to be located.

Centros Ltd v *Erhervs- og Selskabhysstyrelsen* (Case C-212/97)
Judgment of 9 March 1999
Court of Justice of the European Communities

Centros Ltd was a private limited company registered in the UK in accordance with English law. Its shares were held by Mr and Mrs Bryde, who were Danish nationals. Centros did not trade in the UK. It planned to trade in Denmark. Its application to register a branch in Denmark was refused by the other party to the proceedings, the Danish Trade and Companies Board, on the ground that Centros was in fact attempting to establish not a branch but a principal establishment in Denmark, which would have involved subjection to Danish regulatory requirements, including the paying-up of minimum share capital, which were far more onerous than those demanded under English law. Centros was, in short, a consumer of competition between (State) regulators (p. 219 above); but could it rely on EC law to entitle it to act in this way? A preliminary reference seeking an interpretation of Articles 52, 56 and 58 of the EC Treaty (now, after amendment, Articles 43, 46 and 48 BC) was made by a Danish court before which Centros's challenge had been pursued. The European Court treated the refusal to register the branch as an obstacle to the exercise of the freedom of establishment.

[23]   According to the Danish authorities, however, Mr and Mrs Bryde cannot rely on those provisions, since the sole purpose of the company formation which they have in mind is to circumvent the application of the national law governing formation of private limited companies and therefore constitutes abuse of the freedom of establishment. In their submission, the Kingdom of Denmark is therefore entitled to take steps to prevent such abuse by refusing to register the branch.

[24]   It is true that according to the case-law of the Court a Member State is entitled to take measures designed to prevent certain of its nationals from attempting, under cover of the rights created by the Treaty, improperly to circumvent their national legislation or to prevent individuals from improperly or fraudulently taking advantage of provisions of Community law (see, in particular, regarding freedom to supply services, Case 33/74 *Van Binsbergen* v *Bedrijfsvereniging Metaalnijverheid* [1974] ECR 1299, paragraph 13, Case C-148/91 *Veronica Omroep Organisatie* v *Commissariaat voor de Media* [1993] ECR I-487, paragraph 12, and Case C-23/93 *TV 10* v *Commissariaat voor de Media* [1994] ECR I-4795, paragraph 21; regarding freedom of establishment, Case 115/78 *Knoors* [1979] ECR 399, paragraph 25, and Case C-61/89 *Bouchoucha* [1990] ECR I-3551, paragraph 14; regarding the free movement of goods, Case 229/83 *Leclerc and Others* v *'Au Blé Vert' and Others* [1985] ECR 1, paragraph 27; regarding social security, Case C-206/94 *Brennet* v *Paletta* [1996] ECR I-2357, '*Paletta II*', paragraph 24; regarding freedom of movement for workers, Case 39/86 *Lair* v *Universität Hannover* [1988] ECR 3161, paragraph 43; regarding the common agricultural policy, Case C-8/92 *General Milk Products* v *Hauptzollamt Hamburg-Jonas* [1993] ECR I-779, paragraph 21, and regarding company law, Case C-367/96 *Kefalas and Others* v *Greece* [1998] ECR I-2843, paragraph 20).

[25]   However, although, in such circumstances, the national courts may, case by case, take account – on the basis of objective evidence — of abuse or fraudulent conduct on the part of the persons concerned in order, where appropriate, to deny them the benefit of the provisions of Community law on which they seek to rely, they must nevertheless assess such conduct in the light of the objectives pursued by those provisions (*Paletta II*, paragraph 25).

[26]   In the present case, the provisions of national law, application of which the parties concerned have sought to avoid, are rules governing the formation of companies and not rules concerning the carrying on of certain trades, professions or

businesses. The provisions of the Treaty on freedom of establishment are intended specifically to enable companies formed in accordance with the law of a Member State and having their registered office, central administration or principal place of business within the Community to pursue activities in other Member States through an agency, branch or subsidiary.

[27]   That being so, the fact that a national of a Member State who wishes to set up a company chooses to form it in the Member State whose rules of company law seem to him the least restrictive and to set up branches in other Member States cannot, in itself, constitute an abuse of the right of establishment. The right to form a company in accordance with the law of a Member State and to set up branches in other Member States is inherent in the exercise, in a single market, of the freedom of establishment guaranteed by the Treaty.

[28]   In this connection, the fact that company law is not completely harmonised in the Community is of little consequence. Moreover, it is always open to the Council, on the basis of the powers conferred upon it by Article 54(3)(g) of the EC Treaty, to achieve complete harmonisation,

[29]   In addition, it is clear from paragraph 16 of *Segers* [Case 79/85 [1986] ECR 2375] that the fact that a company does not conduct any business in the Member State in which it has its registered office and pursues its activities only in the Member State where its branch is established is not sufficient to prove the existence of abuse or fraudulent conduct which would entitle the latter Member State to deny that company the benefit of the provisions of Community law relating to the right of establishment.

[30]   Accordingly, the refusal of a Member State to register a branch of a company formed in accordance with the law of another Member State in which it has its registered office on the grounds that the branch is intended to enable the company to carry on all its economic activity in the host State, with the result that the secondary establishment escapes national rules on the provision for and the paying-up of a minimum capital, is incompatible with Articles 52 and 58 of the Treaty, in so far as it prevents any exercise of the right freely to set up a secondary establishment which Articles 52 and 58 are specifically intended to guarantee.

[31]   The final question to be considered is whether the national practice in question might not be justified for the reasons put forward by the Danish authorities.

[32]   Referring both to Article 56 of the Treaty and to the case-law of the Court on imperative requirements in the general interest, the Board argues that the requirement that private limited companies provide for and pay up a minimum share capital pursues a dual objective: first, to reinforce the financial soundness of those companies in order to protect public creditors against the risk of seeing the public debts owing to them become irrecoverable since, unlike private creditors, they cannot secure those debts by means of guarantees and, second, and more generally, to protect all creditors, whether public or private, by anticipating the risk of fraudulent bankruptcy due to the insolvency of companies whose initial capitalisation was inadequate.

[33]   The Board adds that there is no less restrictive means of attaining this dual objective. The other way of protecting creditors, namely by introducing rules making it possible for shareholders to incur personal liability, under certain conditions, would be more restrictive than the requirement to provide for and pay up a minimum share capital.

[34] It should be observed, first, that the reasons put forward do not fall within the ambit of Article 56 of the Treaty. Next, it should be borne in mind that, according to the Court's case-law, national measures liable to hinder or make less attractive the exercise of fundamental freedoms guaranteed by the Treaty must fulfil four conditions: they must be applied in a non-discriminatory manner; they must be justified by imperative requirements in the general interest; they must be suitable for securing the attainment of the objective which they pursue; and they must not go beyond what is necessary in order to attain it (see Case C-19/92 *Kraus* v *Land Baden-Württemberg* [1993] ECR I-1663, paragraph 32, and Case C-55/94 *Gebhard* v *Consiglio dell'Ordine degli Avvocati e Procuratori di Milano* [1995] ECR I-4165, paragraph 37).

[35] Those conditions are not fulfilled in the case in the main proceedings. First, the practice in question is not such as to attain the objective of protecting creditors which it purports to pursue since, if the company concerned had conducted business in the United Kingdom, its branch would have been registered in Denmark, even though Danish creditors might have been equally exposed to risk.

[36] Since the company concerned in the main proceedings holds itself out as a company governed by the law of England and Wales and not as a company governed by Danish law, its creditors are on notice that it is covered by laws different from those which govern the formation of private limited companies in Denmark and they can refer to certain rules of Community law which protect them, such as the Fourth Council Directive 78/660/EEC of 25 July 1978 based on Article 54(3)(g) of the Treaty on the annual accounts of certain types of companies (OJ 1978 L 222, p. 11), and the Eleventh Council Directive 89/666/EEC of 21 December 1989 concerning disclosure requirements in respect of branches opened in a Member State by certain types of company governed by the law of another State (OJ 1989 L 395, p. 36).

[37] Second, contrary to the arguments of the Danish authorities, it is possible to adopt measures which are less restrictive, or which interfere less with fundamental freedoms, by, for example, making it possible in law for public creditors to obtain the necessary guarantees.

[38] Lastly, the fact that a Member State may not refuse to register a branch of a company formed in accordance with the law of another Member State in which it has its registered office does not preclude that first State from adopting any appropriate measure for preventing or penalising fraud, either in relation to the company itself, if need be in cooperation with the Member State in which it was formed, or in relation to its members, where it has been established that they are in fact attempting, by means of the formation of the company, to evade their obligations towards private or public creditors established on the territory of a Member State concerned. In any event, combating fraud cannot justify a practice of refusing to register a branch of a company which has its registered office in another Member State.

[39] The answer to the question referred must therefore be that it is contrary to Articles 52 and 58 of the Treaty for a Member State to refuse to register a branch of a company formed in accordance with the law of another Member State in which it has its registered office but in which it conducts no business where the branch is intended to enable the company in question to carry on its entire business in the State in which that branch is to be created, while avoiding the need to form a company there, thus evading application of the rules governing the formation of companies which, in that State, are more restrictive as regards the paying up of a minimum share capital. That interpretation does not, however, prevent the authorities of the Member

State concerned from adopting any appropriate measure for preventing or penalising fraud, either in relation to the company itself, if need be in cooperation with the Member State in which it was formed, or in relation to its members, where it has been established that they are in fact attempting, by means of the formation of a company, to evade their obligations towards private or public creditors established in the territory of the Member State concerned.

Note
This ruling does not set aside the ability of Member States to exercise supervision over companies active on their territory in pursuit of economic freedoms guaranteed by the EC Treaty. Paragraph 34 is familiar territory to the student of EC trade law (p. 218 above). However, the ruling confines the scope of permissible public control in cases of strategic choices about company formation. Moreover, it offers possibilities for future exploitation of patterns of interstate regulatory competition by firms seeking what the judgment refers to as the 'least restrictive' regime (para. 27). More litigation in these realms may be expected (see prognosis by Roth (2000) 37 CML Rev 147; Calral and Cunha (2000) 25 EL Rev 157).

The cases considered above brought the law of market integration into collision with technical national rules. The next case shows how much broader and, arguably, more important national interests may clash with the integrative process.

Society for the Protection of Unborn Children Ireland Ltd (SPUC) v *Grogan (Case C-159/90)*
[1991] ECR I-4685, [1991] 3 CMLR 849
Court of Justice of the European Communities

The litigation arose against the background of the right to life of the unborn under the Irish Constitution. Thousands of Irish women travel annually to London to receive abortion services because they are unable to receive such services in Ireland. A Students' Union in Dublin provided information about services lawfully available in London. This practice was challenged before the Irish courts by SPUC. The Students' Union claimed that as a matter of Community law it was entitled to distribute such information, relying on Articles 59–66 of the EC Treaty (now, after amendment, Articles 49–55 EC).

The European Court accepted that abortion was a commercial service within the meaning of then Article 60 of the EC Treaty (now, after amendment, Article 50 EC). It then observed that the Students' Union did not in any way cooperate with the clinics whose addresses were published. It declared that:

[26]   The information to which the national court's questions refer is not distributed on behalf of an economic operator established in another Member State. On the contrary, the information constitutes a manifestation of freedom of expression and of the freedom to impart and receive information which is independent of the economic activity carried on by clinics established in another Member State.

[27]   It follows that, in any event, a prohibition of the distribution of information in circumstances such as those which are the subject of the main proceedings cannot be regarded as a restriction within the meaning of Article 59 of the Treaty.

This perception that there was no economic motivation in the case allowed the Court to conclude that:

It is not contrary to Community law for a Member State in which medical termination of pregnancy is forbidden to prohibit students associations from distributing information about the identity and location of clinics in another Member State where voluntary termination of pregnancy is lawfully carried out and the means of communicating with those clinics, where the clinics in question have no involvement in the distribution of the said information.

Note
The Court thus sidestepped the need to make an assessment which Advocate-General van Gerven had characterised in his Opinion as a balancing exercise:

The question remains whether it is consonant with the general principles of Community law with regard to fundamental rights and freedoms for a Member State to prohibit the provision and receipt of information by way of assistance about abortions lawfully carried out in other Member States, thereby infringing individuals' freedom of expression. It is a question here of *balancing* two fundamental rights, on the one hand the right to life as defined and declared to be applicable to unborn life by a Member State, and on the other the freedom of expression, which is one of the general principles of Community law on the basis of the constitutional traditions of the Member States and the European and international treaties and declarations on fundamental rights, in particular Article 10 of the European Convention on Human Rights.

The Advocate-General, in contrast to the Court, explored these difficult issues. He concluded his Opinion by proposing that the following answer should be given to the referring court:

The Treaty provisions with regard to the freedom to provide services do not prevent a Member State where the protection of unborn life is recognized in the Constitution and in its legislation as a fundamental principle from imposing a general prohibition, applying to everyone regardless of their nationality or place of establishment, on the provision of assistance to pregnant women, regardless of their nationality, with a view to the termination of their pregnancy, more specifically through the distribution of information as to the identity and location of and method of communication with clinics located in another Member State where abortions are carried out, even though the services of medical termination of pregnancy and the information relating thereto are provided in accordance with the law in force in that second Member State.

The final clause of the Court's ruling clearly indicated the potential for future litigation where the required commercial link is shown to exist. A Protocol annexed to the Maastricht Treaty on European Union declares that nothing therein 'shall affect the application in Ireland' of the relevant provision of the Irish Constitution. The protection which that Protocol afforded Ireland against further EC-derived litigation was soon seen to be a mixed blessing as a combination of domestic and European pressures led to reconsideration of the nature of the Constitutional guarantees (see Pearce, 'Abortion and the Right to Life under the Irish Constitution' [1993] JSWFL 396).

Looking beyond the specific problem of abortion and Irish law, the litigation strikingly illustrates the potential depth of the intrusion of Community law into national life and the potential of the European Court to assume a controversial adjudicative role far beyond the economic sphere as narrowly understood. The following articles draw broader conclusions about the development of Community law from the process of the litigation in *SPUC* v *Grogan* (Case C-159/90):

de Burca, G., 'Fundamental Human Rights and the Reach of EC Law' (1993) 13 OJLS 283.

Hervey, T., 'Buy Baby: The European Union and regulation of human reproduction' (1998) 18 OJLS 207.

O'Leary, S., 'The Court of Justice as a reluctant constitutional adjudicator' (1992) 71 EL Rev 138.

Spalin, E., 'Abortion, Speech and the European Community' (1992) *Journal of Social Welfare and Family Law* 17.

Question

'[R]ights to travel or freedom of information are rights with which men [rather than women] can more easily identify. By focussing on matters which are peripheral to the abortion issue itself, the media, in common with politicians, have sought refuge in the discourse of liberal legalism which more easily accommodates rights to travel or information than rights to abortion' (M. Fox and T. Murphy, 'Irish Abortion: Seeking Refuge in a Jurisprudence of Doubt and Delegation' (1992) 19 *Journal of Law and Society* 454, 457). Might this criticism be extended to apply to the structure of European Community law?

(D) HARMONISATION

The Court, in its judgments discussed in the previous section, recognises, as it did in '*Cassis de Dijon*' (p. 290 above), that where a genuine interest is the subject of protection, national restrictive rules may remain compatible with the Treaty. So professional qualifications, designed to maintain standards and integrity, obstruct free movement but may be lawful. So, too, rules protecting the consumer or the investor, or the reputation of financial markets. Here lie the limits of the Court's role. This suggests a role for legislative harmonisation.

Harmonisation requires all professionals to meet common standards, wherever qualified. There is then no obstruction to free movement (see, e.g., *Auer* v *Ministère Public* (Case 271/82) [1983] ECR 2727). Yet achieving such harmonisation has proved extremely difficult. Profession by profession, progress has been painfully slow, doubtless because vested interests, many of them perfectly legitimate, are at stake. A 'New Approach' has been initiated. This sets broad common standards which must be met, but avoids the detailed, laborious approach of old. Again, an analogy with the free movement of goods is appropriate, for in that field, too, it has been recognised that the inclusion of excessive detail in Community measures is counter-productive (see p. 571).

The first measure which adopted the 'New Approach' to harmonisation in this field is Directive 89/48.

Council Directive 89/48/EEC on a General System for the Recognition of Higher Education Diplomas, Articles 1-4
(1989) OJ L19/16

Article 1
For the purposes of this Directive following definitions shall apply:
(a) diploma: any diploma, certificate or other evidence of formal qualifications or any set of such diplomas, certificates or other evidence:
—which has been awarded by a competent authority in a Member State, designated in accordance with its own laws, regulations or administrative provisions;
—which shows that the holder has successfully completed a post-secondary course of at least three years' duration, or of an equivalent duration part-time, at a university or establishment of higher education or another establishment of similar level and, where appropriate, that he has successfully completed the professional training required in addition to the post-secondary course, and
—which shows that the holder has the professional qualifications required for the taking up or pursuit of a regulated profession in that Member State,
provided that the education and training attested by the diploma, certificate or other evidence of formal qualifications were received mainly in the Community, or the holder thereof has three years' professional experience certified by the Member State which recognised a third-country diploma, certificate or other evidence of formal qualifications.

The following shall be treated in the same way as a diploma, within the meaning of the first sub-paragraph: any diploma, certificate or other evidence of formal qualifications or any set of such diplomas, certificates or other evidence awarded by a competent authority in a Member State if it is awarded on the successful completion of education and training received in the Community and recognised by a competent authority in that Member State as being of an equivalent level and if it confers the same rights in respect of the taking up and pursuit of a regulated profession in that Member State;

(b) host Member State: any Member State in which a national of a Member State applies to pursue a profession subject to regulation in that Member State, other than the State in which he obtained his diploma or first pursued the profession in question;

(c) a regulated profession: the regulated professional activity or range of activities which constitute this profession in a Member State;

(d)   regulated professional activity: a professional activity, in so far as the taking up or pursuit of such activity or one of its modes of pursuit in a Member State is subject, directly or indirectly by virtue of laws, regulations or administrative provisions, to the possession of a diploma. The following in particular shall constitute a mode of pursuit of a regulated professional activity:

—pursuit of an activity under a professional title, in so far as the use of such a title is reserved to the holders of a diploma governed by laws, regulations or administrative provisions,

—pursuit of a professional activity relating to health, in so far as remuneration and/or reimbursement for such an activity is subject by virtue of national social security arrangements to the possession of a diploma.

Where the first subparagraph does not apply, a professional activity shall be deemed to be a regulated professional activity if it is pursued by the members of an association or organisation the purpose of which is, in particular, to promote and maintain a high standard in the professional field concerned and which, to achieve that purpose, is recognised in a special form by a Member State and:

—awards a diploma to its members,

—ensures that its members respect the rules of professional conduct which it prescribes, and

—confers on them the right to use a title or designatory letters, or to benefit from a status corresponding to that diploma.

A non-exhaustive list of associations or organisations which, when this Directive is adopted, satisfy the conditions of the second subparagraph is contained in the Annex. Whenever a Member State grants the recognition referred to in the second subparagraph to an association or organisation, it shall inform the Commission thereof, which shall publish this information in the *Official Journal of the European Communities*.

(e)   professional experience: the actual and lawful pursuit of the profession concerned in a Member State;

(f)   adaptation period: the pursuit of a regulated profession in the host Member State under the responsibility of a qualified member of that profession, such period of supervised practice possibly being accompanied by further training. This period of supervised practice shall be the subject of an assessment. The detailed rules governing the adaptation period and its assessment as well as the status of a migrant person under supervision shall be laid down by the competent authority in the host Member States;

(g)   aptitude test: a test limited to the professional knowledge of the applicant, made by the competent authorities of the host Member State with the aim of assessing the ability of the applicant to pursue a regulated profession in that Member State.

In order to permit this test to be carried out, the competent authorities shall draw up a list of subjects which, on the basis of a comparison of the education and training required in the Member State and that received by the applicant, are not covered by the diploma or other evidence of formal qualifications possessed by the applicant.

The aptitude test must take account of the fact that the applicant is a qualified professional in the Member State of origin or the Member State from which he comes. It shall cover subjects to be selected from those on the list, knowledge of which is essential in order to be able to exercise the profession in the host Member State. The test may also include knowledge of the professional rules applicable to the activities in question in the host Member State. The detailed application of the aptitude test shall be determined by the competent authorities of that State with due regard to the rules of Community law.

The status, in the host Member State, of the applicant who wishes to prepare himself for the aptitude test in that State shall be determined by the competent authorities in that State.

Article 2
This Directive shall apply to any national of a Member State wishing to pursue a regulated profession in a host Member State in a self-employed capacity or as an employed person.

This Directive shall not apply to professions which are the subject of a separate Directive establishing arrangements for the mutual recognition of diplomas by Member States.

Article 3
Where, in a host Member State, the taking up or pursuit of a regulated profession is subject to possession of a diploma, the competent authority may not, on the grounds of inadequate qualifications, refuse to authorise a national of a Member State to take up or pursue that profession on the same conditions as apply to its own nationals:

(a) if the applicant holds the diploma required in another Member State for the taking up or pursuit of the profession in question in its territory, such diploma having been awarded in a Member State; or

(b) if the applicant has pursued the profession in question full-time for two years during the previous ten years in another Member State which does not regulate that profession, within the meaning of Article 1(c) and the first subparagraph of Article 1(d), and possesses evidence of one or more formal qualifications:

—which have been awarded by a competent authority in a Member State, designated in accordance with the laws, regulations or administrative provisions of such State,

—which show that the holder has successfully completed a post-secondary course of at least three years' duration, or of an equivalent duration part-time, at a university or establishment of higher education or another establishment of similar level of a Member State and, where appropriate, that he has successfully completed the professional training required in addition to the post-secondary course and

—which have prepared the holder for the pursuit of his profession.

The following shall be treated in the same way as the evidence of formal qualifications referred to in the first subparagraph: any formal qualifications or any set of such formal qualifications awarded by a competent authority in a Member State if it is awarded on the successful completion of training received in the Community and is recognised by that Member State as being of an equivalent level, provided that the other Member States and the Commission have been notified of this recognition.

Article 4
1. Notwithstanding Article 3, the host Member State may also require the applicant:

(a) to provide evidence of professional experience, where the duration of the education and training adduced in support of his application, as laid down in Article 3(a) and (b), is at least one year less than that required in the host Member State. In this event, the period of professional experience required:

—may not exceed twice the shortfall in duration of education and training where the shortfall relates to post-secondary studies and/or to a period of probationary practice carried out under the control of a supervising professional person and ending with an examination,

—may not exceed the shortfall where the shortfall relates to professional practice acquired with the assistance of a qualified member of the profession.

In the case of diplomas within the meaning of the last subparagraph of Article 1(a), the duration of education and training recognised as being of an equivalent level shall be determined as for the education and training defined in the first subparagraph of Article 1(a).

When applying these provisions, account must be taken of the professional experience referred to in Article 3(b).

At all events, the professional experience required may not exceed four years;

(b)   to complete an adaptation period not exceeding three years or take an aptitude test:

—where the matters covered by the education and training he has received as laid down in Article 3(a) and (b), differ substantially from those covered by the diploma required in the host Member State, or

—where, in the case referred to in Article 3(a), the profession regulated in the host Member State comprises one or more regulated professional activities which are not in the profession regulated in the Member State from which the applicant originates or comes and that difference corresponds to specific education and training required in the host Member State and covers matters which differ substantially from those covered by the diploma adduced by the applicant, or

—where, in the case referred to in Article 3(b), the profession regulated in the host Member State comprises one or more regulated professional activities which are not in the profession pursued by the applicant in the Member State from which he originates or comes, and that difference corresponds to specific education and training required in the host Member State and covers matters which differ substantially from those covered by the evidence of formal qualifications adduced by the applicant.

Should the host Member State make use of this possibility, it must give the applicant the right to choose between an adaptation period and an aptitude test. By way of derogation from this principle, for professions whose practice requires precise knowledge of national law and in respect of which the provision of advice and/or assistance concerning national law is an essential and constant aspect of the professional activity, the host Member State may stipulate either an adaptation period or an aptitude test. Where the host Member State intends to introduce derogations for other professions as regards an applicant's right to choose, the procedure laid down in Article 10 shall apply.

2.   However, the host Member State may not apply the provisions of paragraph 1(a) and (b) cumulatively.

Note

Directive 89/48 is now supplemented by Directive 92/51 (OJ 1992 L209/ 25), which extends beyond training in higher education of at least three years' duration, and further supplemented by Directive 99/42 (OJ 1999 L201/77).

For lawyers, then, as for other professions, cross-border competition should become a reality. The barriers created by long-standing professional requirements should fall. The migrant lawyer must demonstrate a basic ability, but is not to be subjected to the full period of professional training normal in the host State. (Primary law already plays a role; note that the dispute in Case C-340/89 *Vlassopoulou* (p. 381 above) pre-dated the entry into force of Directive 89/48. See also Case C-55/94 *Gebhard* (p. 218 above), annotated from the perspective of its impact on the mobility of lawyers by J. Lonbay, (1996) 33 CML Rev 1073.) UK lawyers can expect to face developing competition from outside the UK; but the process is two-way, and UK lawyers can also look to expand their own activities beyond traditional frontiers. Strictly, the Directive is not of purely internal effect. It is concerned with migration. Yet the Directive is likely to supplement the many factors currently operative as catalysts in the reform of the English legal profession. It would be a strange result indeed if lawyers who are nationals of other Member States enjoy access to all English courts, leaving only English solicitors beyond the pale. The market for legal services will undergo further adjustment as a result of Directive 98/5 (OJ 1998 L77/36), the deadline for implementation of which was 14 March 2000. Lawyers are to be entitled to pursue specified activities on a permanent basis in another Member State while using their home-State professional title. Moreover, a lawyer so practising who has 'effectively and regularly' pursued an activity in the host State in that State's law or Community law for at least three years is exempted from the conditions of Article 4(1)(b) of Directive 89/48 with regard to gaining admission to the profession of lawyer in the host State.

Similar initiatives aim to remove trade barriers resulting from divergent company law and other regulatory regimes, which hinder the free movement of services provided by companies. The Second Banking Directive (Directive 89/646 (1989) OJ L386/1) illustrates the use of the New Approach in this area. Consider also the relevance of the initiative to tackle 'Harmful Tax Competition' (p. 239 above). These issues are considered further in Chapter 15, which discusses some of the policy implications of the new style of harmonisation.

(E) EUROPEAN CITIZENSHIP

As the introduction to Chapter 9 (p. 343 above) explains, the precise nature of citizenship of the Union requires elaboration. For the German Federal Constitutional Court in its *Maastricht* decision, Union citizenship represents 'a lasting legal tie . . . knotted between the nationals of the individual Member States' (p. 16 above). Nevertheless, it remains unclear how far in practical terms citizenship of the Union transcends the pre-existing law, which already conferred on migrants a bundle of rights which *de facto* created a form of Community citizenship (e.g. A. Evans, 'European Citizenship' (1982) 45 MLR 497). Union citizenship seems to lie in a penumbra between the largely economic status sketched in this chapter and the one which precedes it (*cf* p. 358) and one more intricately embroidered with political and social connotations (see M. Everson, 'The Legacy of the Market Citizen' in J. Shaw and G. More (eds), *New Legal Dynamics of European Union* (1995)).

C. Closa, 'The Concept of Citizenship in the Treaty on European Union' (1992) 29 CML Rev 1137, 1159–62

(Footnotes omitted.)

3.3 *Defining citizenship of the Union*
The Treaty establishes that 'Every person holding the nationality of a Member State shall be a citizen of the Union' (Article 8.1 [now 17.1]). This is, essentially, the

wording that the Commission proposed in its contribution. Citizenship had been defined by the Spanish memorandum as 'the personal and inalienable status of citizens of Member States, which by virtue of their membership of the union, have special rights and tasks, inherent in the framework of the Union, which are exercised and protected specifically within the borders of the Community, without this prejudicing the possibility of taking advantage of this same quality of European citizenship outside the said borders'.

The distinctive element of the concept of citizenship of the Union is the enjoyment of rights and the subjection to the obligations granted by the Treaty (Article 8.2 [now 17.2]). This determines the first characteristic of citizenship: additionality. The Spanish proposal had differentiated the definition of the concept of citizenship (which was regarded *per se* as the basis of the democratic legitimacy), from the *status civitatis* which is defined as a set of rights, freedoms and obligations of citizens of the European Union. The *status civitatis* is based on a set of rights additional to another two: national rights and responsibilities stemming from national citizenship at the level of Member States which will subsist in any case, and the set of Community rights and responsibilities stemming from the Rome Treaties for citizens of a Community Member State. The Commission opinion endorsed this additional character and its contribution argued also that this notion was supplementary to rights and obligations attached to every national as a citizen of their own Member State. A subsequent characteristic stems from additionality: citizenship will be an indirect relationship between the individual and the Union since the link which entitles individuals to the enjoyment of rights is the link with a Member State (i.e. nationality). This indirect character will not affect, however, the direct effectiveness of Community law on citizenship.

Lacking a strict definition on what a citizen of the Union is, nationality of any of the Member States becomes the requisite *sine qua* for the enjoyment of citizenship. Union citizenship will not supersede in any case nationality and, therefore, the Final Act of the Conference annexed to the Treaty included a Declaration on nationality. This declaration establishes that settlements on the possession of the nationality of a Member State will be made by reference to the domestic law of the Member State concerned. Member States will decide also who are to be considered their nationals for Community purposes and may amend this whenever they consider it necessary. Differences in naturalization systems do not seem to be an insuperable problem, since there is widespread agreement on preventing any form of 'passport dumping'.

3.4   *Rights of citizenship*
All the rights attached to the condition of citizen of the Union are regulated in Part Two of the Provisions creating the European Community. However, some aspects related to these rights such as the institutions of ombudsman and petition, and provisions to implement diplomatic protection are also contemplated by other Articles of the TEU.

3.4.1   *Rights of freedom of movement and residence*
The Treaty grants the right to move and reside freely within the territory of Member States to every citizen of the Union subject to the limitations and conditions laid down by the Treaty and secondary legislation (Article 8a.1 [now 18.1]). On this point, the Treaty implies a generalization of precedent Community rights and the removal of their attachment to the exercise of economic activity. The proposals to the IGC recognized the Community *acquis*. Thus, the Spanish memorandum considered that the rights of residence and movement were rights stemming from the Treaties which should be extended and applied to all European citizens.

Two provisions of this article are relevant. Firstly, these are not unlimited rights. The subjection to limitations and conditions laid down by the Treaty and secondary legislation gives margin for certain restrictions in both rights, which might follow from intergovernmental arrangements concluded under the Provisions on Home Affairs and Judicial Cooperation [cf the impact of Amsterdam, pp. 192 and 365 above]. Secondly, the remission to secondary legislation is based on a preoccupation to ensure an equitable distribution of charges particularly regarding social protection. This reflected the fears of eventual pressures on the more generous social systems which appeared in the wording of the initial draft. Although this reference was eliminated afterwards, this concern underlies the final wording.

The article proceeds to discuss voting rights under Article 8b of the EC Treaty (now, after amendment, Article 19 EC) (which have been amplified by Directive 94/80 OJ 1994 L368/38 amended by Directive 96/30 OJ 1996 L122, Directive 93/109 OJ 1993 L329), diplomatic protection under Article 8c (now 20) and petition and ombudsman under Article 8d (now 21), before turning to Article 8e of the EC Treaty (now, after amendment, Article 22 EC) and drawing conclusions (pp. 1166–69):

3.5   *Modification of the catalogue of rights*

The catalogue of rights enshrined by the Treaty is not intended to be a definitive one; current rights may be strengthened and/or new ones added (Article 8e [now 22]). The final wording of the Treaty has rejected the restrictive version contained in the first Presidency draft, which empowered the Council to modify the catalogue of rights. Modification meant that the Council could eventually *restrict* the foreseen rights through majority voting. Clearly, this restrictive option was not acceptable to most of the parties and, therefore, the Council will only be allowed to act in a positive way: *the Council may adopt provisions to strengthen or to add to the rights* laid down in Part Two. In any case, future provisions are not automatically binding, since the Council *shall recommend to the Member States for adoption in accordance with their respective constitutional rules*. Therefore, the future development of Union citizenship is left to the discretion of the Member States.

Finally, the Commission has been entrusted with guiding the dynamic evolution of citizenship and its parallel development alongside the Union itself. The Commission would report before the 31 December 1993 [see COM (93) 702] and every three years thereafter on the implementation of the provisions of Part Two [see COM (97) 230]. This Commission report will become a basis for Council decisions acting unanimously on a Commission proposal after consulting the EP.

Therefore, the character of the union citizenship is determined by the progressive acquisition of rights stemming from the dynamic development of the Union. That is, the gradual acquisition by the European citizen of specific rights in new policy-areas transferred to the Union. This evolutive character, which is in itself the most characteristic feature of the citizenship of the Union, was developed by the contributions to the conference as a channel for incorporating controversial socio-economic rights. As it has been recorded above, the Spanish proposal differentiated citizenship from the *status civitatis* which is linked to the degree of union achieved. Lastly, a 'real Union' would require a European citizenship of great content, that is, 'real union' should aim to overcome the inequalities which subsist between Community citizens through the promotion of economic and social cohesion, this being a constant claim of the Spanish government.

The Commission also endorsed this dynamic character (i.e. Citizenship would be progressively developed) in its opinion. Indeed, the Commission included as one element of Union citizenship the establishment of targets for the civic, economic and social rights of the individuals to be properly defined in a later stage. When it presented its contribution to the IGC, the Commission explained that the dynamic character was one of the principles on which Union citizenship was based: it *reflects the aims of the Union, involving as it does an indivisible body of rights and obligations stemming from the gradual and coherent development of the Union's political, economic and social dimension.* The Commission wanted to avoid the concept of citizenship being restricted to economic rights in the framework of the Rome Treaties and, at the same time, it sought to provide the basis for its future updating as the union developed. Therefore, the provisions proposed laid down objectives for the granting of rights in the future and for defining obligations, specially in the social field, with the possibility of eventually *enlarging* (and only enlarging, not reducing) the catalogue of citizens' rights by a unanimous Council vote on a Commission proposal.

4. Conclusions

The concept of union citizenship embodied by the Treaty on European Union has formalized or constitutionalized certain already existing rights within the Community ambit; it has introduced certain new rights and, above all, it has provided a solid basis for further enlargement of the catalogue of rights attached to citizenship. From this point of view, it represents an advance on the situation under the Rome Treaty and the SEA. The institutional role for the development of the dynamic character of citizenship will be the determinant factor to produce a qualitative leap forward.

However, citizenship of the Union has not superseded nationality of the Member States, in much the same way as the European Union has not abolished the sovereign existence of the Member States. This is particularly evident regarding certain political rights not included in the Treaty: national elections – the mechanism to actualize sovereignty and the source of a state policy on the Union itself – are the exclusive domain of *nationals*. The same applies to referendum: without being a procedure common to all twelve Member States, referendums have had a decisive role in Community developments, as the latest Danish and French referendums prove. The important point is that the decisive entitlement for individuals' decisions on the Union is not citizenship but nationality. It remains to be seen whether the basis of citizenship of the Union provided by the Treaty could evolve in the future to develop a political subject for the Union.

H.U. Jessurun D'Oliveira, 'Union Citizenship: Pie in the Sky?'
in A. Rosas & E. Antola (eds), *A Citizen's Europe*
(1995), pp. 82–84

(Footnotes omitted.)

Up till now, as far as citizenship is concerned, the European market is a 'futures' market. Citizenship is, in other words, nearly exclusively a symbolic plaything without substantive content, and in the Maastricht Treaty very little is added to the existing status of nationals of Member States. It is worth noting that, whereas in the Member States the notion of citizenship historically accrued around the *political* rights of the individual, it is around the freedom of movement that the notion of Union citizenship is crystallising.

It is unclear which rights and duties together are connected with Union citizenship because there is no cohesive notion of this new citizenship, and because the political dimension of citizenship here is underdeveloped. The instruments for participation in the public life of the Union are lacking as this public life itself, as distinguished from public life in the Member States, is virtually non-existent: a weak Parliament, next to no direct access to the European Courts, and so on.

Furthermore, the rights and obligations of the European citizen as granted by the Maastricht Treaty do differentiate only very partially between citizens and non-citizens. Several rights, such as the freedom of movement, are granted to large categories of non-nationals, such as nationals of the EFTA countries, or even to 'everyone', or normally to those legally resident in the territory of one of the Member States. Thus, European citizenship is not only severely underdeveloped, but also insufficiently distinctive between those who 'belong' and those who do not. In this situation, and also for policy reasons, it is better to forge a Union citizenship not only for nationals of Member States, but for resident aliens as part of the population of the Member States of the Union as well. This would increase rationality and cohesiveness of such a larger concept, and would reinforce democratic access to participation in the cultural, political and economic life of the Union and Community of the resident population of the Member States.

One must not forget, after all, that the creation, albeit in an as yet very rudimentary form, of a concept of citizenship which is related to a community of states, marks a significant departure from the traditional link between nationality and citizenship in the nation-state. It represents a loosening of the metaphysical ties between persons and a state, and forms a symptom of cosmopolitisation of citizenship. The rising concept of European citizenship is not the concept of national citizenship writ large: its quality has changed in that it does not presuppose any more a large set of common or shared values. It is a clear indication of a phenomenon which is also to be observed in the component parts of the European Community: that the Member States have to a large extent become multicultural and multi-ethnic societies which may be bound together not in the first place by a set of common values, but by a developing competence of persons to deal with differences in their dealing with others who do not necessarily share the same values and with redefined institutions. It is this competence to deal with differences which may be the nucleus of modern active citizenship, and European citizenship may be useful as a laboratory for this procedural concept of proto-cosmopolitan citizenship.

As it stands, Union citizenship is misleading in that it suggests that the Union is a state-like entity. This connotation is less adequate than ever as the Union moves more and more away from federal and supranational aspirations. It is furthermore misleading as the elements added to the European Community, and especially the third pillar of the Union, are inaccessible to the political influence of the so-called citizens. Nobody in his or her right mind would use the word citizen to describe the relationship between people and international organisations like GATT or the Hague Conference for private international law. To indicate the position of people under the Maastricht Treaty as citizenship is nearly as gross a misnomer. The populations of the Member States have not asked for citizenship; it has graciously been bestowed upon them as a cover-up for the still existing democratic deficit. As an alibi it may please Brussels; whether it changes anything in the sceptical attitude and weak position of the populations of the Member States is, in my view, rather improbable.

Notes

1.   One cannot sensibly attempt to get to grips with the nature of citizenship without considering what it is in the EU that people are classified as citizens

of. For a more general discussion of what the Union is and might become, see pp. 13–36 above.

2. Pending elaboration of the content of European citizenship through legislation and/or Treaty revision, it is an intriguing, and familiar, question in EC law and policy whether the Court will employ the admittedly guarded wording of the relevant Treaty provisions as a basis for dynamic interpretation of the law in order to enhance the status of the individual. In Cases C-64/96 and C-65/96 *Land Nordrhein Westfalen* v *Uecker, Jacquet* (p. 350 above) it did not, preferring to adhere to the perceived existing limitations on the scope of the Treaty. In Case C-91/92 *Paola Faccini Dori* (p. 112 above) it declined the invitation of its Advocate General, Mr Lenz, to secure the equality of the European Citizen before the law by embracing the horizontal direct effect of Directives. This would preclude the variation in the impact of Directives State-by-State which is caused by uneven local fidelity to the obligation of timely transposition. But the Court stuck doggedly to its rejection of the phenomenon of horizontal direct effect in the case of Directives. However, a glimpse of a more dynamic role for European citizenship emerges from the Court's ruling in *Maria Martinez Sala* v *Freistaat Bayern* (Case C-85/96) [1998] ECR I-2691. It ruled that a national of a Member State lawfully residing in the territory of another Member State falls within the personal scope of the Treaty provisions on European Citizenship. This triggered a right to, *inter alia*, protection from discrimination on grounds of nationality within the material scope of application of the Treaty. In *Martinez Sala* this allowed the applicant access to benefits which, one might previously have supposed, would have been available to her only had she held a more active economic status than mere lawful residence in the host State. *Martinez Sala* may prove to be the key ruling that breaks the ground between the orthodoxy of economic rights for economic migrants and new horizons lit up by comprehensive rights to equal treatment for Union citizens. See S. Fries and J. Shaw, 'Citizenship of the Union: First Steps in the Court of Justice' (1998) 4 *European Public Law* 533; 5. O'Leary, 'Putting Flesh on the Bones of European Union Citizenship' (1999) 24 EL Rev 68. But what if the applicant had *not* been lawfully resident in Germany? Would the Treaty provisions on citizenship secure that right, even for individuals falling outwith the scope of the familiar economically-focused Treaty provisions and the package of secondary legislation adopted in 1990 (p. 374)? *Martinez Sala* does not answer this question. Closa's prediction at p. 400 above of the 'progressive acquisition of rights [by the Union citizen] stemming from the dynamic development of the Union' invites us, a decade later, to reflect on slow progress in this area.

3. C. Vincenzi made the following far-sighted observations in 1991 (Paper on 'Freedom of Movement Rights of Community Nationals'):

Despite the creative jurisprudence of the European Court of Justice, and the modest successes of the Commission in securing approval for the three new Directives on rights of residence [p. 374 above], much still needs to be done in the area of freedom of movement and citizenship rights. The European Parliament has expressed its support for the enlargement of free movement rights, but the will at Council of Ministers level still seems to be lacking. The danger is that agreement may be reached between the Member States on abolishing frontier controls, and establishing a network of post-entry control, without agreement on positive rights/duties intended to safeguard the interests of those subject to control.

Questions
1.   Do the provisions on Citizenship of the Union (p. 343) address Vincenzi's concerns? Are there better methods for addressing those concerns? Assess the contribution of the Treaty of Amsterdam to freedom of movement (p. 192) and citizenship rights (p. 343).
2.   Wilkinson asserts that 'this mythical European citizen might, to paraphrase Mark Twain, complain that rumours of his or her *birth* have been greatly exaggerated' ((1995) 1 *European Public Law* 417). Do you agree? What suggestions for nurture would you make?

Further Reading
Barnard, C., 'Article 13: Through the Looking Glass of Union Citizenship', in D. O'Keefe and P. Twomey, *Legal Issues of the Amsterdam Treaty* (Oxford, Hart Publishing, 1999).
De Burca, G., 'The Quest for Legitimacy in the European Union' (1996) 59 MLR 349.
Douglas Scott, S., 'In search of Union Citizenship' (1998) 18 YEL 29.
Jessurun d'Oliveira, H., 'Nationality and the European Union after Amsterdam' in D. O'Keefe and P. Twomey, *Legal Issues of the Amsterdam Treaty* (Oxford, Hart Publishing, 1999).
Lardy, H., 'The Political Rights of Union Citizenship' (1996) 2 *European Public Law* 611.
Lyons, C., 'A Voyage around Article 8: an Historical and Comparative Evaluation of the Fate of European Union Citizenship' (1997) 17 YEL 135.
Shaw, J., 'The Many Pasts and Futures of Citizenship in the European Union' (1997) 22 EL Rev 554.
Shaw, J, 'European Union Citizenship: the IGC and Beyond' (1997) 3 *European Public Law* 413.
Wiener, A., and Della Sala, V., 'Constitution-making and Citizenship Practice – Bridging the Democracy Gap in the EU?' (1997) 35 JCMS 595.

11 ARTICLE 81: CARTELS

(A) INTRODUCTION TO COMPETITION LAW

The competition law provisions of the EC Treaty are probably the most important of all from the perspective of the commercial lawyer or business person. Nothing could illustrate this more vividly than the fines, occasionally well in excess of €10 million, which have been imposed on firms by the Commission, which is responsible for the administration of these rules, subject to supervision by the Court (initially, the Court of First Instance).

The function of the competition rules was summarised by the Court in the following dictum:

Metro-SB-Grossmärkte GmbH & Co. KG v *Commission (Case 26/76)*
[1977] ECR 1875; [1978] 2 CMLR 1
Court of Justice of the European Communities

The requirement contained in Articles 3 and 85 of the EEC Treaty [now Articles 3 and 81 of the EC Treaty] that competition shall not be distorted implies the existence on the market of workable competition, that is to say the degree of competition necessary to ensure the observance of the basic requirements and attainment of the objectives of the Treaty, in particular the creation of a single market achieving conditions similar to those of a domestic market.

Note
Two ringing phrases may be extracted from that dictum: *workable competition* and *a single market*.

The first, the notion that the Treaty competition rules are concerned to promote *workable competition*, reflects a kind of economic pragmatism. 'Perfect' competition, where producers respond instantly and inevitably to consumer demand and where the efficient allocation of resources is ensured, is in practice an illusion. 'Workable' competition is concerned to achieve the most efficient resource allocation available, given the constraints of a modern economy where consumer choice cannot be perfectly expressed. So EC competition law controls cartels under Article 81, because such arrangements tend to suppress improvements normally stimulated by competition and to reduce consumer choice. Yet some cartels yield benefits, for example, through the ability of firms to specialise; this is reflected in Article 81(3), which allows exemption from prohibition for economically desirable cartels. Community law accepts that monopolies – 'dominant positions' in Community terminology – exist and may yield inefficient results. So it uses Article 82 to prohibit abuse of that position of economic strength.

The second idea, that of the *single market*, is a familiar one. Here we see the special role of competition law in a common market. Articles 81 and 82 are concerned with market integration as well as with suppressing anti-competitive conduct. In fact, Articles 81 and 82 have much in common with Articles 25, 28, 39, etc., which aim to eliminate State barriers to trade and to convert a fragmented market into a common market. Articles 81 and 82 perform a similar role but they operate in the private sector. It will be seen that firms which agree to carve up the common market along national lines are targets for severe penalties under Community competition law.

Much of the theory and practice of competition law is tied up with economic lore. This contributes to the intellectual challenge of this area of the law. At this stage, no further analysis will be provided in the abstract. However, through the course of the next two chapters, where specific issues are dealt with, references to the relevant general literature which questions the impact of competition law will be provided. It is a matter of personal choice how deeply a student wishes to inquire into the implications of the choice of particular legal rules. However, it is suggested that basic economic theory is not as forbidding as it may first appear, and that study in this area will greatly assist understanding of the application of the legal rules.

(B) ARTICLE 81

Article 81, EC

Article 81

1. The following shall be prohibited as incompatible with the common market: all agreements between undertakings, decisions by associations of undertakings and concerted practices which may affect trade between Member States and which have as their object or effect the prevention, restriction or distortion of competition within the common market, and in particular those which:

    (a)   directly or indirectly fix purchase or selling prices or any other trading conditions;

    (b)   limit or control production, markets, technical development, or investment;

    (c)   share markets or sources of supply;

    (d)   apply dissimilar conditions to equivalent transactions with other trading parties, thereby placing them at a competitive disadvantage;

    (e)   make the conclusion of contracts subject to acceptance by the other parties of supplementary obligations which, by their nature or according to commercial usage, have no connection with the subject of such contracts.

2. Any agreements or decisions prohibited pursuant to this Article shall be automatically void.

3. The provisions of paragraph 1 may, however, be declared inapplicable in the case of:

—any agreement or category of agreements between undertakings;

—any decision or category of decisions by associations of undertakings;

—any concerted practice or category of concerted practices;

which contributes to improving the production or distribution of goods or to promoting technical or economic progress, while allowing consumers a fair share of the resulting benefit, and which does not:

(a) impose on the undertakings concerned restrictions which are not indispensable to the attainment of these objectives;

(b) afford such undertakings the possibility of eliminating competition in respect of a substantial part of the products in question.

Note

The text of this provision was untouched by the Amsterdam Treaty. However, Article 81's pre-Amsterdam number was 85. This must be borne in mind in reading the material contained in this Chapter.

No case better illustrates the nature and purpose of Article 81 than the following:

Établissements Consten SA and Grundig GmbH v *Commission (Cases 56 & 58/64)*
[1966] ECR 299; [1966] CMLR 418
Court of Justice of the European Communities

Consten, a French firm, agreed to handle only German-made Grundig electrical products in France. Grundig agreed to supply only Consten in France and to ensure that its customers outside France were restrained from delivering the goods into France. This was an 'exclusive distribution' deal which conferred 'absolute territorial protection' in France on Consten. The Commission found the agreement unlawful and the parties applied to the Court for annulment of that decision. The Court's ruling deserves close attention. Remember that Article 85 is now, post-Amsterdam, Article 81.

The applicants submit that the prohibition in Article 81(1) applies only to so-called horizontal agreements. The Italian Government submits furthermore that sole distributorship contracts do not constitute 'agreements between undertakings' within the meaning of that provision, since the parties are not on a footing of equality. With regard to these contracts, freedom of competition may only be protected by virtue of Article 86 of the Treaty.

Neither the wording of Article 85 nor that of Article 86 gives any ground for holding that distinct areas of application are to be assigned to each of the two Articles according to the level in the economy at which the contracting parties operate. Article 85 refers in a general way to all agreements which distort competition within the Common Market and does not lay down any distinction between those agreements based on whether they are made between competitors operating at the same level in the economic process or between non-competing persons operating at different levels. In principle, no distinction can be made where the Treaty does not make any distinction.

Furthermore, the possible application of Article 85 to a sole distributorship contract cannot be excluded merely because the grantor and the concessionnaire are not competitors *inter se* and not on a footing of equality. Competition may be distorted within the meaning of Article 85(1) not only by agreements which limit it as between the parties, but also by agreements which prevent or restrict the competition which might take place between one of them and third parties. For this purpose, it is irrelevant whether the parties to the agreement are or are not on a footing of equality as regards their position and function in the economy. This applies all the more, since, by such an agreement, the parties might seek, by preventing or limiting the competition of third parties in respect of the products, to create or guarantee for their benefit an unjustified advantage at the expense of the consumer or user, contrary to the general aims of Article 85.

It is thus possible that, without involving an abuse of a dominant position, an agreement between economic operators at different levels may affect trade between Member States and at the same time have as its object or effect the prevention, restriction or distortion of competition, thus falling under the prohibition of Article 85(1).

In addition, it is pointless to compare on the one hand the situation, to which Article 85 applies, of a producer bound by a sole distributorship agreement to the distributor of his products with on the other hand that of a producer who includes within his undertaking the distribution of his own products by some means, for example, by commercial representatives, to which Article 85 does not apply. These situations are distinct in law and, moreover, need to be assessed differently, since two marketing organizations, one of which is integrated into the manufacturer's undertaking whilst the other is not, may not necessarily have the same efficiency. The wording of Article 85 causes the prohibition to apply, provided that the other conditions are met, to an agreement between several undertakings. Thus it does not apply where a sole undertaking integrates its own distribution network into its business organization. It does not thereby follow, however, that the contractual situation based on an agreement between a manufacturing and a distributing undertaking is rendered legally acceptable by a simple process of economic analogy – which is in any case incomplete and in contradiction with the said Article. Furthermore, although in the first case the Treaty intended in Article 85 to leave untouched the internal organization of an undertaking and to render it liable to be called in question, by means of Article 86, only in cases where it reaches such a degree of seriousness as to amount to an abuse of a dominant position, the same reservation could not apply when the impediments to competition result from agreement between two different undertakings which then as a general rule simply require to be prohibited.

Finally, an agreement between producer and distributor which might tend to restore the national divisions in trade between Member States might be such as to frustrate the most fundamental object of the Community. The Treaty, whose preamble and content aim at abolishing the barriers between States, and which in several provisions gives evidence of a stern attitude with regard to their reappearance, could not allow undertakings to reconstruct such barriers. Article 85(1) is designed to pursue this aim, even in the case of agreements between undertakings placed at different levels in the economic process.

The submissions set out above are consequently unfounded. . . .

The complaints relating to the concept of 'agreements. . .which may affect trade between Member States'
The applicants and the German Government maintain that the Commission has relied on a mistaken interpretation of the concept of an agreement which may affect trade between Member States and has not shown that such trade would have been greater without the agreement in dispute.

The defendant replies that this requirement in Article 85(1) is fulfilled once trade between Member States develops, as a result of the agreement, differently from the way in which it would have done without the restriction resulting from the agreement, and once the influence of the agreement on market conditions reaches a certain degree. Such is the case here, according to the defendant, particularly in view of the impediments resulting within the Common Market from the disputed agreement as regards the exporting and importing of Grundig products to and from France.

The concept of an agreement 'which may affect trade between Member States' is intended to define, in the law governing cartels, the boundary between the areas respectively covered by Community law and national law. It is only to the extent to which the agreement may affect trade between Member States that the deterioration in competition caused by the agreement falls under the prohibition of Community law contained in Article 85; otherwise it escapes the prohibition.

In this connexion, what is particularly important is whether the agreement is capable of constituting a threat, either direct or indirect, actual or potential, to freedom of trade between Member States in a manner which might harm the attainment of the objectives of a single market between States. Thus the fact that an agreement encourages an increase, even a large one, in the volume of trade between States is not sufficient to exclude the possibility that the agreement may 'affect' such trade in the abovementioned manner. In the present case, the contract between Grundig and Consten, on the one hand by preventing undertakings other than Consten from importing Grundig products into France, and on the other hand by prohibiting Consten from re-exporting those products to other countries of the Common Market, indisputably affects trade between Member States. These limitations on the freedom of trade, as well as those which might ensue for third parties from the registration in France by Consten of the GINT trade mark, which Grundig places on all its products, are enough to satisfy the requirement in question.

Consequently, the complaints raised in this respect must be dismissed.

The complaints concerning the criterion of restriction on competition
The applicants and the German Government maintain that since the Commission restricted its examination solely to Grundig products the decision was based upon a false concept of competition and of the rules on prohibition contained in Article 85(1), since this concept applies particularly to competition between similar products of different makes; the Commission, before declaring Article 85(1) to be applicable, should, by basing itself upon the 'rule of reason', have considered the economic effects of the disputed contract upon competition between the different makes. There is a presumption that vertical sole distributorship agreements are not harmful to competition and in the present case there is nothing to invalidate that presumption. On the contrary, the contract in question has increased the competition between similar products of different makes.

The principle of freedom of competition concerns the various stages and manifestations of competition. Although competition between producers is generally more noticeable than that between distributors of products of the same make, it does not thereby follow that an agreement tending to restrict the latter kind of competition should escape the prohibition of Article 85(1) merely because it might increase the former.

Besides, for the purpose of applying Article 85(1), there is no need to take account of the concrete effects of an agreement once it appears that it has as its object the prevention, restriction or distortion of competition.

Therefore the absence in the contested decision of any analysis of the effects of the agreement on competition between similar products of different makes does not, of itself, constitute a defect in the decision.

It thus remains to consider whether the contested decision was right in founding the prohibition of the disputed agreement under Article 85(1) on the restriction on competition created by the agreement in the sphere of the distribution of Grundig products alone. The infringement which was found to exist by the contested decision results from the absolute territorial protection created the said contract in favour of Consten on the basis of French law. The applicants thus wished to eliminate any possibility of competition at the wholesale level in Grundig products in the territory specified in the contract essentially by two methods.

First, Grundig undertook not to deliver even indirectly to third parties products intended for the area covered by the contract. The restrictive nature of that undertaking is obvious if it is considered in the light of the prohibition on exporting which was imposed not only on Consten but also on all the other sole concessionnaires of Grundig, as well as the German wholesalers. Secondly, the registration in France by Consten of the GINT trade mark, which Grundig affixes to all its products, is intended to increase the protection inherent in the disputed agreement, against the risk of parallel imports into France of Grundig products, by adding the protection deriving from the law on industrial property rights. Thus no third party could import Grundig products from other Member States of the Community for resale in France without running serious risks.

The defendant properly took into account the whole distribution system thus set up by Grundig. In order to arrive at a true representation of the contractual position the contract must be placed in the economic and legal context in the light of which it was concluded by the parties. Such a procedure is not to be regarded as an unwarrantable interference in legal transactions or circumstances which were not the subject of the proceedings before the Commission.

The situation as ascertained above results in the isolation of the French market and makes it possible to charge for the products in question prices which are sheltered from all effective competition. In addition, the more producers succeed in their efforts to render their own makes of product individually distinct in the eyes of the consumer, the more the effectiveness of competition between producers tends to diminish. Because of the considerable impact of distribution costs on the aggregate cost price, it seems important that competition between dealers should also be stimulated. The efforts of the dealer are stimulated by competition between distributors of products of the same make. Since the agreement thus aims at isolating the French market for Grundig products and maintaining artificially, for products of a very well-known brand, separate national markets within the Community, it is therefore such as to distort competition in the Common Market.

It was therefore proper for the contested decision to hold that the agreement constitutes an infringement of Article 85(1). No further considerations, whether of economic data (price differences between France and Germany, representative character of the type of appliance considered, level of overheads borne by Consten) or of the corrections of the criteria upon which the Commission relied in its comparisons between the situations of the French and German markets, and no possible favourable effects of the agreement in other respects, can in any way lead, in the face of abovementioned restrictions, to a different solution under Article 85(1).

Note
Was this an *anti-competitive* deal? In one sense it was, because Grundig goods were available in France from just one source, Consten. But did it really matter? After all, if Consten had sold Grundig goods at unreasonably high prices, consumers would simply have bought the electrical products of other manufacturers. Competition between different brands of the goods would restrain Consten.

So, adopting this perspective, the US Supreme Court declared in *Continental TV* v *Sylvania* 433 US 36 (1977) that:

> Interbrand competition . . . is the primary concern of antitrust law . . . When interbrand competition exists . . . it provides a significant check on the exploitation of intrabrand market power because of the ability of consumers to substitute a different brand of the same product.

Question
Explain how and why this perception went largely ignored in *Consten* (Cases 56 & 58/64). Notice the Court's concern to preserve 'parallel trade'; cross-border intrabrand competition must be secured, whatever the interbrand competitive situation may be.

Note
So EC competition law has special objectives. It aims to further *market integration*. It is different from US law, and, for that matter, from UK or German law. *Consten* (Cases 56 & 58/64), then, has caused us to ask some important questions about the *purpose* of competition law. It seems that EC law may have suspicions about 'vertical' deals which improve product distribution which would not be entertained by other competition law systems which are not designed to help market integration.

But *should* it? Is interventionism of this type, even in markets shown to be characterised by interbrand competition, truly justified or is market integration but a shibboleth? Even if such an approach *was* so justified, can it remain so in the post-1992 climate of an internal market? These questions about the shape of EC competition policy were among those that prompted the Commission to publish a Green Paper on *Vertical Restraints in EC Competition Policy* in January 1997 (COM (96) 721), which initiated a wide-ranging review of the application of Article 81 to vertical restraints (those between traders at different points in the supply chain), including distribution agreements of the *Consten and Grundig* type. This review culminated in the adoption of Regulation 2790/1999 on vertical restraints in December 1999, which is examined below at p. 452, after the structure of Article 81 has been placed in its full context, for the pressure for reform is motivated not only by the suspicion that the insistence on using Article 81(1) to drive forward the policy of integration may today prove to be inappropriately intense, but also by concern that a broad reading of Article 81(1) may exaggerate dependence on the Commission in consequence of its exclusive grip over the power to apply Article 81(3) to exempt agreements falling within Article 85(1). Here too the wind of change is blowing: in its 1999 White Paper on *Modernisation of the Rules implementing Articles 85 and 86 [now 81 and 82] of the EC Treaty* (OJ 1999 C132) the Commission airs the suggestion that exemption should also lie in the gift of bodies within the Member States, although consensus has not yet been reached on the desirability of this shift of institutional emphasis (see p. 527 below). That is to say, the thinking about how to modernise the application of Article 81 is motivated by both policy and administrative concerns.

Further reading
The following are of general interest in the area of competition law policy (but see p. 459 below on *Vertical Restraints* and p. 529 below on the White Paper on *Modernisation*):

Ehlermann, C.-D., 'The Contribution of EC Competition Policy to the Single Market' (1992) 29 CML Rev 257.
Frazer, T., 'Competition Policy after 1992 – the next step' (1990) 53 MLR 609.
Gerber, D., 'The Transformation of European Community Competition Law' (1994) 35 Harvard Intl LJ 97.
Snyder, F., 'Ideologies of Competition in European Community Law' (1989) 52 MLR 149.
Van den Bergh, R., 'Modern Industrial Organisation versus Old-Fashioned European Competition Law' [1996] ECLR 75.

(C) JURISDICTION

Community competition law applies only to deals which 'affect trade between Member States'. Most deals which involve parties in more than one State will raise no great difficulty under this head. Obviously, the Consten/Grundig arrangement affected trade between Member States; so too the Dyestuffs concerted practice (*ICI* v *Commission* (Case 48/69)) discussed at p. 417 below. However, the ambit of EC competition law is broad. Two situations may seem prima facie to fall out with Article 81; first, where the parties to the deal are all located within one Member State; secondly, where the parties to the deal are all located outside the Community. Both may nevertheless fall within Article 81.
    The first issue, a deal apparently internal to one Member State, is discussed in the next case.

Cooperatieve Stremsel- en Kleurselfabriek v *Commission*
(Case 61/80)
[1981] ECR 851
Court of Justice of the European Communities

A cooperative of producers in the dairy sector required all its members to buy exclusively from each other. All the members were Dutch. The

Commission held that an effect on inter-State trade had been established. The Court agreed, for the following reasons:

[12] . . . [I]t should be recalled that for the agreement at issue to be caught by the prohibition contained in Article 85(1) it must have 'as its object or effect the prevention, restriction or distortion of competition within the common market'. The Cooperative's rules, which require its members to purchase from the Cooperative all the rennet and colouring agents for cheese which they need, and which reinforce that obligation by stipulating the payment of a not inconsiderable sum in the event of resignation or expulsion, have clearly as their object to prevent members from obtaining supplies from other suppliers of rennet or colouring agents or from making them themselves should those alternatives offer advantages from the point of view of quality or price. Since, according to information which has not been challenged, the members now account for more than 90% of Netherlands cheese output, those provisions in addition contribute to maintaining the present situation, in which the Cooperative is virtually the only supplier of rennet on the Netherlands market.

[13] Those provisions are thus of such a nature as to prevent competition, at the level of the supply of rennet and colouring agents for cheese, between producers holding a large part of the Community market in cheese, and also tend to rule out the possibility of creating a competitive situation on the whole of the Netherlands market in these ancillary substances which are indispensable in the making of cheese. In the circumstances, there is no need to examine the question whether other factors help to maintain the Cooperative's dominant position on the relevant market and whether such factors are sufficient to consolidate that position, even in the absence of the aforesaid provisions.

[14] In order to determine whether the agreement is contrary to Article 85(1) it is also necessary to consider whether it is liable to affect trade between Member States, that is to say whether, according to the consistent case-law of the Court, it is possible to foresee with a sufficient degree of probability that it may have an influence, direct or indirect, actual or potential, on the pattern of trade between Member States, thus rendering more difficult the interpenetration of trade which the Treaty is intended to create.

[15] It emerges from information supplied by the Commission that there is already trade in animal rennet and colouring agents between Member States and no mention has been made of technical or economic difficulties standing in the way of the expansion of such trade. On the other hand, bearing in mind the economic context to which they belong, the obligations contained in the rules of the Cooperative are precisely of such a nature as to reinforce the partitioning of markets on a national basis, thereby holding up the economic interpenetration which the Treaty is designed to bring about.

Note
Notice how the stress on preventing the isolation of national markets has much in common with the rationale of the *'Cassis de Dijon'* (Case 120/78) line of authority under Article 28. It can also be identified in *Keck* (Cases C-267 and 268/91) (p. 316 above). This is the law of market integration rather than a set of individual Treaty provisions.

The second issue, the deal external to the Community's borders, was examined by the Court in the 'Woodpulp' cartel case.

Ahlström Osakyhtio v *Commission*
(Cases 89, 104, 114, 116, 117 & 125–129/85)
[1988] ECR 5193; [1988] 4 CMLR 901
Court of Justice of the European Communities

[12]   It should be noted that the main sources of supply of wood pulp are outside the Community, in Canada, the United States, Sweden and Finland and that the market therefore has global dimensions. Where wood pulp producers established in those countries sell directly to purchasers established in the Community and engage in price competition in order to win orders from those customers, that constitutes competition within the common market.

[13]   It follows that where those producers concert on the prices to be charged to their customers in the Community and put that concertation into effect by selling at prices which are actually coordinated, they are taking part in concertation which has the object and effect of restricting competition within the common market within the meaning of Article 85 of the Treaty.

[14]   Accordingly, it must be concluded that by applying the competition rules in the Treaty in the circumstances of this case to undertakings whose registered offices are situated outside the Community, the Commission has not made an incorrect assessment of the territorial scope of Article 85.

[15]   The applicants have submitted that the decision is incompatible with public international law on the grounds that the application of the competition rules in this case was founded exclusively on the economic repercussions within the common market of conduct restricting competition which was adopted outside the Community.

[16]   It should be observed that an infringement of Article 85, such as the conclusion of an agreement which has had the effect of restricting competition within the common market, consists of conduct made up of two elements, the formation of the agreement, decision or concerted practice and the implementation thereof. If the applicability of prohibitions laid down under competition law were made to depend on the place where the agreement, decision or concerted practice was formed, the result would obviously be to give undertakings an easy means of evading those prohibitions. The decisive factor is therefore the place where it is implemented.

[17]   The producers in this case implemented their pricing agreement within the common market. It is immaterial in that respect whether or not they had recourse to subsidiaries, agents, sub-agents, or branches within the Community in order to make their contacts with purchasers within the Community.

[18]   Accordingly the Community's jurisdiction to apply its competition rules to such conduct is covered by the territoriality principle as universally recognized in public international law.

[19]   As regards the argument based on the infringement of the principle of non-interference, it should be pointed out that the applicants who are members of KEA have referred to a rule according to which where two States have jurisdiction to lay down and enforce rules and the effect of those rules is that a person finds himself subject to contradictory orders as to the conduct he must adopt, each State is obliged to exercise its jurisdiction with moderation. The applicants have concluded that by disregarding that rule in applying its competition rules the Community has infringed the principle of non-interference.

[20] There is no need to enquire into the existence in international law of such a rule since it suffices to observe that the conditions for its application are in any event not satisfied. There is not, in this case, any contradiction between the conduct required by the United States and that required by the Community since the Webb Pomerene Act merely exempts the conclusion of export cartels from the application of United States anti-trust laws but does not require such cartels to be concluded.

[21] It should further be pointed out that the United States authorities raised no objections regarding any conflict of jurisdiction when consulted by the Commission pursuant to the OECD Council Recommendation of 25 October 1979 concerning cooperation between member countries on restrictive business practices affecting international trade (*Acts of the organization*, Vol. 19, p. 376).

[22] As regards the argument relating to disregard of international comity, it suffices to observe that it amounts to calling in question the Community's jurisdiction to apply its competition rules to conduct such as that found to exist in this case and that, as such, that argument has already been rejected.

[23] Accordingly it must be concluded that the Commission's decision is not contrary to Article 85 of the Treaty or to the rules of public international law relied on by the applicants.

Note
The Court, by concentrating on 'implementation' (para. 16), is obviously skirting around an explicit adoption of the 'effects doctrine' of jurisdiction under international law. Advocate-General Darmon, after examining relevant authorities, had concluded ([1988] ECR, at p. 5227) that:

> . . . there is no rule of international law which is capable of being relied upon against the criterion of the direct, substantial and foreseeable effect. Nor does the concept of international comity, in view of its uncertain scope, militate against that criterion either.
>
> In the absence of any such prohibitive rule and in the light of widespread State practice, I would therefore propose that in view of its appropriateness to the field of competition, it be adopted as a criterion for the jurisdiction of the Community.

Question
Has the Court adopted a test which is distinct in practice from the 'effects doctrine'? For comment, read, e.g., J. B. Lange and D. Sandage (1989) 26 CML Rev 137; F. Mann (1989) 38 ICLQ 375; A. V. Lowe (1989) 48 CLJ 9.

(D) AN AGREEMENT

The 'agreement' which may be caught by Article 81 goes beyond the formal contract. Article 81 is aimed at the parties' intent, not the form in which that may be expressed. It covers informal agreements, claimed to be non-binding, secret cartels, and even imposed agreements. The next case involves the uncovering of the multi-faceted 'Quinine Cartel'.

ACF Chemiefarma v *Commission (Cases 41, 44 & 45/69)*
[1970] ECR 661
Court of Justice of the European Communities

[106]   The applicant complains that the Commission considered that the export agreement relating to trade with third countries and the gentlemen's agreement governing the conduct of its members in the Common Market constituted an indivisible entity as far as Article 85 was concerned.

[107]   The applicant states that the gentlemen's agreement, unlike the export agreement, did not constitute an agreement within the meaning of Article 85(1) and in any event it definitively ceased to exist from the end of October 1962.

[108]   The conduct of the parties to the export agreement does not in the applicant's view indicate that they continued the restrictions on competition which were originally provided for in the gentlemen's agreement.

[109]   The opposite conclusions reached by the contested decision are therefore alleged to be vitiated because they are based on incorrect findings.

[110]   The gentlemen's agreement, which the applicant admits existed until the end of October 1962, had as its object the restriction of competition within the Common Market.

[111]   The parties to the export agreement mutually declared themselves willing to abide by the gentlemen's agreement and concede that they did so until the end of October 1962.

[112]   This document thus amounted to the faithful expression of the joint intention of the parties to the agreement with regard to their conduct in the Common Market.

[113]   Furthermore it contained a provision to the effect that infringement of the gentlemen's agreement would *ipso facto* constitute an infringement of the export agreement.

[114]   In those circumstances account must be taken of this connexion in assessing the effects of the gentlemen's agreement with regard to the categories of acts prohibited by Article 85(1).

[115]   The defendant bases its view that the gentlemen's agreement was continued until February 1965 on documents and declarations emanating from the parties to the agreement the tenor of which is indistinct and indeed contradictory so that it is impossible to conclude whether those undertakings intended to terminate the gentlemen's agreement at their meeting on 29 October 1962.

[116]   The conduct of the undertakings in the Common Market after 29 October 1962 must therefore be considered in relation to the following four points: sharing out of domestic markets, fixing of common prices, determination of sales quotas and prohibition against manufacturing synthetic quinidine.

[117]   The gentlemen's agreement guaranteed protection of each domestic market for the producers in the various Member States.

[118]   After October 1962 when significant supplies were delivered on one of those markets by producers who were not nationals, as for example in the case of sales of quinine and quinidine in France, there was a substantial alignment of prices

conforming to French domestic prices which were higher than the export prices to third countries.

[119] It does not appear that there were alterations in the insignificant volume of trade between the other Member States referred to by the clause relating to domestic protection in spite of considerable differences in the prices prevailing in each of those States.

[120] The divergences between the domestic legislation of those States cannot by itself explain those differences in price or the substantial absence of trade.

[121] Obstacles which might arise in the trade in quinine and quinidine from differences between national legislation governing pharmaceutical products under trade-mark cannot relevantly be invoked to explain those facts.

[122] The correspondence exchanged in October and November 1963 between the parties to the export agreement with regard to the protection of domestic markets merely confirmed the intention of those undertakings to allow this state of affairs to remain unchanged.

[123] This intention was subsequently confirmed by Nedchem during the meeting of the undertakings concerned in Brussels on 14 March 1964.

[124] From those circumstances it is clear that with regard to the restriction on competition arising from the protection of the producers' domestic markets the producers continued after the meeting on 29 October 1962 to abide by the gentlemen's agreement of 1960 and confirmed their common intention to do so.

Note
Read also *BMW* v *Belgium* (Case 32/78) [1979] ECR 2435, [1980] 1 CMLR 370.

(E) THE CONCERTED PRACTICE

Even arrangements which are less formal than an agreement are caught by Article 81 if they constitute a 'concerted practice'. In fact, because both the agreement and the concerted practice fall within Article 81, there may be little point distinguishing between them. However, it remains crucial to differentiate collusion, whether agreement or concerted practice, from mere parallel behaviour, for the latter remains perfectly lawful. The next case illustrates the notion of the concerted practice and raises complex questions about the reach of Article 81. It is concerned with the dyestuffs industry and is commonly referred to as the 'Dyestuffs' case. Remember: Article 81 was Article 85 prior to the re-numbering effected by the Amsterdam Treaty (p. 29 above).

ICI v *Commission (Case 48/69)*
[1972] ECR 619
Court of Justice of the European Communities

The Court first examined the concept of a concerted practice.

[64]   Article 85 draws a distinction between the concept of 'concerted practices' and that of 'agreements between undertakings' or of 'decisions by associations of undertakings'; the object is to bring within the prohibition of that article a form of coordination between undertakings which, without having reached the stage where an agreement properly so-called has been concluded, knowingly substitutes practical cooperation between them for the risks of competition.

[65]   By its very nature, then, a concerted practice does not have all the elements of a contract but may *inter alia* arise out of coordination which becomes apparent from the behaviour of the participants.

[66]   Although parallel behaviour may not by itself be identified with a concerted practice, it may however amount to strong evidence of such a practice if it leads to conditions of competition which do not correspond to the normal conditions of the market, having regard to the nature of the products, the size and number of the undertakings, and the volume of the said market.

[67]   This is especially the case if the parallel conduct is such as to enable those concerned to attempt to stabilize prices at a level different from that to which competition would have led, and to consolidate established positions to the detriment of effective freedom of movement of the products in the Common Market and of the freedom of consumers to choose their suppliers.

[68]   Therefore the question whether there was a concerted action in this case can only be correctly determined if the evidence upon which the contested decision is based is considered, not in isolation, but as a whole, account being taken of the specific features of the market in the products in question.

The Court then proceeded to explore the nature of the dyestuffs market.

[69]   The market in dyestuffs is characterized by the fact that 80% of the market is supplied by about ten producers, very large ones in the main, which often manufacture these products together with other chemical products or pharmaceutical specialities.

[70]   The production patterns and therefore the cost structures of these manufacturers are very different, and this makes it difficult to ascertain competing manufacturers' costs.

[71]   The total number of dyestuffs is very high, each undertaking producing more than a thousand.

[72]   The average extent to which these products can be replaced by others is considered relatively good for standard dyes, but it can be very low or even non-existent for speciality dyes.

[73]   As regards speciality products, the market tends in certain cases towards an oligopolistic situation.

[74]   Since the price of dyestuffs forms a relatively small part of the price of the final product of the user undertaking, there is little elasticity of demand for dyestuffs on the market as a whole and this encourages price increases in the short term.

[75]   Another factor is that the total demand for dyestuffs is constantly increasing, and this tends to induce producers to adopt a policy enabling them to take advantage of this increase.

[76]   In the territory of the Community, the market in dyestuffs in fact consists of five separate national markets with different price levels which cannot be explained by differences in costs and charges affecting producers in those countries.

[77]   Thus the establishment of the Common Market would not appear to have had any effect on this situation, since the differences between national price levels have scarcely decreased.

[78]   On the contrary, it is clear that each of the national markets has the characteristics of an oligopoly and that in most of them price levels are established under the influence of a 'priceleader', who in some cases is the largest producer in the country concerned, and in other cases is a producer in another Member State or a third State, acting through a subsidiary.

[79]   According to the experts this dividing-up of the market is due to the need to supply local technical assistance to users and to ensure immediate delivery, generally in small quantities, since, apart from exceptional cases, producers supply their subsidiaries established in the different Member States and maintain a network of agents and depots to ensure that user undertakings receive specific assistance and supplies.

[80]   It appears from the data produced during the course of the proceedings that even in cases where a producer establishes direct contact with an important user in another Member State, prices are usually fixed in relation to the place where the user is established and tend to follow the level of prices on the national market.

[81]   Although the foremost reason why producers have acted in this way is in order to adapt themselves to the special features of the market in dyestuffs and to the needs of their customers, the fact remains that the dividing-up of the market which results tends, by fragmenting the effects of competition, to isolate users in their national market, and to prevent a general confrontation between producers throughout the Common Market.

[82]   It is in this context, which is peculiar to the way in which the dyestuffs market works, that the facts of the case should be considered.

The increases of 1964, 1965 and 1967

[83]   The increases of 1964, 1965 and 1967 covered by the contested decision are interconnected.

[84]   The increase of 15% in the prices of most aniline dyes in Germany on 1 January 1965 was in reality nothing more than the extension to another national market of the increase applied in January 1964 in Italy, the Netherlands, Belgium and Luxembourg.

[85]   The increase in the prices of certain dyes and pigments introduced on 1 January 1965 in all the Member States, except France, applied to all the products which had been excluded from the first increase.

[86]   The reason why the price increase of 8% introduced in the autumn of 1967 was raised to 12% for France was that there was a wish to make up for the increases of 1964 and 1965 in which that market had not taken part because of the price control system.

[87]   Therefore the three increases cannot be isolated from one another, even though they did not take place under identical conditions.

[88] In 1964 all the undertakings in question announced their increases and immediately put them into effect, the initiative coming from Ciba-Italy which, on 7 January 1964, following instructions from Ciba-Switzerland, announced and immediately introduced an increase of 15%. This initiative was followed by the other producers on the Italian market within two or three days.

[89] On 9 January ICI Holland took the initiative in introducing the same increase in the Netherlands, whilst on the same day Bayer took the same initiative on the Belgo-Luxembourg market.

[90] With minor differences, particularly between the price increases by the German undertakings on the one hand and the Swiss and United Kingdom undertakings on the other, these increases concerned the same range of products for the various producers and markets, namely, most aniline dyes other than pigments, food colourings and cosmetics.

[91] As regards the increase of 1965 certain undertakings announced in advance price increases amounting, for the German market, to an increase of 15% for products whose prices had already been similarly increased on the other markets, and to 10% for products whose prices had not yet been increased. These announcements were spread over the period between 14 October and 28 December 1964.

[92] The first announcement was made by BASF, on 14 October 1964, followed by an announcement by Bayer on 30 October and by Casella on 5 November.

[93] These increases were simultaneously applied on 1 January 1965 on all the markets except for the French market because of the price freeze in that State, and the Italian market where, as a result of the refusal by the principal Italian producer, ACNA, to increase its prices on the said market, the other producers also decided not to increase theirs.

[94] ACNA also refrained from putting its prices up by 10% on the German market.

[95] Otherwise the increase was general, was simultaneously introduced by all the producers mentioned in the contested decision, and was applied without any differences concerning the range of products.

[96] As regards the increase of 1967, during a meeting held at Basel on 19 August 1967, which was attended by all the producers mentioned in the contested decision except ACNA, the Geigy undertaking announced its intention to increase its selling prices by 8% with effect from 16 October 1967.

[97] On that same occasion the representatives of Bayer and Francolor stated that their undertakings were also considering an increase.

[98] From mid-September all the undertakings mentioned in the contested decision announced a price increase of 8%, raised to 12% for France, to take effect on 16 October in all the countries except Italy, where ACNA again refused to increase its prices, although it was willing to follow the movement in prices on two other markets, albeit on dates other than 16 October.

[99] Viewed as a whole, the three consecutive increases reveal progressive cooperation between the undertakings concerned.

[100] In fact, after the experience of 1964, when the announcement of the increases and their application coincided, although with minor differences as regards the range

of products affected, the increases of 1965 and 1967 indicate a different mode of operation. Here, the undertakings taking the initiative, BASF and Geigy respectively, announced their intentions of making an increase some time in advance, which allowed the undertakings to observe each other's reactions on the different markets, and to adapt themselves accordingly.

[101] By means of these advance announcements the various undertakings eliminated all uncertainty between them as to their future conduct and, in doing so, also eliminated a large part of the risk usually inherent in any independent change of conduct on one or several markets.

[102] This was all the more the case since these announcements, which led to the fixing of general and equal increases in prices for the markets in dyestuffs, rendered the market transparent as regard the percentage rates of increase.

[103] Therefore, by the way in which they acted, the undertakings in question temporarily eliminated with respect to prices some of the preconditions for competition on the market which stood in the way of the achievement of parallel uniformity of conduct.

[104] The fact that this conduct was not spontaneous is corroborated by an examination of other aspects of the market.

[105] In fact, from the number of producers concerned it is not possible to say that the European market in dyestuffs is, in the strict sense, an oligopoly in which price competition could no longer play a substantial role.

[106] These producers are sufficiently powerful and numerous to create a considerable risk that in times of rising prices some of them might not follow the general movement but might instead try to increase their share of the market by behaving in an individual way.

[107] Furthermore, the dividing-up of the Common Market into five national markets with different price levels and structures makes it improbable that a spontaneous and equal price increase would occur on all the national markets.

[108] Although a general, spontaneous increase on each of the national markets is just conceivable, these increases might be expected to differ according to the particular characteristics of the different national markets.

[109] Therefore, although parallel conduct in respect of prices may well have been an attractive and risk-free objective for the undertakings concerned, it is hardly conceivable that the same action could be taken spontaneously at the same time, on the same national markets and for the same range of products.

[110] Nor is it any more plausible that the increases of January 1964, introduced on the Italian market and copied on the Netherlands and Belgo-Luxembourg markets, which have little in common with each other either as regards the level of prices or the pattern of competition, could have been brought into effect within a period of two to three days without prior concertation.

[111] As regards the increases of 1965 and 1967 concertation took place openly, since all the announcements of the intention to increase prices with effect from a certain date and for a certain range of products made it possible for producers to decide on their conduct regarding the special cases of France and Italy.

422 Article 81: Cartels

[112]   In proceeding in this way, the undertakings mutually eliminated in advance any uncertainties concerning their reciprocal behaviour on the different markets and thereby also eliminated a large part of the risk inherent in any independent change of conduct on those markets.

[113]   The general and uniform increase on those different markets can only be explained by a common intention on the part of those undertakings, first, to adjust the level of prices and the situation resulting from competition in the form of discounts, and secondly, to avoid the risk, which is inherent in any price increase, of changing the conditions of competition.

Note

The key point about the 'Dyestuffs' case is that the Court decided that there was *no* oligopoly. There must, the Court deduced, have been a concerted practice which explained the absence of effective competition. Proof of concertation is problematic. You should carefully examine the 'Dyestuffs' judgment *and the Commission's decision* ([1969] CMLR D23) in order to determine which pieces of evidence you may take into account in locating a concerted practice.

See also *Coöperatieve Vereniging 'Suiker Unie' v Commission* (Cases 40-48, 50, 54-56, 111, 113 & 114/73) [1975] ECR 1663; J. Joshua, 'Proof in Contested EEC Competition Cases' (1987) EL Rev 315; L. Antunes 'Agreements and Concerted Practices under EEC Competition Law' (1991) 11 YEL 57.

The development of the law has been distorted because procedural irregularities have led to the annulment of some Commission Decisions which have found the existence of concerted practices. The 'Woodpulp Cartel' was considered above in connection with jurisdictional aspects (p. 414). The substance was dealt with by the Court in 1993, when it largely annulled the Decision. However, the Court provided important comment on proof of concertation. It said that parallel conduct is not proof of concertation unless concertation represents the only plausible explanation for such conduct. It then applied this principle to the producers' quarterly price announcements which the Commission had used as evidence of concertation:

A Ahlstrom Oy v Commission (Cases C-89, 104, 114,116–7, 125–129/85)
[1993] ECR I-1307, [1993] 4 CMLR 407

[126]   . . . [I]t must be stated that, in this case, concertation is not the only plausible explanation for the parallel conduct. To begin with, the system of price announcements may be regarded as constituting a rational response to the fact that the pulp market constituted a long-term market and to the need felt by both buyers and sellers to limit commercial risks. Further, the similarity in the dates of price announcements may be regarded as a direct result of the high degree of market transparency, which does not have to be described as artificial. Finally, the parallelism of prices and the price trends may be satisfactorily explained by the oligopolistic tendencies of the

market and by the specific circumstances prevailing in certain periods. Accordingly, the parallel conduct established by the Commission does not constitute evidence of concertation.

[127]   In the absence of a firm, precise and consistent body of evidence, it must be held that concertation regarding announced prices has not been established by the Commission. Article 1(1) of the contested decision must therefore be annulled.

Note
See comment by A. Jones (1993) 14 ECLR 273; G. Cumming [1994] JBL 165; C. Osti [1994] ECLR 176.

   Consider also *John Deere* v *Commission* (Case T-35/92) [1994] ECR II-957, for a case in which information exchange was found to violate Article 81, in part because of the confidential nature of the data exchanged. Residual market competition was inhibited by the reduced uncertainty about strategies planned by rival firms. In such litigation the Court of First Instance is today responsible for carrying out the function of checking the compatibility of the Commission's conduct of an investigation with Community law (see, e.g., on concertation, Case T-334/94 *Sarrio* v *Commission* [1998] ECR II-1439). The unsuccessful appeal in *John Deere* v *Commission* (Case C-7/95P) [1998] ECR I-3111 provides an example of the European Court's treatment of appeals against such CFI decisions.

   Where a true oligopoly exists (which in the view of both Court and Commission was *not* the case in 'Dyestuffs'), firms may make parallel decisions without colluding. Yet the observable result on the market would be more or less the same as if they had colluded. The inadequacies of the collusion-based Article 81 as a method for controlling true oligopolies appear to have tempted the Commission to move in the direction of treating firms in an oligopoly as collectively dominant and therefore subject to the prohibition of Article 82 against abusive conduct. (Article 82 is examined in depth in the next chapter.)

   In Commission Decision 89/93, *Flat Glass* [1990] 4 CMLR 535, (1989) OJ L33/44, it found that three Italian glass firms, FP, SIV and VP, had not only established an unlawful cartel but that moreover the firms were 'Participants in a tight oligopoly, [who] enjoy a degree of independence from competitive pressures that enables them to impede the maintenance of effective competition, notably by not having to take account of the behaviour of the other market participants'. The Commission decided that the three firms 'present themselves on the market as a single entity and not as individuals'. (For comment see M. Schodermeier, 'Collective Dominance Revisited' (1990) 11 ECLR 28.)

   In *Società Italiano Vetro SpA et al* v *Commission* (Cases T-68, 77 and 78/89) the Commission's Decision in *Flat Glass* was largely annulled by the Court of First Instance which found serious procedural irregularities in the Commission's handling of the case. However, the notion of collective dominance under Article 82 was not ruled out by the Court even though it was not satisfied that the Commission had shown such to exist in the case:

Società Italiano Vetro SpA et al v Commission
(Cases T-68, 77 and 78/89)
[1992] ECR II-1403, [1992] 5 CMLR 301

[358] . . . There is nothing, in principle, to prevent two or more independent economic entities from being, on a specific market, united by such economic links that, by virtue of that fact, together they hold a dominant position *vis-à-vis* the other operators on the same market. This could be the case, for example, where two or more independent undertakings jointly have, through agreements or licences, a technological lead affording them the power to behave to an appreciable extent independently of their competitors, their customers and ultimately of their consumers . . .

The Court added that:

[360] However, it should be pointed out that for the purposes of establishing an infringement of Article 86 of the Treaty [now Article 82], it is not sufficient, as the Commission's agent claimed at the hearing, to 'recycle' the facts constituting an infringement of Article 85 [now Article 81], deducing from them the finding that the parties to an agreement or to an unlawful practice jointly hold a substantial share of the market, that by virtue of that fact alone they hold a collective dominant position, and that their unlawful behaviour constitutes an abuse of that collective dominant position. Amongst other considerations, a finding of a dominant position which is in any case not in itself a matter of reproach, presupposes that the market in question has been defined . . . .

Note

For comment, see D. Pope (1993) 14 ECLR 172; more broadly on oligopoly control, R. Whish and B. Sufrin, 'Oligopolistic Markets and EC Competition Law' (1992) 12 YEL 59; B. Rodger, 'Market Integration and the Development of European Competition Policy to Meet New Demands' [1994/2] LIEI 1; T. Soames, 'An Analysis of the Principles of Concerted Practice and Collective Dominance: A Distinction without a Difference' [1996] ECLR 24; D. Stevens, 'Covert Collusion and Conscious Parallelism in Oligopolistic Markets: A Comparison of EC and US Competition Law' (1995) 15 YEL 47. Much of the recent debate about collective dominance has occurred in the context of EC merger control; see V. Korah [1999] ECLR 337.

Questions
1.   M. Franzosi has wryly observed (at (1988) 9 ECLR 385) that:

An indirect effect of the antitrust legislation is that its very vagueness will induce oligopolists to conceal their methods. This reduces the function of anti-trust legislation to that of a referee in a sham wrestling contest.

Do you agree?
To what extent is a structural instead of a behavioural approach to oligopolies either feasible or desirable under EC competition law?
2.   You are asked to advise Alpha, a producer in a market which contains only three other producers. Would the following be caught by Article 81?

(a)   Alpha's announcement of a 10% price rise, communicated 14 days in advance through a statement in the trade's leading journal;

(b)   Alpha's Christmas card, sent to the other three producers, which adds to seasonal greetings the comment: 'Life would be so much easier if we simply followed each other's prices! But of course we'd never get away with it.' Alpha's 5% price rise on 1 January is followed by the other three producers on 10 January;

(c)   the establishment of a trade association of which all four producers are members.

(F) MARKET DISTORTION

The deal, having satisfied the preceding requirements, must have as its 'object or effect the prevention, restriction or distortion of competition within the common market'. Each word in this phrase has some independent relevance, but the idea can be summarised as the requirement that *market distortion* be demonstrated.

The classic statement of the requirements of this test was supplied in *Société Technique Minière* v *Maschinenbau Ulm* (Case 56/65) [1966] ECR 235:

It must be possible to foresee with a sufficient degree of probability on the basis of a set of objective factors of law or fact that the agreement in question may have an influence, direct or indirect, actual or potential, on the pattern of trade between Member States.

Often this is not a difficult test to satisfy. In *Consten* (Cases 56 & 58/64), the contract clearly distorted normal competitive conditions. In *Cooperatieve Stremsel-* (Case 61/80), the Court explained how the arrangement distorted patterns of trade between The Netherlands and the rest of the common market.

(i) Preventing or distorting competition
A balance needs to be struck in the legal control of agreements which may contain terms seemingly restrictive of competition, yet which also may serve to promote market integration and product distribution. The next case examines whether the required element of market distortion may be found in an agreement which contributes to furthering competition and distribution in circumstances where both were previously lacking.

Nungesser v Commission (Case 258/78)
[1982] ECR 2015; [1983] 1 CMLR 278
Court of Justice of the European Communities

There is considerable technical expertise involved in the development of new types of seeds. The case involves techniques of cultivating new types of maize varieties. These skills are passed between plant breeders and are valuable. An agreement which may be subject to Article 81 is concluded where technical knowledge is transferred between traders in different Member States. The transfer in this case conferred exclusive rights for Germany on Nungesser. The Court was asked to annul the Commission's decision relating to the lawfulness of the agreement.

[44] . . . [T]he applicants criticize the Commission for wrongly taking the view that an exclusive licence of breeders' rights must by its very nature be treated as an agreement prohibited by Article 85(1) of the Treaty. They submit that the Commission's opinion in that respect is unfounded in so far as the exclusive licence constitutes the sole means, as regards seeds which have been recently developed in a Member State and which have not yet penetrated the market of another Member State, of promoting competition between the new product and comparable products in that other Member State; indeed, no grower or trader would take the risk of launching the new product on a new market if he were not protected against direct competition from the holder of the breeders' rights and from his other licensees.

The Court went on to examine the nature of the licences at issue; there were two distinct types.

[53] . . . The first case concerns a so-called open exclusive licence or assignment and the exclusivity of the licence relates solely to the contractual relationship between the owner of the right and the licensee, whereby the owner merely undertakes not to grant other licences in respect of the same territory and not to compete himself with the licensee on that territory. On the other hand, the second case involves an exclusive licence or assignment with absolute territorial protection, under which the parties to the contract propose, as regards the products and the territory in question, to eliminate all competition from third parties, such as parallel importers or licensees for other territories.

[54] That point having been clarified, it is necessary to examine whether, in the present case, the exclusive nature of the licence, in so far as it is an open licence, has the effect of preventing or distorting competition within the meaning of Article 85(1) of the Treaty.

[55] In that respect the Government of the Federal Republic of Germany emphasized that the protection of agricultural innovations by means of breeders' rights constitutes a means of encouraging such innovations and the grant of exclusive rights for a limited period, is capable of providing a further incentive to innovative efforts.

From that it infers that a total prohibition of every exclusive licence, even an open one, would cause the interest of undertakings in licences to fall away, which would be prejudicial to the dissemination of knowledge and techniques in the Community.

[56] The exclusive licence which forms the subject-matter of the contested decision concerns the cultivation and marketing of hybrid maize seeds which were developed by INRA after years of research and experimentation and were unknown to German farmers at the time when the cooperation between INRA and the applicants was taking shape. For that reason the concern shown by the interveners as regards the protection of new technology is justified.

[57] In fact, in the case of a licence of breeders' rights over hybrid maize seeds newly developed in one Member State, an undertaking established in another Member State which was not certain that it would not encounter competition from other licensees for the territory granted to it, or from the owner of the right himself, might be deterred

from accepting the risk of cultivating and marketing that product; such a result would be damaging to the dissemination of a new technology and would prejudice competition in the Community between the new product and similar existing products.

[58]   Having regard to the specific nature of the products in question, the Court concludes that, in a case such as the present, the grant of an open exclusive licence, that is to say a licence which does not affect the position of third parties such as parallel importers and licensees for other territories, is not in itself incompatible with Article 85(1) of the Treaty.

[59]   Part B of the third submission is thus justified to the extent to which it concerns that aspect of the exclusive nature of the licence.

[60]   As regard to the position of third parties, the Commission in essence criticizes the parties to the contract for having extended the definition of exclusivity to importers who are not bound to the contract, in particular parallel importers. Parallel importers or exporters, such as Louis David KG in Germany and Robert Bomberault in France who offered INRA seed for sale to German buyers, had found themselves subjected to pressure and legal proceedings by INRA, Frasema and the applicants, the purpose of which was to maintain the exclusive position of the applicants on the German market.

[61]   The Court has consistently held (cf. Joined Cases 56 and 58/64 *Consten and Grundig* v *Commission* [1966] ECR 299) that absolute territorial protection granted to a licensee in order to enable parallel imports to be controlled and prevented results in the artificial maintenance of separate national markets, contrary to the Treaty.

Note
The Court is prepared to accept that some apparent restrictions on trade are immune from control under Article 81(1), provided that they are necessary as part of a package for securing the conclusion of desirable deals. Yet a balance must be struck: only reasonable restraints are permitted to escape Article 81. Unduly tight or lengthy restrictions will not escape the prohibition in this way. So in *Nungesser* (Case 258/78) the Court would not countenance a licence which suppressed parallel trade (paras 53, 61). And in *Consten* (Cases 56 & 58/64) itself (p. 407 above), a deal which enhanced product distribution was held incompatible with the Treaty because of the extra clause which forbade parallel trade.

In the following case the Court considered the application of Article 85 of the EC Treaty (now Article 81 EC) to franchising agreements. Once again, it accepted that some apparent restraints on competition are simply part of a wider, desirable deal and therefore unaffected by Article 85 of the EC Treaty (now Article 81 EC).

Pronuptia de Paris GmbH v Pronuptia de Paris Irmgaard Schillgalis
(Case 161/84)
[1986] ECR 353; [1986] 1 CMLR 414
Court of Justice of the European Communities

The first question referred under the preliminary reference procedure (Chapter 4) by the German court asked:

Is Article 85(1) of the Treaty [now Article 81(1)] applicable to franchise agreements such as the contracts between the parties, which have as their object the establishment of a special distribution system whereby the franchisor provides to the franchisee, in addition to goods, certain trade names, trade-marks, merchandising material and services?

[27]   . . . the answer to the first question must be that:

(1)   The compatibility of franchise agreements for the distribution of goods with Article 85(1) depends on the provisions contained therein and on their economic context.
(2)   Provisions which are strictly necessary in order to ensure that the know-how and assistance provided by the franchisor do not benefit competitors do not constitute restrictions of competition for the purposes of Article 85(1).
(3)   Provisions which establish the control strictly necessary for maintaining the identity and reputation of the network identified by the common name or symbol do not constitute restrictions of competition for the purposes of Article 85(1).
(4)   Provisions which share markets between the franchisor and the franchisee or between franchisees constitute restrictions of competition for the purposes of Article 85(1).
(5)   The fact that the franchisor makes price recommendations to the franchisee does not constitute a restriction of competition, so long as there is no concerted practice between the franchisor and the franchisees or between the franchisees themselves for the actual application of such prices.
(6)   Franchise agreements for the distribution of goods which contain provisions sharing markets between the franchisor and the franchisees or between franchisees are capable of affecting trade between Member States.

Note
For a casenote see J. Venit (1986) 11 EL Rev 213. The area is now affected by a Block Exemption Regulation (on which see p. 450 below).

Similarities will be found in the Court's approach to selective distribution arrangements in *Metro* v *Commission* (Case 26/76) [1977] ECR 1875. See R. J. Goebel (1987) 24 CML Rev 605.

The use of this 'rule of reason' approach is common in US antitrust law. There are, however, reasons for doubting whether the US analogy can usefully be transplanted into EC law. The next extract subjects *Nungesser* (Case 258/78) and the rule of reason to close analysis before picking up this comparative issue. Remember that references to Article 85 should be read as Article 81 with post-Amsterdam eyes.

J. Peeters, 'The Rule of Reason Revisited: Prohibition on Restraints of Competition in the Sherman Act and the EEC Treaty'
(1989) 37 *American Journal of Comparative Law*,
pp. 521, 550–557, 568–570

(Most footnotes omitted.)

E.   Economic Policy Rule of Reason Under Article 85
The proponents of an economic policy rule of reason under Article 85(1) invoke the Court's opinion in the *Nungesser* case in support of their theory. The Commission had

refused to grant an exemption under Article 85(3), finding that the agreements between K. Eisele[137] and INRA[138] violated the prohibition of Article 85(1). In its legal analysis of the agreements under Article 85(1), the Commission had found restrictions upon the freedom of action of the parties to the agreement[140] and an effect upon third parties.[141] Its decision implied that every exclusivity would always be restrictive within the meaning of Article 85(1) and could only be exempted by means of Article 85(3). The agreements were denied exemption under Article 85(3). Even though the exclusivity in itself was capable of being considered to have satisfied all the tests for exemption under Article 85(3), the test for exemption of exclusive selling rights and their accompanying export prohibitions was not satisfied. . . . Absolute territorial protection . . . has had the sole and direct consequence of totally preventing imports via other channels of the original products . . . notwithstanding a persistent demand for such imports in Germany . . . such a situation neither constitutes nor contributes to an improvement within the meaning of the first test under Article 85(3) . . . [and] has excluded [the ultimate users] from obtaining a fair share of the benefit as required by the second test of Article 85(3).[144]

Answering the applicant's contention that the Commission's decision had wrongfully taken the view that an exclusive license of breeder's rights must by its very nature be treated as an agreement prohibited by Article 85(1) of the Treaty, the Court referred to the two sets of circumstances the Commission had taken into account in order to justify the application of Article 85(1) to the exclusive license in question and then observed that:

[The article here cites paras. 53-58 of the Court's judgment in *Nungesser* (Case 258/78), set out at p. 426 above.]

The distinction made between 'open' and 'closed' exclusive licenses and the holding that the Commission's decision was void insofar as it found that both violated Article 85(1) and could not be exempted under Article 85(3) should first of all be read as an application of the doctrine of partial illegality as adopted by the Court in the *Grundig* case. With regard to these open exclusive licenses the Court only stated that they were not in themselves incompatible with Article 85(1), leaving open the possibility that such a license can be prohibited. Nowhere does the Court say that this should be read as 'an open exclusive license does not violate Article 85(1) if the grant of the exclusivity is reasonable.'

Before analyzing this language, it is necessary, however, to define what the Court understands by an 'open' exclusive license. Although it defines a closed license as an agreement eliminating all competition from third parties in the licensed territory and

---

[137] The German Breeder and Seed Merchant.

[138] The French State Agency responsible for improving and developing crop production.

[140] These obligations are restrictive in that, by licensing a single undertaking to exploit its breeder's rights in a given territory, the licensor deprives himself for the entire duration of the contract of the ability to issue licenses to other undertakings in the same territory, thereby eliminating them as competing suppliers in that territory . . . by undertaking not to produce or market the product himself in the territory covered by the contract the licensor likewise eliminates himself . . . as supplier in that territory. 21 OJ Eur Comm (No. L 286) 31 (1978).

[141] The fact that third parties may not import the same seed from other Community Countries into Germany or export from Germany to other community countries, makes for market sharing and deprives German farmers of any real room for negotiation since seed is supplied by one supplier and one supplier only. 21 OJ Eur Comm (No. L 286) 31 (1978).

[144] The set of agreements and their manner of enforcement had conferred upon Eisele absolute territorial protection in Germany resulting in higher prices for German farmers than those charged in France for seeds that were absolutely identical. 21 OJ Eur Comm (No. L 286) 29 (1978).

names both parallel importers and licensees for other territories as third parties, in its ultimate holding the Court declares the Commission's decision void:

> in so far as that contract imposes upon INRA or those deriving rights from INRA to refrain from having the relevant seeds provided or sold by other licensees in Germany, and an obligation upon INRA or those deriving rights through INRA to refrain from producing or selling the relevant seeds in Germany themselves, and dismissed the application for the rest.[152]

Axter has argued that there might be a difference between the Court's holding and opinion: the open exclusive licenses would according to the holding, also include the right to exclude direct sales in Germany by licensees for other territories. The open exclusive license thus defined would allow contractual exclusion of all intra-brand trade except by parallel traders.[153] Upholding such an agreement under Article 85(1) departs markedly from the traditional analysis. It would imply that the Court has introduced under Article 85(1) a rule of reason where intra-brand restrictions[154] will be upheld as long as they are balanced by interbrand competition in the relevant market. Axter's reading of the Court's holding edits out however 'or those deriving rights through INRA', a crucial part of the holding since it includes the licensees for other territories. An open exclusive license as defined by the Court therefore not only requires intra-brand competition from parallel traders but also intra-brand competition from licensees for other territories, although perhaps not necessarily direct competition ('to refrain from selling themselves in Germany').

For a proper understanding of the distinction drawn by the Court, it might be interesting to take into account that the Commission wanted to have established whether the granting of a license as such is a 'putting on the market with consent' as defined in the Court's case law with regard to Articles 30 and 36 of the EEC Treaty [now Articles 28 and 30 EC]. If this could be established, it would mean that the granting of an exclusive license for a certain territory would by itself necessarily exclude the possibility of using industrial property rights to prevent export by the licensee to other territories within the Common Market.

The Court's definition of an open exclusive license requires the possibility of competition from both parallel traders and licensees from other territories. Applying the doctrine of partial illegality, the Court upheld the illegality of the 'closed' exclusive license but declared void the Commission's decision with regard to 'open' exclusive licenses as defined. In analyzing whether the Court has further shifted the analysis from Article 85(3) to Article 85(1), one should first establish whether such an 'open' exclusive license can ever be restrictive of competition under the traditional analysis.

The distinction made between restriction on the freedom of the parties to the agreement and effect on a third party reflects the analysis to be used with regard to horizontal agreements in order to find a restriction of competition. Although one can

---

[152] Eur. Ct. Rep. 2015. at s. 2077.

[153] Axter, 'Die Maissaatgutentscheidung des Europäischen Gerichtshof', 84 *GRUR Int.* 646 (1982). The Commission had only dealt with actions taken against independent parallel importers. The Court could thus limit its analysis to such restraints. This might explain the doctrinal dispute on the definition of an 'open' exclusive license. Hoffman, 'Die offene ausschliessliche Lizenz: Tragweite und Konzequenzen', 30 *R Intl Wirt* 93, 96 (1984) and Lutz, 'Lizenzverträge und sachlich notwendige Wettbewerbsbeschränkungen nach EG-Kartellrecht', 29 *R Intl Wirt* 485, 488 (1983).

[154] With the exception of parallel trade by non-licensees to avoid complete market partitioning in violation of the market-integration goal of the EEC.

argue whether the open exclusive license between Eisele and INRA was a horizontal or vertical agreement,[159] it should be noted that both the case-law of the Court of Justice and the decisions of the Commission have in this regard analyzed vertical agreements by looking at their horizontal effects on third parties.

Although reading 'third parties' as 'competitors, suppliers or purchasers', Advocate General VerLoren van Themaat insisted in his conclusion in the *Pronuptia* case, that the case law of the Court had held Article 85(1) applicable only when there had been a showing of injury to the third parties, 'which will seldom be the case where there are adequate alternative chains of distribution for similar products.'

I respectfully disagree. Article 85 was conceived as a prohibition (laid down in paragraph (1)) accompanied by a possibility of exemption (laid down in paragraph (3)). Never was there a need to establish injury. The Commission's case law regarding exclusive licenses reflected this type of analysis, but had never been subjected to the Court since none of the parties had an incentive to lodge an appeal against a decision granting an exemption.

Under the traditional analysis, such an open exclusive license is restrictive of competition within the meaning of Article 85(1) since the licensor undertakes to license no one else for the licensed territory, a restriction on the freedom of action of the parties to the agreement having a perceptible effect on third parties. The Court's holding that such a license is not in itself incompatible with Article 85(1) is, however, in no way based on a balancing of the restrictions imposed on intra-brand competition with the enhancement of inter-brand competition. Rather, the Court refers to the need to protect the licensee against competition from licensees for the same territory or the licensor himself to induce him to make the necessary investments in a new technology being licensed. Only 'in a case such as the present' will an open exclusive license not be incompatible with Article 85(1), implying that the Court has probably applied the doctrine of market opening. This doctrine starts from the premise that introducing a new product in the territory granted to the licensee, implies that the product itself was not yet available in that area, meaning no intrabrand competition could be restricted but inter brand competition will be created. Although one can argue that under such type of analysis the Court should not have objected to absolute territorial protection, including protection against parallel importers, such an argument tends to forget the goal of market integration and should therefore be rejected.[167]

According to the Commission, the *Nungesser* judgment confirmed that exclusive licenses can fall under Article 85(1) and that exclusive licenses which afford absolute

---

[159] If licensor and licensee become competing manufacturers in respect of the licensed technology, the patent license will have an important horizontal element. Where an inventor, who does not himself manufacture or sell, licenses numerous licensees the arrangement will be vertical as between the licensor and his licensees, restrictions imposed on the licensees will, if they use their own individual trade-marks to market the product, affect inter-brand competition in the product-market. Venit, 'In the Wake of Windsurfing — Patent Licensing within the Common Market', in Hawk (ed.), *Annual Proceedings of the Fordham Corporate Law Institute 1986*, 521–603 (1987). However, if the licensees use the licensor's trademark, restrictions imposed upon the licensee will affect intra-brand competition. See, e.g., the *Windsurfing* case.

[167] The *Distiller's* case has shown, however, that the Commission is prepared to give up this market-integration goal if as a result of its insistence on the removal of territorial protection, the manufacturer decides not to market the product at all. Commission Decision, *The Distiller's Company Ltd*, 20 December 1977, 21 OJ Eur Comm (No. L 50) 16 (1978) and Commission Decision, *Distillers Company Ltd Ship Chandlers*, 22 July 1980, 23 OJ Eur Comm (No. L 233) 43 (1980). See also Korah, 'Goodbye Red Label: condemnation of dual pricing by Distillers', 3 *Eur L Rev* 62 (1978); . . .

territorial protection can rarely, if ever, be exempted under Article 85(3).[168] But the Commission nevertheless thought it useful for the purpose of legal certainty to include them in Article 1 of the Group Exemption on Patent Licensing Agreements, insofar as in other cases agreements of this kind may fall within the scope of Article 85(1). The Regulation did not refer however to the distinction traditionally made between the existence of the industrial property right and its exercise.

. . .

CONCLUSION

Both Section 1 of the Sherman Act, as analyzed under a rule of reason standard, and Article 85, with its possibility of exemption under paragraph (3), provide means for limiting the applicability of the prohibition principle to 'unacceptable' restraints of trade. Until recently, both systems used similar policy considerations in administering this 'rule of reason'. But under EEC competition law only the Commission could grant such an 'exemption', leading to an untenable administrative situation.

These administrative concerns, however, are not the only arguments in favor of the introduction of a rule of reason into the analysis under Article 85(1). Invoking the current policy attitude towards vertical restraints under US antitrust law, the European Commission has been urged to give up its concern for vertical restraints and concentrate instead on horizontal restraints. The Commission's stand towards vertical territorial restraints has been criticized for neglecting the free-rider problem.

Several devices have been introduced to cure the administrative problems: group exemptions, comfort letters, short term notification . . .

The *de minimis* concept, as introduced by the Court and followed in the administrative practice of the Commission, shifted the line separating Article 85(1) from Article 85(3): under the *de minimis* concept an agreement will only be within the purview of Article 85(1) if it has a 'quantifiable' effect in the market. This should not be seen, however, as imposing the need for a market-analysis as used in US antitrust practice. The levels at which the agreement can be held to be a restriction of competition are far below the market shares as used in the US rule of reason analysis.

The ancillary restraints concept has been used in cases relating to the transfer of good-will, as in the selective distribution area. These restraints are indeed not restrictions of competition for the purpose of Article 85(1) since they are necessary if the agreements are to exist at all.

Neither are restrictions that are imposed while remaining within the specific object of intellectual and industrial property rights restrictions of competition for the purpose of Article 85. Such exercise of intellectual and industrial property rights remains outside of the reach of the EEC treaty for institutional reasons. However, anything that exceeds the specific object must be analyzed under Article 85(1). The market opening concept used in this regard in the *Nungesser* case, seems to have been abandoned by the Court in the *Pronuptia* case.

No European case has upheld under Article 85(1) an agreement in restraint of trade by taking into account that the restraints on intra-brand competition are outweighed by the enhancement of inter-brand competition. This balancing has always taken place at the level of Article 85(3). If such an economic policy rule of reason would be shifted toward the analysis under Article 85(1) very little would be achieved: current European case law tends to suggest that the Court will insist on the presence of workable competition and a taking into account of distributive concerns.

---

[168] Competition Report EC 1982, at 50–51.

Such a shift might of course solve the administrative problems since both the European commission and the national courts would have jurisdiction to exempt agreements in restraint of trade upon economic grounds. But from such a shift it might also follow that the antitrust plaintiff will have to establish the 'unreasonableness' of the agreement, since the national courts would have no jurisdiction over the exemption possibility of Article 85(3). This can only create new administrative problems and lead to unwanted per se rules!

The foregoing should suggest, however, that if this solution of the administrative problems is the goal of the introduction of a rule of reason in European competition law, it might be preferable to lift the exclusive jurisdiction over Article 85(3) as provided for in Regulation 17. In this way further confusion between solving the administrative problem and changing substantive European competition law would be avoided and the debate could really focus on what type of policy should be conducted under EEC 'competition' law. It is by no means a given fact that such 'policy' should solely by concerned with efficiency. That debate has only just started.

Note

As explained at p. 411 above, Article 81 is under the scrutiny of modernisers in the Commission because of both policy and administrative concerns. The Conclusion to this article by Peeters makes this theme particularly plain. In policy terms, restricting the reach of Article 81(1) would doubtless permit greater commercial freedom, while incidentally reducing the Commission's workload and curtailing the heavy emphasis on the role of exemption under Article 81(3). But such a restriction to Article 81(1)'s scope might damage the balance of interests mapped out for assessment by the Treaty's separation of Article 81's first and third paragraphs. For discussion of the nature of the rule of reason in this context, contrast R. Whish and B. Sufrin, 'Article 85 and the Rule of Reason' (1987) 7 YEL 1 with the approach of B. Hawk, 'System Failure: Vertical restraints and EC competition law' (1995) 32 CML Rev 973. The EC's new regime applicable to *vertical restraints*, discussed at p. 452 below, should be assessed with awareness of this debate.

Several of the administrative and enforcement techniques mentioned in the Conclusion to the extract from this article by Peeters will be examined further in Chapter 13. In particular, the lifting of the Commission's exclusive jurisdiction over Article 81(3), mentioned by Peeters in the final paragraph, is now under serious consideration as a result of the publication of the Commission's 1999 White Paper on Modernisation, discussed at p. 527 below.

In relation to several types of agreement, including distribution and franchising agreements, it has long ago been decided that the uncertainty which surrounds the application of Article 81 can best be allayed by the introduction of Block Exemption Regulations. These constitute, more or less, lists of permissible and impermissible clauses, and are of immense practical importance to the commercial lawyer. Regulation 2790/99 now governs vertical restraints (see below p. 452).

(ii) De minimis

Some agreements have an insignificant economic impact. In such circumstances the market distortion test is not met and Article 81 is inapplicable. The Court accepted the validity of this analysis in *Volk* v *Verwaecke* (Case 5/69)

[1969] ECR 295, and the Commission has sought to bring clarity to its scope by issuing an explanatory Notice. Such a Notice is not legislation, but its terms are influential, particularly in respect of Commission enforcement practice. Remember that Article 85 is, post-Amsterdam, Article 81.

Commission Notice on Agreements of Minor Importance which do not Fall Within the meaning of Article 85(1) of the Treaty Establishing the EC
(1997) OJ C372/13

I.

1.   The Commission considers it important to facilitate cooperation between undertakings where such cooperation is economically desirable without presenting difficulties from the point of view of competition policy. To this end, it published the notice concerning agreements, decisions and concerted practices in the field of cooperation between enterprises ([1]) listing a number of agreements that by their nature cannot be regarded as being in restraint of competition. Furthermore, in the notice concerning its assessment of certain subcontracting agreements ([2]) the Commission considered that that type of contract, which offers all undertakings opportunities for development, does not automatically fall within the scope of Article 85(1). The notice concerning the assessment of cooperative joint ventures pursuant to Article 85 of the EC Treaty ([3]) describes in detail the conditions under which the agreements in question do not fall under the prohibition of restrictive agreements. By issuing this notice which replaces the Commission notice of 3 September 1986 ([4]), the Commission is taking a further step towards defining the scope of Article 85(1), in order to facilitate cooperation between undertakings.

2.   Article 85(1) prohibits agreements which may affect trade between Member States and which have as their object or effect the prevention, restriction or distortion of competition within the common market. The Court of Justice of the European Communities has clarified that this provision is not applicable where the impact of the agreement on intra-Community trade or on competition is not appreciable. Agreements which are not capable of significantly affecting trade between Member States are not caught by Article 85. They should therefore be examined on the basis, and within the framework, of national legislation alone. This is also the case for agreements whose actual or potential effect remains limited to the territory of only one Member State or of one or more third countries. Likewise, agreements which do not have as their object or their effect an appreciable restriction of competition are not caught by the prohibition contained in Article 85(1).

3.   In this notice the Commission, by setting quantitative criteria and by explaining their application, has given a sufficiently concrete meaning to the term 'appreciable' for undertakings to be able to judge for themselves whether their agreements do not fall within the prohibition pursuant to Article 85(1) by virtue of their minor importance. The quantitative definition of appreciability, however, serves only as a guideline: in individual cases even agreements between undertakings which exceed the threshold set out below may still have only a negligible effect on trade between Member States or on competition within the common market and are therefore not

---

([1])   OJ C75, 29.7.1968. p. 3, as corrected in OJ C 84, 28.8.1968, p. 14.
([2])   OJ C1, 3.1.1979, p. 2.
([3])   OJ C43, 16.2.1993, p. 2.
([4])   OJ C231, 12.9.1986, p. 2.

caught by Article 85(1). This notices does not contain an exhaustive description of restrictions which fall outside Article 85(1). It is generally recognized that even agreements which are not of minor importance can escape the prohibition on agreements on account of their exclusively favourable impact on competition.

4. The benchmarks provided by the Commission in this notice should eliminate the need to have the legal status of agreements covered by it established through individual Commission decisions; notification for this purpose will no longer be necessary for such agreements. However, if it is doubtful whether, in an individual case, an agreement is likely to affect trade between Member States or to restrict competition to any significant extent, undertakings are free to apply for negative clearance or to notify the agreement pursuant to Council Regulations No. 17 ([5]), (EEC). No 1017/69 ([6]), (EEC) No. 4056/86 ([7]) and (EEC) No. 3975/87 ([8]).

5. In cases covered by this notice, and subject to points 11 and 20, the Commission will not institute any proceedings either on application or on its own initiative. Where undertakings have failed to notify an agreement falling within the scope of Article 85(1) because they assumed in good faith that the agreement was covered by this notice, the Commission will not consider imposing fines.

6. This notice is likewise applicable to decisions by associations of undertakings and to concerted practices.

7. This notice is without prejudice to the competence of national courts to apply Article 85. However, it constitutes a factor which those courts may take into account when deciding a pending case. It is also without prejudice to any interpretation of Article 85 which may be given by the Court of Justice or the Court of First Instance of the European Communities.

8. This notice is without prejudice to the application of national competition laws.

II.

9. The Commission holds the view that agreements between undertakings engaged in the production or distribution of goods or in the provision of services do not fall under the prohibition in Article 85(1) if the aggregate market shares held by all of the participating undertakings do not exceed, on any of the relevant markets:

(a) the 5% threshold, where the agreement is made between undertakings operating at the same level of production or of marketing ('horizontal' agreement);

(b) the 10% threshold, where the agreement is made between undertakings operating at different economic levels ('vertical' agreement).

In the case of a mixed horizontal/vertical agreement or where it is difficult to classify the agreement as either horizontal or vertical, the 5% threshold is applicable.

10. The Commission also holds the view that the said agreements do not fall under the prohibition of Article 85(1) if the market shares given at point 9 are exceeded by no more than one 10th during two successive financial years.

11. With regard to:

(a) horizontal agreements which have as their object
— to fix prices or to limit production or sales, or
— to share markets or sources of supply,

(b) vertical agreements which have as their object
— to fix resale prices, or

([5]) OJ 13, 21.2.1962, p. 204/62.
([6]) OJ L175, 23.7.1968, p. 1.
([7]) OJ L378, 31.12.1986, p. 4.
([8]) OJ L374, 31.12.1987, p. 1.

— to confer territorial protection on the participating undertakings or third undertakings,

the applicability of Article 85(1) cannot be ruled out even where the aggregate market shares held by all of the participating undertakings remain below the thresholds mentioned in points 9 and 10.

The Commission considers, however, that in the first instance it is for the authorities and courts of the Member States to take action on any agreements envisaged above in (a) and (b). Accordingly, it will only intervene in such cases when it considers that the interest of the Community so demands, and in particular if the agreements impair the proper functioning of the internal market.

12.   For the purposes of this notice, 'participating undertakings' are:

   (a)   undertakings being parties to the agreement;

   (b)   undertakings in which a party to the agreement, directly or indirectly,

— owns more than half of the capital or business assets, or

— has the power to exercise more than half of the voting rights, or

— has the power to appoint more than half of the members of the supervisory board, board of management or bodies legally representing the undertakings, or

— has to the right to manage the undertaking's business;

   (c)   undertakings which directly or indirectly have over a party to the agreement the rights or powers listed in (b);

   (d)   undertakings over which an undertaking referred to in (c) has, directly or indirectly, the rights or powers listed in (b).

Undertakings over which several undertakings as referred to in (a) to (d) jointly have, directly or indirectly, the rights or powers set out in (b) shall also be considered to be participating undertakings.

13.   In order to calculate the market share, it is necessary to determine the relevant market; for this, the relevant product market and the relevant geographic market must be defined.

14.   The relevant product market comprises any products or services which are regarded as interchangeable or substitutable by the consumer, by reason of their characteristics, prices and intended use.

15.   The relevant geographic market comprises the area in which the participating undertakings are involved in the supply of relevant products or services, in which the conditions of competition are sufficiently homogeneous, and which can be distinguished from neighbouring geographic areas because, in particular, conditions of competition are appreciably different in those areas.

16.   When applying points 14 and 15, reference should be had to the notice (on the definition of the relevant market under Community competition law ([9]). [p. 455 of this book]

17.   In the case of doubt about the delimitation of the relevant geographic market, undertakings may take the view that their agreement has no appreciable effect on intra-Community trade or on competition when the market share thresholds indicated in points 9 and 10 are not exceeded in any Member State. This view, however, does not preclude the application of national competition law to the agreements in question.

18.   Chapter II of this notice shall not apply where in a relevant market competition is restricted by the cumulative effects of parallel networks of similar agreements established by several manufacturers or dealers.

([9])   OJ C372, 9.12.1997, p. 5.

III.

19.   Agreements between small and medium-sized undertakings, as defined in the Annex to Commission recommendation 96/280/EC ([10]) are rarely capable of significantly affecting trade between Member States and competition within the common market. Consequently, as a general rule, they are not caught by the prohibition in Article 85(1). In cases where such agreements exceptionally meet the conditions for the application of that provision, they will not be of sufficient Community interest to justify any intervention. This is why the Commission will not institute any proceedings, either on request or on its own initiative, to apply the provisions of Article 85(1) to such agreements, even if the thresholds set out in points 9 and 10 above are exceeded.

20.   The Commission nevertheless reserves the right to intervene in such agreements:

   (a)   where they significantly impede competition in a substantial part of the relevant market,

   (b)   where, in the relevant market, competition is restricted by the cumulative effect of parallel networks of similar agreements made between several producers or dealers.

Notes

1.   This text replaces an earlier version of the Notice, (1986) OJ C231/2, amended (1994) OJ C368/20. There is an important shift of emphasis in the 1997 version of the Notice, for it abandons the previous practice of setting *de minimis* thresholds based on *both* market share *and* aggregate turnover of the participating undertakings. The 1997 Notice focuses on market shares alone.

2.   In assessing the economic impact of an agreement, its wider context must be appraised. An apparently minor agreement may fall foul of Article 81 if in reality it forms part of a network of similar agreements (*cf.* paras 18 and 20 of the Notice).

Brasserie de Haecht SA v *Wilkin (Case 23/67)*
[1967] ECR 407; [1968] CMLR 26
Court of Justice of the European Communities

The agreement was between a brewery and a cafe owner in Belgium. However, a number of similar agreements between the brewery and other cafe owners also existed.

. . . Article 85(1) mentions agreements, decisions and practices. By referring in the same sentence to agreements between undertakings, decisions by associations of undertakings and concerted practices, which may involve many parties, Article 85(1) implies that the constituent elements of those agreements, decisions and practices may be considered together as a whole.

Furthermore, by basing its application to agreements, decisions or practices not only on their subject-matter but also on their effects in relation to competition, Article 85(1) implies that regard must be had to such effects in the context in which they

---

([10])   OJ L107, 30.4.1996, p. 4.

occur, that is to say, in the economic and legal context of such agreements, decisions or practices and where they might combine with others to have a cumulative effect on competition. In fact, it would be pointless to consider an agreement, decision or practice by reason of its effects if those effects were to be taken distinct from the market in which they are seen to operate and could only be examined apart from the body of effects, whether convergent or not, surrounding their implementation. Thus in order to examine whether it is caught by Article 85(1) an agreement cannot be examined in isolation from the above context, that is, from the factual or legal circumstances causing it to prevent, restrict or distort competition. The existence of similar contracts may be taken into consideration for this objective to the extent to which the general body of contracts of this type is capable of restricting the freedom of trade.

Lastly, it is only to the extent to which agreements, decisions or practices are capable of affecting trade between Member States that the alteration of competition comes under Community prohibitions. In order to satisfy this condition, it must be possible for the agreement, decision or practice, when viewed in the light of a combination of the objective, factual or legal circumstances, to appear to be capable of having some influence, direct or indirect, on trade between Member States, of being conducive to a partitioning of the market and of hampering the economic interpenetration sought by the Treaty. When this point is considered the agreement, decision or practice cannot therefore be isolated from all the others of which it is one.

The existence of similar contracts is a circumstance which, together with others, is capable of being a factor in the economic and legal context within which the contract must be judged. Accordingly, whilst such a situation must be taken into account it should not be considered as decisive by itself, but merely as one among others in judging whether trade between Member States is capable of being affected through any alteration in competition.

Note

The link with defining the jurisdictional reach of Article 81 is plain. In similar fashion, an agreement which seems of purely local impact may have cross-border implications if viewed in its true context. See also *Windsurfing v Commission* (Case 193/83) [1986] ECR 611.

The Court pronounced further on this issue in *Stergios Delimitis* v *Henninger Brau* (Case C-234/89). As in the previous case, the litigation involved beer supply agreements.

Stergios Delimitis v *Henninger Brau (Case C-234/89)*
[1991] ECR I-935
Court of Justice of the European Communities

[14] In its judgment in Case 23/67 *Brasserie De Haecht* v *Wilkin* [1967] ECR 407, the Court held that the effects of such an agreement had to be assessed in the context in which they occur and where they might combine with others to have a cumulative effect on competition. It also follows from that judgment that the cumulative effect of several similar agreements constitutes one factor amongst others in ascertaining whether, by way of a possible alteration of competition, trade between Member States is capable of being affected.

[15]   Consequently, in the present case it is necessary to analyse the effects of a beer supply agreement, taken together with other contracts of the same type, on the opportunities of national competitors or those from other Member States, to gain access to the market for beer consumption or to increase their market share and, accordingly, the effects on the range of products offered to consumers.

[16]   In making that analysis, the relevant market must first be determined. The relevant market is primarily defined on the basis of the nature of the economic activity in question, in this case the sale of beer. Beer is sold through both retail channels and premises for the sale and consumption of drinks. From the consumer's point of view, the latter sector, comprising in particular public houses and restaurants, may be distinguished from the retail sector on the grounds that the sale of beer in public houses does not solely consist of the purchase of a product but is also linked with the provision of services, and that beer consumption in public houses is not essentially dependent on economic considerations. The specific nature of the public house trade is borne out by the fact that the breweries organize specific distribution systems for this sector which require special installations, and that the prices charged in that sector are generally higher than retail prices.

[17]   It follows that in the present case the reference market is that for the distribution of beer in premises for the sale and consumption of drinks. That finding is not affected by the fact that there is a certain overlap between the two distribution networks, namely inasmuch as retail sales allow new competitors to make their brands known and to use their reputation in order to gain access to the market constituted by premises for the sale and consumption of drinks.

[18]   Secondly, the relevant market is delimited from a geographical point of view. It should be noted that most beer supply agreements are still entered into at a national level. It follows that, in applying the Community competition rules, account is to be taken of the national market for beer distribution in premises for the sale and consumption of drinks.

[19]   In order to assess whether the existence of several beer supply agreements impedes access to the market as so defined, it is further necessary to examine the nature and extent of those agreements in their totality, comprising all similar contracts tying a large number of points of sale to several national producers (judgment in Case 43/69 *Bilger* v *Jehle* [1970] ECR 127). The effect of those networks of contracts on access to the market depends specifically on the number of outlets thus tied to national producers in relation to the number of public houses which are not so tied, the duration of the commitments entered into, the quantities of beer to which those commitments relate, and on the proportion between those quantities and the quantities sold by free distributors.

[20]   The existence of a bundle of similar contracts, even if it has a considerable effect on the opportunities for gaining access to the market, is not, however, sufficient in itself to support a finding that the relevant market is inaccessible, inasmuch as it is only one factor, amongst others, pertaining to the economic and legal context in which an agreement must be appraised (Case 23/67 *Brasserie De Haecht*, cited above). The other factors to be taken into account are, in the first instance, those also relating to opportunities for access.

[21]   In that connection it is necessary to examine whether there are real concrete possibilities for a new competitor to penetrate the bundle of contracts by acquiring a

brewery already established on the market together with its network of sales outlets, or to circumvent the bundle of contracts by opening new public houses. For that purpose it is necessary to have regard to the legal rules and agreements on the acquisition of companies and the establishment of outlets, and to the minimum number of outlets necessary for the economic operation of a distribution system. The presence of beer wholesalers not tied to producers who are active on the market is also a factor capable of facilitating a new producer's access to that market since he can make use of those wholesalers' sales networks to distribute his own beer.

[22] Secondly, account must be taken of the conditions under which competitive forces operate on the relevant market. In that connection it is necessary to know not only the number and the size of producers present on the market, but also the degree of saturation of that market and customer fidelity to existing brands, for it is generally more difficult to penetrate a saturated market in which customers are loyal to a small number of large producers than a market in full expansion in which a large number of small producers are operating without any strong brand names. The trend in beer sales in the retail trade provides useful information on the development of demand and thus an indication of the degree of saturation of the beer market as a whole. The analysis of that trend is, moreover, of interest in evaluating brand loyalty. A steady increase in sales of beer under new brand names may confer on the owners of those brand names a reputation which they may turn to account in gaining access to the public-house market.

[23] If an examination of all similar contracts entered into on the relevant market and the other factors relevant to the economic and legal context in which the contract must be examined shows that those agreements do not have the cumulative effect of denying access to that market to new national and foreign competitors, the individual agreements comprising the bundle of agreements cannot be held to restrict competition within the meaning of Article 85(1) of the Treaty. They do not, therefore, fall under the prohibition laid down in that provision.

[24] If, on the other hand, such examination reveals that it is difficult to gain access to the relevant market, it is necessary to assess the extent to which the agreements entered into by the brewery in question contribute to the cumulative effect produced in that respect by the totality of the similar contracts found on that market. Under the Community rules on competition, responsibility for such an effect of closing off the market must be attributed to the breweries which make an appreciable contribution thereto. Beer supply agreements entered into by breweries whose contribution to the cumulative effect is insignificant do not therefore fall under the prohibition under Article 85(1).

[25] In order to assess the extent of the contribution of the beer supply agreements entered into by a brewery to the cumulative sealing-off effect mentioned above, the market position of the contracting parties must be taken into consideration. That position is not determined solely by the market share held by the brewery and any group to which it may belong, but also by the number of outlets tied to it or to its group, in relation to the total number of premises for the sale and consumption of drinks found in the relevant market.

[26] The contribution of the individual contracts entered into by a brewery to the sealing-off of that market also depends on their duration. If the duration is manifestly excessive in relation to the average duration of beer supply agreements generally entered into on the relevant market, the individual contract falls under the prohibition

under Article 85(1). A brewery with a relatively small market share which ties its sales outlets for many years may make as significant a contribution to a sealing-off of the market as a brewery in a relatively strong market position which regularly releases sales outlets at shorter intervals.

[27] The reply to be given to the first three questions is therefore that a beer supply agreement is prohibited by Article 85(1) of the EEC Treaty, if two cumulative conditions are met. The first is that, having regard to the economic and legal context of the agreement at issue, it is difficult for competitors who could enter the market or increase their market share to gain access to the national market for the distribution of beer in premises for the sale and consumption of drinks. The fact that, in that market, the agreement in issue is one of a number of similar agreements having a cumulative effect on competition constitutes only one factor amongst others in assessing whether access to that market is indeed difficult. The second condition is that the agreement in question must make a significant contribution to the sealing-off effect brought about by the totality of those agreements in their economic and legal context. The extent of the contribution made by the individual agreement depends on the position of the contracting parties in the relevant market and on the duration of the agreement.

Question
Do you perceive any shift in emphasis in this ruling?

Note
The Commission's view of the implications of the *Delimitis* ruling for beer supply agreements may be found in a Notice published at (1992) OJ C121/2. This a further example of the Commission's work in developing policy from the accidents of litigation, *cf.* pp. 268, 305 and 383 above.

Municipality of Almelo and others v *Energiebedrijf IJsselmij NV* *(Case C–393/92)*
[1994] ECR I–1477
Court of Justice of the European Communities

The Court was asked to consider the application of Article 85 of the EC Treaty (now Article 81 EC) to distribution patterns for electricity in The Netherlands. These included a requirement imposed on local distributors to purchase exclusively from a Dutch supplier, which precluded importation of electricity.

[34] Article 85 of the Treaty applies, in its own terms, to agreements between undertakings which restrict competition and affect trade between Member States.

[35] As regards the existence of an agreement between undertakings, it is to be observed, as the Commission found in the 1991 Decision, that the electricity distribution system in the Netherlands is based on a network of contractual legal relationships between generators, between generators and regional distributors, between regional distributors and local distributors and, finally between local

distributors and end-users. The exclusive purchasing clause in issue before the national court is contained in the general conditions for the supply of electric power by a regional distributor to local distributors and therefore constitutes a clause contained in an agreement as referred to in Article 85 of the Treaty.

[36]   An agreement containing such a clause has a restrictive effect on competition, inasmuch as the clause prohibits the local distributors from obtaining electricity supplies from other suppliers.

[37]   In order to determine whether such an agreement has an appreciable effect on trade between Member States, it is necessary, as the Court observed in its judgments in Case 23/67 *Brasserie de Haecht* [1967] ECR 525 and Case C–234/89 *Delimitis* [1991] ECR I–935, to assess it in its economic and legal context and to take account of any cumulative effect resulting from the existence of other exclusivity agreements.

[38]   In that regard, it appears from the documents before the Court that the general conditions governing the relations between the parties to the main proceedings, which contain the exclusivity clause, follow the model General Terms and Conditions for the supply of electricity drawn up by the Association of Operators of Electricity Undertakings in the Netherlands.

[39]   Those contractual relationships have the cumulative effect of compartmentalising the national market, inasmuch as they have the effect of prohibiting local distributors established in the Netherlands from obtaining supplies of electricity from distributors or producers in other Member States.

Note
For another example of the Court's insistence on appraising the pattern of contractual relationships in their true economic and legal context, see Case C–306/96 *Javico et al* v *Yves St Laurent Parfums* [1998] ECR I-1983.

(iii) State involvement
What if the State is involved in the practice which causes market distortion? The approach of Community law depends on the precise nature of State participation. If the State is simply pursuing a commercial activity in, perhaps, the guise of a nationalised industry, then Article 81 will apply to any agreements struck (e.g. *Aluminium Products* (1985) OJ L92/1). If the body is a public undertaking or an undertaking to which the State grants special or exclusive rights, Article 86 applies. Article 86 requires conformity with the requirements of Article 81, but offers exception in its second paragraph where this is necessary to enable the entity to perform its assigned tasks. This is a narrow exception. Where the State obstructs cross-border trade by legislative or administrative action, Article 28 applies (Chapter 7). So the price-fixing cases such as *Tasca* (Case 65/75) (discussed above, at p. 271) involve obligations imposed on private firms to set prices within certain bands, but the measure caught by Community law is the State compulsion which falls within the definition of Article 28's prohibition on MEQRs. The State which subsidises domestic industry is liable to distort the market. Article 87 controls State aids.

    Where the State legislates to permit or encourage a breach of the competition rules, then not only do the parties to the agreement act in breach of the

Treaty, but also the State has violated its duty to cooperate in the pursuit of the objectives of the Community. It may be in breach of Article 10 (which was Article 5 pre-Amsterdam) read with the competition provisions. In the next case, the issue arose in relation to State approval of airline fare structures.

Ahmed Saeed Flugreisen v Zentrale zur Bekämpfung unlauteren Wettbewerbs (Case 66/86)
[1989] ECR 803; [1990] 4 CMLR 102
Court of Justice of the European Communities

[48] . . . [I]t should be borne in mind in the first place that, as the Court has consistently held, while it is true that the competition rules set out in Articles 85 and 86 concern the conduct of undertakings and not measures of the authorities in the Member States, Article 5 of the Treaty nevertheless imposes a duty on those authorities not to adopt or maintain in force any measure which could deprive those competition rules of their effectiveness. That would be the case, in particular, if a Member State were to require or favour the adoption of agreements, decisions or concerted practices contrary to Article 85 or reinforce their effects (see, most recently, the judgment of 1 October 1987 in Case 311/85 *Vereniging van Vlaamse Reisbureaus v Sociaale Dienst van de plaatselijke en gewestelijke Overheidsdiensten* [1987] ECR 3801).

[49] It must be concluded as a result that the approval by the aeronautical authorities of tariff agreements contrary to Article 85(1) is not compatible with Community law and in particular with Article 5 of the Treaty. It also follows that the aeronautical authorities must refrain from taking any measure which might be construed as encouraging airlines to conclude tariff agreements contrary to the Treaty.

[50] In the specific case of tariffs for scheduled flights that interpretation of the Treaty is borne out by Article 90(1) of the Treaty, which provides that in the case of undertakings to which Member States grant special or exclusive rights – such as rights to operate on an air route alone or with one or two other undertakings – Member States must not enact or maintain in force any measure contrary to the competition rules laid down in Articles 85 and 86. Moreover, it is stated in the preambles to Council Regulations Nos 3975 and 3976/87 that those regulations do not prejudice the application of Article 90 of the Treaty.

[51] Admittedly, in the preamble to Regulation No 3976/87 the Council expressed a desire to increase competition in air transport services between Member States gradually so as to provide time for the sector concerned to adapt to a system different from the present system of establishing a network of agreements between Member States and air carriers. However, that concern can be respected only within the limits laid down by the provisions of the Treaty.

[52] Whilst, as a result, the new rules laid down by the Council and the Commission leave the Community institutions and the authorities in the Member States free to encourage the airlines to organize mutual consultations on the tariffs to be applied on certain routes served by scheduled flights, such as the consultations provided for in Directive 87/601/EEC, the Treaty nevertheless strictly prohibits them from giving encouragement, in any form whatsoever, to the adoption of agreements or concerted practices with regard to tariffs contrary to Article 85(1) or Article 86, as the case may be.

[53] The national court also refers to Article 90(3), but that provision appears to be of no relevance for the purpose of resolving the problems raised by this case. That

provision places the Commission under a duty to ensure the application of the provisions of Article 90 and to address, where necessary, appropriate directives or decisions to Member States; it does not, however, preclude the application of paragraphs (1) and (2) of that article where the Commission fails to act.

[54] In contrast, Article 90(2) might entail consequences for decisions by the aeronautical authorities with regard to the approval of tariffs. That provision provides *inter alia* that undertakings entrusted with the operation of services of general economic interest are to be subject to the competition rules contained in the Treaty, in so far however as the application of such rules does not obstruct the performance of the particular tasks assigned to them.

[55] That provision may be applied to carriers who may be obliged, by the public authorities, to operate on routes which are not commercially viable but which it is necessary to operate for reasons of the general interest. It is necessary in each case for the competent national administrative or judicial authorities to establish whether the airline in question has actually been entrusted with the task of operating on such routes by an act of the public authority (judgment of 27 March 1974 in Case 127/73 *Belgische Radio en Televisie* v *Sabam* ('BRT-II') [1974] ECR 313).

[56] However, for it to be possible for the effect of the competition rules to be restricted pursuant to Article 90(2) by needs arising from performance of a task of general interest, the national authorities responsible for the approval of tariffs and the courts to which disputes relating thereto are submitted must be able to determine the exact nature of the needs in question and their impact on the structure of the tariffs applied by the airlines in question.

[57] Indeed, where there is no effective transparency of the tariff structure it is difficult, if not impossible, to assess the influence of the task of general interest on the application of the competition rules in the field of tariffs. It is for the national court to make the necessary findings of fact in that connection.

[58] It follows from the foregoing considerations that it should be stated in reply to the third question submitted by the national court that Articles 5 and 90 of the EEC Treaty must be interpreted as:

(i) prohibiting the national authorities from encouraging the conclusion of agreements on tariffs contrary to Article 85(1) or Article 86 of the Treaty, as the case may be;

(ii) precluding the approval by those authorities of tariffs resulting from such agreements;

(iii) not precluding a limitation of the effects of the competition rules in so far as it is indispensable for the performance of a task of general interest which air carriers are required to carry out, provided that the nature of that task and its impact on the tariff structure are clearly established.

Note

German legislation which restricted the growth of a market in employment procurement services was at issue in the next case. The Court made it clear that a State which nurtures an uncompetitive market may violate the Treaty rules. The result of the application of the Community rules is market liberalisation.

Höfner v *Macrotron (Case C-41/90)*
[1991] ECR I-1979
Court of Justice of the European Communities

[34] . . . [A] public employment agency engaged in employment procurement activities is subject to the prohibition contained in Article 86 of the Treaty [now Article 82], so long as the application of that provision does not obstruct the performance of the particular task assigned to it. A Member State which has conferred an exclusive right to carry on that activity upon the public employment agency is in breach of Article 90(1) of the Treaty [now Article 86(1)] where it creates a situation in which that agency cannot avoid infringing Article 86 of the Treaty [now Article 82]. That is the case, in particular, where the following conditions are satisfied:

— the exclusive right extends to executive recruitment activities;
— the public employment agency is manifestly incapable of satisfying demand prevailing on the market for such activities;
— the actual pursuit of those activities by private recruitment consultants is rendered impossible by the maintenance in force of a statutory provision under which such activities are prohibited and non-observance of that prohibition renders the contracts concerned void;
— the activities in question may extend to the nationals or to the territory of other Member States.

Note
The profile of EC law's supervision of anticompetitive State laws has increased markedly since the late-1980s. This has given rise to challenges to long-standing national monopolies in areas such as energy supply and telecommunications. It is beyond the scope of this book to provide extended coverage. The following articles offer scope for further reading:

Edward, D. and Hoskins, M., 'Article 90: Deregulation and EC Law. Reflections arising from the XVI FIDE Conference' (1995) 32 CML Rev 157.
Ehlermann, C.-D., 'Managing Monopolies: the Role of the State in Controlling Market Dominance in the European Community' (1993) 14 ECLR 61.
Gyselen, L., 'Anti-Competitive State Measures under the EC Treaty: Towards a Substantive Legality Standard' (1993) EL Rev CC 55.
Ross, M., 'Article 16 EC and Services of general interest: from derogation to obligation' (2000) 25 EL Rev 22.

Note
Nevertheless, the Court does not assert a general power to supervise all State intervention in the market. It is necessary to establish the application of one or more specific Treaty provisions. In the next case the Court picks its way carefully through the Treaty provisions to which reference is made by the

national court and concludes that none prevents the application of the Italian rules in question.

DIP SpA v Comune di Bassano del Grappa (Case C–140/94), LIDL Italia SrL v Comune di Chioggia (Case C–141/94), Lingral SrL v Comune di Chioggia (Case C–142/94)
[1995] ECR I-3257
Court of Justice of European Communities

The three applicants had been refused licences to open retail premises. Under the relevant Italian legislation, opening a new shop is subject to the issue of a licence by the local mayor on the opinion of a municipal committee, taking into account the criteria laid down in a commercial development plan drawn up by each municipality after consulting the committee. The committee membership is determined by law and its precise composition differs depending whether the municipality has more or fewer than 50,000 inhabitants. However, in either instance, members include public officials, an urban planning expert and traffic expert appointed by the town council, experts on distribution problems appointed with the involvement of trade and consumer representative organisations and, finally, workers' representatives. The Court first considered whether the State could be held in violation of Article 5 read with Articles 85 and 86 of the EC Treaty (now Articles 10, 81 and 82 EC) by introducing or maintaining in force measures which may render ineffective the competition rules applicable to undertakings. It stated that:

[15]   The Court has held that Articles 5 and 85 are infringed where a Member State requires or favours the adoption of agreements, decisions or concerted practices contrary to Article 85 or reinforces their effects, or where it deprives its own rules of the character of legislation by delegating to private economic operators responsibility for taking decisions affecting the economic sphere. . . .

The Court continued:

[17]   As regards rules such as those contained in the Italian Law, it should first be pointed out that members appointed or nominated by traders' organisations are in a minority on the municipal committees, side by side with workers' representatives, representatives of public authorities and experts appointed by the latter.

[18]   Moreover, as expressly indicated in that law, the members appointed or nominated by traders' organisations are present as experts on distribution problems and not in order to represent their own business interests, and in drawing up its opinions the municipal committee is to observe the public interest.

[19]   It follows from the foregoing considerations that in a trading licence system such as that established by the Italian Law, the opinions adopted by the municipal committee cannot be regarded as agreements between traders which the public authorities have required or favoured or the effects of which they have reinforced.

[20]   It must next be considered . . . whether the public authorities have delegated their powers in the matter of trading licences to private economic operators.

[21]   The Italian Law provides that licences are to be issued by the mayor of the municipality concerned, taking into account the criteria laid down in the municipal commercial development plan. The purpose of that plan is to provide the best possible service for consumers and the best possible balance between permanent trading establishments and foreseeable demand from the population.

[22]   Furthermore,the municipal committee is called on to give the mayor merely an opinion on individual licenses. It is only where the municipality does not yet have an approved commercial development plan that licences may not be issued unless the committee's opinion is favourable.

[23]   It follows from the foregoing considerations that, in a system such as that established by the Italian Law, the public authorities have not delegated their powers to private economic operators.

[24]   Articles 3(g), 5 and 86 of the Treaty could apply to rules such as those contained in the Italian Law only if it were proved that that law creates a position of economic strength for an undertaking which enables it to prevent effective competition being maintained on the relevant market by affording it the power to behave to an appreciable extent independently of its competitors, its customers and, ultimately, the consumers (judgment in Case 85/76 *Hoffmann-La Roche* v *Commission* [1979] ECR 461, paragraph 38).

[25]   The Court has held that Article 86 of the Treaty prohibits abusive practices resulting from the exploitation, by one or more undertakings, of a dominant position on the common market or in a substantial part of it, in so far as those practices may affect trade between Member States (judgment in Case C–393/92 *Almelo and Others* v *Energiebedriff IJsselmij* [1994] ECR I–1477, paragraph 40).

[26]   In order to find that a collective dominant position exists, the undertakings in question must be linked in such a way that they adopt the same conduct on the market (judgment in *Almelo*, paragraph 42).

[27]   National rules which require a licence to be obtained before a new shop can be opened and limit the number of shops in the municipality in order to achieve a balance between supply and demand cannot be considered to put individual traders in dominant positions or all the traders established in a municipality in a collective dominant position, a salient feature of which would be that traders did not compete against one another.

[28]   It follows that Articles 85 and 86, in conjunction with Articles 3(g) and 5, of the Treaty do not preclude rules such as those contained in the Italian Law.

The Court then completed its exploration of EC trade law by adding reference to Article 30 of the EC Treaty (now, after amendment, Article 28: Chapters 7 and 8):

[29]   On this point, it is sufficient to observe that rules such as those contained in the Italian Law make no distinction according to the origin of the goods distributed by the business concerned, that their purpose is not to regulate trade in goods with other Member States and that the restrictive effects which they might have on the free movement of goods are too uncertain and indirect for the obligation which they impose to be regarded as being capable of hindering trade between Member States (judgment in

Case C–379/92 *Peralta* [1994] ECR I–3453, paragraph 24, and the decisions cited above).

[30]   Article 30 does not therefore preclude legislation such as the Italian Law.

Questions

1.   The referring national court did not ask about the potential application of Articles 52 or 59 of the EC Treaty (now, after amendment, Articles 43 and 49 respectively), which govern establishment and provision of services respectively. What would be the relevance of those Treaty provisions in such circumstances?

2.   Laws such as that in issue in this decision place barriers to entry on to the market by potential new suppliers. Where a licence is refused, this may forestall a widening of consumer choice and may allow existing operators to cushion themselves from (potentially price-cutting) competitors. So is the European Court well advised to decline to take a stand on the permissibility of such a rule?

Note

See also Case C-38/97 *Autotrasporti Librandi Snc di Librandi F & C* [1998] ECR I-5955; Case C-67/96 *Albany International BV*, judgment of 21 September 1999. The market regulation in question is treated by the Court as a matter of national competence untouched by EC trade law. The decision should be read in conjunction with discussion elsewhere of the outer limits to EC trade law (pp. 300, 374). In adopting a relatively narrow focus, the Court has declined the temptation to create a general economic constitutional law for the Community (see N. Bernard, 'Discrimination and Free Movement in EC Law' (1996) 45 ICLQ 82, P. Davies, 'Market Integration and Social Policy' (1995) 25 ILJ 49, D. Gerber, 'Constitutionalising the Economy: German Neo-Liberalism, Competition law and the "New" Europe' (1994) 42 AJCL 25, T. Hervey, 'Social Solidarity: a buttress against internal market' in J. Shaw (ed.), *Social Law and policy in an Evolving European Union* (2000), B. Van Der Esch, 'Loyauté Fédérale et Subsidiarité' (1994) 30 CDE 523).

(G) EXEMPTION

Article 81(3) permits exemption of agreements falling within Article 81(1). It is set out at p. 407 above. It implies a cost-benefit assessment, whereby the advantages of collaboration are balanced against the disadvantages of impeded competition. However, the terms of Article 81(3) are rather more specific than general economic cost-benefit. The provision contains four elements; two positive conditions and two negative conditions. All must be satisfied. The two positive conditions demand a yield of economic progress, a fair share of which must percolate to the consumer; the two negative conditions forbid unnecessary extra restraints and the elimination of competition.

Typically, a Commission Decision relating to Article 81(3) will appraise the general economic context of an agreement and then proceed to apply these four elements. Despite this step-by-step approach, all four elements are inter-linked. The following Decision illustrates the types of argument relevant under Article 81(3) and the application of the conditions, two positive, two negative.

Prym-Werke
[1973] CMLR D250; (1973) OJ L296/24
Commission Decision 73/323

Prym agreed to give up making needles. It agreed to buy its needle needs from Beka. Beka agreed to supply Prym. Beka could then specialise in needle production. The Commission decided to exempt the agreement after the following analysis.

. . . [T]he concentration of manufacturing agreed on by Prym and Beka has, from the point of view of the improvement of production, favourable effects analogous to those of specialisation; it causes an increase of at least 50 per cent in the quantity of needles to be manufactured in the Eupen factory, which makes it possible to make more intensive use of the existing plant and to introduce production-line manufacture.

This rationalisation of production has in particular made it possible to reduce the very large proportion of labour costs in the producer's cost price. The producer's cost price of 'Standard' quality needles, which fell by some 20 per cent in 1970 after the concentration of production at Eupen, was still lower at the end of 1972 than in 1969 in spite of the increases in wages and in the cost of raw materials which had occurred during those four years. The introduction of mechanised production-line manufacture with increased productive capacity also makes it possible to manufacture articles of a more even quality.

The agreement allows consumers a fair share of the benefit resulting from it, as it must be supposed that because of the pressure of competition existing on the needle market the advantages resulting from rationalisation will be passed on to consumers.

The agreement does not contain restrictions which are not indispensable to the attainment of the said advantages. The favourable effects of the agreement are due essentially to the improvement in productivity resulting from a more intensive utilisation of productive capacity, and that more intensive utilisation is only possible if the quantities of needles to be manufactured are, and are to remain, considerably larger than before. That being so, it is essential that Prym should enter into a commitment for a long period, not only to cease manufacture, but also to purchase all its requirements of needles for domestic sewing machines from Beka, so as to provide a guarantee for an increased output by the latter.

The long-term commitments by Prym to obtain its supplies exclusively from Beka thus represents an indispensable restriction if the favourable effects of the agreement are to be achieved and, moreover, maintained. That commitment, moreover, does not go beyond what is strictly necessary, since it allows Prym the possibility, in the event of Beka being unable to meet its commitments, of buying from other sources and since, in any case, Prym gets the benefit of preferential prices.

The agreement does not afford the parties the possibility of eliminating competition in respect of a substantial part of the products in question. In the amended version in force since 10 October 1972 the agreement no longer prevents Beka and Prym from competing with each other on any EEC market, whether geographic or sectoral. Both undertakings rest exposed to the keen competition from other, sometimes larger, producers who appear as sellers within the EEC.

All the conditions necessary for the application of Article 85(3) of the Treaty [now Article 81(3) are thus fulfilled.

Question
Why was exemption unavailable to the Consten/Grundig deal (p. 407 above)?
After all, it improved product distribution; German goods were available in
France. Consider each of the four elements of Article 81(3).

Note
It is relatively uncommon for an agreement to be denied exemption due to
failure to satisfy one element only. See, e.g., *WANO Schwarzpulver* (1978) OJ
L322/26, [1979] 1 CMLR 403, for an example of a Commission Decision
which finds several reasons for refusal and illustrates how the four elements
of Article 81(3) are connected.

(H) BLOCK EXEMPTION

The four elements of Article 81(3) find practical expression in Block Exemption
Regulations. These measures apply the criteria for exemption to particular types
of collaboration. As charters for lawful agreements, they assist in the practical
administration of the competition rules by the Commission; and in commercial
planning by firms. At the beginning of 2000 there were several Block Exemption
Regulations in force. They covered several types of agreement. Some regulations
dealt with agreements of a vertical type (those between traders at different points
in the supply chain, e.g., Regulation 1983/83 on exclusive distribution,
Regulation 1984/83 on exclusive purchasing and Regulation 4087/88 on
franchising). Others covered agreements more typically struck on a horizontal
basis (between traders at the same point on the supply chain, e.g., Regulation
418/85 on research and development, Regulation 417/85 on specialisation). But
the Commission's approach to block exemptions is currently undergoing a
radical overhaul. The Commission launched an extensive review of its treatment
of vertical restraints in its Green Paper on *Vertical Restraints in EC Competition
Policy*, published in January 1997 (COM (96) 721. As already mentioned at pp.
411 and 433 above, this review was initiated against a background of increasing
pressure from commercial interests and from some academics in favour of
relaxing the grip of Article 81 on private contractual autonomy. Concerns rooted
in both policy and administration underpin the review. 'Background and reasons
for the Green Paper' form the opening section of its Executive Summary:

Green Paper on Vertical Restraints in EC Competition Policy
Executive Summary

Background and reasons for Green Paper[1]
1.   The creation of a single market is one of the main objectives of the European
Union's competition policy. Whilst great progress has been made further efforts are
still necessary if the full economic advantages of integration are to be realised.
2.   The single market represents an opportunity for EU firms to enter new markets
that may have been previously closed to them because of government barriers. This
penetration of new markets takes time and investment and is risky. The process is

---

[1]   Each heading in this executive summary corresponds to a chapter in this Green Paper.

often facilitated by agreements between producers who want to break into a new market and local distributors. Efficient distribution with appropriate pre- and after-sales support is part of the competitive process that brings benefits to consumers.

However, arrangements between producers and distributors can also be used to continue the partitioning of the market and exclude new entrants who would intensify competition and lead to downward pressure on prices. Agreements between producers and distributors (vertical restraints) can therefore be used pro-competitively to promote market integration and efficient distribution or anti-competitively to block integration and competition. The price differences between Member States that are still found provide the incentive for companies to enter new markets as well as to erect barriers against new competition.

3.   Because of their strong links to market integration that can be either positive or negative, vertical restraints have been of particular importance to the Union's competition policy. Whilst this policy has been successful in over 30 years of application a review is now necessary because

- the single market legislation for the free movement of products is now largely in place
- the Regulations governing vertical restraints expire, and
- there have been major changes in methods of distribution that may have implications for policy.

4.   In addition, as the world's largest trading block, the Union is committed to the development of open and fair international trade. Just as vertical restraints can either promote or hinder the creation of a real single market, they can be either beneficial or detrimental to international trade. The Union's policy in this area is therefore of wider international importance. Our experience may be useful for analysing market access impediments in third countries.

5.   The review of policy takes the form of a Green Paper, which sets out the relevant issues as understood by the Commission[2]. Several policy options (point VIII below) are set out which will form the basis for a wide reaching public consultation involving Parliament, Member States, the Economic and Social Committee and Committee of Regions as well as all interested parties (producers, distributors, workers' representatives and consumers). This consultation will allow the Commission to decide on the direction and form of future policy in the full light of all the facts. This review and consultation also constitute the Commission's response to the exciting challenge of taking forward this key area of competition policy into the next millennium.

The Green Paper generated the lively debate that one would expect of a document which represented an invitation to consider the 'modernisation' of EC competition law after almost 40 years of experience.

Reading on the Green Paper on Vertical Restraints
Bright, C., 'EU Competition Policy: Rules, Objectives and Deregulation' (1996) 16 OxJLS 535.

---

[2]   This Green Paper does not cover motor vehicles, commercial agents or licensing of intellectual property which have been or are the object of separate exercises. The focus is primarily on vertical restraints in the distribution chain. However, comments are also invited in relation to upstream linkages in the supply chain between producers and suppliers of intermediary inputs.

Schroeder, D., 'The Green Paper on Vertical Restraints: Beware of Market Share Thresholds' [1997] 7 ECLR 430.

Wesseling, R., 'Subsidiarity in Community Antitrust Law: Setting the Right Agenda' (1997) 22 EL Rev 35.

After an intense period of consultation, the main lines of planned reform were set out in the Commission *Communication on the application of EC competition rules to vertical restraints*, COM (98) 544. Council Regulation 1215/99 then amended Regulation 19/65 to empower the Commission to adopt a block exemption for vertical restraints. It duly adopted Regulation 2790/1999 on the application of Article 81(3) of the Treaty to categories of vertical agreements and concerted practices, which is set out below. This alters the law by adjusting the conditions for exempting vertical deals (as defined) from the prohibition in Article 81. The Regulation entered into force on 1 January 2000, but its key provisions applied from 1 June 2000 (Article 13). It replaces the block exemptions governing exclusive distribution, exclusive purchasing and franchising (although existing agreements made in accordance with those Regulations continue to benefit from exemption until the end of 2001; Article 12(2)).

Commission Regulation (EC) 2790/1999 of 22 December 1999 on the application of Article 81(3) of the Treaty to categories of vertical agreements and concerted practices (OJ 1999 L336/21)

THE COMMISSION OF THE EUROPEAN COMMUNITIES,
Having regard to the Treaty establishing the European Community, Having regard to Council Regulation No 19/65/EEC of 2 March 1965 on the application of Article 85(3) of the Treaty to certain categories of agreements and concerted practices [OJ 36, 6.3.1965, p. 533/65], as last amended by Regulation (EC) No 1215/1999 [OJ L 148, 15.6.1999, p. 1], and in particular Article 1 thereof,
Having published a draft of this Regulation [OJ C 270, 24.9.1999, p. 7],
Having consulted the Advisory Committee on Restrictive Practices and Dominant Positions,
Whereas:
(1)   Regulation No 19/65/EEC empowers the Commission to apply Article 81(3) of the Treaty (formerly Article 85(3)) by regulation to certain categories of vertical agreements and corresponding concerted practices falling within Article 81(1).
(2)   Experience acquired to date makes it possible to define a category of vertical agreements which can be regarded as normally satisfying the conditions laid down in Article 81(3).
(3)   This category includes vertical agreements for the purchase or sale of goods or services where these agreements are concluded between non-competing undertakings, between certain competitors or by certain associations of retailers of goods; it also includes vertical agreements containing ancillary provisions on the assignment or use of intellectual property rights; for the purposes of this Regulation, the term 'vertical agreements' includes the corresponding concerted practices.
(4)   For the application of Article 81(3) by regulation, it is not necessary to define those vertical agreements which are capable of falling within Article 81(1); in the

individual assessment of agreements under Article 81(1), account has to be taken of several factors, and in particular the market structure on the supply and purchase side.

(5)   The benefit of the block exemption should be limited to vertical agreements for which it can be assumed with sufficient certainty that they satisfy the conditions of Article 81(3).

(6)   Vertical agreements of the category defined in this Regulation can improve economic efficiency within a chain of production or distribution by facilitating better coordination between the participating undertakings; in particular, they can lead to a reduction in the transaction and distribution costs of the parties and to an optimisation of their sales and investment levels.

(7)   The likelihood that such efficiency-enhancing effects will outweigh any anti-competitive effects due to restrictions contained in vertical agreements depends on the degree of market power of the undertakings concerned and, therefore, on the extent to which those undertakings face competition from other suppliers of goods or services regarded by the buyer as interchangeable or substitutable for one another, by reason of the products' characteristics, their prices and their intended use.

(8)   It can be presumed that, where the share of the relevant market accounted for by the supplier does not exceed 30%, vertical agreements which do not contain certain types of severely anti-competitive restraints generally lead to an improvement in production or distribution and allow consumers a fair share of the resulting benefits; in the case of vertical agreements containing exclusive supply obligations, it is the market share of the buyer which is relevant in determining the overall effects of such vertical agreements on the market.

(9)   Above the market share threshold of 30%, there can be no presumption that vertical agreements falling within the scope of Article 81(1) will usually give rise to objective advantages of such a character and size as to compensate for the disadvantages which they create for competition.

(10)   This Regulation should not exempt vertical agreements containing restrictions which are not indispensable to the attainment of the positive effects mentioned above; in particular, vertical agreements containing certain types of severely anti-competitive restraints such as minimum and fixed resale-prices, as well as certain types of territorial protection, should be excluded from the benefit of the block exemption established by this Regulation irrespective of the market share of the undertakings concerned.

(11)   In order to ensure access to or to prevent collusion on the relevant market, certain conditions are to be attached to the block exemption; to this end, the exemption of non-compete obligations should be limited to obligations which do not exceed a definite duration; for the same reasons, any direct or indirect obligation causing the members of a selective distribution system not to sell the brands of particular competing suppliers should be excluded from the benefit of this Regulation.

(12)   The market-share limitation, the non-exemption of certain vertical agreements and the conditions provided for in this Regulation normally ensure that the agreements to which the block exemption applies do not enable the participating undertakings to eliminate competition in respect of a substantial part of the products in question.

(13)   In particular cases in which the agreements falling under this Regulation nevertheless have effects incompatible with Article 81(3), the Commission may withdraw the benefit of the block exemption; this may occur in particular where the buyer has significant market power in the relevant market in which it resells the goods or provides the services or where parallel networks of vertical agreements have similar effects which significantly restrict access to a relevant market or competition therein;

such cumulative effects may, for example, arise in the case of selective distribution or non-compete obligations.

(14)   Regulation No 19/65/EEC empowers the competent authorities of Member States to withdraw the benefit of the block exemption in respect of vertical agreements having effects incompatible with the conditions laid down in Article 81(3), where such effects are felt in their respective territory, or in a part thereof; and where such territory has the characteristics of a distinct geographic market; Member States should ensure that the exercise of this power of withdrawal does not prejudice the uniform application throughout the common market of the Community competition rules or the full effect of the measures adopted in implementation of those rules.

(15)   In order to strengthen supervision of parallel networks of vertical agreements which have similar restrictive effects and which cover more than 50% of a given market, the Commission may declare this Regulation inapplicable to vertical agreements containing specific restraints relating to the market concerned, thereby restoring the full application of Article 81 to such agreements.

(16)   This Regulation is without prejudice to the application of Article 82.

(17)   In accordance with the principle of the primacy of Community law, no measure taken pursuant to national laws on competition should prejudice the uniform application throughout the common market of the Community competition rules or the full effect of any measures adopted in implementation of those rules, including this Regulation,

HAS ADOPTED THIS REGULATION:

Article 1

For the purposes of this Regulation:

(a)   'competing undertakings' means actual or potential suppliers in the same product market; the, product market includes goods or services which are regarded by the buyer as interchangeable with or substitutable for the contract goods or services, by reason of the products' characteristics, their prices and their intended use;

(b)   'non-compete obligation' means any direct or indirect obligation causing the buyer not to manufacture, purchase, sell or resell goods or services which compete with the contract goods or services, or any direct or indirect obligation on the buyer to purchase from the supplier or from another undertaking designated by the supplier more than 80% of the buyer's total purchases of the contract goods or services and their substitutes on the relevant market, calculated on the basis of the value of its purchases in the preceding calendar year;

(c)   'exclusive supply obligation' means any direct or indirect obligation causing the supplier to sell the goods or services specified in the agreement only to one buyer inside the Community for the purposes of a specific use or for resale;

(d)   'Selective distribution system' means a distribution system where the supplier undertakes to sell the contract goods or services, either directly or indirectly, only to distributors selected on the basis of specified criteria and where these distributors undertake not to sell such goods or services to unauthorised distributors;

(e)   'intellectual property rights' includes industrial property rights, copyright and neighbouring rights;

(f)   'know-how' means a package of non-patented practical information, resulting from experience and testing by the supplier, which is secret, substantial and identified: in this context, 'secret' means that the know-how, as a body or in the precise configuration and assembly of its components, is not generally known or easily accessible; 'substantial' means that the know-how includes information which is indispensable to the buyer for the use, sale or resale of the contract goods or services;

'identified' means that the know-how must be described in a sufficiently comprehensive manner so as to make it possible to verify that it fulfils the criteria of secrecy and substantiality;

(g) 'buyer' includes an undertaking which, under an agreement falling within Article 81(1) of the Treaty, sells goods or services on behalf of another undertaking.

Article 2

1. Pursuant to Article 81(3) of the Treaty and subject to the provisions of this Regulation, it is hereby declared that Article 81(1) shall not apply to agreements or concerted practices entered into between two or more undertakings each of which operates, for the purposes of the agreement, at a different level of the production or distribution chain, and relating to the conditions under which the parties may purchase, sell or resell certain goods or services ('vertical agreements').

This exemption shall apply to the extent that such agreements contain restrictions of competition falling within the scope of Article 81(1) ('vertical restraints').

2. The exemption provided for in paragraph 1 shall apply to vertical agreements entered into between an association of undertakings and its members, or between such an association and its suppliers, only if all its members are retailers of goods and if no individual member of the association, together with its connected undertakings, has a total annual turnover exceeding EUR 50 million; vertical agreements entered into by such associations shall be covered by this Regulation without prejudice to the application of Article 81 to horizontal agreements concluded between the members of the association or decisions adopted by the association.

3. The exemption provided for in paragraph 1 shall apply to vertical agreements containing provisions which relate to the assignment to the buyer or use by the buyer of intellectual property rights, provided that those provisions do not constitute the primary object of such agreements and are directly related to the use, sale or resale of goods or services by the buyer or its customers. The exemption applies on condition that, in relation to the contract goods or services, those provisions do not contain restrictions of competition having the same object or effect as vertical restraints which are not exempted under this Regulation.

4. The exemption provided for in paragraph 1 shall not apply to vertical agreements entered into between competing undertakings; however, it shall apply where competing undertakings enter into a non-reciprocal vertical agreement and:

(a) the buyer has a total annual turnover not exceeding EUR 100 million, or

(b) the supplier is a manufacturer and a distributor of goods, while the buyer is a distributor not manufacturing goods competing with the contract goods, or

(c) the supplier is a provider of services at several levels of trade, while the buyer does not provide competing services at the level of trade where it purchases the contract services.

5. This Regulation shall not apply to vertical agreements the subject matter of which falls within the scope of any other block exemption regulation.

Article 3

1. Subject to paragraph 2 of this Article, the exemption provided for in Article 2 shall apply on condition that the market share held by the supplier does not exceed 30% of the relevant market on which it sells the contract goods or services.

2. In the case of vertical agreements containing exclusive supply obligations, the exemption provided for in Article 2 shall apply on condition that the market share held by the buyer does not exceed 30% of the relevant market on which it purchases the contract goods or services.

Article 4

The exemption provided for in Article 2 shall not apply to vertical agreements which, directly or indirectly, in isolation or in combination with other factors under the control of the parties, have as their object:

(a) the restriction of the buyer's ability to determine its sale price, without prejudice to the possibility of the supplier's imposing a maximum sale price or recommending a sale price, provided that they do not amount to a fixed or minimum sale price as a result of pressure from, or incentives offered by, any of the parties;

(b) the restriction of the territory into which, or of the customers to whom, the buyer may sell the contract goods or services, except:

— the restriction of active sales into the exclusive territory or to an exclusive customer group reserved to the supplier or allocated by the supplier to another buyer, where such a restriction does not limit sales by the customers of the buyer,

— the restriction of sales to end users by a buyer operating at the wholesale level of trade,

— the restriction of sales to unauthorised distributors by the members of a selective distribution system, and

— the restriction of the buyer's ability to sell components, supplied for the purposes of incorporation, to customers who would use them to manufacture the same type of goods as those produced by the supplier;

(c) the restriction of active or passive sales to end users by members of a selective distribution system operating at the retail level of trade, without prejudice to the possibility of prohibiting a member of the system from operating out of an unauthorised place of establishment;

(d) the restriction of cross-supplies between distributors within a selective distribution system, including between distributors operating at different level of trade;

(e) the restriction agreed between a supplier of components and a buyer who incorporates those components, which limits the supplier to selling the components as spare parts to end-users or to repairers or other service providers not entrusted by the buyer with the repair or servicing of its goods.

Article 5

The exemption provided for in Article 2 shall not apply to any of the following obligations contained in vertical agreements:

(a) any direct or indirect non-compete obligation, the duration of which is indefinite or exceeds five years. A non-compete obligation which is tacitly renewable beyond a period of five years is to be deemed to have been concluded for an indefinite duration. However, the time limitation of five years shall not apply where the contract goods or services are sold by the buyer from premises and land owned by the supplier or leased by the supplier from third parties not connected with the buyer, provided that the duration of the non-compete obligation does not exceed the period of occupancy of the premises and land by the buyer;

(b) any direct or indirect obligation causing the buyer, after termination of the agreement, not to manufacture, purchase, sell or resell goods or services, unless such obligation:

— relates to goods or services which compete with the contract goods or services, and

— is limited to the premises and land from which the buyer has operated during the contract period, and

— is indispensable to protect know-how transferred by the supplier to the buyer, and provided that the duration of such non-compete obligation is limited to a period of one year after termination of the agreement; this obligation is without prejudice to the possibility of imposing a restriction which is unlimited in time on the use and disclosure of know-how which has not entered the public domain;

(c)   any direct or indirect obligation causing the members of a selective distribution system not to sell the brands of particular competing suppliers.

Article 6

The Commission may withdraw the benefit of this Regulation, pursuant to Article 7(1) of Regulation No 19/65/EEC, where it finds in any particular case that vertical agreements to which this Regulation applies nevertheless have effects which are incompatible with the conditions laid down in Article 81(3) of the Treaty, and in particular where access to the relevant market or competition therein is significantly restricted by the cumulative effect of parallel networks of similar vertical restraints implemented by competing suppliers or buyers.

Article 7

Where in any particular case vertical agreements to which the exemption provided for in Article 2 applies have effects incompatible with the conditions laid down in Article 81(3) of the Treaty in the territory of a Member State, or in a part thereof; which has all the characteristics of a distinct geographic market, the competent authority of that Member State may withdraw the benefit of application of this Regulation in respect of that territory, under the same conditions as provided in Article 6.

Article 8

1.   Pursuant to Article 1 a of Regulation No 19/65/EEC, the Commission may by regulation declare that, where parallel networks of similar vertical restraints cover more than 50% of a relevant market, this Regulation shall not apply to vertical agreements containing specific restraints relating to that market.

2.   A regulation pursuant to paragraph 1 shall not become applicable earlier than six months following its adoption.

Article 9

1.   The market share of 30% provided for in Article 3(1) shall be calculated on the basis of the market sales value of the contract goods or services and other goods or services sold by the supplier, which are regarded as interchangeable or substitutable by the buyer, by reason of the products' characteristics, their prices and their intended use; if market sales value data are not available, estimates based on other reliable market information, including market sales volumes, may be used to establish the market share of the undertaking concerned. For the purposes of Article 3(2), it is either the market purchase value or estimates thereof which shall be used to calculate the market share.

2.   For the purposes of applying the market share, threshold provided for in Article 3 the following rules shall apply:

(a)   the market share shall be calculated on the basis of data relating to the preceding calendar year;

(b)   the market share shall include any goods or services supplied to integrated distributors for the purposes of sale;

(c)   if the market share is initially not more than 30% but subsequently rises above that level without exceeding 35%, the exemption provided for in Article 2 shall continue to apply for a period of two consecutive calendar years following the year in which the 30% market share threshold was first exceeded;

(d)   if the market share is initially not more than 30% but subsequently rises above 35%, the exemption provided for in Article 2 shall continue to apply for one calendar year following the year in which the level of 35% was first exceeded;

(e)   the benefit of points (c) and (d) may not be combined so as to exceed a period of two calendar years.

Article 10

1.   For the purpose of calculating total annual turnover within the meaning of Article 2(2) and (4), the turnover achieved during the previous financial year by the relevant party to the vertical agreement and the turnover achieved by its connected undertakings in respect of all goods and services, excluding all taxes and other duties, shall be added together. For this purpose, no account shall be taken of dealings between the party to the vertical agreement and its connected undertakings or between its connected undertakings.

2.   The exemption provided for in Article 2 shall remain applicable where, for any period of two consecutive financial years, the total annual turnover threshold is exceeded by no more than 10%.

Article 11

1.   For the purposes of this Regulation, the terms 'undertaking', 'supplier' and 'buyer' shall include their respective connected undertakings.

2.   'Connected undertakings' are:

(a)   undertakings in which a party to the agreement, directly or indirectly:

— has the power to exercise more than half the voting rights, or

— has the power to appoint more than half the members of the supervisory board, board of management or bodies legally representing the undertaking, or

— has the right to manage the undertaking's affairs;

(b)   undertakings which directly or indirectly have, over a party to the agreement, the rights or powers listed in (a);

(c)   undertakings in which an undertaking referred to in (b) has, directly or indirectly, the rights or powers listed in (a);

(d)   undertakings in which a party to the agreement together with one or more of the undertakings referred to in (a), (b) or (c), or in which two or more of the latter undertakings, jointly have the rights or powers listed in (a);

(e)   undertakings in which the rights or the powers listed in (a) are jointly held by:

— parties to the agreement or their respective connected undertakings referred to in (a) to (d), or

— one or more of the parties to the agreement or one or more of their connected undertakings referred to in (a) to (d) and one or more third parties.

3.   For the purposes of Article 3, the market share held by the undertakings referred to in paragraph 2(e) of this Article shall be apportioned equally to each undertaking having the rights or the powers listed in paragraph 2(a).

Article 12

1.   The exemptions provided for in Commission Regulations (EEC) No 1983/83 [OJ L 173, 30.6.1983, p. 1], (EEC) No 1984/83 [OJ L 173, 30.6.1983, p. 5] and (EEC) No 4087/88 [OJ L 359, 28.12.1988, p. 46] shall continue to apply until 31 May 2000.

2.   The prohibition laid down in Article 81(1) of the EC Treaty shall not apply during the period from 1 June 2000 to 31 December 2001 in respect of agreements already in force on 31 May 2000 which do not satisfy the conditions for exemption

provided for in this Regulation but which satisfy the conditions for exemption provided for in Regulations (EEC) No 19 83/83, (EEC) No 1984/83 or (EEC) No 4087/88.

Article 13
This Regulation shall enter into force on 1 January 2000.
It shall apply from 1 June 2000, except for Article 12(1) which shall apply from 1 January 2000.
This Regulation shall expire on 31 May 2010.

This Regulation shall be binding in its entirety and directly applicable in all Member States.
Done at Brussels, 22 December 1999.

Questions
1.   Explain, with reference to particular clauses, how the requirements of Article 81(3) are reflected in this Block Exemption Regulation.
2.   A major element in the Commission's modernisation programme is the drive to ensure the efficient allocation of its scarce enforcement resources while also reducing burdens on business. The use of market share threshold criteria (Articles 3, 8, 9 of Regulation 2790/1999; and *cf.* the Notice on Agreements of Minor Importance, p. 434 above) is part of this strategy. It is hoped to set aside the task of scrutinising deals with an insignificant impact on market competition in favour of a focus on agreements with seriously prejudicial potential. Do 'safe havens' defined by market share criteria serve this purpose? What are their limitations? (Consider also the Commission *Notice on the Definition of the Relevant Market*, extracted at p. 469 below.)
3.   Could the Commission have achieved its objects in the area of control of vertical restraints simply by adopting a narrower interpretation of the scope of Article 81(1)? To what extent is the rule of reason approach, discussed at p. 428 above, relevant in assessing the contribution of this Regulation to the modernisation of EC competition law and policy?
4.   How is the golden thread of market integration in EC law reflected in Regulation 2790/1999?

Further reading
Nazerali, J., and Cowan, D., 'Unlocking EU Distribution Rules – has the European Commission found the Right Keys?' [2000] ECLR 50.
Neubauer, S. and Lever, J., 'Vertical Restraints, their Motivation and Justification' [2000] ECLR 7.

Note
The Commission spent time in 1999 and 2000 pursuing consultation on its treatment of horizontal restraints. Here too modernisation is in the air. The Commission aims to develop a new approach that will allow a regime contained within a single Regulation to be adopted in time to replace the existing Block Exemption Regulations on specialisation and research-and-development (p. 450 above) which expire at the end of 2000. Here too the

Commission wishes to free both itself and commercial actors of burdens
associated with supervision of deals that are insignificant in competition terms
in order to target resources more efficiently on more serious cases. A more
flexible regime is anticipated.

Question
Pursuit of market integration has served as a canon of interpretation in EC
competition law in the past; in the light of the likely accession of Central and
Eastern European countries lacking developed economic links with Western
Europe, ought market integration to retain its leading role also in the future?

12 ARTICLE 82: DOMINANT POSITIONS

Article 82 EC

Article 82

Any abuse by one or more undertakings of a dominant position within the common market or in a substantial part of it shall be prohibited as incompatible with the common market in so far as it may affect trade between Member States.

Such abuse may, in particular, consist in:

(a)   directly or indirectly imposing unfair purchase or selling prices or other unfair trading conditions;

(b)   limiting production, markets or technical development to the prejudice of consumers;

(c)   applying dissimilar conditions to equivalent transactions with other trading parties, thereby placing them at a competitive disadvantage;

(d)   making the conclusion of contracts subject to acceptance by the other parties of supplementary obligations which, by their nature or according to commercial usage, have no connection with the subject of such contracts.

The text of Article 82 was untouched by the Amsterdam Treaty, but it must be borne in mind in reading the material in this Chapter that what is now Article 82 was numbered Article 86 until the entry into force of the Amsterdam Treaty on 1 May 1999 (p. 29 above).

Article 82 stands alongside Article 81 as the second of the twin pillars of the Community's competition law system. Like Article 81, it controls undertakings, depends on an effect on trade between Member States and has as its objective the control of market distortion. However, unlike Article 81, it controls the conduct of a single firm, rather than two or more firms. Articles 81 and 82 complement each other and should be read together as a competition law regime, not as two independent provisions.

The rationale for controlling the conduct of a single firm is found in the damage which it can wreak on the market. The firm may charge high prices, or it may refuse to supply customers. None of this matters in a competitive market. Our firm will simply lose business. But where our firm is economically powerful, it may be able to distort the market without fear of effective competition. The result may be inefficiency as a result of mismatch between the influence of supply and demand. The law, then, has reason to control the conduct of a single firm, but only where the firm has passed a threshold of economic power. English law calls that threshold the monopoly; Article 82 refers to it as the dominant position.

But it is not the dominant position that is condemned. It is the *abuse* of a dominant position, not its existence, which is unlawful. Article 82, set out above, supplies an illustrative list of the type of practice which may be held abusive.

Logically, there are two elements to an analysis under Article 82, First, is the firm *in a dominant position*? If so, secondly, has it *abused* that dominant position? The discussion uses as its framework the Court's decision in *United Brands* v *Commission* (Case 27/76), a famous case which touches on many of the issues of law and policy in this area.

(A) THE DOMINANT POSITION: DEFINING THE MARKET

The question, 'Is this firm in a dominant position?,' is simply answered: 'It depends!' And it depends on exactly what it is that the firm is alleged to be dominating. The producer of 80 per cent of a nation's ox liver dominates the ox liver market. But there is no lack of competition if the consumer will freely switch preference to lamb's liver in the event of the ox liver producer raising prices. The breadth of the market, then, has to be defined accurately before one can logically accuse a firm of dominance on that market, and before one can claim a rationale for intervention to control dominance.

United Brands v *Commission (Case 27/76)*
[1978] ECR 207; [1978] 1 CMLR 429
Court of Justice of the European Communities

The United Brands Company (UBC) was found by the Commission to have abused a dominant position in the banana market. The firm sought annulment of that Decision before the Court. The following extract involves assessment of the market, defined according to product.

[12]   As far as the product market is concerned it is first of all necessary to ascertain whether, as the applicant maintains, bananas are an integral part of the fresh fruit market, because they are reasonably interchangeable by consumers with other kinds of fresh fruit such as apples, oranges, grapes, peaches, strawberries, etc. or whether the relevant market consists solely of the banana market which includes both branded bananas and unlabelled bananas and is a market sufficiently homogeneous and distinct from the market of other fresh fruit.

[13]   The applicant submits in support of its argument that bananas compete with other fresh fruit in the same shops, on the same shelves, at prices which can be compared, satisfying the same needs: consumption as a dessert or between meals.

[14]   The statistics produced show that consumer expenditure on the purchase of bananas is at its lowest between June and December when there is a plentiful supply of domestic fresh fruit on the market.

[15]   Studies carried out by the Food and Agriculture Organization (FAO) (especially in 1975) confirm that banana prices are relatively weak during the summer months and that the price of apples for example has a statistically appreciable impact on the consumption of bananas in the Federal Republic of Germany.

[16]   Again according to these studies some easing of prices is noticeable at the end of the year during the 'orange season'.

[17]   The seasonal peak periods when there is a plentiful supply of other fresh fruit exert an influence not only on the prices but also on the volume of sales of bananas and consequently on the volume of imports thereof.

[18]   The applicant concludes from these findings that bananas and other fresh fruit form only one market and that UBC's operations should have been examined in this context for the purpose of any application of Article 86 of the Treaty.

[19]   The Commission maintains that there is a demand for bananas which is distinct from the demand for other fresh fruit especially as the banana is a very important part of the diet of certain sections of the community.

[20]   The specific qualities of the banana influence customer preference and induce him not to readily accept other fruits as a substitute.

[21]   The Commission draws the conclusion from the studies quoted by the applicant that the influence of the prices and availabilities of other types of fruit on the prices and availabilities of bananas on the relevant market is very ineffective and that these effects are too brief and too spasmodic for such other fruit to be regarded as forming part of the same market as bananas or as a substitute therefor.

[22]   For the banana to be regarded as forming a market which is sufficiently differentiated from other fruit markets it must be possible for it to be singled out by such special features distinguishing it from other fruits that it is only to a limited extent interchangeable with them and is only exposed to their competition in a way that is hardly perceptible.

[23]   The ripening of bananas takes place the whole year round without any season having to be taken into account.

[24]   Throughout the year production exceeds demand and can satisfy it at any time.

[25]   Owing to this particular feature the banana is a privileged fruit and its production and marketing can be adapted to the seasonal fluctuations of other fresh fruit which are known and can be computed.

[26]   There is no unavoidable seasonal substitution since the consumer can obtain this fruit all the year round.

[27]   Since the banana is a fruit which is always available in sufficient quantities the question whether it can be replaced by other fruits must be determined over the whole

of the year for the purpose of ascertaining the degree of competition between it and other fresh fruit.

[28]   The studies of the banana market on the Court's file show that on the latter market there is no significant long term cross-elasticity any more than – as has been mentioned – there is any seasonal substitutability in general between the banana and all the seasonal fruits, as this only exists between the banana and two fruits (peaches and table grapes) in one of the countries (West Germany) of the relevant geographic market.

[29]   As far as concerns the two fruits available throughout the year (oranges and apples) the first are not interchangeable and in the case of the second there is only a relative degree of substitutability.

[30]   This small degree of substitutability is accounted for by the specific features of the banana and all the factors which influence consumer choice.

[31]   The banana has certain characteristics, appearance, taste, softness, seedless-ness, easy handling, a constant level of production which enable it to satisfy the constant needs of an important section of the population consisting of the very young, the old and the sick.

[32]   As far as prices are concerned two FAO studies show that the banana is only affected by the prices – falling prices – of other fruits (and only of peaches and table grapes) during the summer months and mainly in July and then by an amount not exceeding 20%.

[33]   Although it cannot be denied that during these months and some weeks at the end of the year this product is exposed to competition from other fruits, the flexible way in which the volume of imports and their marketing on the relevant geographic market is adjusted means that the conditions of competition are extremely limited and that its price adapts without any serious difficulties to this situation where supplies of fruit are plentiful.

[34]   It follows from all these considerations that a very large number of consumers having a constant need for bananas are not noticeably or even appreciably enticed away from the consumption of this product by the arrival of other fresh fruit on the market and that even the personal peak periods only affect it for a limited period of time and to a very limited extent from the point of view of substitutability.

[35]   Consequently the banana market is a market which is sufficiently distinct from the other fresh fruit markets.

Note

The Commission had adopted a narrower market definition than that advocated by United Brands. The narrower the definition, the more likely that dominance will be established. Disagreement between Commission and undertaking in this fashion is a common feature of Article 82 cases.

Markets may also be defined by reference to their territorial scope. Even if consumers will not switch from ox liver to other types of liver, the single national ox liver producer is not dominant if producers of ox liver in other States can import their produce as competition.

United Brands v Commission (Case 27/76)
[1978] ECR 207; [1978] 1 CMLR 429
Court of Justice of the European Communities

The Commission had analysed UBC's conduct in a market comprising Germany, Ireland, Denmark, Belgium, The Netherlands and Luxembourg, but excluding the other three Member States at that time, the UK, France and Italy. UBC argued that the geographic market 'should only comprise areas where the conditions of competition are homogenous' and that this test was not satisfied by the Commission's chosen market. The Court, however, agreed with the Commission:

[44] The conditions for the application of Article 86 to an undertaking in a dominant position presuppose the clear delimitation of the substantial part of the Common Market in which it may be able to engage in abuses which hinder effective competition and this is an area where the objective conditions of competition applying to the product in question must be the same for all traders.

[45] The Community has not established a common organization of the agricultural market in bananas.

[46] Consequently import arrangements vary considerably from one Member State to another and reflect a specific commercial policy peculiar to the States concerned.

[47] This explains why for example the French market owing to its national organization is restricted upstream by a particular import arrangement and obstructed downstream by a retail price monitored by the Administration.

[48] This market, in addition to adopting certain measures relating to a 'target price' ('prix objectif') fixed each year and to packaging and grading standards and the minimum qualities required, reserves about two thirds of the market for the production of the overseas departments and one third to that of certain countries enjoying preferential relations with France (Ivory Coast, Madagascar, Cameroon) the bananas whereof are imported duty-free, and it includes a system the running of which is entrusted to the 'Comité interprofessionnel bananier' ('CIB').

[49] The United Kingdom market enjoys 'Commonwealth preferences', a system of which the main feature is the maintenance of a level of production favouring the developing countries of the Commonwealth and of a price paid to the associations of producers directly linked to the selling price of the green banana charged in the United Kingdom.

[50] On the Italian market, since the abolition in 1965 of the State Monopoly responsible for marketing bananas, a national system of quota restrictions has been introduced, the Ministry for Shipping and the Exchange Control Office supervising the imports and the charterparties relating to the foreign ships which carry the bananas.

[51] The effect of the national organization of these three markets is that the applicant's bananas do not compete on equal terms with the other bananas sold in these States which benefit from a preferential system and the Commission was right to exclude these three national markets from the geographic market under consideration.

[52]   On the other hand the six other States are markets which are completely free, although the applicable tariff provisions and transport costs are of necessity different but not discriminatory, and in which the conditions of competition are the same for all.

[53]   From the standpoint of being able to engage in free competition these six States form an area which is sufficiently homogeneous to be considered in its entirety.

[54]   UBC has arranged for its subsidiary in Rotterdam – UBCBV – to market its products. UBCBV is for this purpose a single centre for the whole of this part of the Community.

[55]   Transport costs do not in fact stand in the way of the distribution policy chosen by UBC which consists in selling f.o.r. Rotterdam and Bremerhaven, the two ports where the bananas are unloaded.

[56]   These are factors which go to make relevant market a single market.

[57]   It follows from all these considerations that the geographic market as determined by the Commission which constitutes a substantial part of the common market must be regarded as the relevant market for the purpose of determining whether the applicant may be in a dominant position.

The defined market, then, was internally more or less homogenous and distinct in material respects from the wider market, defined by product and by territory. The next question was whether United Brands dominated that market. The Court established its test:

[65]   The dominant position referred to in this article relates to a position of economic strength enjoyed by an undertaking which enables it to prevent effective competition being maintained on the relevant market by giving it the power to behave to an appreciable extent independently of its competitors, customers and ultimately of its consumers.

[66]   In general a dominant position derives from a combination of several factors which, taken separately, are not necessarily determinative.

The first set of factors then analysed relate to the structure of UBC.

[69]   It is advisable to examine in turn UBC's resources for and methods of producing, packaging, transporting, selling and displaying its product.

[70]   UBC is an undertaking vertically integrated to a high degree.

[71]   This integration is evident at each of the stages from the plantation to the loading on wagons or lorries in the ports of delivery and after those stages, as far as ripening and sale prices are concerned, UBC even extends its control to ripener/distributors and wholesalers by setting up a complete network of agents.

[72]   At the production stage UBC owns large plantations in Central and South America.

[73]   In so far as UBC's own production does not meet its requirements it can obtain supplies without any difficulty from independent planters since it is an established fact that unless circumstances are exceptional there is a production surplus.

[74]   Furthermore several independent producers have links with UBC through contracts for the growing of bananas which have caused them to grow the varieties of bananas which UBC has advised them to adopt.

[75]   The effects of natural disasters which could jeopardize supplies are greatly reduced by the fact that the plantations are spread over a wide geographic area and by the selection of varieties not very susceptible to diseases.

[76]   This situation was born out by the way in which UBC was able to react to the consequences of hurricane 'Fifi' in 1974.

[77]   At the production stage UBC therefore knows that it can comply with all the requests which it receives.

[78]   At the stage of packaging and presentation on its premises UBC has at its disposal factories, manpower, plant and material which enable it to handle the goods independently.

[79]   The bananas are carried from the place of production to the port of shipment by its own means of transport including railways.

[80]   At the carriage by sea stage it has been acknowledged that UBC is the only undertaking of its kind which is capable of carrying two thirds of its exports by means of its own banana fleet.

[81]   Thus UBC knows that it is able to transport regularly, without running the risk of its own ships not being used and whatever the market situation may be, two thirds of its average volume of sales and is alone able to ensure that three regular consignments reach Europe each week, and all this guarantees it commercial stability and well being.

[82]   In the field of technical knowledge and as a result of continual research UBC keeps on improving the productivity and yield of its plantations by improving the draining system, making good soil deficiencies and combating effectively plant disease.

[83]   It has perfected new ripening methods in which its technicians instruct the distributor/ripeners of the Chiquita banana.

[84]   That is another factor to be borne in mind when considering UBC's position since competing firms cannot develop research at a comparable level and are in this respect at a disadvantage compared with the applicant.

[85]   It is acknowledged that at the stage where the goods are given the final finish and undergo quality control UBC not only controls the distributor/ripeners which are direct customers but also those who work for the account of its important customers such as the Scipio group.

[86]   Even if the object of the clause prohibiting the sale of green bananas was only strict quality control, it in fact gives UBC absolute control of all trade in its goods so long as they are marketable wholesale, that is to say before the ripening process begins which makes an immediate sale unavoidable.

[87]   This general quality control of a homogeneous product makes the advertising of the brand name effective.

[88]   Since 1967 UBC has based its general policy in the relevant market on the quality of its Chiquita brand banana.

[89]   There is no doubt that this policy gives UBC control over the transformation of the product into bananas for consumption even though most of this product no longer belongs to it.

[90]   This policy has been based on a thorough reorganization of the arrangements for production, packaging, carriage, ripening (new plant with ventilation and a cooling system) and sale (a network of agents).

[91]   UBC has made this product distinctive by large-scale repeated advertising and promotion campaigns which have induced the consumer to show a preference for it in spite of the difference between the price of labelled and unlabelled bananas (in the region of 30 to 40%) and also of Chiquita bananas and those which have been labelled with another brand name (in the region of 7 to 10%).

[92]   It was the first to take full advantage of the opportunities presented by labelling in the tropics for the purpose of large-scale advertising and this, to use UBC's own words, has 'revolutionized the commercial exploitation of the banana' (Annex II (a) to the application, p. 10).

[93]   It has thus attained a privileged position by making Chiquita the premier banana brand name on the relevant market with the result that the distributor cannot afford not to offer it to the consumer.

[94]   At the selling stage this distinguishing factor – justified by the unchanging quality of the banana bearing this label – ensures that it has regular customers and consolidates its economic strength.

[95]   The effect of its sales networks only covering a limited number of customers, large groups or distributor/ripeners, is a simplification of its supply policy and economies of scale.

[96]   Since UBC's supply policy consists – in spite of the production surplus – in only meeting the requests for Chiquita bananas parsimoniously and sometimes incompletely UBC is in a position of strength at the selling stage.

The Court went on to examine the competitive situation on the market. UBC was by no means the only active trader. The Court declared that 'an undertaking does not have to have eliminated all opportunity for competition in order to be in a dominant position'; and it observed that UBC's market share, fixed by the Court at 40–45%, was several times greater than its nearest rival. Limited price wars had not altered market shares. The Court came to the conclusion that:

[121]   UBC's economic strength has thus enabled it to adopt a flexible overall strategy directed against new competitors establishing themselves on the whole of the relevant market.

[122]   The particular barriers to competitors entering the market are the exceptionally large capital investments required for the creation and running of banana plantations, the need to increase sources of supply in order to avoid the effects of fruit diseases and bad weather (hurricanes, floods), the introduction of an essential system of logistics which the distribution of a very perishable product makes necessary, economies of scale from which newcomers to the market cannot derive any immediate

benefit and the actual cost of entry made up *inter alia* of all the general expenses incurred in penetrating the market such as the setting up of an adequate commercial network, the mounting of very large-scale advertising campaigns, all those financial risks, the costs of which are irrecoverable if the attempt fails.

[123]   Thus, although, as UBC has pointed out, it is true that competitors are able to use the same methods of production and distribution as the applicant, they come up against almost insuperable practical and financial obstacles.

[124]   That is another factor peculiar to a dominant position.

[125]   However UBC takes into account the losses which its banana division made from 1971 to 1976 – whereas during this period its competitors made profits – for the purpose of inferring that, since dominance is in essence the power to fix prices, making losses is inconsistent with the existence of a dominant position.

[126]   An undertaking's economic strength is not measured by its profitability; a reduced profit margin or even losses for a time are not incompatible with a dominant position, just as large profits may be compatible with a situation where there is effective competition.

[127]   The fact that UBC's profitability is for a time moderate or non-existent must be considered in the light of the whole of its operations.

[128]   The finding that, whatever losses UBC may make, the customers continue to buy more goods from UBC which is the dearest vendor, is more significant and this fact is a particular feature of the dominant position and its verification is determinative in this case.

[129]   The cumulative effect of all the advantages enjoyed by UBC thus ensures that it has a dominant position on the relevant market.

Note

Of course, the bigger the market share, the more likely that dominance is established. But *United Brands* (Case 27/76) emphasises that each market requires special attention and must be judged according to its own peculiarities.

In 1997, the Commission sought to make its approach to market definition more transparent. In reading this text, remember it is a pre-Amsterdam document. Articles 81 and 82 are the post-Amsterdam numbers of Articles 85 and 86 respectively.

Commission Notice on the Definition of the Relevant Market for the Purposes of Community Competition Law
(1997) OJ C372

I.   INTRODUCTION

1.   The purpose of this notice is to provide guidance as to how the Commission applies the concept of relevant product and geographic market in its ongoing enforcement of Community competition law, in particular the application of Council Regulation No. 17 and (EEC) No. 4064/89, their equivalents in other sectoral applications such as transport, coal and steel, and agriculture, and the relevant

provisions of the EEA Agreement[1]. Throughout this notice, references to Articles 85 and 86 of the Treaty and to merger control are to be understood as referring to the equivalent provisions in the EEA Agreement and the ECSC Treaty.

2.   Market definition is a tool to identify and define the boundaries of competition between firms. It serves to establish the framework within which competition policy is applied by the Commission. The main purpose of market definition is to identify in a systematic way the competitive constraints that the undertakings involved[2] face. The objective of defining a market in both its product and geographic dimension is to identify those actual competitors of the undertakings involved that are capable of constraining those undertakings' behaviour and of preventing them from behaving independently of effective competitive pressure. It is from this perspective that the market definition makes it possible *inter alia* to calculate market shares that would convey meaningful information regarding market power for the purposes of assessing dominance or for the purposes of applying Article 85.

3.   It follows from point 2 that the concept of 'relevant market' is different from other definitions of market often used in other contexts. For instance, companies often use the term 'market' to refer to the area where it sells its products or to refer broadly to the industry or sector where it belongs.

4.   The definition of the relevant market in both its product and its geographic dimensions often has a decisive influence on the assessment of a competition case. By rendering public the procedures which the Commission follows when considering market definition and by indicating the criteria and evidence on which it relies to reach a decision, the Commission expects to increase the transparency of its policy and decision-making in the area of competition policy.

5.   Increased transparency will also result in companies and their advisers being able to better anticipate the possibility that the Commission may raise competition concerns in an individual case. Companies could, therefore, take such a possibility into account in their own internal decision-making when contemplating, for instance, acquisitions, the creation of joint ventures, or the establishment of certain agreements. It is also intended that companies should be in a better position to understand what sort of information the Commission considers relevant for the purposes of market definition.

6.   The Commission's interpretation of 'relevant market' is without prejudice to the interpretation which may be given by the Court of Justice or the Court of First Instance of the European Communities.

II.   DEFINITION OF RELEVANT MARKET

Definition of relevant product market and relevant geographic market

7.   The Regulations based on Article 85 and 86 of the Treaty, in particular in section 6 of Form A/B with respect to Regulation No. 17, as well as in section 6 of Form CO with respect to Regulation (EEC) No. 4064/89 on the control of

---

[1]   The focus of assessment in State aid cases is the aid recipient and the industry/sector concerned rather than identification of competitive constraints faced by the aid recipient. When consideration of market power and therefore of the relevant market are raised in any particular case, elements of the approach outlined here might serve as a basis for the assessment of State aid cases.

[2]   For the purposes of this notice, the undertakings involved will be, in the case of a concentration, the parties to the concentration; in investigations within the meaning of Article 86 of the Treaty, the undertaking being investigated or the complainants; for investigations within the meaning of Article 85, the parties to the Agreement.

concentrations having a Community dimension have laid down the following definitions, 'Relevant product markets' are defined as follows:

'A relevant product market comprises all those products and/or services which are
regarded as interchangeable or substitutable by the consumer, by reason of the
products' characteristics, their prices and their intended use'.

8.   'Relevant geographic markets' are defined as follows:

'The relevant geographic market comprises the area in which the undertakings
concerned are involved in the supply and demand of products or services, in which
the conditions of competition are sufficiently homogeneous and which can be
distinguished from neighbouring areas because the conditions of competition are
appreciably different in those area'.

9.   The relevant market within which to assess a given competition issue is
therefore established by the combination of the product and geographic markets. The
Commission interprets the definitions in paragraphs 7 and 8 (which reflect the
case-law of the Court of Justice and the Court of First Instance as well as its own
decision-making practice) according to the orientations defined in this notice.

Concept of relevant market and objectives of Community competition policy

10.   The concept of relevant market is closely related to the objectives pursued
under Community competition policy. For example, under the Community's merger
control, the objective in controlling structural changes in the supply of a product/
service is to prevent the creation or reinforcement of a dominant position as a result
of which effective competition would be significantly impeded in a substantial part of
the common market. Under the Community's competition rules, a dominant position
is such that a firm or group of firms would be in a position to behave to an appreciable
extent independently of its competitors, customers and ultimately of its consumers[3].
Such a position would usually arise when a firm or group of firms accounted for a
large share of the supply in any given market, provided that other factors analysed in
the assessment (such as entry barriers, customers' capacity to react, etc.) point in the
same direction.

11.   The same approach is followed by the Commission in its application of Article
86 of the Treaty to firms that enjoy a single or collective dominant position. Within
the meaning of Regulation No. 17, the Commission has the power to investigate and
bring to an end abuses of such a dominant position, which must also be defined by
reference to the relevant market. Markets may also need to be defined in the
application of Article 85 of the Treaty, in particular, in determining whether an
appreciable restriction of competition exists or in establishing if the condition
pursuant to Article 85(3)(b) for an exemption from the application of Article 85(1) is
met.

12.   The criteria for defining the relevant market are applied generally for the
analysis of certain types of behaviour in the market and for the analysis of structural
changes in the supply of products. This methodology, though, might lead to different
results depending on the nature of the competition issue being examined. For
instance, the scope of the geographic market might be different when analysing a
concentration, where the analysis is essentially prospective, from an analysis of past
behaviour. The different time horizon considered in each case might lead to the result

---

[3]   Definition given by the Court of Justice in its judgment of 13 February 1979 in Case 85/76,
Hoffmann-La Roche [1979] ECR 461, and confirmed in subsequent judgments.

that different geographic markets are defined for the same products depending on whether the Commission is examining a change in the structure of supply, such as a concentration or a cooperative joint venture, or examining issues relating to certain past behaviour.

Basic principles for market definition

Competitive constraints

13.   Firms are subject to three main sources or competitive constraints: demand substitutability, supply substitutability and potential competition. From an economic point of view, for the definition of the relevant market, demand substitution constitutes the most immediate and effective disciplinary force on the suppliers of a given product, in particular in relation to their pricing decisions. A firm or a group of firms cannot have a significant impact on the prevailing conditions of sale, such as prices, if its customers are in a position to switch easily to available substitute products or to suppliers located elsewhere. Basically, the exercise of market definition consists in identifying the effective alternative sources of supply for the customers of the undertakings involved, in terms both of products/services and of geographic location of suppliers.

14.   The competitive constraints arising from supply side substitutability other then those described in paragraphs 20 to 23 and from potential competition are in general less immediate and in any case require an analysis of additional factors. As a result such constraints are taken into account at the assessment stage of competition analysis.

Demand substitution

15.   The assessment of demand substitution entails a determination of the range of products which are viewed as substitutes by the consumer. One way of making this determination can be viewed as a speculative experiment, postulating a hypothetical small, lasting change in relative prices and evaluating the likely reactions of customers to that increase. The exercise of market definition focuses on prices for operational and practical purposes, and more precisely on demand substitution arising from small, permanent changes in relative prices. This concept can provide clear indications as to the evidence that is relevant in defining markets.

16.   Conceptually, this approach means that, starting from the type of products that the undertakings involved sell and the area in which they sell them, additional products and areas will be included in, or excluded from, the market definition depending on whether competition from these other products and areas affect or restrain sufficiently the pricing of the parties' products in the short term.

17.   The question to be answered is whether the parties' customers would switch to readily available substitutes or to suppliers located elsewhere in response to a hypothetical small (in the range 5% to 10%) but permanent relative price increase in the products and areas being considered. If substitution were enough to make the price increase unprofitable because of the resulting loss of sales, additional substitutes and areas are included in the relevant market. This would be done until the set of products and geographical areas is such that small, permanent increases in relative prices would be profitable. The equivalent analysis is applicable in cases concerning the concentration of buying power, where the starting point would then be the supplier and the price test serves to identify the alternative distribution channels or outlets for the supplier's products. In the application of these principles, careful account should be taken of certain particular situations as described within paragraphs 56 and 58.

18.   A practical example of this test can be provided by its application to a merger of, for instance, soft-drink bottlers. An issue to examine in such a case would be to decide whether different flavours of soft drinks belong to the same market. In practice, the question to address would be whether consumers of flavour A would switch to other flavours when confronted with a permanent price increase of 5% to 10% for flavour A. If a sufficient number of consumers would switch to, say, flavour B, to such an extent that the price increase for flavour A would not be profitable owing to the resulting loss of sales, then the market would comprise at least flavours A and B. The process would have to be extended in addition to other available flavours until a set of products is identified for which a price rise would not induce a sufficient substitution in demand.

19.   Generally, and in particular for the analysis of merger cases, the price to take into account will be the prevailing market price. This may not be the case where the prevailing price has been determined in the absence of sufficient competition. In particular for the investigation of abuses of dominant positions, the fact that the prevailing price might already have been substantially increased will be taken into account.

Supply substitution

20.   Supply-side substitutability may also be taken into account when defining markets in those situations in which its effects are equivalent to those of demand substitution in terms of effectiveness and immediacy. This means that suppliers are able to switch production to the relevant products and market them in the short term[4] without incurring significant additional costs or risks in response to small and permanent changes in relative prices. When these conditions are met, the additional production that is put on the market will have a disciplinary effect on the competitive behaviour of the companies involved. Such an impact in terms of effectiveness and immediacy is equivalent to the demand substitution effect.

21.   These situations typically arise when companies market a wide range of qualities or grades of one product; even if, for a given final customer or group of consumers, the different qualities are not substitutable, the different qualities will be grouped into one product market, provided that most of the suppliers are able to offer and sell the various qualities immediately and without the significant increases in costs described above. In such cases, the relevant product market will encompass all products that are substitutable in demand and supply, and the current sales of those products will be aggregated so as to give the total value or volume of the market. The same reasoning may lead to group different geographic areas.

22.   A practical example of the approach to supply-side substitutability when defining product markets is to be found in the case of paper. Paper is usually supplied in a range of different qualities, from standard writing paper to high quality papers to be used, for instance, to publish art books. From a demand point of view, different qualities of paper cannot be used for any given use, i.e. an art book or a high quality publication cannot be based on lower quality papers. However, paper plants are prepared to manufacture the different qualities, and production can be adjusted with negligible costs and in a short time-frame. In the absence of particular difficulties in distribution, paper manufacturers are able therefore, to compete for orders of the various qualities, in particular if orders are placed with sufficient lead time to allow for modification of production plans. Under such circumstances, the Commission

---

[4]   That is such a period that does not entail a significant adjustment of existing tangible and intangible assets (see paragraph 23).

would not define a separate market for each quality of paper and its respective use. The various qualities of paper are included in the relevant market, and their sales added up to estimate total market value and volume.

23. When supply-side substitutability would entail the need to adjust significantly existing tangible and intangible assets, additional investments, strategic decisions or time delays, it will not be considered at the stage of market definition. Examples where supply-side substitution did not induce the Commission to enlarge the market are offered in the area of consumer products, in particular for branded beverages. Although bottling plants may in principle bottle different beverages, there are costs and lead times involved (in terms of advertising, product testing and distribution) before the products can actually be sold. In these cases, the effects of supply-side substitutability and other forms of potential competition would then be examined at a later stage.

Potential competition

24. The third source of competitive constraint, potential competition, is not taken into account when defining markets, since the conditions under which potential competition will actually represent an effective competitive constraint depend on the analysis of specific factors and circumstances related to the conditions of entry. If required, this analysis is only carried out at a subsequent stage, in general once the position of the companies involved in the relevant market has already been ascertained, and when such position gives rise to concerns from a competition point of view.

III. EVIDENCE RELIED ON TO DEFINE RELEVANT MARKETS

The process of defining the relevant market in practice

Product dimension

25. There is a range of evidence permitting an assessment of the extent to which substitution would take place. In individual cases, certain types of evidence will be determinant, depending very much on the characteristics and specificity of the industry and products or services that are being examined. The same type of evidence may be of no importance in other cases. In most cases, a decision will have to be based on the consideration of a number of criteria and different items of evidence. The Commission follows an open approach to empirical evidence, aimed at making an effective use of all available information which may be relevant in individual cases. The Commission does not follow a rigid hierarchy of different sources of information or types of evidence.

26. The process of defining relevant markets may be summarized as follows: on the basis of the preliminary information available or information submitted by the undertakings involved, the Commission will usually be in a position to broadly establish the possible relevant markets within which, for instance, a concentration or a restriction of competition has to be assessed. In general, and for all practical purposes when handling individual cases, the question will usually be to decide on a few alternative possible relevant markets. For instance, with respect to the product market, the issue will often be to establish whether product A and product B belong or do not belong to the same product market. It is often the case that the inclusion of product B would be enough to remove any competition concerns.

27. In such situations it is not necessary to consider whether the market includes additional products, or to reach a definitive conclusion on the precise product market. If under the conceivable alternative market definitions the operation in question does

not raise competition concerns, the question of market definition will be left open, reducing thereby the burden on companies to supply information.

Geographic dimension
28. The Commission's approach to geographic market definition might be summarized as follows: it will take a preliminary view of the scope of the geographic market on the basis of broad indications as to the distribution of market shares between the parties and their competitors, as well as a preliminary analysis of pricing and price differences at national and Community or EEA level. This initial view is used basically as a working hypothesis to focus the Commission's enquiries for the purposes of arriving at a precise geographic market definition.

29. The reasons behind any particular configuration of prices and market shares need to be explored. Companies might enjoy high market shares in their domestic markets just because of the weight of the past, and conversely, a homogeneous presence of companies throughout the EEA might be consistent with national or regional geographic markets. The initial working hypothesis will therefore be checked against an analysis of demand characteristics (importance of national or local preferences, current patterns of purchases of customers, product differentiation/brands, other) in order to establish whether companies in different areas do indeed constitute a real alternative source of supply for consumers. The theoretical experiment is again based on substitution arising from changes in relative prices, and the question to answer is again whether the customers of the parties would switch their orders to companies located elsewhere in the short term and at a negligible cost.

30. If necessary, a further check on supply factors will be carried out to ensure that those companies located in differing areas do not face impediments in developing their sales on competitive terms throughout the whole geographic market. This analysis will include an examination of requirements for a local presence in order to sell in that area the conditions of access to distribution channels, costs associated with setting up a distribution network, and the presence or absence of regulatory barriers arising from public procurement, price regulations, quotas and tariffs limiting trade or production, technical standards, monopolies, freedom of establishment, requirements for administrative authorizations, packaging regulations, etc. In short, the Commission will identify possible obstacles and barriers isolating companies located in a given area from the competitive pressure of companies located outside that area, so as to determine the precise degree of market interpenetration at national, European or global level.

31. The actual pattern and evolution of trade flows offers useful supplementary indications as to the economic importance of each demand or supply factor mentioned above, and the extent to which they may or may not constitute actual barriers creating different geographic markets. The analysis of trade flows will generally address the question of transport costs and the extent to which these may hinder trade between different areas, having regard to plant location, costs of production and relative price levels.

Market integration in the Community
32. Finally, the Commission also takes into account the continuing process of market integration, in particular in the Community, when defining geographic markets, especially in the area of concentrations and structural joint ventures. The measures adopted and implemented in the internal market programme to remove barriers to trade and further integrate the Community markets cannot be ignored when assessing the effects on competition of a concentration or a structural joint

venture. A situation where national markets have been artifically isolated from each other because of the existence of legislative barriers that have now been removed will generally lead to a cautious assessment of past evidence regarding prices, market shares or trade patterns. A process of market integration that would, in the short term, lead to wider geographic markets may therefore be taken into consideration when defining the geographic market for the purposes of assessing concentrations and joint ventures.

The process of gathering evidence

33. When a precise market definition is deemed necessary, the Commission will often contact the main customers and the main companies in the industry to enquire into their views about the boundaries of product and geographic markets and to obtain the necessary factual evidence to reach a conclusion. The Commission might also contact the relevant professional associations, and companies active in upstream markets, so as to be able to define, in so far as necessary, separate product and geographic markets, for different levels of production or distribution of the products/ services in question. It might also request additional information to the undertakings involved.

34. Where appropriate, the Commission will address written requests for information to the market players mentioned above. These requests will usually include questions relating to the perceptions of companies about reactions to hypothetical price increases and their views of the boundaries of the relevant market. They will also ask for provision of the factual information the Commission deems necessary to reach a conclusion on the extent of the relevant market. The Commission might also discuss with marketing directors or other officers of those companies to gain a better understanding on how negotiations between suppliers and customers take place and better understand issues relating to the definition of the relevant market. Where appropriate, they might also carry out visits or inspections to the premises of the parties, their customers and/or their competitors, in order to better understand how products are manufactured and sold.

35. The type of evidence relevant to reach a conclusion as to the product market can be categorized as follows:

Evidence to define markets – product dimension

36. An analysis of the product characteristics and its intended use allows the Commission, as a first step, to limit the field of investigation of possible substitutes. However, product characteristics and intended use are insufficient to show whether two products are demand substitutes. Functional interchangeability or similarity in characteristics may not, in themselves, provide sufficient criteria, because the responsiveness of customers to relative price changes may be determined by other considerations as well. For example, there may be different competitive constraints in the original equipment market for car components and in spare parts, thereby leading to a separate delineation of two relevant markets. Conversely, differences in product characteristics are not in themselves sufficient to exclude demand substitutability, since this will depend to a large extent on how customers value different characteristics.

37. The type of evidence the Commission considers relevant to assess whether two products are demand substitutes can be categorized as follows:

38. *Evidence of substitution in the recent past.* In certain cases, it is possible to analyse evidence relating to recent past events or shocks in the market that offer actual examples of substitution between two products. When available, this sort of information will normally be fundamental for market definition. If there have been changes

in relative prices in the past (all else being equal), the reactions in terms of quantities demanded will be determinant in establishing substitutability. Launches of new products in the past can also offer useful information, when it is possible to precisely analyse which products have lost sales to the new product.

39.   There are a number of *quantitative tests* that have specifically been designed for the purpose of delineating markets. These tests consist of various econometric and statistical approaches, estimates of elasticities and cross-price elasticities[5] for the demand of a product, tests based on similarity of price movements over time, the analysis of causality between price series and similarity of price levels and/or their convergence. The Commission takes into account the available quantitative evidence capable of withstanding rigorous scrutiny for the purposes of establishing patterns of substitution in the past.

40.   *Views of customers and competitors.* The Commission often contacts the main customers and competitors of the companies involved in its enquiries, to gather their views on the boundaries of the product market as well as most of the factual information it requires to reach a conclusion on the scope of the market. Reasoned answers of customers and competitors as to what would happen if relative prices for the candidate products were to increase in the candidate geographic area by a small amount (for instance of 5% to 10%) are taken into account when they are sufficiently backed by factual evidence.

41.   *Consumer preferences.* In the case of consumer goods, it may be difficult for the Commission to gather the direct views of end consumers about substitute products. *Marketing studies* that companies have commissioned in the past and that are used by companies in their own decision-making as to pricing of their products and/or marketing actions may provide useful information for the Commission's delineation of the relevant market. Consumer surveys on usage patterns and attitudes, data from consumer's purchasing patterns, the views expressed by retailers and more generally, market research studies submitted by the parties and their competitors are taken into account to establish whether an economically significant proportion of consumers consider two products as substitutable, also taking into account the importance of brands for the products in question. The methodology followed in consumer surveys carried out *ad hoc* by the undertakings involved or their competitors for the purposes of a merger procedure or a procedure pursuant to Regulation No. 17 will usually be scrutinized with utmost care. Unlike pre-existing studies, they have not been prepared in the normal course of business for the adoption of business decisions.

42.   *Barriers and costs associated with switching demand to potential substitutes.* There are a number of barriers and costs that might prevent the Commission from considering two *prima facie* demand substitutes as belonging to one single product market. It is not possible to provide an exhaustive list of all the possible barriers to substitution and of switching costs. These barriers or obstacles might have a wide range of origins, and in its decisions, the Commission has been confronted with regulatory barriers or other forms of State intervention, constraints arising in downstream markets, need to incur specific capital investment or loss in current output in order to switch to alternative inputs, the location of customers, specific investment in production process, learning and human capital investment, retooling costs or other investments, uncertainty about quality and reputation of unknown suppliers, and others.

---

[5]   Own-price elasticity of demand for product X is a measure of the responsiveness of demand for X to percentage change in its own price. Cross-price elasticity between products X and Y is the responsiveness of demand for product X to percentage change in the price of product Y.

43. *Different categories of customers and price discrimination.* The extent of the product market might be narrowed in the presence of distinct groups of customers. A distinct group of customers for the relevant product may constitute a narrower, distinct market when such a group could be subject to price discrimination. This will usually be the case when two conditions are met: (a) it is possible to identify clearly which group an individual customer belongs to at the moment of selling the relevant products to him, and (b) trade among customers or arbitrage by third parties should not be feasible.

Evidence for defining markets – geographic dimension

44. The type of evidence the Commission considers relevant to reach a conclusion as to the geographic market can be categorized as follows:

45. *Past evidence of diversion of orders to other areas.* In certain cases, evidence on changes in prices between different areas and consequent reactions by customers might be available. Generally, the same quantitative tests used for product market definition might as well be used in geographic market definition, bearing in mind that international comparisons of prices might be more complex due to a number of factors such as exchange rate movements, taxation and product differentiation.

46. *Basic demand characteristics.* The nature of demand for the relevant product may in itself determine the scope of the geographical market. Factors such as national preferences or preferences for national brands, language, culture and life style, and the need for a local presence have a strong potential to limit the geographic scope of competition.

47. *Views of customers and competitors.* Where appropriate, the Commission will contact the main customers and competitors of the parties in its enquiries, to gather their views on the boundaries of the geographic market as well as most of the factual information it requires to reach a conclusion on the scope of the market when they are sufficiently backed by factual evidence.

48. *Current geographic pattern of purchases.* An examination of the customers' current geographic pattern of purchases provides useful evidence as to the possible scope of the geographic market. When customers purchase from companies located anywhere in the Community or the EEA on similar terms, or they procure their supplies through effective tendering procedures in which companies from anywhere in the Community or the EEA submit bids, usually the geographic market will be considered to be Community-wide.

49. *Trade flows/pattern of shipments.* When the number of customers is so large that it is not possible to obtain through them a clear picture of geographic purchasing patterns, information on trade flows might be used alternatively, provided that the trade statistics are available with a sufficient degree of detail for the relevant products. Trade flows, and above all, the rationale behind trade flows provide useful insights and information for the purpose of establishing the scope of the geographic market but are not in themselves conclusive.

50. *Barriers and switching costs associated to divert orders to companies located in other areas.* The absence of trans-border purchases or trade flows, for instance, does not necessarily mean that the market is at most national in scope. Still, barriers isolating the national market have to identified before it is concluded that the relevant geographic market in such a case is national. Perhaps the clearest obstacle for a customer to divert its orders to other areas is the impact of transport costs and transport restrictions arising from legislation or from the nature of the relevant products. The impact of transport costs will usually limit the scope of the geographic market for bulky, low-value products, bearing in mind that a transport disadvantage might also be compensated by a comparative advantage in other costs (labour costs

or raw materials). Access to distribution in a given area, regulatory barriers still existing in certain sectors, quotas and custom tariffs might also constitute barriers isolating a geographic area from the competitive pressure of companies located outside that area. Significant switching costs in procuring supplies from companies located in other countries constitute additional sources of such barriers.

51.   On the basis of the evidence gathered, the Commission will then define a geographic market that could range from a local dimension to a global one, and there are examples of both local and global markets in past decisions of the Commission.

52.   The paragraphs above describe the different factors which might be relevant to define markets. This does not imply that in each individual case it will be necessary to obtain evidence and assess each of these factors. Often in practice the evidence provided by a subset of these factors will be sufficient to reach a conclusion, as shown in the past decisional practice of the Commission.

IV.   CALCULATION OF MARKET SHARE

53.   The definition of the relevant market in both its product and geographic dimensions allows the identification of the suppliers and the customers/consumers active on that market. On that basis, a total market size and market shares for each supplier can be calculated on the basis of their sales of the relevant products in the relevant area. In practice, the total market size and market shares are often available from market sources, i.e. companies' estimates, studies commissioned from industry consultants and/or trade associations. When this is not the case, or when available estimates are not reliable, the Commission will usually ask each supplier in the relevant market to provide its own sales in order to calculate total market size and market shares.

54.   If sales are usually the reference to calculate market shares, there are nevertheless other indications that, depending on the specific products or industry in question, can offer useful information such as, in particular, capacity, the number of players in bidding markets, units of fleet as in aerospace, or the reserves held in the case of sectors such as mining.

55.   As a rule of thumb, both volume sales and value sales provide useful information. In cases of differentiated products, sales in value and their associated market share will usually be considered to better reflect the relative position and strength of each supplier.

V.   ADDITIONAL CONSIDERATIONS

56.   There are certain areas where the application of the principles above has to be undertaken with care. This is the case when considering primary and secondary markets, in particular, when the behaviour of undertakings at a point in time has to be analysed pursuant to Article 86. The method of defining markets in these cases is the same, i.e. assessing the responses of customers based on their purchasing decisions to relative price changes, but taking into account as well, constraints on substitution imposed by conditions in the connected markets. A narrow definition of market for secondary products, for instance, spare parts, may result when compatibility with the primary product is important. Problems of finding compatible secondary products together with the existence of high prices and a long lifetime of the primary products may render relative price increases of secondary products profitable. A different market definition may result if significant substitution between secondary products is possible or if the characteristics of the primary products make quick and direct consumer responses to relative price increases of the secondary products feasible.

57. In certain cases, the existence of chains of substitution might lead to the definition of a relevant market where products or areas at the extreme of the market are not directly substitutable. An example might be provided by the geographic dimension of a product with significant transport costs. In such cases, deliveries from a given plant are limited to a certain area around each plant by the impact of transport costs. In principle, such an area could constitute the relevant geographic market. However, if the distribution of plants is such that there are considerable overlaps between the areas around different plants, it is possible that the pricing of those products will be constrained by a chain substitution effect, and lead to the definition of a broader geographic market. The same reasoning may apply if product B is a demand substitute for products A and C. Even if products A and C are not direct demand substitutes, they might be found to be in the same relevant product market since their respective pricing might be constrained by substitution to B.

58. From a practical perspective, the concept of chains of substitution has to be corroborated by actual evidence, for instance related to price interdependence at the extremes of the chains of substitution, in order to lead to an extension of the relevant market in an individual case. Price levels at the extremes of the chains would have to be of the same magnitude as well.

Note

It is constitutionally plain that the Court, not the Commission, serves as the authoritative source of interpretation of Community law. This is made explicit in para. 6 of the Notice. However, the Commission's direct control over the practical administration of competition policy (examined in the next chapter) ensures that this Notice will have considerable influence in the treatment of cases. A test for determining substitutability based on on customer reaction to a 'small [5–10%], non-transitory change in relative prices' (paras 15, 17) is not to be found in such terms in judgments delivered by the European Court, but is instead drawn directly from North American practice. An illustration of the application of this test by the Commission is provided by Commission Decision 2000/12 *1998 Football World Cup* (2000) OJ L5/55. The market for match tickets for the tournament stood alone from the perspective of the consumer.

It should be obvious from the approach taken in *United Brands* (Case 27/76), that defining a market involves a calculation of the barriers which surround that market (see para. 122). At one extreme, even 100% occupation of a market is not a cause for concern where any other firm is able freely to enter that market. Potential competition controls the liberty of the firm in occupation. (See the annulment of an economically inadequate Commission Decision in *Continental Can* v *Commission* (Case 6/72) [1973] ECR 215.) However, the Commission's Notice prefers to treat this not as a matter of market definition, but rather as a (logically subsequent) matter of market power (para. 24). The stage at which the role of potential competition is taken into account in the analysis should not be of any practical significance to the outcome.

Should you wish to explore economic theory in this area, the classic work is J. S. Bain, *Barriers to New Competition* (1956). Try also W. Baumol, J. Panzar and R. Willig, *Contestable Markets and the Theory of Industrial*

Structure (1982). P. A. Geroski and A. Jacquemin, 'Industrial change, barriers to mobility and European industrial policy' (1985) 1 *Economic Policy* 170 provide a useful synthesis.

Over-estimation of entry barriers leads to unduly narrow market definition, which leads to unnecessary intervention in markets which would correct themselves. The next case has been criticised from this perspective.

Hugin Kassaregister AB v *Commission (Case 22/78)*
[1979] ECR 1869; [1979] 3 CMLR 345
Court of Justice of the European Communities

The Commission held Hugin in breach of Article 86 of the EC Treaty (now Article 82 EC) for refusal to supply spare parts for Hugin cash registers to Liptons. It defined the market as comprising spare parts for Hugin machines needed by independent repairers. Hugin argued the proper market definition covered the fiercely competitive cash register market in general. The Court dealt with the dispute as follows.

[5]   To resolve the dispute it is necessary, first, to determine the relevant market. In this respect account must be taken of the fact that the conduct alleged against Hugin consists in the refusal to supply spare parts to Liptons and, generally, to any independent undertaking outside its distribution network. The question is, therefore, whether the supply of spare parts constitutes a specific market or whether it forms part of a wider market. To answer that question it is necessary to determine the category of clients who require such parts.

[6]   In this respect it is established, on the one hand, that cash registers are of such a technical nature that the user cannot fit the spare parts into the machine but requires the services of a specialized technician and, on the other, that the value of the spare parts is of little significance in relation to the cost of maintenance and repairs. That being the case, users of cash registers do not operate on the market as purchasers of spare parts, however they have their machines maintained and repaired. Whether they avail themselves of Hugin's after-sales service or whether they rely on independent undertakings engaged in maintenance and repair work, their spare part requirements are not manifested directly and independently on the market. While there certainly exists amongst users a market for maintenance and repairs which is distinct from the market in new cash registers, it is essentially a market for the provision of services and not for the sale of a product such as spare parts, the refusal to supply which forms the subject-matter of the Commission's decision.

[7]   On the other hand, there exists a separate market for Hugin spare parts at another level, namely that of independent undertakings which specialize in the maintenance and repair of cash registers, in the reconditioning of used machines and in the sale of used machines and the renting out of machines. The rôle of those undertakings on the market is that of businesses which require spare parts for their various activities. They need such parts in order to provide services for cash register users in the form of maintenance and repairs and for the reconditioning of used machines intended for re-sale or renting out. Finally, they require spare parts for the maintenance and repair of new or used machines belonging to them which are rented out to their clients. It is, moreover, established that there is a specific demand for

Hugin spare parts, since those parts are not interchangeable with spare parts for cash registers of other makes.

[8]   Consequently the market thus constituted by Hugin spare parts required by independent undertakings must be regarded as the relevant market for the purposes of the application of Article 86 of the facts of the case. It is in fact the market on which the alleged abuse was committed.

[9]   It is necessary to examine next whether Hugin occupies a dominant position on that market. In this respect Hugin admits that it has a monopoly in new spare parts. For commercial reasons any competing production of spare parts which could be used in Hugin cash registers is not conceivable in practice. Hugin argues nevertheless that another source of supply does exist, namely the purchase and dismantling of used machines. The value of that source of supply is disputed by the parties. Although the file appears to show that the practice of dismantling used machines is current in the cash register sector it cannot be regarded as constituting a sufficient alternative source of supply. Indeed the figures relating to Liptons' turnover during the years when Hugin refused to sell spare parts to it show that Liptons' business in the selling, renting out and repairing of Hugin machines diminished considerably, not only when expressed in absolute terms but even more so in real terms, taking inflation into account.

Note

So Hugin dominated the market for its own spare parts. However, the Court went on to annul the Decision because it was not satisfied that any impact on trade between Member States had been shown.

The finding of dominance in *Hugin* (Case 22/78) is challenged in the next extract.

E. Fox, 'Monopolization and Dominance in the US and the EC: Efficiency, Opportunity and Fairness' (1986) 61 Notre Dame Law Rev 981, at pp. 1003, 1004
[© 1983 by Matthew Bender & Co. Inc., and reproduced by permission of 1983 Fordham Corporate Law Institute]

Having analysed *United Brands* (Case 27/76) and uncovered discrepancies between US and EC law, Fox continues:

In *Hugin-Liptons*, we find an even greater gap between US and Common Market law. First, in the United States, a company's own brand of product is almost never a market.[89] Under Community law, customer dependence may qualify a brand as a market. In *Hugin-Liptons*, the Court of Justice defined the market as spare parts for Hugin machines in view of the demand by independent servicers and renting agents. In doing so it ignored facts that US courts would deem material; namely, that the independents could get spare parts for the other cash registers from their producers and that Liptons could be expected to shift its business to the servicing and renting

---

[89] See *Calculators Hawaii, Inc.* v *Brandt, Inc.*, 724 F 2d 1332, 1337 (9th Cir 1983); *Telex Corp* v *IBM Corp* 510 F 2d 894,914–19 (10th Cir 1975), *cert. dismissed*, 423 US 802 (1975); *Rea* v *Ford Motor Co.*, 497 F 2d 577, 590 n 28 (3d Cir 1974), *cert. denied*, 419 US 868 (1974).

of more cash registers produced by other firms. A healthy market of independents who serviced and rented cash registers (made by other producers) would have remained.

When one asks whether Hugin's termination of Liptons was an effort to monopolize, the misfit of the monopoly framework becomes plain. Hugin was not a dominant cash register firm. It surely could not get a monopoly by charging a supracompetitive price for spare parts, and it would undercut its competitive attractiveness as a supplier of new machines if it developed a reputation for overcharging for repairs. Only two hypotheses seem plausible. Either Hugin was charging a low price for service and was providing rapid reliable service itself or through its authorized distributors, so as to wage more effective competition against its highly aggressive competitors, or Hugin wanted to keep the servicing business for itself and its authorized distributors and they were providing at least as good a price/service package as Liptons. Both for lack of dominance and lack of anticompetitive conduct, American courts would dismiss the case against Hugin. . . .

One suspects that the Court of Justice concludes too quickly that refusals to deal harm consumers. To base a result on harm to consumers where neither evidence nor theory indicates that such harm exists undermines the legitimacy of Court of Justice judgments, although those judgments might have been justified by an interest in protecting entrepreneurs.

Note

The economic analysis remains instructive, even though practice in this area in both jurisdictions has moved on; see, in the US, the Supreme Court's ruling in *Eastman Kodak Co.* v *Image Technical Services, Inc* 112 S. Ct. 2072 (1992) and, in the EC, the Commission's decision in *Pelikan* (XXVth Report on Competition on Policy, para. 87, 1995), both of which are noted by D. Maldoom [1996] 8 ECLR 473. See also on markets for spare parts, para. 56 of the Notice, p. 479 above. Refusal to deal is discussed further at p. 488.

Other cases which deserve attention for their approach to market definition include: *Hoffman la Roche* v *Commission* (Case 85/76) [1979] ECR 461; *Michelin* v *Commission* (Case 322/81) [1983] ECR 3461; *Continental Can* v *Commission* (Case 6/72), above.

Comparable issues arise in EC merger control which, since 21 September 1990, has been dealt with under the 'Merger Regulation', Regulation 4064/89 ((1989) OJ L395/1, corrected version published (1990) OJ L257/14), amended with effect from 1 March 1998 by Regulation 1310/97 ((1997) OJ L180/1, corrig. *ibid.* L199/69). (For treatment of the Regulation, see J. Cook and C. Kerse, *EC Merger Control* (3rd ed., 1999).) Like Article 82, merger control is motivated by the need to keep a check on market power and the specialised merger regime has many features in common with Article 82. This is evident from the cross-references in the Commission's Notice on Definition of the Relevant Market, p. 469 above. Article 2(3) of the Regulation provides that:

A concentration which creates or strengthens a dominant position as a result of which effective competition would be significantly impeded in the common market or in a substantial part of it shall be declared incompatible with the common market.

The Commission Decision in M053 *Aerospatiale Alenia/De Havilland* (1991) OJ L334/42, [1992] 4 CMLR M2, provides a good example of the process of market definition under the Regulation, covering matters such as substitutability and the impact of governmental regulation of airlines. Once the market was defined to cover specific types of short haul commuter aircraft the merger was blocked as incompatible with the Regulation. (See A. Downes and D. MacDougall, 'Significantly Impeding Effective Competition: Substantive Appraisal under the Merger Regulation' (1994) 19 EL Rev 286.)

Question
Are the Community institutions consistent in these cases in their approach to the role of potential competition brought about by adaptation of existing techniques? Are they too ready to permit intervention in the market?

Further reading
Further reading which takes account of the interweaving of law and economics in this field includes:

Baden Fuller, C. W., 'Article 86 EEC: Economic Analysis of the Existence of a Dominant Position' (1979) 4 EL Rev 423.
Gyselen, L., and Kyriazis, N., 'Article 86: Monopoly Power Measurement Issue Revisited' (1986) 11 EL Rev 134.

US law analogies are useful; see, for example:

G. Stigler and G. Sherwin, 'The Extent of the Market' 28 J Law and Econ 555 (1985).
Pitofsky, R., 'New Definitions of Relevant Market and the Assault on Antitrust' 90 *Columbia Law Rev* 1806 (1990).

(B) ABUSE

Dominance is not unlawful. Once the firm has been held dominant, it is necessary to decide whether it has abused that dominance. Again, *United Brands* (Case 27/76) provides an example of the types of conduct subject to control.

United Brands v *Commission (Case 27/76)*
[1978] ECR 207; [1978] 1 CMLR 429
Court of Justice of the European Communities

First, UBC forbade its distributors from reselling bananas when still green. The Commission considered this an abusive tactic, because it effectively prohibited cross-border trade in green bananas. UBC also routinely undersupplied in response to orders so as to force distributors to sell locally rather than seek to penetrate new markets. UBC was controlling the structure of the market.

Secondly, UBC cut off supply of Chiquita bananas to Olesen, a Danish distributor, in response to Olesen's participation in a promotion of Dole bananas, a rival brand.

The third practice condemned by the Commission related to UBC's selling prices, which differed dependent on the customer's Member State. These price differences were imposed at the banana's port of entry into the Community, before any supplement based on transport costs within the Community might have caused such discrepancy.

Finally, the Commission accused UBC of charging unfair prices; prices 'excessive in relation to the economic value of the product supplied'.

[157]   [In response to the first practice.] To impose on the ripener the obligation not to resell bananas so long as he has not had them ripened and to cut down the operations of such a ripener to contacts only with retailers is a restriction of competition.

[158]   Although it is commendable and lawful to pursue a policy of quality, especially by choosing sellers according to objective criteria relating to the qualifications of the seller, his staff and his facilities, such a practice can only be justified if it does not raise obstacles, the effect of which goes beyond the objective to be attained.

[159]   In this case, although these conditions for selection have been laid down in a way which is objective and not discriminatory, the prohibition on resale imposed upon duly appointed Chiquita ripeners and the prohibition of the resale of unbranded bananas – even if the perishable nature of the banana in practice restricted the opportunities of reselling to the duration of a specific period of time – when without any doubt an abuse of the dominant position since they limit markets to the prejudice of consumers and affects trade between Member States, in particular by partitioning national markets.

[160]   Thus UBC's organization of the market confined the ripeners to the role of suppliers of the local market and prevented them from developing their capacity to trade *vis-à-vis* UBC, which moreover tightened its economic hold on them by supplying less goods than they ordered.

[161]   It follows from all these considerations that the clause at issue forbidding the sale of green bananas infringes Article 86 of the Treaty.
. . .

[182]   [In response to the second practice.] . . . [I]t is advisable to assert positively from the outset that an undertaking in a dominant position for the purpose of marketing a product – which cashes in on the reputation of a brand name known to and valued by the consumers – cannot stop supplying a long standing customer who abides by regular commercial practice, if the orders placed by that customer are in no way out of the ordinary.

[183]   Such conduct is inconsistent with the objectives laid down in Article 3 (f) of the Treaty, which are set out in detail in Article 86, especially in paragraphs (b) and (c), since the refusal to sell would limit markets to the prejudice of consumers and would amount to discrimination which might in the end eliminate a trading party from the relevant market.

[184]   It is therefore necessary to ascertain whether the discontinuance of supplies by UBC in October 1973 was justified.

[185]   The reason given is in the applicant's letter of 11 October 1973 in which it upbraided Olesen in no uncertain manner for having participated in an advertising campaign for one of its competitors.

[186]   Later on UBC added to this reason a number of complaints, for example, that Olesen was the exclusive representative of its main competitor on the Danish market.

[187]   This was not a new situation since it goes back to 1969 and was not in any case inconsistent with fair trade practices.

[188]   Finally UBC has not put forward any relevant argument to justify the refusal of supplies.

[189]   Although it is true, as the applicant points out, that the fact that an undertaking is in a dominant position cannot disentitle it from protecting its own commercial interests if they are attacked, and that such an undertaking must be conceded the right to take such reasonable steps as it deems appropriate to protect its said interests, such behaviour cannot be countenanced if its actual purpose is to strengthen this dominant position and abuse it.

[190]   Even if the possibility of a counter-attack is acceptable that attack must still be proportionate to the threat taking into account the economic strength of the undertakings confronting each other.

[191]   The sanction consisting of a refusal to supply by an undertaking in a dominant position was in excess of what might, if such a situation were to arise, reasonably be contemplated as a sanction for conduct similar to that for which UBC blamed Olesen.

[192]   In fact UBC could not be unaware of that fact that by acting in this way it would discourage its other ripener/distributors from supporting the advertising of other brand names and that the deterrent effect of the sanction imposed upon one of them would make its position of strength on the relevant market that much more effective.

[193]   Such a course of conduct amounts therefore to a serious interference with the independence of small and medium sized firms in their commercial relations with the undertaking in a dominant position and this independence implies the right to give preference to competitors' goods.

[194]   In this case the adoption of such a course of conduct is designed to have a serious adverse effect on competition on the relevant banana market by only allowing firms dependant upon the dominant undertaking to stay in business.
. . .

[227]   [In response to the third practice.] Although the responsibility for establishing the single banana market does not lie with the applicant, it can only endeavour to take 'what the market can bear' provided that it complies with the rules for the regulation and coordination of the market laid down by the Treaty.

[228]   Once it can be grasped that differences in transport costs, taxation, customs duties, the wages of the labour force, the conditions of marketing, the differences in the parity of currencies, the density of competition may eventually culminate in different retail selling price levels according to the Member States, then it follows those differences are factors which UBC only has to take into account to a limited extent since it sells a product which is always the same and at the same place to ripener/distributors who – alone – bear the risks of the consumers' market.

[229] The interplay of supply and demand should, owing to its nature, only be applied to each stage where it is really manifest.

[230] The mechanisms of the market are adversely affected if the price is calculated by leaving out one stage of the market and taking into account the law of supply and demand as between the vendor and the ultimate consumer and not as between the vendor (UBC) and the purchaser (the ripener/distributors).

[231] Thus, by reason of its dominant position UBC, fed with information by its local representatives, was in fact able to impose its selling price on the intermediate purchaser. This price and also the 'weekly quota allocated' is only fixed and notified to the customer four days before the vessel carrying the bananas berths.

[232] These discriminatory prices, which varied according to the circumstances of the Member States, were just so many obstacles to the free movement of goods and their effect was intensified by the clause forbidding the resale of bananas while still green and by reducing the deliveries of the quantities ordered.

[233] A rigid partitioning of national markets was thus created at price levels, which were artificially different, placing certain distributor/ripeners at a competitive disadvantage, since compared with what it should have been competition had thereby been distorted.

[234] Consequently the policy of differing prices enabling UBC to apply dissimilar conditions to equivalent transactions with other trading parties, thereby placing them at a competitive disadvantage, was an abuse of a dominant position.

. . .

[248] [In response to the last practice.] The imposition by an undertaking in a dominant position directly or indirectly of unfair purchase or selling prices is an abuse to which exception can be taken under Article 86 of the Treaty.

[249] It is advisable therefore to ascertain whether the dominant undertaking has made use of the opportunities arising out of its dominant position in such a way as to reap trading benefits which it would not have reaped if there had been normal and sufficiently effective competition.

[250] In this case charging a price which is excessive because it has no reasonable relation to the economic value of the product supplied would be such an abuse.

[251] This excess could, *inter alia*, be determined objectively if it were possible for it to be calculated by making a comparison between the selling price of the product in question and its cost of production, which would disclose the amount of the profit margin; however the Commission has not done this since it has not analysed UBC's costs structure.

[252] The questions therefore to be determined are whether the difference between the costs actually incurred and the price actually charged is excessive, and, if the answer to this question is in the affirmative, whether a price has been imposed which is either unfair in itself or when compared to competing products.

The Court decided that the Commission had not proved this last allegation and annulled this part of the Decision.

Note

Unfairness in pricing is obviously hard to pin down. For discussion see R. Whish, *Competition Law*, Ch. 15.

Question

Consider which aspects of United Brands' policy were likely to exploit consumers directly; and which were more indirect in that they served to reduce or suppress competition. Article 82 is broad enough to cover both types of practice.

Note

One of the several matters considered in *United Brands* (Case 27/76) was the conduct of a dominant firm towards the supply of its customers. The Court accepts that the dominant firm is precluded from arbitrary conduct (paras 182–89). The precise nature of the control exercised in this area depends on the nature of the market in issue. The next case is an important decision on abusive refusal to supply.

Istituto Chemicoterapico Italiano SpA and Commercial Solvents Corporation (Cases 6 & 7/73) v Commission
[1974] ECR 223; [1974] 1 CMLR 309
Court of Justice of the European Communities

Commercial Solvents (CSC) stopped supplying Zoja with aminobutanol, a raw material used in the production of ethambutol. The Commission held CSC dominant in the market for aminobutanol. The firm challenged the subsequent finding that it had abused that dominance by refusing to continue supplies to Zoja.

[23] The applicants state that they ought not to be held responsible for stopping supplies of aminobutanol to Zoja for this was due to the fact that in the spring of 1970 Zoja itself informed Istituto that it was cancelling the purchase of large quantities of aminobutanol which had been provided for in a contract then in force between Istituto and Zoja. When at the end of 1970 Zoja again contacted Istituto to obtain this product, the latter was obliged to reply, after consulting CSC, that in the meantime CSC had changed its commercial policy and that the product was no longer available. The change of policy by CSC was, they claim, inspired by a legitimate consideration of the advantage that would accrue to it of expanding its production to include the manufacture of finished products and not limiting itself to that of raw material or intermediate products. In pursuance of this policy it decided to improve its product and no longer to supply aminobutanol save in respect of commitments already entered into by its distributors.

[24] It appears from the documents and from the hearing that the suppliers of raw material are limited, as regards the EEC, to Istituto, which, as stated in the claim by CSC, started in 1968 to develop its own specialities based on ethambutol, and in November 1969 obtained the approval of the Italian government necessary for the manufacture and in 1970 started manufacturing its own specialities. When Zoja

sought to obtain further supplies of aminobutanol, it received a negative reply. CSC had decided to limit, if not completely to cease, the supply of nitropropane and aminobutanol to certain parties in order to facilitate its own access to the market for the derivatives.

[25]   However, an undertaking being in a dominant position as regards the production of raw material and therefore able to control the supply to manufacturers of derivatives, cannot, just because it decides to start manufacturing these derivatives (in competition with its former customers) act in such a way as to eliminate their competition which in the case in question, would amount to eliminating one of the principal manufacturers of ethambutol in the Common Market. Since such conduct is contrary to the objectives expressed in Article 3(f) of the Treaty and set out in greater detail in Articles 85 and 86, it follows that an undertaking which has a dominant position in the market in raw materials and which, with the object of reserving such raw material for manufacturing its own derivatives, refuses to supply a customer, which is itself a manufacturer of these derivatives, and therefore risks eliminating all competition on the part of this customer, is abusing its dominant position within the meaning of Article 86. In this context it does not matter that the undertaking ceased to supply in the spring of 1970 because of the cancellation of the purchases by Zoja, because it appears from the applicants' own statement that, when the supplies provided for in the contract had been completed, the sale of aminobutanol would have stopped in any case.

[26]   It is also unnecessary to examine, as the applicants have asked, whether Zoja had an urgent need for aminobutanol in 1970 and 1971 or whether this company still had large quantities of this product which would enable it to reorganize its production in good time, since that question is not relevant to the consideration of the conduct of the applicants.

The Court upheld the finding of abuse.

Note
A different market yielded a different result in the next case.

BP v Commission (Case 77/77)
[1978] ECR 1511
Court of Justice of the European Communities

The Commission found abusive BP's reduction in supply of oil to ABG, a Dutch customer, during the oil crisis of the early-1970s. The Court disagreed.

[28]   It emerges from the contested decision that the fact that BP in November 1972 terminated its commercial relations with ABG was connected with the regrouping of BP's operational activities which was made necessary by the nationalization of a large part of that company's interests in the production sector and by the participation of the producer countries in its extracting activities and is thus explained by considerations which have nothing to do with its relations with ABG.

[29]   It therefore follows that at the time of the crisis and even from November 1972, ABG's position in relation to BP was no longer, as regards the supply of motor spirit, that of a contractual customer but that of an occasional customer.

[30] The principle laid down by the contested decision that reductions in supplies ought to have been carried out on the basis of a reference period fixed in the year before the crisis, although it may be explicable in cases in which a continued supply relationship has been maintained, during that period, between seller and purchaser, cannot be applied when the supplier ceased during the course of that same period to carry on such relations with its customer, regard being had in particular to the fact that the plans of any undertaking are normally based on reasonable forecasts.

[31] Moreover, the advances in petrol against crude oil agreed to by BP in pursuance of the processing agreement, as they occur within the context of an agreement whose purpose was solely the refining of crude oil supplied by ABG and not the supplying of ABG with motor spirit, cannot serve as a valid argument to compare ABG's position in this case in relation to BP with that of a traditional customer of BP during the above-mentioned reference period.

[32] For all these reasons, since ABG's position in relation to BP had been, for several months before the crisis occurred, that of an occasional customer, BP cannot be accused of having applied to it during the crisis less favourable treatment than that which it reserved for its traditional customers.

Question
Explain the major features which distinguish these two cases. You might also look at the decision of the Court of First Instance in *BPB Industries and British Gypsum Ltd* v *Commission* (Case T-65/89) [1993] ECR II-389, [1993] 5 CMLR 32 (the subject of an unsuccessful appeal dealing only with procedural matters in *BPB Industries and British Gypsum Ltd* v *Commission* (Case C-310/93 P) [1995] ECR I-865) and that of the Court of Justice in Case C-333/94 P *Tetra Pak* v *Commission* [1996] ECR I-5951.

Note
Broadly, this type of intervention can be justified as an attempt to preserve vestiges of competition and to curb potential inefficiencies flowing from the dominator's tactics. The cases have, not surprisingly, aroused some concern about the nature of the policy pursued. Read, for example, A. Pathak, 'Vertical Restraints in EEC Competition Law' [1988/2] LIEI 15, who questions whom the Commission is trying to protect in this area; consumer, small trader . . . ?

In the next case the Court upheld the Commission's extension of control to cover a refusal to supply a first-time customer.

Radio Téléfis Eireann and Independent Television Publications v Commission (Cases C–241/91P, C–242/91P)
[1995] ECR I–801, [1995] 4 CMLR 718
Court of Justice of the European Communities

Three British and Irish television companies, RTE, BBC and ITP, held copyright over programme listings. Each produced a guide to its own programmes, but they did not produce a single guide available to Irish consumers containing the combined listings. Third party publishers were unable to produce a comprehensive guide, because the companies refused to license use of the copyright-protected material. The Court of First Instance rejected an application for the annulment of the Commission Decision that the companies were abusing their dominant position (Case T–69/89 [1991] ECR II–485). The companies' appeal to the European Court was also unsuccessful. In reading this extract from the judgment remember that Article 86 should be read with post-Amsterdam eyes as Article 82.

[52]   Among the circumstances taken into account by the Court of First Instance in concluding that such conduct was abusive was, first, the fact that there was, according to the findings of the Court of First Instance, no actual or potential substitute for a weekly television guide offering information on the programmes for the week ahead. On this point, the Court of First Instance confirmed the Commission's finding that the complete lists of programmes for a 24-hour period – and for a 48-hour period at weekends and before public holidays – published in certain daily and Sunday newspapers, and the television sections of certain magazines covering, in addition, 'highlights' of the week's programmes, were only to a limited extent substitutable for advance information to viewers on all the week's programmes. Only weekly television guides containing comprehensive listings for the week ahead would enable users to decide in advance which programmes they wished to follow and arrange their leisure activities for the week accordingly. The Court of First Instance also established that there was a specific, constant and regular potential demand on the part of consumers (see the *RTE* judgment, paragraph 62, and the *ITP* judgment, paragraph 48).

[53]   Thus the appellants – who were, by force of circumstances, the only sources of the basic information on programme scheduling which is the indispensable raw material for compiling a weekly television guide – gave viewers wishing to obtain information on the choice of programmes for the week ahead no choice but to buy the weekly guides for each station and draw from each of them the information they needed to make comparisons.

[54]   The appellants' refusal to provide basic information by relying on national copyright provisions thus prevented the appearance of a new product, a comprehensive weekly guide to television programmes, which the appellants did not offer and for which there was a potential consumer demand. Such refusal constitutes an abuse under heading (b) of the second paragraph of Article 86 of the Treaty.

[55]   Second, there was no justification for such refusal either in the activity of television broadcasting or in that of publishing television magazines (*RTE* judgment, paragraph 73, and *ITP* judgment, paragraph 58).

[56]   Third, and finally, as the Court of First Instance also held, the appellants, by their conduct, reserved to themselves the secondary market of weekly television guides by excluding all competition on that market (see the judgment in Joined Cases 6/73 and 7/73 *Commercial Solvents* v *Commission* [1974] ECR 223, paragraph 25) since they denied access to the basic information which is the raw material indispensable for the compilation of such a guide.

[57]   In the light of all those circumstances, the Court of First Instance did not err in law in holding that the appellants' conduct was an abuse of a dominant position within the meaning of Article 86 of the Treaty.

Note and Question
The decision is remarkable for its assertion of control of the firms' exercise of exclusive rights under national copyright law; see p. 564 below. P. Crowther comments that '[t]aken literally, the court's pronouncement on the fact that the copyright was used to restrict competition on a derivative market leaves the owner of an intellectual property right in a very precarious position . . . the upshot . . . is that owners of intellectual property rights, controlling "indispensable raw materials", might think twice about launching expensive R[esearch] & D[evelopment] programmes' ((1995) 20 EL Rev 521, 528). Has the Court established a satisfactory balance between the consumer interest in a market that is currently competitive and the consumer interest in a market which encourages innovators by rewarding them through shelter from competition? The Court of First Instance subsequently ruled that a refusal to supply may be condemned under Article 82 only where supply is essential to the activity in question or where the refusal prevents the introduction of a new product subject to consumer demand (Case T-504/93 *Tiercé Ladbroke* v *Commission* [1997] ECR II-923). And in the next case the European Court offered a further hint that the treatment of the market for television listings which led it to impose an obligation to contract on the dominant firm is likely to be regarded as exceptional.

Oscar Bronner GmbH & Co. KG v *Mediaprint* (Case C-7/97)
[1998] ECR I-7791
Court of Justice of the European Communities

This was a preliminary reference made by an Austrian court. Mediaprint, a publisher, had established a nationwide home-delivery scheme for newspapers. No competing facility existed in Austria. Oscar Bronner claimed that Mediaprint was acting in breach of Article 86 of the EC Treaty (now Article 82 EC) by refusing to include Bronner's newspaper, *Der Standard*, in the delivery service (for which Bronner was prepared to pay). Mediaprint pointed to the considerable investment it had made in developing the service and submitted that even though it held considerable market power in the Austrian daily newspaper market, it was not obliged to assist competing companies by allowing access to its facility. The Court agreed with Mediaprint.

[32.]   In examining whether an undertaking holds a dominant position within the meaning of Article 86 of the Treaty, it is of fundamental importance, as the Court has emphasised many times, to define the market in question and to define the substantial part of the common market in which the undertaking may be able to engage in abuses which hinder effective competition (Case C-242/95 *GT-Link* v *DSB* [1997] ECR I-4449, paragraph 36).

[33.]   It is settled case-law that, for the purposes of applying Article 86 of the Treaty, the market for the product or service in question comprises all the products or services which in view of their characteristics are particularly suited to satisfy constant needs and are only to a limited extent interchangeable with other products or services (Case 31/80 *L'Oréal v De Nieuwe AMCK* [1980] ECR 3775, paragraph 25; Case C-62/86 *AKZO v Commission* [1991] ECR I-3359, paragraph 51).

[34.] As regards the definition of the market at issue in the main proceedings, it is therefore for the national court to determine, *inter alia*, whether home-delivery schemes constitute a separate market, or whether other methods of distributing daily newspapers, such as sale in shops or at kiosks or delivery by post, are sufficiently interchangeable with them to have to be taken into account also. In deciding whether there is a dominant position the court must also take account, as the Commission has emphasised, of the possible existence of regional home-delivery schemes.

[35.] If that examination leads the national court to conclude that a separate market in home-delivery schemes does exist, and that there is an insufficient degree of interchangeability between Mediaprint's nationwide scheme and other, regional, schemes, it must hold that Mediaprint, which according to the information in the order for reference operates the only nationwide home-delivery service in Austria, is *de facto* in a monopoly situation in the market thus defined, and thus holds a dominant position in it.

[36.] In that event, the national court would also have to find that Mediaprint holds a dominant position in a substantial part of the common market, since the case-law indicates that the territory of a Member State over which a dominant position extends is capable of constituting a substantial part of the common market (see, to that effect, Case 322/81 *Michelin v Commission* [1983] ECR 3461, paragraph 28; Case C-323/93 *Centre d'Insémination de la Crespelle* [1994] ECR I-5077, paragraph 17).

[37.] Finally, it would need to be determined whether the refusal by the owner of the only nationwide home-delivery scheme in the territory of a Member State, which uses that scheme to distribute its own daily newspapers, to allow the publisher of a rival daily newspaper access to it constitutes an abuse of a dominant position within the meaning of Article 86 of the Treaty, on the ground that such refusal deprives that competitor of a means of distribution judged essential for the sale of its newspaper.

[38.] Although in *Commercial Solvents v Commission* [Cases 6 & 7/73 p. 488 above] and CBEM [v *CLT and IPB* Case 311/84 [1985] ECR 3261] cited above, the Court of Justice held the refusal by an undertaking holding a dominant position in a given market to supply an undertaking with which it was in competition in a neighbouring market with raw materials (*Commercial Solvents v Commission*, paragraph 25) and services (*CBEM*, paragraph 26) respectively, which were indispensable to carrying on the rival's business, to constitute an abuse, it should be noted, first, that the Court did so to the extent that the conduct in question was likely to eliminate all competition on the part of that undertaking.

[39.] Secondly, in *Magill* [Cases C-241/91 P, C-242/91 P *RTE and ITP v Commission*, above], at paragraphs 49 and 50, the Court held that refusal by the owner of an intellectual property right to grant a licence, even if it is the act of an undertaking holding a dominant position, cannot in itself constitute abuse of a dominant position, but that the exercise of an exclusive right by the proprietor may, in exceptional circumstances, involve an abuse.

[40.] In *Magill*, the Court found such exceptional circumstances in the fact that the refusal in question concerned a product (information on the weekly schedules of certain television channels) the supply of which was indispensable for carrying on the business in question (the publishing of a general television guide), in that, without that information, the person wishing to produce such a guide would find it impossible to publish it and offer it for sale (paragraph 53), the fact that such refusal prevented the appearance of a new product for which there was a potential consumer demand (paragraph 54), the fact that it was not justified by objective considerations (paragraph 55), and that it was likely to exclude all competition in the secondary market of television guides (paragraph 56).

[41.]   Therefore, even if that case-law on the exercise of an intellectual property right were applicable to the exercise of any property right whatever, it would still be necessary, for the *Magill* judgment to be effectively relied upon in order to plead the existence of an abuse within the meaning of Article 86 of the Treaty in a situation such as that which forms the subject-matter of the first question, not only that the refusal of the service comprised in home delivery be likely to eliminate all competition in the daily newspaper market on the part of the person requesting the service and that such refusal be incapable of being objectively justified, but also that the service in itself be indispensable to carrying on that person's business, inasmuch as there is no actual or potential substitute in existence for that home-delivery scheme.

[42.]   That is certainly not the case even if, as in the case which is the subject of the main proceedings, there is only one nationwide home-delivery scheme in the territory of a Member State and, moreover, the owner of that scheme holds a dominant position in the market for services constituted by that scheme or of which it forms part.

[43.]   In the first place, it is undisputed that other methods of distributing daily newspapers, such as by post and through sale in shops and at kiosks, even though they may be less advantageous for the distribution of certain newspapers, exist and are used by the publishers of those daily newspapers.

[44.]   Moreover, it does not appear that there are any technical, legal or even economic obstacles capable of making it impossible, or even unreasonably difficult, for any other publisher of daily newspapers to establish, alone or in cooperation with other publishers, its own nationwide home-delivery scheme and use it to distribute its own daily newspapers.

[45.]   It should be emphasised in that respect that, in order to demonstrate that the creation of such a system is not a realistic potential alternative and that access to the existing system is therefore indispensable, it is not enough to argue that it is not economically viable by reason of the small circulation of the daily newspaper or newspapers to be distributed.

[46.]   For such access to be capable of being regarded as indispensable, it would be necessary at the very least to establish, as the Advocate General has pointed out at point 68 of his Opinion, that it is not economically viable to create a second home-delivery scheme for the distribution of daily newspapers with a circulation comparable to that of the daily newspapers distributed by the existing scheme.

[47.]   In the light of the foregoing considerations, the answer to the first question must be that the refusal by a press undertaking which holds a very large share of the daily newspaper market in a Member State and operates the only nationwide newspaper home-delivery scheme in that Member State to allow the publisher of a rival newspaper, which by reason of its small circulation is unable either alone or in cooperation with other publishers to set up and operate its own home-delivery scheme in economically reasonable conditions, to have access to that scheme for appropriate remuneration does not constitute abuse of a dominant position within the meaning of Article 86 of the Treaty.

Question

Alpha plc is the sole UK manufacturer of Brillyarn, and its output of Brillyarn constitutes 50 per cent of production of the fibre in the EC. There are only two other EC producers: Heinz, a German firm responsible for 30 per cent of the EC output; and Ventoux, a French firm responsible for the remaining 20 per cent of EC production.

Brillyarn cannot be manufactured without the constituent material, 'Coralfoam'. The only supplier of 'Coralfoam' presently active in the EC is an Italian firm, Donadoni, although several American companies also produce 'Coralfoam', but have not attempted to enter the European market due to the costs of transporting 'Coralfoam' across the Atlantic.

Donadoni has supplied Alpha with 'Coralfoam' for six years, since the discovery of the process for manufacturing Brillyarn. However, when Alpha orders an increase in supplies of 'Coralfoam' as part of an expansion programme, Donadoni rejects the order and informs Alpha that it no longer intends to do business with it. Donadoni explains that it has concluded an exclusive dealing contract with Heinz, designed to permit Heinz to purchase all Donadoni's supplies of 'Coralfoam' with a view to rapid expansion.

Alpha seeks your advice as to whether any infringements of the EC Treaty have been committed.

Advise Alpha.

How, if at all, would your answer differ if Donadoni had agreed to continue supplying Alpha but had insisted on an immediate 50 per cent price increase?

13 THE ENFORCEMENT OF THE COMPETITION RULES

(A) ENFORCEMENT BY THE COMMISSION

Article 87 of the EC Treaty (now, after amendment, Article 83 EC) empowers the Council to adopt measures to give effect to the principles contained in Articles 85 and 86 of the EC Treaty (now Article 81 and 82 EC). It did so in Regulation 17/62.

Regulation 17/62/EEC, First Regulation Implementing Articles 85 and 86 [now 81 and 82] of the Treaty, Articles 1–25
(1959–62) OJ (Special Edition), 87

Article 1 Basic provision
Without prejudice to Articles 6,7 and 23 of this Regulation, agreements, decisions and concerted practices of the kind described in Article 85(1) of the Treaty and the abuse of a dominant position in the market, within the meaning of Article 86 of the Treaty, shall be prohibited, no prior decision to that effect being required.

Article 2 Negative clearance
Upon application by the undertakings or associations of undertakings concerned, the Commission may certify that, on the basis of the facts in its possession, there are no grounds under Article 85(1) or Article 86 of the Treaty for action on its part in respect of an agreement, decision or practice.

Article 3 Termination of infringements
1. Where the Commission, upon application or upon its own initiative, finds that there is infringement of Article 85 or Article 86 of the Treaty, it may by decision require the undertakings or associations of undertakings concerned to bring such infringement to an end.
2. Those entitled to make application are:
   (a) Member States;
   (b) natural or legal persons who claim a legitimate interest.
3. Without prejudice to the other provisions of this Regulation, the Commission may, before taking a decision under paragraph 1, address to the undertakings or

associations of undertakings concerned recommendations for termination of the infringement.

Article 4 Notification of new agreements, decisions and practices

1. Agreements, decisions and concerted practices of the kind described in Article 85(1) of the Treaty which come into existence after the entry into force of this Regulation and in respect of which the parties seek application of Article 85(3) must be notified to the Commission. Until they have been notified, no decision in application of Article 85(3) may be taken.

2. Paragraph 1 shall not apply to agreements, decisions or concerted practices where:

(1) the only parties thereto are undertakings from one Member State and the agreements, decisions or practices do not relate either to imports or to exports between Member States;

2. *(a) the agreements or concerted practices are entered into by two or more undertakings, each operating, for the purposes of the agreement, at a different level of the production or distribution chain, and relate to the conditions under which the parties may purchase, sell or resell certain goods or services;*

(b) not more than two undertakings are party thereto, and the agreements only impose restrictions on the exercise of the rights of the assignee or user of industrial property rights, in particular patents, utility models, designs or trade marks, or of the person entitled under a contract to the assignment, or grant, of the right to use a method of manufacture or knowledge relating to the use and to the application of industrial processes.

This paragraph was introduced by amending Regulation 1216/1999 OJ 1999 L 148/5: see further on its intent, p. 527 below.

(3) they have as their sole object:

(a) the development or uniform application of standards or types; or

(b) joint research for improvement of techniques, provided the results are accessible to all parties thereto and may be used by each of them.

These agreements, decisions and practices may be notified to the Commission.

Article 5 Notification of existing agreements, decisions and practices

1. Agreements, decisions and concerted practices of the kind described in Article 85(1) of the Treaty which are in existence at the date of entry into force of this Regulation and in respect of which the parties seek application of Article 85(3) shall be notified to the Commission before 1 August 1962.

2. Paragraph 1 shall not apply to agreements, decisions or concerted practices falling within Article 4(2); these may be notified to the Commission.

Article 6 Decisions pursuant to Article 85(3)

1. Whenever the Commission takes a decision pursuant to Article 85(3) of the Treaty, it shall specify therein the date from which the decision shall take effect. Such date shall not be earlier than the date of notification.

2. The second sentence of paragraph 1 shall not apply to agreements, decisions or concerted practices falling within Article 4(2) and Article 5(2), nor to those falling within Article 5(1) which have been notified within the time limit specified in Article 5(1).

Article 7 Special provisions for existing agreements, decisions and practices

1. Where agreements, decisions and concerted practices in existence at the date of entry into force of this Regulation and notified before 12 August 1962 do not satisfy

the requirements of Article 85(3) of the Treaty and the undertakings or associations of undertakings concerned cease to give effect to them or modify them in such manner that they no longer fall within the prohibition contained in Article 85(1) or that they satisfy the requirements of Article 85(3), the prohibition contained in Article 85(1) shall apply only for a period fixed by the Commission. A decision by the Commission pursuant to the foregoing sentence shall not apply as against undertakings and associations of undertakings which did not expressly consent to the notification.

2. Paragraph 1 shall apply to agreements, decisions and concerted practices falling within Article 4(2) which are in existence at the date of entry into force of this Regulation if they are notified before 1 January 1964.

Article 8 Duration and revocation of decisions under Article 85(3)

1. A decision in application of Article 85(3) of the Treaty shall be issued for a specified period and conditions and obligations may be attached thereto.

2. A decision may on application be renewed if the requirements of Article 85(3) of the Treaty continue to be satisfied.

3. The Commission may revoke or amend its decision or prohibit specified acts by the parties:

(a) where there has been a change in any of the facts which were basic to the making of the decision;

(b) where the parties commit a breach of any obligation attached to the decision;

(c) where the decision is based on incorrect information or was induced by deceit;

(d) where the parties abuse the exemption from the provisions of Article 85(1) of the Treaty granted to them by the decision.

In cases to which subparagraphs (b), (c) or (d) apply, the decision may be revoked with retroactive effect.

Article 9 Powers

1. Subject to review of its decision by the Court of Justice, the Commission shall have sole power to declare Article 85(1) inapplicable pursuant to Article 85(3) of the Treaty.

2. The Commission shall have power to apply Article 85(1) and Article 86 of the Treaty; this power may be exercised notwithstanding that the time limits specified in Article 5(1) and in Article 7(2) relating to notification have not expired.

3. As long as the Commission has not initiated any procedure under Articles 2, 3 or 6, the authorities of the Member States shall remain competent to apply Article 85(1) and Article 86 in accordance with Article 88 of the Treaty; they shall remain competent in this respect notwithstanding that the time limits specified in Article 5(1) and in Article 7(2) relating to notification have not expired.

Article 10 Liaison with the authorities of the Member States

1. The Commission shall forthwith transmit to the competent authorities of the Member States a copy of the applications and notifications together with copies of the most important documents lodged with the Commission for the purpose of establishing the existence of infringements of Articles 85 or 86 of the Treaty or of obtaining negative clearance or a decision in application of Article 85(3).

2. The Commission shall carry out the procedure set out in paragraph 1 in close and constant liaison with the competent authorities of the Member States; such authorities shall have the right to express their views upon the procedure.

3. An Advisory Committee on Restrictive Practices and Monopolies shall be consulted prior to the taking of any decision following upon a procedure under paragraph 1, and of any decision concerning the renewal, amendment or revocation of a decision pursuant to Article 85(3) of the Treaty.

4. The Advisory Committee shall be composed of officials competent in the matter of restrictive practices and monopolies. Each Member State shall appoint an official to represent it who, if prevented from attending, may be replaced by another official.

5. The consultation shall take place at a joint meeting convened by the Commission; such meeting shall be held not earlier than fourteen days after dispatch of the notice convening it. The notice shall, in respect of each case to be examined, be accompanied by a summary of the case together with an indication of the most important documents, and a preliminary draft decision.

6. The Advisory Committee may deliver an opinion notwithstanding that some of its members or their alternates are not present. A report of the outcome of the consultative proceedings shall be annexed to the draft decision. It shall not be made public.

Article 11 Requests for information

1. In carrying out the duties assigned to it by Article 89 and by provisions adopted under Article 87 of the Treaty, the Commission may obtain all necessary information from the Governments and competent authorities of the Member States and from undertakings and associations of undertakings.

2. When sending a request for information to an undertaking or association of undertakings, the Commission shall at the same time forward a copy of the request to the competent authority of the Member State in whose territory the seat of the undertaking or association of undertakings is situated.

3. In its request the Commission shall state the legal basis and the purpose of the request and also the penalties provided for in Article 15(1)(b) for supplying incorrect information.

4. The owners of the undertakings or their representatives and, in the case of legal persons, companies or firms, or of associations having no legal personality, the persons authorised to represent them by law or by their constitution shall supply the information requested.

5. Where an undertaking or association of undertakings does not supply the information requested within the time limit fixed by the Commission, or supplies incomplete information, the Commission shall by decision require the information to be supplied. The decision shall specify what information is required, fix an appropriate time limit within which it is to be supplied and indicate the penalties provided for in Article 15(1)(b) and Article 16(1)(c) and the right to have the decision reviewed by the Court of Justice.

6. The Commission shall at the same time forward a copy of its decision to the competent authority of the Member State in whose territory the seat of the undertaking or association of undertakings is situated.

Article 12 Inquiry into sectors of the economy

1. If in any sector of the economy the trend of trade between Member States, price movements, inflexibility of prices or other circumstances suggest that in the economic sector concerned competition is being restricted or distorted within the common market, the Commission may decide to conduct a general inquiry into that economic sector and in the course thereof may request undertakings in the sector concerned to supply the information necessary for giving effect to the principles formulated in

Article 85 and 86 of the Treaty and for carrying out the duties entrusted to the Commission.

2.   The Commission may in particular request every undertaking or association of undertakings in the economic sector concerned to communicate to it all agreements, decisions and concerted practices which are exempt from notification by virtue of Article 4(2) and Article 5(2).

3.   When making inquiries pursuant to paragraph 2, the Commission shall also request undertakings or groups of undertakings whose size suggests that they occupy a dominant position within the common market or a substantial part thereof to supply to the Commission and such particulars of the structure of the undertakings and of their behaviour as are requisite to an appraisal of their position in the light of Article 86 of the Treaty.

4.   Article 10(3) to (6) and Articles 11, 13 and 14 shall apply correspondingly.

Article 13   Investigations by the authorities of the Member States

1.   At the request of the Commission, the competent authorities of the Member States shall undertake the investigations which the Commission considers to be necessary under Article 14(1), or which it has ordered by decision pursuant to Article 14(3). The officials of the competent authorities of the Member States responsible for conducting these investigations shall exercise their powers upon production of an authorisation in writing issued by the competent authority of the Member State in whose territory the investigation is to be made. Such authorisation shall specify the subject matter and purpose of the investigation.

2.   If so requested by the Commission or by the competent authority of the Member State in whose territory the investigation is to be made, the officials of the Commission may assist the officials of such authorities in carrying out their duties.

Article 14   Investigating powers of the Commission

1.   In carrying out the duties assigned to it by Article 89 and by provisions adopted under Article 87 of the Treaty, the Commission may undertake all necessary investigations into undertakings and associations of undertakings. To this end the officials authorised by the Commission are empowered:
  (a)   to examine the books and other business records;
  (b)   to take copies of or extracts from the books and business records;
  (c)   to ask for oral explanations on the spot;
  (d)   to enter any premises; land and means of transport of undertakings.

2.   The officials of the Commission authorised for the purpose of these investigations shall exercise their powers upon production of an authorisation in writing specifying the subject matter and purpose of the investigation and the penalties provided for in Article 15(1)(c) in cases where production of the required books or other business records is incomplete. In good time before the investigation, the Commission shall inform the competent authority of the Member State in whose territory the same is to be made of the investigation and of the identity of the authorised officials.

3.   Undertakings and associations of undertakings shall submit to investigations ordered by decision of the Commission. The decision shall specify the subject matter and purpose of the investigation, appoint the date on which it is to begin and indicate the penalties provided for in Article 15(1)(c) and Article 16(1)(d) and the right to have the decision reviewed by the Court of Justice.

4.   The Commission shall take decisions referred to in paragraph 3 after consultation with the competent authority of the Member State in whose territory the investigation is to be made.

5. Officials of the competent authority of the Member State in whose territory the investigation is to be made may, at the request of such authority or of the Commission, assist the officials of the Commission in carrying out their duties.

6. Where an undertaking opposes an investigation ordered pursuant to this Article, the Member State concerned shall afford the necessary assistance to the officials authorised by the Commission to enable them to make their investigation. Member States shall, after consultation with the Commission, take the necessary measures to this end before 1 October 1962.

Article 15   Fines

1. The Commission may by decision impose on undertakings or associations of undertakings fines of from 100 to 5,000 units of account where, intentionally or negligently:

(a)   they supply incorrect or misleading information in an application pursuant to Article 2 or in a notification pursuant to Articles 4 or 5; or

(b)   they supply incorrect information in response to a request made pursuant to Article 11(3) or (5) or to Article 12, or do not supply information within the time limit fixed by a decision taken under Article 11(5); or

(c)   they produce the required books or other business records in incomplete form during investigations under Article 13 or 14, or refuse to submit to an investigation ordered by decision issued in implementation of Article 14(3).

2. The Commission may by decision impose on undertakings or associations of undertakings fines of from 1,000 to 1,000,000 units of account, or a sum in excess thereof but not exceeding 10% of the turnover in the preceding business year of each of the undertakings participating in the infringement where, either intentionally or negligently:

(a)   they infringe Article 85(1) or Article 86 of the Treaty; or

(b)   they commit a breach of any obligation imposed pursuant to Article 8(1). In fixing the amount of the fine, regard shall be had both to the gravity and to the duration of the infringement.

3. Article 10(3) to (6) shall apply.

4. Decisions taken pursuant to paragraphs 1 and 2 shall not be of a criminal law nature.

5. The fines provided for in paragraph 2(a) shall not be imposed in respect of acts taking place:

(a)   after notification to the Commission and before its decision in application of Article 85(3) of the Treaty, provided they fall within the limits of the activity described in the notification;

(b)   before notification and in the course of agreements, decisions or concerted practices in existence at the date of entry into force of this Regulation, provided that notification was effected within the time limits specified in Article 5(1) and Article 7(2).

6. Paragraph 5 shall not have effect where the Commission has informed the undertakings concerned that after preliminary examination it is of opinion that Article 85(1) of the Treaty applies and that application of Article 85(3) is not justified.

Article 16   Periodic penalty payments

1. The Commission may by decision impose on undertakings or associations of undertakings periodic penalty payments of from 50 to 1,000 units of account per day, calculated from the date appointed by the decision, in order to compel them:

(a)   to put an end to an infringement of Article 85 or 86 of the Treaty, in accordance with a decision taken pursuant to Article 3 of this Regulation;

(b)   to refrain from any act prohibited under Article 8(3);

(c)   to supply complete and correct information which it has requested by decision taken pursuant to Article 11(5);

(d)   to submit to an investigation which it has ordered by decision taken pursuant to Article 14(3).

2.   Where the undertakings or associations of undertakings have satisfied the obligation which it was the purpose of the periodic penalty payment to enforce, the Commission may fix the total amount of the periodic penalty payment at a lower figure than that which would arise under the original decision.

3.   Article 10(3) to (6) shall apply.

Article 17   Review by the Court of Justice

The Court of Justice shall have unlimited jurisdiction within the meaning of Article 172 of the Treaty to review decisions whereby the Commission has fixed a fine or periodic penalty payment; it may cancel, reduce or increase the fine or periodic penalty payment imposed.

Article 18   Unit of account

For the purposes of applying Articles 15 to 17 the unit of account shall be that adopted in drawing up the budget of the Community in accordance with Articles 207 and 209 of the Treaty.

Article 19   Hearing of the parties and of third persons

1.   Before taking decisions as provided for in Articles 2, 3, 6, 7, 8, 15 and 16, the Commission shall give the undertakings or associations of undertakings concerned the opportunity of being heard on the matters to which the Commission has taken objection.

2.   If the Commission or the competent authorities of the Member State consider it necessary, they may also hear other natural or legal persons. Applications to be heard on the part of such persons shall, where they show a sufficient interest be granted.

3.   Where the Commission intends to give negative clearance pursuant to Article 2 or take a decision in application of Article 85(3) of the Treaty, it shall publish a summary of the relevant application or notification and invite all interested third parties to submit their observations within a time limit which it shall fix being not less than one month. Publication shall have regard to the legitimate interest of undertakings in the protection of their business secrets.

Article 20   Professional secrecy

1.   Information acquired as a result of the application of Articles 11, 12, 13 and 14 shall be used only for the purpose of the relevant request or investigation.

2.   Without prejudice to the provisions of Articles 19 and 21, the Commission and the competent authorities of the Member States, their officials and other servants shall not disclose information acquired by them as a result of the application of this Regulation and of the kind covered by the obligation of professional secrecy.

3.   The provisions of paragraphs 1 and 2 shall not prevent publication of general information or surveys which do not contain information relating to particular undertakings or associations of undertakings.

Article 21   Publication of decisions

1.   The Commission shall publish the decisions which it takes pursuant to Articles 2, 3, 6, 7 and 8.

2.   The publication shall state the names of the parties and the main content of the decisions; it shall have regard to the legitimate interest of undertakings in the protection of their business secrets.

Article 22   Special provisions

1.   The Commission shall submit to the Council proposals for making certain categories of agreement, decision and concerted practice falling within Article 4(2) or Article 5(2) compulsorily notifiable under Article 4 or 5.

2.   Within one year from the date of entry into force of this Regulation, the Council shall examine, on a proposal from the Commission, what special provisions might be made for exempting from the provisions of this Regulation agreements, decisions and concerted practices falling within Article 4(2) or Article 5(2).

Article 23   Transitional provisions applicable to decisions of authorities of the Member States

1.   Agreements, decisions and concerted practices of the kind described in Article 85(1) of the Treaty to which, before the entry into force of this Regulation, the competent authority of a Member State has declared Article 85(1) to be inapplicable pursuant to Article 85(3) shall not be subject to compulsory notification under Article 5. The decision of the competent authority of the Member State shall be deemed to be a decision within the meaning of Article 6; it shall cease to be valid upon expiration of the period fixed by such authority but in any event not more than three years after the entry into force of this Regulation. Article 8(3) shall apply.

2.   Applications for renewal of decisions of the kind described in paragraph 1 shall be decided upon by the Commission in accordance with Article 8(2).

Article 24   Implementing provisions

The Commission shall have power to adopt implementing provisions concerning the form, content and other details of applications pursuant to Articles 2 and 3 and of notifications pursuant to Articles 4 and 5, and concerning hearings pursuant to Article 19(1) and (2).

Article 25

1.   As regards agreements, decisions and concerted practices to which Article 85 of the Treaty applies by virtue of accession, the date of accession shall be substituted for the date of entry into force of this Regulation in every place where reference is made in this Regulation to this latter date.

2.   Agreements, decisions and concerted practices existing at the date of accession to which Article 85 of the Treaty applies by virtue of accession shall be notified pursuant to Article 5(1) or Article 7(1) and (2) within six months from the date of accession.

3.   Fines under Article 15(2)(a) shall not be imposed in respect of any act prior to notification of the agreements, decisions and practices to which paragraph 2 applies and which have been notified within the period therein specified.

4.   New Member States shall take the measures referred to in Article 14(6) within six months from the date of accession after consulting the Commission.

5.   The provisions of paragraphs 1 to 4 above still apply in the same way in the case of the accession of the Hellenic Republic, the Kingdom of Spain and the Portuguese Republic.

Note

These powers are exercised by the Directorate General for Competition in the Commission. The Regulation itself contains safeguards for the firm under investigation, e.g., Articles 19 and 20. These rights were supplemented by Regulation 99/63 which concerned hearings. This has now been repealed and replaced by Regulation 2842/98.

Commission Regulation (EC) No. 2842/98 of 22 December 1998 on the hearing of parties in certain proceedings under Articles 85 and 86 [now 81 and 82] of the EC Treaty
(OJ 1998 L 354/18)

CHAPTER 1   SCOPE

Article 1

This Regulation shall apply to the hearing of parties under Article 19(1) and (2) of Regulation No 17, Article 26(1) and (2) of Regulation (EEC) No 1017/68, Article 23(1) and (2) of Regulation (EEC) No 4056/86 and Article 16(1) and (2) of Regulation (EEC) No 3975/87.

CHAPTER II   HEARING OF PARTIES TO WHICH THE COMMISSION HAS ADDRESSED OBJECTIONS

Article 2

1.   The Commission shall hear the parties to which it has addressed objections before consulting the appropriate Advisory Committee under Article 10(3) of Regulation No 17, Article 16(3) of Regulation (EEC) No 1017/68, Article 15(3) of Regulation (EEC) No 4056/86 or Article 8(3) of Regulation (EEC) No 3975/87.

2.   The Commission shall in its decisions deal only with objections in respect of which the parties have been afforded the opportunity of making their views known.

Article 3

1.   The Commission shall inform the parties in writing of the objections raised against them. The objections shall be notified to each of them or to a duly appointed agent.

2.   The Commission may inform the parties by giving notice in the Official Journal of the European Communities, if from the circumstances of the case this appears appropriate, in particular where notice is to be given to a number of undertakings but no joint agent has been appointed. The notice shall have regard to the legitimate interests of the undertakings in the protection of their business secrets and other confidential information.

3.   A fine or a periodic penalty payment may be imposed on a party only if the objections have been notified in the manner provided for in paragraph 1.

4.   The Commission shall, when giving notice of objections, set a date by which the parties may inform it in writing of their views.

5.   The Commission shall set a date by which the parties may indicate any parts of the objections which in their view contain business secrets or other confidential material. If they do not do so by that date, the Commission may assume that the objections do not contain such information.

Article 4

1.   Parties which wish to make known their views on the objections raised against them shall do so in writing and by the date referred to in Article 3(4). The Commission shall not be obliged to take into account written comments received after that date.

2.   The parties may in their written comments set out all matters relevant to their defence. They may attach any relevant documents as proof of the facts set out and may also propose that the Commission hear persons who may corroborate those facts.

Article 5
The Commission shall afford to parties against which objections have been raised the opportunity to develop their arguments at an oral hearing, if they so request in their written comments.

CHAPTER III   HEARING OF APPLICANTS AND COMPLAINANTS

Article 6
Where the Commission, having received an application made under Article 3(2) of Regulation No 17 or a complaint made under Article 10 of Regulation (EEC) No 1017/68, Article 10 of Regulation (EEC) No 4056/86 or Article 3(1) of Regulation (EEC) No 3975/87, considers that on the basis of the information in its possession there are insufficient grounds for granting the application or acting on the complaint, it shall inform the applicant or complainant of its reasons and set a date by which the applicant or complainant may make known its views in writing.

Article 7
Where the Commission raises objections relating to an issue in respect of which it has received an application on a complaint as referred to in Article 6, it shall provide an applicant or complainant with a copy of the non-confidential version of the objections and set a date by which the applicant or complainant may make known its views in writing.

Article 8
The Commission may, where appropriate, afford to applicants and complainants the opportunity of orally expressing their views, if they so request in their written comments.

CHAPTER IV   HEARING OF OTHER THIRD PARTIES

Article 9
1.   If parties other than those referred to in Chapters II and III apply to be heard and show a sufficient interest, the Commission shall inform them in writing of the nature and subject matter of the procedure and shall set a date by which they may make known their views in writing.
2.   The Commission may, where appropriate, invite parties referred to in paragraph 1 to develop their arguments at the oral hearing of the parties against which objections have been raised, if they so request in their written comments.
3.   The Commission may afford to any other third parties the opportunity of orally expressing their views.

CHAPTER V   GENERAL PROVISIONS

Article 10
Hearings shall be conducted by the Hearing Officer.

Article 11
1.   The Commission shall invite the persons to be heard to attend the oral hearing on such date as it shall appoint.
2.   The Commission shall invite the competent authorities of the Member States to take part in the oral hearing.

Article 12

1.   Persons invited to attend shall either appear in person or be represented by legal representatives or by representatives authorised by their constitution as appropriate.

Undertakings and associations of undertakings may be represented by a duly authorised agent appointed from among their permanent staff.

2.   Persons heard by the Commission may be assisted by their legal advisers or other qualified persons admitted by the Hearing Officer.

3.   Oral hearings shall not be public. Each person shall be heard separately or in the presence of other persons invited to attend. In the latter case, regard shall be had to the legitimate interest of the undertakings in the protection of their business secrets and other confidential information.

4.   The statements made by each person heard shall be recorded on tape. The recording shall be made available to such persons on request, by means of a copy from which business secrets and other confidential information shall be deleted.

Article 13

1.   Information, including documents, shall not be communicated or made accessible in so far as it contains business secrets of any party, including the parties to which the Commission has addressed objections, applicants and complainants and other third parties, or other confidential information or where internal documents of the authorities are concerned. The Commission shall make appropriate arrangements for allowing access to the file, taking due account of the need to protect business secrets, internal Commission documents and other confidential information.

2.   Any party which makes known its views under the provisions of this Regulation shall clearly identify any material which it considers to be confidential, giving reasons, and provide a separate non-confidential version by the date set by the Commission. If it does not do so by the set date, the Commission may assume that the submission does not contain such material.

Article 14

In setting the dates provided for in Articles 3(4), 6, 7 and 9(1), the Commission shall have regard both to the time required for preparation of the submission and to the urgency of the case. The time allowed in each case shall be at least two weeks; it may be extended.

CHAPTER VI   FINAL PROVISIONS

Article 15

1.   Regulations No 99/63/EEC and (EEC) No 1630/69 are repealed.

2.   Sections II of Regulations (EEC) No 4260/88 and (EEC) No 4261/88 are deleted.

Article 16

This Regulation shall enter into force on 1 February 1999.

This Regulation shall be binding in its entirety and directly applicable in all Member States.

Note

Both Regulations also confer rights on third parties with an interest; see, e.g., Articles 3(2) and 19 of Regulation 17/62 and Article 6–9 of Regulation 2842/98. Achieving a balance between the needs of effective enforcement of the competition rules and the protection of firms subject to the rules is a difficult but vital issue. The Court has played an important part. Its cases in this area are important in competition law, but also reflect more generally the development of Community notions of fundamental rights (p. 66 above). Its major decisions include *National Panasonic* v *Commission* (Case 136/79) [1980] ECR 2033; *Musique Diffusion Française* v *Commission* (Cases 100–103/80) [1983] ECR 1825; *Transocean Marine Paint* v *Commission* (Case 17/74) [1974] ECR 1063, discussed at p. 73 above for its value as an example of Community legal technique; and *AKZO* v *Commission* (Case 5/85) [1986] ECR 2585.

The Court of First Instance has now assumed jurisdiction in this area and it too has begun to establish important ground rules. However, the following decision of the Court of Justice remains highly significant.

Hoechst v *Commission (Case 46/87)*
[1989] ECR 2859
Court of Justice of the European Communities

The Commission suspected Hoechst was implicated in a cartel. Seeking information, it arrived unannounced at Hoechst's premises, as it is entitled to do under Article 14 of Regulation 17/62. This is the so-called 'dawn raid', which, since the Commission prefers to find the building open, does not take place at dawn. Hoechst refused to admit the Commission officials and argued that it was entitled to exclude them until a search warrant had been obtained through national procedures. The Commission eventually obtained access using this route, but imposed financial penalties on Hoechst for refusal to comply with the original decision under Article 14. Hoechst sought the annulment of that decision before the Court. The extract below covers Hoechst's submissions relating, first, to the scope of the Commission's powers of investigation; and, secondly, to the adequacy of the reasons for the decision supplied by the Commission.

(a) *The Commission's powers of investigation*

[10] The applicant considers that the contested decision is unlawful inasmuch as it permitted the Commission's officials to take steps which the applicant describes as a search, which are not provided for under Article 14 of Regulation No 17 and which infringe fundamental rights recognized by Community law. It adds that if that provision is to be interpreted as empowering the Commission to carry out searches, it is unlawful on the ground that it is incompatible with fundamental rights, for the protection of which it is necessary that searches should be carried out only on the basis of a judicial warrant issued in advance.

[11] The Commission contends that its powers under Article 14 of Regulation No 17 extend to the adoption of measures which, under the law of some Member States, would be regarded as searches. It none the less considers that the requirements of judicial protection deriving from fundamental rights, which it does not contest in principle, are fulfilled in so far as the addressees of decisions ordering investigations have an opportunity, on the one hand, to contest those decisions before the Court

and, on the other, to apply for suspension of their operation by way of interim order, which permits the Court to check rapidly that the investigations ordered are not arbitrary in nature. Such review is equivalent to a judicial warrant issued in advance.

[12]   It should be noted, before the nature and scope of the Commission's powers of investigation under Article 14 of Regulation No 17 are examined, that that article cannot be interpreted in such a way as to give rise to results which are incompatible with the general principles of Community law and in particular with fundamental rights.

[13]   The Court has consistently held that fundamental rights are an integral part of the general principles of law the observance of which the Court ensures, in accordance with constitutional traditions common to the Member States, and the international treaties on which the Member States have collaborated or of which they are signatories (see, in particular, the judgment of 14 May 1974 in Case 4/73 *Nold* v *Commission* [1974] ECR 491). The European Convention for the Protection of Human Rights and Fundamental Freedoms of 4 November 1950 (hereinafter referred to as 'the European Convention on Human Rights') is of particular significance in that regard (see, in particular, the judgment of 15 May 1986 in Case 222/84 *Johnston* v *Chief Constable of the Royal Ulster Constabulary* [1986] ECR 1651).

[14]   In interpreting Article 14 of Regulation No 17, regard must be had in particular to the rights of the defence, a principle whose fundamental nature has been stressed on numerous occasions in the Court's decisions (see, in particular, the judgment of 9 November 1983 in Case 322/81 *Michelin* v *Commission* [1983] ECR 3461, paragraph 7).

[15]   In that judgment, the Court pointed out that the rights of the defence must be observed in administrative procedures which may lead to the imposition of penalties. But it is also necessary to prevent those rights from being irremediably impaired during preliminary inquiry procedures including, in particular, investigations which may be decisive in providing evidence of the unlawful nature of conduct engaged in by undertakings for which they may be liable.

[16]   Consequently, although certain rights of the defence relate only to the contentious proceedings which follow the delivery of the statement of objections, other rights, such as the right to legal representation and the privileged nature of correspondence between lawyer and client (recognized by the Court in the judgment of 18 May 1982 in Case 155/79 *AM & S* v *Commission* [1982] ECR 1575) must be respected as from the preliminary-inquiry stage.

[17]   Since the applicant has also relied on the requirements stemming from the fundamental right to the inviolability of the home, it should be observed that, although the existence of such a right must be recognized in the Community legal order as a principle common to the laws of the Member States in regard to the private dwellings of natural persons, the same is not true in regard to undertakings, because there are not inconsiderable divergences between the legal systems of the Member States in regard to the nature and degree of protection afforded to business premises against intervention by the public authorities.

[18]   No other inference is to be drawn from Article 8(1) of the European Convention on Human Rights which provides that: 'Everyone has the right to respect for his private and family life, his home and his correspondence'. The protective scope of that article is concerned with the development of man's personal freedom and may not

therefore be extended to business premises. Furthermore, it should be noted that there is no case-law of the European Court of Human Rights on that subject.

[19]   None the less, in all the legal systems of the Member States, any intervention by the public authorities in the sphere of private activities of any person, whether natural or legal, must have a legal basis and be justified on the grounds laid down by law, and, consequently, those systems provide, albeit in different forms, protection against arbitrary or disproportionate intervention. The need for such protection must be recognized as a general principle of Community law. In that regard, it should be pointed out that the Court has held that it has the power to determine whether measures of investigation taken by the Commission under the ECSC Treaty are excessive (judgment of 14 December 1962 in Joined Cases 5 to 11 and 13 to 15/62 *San Michele and Others* v *Commission* [1962] ECR 449).

[20]   The nature and scope of the Commission's powers of investigation under Article 14 of Regulation No 17 should therefore be considered in the light of the general principles set out above.

[21]   Article 14(1) authorizes the Commission to undertake all necessary investigations into undertakings and associations of undertakings and provides that: 'To this end the officials authorized by the Commission are empowered:

(a)   to examine the books and other business records;
(b)   to take copies of or extracts from the books and business records;
(c)   to ask for oral explanations on the spot;
(d)   to enter any premises, land and means of transport of undertakings'.

[22]   Article 14(2) and (3) provide that investigations may be carried out upon production of an authorization in writing or of a decision requiring undertakings to submit to the investigation. As the Court has already decided, the Commission may choose between those two possibilities in the light of the special features of each case (judgment of 26 June 1980 in Case 136/79 *National Panasonic* v *Commission* [1980] ECR 2033). Both the written authorizations and the decisions must specify the subject-matter and purpose of the investigation. Whichever procedure is followed, the Commission is required to inform, in advance, the competent authority of the Member State in whose territory the investigation is to be carried out and, according to Article 14(4), that authority must be consulted before the decision ordering the investigation is adopted.

[23]   According to Article 14(5), the Commission's officials may be assisted in carrying out their duties by officials of the competent authority of the Member State in whose territory the investigation is to be made. Such assistance may be provided either at the request of that authority or of the Commission.

[24]   Finally, according to Article 14(6), the assistance of the national authorities is necessary for the carrying out of the investigation where it is opposed by an undertaking.

[25]   As the Court pointed out in the abovementioned judgment of 26 June 1980 (paragraph 20), it follows from the seventh and eighth recitals in the preamble to Regulation No 17 that the aim of the powers given to the Commission by Article 14 of that regulation is to enable it to carry out its duty under the EEC Treaty of ensuring that the rules on competition are applied in the common market. The function of those rules is, as follows from the fourth recital in the preamble to the Treaty, Article 3(f) and Articles 85 and 86, to prevent competition from being distorted to the

detriment of the public interest, individual undertakings and consumers. The exercise of the powers given to the Commission by Regulation No 17 thus contributes to the maintenance of the system of competition intended by the Treaty with which undertakings are absolutely bound to comply. The eighth recital states that for that purpose the Commission must be empowered, throughout the common market, to require such information to be supplied and to undertake such investigations 'as are necessary' to bring to light any infringement of Articles 85 or 86.

[26]   Both the purpose of Regulation No 17 and the list of powers conferred on the Commission's officials by Article 14 thereof show that the scope of investigations may be very wide. In that regard, the right to enter any premises, land and means of transport of undertakings is of particular importance inasmuch as it is intended to permit the Commission to obtain evidence of infringements of the competition rules in the places in which such evidence is normally to be found, that is to say, on the business premises of undertakings.

[27]   That right of access would serve no useful purpose if the Commission's officials could do no more than ask for documents or files which they could identify precisely in advance. On the contrary, such a right implies the power to search for various items of information which are not already known or fully identified. Without such a power, it would be impossible for the Commission to obtain the information necessary to carry out the investigation if the undertakings concerned refused to cooperate or adopted an obstructive attitude.

[28]   Although Article 14 of Regulation No 17 thus confers wide powers of investigation on the Commission, the exercise of those powers is subject to conditions serving to ensure that the rights of the undertakings concerned are respected.

[29]   In that regard, it should be noted first that the Commission is required to specify the subject-matter and purpose of the investigation. That obligation is a fundamental requirement not merely in order to show that the investigation to be carried out on the premises of the undertakings concerned is justified but also to enable those undertakings to assess the scope of their duty to cooperate while at the same time safeguarding the rights of the defence.

[30]   It should also be pointed out that the conditions for the exercise of the Commission's investigative powers vary according to the procedure which the Commission has chosen, the attitude of the undertakings concerned and the intervention of the national authorities.

[31]   Article 14 of Regulation No 17 deals in the first place with investigations carried out with the cooperation of the undertakings concerned, either voluntarily, where there is a written authorization, or by virtue of an obligation arising under a decision ordering an investigation. In the latter case, which is the situation here, the Commission's officials have, *inter alia*, the power to have shown to them the documents they request, to enter such premises as they choose, and to have shown to them the contents of any piece of furniture which they indicate. On the other hand, they may not obtain access to premises or furniture by force or oblige the staff of the undertaking to give them such access, or carry out searches without the permission of the management of the undertaking.

[32]   The situation is completely different if the undertakings concerned oppose the Commission's investigation. In that case, the Commission's officials may, on the basis of Article 14(6) and without the cooperation of the undertakings, search for any

information necessary for the investigation with the assistance of the national authorities, which are required to afford them the assistance necessary for the performance of their duties. Although such assistance is required only if the undertaking expresses its opposition, it may also be requested as a precautionary measure, in order to overcome any opposition on the part of the undertaking.

[33] It follows from Article 14(6) that it is for each Member State to determine the conditions under which the national authorities will afford assistance to the Commission's officials. In that regard, the Member States are required to ensure that the Commission's action is effective, while respecting the general principles set out above. It follows that, within those limits, the appropriate procedural rules designed to ensure respect for undertakings' rights are those laid down by national law.

[34] Consequently, if the Commission intends, with the assistance of the national authorities, to carry out an investigation other than with the cooperation of the undertakings concerned, it is required to respect the relevant procedural guarantees laid down by national law.

[35] The Commission must make sure that the competent body under national law has all that it needs to exercise its own supervisory powers. It should be pointed out that that body, whether judicial or otherwise, cannot in this respect substitute its own assessment of the need for the investigations ordered for that of the Commission, the lawfulness of whose assessments of fact and law is subject only to review by the Court of Justice. On the other hand, it is within the powers of the national body, after satisfying itself that the decision ordering the investigation is authentic, to consider whether the measures of constraint envisaged are arbitrary or excessive having regard to the subject-matter of the investigation and to ensure that the rules of national law are complied with in the application of those measures.

[36] In the light of the foregoing, it must be held that the measures which the contested decision ordering the investigation permitted the Commission's officials to take did not exceed their powers under Article 14 of Regulation No 17. Article 1 of that decision merely requires the applicant 'to permit officials authorized by the Commission to enter its premises during normal office hours, to produce for inspection and to permit copies to be made of business documents related to the subject-matter of the enquiry which are requested by the said officials and to provide immediately any explanations which those officials may seek'.

[37] During the proceedings before the Court, the Commission did indeed argue that its officials are entitled, when making investigations, to carry out searches without the assistance of the national authorities and without respecting the procedural guarantees provided for under national law. However, that misinterpretation of Article 14 of Regulation No 17 cannot render unlawful decisions adopted on the basis of that provision.

[38] The submission alleging that the Commission exceeded its powers of investigation must therefore be rejected.

(b) *The statement of reasons*

[39] According to the applicant, the decision ordering the investigation infringes Article 190 of the Treaty and Article 14(3) of Regulation No 17 on the ground that it is imprecise, in particular in regard to the subject-matter and purpose of the investigation.

[40]　It should be pointed out that, as the Court held in its abovementioned judgment of 26 June 1980 (*National Panasonic*, paragraph 25), Article 14(3) of Regulation No 17 itself lays down the essential constituents of the statement of the reasons upon which a decision ordering an investigation is based by providing that it 'shall specify the subject-matter and the purpose of the investigation, appoint the date on which it is to begin and indicate the penalties provided for in Article 15(1)(c) and Article 16(1)(d) and the right to have the decision reviewed by the Court of Justice'.

[41]　As has been stated above, the Commission's obligation to specify the subject-matter and purpose of the investigation constitutes a fundamental guarantee of the rights of the defence of the undertakings concerned. It follows that the scope of the obligation to state the reasons on which decisions ordering investigations are based cannot be restricted on the basis of considerations concerning the effectiveness of the investigation. Although the Commission is not required to communicate to the addressee of a decision ordering an investigation all the information at its disposal concerning the presumed infringements, or to make a precise legal analysis of those infringements, it must none the less clearly indicate the presumed facts which it intends to investigate.

[42]　Although the statement of the reasons on which the contested decision is based is drawn up in very general terms which might well have been made more precise, and is therefore open to criticism in that respect, it none the less contains the essential indications prescribed by Article 14(3) of Regulation No 17. The decision at issue refers in particular to information suggesting the existence and application of agreements or concerted practices between certain producers and suppliers of PVC and polyethylene (including, but not limited to, LdPE) in the EEC, concerning prices, quantities or sales targets for those products. It states that those agreements and practices may constitute a serious infringement of Article 85(1) of the Treaty. According to Article 1 of the decision in question, the applicant 'is required to submit to an investigation concerning its possible participation' in those agreements or concerted practices and, consequently, to give the Commission's officials access to its premises and to produce or allow copies to be made for the purpose of inspection of business documents 'related to the subject-matter of the investigation'.

[43]　In those circumstances, the submission alleging that the statement of reasons is insufficient must be rejected.

Question
How successful is the Court's balance between the interests of the Commission and of the firm under investigation? Is there any contradiction between accepting on the one hand that the firm is entitled to the procedural protection of national law in proceedings to gain access, while on the other hand allowing the firm to be fined while those procedural guarantees are in the process of being respected?

　　For notes of the case see J. Shaw (1990) 15 EL Rev 326, R. Lauwaars (1990) 27 CML Rev 355. See more generally C.S. Kerse, *EC Antitrust Procedure* (1998) and also I. Van Bael, 'The Antitrust Settlement Practice of the EC Commission' (1986) 23 CML Rev 61; D. Curtin, 'Constitutionalism in the European Community: The Right to Fair Proceedings in Administrative Law' in J. O'Reilly (ed.) *Human Rights and Constitutional Law*;

C. Harding, *EC Investigations and Sanctions* (1993); K. Lenaerts and L. Vandamme, 'Procedural rights of private parties in the Community administrative process' (1997) 34 CML Rev 531.

Note

The Court also accepts that the firm may enjoy some protection from Commission scrutiny of documents. Notice particularly how in the following case the Court develops Community law by reference to national law.

Australian Mining & Smelting Europe Ltd v *Commission*
(Case 155/79)
[1982] ECR 1575
Court of Justice of the European Communities

[18] . . . Community law, which derives from not only the economic but also the legal interpenetration of the Member States, must take into account the principles and concepts common to the laws of those States concerning the observance of confidentiality, in particular, as regards certain communications between lawyer and client. That confidentiality serves the requirements, the importance of which is recognized in all of the Member States, that any person must be able, without constraint, to consult a lawyer whose profession entails the giving of independent legal advice to all those in need of it.

[19] As far as the protection of written communications between lawyer and client is concerned, it is apparent from the legal systems of the Member States that, although the principle of such protection is generally recognized, its scope and the criteria for applying it vary, as has, indeed, been conceded both by the applicant and by the parties who have intervened in support of its conclusions.

[20] Whilst in some of the Member States the protection against disclosure afforded to written communications between lawyer and client is based principally on a recognition of the very nature of the legal profession, inasmuch as it contributes towards the maintenance of the rule of law, in other Member States the same protection is justified by the more specific requirement (which, moreover, is also recognized in the first-mentioned States) that the rights of the defence must be respected.

[21] Apart from these differences, however, there are to be found in the national laws of the Member States common criteria inasmuch as those laws protect, in similar circumstances, the confidentiality of written communications between lawyer and client provided that, on the one hand, such communications are made for the purposes and in the interests of the client's rights of defence and, on the other hand, they emanate from independent lawyers, that is to say, lawyers who are not bound to the client by a relationship of employment.

[22] Viewed in that context Regulation No 17 must be interpreted as protecting, in its turn, the confidentiality of written communications between lawyer and client subject to those two conditions, and thus incorporating such elements of that protection as are common to the laws of the Member States.

[23]   As far as the first of those two conditions is concerned, in Regulation No 17 itself, in particular in the eleventh recital in its preamble and in the provisions contained in Article 19, care is taken to ensure that the rights of the defence may be exercised to the full, and the protection of the confidentiality of written communications between lawyer and client is an essential corollary to those rights. In those circumstances, such protection must, if it is to be effective, be recognized as covering all written communications exchanged after the initiation of the administrative procedure under Regulation No 17 which may lead to a decision on the application of Articles 85 and 86 of the Treaty or to a decision imposing a pecuniary sanction on the undertaking. It must also be possible to extend it to earlier written communications which have a relationship to the subject-matter of that procedure.

[24]   As regards the second condition, it should be stated that the requirement as to the position and status as an independent lawyer, which must be fulfilled by the legal adviser from whom the written communications which may be protected emanate, is based on a conception of the lawyer's role as collaborating in the administration of justice by the courts and as being required to provide, in full independence, and in the overriding interests of that cause, such legal assistance as the client needs. The counterpart of that protection lies in the rules of professional ethics and discipline which are laid down and enforced in the general interest by institutions endowed with the requisite powers for that purpose. Such a conception reflects the legal traditions common to the Member States and is also to be found in legal order of the Community, as is demonstrated by Article 17 of the Protocols on the Statutes of the Court of Justice of the EEC and the EAEC, and also by Article 20 of the Protocol on the Statute of the Court of Justice of the ECSC.

[25]   Having regard to the principles of the Treaty concerning freedom of establishment and the freedom to provide services the protection thus afforded by Community law, in particular in the context of Regulation No 17, to written communications between lawyer and client must apply without distinction to any lawyer entitled to practise his profession in one of the Member States, regardless of the Member State in which the client lives.

[26]   Such protection may not be extended beyond those limits, which are determined by the scope of the common rules on the exercise of the legal profession as laid down in Council Directive 77/249/EEC of 22 March 1977 (OJ L 78, p. 17), which is based in its turn on the mutual recognition by all the Member States of the national legal concepts of each of them on this subject.

[27]   In view of all these factors it must therefore be concluded that although Regulation No 17, and in particular Article 14 thereof, interpreted in the light of its wording, structure and aims, and having regard to the laws of the Member States, empowers the Commission to require, in the course of an investigation within the meaning of that article, production of the business documents the disclosure of which it considers necessary, including written communications between lawyer and client, for proceedings in respect of any infringements of Articles 85 and 86 of the Treaty, that power is, however, subject to a restriction imposed by the need to protect confidentiality, on the conditions defined above, and provided that the communications in question are exchanged between an independent lawyer, that is to say one who is not bound to his client by a relationship of employment, and his client.

[28]   Finally, it should be remarked that the principle of confidentiality does not prevent a lawyer's client from disclosing the written communications between them if he considers that it is in his interests to do so.

Note
See also *Samenwerkende Elektriciteits-produktiebedrijven NV* v *Commission* (Case C-36/92) [1994] ECR I-1911; Cases T-25/95 et al *Cimentières et al* v *Commission* judgment of 15 March 2000.

The scope of the Commission's powers and the severity of potential sanctions (see below) mean that an awareness of the rules is essential. Advice to clients in this area is an important function of any practising commercial lawyer.

Allen and Overy (Solicitors), *The EU Inspector at the Door: A Practical Guide on how to deal with On-the-Spot Investigations by the European Commission* (2000), pp. 1–3, 16–17

I. INTRODUCTION . . .

1. JURISDICTION

The Commission has jurisdiction to carry out investigations at the premises of companies located within the territory of the European Union. The Commission does not have jurisdiction to carry out on-the-spot inspections outside the territory of the EU. However, where a company established outside the EU has offices within the EU, the Commission may issue a decision against that part of the company within the EU and may require the production of documents located outside the territory of the EU. A company may be fined for failure to produce such documents.

2. INSPECTIONS GENERALLY

The Directorate General Competition ('DG Competition'), the department of the Commission which investigates suspected infringements of Articles 81 and 82 of the EU Treaty, has formidable investigatory powers to seek out violations of the EU competition rules and does not hesitate to use them in appropriate cases. The powers are basically threefold: to search companies' premises for relevant documents, to examine and take copies of documents and to ask officers of the company to answer specific questions.

An inspection team generally consists of the rapporteur dealing with the case, together with other members of the case team from DG Competition and one or more representatives of the national competition authorities. The rapporteur, being familiar with the case, is well placed to ask relevant questions and identify relevant documents. Many of the staff of DG Competition are legally qualified and were formerly in private practice or attached to national competition authorities. Members of DG Competition's Cartel Unit, Directorate E, undertake investigations into alleged cartel behaviour.

The Commission works in close liaison with national competition authorities and they will often share information, although material received from one body cannot be used directly by the other as evidence. The competent national authority in the UK is the Office of Fair Trading (the 'OFT'). National competition authorities are often requested by the Commission to assist in inspections and they also have the right to take part if they wish. The national officials will take an active part in the investigation and are not there as umpires or guardians of the undertaking's interests. The Commission can also request national competition authorities to undertake an investigation.

3. WAYS OF OBTAINING EVIDENCE

The Commission's investigatory powers are contained in Articles 11 and 14 of Regulation 17/62 which implements Articles 81 and 82 of the EU Treaty. Article 11 relates to written requests for information and Article 14 to on-the-spot investigations. This Memorandum deals primarily with Article 14 investigations. However, for the sake of completeness we set out below a brief description of the Commission's powers under Article 11.

3.1   Article 11

Information about a market and about the conduct of a company suspected of an infringement can be, and often is, informally obtained from the parties, complainants, national authorities or other sources. Thus, the Commission often first makes a written request for information under Article 11(1). Such a request is voluntary and attracts no penalty for failure to comply. However, if a company does provide the Commission with information it must ensure that the information supplied is correct. The Commission may impose fines of between EUR 100 and 5,000 for supplying incorrect information, whether intentionally or negligently, under Article 15(1)(b).

If a company fails to reply to an Article 11(1) request for information within the specified time limit, it can then be served with a mandatory decision under Article 11(5) requiring the information to be produced by a given date. Failure to comply with this request may lead to the imposition of fines of between EUR 100 and 5,000 by the Commission. The White Paper on Modernisation of the Rules Implementing Articles 81 and 82 of the EC Treaty (the 'White Paper' [OJ C132, 12.5.1999, p. 1]) recommends increasing this figure to a minimum of EUR 1,000 and a maximum of EUR 50,000 in line with the fining powers under the EU Merger Regulation.

3.2   Article 14 – Two types of investigation defined

The Commission may also obtain evidence under Article 14 by way of an investigation at the premises of a company either instead of or in addition to its powers under Article 11. Investigations under Article 14 may be either voluntary or compulsory. The choice of procedure will depend upon the circumstances of the individual case and a compulsory inspection will not normally be preceded by attempts to carry out a voluntary inspection.

(i)   Voluntary

The Commission's officials may exercise their investigatory powers upon production of a written mandate of authorisation in accordance with Article 14(2). There is no legal obligation on a company to allow the Commission to investigate. These inspections are usually arranged a week or two in advance, although they may be unannounced.

(ii)   Compulsory

Where an investigation is ordered by a formal decision under Article 14(3), the company named therein is under a legal obligation to comply with the terms of the decision and the inspectors are not required to obtain a court order before carrying out an investigation. Companies may well receive no prior warning of such an inspection.

The Commission has made increasing use of its power to conduct surprise investigations over recent years. For example in each of the polypropylene, PVC and polyethylene cartel cases, as well as the MEWAC and UKWAL shipping conferences cases, the Commission conducted simultaneous unannounced investigations at the premises of undertakings suspected of participating in the cartels. Each of these investigations led to Commission decisions imposing fines for infringement of the EU competition rules. . . .

V. PRACTICAL TIPS

Set out below are some suggested steps which can be taken in advance to ensure that, if a company is subjected to a surprise investigation by the Commission, it is ready to deal with it.

An agreed procedure can be adopted by companies so that it is clear to everyone in the company, from the receptionists to the Chief Executive Officer, what investigations are and how they should be handled; who should be contacted and in what order; and what else should be done to ensure that the investigation is carried out as quickly and with as little disruption as possible. In the case of a voluntary investigation, there is usually prior warning and the company will have time to prepare. The procedure suggested below is therefore primarily designed for dealing with unannounced and compulsory investigations. However, the steps will be broadly similar in both types of investigation.

The agreed company procedure should incorporate the following practical steps:

1. The receptionist should contact a previously nominated executive, or an agreed cover in case of unavailability, to greet the inspectors (even if they ask for a specific employee by name). That person should ascertain whether they have a decision or a mandate of authorisation. The person nominated should contact the company's legal advisers and/or in-house counsel immediately.

2. If the inspectors' authorisation is a mandate of authorisation, senior company representatives together with counsel should check its terms and consider whether to permit entry. If it is decided not to permit entry, a record should be kept of any explanations given to the inspectors.

3. If the authorisation is a decision, its terms should be examined carefully to determine the scope of the investigation but, essentially, the company is obliged to submit to the investigation.

4. Assuming that the company submits to the investigation, it is best to direct the inspectors to a board room or conference room where at least the preliminary steps of the investigation can be carried out. Appoint one or more secretaries to take a full record of the questions asked and the answers given during the course of the investigation. Assemble a team of executives and secretaries to deal with the inspectors' requests for production of documents, etc. (if necessary arranging for staff to stay late), appoint one or several executives to answer all requests for oral explanations, inform the inspectors that all such requests should be directed to those representatives, and inform all relevant employees.

5. If necessary, request the inspectors to delay commencing the investigation until legal advisers arrive. They may be prepared to wait for a short time but the investigation cannot be unreasonably delayed. In the meantime, find out the purpose of the investigation, ask relevant questions about the authorisation or decision, ask the inspectors to estimate how long the inspection will take and check that the dates on the authorising document cover the relevant days.

6. It will then be helpful to decide on an appropriate strategy for the inspection, and the inspectors will probably want to know how the company is organised, who is responsible for various files and where those files are to be found. It can then be agreed which inspectors will cover which offices or files; sometimes the inspectors may agree to stay in the room whilst documents are brought in to them and may be satisfied with a brief tour around the company's premises later in the day; often, however, they will

insist on being taken to the actual filing cabinets and offices where the relevant documents are stored.

7.   Agree to copy all documents requested by the inspectors, consider asking for reasonable payment for all such copies, keep a record and at least one spare copy of all copied documents, preferably two, one for the company and one for its lawyers. Request a signed inventory of the copies and extracts taken by the Commission officials during the investigation.

8.   Keep a detailed note of anything said during the investigation for future reference.

9.   Make sure as a matter of everyday practice that all documents which may come within the scope of legal professional privilege (see Part III above) are kept on separate files, retained preferably by in-house counsel and away from other documents. A schedule should be kept briefly describing the privileged documents. Only this list should be given to the inspector and not the privileged file itself. It is helpful if all correspondence between a company and its outside lawyers is marked '(Request for) Legal Advice – Privileged and Confidential', so that is easily identified as such without its contents having to be read.

Note

Having obtained the necessary information, the Commission is then able to conclude the matter. The requirements of Regulation 2842/98 (p. 504 above) must be respected. The matter may be concluded formally. Article 3 of Regulation 17/62 refers to termination of the practice. Exemption is covered by Articles 4–9 of Regulation 17/62. Notice, particularly, that Article 4 provides that exemption is unavailable without notification subject to the exceptional cases in Article 4(2) where notification is not required. Notification is not necessary where the agreement falls within a block exemption. This reduces the Commission's workload and constitutes a major motivation for the adoption of block exemptions.

The Commission's preference for informal settlement may encompass negative clearance (Regulation 17/62, Article 2) and comfort letters, administrative notices which are not referred to in the Regulation. These measures reduce the Commission's workload and allow the parties to proceed with confidence that the Commission will not interfere. Their relevance at national level may be controversial (see p. 526 below).

The Court believes that interim relief is a key component in any effective system of remedies (*cf.* the *Factortame* litigation, at p. 729 below). Therefore the Court has held that the Commission has powers to adopt interim measures forbidding particular practices, even though that power is missing from Regulation 17/62.

Camera Care Ltd v *Commission (Case 792/79R)*
[1980] ECR 119; [1980] 1 CMLR 334
Court of Justice of the European Communities

[14]   It is obvious that in certain circumstances there may be a need to adopt interim protective measures when the practice of certain undertakings in competition matters has the effect of injuring the interests of some Member States, causing damage to

other undertakings, or of unacceptably jeopardizing the Community's competition policy. In such circumstances it is important to ensure that, whilst inquiries are being carried out no irreparable damage is caused such as could not be remedied by any decision which the Commission might take at the conclusion of the administrative procedure.

[15] Although it is true that, from the point of view of both the efficacy of competition law and the protection of the legitimate interests of the Member States or undertakings concerned, the adoption of protective measures may seem to be necessary in certain circumstances, the provisions of Regulation No 17 must nevertheless be examined to see whether they can accommodate this legal requirement.

[16] It is as well to observe on this point that Article 3 of the Regulation entitles the Commission to take two types of action in order to bring to an end any infringements that it finds: first, the Commission may take 'decisions' which, according to Article 189 of the Treaty, are binding upon those to whom they are addressed and which, according to Articles 15 and 16 of Regulation No 17, may be accompanied by fines and periodic penalty payments; secondly, before taking a binding decision, the Commission is always entitled under Article 3(3) to address to the undertakings concerned 'recommendations for termination of the infringement'. The object of this last provision is to enable the Commission to inform the undertakings concerned of its assessment of the situation with regard to Community law in order to persuade them to comply with its point of view without immediately resorting to legal enforcement. It cannot, however, be construed as a limitation upon the practical ways in which the power to take a decision, which is the core of Article 3, may be exercised.

[17] As regards the right to take decisions conferred upon the Commission by Article 3(1), it is essential that it should be exercised in the most efficacious manner best suited to the circumstances of each given situation. To this end the possibility cannot be excluded that the exercise of the right to take decisions conferred upon the Commission should comprise successive stages so that a decision finding that there is an infringement may be preceded by any preliminary measures which may appear necessary at any given moment.

[18] From this point of view the Commission must also be able, within the bounds of its supervisory task conferred upon it in competition matters by the Treaty and Regulation No 17, to take protective measures to the extent to which they might appear indispensable in order to avoid the exercise of the power to make decisions given by Article 3 from becoming ineffectual or even illusory because of the action of certain undertakings. The powers which the Commission holds under Article 3(1) of Regulation No 17 therefore include the power to take interim measures which are indispensable for the effective exercise of its functions and, in particular, for ensuring the effectiveness of any decisions requiring undertakings to bring to an end infringements which it has found to exist.

[19] However, the Commission could not take such measures without having regard to the legitimate interests of the undertaking concerned by them. For this reason it is essential that interim measures be taken only in cases proved to be urgent in order to avoid a situation likely to cause serious and irreparable damage to the party seeking their adoption, or which is intolerable for the public interest. A further requirement is that these measures be of a temporary and conservatory nature and restricted to what is required in the given situation. When adopting them the Commission is bound to maintain the essential safeguards guaranteed to the parties concerned by Regulation No 17, in particular by Article 19. Finally, the decisions must be made in such a form

that an action may be brought upon them before the Court of Justice by any party who considers he has been injured.

[20]   As the President of the Court has indicated, in the context of the ECSC Treaty, in his interlocutory order of 22 October 1975 in Case 109/75R (*National Carbonising Company*, [1975] ECR 1193), it is in accordance with the key principles of the Community that any interim measures which prove to be necessary should be taken by the Community institution which is given the task of receiving complaints by governments or individuals, of making inquiries and of taking decisions in regard to infringements which are found to exist, whilst the role of the Court of Justice consists in undertaking the legal review of the action taken by the Commission in these matters. In this regard, the rights of those concerned are safeguarded by the fact that if interim measures decided upon by the Commission adversely affect the legitimate interests of any party the person concerned may always obtain the revision of the decision made, by the appropriate judicial recourse, applying if necessary for emergency measures under Article 185 or Article 186 of the EEC Treaty.

Note

Article 15 of Regulation 17/62 (p. 501 above) adds the power to fine to the Commission's arsenal; as a deterrent, this power is a key element in an effective system. However, the Regulation offers little guidance to the Commission on how to fix fines. The Commission has sought to improve transparency by issuing a Notice outlining its fining policy. The use of explanatory Notices conforms with practice visible elsewhere in the competition field, e.g. in relation to market definition, (p. 469), and enforcement cooperation (p. 530). A Notice on the non-imposition of fines in cartel cases was published in July 1996, (1996) OJ C207/4. This is especially designed to offer inducements to firms to cooperate with the Commission (see W. Wils, (1997) 22 EL Rev 125). This was followed by the Guidelines set out below, which were published in late 1997.

Guidelines on the method of setting fines imposed pursuant to Article 15(2) of Regulation No. 17 and Article 65(5) of the ECSC Treaty
(1998) OJ C9/3

The principles outlined here should ensure the transparency and impartiality of the Commission's decisions, in the eyes of the undertakings and of the Court of Justice alike, while upholding the discretion which the Commission is granted under the relevant legislation to set fines within the limit of 10% of overall turnover. This discretion must, however, follow a coherent and non-discriminatory policy which is consistent with the objectives pursued in penalizing infringements of the competition rules.

The new method of determining the amount of a fine will adhere to the following rules, which start from a basic amount that will be increased to take account of aggravating circumstances or reduced to take account of attenuating circumstances.

1.   Basic amount

The basic amount will be determined according to the gravity and duration of the infringement, which are the only criteria referred to in Article 15(2) of Regulation No. 17.

A. *Gravity*

In assessing the gravity of the infringement, account must be taken of its nature, its actual impact on the market, where this can be measured, and the size of the relevant geographic market.

Infringements will thus be put into one of three categories: minor infringements, serious infringements and very serious infringements.

— *minor infringements:*
These might be trade restrictions, usually of a vertical nature, but with a limited market impact and affecting only a substantial but relatively limited part of the Community market.
Likely fines: €1,000 to €1 million.

— *serious infringements:*
These will more often than not be horizontal or vertical restrictions of the same type as above, but more rigorously applied, with a wider market impact, and with effects in extensive areas of the common market. There might also be abuse of a dominant position (refusals to supply, discrimination, exclusion, loyalty discounts made by dominant firms in order to shut competitors out of the market, etc.).
Likely fines: €1 million to €20 million.

— *very serious infringements:*
These will generally be horizontal restrictions such as price cartels and market-sharing quotas, or other practices which jeopardize the proper functioning of the single market, such as the partitioning of national markets and clear-cut abuse of a dominant position by undertakings holding a virtual monopoly (see Decisions 91/297/EEC, 91/298/EEC, 91/299/EEC, 91/300/EEC and 91/301/EEC[1] – Soda Ash, 94/815/EC[2] – Cement, 94/601/EC[3] – Cartonboard, 92/163/EC[4] – Tetra Pak, and 94/215/ ECSC[5] – Steel beams).
Likely fines: above €20 million

Within each of these categories, and in particular as far as serious and very serious infringements are concerned, the proposed scale of fines will make it possible to apply differential treatment to undertakings according to the nature of the infringement committed.

It will also be necessary to take account of the effective economic capacity of offenders to cause significant damage to other operators, in particular consumers, and to set the fine at a level which ensures that it has a sufficiently deterrent effect.

Generally speaking, account may also be taken of the fact that large undertakings usually have legal and economic knowledge and infrastructures which enable them more easily to recognize that their conduct constitutes an infringement and be aware of the consequences stemming from it under competition law.

Where an infringement involves several undertakings (e.g. cartels), it might be necessary in some cases to apply weightings to the amounts determined within each of the three categories in order to take account of the specific weight and, therefore, the real impact of the offending conduct of each undertaking on competition, particularly where there is considerable disparity between the sizes of the undertakings committing infringements of the same type.

---

[1]   OJ L152, 15.6.1991, p. 54.
[2]   OJ L343, 30.12.1994, p. 1.
[3]   OJ L243, 19.9.1994, p. 1.
[4]   OJ L72, 18.3.1992, p. 1.
[5]   OJ L116, 6.5.1994, p. 1.

Thus, the principle of equal punishment for the same conduct may, if the circumstances so warrant, lead to different fines being imposed on the undertakings concerned without this differentiation being governed by arithmetic calculation.

B. *Duration*

A distinction should be made between the following:

— infringements of short duration (in general, less than one year): no increase in amount,
— infringements of medium duration (in general, one to five years): increase of up to 50% in the amount determined for gravity
— infringements of long duration (in general, more than five years): increase of up to 10% per year in the amount determined for gravity.

This approach will therefore point to a possible increase in the amount of the fine.

Generally speaking, the increase in the fine for long-term infringements represents a considerable strengthening of the previous practice with a view to imposing effective sanctions on restrictions which have had a harmful impact on consumers over a long period. Moreover, this new approach is consistent with the expected effect of the notice of 18 July 1996 on the non-imposition or reduction of fines in cartel cases.[6] The risk of having to pay a much larger fine, proportionate to the duration of the infringement, will necessarily increase the incentive to denounce it or to cooperate with the Commission.

The basic amount will result from the addition of the two amounts established in accordance with the above:

$$\times \text{ gravity} + \text{y duration} = \text{basic amount}$$

2. Aggravating circumstances

The basic amount will be increased where there are aggravating circumstances such as:

— repeated infringement of the same type by the same undertaking(s),
— refusal to cooperate with or attempts to obstruct the Commission in carrying out its investigations,
— role of leader in, or instigator of the infringement,
— retaliatory measures against other undertakings with a view to enforcing practices which constitute an infringement,
— need to increase the penalty in order to exceed the amount of gains improperly made as a result of the infringement when it is objectively possible to estimate that amount,
— other.

3. Attenuating circumstances

The basic amount will be reduced where there are attenuating circumstances such as:

— an exclusively passive or 'follow-my-leader' role in the infringement,
— non-implementation in practice of the offending agreements or practices,
— termination of the infringement as soon as the Commission intervenes (in particular when it carries out checks),
— existence of reasonable doubt on the part of the undertaking as to whether the restrictive conduct does indeed constitute an infringement,
— infringements committed as a result of negligence or unintentionally,

---

[6] OJ C207, 18.7.1996, p. 4.

— effective cooperation by the undertaking in the proceedings, outside the scope of the Notice of 18 July 1996 on the non-imposition or reduction of fines in cartel cases,
— other.

4. Application of the Notice of 18 July 1996 on the non-imposition or reduction of fines[7]

5. General comments

(a) It goes without saying that the final amount calculated according to this method (basic amount increased or reduced on a percentage basis) may not in any case exceed 10% of the worldwide turnover of the undertakings, as laid down by Article 15(2) of Regulation No. 17. In the case of agreements which are illegal under the ECSC Treaty, the limit laid down by Article 65(5) is twice the turnover on the products in question, increased in certain cases to a maximum of 10% of the undertaking's turnover on ECSC products.

The accounting year on the basis of which the worldwide turnover is determined must, as far as possible, be the one preceding the year in which the decision is taken or, if figures are not available for that accounting year, the one immediately preceding it.

(b) Depending on the circumstances, account should be taken, once the above calculations have been made, of certain objective factors such as a specific economic context, any economic or financial benefit derived by the offenders (see Twenty-first report on competition policy, point 139), the specific characteristics of the undertakings in question and their real ability to pay in a specific social context, and the fines should be adjusted accordingly.

(c) In cases involving associations of undertakings, decisions should as far as possible be addressed to and fines imposed on the individual undertakings belonging to the association. If this is not possible (e.g. where there are several thousands of affiliated undertakings), and except for cases falling within the ECSC Treaty, an overall fine should be imposed on the association, calculated according to the principles outlined above but equivalent to the total of individual fines which might have been imposed on each of the members of the association.

(d) The Commission will also reserve the right, in certain cases, to impose a 'symbolic' fine of €1,000, which would not involve any calculation based on the duration of the infringement or any aggravating or attenuating circumstances. The justification for imposing such a fine should be given in the text of the decision.

Question

Do you think the following factors are likely to increase or decrease the fine imposed?:

(a) The firm had been told by its lawyers that it was acting illegally, but pressed ahead anyway.

(b) The unlawful agreement was of a type condemned by the Commission many times in the past.

(c) As soon as the Commission suggested to the firm it was acting unlawfully, the firm cooperated, helped the Commission with its enquiries and changed its practices.

---

[7] See footnote 6.

(d)   The firm is a small Scottish toy manufacturer. The offence relates to its first ever agreement with a foreign firm.

(e)   The firm was forced unwillingly to participate in the illegal agreement by a much bigger firm which threatened to cut off its supplies unless it agreed to participate.

(f)   The unlawful agreement was secret and had been in operation for 15 years.

(g)   The firm is a United States-based firm which explains that the agreement would be lawful under US anti-trust law and that it believed the same would be true under EC law.

Read, e.g., *Polistil/Arbois* (1984) OJ L136/9, [1984] 2 CMLR 594; *John Deere* (1985) OJ L35/58, [1985] 2 CMLR 554 and, after the adoption of the Guidelines, *Preinsulated pipes* (1999) OJ L24. See also I. Van Bael, 'Fining *à la Carte*: the Lottery of EU Competition Law' [1995] ECLR 237; W. Wils, 'EC Competition Fines: to deter or not to deter' (1995) 15 YEL 17; P. Spink, 'Enforcing EC Competition Law: Fixing the Quantum of Fines' [1999] JBL 219.

Note

The structure explained above is based on a striking concentration of function in the hands of the Commission in Brussels. The next case is a decision of the European Commission on Human Rights – *it is outside the formal sphere of Community law*. However, not only does it provide an academically interesting analogy, it is also likely to come to exert practical influence on the Community system.

Société Stenuit v France
Judgment of 27 February 1992, Series A no. 232–A
European Commission on Human Rights

A firm party to an alleged cartel was fined 50,000 FF by the Minister of Economic and Financial Affairs under French competition law. The fine was characterised under French law as administrative rather than criminal. A complaint was made to the European Commission on Human Rights of violation of Article 6(1) of the European Convention. The relevant section reads:

> In the determination of his civil rights and obligations or of any criminal charge against him, everyone is entitled to a fair and public hearing within a reasonable time by an independent and impartial tribunal established by law.

The Human Rights Commission decided the fine was of a criminal nature and considered that there was a violation of Article 6(1) in the absence of a separate tribunal which determined the criminal charge (the Conseil d'Etat's review function was in this respect considered inadequate). The reasoning which led to the conclusion that this was a criminal matter was as follows:

62. The Commission observes in this connection that the aim pursued by the impugned provisions of the Order of 30 June 1945 was to maintain free competition within the French market. The Order thus affected the general interests of society normally protected by criminal law (application no. 7341/76, case of *Eggs v Switzerland*, Commission's report of 4 March 1978, Decisions and Reports (DR) no. 15, p. 35, § 79). The penalties imposed by the Minister were measures directed against firms or corporate bodies which had committed acts constituting '*infractions*'. The Commission further points out that the Minister could refer the case to the prosecuting authorities with a view to their instituting criminal proceedings against the '*contrevenant*'. Furthermore, after transmitting the file to the prosecuting authorities, the Minister could no longer impose a fine. A fine was therefore a substitute for the penalty the criminal courts might have imposed if the case had been referred to the prosecuting authorities.

63. With regard to the nature and severity of the penalty to which those responsible for infringements made themselves liable, the Commission observes first of all that 'according to the ordinary meaning of the terms, there generally come within the ambit of the criminal law offences that make their perpetrator liable to penalties intended [. . .] to be deterrent and usually consisting of fines and of measures depriving the person of his liberty' (Eur. Court H. R., above-mentioned Öztürk judgment, p. 20, § 53 *Öztürk* v *Germany*, judgment of 21 February 1984, Series A no. 73). However, that does not imply that every penalty involving deprivation of liberty or every fine necessarily belongs to the criminal law (Eur. Court H. R., above-mentioned Engel judgment, p. 36, § 85 *Engel and others* v *The Netherlands*, judgment of 8 June 1976, Series A no. 22).

64. In the present case the penalty imposed by the Minister was a fine of 50,000 FRF, a sum which, in itself, is not negligible. But it is above all the fact that the maximum fine, i.e. the penalty to which those responsible for infringements made themselves liable, was 5% of the annual turnover for a firm and 5,000,000 FRF for other '*contrevenants*' (see paragraph 32 of the report) which shows quite clearly that the penalty in question was intended to be deterrent.

65. In the Commission's view the criminal aspect of the case for the purposes of the Convention is revealed unambiguously by the combination of concordant factors noted above. The Commission points out that in certain circumstances a charge could, for the purposes of Article 6 § 1 of the Convention, be defined as the official notification given to an individual by the competent authority, of an allegation that he has committed a criminal offence (see paragraph 55 of the Commission's opinion). This had already taken place in the present case when the Minister consulted the Competition Commission and when the latter recommended that the applicant be fined 100,000 FRF. In any case, the Minister's decision to impose a fine constituted, for the purposes of the Convention, determination of a criminal charge, and the fine had all the aspects of a criminal penalty.

66. However, the Government seem to raise an objection, albeit indirectly, by maintaining that corporate bodies cannot be liable under criminal law. The Commission observes in the first place that the Convention contains no provision to that effect. It further observes that the question of the criminal liability of corporate bodies is dealt with in different ways in the various legal systems of the member countries of the

Council of Europe. It points out that French law establishes exceptions to the principle that corporate bodies may not be held criminally liable. The Court of Cassation has recognised the existence of such exceptions where they are prescribed by law (see paragraph 47 of the report). Lastly, the Commission notes that there is no doubt that the penalty imposed in this case was imposed on a corporate body. The Commission therefore takes the view that in a situation such as the one under consideration in this case, it is possible under French law for a corporate body to face a criminal charge. Consequently, the question which arises under the Convention is whether the guarantees it confers on natural persons may or may not be afforded to corporate bodies which suffer a violation of its provisions. In this connection the Commission points out that the institutions of the Convention have already recognised in the past that corporate bodies can exercise a number of rights usually enjoyed by natural persons, such as the right to freedom of expression (Eur. Court H. R., *Sunday Times* v *the United Kingdom* judgment of 26 April 1979, Series A no. 30; application no. 13166/86, *Times Newspapers Ltd and Andrew Neil* v *the United Kingdom*. Commission's report of 12 July 1990) or the rights set forth in Article 9 of the Convention (application no. 8118/77, decision of 19 March 1981, DR 25, pp. 105–117). Lastly, the Commission points out that the institutions of the Convention have consistently emphasised the importance of Article 6 of the Convention, which reflects 'the fundamental principle of the rule of law' (Eur. Court H. R., above-mentioned *Sunday Times* judgment, p. 34. § 55) and that a restrictive interpretation of that article 'would not be consonant with the object and purpose of the provision' (Eur. Court H. R., *De Cubber* v *Belgium* judgment of 26 October 1984, Series A no. 86, p. 16, § 30). In the light of the above considerations, the Commission considers that a corporate body can claim the protection of Article 6 of the Convention when a 'criminal charge' has been made against it.

67.   In conclusion, Article 6 was applicable in this case.

Note
A friendly settlement was reached before the European Court of Human Rights came to rule on the matter. The case was accordingly struck from the list.

Question
In Community law, Article 15(4) of Regulation 17/62 denies the criminal nature of fining decisions taken by the Commission in Brussels. But could the Community's competition law procedures be classified as criminal on the reasoning offered in *Société Stenuit* by the Human Rights Commission? If the answer is 'Yes', would the Community's structure conform to Article 6(1) of the Convention? If the answer to that second question is 'No', how might a challenge to the Community system's compatibility with the Convention be brought (*cf.* pp. 66–73 above)?

(B) ENFORCEMENT AT NATIONAL LEVEL

Enforcement at two levels is a familiar feature of the Community legal order. Action may be taken both by the Commission at Community level and by private individuals relying on the direct effect of Community law before national courts. The competition rules are in this respect no different from provisions such as Articles 25, 28 and 90 considered elsewhere in this book. However, there is a partial interdependence between the two levels peculiar to competition law, which arises from the problem that Article 81(3) is *not* directly effective. This may leave the individual dependent on the Commission. In any event the Commission's powers are such that an individual faced by suspected anti-competitive conduct will be eager to alert the Commission (see Regulation 17/62, Article 3, at p. 496 above). In practice, both routes of enforcement may be commercially valuable.

The Commission's quest to 'modernise' EC competition law and practice was encountered in Chapter 11 in connection with the new approach to vertical restraints (p. 450) and the proposed changes to the treatment of horizontal arrangements. In the field of enforcement too the wind of change is blowing, although reform is as yet proposed rather than than agreed. The Commission in 1999 proposed radical and controversial changes to its supervisory system in the White Paper on *Modernisation of the Rules Implementing Articles 85 and 86 of the EC Treaty* (OJ 1999 C132). Decentralisation to national level is the aim. The core of the long-established scheme is the requirement imposed on collaborating firms to notify agreements falling within the Article 81(1) prohibition to the Commission, so that it can consider whether or not to grant an exemption under Article 81(3). In practice much reliance is placed on block exemptions (p. 450), which allow restrictive agreements to be struck without the need for individual exemption provided the terms fit the mould set by the Block Exemption Regulation. However, outside the scope of the Block Exemptions, individual exemption without notification is unavailable, except in a small number of exceptional cases (Article 4(2) Regulation 17/62, p. 497 above: although already here, in line with the adjustment of the regime governing vertical restraints (p. 450 above), Council Regulation 1216/99 has amended Article 4(2) of Regulation 17/62 to allow the Commission to grant individual exemption for vertical agreements caught by Article 81(1) from the date on which they were entered into without the need for prior notification). Moreover, the Commission enjoys exclusive power to grant an exemption (Article 9, Regulation 17/62); the power to exempt is *not* within the competence of national competition authorities or national courts. Article 81(3) is *not* directly effective, although Articles 81(1) and (2) are. This restricts the scope of effective national level application of the Treaty rules, and puts great demands on the Commission. Its workload is huge.

In practice the system has come under increasing strain. It is well known that many agreements simply are not notified. The Commission, for its part, is unable to issue more than a handful of formal decisions annually. Much of its work is informal. Change is needed. But shaping the detail of that change is controversial. It is necessary to address the pragmatic problem of excessive Commission workload, but to preserve the spirit of EC competition law and policy with which the Commission has infused its practice over 40 years. One device is to improve the shaping of Block Exemption Regulations, so that they allow greater flexibility to business while diminishing areas requiring the individual attention of the Commission. The adjustments in the sphere of vertical restraints are underpinned in part by this motivation (p. 450 above). More fundamentally, in the 1999 Modernisation White Paper the Commission proposes the abandonment of the prior notification system in favour of a system in which it would intervene in cases of sufficient importance to merit individual scrutiny. Otherwise firms making agreements could proceed by aligning their arrangements with published guidelines. Deals would be valid from the date of conclusion provided they satisfy the Article 81(3) criteria without the need for notification to the Commission. There would no longer be any requirement of an administrative decision confirming exemption. The Commission, freed of the notification burden, could concentrate on unearthing serious infringements (which are hardly likely ever to have been notified!). The Commission has also expressed itself receptive to surrender of its monopoly over Article 81(3) exemption. It has sought in recent years to deepen its collaboration with national courts and national competition authorities. A Commission Notice on cooperation with the former was published in 1993 (set out at p. 530 below), and with the latter in 1997 (mentioned at p. 538 below). Moreover, the Court of First Instance has confirmed that the Commission is not obliged to commence proceedings which seek to establish violations of Community law (cf. p. 682 below in relation to Article 226 EC), but rather it may prioritise complaints according to the 'Community interest' in their investigation (Cases T-24/90 and T-28/90 *Automec and Asia Motor France* v *Commission* [1992] ECR II-2223, see para. 13 of the 1993 Notice, p. 532 below).

These initiatives reflect the Commission's desire to secure a decentralisation of enforcement, both as a means of reducing pressure on its own scarce resources and as a basis for improving policing of the Treaty competition rules by increasing the likelihood of local-level detection and penalising of infringements. This strategy of cooperation with national actors was always incomplete because of the Commission's refusal to share the jewel in its crown, the exclusive power to exempt agreements according to the criteria in Article 81(3). Now, however, the 1999 Modernisation White Paper reveals the Commission to be ready to deepen the decentralisation of enforcement of EC competition policy by accepting the possibility that decisions on whether the Article 81(3) exemption criteria are satisfied may be taken by national courts and/or competition authorities. This is by no means a cost-free option. It raises the spectre of uneven approaches to exemption State-by-State. Commission exclusivity enjoys the major advantage of allowing the Commission to oversee the development of a competition policy for the whole territory of the Community. For 40 years this has been treated by the Commission as non-negotiable. No longer. The stability of this genuinely 'Europeanised' competition law is jeopardised by the shift to supplementary national-level enforcement and exemption. In its 1999 proposals the Commission's response to this anxiety is a promise that it will intervene if local misapplication of the rules is detected. Intensified collaboration between competition authorities in Europe is envisaged. The substantive alignment of national competition law with the EC model has been a feature of recent years (see I. Maher, 'Alignment of Competition Laws in the European Community' (1996) 16 YEL 223; for the UK, the Competition Act 1998) and this should serve to diminish the risk of misunderstanding of EC practice by national courts and administrators. Nevertheless, the construction of effective 'networks' of competition authorities in Europe, though appealing, is a major challenge, likely to become even stiffer on enlargement.

Further reading
The debate on the 1999 White Paper continues. For further reading see:

'Reforming EC Competition Law Procedures', report of the House of Lords Select Committee, HL 33 1999-2000.
Klimisch, A., and Krueger, B., 'Decentralised application of EC competition law: current practice and future prospects' (1999) 24 EL Rev 463.
Rodger, B., 'The Commission White Paper on modernisation of the rules implementing Articles 81 and 82 of the EC Treaty' (1999) 24 EL Rev 653.
Wesseling, R., 'The Commission White Paper on Modernisation of EC Antitrust Law' [1999] ECLR 420.

It is desirable that scarce Commission enforcement resources be focused on matters of major significance and that EC competition law becomes more deeply absorbed into the legal and administrative culture of the Member States, but agreement on the the detailed changes required remains elusive. It seems probable that the Commission's 1999 White Paper proposals for change will be accepted in part or in whole. If so, a Council Regulation would be required. In the meantime enforcement at national level occurs against a background of increasing emphasis on the importance of such decentralised control.

In *Stergios Delimitis* v *Henninger Brau* (Case C-234/89) [1991] ECR I-935 (p. 438 above) the Court commented that the Commission's powers are shared with the national courts. It added that account must be taken of the risk of conflict. It envisaged cooperation between the two sets of authorities:

[53] It should be noted in this context that it is always open to a national court, within the limits of the applicable national procedural rules and subject to Article 214 [now 287] of the Treaty, to seek information from the Commission on the state of any procedure which the Commission may have set in motion and as to the likelihood of its giving an official ruling on the agreement in issue pursuant to Regulation No 17. Under the same conditions, the national court may contact the Commission where the concrete application of Article 85(1) [now 81(1)] or of Article 86 [now 82] raises particular difficulties, in order to obtain the economic and legal information which that institution can supply to it. Under Article 5 [now 10] of the Treaty, the Commission is bound by a duty of sincere cooperation with the judicial authorities of the Member State, who are responsible for ensuring that Community law is applied and respected in the national legal system (Order of 13 July 1990 in Case C-2/88, *Zwartveld* [1990] ECR I-3365, paragraph 18).

If this policy of cooperation and decentralisation is to prove effective, national courts will need support. In *Automec* (Case T-24/90 p. 528 above), the Court commented on the obligation of 'loyal cooperation' between the Commission and national courts drawn from Article 5 of the EC Treaty (now Article 10 EC), and referred explicitly to *Delimitis*. In February 1993, the Commission published a Notice on such cooperation. Paragraph 47 shows that the formal legal effect of the Notice is limited, although the Commission has plainly tried to base it on the existing jurisprudence of the Court. The Notice constitutes an important statement of Commission practice. It carries weight in national proceedings. Remember that references to Articles 85 and 86 should now, post-Amsterdam, be treated as references to Articles 81 and 82.

Notice on cooperation between national courts and the Commission in applying Articles 85 and 86 of the EEC Treaty
(1993) OJ C39/5)

I. INTRODUCTION

1.   The abolition of internal frontiers enables firms in the Community to embark on new activities and Community consumers to benefit from increased competition. The Commission considers that these advantages must not be jeopardized by restrictive or abusive practices of undertakings and that the completion of the internal market thus reaffirms the importance of the Community's competition policy and competition law.

2.   A number of national and Community institutions have contributed to the formulation of Community competition law and are responsible for its day-to-day application. For this purpose, the national competition authorities, national and Community courts and the Commission each assume their own tasks and responsibilities, in line with the principles developed by the case-law of the Court of Justice of the European Communities.

3.   If the competition process is to work well in the internal market, effective cooperation between these institutions must be ensured. The purpose of this Notice is to achieve this in relations between national courts and the Commission. It spells out how the Commission intends to assist national courts by closer cooperation in the application of Articles 85 and 86 of the EEC Treaty in individual cases.

II. POWERS

4.   The Commission is the administrative authority responsible for the implementation and for the thrust of competition policy in the Community and for this purpose has to act in the public interest. National courts, on the other hand, have the task of safeguarding the subjective rights of private individuals in their relations with one another [1].

5.   In performing these different tasks, national courts and the Commission possess concurrent powers for the application of Article 85(1) and Article 86 of the Treaty. In the case of the Commission, the power is conferred by Article 89 and by the provisions adopted pursuant to Article 87. In the case of the national courts, the

---

[1] Case C-234/89, *Delimitis* v *Henninger Bräu*, [1991] ECR I-935, paragraph 44; Case T-24/90, *Automec* v *Commission*, judgment of 17 September 1992, paragraphs 73 and 85 [[1992] ECR II-2233].

power derives from the direct effect of the relevant Community rules. In *BRT* v *Sabam*, the Court of Justice considered that 'as the prohibitions of Articles 85(1) and 86 tend by their very nature to produce direct effects in relations between individuals, these Articles create direct rights in respect of the individuals concerned which the national courts must safeguard' (²).

6. In this way, national courts are able to ensure, at the request of the litigants or on their own initiative, that the competition rules will be respected for the benefit of private individuals. In addition, Article 85(2) enables them to determine, in accordance with the national procedural law applicable, the civil law effects of the prohibition set out in Article 85 (³).

7. However, the Commission, pursuant to Article 9 of Regulation No 17 (⁴), has sole power to exempt certain types of agreements, decisions and concerted practices from this prohibition. The Commission may exercise this power in two ways. It may take a decision exempting a specific agreement in an individual case. It may also adopt regulations granting block exemptions for certain categories of agreements, decisions or concerted practices, where it is authorized to do so by the Council, in accordance with Article 87.

8. Although national courts are not competent to apply Article 85(3), they may nevertheless apply the decisions and regulations adopted by the Commission pursuant to that provision. The Court has on several occasions confirmed that the provisions of a regulation are directly applicable (⁵). The Commission considers that the same is true for the substantive provisions of an individual exemption decision.

9. The powers of the Commission and those of national courts differ not only in their objective and content, but also in the ways in which they are exercised. The Commission exercises its powers according to the procedural rules laid down by Regulation No 17, whereas national courts exercise theirs in the context of national procedural law.

10. In this connection, the Court of Justice has laid down the principles which govern procedures and remedies for invoking directly applicable Community law.

Although the Treaty has made it possible in a number of instances for private persons to bring a direct action, where appropriate, before the Court of Justice, it was not intended to create new remedies in the national courts to ensure the observance of Community law other than those already laid down by national law. On the other hand . . . it must be possible for every type of action provided for by national law to be available for the purpose of ensuring observance of Community provisions having direct effect, on the same conditions concerning the admissibility and procedure as would apply were it a question of ensuring observance of national law (⁶).

11. The Commission considers that these principles apply in the event of breach of the Community competition rules; individuals and companies have access to all

---

(²) Case 127/73, *BRT* v *Sabam*, [1974] ECR 51, paragraph 16.
(³) Case 56/65, *LTM* v *MBU*, [1966] ECR 337; Case 48/72, *Brasserie De Haecht* v *Wilkin-Janssen*, [1973] ECR 77; Case 319/82, *Ciments et Bétons* v *Kerpen & Kerpen*, [1983] ECR 4173.
(⁴) Council Regulation No 17 of 6 February 1962: First Regulation implementing Articles 85 and 86 of the Treaty (OJ No 13, 21.2.1962, p. 204/62; Special Edition 1959-62, p. 87).
(⁵) Case 63/75, *Fonderies Roubaix* v *Fonderies Roux*, [1976] ECR 111; Case C-234/89, *Delimitis* v *Henninger Bräu*, [1991] ECR I-935.
(⁶) Case 158/80, *Rewe* v *Hauptzollamt Kiel*, [1981] ECR 1805, paragraph 44; see also Case 33/76, *Rewe* v *Landwirtschaftskammer Saarland*, [1976] ECR 1989; Case 79/83, *Hartz* v *Deutsche Tradax*, [1984] ECR 1921; Case 199/82, *Amministrazione delle Finanze dello Stato* v *San Giorgio* [1983] ECR 3595.

procedural remedies provided for by national law on the same conditions as would apply if a comparable breach of national law were involved. This equality of treatment concerns not only the definitive finding of a breach of competition rules, but embraces all the legal means capable of contributing to effective legal protection. Consequently, it is the right of parties subject to Community law that national courts should take provisional measures, that an effective end should be brought, by injunction, to the infringement of Community competition rules of which they are victims, and that compensation should be awarded for the damage suffered as a result of infringements, where such remedies are available in proceedings relating to similar national law.

12.   Here the Commission would like to make it clear that the simultaneous application of national competition law is compatible with the application of Community law, provided that it does not impair the effectiveness and uniformity of Community competition rules and the measures taken to enforce them. Any conflicts which may arise when national and Community competition law are applied simultaneously must be resolved in accordance with the principle of the precedence of Community law ([7]). The purpose of this principle is to rule out any national measure which could jeopardize the full effectiveness of the provisions of Community law.

III.   THE EXERCISE OF POWERS BY THE COMMISSION

13.   As the administrative authority responsible for the Community's competition policy, the Commission must serve the Community's general interest. The administrative resources at the Commission's disposal to perform its task are necessarily limited and cannot be used to deal with all the cases brought to its attention. The Commission is therefore obliged, in general, to take all organizational measures necessary for the performance of its task and, in particular, to establish priorities ([8]).

14.   The Commission intends, in implementing its decision-making powers, to concentrate on notifications, complaints and own-initiative proceedings having particular political, economic or legal significance for the Community. Where these features are absent in a particular case, notifications will normally be dealt with by means of comfort letter and complaints should, as a rule, be handled by national courts or authorities.

15.   The Commission considers that there is not normally a sufficient Community interest in examining a case when the plaintiff is able to secure adequate protection of his rights before the national courts ([9]). In these circumstances the complaint will normally be filed.

16.   In this respect the Commission would like to make it clear that the application of Community competition law by the national courts has considerable advantages for individuals and companies:

— the Commission cannot award compensation for loss suffered as a result of an infringement of Article 85 or Article 86. Such claims may be brought only before the national courts. Companies are more likely to avoid infringements of the Community competition rules if they risk having to pay damages or interest in such an event,

— national courts can usually adopt interim measures and order the ending of infringements more quickly than the Commission is able to do,

---

([7]) Case 14/68, *Walt Wilhelm and Others* v *Bundeskartellamt*, [1969] ECR 1; Joined Cases 253/78 and 1 to 3/79, *Procureur de la République* v *Giry and Guerlain*, [1980] ECR 2327.

([8]) Case T-24/90, *Automec* v *Commission*, judgment of 17 September 1992, paragraph 77 [[1992] ECR II-2223].

([9]) Case T-24/90, cited above, paragraphs 91 to 94.

— before national courts, it is possible to combine a claim under Community law with a claim under national law. This is not possible in a procedure before the Commission,
— in some Member States, the courts have the power to award legal costs to the successful applicant. This is never possible in the administrative procedure before the Commission.

IV. APPLICATION OF ARTICLES 85 AND 86 BY NATIONAL COURTS

17. The national court may have to reach a decision on the application of Articles 85 and 86 in several procedural situations. In the case of civil law proceedings, two types of action are particularly frequent: actions relating to contracts and actions for damages. Under the former, the defendant usually relies on Article 85(2) to dispute the contractual obligations invoked by the plaintiff. Under the latter, the prohibitions contained in Articles 85 and 86 are generally relevant in determining whether the conduct which has given rise to the alleged injury is illegal.

18. In such situations, the direct effect of Article 85(1) and Article 86 gives national courts sufficient powers to comply with their obligation to hand down judgment. Nevertheless, when exercising these powers, they must take account of the Commission's powers in order to avoid decisions which could conflict with those taken or envisaged by the Commission in applying Article 85(1) and Article 86, and also Article 85(3) ([10]).

19. In its case-law the Court of Justice has developed a number of principles which make it possible for such contradictory decisions to be avoided ([11]). The Commission feels that national courts could take account of these principles in the following manner.

1. *Application of Article 85(1) and (2) and Article 86*

20. The first question which national courts have to answer is whether the agreement, decision or concerted practice at issue infringes the prohibitions laid down in Article 85(1) or Article 86. Before answering this question, national courts should ascertain whether the agreement, decision or concerted practice has already been the subject of a decision, opinion or other official statement issued by an administrative authority and in particular by the Commission. Such statements provide national courts with significant information for reaching a judgment, even if they are not formally bound by them. It should be noted in this respect that not all procedures before the Commission lead to an official decision, but that cases can also be closed by comfort letters. Whilst it is true that the Court of Justice has ruled that this type of letter does not bind national courts, it has nevertheless stated that the opinion expressed by the Commission constitutes a factor which the national courts may take into account in examining whether the agreements or conduct in question are in accordance with the provisions of Article 85 ([12]).

21. If the Commission has not ruled on the same agreement, decision or concerted practice, the national courts can always be guided, in interpreting the Community law in question, by the case-law of the Court of Justice and the existing decisions of the Commission. It is with this in view that the Commission has, in a

---

([10]) Case C-234/89, *Delimitis* v *Henninger Bräu*, [1991] ECR I-935, paragraph 47.
([11]) Case 48/72, *Brasserie de Haecht* v *Wilkin-Janssen*, [1973] ECR 77; Case 127/73, *BRT* v *Sabam*, [1974] ECR 51; Case C-234/89; *Delimitis* v *Henninger Bräu*, [1991] ECR I-935.
([12]) Case 99/79, *Lancôme* v *Etos*, (1980) ECR 2511, paragraph 11.

number of general notices ([13]), specified categories of agreements that are not caught by the ban laid down in Article 85(1).

22.   On these bases, national courts should generally be able to decide whether the conduct at issue is compatible with Article 85(1) and Article 86. Nevertheless, if the Commission has initiated a procedure in a case relating to the same conduct, they may, if they consider it necessary for reasons of legal certainty, stay the proceedings while awaiting the outcome of the Commission's action ([14]). A stay of proceedings may also be envisaged where national courts wish to seek the Commission's views in accordance with the arrangements referred to in this Notice ([15]). Finally, where national courts have persistent doubts on questions of compatibility, they may stay proceedings in order to bring the matter before the Court of Justice, in accordance with Article 177 of the Treaty.

23.   However, where national courts decide to give judgment and find that the conditions for applying Article 85(1) or Article 86 are not met, they should pursue their proceedings on the basis of such a finding, even if the agreement, decision or concerted practice at issue has been notified to the Commission. Where the assessment of the facts shows that the conditions for applying the said Articles are met, national courts must rule that the conduct at issue infringes Community competition law and take the appropriate measures, including those relating to the consequences that attach to infringement of a statutory prohibition under the civil law applicable.

2.   *Application of Article 85(3)*

24.   If the national court concludes that an agreement, decision or concerted practice is prohibited by Article 85(1), it must check whether it is or will be the subject of an exemption by the Commission under Article 85(3). Here several situations may arise.

25.(a)   The national court is required to respect the exemption decisions taken by the Commission. Consequently, it must treat the agreement, decision or concerted practice at issue as compatible with Community law and fully recognize its civil law effects. In this respect mention should be made of comfort letters in which the Commission services state that the conditions for applying Article 85(3) have been met. The Commission considers that national courts may take account of these letters as factual elements.

26.(b)   Agreements, decisions and concerted practices which fall within the scope of application of a block exemption regulation are automatically exempted from the prohibition laid down in Article 85(1) without the need for a Commission decision or comfort letter ([16]).

([13]) See the notices on:
— exclusive dealing contracts with commercial agents (OJ No 139, 24.12.1962, p. 2921/
    62),
— agreements, decisions and concerted practices in the field of cooperation between
    enterprises (OJ No C 75, 29.7.1968, p. 3, as corrected in OJ No C 84, 28.8. 1968, p. 14),
— assessment of certain subcontracting agreements (OJ No C 1, 3.1. 1979, p. 2),
— agreements of minor importance (OJ No C 231, 12.9. 1986, p. 2).

([14]) Case 127/73, *BRT* v *Sabam*, [1974] ECR 51, paragraph 21. The procedure before the Commission is initiated by an authoritative act. A simple acknowledgement of receipt cannot be considered an authoritative act as such; Case 48/72, *Brasserie de Haecht* v *Wilkin-Janssen*, [1973] ECR 77, paragraphs 16 and 17.

([15]) Case C-234/89, *Delimitis* v *Henninger Bräu*, [1991] ECR I-935, paragraph 53, Part V of this Notice.

([16]) A list of the relevant regulations and of the official explanatory comments relating to them is given in the Annex to this Notice.

27.(c) Agreements, decisions and concerted practices which are not covered by a block exemption regulation and which have not been the subject of an individual exemption decision or a comfort letter must, in the Commission's view, be examined in the following manner.

28. The national court must first examine whether the procedural conditions necessary for securing exemption are fulfilled, notably whether the agreement, decision or concerted practice has been duly notified in accordance with Article 4(1) of Regulation No 17. Where no such notification has been made, and subject to Article 4(2) of Regulation No 17, exemption under Article 85(3) is ruled out, so that the national court may decide, pursuant to Article 85(2), that the agreement, decision or concerted practice is void.

29. Where the agreement, decision or concerted practice has been duly notified to the Commission, the national court will assess the likelihood of an exemption being granted in the case in question in the light of the relevant criteria developed by the case law of the Court of Justice and the Court of First Instance and by previous regulations and decisions of the Commission.

30. Where the national court has in this way ascertained that the agreement, decision or concerted practice at issue cannot be the subject of an individual exemption, it will take the measures necessary to comply with the requirements of Article 85(1) and (2). On the other hand, if it takes the view that individual exemption is possible, the national court should suspend the proceedings while awaiting the Commission's decision. If the national court does suspend the proceedings, it nevertheless remains free, according to the rules of the applicable national law, to adopt any interim measures it deems necessary.

31. In this connection, it should be made clear that these principles do not apply to agreements, decisions and concerted practices which existed before Regulation No 17 entered into force or before that Regulation became applicable as a result of the accession of a new Member State and which were duly notified to the Commission. The national courts must consider such agreements, decisions and concerted practices to be valid so long as the Commission or the authorities of the Member States have not taken a prohibition decision or sent a comfort letter to the parties informing them that the file has been closed ([17]).

32. The Commission realizes that the principles set out above for the application of Articles 85 and 86 by national courts are complex and sometimes insufficient to enable those courts to perform their judicial function properly. This is particularly so where the practical application of Article 85(1) and Article 86 gives rise to legal or economic difficulties, where the Commission has initiated a procedure in the same case or where the agreement, decision or concerted practice concerned may become the subject of an individual exemption within the meaning of Article 85(3). National courts may bring such cases before the Court of Justice for a preliminary ruling, in accordance with Article 177. They may also avail themselves of the Commission's assistance according to the procedures set out below.

V. COOPERATION BETWEEN NATIONAL COURTS AND THE COMMISSION

33. Article 5 of the EEC Treaty establishes the principle of constant and sincere cooperation between the Community and the Member States with a view to attaining the objectives of the Treaty, including implementation of Article 3(f), which refers to the establishment of a system ensuring that competition in the common market is not

---

([17]) Case 48/72, *Brasserie de Haecht* v *Wilkin-Janssen*, [1973] ECR 77; Case 59/77, *De Bloss* v *Bouyer*, [1977] ECR 2359; Case 99/79, *Lancôme* v *Etos*, [1980] ECR 2511.

distorted [now Art. 3(g) EC]. This principle involves obligations and duties of mutual assistance, both for the Member States and for the Community institutions. The Court has thus ruled that, under Article 5 of the EEC Treaty, the Commission has a duty of sincere cooperation *vis-à-vis* judicial authorities of the Member States, who are responsible for ensuring that Community law is applied and respected in the national legal system ([18]).

34.   The Commission considers that such cooperation is essential in order to guarantee the strict, effective and consistent application of Community competition law. In addition, more effective participation by the national courts in the day-to-day application of competition law gives the Commission more time to perform its administrative task, namely to steer competition policy in the Community.

35.   In the light of these considerations, the Commission intends to work towards closer cooperation with national courts in the following manner.

36.   The Commission conducts its policy so as to give the parties concerned useful pointers to the application of competition rules. To this end, it will continue its policy in relation to block exemption regulations and general notices. These general texts, the case-law of the Court of Justice and the Court of First Instance, the decisions previously taken by the Commission and the annual reports on competition policy are all elements of secondary legislation or explanations which may assist national courts in examining individual cases.

37.   If these general pointers are insufficient, national courts may, within the limits of their national procedural law, ask the Commission and in particular its Directorate-General for Competition for the following information.

First, they may ask for information of a procedural nature to enable them to discover whether a certain case is pending before the Commission, whether a case has been the subject of a notification, whether the Commission has officially initiated a procedure or whether it has already taken a position through an official decision or through a comfort letter sent by its services. If necessary, national courts may also ask the Commission to give an opinion as to how much time is likely to be required for granting or refusing individual exemption for notified agreements or practices, so as to be able to determine the conditions for any decision to suspend proceedings or whether interim measures need to be adopted ([19]). The Commission, for its part, will endeavour to give priority to cases which are the subject of national proceedings suspended in this way, in particular when the outcome of a civil dispute depends on them.

38.   Next, national courts may consult the Commission on points of law. Where the application of Article 85(1) and Article 86 causes them particular difficulties, national courts may consult the Commission on its customary practice in relation to the Community law at issue. As far as Articles 85 and 86 are concerned, these difficulties relate in particular to the conditions for applying these Articles as regards the effect on trade between Member States and as regards the extent to which the restriction of competition resulting from the practices specified in these provisions is appreciable. In its replies, the Commission does not consider the merits of the case. In addition, where they have doubts as to whether a contested agreement, decision or concerted practice is eligible for an individual exemption, they may ask the Commission to provide them with an interim opinion. If the Commission says that the case in question is unlikely to qualify for an exemption, national courts will be able to waive a stay of proceedings and rule on the validity of the agreement, decision or concerted practice.

([18]) Case C-2/88 Imm., *Zwartveld*, [1990] ECR I-3365, paragraph 18; Case C-234/89, *Delimitis* v *Henninger Bräu*, [1991] ECR I-935, paragraph 53.
([19]) See paragraphs 22 and 30 of this Notice.

39.   The answers given by the Commission are not binding on the courts which have requested them. In its replies the Commission makes it clear that its view is not definitive and that the right for the national court to refer to the Court of Justice, pursuant to Article 177, is not affected. Nevertheless, the Commission considers that it gives them useful guidance for resolving disputes.

40.   Lastly, national courts can obtain information from the Commission regarding factual data: statistics, market studies and economic analyses. The Commission will endeavour to communicate these data, within the limits laid down in the following paragraph, or will indicate the source from which they can be obtained.

41.   It is in the interests of the proper administration of justice that the Commission should answer requests for legal and factual information in the shortest possible time. Nevertheless, the Commission cannot accede to such requests unless several conditions are met. First, the requisite data must actually be at its disposal. Secondly, the Commission may communicate this data only in so far as permitted by the general principle of sound administrative practice.

42.   For example, Article 214 of the Treaty, as spelt out in Article 20 of Regulation No 17 for the purposes of the competition rules, requires the Commission not to disclose information of a confidential nature. In addition, the duty of sincere cooperation deriving from Article 5 is one applying to the relationship between national courts and the Commission and cannot concern the position of the parties to the dispute pending before those courts. As *amicus curiae*, the Commission is obliged to respect legal neutrality and objectivity. Consequently, it will not accede to requests for information unless they come from a national court, either directly, or indirectly through parties which have been ordered by the court concerned to provide certain information. In the latter case, the Commission will ensure that its answer reaches all the parties to the proceedings.

43.   Over and above such exchange of information, required in specific cases, the Commission is anxious to develop as far as possible a more general information policy. To this end, the Commission intends to publish an explanatory booklet regarding the application of the competition rules at national level.

44.   Lastly, the Commission also wishes to reinforce the effect of national competition judgments. To this end, it will study the possibility of extending the scope of the Convention on jurisdiction and the enforcement of judgments in civil and commercial matters to competition cases assigned to administrative courts [20]. It should be noted that, in the Commission's view, competition judgments are already governed by this Convention where they are handed down in cases of a civil and commercial nature.

VI.   FINAL REMARKS

45.   This Notice does not relate to the competition rules governing the transport sector [21]. Nor does it relate to the competition rules laid down in the Treaty establishing the European Coal and Steel Community.

---

[20] Convention of 27 September 1968 (OJ No L 304, 30.10.1978, p. 77).

[21] Regulation No 141/62 of the Council of 26 November 1962 exempting transport from the application of Council Regulation No 17 (OJ No 124, 28.11. 1962, p. 2751/62), as amended by Regulations Nos 165/65/EEC (OJ No 210, 11.12. 1965, p. 3141/65) and 1002/67/EEC (OJ No 306, 16.12. 1967, p. 1); Regulation (EEC) No 1017/68 of the Council of 19 July 1968 applying rules of competition to transport by rail, road and inland waterway (OJ No L 175, 23.7. 1968, p. 1); Council Regulation (EEC) No 4056/86 of 22 December 1986 laying down detailed rules for the application of Articles 85 and 86 of the Treaty to maritime transport (OJ No L 378, 31.12. 1986, p. 4); Council Regulation (EEC) No 3975/87 of 14 December 1987 laying down the procedure for the application of the rules on competition to undertakings in the air transport sector (OJ No L 374, 31.12. 1987, p. 1).

46. This Notice is issued for guidance and does not in any way restrict the rights conferred on individuals or companies by Community law.

47. This Notice is without prejudice to any interpretation of the Community competition rules which may be given by the Court of Justice of the European Communities.

48. A summary of the answers given by the Commission pursuant to this Notice will be published annually in the Competition Report.

Question
In *BEMIM* v *Commission* (Case T–114/92) [1995] ECR II–147, the Court of First Instance accepted that the Commission had acted properly in declining to pursue a complaint relating to practices that were essentially confined to the territory of a single Member State, France. The Court stated 'that the rights of a complainant could not be regarded as sufficiently protected before the national court if the court were not reasonably able, in view of the complexity of the case, to gather the factual information necessary in order to determine whether the practices criticised in the complaint constituted an infringement of the said Treaty provisions', but in the case the Court concluded there was no specific evidence of inadequacy within the French system. What difference would it have made to the Court's approach to Commission practice had *BEMIM* been able to show an absence under French law of a satisfactory remedy? You should consider J. Shaw's regret that the final version of the Notice contains no mention of 'the Commission actively policing compliance by national courts with *their* obligations under Article 5 [now 10 EC] to ensure the effective enforcement of the competition rules' ((1993) 18 EL Rev 427, at p. 471). Consider also the commentary, reading list and questions which conclude this chapter.

In late 1997, the Commission's desire to draw on enforcement resources at national level to police infraction of EC competition rules led it to publish a 'Notice on cooperation between national competition authorities and the Commission in handling cases falling within the scope of Articles 85 or 86 of the Treaty' (1997) OJ C313/3. Decentralisation to national administrative bodies offers the potential to maximise the efficient use of finite enforcement resources. However, although the Notice is presented as a counterpart to the 1993 Notice on cooperation between the Commission and national courts, set out above, a distinct problem arises. National administrative authorities, unlike national courts, are not obliged as a matter of Community law to enforce the EC rules: they are dependent on empowerment by the national system. In 1997 the Commission reported that administrative authorities in only seven of the 15 Member States are able directly to apply (what are now) Articles 81 and 82. It is also notable that in neither the 1993 nor the 1997 Notices did the Commission evince any intention to surrender its exclusive competence to grant exemptions. Similarly, in its 1997 Green Paper on *Vertical Restraints*, (p. 450 above) the Commission excluded the ceding of exclusive competence over exemption from available policy options. The Commission's mood has now altered and, as explained at p. 528

above, the 1999 Modernisation White Paper expresses a readiness to decentralise even the power to decide on exemption under Article 81(3).

Note
A third-party victim of anti-competitive conduct may be interested not merely in putting an end to the practice but in claiming compensation for loss suffered. It is plain from the 1993 Notice (e.g. paras 11, 16) that this can be secured only by proceedings at national level. The leading case in English law is *Garden Cottage Foods* v *Milk Marketing Board*.

Garden Cottage Foods v *Milk Marketing Board*
[1983] 3 WLR 143; [1984] AC 130
House of Lords

The action was an application for an interlocutory injunction to restrain a refusal to supply milk which was alleged to constitute an abuse of a dominant position contrary to Article 86 of the EC Treaty (now Article 82 EC). The fullest speech was that of Lord Diplock, who, in the extract below, begins by examining Article 86 of the EC Treaty (now Article 82 EC).

LORD DIPLOCK: . . . This article of the Treaty of Rome (the EEC Treaty) was held by the European Court of Justice in *Belgische Radio en Televisie* v *SV SABAM* (Case 127/73) [1974] 1 ECR 51, 62, to produce direct effects in relations between individuals and to create direct rights in respect of the individuals concerned which the national courts must protect. This decision of the European Court of Justice as to the effect of article 86 is one which section 3(1) of the European Communities Act 1972 requires your Lordships to follow. The rights which the article confers upon citizens in the United Kingdom accordingly fall within section 2(1) of the Act. They are without further enactment to be given legal effect in the United Kingdom and enforced accordingly.

A breach of the duty imposed by article 86 not to abuse a dominant position in the common market or in a substantial part of it, can thus be categorised in English law as a breach of statutory duty that is imposed not only for the purpose of promoting the general economic prosperity of the common market but also for the benefit of private individuals to whom loss or damage is caused by a breach of that duty.

If this categorisation be correct, and I can see none other that would be capable of giving rise to a civil cause of action in English private law on the part of a private individual who sustained loss or damage by reason of a breach of a directly applicable provision of the Treaty of Rome, the nature of the cause of action cannot, in my view, be affected by the fact that the legislative provision by which the duty is imposed takes the negative form of a prohibition of particular kinds of conduct rather than the positive form of an obligation to do particular acts. Of the many statutory duties imposed upon employers under successive Factories Acts and regulations made thereunder, which have provided far and away the commonest cases of this kind of action, some take the form of prohibitions, others positive obligations to do something: yet it has never been suggested that it makes any difference to the cause of action whether the breach relied on was a failure to perform a positive duty or the doing of a prohibited act.

My Lords, when faced with the company's application for an interlocutory injunction, the first task of the judge was to make up his mind whether there was a serious question to be tried. Plainly a number of difficult and doubtful questions would be involved in any trial of the action. The jurisprudence of the European Court of Justice, which in this field of law is well settled, indicates that there are three matters that must be proved to constitute a contravention of article 86. First, the contravenor must be in a dominant position in a substantial part of the common market; and this involves as a preliminary question the identification of the 'relevant market' – not necessarily an easy task as *Europemballage Corporation and Continental Can Co. Inc.* v *Commission of the European Communities* (Case 6/72) [1973] 1 ECR 215 shows. Secondly, there must be shown an 'abuse' of that dominant position. The particular examples in paragraphs (b) and (c) of article 86 upon which the company principally relies *may* constitute an abuse but do not necessarily do so, and in this connection it may be necessary to take into account the interaction between the Community rules on competition and the CAP. Thirdly, it must be shown that the abuse affects trade between member states.

My Lords, I express no view as to what is likely to be the answer to any of those questions, save to observe that it would be quite impossible at this stage and, probably, at any stage until after a reference under article 177 of the Treaty to the European Court of Justice, to say on the one hand that MMB's behaviour that forms the subject matter of the action is clearly not capable of having any appreciable effect on competition or on trade between member states, or, on the other hand, that there is no doubt of the incompatibility of that behaviour with article 86. I mention this because, your Lordships having been informed that the company, since the judgment of the Court of Appeal, has also made a complaint to the Commission under article 3 of Council Regulation (EEC) No. 17/62 (Official Journal, English Special Edition 1959–62, p. 87), the judgment of the European Court in *Belgische Radio en Televisie* v *SV SABAM* (Case 127/73) [1974] 1 ECR 51 indicates that it may have some relevance to the future progress of the present action in the High Court.

My Lords, Parker J having rightly, indeed inevitably, decided that there were serious questions to be tried, next turned, as directed by *American Cyanamid Co.* v *Ethicon Ltd* [1975] AC 396, to consider whether if the company were to succeed at the trial in establishing its right to a permanent injunction (if a permanent injunction in some appropriate form could be devised) it would be adequately compensated by an award of damages for the loss it would have sustained as a result of MMB's continuing to do what was sought to be enjoined between the time of the application for the interim injunction and the time of the trial.

Parker J was of opinion that an award of damages would provide adequate compensation for any such loss if MMB's refusal to accept direct tenders from it for bulk butter should be held to be a contravention of article 86. So far as the business of the company, conducted as it was entirely by Mr and Mrs Bunch from their own home, consisted of dealing in bulk butter it appears to have involved no more than acting as a middleman who transferred to traders in the bulk market immediately upon delivery by the MMB ex-creamery or ex-coldstore consignments of butter that the company had itself bought on seven-day credit terms, and taking its own 'cut' out of the price at which it passed on the consignment to the trader. If it were compelled to buy bulk butter from one or other of four distributors referred to in the letter of March 24, 1982, instead of directly from MMB this would be likely to reduce the amount of the company's cut; or even to eliminate the possibility of retaining one, so that the sensible course would be to suspend until trial of the action this part of the company's business. But if that were the course adopted, all that the company would lose by such suspension of business would be the opportunity of obtaining the sums of money represented by that cut. There could hardly be a clearer case of damages being an adequate remedy unless insuperable difficulties of estimation could be foreseen; but any difficulties of estimation would be greatly reduced by the fact that the company had only one substantial customer, JWBV, with whom 95 per cent of the company's business in bulk butter was transacted, and that one customer, as appears from an affidavit of Mr J. Wijffels that was before the Court of Appeal, during the period that the company was obtaining butter from MMB, purchased from the company about one-third of its requirements for bulk butter originating in the United Kingdom.

Difficulties of estimation, however, were not the ground on which the Court of Appeal overruled the judge's opinion that damages would be an adequate remedy. Neither Lord Denning MR nor Sir Sebag Shaw made any mention of this topic; nor does a passing reference by May LJ at p. 1126 to possible difficulties of assessment of the proper measure of damages 'in cases such as this,' without any reference to the special characteristics of the company's business to which I have just drawn attention, appear to play a significant role in his ratio decidendi. It was for an entirely different reason that the Court of Appeal rejected the view of the learned judge that damages would provide an adequate remedy.

To that reason I must shortly come; but, before doing so, I should refer to another aspect of the difficulty of estimating damages, which the judge also took into account in exercising his discretion in favour of refusing to grant an interlocutory injunction. That was: the damage that would be caused to the business of MMB and the business of the four distributors to whom it had already made commitments. For that disturbance, in the event of the company failing in the action, MMB's only remedy would be the recovery of damages from the company under the cross-undertaking which it would be required to give. This is a matter which, it was said by this House in *American Cyanamid Co.* v *Ethicon Ltd* [1975] AC 396, a judge ought to take into consideration in deciding how to exercise his discretion. No consideration appears to have been given to it by the Court of Appeal, save that it evoked the procrustean comment from the Master of the Rolls [1982] QB 1114, 1125H; 'I am afraid that that is a bed of their own making and they must deal with it as best they can.'

The only reason why the Court of Appeal held that the judge was wrong in his view that damages would provide an adequate remedy to the company for any interference with its bulk butter business pending the trial of the action, appears to have been that each member of the court felt doubt, in varying degrees, as to whether the company's cause of action sounded in damages at all. Sir Sebag Shaw, at p. 1126G, expressed considerable misgivings as to whether a remedy in damages lies for a contravention of article 86 of the Treaty. Lord Denning MR at p. 1125A, thought there was a good deal to be said for there being a remedy in damages, but that it was not altogether certain. May LJ, though less doubtful than the Master of the Rolls as to the availability of a remedy in damages, considered that the contrary was certainly arguable: p. 1126B-D.

My Lords, in the light (a) of the uniform jurisprudence of the European Court of Justice, of which it is sufficient to mention *Belgische Radio en Televisie* v *SV SABAM* (Case 127/73) [1974] 1 ECR 51 (which I have already cited) and the subsequent case of *Rewe-Zentralfinanz eG* v *Landwirtschaftskammer für das Saarland* (Case 33/76) [1976] 3 ECR 1989, which was to the same effect as respects the duty of national courts to protect rights conferred on individual citizens by directly applicable provisions of the Treaty; and (b) of sections 2 (1) and 3 (1) of the European Communities Act 1972, I, for my own part, find it difficult to see how it can ultimately be successfully argued, as MMB will seek to do, that a contravention of article 86 which causes damage to an individual citizen does not give rise to a cause of action in English law of the nature of a cause of action for breach of statutory duty; but since it cannot be regarded as unarguable that is not a matter for final decision by your Lordships at the interlocutory stage that the instant case has reached. What, with great respect to those who think otherwise, I *do* regard as quite unarguable is the proposition, advanced by the Court of Appeal itself but disclaimed by both parties to the action: that if such a contravention of article 86 gives rise to any cause of action at all, it gives rise to a cause of action for which there is no remedy in damages to compensate for loss already caused by that contravention but only a remedy by way of injunction to prevent future loss being caused. A cause of action to which an unlawful act by the defendant causing pecuniary loss to the plaintiff gives rise, if it possessed those characteristics as respects the remedies available, would be one which, so far as my understanding goes, is unknown in English private law, at any rate since 1875 when the jurisdiction conferred upon the Court of Chancery by Lord Cairns' Act passed to the High Court. I leave aside as irrelevant for present purposes injunctions granted in matrimonial causes or wardship proceedings which may have no connection with pecuniary loss. I likewise leave out of account injunctions obtainable as remedies in public law whether upon application for judicial review or in an action brought by the Attorney-General ex officio or ex relatione some private individual. It is private law, not public law, to which the company has had recourse. In its action it claims damages as well as an injunction. No reasons are to be found in any of the judgments of the Court of Appeal and none has been advanced at the hearing before your Lordships, why in law, in logic or in justice, if contravention of article 86 of the Treaty of Rome is capable of giving rise to a cause of action in English private law at all, there is any need to invent a cause of action with characteristics that are wholly novel as respects the remedies that it attracts, in order to deal with breaches of articles of the Treaty of Rome which have in the United Kingdom the same effect as statutes.

The notion that it is seriously arguable that a contravention of article 86 may give rise to a cause of action possessing such unique characteristics appears to have been based upon a misunderstanding by the Court of Appeal of a cautionary obiter dictum of my noble and learned friend, Lord Roskill (then Roskill LJ) in *Valor International Ltd* v *Application des Gaz SA* [1978] 3 CMLR 87. In a previous decision of the Court of Appeal, *Application des Gaz SA* v *Falks Veritas Ltd* [1974] Ch 381, 396, Lord Denning MR had stated that 'articles 85 and 86 are part of our law. They create new torts or wrongs.' The issue in that case, however, which was one for breach of copyright in a drawing of a tin for holding liquid gas, was whether a defendant could plead breaches by the plaintiff of article 85 or 86 as a defence to the plaintiff's claim. The court was unanimous in holding that the defendant could so plead but only the Master of the Rolls expressed any view as to whether those articles created new torts or wrongs in English law. It was unnecessary for the purposes of that case to do more than to decide that it was arguable that those articles could be used as a shield, whether or not they could also be used as a sword; and in the *Valor International* case [1978] 3 CMLR 87, Roskill LJ, who had been a member of the court in the *Falks Veritas* case, pointed this out and said, at p. 100, that there were 'many questions which will have to be argued in this court or elsewhere in this country or at Luxembourg, before it can be stated categorically . . . that articles 85 and 86 create new torts or wrongs . . .'

The concept of conduct by a plaintiff in legal proceedings that may be relied upon by the defendant as a defence to the plaintiff's claim although it *does not* give rise to a cause of action on the part of the defendant against the plaintiff, is one with which

English law is familiar. Examples of the application of this concept are provided by estoppel and, what my noble and learned friend may have had in mind as presenting the closest analogy to a contravention of article 85 or 86, the application of the maxim ex turpi causa non oritur actio. There is nothing whatever in his observations to suggest that it had ever crossed his mind that if article 86 *did* give rise to a cause of action in English private law on the part of an individual citizen who suffered pecuniary loss as a result of another individual's contravention of that article, the resulting cause of action might have the unique and heterodox characteristics that it gave a remedy by injunction to prevent future pecuniary loss but none in damages for loss that had already been sustained.

To summarise, the Court of Appeal was in my view wrong in suggesting that if it were established at the trial (a) that MMB had contravened article 86, and (b) that such contravention had (i) caused the company pecuniary loss and (ii) thereby given rise to a cause of action in English law on the part of the company against MMB, it was a seriously arguable proposition that such cause of action did not entitle the company to a remedy in damages although it did entitle the company to a remedy by injunction. Parker J did not misunderstand the law in this respect. He was entitled to take the view that a remedy in damages would be available and, for the reasons I have stated earlier, that such remedy would be adequate.

LORD WILBERFORCE (dissenting): It can I think be accepted that a private person can sue in this country to prevent an infraction of article 86. This follows from the fact, which is indisputable, that this article is directly applicable in member states. The European Court of Justice has moreover decided in *Belgische Radio en Televisie* v *SV SABAM* (Case 127/73) [1974] 1 ECR 51, in connection with article 86, that it is for the national courts of member states to safeguard the rights of individuals: paragraph 16, at p. 62. Since article 86 says that abuses of a dominant position are prohibited, and since prohibited conduct in England is sanctioned by an injunction, it would seem to follow that an action lies, at the instance of a private person, for an injunction to restrain the prohibited conduct. But can he recover damages? Your Lordships, I understand, regard the contrary as 'unarguable' or indeed 'quite unarguable' – a bold proposition in the face of doubts expressed by the learned Lords Justices and one whose confidence I do not share. So far as the Community is concerned, article 86 is enforced under Regulation No 17 by orders to desist (article 3), and if necessary by fines (article 15), and the Court of Justice has similar powers on review. Fines are not payable to persons injured by the prohibited conduct, and there is no way under Community law by which such persons can get damages. So the question is, whether the situation is changed, and the remedy extended, by the incorporation of article 86 into our law by section 2 of the European Communities Act 1972. To say that thereby what is prohibited action becomes a tort or a 'breach of statutory duty' is, in my opinion, a conclusionary statement concealing a vital and unexpressed step. All that section 2 says (relevantly) is that rights arising under the Treaty are to be available in law in the United Kingdom, but this does not suggest any transformation or enlargement in their character. Indeed the section calls them 'enforceable Community rights' – not rights arising under United Kingdom law. All that the relevant cases (*Rewe-Zentralfinanz eG* v *Landwirtschaftskammer für das Saarland* (Case 33/76) [1976] 3 ECR 1989, *Amministrazione delle Finanze dello Stato* v *MIRECO* (Case 826/79) [1980] 3 ECR 2559) tell us is that it is for national laws to designate the appropriate courts having jurisdiction, and to establish the procedural conditions. Does this enable national laws to define the remedy? There is of course nothing illogical or even unusual in a situation in which a person's rights extend to an injunction but not to damages – many such exist in English law. Community law which is what the English court would be applying is, in any case, sui generis and the wording used in article 86 'prohibited' and 'so far as it may affect trade' 'between member states' suggest that this may be such a case – the purpose of this article in the Treaty being, so far as necessary, to stop such practices continuing. No doubt there are arguments the other way; I am certainly not contending for reverse unarguability, but I regret that this House should take a position on this point, which was only skeletally argued, in an interlocutory proceeding. It seems to me, with respect, and I am supported by Lord Denning MR, to deserve consideration in greater depth, and, if I may invoke *American Cyanamid Co.* v *Ethicon Ltd* [1975] AC 396, 407, the court should not in an interlocutory proceeding 'decide difficult questions of law which call for detailed argument and mature considerations.'

Note
The majority decision, 4 to 1 in favour of the availability of damages, reduces the opportunities for the award of interim relief by English courts (but see *Cutsforth* v *Mansfield Inns* [1986] 1 CMLR 1). However, the prospect of an award of damages could be a very significant one. Such a remedy cannot be obtained through the exercise of the Commission's powers.

The fuller implications of *Garden Cottage* will require judicial elaboration. Its complexity is indicated by the absence of unanimity in the House of Lords. In fact, *Garden Cottage* provides a case study in the difficulties of absorbing EC law into domestic law, an enduring problem. Chapter 17 explores further the obligations cast on national courts to provide remedies in the event of violation of EC law rights.

Question
What are the implications for domestic enforcement of competition law of the Community law requirement that there be effective remedies at national level?

Note
Were *Francovich* liability (Cases C–6, C–9/90, p. 128 above) to be developed in the context of the competition rules it would represent a significant intrusion of EC law into legal rules governing relationships between *private* parties. The preliminary reference in *H. Banks & Co. Ltd* v *British Coal Corporation* (Case C–128/92) [1994] ECR I–1209 related to a damages claim arising out of alleged infringements of the competition rules of the European Coal and Steel Community Treaty. Advocate-General Van Gerven analysed *Francovich* liability as part of the general system of Community law and, in pursuit of effective protection of Community law rights against both public and private sector defendants, he favoured its application to violations by private parties. However, the Court, in a cautious ruling carefully confined to the Coal and Steel Treaty, held that an action for damages before a national court could not be pursued in the absence of a Commission finding of violation. In its subsequent rulings in March 1996, including '*Factortame III*' (Case C–48/93, p. 136 above, p. 737 below), the Court was also able to avoid

ruling directly on the impact on private law of its principle that Community law rights shall be effectively protected.

Further reading on patterns of private enforcement
(In consulting these sources, bear in mind the potential impact of the 1999 Modernisation White Paper (p. 527), especially the proposed decentralisation of power to find a practice falling within Article 81(1) capable of exemption under Article 81(3).)

Brent, R., 'The Binding of Leviathan? The Changing Role of the European Commission in Competition Cases' (1995) 44 ICLQ 255.

Hiljemark, L., 'Enforcement of EC Competition Law in National Courts – the Perspective of Judicial Protection' (1997) 17 YEL 83.

Jones, C., *Private Enforcement of Antitrust Law in the EU, UK and USA* (Oxford, OUP, 1999).

Shaw, J., 'Decentralised Law Enforcement in EC Competition Law' (1995) 15 *Legal Studies* 128.

Waller, A., 'Decentralization of the Enforcement Process of EC Competition Law – The Greater Role of National Courts' [1996/2] LIEI 1.

Yeung, K., 'Privatising Competition Regulation' (1998) 18 OxJLS 581.

14   THE PROTECTION OF INTELLECTUAL PROPERTY

The most familiar forms of 'intellectual (or industrial) property' are patents, copyrights and trademarks. They exist to reward, and therefore to encourage, innovation. If Catherine devises a new gadget, she can take out a patent in the UK, which gives her the exclusive right to exploit her invention in the UK for a statutory period. Patent law protects her from competitors who might steal her idea – and her profits. The patent system induces talented people to create new products for the benefit of society, secure in the knowledge that their efforts will be financially worthwhile.

(A) FREE TRADE OR TERRITORIAL PROTECTION?

Community law is confronted by a particular problem in the area of intellectual property. Patents, copyrights and trademarks typically provide protection for the inventor within a single Member State. Catherine has a UK patent and can keep similar German and French products off the UK market. 'Geographical exclusivity' is a key feature of national intellectual property law. This runs contrary to the Community objective of economic integration. The Court has long recognised this problem.

Parke Davis v Probel & Centrafarm (Case 24/67)
[1968] ECR 55
Court of Justice of the European Communities

The national rules relating to the protection of industrial property have not yet been unified within the Community. In the absence of such unification, the national character of the protection of industrial property and the variations between the different legislative systems on this subject are capable of creating obstacles both to the free movement of the patented products and to competition within the common market.

Note

The Treaty of Rome provides no simple answer. Article 28 seems to suggest that economic integration must prevail; that national intellectual property rights (patents, copyrights, trademarks) are unlawful barriers to trade.

Article 28 EC

Article 28

Quantitative restrictions on imports and all measures having equivalent effect shall be prohibited between Member States.

Note

As is explained in Chapter 7, this has been interpreted by the Court in *Dassonville* (Case 8/74), as prohibiting 'all trading rules enacted by Member States which are capable of hindering, directly or indirectly, actually or potentially, intra-Community trade'.

On the other hand, Article 30 and Article 295 seem to uphold national territorial protection of intellectual property as a lawful obstacle to free trade.

Articles 30 and 295 EC

Article 30

The provisions of Articles 28 and 29 shall not preclude prohibitions or restrictions on imports,exports or goods in transit justified on grounds of [*inter alia*] . . . the protection of industrial and commercial property. Such prohibitions or restrictions shall not, however, constitute a means of arbitrary discrimination or a disguised restriction on trade between Member States.

Article 295

The Treaty shall in no way prejudice the rules in Member States governing the system of property ownership.

Note

Pre-Amsterdam (p. 29 above), Article 28 was Article 30; Article 30 was Article 36; and Article 295 was Article 222. This must be remembered when reading the material contained in this chapter. The Amsterdam Treaty made minor textual adjustments to (what are now) Articles 28 and 30 EC (Chapter 8). Article 295 was untouched.

(B) THE APPROACH OF THE EUROPEAN COURT

The Court's solution to this clash between free trade and national protection is based on a distinction between the *existence* of national intellectual property rights and their *exercise*. It cannot question their existence, but it will control their exercise. In this way, a balance between economic integration and national territorial protection is achieved.

The Court has adopted some rather confusing jargon in this area. You might suppose that this is evidence of judicial sleight of hand in the attempt to reconcile Article 28 (free trade) with Articles 30 and 295 (national protection). The Court believes that the owner of an intellectual property right can lawfully protect the *specific subject matter* of the right. The specific subject matter of the patent was defined in *Centrafarm BV* v *Sterling Drug Inc.* (Case 15/74), as:

> the guarantee that the patentee, to reward the creative effort of the inventor, has the exclusive right to use an invention with a view to manufacturing industrial products and putting them into circulation for the first time, either directly or by the grant of licences to third parties as well as the right to oppose infringements.

Within the scope of that specific subject matter, free trade can be restricted through the exercise of the national intellectual property right.

(C) EXHAUSTION OF RIGHTS

The easiest way to understand the meaning of the 'specific subject matter' is to examine its application in particular cases. The most important and most illuminating area is the *exhaustion of rights* principle. The Court has decided that Catherine, our UK patent holder, has a choice. She can exploit the UK market alone, when she is entitled to rely on her UK patent to exclude goods from other Member States (Articles 30 and 295 override Article 28). But if she chooses to sell her patented product in another Member State, she cannot then prevent the reimport of that product into the UK. Her consent to its marketing outside the UK 'exhausts her rights' under UK patent law (Article 28 overrides Articles 30 and 295). In the Court's jargon, the specific subject matter of the right is spent once she consents to the marketing of her patented product outside the UK.

Centrafarm BV v *Sterling Drug Inc. (Case 15/74)*
[1974] ECR 1147; [1974] 2 CMLR 480
Court of Justice of the European Communities

Sterling Drug held parallel patents in several Member States for certain pharamaceuticals, including the drug NEGRAM. The products protected by those patents were lawfully marketed in those Member States either by Sterling Drug or by undertakings to which Sterling Drug had granted licences. Centrafarm, a third party, bought up stocks of NEGRAM in the UK and exported them to the Netherlands. There, they were able to make a substantial profit, because the cost of NEGRAM on the Dutch market was far higher than its cost in the UK. Sterling Drug initiated patent infringement proceedings to prevent NEGRAM being marketed in the Netherlands by Centrafarm. Centrafarm argued that they had a right under Community law to export the drug from one Member State to another, given that Sterling Drug had consented to the marketing of the product in both States. The Dutch court referred questions about the relevance of

Community law to Luxembourg. The European Court gave the definition of the specific subject matter of the patent set out above, and continued:

[10] An obstacle to the free movement of goods may arise out of the existence, within a national legislation concerning industrial and commercial property, of provisions laying down that a patentee's right is not exhausted when the product protected by the patent is marketed in another Member State, with the result that the patentee can prevent importation of the product into his own Member State when it has been marketed in another State.

[11] Whereas an obstacle to the free movement of goods of this kind may be justified on the ground of protection of industrial property where such protection is invoked against a product coming from a Member State where it is not patentable and has been manufactured by third parties without the consent of the patentee and in cases where there exist patents, the original proprietors of which are legally and economically independent, a derogation from the principle of the free movement of goods is not, however, justified where the product has been put onto the market in a legal manner, by the patentee himself or with his consent, in the Member State from which it has been imported, in particular in the case of a proprietor of parallel patents.

[12] In fact, if a patentee could prevent the import of protected products marketed by him or with his consent in another Member State, he would be able to partition off national markets and thereby restrict trade between Member States, in a situation where no such restriction was necessary to guarantee the essence of the exclusive rights flowing from the parallel patents.

[13] The plaintiff in the main action claims, in this connection, that by reason of divergences between national legislations and practice, truly identical or parallel patents can hardly be said to exist.

[14] It should be noted here that, in spite of the divergences which remain in the absence of any unification of national rules concerning industrial property, the identity of the protected invention is clearly the essential element of the concept of parallel patents which it is for the courts to assess.

[15] The question referred should therefore be answered to the effect that the exercise, by a patentee, of the right which he enjoys under the legislation of a Member State to prohibit the sale, in the State, of a product protected by the patent which has been marketed in another Member State by the patentee or with his consent is incompatible with the rules of the EEC Treaty concerning the free movement of goods within the Common Market.

Question
Do you think that there is a risk that firms eager to retain protection on their home markets might react by refusing to cross frontiers in order to avoid exhausting their rights under national law? If this happens, economic interpenetration will be hindered.

Note
For a recent exposé of these issues, in which the Court resisted the encouragement of its Advocate General, Mr Fennelly, to reconsider the

ruling in *Merck* v *Stephar* (Case 187/80) [1981] ECR 2063, that a right holder in State X who markets a product in State Y may not prevent parallel trade in the goods from State Y to State X *even if* protection is not available under State Y's legal system, see Cases C-267/95 & C-268/95 *Merck and others* v *Primecrown Ltd* [1996] ECR I-6285. The Court adhered to its view that consenual marketing in State Y is the trigger to exhaustion of the patentee's rights to prevent the goods finding their way back on to the home market. However, it also noted that pharmaceutical products are now patentable throughout the EC, so the clash between free trade and national patent protection will not recur in its *Merck* v *Stephar* form.

Rights are exhausted once the patented product is marketed with the right holder's consent in another Member State. National patent infringement proceedings brought against reimports will be defeated by reliance on Article 28, as Sterling Drug and Merck discovered. It is therefore vital to decide exactly what 'consent' means in this area. The next case is on this point.

Pharmon BV v *Hoechst AG (Case 19/84)*
[1985] ECR 2281; [1985] 3 CMLR 775
Court of Justice of the European Communities

Hoechst, a German company, was the owner of a patent in the Federal Republic of Germany and of parallel patents in both Holland and the United Kingdom in respect of a process for the manufacture of a drug called 'Frusemide'. Despite holding the patent, Hoechst had never manufactured 'Frusemide' in the UK. However, the drug had been manufactured in the UK by a third party, DDSA, as a result of the grant to them of a compulsory licence under UK legislation. Compulsory licences permit the licensee to manufacture the product without the consent of the patent holder, albeit on condition that a royalty be paid to the holder. Batches of 'Frusemide' made by DDSA in the UK reached the Dutch market, where Pharmon, a Dutch firm, wished to sell them. Hoechst sought to rely on its Dutch patent to exclude the goods. Now, Hoechst had not consented to the manufacture or marketing of the drug in the UK. But it had freely taken out a patent there. Pharmon argued Hoechst had exhausted its rights; Hoechst denied it. The European Court set out the competing arguments.

[16]   Pharmon puts forward several arguments in support of its view. It claims that the nature of a compulsory licence is not appreciably different from that of a licence freely granted, in view of the procedural rules concerning the grant of compulsory licences, the legal protection provided for the patent proprietor and the fact that he receives reasonable compensation. With regard to the problem of the patent proprietor's consent, it claims that the decision of the national authorities may be deemed to replace the consent of the patent proprietor, and that, in any event, the exhaustion of patent rights is also applicable where the product has been marketed in the Member State where the compulsory licence was granted. Pharmon takes the view, in addition, that several judgments of the Court of Justice corroborate its view, in particular the judgments of 3 July 1974 (Case 192/73 *Van Zuylen Frères* v *Hag AG* [1974] ECR 731),

20 January 1981 (Joined Cases 55 and 57/80 *Musik-Vertrieb Membran* v *GEMA* [1981] ECR 147) and 14 July 1981 (Case 187/80 *Merck* v *Stephar* [1981] ECR 2063 [mentioned in the text at p. 528 above]). It follows from those judgments that a person who decides to avail himself of the possibility of seeking a parallel patent in the United Kingdom, by the same token accepts the whole body of the relevant British legislation with all the consequences which that implies, including the possibility that a compulsory licence may be granted in respect of that parallel patent.

[17]   Hoechst, the six Member States which have submitted observations, and the Commission largely concur in their view that the holder of a compulsory licence is not entitled to deliver the product directly in the territory of a Member State where a parallel patent exists. Consequently, they consider that it is not incompatible with the rules on the free movement of goods for a patent proprietor to exercise his rights under the law of a Member State to oppose the putting into circulation in the abovementioned circumstances, in that State, of a product protected by the patent of which he is the proprietor.

[18]   In the first place it is contended that the nature of a compulsory licence is different to that of a licence freely granted because, in particular, there are no real negotiations between the compulsory licensee and the patentee, neither the licensee nor the patentee sign the document, which remains a measure adopted by a public authority, and the relationship which in normal circumstances exists between a patentee and a contractual licensee is lacking.

[19]   Secondly, it is argued that the objectives of a compulsory licence and a licence freely granted are different. Whilst a licence freely granted is a means of exploitation which goes to the specific subject-matter of the patent right as defined by the Court, a compulsory licence, on the other hand, is essentially intended to meet the special needs of a Member State. Accordingly, it would be unfair, and even dangerous, to accord that Member State a further advantage by allowing a product manufactured under the compulsory licences granted by it to be delivered directly in Member States where a parallel patent exists.

[20]   Thirdly, all the abovementioned observations emphasize in particular the lack of direct or indirect consent on the part of the patent proprietor in the case of compulsory licences. Referring to the decisions of the Court (in particular the judgment of 31 October 1974, Case 15/74 *Centrafarm* v *Sterling Drug* [1974] ECR 1147; the judgment of 14 July 1981, Case 187/80, *Merck* v *Stephar*, cited above; and the judgment of 14 September 1982, Case 144/81 *Keurkoop* v *Nancy Kean Gifts* [1982] ECR 2853), they stress the fact that in the case of a compulsory licence none of the conditions which, according to the Court's case-law, fix the limits laid down by Community law on the exercise of an industrial and commercial property right protected at national level are satisfied. It follows that the theory of the exhaustion of patent rights which presupposes that the product in question has been marketed freely and voluntarily by the patent proprietor, or by a third party with the proprietor's consent, does not apply in the case of a compulsory licence. That view is confirmed by the provisions of the Convention for the European Patent for the Common Market (Community Patent Convention) (Official Journal 1976, L 17, p. 1), in particular Article 81(3) thereof which, although it has not yet come into force, nevertheless expresses the position of the Member States in that respect.

[21]   Fourthly, Hoechst and all the Member States which have submitted observations claim that, in accordance with the principle of the territoriality of the acts of the

public authorities of a Member State, a compulsory licence cannot confer on its holder rights in the territories of the other Member States. Since a compulsory licence is an exceptional measure and is often in the nature of a penalty for the patentee, it must be applied restrictively and its effects should not be extended beyond its inherent purpose, that is to say the public interest in general and, with regard to medicines in particular, the maintenance of supplies to the internal market under satisfactory conditions.

The Court then repeated its 'exhaustion of rights' principle and proceeded to apply it to the circumstances of a compulsory licence:

[25] It is necessary to point out that where, as in this instance, the competent authorities of a Member State grant a third party a compulsory licence which allows him to carry out manufacturing and marketing operations which the patentee would normally have the right to prevent, the patentee cannot be deemed to have consented to the operation of that third party. Such a measure deprives the patent proprietor of his right to determine freely the conditions under which he markets his products.

[26] As the Court held most recently in its judgment of 14 July 1981 (*Merck* v *Stephar*, cited above), the substance of a patent right lies essentially in according the inventor an exclusive right of first placing the product on the market so as to allow him to obtain the reward for his creative effort. It is therefore necessary to allow the patent proprietor to prevent the importation and marketing of products manufactured under a compulsory licence in order to protect the substance of his exclusive rights under his patent.

Note

The Court then proceeded to declare that the application of Community law to the national legislation in question does not depend on the conditions to which the competent authorities in the Member State of export have subjected the grant of the compulsory licence. It was therefore irrelevant 'whether a prohibition on exportation is attached to the compulsory licence, whether that licence fixes royalties payable to the patentee or whether the patentee has accepted or refused such royalties'.

The Court's view of 'consent' in this case is narrow. It favours the right holder; it weakens free trade. *Consensual registration* of the patent in the UK was not held to exhaust rights. The Court placed its emphasis on the need for *consensual marketing*. Hoechst had not given such consent, which distinguished its conduct from that of Sterling Drug.

(D) EXHAUSTION OF RIGHTS: TRADEMARKS

In connection with trademarks, the Court has adopted an approach to exhaustion of rights which parallels that observed in connection with patents. In *Centrafarm BV* v *Winthrop BV* (Case 16/74) [1974] ECR 1183, the Court defined the *specific subject matter* of a trademark and explained that the right to rely on the national right expired once the product had been marketed in another Member State.

Suppose the reimporter does not simply buy up the goods and resell them unaltered in the country of origin, as Centrafarm did in the cases mentioned so far, but instead alters the packaging of the goods before reapplying the original trademark and reimporting the goods. Can the national intellectual property right holder, who has admittedly chosen to expand beyond the home State, now claim that rights to exclude reimports can be asserted because the original trademark has been removed in the course of repackaging only to be replaced later?

Hoffman-La Roche & Co. AG v Centrafarm Vertriebsgesellschaft Pharmazeutischer Erzeugnisse GmbH (Case 102/77)
[1978] ECR 1139; [1978] 3 CMLR 217
Court of Justice of the European Communities

The product was 'Valium'. It was marketed in Germany by Hoffmann-La Roche for individual consumers in packages of 20 or 50 tablets, and for hospitals in batches of five packages of 100 or 250 tablets. The UK subsidiary of the Roche group marketed the same product in packages of 100 or 500 tablets at lower prices than those in Germany. Centrafarm (again!) marketed in Germany 'Valium' purchased in the UK in the original packages, which it put up into new packages of 1,000 tablets. It affixed the trademark of Hoffman-La Roche and also a notice that the product had been marketed by Centrafarm. Centrafarm also gave notice of its intention to repack the tablets into smaller packages intended for sale to individuals. Roche argued before German courts that Centrafarm had infringed its rights under the German trademark law. The matter reached the European Court via the preliminary reference procedure (Chapter 4). It applied its notion of specific subject matter and the exhaustion of rights principle to the new situation of repackaged goods. Remember that Article 36 is now, post-Amsterdam, Article 30; and that what was Article 30 is now Article 28

[7]   . . . [R]egard must be had to the essential function of the trademark, which is to guarantee the identity of the origin of the trademarked product to the consumer or ultimate user, by enabling him without any possibility of confusion to distinguish that product from products which have another origin. This guarantee of origin means that the consumer or ultimate user can be certain that a trademarked product which is sold to him has not been subject at a previous stage of marketing to interference by a third person, without the authorization of the proprietor of the trademark, such as to affect the original condition of the product.

This led the Court to conclude:

[8]   It is accordingly justified under the first sentence of Article 36 to recognize that the proprietor of a trademark is entitled to prevent an importer of a trademarked product, following repackaging of that product, from affixing the trademark to the new packaging without the authorization of the proprietor.

Then, however, the Court qualified this approach, which is so far plainly favourable to the right holder:

[9] It is, however, necessary to consider whether the exercise of such a right may constitute a disguised restriction on trade between Member States within the meaning of the second sentence of Article 36. Such a restriction might arise, *inter alia*, from the proprietor of the trademark putting onto the market in various Member States an identical product in various packages while availing himself of the rights inherent in the trademark to prevent repackaging by a third person even if it were done in such a way that the identity of origin of the trademarked product and its original condition could not be affected. The question, therefore, in the present case is whether the repackaging of a trademarked product such as that undertaken by Centrafarm is capable of affecting the original condition of the product.

[10] In this respect the answer must vary according to the circumstances and in particular according to the nature of the product and the method of repackaging. Depending on the nature of the product repackaging in many cases inevitably affects its condition, while in others repackaging involves a more or less obvious risk that the product might be interfered with or its original condition otherwise affected. Nevertheless, it is possible to conceive of the repackaging being undertaken in such a way that the original condition of the product cannot be affected. This may be so where, for example, the proprietor of the trademark has marketed the product in a double packaging and the repackaging affects only the external packaging, leaving the internal packaging intact, or where the repackaging is inspected by a public authority for the purpose of ensuring that the product is not adversely affected. Where the essential function of the trademark to guarantee the origin of the product is thus protected, the exercise of his rights by the proprietor of the trademark in order to fetter the free movement of goods between Member States may constitute a disguised restriction within the meaning of the second sentence of Article 36 of the Treaty if it is established that the use of the trademark right by the proprietor, having regard to the marketing system which he has adopted, will contribute to the artificial partitioning of the markets between Member States.

[11] Although this conclusion is unavoidable in the interests of freedom of trade, it amounts to giving the trader, who sells the imported product with the trademark affixed to the new packaging without the authorization of the proprietor, a certain licence which in normal circumstances is reserved to the proprietor himself. In the interests of the proprietor as trademark owner and to protect him against any abuse it is therefore right to allow such licence only where it is shown that the repackaging cannot adversely affect the original condition of the product.

[12] Since it is in the proprietor's interest that the consumer should not be misled as to the origin of the product, it is moreover right to allow the trader to sell the imported product with the trademark affixed to the new packaging only on condition that he gives the proprietor of the mark prior notice and that he states on the new packaging that the product has been repackaged by him . . .

The Court concluded that:

(a) The proprietor of a trademark right which is protected in two Member States at the same time is justified pursuant to the first sentence of Article 36 of the EEC Treaty in preventing a product to which the trademark has lawfully been applied in one of those States from being marketed in the other Member State after it has been repacked in new packaging to which the trademark has been affixed by a third party.

(b) However, such prevention of marketing constitutes a disguised restriction on trade between Member States within the meaning of the second sentence of Article 36 where:

— It is established that the use of the trademark right by the proprietor, having regard to the marketing system which he has adopted, will contribute to the artificial partitioning of the markets between Member States;

— It is shown that the repackaging cannot adversely affect the original condition of the product;

— The proprietor of the mark receives prior notice of the marketing of the repackaged product; and

— It is stated on the new packaging by whom the product has been repackaged.

Note

The Court's decision effectively lays down conditions which, if met, mean that the repackager cannot be restrained by the trademark holder from reimporting the product. The Court thus provides a 'blueprint' for the importer, and thus for market integration. The judgment is free, rather precise legal advice. For a case where the importer acted on this advice, see *Pfizer Inc.* v *Eurim-Pharm GmbH* (Case 1/81) [1981] ECR 2913.

If the judgment in *Hoffman-La Roche* v *Centrafarm* (Case 102/77) is a blueprint for importers, it also allows holders of intellectual property rights to plan their marketing strategies in order to try to prevent repackagers competing with them.

The Court has lately been invited to re-visit the balance it seeks to draw between the interests of integration and the exclusive rights of proprietors of national intellectual property in the context of appeals by traders to the importance of quality control over 'their' products as a basis for impeding trade in repackaged goods. Such appeals, if upheld, improve the protection of the remuneration of trademark holders. See Cases C-427/93, C-429/93 and C-436/93 *Bristol-Myers Squibb and others* v *Paranova A/S* [1996] ECR I-3457; Case C-352/95 *Phytheron International SA* v *Jean Bordon SA* [1997] ECR I-1729; Case C-349/95 *Frits Loendersloot* v *George Ballantine & Sons Ltd* [1997] ECR I-6227 (applying the principles to alcoholic drinks rather than pharmaceuticals, where litigation has been most common); and, concerning the use of a trademark in an advertising campaign by a re-importer, Case C-337/95 *Parfums Christian Dior SA and Parfums Christian Dior BV* v *Evora BV* [1997] ECR I-6013.) Read F. Urlesberger, 'Legitimate reasons for the proprietor of a trade mark registered in the EU to oppose further dealings in the goods after they have been put on the market for the first time' (1999) 36 CML Rev 1195.

Consider the case of different trademarks registered in different States for the same drug by the same firm. Repackaging in order to apply the trademark familiar in the State of sale could be very difficult if, say, the trademark held in the State of export is stamped on the blister strips containing the drug. If the registration of different trademarks in different States partitions the market, would the holder of the right be prevented from relying on the right?

The basis for assessment of 'artificial partitioning of the markets between the Member States', to which the Court refers in its conclusion in *Hoffman La Roche* v *Centrafarm* (Case 102/77), p. 553 above, is addressed by the Court in the next case. A finding of *artificial* market partitioning undermines the right-holder's position. But is this an objective or a subjective test? The Court first states that, in assessing the artificial nature of market partitioning, there is no difference in principle between situations where the repackager re-affixes the original trademark (as in Case 102/77) and situations where the original trademark is replaced by another trademark apt to suit the market conditions of the importing State (as in this case).

Pharmacia & Upjohn SA v *Paranova A/S* (*Case C-379/97*)
Judgment of 12 October 1999
Court of Justice of the European Communities

[38] In the first place, the practice of using different packaging and that of using different trade marks for the same product, in contributing similarly to the partitioning of the single market, adversely affect intracommunity trade in the same way; secondly, the reaffixing of the original trade mark on the repackaged product and its replacement by another trade mark both represent a use by the parallel importer of a trade mark which does not belong to him.

[39] Consequently, where the trade-mark rights in the importing Member State allow the proprietor of the trade mark to prevent it being reaffixed after repackaging of the product or being replaced, and where the repackaging with reaffixing or the replacement of the trade mark are necessary to enable the products to be marketed by the parallel importer in the importing Member State, there are obstacles to intracommunity trade giving rise to artificial partitioning of the markets between Member States within the meaning of the case-law cited, whether or not the proprietor intended such partitioning.

[40] The condition of artificial partitioning of the markets between Member States, as defined by the Court in *Bristol-Myers Squibb*, thus applies where a parallel importer replaces the original trade mark by that used by the proprietor in the Member State of import.

[41] Furthermore, as the Advocate General notes in paragraphs 40 to 42 of his Opinion, this solution also has the practical advantage that it does not require national courts to assess evidence of intention, which is notoriously difficult to prove.

[42] The view that the condition of market partitioning defined in *Bristol-Myers Squibb* applies to the case where a trade mark is replaced also implies, contrary to what Paranova argues, that this replacement of the trade mark must be objectively necessary within the meaning of that judgment if the proprietor is to be precluded from opposing it.

[43] It follows that it is for the national courts to examine whether the circumstances prevailing at the time of marketing made it objectively necessary to replace the original trade mark by that of the importing Member State in order that the product in question could be placed on the market in that State by the parallel importer. This condition of necessity is satisfied if, in a specific case, the prohibition imposed on the importer against replacing the trade mark hinders effective access to the markets of the importing Member State. That would be the case if the rules or practices in the importing Member State prevent the product in question from being marketed in that State under its trade mark in the exporting Member State. This is so where a rule for the protection of consumers prohibits the use, in the importing Member State, of the

trade mark used in the exporting Member State on the ground that it is liable to mislead consumers.

[44] In contrast, the condition of necessity will not be satisfied if replacement of the trade mark is explicable solely by the parallel importer's attempt to secure a commercial advantage.

[45] It is for the national courts to determine, in each specific case, whether it was objectively necessary for the parallel importer to use the trade mark used in the Member State of import in order to enable the imported products to be marketed.

[46] In light of the foregoing, the answer to the questions submitted is that the condition of artificial partitioning of the markets between Member States, as laid down in the judgments in *Hoffmann-La Roche* and *Bristol-Myers Squibb*, means that it is necessary, in order to determine whether the proprietor of a trade mark may, under national law, prevent a parallel importer of pharmaceutical products from replacing the trade mark used in the Member State of export by that which the proprietor uses in the Member State of import, to assess whether the circumstances prevailing at the time of marketing in the Member State of import make it objectively necessary to replace the original trade mark by that used in the Member State of import in order that the product in question may be marketed in that State by the parallel importer.

(E) EXHAUSTION OF RIGHTS: COPYRIGHT

The exhaustion of rights principle applies also to copyright.

Musik-Vertrieb Membran v *GEMA (Cases 55 & 57/80)*
[1981] ECR 147; [1981] 2 CMLR 44
Court of Justice of the European Communities

The dispute in this case arose between GEMA, a German copyright management society, and two firms which imported protected musical works on tape and record into the Federal Republic from the UK. 'Consent' was not disputed here: the German copyright holders had certainly consented to the marketing of the goods in the UK. GEMA sought *not* to exclude the imports, the rights being unarguably exhausted, but *instead* to claim payment of the difference between the royalties payable on recordings marketed in Germany and the (much lower) rate of royalties required in the UK.

[10] It is apparent from the well-established case-law of the Court and most recently from the judgment of 22 June 1976 in Case 119/75 *Terrapin* v *Terranova* [1976] ECR 1039 that the proprietor of an industrial or commercial property right protected by the law of a Member State cannot rely on that law to prevent the importation of a product which has been lawfully marketed in another Member State by the proprietor himself or with his consent.

. . .

[16] . . . GEMA has argued that such an interpretation of Articles 30 and 36 of the Treaty is not sufficient to resolve the problem facing the national court since GEMA's application to the German courts is not for the prohibition or restriction of the

marketing of the gramophone records and tape cassettes in question on German territory but for equality in the royalties paid for any distribution of those sound recordings on the German market. The owner of a copyright in a recorded musical work has a legitimate interest in receiving and retaining the benefit of his intellectual or artistic effort regardless of the degree to which his work is distributed and consequently it is maintained that he should not lose the right to claim royalties equal to those paid in the country in which the recorded work is marketed.

[17]   It should first be observed that the question put by the national court is concerned with the legal consequences of infringement of copyright. GEMA seeks damages for that infringement pursuant to the applicable national legislation and it is immaterial whether the quantum of damages which it seeks is calculated according to the difference between the rate of royalty payable on distribution in the national market and the rate of royalty paid in the country of manufacture or in any other manner. On any view its claims are in fact founded on the copyright owner's exclusive right of exploitation, which enables him to prohibit or restrict the free movement of the products incorporating the protected musical work.

[18]   It should be observed next that no provision of national legislation may permit an undertaking which is responsible for the management of copyrights and has a monopoly on the territory of a Member State by virtue of that management to charge a levy on products imported from another Member State where they were put into circulation by or with the consent of the copyright owner and thereby cause the Common Market to be partitioned. Such a practice would amount to allowing a private undertaking to impose a charge on the importation of sound recordings which are already in free circulation in the Common Market on account of their crossing a frontier; it would therefore have the effect of entrenching the isolation of national markets which the Treaty seeks to abolish.

[19]   It follows from those considerations that this argument must be rejected as being incompatible with the operation of the Common Market and with the aims of the Treaty.

. . .

[24]   . . . As the Court has already stated in its judgment of 31 October 1974 in Case 15/74 *Centrafarm* v *Sterling Drug* [1974] ECR 1147, the existence of a disparity between national laws which is capable of distorting competition between Member States cannot justify the maintenance or introduction by a Member State of measures which are incompatible with the rules concerning the free movement of goods. Such disparities must be abolished by the means provided for to that end by the Treaty, and in particular through the harmonization of national laws.

[25]   It should further be observed that in a common market distinguished by free movement of goods and freedom to provide services an author, acting directly or through his publisher, is free to choose the place, in any of the Member States, in which to put his work into circulation. He may make that choice according to his best interests, which involve not only the level of remuneration provided in the Member State in question but other factors such as, for example, the opportunities for distributing his work and the marketing facilities which are further enhanced by virtue of the free movement of goods within the Community. In those circumstances, a copyright management society may not be permitted to claim, on the importation of sound recordings into another Member State, payment of additional fees

based on the difference in the rates of remuneration existing in the various Member States.

Note
This decision is based on the idea that the right holder must accept the full consequences of expanding the market for the protected product. The German right holder had to accept the UK market with all its peculiarities.

Question
Can you reconcile this decision (and that in Cases C-267/95 & C-268/95 *Primecrown*, p. 550 above) with *Pharmon* v *Hoechst* (Case 19/84) (p. 550) which allowed Hoechst to avoid the unpleasant (for it) consequences of the UK's compulsory licensing system? Was the system in that case a materially distinct interference with the right holder's 'consent' compared with the UK legal rules in *Musik-Vertrieb Membran* v *GEMA* (Cases 55 & 57/80)?

You might also look at *EMI Electrola* v *Patricia Import* (Case 341/87) [1989] ECR 79, for a case in which the Court took a rather restricted view of the notion of 'consent to marketing' in another Member State, with the result that the national right holder was able to restrict free trade. Consider also *Warner Bros* v *Christiansen* (Case 158/86) [1988] ECR 2605; and *CNL Sucal* v *Hag* (Case C-10/89) [1990] ECR I-3711, in which the Court, rejecting its own 15-year-old 'common origin' doctrine, reasserted the importance of consensual participation in the broader market before rights to protect a territory are lost; but, as G. Metaxas (1991) 16 EL Rev 128 notes, it left open many arguments about the true nature of 'consent' in this context.

Some further light was shed on the issue in the next case, which concerns trade marks. It continues the recent trend of a narrow reading of the 'consent' to marketing required before the right to assert territorial protection is lost – the corollary of which is that the Court respects the scope of Article 36 of the EC Treaty (now, after amendment, Article 30 EC) as a limit to market integration driven by Article 30 of the EC Treaty (now, after amendment, Article 28 EC).

IHT Internationale Heiztechnik GmbH v *Ideal Standard GmbH* (*Case C–9/93*)
[1994] ECR I–2789
Court of Justice of the European Communities

The American Standard group held the trade mark 'Ideal Standard' through subsidiaries in France and Germany. Its French subsidiary sold the trade mark in 1984 to an independent third party. IHT, a German subsidiary of the buyer, sold the French-made goods in Germany bearing the French 'Ideal Standard' trade mark. It was then the subject of proceedings before the German courts brought by Ideal Standard alleging infringement of the German 'Ideal Standard' trade mark. There were 'Ideal Standard' marks in both France and Germany and they had the same

source – a 'common origin'—yet they were held by economically independent firms. The Court had already held in *CNL Sucal* v *Hag* (Case
C–10/89), mentioned above, that where the trade marks derived from a
common origin but had been split by an act of the *public authorities*, the
right-holder in one State should not be treated as having consented to
marketing of goods in another State by the economically independent
owner of the mark in that other State. So the mark could be relied on to
exclude imported goods. The Court in the *Ideal Standard* case decided that
even where the division of the trade mark was the result of a *private
agreement*, the owner in one State should not be taken to have consented
to marketing of goods in another State by the 'other' owner.

[51]   First of all, the assignment was made only for France. The effect of that
argument if it were accepted, would, as the German Government points out, be that
assignment of the right for France would entail permission to use the device in
Germany, whereas assignments and licences always relate, having regard to the
territorial nature of national trade mark rights, to a specified territory.

[52]   Moreover, and most importantly, French law, which governs the assignment in
question here, permits assignments of trade marks confined to certain products, with
the result that similar products from different sources may be in circulation on French
territory under the same trade mark, whereas German law, by prohibiting assignments
of trade marks confined to certain products, seeks to prevent such co-existence. The
effect of IHT's argument, if it were accepted, would be to extend to the importing
State whose law opposes such co-existence the solution prevailing in the exporting
State despite the territorial nature of the rights in question.

[53]   Starting from the position that assignment to an assignee having no links with
the assignor would lead to the existence of separate sources within a single territory
and that, in order to safeguard the function of the trade mark, it would then be
necessary to allow prohibition of export of the assignee's products to the assignor's
territory and vice versa, unified laws, to avoid creating such obstacles to the free
movement of goods, render void assignments made for only part of the territory
covered by the rights they create. By limiting the right to dispose of the trade mark in
this way, such unified laws ensure single ownership throughout the territory to which
they apply and guarantee free movement of the product.

The Court proceeded to state that the Regulation on the Community trade
mark (Reg. 40/94 OJ 1994 L11/1) does not render void assignments of
national marks which are confined to some Member States only, and
concluded:

[57]   That sanction cannot be introduced through case-law. To hold that the national
laws are measures having equivalent effect which fall under Article 30 and are not
justified by Article 36, in that, given the independence of national rights (see
paragraphs 25 to 32 above), they do not, at present, make the validity of assignments
for the territories to which they apply conditional on the concomitant assignment of the
trade mark for the other States of the Community, would have the effect of imposing on
the States a positive obligation, namely to embody in their laws a rule rendering void
assignments of national trade marks made for part only of the Community.

[58] It is for the Community legislature to impose such an obligation on the Member States by a directive adopted under Article 100a of the EEC Treaty, elimination of the obstacles arising from the territoriality of national trade marks being necessary for the establishment and functioning of the internal market, or itself to enact that rule directly by a regulation adopted under the same provision.

[59] It should be added that, where undertakings independent of each other make trade mark assignments following a market-sharing agreement, the prohibition of anti-competitive agreements under Article 85 applies and assignments which give effect to that agreement are consequently void. However, as the United Kingdom rightly pointed out, that rule and the accompanying sanction cannot be applied mechanically to every assignment. Before a trade mark assignment can be treated as giving effect to an agreement prohibited under Article 85, it is necessary to analyse the context, the commitments underlying the assignment, the intention of the parties and the consideration for the assignment.

[60] In view of the foregoing, the answer to the Oberlandesgericht Düsseldorf's question must be that there is no unlawful restriction on trade between Member States within the meaning of Articles 30 and 36 where a subsidiary operating in Member State A of a manufacturer established in Member State B is to be enjoined from using as a trade mark the name 'Ideal Standard' because of the risk of confusion with a device having the same origin, even if the manufacturer is lawfully using that name in his country of origin under a trade mark protected there, he acquired that trade mark by assignment and the trade mark originally belonged to a company affiliated to the undertaking which, in Member State A, opposes the importation of goods bearing the trade mark 'Ideal Standard'.

Note

So imports of French-made goods into Germany could be restrained at the behest of the German right-holder. The assignor's right to protect its home (German) territory from goods made by the assignee was not exhausted. The trade restriction was justified under Article 36 of the EC Treaty (now, after amendment, Article 30 EC). Read W. Alexander (1995) 32 CML Rev 327.

Paragraph 58 of the *Ideal Standard* ruling shows the Court's reluctance to employ the law of free movement to solve problems of legal disparity between States which it regards as lying in the province of the Community legislature (see p. 569 below on Article 100a, which has become, in amended form, Article 95 post-Amsterdam). The Court chose to make explicit its perception of the margin between its own role and that of the Community legislature.

Question

Is the Court's balance between free trade and national protection successful? To what extent is legislation in this area essential in order to achieve a common market?

(F) UNFAIR COMPETITION RULES

A producer in one Member State may wish to exclude a product imported from another Member State *not* through reliance on an intellectual property right (because the producer has no exclusive right), but *instead* by relying on more general laws against unfair competition. Our producer may, for example, claim that the importer is deliberately imitating the product. In English law, a passing-off action against the unfair competition posed by the import would be appropriate. Such rules may lawfully restrict inter-State trade if they comply with the '*Cassis de Dijon*' (Case 120/78) formula (Chapter 8).

Rewe-Zentrale AG v *Bundesmonopolverwaltung für Branntwein (Case 120/78)*
[1979] ECR 649; [1979] 3 CMLR 494
Court of Justice of the European Communities

Obstacles to movement within the Community resulting from disparities between the national laws relating to the marketing of the products in question must be accepted in so far as those provisions may be recognised as being necessary in order to satisfy mandatory requirements relating to [*inter alia*] . . . the fairness of commercial transactions and the defence of the consumer . . .

Criminal proceedings against Karl Prantl (Case 16/83)
[1984] ECR 1299; [1985] 2 CMLR 238
Court of Justice of the European Communities

The 'Bocksbeutel' wine bottle has a characteristic bulbous shape. Under the German *Wein-Verordnung* (Wine Regulation) its use is limited to wine producers in Franconia and Baden, where the shape has been in use for centuries. In Bolzano, in northern Italy, the use of a similarly shaped bottle has a tradition going back more than one hundred years. Karl Prantl, an Italian national, imported the Italian product into the Federal Republic and found himself prosecuted under the *Wein-Verordnung*. The criminal sanction existed under German law in order to deter unfair imitation of the typical regional German product. (It is *not* strictly an intellectual property right, for no single producer enjoyed the right to use the 'Bocksbeutel'.) Prantl sought to defend himself on the basis that the *Wein-Verordnung* infringed the Treaty, in so far as it restricted him from importing a product from Italy. The *Landgericht* in Munich referred questions concerning the interpretation of Article 30 of the EC Treaty (now, after amendment, Article 28 EC) to the Court.

[26] In principle, the justification for adopting legislation designed to prevent customers from confusing wines of different quality and origin cannot be denied. That concern is particularly worthy in the case of wines, for traditions and peculiarities play an important role in this field . . .

[27] Where, however, it is a matter of determining whether the legislation of a Member State may, in order to protect an indirect designation of geographical origin in the interests of consumers, prohibit the marketing of wines imported in a certain

type of bottle, it must be observed that in the system of the Common Market consumer protection and fair trading as regards the presentation of wines must be guaranteed with regard on all sides for the fair and traditional practices observed in the various Member States.

[28] In this regard the arguments advanced before the Court have revealed that bottles which are identical in shape to the Bocksbeutel bottle or differ from it only in ways imperceptible to the consumer are traditionally used to market wines originating in certain regions of Italy. An exclusive right to use a certain type of bottle granted by national legislation in a Member State may not therefore be used as a bar to imports of wines originating in another Member State put up in bottles of the same or similar shape in accordance with a fair and traditional practice observed in that Member State.

[29] The Government of the Federal Republic of Germany maintains that consumers might be misled if wines from different regions were marketed in the same type of bottle. In answer to that point it must be observed, however, that the provisions of Community law on the labelling of wines, particularly Articles 12 to 18 of Regulation No. 355/79 concerning the labelling of quality wines psr, are particularly comprehensive and enable the feared confusion to be avoided.

The Court ruled out justifications based on Article 36 of the EC Treaty (now, after amendment, Article 30 EC).

Question
What do you understand by a 'fair and traditional practice' (para. 28 of the judgment)? Is it a subjective or an objective test? Would it be compatible with Community law to apply the German rule to the importer of wines made lawfully in Italy purely as a means of penetrating the lucrative German wine market?
    You might also read *Dansk Supermarked* v *Imerco* (Case 58/80) [1981] ECR 181; *Diensten Groep* v *Beele* (Case 6/81) [1982] ECR 707. Compare also *Mars* (Case C-470/93), p. 327 above, and cases at p. 310, dealing with broader aspects of national unfair competition law in the light of Article 28.

(G) INTELLECTUAL PROPERTY RIGHTS AND THE EC COMPETITION RULES

(i) Article 82
See Chapter 12.
    A market analysis may reveal that the holder of an intellectual property right occupies a dominant position. If so, the right holder may be accused of abuse by, for example, excessive pricing or refusal to licence the right. In this area, the Court has again sought to achieve a balance between the *existence* of the right (which it acknowledges) and its *exercise* (which it controls).
    In *Hoffmann-La Roche* v *Centrafarm* (Case 102/77) (p. 553 above), the Court declared that:

It is sufficient to observe that to the extent to which the exercise of a trademark right is lawful in accordance with the provisions of Article 36 [now 30] of the Treaty, such exercise is not contrary to Article 86 [now 82] of the Treaty on the sole ground that it is the act of an undertaking occupying a dominant position on the market if the trademark right has not been used as an instrument for the abuse of such a position.

But what if there *is* an abuse? It appears that in certain circumstances a dominant intellectual property right holder will be unable to stand aloof from would-be customers. The Court faced the problem in the following case.

Volvo v Erik Veng Ltd (Case 238/87)
[1988] ECR 6211; [1989] 4 CMLR 122
Court of Justice of the European Communities

Volvo held registered design rights in the UK for the front wings of Volvo cars. It instituted proceedings against an importer, Veng, for infringement of its exclusive rights. The High Court sought the European Court's advice on the applicability of Article 86 of the EC Treaty (now Article 82 EC).

[8] . . . It must. . . be emphasised that the right of the proprietor of a protected design to prevent third parties from manufacturing and selling or importing, without its consent, products incorporating the design constitutes the very subject-matter of his exclusive right. It follows that an obligation imposed upon the proprietor of a protected design to grant to third parties, even in return for a reasonable royalty, a licence for the supply of products incorporating the design would lead to the proprietor thereof being deprived of the substance of his exclusive right, and that a refusal to grant such a licence cannot in itself constitute an abuse of a dominant position.

[9] It must however be noted that the exercise of an exclusive right by the proprietor of a registered design in respect of car body panels may be prohibited by Article 86 if it involves, on the part of an undertaking holding a dominant position, certain abusive conduct such as the arbitrary refusal to supply spare parts to independent repairers, the fixing of prices for spare parts at an unfair level or a decision no longer to produce spare parts for a particular model even though many cars of that model are still in circulation, provided that such conduct is liable to affect trade between Member States.

Note
You might also look at *Ministère Public* v *Tournier* (Case 395/87) [1989] ECR 2521; and see also the decision of the Court in relation to television guides (Cases C-241/91P, C-242/91P), p. 490 above, in which refusal to license copyright held over listings was ruled abusive where it 'stifled the emergence on the market of a certain type of product' and failed 'to take consumer needs into consideration'. The exceptional nature of this interventionist decision is discussed at p. 492 above.

(ii) Article 81
See Chapter 11.
Where the patent holder agrees to license the technology, Article 81 is in issue. The Commission has acknowledged the importance of this field of collaboration by issuing a block exemption. This is currently found in the Technology Transfer Block Exemption (Regulation 240/96, (1996) OJ L31/2).

(H) LEGISLATION

An ultimate solution to the problems in this area would involve the grant of intellectual property rights covering the territory of the whole Community. A complete transfer from national to Community level lies in the distant future, although some progress has been made. A first step may be made by harmonising national rules. Much effort has been spent in achieving limited progress in this area too.

See, for example, Directive 98/44 (biotechnological inventions), Directive 89/104 (Trade marks), Regulation 40/94 on the Community Trade Mark and Directive 96/9 on the legal protection of databases. Several of the more recent cases referred to in this chapter were decided in the light of both the relevant Treaty provisions and secondary legislation which the Court interprets to conform with its established approach under the Treaty; e.g. Cases C-427/93, C-429/93 & C-436/93 *Bristol-Myers Squibb*, p. 555 above.

In appreciating the absence of comprehensive solutions introduced through these measures, it is instructive to recall that in Case C-9/93 (p. 559 above) the Court's reference to Regulation 40/94 was made in the context of that measure's inability to provide the basis for a fully integrated market. For comment on recent progress consult the monthly *European Intellectual Property Review* and consult also the home page of the Internal Market Directorate-General in the Commission, currently at http://europa.eu.int/comm/internal_market/en/intprop/index.htm.

Questions
1. Jeff holds a UK patent for a product. Explain to him the implications for his rights under UK patent law of selling the product in France.
2. The European Court's Article 28 case law on intellectual property falls into two camps – the cases which uphold national (market partitioning) rights, and the cases which insist on free trade. Which cases do you think come closest to the boundary between the two camps; and are there any cases you think the Court despatched to the wrong camp?

15   COMMUNITY POLICY MAKING

(A) INTRODUCTION

Much – perhaps too much – of this book has concentrated on the *negative* aspects of the Community's substantive law. Articles 25, 28, 39 and 90, for example, all forbid the maintenance of national rules which restrict free movement. The suppression by law of trade barriers assists in market integration. Yet the development of the Community is also dependent on a *positive* contribution by the law. A common market can only be fully realised by common policy making; by creating positive Community rules. Both Articles 2 and 3 of the EC Treaty, set out at pp. 168 and 172 above, insist on the importance of both negative and positive action. The positive elements of Community policy making may assume many forms and may be adopted under a wide range of Treaty provisions. This chapter is by no means an exhaustive survey of Community policy making. Instead, it selects particular areas as illustrations and endeavours to extract and illuminate key themes and endemic problems in the shaping of Community policies.

The first extract presents a useful overview of the issues. It reintroduces some aspects already touched on in Chapter 5.

J. Lodge, *The European Community and the Challenge of the Future* (1989), pp. 83–85

(Footnote omitted.)

The 1990s are clearly going to be preoccupied with issues arising out of the attempt to realize the Single European Market (SEM). An artificial distinction can be made between what might loosely be defined as 'internal' and 'external' policies. However, it must be remembered that internal policies have external effects and the idea of an impenetrable barrier separating the two is misleading. By 'internal' policies, we mean that group of policies whose goals are directly related to the accomplishment of targets within the EC: they are inner-directed; they seek to modify in some way policy activities within the domestic settings of the EC and its member states. 'External policies' are outer-directed and aim at producing a degree of agreement and/or consensual policies among the Twelve towards non-EC, often known as 'third', states. An example of the latter would be the Lomé Conventions.

However, 'domestic' policies like the CAP, attempts to manage difficult sectoral areas (like steel and textiles) and to advance EC monetary integration, fiscal harmonization and capital and labour mobility as well as new efforts in the environmental and information technology (IT) trade spheres spill-out into the external arena. As a result, the EC's own arrangements for initiating, managing and executing policies in those sectors become stressed by the absence of appropriate mechanisms to manage effectively external effects of domestic policies that are often highly sensitive. Moreover, the goal of achieving a common market (as in the 1950s) and now a SEM inadvertently encourages policymakers at all levels from the EC itself through national government down to local government to focus on internal problems and on the difficulties associated with member states having to adjust to new policy environments and conditions. Since the effects of policies are largely unknown at the outset, and since subsequent wrangling is likely to result from unpalatable effects within certain sectors or member states, it is to be expected that policymakers will not necessarily anticipate possibly deleterious external effects. Moreover, in dealing with them (as in the case of Mediterranean enlargement), they have to adopt some means of prioritizing the claims of those who feel that their interests usually trade interests) have been harmed as a result. The criteria they choose will almost always be contested.

It is obvious that neither a common market nor the SEM can be established without often unwelcome consequences for third states. The mere establishment of a Common External Tariff demands adjustments both by members of the bloc applying that tariff and by those who export to the bloc. Various forms of protectionism and market support also have trade diversifying effects. The year 1992 has become shorthand for the completion of the SEM. While its consolidation will extend beyond the 1990s, many third states and commercial interests within them are operating as if the SEM will assume concrete shape by 1992. This is especially true of the EC's major trading partners, including the rump EFTA . . . Third states are forced to adapt to the EC's policies and its anticipated effects. EC rim states seem to be following parallel actions, at a minimum, to minimize anticipated difficulties from the SEM's establishment.

While such effects are largely an unknown quantity, they are recognized. Predicting and managing them is, however, difficult. Equally, the internal consequences of a limited range of inner-directed policies are often overlooked, or insufficient resources are set aside to encourage appropriate supranantional-led action. Economic and political considerations explain this. Certainly this has been the EC's experience. The accent on the removal of obstacles to trade within the EC led, for example, to the EC being castigated as a 'rich man's club'. The SEM has been similarly construed as a commercial ploy whose uncertain benefits would gravitate towards already rich centres – the Golden Triangle – wealthy elites and powerful companies already in a position to benefit from the hypothesized economies of scale consequent upon the SEM . . . . Whereas the Rome Treaty establishing the EEC made some provisions to assist poorer sectors, it did not 'flag' them in the way in which Commission President Delors did.

The qualitative difference to European integration in the 1990s inheres not simply in the modifications to the Rome Treaty introduced through the Single European Act, but in the way in which they have been interpreted in the public domaine. The politico-economic context in which the SEA unfurled partly accounts for this. The era of Green parties on mainland Europe and generalized high unemployment with its attendant social problems meant that something more than mere lip-service had to be paid to sectors that clearly were high on the Member States' domestic political agenda.

Equally important, however, was M. Delors's intention to define the EC's *raison d'être*. Since its inception, this issue had been side-stepped . . . . The Monnet-Schuman visions and methods stressed the establishment of concrete achievements to create real solidarity and to realize the common good. However, the goal of European Union had been obfuscated by the process. Gradualism reigned supreme: indeed, had to assume centre stage at a time when national sovereignty was not only sorely tried but was still being slowly granted to the new West German state by its Western allies.

The phrase 'an ever closer union' disguised or hid the likely extensive implications of the creation of a common market for thirty years. National governments occasionally protested loudly at steps likely to augment the authority and competence of the EC's institutions. Such protestations seemed to reflect anxiety over an inability to make others in the EC follow a line prescribed by one state's national interest. A well thought-out understanding of what the various sectoral policy measures to advance integration implied in the longer term for both the Member States' and the EC's capacity to deliver the goods proved elusive. No matter how serious and protracted disagreements among the Member States, it was clear that the EC was not only an acceptable forum for the pursuit of goals but one which soon attracted more members. The effect on the EC of many states using it instrumentally to advance national interests was, paradoxically and contrary to the assumptions implicit in many integration theories, to reinforce and consolidate rather than weaken it. Many appreciated that the political implications of the processes of economic integration could not be forever ignored. Few appreciated that greater political integration would have consequences for macro and microeconomic sectoral integration.

It was comparatively easy in the early stages of European integration to deride and dismiss the future visions as 'federalist rantings'. By the 1980s, as Mrs Thatcher was to learn, this ceased to be the case. Many still abhor 'federalism' (often without understanding what it implies). But it is also clear that the EC's *raison d'être* needs some clarification. Public and elite expectations of what it can deliver exceed its capacity. The notion that the EC is a political animal is accepted. M. Delors tried to set out some parameters and to project a vision of a future EC. The precise details of the vision are less important than the fact that the vision makes clear that domestic and external policy sectors are irrevocably intertwined; that any benefits from economic integration must be shared in the name of social justice and its disadvantages offset. While the 'Social Europe' package was disappointing, the highlighting of different tranches of the SEM has imprinted a socialist element firmly on the EC.

A faint socialist watermark is clear in the Rome Treaty. Conscience calls for measures to deal with the negative effects of integration. Some incentives exist for labour mobility. By and large, however, the 'social' aspects of integration have played a secondary role. Attention has focused on removing barriers to trade and other forms of economic discrimination that might adversely affect intra-EC trade. The creation of the SEM and an industrial base for the EC remains frustrated by weaknesses in the EC's policy processes, the absence of consensus over macroeconomic goals and the continuing wrangling among the Twelve over the locus of authority.

Problems also inhere in the piecemeal approach to policymaking, the identification and implementation of sectoral policy goals that require a horizontal rather than a vertical approach to ensure rational and optimal outcomes. Moreover, the domestic organization and funding of agencies and departments charged with implementing and enforcing EC policy varies so greatly as to further frustrate rational and approximately common outcomes. Moreover, the EC lacks an overall economic plan (the SEM only partly disguises this). Instead of coherent over-arching economic policy, the EC has a series of economic instruments, often designed to prevent national actions that will distort competition (such as non-tariff and technical barriers to trade, state aids, export premiums, preferential energy and freight rates for exports, for example) or that unfairly give or allow companies to abuse a dominant position . . .

Note
Although Professor Lodge's book was published in a 2nd edition in 1993, the above extract from the 1st edition has been retained as an introduction to this chapter in order to emphasise the enduring nature of the problems that confront the EC. The reader who has reached this stage of the book will have no difficulty in identifying how these comments may be extended beyond the SEM project to the prospects for Economic and Monetary Union and Enlargement.

(B) HARMONISATION POLICY

Even at the simple level of the quest for market access, it is obvious that not just *negative* but also *positive* rule making is required. Articles 28 and 39, for example, do not forbid all national rules which partition the market. There are derogations in Article 30 and Article 39(3) which envisage the maintenance of lawful trade barriers. Article 90 forbids discriminatory internal taxation, but the tax systems of the Member States remain different, and consequently trade barriers may remain justified in order to allow the collection of taxes. A *positive* set of rules is needed to remove such lawful trade barriers. This explains the need for the Community's harmonisation programme. (For a simple introduction, read D. Vignes, 'The Harmonisation of National Legislation and the EEC' (1990) 15 EL Rev 358; and see p. 288 above.) Harmonisation sets common Community standards of, for example, health protection, which deprive States of the ability to take unilateral action in defence of such interests which would inhibit free trade.

The old Article 100a served as the legal base for a wide variety of harmonisation Directives connected with the process of building the internal market, stretching from, for example, procedures for the award of public works contracts (Dir. 93/37 OJ 1993 L199/54) to unfair terms in consumer contracts (Dir. 93/13 OJ 1993 L95/29). On the entry into force of the Amsterdam Treaty (p. 29 above), Article 100a was amended and re-numbered Article 95 EC.

Article 95 EC

Article 95
1. By way of derogation from Article 94 and save where otherwise provided in this Treaty, the following provisions shall apply for the achievement of the objectives set out in Article 14. The Council shall, acting in accordance with the procedure referred to in Article 251 and after consulting the Economic and Social Committee, adopt the measures for the approximation of the provisions laid down by law, regulation or administrative action in Member States which have as their object the establishment and functioning of the internal market.

2. Paragraph 1 shall not apply to fiscal provisions, to those relating to the free movement of persons nor to those relating to the rights and interests of employed persons.

3. The Commission, in its proposals envisaged in paragraph 1 concerning health, safety, environmental protection and consumer protection, will take as a base a high level of protection, taking account in particular of any new development based on scientific facts. Within their respective powers, the European Parliament and the Council will also seek to achieve this objective.

4. If, after the adoption by the Council or by the Commission of a harmonisation measure, a Member State deems it necessary to maintain national provisions on grounds of major needs referred to in Article 30, or relating to the protection of the environment or the working environment, it shall notify the Commission of these provisions as well as the grounds for maintaining them.

5. Moreover, without prejudice to paragraph 4, if, after the adoption by the Council or by the Commission of a harmonisation measure, a Member State deems it necessary to introduce national provisions based on new scientific evidence relating to the protection of the environment or the working environment on grounds of a problem specific to that Member State arising after the adoption of the harmonisation measure, it shall notify the Commission of the envisaged provisions as well as the grounds for introducing them.

6. The Commission shall, within six months of the notifications as referred to in paragraphs 4 and 5, approve or reject the national provisions involved after having verified whether or not they are a means of arbitrary discrimination or a disguised restriction on trade between Member States and whether or not they shall constitute an obstacle to the functioning of the internal market.

In the absence of a decision by the Commission within this period the national provisions referred to in paragraphs 4 and 5 shall be deemed to have been approved.

When justified by the complexity of the matter and in the absence of danger for human health, the Commission may notify the Member State concerned that the period referred to in this paragraph may be extended for a further period of up to six months.

7. When, pursuant to paragraph 6, a Member State is authorised to maintain or introduce national provisions derogating from a harmonisation measure, the Commission shall immediately examine whether to propose an adaptation to that measure.

8. When a Member State raises a specific problem on public health in a field which has been the subject of prior harmonisation measures, it shall bring it to the attention of the Commission which shall immediately examine whether to propose appropriate measures to the Council.

9. By way of derogation from the procedure laid down in Articles 226 and 227, the Commission and any Member State may bring the matter directly before the Court of Justice if it considers that another Member State is making improper use of the powers provided for in this Article.

10. The harmonisation measures referred to above shall, in appropriate cases, include a safeguard clause authorising the Member States to take, for one or more of the non-economic reasons referred to in Article 30, provisional measures subject to a Community control procedure.

There are important policy issues which emerge from the harmonisation programme. Harmonisation is designed to protect interests such as public health in the framework of an integrating Community in which the advantages of free trade will be secured. Harmonisation, then, has a dual aim: protection of the citizen and facilitation of free trade. The difficulty of achieving both objectives was discussed in the context of the free movement of goods in the several extracts presented at pp. 336–42 above. The problems of fiscal harmonisation were discussed at p. 236 above. In Article 95 itself, the tensions involved in attempting to satisfy all interests affected by harmonisation emerge in the procedure found in paras (4) *et seq.*

(i)   The new approach to harmonisation policy

The difficulty in achieving the harmonisation of technical rules relating to products has led to a new impetus in Community harmonisation policy. The problems of old style harmonisation are well explained in the following extract.

J. Pelkmans, 'The New Approach to Technical Harmonization and Standardization' (1986–87) 25 JCMS 249, at pp. 251–253

(Footnote omitted.)

The 'Traditional' Approach of the Policy Regime

For more than one and a half decades the European Commission has tried to pursue an ambitious harmonization programme. Following a few ad hoc cases, and a prudent first step towards the harmonization of the national regulations concerning pharmaceutical products, in March 1968, the Commission proposed a General Programme. From that time until the so-called Mutual Information Directive 83/189/EEC [p. 335 above], an incredible amount of energy on the part of civil servants and experts had been devoted to the production of an extremely limited number of Council Directives. Many of these directives focus on specific technical *aspects* of products and they therefore fail to solve all the problems of access in product markets. During these fifteen years the EC has adopted on average only a little over ten technical directives a year.

It is doubtful, to say the least, whether such a slow speed can actually bring about a net reduction in the technical barriers to trade in the Community in view of the simultaneous accretion of regulations in Member States. To put it more strongly, given the increase in bureaucratic regulatory capacity in recent decades in all Member States and the greater societal preference for environmental and consumer protection, it can safely be presumed that the tempo of national regulation has, for many years, exceeded by far that of the annual output of 'aspect-directives' at EC level with respect to a rather limited group of products. Apart from being *inefficient* – due to extensive and drawn out consultations on technical specifications – the method was *ineffective* as well: a general improvement of mutual market access was not achieved, at best there was only a slowing down of the rate of increase of technical barriers.

Nor did the wider European standardization processes proceed smoothly. The history of CEN (European Standardization Committee) shows clearly that, without some connection with the EC's own harmonization policy, progress at the wider European level tends to be exceedingly difficult. A serious drawback of the functioning of CEN is that no long-term programmes are being developed to remove the trade-impeding effects of different national standards (notwithstanding their private and voluntary character). . . .

Drawbacks of the 'Traditional' Approach

In earlier work I have analysed extensively the considerable disadvantages and shortcomings of the traditional strategy of technical harmonization (and standardization) of the Community. Briefly these consist of:

1. time-consuming and cumbersome procedures
2. excessive uniformity
3. unanimity (ex Art. 100, EEC) [now 94 EC]
4. the failure, except rarely, to develop a linkage between the harmonization of technical regulations and European standardization, leading to wasteful duplication, useless inconsistencies and time lost
5. the slowness of European harmonization and standardization relative to national regulation and standardization
6. a neglect of the problems of certification and testing
7. the incapacity to solve the third country problem
8. implementation problems in Member States
9. a lack of political interest by the Ministers.

It is not surprising that by the early 1980s the question of the removal of technical barriers to trade in the EC had led to profound feelings of frustration and disappointment.

The policy climate in which the elimination of technical barriers to trade in the EC had to be realized was such that the individual protectionist was thriving whereas the dynamic exporter, attempting to encroach upon other markets, was hampered. Of course, the opposite climate should characterize European market integration for the benefit of the Community's economy at large.

Note

Consequently, the Council adopted in 1985 a Resolution approving a *New Approach* to technical harmonisation.

Council Resolution of 7 May 1985 on a new approach to technical harmonisation and standards (1985) OJ C136/1; Annex, 'Guidelines for a New Approach to Technical Harmonization and Standards'

The following are the four fundamental principals [sic] on which the new approach is based:

(i)   legislative harmonization is limited to the adoption, by means of Directives based on Article 100 of the EEC Treaty, of the essential safety requirements (or other requirements in the general interest) with which products put on the market must conform, and which should therefore enjoy free movement throughout the Community.

(ii)   the task of drawing up the technical specifications needed for the production and placing on the market of products conforming to the essential requirements established by the Directives, while taking into account the current stage of technology, is entrusted to organizations competent in the standardization area,

(iii)   these technical specifications are not mandatory and maintain their status of voluntary standards,

(iv)   but at the same time national authorities are obliged to recognize that products manufactured in conformity with harmonized standards (or, provisionally, with national standards) are presumed to conform to the 'essential requirements' established by the Directive. (This signifies that the producer has the choice of not manufacturing in conformity with the standards but that in this event he has an obligation to prove that his products conform to the essential requirements of the Directive).

In order that this system may operate it is necessary:

(i)   on the one hand that the standards offer a guarantee of quality with regard to the 'essential requirements' established by the Directives.

(ii)   on the other hand that the public authorities keep intact their responsibility for the protection of safety (or other requirements envisaged) on their territory.

The quality of harmonized standards must be ensured by standardization mandates, conferred by the Commission, the execution of which must conform to the general guidelines which have been the subject of agreement between the Commission and the European standardization organizations. In so far as national standards are concerned their quality must be verified by a procedure at Community level managed by the Commission, assisted by a standing committee composed of officials from national administrations.

At the same time safeguard procedures must be provided for, under the management of the Commission assisted by the same committee, in order to allow the competent public authorities the possibility of contesting the conformity of a product, the validity of a certificate or the quality of a standard.

In following this system of legislative harmonization in each area in which it is feasible, the Commission intends to be able to halt the proliferation of excessively technical separate Directives for each product. The scope of Directives according to the 'general reference to standards' formula should encompass wide product categories and types of risk.

The Community could on the one hand, therefore, complete the extremely complex undertaking of harmonizing technical legislation and on the other hand promote the development and application of European standards. These are essential conditions for the improvement of the competitiveness of its industry.

Note

Accordingly, Directives conforming to the New Approach need not include detailed specifications. They instead set broad performance standards. Products meeting those standards are entitled to access to the markets of all the Member States. See, for example, Directive 92/59, the Directive on General Product Safety (1992) OJ L228/24.

Note

The advantages of the New Approach are manifold.

J. Pelkmans, 'The New Approach to Technical Harmonization and Standardization'
(1986–87) 25 JCMS 249, at pp. 257–261

(Footnotes omitted.)

Advantages of the 'New Approach'

The most important potential advantages of the 'new approach' are (i) greater coherence between the policy regime and the legal regime to eliminate technical barriers, and (ii) the better conveyance between European harmonization of technical regulations and European standardization. As stated earlier, the Council will have to assume the task of reaching a 'European doctrine' in the fields of safety, health, etc., so that the technical barriers to intra-EC free movement can disappear. The new approach is a serious attempt to achieve this coherence by combining *total harmonization* of the objectives at issue (safety, etc.) with a *flexible approach* of the means (standardization). It also improves the scope for a timely interchange of information so that national draft-standards and technical draft-regulations can be altered or converted into European ones before formally taking effect.

These advantages are commendable and may explain the willingness in Member States and in various circles to view the new approach with a 'préjugé favourable'. They are however *potential* advantages because a great deal depends on the actual results, both in the Council, with respect to the total harmonization of objectives of health, safety, etc., and also from the standardization processes in the CEN/CENELEC framework.

The advantages can be formulated in a less abstract way by examining which *dis*advantages of the traditional approach, as mentioned before, will be reduced or eliminated by the new approach. The effects on these nine disadvantages and deficiencies are summed up below. The reader is warned that for the time being a speculative evaluation concerning the 'quality policy' is needed in some cases. The author considers the model directive to be a sufficient basis to develop an adequate quality policy from the coordinated work of the Commission, the Standing Committee 'Reference to Standards' and CEN/CENELEC. Given this presumption, the effects on the 'old' approach disadvantages are summarized as follows:

1. *Time-consuming and laborious procedures.*
Both the Commission and the Council (and the Coreper bodies) could save a considerable amount of time, not only because technical specifications do not need to be approved twice, but also because technical aspects – within the quality policy – are in fact delegated. Whether this time-saving can be transformed into acceleration depends on the speed of standardization. Standardization speed can be increased by pressure originating from the procedures under the Mutual Information Directive and by apportioning Commission payments for the implementation of mandates to CEN and CENELEC. It is not precluded (indeed, it is implicit in the new approach) that, should the safety objectives, etc., be agreed, legislation can also lead to greater pressure being exerted to speed up standardization.

2. *Uniformity.*
The advantage here has already been reported: the combination of uniform safety objectives (etc.) with the desired variability in the means for industry or for the consumers. Moreover, the fact that no mandatory reference takes place leaves room for original solutions in existing products and for product innovation.

3. *Unanimity.*
The central question remains whether unanimity with respect to the objectives, including the demands on the quality policy, will always be achieved so easily. This question is even more pressing because the new approach is applied to relatively comprehensive product groups. The way out in the Council that is apparently used with the first 'new approach' proposals of the Commission is to negotiate 'mixed forms' of the old and the new approach, with some technical specification in the directive itself but not as detailed as before. The 'traditional' approach will not completely disappear: the White Paper contains some 90 industrial and 60 agricultural proposals of the traditional type. Recent experience with lead-free petrol and with the reduction of exhaust gases of motor vehicles has shown that even unanimity *can* lead

to decisions if the pressure of time arising from the Mutual Information Directive together with economic (export) interests increase the willingness to reach compromises.

The newly agreed Art. 100–A [now Art. 95 EC], included in the Single European Act and providing for qualified majority voting, could constitute a significant boost in overcoming the resistance of a single country. It is expected to enhance the room for manoeuvre of the Commission, which was almost non-existent under unanimity. Nevertheless, the usage of products for workers and the possibility of safeguards (subject to Court review) may continue to cause occasional problems in case of majority voting (given paragraphs 3, 4 and 5 of this new Article).

4. *Harmonization not related to standardization.*
For every case in which the 'new approach' is applied, this problem is by definition solved.

5. *EC standardization slower than national standardization.*
Because standards are included in the Mutual Information Directive, and because 'reference to standards' will be used in directives, an increase in the tempo and in the volume of European standardization can reasonably be expected.

With regard to the short-term, it is doubtful whether this acceleration and volume increase is sufficient to bring about a net reduction in the barriers; in the long run this is certainly possible. It should be ensured that the volume increase does not merely consist of CEN approval of all sorts of sectoral standards which in certain sectors have already been agreed at European level for a long time. Indeed, to the extent that this is a 'cosmetic' operation, little value can be attached to it. To the extent that the standards were not actually followed, it does have significance. Moreover, where government contracts are at stake, the European Commission can possibly extend the significance further. Ultimately a strong tempo and volume increase by CEN and CENELEC depends on capacity limitations and the rapidity with which these can be overcome.

6. *Limited attention to tests and certification.*
Except for a vague promise nothing can be found on this in the new approach. This serious weakness of the new approach must be dealt with soon . . . .

7. *The third country problem.*
Here also the effect of the new approach is still not clear.

8. *Application and implementation.*
It seems reasonable to accept that the combination of total harmonization of health/safety objectives, European standards linked to an adequate quality policy of the Council and the already existing legislation, will have a favourable effect on the actual application of the directives in the Member States. Of course, it is the details of application that will be decisive for the economic agents in the market. Proper implementation is, however, a slow process and substantial improvement is not to be expected before the 1990s [for practice in the 1990s, see p. 201 above]. It can be speeded up by the greater potential which careful total harmonization of objectives offers for the national judicial process. However the real problems are sometimes deep seated, for instance, reference to national standards in insurance contracts, in the conditions for connection imposed by public utilities or in local delivery conditions.

9. *Lack of political interest.*
Total harmonization of the objectives as well as the comprehensiveness of the product groups form the arguments which give rise to the presumption that *more* political interest in the Internal Market Council and in the Commission will be mustered.

Taking everything together, improvements can be perceived with respect to seven of the nine disadvantages of the 'traditional' approach. The extent of these advantages, however, is at the moment far from obvious and the length of time before they will be felt by industry and consumers could be considerable. Nevertheless this does not detract from the fact that the 'new approach' looks as though it will be *qualitatively an enormous improvement* over the traditional approach.

Finally, two advantages must be pointed out which are directly connected with the nine points just mentioned, but are of such potential importance that they deserve to be mentioned separately and emphatically.

In the first place the new approach is linked to the issue of *improvement in the competitiveness of European industry*. Harmonization and standardization are still viewed in many branches of industry or in individual companies as a potential threat to the market position or a cause of unwanted adaptation costs. Except for extremely specific conditions in a large market, however, protectionism leads in due course to a worsening international competitiveness.

If, on the other hand, *standard quality* is such that penetration into many foreign markets is possible, then standardization can be seen in quite another light. Because specialization is becoming ever more refined, and scale effects in many cases form an important determinant of the export position, the quality approach offers a much better perspective, not only for industry and the consumer but also for the economy as a whole. Seen in this way, emphasis will come to lie on quality and international acceptance of the standard, two matters which – except in the case of far-fetched protectionism – are closely connected. The new approach stimulates this because it aims at making market penetration easier and at the same time at pursuing a quality policy. This is further stimulated by Art. 100–A, sub 3 of the Single European Act. Considering the weaknesses widely observed in the competitiveness of European industry, this advantage can be described as carrying some weight.

In some branches of industry the positive impact of European standardization on competitiveness will weigh even more heavily. Standards can have a market-creating effect or, in other words, the lack of a standard between adjoining countries can make the Euromarket (i.e. trade between Member States) impossible, as is for instance the case with car telephones. Standards can also have an anticipatory effect. For instance, sufficient investment in product development, process technology and further innovations takes place in some products only when compatibility is secured first. Interesting examples of this are the recently proposed Council directives concerning standardization in the field of information technologies and telecom and concerning the mutual recognition of type approval of terminal equipment for telecommunication, the latter now having been adopted. Given the very close relationship between telecom and information technologies, the key to promoting European product development and greater intra-EC trade is a system of European standards which provides specifications in much more detail than the CCITT world standards. When (different) computers or word processors communicate at a distance, compatibility standards require precise conventions (on the basis of which information exchange takes place) while safeguarding the inter-operability of the systems for processing and communicating the information. European industry lacks these standards and, thereby, a necessary condition for maintaining and improving its world competitive position.

Secondly, it can be expected that the workload on some Commission services will be considerably reduced by the new approach and that the excessively detailed regulations will gradually become of lesser importance. The Commission has already withdrawn various draft directives which were laid before the Council in the context of the traditional approach. *The reduction in the Commission's workload* is welcome because attention can then be given to more urgent problems in the field of technical trade barriers which have a more direct and greater effect on the free intra-EC movement of goods. A couple of urgent problems ask for that attention: the whole set of problems concerning testing, inspections and certification marks; and the consultation procedures in the framework of the Mutual Information Directive which are labour intensive but prevent many potential bottlenecks in the national draft regulations at an early stage.

Reduction in the Commission's workload can also lead to more attention being given to implementation and enforcement questions in the Member States. For many years responses have only been made to complaints and the question is whether even these have been pursued adequately.

Note
Many of the perceived economic advantages of the New Approach should be familiar from the material found in Chapter 5. See also G. Bermann, 'The Single European Act: A New Constitution for the Community?' 27 *Columbia Journal of Transnational Law* 529 (1989); D. Waelbroeck, 'L'harmonisation des règles et normes téchniques dans la CEE' (1988) CDE 243.

(ii)   Questioning the new approach
Nonetheless, fears have been expressed on several levels about the desirability of the New Approach. First, it has been alleged that the New Approach is liable to reduce effective protection of the citizen by diminishing the explicit detailed commitment to social protection. A connection should here be made with the discussion at p. 336 above of the arguably related shift in balance in favour of free trade achieved by the '*Cassis de Dijon*' (Case 120/78) judgment and its subsequent interpretation. The following extract discusses the matter in connection with the free movement of foodstuffs.

> **O. Brouwer, '*Free Movement of Foodstuffs and Quality*
> *Requirements; Has the Commission got it Wrong?*'**
> **(1988) 25 CML Rev 237, at pp. 248–252**

(Some footnotes omitted)

4.   Critical remarks
The Commission's rejection of detailed recipes in Community legislation can be qualified as a minimalist approach; the Commission leaves quality policy with regard to foodstuffs to the Member States and leaves the enforcement and further realisation of the free movement of foodstuffs in this respect to the judiciary. A minimalist approach is not necessarily a bad one; however, in the present case, the foundations for the adoption of this approach are shaky, for the reasons discussed below.

4.1   *The borderline between quality requirements and public health requirements*
It must first of all be noted that, in general, the composition or manufacturing characteristics of a foodstuff cannot be isolated from matters which are covered by public health requirements. The use of certain ingredients may have as a corollary the use of certain pesticides or additives (the German beer case provides a striking example in this respect [p. 297 above]), or the prescription of a certain manufacturing process or treatment which is regulated by law to protect public health (e.g., a biotechnological process). In consequence, the mutual recognition

of quality requirements is often only one aspect when the question arises whether a foodstuff, which is lawfully manufactured and marketed in one Member State, may be marketed in another Member State. In any event, it seems inevitable that the free movement of foodstuffs within the Community will remain dependent on the harmonisation of public health requirements (and methods of inspection, analysis and sampling) and the further development and coordination of a public health policy with regard to foodstuffs at Community level.

However, the point at issue is that difficulties may arise as to the borderline between quality requirements and issues of public health even with regard to recipe laws as such. The Commission rightly admits in its Communication that it may be necessary, in the interest of public health, to define in law the nature and composition of a foodstuff, even if the purchaser is adequately informed, by a label, of these elements. The fear then arises that the new legislative approach of the Commission, as set out in its Communication, may partly be jeopardised; after all, who is going to establish whether a given composition of a foodstuff, despite the fact that it may have been lawfully produced and marketed in the exporting Member State, may be undesirable from the point of view of public health in the Member State of import? It must be borne clearly in mind that the Court has in this respect consistently held that the eating habits in the Member State of import comprise one of the elements which may be taken into account when considering potential dangers for public health.

The Commission's viewpoint seems to indicate that it is the task of national courts and the Court of Justice to assess this matter. In fact, the judiciary has been able in a number of cases to dismiss the plea of public health when manifestly ill-founded or when the national legislation in question was clearly disproportionate.[29] However, apart from these situations, the general problem arises to what extent the judiciary is equipped to assess whether products are or may be positively harmful to health. Often scientists, who have been called as expert witnesses in legal proceedings, do not agree, or, findings of scientific research show that uncertainties remain. If one adds to this difficulty the fact that the Court has consistently held that, insofar as scientific uncertainties remain, it is in principle for the Member States, in the absence of harmonisation, to decide what degree of protection of public health they intend to assure,[31] it seems justified to conclude that the judiciary may often not be in a position to overrule the view of the national legislator.

4.2   Is the Commission's approach desirable?

Apart from the preceding observations, it is submitted that the rigorousness of the Commission's new approach is not desirable. The absolute priority accorded to the principle of free movement of goods, and the abandonment, as a matter of principle, of further harmonisation, is undesirable for several reasons.

4.2.1   The protection of the consumer

4.2.1.1   Foodstuffs which lack essential characteristics

It is not my intention to rehearse once again the frequent criticism that the *Cassis de Dijon* ruling will automatically lead to a general reduction in quality, since the most liberal national rule will become general practice. This question has already been discussed *in extenso* on many occasions and the Commission is probably right to reject this criticism in general. The Commission is equally right to reject the similar criticism that a lack of Community compositional rules will automatically lead to a general reduction in quality.

---

[29] The German beer case is a clear example in this respect [Case 178/84, p. 297 above].
[31] See in particular Case 174/82, *Sandoz*, [1983] ECR 2445.

However, the question which seems more appropriate in the context of its Communication and which the Commission does not discuss, is whether the Commission should, as a matter of principle, abandon the introduction of any Community legislation in this field. It may turn out in the end to be highly undesirable with regard to the protection of the consumer to abandon such legislation. In particular, if foodstuffs are brought on the market which lack essential characteristics and are nutritionally inferior, the argument that the choice should be left to the consumer comes across as a bromide. Such situations do not necessarily stem from the disparity in national recipe laws, but may stem from the fact that a foodstuff is not subject to any regulation in the exporting Member State or has been exempted therefrom.

The food laws of the Member States provide numerous exemptions for the manufacturing of foodstuffs which are intended for export. An illustration of this can be found again in the Italian pasta cases: the mandatory use of durum wheat meal is not prescribed for pasta intended for export. Moreover, it may be noted that a number of Member States have exempted products which are intended for export from the official inspections which are prescribed by national legislation with regard to foodstuffs, to ensure protection against public health risks and fraud. But apparently, even if there is no such exemption, the competent authorities of Member States do often, in practice, not carry out any inspections with regard to foodstuffs intended for export.

Note

Also worth reading in this area is H.-C. Von Heydebrand u.d. Lasa, 'Free Movement of Foodstuffs, Consumer Protection and Food Standards in the European Community: has the Court of Justice got it wrong?' (1991) 16 EL Rev 391.

Concern has also been expressed about what has been seen as the privatisation of the standards making process under the New Approach. The next extract addresses some questions about the democratic accountability of aspects of the legislative process which emerges from the New Approach's shift in emphasis.

R. Dehousse, '1992 and Beyond: the Institutional Dimension of the Internal Market Programme' [1989/1] LIEI 109, at pp. 125–127

(Footnotes omitted.)

A. DELEGATION OF POWERS: EFFICIENCY v DEMOCRACY?

We have seen that the internal market programme was framed under the assumption that no major alteration to the key principle of decision-making by consensus was likely to take place in the near future. In spite of the long-term effects they might possibly have, the modifications contained in the Single Act did not fundamentally change the nature of the problem. If a leap forward is to be realized, it is therefore necessary to think of alternative ways of avoiding the protracted bargaining to which decision-making by consensus amounts most of the time.

One such way is of course to reduce the legislative agenda, which is as we saw one of the main advantages of the principle of mutual recognition. Another way is to limit the Council's work-load by delegating more decision-making powers to other bodies.

This latter way has been more actively explored at Community level in recent years, be it in the field of standardisation or through an increase in the Commission's powers as regards the implementation of Community legislation. Although these two techniques involve different kinds of problems, they raise similar political issues.

The new strategy defined by the Commission in the wake of *Cassis de Dijon* not only limits the extent to which harmonisation is necessary, but also involves a new approach to ways of harmonisation. The basic feature of this new line is the distinction drawn between essential safety requirements, which must be adopted at Community level, and technical specifications, the defining of which can be entrusted to private standardisation bodies. This new approach was defined by the Council even before the White Paper on the internal market was finalised. Later on, the 'Model directive' on technical harmonisation made it clear that although standards defined by European bodies like CEN or CENELEC – or, in their absence, by national bodies – were to retain their non-mandatory character, products manufactured according to these technical specifications were to be regarded as conforming to the essential requirements laid down by the directives.

One of the reasons used to justify this mechanism is that since harmonisation is of direct interest to the industry and industrialists have a more direct knowledge of the technical problems involved, it would be unwise to give this task to an already overburdened Community legislator. It is clear that the reference to standards can also ease the updating of technical regulations, which is often a delicate matter. But this search for greater efficiency cannot ignore the basic requirements of the Commission legal system. It has been stressed that since compliance with standards entitles a product to free movement, the reference to standards in directives amounts to a delegation of competence from the Council to private bodies. It can therefore only be made in accordance with the general principles laid down by the Court of Justice: delegated powers must be of a clearly defined executive nature and subject to the same conditions as those imposed on the delegating institution, such as the duty to state reasons and the necessary [sic] of judicial control [*Meroni* (Case 9/56)]. These requirements are in a way the transportation in legal terms of more general concerns. If reference to standards is to become a permanent feature of Community regulatory policy, the transparency of this process must be ensured so as to guarantee that the interests of all parties concerned (the industry, of course, but consumers as well, for instance) are duly taken into account. In other words, a balance must be struck between public and private concerns.

How could the requirements laid down by the Court be satisfied? It has been suggested that standards could be published as an annex to which harmonisation directives will refer, in order to make judicial control possible. To some extent, the difficulty was also anticipated by the Model Directive. The need to assign clear limits to the delegated powers surfaces in the description which is given of the essential requirements to be covered by harmonisation directives:

> 'The essential safety requirements . . . shall be worded precisely enough in order to create, on transposition into national law, legally binding obligations which can be enforced. They should be so formulated as to enable the certifications straight away to certify products as being in conformity, having regard to those requirements in the absence of standards.'

While this line of conduct is probably able to reconcile the somewhat contradictory requirements of legitimacy and efficiency, the practical difficulties should not be underestimated: whereas too much discretion given to private bodies could be regarded as incompatible with the guidelines given by the Court, a too detailed directive would amount to no less than a return to the 'old approach'. The implementation of the new approach will therefore be no easy task.

Question
P. Birkenshaw, I. Harden and N. Lewis, in *Government by Moonlight* (1990), conclude a survey of the implications for democratic accountability of privatisation in the UK context as follows:

> It would be a fine irony if British citizens were to get a bill of rights only to find that the 'public' authorities against which the rights might be impleaded had largely been replaced by 'private' bodies, which can be rendered accountable only through private law mechanisms.

To what extent do you think that the privatisating trend of the New Approach yields a parallel (and perhaps greater) democratic deficit at Community level?

Notes
1.   See R. Lauwaars in R. Bieber, et al. (eds), at p. 175 above; S. Weatherill and A. McGee (1990) 53 MLR 578, at pp. 582–87; N. Burrows, *ibid.* at p. 597. But contrast L. Gormley [1989/1] LIEI 9, esp. p. 13, n. 18; J. Stoodley, quoted in N. Burrows, at pp. 601–02. For more recent debate in related areas, see G. Spindler, 'Market Processes, Standardisation, and Tort Law' (1998) 4 ELJ 316; E. Vos, *Institutional Frameworks of Community Health and Safety Regulation: Committees, Agencies and Private Bodies* (1999).
    In conclusion, it should be pointed out that the New Approach, although now firmly embedded within Community regulatory strategy, is not seen as appropriate for *all* future harmonisation. The realisation of economies of scale within the wider market will sometimes be dependent on effective Community-wide harmonisation. In the absence of uniformity, as H. von Sydow has observed (in R. Bieber et al., at p. 97), 'it will be possible to buy an electrical appliance in any part of the Community and to take it across the border without restriction, but, once at home, it may still prove impossible to plug it into the wall socket'.
2.   The second important component in the shift of emphasis in the Commission's harmonisation programme was the change in voting rules introduced by the Single European Act. In Article 100a, an important move towards qualified majority voting in place of unanimity was made. This is now found in Article 95 post-Amsterdam. Yet States still retain some protection against the risk that their standards would be lowered by the harmonised rule (Article 95(3) and (4) *et seq.*). See p. 569 above.

(C) METHODS OF HARMONISATION

(i)   *The uniform rule*
The simplest model of Community harmonisation involves the replacement of diverse national rules by a common Community rule applicable

throughout the 15 Member States. Free trade proceeds on the basis of a rule which is identical throughout the Community. States are deprived of the ability to set standards which diverge from the Community norm.

The following case is a simple example of this approach. The UK is held to have acted in breach of the Treaty by imposing a requirement not included in the exhaustive list of requirements permissible under the relevant Directive. It prohibited the use of motor vehicles not equipped with dim dip lighting.

Commission v *UK (Case 60/86)*
[1988] ECR 3921
Court of Justice of the European Communities

[10]   It is clear from the documents before the Court that the reason for which dim-dip devices were not included in the provisions, even as optional devices, is that the technical committee of national experts did not consider them acceptable given the state of technical progress at the time. In addition, it was not considered appropriate to adapt Directive 76/756/EEC, after its entry into force, so as to take account of technical progress in accordance with the procedure laid down in Article 13 of Directive 70/156/EEC and Article 5 of Directive 76/756/EEC, by bringing dim-dip devices within the scope of the latter directive.

[11]   Such an interpretation of the exhaustive nature of the list of lighting and light-signalling devices set out in Annex I to the directive is consistent with the purpose of Directive 70/156/EEC which is to reduce, and even eliminate, hindrances to trade within the Community resulting from the fact that mandatory technical requirements differ from one Member State to another (see the first and second recitals in the preamble to Directive 70/156/EEC). In the context of Directive 76/756/EEC that objective is reflected in the obligation imposed on the Member States to adopt the same requirements 'either in addition to or in place of their existing rules' (second recital).

[12]   It follows that the Member States cannot unilaterally require manufacturers who have complied with the harmonized technical requirements set out in Directive 76/756/EEC to comply with a requirement which is not imposed by that directive, since motor vehicles complying with the technical requirements laid down therein must be able to move freely within the common market.

[13]   It must therefore be declared that, by prohibiting, in breach of Council Directive 76/756/EEC of 27 July 1976, the use of motor vehicles manufactured after 1 October 1986 and put into service after 1 April 1987 which are not equipped with a dim-dip device, the United Kingdom has failed to fulfil its obligations under Community law.

Note

The principle of *Commission* v *UK* (Case 60/86) is obviously of relevance beyond its facts. The same approach might be taken, for example, to rules relating to the quality of goods or the qualifications which a migrant professional must possess.

Consider, however, the argument that this style of harmonisation is undesirable. At least two arguments may be advanced:

(a)   Harmonisation of this nature is *conservative*. The standard is fixed until such time as the legislator is able to alter it – a laborious process, especially at Community level. The inflexible, rigid standard hinders innovation (e.g. in respect of cheaper or safer lighting devices), and is consequently inefficient.

(b)   Harmonisation of this nature suppresses national tradition. Why should one single Community rule replace national preference? Is free trade a goal which overrides the capacity of individual States to retain higher standards of, say, environmental and consumer protection?

You should consider how this argument has already been addressed in the context of the application of Article 28 to indistinctly applicable rules (p. 329 above); *and* in relation to harmonisation by qualified majority vote under Article 95 (p. 581, above).

Partly in consequence of such reservations, harmonisation is frequently less simple than the model of Directive 76/756 which was at issue in *Commission v UK* (Case 60/86). Community measures are capable of taking account of national concerns by permitting derogations. The legal aspects of this issue under Articles 28 to 30 are discussed in *Rewe* (Case 4/75) and *Moormann* (Case 190/87), at p. 285 above.

(ii)   Differentiated and flexible integration
The existence of optional clauses in Directives raises the issue of 'differentiated integration' – the 'two (or more)-speed Europe'. An absence of uniformity even post-harmonisation is assumed. As already mentioned in Chapter 5 (p. 219 above), pressures in this direction increase as the Community enlarges. They also played a part in the Maastricht negotiations which shaped the Treaty on European Union and are prominent too in the Treaty of Amsterdam.

J. Harrop, *The Political Economy of Integration in the EC* (2nd edn 1992), 262–7

B   Differentiated and flexible integration
Enlargement is likely to accelerate the more pragmatic and flexible approach to integration. However, a range of basic common policies have formed the building blocks of the Community. Countries have to conform to the Treaties and to the ongoing legislation from Community institutions. The basic foundations of the EC, such as the principle of non-discrimination against its members, have to be respected and countries cannot reimpose trading barriers against other members of the Community. Unless these principles are applied, the EC cannot operate effectively and will be undermined. Nevertheless, a pursuit of excessive common standardisation and an attempt to impose uniformity for its own sake is undesirable and certainly less practicable for a Community of twelve different countries. The Community has acknowledged this, using various instruments such as gradual and phased directives, plus some derogations, and some national discretion in how measures are to be applied. . . .

Some differentiation in approach has also existed in other organisations, such as French and Spanish arrangements in NATO. The crucial issue, however, is how much flexibility is possible and whether it can be provided without creating so many exceptions and special cases that ultimately it distorts and discredits the whole organisation. In the new Community the less standard and more diverse pattern of integration which has had to emerge is likely to be reinforced in the future. The first enlargement of the EC in 1973 created a situation of differential treatment by the transition phases of adjustment. It is no coincidence that this first enlargement resulted in greater discussion about a two-speed Europe which was suggested by W. Brandt in West Germany in 1974; this was followed by the Tindemans Report in 1976 in which there were further proposals for differentiated development. In a two-speed Europe at least there is an obligation on those countries which are forging ahead faster to help the weaker countries, for example, by greater regional assistance.

There is little doubt that since enlargement the EC has shown a tendency to split into at least two tiers. There is not only a reluctance to support weaker countries sufficiently, but also doubts about whether such fiscal transfers would actually produce long-run convergence. The pattern that is inevitably emerging is one in which some countries, usually the original Six, are better able to push forward with policies in new areas. The two countries, France and Germany, which have taken most initiatives have provided the momentum in fields such as the EMS, though the Bundesbank since German reunification has become conscious of the costs imposed on the real economy for weaker areas. Countries not participating in new initiatives are free to join and encouraged to take up the option when conditions become more propitious for them . . .

The Community is likely to be confined to core policies, though there is no consensus over what they should be; for example, R. Dahrendorf's list in a Europe *à la carte* included foreign policy, trade, monetary policy and overseas development. France approved a variable-geometry Community in the 1970's, particularly in industrial and technological policy. The *'acquis communautaire'* applies to core policies, but in other areas countries may choose whether to participate or not. Even some non-members of the EC have participated in the EUREKA project and projects of nuclear fusion, such as the Joint European Torus (JET).

The new Community of twelve cannot be optimal for all activities. It has striven hard to obtain basic agreement in key areas and indeed it is surprising in some respects that the Community has been able to make as much progress as it has, given the differences and at times the unco-operativeness of new members. A much looser pattern of integration seems inevitable in the future and the UK may look back wistfully on why it could not attain flexibility to a greater extent in the first place in sectors such as agriculture. A more variegated pattern of integration enables the more dynamic countries to press on ahead, acting as catalysts to new policy areas and providing a way of breaking the soul-destroying deadlock and paralysis of the EC . . . Perhaps the SEA, with more use of majority voting, will help to overcome a damaging split of the Community into two groups.

C The EC: prospect and retrospect

. . . Any temporary loss of momentum towards integration is inevitable at times, and especially after the early idealism and the dynamism of super-economic growth of the 1960s. The most recent attempt to restore a new sense of direction to the Community has been provided by the Single European Act which came into force in 1987. This is much less ambitious than many supporters of European union had hoped for, and in some respects is the lowest common denominator which could be agreed by the Twelve. Even so, it represents a recommitment to real completion of the internal market; to co-operation in economic and monetary policy; economic and social cohesion;

research and technological development; the environment; and greater political co-operation, leading towards a common foreign policy. It became necessary to refocus the Community's activities, since some new policies had begun to operate outside the Community's framework, with also a trend towards inter-governmental integration. A greater use of majority voting became a prime requirement if the enlarged Community were to work more effectively and not become almost paralysed in its decision-making. Majority voting has been introduced in areas which are important in revitalising the EC, such as the internal market. The fact that a vote can be taken is likely to encourage compromise, though there are still many areas where unanimity is necessary. . . .

The EC is aware that it needs to confine itself to those areas where it can demonstrate clear superiority of competence and performance over nation states. The principle of subsidiarity needs to be enshrined to determine their different levels of activity. In moving forward into new areas the Community cannot assume or take for granted that all the problems have been solved in existing areas of integration. In addition, the enlarged Community is likely to experience greater internal problems since it now comprises a much less optimal grouping in its membership; for example, doubts remain about whether sufficient structural funding will be forthcoming for the weakest Southern European economies to enable them to participate fully in EMU. It would appear that only a looser pattern of integration is compatible and suitable for the new Community in the future, particularly if it is to see continuing enlargement, such as that incorporating additional membership by some countries in Eastern Europe.

Notes

1.   This discussion invites a widening of the debate. There are fundamentally important questions about the extent to which the EC should develop common policies designed to regulate the market in the wake of the process of integration. Some States, most notably the UK, have expressed fears about perceived 'over-regulation' of the European market. This anxiety has by no means vanished from the agenda since the Labour government took power in May 1997. A further element in this volatile debate relates to the question of whether a majority decision among the Member States in favour of pursuit of a particular common policy should bind all participants, or whether dissentient States can be permitted to 'opt-out' (and thereby to 'compete' against the standards chosen by the majority). Such issues are critical in the shaping of a Union pursuing a path of both functional and geographic expansion. The question whether the emerging structure of a two (or more)-speed Europe represents a fragmentation or an evolution in the entity's endeavours already deserves the reader's attention. 'Flexibility' as a catch-phrase encompasses not only constructive but also perilous trends for the Union. This matter will be re-addressed at a more general level in the final section of this chapter, at p. 625 below, which includes the text of the arrangements for 'enhanced cooperation' agreed at Amsterdam, following discussion of specific manifestations of differentiated integration.

2.   One aspect of differentiated integration is the technique of minimum harmonisation. This sets a basic Community level of regulation but permits States to set rules at a stricter level if so desired. The next extract examines minimum harmonisation in the context of the harmonisation of consumer protection laws.

K. Mortelmans, 'Minimum Harmonization and Consumer Law' [1988] ECLJ 2, at pp. 5–7

(Some footnotes omitted.)

The double objective of harmonization, i.e. the establishment of a Common Market and the protection of the interests of the consumer, may be related to the technique of minimum harmonization. Free movement is facilitated as the harmonization of legislation removes distortions in competition; but, since consumer legislation in a number of Member States provides more stringent safeguards, such Member States regard harmonization as a minimum and, on the basis of a provision in the directive, they are authorized to introduce more stringent national measures.

The technique of minimum harmonization is explicitly provided for in the Single European Act, in so far as it concerns the safety and health of workers and the protection of the environment. According to Article 118a, paragraph 3 [see now the broader post-Amsterdam provision, Art. 137 EC], the Council establishes minimum provisions taking into account the circumstances and technical rules obtaining in each of the Member States. These provisions do not prevent a Member State from maintaining and introducing more stringent measures of protection for working conditions, compatible with the Treaty. Article 130t [now Art. 176] states that environmental protection measures established by the Community do not prevent Member States from maintaining or introducing more stringent measures compatible with the Treaty. Directives do not therefore have to contain explicit minimum harmonization provisions where measures have been based on Article 118, paragraph 2 or Article 130s. They do however where measures are based on Article 100a . . .

As far as the consumer protection is considered, there is no explicit treaty provision for minimum harmonization [see note below for the changes made at Maastricht]. The protection of the consumer is, pursuant to the [pre-Maastricht] Treaty, viewed from the perspective of the establishment of the internal market (Article 100a) and not from that of a separate consumer policy. Article 100a, paragraph 3 provides that the Commission in its proposals for harmonization in the area of consumer protection shall proceed from an assumption of a high level of protection. . . .

The provisions for minimum harmonization arise primarily in directives aimed specifically at the protection of the consumer, the environment or other justified interests and where the abolition of obstacles to free movement of goods comes in second place. In such cases the public interest, in this context in terms of consumer protection, acquires relative precedence over the free movement of goods. More stringent national measures most often arise when scholarly or legal doubts obtain in respect of the protection required for certain specific situations, persons or geographical areas. This then leads to national legislation with different levels of protection.

Minimum harmonization is sometimes applied to products, such as lead in petrol and water intended for human consumption, but more often to market practices, for example driver training for road transport vehicles or to process regulation as for example in the protection of groundwater.[17]

As a rule, more stringent national measures are taken by Member States separately. It is however possible for various Member States to establish these measures jointly.

---

[17] The directive of February 14, 1977 concerning the rights of employees in the case of business takeovers (OJ, 1977, L 61/26); directive of December 16, 1976 concerning the minimum level of training for drivers of road transport vehicles (OJ, 1976 L 357/36); directive of March 20, 1985 in respect of the lead context [sic] of petrol (OJ, 1985, L 96/25); directive of July 15, 1980 concerning the quality of water intended for human consumption (OJ, 1980, L 229/11).

Harmonization provisions are also incorporated in regulations. An example may be found in the Regulation laying down certain technical measures for the conservation of fishery resources. From the viewpoint of the Community, the use of minimum measures is a second best solution. It is however doubtful whether some Member States would be prepared to sacrifice acquired 'social rights' such as consumer protection for the achievement of a common market. The technique of minimum harmonization is consequently [a more] than honourable means of reconciling the common market with consumer interests. . . .

Question
In contrast K. Taschner 'regards minimum directives as a sign of the decreasing integrative force of Member States, because they are often only an easy way to evade the inconvenient necessity of finding an agreement' (in L. Kramer, *EEC Consumer Law*, para. 86). Which view accords more closely with your perception of the proper development of the Community? (You should return to this question after completing reading this chapter.)

See also, e.g., N. Reich, 'Some Remarks on the Theory of European Consumer Law' (1995) 3 Euro Rev Private Law 285. More generally see J. Currall, 'Some Aspects of the Relation between Articles 30–36 and Article 100 of the EEC Treaty, with a Closer Look at Optional Harmonisation' (1984) 4 YEL 169; E. Cross, 'Pre-emption of Member State Law in the European Economic Community: A Framework for Analysis' (1992) 29 CML Rev 447; P.-J. Slot 'Harmonisation' (1996) 21 EL Rev 378 and further at p. 634 below.

Note
As Mortelmans explains in the above extract, Article 100a does not specify that Directives made under it achieve only minimum harmonisation; the same is true of the post-Amsterdam version, Article 95 (p. 569). However, many Directives dealing with the harmonisation of consumer law have been adopted under this legal base, and in particular where protection of the economic interests of consumers has been at stake the minimum formula has been explicitly included in the secondary legislation. Examples include Directive 93/13 on unfair terms in consumer contracts and Directive 94/46 on timeshare ((1993) OJ L95/29 and (1994) OJ L280/83 respectively; see further S. Weatherill, *EC Consumer Law and Policy* (1997)). The scope of EC competence in the field was extended by the Maastricht Treaty, which inserted a new title devoted to consumer protection into the EC Treaty. This is Article 153 post-Amsterdam. The minimum harmonisation model is explicitly adopted. Article 153(5) EC provides that:

Action adopted [by the Council and Parliament] pursuant to paragraph 4 shall not prevent any Member State from maintaining or introducing more stringent protective measures. Such measures must be compatible with this Treaty. The Commission shall be notified of them.

It was noted at p. 52 above that the demarcation between legal bases in the Treaty is enduringly complex and fixing that between Article 153 and Article 95 is capable of proving troublesome, but as a general observation this provision offers scope for deeper policy-making in this sphere (S. Weatherill and H. Micklitz, 'Consumer Policy in the EC before and after Maastricht' ((1993) 16 JCP 285).

In December 1992, the Edinburgh European Council concluded that:

> . . . where it is necessary to set standards at Community level, consideration should be given to setting minimum standards, with freedom for Member States to set higher standards, not only in the areas where the Treaty so requires . . . but also in other areas where this would not conflict with the objectives of the proposed measure or with the Treaty.

The increasingly prominent phenomenon of minimum harmonisation puts in place a floor of regulatory standards below which Member States may not drop. However, the technique leaves open the possibility of an uneven 'playing field' for traders in so far as States choose to set rules above the Community minimum. The Court expressly accepted this result in the next case, in rejecting a submission that a Directive should be interpreted as setting both floor and ceiling (total harmonisation) and finding instead that it fixed a floor only (minimum harmonisation). Stricter State rules were therefore not pre-empted by the Directive.

Hans Hönig v Stadt Stockach (Case C–128/94)
[1995] ECR I-3389
Court of Justice of the European Communities

Directive 88/166 lays down standards for the protection of laying hens kept in battery cages. German rules required larger cages than were provided for under the Directive. Hönig, a German farmer, submitted that to allow a State to set a stricter rule would frustrate the Directive's capacity to achieve uniform conditions of competition in the EC. Via the preliminary reference procedure, a German court sought the European Court's interpretation of the leeway permitted to Member States under the Directive. The Court based its ruling on both the text and the purpose of the Directive.

[9]   As the Court has emphasised in its decisions, it is necessary in interpreting a provision of Community law to consider not only its wording but also the context in which it occurs and the objects of the rules of which it is part (judgment in Case 292/82 *Merck* v *Hauptzollamt Hamburg-Jonas* [1983] ECR 3781, paragraph 12, and in Case 337/82 *St Nikolaus Brennerei* v *Hauptzollamt Krefeld* [1984] ECR 1051, paragraph 10).

[10]   As regards in the first place the wording of the directive, Article 3(1)(a) of the Annex provides as follows:

Member States shall ensure that from 1 January 1988:
— all newly built cages for use within the Community,
— all cages brought into use for the first time,

at least comply with the following requirements:

(a)   at least 450cm^2 of cage area . . . shall be provided for each laying hen. . . .

[11]   On the wording of the provision, therefore, the Member States may not lay down a minimum surface area of less the 450cm^2 per cage, but may lay down a minimum cage area per hen greater than that provided for; that is shown, moreover, by the title of the directive and Article 1 thereof, which provides that 'this directive lays down the minimum standards for the protection of laying hens kept in battery cages'.

[12]   The minimum standards contained in the directive were laid down as a consequence of the Council Resolution of 22 July 1980 on the protection of laying hens in cages (OJ 1980 C 196, p.1) and in Council Decision 78/923/EEC of 19 June 1978 approving the European Convention for the Protection of Animals kept for Farming Purposes (OJ 1978 L 323, p.12).

[13]   Next, the purpose of the directive must be considered.

[14]   As the Advocate General pointed out in paragraph 13 of his Opinion, the directive seeks first to provide protection for animals kept for farming purposes and secondly to reduce the disparities in conditions of competition as between Member States on the market in eggs and poultry.

[15]   The Community legislature therefore sought to reconcile the interests of the proper functioning of the organisation of the market in eggs and poultry with those of animal protection by laying down, according to the third recital in the preamble to the directive, common minimum requirements applicable to all intensive housing systems, including those for laying hens kept in battery cages.

[16]   Lastly, the use of the words 'as a first step' in the third recital, and the content of the fourth recital in the preamble to the directive, indicate that the latter seeks only a certain degree of harmonisation in the protection of hens by means of provisions laying down minimum standards.

[17]   Admittedly, that interpretation of the directive's provisions may lead, as the plaintiff in the main action has pointed out, to battery hen farmers in one Member State receiving less favourable treatment than those in other Member States, thus allowing some inequalities in competition to persist. However, those are the consequences of the level of harmonisation sought by those provisions, which lay down minimum standards.

Note
The next section concerns a derogation in a Directive concerned with the harmonisation of civil liability rules. Once again, the policy issue relates to the accommodation of diffuse aspirations within a regime devoted to free trade.

(iii)   The Product Liability Directive
Directive 85/374 ((1985) OJ L210/29 as amended by Directive 99/34 (1999) L141/20) harmonises the rules on liability for injury caused by defective consumer products. Article 1 provides that, 'The producer shall be liable for damage caused by a defect in his product.' The Directive is a classic 'dual aim' harmonisation measure.

R. Merkin, *A Guide to the Consumer Protection Act 1987* (1987), pp. 4–5

. . . Reasons for the Directive

The introduction of a uniform code of product liability within the European Community is perceived by the Community authorities as being necessary to bring about two broad sets of objectives: consumer protection objectives and market unity objectives.

The importance of consumer protection is recognised by the second recital of the product liability Directive, which states that:

> . . . liability without fault on the part of the producer is the sole means of adequately solving the problem, peculiar to our age of increasing technicality, of a fair apportionment of the risks inherent in modern technological production.

This broad statement encompasses a number of distinct arguments in favour of strict liability:

(a)   The general desire to spread loss throughout society rather than to allow it to fall on individual consumers.

(b)   The belief that producers can insure against third-party risks at a lower cost than individual consumers could insure against first-party risks, so that strict liability is the cheapest form of risk-spreading.

(c)   The possibility that strict liability will provide manufacturers with the incentive to increase safety and standards generally, an incentive which is not diminished by the probable existence of liability insurance, given the dangers of premium-rating and of adverse publicity.

(d)   The illogicality and expense of maintaining a fault-based system.

The market unity arguments for strict liability are rather more subtle. The first recital of the Directive asserts that:

> . . . the existing divergences [between the laws of Member States] may distort competition and affect the movement of goods within the common market and entail a differing degree of protection of the consumer.

Two distinct issues are at stake here:

(a)   The principle that goods must be allowed to move freely between Member States, enshrined in articles 30 to 36 [now 28–30] of the Treaty of Rome, is overridden by mandatory consumer protection laws which prevent the sale of dangerous goods, imported or otherwise. By imposing strict liability, standards will improve and goods will be permitted to circulate more freely as between Member States.

(b)   If the laws of one Member State are less generous to manufacturers than the laws of other Member States, by the imposition of strict liability, those manufacturers subject to strict liability will be at a competitive disadvantage when exporting to Member States offering a lesser degree of consumer protection. This is so because their products will be more expensive, either as a result of the costs of higher safety standards or as a result of the price of the goods containing an element representing domestic liability insurance premiums. Failure to implement strict liability is thus seen as a form of indirect protectionism.

Note

Yet it was not possible to achieve unanimity in drafting a final version of the Directive which would apply without derogation to all Member States.

R. Merkin, *A Guide to the Consumer Protection Act 1987*
(1987), pp. 6–7

One interesting feature of the Directive is that it permits three 'derogations', i.e., matters in respect of which each Member State is free to determine whether or not it wishes to follow the terms of the Directive. The derogations are as follows:

(a)   Agricultural products and game. Article 1 of the Directive provides that there is to be no strict liability upon the producers of these products, although Article 15.1(a) permits Member States to impose such liability if they so wish. . . .

(b)   A 'development risks' defence. The Directive contains, in Article 7(e), a defence open to a manufacturer to the effect that the state of scientific and technical knowledge was not such as to enable the defect to be discovered when the product was put into circulation. However, Article 15.1(b) allows Member States to extend strict liability to cover development risks of this nature. It would appear that the majority of Member States intend to avail themselves of the derogation, but the UK has again opted to follow the Directive and to retain the defence (see Chapter 3). [In fact, it emerged that most Member States permit the defence; COM (95) 617, Commission's first report on the Directive.]

(c)   Maximum liability. Article 16 allows the imposition of a maximum liability in respect of individual claims or in respect of aggregate claims arising out of a particular defect in a product, of some £40 million. The UK did not think it necessary to limit liability in this way . . .

The operation of these three derogations is to be assessed in July 1995 to determine whether they should be abandoned or made mandatory. . . . [In COM (95) 617, the Commission proposed no modification to the Directive. However, agricultural products and game (point (a)) *are* now subject to the liability régime as a result of amending Directive 99/34.]

Note

A major stumbling block was the argument over whether or not to include the 'development risks' defence; derogation (b) in the preceding extract. Its absence would, it was alleged, lead, *inter alia*, to undesirable inhibition of technical innovation.

R. Merkin, *A Guide to the Consumer Protection Act 1987*
(1987), pp. 35–36

. . . The most important justification of the development risks defence is that it encourages research into new products. The argument runs that a producer facing absolute liability for unforeseeable defects will simply not risk marketing new products, to the ultimate detriment of all consumers, because of the cost of potential liability from doing so and because of the danger of damage to reputation resulting from widely publicised successful proceedings.

The validity of the cost approach rests upon two assumptions. First, it presupposes that insurance will not be available for development risk liability. The preliminary view of the Association of British Insurers is, as already noted, that premiums will not be increased significantly by the imposition of strict liability as long as the development risks defence is available, but that there will be a substantial rise if absolute liability is imposed. Given, however, that insurance is available – albeit at a price – the question becomes whether it is proper to allow loss by development risks to fall upon individuals, or whether it is more desirable to require all consumers to contribute to the costs of insurance when making their purchases.

The underlying assumption of product liability is that the latter option is the most desirable. It might also be questioned whether premiums would in fact have to rise as steeply as has been predicted by the Association of British Insurers: most of the calculations were done by assessing the American experience, although the high levels of damages there awarded and the contingency fee system may both render any comparison with the UK misleading.

The second assumption is that producers will not face development risk liability if a development risks defence is included. This, however, is not the case. First, an exporter to other Member States of the EEC may, depending upon the conflict of laws rules prevailing in those States, face absolute liability. Secondly, the original producer may face liability in the UK under the Sale of Goods Act 1979, where a chain action is commenced. Finally, there is always the possibility that, following expensive litigation, the defence cannot be made out. Consequently, it would appear that UK suppliers would be unwise not to carry development risk cover irrespective of the position under the Consumer Protection Act 1987.

The reputation argument would not appear to be significant. In the absence of a development risks defence there would appear not to be a need for litigation, and all manufacturers would in any event face the same liability, so that there ought not be a fear of competitive disadvantage. In addition, reputation may be lost as much in successfully defending litigation as in accepting liability quietly.

Note

The existence of the development risk defence has been criticised as a severe curtailment of the ability of the measure to provide effective consumer protection. For example, a modern parallel to the thalidomide tragedy would probably still go uncompensated in the UK because of the producer's ability to rely on the defence. See Cmnd. 7054 (1978), para. 1259, *Report of the Pearson Commission on Civil Liability and Compensation for Personal Injury*. See also C. Newdick, 'The Future of Negligence in Product Liability' (1987) 103 LQR 288; M. Shapo, 'Comparing Products Liability: Concepts in European and American Law' (1993) 26 Cornell Intl LJ 279; G. Howells and T. Wilhelmsson, 'EC and US Approaches to Consumer Protection – Should the Gap be Bridged?' (1997) 17 YEL 207; and, more broadly J. Stapleton, *Product Liability* (1994).

Furthermore, the nature of the defence and its implementation in the UK has provoked controversy; Article 7(e) of Directive 85/374 provides that 'the producer shall not be liable as result of this Directive if he proves that the state of scientific and technical knowledge at the time when he put the product into circulation was not such as to enable the existence of the defect to be discovered'. The UK's implementing Consumer Protection Act 1987, s. 4(1)(e), provides that it is a defence to show 'that the state of scientific and technical knowledge at the relevant time was not such that a producer of products of the same description as the product in question might be expected to have discovered the defect if it had existed in his products while they were under his control'. For a challenging argument that the UK's implementation is in fact correct, notwithstanding the textual discrepancy, see C. Newdick, 'The Development Risk Defence of the Consumer Protection Act 1987' (1988) 47 CLJ 455 and 'Risk, Uncertainty and "Knowledge" in the Development Risk Defence' [1991] Anglo-Amer LR 127. The Court was provided with the opportunity to clarify the position by Commission infringement proceedings brought against the United Kingdom under Article 169 EC, but the Court's ruling did not entirely resolve the matters of substance.

Commission v United Kingdom (Case C-300/95)
[1997] ECR I-2649
Court of Justice of the European Communities

The core of the Commission's complaint is summarised as follows:

[16] In its application, the Commission argues that the United Kingdom legislature has broadened the defence under Article 7(e) of the Directive to a considerable degree and converted the strict liability imposed by Article 1 of the Directive into mere liability for negligence.

[17] The Commission submits that the test in Article 7(e) of the Directive is objective in that it refers to a state of knowledge, and not to the capacity of the producer of the product in question, or to that of another producer of a product of the same description, to discover the defect. However, by its use of the words 'a producer of products of the same description as the product in question [who] might be expected to have discovered the defect', section 4(1)(e) of the Act presupposes a subjective assessment based on the behaviour of a reasonable producer. It is easier for the producer of a defective product to demonstrate, under section 4(1)(e), that neither he nor a producer of similar products could have identified the defect at the material time, provided that the standard precautions in the particular industry were taken and there was no negligence, than to show, under Article 7(e), that the state of scientific and technical knowledge was such that no-one would have been able to discover the defect.

The Court proceeded to reject the Commission's application:

[23] In order to determine whether the national implementing provision at issue is clearly contrary to Article 7(e) as the Commission argues, the scope of the Community provision which it purports to implement must first be considered.

[24] In order for a producer to incur liability for defective products under Article 4 of the Directive, the victim must prove the damage, the defect and the causal relationship between defect and damage, but not that the producer was at fault. However, in accordance with the principle of fair apportionment of risk between the injured person and the producer set forth in the seventh recital in the preamble to the Directive, Article 7 provides that the producer has a defence if he can prove certain facts exonerating him from liability, including 'that the state of scientific and technical knowledge at the time when he put the product into circulation was not such as to enable the existence of the defect to be discovered' (Article 7(e)).

[25]   Certain general observations can be made as to the wording of Article 7(e) of the Directive.

[26]   First, as the Advocate General rightly observes in paragraph 20 of his Opinion, since that provision refers to 'scientific and technical knowledge at the time when [the producer] put the product into circulation', Article 7(e) is not specifically directed at the practices and safety standards in use in the industrial sector in which the producer is operating, but, unreservedly, at the state of scientific and technical knowledge, including the most advanced level of such knowledge, at the time when the product in question was put into circulation.

[27]   Second, the clause providing for the defence in question does not contemplate the state of knowledge of which the producer in question actually or subjectively was or could have been apprised, but the objective state of scientific and technical knowledge of which the producer is presumed to have been informed.

[28]   However, it is implicit in the wording of Article 7(e) that the relevant scientific and technical knowledge must have been accessible at the time when the product in question was put into circulation.

[29]   It follows that, in order to have a defence under Article 7(e) of the Directive, the producer of a defective product must prove that the objective state of scientific and technical knowledge, including the most advanced level of such knowledge, at the time when the product in question was put into circulation was not such as to enable the existence of the defect to be discovered. Further, in order for the relevant scientific and technical knowledge to be successfully pleaded against the producer, that knowledge must have been accessible at the time when the product in question was put into circulation. On this last point, contrary to what the Commission seems to consider, Article 7(e) of the Directive raises difficulties of interpretation which, in the event of litigation, the national courts will have to resolve having recourse, if necessary, to Article 177 of the EC Treaty.

[30]   For the present, it is the heads of claim raised by the Commission in support of its application that have to be considered.

[31]   In proceedings brought under Article 169 of the Treaty the Commission is required to prove the alleged infringement. The Commission must provide the Court with the material necessary for it to determine whether the infringement is made out and may not rely on any presumption (see, in particular, Case C-62/89 *Commission v France* [1990] ECR I-925, paragraph 37).

[32]   The Commission takes the view that inasmuch as section 4(1)(e) of the Act refers to what may be expected of a producer of products of the same description as the product in question, its wording clearly conflicts with Article 7(e) of the Directive in that it permits account to be taken of the subjective knowledge of a producer taking reasonable care, having regard to the standard precautions taken in the industrial sector in question.

[33]   That argument must be rejected in so far as it selectively stresses particular terms used in section 4(1)(e) without demonstrating that the general legal context of the provision at issue fails effectively to secure full application of the Directive. Taking that context into account, the Commission has failed to make out its claim that the result intended by Article 7(e) of the Directive would clearly not be achieved in the domestic legal order.

[34]   First, section 4(1)(e) of the Act places the burden of proof on the producer wishing to rely on the defence, as Article 7 of the Directive requires.

[35]   Second, section 4(1)(e) places no restriction on the state and degree of scientific and technical knowledge at the material time which is to be taken into account.

[36]   Third, its wording as such does not suggest, as the Commission alleges that the availability of the defence depends on the subjective knowledge of a producer taking reasonable care in the light of the standard precautions taken in the industrial sector in question.

[37]   Fourth, the Court has consistently held that the scope of national laws, regulations or administrative provisions must be assessed in the light of the interpretation given to them by national courts (see, in particular, Case C-382/92 *Commission v United Kingdom* [1994] ECR I-2435, paragraph 36). Yet in this case the Commission has not referred in support of its application to any national judicial decision which, in its view, interprets the domestic provision at issue inconsistently with the Directive.

[38]   Lastly, there is nothing in the material produced to the Court to suggest that the courts in the United Kingdom, if called upon to interpret section 4(1)(e), would not do so in the light of the wording and the purpose of the Directive so as to achieve the result which it has in view and thereby comply with the third paragraph of Article 189 of the Treaty (see, in particular, Case C-91/92 *Faccini Dori* v *Recreb* [1994) ECR I-3325, paragraph 26). Moreover, section 1(1) of the Act expressly imposes such an obligation on the national courts.

[39]   It follows that the Commission has failed to make out its allegation that, having regard to its general legal context and especially section 1(1) of the Act, section 4(1)(e) clearly conflicts with Article 7(e) of the Directive. As a result, the application must be dismissed.

Question
How does one determine when knowledge is 'accessible'? Is such an issue apt for preliminary reference to the European Court, as suggested in para. 29 of the ruling above?

Note
For our purposes the central question must be whether the existence of such options in the Directive represents a satisfactory compromise between the demands of free trade and consumer protection.

G. Howells, 'Implications of the Implementation and Non-Implementation of the EC Products Liability Directive' (1990) 41 NILQ 22, at pp. 25–27

(Footnotes omitted.)

THE THREAT TO HARMONISATION

The goal of approximation is clearly threatened by the failure of Member States to comply with the Directive or to implement it correctly. However, as a harmonising measure, the Directive was in any event inherently flawed. Article 13 of the Directive provides:

> 'This Directive shall not affect any rights which an injured person may have according to the rules of the law of contractual or non-contractual liability or a special liability system existing at the moment when this Directive is notified.'

Thus not only are special liability systems like the West German pharmaceutical liability regime preserved, but so also is domestic contractual and tortious liability. This will make a serious inroad into the goal of approximation, for legal advisers must continue to be alert to domestic rules which may afford better protection than the Directive. For example, in the United Kingdom an action for breach of the implied condition of merchantable quality may be preferable to having to prove that the product is defective – provided, of course, that the plaintiff has privity of contract with the defendant. In France a contractual action for '*vice cachée*' (hidden defect) may be the preferred option. Furthermore the possibility of an '*action directe*' against a manufacturer has freed the plaintiff from the shackles of the privity of contract doctrine, while the assimilation of a professional seller with a seller in bad faith permits recovery for consequential loss. Similarly, in West Germany, tortious liability has been developed to such an extent (for example, by the reversal of the burden of proof and the imposition of the obligation to monitor products) that better protection may be available under domestic West German law. These are merely a few examples, from just three Member States, which serve to make the point that the Directive is not the only source of protection for the Community's consumers.

The different language versions of the Directive are openly contradictory. Article 9(b) of the English language version talks of 'a lower threshold of 500 ECU' which clearly contemplates claims for higher amounts being compensated in full. The French and German versions, however, envisage this amount being deducted from larger claims. The Dutch version is ambiguous, but their draft Bill appears to follow the United Kingdom approach. Apparently the United Kingdom's divergent text is to be explained by a misunderstanding on the part of the United Kingdom delegation. This is perhaps understandable, for recital 9 of the preamble to the Directive states that the policy is 'to avoid litigation in an excessive number of cases'. The number of potential cases could have been further reduced if a higher threshold had been set; but deducting a specified amount simply means that there will continue to be potential litigation over small amounts. Against this it should be remembered that the preamble does talk about 'a *deduction* of a lower threshold'.

The three optional elements mentioned earlier will lead to additional inconsistencies if Member States adopt different positions thereon. Although it is too early to know how the final picture will look, it is clear that on each of the options (agricultural produce [this option has now been deleted by Dir. 99/34, above], development risks and global limits for personal injury damages) at least one Member State will derogate from the Directive. The options resulted, of course, from compromises which had to be reached in order for the Directive to be acceptable to all the Member States in the first place. Article 15(2) does provide a partial safeguard, in that it provides that a Member State wishing to derogate from Article 7(e) (the development risks defence) must communicate the proposed text to the Commission, who must then inform the other Member States. In general, however, the problem of not knowing how other Member States will decide on the optional provisions has been a disincentive to Member States to provide more than a minimalist level of consumer protection. Thus it was argued that if primary agricultural produce was included within the United

Kingdom's provisions, it would place our farmers at a disadvantage to French farmers. Ironically, it is likely that the French *will* include agricultural produce within their regime. However, with so many rumours abounding about the form which implementing legislation would take across the Community, it is easy to understand the confusion.

It is, however, possible that by the end of the century these options will have been removed. The Commission has to submit a report to the Council on the application of the Directive every five years, together with appropriate proposals. More specifically, the Commission has to report to the Council on the effect on consumer protection and the functioning of the common market of both rulings of the courts on the development risks defence (and derogations therefrom) and the financial limits on liability. The Council has then to decide whether to repeal these provisions.

There also seems to be a more subtle threat to harmonisation implicit in the Directive's definition of 'defect' as including a product which does not provide 'the safety which a person is entitled to expect'. Although the same test will be applied in each Member State, will the answer vary between them? One might wonder, for example, whether a Greek consumer has the same expectations as a West German?

Note

The Commission's first report, issued in 1995 pursuant to the requirements mentioned in the penultimate paragraph of this extract, proposed no change for the time being (COM (95) 617). A further Commission report published as a Green Paper in 1999 is undergoing a process of consultation and may generate more radical proposals about the future of the 'development risk' defence (COM (99) 396; see Izquierdo Peris [1999] Cons Law Jnl 331).

The final paragraph of this extract raises a connected point of great significance. Beyond the existence of options, one can legitimately question whether the terms of the Directive are sufficiently clear and precise to lead to effective harmonisation. (*Cf.* Brouwer's discussion of food law, at p. 577 above.)

Given such ambiguity, which will suffer – free trade or consumer protection? It would be foolish to underestimate the extent to which an erosion of consumer confidence in the safety of imported goods will jeopardise the realisation of market integration.

Question

The development risk defence is an example of optional differentiated integration within a Community measure. The legal base of a measure may permit optional derogation – see Article 95, at p. 569 above. Might one see failure to implement Directives in the national legal order as a further means of choosing differentiated integration? How effective are the Community rules on the direct and indirect effect of Directives (see p. 103 above) as controls over inadequate national implementation of Directives? What might be the impact of the ruling in *Francovich* (Cases C-6, C-9/90), p. 128 above?

Note

The Product Liability Directive seeks to harmonise national liability rules. More generally, the Community is engaged in developing a regulatory strategy for defective products, which encompasses both private and public law.

Directive 92/59 on General Product Safety (1992) OJ L228/24 was made under Article 100a of the EC Treaty (now, after amendment, Article 95 EC) and operates without prejudice to the Product Liability Directive. Article 1(1) of Directive 92/59 declares that 'The purpose of the provisions of this Directive is to ensure that products placed on the market are safe'. According to Article 3, 'Producers shall be obliged to place only safe products on the market'. A safe product is one which 'under normal or reasonably foreseeable conditions of use, including duration, does not present any risk or only the minimum risks compatible with the product's use' (Article 2). As indicated at p. 573 above, Directive 92/59 is a classic 'New Approach' Directive. It does not seek to harmonise laws relating to a particular type of product, but instead seeks to establish 'horizontal' rules setting broad Community standards across a wide range of products. (See further S. Weatherill, *EC Consumer Law and Policy* (1997), Ch. 7; G. Howells, *Consumer Product Safety* (1998), Ch. 2.) Is the notion of an unacceptable risk on which the Directive is based capable of similar interpretation in every Member State? (*Cf.* the Product Liability Directive, above.) If not, what are the consequences for the proposal's capacity to create (i) effective consumer protection, (ii) unrestricted free trade?

It may seem a simple proposition that where national markets are integrated into a Community market, the regulatory structure affecting that market should also transfer to the Community level. Yet although certain aspects of regulatory policy are held to be efficiently controlled at Community level (e.g., agricultural policy, competition policy – although even in that field there exist complicated overlaps of competence between national and EC level, the precise patterns of which remain a matter of debate (p. 527 above)), other aspects may more efficiently be devolved to national or local level. For example, although there may be a case for overall policy making in relation to the control of unsafe products being undertaken at Community level, enforcement activity will inevitably and efficiently be performed at local level. The appropriate division of function was an issue of fierce debate in relation to Directive 92/59. Articles 5–6 are directed at enforcement by national authorities, but the Directive also confers powers on the Commission. Title V covers 'Emergency situations and action at Community level'.

Directive 92/59/EEC on General Product Safety
(1992) OJ L228/24

Article 8

1. Where a Member State adopts or decides to adopt emergency measures to prevent, restrict or impose specific conditions on the possible marketing or use, within its own territory, of a product or product batch by reason of a serious and immediate risk presented by the said product or product batch to the health and safety of consumers, it shall forthwith inform the Commission thereof, unless provision is made

for this obligation in procedures of a similar nature in the context of other Community instruments.

This obligation shall not apply if the effects of the risk do not, or cannot, go beyond the territory of the Member State concerned.

Without prejudice to the provisions of the first subparagraph, Member States may pass on to the Commission any information in their possession regarding the existence of a serious and immediate risk before deciding to adopt the measures in question.

2.   On receiving this information, the Commission shall check to see whether it complies with the provisions of this Directive and shall forward it to the other Member States, which, in turn, shall immediately inform the Commission of any measures adopted.

3.   Detailed procedures for the Community information system described in this Article are set out in the Annex. They shall be adapted [sic] by the Commission in accordance with the procedure laid down in Article 11.

Article 9

If the Commission becomes aware, through notification given by the Member States or through information provided by them, in particular under Article 7 or Article 8, of the existence of a serious and immediate risk from a product to the health and safety of consumers in various Member States and if:

(a)   one or more Member States have adopted measures entailing restrictions on the marketing of the product or requiring its withdrawal from the market, such as those provided for in Article 6(1)(d) to (h);

(b)   Member States differ on the adoption of measures to deal with the risk in question;

(c)   the risk cannot be dealt with, in view of the nature of the safety issue posed by the product and in a manner compatible with the urgency of the case, under the other procedures laid down by the specific Community legislation applicable to the product or category of products concerned; and

(d)   the risk can be eliminated effectively only by adopting appropriate measures applicable at Community level, in order to ensure the protection of the health and safety of consumers and the proper functioning of the common market, the Commission, after consulting the Member States and at the request of at least one of them, may adopt a decision, in accordance with the procedure laid down in Article 11, requiring Member States to take temporary measures from among those listed in Article 6(1)(d) to (h).

Article 10

1.   The Commission shall be assisted by a Committee on Product Safety Emergencies, hereinafter referred to as 'the Committee', composed of the representatives of the Member States and chaired by a representative of the Commission.

2.   Without prejudice to Article 9(c), there shall be close cooperation between the Committee referred to in paragraph 1 and the other Committees established by specific rules of Community law to assist the Commission as regards the health and safety aspects of the product concerned.

Article 11

1.   The Commission representative shall submit to the Committee a draft of the measures to be taken. The Committee, having verified that the conditions listed in Article 9 are fulfilled, shall deliver its opinion on the draft within a time limit which the Chairman may lay down according to the urgency of the matter but which may

not exceed one month. The opinion shall be delivered by the majority laid down in Article 148(2) of the Treaty for adoption of decisions by the Council on a proposal from the Commission. The votes of the representatives of the Member States within the Committee shall be weighted in the manner set out in that Article. The Chairman shall not vote.

The Commission shall adopt the measures in question, if they are in accordance with the opinion of the Committee. If the measures proposed are not in accordance with the Committee's opinion, or in the absence of an opinion, the Commission shall forthwith submit to the Council a proposal regarding the measures to be taken. The Council shall act by a qualified majority.

If the Council has not acted within 15 days of the date on which the proposal was submitted to it, the measures proposed shall be adopted by the Commission unless the Council has decided against them by a simple majority.

2. Any measure adopted under this procedure shall be valid for no longer than three months. That period may be prolonged under the same procedure.

3. Member States shall take all necessary measures to implement the decisions adopted under this procedure within less than 10 days.

4. The competent authorities of the Member States responsible for carrying out measures adopted under this procedure shall, within one month, give the parties concerned an opportunity to submit their views and shall inform the Commission accordingly.

Article 12
The Member States and the Commission shall take the steps necessary to ensure that their officials and agents are required not to disclose information obtained for the purposes of this Directive which, by its nature, is covered by professional secrecy, except for information relating to the safety properties of a given product which must be made public if circumstances so require, in order to protect the health and safety of persons.

Note
The list referred to at the end of Article 9, contained in Article 6(1)(d) to (h), reads as follows:

(d) subjecting product marketing to prior conditions designed to ensure product safety and requiring that suitable warnings may be affixed regarding the risks which the product may present;

(e) making arrangements to ensure that persons who might be exposed to a risk from a product are informed in good time and in a suitable manner of the said risk by, *inter alia*, the publication of special warnings;

(f) temporarily prohibiting, for the period required to carry out the various checks, anyone from supplying, offering to supply or exhibiting a product or product batch, whenever there are precise and consistent indications that they are dangerous;

(g) prohibiting the placing on the market of a product or product batch which has proved dangerous and establishing the accompanying measures needed to ensure that the ban is complied with;

(h) organising the effective and immediate withdrawal of a dangerous product or product batch already on the market and, if necessary, its destruction under appropriate conditions.

For an example of the exercise of the Commission's powers under Article 9 of the Directive, see Decisions 99/815 *Soft PVC Toys* (1999) OJ L315/46, requiring the prohibition of the placing on the market of certain toys.

Earlier drafts of the Directive contained less stringent criteria which had to be met before the Commission could act. The Commission's 1989 draft (OJ 1989 C193/1) required neither prior action to have been taken against the product by at least one Member State nor divergence between Member States on the adoption of measures. However, even the relatively narrow competence to act conferred on the Commission by Article 9 of the Directive as adopted provoked a challenge under Article 173 of the EC Treaty (now, after amendment, Article 230 EC: see Chapter 16) to the validity of the measure.

Germany v *Council (Case C–359/92)*
[1994] ECR I–3681
Court of Justice of the European Communities

Germany submitted that the Community was not competent to adopt Article 9 of the Directive on the basis of Article 100a of the EC Treaty (now, after amendment, Article 95: though the amendments are not relevant to the subject matter of this litigation). The Court rejected the application for annulment.

[32] The Community legislature therefore considered it necessary, in order to cope with a serious and immediate risk to the health and safety of consumers, to provide for an adequate mechanism allowing, in the last resort, for the adoption of measures applicable throughout the Community, in the form of decisions addressed to the Member States (see the twentieth recital in the preamble to the directive).

[33] For that purpose, Article 9 of the directive empowers the Commission, on the basis of the information received, to act in cases where a product placed on the market puts in serious and immediate jeopardy the health and safety of consumers in a number of Member States and those States differ with respect to the measures adopted or planned with regard to that product, that is to say, where such measures do not provide the same level of protection and thereby prevent the product from moving freely within the Community. Article 9 provides that, to the extent that effective protection can be ensured only by action at Community level and no other procedure specifically applicable to the product can be used, the Commission may adopt a decision requiring Member States to take temporary measures from among those listed in Article 6(1)(d) to (h).

[34] As is apparent from the eighteenth, nineteenth and twentieth recitals of the preamble to the directive and from the structure of Article 9, the purpose of that provision is to enable the Commission to adopt, as promptly as possible, temporary measures applicable throughout the Community with respect to a product which presents a serious and immediate risk to the health and safety of consumers, so as to ensure compliance with the objectives of the directive. The free movement of goods can be secured only if product safety requirements do not differ significantly from one Member State to another. A high level of protection can be achieved only if dangerous products are subject to appropriate measures in all the Member States.

[35] Such action must be taken by the Commission in close cooperation with Member States. For one thing, decisions taken at Community level may be adopted by the Commission only after consulting the Member States and at the request of a Member State. For another, such measures may be adopted by the Commission only if they are in accordance with the opinion of a committee composed of the Member States' representatives and a Commission representative. Otherwise the measure must be adopted by the Council within a specified period. Lastly, those decisions are addressed only to the Member States. The twentieth recital in the preamble to the directive states that such decisions are not of direct application to traders in the Community and must be incorporated in a national measure.

[36] Thus, in the circumstances set out in Article 9, action by the Community authorities is justified by the fact that, in the terms used in Article 9(d), 'the risk can be eliminated effectively only by adopting appropriate measures at Community level, in order to ensure the protection of the health and safety of consumers and the proper functioning of the Common Market'.

[37] Such action is not contrary to Article 100a (1) of the Treaty. The measures which the Council is empowered to take under that provision are aimed at 'the establishment and functioning of the internal market'. In certain fields, and particularly in that of product safety, the approximation of general laws alone may not be sufficient to ensure the unity of the market. Consequently, the concept of 'measures for the approximation' of legislation must be interpreted as encompassing the Council's power to lay down measures relating to a specific product or class of products and, if necessary, individual measures concerning those products.

[38] So far as concerns the argument that the power thus conferred on the Commission goes beyond that which, in a federal state such as the Federal Republic of Germany, is enjoyed by the *Bund* in relation to the *Länder*, it must be borne in mind that the rules governing the relationship between the Community and its Member States are not the same as those which link the *Bund* with the *Länder*. Furthermore, the measures taken for the implementation of Article 100a of the Treaty are addressed to Member States and not to their constituent entities. Nor do the powers conferred on the Commission by Article 9 of the directive have any bearing upon the division of powers within the Federal Republic of Germany.

Note

The Court concluded that the legal base for the conferral of powers on the Commission by Article 9 was (what was then) Article 100a(1). It proceeded to dismiss further submissions based on violation of the principle of proportionality (*cf.* p. 61 above). Germany lost the case, but the very fact that it was prepared to bring the matter before the Court emphasises the sensitivity of issues of competence. In this ruling, the Court has left open the possibility for future use of Article 95 (p. 569 above), to build institutional structures at Community level, instead of simply relying on national systems. This is of critical importance to the question of the extent to which European market-building carries with it a need for European institution-building, which is highly significant in tracing the shaping of the institutional architecture of the Union. At the general level, this recurring issue of policy was addressed above at pp. 13, 342 and it will be considered once again in this chapter at p. 625 below.

(D) SUBSIDIARITY

The preceding subsection leads on to the debate about the *principle of subsidiarity*. The principle can be used to assess the appropriateness of a wide range of Community policy making.

Neither the Treaty of Rome nor the Single European Act contained explicit reference to the principle of subsidiarity. Its essence appears, however, in (what was) Article 130r(4), a provision inserted by the Single European Act.

4. The Community shall take action relating to the environment to the extent to which the objectives referred to in paragraph 1 *can be attained better at Community level than at the level of the individual Member States.* (emphasis added)

Note
The Maastricht Treaty introduced a broader formulation of the principle of subsidiarity. It was Article 3b EC and is now, in unamended form, Article 5 post-Amsterdam.

Article 5 EC

Article 5
The Community shall act within the limits of the powers conferred upon it by this Treaty and of the objectives assigned to it therein.

In areas which do not fall within its exclusive competence, the Community shall take action, in accordance with the principle of subsidiarity, only if and in so far as the objectives of the proposed action cannot be sufficiently achieved by the Member States and can therefore, by reason of the scale or effects of the proposed action, be better achieved by the Community.

Any action by the Community shall not go beyond what is necessary to achieve the objectives of this Treaty.

Note
The principle of subsidiarity has been cited in connection with the withdrawal of a number of legislative proposals in recent years. The Product Liability Directive (85/374) was examined in the preceding subsection. The Commission proposed that this liability system for the supply of defective goods should by complemented by a Directive governing liability for supply of defective services (COM (90) 482). In the Commission's report submitted to the Edinburgh European Council in December 1992, which reviewed existing and proposed legislation in the light of the subsidiarity principle, the Commission included the draft Directive in its list of excessively detailed instruments which required revision. It became plain that there was an absence of political will behind the proposed Directive. Eventually, in a Communication on new directions on the liability of suppliers of services (COM (94) 260), the Commission concluded that its 'proposal stands no chance of being adopted without sweeping changes which would risk voiding it of much of its substance'. It therefore withdrew it.

'Subsidiarity' has been employed as a slogan for challenging the expansion of Community activity. Yet the wording of Article 5 is directed

at identification of the appropriate level at which action should be taken. It
is not based on any entrenched preconception in favour of State action at the
expense of the Community. The nature and purpose of the principle of
subsidiarity in the context of allocating competences between States and
Community has been subjected to increasing scrutiny as the Community
continues to develop.

M. Wilke and H. Wallace, 'Subsidiarity: Approaches to Power-Sharing in the European Community' *RIIA Discussion Paper No. 27* (1990) pp. 21, 30–31

(Some footnotes omitted.)

The current British political debate links the principle of subsidiarity exclusively to the
debate about the European Community. Policy-makers and academics are attempting
to develop new definitions of the concept, recognizing that Roman Catholic sources
have supplied the basic foundations. It is not surprising, however, given that British
experience is different from Dutch or German, that a considerable confusion persists
when it comes to 'pinning down' the principle of subsidiarity.

In February 1990, the Legal Adviser of the Select Committee on European
Legislation of the House of Commons was asked to produce a note on subsidiarity.[23]
Mentioning the Madrid European Council and the different interventions on the
subject made by Jacques Delors, the note states that, in absence of a 'precise identity',
it is time 'to start with . . . a clean sheet of paper' as 'the concept of subsidiarity is
assigned a major constitutional role'. This last assumption necessitates a clarification
of the subsidiarity concept, which is 'clearly established as a manufactured term; and
accordingly there is ample scope for argument about the meaning to be ascribed to it
today'.

The note attempts to clarify the political function of the principle of subsidiarity.
The concept might facilitate more efficient and productive policy-making and implementation, thus following the exhortation given by the House of Lords Select
Committee on the EC, in its *Report on the Community Social Charter*, which stated that
'the Community should act only where objectives can be attained better at Community level than at the level of the individual Member States'?[26] If so, 'the Commission
is likely to take a more generous view of the benefits of Community action and of its
own capability than Member States may be disposed to do'. Does the principle of
subsidiarity serve the common interest, as mentioned the Commission's Programme
for 1989? Is the principle to add to democratic accountability, as Leon Brittan
suggested in his speech of 13 July 1989? If so, stated the note, 'little would be
appropriate for Community action because ordinarily Member States will be much
closer to the people affected'. Or is it Francis Maude's definition of subsidiarity that
should stand, namely 'that things should not be done at Community level unless they
cannot be done at national level'? This definition, the note concludes, 'would raise
substantially the barrier which the Community must cross'. Its author believed,

---

[23] See the House of Commons Foreign Affairs Committee, *The Operation of the Single European
Act: Minutes of Evidence,* 17 January 1990, Select Committee on European Legislation, House
of Commons, Session 1989–1990, pp. 68–72.
[26] House of Lords Select Committee of the European Communities, *Report on a Community
Social Charter,* House of Lords Paper 6 (1989–90), 5 December 1989, p, 26.

however, that the definition given by House of Lords Select Committee on the EC, using the wording 'attained better', would 'command the greatest measure of support'.

The issue which justifies these speculations, and which 'is in the air' remains: whether to incorporate the principle of subsidiarity into the EC Treaties. 'Any such suggestion', states the note 'would be received with alarm by lawyers brought up in the common law tradition. For if written in as a pure statement of principle, it would serve no purpose. And if written in as something more, it could do great harm'.

. . .

Subsidiarity has thus been introduced into the debate about EC institutions and policies. Its wide-ranging character has not, however, been derived from a concrete formulation of the principle. The Commission has over the last two years attempted to clarify, define and explore how it might help to identify the appropriate level of policy competence. But so far each case for its application has rested on a separate analysis, in relation to criteria of efficiency, proportionality and judicial soundness.

Jacques Delors has become the leading exponent of the principle of subsidiarity. His political, philosophical and social background suggests some familiarity with the concept. Through his readings of Emmanuel Mounier, Jacques Delors acquired a specific perception of the individual in society. Mounier, born in Grenoble in 1905 and founder of the prestigious review *Esprit*, became a major spokesman for the so-called *personalisme* movement, which sought to reconcile Christianity and socialism.

Jacques Delors was inspired by the idea that a global approach rather than particular solutions was needed to define the proper place of the individual in society. As a member of a community, the individual was enabled to participate in the creation of a growing socio-economical world. Finding and implementing the 'difficile équilibre entre la nécessaire affirmation de la volonté collective par l'Etat et le libre jeu de tous les centres de décisions' became a leading objective of Jacques Delors' political career. Any member of society is to be allocated a considerable autonomy in his activities, an idea cherished by Jacques Delors since his earliest participation in the semi-religious movement *Vie Nouvelle*. These thoughts were further elaborated during his first encounters with socialism, which focused on the development of the so-called 'communautés de base', as an alternative to the omnipresent state.

Jacques Delors links the principle of subsidiarity to the co-existence of federalism and sovereignty. Last autumn, speaking in Bruges, he declared:

j'ai souvent l'occasion de recourir au fédéralisme comme méthode, en y incluant le principe de subsidiarité. J'y vois l'inspiration pour concilier ce qui apparait à beaucoup comme inconciliable: l'emergence de l'Europe unie et la fidelité à notre nation, à notre patrie; la nécessité d'un pouvoir européen à la dimension des problémes de notre temps, et l'impératif vital de conserver nos nations et nos régions . . .'.

The scaffolding of European architecture offers the possibility 'd'un exercice en commun de la souveraineté, tout en respectant nos diversités et donc les principes de pluralisme et de subsidiarité'. He also insisted that the Commission 'ne doit jamais succomber à l'ivresse de ses pouvoirs' and, consequently, 'applique rigoureusement le principe de subsidiarité'. In the case of EMU 'le principe [de subsidiarité] est clair, il reste à en definir, en l'espèce, les modalités d'application'.

Leon Brittan, in his Granada lecture of November 1989, stated that it was 'impossible to set down in advance clear guidelines as to when the subsidiarity principle should apply'. Nevertheless if the EC is to prove a liberating influence and not a centralizing and corporatist one, we must further develop and apply the principle that decisions should be taken at the lowest appropriate level: as close as possible, that is, to the people who are affected by them.

There is a challenge involved here, Brittan believed, as

we should ask ourselves, particularly in the social domain, is this really a decision that needs to be taken at Community level? If it is not, the Community would be wise to set out the general objective, but leave it to the individual Member State to achieve that as they wish, according to their own traditions and their own laws.

Leon Brittan, a lawyer himself, argued that subsidiarity 'should not be seen as something for the theologians of Community law, but as something *intensely practical*: where to draw the dividing line between what is best done by the Community and what is best done by national governments'. Subsidiarity 'needs to be developed and applied with much more vigour in practice'.

Note

The frequently-observed British tendency to view European federalism as a centralising process may be corrected by a fuller understanding of the implications of the principle of subsidiarity. Indeed, far from leading inevitably to centralisation, Community development may have quite the reverse effect.

M. Wilke and H. Wallace, 'Subsidiarity: Approaches to Power-Sharing in the European Community' *RIIA Discussion Paper No. 27* (1990), p. 8

In addition it should be borne in mind that the concern of the German Länder is not about the balance of powers between the Community and the Member States, but about the impact on the regional level of government for a country with a federal constitution. The logic of their complaint is that the EC should not be empowered to make EC legislation in areas of Länder competence, unless the Länder themselves have endorsed the measure. One can envisage similar arguments being made in Belgium, Italy or Spain. To follow this logic would be enormously to complicate the EC process and would also set a model which could become an issue in other Member States with rather different internal arrangements. Thus within the UK one could envisage the supporters of Scottish devolution, who in any event can also plead differences between Scottish and English law, rushing to exploit the precedent. There is an important question here about whether this regional dimension should be recognized in any way at the EC level or left to the constitutional rules and political practice of individual Member States.

Note

The adoption of the principle of subsidiarity as a guide is only the starting point. As the above extracts suggest, immense problems surround the proper interpretation of the principle in particular circumstances. Once the decision had been taken at Maastricht in December 1991 formally to incorporate the principle into the Treaty as Article 3b of the EC Treaty (now Article 5 EC), debate began in earnest about its nature and purpose.

W. Robinson, 'The Court of Justice after Maastricht' in D. O'Keeffe and P. Twomey (eds), *Legal Issues of the Maastricht Treaty* (1994), 187–9

The principle of subsidiarity has been described as a 'national precedence',[43] a 'best level' test,[44] 'an anti-competitive arrangement among executive branches',[45] 'an elementary principle of good government'[46] and 'a principle of social organisation developed to be used in combination with other principles of collective and individual action'.[47] Any definition of 'subsidiarity' will therefore include an ideological under-pinning. It serves for the purposes of this article merely to cite the second paragraph of Article 3b as a working definition of the inherently imprecise principle:

> In areas which do not fall within its exclusive competence, the Community shall take action, in accordance with the principle of subsidiarity, only if and in so far as the objectives of the proposed action cannot be sufficiently achieved by the Member States and can therefore, by reason of the scale or effects of the proposed action, be better achieved by the Community.

Whilst it is clear therefore that all parties accept the binding nature of Article 3b EC, their purposes for such acceptance are markedly different. The political moti-vations range the *Länder*'s fear of the extension of Community responsibility into areas within their exclusive competence under the *Grundgesetz*, through the UK's desire to preserve 'sovereignty' at a national level to the introduction of subsidiarity as an acceptance of federalism. Article 3b has enabled national politicians to claim that the Treaty of European Union, and Community law, will serve their requirements. Clearly, the uniformity of interpretation which will arise from the Court of Justice's jurisprudence on the principle will not enable the expectations of all the Member States to be met. Professor Curtin's statement that 'subsidiarity is presented in terms capable of papering over any number of cracks and crevices in the structure of the Maastricht Treaty'[48] reflects the difference between the political and legal implications of the principle.

The Treaty on European Union has increased the use of qualified majority voting in the Council. This follows the precedent set by the Single European Act. The combination of varying political perceptions of the principle of subsidiarity and the increase in qualified majority voting is likely to result in litigation. Member States who argued, unsuccessfully, within the Council that the Community should not act on a particular matter may challenge the adopted legislation before the Court on the principle of subsidiarity. The Court of Justice will, seemingly inevitably, be drawn into political dispute resolution which has arisen within one institution, rather than between institutions. This may be regarded as the first significant difference from the Court's existing constitutional jurisprudence.

---

[43] Major, speech to the Conservative Group for Europe, 22 April 1993.
[44] Brittan, 'Institutional Developments of the European Community' (1992) *Public Law*, 567-579 at 574.
[45] Allott, 'Europe after Maastricht: Interim Report', First Report from the foreign Affairs Committee, HC 205, 1992-93, Ev at 51.
[46] MacKenzie-Stuart, 'Assessment of the view expressed and introduction to a panel discussion' in *Subsidiarity: the Challenge of Change* (1991), European Institute of Public Administration at 38.
[47] Wilke and Wallace, *Subsidiarity: Approaches to Power-Sharing in the European Community* (1990) at 11.
[48] Curtin, *The Irish Times*, 16 October 1992 at 16.

Secondly, the Court of Justice has determined the majority of its constitutional cases on the interpretation of the aim and content of the particular legislative act, as seen above, the text and spirit of the Treaties and the general principles of law. Challenges by Member States to enacted legislation on the principle of subsidiarity will not, however, seek to annul legislation on the determination of the aim and content of the measure itself, but upon the question whether those aims should be pursued at a Community level at all. Put another way, should those aims exist at all at the Community level within Community legislation?

The way a particular act is phrased will suggest that the Community is indeed both competent in that area and should enact legislation. The adopted act must state the reasons for its adoption. These will have been drafted in order to give effect to the wishes of the majority. The reasons for Community action will therefore be stated on the face of the act. The arguments of the dissenting voices will not appear. The content and aim of the act is therefore unlikely to assist the Court. The Court would consider the Treaty provisions upon which basis the act was adopted. Unless the act is *ultra vires*, the provision will provide jurisdiction for the Community to act, albeit concurrently with Member States. This is unlikely to provide guidance for the level of action. Similarly, the spirit of the Treaty has been interpreted, to date, as integrating action at a Community level in the pursuit of an 'ever closer union among the peoples of Europe'. The existing *acquis communautaire* and the drafting of the disputed act are unlikely to assist the Court. The applicants would, however, argue that the Community should not have acted at all. The general principle of subsidiarity will require the Court to 'step back' from the particular act and the existing *acquis communautaire* to consider the level at which the measure should have been adopted. This is an almost unprecedented task, which requires the Court to place constraints upon its methods of interpretation and to consider arguments based on a general principle against an adopted act and the spirit of the Treaty itself.

Note

William Robinson accurately predicts the emergence of *subsidiarity* in challenges to the validity of adopted legislation before the Court. The lack of clarity in such litigation thus far is instructive. In Case C-84/94 *UK* v *Council* [1996] ECR I-5755, the almost entirely unsuccessful challenge to the 'Working Time' Directive extracted at p. 52 above, the Court felt able to reject the argument based on subsidiarity 'at the outset'. Advocate-General Leger was more blunt: the UK 'created some confusion by regularly invoking the principle of subsidiarity in the course of the proceedings – without, however, relying on it as a ground of annulment – and seemingly equating it with the principle of proportionality'. The applicant was also unsuccessful in Case C-223/94 *Germany* v *Parliament and Council* [1997] ECR I-2304.

Question

'. . . the chief advantage of [subsidiarity] seems to be its capacity to mean all things to all interested parties – simultaneously' (Mary Robinson [when President of Ireland], 'Constitutional Shifts in Europe and the US: Learning from each other' (1996) 32 Stanford Jnl Int L 1, 10). Is this a good thing or a bad thing? Is this law or politics?

Further reading

For further reading, it is possible to refer to only a selection of the enormous range of comment which has been published in this area:

Bernard, N., 'The Future of European Economic Law in the Light of the Principle of Subsidiarity' (1996) 33 CML Rev 633.

Cass, D., 'The Word that Saves Maastricht? The Principle of Subsidiarity and the Division of Powers within the European Community' (1992) 29 CML Rev 1107.

Edwards, D., 'Fearing Federalism's Failure: Subsidiarity in the EU' (1996) 44 AJCL 537.

Emiliou, N., 'Subsidiarity: An Effective Barrier against "the Enterprises of Ambition"?' (1992) 17 EL Rev 383.

González, J. P., 'The Principle of Subsidiarity' (1995) 20 EL Rev 355.

Peterson, J., 'Subsidiarity: a Definition to Suit any Vision' (1994) 47 *Parliamentary Affairs* 116.

Timmermans, C., 'Subsidiarity and Transparency' (1999) 22 Fordham Intl Law Jnl 5106.

Wyatt, D., 'Is subsidiarity justiciable?' in O'Keeffe, D. (ed.), *Liber Amicorum Gordon Slynn* (2000).

In addition, several essays (not just those explicitly entitled as examinations of subsidiarity) in D. O'Keeffe and P. Twomey, *Legal Issues of the Maastricht Treaty* (1994) provide wide-ranging (and, instructively, far from harmonious!) discussion of subsidiarity. The general issue of competence allocation and identification of the appropriate respective contributions of the Community and the Member States to the evolution of the Community/Union is quite fundamental to any perspective on the future of Europe. Subsidiarity acts as a catchphrase for that debate and its high profile is accordingly hardly surprising. Its continued prominence is ensured by the attachment of a Protocol on the application of the principles of subsidiarity and proportionality to the EC Treaty by the Treaty of Amsterdam. Does this Protocol help you to grasp the intended impact of subsidiarity on the EC's institutional culture?

PROTOCOL ON THE APPLICATION OF THE PRINCIPLES OF SUBSIDIARITY AND PROPORTIONALITY

THE HIGH CONTRACTING PARTIES,

DETERMINED to establish the conditions for the application of the principles of subsidiarity and proportionality enshrined in Article 3b of the Treaty establishing the European Community with a view to defining more precisely the criteria for applying them and to ensure their strict observance and consistent implementation by all institutions;

WISHING to ensure that decisions are taken as closely as possible to the citizens of the Union;

TAKING ACCOUNT of the Interinstitutional Agreement of 25 October 1993 between the European Parliament, the Council and the Commission on procedures for implementing the principle of subsidiarity;

HAVE CONFIRMED that the conclusions of the Birmingham European Council on 16 October 1992 and the overall approach to the application of the subsidiarity principle agreed by the European Council meeting in Edinburgh on 11–12 December 1992 will continue to guide the action of the Union's institutions as well as the development of the application of the principle of subsidiarity, and, for this purpose,

HAVE AGREED UPON the following provisions which shall be annexed to the Treaty establishing the European Community:

(1)   In exercising the powers conferred on it, each institution shall ensure that the principle of subsidiarity is complied with. It shall also ensure compliance with the principle of proportionality, according to which any action by the Community shall not go beyond what is necessary to achieve the objectives of the Treaty.

(2)   The application of the principles of subsidiarity and proportionality shall respect the general provisions and the objectives of the Treaty, particularly as regards the maintaining in full of the acquis communautaire and the institutional balance; it shall not affect the principles developed by the Court of Justice regarding the relationship between national and Community law, and it should take into account Article F(4) of the Treaty on European Union, according to which 'the Union shall provide itself with the means necessary to attain its objectives and carry through its policies'.

(3)   The principle of subsidiarity does not call into question the powers conferred on the European Community by the Treaty, as interpreted by the Court of Justice. The criteria referred to in the second paragraph of Article 3b of the Treaty shall relate to areas for which the Community does not have exclusive competence. The principle of subsidiarity provides a guide as to how those powers are to be exercised at the Community level. Subsidiarity is a dynamic concept and should be applied in the light of the objectives set out in the Treaty. It allows Community action within the limits of its powers to be expanded where circumstances so require, and conversely, to be restricted or discontinued where it is no longer justified.

(4)   For any proposed Community legislation, the reasons on which it is based shall be stated with a view to justifying its compliance with the principles of subsidiarity and proportionality; the reasons for concluding that a Community objective can be better achieved by the Community must be substantiated by qualitative or, wherever possible, quantitative indicators.

(5)   For Community action to be justified, both aspects of the subsidiarity principle shall be met: the objectives of the proposed action cannot be sufficiently achieved by Member States' action in the framework of their national constitutional system and can therefore be better achieved by action on the part of the Community.

The following guidelines should be used in examining whether the abovementioned condition is fulfilled:

— the issue under consideration has transnational aspects which cannot be satisfactorily regulated by action by Member States;

— actions by Member States alone or lack of Community action would conflict with the requirements of the Treaty (such as the need to correct distortion of competition or avoid disguised restrictions on trade or strengthen economic and social cohesion) or would otherwise significantly damage Member States' interests;

— action at Community level would produce clear benefits by reason of its scale or effects compared with action at the level of the Member States.

(6)   The form of Community action shall be as simple as possible, consistent with satisfactory achievement of the objective of the measure and the need for effective enforcement. The Community shall legislate only to the extent necessary. Other things being equal, directives should be preferred to regulations and framework

directives to detailed measures. Directives as provided for in Article 189 of the Treaty, while binding upon each Member State to which they are addressed as to the result to be achieved, shall leave to the national authorities the choice of form and methods.

(7) Regarding the nature and the extent of Community action, Community measures should leave as much scope for national decision as possible, consistent with securing the aim of the measure and observing the requirements of the Treaty. While respecting Community law, care should be taken to respect well established national arrangements and the organisation and working of Member States' legal systems. Where appropriate and subject to the need for proper enforcement; Community measures should provide Member States with alternative ways to achieve the objectives of the measures.

(8) Where the application of the principle of subsidiarity leads to no action being taken by the Community, Member States are required in their action to comply with the general rules laid down in Article 5 of the Treaty, by taking all appropriate measures to ensure fulfilment of their obligations under the Treaty and by abstaining from any measure which could jeopardise the attainment of the objectives of the Treaty.

(9) Without prejudice to its right of initiative, the Commission should:
— except in cases of particular urgency or confidentiality, consult widely before proposing legislation and, wherever appropriate, publish consultation documents;
— justify the relevance of its proposals with regard to the principle of subsidiarity: whenever necessary, the explanatory memorandum accompanying a proposal will give details in this respect. The financing of Community action in whole or in part from the Community budget shall require an explanation;
— take duly into account the need for any burden, whether financial or administrative, falling upon the Community, national governments, local authorities, economic operators and citizens, to be minimised and proportionate to the objective to be achieved;
— submit an annual report to the European Council, the European Parliament and the Council on the application of Article 3b of the Treaty. This annual report shall also be sent to the Committee of the Regions and to the Economic and Social Committee.

(10) The European Council shall take account of the Commission report referred to in the fourth indent of point 9 within the report on the progress achieved by the Union which it is required to submit to the European Parliament in accordance with Article D of the Treaty on European Union.

(11) While fully observing the procedures applicable, the European Parliament and the Council shall, as an integral part of the overall examination of Commission proposals, consider their consistency with Article 3b of the Treaty. This concerns the original Commission proposal as well as amendments which the European Parliament and the Council envisage making to the proposal.

(12) In the course of the procedures referred to in Articles 189b and 189c of the Treaty, the European Parliament shall be informed of the Council's position on the application of Article 3b of the Treaty, by way of a statement of the reasons which led the Council to adopt its common position. The Council shall inform the European Parliament of the reasons on the basis of which all or part of a Commission proposal is deemed to be inconsistent with Article 3b of the Treaty.

(13) Compliance with the principle of subsidiarity shall be reviewed in accordance with the rules laid down by the Treaty.

Question
The idea of subsidiarity, if not the word, has been familiar for decades in the Community. Consider, for example, how you might use subsidiarity to analyse:

(a)   The division of function between national and Community courts under the Article 234 preliminary reference procedure (Chapter 4).

(b)   The distinction between the Regulation and the Directive under Article 249; p. 40 above).

(c)   The scope of Article 28, as illuminated by the rulings of the European Court in *Torfaen* v *B & Q plc* (Case 145/88); *Stoke-on-Trent and Norwich City Councils* v *B & Q* (Case C-169/91); and *Keck and Mithouard* (Joined Cases C-267 and C-268/91) (Chapter 8).

(d)   The structure of administration and enforcement of Directive 92/59 on General Product Safety and the Court's ruling in Case C-359/92 (in which, at para. 38, it declines to engage in 'comparative federalism') (p. 601 above).

(e)   The enforcement of competition law envisaged in the Commission's Notice of February 1993 relating to cooperation with national courts; and in that of November 1997 relating to cooperation with national competition authorities; and in the 1999 White Paper on Modernisation (pp. 530, 538 and 527 above).

To what extent is it possible for the European Court to use subsidiarity under Article 5 as an enforceable legal rule in adjudication in these or other areas? Do you agree with the Commission's view that 'subsidiarity cannot be reduced to a set of procedural rules; it is primarily a state of mind' (COM (93) 545)? What, then, of the Amsterdam Protocol? You might also consider the Commission's tart comment in its first annual report on the subsidiarity principle that 'one cannot help observing that principle and practice are often far apart with Member States meeting within the Council often adopting positions on individual cases at variance with their respect in principle for Article 3b' (COM (94) 533; see subsequently COM (98) 715, COM (99) 562).

(E) COMMUNITY SOCIAL POLICY

Why does the Community possess a social policy? In many areas there is much controversy about the need for harmonisation and/or the form it should take. However, both a social protection rationale and a market integration rationale for social policy may be extracted from Article 2 of the Treaty (p. 168 above).

The next extract explains the policy choices more fully. It uses the numbers for the Treaty Articles applicable pre-Amsterdam. The post-Amsterdam provisions, which are much amended, are set out at p. 622 below.

Edward Moxon-Browne, 'Social Europe' in J. Lodge (ed.),
The European Community and the Challenge of the Future
(2nd ed., 1993) pp. 152–7

Introduction

The origins of the Community's social policy can be traced back to the European Coal and Steel Community (ECSC) where special provisions were made for the re-training of coal miners who had been made redundant as a result of the inevitable closure of the less competitive pits. In the Rome Treaty, social policy is almost entirely conceived in terms of correcting distortions resulting from the operation of the common market/customs union. Thus 'free movement of workers' (Article 48) is logically complemented by the increasing harmonisation of social security provision throughout the Community (Article 121); and the guarantee of equal pay for men and women in Article 119 had as its underlying motive the avoidance of cheap labour being used to secure competitive advantage in free-market conditions.

At the outset, therefore, the EC's social policy was essentially ancillary and corrective: its aim was to render more acceptable the occasionally harsh realities of market forces. From about 1972 onwards, the concerns of social policy became less passive and increasingly comprehensive in scope. The evolution of social policy within the EC reflects an increasing concern with the inhabitants of the EC as individuals in an increasingly diverse panoply of roles: as unemployed, as women, as workers, as handicapped, as students, as consumers and as citizens of an emergent political union. Social policy, therefore, has been transformed from being merely reactive to a situation today where it has become one of the more pervasive concerns of the EC and where, in contrast to its earlier technical and uncontroversial nature, it has become politically sensitive by expanding awkwardly into the domain of domestic politics and challenging party political dogma.

Today, the advent of the Single European Market has imposed new demands and new priorities on the EC's social policy. In his opening address to the European Parliament, Delors called for a 'social Europe' to support the achievement of the single market for goods and services. Behind the Commission's thinking is the view that the single market creates new conditions requiring regulation of social policy. In the absence of Community norms, for example, firms might be tempted to locate in parts of the EC where social security legislation is more lax and, by implication, less costly, thus distorting the conditions of free competition. If the single market is to work effectively, the European workforce must be considered as integrated and mobile, implying common conditions of employment, mutual recognition of qualifications and equal benefits for workers and their families. The acquisition of skills in the new technologies must keep pace with competitors in Japan and the US: hence the development of EC-sponsored programmes in the areas of training and research.

From the Rome Treaty to the SEA

However, before examining the array of social policy issues facing the EC today, it is worth reminding ourselves, briefly, of the extent to which social policy has evolved from the constraints of the Rome Treaty to its broader interpretation in the Single European Act of 1986. As we have seen already, the Rome Treaty had foundations to build on in the field of social policy. The High Authority of the ECSC was able to give grants for the re-training of redundant workers in the coal and steel industries; and in the Rome Treaty itself there are specific commitments to improve health and safety at work (Article 118), harmonise social security provision for migrant workers

(Article 121) and achieve equality between males and females in the workplace (Article 119). The Rome Treaty also established the Social Fund (Article 123, 128), but its functions were limited to (i) vocational retraining or resettlement allowances and (ii) the maintenance of income levels of workers temporarily out of work. The Fund financed up to half the cost of these schemes. The 1960s were a period of full employment, rising wages in real terms and growth in GNP of the Six. At the same time, it is difficult to describe the modest advances made, or indeed the modest initiatives undertaken, as a social policy. By the end of the 1960s it was still true that social policy played a relatively minor role in the EC's development, and the belief still held sway that market forces would iron out the discrepancies between social groups. However, despite the aspirations of Article 119, for example, the wages gap between male and female workers did not diminish and despite the achievement, formally, of the common market in 1968, real labour mobility was still frustrated by administrative barriers and legislative differences between the member states.

From the time of the 1969 Hague Summit, and more particularly with the prospect of three new member states joining the EC in 1973, it became clear that free-market forces were an insufficient bulwark against inflation, monetary instability and socioeconomic divergence. The Paris Summit of 1972 proved to be a turning-point when the assembled leaders of the Nine committed themselves to establishing a Regional Fund and a Social Action Programme. The latter was adopted in 1974 and was directed towards three major goals: the attainment of full employment in the EC, the improvement of living and working conditions and the increased involvement of management and labour in the economic and social decisions of the EC. Even if the 1970s had not proved to be a decade of monetary instability and high inflation, these targets would have been difficult to attain. As it was, they had to be tackled against a sombre background of rising unemployment. The numbers out of work in the EC rose from 2.6 million in 1973 to 5.2 million in 1976 and 6.5 million in 1980.

The European Social Fund (ESF) was to be the principal vehicle through which unemployment was confronted. In 1972, its role was broadened in such a way that it came to deal with the effects of other EC policies. Thus it came to co-finance the vocational training of persons wishing or forced to leave agriculture or the textile and clothing sector; and, second, to overcome the difficulties experienced by certain backward regions or disadvantaged groups in the population such as migrant workers (from 1974), young unemployed (from 1975), women (1978) and handicapped people. Despite quadrupling its budget between 1973 and 1979, the ESF was unable to reverse the rising tide of unemployment which continued unabated until the end of the 1980s. In 1983, in a further attempt to deploy the Fund's resources more effectively, a new set of priorities was earmarked: 75 per cent of funds were now to be concentrated on the young (under twenty-five) unemployed, and 40 per cent of funds available for operations of a general nature were to go to the least-favoured regions of the Community, among them Northern Ireland, Greece and the Italian Mezzogiorno (all of Portugal and most of Spain were added to this category on their accession in 1986).

In 1975, to complement the work of the ESF in the fight against unemployment, the EC created two institutions. The European Centre for the Development of Vocational Training (Cedefop) is located in Berlin and has a quadripartite administrative structure consisting of representatives of governments, employers, workers and the Commission. The emphasis of its work is on documentation, information and research. Its sister institution the European Foundation for the Improvement of Living and Working Conditions, was established in Dublin and is also mainly a research body focusing on questions connected with working conditions and work organisation, improvement of the environment and the distribution in time and space of human activities.

While losing the battle against unemployment, the Commission succeeded in the 1970s in implementing Directives that aimed to protect those in employment. In 1975, a Directive designed to mitigate the effects of collective redundancies required employers to consult workers through staff representatives (Directive 75/129/EEC); two years later saw a Directive safeguarding employees' rights in the event of a transfer of company ownership (77/187/EEC); and in 1980 the protection of employees in the event of their employer becoming insolvent was the subject of a further Directive (80/987/EEC).

If the 1970s were a time of economic despondency, the decade also saw the EC's ideals under threat. The rejection of membership by the Norwegians in 1972, and the 'renegotiation' of their membership by the British in 1974–5 caused the Commission to become more self-critical. The impact of the oil price 'shock' in 1973–4 and the failure of the monetary 'snake' experiment by 1977 added to the general mood of pessimism. It was in these circumstances that the Community's social policy assumed an important political role: it was intended partly as a way of bolstering the faltering legitimacy of the EC's institutions. In this sense, it mattered less what the social policy actually achieved in redistributive terms, if the broad thrust was seen to be a concern with the quality of life of ordinary citizens and not simply the creation of wealth for a privileged few. By the end of the 1970s, one writer was able to see social policy as:

. . . no longer concerned with rectifying and redressing negative efforts of integration. Instead, it provides the context in which a new image of the EEC may be articulated and projected. The awareness-creating and image-building tactics associated with the social policy may well be more important than the actual 'goods' disbursed to relatively small numbers of EEC citizens under this policy; and may well be a way of promoting transnational socio-psychological community formation and increasing public support for – or at least lessening public disaffection from – the EEC. [Lodge, 1978: 132]

The Single European Act
The SEA extended the EC's formal powers in the field of social policy. In Article 118b the 'Val Duchesse' idea is expressed as a 'dialogue between management and labour at European level which could, if the two sides consider it desirable, lead to relations based on agreement'. In Articles 130a–e the goal of economic and social cohesion becomes an important determining theme for a range of Community policies for example the common agricultural policy, regional policy and loans from the EIB. The SEA thus goes much further than the Rome Treaty in acknowledging (a) the disparities between regions and (b) the need to tackle these disparities by harnessing in a mutually reinforcing manner the EC's policies.

The major reform of the structural funds which followed the signing of the SEA not only doubled the resources allocated to them in the period up to 1993 but also ensured that they were deployed in such a way as to concentrate on the groups in society, and the regions in the EC, that were most seriously disadvantaged. At the same time, Marin (the Social Affairs Commissioner) presented, in January 1988, a document that marked out the evolution of the 'social dimension of the internal market'. It proposed a number of measures, some of them new, that collectively sought to balance the purely economic objectives of the Single Market with concern for employees, their families and the rights of the individual. Social policy became politicised partly because it now sought to appease the fears of those countries, and those groups in society, who felt they had the most to lose from the successful completion of the Single Market, and partly because it touches sensitive issues, like working hours and maternity leave, which affect both sides of industry and worry both, since the trade unions feel that some proposals do not go far enough, and management fear that they are too restrictive.

In May 1989, the Commission published its first draft of the document that became known as the Social Charter, a document that attempted to define in more detail the principles enshrined in the SEA. While the social policy sections of the SEA had been couched in deliberately cautious language, the Charter was more precise and covered a number of issues that were not specifically mentioned, or even hinted at, in the SEA. The Charter was, however, a framework for future Community legislation. Social policy had been fairly low key in the SEA so as to guarantee its acceptance by all member states, but the Charter's acceptability was assumed as the trade-off for the inclusion of social policy, *sotto voce*, in the SEA. In June 1989 the Charter was discussed at the Madrid European Council Summit but was rejected by Britain. The Charter was then amended in the hope of winning British approval but to no avail. The British government refused to accept the final version of the Charter at the Strasbourg Summit in December 1989.

Although the British government appeared to be alone in its opposition to the Charter, it is worth remembering that other governments had reservations about some of the items in the document and were happy to let the British take most of the flak. In any event, British opposition was part of a broader antipathy towards any strengthening of the EC social policy. Despite signing the SEA which committed the signatories to the extension of social policy, the British have consistently opposed all attempts to introduce new Community policies in the social field. In 1989, the UK was the only Community country to oppose the mandatory printing of health warnings on cigarette packets despite the fact that, and perhaps because, such warnings were already required by British law; and the Lingua programme was successfully excluded from secondary schools, despite the low level of foreign language competence evident in Britain.

British opposition to the extension of EC social policy stems partly from an ideological belief that the unfettered operation of the free market will itself guarantee prosperity and employment – a belief, incidentally, that mirrors the thinking behind Article 117 of the Rome Treaty – and partly from a conviction that trade-union power, already successfully curbed by the cumulative impact of industrial relations legislation, would enjoy an unwelcome renaissance.

The inclusion of social policy in the SEA was, however, more than window-dressing: it was perceived as an integral part of the process towards the completion of the single market. In particular, if divergent conditions of employment were allowed to persist, there was a risk that governments with inferior standards would not only exploit workers but could also derive cost advantages by spending less on employee welfare. This so-called 'social dumping' would encourage multinational firms to concentrate their investment in parts of the EC where 'social costs' were lower. At the same time, leaving social policy largely in the hands of national governments would continue the fragmentation of the EC labour market in terms of social security provision, training schemes and measures designed to combat unemployment. If the single market is to mean anything, it must mean that workers are able to move freely between member states: but this will not be a reality as long as qualifications for employment, and conditions in employment, vary significantly between different parts of the Community.

The impact of Maastricht

In the Maastricht Treaty, social policy was given more publicity than might have been the case because it became the issue on which Britain again parted company with the other member states; and this disagreement led to a unique solution: the other eleven member states agreed a protocol on social policy between them whereby they would make progress 'borrowing' the EC's institutions to do so. The isolation of the UK on the social chapter of the Maastricht Treaty was simply the reflection of very different traditions and policies in the field of labour law. Britain is unusual in the EC in the degree of which hours of work, overtime, holidays and employment contracts are left to employers or collective bargaining (Towers, 1992: 85). Among other member states, however, there was the suspicion that the UK, by opting out of the Maastricht section on social policy, was in fact seeking an unfair advantage over its partners: 'A UK outside the Social Chapter but within the EC tariff wall could become very attractive to inward investors capable of raising productivity to European levels without paying the full labour cost price' (Towers, 1992: 83).

In other, more important, respects Maastricht broke new ground in the field of social policy. First, the scope of social policy was considerably broadened. The ESF will be expected to take into account the goal of 'economic and social cohesion', thus widening the areas in which it may intervene. A new legal basis is provided for covering education and public health: in the case of the former the emphasis is on promoting the European dimension in national educational curricula, and in the case of the latter the aim is simply to exploit the advantages of transnational co-operation. Since the combating of 'social exclusion' (for example from the labour force) is written into EC objectives, EC policies can now be geared more openly towards the tackling of both unemployment and poverty.

Although Maastricht undoubtedly reinforces the position of social policy within the framework of the EC's development, it also complicates it. The Prime Minister, John Major, was under strong political pressure from within his own party to bring back visible evidence of having secured a treaty favourable to Britain. What *The Economist* (14 December 1991) referred to as the 'unprecedented institutional fix' relating to the Social Chapter of the treaty, coupled with the loophole for Britain on EMU, provided this evidence. The resulting formula may have long-term consequences for the EC inasmuch as other member states in the future may adopt an *à la carte* attitude towards extensions of the EC's competence. A protocol attached to the Treaty states that eleven countries will make social policy legislation on the basis of the Maastricht text. The Commission, the EP and the Court of Justice play the roles they would in normal EC legislation, with their British members playing a full part. However, Britain will be absent from the Council of Ministers so that a qualified majority of forty-four votes out of sixty-six instead of the usual fifty-four out of seventy-six votes will be required [cf. p. 8 above]. In future, if the Commission proposes a new piece of legislation in the social policy field, it will be dealt with either on the basis of the Rome Treaty (plus SEA) or by the Eleven based on the Maastricht procedure. Inevitably, in some areas, there will be ambiguity as to whether new legislation is to be dealt with under the normal or 'Maastricht' procedure. Social security issues will continue to be dealt with on the basis of unanimity, while those relating to equality between men and women will be decided on the basis of a qualified majority. Thus future progress in the social policy arena is likely to be piecemeal, uneven and disconnected; and much will hinge on the legal interpretation of draft proposals and, in particular, the legal basis on which they are to be processed. A separate issue, and one that is not yet resolved is the status of legislation adopted by the Eleven (under the Maastricht procedure); and any resolution of the issue by the ECJ in a test case could have far-reaching implications for the future development of the EC's social policy. The progress of social policy, so far, has clearly been patchy . . .

Notes

1. The references in the above extract are to the following:

Lodge 'Towards a Human Union: EEC Social Policy and European Integration' (1978) *British Journal of International Studies*, 4, 107–134;

Towers, 'Two Speed ahead: social Europe and the UK after Maastricht' (1992) *Industrial Relations Journal*, 23(2), 83–9.

See also M. Wise and R. Gibb, *Single Market to Social Europe* (1993).
2. The field of sex discrimination has generated much debate about the nature of the Community's role in pursuing social policy. The Community has developed its policy in this area primarily under what was Article 119 and is now, in amended form, Article 141 post-Amsterdam, which concerns equal pay, and a range of associated secondary legislation.

Article 141 EC

Article 141
Each Member State shall ensure that the principle of equal pay for male and female workers for equal work or work of equal value is applied.

Note
The Court explained the double function of what was then Article 119 in *Defrenne* v *SABENA* (Case 43/75) (on which see p. 95 above).

Defrenne v SABENA (Case 43/75)
[1976] ECR 455
Court of Justice of the European Communities

[8]   Article 119 pursues a double aim.

[9] First, in the light of the different stages of the development of social legislation in the various Member-States, the aim of Article 119 is to avoid a situation in which undertakings established in States which have actually implemented the principle of equal pay suffer a competitive disadvantage in intra-Community competition as compared with undertakings established in States which have not yet eliminated discrimination against women workers as regards pay.

[10] Secondly, this provision forms part of the social objectives of the Community, which is not merely an economic union, but is at the same time intended, by common action, to ensure social progress and seek the constant improvement of the living and working conditions of their peoples, as is emphasised by the Preamble to the Treaty. . . .

Note
The Court has been extremely active in extending the scope of the principle of equality. The Treaty is capable of prohibiting not only direct but also indirect discrimination on grounds of sex.

Jenkins v Kingsgate (Clothing Productions) Ltd (Case 96/80)
[1981] ECR 911
Court of Justice of the European Communities

The Court was asked whether a difference in pay rates between part-time and full-time work may violate (what was then) Article 119 where the part-time workers are mainly female.

[10] The answer to the questions thus understood is that the purpose of Article 119 is to ensure the application of the principle of equal pay for men and women for the same work. The differences in pay prohibited by that provision are therefore exclusively those based on the difference of the sex of the workers. Consequently the fact that part-time work is paid at an hourly rate lower than pay for full-time work does not amount *per se* to discrimination prohibited by Article 119 provided that the hourly rates are applied to workers belonging to either category without distinction based on sex.

[11] If there is no such distinction, therefore, the fact that work paid at time rates is remunerated at an hourly rate which varies according to the number of hours worked per week does not offend against the principle of equal pay laid down in Article 119 of the Treaty in so far as the difference in pay between part-time work and full-time work is attributable to factors which are objectively justified and are in no way related to any discrimination based on sex.

[12] Such may be the case, in particular, when by giving hourly rates of pay which are lower for part-time work than those for full-time work the employer is endeavouring, on economic grounds which may be objectively justified, to encourage full-time work irrespective of the sex of the worker.

[13] By contrast, if it is established that a considerably smaller percentage of women than of men perform the minimum number of weekly working hours required in order to be able to claim the full-time hourly rate of pay, the inequality in pay will be contrary to Article 119 of the Treaty where, regard being had to the difficulties encountered by women in arranging to work that minimum number of hours per week, the pay policy of the undertaking in question cannot be explained by factors other than discrimination based on sex.

Note
The ability objectively to justify indirect discrimination is a theme of substantive Community law. See, e.g., p. 231 above on Article 90.

The secondary legislation in this area comprises *inter alia*:

Directive 75/117 – equal pay for work of equal value
Directive 76/207 – equal treatment for men and women
Directive 79/7 – equal treatment in respect of social security
Directive 86/378 – equal treatment in occupational pension schemes
Directive 86/613 – equal treatment for the self-employed.

Inadequate implementation of these Directives at national level has given rise to many cases in which litigants have sought to rely on their direct effect. Some of these cases are dealt with in Chapter 3 because they have yielded much of constitutional interest. At the substantive level, however, they are also important cases relating to the scope of the Community's social policy. Several cases in this area have been criticised as instances of the Court treading in areas which should be left to the legislator, Community or national. See, e.g., *Rinner-Kuhn* v *FWW GmbH* (Case 171/88) [1989] ECR 2743; *Barber* v *GRE* (Case C-262/88) [1990] ECR I-1889 (on which see, e.g., D. Curtin, 'Scalping the Community Legislator' (1990) 27 CML Rev 475). The Court's approach is, however, widely regarded as rather erratic and it is also possible to identify decisions that have attracted criticism for their reticence to exercise control over perceived discrimination, thereby undermining the construction of an effective equality law. See, e.g., *Enderby v Frenchay Health Authority and the Secretary of State for Health* (Case C–127/92) [1993] ECR I–5535; *Maria Van den Akker v Stichting Shell Pensioenfonds* (Case C–28/93) [1994] ECR I–4527; and critique by E. Whiteford (1995) 32 CML Rev 801; H. Fenwick [1995/1] Euro Public Law 331; H. Fenwick and T. Hervey (1995) 32 CML Rev 443. The law is too elaborate for in-depth examination here; see generally R. Nielsen and E. Szyszczak, *The Social Dimension of the European Community* (3rd ed., 1997), C. Barnard, *EC Employment Law* (1996); T. Hervey and D. O'Keeffe, *Sex Equality Law in the EU* (1996).

A similarly ambiguous pattern of judicial readiness to develop the principle of equality may be detected in the contrasting decisions in *P v S and Cornwall County Council* (Case C–13/94) [1996] ECR I–2143 and *Grant v South West Trains Ltd* (Case C–249/96) [1998] ECR I–621. In the former the Court felt able to bring discrimination against transsexuals within the scope of EC sex discrimination law under the Equal Treatment Directive 76/207, but in the latter discrimination on the grounds of sexual orientation was treated as falling outwith the scope of protection under what was then Article 119 EC. For comment see, e.g., E. Ellis, 'Recent Developments in European Community Sex Equality Law' (1998) 35 CML Rev 379; C. Barnard, 'The Principle of Equality in the Community context: *P*, *Grant*, *Kalanke* and *Marschall*: Four Uneasy Bedfellows' (1998) 57 CLJ 352. In *Grant* (Case C–249/96), the Court referred to the prospects for legislative action to bring such discrimination within the scope of conduct prohibited by Community law. The relevant provision was an Amsterdam innovation, not yet in force at the time the Court decided *Grant*. It is now Article 13, EC and proposals have been advanced by the Commission for legislation to combat discrimination based on sex, racial or ethnic origin, religion or belief, disability, age or sexual orientation. For discussion of the potential role of Article 13, see C. Barnard, 'Article 13: through the looking glass of Union Citizenship', in D. O'Keeffe and P. Twomey (eds), *Legal Issues of the Amsterdam Treaty* (Hart Publishing, 1999), Ch. 22; L. Flynn, 'The implications of Article 13 – after Amsterdam, will some forms of discrimination be more equal than others?, (1999) 36 CML Rev 1127; L. Waddington, 'Testing the Limits of the EC Treaty Article on non-discrimination' (1999) 28 ILJ 133.

A firm in State A which is able to underpay its female workers enjoys a competitive advantage over a firm in State B which is obliged by law to pay its female workers the same rate as its men. Yet it may be argued that such differences, far from being undesirable distortions, are the very lifeblood of the competitive structure of the Community. Harmonisation is undesirable, for it suppresses national preference. The operation of the market is stifled by such regulation.

Such arguments have been fundamental to the intense debate about how much further the social policy of the Community should intrude on national competence.

At Maastricht, there proved to be an irreconcilable gulf between the United Kingdom and its partners. The result was a Protocol and an Agreement annexed to the EC Treaty. The election of a Labour government in the UK in May 1997 as consigned the Maastricht pattern to history via the Amsterdam Treaty (below), but its extraordinary character deserves brief attention. As already mentioned in the extract at p. 617 above, this was, in Community law terms, odd indeed. It was widely described as the UK's 'opt-out' from deeper EC social policy-making, although a strict reading might label it as an 'opt-in' by the other 11 (now 14) Member States. Whichever formulation is preferred, the structure envisaged the uneven development of social policy among the 12 (now 15) Member States of the Community.

Protocol on social policy

THE HIGH CONTRACTING PARTIES,

NOTING that eleven Member States, that is to say the Kingdom of Belgium, the Kingdom of Denmark, the Federal Republic of Germany, the Hellenic Republic, the Kingdom of Spain, the French Republic, Ireland, the Italian Republic, the Grand Duchy of Luxembourg, the Kingdom of the Netherlands, the Portuguese Republic, wish to continue along the path laid down in the 1989 Social Charter; that they have adopted among themselves an Agreement to this end; that this Agreement is annexed to this Protocol; that this Protocol and the said Agreement are without prejudice to the provisions of this Treaty, particularly those which relate to social policy which constitute an integral part of the 'acquis communautaire':

1. Agree to authorise those eleven Member States to have recourse to the institutions, procedures and mechanisms of the Treaty for the purposes of taking among themselves and applying as far as they are concerned the acts and decisions required for giving effect to the above-mentioned Agreement.

2. The United Kingdom of Great Britain and Northern Ireland shall not take part in the deliberations and the adoption by the Council of Commission proposals made on the basis of this Protocol and the above-mentioned Agreement.

By way of derogation from Article 148(2) of the Treaty, acts of the Council which are made pursuant to this Protocol and which must be adopted by a qualified majority shall be deemed to be so adopted if they have received at least forty-four votes in favour. The unanimity of the members of the Council, with the exception of the United Kingdom of Great Britain and Northern Ireland, shall be necessary for acts of the Council which must be adopted unanimously and for those amending the Commission proposal.

Acts adopted by the Council and any financial consequences other than administrative costs entailed for the institutions shall not be applicable to the United Kingdom of Great Britain and Northern Ireland.

3. This Protocol shall be annexed to the Treaty establishing the European Community.

Further reading

Deakin, S., 'Social Policy in Search of a Role: Integration, Cohesion and Citizenship' in A. Caiger and D. Floudas, *1996 Onwards* (1996).

McGlynn, C., 'An Exercise in Futility: the practical effects of the social policy opt-out' (1998) 49 NILQ 60.

Sciarra, S., 'Social Values and the Multiple Sources of European Social Law' (1995) 1 Euro Law Jnl 60.

Szyszczak, E., 'Future Directions in European Union Social Policy Law' (1995) 24 ILJ 19.

Whiteford, E., 'Social Policy after Maastricht' (1993) 18 EL Rev 202.

Note

The new route offered by the Protocol-plus-Agreement was used sparingly. Few Directives were adopted. This type of 'flexibility' within the EU appeared to be more symbol than reality. The Labour government, having taken power in the UK in May 1997, was receptive the following month in Amsterdam to the abandonment of this two-speed pattern. Accordingly, the modestly ambitious social policy arrangements found in the Protocol-plus-Agreement were amalgamated with the existing, and in part modified, long-standing provisions on social policy found in the Treaty 'proper'. They have become Chapter 1, 'Social Provisions', of Title XI, 'Social Policy, Education, Vocational Training and Youth', comprising Articles 136–145 of the re-numbered Treaty. In this sphere, 'variable integration' is at an end.

TITLE XI   SOCIAL POLICY, EDUCATION, VOCATIONAL TRAINING AND YOUTH

CHAPTER 1   SOCIAL PROVISIONS

Article 136

The Community and the Member States, having in mind fundamental social rights such as those set out in the European Social Charter signed at Turin on 18 October 1961 and in the 1989 Community Charter of the Fundamental Social Rights of Workers, shall have as their objectives the promotion of employment, improved living and working conditions, so as to make possible their harmonisation while the improvement is being maintained, proper social protection, dialogue between management and labour, the development of human resources with a view to lasting high employment and the combating of exclusion.

To this end the Community and the Member States shall implement measures which take account of the diverse forms of national practices, in particular in the field of contractual relations, and the need to maintain the competitiveness of the Community economy.

They believe that such a development will ensue not only from the functioning of the common market, which will favour the harmonisation of social systems, but also from the procedures provided for in this Treaty and from the approximation of provisions laid down by law, regulation or administrative action.

Article 137

1.   With a view to achieving the objectives of Article 136, the Community shall support and complement the activities of the Member States in the following fields:
—   improvement in particular of the working environment to protect workers' health and safety;
—   working conditions;
—   the information and consultation of workers;
—   the integration of persons excluded from the labour market, without prejudice to Article 150;

— equality between men and women with regard to labour market opportunities and treatment at work.

2. To this end, the Council may adopt, by means of directives, minimum requirements for gradual implementation, having regard to the conditions and technical rules obtaining in each of the Member States. Such directives shall avoid imposing administrative, financial and legal constraints in a way which would hold back the creation and development of small and medium-sized undertakings.

The Council shall act in accordance with the procedure referred to in Article 251 after consulting the Economic and Social Committee and the Committee of the Regions.

The Council, acting in accordance with the same procedure, may adopt measures designed to encourage cooperation between Member States through initiatives aimed at improving knowledge, developing exchanges of information and best practices, promoting innovative approaches and evaluating experiences in order to combat social exclusion.

3. However, the Council shall act unanimously on a proposal from the Commission, after consulting the European Parliament, the Economic and Social Committee and the Committee of the Regions in the following areas:

— social security and social protection of workers;
— protection of workers where their employment contract is terminated;
— representation and collective defence of the interests of workers and employers, including co-determination, subject to paragraph 6;
— conditions of employment for third country nationals legally residing in Community territory;
— financial contributions for promotion of employment and job creation, without prejudice to the provisions relating to the Social Fund.

4. A Member State may entrust management and labour, at their joint request, with the implementation of directives adopted pursuant to paragraphs 2 and 3.

In this case, it shall ensure that, no later than the date on which a directive must be transposed in accordance with Article 249, management and labour have introduced the necessary measures by agreement, the Member State concerned being required to take any necessary measure enabling it at any time to be in a position to guarantee the results imposed by that directive.

5. The provisions adopted pursuant to this Article shall not prevent any Member State from maintaining or introducing more stringent protective measures compatible with this Treaty.

6. The provisions of this Article shall not apply to pay, the right of association, the right to strike or the right to impose lock-outs.

Article 138

1. The Commission shall have the task of promoting the consultation of management and labour at Community level and shall take any relevant measure to facilitate their dialogue by ensuring balanced support for the parties.

2. To this end, before submitting proposals in the social policy field, the Commission shall consult management and labour on the possible direction of Community action.

3. If, after such consultation, the Commission considers Community action advisable, it shall consult management and labour on the content of the envisaged proposal. Management and labour shall forward to the Commission an opinion or, where appropriate, a recommendation.

4. On the occasion of such consultation, management and labour may inform the Commission of their wish to initiate the process provided for in Article 139. The

duration of the procedure shall not exceed nine months, unless the management and labour concerned and the Commission decide jointly to extend it.

Article 139

1. Should management and labour so desire, the dialogue between them at Community level may lead to contractual relations, including agreements.

2. Agreements concluded at Community level shall be implemented either in accordance with the procedures and practices specific to management and labour and the Member States or, in matters covered by Article 137, at the joint request of the signatory parties, by a Council decision on a proposal from the Commission.

The Council shall act by qualified majority, except where the agreement in question contains one or more provisions relating to one of the areas referred to in Article 137(3), in which case it shall act unanimously.

Article 140

With a view to achieving the objectives of Article 136 and without prejudice to the other provisions of this Treaty, the Commission shall encourage cooperation between tine Member States and facilitate the coordination of their action in all social policy fields under this chapter, particularly in matters relating to:

— employment;
— labour law and working conditions;
— basic and advanced vocational training;
— social security
— prevention of occupational accidents and diseases;
— occupational hygiene;
— the right of association and collective bargaining between employers and workers.

To this end, the Commission shall act in close contact with Member States by making studies, delivering opinions and arranging consultations both on problems arising at national level and on those of concern to international organisations.

Before delivering the opinions provided for in this Article, the Commission shall consult the Economic and Social Committee.

Article 141

1. Each Member State shall ensure that the principle of equal pay for male and female workers for equal work or work of equal value is applied.

2. For the purpose of this Article, 'pay' means the ordinary basic or minimum wage or salary and any other consideration, whether in cash or in kind, which the worker receives directly or indirectly, in respect of his employment, from his employer.

Equal pay without discrimination based on sex means:

(a) that pay for the same work at piece rates shall be calculated on the basis of the same Unit of measurement;

(b) that pay for work at time rates shall be the same for the same job.

3. The Council, acting in accordance with the procedure referred to in Article 251, and after consulting the Economic and Social Committee, shall adopt measures to ensure tine application of the principle of equal opportunities and equal treatment of men and women in matters of employment and occupation, including the principle of equal pay for equal work or work of equal value.

4. With a view to ensuring full equality in practice between men and women in working life, the principle of equal treatment shall not prevent any Member State from maintaining or adopting measures providing for specific advantages in order to make

it easier for the under-represented sex to pursue a vocational activity or to prevent or compensate for disadvantages in professional careers.

Article 142
Member States shall endeavour to maintain the existing equivalence between paid holiday schemes.

Article 143
The Commission shall draw up a report each year on progress in achieving the objectives of Article 136, including the demographic situation in the Community. it shall forward the report to the European Parliament, the Council and tine Economic and Social Committee.

The European Parliament may invite the Commission to draw up reports on particular problems concerning the social situation.

Article 144
The Council may, acting unanimously and after consulting the Economic and Social Committee, assign to the Commission tasks in connection with the implementation of common measures, particularly as regards social security for the migrant workers referred to in Articles 39 to 42.

Article 145
The Commission shall include a separate chapter on social developments within the Community in its annual report to the European Parliament.

The European Parliament may invite the Commission to draw up reports on any particular problems concerning social conditions.

Question
Do the Social Provisions found in the Treaty since the entry into force of the Amsterdam Treaty, which apply in common to all 15 Member States, represent a continuation or a break with the historical trends in European social policy mapped by Moxon-Browne in the extract that begins at p. 613 above? Do they clarify the mission of the Community as an actor in the social policy field? (See E. Szyszczak, 'The New Parameters of European Labour Law' in D. O'Keeffe and P. Twomey (eds), *Legal Issues of the Amsterdam Treaty* (1999).) Consider also Articles 125–130 EC, the Title on Employment which is an Amsterdam innovation (on which see S. Sciarra, in D. O'Keeffe and P. Twomey (eds), *Legal Issues of the Amsterdam Treaty* (1999)).

(F) THE FUTURE OF VARIABLE INTEGRATION

As the comments by J. Harrop (p. 583 above) and E. Moxon-Browne (p. 613 above) suggest, the critical question for the future is the extent to which willingness in the social policy sphere to allow a dissenting minority to opt out of common policy making will become a model for resolving disagreements about the path the Union should follow. In times of geographic and functional expansion, there is a probability that consensus will be increasingly elusive. The temptation for a majority to push ahead, without waiting to persuade a reluctant minority, will be powerful. Yet, for some, such variable integration undermines the traditional notions of the European common market.

At stake is the identification of the proper and achievable scope of Community intervention into the market. There is a fierce debate about the extent to which the Community should combine a commitment to market liberalisation with a readiness to establish a common basis for the regulation of the market. As mentioned in Chapter 5 (p. 219 above), this is reducible (with a risk of oversimplification) to the battle between a 'competition between regulators' (which favours a basic rule of mutual market access against a background of regulatory diversity which breeds competition and releases comparative advantage) and the 'level playing field' (which prefers a greater degree of rule making in common in order to equalise competitive conditions and deepen interdependence between the Member States).

This debate is being conducted in many sectors. For example, in the social policy field, anxiety is frequently expressed that inadequate common rules will release a market for regulation in which firms will re-locate to jurisdictions offering them the cheapest regime, thereby driving down social standards in Europe. From another perspective, this is precisely the sort of competition that will equip European firms with the efficiency required to succeed in global markets, thereby enhancing job creation. For discussion, see C. Barnard, 'Social dumping and race to the bottom: some lessons for the EU from Delaware?' (2000) 25 EL Rev 57. In another sector: to what extent should the liberalisation of the market for financial services be accompanied by the fixing of standards that must be met before a provider may claim access to the integrated market? And should any Community standards that are set be minimum standards only? See Chapter 10; and for an overview of the policy issues, M. Cremona, 'Freedom of Movement of Financial Services' in A. Caiger and D. Floudas, *1996 Onwards* (1996).

The significance of developments in the social policy sphere is that the Member States at Maastricht were prepared to abandon the search for an agreed common path through this policy maze. One State, the UK, was allowed to opt out; one State, the UK, was allowed to maintain regulatory diversity and compete with its partners by offering firms a lighter regulatory regime. Elsewhere, in relation to the third stage of Economic and Monetary Union, two States, Denmark and the UK, have been allowed to choose whether or not to proceed, whereas all other Member States are committed according to the Treaty.

Such variable integration – or 'flexibility' – raises questions of the highest significance in judging the future institutional and constitutional shaping of the Union. The two extracts that follow should be read with regard both to 'agenda-setting' for the 1996 Intergovernmental Conference which generated the Treaty of Amsterdam in 1997 and, looking further ahead, to the structures needed for the potential growth of the Union to embrace most of Europe early in the new millennium. The chapter then concludes with the provisions found in the Treaty of Amsterdam designed to provide a general framework for integration at different speeds – so-called 'closer cooperation', p. 635 below.

D. Curtin, 'The Shaping of a European Constitution and the 1996 IGC' (1995) 50 *Aussenwirtschaft* 237, 244–9

4. Towards a systematisation of 'flexibility'

In many respects the EC has always been a multi-speed phenomenon and multiple speed integration in this almost classic sense can be defined as integration whereby the policy objective is the same for all the Member States and has been agreed to by all of them: it is only the speed at which it is achieved which varies.[23] Generally such differentiation must be capable of objective justification and be temporary in nature. The reason for the introduction of this type of divergence which is mainly to be found in the application of secondary Community law is to account for internal (social or economic) difficulties of one or several Member States which are expected to be overcome during the period of exception.[24] Nevertheless the underlying legislative act (often a harmonising directive) is based on the principle of unanimous will of all the Member States including the declared intention of the excluded Member State(s) to introduce the harmonised standard at the agreed and fixed date. The ultimate aim is clearly a *uniform rule* for a fully integrated market.[25]

The transition to the third stage of EMU as regulated in the TEU is another example of multiple speed integration more or less in the classic sense, albeit regulated via a Treaty amendment: it does not undermine the Community legal order as such nor arguably impair the cohesion of the internal market. Rather it enables a leading group of Member States to proceed with further cooperation and integration on the basis of objectively defined criteria with the intention that the other Member States will in principle, in the ripeness of time, join this leading group in the path ahead which has been forged. The controversial point is the inevitable creation of two classes of membership without adequate provision for common action to enable weaker economies to catch up and earn their membership of the common currency regime.

In the EMU system, the possibility of a leading group is explicitly accepted by *all* the EU Member States in the TEU, including the UK and Denmark, although they have secured an opt-out for themselves. It can be argued however that the emergence of an EMU leading group is not only compatible with the internal market but enables additional profit to be obtained from it.[26] The quibble one can have with the opt-out's which Denmark and the UK obtained in Maastricht and Edinburgh regarding the move to the final stage of the EMU is that they provide the possibility of *permanently* 'opting out' of the provisions laid down in the Treaty on the third stage of the EMU (in the sense of an indefinite period as opposed to a merely undefined period) and that they were obtained for purely political reasons (as opposed to social and economic factors which were the only objective justification in the classic approach[27]). To this

---

[23] See, in general, Feenstra and Mortelmans. Gedifferentieerde integratie en Gemeenschapstecht. Institutioneel – en materieel-rechtelijke aspecten. (The Hague, 1985).

[24] See further, Feenstra and Mortelmans. 33–34. See too, Article 35 of the European Parliaments Draft Treaty on European Union, 1984 which accepted the idea of the differentiated application of Community rules provided that such differentiation was limited in time, being 'designed to facilitate the subsequent application of all the provisions of the law to all of its addressees'. See further, Louis, 'Europese Unie en gedifferentieerde integratie', SEW 6 (1985) 410.

[25] Feenstra and Mortelmans, *op. cit.* 33.

[26] See too the view of the Dutch Government in their enlargement policy document. [Second Chamber of the Dutch Parliament, 1994–95, 23 987, no. 2]

[27] See, in general Ehlermann, 'How flexible is Community law? An unusual approach to the concept of "two speeds"' in (1984) Michigan Law Review. 136, 151.

extent one can indeed claim that the opt-outs do in fact contribute to the undermining of the Community legal order.

The bottom line in a multiple (or two) speed approach such as that encapsulated in the EMU is that it probably is possible to a considerable extent to maintain the principle of the single institutional framework as enshrined in article C of the Treaty [now Art. 3 EU] on the assumption that, although temporary derogations or special arrangements might be granted, 'all those who are party to the single institutional framework share the same framework and are ready in time to conform to the same system'.[28]

However another different form of graduated integration may also be distinguished and this is one which gives rise to more serious problems. *Variable geometry* is quite different from variable speeds in the sense that the group of Member States deciding to proceed with closer integration actually agree *among themselves* their policy objectives as well as the tempo for their realisation.[29] In this construction those left 'behind' are not at all involved and simply 'opt out' of any agreement as to the policy objectives. So it is not only the speed but also the specific policy objectives and the means of achieving these which varies for different groups of countries.

It is submitted that this (disintegrative) formula should *not* be applied to the so-called 'hard core' of Community law and in particular not to those policy areas which might impair the cohesion of the internal market. The same is arguably also true with regard to the organisation of the Union's external economic relations as well as solidarity within the Union.[30]

The substantive *hard core* of the Union can be tentatively defined for present purposes as the rules and obligations entailed in the establishment of the internal market including the necessary harmonisation of legislation, the five freedoms and the common competition, agriculture, transport and trade policies as well as certain aspects of the EMU which constitute a necessary addition to the internal market.[31] This definition does not necessarily exclude the right for small groups of countries to take more *far-reaching measures* in certain areas of 'supplementary policy' which essentially seek to establish *minimum* norms (for example, environmental policy, social policy, research and technological policy, etc).[32]

For the internal market and the foundations of the Community system (the substantive 'hard core' and the institutional core *acquis*), it is mandatory, at least from the perspective of the *acquis communautaire*, that the Community decision making procedure as such is followed and that *all* Member States *participate* (albeit with the possibility of different speeds, see *supra*) with regard to Community policy. Moreover, when action is envisaged in the so-called 'hard core' of the Community then the principle of institutional unity and balance as envisaged in the Treaty itself must be respected. Finally, the fundamental rule is that of the equality of the Member States, thereby prohibiting the exclusion of one or more Member States from a particular

---

[28] Ludlow, Beyond Maastricht, Brussels. 1993. p. 70.
[29] See, in general, Maillet and Velo, (eds.), *L'Europe a geometrie variable. Transition vers l'integration* (Paris, 1994)
[30] See, Maillet and Velo, *op. cit.*, 125.
[31] See further, the interesting discussion by Verloren van Themaat. 'Epiloog, De horizon 2000', in: Kapteyn, Verloren van Themaat et al., *Jnleiding tot het Recht van de Europese Gemeenschappen*, 5th ed., 1995, forthcoming.
[32] See, Dutch Government policy document on enlargement, *op. cit* where it suggests the test in each case whether the differentiation of norms and policy in this way will gradually undermine the level playing field of the internal market.

policy area. These are the three fundamental rules mandated by the *acquis commu-nautaire* with regard to the substantive 'hard core' of the Community.[33]

A prominent example of variable geometry in the TEU is the controversial Protocol and Agreement on Social Policy which granted the United Kingdom an unlimited 'opt-out' from amended social policy provisions for an undefined period and main-tained, in tandem, the unamended social policy provisions in the body of the EC Treaty. Another example is constituted by the Schengen process which aims to bring about the free movement of persons, one of the objectives of the EC. This example is also problematic in the sense that the treatment of these objectives in an intergovern-mental context as opposed to the Community one has certainly led to a significant *democratic retrogression*,[34] moreover the risk clearly is of a lack of uniformity in the implementation of the third pillar and the legal protection of the vital human interests involved in this area. The Schengen process of cooperation is – implicitly – legitimated by Article K.7 of the TEU. The Schengen Convention also explicitly states that the intergovernmental Schengen rules will disappear as soon as there are Community/ Union rules to the same effect.

Outside the scope of the so-called 'hard core' there is certainly room for the application of the 'variable geometry' model of integration provided that certain minimum rules are respected.[35] The option of variable geometry in fields that are not directly related to the internal market, such as the two inter-governmental pillars envisaged in the TEU, is likely to be the subject of extensive debate in the run-up to the 1996 IGC. An example is constituted by the arrangements which the second pillar of the TEU contains with regard to the security arm of the Union, the WEU, an international organisation of which not all Member States are members. This arrangement may well be further elaborated and refined in 1996. Moreover, it must be considered highly probable that in the field of CFSP the creation of one or more institutionalised 'core groups' may be envisaged, provided that membership is in fact open to all interested Member States. Another form of differentiation may also be considered in 1996, as part and parcel of a type of second generation CFSP reinvigorating the integration process in this important field of Union policy making. In the (necessary) movement away from unanimous decision-making by the Council with regard to decisions for joint action towards qualified majority decisions, it might be envisaged that objecting Member States could simply 'opt-out' in practice (on an entirely *ad hoc* basis) from any legally binding effects of certain decisions for 'joint action'.[36]

---

[33] See further, Feenstra and Mortelmans, *op. cit.*
[34] See further, Curtin and Meijers, 'Openbaarheid in Europa. Geheim bestuur door "Schengen" en "Maastricht"?' (1995) NJB, forthcoming [*cf.* Curtin and Meijers (1995) 32 CML Rev 391].
[35] This seems to be the view too of Balladur, op. cit., who speaks of various 'inner circles', subsumed within his grand design of a 'Europe of concentric circles', but enabling (separate) deeper fast track integration in areas such as, for example, monetary and military integration. On the other hand his 'cercle de droit commun' comprising the internal market, common policies and external and security policies amounts to a type of 'hard core' which all Member States of the Union would have to equally subscribe to (presumably with some classic multiple speed possibilities, although this is not referred to by Balladur in his analysis). Membership of the fast track inner circles would be open to all Member States willing and able to subscribe to the commitments in question, an important difference with the approach adopted in the German CDU/CSU document. op. cit.
[36] This suggestion has been made by Commissioner van den Brock in a speech, 'Het Gemeenschappelijk buitenlands en veiligheidsbeleid van de Europese Unie - een eerste balans', delivered to the Clingendael Institute, The Hague, 24 May 1994.

With regard to the third pillar, justice and home affairs, it can be submitted that because of the close links of many of the policy areas outlined in Article K.1 with the completion of the internal market and in particular the free movement of persons that a system of institutionalised variable geometry might be objectionable from the point of view of the *acquis communautaire*. Nevertheless it cannot be excluded out of hand that it may be possible to envisage some limited form of modified variable geometry in the context of this pillar of the Union, in an attempt to ensure a rite of passage to the second generation of integration away from the purely intergovernmental and injecting more democratic content into the decision making processes as such.

As is well known, one of the most heinous defects in this area of intergovernmental decision making is the lack of any judicial control and this defect must be a major item on the 1996 revision agenda, certainly if there is to be any semblance of shaping a veritable 'Constitution' based on the rule of law. It is not unrealistic to expect that certain Member States (and in any event the United Kingdom) will continue to vigorously oppose a role for the Court of Justice given the unhappy recent debates on this subject in the context of the Europol Treaty.[37] In these circumstances might it not be conceivable to include in the text of the revision treaty a new article which in essence envisages a type of 'optional clause' enabling Member States to accept (on an *ad hoc* basis) the Court of Justice's jurisdiction over (legally binding) Conventions in the sense of Article K.3.2.c., in spite of a failure to reach unanimous agreement on this subject in each individual Convention?

Note

The extent to which the Treaty of Amsterdam adjusts the relationship between the first (EC) and the third pillar, referred to in the concluding two paragraphs of this extract, is examined above at pp. 192 and 365.

R. Harmsen, 'A European Union of Variable Geometry: Problems and Perspectives' (1994) 45 NILQ 109, 129–33

IV.   THE LIMITS OF VARIABILITY

If 'variable geometry' corresponds to deep-seated political trends, it nonetheless also poses significant problems with respect to both the maintenance of system legitimacy and the practical functioning of institutions. As regards the legitimacy of the politico-legal system, extensive recourse to variable institutional structures risks undermining the minimal sense of 'community' necessary for the creation or maintenance of a cohesive political unit. At a more practical level, problems are presented by the coexistence of parallel legal orders as well as by the need to redesign common political institutions in a way which corresponds to jurisdictional variations. Straddling the line between abstract considerations of legitimacy and more practical problems of institutional design, the overall level of systemic complexity further gives cause for concern.

Potential problems of legitimacy most obviously attach to national opt-outs, given that they may easily be perceived as unfairly benefiting a particular Member State. The case of the British Social Protocol opt-out is paradigmatic. As pointedly demonstrated by the so-called 'Hoover Affair' of 1992, British non-participation in the new areas of common social policy rapidly sparks allegations in other Member States

---

[37] See, Agence Europe, 2 December 1994.

of a fundamental inequity.[66] In effect, a situation has been created in which either the UK is allowed to enjoy the perceived relative advantage of lower social costs or the other Member States must accept a lower level of social protection so as not to be at a competitive disadvantage. In either case a highly corrosive dynamic is produced. The logic of the integration process to date has been very much one of complex political trade-offs resulting in 'package deals' which, though far from seamless webs, ensure a minimum of cohesion. A simple 'agreement to disagree' breaks with even this minimalist search for cohesiveness and, consequently, risks a more general unravelling of the overarching political compromises which define the Community. Indeed, in this light, it is difficult to envisage the UK's social policy opt-out being a workable long-term arrangement.[67] The opening of a substantial breach may perhaps be avoided in the short term only because of a quite limited enthusiasm on the part of the 11 participatory States to move much beyond the level of a declaration of principles.[68]

Graduated integration on the EMU model avoids some of the pitfalls associated with opt-outs of the Social Protocol type. In so far as the graduated EMU model appears to differentiate States on the basis of 'objective' criteria rather than subjective political will it is unlikely to provoke similar sentiments of fundamental unfairness. However, as already became clear when the idea was first mooted by Brandt and Tindemans in the 1970s, graduated integration does threaten to marginalise those States relegated to the 'second tier'. For example, in the specific case of EMU, the fears of the Union's poorer Member States that their transitional 'derogations' may become a form of permanent 'second-class' status have been strongly and repeatedly voiced.[69] In this way, questions of system legitimacy may also be raised. Involuntary exclusion, no less than the perceived inequities of voluntary non-participation, may tear at the fabric of political community.

At the level of institutional practice, the logic of 'variable geometry' poses the problem of co-ordinating parallel legal orders. Jurisdictional variability, by definition, involves the creation of parallel legislative or regulatory regimes. Nevertheless, the differentiation thus admitted must in some way be controlled if it is not to vitiate or distort the core principles upon which the Union is based. This problem was quite explicitly addressed, and in good part resolved, by the negotiators of the EEA Agreement, albeit at the cost of severely limiting the input of the EFTA States into the decision-making process. In worrying contrast, however, no mechanism has been

---

[66] The incident centred on the relocation of a Hoover factory from France to Scotland, essentially because of the lower labour and social security costs in the UK. See, for example, the editorial comment, 'Are European Values being Hoovered Away?' (1993) 29 *CML Rev* 445. [See now the article by Barnard (2000), cited at p. 626 above.]

[67] The European Commission appears set to make a bid for the termination of the British social opt-out in 1996 as part of the next round of negotiation on institutional reform (reported in Taylor, 'Brussels wants to stop UK social policy opt-out', *Financial Times*, 21 January 1994).

[68] See, for example, Lange, 'Maastricht and the Social Protocol: Why Did They Do It?' (1993) 21 *Politics and Society* 5. Lange argues that the social dimension has been and is likely to remain a 'sideshow' to the central process of market integration for reasons to do with the interests of national governments, the fragmentation of social interests and the Community's own policy-making rules.

[69] Most recently, the Spanish government has insisted that the EMU convergence criteria not take into account the economic performance of any of the EFTA countries which may accede to the Union prior to the turn of the century, in good part for fear that a Northern European group of EMU 'hard core' States may form around Germany. See Gardner, 'Spanish demand upsets EU enlargement talks'. *Financial Times*, 21 December 1993.

envisaged to deal with the potential emergence of competing social policy regimes under the terms of the Social Protocol.

'Variable geometry' also presents clear and as yet only partially resolved problems for the structure of the Union's political institutions. Some forms of institutional asymmetry have already been adopted which correspond to the jurisdictional asymmetry accepted as part of the Maastricht process. Thus, for example, the UK has no voting rights on matters decided under the Social Protocol Agreement, with the arithmetic of the qualified majority being adjusted accordingly. Similarly, as noted earlier, Denmark has renounced its right to exercise the Union Presidency when defence matters are under consideration. Nevertheless, other questions raised by such opt-outs remain unresolved. For example, no clear decision has been taken (at the time of writing) concerning the extent to which British MEPs may properly participate in parliamentary deliberations concerning social-policy matters covered by the opt-out.[70] It might also be asked if the Danish renunciation of the Union Presidency with respect to defence matters is at all a viable model for dealing with future opt-outs. If this single case is in itself relatively unproblematic, it is difficult to imagine the operation of an indefinite number of such variations within the rotating structure of the Union Presidency.

It is at this point that considerations of legitimacy and practicality overlap. In part, as suggested by the preceding discussion of institutional mechanics, the limits of variability are set by the practical capacity of a legal or political system to cope with complexity. However, beyond the internal manageability of the system, attention must be paid to its external intelligibility. Simply put, institutional variability, though it may correspond to very real political necessity, also renders the politico-legal system as a whole exceptionally opaque. For the European Union, already sharply criticised for a relatively low degree of intelligibility, there is a very real danger that further moves down the path of 'variable geometry' will render still more difficult its legitimation in the eyes of often sceptical national publics.

CONCLUSION

It has clearly emerged in the preceding sections that multiple forms of both 'structural' and 'jurisdictional' variability have been accepted within the European Union and that these variable institutional structures correspond to deeply embedded political imperatives. It is equally clear, however, that such differentiated institutional structures pose significant problems, potentially even calling into question basic precepts of the entire integration project. More than most problems of institutional design, there is no readily apparent way of resolving this tension between strong demands for diversity and an equally compelling logic of uniformity. Nevertheless, a promising path forward has been sketched out by the Court of Justice, with its tentative acceptance of a notion of 'supraconstitutionality' at the supranational level.

Although essentially unknown in the common-law world, the idea of 'supraconstitutionality' has been a staple of post-war public-law theory in much of continental

---

[70] Watson. *op cit.* 504-5 concludes that 'since neither the Commissioners nor the members of the European Parliament represent the United Kingdom it is not unreasonable that they should participate in the making of measures based upon the Agreement'. Duverger, 'L'heure de vérité', *Le Monde*, 19 June 1992, conversely argues that neither British Commissioners nor British MEPs may participate in deliberations on matters raised under the Social Protocol Agreement. I would argue that a median position between the two is perhaps most justifiable. If Commissioners are by Treaty obligation 'servants of the Community', whose nationality should not affect their participation in all Community activities, parliamentarians are political representatives who cannot legitimately 'legislate' in areas from which their own constituents are exempt.

Western Europe.[71] As the term implies, 'supraconstitutionality' refers to the existence of principles or positive law norms which are logically prior to and therefore in some sense 'above' the written constitution. It follows that these principles or norms must be respected by every governmental and legislative act, including constitutional amendment. Most simply, one notes the prohibition on the abolition of the Republican form of government contained in both the French and the Italian Constitutions; 'Republicanism' is defined as a prior value which even the constitutional legislator must respect.[72] In a more elaborate fashion, Article 79(3) of the German Basic Law enumerates a number of 'unrevisable' provisions, placing certain basic individual rights and the federal character of the State beyond the realm of constitutional amendment. In each case, while one may question the practical effectiveness of such provisions, they unquestionably make explicit the core or constitutive values of the regime.

In the Community context, the Court of Justice broached the idea of supraconstitutionality in its first decision concerning the EEA Agreement, handed down on 14 December 1991.[73] Specifically, the Commission asked the Court to rule on whether any incompatibilities found to exist between the judicial mechanism provided for in the EEA Agreement and the EC founding treaties might be resolved by way of amendment to the Treaty of Rome. The Commission envisaged a simple amendment to Article 238, permitting the establishment of the court system agreed. The Court of Justice, in response, ruled that even Treaty amendment would 'not cure the incompatibility', as the proposed system of courts (functionally integrating the CJEC and the Court of First Instance into EEA courts for EEA purposes) conflicted 'with the very foundations of the Community.'[74] In other words, the autonomy and integrity of the Community legal system has been held by the Court of Justice to constitute a 'prior' or 'supraconstitutional' value of the Community order, which even Treaty amendment should not be allowed to violate.

Relative to the present concern with 'variable geometry', the CJEC's decision crucially underlines the need for variable or asymmetrical structures to be conceived with reference to a Community 'core'.[75] Simply put, increased institutional variability must inevitably call forward a stronger and more explicit conception of which principles, values, and policies integrally define the Community. Although the exact parameters of such a core can emerge only gradually, its constituent elements must reasonably include the basic precepts of the common market, the underlying principles of the legal order, and some sense of a common political destiny (paralleling, at the supranational level, Renan's classic definition of a nation in terms of a *vouloir vivre ensemble*).

At the same time, the limits of a Community-level reliance on the notion of supraconstitutionality must also be underlined. First, concerning the substantive

---

[71] The doctrinal background is discussed in Stéphane Rials. 'Supraconstitutionnalité et systématicité du droit' [1986] 31 *Archives de Philosophie du Droit* 57. A somewhat more empirical survey may be found in Arne. 'Existe-t-il des normes supra-constitutionnelles? Contribution à l'étude des fondamentaux et de la constitutionnalité' (1993) 205 *Revue du Droit public* 459.

[72] Art 89 of the Constitution of the French Fifth Republic: Art 139 of the present Italian Constitution.

[73] *Re The Draft Treaty on a European Economic Area.* Opinion 1/91. [1992] 1 CMLR 245. Commentaries and follow-up are cited *supra*, n45. The 'supraconstitutional' dimension of the decision is discussed in Dutheil de la Rochère, *supra*, n52, at 607.

[74] Opinion 1/91 at 275.

[75] It may be argued that the European Convention on Human Rights already has such a core, in so far as contracting States may not derogate, even in time of emergency, from specified central Articles (*viz* 2, 3, 4/1 and 7). See Arné, *op. cit.*, p. 466.

definition of a Community core, it is essential that the *noyau communautaire* not be confused with the *acquis communautaire*. The core, by definition, must include only those principles which are constitutive of the Community order, not the sum total of all policies and practices which might have developed under the Community rubric. Second, at a procedural level, the part played by the Court of Justice in defining this supraconstitutional core must be carefully limited relative to the role of political actors. In this regard, it should be borne in mind that a Community supracon- stitutionality lacks the inherent legitimacy of its national counterparts, as it refers only to fairly abstract concepts of 'order', rather than to basic human rights or founding principles of liberal democracy.

In sum, a logic of supraconstitutionality would appear to offer a conceptual framework within which an increasing variability of institutional structures might be reconciled with the need to preserve the basic tenets of the Union as an economic, legal, and political order. Nevertheless, whether through the adoption of such a framework or through another means, it is clear that an increasing structural and jurisdictional variability must be accompanied by a more explicit definition of the Union's invariable core. Therein lies a task, whatever their initial differences, which would seem singularly well suited to a co-operative effort on the part of lawyers and political scientists.

Question
Do you find attractive the attempt in these two extracts to identify a 'hard core' of Community obligations? What machinery could be used to define the content and to secure the inviolability of such a hard core?

Further reading
Bieber, R., 'On the Mutual Completion of Overlapping Legal Systems: the Case of the European Communities and the National Legal Orders' (1988) 13 EL Rev 147.
Dehousse, R., 'Community Competence: Are there Limits to Growth' in R. Dehousse (ed.), *Europe After Maastricht* (Munich, Law Books, 1994).
Ehlermann, C.D., 'How Flexible is Community Law? An Unusual Approach to the Concept of "Two Speeds"' (1984) 82 Michigan Law Rev 1274.
Jachtenfuchs, M., 'Theoretical Perspectives on European Governance' (1995) 1 *European Law Journal* 115.
McGee, A. and Weatherill, S., 'The Evolution of the Single Market – Harmonisation or Liberalisation' (1990) 53 MLR 578.
Reich, N., 'Competition Between Legal Orders: A New Paradigm of EC Law' (1992) 29 CML Rev 861.
Scharpf, F., 'The problem-solving capacity of multi-level governance' (1997) 4 *Journal of European Public Policy* 520.
Stubb, A., 'The 1996 Intergovernmental Conference and the management of flexible integration' (1997) 4 *Journal of European Public Policy* 37.
Usher, J., 'Variable Geometry or Concentric Circles: Patterns for the EU' (1997) 46 ICLQ 243.
Weatherill, S., 'Preemption and Competence in a Wider and Deeper Union', Ch 5 in *Law and Integration in the European Union* (Oxford, Oxford University Press, 1995).

Note

One of the more innovative amendments made by the Treaty of Amsterdam is the introduction of new provisions designed to permit 'closer cooperation', through which some, but not all, Member States may choose to deepen their mutual interdependence. These provisions are by no means exhaustive of the models of 'flexibility' available to the Member States, but they represent an illuminating attempt to chart a course in the Treaty for forms of action that may be thought to carry a disturbing momentum towards fragmentation of the unity of the legal order. Rigorous criteria must be satisfied before 'enhanced cooperation' is permitted; and tight institutional control is also envisaged. The 'master' provisions governing 'closer cooperation' are Articles 43 and 44 of the Treaty on European Union.

Treaty on European Union

TITLE VII
PROVISIONS ON CLOSER COOPERATION

Article 43

1. Member States which intend to establish closer cooperation between themselves may make use of the institutions, procedures and mechanisms laid down by this Treaty and the Treaty establishing the European Community provided that the cooperation:

(a) is aimed at furthering the objectives of the Union and at protecting and serving its interests;

(b) respects the principles of the said Treaties and the single institutional framework of the Union;

(c) is only used as a last resort, where the objectives of the said Treaties could not be attained by applying the relevant procedures laid down therein;

(d) concerns at least a majority of Member States;

(e) does not affect the '*acquis communautaire*' and the measures adopted under the other provisions of the said Treaties;

(f) does not affect the competences, rights, obligations and interests of those Member States which do not participate therein;

(g) is open to all Member States and allows them to become parties to the cooperation at any time, provided that they comply with the basic decision and with the decisions taken within that framework;

(h) complies with the specific additional criteria laid down in Article 11 of the Treaty establishing the European Community and Article 40 of this Treaty, depending, on the area concerned, and is authorised by the Council in accordance with the procedures laid down therein.

2. Member States shall apply, as far as they are concerned, the acts and decisions adopted for the implementation of the cooperation in which they participate. Member States not participating in such cooperation shall not impede the implementation thereof by the participating Member States.

Article 44

1. For the purposes of the adoption of the acts and decisions necessary for the implementation of the cooperation referred to in Article 43, the relevant institutional provisions of this Treaty and of the Treaty establishing the European Community shall

apply. However, while all members of the Council shall be able to take part in the deliberations, only those representing participating Member States shall take part in the adoption of decisions. The qualified majority shall be defined as the same proportion of the weighted votes of the members of the Council concerned as laid down in Article 205(2) of the Treaty establishing the European Community. Unanimity shall be constituted by only those Council members concerned.

2. Expenditure resulting from implementation of the cooperation, other than administrative costs entailed for the institutions, shall be borne by the participating Member States, unless the Council, acting unanimously, decides otherwise.

Provisions in both the TEU and in the EC Treaty build on this base. In the former instance, Article 40 EU permits closer cooperation between some, but not all, Member States in pursuit of accelerated development towards an area of freedom, security and justice. This provision's cousin in the EC Treaty as amended by the Treaty of Amsterdam is Article 11 EC.

Article 11

1. Member States which intend to establish closer cooperation between themselves may be authorised, subject to Articles 43 and 44 of the Treaty on European Union, to make use of the institutions, procedures and mechanisms laid down by this Treaty, provided that the cooperation proposed:

    (a)   does not concern areas which fall within the exclusive competence of the Community;

    (b)   does not affect Community policies, actions or programmes;

    (c)   does not concern the citizenship of the Union or discriminate between nationals of Member States;

    (d)   remains within the limits of the powers conferred upon the Community by this Treaty; and

    (e)   does not constitute a discrimination or a restriction of trade between Member States and does not distort the conditions of competition between the latter.

2. The authorisation referred to in paragraph 1 shall be granted by the Council, acting by a qualified majority on a proposal from the Commission and after consulting the European Parliament.

If a member of the Council declares that, for important and stated reasons of national policy, it intends to oppose the granting of an authorisation by qualified majority, a vote shall not be taken. The Council may, acting by a qualified majority, request that the matter be referred to the Council, meeting in the composition of the Heads of State or Government, for decision by unanimity.

Member States which intend to establish closer cooperation as referred to in paragraph 1 may address a request to the Commission, which may submit a proposal to the Council to that effect. In the event of the Commission not submitting a proposal, it shall inform the Member States concerned of the reasons for not doing so.

3. Any Member State which wishes to become a party to cooperation set up in accordance with this Article shall notify its intention to the Council and to the Commission, which shall give an opinion to the Council within three months of receipt of that notification. Within four months of the date of that notification, the Commission shall decide on it and on such specific arrangements as it may deem necessary.

4. The acts and decisions necessary for the implementation of cooperation activities shall be subject to all the relevant provisions of this Treaty, save as otherwise

provided for in this Article and in Articles 43 and 44 of the Treaty on European Union.
5. This Article is without prejudice to the provisions of the Protocol integrating the Schengen acquis into the framework of the European Union.

Questions
1. Try to construct a form of closer cooperation which would satisfy all the criteria imposed by Articles 43, 44 EU and Article 11 EC.
2. Would the Maastricht pattern of two-speed social policy (p. 621 above) comply with the Amsterdam model establishing a framework for closer co-operation between some, but not all, Member States?
3. Review the new provisions on closer cooperation in the light of the two extracts above, pp. 627–634. Are the anxieties and suggestions expounded by Curtin and Harmsen reflected in these provisions?

G. Edwards and E. Philippart, *Flexibility and the Treaty of Amsterdam: Europe's New Byzantium?*
(1997) University of Cambridge, Centre for European Legal Studies (CELS), Occasional Paper No. 3, pp. 19–22

3.2 Provisions specific to the TEC
Article 5a [now 11] TEC contains the provisions specific to the First Pillar. It sets out a number of additional conditions and procedures for closer cooperation in the realm of the TEC. The underlying philosophy of the Article is clearly defensive in so far as it reinforces the limiting factors governing any move towards closer cooperation. Authorization may be given, so long as the cooperation: does not concern areas within the exclusive competence of the Community; does not affect Community policies, actions or programmes; does not concern the citizenship of the Union or discriminate between nationals of the Member States; remains within the limits of the powers conferred on the Community by the Treaty; and does not distort trade or competition between the Member States.

During the IGC negotiations, the alternatives contemplated were a negative list of areas excluded from closer cooperation and a positive list of areas potentially open for closer cooperation. As the former was not particularly precise and was therefore more open-ended, it was regarded as more threatening for those Governments with reservations about the idea and its potential consequences in terms of hard core or multi-tier Europe. A unanimous decision to authorize cooperation was seen as necessary. The final choice of QMV but with the possibility of a veto was made because it offered a balance between protecting the core elements of the Union, reassurance for non-participating Member States and political versatility.

The solution of a negative list does not however add greatly to improving the justiciability of flexibility. For instance, under Article 5a(1) [now 11], closer cooperation shall not 'concern areas which fall within the exclusive competence of the Community'. This adds little in terms of clarity since, as Jo Shaw puts it, 'despite the reference to exclusive competence in Article 3B [now 5] TEC, the balance of exclusive and shared powers is not easy to determine in EC law' (Shaw, *Law of the EU* 1996, p. 79).

In any case, such a list, combined with the flexibility already introduced through 'predetermined flexibility', had already reduced the potential for closer cooperation.

For example, commercial policy is sometimes suggested as a possible area for closer cooperation; especially if the Member States are unable to make use of the fifth paragraph added to Article 113 [now 133] TEC, which opens the possibility of extending the application of the first four paragraphs to 'international negotiations and agreements on services and intellectual property'. The conditions set by Article 5a [now 11] TEC seem nevertheless to constitute a serious obstacle to closer cooperation in that it is difficult to envisage cooperation that would not affect the common commercial policy or distort competition.

The procedure for moving to closer cooperation is by the interested Member States' addressing a request to the Commission, which submits a proposal to the Council. Provision is made for the Commission to refuse to do so, provided that it informs the Member States of its reasons. After consultation of the European Parliament, the Council decides on the proposal by QMV. Any Member State may, nevertheless, prevent the vote being taken by declaring that it intends to oppose the authorization on grounds of 'important and stated reasons of national policy' (Article 5a(2) [now 11(2)]). The Council may then, acting by a qualified majority, refer the matter to 'the Council meeting in the composition of the Heads of State or Government' where a decision has to be taken unanimously. If a Member State wishes to become a party to cooperation subsequently, it notifies the Council and the Commission. Within three months of that notification, the Commission gives an opinion to the Council and then, within four months, takes the decision on it.

This final codification of the Luxembourg Compromise within the TEC is of considerable symbolic importance. Its seemingly easy passage through the final negotiations brought to an end some thirty years of dispute, even while providing a possibly important hostage to fortunate. But it allays some of the fears both of those more sceptical of further integration and those hostile to fragmentation. The use of the veto means that proposed areas for closer cooperation are necessarily aired at the highest level, with all the additional publicity that surrounds meetings of Heads of State and of Government. But the way in which the veto will then be managed is interesting, even if as yet highly speculative. It may be, for example, that at that point the minority State(s) are content, as were the British on social policy with their opt-out. Their point has been made, whether for ideological reasons or more prosaic considerations of domestic party politics, and closer cooperation may then be allowed to take place. On the other hand, if the issue is regarded as so vital and of such profound implications that flexibility is not tolerable, it is up to the majority either to defer or to take the 'extra-EU' option. In between the extremes, there is clearly the opportunity for intense bargaining.

The Commission has not been endowed with a monopoly of initiative, but is clearly closely involved in the procedure. It is firmly empowered as an umpire, largely to answer the concerns of Member States who fear the use of closer cooperation to solve the problem of the unfit at no cost. The Commission has the power to block the authorization procedure insofar as its decision not to submit a proposal would appear to be final. No Member State can, for its own political convenience, prevent another from joining at a later stage because the Commission takes the final decision alone.

The role of the Commission – and the Court of Justice – may also be as critical at later stages in the process of closer cooperation. Both will have a vital part in ensuring the compatibility of subsequent but related legislation among those cooperating more closely. This is especially important because in the decisionmaking process, those not participating in the closer cooperation cannot take part in the adoption of legislation. It can be argued that the Member States themselves who are not participating in the closer cooperation should remain responsible for safeguarding their interests, but hitherto Member States have been able to rely ultimately on the Court for protection where, for instance, distortions in the market have been the result of partial or non-implementation of legislation. Will those who might be affected by the legislation in the Member States not cooperating still be able to rely on the Court? Several general provisions of the TEC seem to provide some protection, , but as we have seen, not all the provisions of Amsterdam point in the same direction.

Further reading on closer cooperation under the Amsterdam Treaty and the broader phenomenon of 'flexibility'

Constantinesco, V., 'Les clauses de coopération renforcée' (1997) 33 RTDE 751.

Ehlermann, C.-D., 'Differentiation, Flexibility, Closer Co-operation: The New Provisions of the Amsterdam Treaty' (1998) 4 ELJ 246.

Gaja, G., 'How flexible is flexibility under the Amsterdam Treaty?' (1998) 35 CML Rev 855.

Shaw, J., 'The Treaty of Amsterdam: Challenges of Flexibility and Legit-imacy' (1998) 4 ELJ 63.

Tuytschaever, F., *Differentiation in European Union Law* (Oxford, Hart Publishing, 1999).

Usher, J., 'Flexibility and Enhanced Cooperation', in T. Heukels, N. Blokker and M. Brus (eds), *The European Union after Amsterdam* (Kluwer, 1998), Ch. 14.

Walker, N., 'Sovereignty and Differentiated Integration in the European Union' (1998) 4 ELJ 355.

Weatherill, S., ' "If I'd wanted you to understand I would have explained it better": what is the purpose of the provisions on closer co-operation introduced by the Treaty of Amsterdam?' in D. O'Keeffe and P. Twomey (eds), *Legal Issues of the Amsterdam Treaty* (Oxford, Hart Publishing, 1999).

Weatherill, S., 'Flexibility or Fragmentation: Trends in European Integra-tion', in J. Usher (ed.), *The State of the European Union* (Harlow, Longman, 2000), Ch. 1.

Question

Norbert Reich has commented that 'the more competences the Community is acquiring, the less exclusive will be its jurisdiction' ((1992) 29 CML Rev 861, 895). What are the manifestations of this development? Is it desirable?

PART THREE:
ENFORCEMENT OF
COMMUNITY LAW

INTRODUCTION

All legal systems contain administrative law and a law of remedies in some form. The substance of the Community's system therefore deserves attention, but it should neither be considered unique nor be viewed in isolation. Its study can be enriched by drawing comparisons with other national and international systems. However, what is of especial interest is the pattern of development of the Community legal order. This has occurred in a fashion which *is* peculiar to the Community. The original structure owed a great deal to French administrative law traditions. The Community legal order still retains many of these features but has increasingly developed a life of its own, drawing on diverse national tradition. Under the influence of the Court, it has evolved along distinctive lines in response to the needs of the institutional and constitutional structures of the maturing Community.

Much of Part Three of this book in fact comprises a closer examination of territory that is already familiar. The Article 230 procedure (Article 173 pre-Amsterdam, p. 29 above) whereby acts of the Community institutions may be reviewed by the Court has frequently been encountered. So too the Article 226 procedure (Article 169 pre-Amsterdam) whereby States acting in violation of Community law may be brought before the Court. The principles of direct effect and the Article 234 preliminary reference procedure (Article 177 pre-Amsterdam) are similarly already understood – such pillars of the Community legal order could hardly be ignored at the outset. In Part Three, however, the purposes to which these provisions and principles are put are examined in the particular context of the enforcement of Community law.

Community law may be enforced at Community level through proceedings before the Court of Justice of the European Communities or, since 1989, the

Court of First Instance, which enjoys only limited jurisdiction. Community law may also be enforced at national level by virtue of the principle of direct effect, which converts national courts and tribunals into bodies responsible for the vindication of Community law rights.

There are also distinct categories of natural or legal persons against which Community law may be enforced. First, the Community institutions; secondly, the Member States; thirdly, private firms or individuals.

These two levels of enforcement, Community and national, allied to the triple focus, Community authorities, national authorities and private undertakings, serve to increase the practical vitality of Community law. The result is, however, a rather complicated range of available remedies in the event of breach of Community law. There may be several possible forums; there may be several possible defendants. The enforcement devices interrelate. Confusion is easy. One must carefully identify who the alleged defaulter is and before which court control will be exercised.

Community institutions may be controlled at Community level by proceedings before the European Court or, in defined circumstances, the Court of First Instance. Article 230 (Article 173 pre-Amsterdam) provides an action to annul Community acts. Article 232 (Article 175 pre-Amsterdam) provides a complementary action for failure to act. Article 241 (Article 184 pre-Amsterdam) allows a measure to be challenged indirectly in an action against another measure. Articles 235 and 288 (Articles 178 and 215 respectively pre-Amsterdam) allow claims to be brought against the Community institutions for compensation for loss suffered as a result of unlawful action. In some circumstances, however, it will be possible to challenge the validity of Community acts without the need to institute a direct challenge before the Court in Luxembourg. Provided a national cause of action can be established, it may be possible to claim before a national tribunal that a relevant Community act is unlawful. Typically this will arise where national authorities are responsible for the implementation of Community legislation. A challenge at national level to the national authorities' acts will involve a plea that the legal basis for the act, Community legislation, is invalid. This will then be determined by the European Court in the context of an Article 234 reference (Article 177 pre-Amsterdam). The system of control of Community institutions, briefly described in this paragraph, is the subject of Chapter 16.

Chapter 17 examines control of Member States. The dual approach to enforcement applies in relation to violations of Community law perpetrated by Member States. At Community level the State in breach of the Treaty may be brought before the European Court by the Commission in the context of the Article 226 procedure (Article 169 pre-Amsterdam), or, less common, by another Member State in reliance on Article 227 (Article 170 pre-Amsterdam). However, the State may also be challenged at national level by litigants relying on the direct effect of Community law. It is then for national courts to grant appropriate remedies against the State in breach, if necessary after seeking the assistance of the European Court in matters of interpretation of Community law via an Article 234 reference (Article 177 pre-Amsterdam).

Enforcement at national level is an area in which Community rules governing procedure have long been conspicuously underdeveloped, but where recent case law has significantly increased the impact of Community law.

Where enforcement before a national court is in issue, whether the challenge is to a Community act or to a Member State practice, the bridge between the action at national level and proceedings at Community level is the Article 234 procedure (Article 177 pre-Amsterdam). It will be recalled from Chapter 4 that Article 234 ensures that points of Community law raised at national level are interpreted authoritatively at Community level. This is essential in order to preserve the uniformity and integrity of the Community legal order. Article 234 is vital to the private individual wishing to enforce Community law, for the private individual enjoys no direct access to the European Court to control either a State or another private party and has limited direct access to control the Community institutions. The action at national level plus Article 234 is thus the individual's legal lifeline.

Throughout this Part of the book, the interrelation of the remedies needs to be appreciated. After each case – even where comment is not explicit – consider what alternative approaches might have been available to the applicant wishing to establish the invalidity of a Community act or a State practice. And – although the reader may be forgiven for weariness at the repetition of this point – remember that in reading pre-Amsterdam material, the numerical changes to the Treaty effected by the Amsterdam Treaty with effect from 1 May 1999 must be kept in mind (p. 29 above).

16 CONTROL OF COMMUNITY INSTITUTIONS

(A) ARTICLE 230

Article 230 provides a procedure whereby Community acts may be annulled by the European Court.

Article 230 EC

Article 230
The Court of Justice shall review the legality of acts adopted jointly by the European Parliament and the Council, of acts of the Council, of the Commission and of the ECB, other than recommendations and opinions, and of acts of the European Parliament intended to produce legal effects *vis-à-vis* third parties.

It shall for this purpose have jurisdiction in actions brought by a Member State, the Council or the Commission on grounds of lack of competence, infringement of an essential procedural requirement, infringement of this Treaty or of any rule of law relating to its application, or misuse of powers.

The Court of Justice shall have jurisdiction under the same conditions in actions brought by the European Parliament, by the Court of Auditors and by the ECB for the purpose of protecting their prerogatives.

Any natural or legal person may, under the same conditions, institute proceedings against a decision addressed to that person or against a decision which, although in the form of a regulation or a decision addressed to another person, is of direct and individual concern to the former.

The proceedings provided for in this Article shall be instituted within two months of the publication of the measure, or of its notification to the plaintiff, or, in the absence thereof, of the day on which it came to the knowledge of the latter, as the case may be.

Article 231 specifies the consequences and offers the Court some flexibility in its rulings.

Article 231 EC

Article 231
If the action is well founded, the Court of Justice shall declare the act concerned to be void.

In the case of a regulation, however, the Court of Justice shall, if it considers this necessary, state which of the effects of the regulation which it has declared void shall be considered as definitive.

Note

The case law which has arisen under Article 230 is vast, and this selection is designed merely to draw out the main principles. However, perhaps the most useful starting point is the general observation that most applications for the annulment of acts of the Community institutions fail. This is especially striking in relation to the fourth paragraph of Article 230, which contains restrictive standing rules which must be satisfied before the merits of an application for annulment will be heard.

(i)   Article 230, first to third paragraphs

It is useful first to return to a case already considered in Chapter 1, in order to appreciate the nature of acts susceptible to review by the Court under this procedure.

Commission v Council (Case 22/70)
[1971] ECR 263
Court of Justice of the European Communities

The Member States had participated in the conclusion of the AETR/ERTA (European Road Transport Agreement). They had expressed agreement to coordinate their approach to the ERTA in a resolution adopted at an EEC Council meeting on 20 March 1970. The Commission formed the view that the matter fell within the competence of the Community, not the individual Member States. In order to test its view of the correct allocation of competence in this field, it brought proceedings to annul the Council resolution. However, the resolution was not a Regulation, a Directive or a Decision, acts mentioned in Article 189 of the EC Treaty (now Article 249 EC) which are clearly reviewable by the Court under Article 173 of the EC Treaty (now, after amendment, Article 230 EC). Was the resolution susceptible to review?

[34]   The Council considers that the proceedings of 20 March 1970 do not constitute an act, within the meaning of the first sentence of the first paragraph of Article 173, the legality of which is open to review.

[35]   Neither by their form nor by their subject-matter or content, it is argued, were these proceedings a regulation, a decision or a directive within the meaning of Article 189.

[36]   They were really nothing more than a coordination of policies amongst Member States within the framework of the Council, and as such created no rights, imposed no obligations and did not modify any legal position.

[37]   This is said to be the case more particularly because in the event of a dispute between the institutions admissibility has to be appraised with particular rigour.

[38]   Under Article 173, the Court has a duty to review the legality 'of acts of the Council . . . other than recommendations or opinions'.

[39]   Since the only matters excluded from the scope of the action for annulment open to the Member States and the institutions are 'recommendations or opinions' – which by the final paragraph of Article 189 are declared to have no binding force – Article 173 treats as acts open to review by the Court all measures adopted by the institutions which are intended to have legal force.

[40]   The objective of this review is to ensure, as required by Article 164, observance of the law in the interpretation and application of the Treaty.

[41]   It would be inconsistent with this objective to interpret the conditions under which the action is admissible so restrictively as to limit the availability of this procedure merely to the categories of measures referred to by Article 189.

[42]   An action for annulment must therefore be available in the case of all measures adopted by the institutions, whatever their nature or form, which are intended to have legal effects.

Note
The Court then proceeded to determine that the resolution was of this character (see the extract at p. 41 above). Remember also the Court's willingness to review (and annul) a Commission 'communication' in Case C-57/95 *France* v *Commission* [1997] ECR I-1627, p. 270 above.

We here now appreciate the full significance of designating the resolution a legal 'act'; it was therefore susceptible to review. Several of the constitutional cases discussed in Part One of this book will be seen in this Part in the broader context of judicial review.

The third paragraph of Article 230 makes it clear that the Parliament has a limited right to challenge acts (p. 643 above). The Parliament makes particular use of its right in relation to wrangles about choice of legal base. Selection of the correct legal base affects the role of the several EC institutions in the legislative procedure and, as explained at p. 52 above, is a political and legal flashpoint; see, e.g. the successful (pre-Maastricht) application for annulment in *Parliament* v *Council* (Case C-295/90), referred to at p. 374 above, and *Parliament* v *Council* (Case C–187/93) [1994] ECR I–2857, in which an application was held part admissible, part inadmissible, according to whether the Parliament's prerogatives were affected by the choice between different legal bases.

In contrast, the Parliament was completely absent from the list of privileged applicants under (what was then) Article 173 prior to the amendments made to it by the Maastricht Treaty. The European Court responded to the Parliament's weak position pre-Maastricht by developing for the Parliament limited rights of standing. The Parliament seemed to have lost the argument when its application was held inadmissible in *Parliament* v *Council* (Case 302/87) [1988] ECR 5615 (known as '*Comitology*', in accordance with the subject matter of the case), but shortly afterwards the Court accepted that in some circumstances the Parliament is entitled to special status in seeking annulment. This occurred in the *'Chernobyl'* case – again, the name refers to the subject matter, measures adopted in respect of the Chernobyl Nuclear Power Plant disaster in the Ukraine.

Although the specific obstacle to standing at issue in this case was removed at Maastricht, it remains important to be aware that what is now the third paragraph of Article 230 represents a codification of the Court's case law. The *'Chernobyl'* ruling was a remarkable example of the Court's 'constitutionalisation' of the Treaty (p. 79 above); its readiness to fill (what *it* perceives as) gaps.

Parliament v *Council (Case C-70/88)*
[1990] ECR I-2041
Court of Justice of the European Communities

[21]   . . . The Treaties set up a system for distributing powers among the different Community institutions, assigning to each institution its own role in the institutional structure of the Community and the accomplishment of the tasks entrusted to the Community.

[22]   Observance of the institutional balance means that each of the institutions must exercise its powers with due regard for the powers of the other institutions. It also requires that it should be possible to penalize any breach of that rule which may occur.

[23]   The Court, which under the Treaties has the task of ensuring that in the interpretation and application of the Treaties the law is observed, must therefore be able to maintain the institutional balance and, consequently, review the observance of the Parliament's prerogatives when called upon to do so by the Parliament, by means of a legal remedy which is suited to the purpose which the Parliament seeks to achieve.

[24]   In carrying out that task the Court cannot, of course, include the Parliament among the institutions which may bring an action under Article 173 of the EEC Treaty or Article 146 of the Euratom Treaty without being required to demonstrate an interest in bringing an action.

[25]   However, it is the Court's duty to ensure that the provisions of the Treaties concerning the institutional balance are fully applied and to see to it that the Parliament's prerogatives, like those of the other institutions, cannot be breached without it having available a legal remedy, among those laid down in the Treaties, which may be exercised in a certain and effective manner.

[26]   The absence in the Treaties of any provision giving the Parliament the right to bring an action for annulment may constitute a procedural gap, but it cannot prevail over the fundamental interest in the maintenance and observance of the institutional balance laid down in the Treaties establishing the European Communities.

[27]   Consequently, an action for annulment brought by the Parliament against an act of the Council or the Commission is admissible provided that the action seeks only to safeguard its prerogatives and that it is founded only on submissions alleging their infringement. Provided that condition is met, the Parliament's action for annulment is subject to the rules laid down in the Treaties for actions for annulment brought by the other institutions.

Note

Applying these criteria, the action was ruled admissible. For comment on the case, read K. Bradley, 'Sense and Sensibility: *Parliament* v *Council* continued' (1991) 16 EL Rev 245, A. Arnull, 'Does the Court of Justice have Inherent Jurisdiction?' (1990) 27 CML Rev 683; and on the impact of the Maastricht Treaty on the Parliament's position, unaffected at Amsterdam, K. Bradley, 'Better Rusty than Missin'?' in D. O'Keeffe and P. Twomey (eds), *Legal Issues of the Maastricht Treaty* (1994). It cannot be left out of account that the Court might in future once again be prepared to look beyond the precise terms of the Treaty in defining the scope of judicial review where it perceives an insufficiency of legal protection, *inter alia* with regard to a perceived need to maintain the institutional balance.

(ii)   Article 230, non-privileged applicants

Whereas the first three paragraphs of Article 230 confer a special status on privileged applicants, most applicants for annulment must use the non-privileged route. The efficacy of this route is heavily qualified by the standing rules. The relevant paragraph of Article 230 is the fourth (p. 643 above). Between 1993 and 1999 this was the fourth paragraph of Article 173. However, prior to the Maastricht amendments that paragraph was the second. Therefore references in the following cases and discussion to Article 173(2) EEC or to the second paragraph of Article 173 EEC should be read with an awareness that this became Article 173(4) EC in 1993; and that in turn this became Article 230(4) EC on the entry into force of the Amsterdam Treaty on 1 May 1999.

It should also be added at this point that in 1993 the Court of First Instance had transferred to it jurisdiction to hear applications brought by natural or legal persons except those concerned with anti-dumping matters (Dec 93/350 (1993) OJ L144/21). In 1994 jurisdiction over anti-dumping matters too was transferred to the CFI (Dec 94/149 (1994) OJ L66/29).

Not every act can be challenged. The act under attack must be defined carefully.

International Fruit Company v *Commission (Cases 41–44/70)*
[1971] ECR 411
Court of Justice of the European Communities

According to the Commission, the acts in question were of general application to the importation of dessert apples into the Community. They were Regulations. The applicant argued that it was picked out specially by the terms of the measures. When adopted, they referred back to importers who had already applied for import licences. The 'class' was closed and the applicant was within it. These were Decisions. The terms of what was the second paragraph of Article 173 EEC and is now the fourth paragraph of Article 230 EC (p. 643 above) make it plain that it was essential to classify the act correctly in order to establish whether the applicant had standing to bring its challenge.

[16]   It is indisputable that Regulation No 983/70 was adopted [on 28 May 1970] with a view on the one hand to the state of the market and on the other to the quantities of dessert apples for which applications for import licences had been made in the week ending on 22 May 1970.

[17]   It follows that when the said regulation was adopted, the number of applications which could be affected by it was fixed.

[18]   No new application could be added.

[19]   To what extent, in percentage terms, the applications could be granted, depended on the total quantity in respect of which applications had been submitted.

[20]   Accordingly, by providing that the system introduced by Article 1 of Regulation No 565/70 should be maintained for the relevant period, the Commission decided, even though it took account only of the quantities requested, on the subsequent fate of each application which had been lodged.

[21]   Consequently, Article 1 of Regulation No 983/70 is not a provision of general application within the meaning of the second paragraph of Article 189 of the Treaty, but must be regarded as a conglomeration of individual decisions taken by the Commission under the guise of a regulation pursuant to Article 2(2) of Regulation No 459/70, each of which decisions affects the legal position of each author of an application for a licence.

[22]   Thus, the decisions are of individual concern to the applicants.

Note
Here, again, one returns to the different types of Community legislation examined in Chapter 1, and realises the true significance of the distinctions.
   In addition to the fact that not every act can be challenged, the non-privileged route under Article 230 makes it clear that not every applicant is capable of making a challenge. Unless the addressee of a Decision, the applicant needs to establish 'direct and individual concern'. Unless this standing requirement is satisfied, the Court will not even examine the merits of the action for annulment.

(iii)   Individual concern
The phrase is already familiar from the extract from *International Fruit Company* (Cases 41–44/70) above. The problem of defining 'individual concern' has been addressed in a string of cases arising out of *general* market regulation by the Community which adversely affects *individual* firms.

Plaumann v *Commission (Case 25/62)*
[1963] ECR 95
Court of Justice of the European Communities

Plaumann was a German importer of clementines. In importing clementines from third countries outside the Community, it had to pay a customs duty of 13 per cent. This sum was due under the Community's Common Customs Tariff, part of the uniform trade policy which the Community presents to the wider world. The German Government asked the Commission to authorise it to levy only 10 per cent duty. The Commission refused. That refusal became the act challenged by Plaumann. No doubt Plaumann was prejudiced by it. But could it challenge it before the European Court given the limitations contained in what was then Article 173(2) EEC, now Article 230(4) EC?

Admissibility

Under the second paragraph of Article 173 of the EEC Treaty 'any natural or legal person may . . . institute proceedings against a decision . . . which, although in the form of . . . a decision addressed to another person, is of direct and individual concern to the former'. The defendant contends that the words 'other person' in this paragraph do not refer to Member States in their capacity as sovereign authorities and that individuals may not therefore bring an action for annulment against the decisions of the Commission or of the Council addressed to Member States.

However the second paragraph of Article 173 does allow an individual to bring an action against decisions addressed to 'another person' which are of direct and individual concern to the former, but this Article neither defines nor limits the scope of these words. The words and the natural meaning of this provision justify the broadest interpretation. Moreover provisions of the Treaty regarding the right of interested parties to bring an action must not be interpreted restrictively. Therefore, the Treaty being silent on the point, a limitation in this respect may not be presumed.

It follows that the defendant's argument cannot be regarded as well founded.

The defendant further contends that the contested decision is by its very nature a regulation in the form of an individual decision and therefore action against it is no more available to individuals than in the case of legislative measures of general application.

It follows however from Articles 189 and 191 of the EEC Treaty that decisions are characterized by the limited number of persons to whom they are addressed. In order to determine whether or not a measure constitutes a decision one must enquire whether that measure concerns specific persons. The contested Decision was addressed to the government of the Federal Republic of Germany and refuses to grant it authorization for the partial suspension of customs duties on certain products imported from third countries. Therefore the contested measure must be regarded as a decision referring to a particular person and binding that person alone.

Under the second paragraph of Article 173 of the Treaty private individuals may institute proceedings for annulment against decisions which, although addressed to another person, are of direct and individual concern to them, but in the present case the defendant denies that the contested decision is of direct and individual concern to the applicant.

It is appropriate in the first place to examine whether the second requirement of admissibility is fulfilled because, if the applicant is not individually concerned by the decision, it becomes unnecessary to enquire whether he is directly concerned.

Persons other than those to whom a decision is addressed may only claim to be individually concerned if that decision affects them by reason of certain attributes which are peculiar to them or by reason of circumstances in which they are differentiated from all other persons and by virtue of these factors distinguishes them individually just as in the case of the person addressed. In the present case the applicant is affected by the disputed Decision as an importer of clementines, that is to say, by reason of a commercial activity which may at any time be practised by any person and is not therefore such as to distinguish the applicant in relation to the contested Decision as in the case of the addressee.

For these reasons the present action for annulment must be declared inadmissible.

Note

A string of cases have been decided in similar fashion, to the detriment of the applicant.

Calpak SpA v *Commission (Cases 789 & 790/79)*
[1980] ECR 1949
Court of Justice of the European Communities

The applicant, an Italian firm, sought annulment under Article 173 of the EC Treaty (now, after amendment, Article 230 EC) of Regulations governing the grant of production aid for Williams pears preserved in syrup. It observed that an identifiable class of producers, including the applicant itself, was affected by the measure. It added that, even within that group it was especially prejudiced, because the Commission's aid was fixed according to production in 1978/79 when Italian production was unusually low. *Plaumann* was a Decision addressed to another; here is a prima facie Regulation. The issue, however, is the same; does the applicant have individual concern in the matter? The Court first explains the Commission's view and then disposes of the application.

[6] The Commission's main contention is that as the disputed provisions were adopted in the form of regulations their annulment may only be sought if their content shows them to be, in fact, decisions. But in the Commission's view the provisions in question, which lay down rules of general application, are truly in the nature of regulations within the meaning of Article 189 of the Treaty. By selecting the 1978/79 marketing year as the reference period the Commission's intention was to limit and stabilize production at a level as low as that of that year. It is said to be possible, but certainly not indefensible that such a restriction has a greater incidence upon marginal producers such as the applicants than, for example, upon co-operatives, but that does not mean that the applicants are individually concerned within the meaning of the second paragraph of Article 173, which hypothesis the Commission denies in any case.

[7] The second paragraph of Article 173 empowers individuals to contest, *inter alia*, any decision which, although in the form of a regulation, is of direct and individual concern to them. The objective of that provision is in particular to prevent the Community institutions from being in a position, merely by choosing the form of a regulation, to exclude an application by an individual against a decision which concerns him directly and individually; it therefore stipulates that the choice of form cannot change the nature of the measure.

[8] By virtue of the second paragraph of Article 189 of the Treaty the criterion for distinguishing between a regulation and a decision is whether the measure at issue is of general application or not.

As the amendment to Regulation No 1530/78 made by Article 1(3) of Regulation No 1732/79 concerning the information to be submitted in support of the application for aid is merely the natural consequence of the limitation imposed by Article 1 of Regulation No 1731/79, consideration need only be given to the nature of the latter provision.

[9]   A provision which limits the granting of production aid for all producers in respect of a particular product to a uniform percentage of the quantity produced by them during a uniform preceding period is by nature a measure of general application within the meaning of Article 189 of the Treaty. In fact the measure applies to objectively determined situations and produces legal effects with regard to categories of persons described in a generalized and abstract manner. The nature of the measure as a regulation is not called in question by the mere fact that it is possible to determine the number or even the identity of the producers to be granted the aid which is limited thereby.

[10]   Nor is the fact that the choice of reference period is particularly important for the applicants, whose production is subject to considerable variation from one marketing year to another as a result of their own programme of production, sufficient to entitle them to an individual remedy. Moreover, the applicants have not established the existence of circumstances such as to justify describing that choice – the conformity of which with the Council's regulations, and especially with the basic regulation, is only relevant to the substantive issues of the case – as a decision adopted specifically in relation to them and, as such, entitling them to institute proceedings under the second paragraph of Article 173.

[11]   It follows that the objection raised by the Commission must be accepted as regards the applications for the annulment of the provisions in the two regulations in question.

[Accordingly:]

THE COURT hereby:

1.   Dismisses the applications as inadmissible;
2.   Orders the applicants to pay the costs.

Union Deutsche Lebensmittelwerke v Commission (Case 97/85)
[1987] ECR 2265
Court of Justice of the European Communities

By a Decision addressed to Germany, the Commission authorised a scheme for selling cheap butter for a short period on the West Berlin market. The object was market research into consumer demand for butter. However, promoting butter hurt sales of margarine. The applicant was a German margarine producer active on the Berlin market. It sought annulment of the Decision addressed to Germany under the second paragraph of Article 173 EEC (now the fourth paragraph of Article 230 EC).

[9]   It should be noted that, according to the second paragraph of Article 173 of the EEC Treaty, proceedings instituted by a natural or legal person against a decision addressed to another person are admissible only if that decision is of direct and individual concern to the applicant.

[10]   The Court has consistently held, since its judgment of 15 July 1963 in Case 25/62 Plaumann [1963] ECR 95, that a decision addressed to a Member State is of

direct and individual concern to natural or legal persons only if that decision affects them by reason of certain attributes which are peculiar to them, or by reason of circumstances in which they are differentiated from all other persons, and by virtue of these factors distinguishes them individually just as in the case of the person addressed.

[11] In this case it must be stated that the contested decision does not apply to a closed circle of persons who were known at the time of its adoption and whose rights the Commission intended to regulate. Although the contested decision affects the applicants, that is only because of the effects it produces on their position on the market. In that regard, the decision is of concern to the applicants just as it was to any other person supplying margarine on the West Berlin market while the contested operation was in progress, and it is not therefore of individual concern to them for the purposes of the second paragraph of Article 173 of the EEC Treaty.

[12] The applicants' argument to the effect that this application should be declared admissible so as to enable them to enjoy full legal protection must be rejected. It must be pointed out that, in support of an action challenging a national measure implementing a Community decision, the applicant may plead the illegality of that decision and thereby require the national court to adjudicate on all the allegations formulated in that respect, if necessary after making a reference to the Court of Justice for a ruling on the validity of the decision in question. The fact that the national court is empowered to determine which questions it intends to submit to the Court is an inherent feature of the system of means of redress established by the Treaty and is not therefore an argument which is capable of justifying a broad interpretation of the conditions of admissibility laid down in the second paragraph of Article 173 of the EEC Treaty.

Note

Paragraph 12 of the judgment indicates that this was not the only avenue of redress open to the applicant. The telling of the tale of the Berlin butter will be resumed later in this chapter. It provides a fine illustration of the pattern of interrelation of the remedies in the Community system, mentioned in the introduction to Part Three of this book.

Note that the Court never even reaches the merits of the challenge to the contested act in these cases.

These decisions indicate that the issue of individual concern and the issue whether the measure is a true Regulation or in reality a Decision (*International Fruit Company* (Cases 41–44/70) at p. 647 above) are conceptually similar. A genuinely normative measure is not susceptible to challenge.

The next case arose from the enforcement of the competition rules and should already be familiar from Chapter 13. It clearly involves a Decision addressed to another person, and the Court focuses on the problem of individual concern.

Metro-SB-Grossmärkte GmbH & Co. KG v *Commission (Case 26/76)*
[1977] ECR 1875
Court of Justice of the European Communities

Metro complained to the Commission under Article 3(2) of Regulation 17/62 about SABA's distributorship network. Metro had been excluded from it, and suggested that SABA was acting in violation of the Treaty competition rules. Contrary to Metro's hopes, the Commission ruled that some terms of SABA's system did not violate Article 85(1) of the EC Treaty (now Article 81(1) EC); others were exemptable under Article 85(3) (now Article 81(3) of the EC Treaty, see Chapter 11)). That ruling became the contested act. Metro wished to challenge under Article 173 of the EC Treaty (now, after amendment, Article 230 EC) the Decision addressed to SABA giving it a clean bill of health.

. . . [T]he contested decision was adopted in particular as the result of a complaint submitted by Metro and that it relates to the provisions of SABA's distribution system, on which SABA relied and continues to rely as against Metro in order to justify its refusal to sell to the latter or to appoint it as a wholesaler, and which the applicant had for this reason impugned in its complaint.

It is in the interests of a satisfactory administration of justice and of the proper application of Articles 85 and 86 that natural or legal persons who are entitled, pursuant to Article 3(2)(b) of Regulation No 17, to request the Commission to find an infringement of Articles 85 and 86 should be able, if their request is not complied with either wholly or in part, to institute proceedings in order to protect their legitimate interests.

In those circumstances the applicant must be considered to be directly and individually concerned, within the meaning of the second paragraph of Article 173, by the contested decision and the application is accordingly admissible.

Note
Looking at all the cases so far considered, the Court's choice of policy is the key feature. The terms of Article 230 invite a creative approach, for they do not lay down a detailed set of rules. The Court is perfectly willing to adjust its approach in accordance with the nature of the challenge before it. The next case arose in special circumstances which persuaded the Court to be receptive to the applicant.

Like Case C-70/88 (p. 646 above), it is a case overtaken by the Maastricht amendments, yet one which remains an important window on European Court interpretative technique. Unlike the present text of Article 230 EC (p. 643 above), the pre-Maastricht Article 173 EEC did not mention review of the acts of the Parliament. This did not deter the Court.

Parti Ecologiste 'Les Verts' v Parliament (Case 294/83)
[1986] ECR 1339
Court of Justice of the European Communities

The applicant, the 'Green Party', wished to challenge the Parliament's allocation of funds to reimburse costs incurred by political groupings which had participated in the 1984 European elections. It felt itself unfairly treated. But first it had to establish its standing. The Court first satisfied itself that, despite the terms of Article 173 of the EEC Treaty (now, after amendment, Article 230 EC), it had jurisdiction to annul measures adopted by the Parliament which were intended to have legal effects *vis-à-vis* third parties. It ruled that the case in issue involved such a measure. Then it turned to examine the issue of individual concern.

[29]   The applicant association emphasizes that it has legal personality and that the contested decisions, entailing as they do a grant of aid to rival political groupings, is certainly of direct and individual concern to it.

[30]   The European Parliament considers that, as the Court's case-law concerning that condition stands at present, the applicant association's action is inadmissible. However, it raises the question whether a wide interpretation of the first paragraph of Article 173 of the Treaty would not affect the interpretation to be given to the second paragraph of that article. It emphasizes in that regard that the applicant association is not an ordinary third party but, as a political party, occupies an intermediate position between the privileged applicants and private individuals. In its view, the special function of political parties must be taken into consideration at Community level. It considers that their special status justifies their being accorded a right of action under the second paragraph of Article 173 of the Treaty against measures which determine under what conditions and in what amount they are to receive, on the occasion of the direct elections, funds from the European Parliament for the purpose of making the latter more widely known. In its defence, the European Parliament concludes from that line of reasoning that political parties are directly and individually concerned by the 1983 Rules.

[31]   It must first be pointed out that the contested measures are of direct concern to the applicant association. They constitute a complete set of rules which are sufficient in themselves and which require no implementing provisions, since the calculation of the share of the appropriations to be granted to each of the political groupings concerned is automatic and leaves no room for any discretion.

[32]   It remains to be examined whether the applicant association is individually concerned by the contested measures.

[33]   That examination must be centred on the 1982 Decision. That decision approved the principle of granting the appropriations entered under Item 3708 to the political groupings; it then determined the share of those appropriations to be paid to the political groups in the Assembly elected in 1979 and to the non-attached members of that Assembly (69%) and the share of the appropriations to be distributed among all the political groupings, whether or not represented in the Assembly elected in 1979, which took part in the 1984 elections (31%); finally, it divided the 69% between the political groups and the non-attached members. The 1983 Rules merely confirmed the 1982 Decision and completed it by setting out the formula for the division of the 31% reserve fund. They must therefore be regarded as an integral part of the original decision.

[34]   The 1982 Decision concerns all the political groupings, even though the treatment they receive differs according to whether or not they were represented in the Assembly elected in 1979.

[35]   This action concerns a situation which has never before come before the Court. Because they had representatives in the institution, certain political groupings took part in the adoption of a decision which deals both with their own treatment and with that accorded to rival groupings which were not represented. In view of this, and in view of the fact that the contested measure concerns the allocation of public funds for the purpose of preparing for elections and it is alleged that those funds were allocated unequally, it cannot be considered that only groupings which were represented and which were therefore identifiable at the date of the adoption of the contested measure are individually concerned by it.

[36]   Such an interpretation would give rise to inequality in the protection afforded by the Court to the various groupings competing in the same elections. Groupings not represented could not prevent the allocation of the appropriations at issue before the beginning of the election campaign because they would be unable to plead the illegality of the basic decision except in support of an action against the individual decisions refusing to reimburse sums greater than those provided for. It would therefore be impossible for them to bring an action for annulment before the Court prior to the elections or to obtain an order from the Court under Article 185 of the Treaty suspending application of the contested basic decision.

[37]   Consequently, it must be concluded that the applicant association, which was in existence at the time when the 1982 Decision was adopted and which was able to present candidates at the 1984 elections, is individually concerned by the contested measures.

[38]   In the light of all those considerations, it must be concluded that the application is admissible.

Note
In *Parti Ecologiste 'Les Verts'* v *Parliament* (Case 190/84) [1988] ECR 1017, the Court was significantly less receptive to the admissibility of the claim. These cases again touch on institutional balance; see, on the impact of the Maastricht Treaty, Bradley's 'Better Rusty than Missin?' mentioned at p. 647 above.

It is notable throughout '*Les Verts*' (Case 294/83) that the Parliament was not prepared vigorously to contest the standing of its challenger. This is explicable with reference to its own strategic interest in achieving a broadening of the standing rules (see p. 645 above).

(iv)   Direct concern
This additional element of the Article 230, fourth paragraph standing rules, mentioned in para. 31 of the previous case, requires the existence of a direct causal link between the challenged Community act and the impact on the applicant.

International Fruit Company v Commission (Cases 41–44/70)
[1971] ECR 411
Court of Justice of the European Communities

The case has already been examined above, at p. 647. Individual concern was there established. In the following extract the Court looks for the applicant's direct concern in the matter.

[23]   Moreover, it is clear from the system introduced by Regulation No 459/70, and particularly from Article 2(2) thereof, that the Decision on the grant of import licences is a matter for the Commission.

[24]   According to this provision, the Commission alone is competent to assess the economic situation in the light of which the grant of import licences must be justified.

[25]   Article 1(2) of Regulation No 459/70, by providing that 'the Member States shall in accordance with the conditions laid down in Article 2, issue the licence to any interested party applying for it', makes it clear that the national authorities do not enjoy any discretion in the matter of the issue of licences and the conditions on which applications by the parties concerned should be granted.

[26]   The duty of such authorities is merely to collect the data necessary in order that the Commission may take its Decision in accordance with Article 2(2) of that Regulation, and subsequently adopt the national measures needed to give effect to that Decision.

[27]   In these circumstances as far as the interested parties are concerned, the issue of or refusal to issue the import licences must be bound up with this Decision.

[28]   The measure whereby the Commission decides on the issues of the import licences thus directly affects the legal position of the parties concerned.

[29]   The applications thus fulfil the requirements of the second paragraph of Article 173 of the Treaty, and are therefore admissible.

Note
Typically, the insertion of a discretionary power vested by Community legislation in national authorities will preclude a direct challenge to the Community act establishing the general system.

Municipality of Differdange v *Commission* (Case 222/83)
[1984] ECR 2889
Court of Justice of the European Communities

The contested act was addressed by the Commission to Luxembourg. It authorised Luxembourg to grant aids to steel firms, provided they undertook reductions in capacity. The applicant municipality argued it was directly and individually concerned by the Commission's Decision on the following grounds:

[5]   . . . Although the contested decision is addressed to the Grand Duchy of Luxembourg it is, from two points of view, of direct and individual concern to the applicants within the meaning of the second paragraph of Article 173 of the EEC Treaty. In the first place the reduction of production capacity and the closure of factories located in their municipal territory results, they claim, in a reduction of the yield from local taxes. In the second place, they contend that according to a principle of administrative law known to several Member States, which also applies in Community law, the interests of the inhabitants of a municipality and the interests of the undertakings established in the municipal territory must be regarded as the municipalities' own interests.

The Court found the applicant had no standing under the ECSC Treaty and turned to the EEC rules:

[9]   With regard, secondly, to the admissibility of the action under the EEC Treaty it must be recalled that the second paragraph of Article 173 of the Treaty makes the admissibility of an action brought by a natural or legal person other than the person

to whom a Council or Commission Decision is addressed, for a declaration that the measure in question is void, subject to the requirement that the contested Decision is of direct and individual concern to him. The purpose of that provision is to ensure that legal protection is also available to a person who, whilst not the person to whom the contested measure is addressed, is in fact affected by it in the same way as is the addressee.

[10]   In this case the contested measure, which is addressed to the Grand Duchy of Luxembourg, authorizes it to grant certain aids to the undertakings named therein provided that they reduce their production capacity by a specified amount. However, it neither identifies the establishments in which the production must be reduced or terminated nor the factories which must be closed as a result of the termination of production. In addition, the Decision states that the Commission was to be notified of the closure dates only by 31 January 1984 so that the undertakings affected were free until that date to fix, where necessary with the agreement of the Luxembourg Government, the detailed rules for the restructuring necessary to comply with the conditions laid down in the Decision.

[11]   That conclusion is, moreover, confirmed by Article 2 of the Decision according to which the capacity reductions may also be carried out by other undertakings.

[12]   It follows that the contested Decision left to the national authorities and undertakings concerned such a margin of discretion with regard to the manner of its implementation and in particular with regard to the choice of the factories to be closed, that the Decision cannot be regarded as being of direct and individual concern to the municipalities with which the undertakings affected, by virtue of the location of their factories, are connected.

[13]   Since the action is therefore inadmissible also to the extent to which it is based on the provisions of the EEC Treaty, it must be dismissed.

Note
See also *Alcan Aluminium Raeren* v *Commission* (Case 69/69) [1970] ECR 385; *Bock* v *Commission* (Case 62/70) [1971] ECR 897; *ARPOSOL* v *Council* (Case 55/86) [1988] ECR 13; *ASPEC* v *Commission* (Case T-435/93) [1995] ECR II-1281.
   Notice that where the intervention of the national authorities prevents an Article 230 action against the Community act, it may instead be possible to challenge the acts of the national authorities at national level, p. 693 below. Indirectly this may permit a challenge to the Community act. Here, then, is a further example of the construction of a complete system of remedies through the interrelation of the several Treaty provisions. This structure will become clearer once the material in this chapter is fully understood.

Further reading
Craig, P., 'Legality, Standing and Substantive Review in Community Law' (1994) 14 Ox JLS 507.
Harlow, C., 'Towards a Theory of Access for the European Court of Justice' (1992) 12 YEL 213.
Rasmussen, H., 'Why is Article 173 Interpreted against Private Plaintiffs?' (1980) 5 EL Rev 112.

(v)   The example of the anti-dumping cases

Anti-dumping procedures are taken where the Commission determines that goods are being dumped on the Community market by traders in third States at unfairly low prices. In order to prevent distortion of the Community market, action is taken in the form of anti-dumping duties imposed by Regulation. These are levies imposed on the products being dumped, thereby raising their price. There is, then, a *general* policy; but it affects *particular* traders. Those traders are naturally eager to protect their interests by challenging the Community measure imposing the duty. But do they have standing? They must show that the act is challengeable *and* that they have standing; two procedural hurdles which are to some extent interdependent. Several important cases have been fought on the issue. All four cases extracted in this sub-section are from the pre-Maastricht era. Consequently they refer to Article 173(2) EEC. Post-Amsterdam, this is Article 230(4) EC (p. 647 above).

NTN Toyo Bearing Co. v *Council (Case 113/77)*
[1979] ECR 1185
Court of Justice of the European Communities

A Regulation imposed an anti-dumping duty on ball-bearings originating in Japan. NTN, a Japanese ball-bearing producer, and its subsidiary companies sought annulment of the measure in so far as it affected them.

The admissibility of the application

[7]   The Council has raised an objection of inadmissibility claiming that the contested Article forms part of a Regulation and that the applicants are therefore not entitled to request annulment of it under the second paragraph of Article 173 of the Treaty. It claims that in the present case this is not a Decision adopted in the guise of a Regulation since Regulation No 1778/77 in fact constitutes a general rule which affects all the products in question originating in Japan and which must, according to Article 19(1) of Regulation No 459/68 of the Council of 5 April 1968 on protection against dumping or the granting of bounties or subsidies by countries which are not members of the European Economic Community (Official Journal, English Special Edition 1968 (I), p. 80), be adopted in the form of a Regulation.

[8]   The applicants reply that the contested Article, although drafted in abstract terms, in fact affects only the first applicant and three other Japanese undertakings which produce the products in question (hereinafter referred to as 'the major producers'), as well as their subsidiaries in the Community. The preliminary investigation carried out before the adoption of Regulation No 1778/77 was limited to inquiries made first at the premises of the European subsidiaries and then at the premises of the major producers in Japan. The specific nature of the measure is confirmed by Article 3 of Regulation No 1778/77 which provides for the collection of the amounts secured by way of provisional duty only as regards the products manufactured and exported by the major producers. The contested Article therefore constitutes a Decision which affects only the major producers and their subsidiaries and must therefore be considered to be a Decision concerning them adopted in the guise of a Regulation.

[9]   Before commencing the examination of the admissibility of the application, it should be stated that NTN and its subsidiaries are sufficiently closely associated for the Commission to have considered, during its examination of the matter, that it was necessary to apply to them the special provisions concerning export prices laid down in Article 3(3) of the basic Regulation, Regulation No 459/68. In these circumstances there is no need, as regards the question whether the contested measure is of direct and individual concern to the applicants, to make a distinction in relation to them between producers on the one hand and importers on the other.

[10]   Regulation No 1778/77 contains essentially three provisions:
     (i)   Article 1 imposes a definitive anti-dumping duty of 15% on the products in question originating in Japan and suspends the application of that duty without prejudice to Article 2;
     (ii)   Article 2 regulates the monitoring of the undertakings given by the major Japanese producers and empowers the Commission to terminate the suspension of the application of the duty if it finds that these undertakings are being evaded, not being observed or have been withdrawn;
     (iii)   Article 3 provides, in respect of the products manufactured by the major producers, for the collection of the amounts secured by way of provisional duty in application of the imposition by previous Regulations of a provisional duty.

[11]   Article 3 constitutes accordingly a collective Decision relating to named addressees. Although the collection of the amounts secured by way of provisional anti-dumping duty is *per se* of direct concern to any importer who has imported the products in question subject to such duty, the special feature of Article 3 which sets it apart is that it does not concern all importers but only those who have imported the products manufactured by the four major Japanese producers named in that Article. The allegation of the Council and the intervener that only implementing measures adopted by the national authorities are of direct concern to the importers and that these importers should therefore, where appropriate, bring the matter before the national courts having jurisdiction disregards the fact that such implementation is purely automatic and, moreover, in pursuance not of intermediate national rules but of Community rules alone.

[12]   Article 3 of Regulation No 1778/77 is therefore of direct and individual concern to those importers and consequently the applications lodged by the susidiaries, as importers of NTN products, are admissible. As a result the application lodged by NTN against that Article is also admissible.

Note
The applicants in the next case were less successful. You will obtain valuable insight into the Court's approach by carefully contrasting this decision with *NTN Toyo Bearing*, above.

Alusuisse Italia SpA v *Council and Commission (Case 307/81)*
[1982] ECR 3463
Court of Justice of the European Communities

The Regulation imposed an anti-dumping duty on orthoxylene originating in Puerto Rico and the USA. The applicant, a company based in Milan, needed orthoxylene as a raw material in its production processes. It imported orthoxylene independently – it was not linked to a manufacturer or an exporting firm. Did it have standing to challenge the measure imposing the duty, which had affected it by raising the prices it had to pay?

[7]   The second paragraph of Article 173 of the Treaty makes the admissibility of proceedings instituted by an individual for a declaration that a measure is void dependent on fulfilment of the condition that the contested measure, although in the form of a Regulation, in fact constitutes a Decision which is of direct and individual concern to him. The objective of that provision is in particular to prevent the Community institutions, merely by choosing the form of a Regulation, from being able to exclude an application by an individual against a Decision of direct and individual concern to him and thus to make clear that the choice of form may not alter the nature of a measure.

[8]   Nevertheless an action brought by an individual is not admissible in so far as it is directed against a Regulation having general application within the meaning of the second paragraph of Article 189 of the Treaty, the test for distinguishing between a Regulation and a Decision, according to the settled case-law of the Court, being whether or not the measure in question has general application. It is therefore necessary to appraise the nature of the contested measures and in particular the legal effects which they are intended to produce or in fact produce.

[9]   In that connection it should be borne in mind that the Regulations at issue have as their object the imposition of an anti-dumping duty on all imports of orthoxylene originating in the United States of America and Puerto Rico, subject to certain exemptions laid down for products exported by undertakings expressly named. Consequently, such measures constitute, as regards independent importers who, in contrast to exporters, are not expressly named in the Regulations, measures having general application within the meaning of the second paragraph of Article 189 of the Treaty, because they apply to objectively determined situations and entail legal effects for categories of persons regarded generally and in the abstract.

[10]   The applicant claims in that connection that, although the contested measures were adopted in the form of Regulations, they in fact constitute Decisions concerning it since importers of orthoxylene who are also users of that substance form a closed category of traders of a limited number whose identity was known at the date when the Regulations were adopted.

[11]   That argument must be rejected. As the Court has already stated, a measure does not cease to be a regulation because it is possible to determine the number or even the identity of the persons to whom it applies at any given time as long as it is established that such application takes effect by virtue of an objective legal or factual situation defined by the measure in relation to its purpose. That applies to independent importers of orthoxylene. Under the Regulations the anti-dumping duty is imposed on persons importing the product from the countries in question solely by reference to the objective criterion that they are importers of that product. Consequently, the Regulations at issue constitute, as regard such importers, measures having general application within the meaning of the second paragraph of Article 189 of the Treaty and not Decisions of direct and individual concern to them.

[12]   In favour of the admissibility of its application the applicant also argues that the particular features of the procedure leading to the adoption of the anti-dumping

Regulations, in particular the participation of the various interested parties in the successive stages of that procedure, lead to the conclusion that the measures in question constitute individual administrative measures which may be contested by individuals under the second paragraph of Article 173 of the Treaty.

[13]   That argument must also be rejected since the distinction between a Regulation and a Decision may be based only on the nature of the measure itself and the legal effects which it produces and not on the procedures for its adoption. That solution is furthermore in conformity with the system of remedies provided for by Community law since importers may contest before the national courts individual measures taken by the national authorities in application of the Community Regulations.

[14]   For all those reasons, it must be concluded that the contested measures are Regulations and not Decisions within the meaning of the second paragraph of Article 173 of the Treaty, so that the application must be dismissed as inadmissible.

Note
The next case confirms, as in *Metro* v *Commission* (Case 26/76), at p. 652 above, that complainants enjoy a special status. However, unlike in *Metro*, the challenged act seems to be a Regulation, not a Decision. The Court here appears ready to hold a measure a Regulation, but a Decision as far as the applicant is concerned – a hybrid measure.

Timex v *Council and Commission (Case 264/82)*
[1985] ECR 849
Court of Justice of the European Communities

A Regulation imposed an anti-dumping duty on wrist watches from the Soviet Union. Timex sought annulment for reasons quite distinct from those motivating the applicants in the previous two cases. As a producer of watches based in the Community, it wanted the duties annulled because they were too *low* to protect it from unfair Soviet competition. But did it have standing?

[9]   In support of their objection of inadmissibility the defendants argue that the contested Regulation is not addressed to Timex, that Timex is not mentioned by name in its Articles and that Timex is not directly and individually concerned by the Regulation, which in their view affects all manufacturers of mechanical wrist-watches in the Community alike. That view is not altered by the fact that Timex may be entitled to request the opening of an anti-dumping proceeding, since, according to the Decisions of the Court, the distinction between a Regulation and a Decision depends solely on the nature of the measure itself and its consequences in law.

[10]   On the other hand, Timex and the parties intervening in its support contend that the action is admissible because the contested Regulation constitutes in reality a Decision which is of direct and individual concern to Timex within the meaning of the second paragraph of Article 173 of the EEC Treaty. They submit that the Regulation was adopted as a result of a complaint lodged on behalf of Timex, amongst others, and that it therefore constitutes the culmination of an administrative proceeding initiated at Timex's request. Its interest in bringing proceedings is all the more

evident in so far as it is the only remaining manufacturer of mechanical wrist-watches in the United Kingdom and the anti-dumping duty in question was fixed exclusively by reference to its economic situation.

[11]   The questions of admissibility raised by the Council and the Commission must be resolved in the light of the system established by Regulation No 3017/79 and, more particularly, of the nature of the anti-dumping measures provided for by that Regulation, regard being had to the provisions of the second paragraph of Article 173 of the EEC Treaty.

[12]   Article 13(1) of Regulation No 3017/79 provides that 'Anti-dumping or countervailing duties, whether provisional or definitive, shall be imposed by Regulation'. In the light of the criteria set out in the second paragraph of Article 173, the measures in question are, in fact, legislative in nature and scope, inasmuch as they apply to traders in general; nevertheless, their provisions may be of direct and individual concern to some of those traders. In this regard, it is necessary to consider in particular the part played by the applicant in the anti-dumping proceedings and its position on the market to which the contested legislation applies.

[13]   It should be pointed out first of all that the complaint under Article 5 of Regulation No 3017/79 which led to the adoption of Regulation No 1882/82 was lodged by the British Clock and Watch Manufacturers' Association Limited on behalf of manufacturers of mechanical watches in France and the United Kingdom, including Timex. According to the documents before the Court, that association took action because a complaint which Timex had itself lodged in April 1979 had been rejected by the Commission on the ground that it came from only one Community manufacturer.

[14]   The complaint which led to the opening of the investigation procedure therefore owes its origin to the complaints originally made by Timex. Moreover, it is clear from the preamble to Commission Regulation No 84/82 and the preamble to Council Regulation No 1882/82 that Timex's views were heard during that procedure.

[15]   It must also be remembered that Timex is the leading manufacturer of mechanical watches and watch movements in the Community and the only remaining manufacturer of those products in the United Kingdom. Furthermore, as is also clear from the preambles to Regulations Nos 84/82 and 1882/82, the conduct of the investigation procedure was largely determined by Timex's observations and the anti-dumping duty was fixed in the light of the effect of the dumping on Timex. More specifically, the preamble to Regulation No 1882/82 makes it clear that the definitive anti-dumping duty was made equal to the dumping margin which was found to exist 'taking into account the extent of the injury caused to Timex by the dumped imports'. The contested Regulation is therefore based on the applicant's own situation.

[16]   It follows that the contested Regulation constitutes a Decision which is of direct and individual concern to Timex within the meaning of the second paragraph of Article 173 of the EEC Treaty. As the Court held in its judgment of 4 October 1983 in Case 191/82 *EEC Seed Crushers' and Oil Processors' Federation (FEDIOL)* v *Commission* ([1983] ECR 2913), the applicant is therefore entitled to put before the Court any matters which would facilitate a review as to whether the Commission has observed the procedural guarantees granted to complainants by Regulation No 3017/79 and whether or not it has committed manifest errors in its assessment of the facts, has omitted to take any essential matters into consideration or has based the reasons for its Decision on considerations amounting to a misuse of powers. In that

respect, the Court is required to exercise its normal powers of review over a discretion granted to a public authority, even though it has no jurisdiction to intervene in the exercise of the discretion reserved to the Community authorities by the aforementioned Regulation.

[17] Since the action is therefore admissible, the objection of inadmissibility raised by the Council and the Commission must be dismissed.

Note
R. Greaves, writing in 1986, surveyed *NTN Toyo Bearing* (Case 113/77) and *Alusuisse* (Case 307/81) and other cases in the area ('Locus Standi under Article 173 EEC when seeking Annulment of a Regulation' (1986) 11 EL Rev 119). She concluded:

What of the future? The Decisions of the Court seem to suggest that cases concerning particular areas of EEC Law such as the competition rules and dumping rules may well encourage a more flexible approach from the Court where admissibility under Article 173, second paragraph, is in dispute. This will be so particularly where the applicant not only has to show direct and individual concern but also that the Regulation is really a Decision within the measure of that Article. How far it will be possible to transpose the Court's rulings in these specific areas to the general body of Community law one can only guess. It would not be surprising if the Court, encouraged by its Advocate Generals and by commentators, took a much more liberal approach in the future and gave Article 173, second paragraph, a more vital role in assisting individuals to subject more of the Community acts to judicial review.

Note
This area of the law continues to provide the Court with a fertile field of litigation. As Greaves indicates, the Court's policy is in a state of flux and is only partly predictable. It is a policy which is susceptible to adjustment. The next case, a 1991 decision, follows neatly from Greaves's concluding sentence, and suggests the Court decided to take a more liberal approach to the standing rules.

Extramet v *Council (Case C-358/89)*
[1991] ECR I-2501
Court of Justice of the European Communities

Extramet, a French firm, sought the annulment of a Regulation imposing an anti-dumping duty on imports of calcium metal from China and the Soviet Union. The Council disputed the admissibility of the application on the basis that Extramet was an independent importer lacking individual concern. The Council referred to the Court's line of authority which, it submitted, showed Extramet had no standing.

[14] . . . [M]easures imposing anti-dumping duties may, without losing their character as regulations, be of individual concern in certain circumstances to certain traders who therefore have standing to bring an action for their annulment.

[15]   The Court has acknowledged that this was the case, in general, with regard to producers and exporters who are able to establish that they were identified in the measures adopted by the Commission or the Council or were concerned by the preliminary measures (see the judgments in Joined Cases 239/82 and 275/82 *Allied Corporation* v *Commission* [1984] ECR 1005, and in Joined Cases C-133/87 and C-150/87 *Nashua Corporation* v *Commission and Council* [1990] ECR I-719, and in Case C-156/87 *Gestetner Holdings* v *Council and Commission* [1990] ECR I-781), and with regard to importers whose retail prices for the goods in question have been used as a basis for establishing the export prices (see, most recently, the judgments in Case C-304/86 *Enital* v *Commission and Council* [1990] ECR I-2939, Case C-305/86 *Neotype Techmashexport* v *Commission and Council* [1990] ECR I-2945, and Case C-157/87 *Electroimpex* v *Council* [1990] ECR I-3021).

[16]   Such recognition of the right of certain categories of traders to bring an action for the annulment of an anti-dumping regulation cannot, however, prevent other traders from also claiming to be individually concerned by such a regulation by reason of certain attributes which are peculiar to them and which differentiate them from all other persons (see the judgment in Case 25/62 *Plaumann* v *Commission* [1963] ECR 95).

[17]   The applicant has established the existence of a set of factors constituting such a situation which is peculiar to the applicant and which differentiates it, as regards the measure in question, from all other traders. The applicant is the largest importer of the product forming the subject-matter of the anti-dumping measure and, at the same time, the end-user of the product. In addition, its business activities depend to a very large extent on those imports and are seriously affected by the contested regulation in view of the limited number of manufacturers of the product concerned and of the difficulties which it encounters in obtaining supplies from the sole Community producer, which, moreover, is its main competitor for the processed product.

[18]   It follows that the objection of inadmissibility raised by the Council must be dismissed.

Note

The novel feature of the decision is that the Court held admissible an action by an independent importer unconnected with any producer or exporter subject to the anti-dumping duty. Subsequently the measure was declared void ([1992] ECR I-3813), although the dispute continued (Case T-2/95 *Industrie des poudres sphériques* v *Council* [1998] ECR I-3939).

Questions
1.   What factors peculiar to the case induced the Court to hear Extramet's application? Can you distinguish this case from *Alusuisse* (Case 307/81) at p. 659 above?
2.   Was the measure in *Extramet* a Regulation or a Decision? Does it matter?

(vi)   Towards a general liberalisation of the standing rules?
The Court's willingness to adjust its stance did not end with *Extramet* (Case C-358/89). Perhaps the liberal attitude in that case could be attributed to the

special circumstances prevailing in the sphere of anti-dumping. However, in the next case the Court seems prepared to transplant the liberal approach accepted in specific sectors such as anti-dumping into the broad area of challenges to general market regulation. The ruling has the appearance of a landmark in the Court's interpretation of the standing rules under Article 173 of the EC Treaty (now, after amendment, Article 230 EC) applicable to non-privileged applicants.

Codorniu SA v *Council (Case C–309/89)*
[1994] ECR I–1853
Court of Justice of the European Communities

Codorniu, a Spanish producer of sparkling wines, sought to annul a provision in Council Regulation 2045/89, amending Regulation 3309/85, laying down general rules for the description and presentation of sparkling wines. The measure reserved the term *crémant* for certain quality sparkling wines manufactured in France and Luxembourg. It was explained in the recitals to the Regulation that this protected traditional descriptions used in those two countries. Codorniu had held and, since 1924, had used the Spanish trade mark *Gran Crémant de Codorniu* to designate one of its wines. It wished to challenge the Regulation. The Council objected to the admissibility of the application.

[14]   In support of its objection of inadmissibility the Council states that it did not adopt the contested provision on the basis of the circumstances peculiar to certain producers but on the basis of a choice of wine-marketing policy in relation to a particular product. The contested provision reserves the use of the term 'crémant' to quality sparkling wines psr manufactured under specific conditions in certain Member States. It thus constitutes a measure applicable to an objectively determined situation which has legal effects in respect of categories of persons considered in a general and abstract manner.

[15]   According to the Council, Codorniu is concerned by the contested provision only in its capacity as a producer of quality sparkling wine psr using the term 'crémant', like any other producer in an identical situation. Even if when that provision was adopted the number or identity of producers of sparkling wines using the term 'crémant' could theoretically be determined, the measure in question remains essentially a regulation inasmuch as it applies on the basis of an objective situation of law or fact defined by the measure in relation to its objective.

[16]   Codorniu alleges that the contested provision is in reality a decision adopted in the guise of a regulation. It has no general scope but affects a well-determined class of producers which cannot be altered. Such producers are those who on 1 September 1989 traditionally designated their sparkling wines with the term 'crémant'. For that class the contested provision has no general scope. Furthermore, the direct result of the contested provision will be to prevent Codorniu from using the term 'Gran Cremant' which will involve a loss of 38% of its turnover. The effect of that damage is to distinguish it, within the meaning of the second paragraph of Article 173 of the Treaty, from any other trader. Codorniu alleges that the Court has already recognised the admissibility of an action for annulment brought by a natural or legal person

against a regulation in such circumstances (see the judgment in Case C–358/89 *Extramet Industrie* v *Council* [1991] ECR I–2501).

[17] Under the second paragraph of Article 173 of the Treaty the institution of proceedings by a natural or legal person for a declaration that a regulation is void is subject to the condition that the provisions of the regulation at issue in the proceedings constitute in reality a decision of direct and individual concern to that person.

[18] As the Court has already held, the general applicability, and thus the legislative nature, of a measure is not called in question by the fact that it is possible to determine more or less exactly the number or even the identity of the persons to whom it applies at any given time, as long as it is established that it applies to them by virtue of an objective legal or factual situation defined by the measure in question in relation to its purpose (see most recently the judgment in Case C–298/89 *Gibraltar* v *Council* [1993] ECR I–3605, paragraph 17).

[19] Although it is true that according to the criteria in the second paragraph of Article 173 of the Treaty the contested provision is, by nature and by virtue of its sphere of application, of a legislative nature in that it applies to the traders concerned in general, that does not prevent it from being of individual concern to some of them.

[20] Natural or legal persons may claim that a contested provision is of individual concern to them only if it affects them by reason of certain attributes which are peculiar to them or by reason of circumstances in which they are differentiated from all other persons (see the judgment in Case 25/62 *Plaumann* v *Commission* [1963] ECR 95).

[21] Codorniu registered the graphic trade mark 'Gran Cremant de Codorniu' in Spain in 1924 and traditionally used that mark both before and after registration. By reserving the right to use the term 'crémant' to French and Luxembourg producers, the contested provision prevents Codorniu from using its graphic trade mark.

[22] It follows that Codorniu has established the existence of a situation which from the point of view of the contested provision differentiates it from all other traders.

[23] It follows that the objection of inadmissibility put forward by the Council must be dismissed.

Note
The Court proceeded to determine that the measure's discrimination between producers from different countries lacked objective justification. The contested provision was accordingly declared void. The ruling is more generous to the admissibility of an application by an individual firm affected by a measure of market regulation than past European Court practice might have led one to expect.

D. Waelbroeck and D. Fosselard, 'Annotation of Case C–309/89, *Codorniu SA* v *Council*', (1995) 32 CML Rev 257, 268–9.

(Footnote omitted.)

The Court's judgment in *Codorniu* certainly marks an important evolution in the case law on admissibility of direct appeals by individuals against regulations.

First, the Court seems to have accepted that the nature of the contested provision was not an important issue in order to determine if a private applicant must be granted *locus standi* under Article 173. Even true legislative measures may be challenged if the applicant is capable of demonstrating that he is individually and directly concerned by them.

The second evolution relates to the notion of 'individual concern'. The Court seems to have made a decisive step in enlarging that notion. Previously, an individual could show that he was individually concerned by a provision only by demonstrating that he had in some way prompted the adoption of the contested measure. In *Codorniu*, the Court indicated that an applicant may be individually concerned by a regulation if that regulation has special and serious economic consequences for him. However, the Court made clear in *Codorniu* that these economic consequences must be of such a nature as to differentiate the applicant from all other persons affected by the contested provision.

Firstly, the contested provision must place the applicant at a disadvantage on the market or, in other words, affect its competitive position on the market.

Secondly, the contested provision must concern an important part of the applicant's economic activities and must represent a serious risk for the profitability of the applicant's business.

Although the reasoning of *Codorniu* is scarce, one might be tempted to conclude that if a measure creates a burden that is particularly heavy for some persons compared to the usual burden supported by the persons affected by that kind of measure, the individuals that support these particular heavy consequences are to be considered as individually concerned by the measure in question.

In conclusion, the Court's judgment in *Codorniu* certainly gives new hopes for private individuals wanting to challenge the legality of EC regulations. However, it is important to underline that the *Codorniu* judgment is barely reasoned and that, therefore, too much hope may not be laid on the judgment at this stage. At most, it can be read as granting *locus standi* to individuals that are specially affected by a legislative measure. *Prima facie*, it should not be sufficient for an applicant to demonstrate that he supported some kind of prejudice following the adoption of a regulation, in order to be granted *locus standi* against a regulation. It must be demonstrated that the applicant is supporting an abnormally heavy prejudice following the adoption of the contested measure, a prejudice peculiar to the applicant and which is not supported by other traders. It will be for the Court of First Instance which has recently been given jurisdiction over all actions brought by private parties to seize the opportunities opened by the *Codorniu* judgment in order to improve judicial protection in the Community. *Codorniu* will certainly serve as a stepping stone to future developments in the case law on this issue.

Note
Read also A. Arnull, 'Private applicants and the action for annulment under Article 173 of the EC Treaty' (1995) 32 CML Rev 7; J. Usher, 'Individual concern in general legislation – 10 years on' (1994) 19 EL Rev 636; N. Neuwahl, 'Article 173 Paragraph 4 EC: Past, Present and Possible Future' (1996) 21 EL Rev 17. More generally, a collection of 24 relevant essays is contained in H.-W. Micklitz and N. Reich, *Public Interest Litigation before European Courts* (Nomos, 1996).

As comment in the final paragraph of the above extract suggests, the development of the law now rests initially with the Court of First Instance

(p. 647 above), which will be asked to determine how far the floodgates of admissibility should be thrown open. *Codorniu* is plainly a significant ruling, but there were special factors affecting the applicant's position, most notably its property right in the trade mark, which could conceivably be used as a basis for limiting the decision's contribution to the general liberalisation of the rules affecting non-privileged applicants under Article 173 of the EC Treaty (now, after amendment, Article 230 EC) (and see para. 72 of the order in Case T–219/95R, below). In itself, *Codorniu* is no mandate for using Article 230 as an avenue for general challenges to legislation brought in the 'public interest' by parties unable to show some special interest in the matter. (As shown at p. 645 above, the Parliament too is inhibited from acting as guardian of the public interest.) This is well illustrated by the next case. Although arising out of a mere application for an interim order, the restrictive approach taken by the President of the Court of First Instance is instructive.

Danielsson, Largenteau and Haoa v *Commission (Case T–219/95R)*
[1995] ECR II-3051
Order of the President of the Court of First Instance

The applicants were residents of Tahiti in French Polynesia. The dispute arose out of well-publicised French nuclear tests carried out on Mururoa atoll in the South Pacific in the summer of 1995. Article 34 of the EURATOM Treaty provides, *inter alia*, that any Member State in whose territories particularly dangerous experiments are to take place shall take health and safety measures on which it shall first obtain the Commission's opinion. A Commission decision of 23 October 1995 stated that, according to information supplied by France, the tests did not present a perceptible risk of significant exposure of workers or the general public to ionizing radiation. The applicants sought suspension of the operation of this Commission decision. They also sought an order that the Commission take all measures necessary to preserve and protect the applicant's rights under the EURATOM Treaty. The application for interim measures was dealt with by the President of the Court of First Instance. The application was formally pursued under the EURATOM Treaty, but the principles are equally applicable to the EC Treaty, and indeed case law including *Codorniu* (Case C–309/89) itself was cited. In accordance with settled case law relating to interim measures, admissibility is precluded only if the application is at first sight manifestly inadmissible. The applicants failed at this hurdle.

63.   It must be determined here whether, at first sight, the main application for annulment may be considered to meet the conditions for admissibility as regards both the nature of the contested act and the locus standi of the applicants.

64.   First, as regards the nature of the contested act of the Commission, it appears, prima facie, both from the tenor of that act and from the legal and factual context in which it was adopted that it may be construed, with a certain probability and in

accordance with well-established case-law, as being in the nature of a decision in that it embodies the final position adopted by the Commission, which is intended to have legal effects (see Case 22/70 *Commission* v *Council* [1971] ECR 263, paragraphs 38 to 42), in so far as, in any event, it has the effect of ruling out the application of Article 34 of the [EURATOM] Treaty, which requires the Member State concerned to take additional health and safety measures on which it must first obtain the opinion of the Commission.

65.   The contested act may therefore be considered, prima facie, a being in the nature of a decision.

66.   Secondly, as regards the locus standi of the applicants, under the fourth paragraph of Article 146 of the Treaty, any natural or legal person may, under the conditions laid down in the first paragraph of that article, institute proceedings against a decision addressed to that person or against a decision which, although in the form of a regulation or a decision addressed to another person, is of direct and individual concern to the former.

67.   In the present case, the contested decision was not addressed to the applicants but to the French Government. It must therefore be determined whether it is none the less of direct and individual concern to them.

68.   As regards, first, the question whether the contested decision is of individual concern to the applicants, it has consistently been held that 'persons other than those to whom a decision is addressed may claim to be individually concerned by that decision only if it affects them by reason of certain attributes which are peculiar to them or by reason of circumstances in which they are differentiated from all other persons and if by virtue of those factors it distinguishes them individually just as in the case of the person addressed' (see Case 25/62 *Plaumann* v *Commission* [1963] ECR 95, Joined Cases 67/85, 68/85 and 70/85 *van der Kooy* v *Commission* [1988] ECR 219, paragraph 14, and the order of 6 July 1995 in Joined Cases T–447/93, T–448/93 and T–449/93 *AITEC* v *Commission*, not yet published in the ECR, paragraph 34).

69.   In the present case, the applicants submit that they meet the condition set out above because, essentially the contested decision affects them in a particularly serious manner and does not properly take into consideration the harmful effects of the nuclear tests in issue on their health, although they are members of the general public referred to in Article 30 of the Treaty, whose health must be protected, inter alia, pursuant to Article 34.

70.   The argument cannot be accepted because, at first sight, the contested decision concerns the applicants only in their objective capacity as residents of Tahiti, in the same way as any other person residing in Polynesia.

71.   Even on the assumption that the applicants might suffer personal damage linked to the alleged harmful effects of the nuclear tests in question on the environment or on the health of the general public, that circumstance alone would not be sufficient to distinguish them individually in the same way as a person to whom the contested decision is addressed, as is required by the fourth paragraph of Article 146 of the Treaty, since damage of the kind they cite could affect, in the same way, any person residing in the area in question (see Case T–585/93 *Greenpeace International*, cited above [order of 9 August 1995] paragraphs 49 to 55).

72.   The applicants have not adduced any evidence capable of showing that, prima facie, the contested decision affects them by reason of certain attributes or circumstances which are peculiar to them. Nor do they allege that the decision encroaches on a right which is specific to them and which, with regard to that decision, differentiates them from all other persons residing in Polynesia (see Case C–309/89 *Codorniu*, cited above, paragraphs 20 to 22, and the order of 23 November 1995 in Case C–10/95 P *Asocarne* v *Council*, not yet published in the ECR, paragraph 43).

73.   In particular, in the legal context of the present dispute, it is necessary to reject the applicants' argument that the Commission was, by virtue of certain specific provisions of the Treaty, under a duty to take account of the consequences for their situation of the measure which it envisaged adopting, in accordance with settled case-law (see Case 11/82 *Piraiki-Patraiki* v *Commission* [1985] ECR 207, paragraph 28 et seq., Case C–152/88 *Sofrimport* v *Commission* [1990] ECR I–2477, paragraphs 11 and 12, and Joined Cases T–480/93 and T–483/93 *Antillean Rice Mills*, cited above [Judgment of 14 September 1995], paragraph 67).

74.   No such obligation is apparent at first sight from the Treaty provisions on which the applicants rely. On the contrary, analysis of the relevant provisions of Chapter 3 of the Treaty shows clearly that, in the context of Article 34, the Commission is under an obligation to assess the effects capable of being caused by the nuclear tests in issue on all members of the general public and workers concerned. Interpreted within the scheme of Chapter 3, in particular in relation to Article 30, which concerns specifically 'the protection of the health of workers and the general public', Article 34 requires the Commission to make its assessment of whether the experiments which a Member State intends to carry out are dangerous within the context of the general objective of protecting the health of workers and the general public as a whole, by means of general preventive action based on considerations of public interest. When it takes such action, the Commission cannot be required to take into consideration the particular situation of each individual resident and worker within the geographical area concerned by a given experiment unless there are specific grounds for taking such considerations into account in the light of the objectives envisaged.

75.   In the present case, therefore, the Commission was prima facie not under an obligation to single out for consideration the applicants' situation from that of the other inhabitants of Polynesia when assessing the risks connected with the nuclear tests in issue in order to determine whether those tests were particularly dangerous within the meaning of Article 34 of the Treaty.

76.   In those circumstances, the applicants cannot be regarded as being prima facie individually concerned by the contested decision. It is thus apparent at first sight that the main action is manifestly inadmissible, without there being any need to consider whether the applicants meet the other condition for admissibility in the fourth paragraph of Article 146 of the Treaty, that the contested decision must be of direct concern to them.

77.   Contrary to the applicants' arguments, that conclusion is not incompatible with their right of access to the courts, since the judicial protection of individuals is ensured, in the Community system of remedies, not only by the various rights of direct action which they enjoy before the Community judicature under the conditions laid down in the Treaty but also by the procedure for seeking a preliminary ruling under Article 150 of the Treaty [EURATOM's version of Article 234, EC] in the context of actions brought before the national courts, which are the ordinary courts of Community law.

78.   The present application for interim measures must therefore be dismissed.

Notes
1.   The French tests were brought to an end by the start of 1996.

Question
Could decisions by EC institutions affecting the environment *ever* be of individual concern to individuals or groups concerned to secure protection of the environment? (See also the *Greenpeace* case, below.)

Note

The factual circumstances of the French nuclear tests case, though fascinating, are not typical of those giving rise to Article 230 applications. But even in more orthodox challenges to forms of Community economic regulation there is scant evidence that the Court of First Instance is prepared to apply *Codorniu* in a fashion apt radically to broaden individual access to justice under the fourth paragraph of Article 230 EC. The important statement at para. 19 of the ruling in *Codorniu* (p. 666 above), that a measure may be 'of a legislative nature in that it applies to the traders concerned in general' yet simultaneously of 'individual concern to some of them', is rehearsed in CFI rulings, yet applicants have consistently found it very difficult to persuade the CFI that their situation falls within this hybrid pattern.

Terres Rouges v *Commission (Case T-47/95)*
[1997] ECR II-481
Court of First Instance of the European Communities

Challenge was directed at Regulation 3224/94, which amended Regulation 404/93 and in doing so significantly reduced the tariff quota entitlement for non-traditional ACP (African, Caribbean and Pacific) bananas from Côte d'Ivoire (Ivory Coast). The applicants submitted that they, as importers into the EU of 70% of the banana production of Côte d'Ivoire, would be prejudiced by the downwards adjustment of the figure and that they were therefore directly and individually concerned.

[41]   In this case the contested regulation does not have any features which would enable it to be classed as a decision taken in the form of a regulation. It is drafted in general and abstract terms and is applicable in all the Member States, without any regard being had to the situation of individual producers. It is designed to amend the arrangements for the import of bananas laid down by Regulation No. 404/93 in order to adapt them to the changes introduced by the Framework Agreement entered into with the Latin American countries concerned.

[42]   It follows that the contested regulation applies to situations which have been determined objectively and has legal effects with respect to a category of persons viewed in a general and abstract manner.

[43]   As regards the question whether the applicants are individually concerned by the contested regulation, it is settled law that, in certain circumstances, even a legislative measure applying to the traders concerned in general may concern some of them individually (judgments in Case C-358/89 *Extramet Industrie* v *Council* [1991] ECR I-2501, paragraph 13, and Case C-309/89 *Codorniu* v *Council* [1994] ECR I-1853, paragraph 19, and order of 11 January 1995 in Case T-116/94 *Cassa Nazionale di Previdenza ed Assistenza a favore degli Avvocati e Procuratori* v *Council* [1995] ECR II-1, paragraph 26). In such circumstances, a Community measure could be of a legislative nature and, at the same time, in the nature of a decision *vis-à-vis* some of the traders concerned (Joined Cases T-481/93 and T-484/93 *Exporteurs in Levende Varkens and Others* v *Commission* [1995] ECR II-2941, paragraph 50).

[44]   However, the possibility of determining more or less precisely the number or even the identity of the persons to whom a measure applies by no means implies that it must be regarded as being of individual concern to them (Case 123/77 *UNICME* v *Council* [1978] ECR 845, paragraph 16).

[45]   In that regard, the legislative provisions relevant to this dispute should be borne in mind. Article 19 of Regulation No 404/93 provides that the tariff quota is to be opened as to 66.5% for the category of operators who marketed third-country and/or non-traditional ACP bananas (category A); as to 30% for the category of operators who marketed Community and/or traditional ACP bananas (category B); and as to 3.5% for the category of operators established in the Community who started marketing bananas other than Community and/or traditional ACP bananas from 1992 (category C). Supplementary criteria to be met by operators are to be laid down in accordance with the procedure provided for in Article 27 of the regulation. Operators who satisfy those conditions and who are granted import licences by the competent authorities of the relevant Member State may import third-country or non-traditional ACP bananas within the tariff quota, whatever category of importer they fall within.

[46]   In addition, the Court of Justice has held that the purpose of Articles 18 and 19 of Regulation No 404/93 is to establish arrangements for trade in bananas with third countries and a mechanism for the allocation of the tariff quota between categories of traders defined according to objective criteria. Those provisions accordingly apply to situations which have been determined objectively and have legal effects as regards categories of persons viewed in a general and abstract manner. It follows that the contested measure is of concern to the applicants only in their objective capacity as traders engaged in the marketing of bananas from third countries in the same way as any other trader in an identical position (order of 21 June 1993 in Case C-276/93 *Chiquita Banana Company and Others* v *Council* [1993] ECR I-3345, paragraphs 10, 11 and 12).

[47]   Regulation No 3224/94 admittedly restricted the quantity of non-traditional ACP bananas that Côte d'Ivoire could export within the tariff quota. However, under Regulation No 404/93 (see paragraph 45 of this judgment), all importers in categories A, B and C are entitled to import bananas from Côte d'Ivoire. Regulation No 3224/94 thus affects every importer wishing to import bananas from Côte d'Ivoire and the fact that the applicants currently import a large proportion of Côte d'Ivoire's bananas does not amount to circumstances differentiating them from other importers.

[48]   The applicants' argument that Regulation No 3224/94 fundamentally altered the rights conferred by Regulation No 404/93 must be rejected.

[49]   It is based on the premiss that, before Regulation No 3224/94 was adopted, Côte d'Ivoire could have placed approximately 50,000 tonnes of non-traditional ACP bananas on the Community market in addition to the 155,000 tonnes of traditional ACP bananas allocated to it by Regulation No 404/93 (see paragraphs 34 to 38 of this judgment).

[50]   First, Regulation No 3224/94 does not in any way preclude the applicants from importing into the Community traditional ACP bananas from Côte d'Ivoire. They can still import 70%, or even more, of the 155,000 tonnes of traditional ACP bananas allocated to that country.

[51]   Secondly, as the Commission stated at the hearing and the applicants did not dispute, the total amount of traditional ACP and non-traditional ACP bananas exported from Côte d'Ivoire in 1993 and 1994 after the new arrangements had been established by Regulation No 404/93 did not exceed 160,000 tonnes per year. Those

exports did not therefore exceed the quantity of 162,500 tonnes constituted by the reserve of 155,000 tonnes of traditional ACP bananas and the share of 7,500 tonnes of non-traditional ACP bananas reserved for Côte d'Ivoire by Regulation No 3224/94, The truth is that the figure of 50,000 tonnes quoted by the applicants is only an estimate of the potential production of Côte d'Ivoire's plantations and does not refer to current exports. Contrary to the applicants' submissions, therefore, their position has not in actual fact been affected by the adoption of Regulation No 3224/94.

The Court of First Instance concluded that Regulation 3224/94 concerned the applicants only in their objective capacity as importers of third-country bananas, and that their legal position was not affected by circumstances in which they were differentiated from the other traders in the same position. It was therefore not of individual concern to them. The CFI added that under Regulation 404/93 importers of third-country bananas must obtain an import licence from the authorities of a Member State, and that only decisions on whether or not to grant a licence affect the applicants directly. The quota allocated by Regulation 3224/94 was therefore not capable of affecting the applicants' legal position directly, as was required under Article 173(4) of the EC Treaty (now, after amendment, Article 230(4) EC), p. 655 above. The Court dismissed the application as inadmissible after commenting:

[59] Nor have the applicants established that in appropriate circumstances it would be impossible for them to challenge the validity of Regulation No 3224/94 before a national court, for example in an action brought against a refusal by the competent national authorities to issue them with import licences for non-traditional ACP bananas from Côte d'Ivoire, and to request the national court to seek a preliminary ruling in that regard from the Court of Justice pursuant to Article 177 [now 234] of the Treaty.

Note

Reviewing the restrictive approach apparent in the CFI's case law, A. Arnull in 1996 'hoped that the Court of Justice will soon take the opportunity, in the exercise of its appellate jurisdiction, to reinforce the message of *Codorniu*' (in 'Challenging Community Acts', in H.-W. Micklitz and N. Reich, *Public Interest Litigation before European Courts* (Nomos, 1996), Ch. 3 at p. 53). In the final case in this section the Court of Justice declined such an opportunity.

Stichting Greenpeace Council (Greenpeace International) and others v *Commission (Case C-321/95 P)*
[1998] ECR I-1651
Court of Justice of the European Communities

In Case T-585/93 *Greenpeace and others* v *Commission* [1995] ECR II-2205, the CFI held inadmissible an action for the annulment of a Commission decision to allocate funds to Spain within the framework of the European Regional Development Fund for the construction of two power stations in the Canary Islands. It was alleged that EC rules on environmental protection had been neglected, but the CFI adhered to existing case law and treated the applicants, who included associations concerned with the protection of the environment, as lacking any distinct interest in the matter of the type necessary to establish 'individual concern' within the meaning of Article 173 of the EC Treaty (now, after amendment, Article 230 EC). On appeal to the Court of Justice, the applicants observed *inter alia* that the CFI's approach 'creates a legal vacuum in ensuring compliance with Community environmental legislation, since in this area the interests are, by their very nature, common and shared, and the rights relating to those interests are liable to be held by a potentially large number of individuals so that there could never be a closed class of applicants satisfying the criteria adopted by the Court of First Instance'. The Court of Justice was then pressed to take the lead in relaxing the strict approach. The Court's 'Findings' occupy no more than nine short paragraphs.

Findings of the Court

27.   The interpretation of the fourth paragraph of Article 173 of the Treaty that the Court of First Instance applied in concluding that the appellants did not have *locus standi* is consonant with the settled case-law of the Court of Justice.

28.   As far as natural persons are concerned, it follows from the case-law, cited at both paragraph 48 of the contested order and at paragraph 7 of this judgment, that where, as in the present case, the specific situation of the applicant was not taken into consideration in the adoption of the act, which concerns him in a general and abstract fashion and, in fact, like any other person in the same situation, the applicant is not individually concerned by the act.

29.   The same applies to associations which claim to have *locus standi* on the basis of the fact that the persons whom they represent are individually concerned by the contested decision. For the reasons given in the preceding paragraph, that is not the case.

30.   In appraising the appellants' arguments purporting to demonstrate that the case-law of the Court of Justice, as applied by the Court of First Instance, takes no account of the nature and specific characteristics of the environmental interests underpinning their action, it should be emphasised that it is the decision to build the two power stations in question which is liable to affect the environmental rights arising under Directive 85/337 that the appellants seek to invoke.

31.   In those circumstances, the contested decision, which concerns the Community financing of those power stations, can affect those rights only indirectly.

32.   As regards the appellants' argument that application of the Court's case-law would mean that, in the present case, the rights which they derive from Directive 85/337 would have no effective judicial protection at all, it must be noted that, as is clear from the file, Greenpeace brought proceedings before the national courts challenging the administrative authorisations issued to Unelco concerning the construction of those power stations. TEA and CIC also lodged appeals against CUMAC's declaration of environmental impact relating to the two construction projects (see paragraphs 6 and 7 of the contested order, reproduced at paragraph 2 of this judgment).

33. Although the subject-matter of those proceedings and of the action brought before the Court of First Instance is different, both actions are based on the same rights afforded to individuals by Directive 85/337, so that in the circumstances of the present case those rights are fully protected by the national courts which may, if need be, refer a question to this Court for a preliminary ruling under Article 177 of the Treaty.

34. The Court of First Instance did not therefore err in law in determining the question of the appellants' *locus standi* in the light of the criteria developed by the Court of Justice in the case-law set out at paragraph 7 of this judgment.

35. In those circumstances the appeal must be dismissed.

Note
Although the applicants in *Greenpeace* referred to *Codorniu* in urging that a restrictive interpretation of Article 173 of the EC Treaty (now, after amendment, Article 230 EC) be eschewed, it will be noted that the Court made no direct mention of it, or any other decision, in these 'Findings'. Moreover, although environmental cases may in principle be decided according to generally applicable rules of law, the dispersed impact of acts affecting the environment creates special problems in determining standing (especially where, as in *Greenpeace*, both national and EC acts are involved). Consequently, the outcome of such cases may not be indicative of trends in the wider arena of challenge to forms of economic regulation. However, even with those *caveats*, *Greenpeace*, in its style and brevity, offers no encouragement to those seeking a hint that the Court of Justice is currently inclined to issue any corrective to the CFI's doggedly restrictive reading of *Codorniu*.

Questions
1. In *Plaumann* v *Commission* (Case 25/62) (p. 648 above) the Court commented that 'provisions of the Treaty regarding the right of interested parties to bring an action must not be interpreted restrictively'. Has the Court adhered to this view in its treatment of applications for annulment of the acts of the Community institutions? Should it?
2. 'It is ill-advised to consider whether natural and legal persons should enjoy more generous rules on standing in order to enhance their capacity to control acts of Community institutions in isolation from questions about the adequacy of the systems of accountability to citizens to which EC institutions are subject and the propensity of those systems for securing representative and responsive governance in the Union.' Discuss.
3. To what extent would the introduction of a new hierarchy of norms within Article 249 EC, based on a clearer separation of constitutional provisions, legislative acts and administrative acts, assist in the development of a coherent approach to the admissibility of individual challenges to Community acts?

(vii)   Grounds for annulment
Having established sufficient standing, the applicant must show the measure is flawed in order to win annulment. The grounds for review are made clear in the Article itself:

. . . lack of competence, infringement of an essential procedural requirement, infringement of this Treaty or of any rule of law relating to its
application, or misuse of powers.

These grounds seem broad. Of particular interest is 'any rule of law relating
to [the Treaty's] application'. It is here that the significance of the Court's
development of the general principles of Community law referred to in
Chapter 1 becomes apparent. The validity of Community acts can be tested
against these principles. Indeed, many of the principles have been developed
by the Court in the context of Article 173 of the EC Treaty (now, after
amendment, Article 230 EC) applications.

International Fruit Company v *Commission (Cases 41–44/70)*
[1971] ECR 411
Court of Justice of the European Communities

(The facts are set out at p. 647 above.) The Court, having held the
application admissible, proceeded to examine the merits. It held the
application unfounded. The next extract explains the Court's rejection of
one of the grounds of complaint.

[66]   . . . [T]he applicants claim that Regulations Nos 565/70 and 686/70 are void
or at least are not applicable to them, inasmuch as they establish a system of import
licences which is in conflict with Articles 3(f), 85 and 96 of the Treaty.

[67]   Moreover, these regulations are said to be insufficiently supported by reasons,
inasmuch as the grounds on which the system was necessary or at least permissible
under the said articles and under Article 39 of the Treaty are not stated.

[68]   Article 3 of the Treaty lists several general objectives, towards the attainment
and harmonization of which the Commission has to direct its activities.

[69]   Amongst these objectives Article 3 specifies not only 'the institution of a system
ensuring that competition in the common market is not distorted', but also (subparagraph (d)) 'the adoption of a common policy in the sphere of agriculture'.

[70]   The Treaty attaches very great importance to the attainment of this latter
objective in the sphere of agriculture, devoting Article 39 to it and providing, in the
first paragraph of Article 42, that the provisions relating to competition shall apply to
agricultural products only to the extent determined by the Council, account being
taken of the objectives set out in Article 39.

[71]   It follows from this that the application of protective measures in the form of a
restriction of imports from third countries might in the present case prove to be
necessary with a view to preventing, in the market in the products in question, serious
disturbances capable of endangering the objectives of Article 39.

[72]   In these circumstances an explicit statement of the reasons for the measures in
question, in relation to Articles 85 and 86 of the Treaty, was not indispensable.

[73]   It may well be that the grant of import licences according to the criterion of a reference quantity led in the present case to a crystallization of the previously existing trade relations with third countries. Yet, on the other hand, the laying down of objective criteria for calculating the quantities of which import was permitted made it possible to avoid discrimination among those who received licences on the basis of previously existing trade relations with third countries.

[74]   This system was the one best adapted to distort competition to the smallest possible extent.

[75]   For these reasons, the submissions directed against Regulations Nos 459/70, 565/70 and 686/70 must be rejected.

Note

In *Timex* v *Council* (Case 264/82) (p. 661 above) the measure was annulled, for Timex had been inadequately involved in the inquiry in breach of relevant Community legislation; an infringement of an essential procedural requirement. In *Codorniu* (Case C-309/89) (p. 665 above) the Court found a breach of the rule of law forbidding unjustified discrimination. The act in '*Les Verts*' (Case 294/83) (p. 653 above) was annulled because it fell within an area reserved to the Member States under the relevant provisions. In *Commission* v *Council* (Case 22/70) (p. 644 above), however, the application for annulment was rejected. In *UK* v *Council* (Case C-84/94) (p. 52 above) the Court rejected the UK's application for annulment of the 'Working Time' Directive almost in its entirety, but it should be noted that in para. 58 (p. 65 above) the Court observed that its review of compliance with the principle of proportionality would be confined to examining whether the legislature's 'wide discretion' had been vitiated by manifest error or misuse of powers, or whether the limits of that discretion had been manifestly exceeded.

(viii)   Interim measures

Articles 242 and 243 EC

Article 242

Actions brought before the Court of Justice shall not have suspensory effect. The Court of Justice may, however, if it considers that circumstances so require, order that application of the contested act be suspended.

Article 243

The Court of Justice may in any cases before it prescribe any necessary interim measures.

These provisions, which were Articles 185 and 186 EC respectively pre-Amsterdam, confer a wide discretion on the Court. It has generally been slow to grant interim relief from Community acts. Here, however, is a successful interim application made in respect of anti-dumping duties imposed on Japanese ball bearings under Regulation 1778/77.

NTN Toyo Bearing Co. v *Council (Case 113/77R)*
[1977] ECR 1721
Court of Justice of the European Communities

[4]   . . . The Council has not contested that the competent British, French and German customs authorities are insisting that the payments required under Article 3 of Regulation No 1778/77 shall be made forthwith. Nor has it contested that the NTN Group will incur the additional charges referred to by NTN in the event of the dismissal of the latter's application for the adoption of interim measures.

[5]   It has not been possible to establish conclusively within the context of the present proceedings whether, in the event of NTN's being successful in the main action, this expenditure would be wholly recouped.

[6]   Having regard to the probable duration of the procedure in the main action, charges at the rate quoted by the applicant cannot be regarded as negligible.

[7]   On the other hand the Council has not been able to demonstrate that the adoption of the interim measures applied for would cause appreciable detriment to the European Economic Community if the NTN Group were to maintain the existing bank guarantees in the sums to be paid in accordance with Article 3 of Regulation No 1778/77 and if NTN were to be unsuccessful in the main action.

[8]   NTN has thus substantiated the circumstances giving rise to urgency and the factual and legal grounds establishing a prima facie case for the suspension of the application, as far as the NTN Group is concerned, of the abovementioned Article 3 (Article 83(2) of the Rules of Procedure of the Court of Justice).

[9]   To that extent therefore the application of the said Article must be suspended until the final judgment in the case of *NTN* v *Council* (Case 113/77) on condition that and for so long as the NTN Group continues to provide security for the performance of its obligation in the amounts which it is required to pay in pursuance of Article 3 of Regulation No 1778/77.

Note
Case 113/77 subsequently reached full trial (see p. 658 above).

Question
Compare and contrast the Community's rules on judicial review, especially those relating to standing, with those of any other administrative law system with which you are familiar.

(B) ARTICLE 232

Article 232 EC

Article 232
Should the European Parliament, the Council or the Commission, in infringement of this Treaty, fail to act, the Member States and the other institutions of the Community may bring an action before the Court of Justice to have the infringement established.

The action shall be admissible only if the institution concerned has first been called upon to act. If, within two months of being so called upon, the institution concerned has not defined its position, the action may be brought within a further period of two months.

Any natural or legal person may, under the conditions laid down in the preceding paragraphs, complain to the Court of Justice that an institution of the Community has failed to address to that person any act other than a recommendation or an opinion.

The Court of Justice shall have jurisdiction, under the same conditions, in actions or proceedings brought by the ECB in the areas falling within the latter's field of competence and in actions or proceedings brought against the latter.

Whereas Article 230 concerns challenges to acts, Article 232 concerns challenges to omissions. It complements Article 230. While Article 230 was numbered Article 173 pre-Amsterdam, Article 175 has become Article 232. In the next case the Parliament obtained a ruling that the Council had unlawfully remained inactive.

Parliament v *Council (Case 13/83)*
[1985] ECR 1513
Court of Justice of the European Communities

The matter concerned the Council's alleged failure to ensure freedom to provide services in the sphere of international transport, and to lay down the conditions under which non-resident carriers may operate transport services in a Member State.

[59]   The Commission and the Netherlands Government point out that the Court has held the provisions of Articles 59 and 60 to be directly applicable since the expiry of the transitional period. They both contend that the fact that Article 61 requires the provision of services in relation to transport to be liberalized within the framework of a common transport policy does not in itself constitute a sufficient ground for suspending indefinitely the effect of the provisions relating to services when the Council has for years failed to introduce a common policy.

[60]   The Netherlands Government states that according to Article 8(7) of the Treaty the expiry of the transitional period is to constitute the latest date by which all the measures required for establishing the common market must be implemented; there is no ground for making the transport market an exception thereto. It also points out that the absence of express implementing provisions in the Treaty has never prevented the application of the general rules of the Treaty or its basic principles. From this it concludes that since the end of the transitional period freedom to provide services must apply even in the transport sector. Since the direct application of the provisions of Articles 59 and 60 is sufficient to achieve the aims of a common transport policy without any further intervention by the Council, that institution cannot be said to have failed to act.

[61]   The Commission, on the other hand, considers that Articles 59 and 60 are not directly applicable in the transport sector. Pursuant to Article 61 freedom to provide services in relation to transport must be achieved within the framework of the rules provided for by Article 75(1)(a) and (b). The aim of that provision is to allow the Council an appropriate period, extending if necessary beyond the expiry of the transitional period, within which to achieve freedom to provide services in relation to

transport within the framework of a common policy. That appropriate period cannot, however, extend indefinitely, and now that more than 15 years have elapsed since the end of the transitional period it must almost have reached its end; if it were otherwise freedom to provide services, although guaranteed by the Treaty, would apply in all but one sector of activity, a situation which in the long term would be likely to cause distortion of competition. In those circumstances the Court should indicate by way of a warning in the present judgment what is a reasonable period for the purposes of Article 61.

[62]   It should first be borne in mind that Article 61(1) provides that freedom to provide services in the field of transport is to be governed by the provisions of the Title relating to transport. Application of the principles governing freedom to provide services, as established in particular by Articles 59 and 60 of the Treaty, must therefore be achieved, according to the Treaty, by introducing a common transport policy and, more particularly, by laying down common rules applicable to international transport and the conditions under which non-resident carriers may operate transport services, the rules and conditions of which are referred to in Article 75(1)(a) and (b) and necessarily affect freedom to provide services.

[63]   Accordingly, the argument of the Netherlands Government to the effect that on the expiry of the transitional period the provisions of Articles 59 and 60 are of direct application even in the transport sector cannot be accepted.

[64]   However, the Parliament, the Commission and the Netherlands Government have rightly contended that the obligations imposed on the Council by Article 75(1)(a) and (b) include the introduction of freedom to provide services in relation to transport, and that the scope of that obligation is clearly defined by the Treaty. Pursuant to Articles 59 and 60 the requirements of freedom to provide services include, as the Court held in its judgment of 17 December 1981 (Case 279/80 *Webb* [1981] ECR 3305), the removal of any discrimination against the person providing services based on his nationality or the fact that he is established in a Member State other than that where the services are to be provided.

[65]   It follows that in that respect the Council does not have the discretion on which it may rely in other areas of the common transport policy. Since the result to be achieved is determined by the combined effect of Articles 59, 60, 61 and 75(1)(a) and (b), the exercise of a certain measure of discretion is allowed only as regards the means employed to obtain that result, bearing in mind, as required by Article 75, those features which are special to transport.

[66]   In so far as the obligations laid down in Article 75(1)(a) and (b) relate to freedom to provide services, therefore, they are sufficiently well-defined for disregard of them to be the subject of a finding of failure to act pursuant to Article 175.

[67]   The Council was required to extend freedom to provide services to the transport sector before the expiry of the transitional period, pursuant to Article 75(1)(a) and (2), in so far as the extension related to international transport to or from the territory of a Member State or across the territory of one or more Member States and, within the framework of freedom to provide services in the transport sector, to lay down, pursuant to Article 75(1)(b) and (2), the conditions under which non-resident carriers may operate transport services within a Member State. It is common ground that the necessary measures for that purpose have not yet been adopted.

[68]   On that point the Court must therefore hold that the Council has failed to act since it has failed to adopt measures which ought to have been adopted before the

expiry of the transitional period and whose subject-matter and nature may be determined with a sufficient degree of precision.

[69]   The Parliament, the Commission and the Netherlands Government also refer to the legal situation which would arise if, after judgment against it, the Council still failed to act. That problem is, however, hypothetical. Article 176 requires the Council to take the measures necessary to comply with this judgment; since that provision does not prescribe a time-limit for such compliance it must be inferred that the Council has a reasonable period for that purpose. It is not necessary in the present judgment to consider what would be the consequences if the Council still fails to act.

[70]   Accordingly, the Court must find that in breach of the Treaty the Council has failed to ensure freedom to provide services in the sphere of international transport and to lay down the conditions under which non-resident carriers may operate transport services in a Member State.

[71]   The Council is at liberty to adopt, in addition to the requisite measures of liberalization, such accompanying measures as it considers necessary and to do so in the order it holds to be appropriate.

Note

The case is a good illustration of the nature and purpose of Article 232. It might also be noted as an example of inter-institutional wrangling in the quest to develop Community policy-making in an important sector.

The next case demonstrates that although Article 232 complements Article 230, it does not offer a method of outflanking the limitations to Article 230. An applicant may find one available, but not both.

Società 'Eridania' Zuccherifici Nazionali v *Commission* ### (*Cases 10 & 18/68*)
[1969] ECR 459
Court of Justice of the European Communities

The application for annulment of Commission Decisions had failed to clear the standing hurdles in Article 173 of the EC Treaty (now, after amendment, Article 230 EC). It was then argued that the Commission's failure to revoke the Decisions despite the applicant's requests was challengeable under Article 175 of the EC Treaty (now, after amendment, Article 232 EC) as a failure to act. On admissibility, the Court held as follows:

[16]   The action provided for in Article 175 is intended to establish an illegal omission as appears from that article, which refers to a failure to act 'in infringement of this Treaty' and from Article 176 which refers to a failure to act declared to be 'contrary to this Treaty'.

Without stating under which provision of Community law the Commission was required to annul or to revoke the said decisions, the applicants have confined themselves to alleging that those decisions were adopted in infringement of the Treaty and that this fact alone would thus suffice to make the Commission's failure to act subject to the provisions of Article 175.

[17]   The Treaty provides, however, particularly in Article 173, other methods of recourse by which an allegedly illegal Community measure may be disputed and if necessary annulled on the application of a duly qualified party.

To admit, as the applicants wish to do, that the parties concerned could ask the institution from which the measure came to revoke it and, in the event of the Commission's failing to act, refer such failure to the Court as an illegal omission to deal with the matter would amount to providing them with a method of recourse parallel to that of Article 173, which would not be subject to the conditions laid down by the Treaty.

[18]   This application does not therefore satisfy the requirements of Article 175 of the Treaty and must thus be held to be inadmissible.

Note

Article 232, as a complement to Article 230, is limited in its scope in a manner comparable to Article 230. As a careful reading of the third paragraph of Article 232 makes clear, the challenged failure to act must be of a particular nature. The applicant's lack of success in the next case is a useful illustration.

Star Fruit Co. v Commission (Case 247/87)
[1989] ECR 291
Court of Justice of the European Communities

Star Fruit, a Belgian banana trader, felt itself prejudiced by French banana market regulation which it believed to be contrary to the Treaty. It considered that the Commission's failure to institute infringement proceedings under Article 169 of the EC Treaty (now Article 226 EC) against France constituted a failure to act, which it was entitled to challenge under Article 175 of the EC Treaty (now, after amendment, Article 232 EC).

[10]   In so far as it is based on the third paragraph of Article 175 of the Treaty, the purpose of the application is to obtain a declaration that in not commencing against the French Republic proceedings to establish its breach of obligations the Commission infringed the Treaty by failing to take a decision.

[11]   However, it is clear from the scheme of Article 169 of the Treaty that the Commission is not bound to commence the proceedings provided for in that provision but in this regard has a discretion which excludes the right for individuals to require that institution to adopt a specific position.

[12]   It is only if it considers that the Member State in question has failed to fulfil one of its obligations that the Commission delivers a reasoned opinion. Furthermore, in the event that the State does not comply with the opinion within the period allowed, the institution has in any event the right, but not the duty, to apply to the Court of Justice for a declaration that the alleged breach of obligations has occurred.

[13]   It must also be observed that in requesting the Commission to commence proceedings pursuant to Article 169 the applicant is in fact seeking the adoption of acts which are not of direct and individual concern to it within the meaning of the

second paragraph of Article 173 and which it could not therefore challenge by means of an action for annulment in any event.

[14]   Consequently, the applicant cannot be entitled to raise the objection that the Commission failed to commence proceedings against the French Republic pursuant to Article 169 of the Treaty.

[15]   It follows that the application is inadmissible in its entirety.

Note
Article 226 is examined in the next chapter. The Court in *Star Fruit* (Case 247/87) never reached the stage of examining the compatibility of the French banana rules with Community law. However, Star Fruit might have enjoyed more success by challenging the alleged illegality perpetrated by the State rather than that of the inactive Commission. This point, which relates to the interrelation of remedies, will be readdressed in Chapter 17.

(C) ARTICLE 241

Article 241 EC

Article 241
Notwithstanding the expiry of the period laid down in the fifth paragraph of Article 230, any party may, in proceedings in which a regulation adopted jointly by the European Parliament and the Council, or a regulation of the Council, of the Commission, or of the ECB is at issue, plead the grounds specified in the second paragraph of Article 230 in order to invoke before the Court of Justice the inapplicability of that regulation.

Article 241 was re-numbered from Article 184 on the entry into force of the Treaty of Amsterdam. The nature and purpose of Article 241 would be immediately apparent to a lawyer familiar with French administrative law, which contains the similar *exception d'illegalité*. Article 241 is, however, initially peculiar to British eyes. It is commonly referred to as the 'plea of illegality', which hardly invites instant recognition of its function. The following extract from '*Les Verts*' v *Parliament* (Case 294/83) (p. 653 above) provides an explanation of the place of Article 241 in the system of judicial remedies instituted by the Treaty.

Parti Ecologiste 'Les Verts' v Parliament (Case 294/83)
[1986] ECR 1339
Court of Justice of the European Communities

[23]   . . . Natural and legal persons are . . . protected against the application to them of general measures which they cannot contest directly before the Court by reason of the special conditions of admissibility laid down in the second paragraph of Article 173 [now the fourth paragraph of Article 230] of the Treaty. Where the Community institutions are responsible for the administrative implementation of such measures, natural or legal persons may bring a direct action before the

Court against implementing measures which are addressed to them or which are of direct and individual concern to them and, in support of such an action, plead the illegality of the general measure on which they are based. . . .

Note

This, then, is the plea of illegality – Article 241. It is a form of indirect challenge to a measure which the applicant is unable to challenge directly.
Article 241's operation may be explained with reference to the next case.

Simmenthal SpA v Commission (Case 92/78)
[1979] ECR 777
Court of Justice of the European Communities

The applicant sought annulment of a February 1978 Decision. The basis of the challenge was the alleged invalidity of several Regulations and Notices from which that Decision of February 1978 derived. The limitations in Article 173 of the EC Treaty (now, after amendment, Article 230 EC), relating to standing and time limits, impeded direct challenge to those 'parent' measures. This application challenged those measures indirectly via a direct challenge to the February 1978 measure which stemmed from them. The Court explained the nature of Article 184 of the EC Treaty (now Article 241 EC) in these circumstances.

[34]   While the applicant formally challenges Commission Decision No 78/258 it has at the same time criticized, in reliance on Article 184 of the EEC Treaty, certain aspects of the 'linking' system in the form in which it has been implemented pursuant to the new Article 14 of Regulation No 805/68, by Regulation No 2900/77 and No 2901/77 and also by the notices of invitations to tender of 13 January 1978.

[35]   Article 184 reads: 'Notwithstanding the expiry of the period laid down in the third paragraph of Article 173, any party may, in proceedings in which a Regulation of the Council or the Commission is in issue, plead the grounds specified in the first paragraph of Article 173, in order to invoke before the Court of Justice the inapplicability of that Regulation'.

[36]   There is no doubt that this provision enables the applicant to challenge indirectly during the proceedings, with a view to obtaining the annulment of the contested Decision, the validity of the measures laid down by Regulation which form the legal basis of the latter.

[37]   On the other hand there are grounds for questioning whether Article 184 applies to the notices of invitations to tender of 13 January 1978 when according to its wording it only provides for the calling in question of 'Regulations'.

[38]   These notices are general acts which determine in advance and objectively the rights and obligations of the traders who wish to participate in the invitations to tender which these notices make public.

[39]   As the Court in its judgment of 12 June 1958 in Case 15/57, *Compagnie des Hauts Fourneaux de Chasse v High Authority of the European Coal and Steel Community* [1957 and 1958] ECR 211, and in its judgment of 13 June 1956 in Case 9/56,

Meroni & Co., Industrie Metallurgische SpA v *High Authority of the European Coal and Steel Community* [1957 and 1958] ECR 133, has already held in connexion with Article 36 of the ECSC Treaty, Article 184 of the EEC Treaty gives expression to a general principle conferring upon any party to proceedings the right to challenge, for the purpose of obtaining the annulment of a Decision of direct and individual concern to that party, the validity of previous acts of the institutions which form the legal basis of the Decision which is being attacked, if that party was not entitled under Article 173 of the Treaty to bring a direct action challenging those acts by which it was thus affected without having been in a position to ask that they be declared void.

[40]   The field of application of the said Article must therefore include acts of the institutions which, although they are not in the form of a Regulation, nevertheless produce similar effects and on those grounds may not be challenged under Article 173 by natural or legal persons other than Community institutions and Member States.

[41]   This wide interpretation of Article 184 derives from the need to provide those persons who are precluded by the second paragraph of Article 173 from instituting proceedings directly in respect of general acts with the benefit of a judicial review of them at the time when they are affected by implementing Decisions which are of direct and individual concern to them.

[42]   The notices of invitations to tender of 13 January 1978 in respect of which the applicant was unable to initiate proceedings are a case in point, seeing that only the Decision taken in consequence of the tender which it had submitted in answer to a specific invitation to tender could be of direct and individual concern to it.

[43]   There are therefore good grounds for declaring that the applicant's challenge during the proceedings under Article 184, which relates not only to the above-mentioned Regulations but also to the notices of invitations to tender of 13 January 1978, is admissible, although the latter are not in the strict sense measures laid down by Regulation.

Note
On the merits the application succeeded. The grounds for review under Article 241 are the same as those applicable to Article 230 (see p. 675 above).

(D) ARTICLES 235 AND 288

Articles 135 and 288 EC

Article 235
The Court of Justice shall have jurisdiction in disputes relating to the compensation for damage provided for in the second paragraph of Article 288.

Article 288
The contractual liability of the Community shall be governed by the law applicable to the contract in question.

In the case of non-contractual liability, the Community shall, in accordance with the general principles common to the laws of the Member States, make good any damage caused by its institutions or by its servants in the performance of their duties.

The preceding paragraph shall apply under the same conditions to damage caused by the ECB or by its servants in the performance of their duties.

The personal liability of its servants towards the Community shall be governed by the provisions laid down in their Staff Regulations or in the Conditions of Employment applicable to them.

Articles 235 and 288 EC were Articles 178 and 215 EC respectively prior to the entry into force of the Treaty of Amsterdam, p. 29 above.

Aktien-Zuckerfabrik Schöppenstedt v *Council (Case 5/71)*
[1971] ECR 975
Court of Justice of the European Communities

[1]   By application filed at the Registry on 13 February 1971 the undertaking Aktien-Zuckerfabrik Schöppenstedt asks the Court under the second paragraph of Article 215 of the EEC Treaty to order the Council to make good the damage which it caused the applicant by adopting Regulation No 769/68 of 18 June 1968 (OJ 1968, L 143) laying down the measures needed to offset the difference between national sugar prices and prices valid from 1 July 1968. Its principal claim is for the payment by the Council of 38 852.78 u.a., that is DM 155 411.13, representing the loss of income which it suffered in relation to the former German price of raw sugar. In the alternative it seeks moreover to be compensated otherwise for the damage which it has suffered.

Admissibility

[2]   The Council contests the admissibility of the application contending in the first place that it is aimed in fact not at compensation for damage due to its wrongful act or omission but to the removal of the legal effects arising from the contested measure. To recognize the admissibility of the application would frustrate the contentious system provided for by the Treaty in particular in the second paragraph of Article 173, under which individuals are not entitled to bring applications for annulment of regulations.

[3]   The action for damages provided for by Articles 178 and 215, paragraph 2, of the Treaty was introduced as an autonomous form of action, with a particular purpose to fulfil within the system of actions and subject to conditions on its use dictated by its specific nature. It differs from an application for annulment in that its end is not the abolition of a particular measure, but compensation for damage caused by an institution in the performance of its duties.

[4]   The Council further contends that the principal conclusions are inadmissible in that they involve the substitution of new rules, in accordance with the criteria described by the applicant, for the rules in question, a substitution which the Court has not the power to order.

[5]   The principal conclusions seek only an award of damages and, therefore, a benefit intended solely to produce effects in the case of the applicant. Therefore this submission must be dismissed.

[6]   The defendant then maintains that if the claim for damages is accepted the Court, in order to determine the amount of the damage in question, would have to fix criteria according to which the compensation with regard to prices would have had to be fixed and would thus encroach upon the discretion which the Council has in adopting legislative measures.

[7]   The determination of the criteria applicable to the calculation of the compensation in question relates not to admissibility but to the substance of the case.

[8]   The defendant pleads that the alternative claim is inadmissible since its subject-matter is unclear and since it is wholly lacking in a statement of the grounds relied on.

[9]   A claim for any unspecified form of damages is not sufficiently concrete and must therefore be regarded as inadmissible.

[10]   Only the principal claim is therefore admissible.

The substance of the case
[11]   In the present case the non-contractual liability of the Community pre-supposes at the very least the unlawful nature of the act alleged to be the cause of the damage. Where legislative action involving measures of economic policy is concerned, the Community does not incur noncontractual liability for damage suffered by individuals as a consequence of that action, by virtue of the provisions contained in Article 215, second paragraph, of the Treaty, unless a sufficiently flagrant violation of a superior rule of law for the protection of the individual has occurred. For that reason the Court, in the present case, must first consider whether such a violation has occurred.

[12]   Regulation No 769/68 was adopted pursuant to Article 37(1) of Regulation No 1009/67 which requires the Council to adopt provisions concerning the measures needed to offset the difference between national sugar prices and prices valid from 1 July 1968, and it authorizes the Member State in which the price of white sugar is higher than the target price to grant compensation for such quantities of white sugar and raw sugar which are in free circulation in its territory at 0.00 hours on 1 July 1968. The applicant points out that as regards Member States with a low price this regulation provides for the payment of dues on sugar stocks only if the previous prices were less than the intervention price valid from 1 July 1968 and concludes from this that by adopting different criteria for the right to compensation of sugar producers in a Member State with high prices, the regulation infringes the provision of the last subparagraph of Article 40(3) of the Treaty according to which any common price policy shall be based on common criteria and uniform methods of calculation.

[13]   The difference referred to does not constitute discrimination because it is the result of a new system of common organization of the market in sugar which does not recognize a single fixed price but has a maximum and minimum price and lays down a framework of prices within which the level of actual prices depends on the development of the market. Thus it is not possible to challenge the justification of transitional rules which proceeded on the basis that where the previous prices were already within the framework set up they must be governed by market forces and which therefore required the payment of dues only in cases where the previous prices were still too low to come within the new framework of prices and authorized compensation only in cases where the previous prices were too high to come within the said framework.

[14]   In addition, having regard to the special features of the system established with effect from 1 July 1968, the Council by adopting Regulation No 769/68 satisfied the requirements of Article 37 of Regulation No 1009/67.

[15]   It is also necessary to dismiss the applicant's claim that Regulation No 769/68 infringed the provisions of Article 40 of the Treaty because the method of calculating the compensation and dues for the raw sugar stocks was derived from that adopted

for white sugar, which could, according to the applicant, result in the unequal treatment of the producers of raw sugar. Although, relying on hypothetical cases, the applicant stated that the calculation methods selected did not necessarily lead to uniform results with regard to producers of raw sugar, it was not proved that this could have been the case on 1 July 1968.

[16]   The applicant's action founded upon the Council's liability does not therefore satisfy the first condition mentioned above and must be dismissed.

Note

The Court's test in para. 11 of the judgment appears extremely difficult to satisfy. This is borne out by subsequent case law in which claims for compensation have been regularly rejected. See also, e.g., *Bayerische HNL Vermehrungsbetriebe GmbH & Co. KG* v *Council* (Case 83/76) [1978] ECR 1209; *Koninklijke Scholten-Honig NV* v *Council and Commission* (Case 143/77) [1979] ECR 3583. There have been occasional successes; see, e.g., *Mulder et al* v *Council & Commission* (Cases C-104/89 and C-37/90) [1992] ECR I-3061, noted by T. Heukels (1993) 30 CML Rev 368.

Question

Article 288, second paragraph, requires the Court to develop Community law in this area in accordance with the general principles common to the law of the Member States. Consider with reference to systems of administrative liability with which you are familiar whether the Court's test in *Schöppenstedt* (Case 5/71) is appropriate. See further p. 737 below on the relationship between principles of liability under Article 288 applicable to *Community* institutions and those developed under Community law applicable to *national* institutions.

Note

Outside the field of legislative economic policy making which was at issue in *Schöppenstedt* (Case 5/71), the Court seems a little more receptive to claims under this head. The Court of First Instance too has explicitly distinguished between 'administrative illegality' and 'legislative illegality' for the purposes of Article 215(2) of the EC Treaty (now Article 288(2) EC), applying strict criteria of the type referred to in para. 11 of Case 5/71 above that will rarely be satisfied only to the latter: Case T-390/94 *Schröder & Thamann* v *Commission* [1997] ECR II-501. The next case, which involves 'administrative illegality', tells a tragic tale. It is thankfully outside the mainstream of Community practice, but deserves attention as an example of how the Court can adopt a flexible approach to these rules.

Adams v *Commission (No. 1) (Case 145/83)*
[1985] ECR 3539
Court of Justice of the European Communities

Stanley Adams sought compensation for damage he claimed to have suffered as a result of wrongful acts on the part of the Commission. Adams, an employee of the Swiss firm Hoffman-La Roche, had 'leaked' to the Commission documents which showed that Roche had been acting contrary to the Treaty competition rules. He requested the Commission to keep his identity secret. In the course of the inquiry, which culminated in the imposition of a fine on Roche, the Commission had let the firm see documents which indicated its participation in unlawful practices. Roche was able to deduce from the documents that the Commission's informant was Adams. Adams was charged with economic espionage under the Swiss Penal Code. He had left Roche and moved to Italy, but in 1974 he was arrested as he crossed the Swiss/Italian border. He was held in solitary confinement. He was not allowed to communicate with his family. His wife committed suicide. He received a one-year suspended prison sentence.

In the following extract from the judgment the Court examines breaches of the duty of confidentiality and the duty to warn Adams as the basis for the Commission's liability to him.

[28] The applicant claims that the relationship between the Commission and himself was in fact confidential in nature, as is clear both from his first letter to the Commission, dated 25 February 1973, and the discussion which he had with the Commission officials at the meeting on 9 April 1973. The existence of a duty of confidentiality follows, moreover, from the general principles common to the laws of the Member States and from the obligations imposed on the Commission by Article 214 of the EEC Treaty and by Article 20 of Regulation No 17 of the Council of 6 February 1962 (Official Journal, English Special Edition 1959–1962, p. 87).

[29] In particular the applicant points out that the fact that he indicated in his letter of 25 February 1973 that he would be prepared to give evidence on oath before the Court as to the accuracy of his statements showed that his identity was to be disclosed by himself alone after the Commission investigation had been completed and the proceedings before the Court initiated. The applicant maintains that he never gave the Commission to understand that after he had left Roche he would no longer insist on that duty of confidentiality in regard to him. Finally, in the applicant's view, the Commission's conduct proved that it considered itself bound by such a duty. Thus on several occasions, both before and after the applicant had left Roche, the Commission deliberately refused to name its informant – until the beginning of 1975 when Mr Schlieder disclosed his name.

[30] Although the Commission was therefore bound by a duty of confidentiality towards the applicant, in his view it acted in breach of that obligation on three occasions in particular. In the first place, the disclosure of the copies of the documents to the Roche employees in October 1974 enabled Roche to infer therefrom that the applicant was the most likely informant. Secondly, the Commission failed to warn the applicant of the risk that he would inevitably run if he returned to Switzerland. In the applicant's view, it was the Commission's duty to warn him of that risk, either after the documents had been handed over to the Roche employees or, and in any event, after Dr Alder's first visit to the Commission in November 1974, when the Commission was made fully aware of the gravity of that risk. In that respect, the applicant points out that Dr Alder had told the Commission officials that Roche was considering the possibility of criminal proceedings against the informant and that the lawyer had even explained the contents of the relevant provision of the Swiss Penal Code.

Thirdly, and finally, in February 1975 Mr Schlieder named the applicant as the Commission's informant.

[31]   The Commission denies that it was bound by a duty of confidentiality towards the applicant after he had left his employment with Roche. It bases its contention in particular on the applicant's express statement in his letter of 25 February 1973 that, after he had left Roche, he would be willing to appear before any court, in other words not only before the Court of Justice, to confirm on oath the statements he had made. Moreover, the applicant's conduct after he had left Roche gave the Commission good reason to believe that it was a matter of indifference to him whether he was identified as the informant, since he had not even informed the Commission of his new address. According to the Commission the fact that it repeatedly declined to identify its informant in no way establishes that it considered itself bound by a duty of confidentiality. Its conduct was dictated entirely by its general practice of not divulging the identity of its informants.

[32]   In any event the Commission contends that even if it were under a duty of confidentiality regarding the applicant's identity, it did not act in breach of that duty. The fact that it handed over photocopies to the Roche employees did not amount to such a breach, since it could not possibly have been foreseen that Roche would be able to identify the source of the documents by examining the copies. The applicant never requested the Commission not to disclose those documents to Roche. On the other hand, he agreed that the Commission could use the documents in connection with an investigation of that firm. The Commission had considered that it was necessary to disclose them to Roche but it nevertheless took care to remove anything which looked as though it might indicate their specific source. Moreover, the documents in question had no evident connection with the applicant, who could have been identified only by someone with a highly detailed knowledge of the organization and the operation of Roche. The applicant had never warned the Commission of such a risk.

[33]   As regards the possible existence of a duty on the part of the Commission to warn the applicant, the Commission contends that such a duty cannot be inferred from any duty of confidentiality which may have existed. In so far as the applicant is putting forward a separate submission in this respect, the Commission adds that it is impossible to establish in law that, following Dr Alder's visit, it was under a duty to warn the applicant of the risks that he would run if he returned to Switzerland. In addition, the Commission had no reason to believe that Roche would be able to identify the applicant as the informant. Finally, during his telephone conversation with Dr Alder at the beginning of February 1975, Mr Schlieder revealed nothing that Roche and the Swiss authorities did not already know, since by then the applicant had already admitted that he was the Commission's informant.

[34]   As regards the existence of a duty of confidentiality it must be pointed out that Article 214 of the EEC Treaty lays down an obligation, in particular for the members and the servants of the institutions of the Community 'not to disclose information of the kind covered by the obligation of professional secrecy, in particular information about undertakings, their business relations or their cost components'. Although that provision primarily refers to information gathered from undertakings, the expression 'in particular' shows that the principle in question is a general one which applies also to information supplied by natural persons, if that information is 'of the kind' that is confidential. That is particularly so in the case of information supplied on a purely

voluntary basis but accompanied by a request for confidentiality in order to protect the informant's anonymity. An institution which accepts such information is bound to comply with such a condition.

[35]   As regards the case before the Court, it is quite clear from the applicant's letter of 25 February 1973 that he requested the Commission not to reveal his identity. It cannot therefore be denied that the Commission was bound by a duty of confidentiality towards the applicant in that respect. In fact the parties disagree not so much as to the existence of such a duty but as to whether the Commission was bound by a duty of confidentiality after the applicant had left his employment with Roche.

[36]   In that respect it must be pointed out that the applicant did not qualify his request by indicating a period upon the expiry of which the Commission would be released from its duty of confidentiality regarding the identity of its informant. No such indication can be inferred from the fact that the applicant was prepared to appear before any court after he had left Roche. The giving of evidence before a court implies that the witness has been duly summoned, that he is under a duty to answer the questions put to him, and is, in return, entitled to all the guarantees provided by a judicial procedure. The applicant's offer to confirm the accuracy of his information under such conditions cannot therefore be interpreted as a general statement releasing the Commission from its duty of confidentiality. Nor can any such intention be inferred from the applicant's subsequent conduct.

[37]   It must therefore be stated that the Commission was under a duty to keep the applicant's identity secret even after he had left his employer.

[38]   Of the events mentioned by the applicant, the only occasion on which the Commission directly revealed the identity of its informant was the telephone conversation between Mr Schlieder and Dr Alder at the beginning of February 1975. However, that conversation took place after the applicant had caused an anonymous letter to be sent to the Commission informing it of his detention and seeking its help. It is difficult to see how the Commission could have acted on that request without confirming, at least by implication, that the applicant was indeed its informant. Moreover, it transpired subsequently that at that time the applicant had already admitted to the Swiss police that he had given information, at least orally, to the Commission and it is clear from the decisions of the Swiss courts that the confirmation of that fact by Mr Schlieder did not have a decisive bearing on the applicant's conviction. The disclosure of the applicant's identity at that time and in those circumstances cannot be regarded as constituting a breach of the duty of confidentiality which could give rise to the Commission's liability *vis-à-vis* the applicant.

[39]   On the other hand, it is clear that the handing over of the edited photocopies to members of the staff of the Roche subsidiaries enabled Roche to identify the applicant as the main suspect in the complaint which it lodged with the Swiss Public Prosecutor's Office. It was therefore that handing over of the documents which led to the applicant's arrest and which in addition supplied the police and the Swiss courts with substantial evidence against him.

[40]   It appears from the documents before the Court that the Commission was fully aware of the risk that the handing over to Roche of the photocopies supplied by the applicant might reveal the informant's identity to the company. For that reason the Commission officials first attempted to obtain other copies of the documents in question from the Roche subsidiaries in Paris and Brussels. When that attempt failed,

the Commission prepared new copies of the documents which it considered were the least likely to lead to the discovery of the applicant's identity and it took care to remove from those copies any indication which it considered might reveal the source of the documents. However, since it was not familiar with Roche's practices regarding the distribution of the documents in question within the company, the Commission could not be sure that those precautions were sufficient to eliminate all risk of the applicant's being identified by means of the copies handed over to Roche. The Commission was therefore, in any event, imprudent in handing over those copies to Roche without having consulted the applicant.

[41]   It is not however necessary to decide whether, in view of the situation at the time and in particular of the information in the Commission's possession, the handing over of the documents is sufficient to give rise to the Commission's liability regarding the consequences of the applicant's being identified as the informant. Although the Commission was not necessarily aware, when those documents were handed over, of the gravity of the risk to which it was exposing the applicant, Dr Alder's visit on 8 November 1974, on the other hand, provided it with all the necessary information in that respect. Following that visit the Commission knew that Roche was determined to discover how the Commission had come into possession of the documents in question and that it was preparing to lay a complaint against the informant under Article 273 of the Swiss Penal Code, the contents of which Dr Alder even took care to explain. The Commission also knew that there was a possibility of obtaining from Roche, in return for the disclosure of the informant's identity, an undertaking not to take action against him. It could not however pursue that possibility without the applicant's consent.

[42]   In those circumstances it was not at all sufficient for the Commission merely to take the view that it was unlikely that the applicant would be identified, that he was probably never going to return to Switzerland and that, in any event, the Swiss authorities did not intend to institute criminal proceedings against him. On the contrary, the Commission was under a duty to take every possible step to warn the applicant, thereby enabling him to make his own arrangements in the light of the information given by Dr Alder, and to consult him as to the approach to be adopted in relation to Dr Alder's proposals.

[43]   Although the applicant had not left any precise address making it possible for the Commission to contact him easily, in his letter of 25 February 1973 he had already indicated his intention of setting up his own meat business in Italy, near Rome. Even in the absence of other indications, that information would have enabled the Commission to make inquiries with a view to discovering where the applicant was staying. It is common ground that the Commission did not even attempt to find the applicant although it allowed almost one month to elapse before communicating to Dr Alder its final refusal to discuss the origin of the documents in its possession, a refusal which was followed by the lodging of Roche's complaint at the Swiss Public Prosecutor's Office.

[44]   It must therefore be concluded that, by failing to make all reasonable efforts to pass on to the applicant the information which was available to it following Dr Alder's visit of 8 November 1974, even though the communication of that information might have prevented, or at least limited, the damage which was likely to result from the discovery of the applicant's identity by means of the documents which it had handed over to Roche, the Commission has incurred liability towards the applicant in respect of that damage.

The Court then rejected the Commission's submission that the action was time-barred. In what may seem a cruel concluding twist, it awarded Adams compensation, but halved the sum payable on the following basis:

[53]   It must therefore be concluded that in principle the Community is bound to make good the damage resulting from the discovery of the applicant's identity by means of the documents handed over to Roche by the Commission. It must however be recognized that the extent of the Commission's liability is diminished by reason of the applicant's own negligence. The applicant failed to inform the Commission that it was possible to infer his identity as the informant from the documents themselves, although he was in the best position to appreciate and to avert that risk. Nor did he ask the Commission to keep him informed of the progress of the investigation of Roche, and in particular of any use that might be made of the documents for that purpose. Lastly, he went back to Switzerland without attempting to make any inquiries in that respect, although he must have been aware of the risks to which his conduct towards his former employer had exposed him with regard to Swiss legislation.

[54]   Consequently, the applicant himself contributed significantly to the damage which he suffered. In assessing the conduct of the Commission on the one hand and that of the applicant on the other, the Court considers it equitable to apportion responsibility for that damage equally between the two parties.

Notes
On this case read J. Meade (1986) 37 NILQ 370; N. March Hunnings (1987) 24 CML Rev 65.

On aspects of Article 288, read the several essays in H. Schermers, P. Mead, T. Heukels (eds), *Non-Contractual Liability of the European Communities*. See also F. Schockweiler, 'La régime de la résponsibilité extra-contractuelle du fait d'actes juridiques dans la Communauté Européenne' (1990) 26 RTDE 27.

(E) ARTICLE 234

(i)   The function of Article 234 in judicial review
The restrictive standing rules under the fourth paragraph of Article 230 and the time limit in its fifth paragraph conspire to diminish the efficacy of direct challenge to Community legislation before the European Court. However, the existence of the Article 234 preliminary reference procedure allows indirect challenge to be brought before national courts. In practice, this is of immense value to the private litigant.

R v Intervention Board, ex parte Man (Sugar) Ltd (Case 181/84) was examined in Chapter 1 and deserves re-reading (p. 62 above). It is an example of an action instituted at national level in which the validity of Community legislation is called into question. The Article 234 reference allows the Court to rule on the Community measure's validity. So, once Community legislation finds expression in national implementing legislation, a challenge to the validity of the Community legislation may be achieved via a challenge at national level to the national implementing acts.

Universität Hamburg v *HZA Hamburg-Kehrwieder (Case 216/82)*
[1983] ECR 2771
Court of Justice of the European Communities

The dispute between the University and the German customs authorities related to the levy due on a Spectrometer imported from the USA for use in laboratory experiments on animals. A Commission Decision addressed to all Member States indicated an outcome unfavourable to the University, and the German authorities confirmed this. The University then brought proceedings at national level against the German authorities. The Finance Court in Hamburg made a preliminary reference questioning the lawfulness of the Commission Decision, but first it asked whether Article 177 of the EC Treaty (now Article 234 EC) could be used in this fashion. After all, the University had failed to use Article 173 of the EC Treaty (now, after amendment, Article 230 EC) directly to challenge the Commission's Decision before the European Court.

The first two questions
[5]   By these questions the national court in substance seeks to ascertain whether, by not having brought proceedings under the second paragraph of Article 173 against a Decision of the Commission of the type in question within the periods stipulated in the third paragraph of that Article, the person or persons concerned by that Decision are, according to Community law, precluded from relying upon the invalidity of that Decision in proceedings before a national court. For the purpose of resolving that issue the procedure established by the aforesaid Regulations should be considered.

[6]   Article 3 of Regulation No 3195/75 requires an application for duty-free admission to be submitted to the competent authority of the Member State in which the scientific establishment in question is situated. Article 4 requires that national authority to give a direct Decision on applications in all cases where the information at its disposal enables it to decide whether or not there exist apparatus of equivalent scientific value which are currently manufactured in the Community. Only if the national authority considers that it is unable to decide that question for itself is it therefore bound to refer it to the Commission and Community law does not require the applicant to be informed of that reference.

[7]   The Decision adopted by the Commission is addressed to all the Member States. By virtue of Article 191 of the Treaty it must therefore be notified to the Member States and it takes effect upon such notification. However, it does not have to be notified to the person applying for exemption from customs duty and it is not one of the measures which the Treaty requires to be published. Even if in practice the Decision is in fact published in the *Official Journal of the European Communities*, its wording does not necessarily enable the applicant to ascertain whether it was adopted in relation to the procedure which he initiated.

[8]   Since the Decision is binding on the Member States, the national authority must reject the application for duty-free admission in the event of a negative Decision on the part of the Commission; however, Community law does not require it to refer to the Commission's Decision in its own Decision rejecting the application. Furthermore, as this case demonstrates, the national authority's Decision may be adopted some time after the notification of the Commission's Decision.

[9]   Finally, as the Finanzgericht rightly points out, for the purpose of bringing an action under the second paragraph of Article 173 of the Treaty against the Commission's Decision, the scientific establishment in question must demonstrate that the Decision is of direct and individual concern to it.

[10]   In those circumstances the rejection by the national authority of the scientific establishment's application is the only measure which is directly addressed to it, of which it has necessarily been informed in good time and which the establishment may challenge in the courts without encountering any difficulty in demonstrating its interest in bringing proceedings. According to a general principle of law which finds its expression in Article 184 of the EEC Treaty, in proceedings brought under national law against the rejection of his application the applicant must be able to plead the illegality of the Commission's Decision on which the national Decision adopted in his regard is based.

[11]   That statement is sufficient to provide an answer capable of dispelling the doubts expressed by the national court without there being any need to consider the wider issue of the general relationship between Articles 173 and 177 of the Treaty or to give a separate answer to the first question.

[12]   The answer to the first two questions of the Finanzgericht should therefore be that the person or persons concerned by a Decision adopted by the Commission pursuant to Article 4 of Regulation No 3195/75 may plead the illegality of the Decision before the national court in proceedings against the fixing of customs duty and that the question of the validity of the Decision may therefore be referred to the Court in proceedings for a preliminary ruling.

On the merits, however, the Court found no reason to impugn the validity of the Decision.

Walter Rau v BALM (Case 133/85)
[1987] ECR 2289
Court of Justice of the European Communities

The Community instituted a scheme whereby cheap butter was sold on the West Berlin market in order to test consumer reaction. German margarine producers challenged the scheme before German courts arguing that the German implementing measures were unlawful because their source, the Community scheme, was unlawful. The national court was immediately concerned whether this line of argument could properly be advanced before it, given the existence of the direct action to challenge Community acts before the European Court under Article 173 of the EC Treaty (now, after amendment, Article 230 EC).

[11]   It must be emphasized that there is nothing in Community law to prevent an action from being brought before a national court against a measure implementing a Decision adopted by a Community institution where the conditions laid down by national law are satisfied. When such an action is brought, if the outcome of the dispute depends on the validity of that Decision the national court may submit questions to the Court of Justice by way of a reference for a preliminary ruling, without there being any need to ascertain whether or not the plaintiff in the main proceedings has the possibility of challenging the Decision directly before the Court.

[12]　The answer to the first question must therefore be that the possibility of bringing a direct action under the second paragraph of Article 173 of the EEC Treaty against a Decision adopted by a Community institution does not preclude the possibility of bringing an action in a national court against a measure adopted by a national authority for the implementation of that Decision on the ground that the latter Decision is unlawful.

However, the Court held that none of several submissions provided a basis for holding the Community scheme invalid. On the issue of proportionality, for example, the Court held:

[33]　In its eighth question the national court asks whether the Decision of 25 February 1985 is compatible with the principle of proportionality in so far as the expansion of the markets or the search for new outlets may be achieved by action which has less impact on the workings of the market.

[34]　By way of explanation, the national court states that rules which interfere with the fundamental right to exercise a trade or profession are justified only if they are dictated by objectives in the general interest which are of such overriding importance that they deserve to take precedence over that fundamental right. The national court considers that that is not the case in this instance. If, on the one hand, the purpose of the operation was to reduce public stocks by 900 tonnes of butter, it could have been achieved by measures which had a less serious effect on the position of competitors protected by fundamental rights. Thus the 900 tonnes of butter could have been distributed over a longer period or over a wider area. If, on the other hand, the purpose of the operation was the search for new outlets, the national court doubts whether the operation is capable of yielding useful results. A measure which is such as to interfere with fundamental rights but not such as to help achieve the aim pursued can never be justified by overriding considerations pertaining to the general interest.

[35]　It follows from those considerations that the question raised by the national court was, more precisely, whether the principle of proportionality had been contravened on the ground that the aim of reducing public stocks by 900 tonnes of butter was attainable by methods which had a serious effect on the position of competitors and that it was doubtful whether a test market such as West Berlin was capable of yielding useful results.

[36]　It must be remembered in the first place that, as the Court stated in reply to the third question, the operation did not have as its purpose to reduce intervention stocks by 900 tonnes of butter and did not conflict with the principle of freedom to pursue a trade or profession, the principle of general freedom to pursue any lawful activity and the principle of freedom of competition.

[37]　Next, it must be emphasized that the operation constituted, as it was intended to, the basis of a scientific survey from which the Commission was able to derive useful information. Furthermore, the Commission chose the West Berlin market because of its isolated geographical location and the possibility of carrying out there, in view of its limited size, an operation at relatively low cost. In so doing, the Commission would not appear to have exceeded the discretion conferred upon it by the Council in Article 4 of Regulation No 1079/77.

[38]　Accordingly, the answer to the eighth question must be that consideration of the decision of 25 February 1985 has not disclosed any evidence of a breach of the principle of proportionality.

Note

The value of the preliminary reference procedure to the applicant is clear when it is appreciated that the applicant's direct action was doomed to fail as inadmissible without any examination of the merits of the claim; it was *Union Deutsche Lebensmittelwerke* (Case 97/85) (p. 651 above), and this is the promised next episode in the saga of the Berlin butter.

Read G. Bebr (1988) 25 CML Rev 684, who points out that it would be misleading to see the Court's willingness to allow the preliminary reference procedure to outflank the direct action for annulment as generosity to the individual applicant. It is more accurate to concentrate on the key role which the preliminary reference procedure plays in helping *courts* to maintain the uniformity and integrity of Community law (see Chapter 4 generally).

Resort to the Article 234 'indirect' route for challenging Community acts has real attractions for the individual confronted by the high hurdles of Article 230. Moreover, the process emphasises the role of national courts acting for these purposes as ordinary courts of Community law. It has a flavour of subsidiarity (p. 603 above). The availability of Article 234 in addition to Article 230 gives the individual flexibility in acting to secure protection of interests affected by EC acts, although the value of Article 234 is limited, *inter alia*, by the individual's inability to *require* that a referral be made. One might be tempted to make the case that the Court's restrictive approach to standing under Article 230 is justified by the open access of individuals to Article 234 via national courts. In this vein, it is notable that in the French nuclear tests case (Case T-219/95 R, p. 668 above), *Terres Rouges* (Case T-47/95, p. 671 above) and in *Greenpeace* (Case C-321/95 P, p. 673 above) a finding of inadmissibility was accompanied by comment on the availability of judicial protection before national courts able to make preliminary references. Nevertheless, the next ruling amounts to a sharp rejection of any notion that an individual is entitled to choose to surrender an opportunity to sue under Article 230 and subsequently await reliance on on Article 234.

TWD Textilwerke Deggendorf GmbH v *Germany (Case C–188/92)*
[1994] ECR I–833
Court of Justice of the European Communities

A Commission Decision addressed to Germany declared that aid paid to TWD Textilwerke Deggendorf GmbH, a Bavarian producer of polyamide and polyester yarn, was incompatible with the rules on State aid, Articles 92–94 of the EC Treaty (now, after amendment, Article 87–89 EC). Germany was required to recover the aid. No direct action was initiated by either Germany or the firm, TWD, even though TWD had received a copy of the Commission Decision from the relevant German Ministry, which had also informed TWD that it could employ Article 173 of the EC Treaty (now, after amendment, Article 230 EC) to challenge the Decision (circumstances emphasised by the referring court). Subsequently in national proceedings to recover the aid, TWD raised challenges to the validity of the Commission Decision on which the national action was based. This led to a preliminary reference relating to the validity of the Commission Decision. But the European Court focused on TWD's tactics in selecting remedies.

[14]   The undertaking in receipt of individual aid which is the subject-matter of a Commission decision adopted on the basis of Article 93 of the Treaty has the right to bring an action for annulment under the second paragraph of Article 173 of the Treaty even if the decision is addressed to a Member State (judgment in Case 730/79 *Philip Morris* v *Commission* [1980] ECR 2671). By virtue of the third paragraph of that article, the expiry of the time-limit laid down in that provision has the same time-barring effect vis-à-vis such an undertaking as it does vis-à-vis the Member State which is the addressee of the decision.

[15]   It is settled law that a Member State may no longer call in question the validity of a decision addressed to it on the basis of Article 93(2) of the Treaty once the time-limit laid down in the third paragraph of Article 173 of the Treaty has expired (see the judgments in Case 156/77 *Commission* v *Belgium* [1978] ECR 1881 and Case C–183/91 *Commission* v *Greece* [1993] ECR I–3131).

[16]   That case-law, according to which it is impossible for a Member State which is the addressee of a decision taken under the first paragraph of Article 93(2) of the Treaty to call in question the validity of the decision in the proceedings for non-compliance provided for in the second paragraph of that provision, is based in particular on the consideration that the periods within which applications must be lodged are intended to safeguard legal certainty by preventing Community measures which involve legal effects from being called in question indefinitely.

[17]   It follows from the same requirements of legal certainty that it is not possible for a recipient of aid, forming the subject-matter of a Commission decision adopted on the basis of Article 93 of the Treaty, who could have challenged that decision and who allowed the mandatory time-limit laid down in this regard by the third paragraph of Article 173 of the Treaty to expire, to call in question the lawfulness of that decision before the national courts in an action brought against the measures taken by the national authorities for implementing that decision.

[18]   To accept that in such circumstances the person concerned could challenge the implementation of the decision in proceedings before the national court on the ground that the decision was unlawful would in effect enable the person concerned to overcome the definitive nature which the decision assumes as against that person once the time-limit for bringing an action has expired.

[19]   It is true that in its judgment in Joined Cases 133 to 136/85 *Rau* v *BALM* [1987] ECR 2289, on which the French Government relies in its observations, the Court held that the possibility of bringing a direct action under the second paragraph of Article 173 of the EEC Treaty against a decision adopted by a Community institution did not preclude the possibility of bringing an action in a national court against a measure adopted by a national authority for the implementation of that decision, on the ground that the latter decision was unlawful.

[20]   However, as is clear from the Report for the Hearing in those cases, each of the plaintiffs in the main proceedings had brought an action before the Court of Justice for the annulment of the decision in question. The Court did not therefore rule, and did not have to rule, in that judgment on the time-barring effects of the expiry of time-limits. It is precisely that issue with which the question referred by the national court in this case is concerned.

[21]   This case is also distinguishable from Case 216/82 *Universität Hamburg* v *Hauptzollamt Hamburg-Kehrwieder* [1983] ECR 2771.

[22]   In the judgment in that case the Court held that a plaintiff whose application for duty-free admission had been rejected by a decision of a national authority taken on the basis of a decision of the Commission addressed to all the Member States had to be able to plead, in proceedings brought under national law against the rejection of his application, the illegality of the Commission's decision on which the national decision adopted in his regard was based.

[23]   In that judgment the Court took into account the fact that the rejection of the application by the national authority was the only measure directly addressed to the person concerned of which it had necessarily been informed in good time and which it could challenge in the courts without encountering any difficulty in demonstrating its interest in bringing proceedings. It held that in those circumstances the possibility of pleading the unlawfulness of the Commission's decision derived from a general principle of law which found its expression in Article 184 of the EEC Treaty, namely the principle which confers upon any party to proceedings the right to challenge, for the purpose of obtaining the annulment of a decision of direct and individual concern to that party, the validity of previous acts of the institutions which form the legal basis of the decision which is being attacked, if that party was not entitled under Article 173 of the Treaty to bring a direct action challenging those acts by which it was thus affected without having been in a position to ask that they be declared void (see the judgment in Case 92/78 *Simmenthal* v *Commission* [1979] ECR 777).

[24]   In the present case, it is common ground that the applicant in the main proceedings was fully aware of the Commission's decision and of the fact that it could without any doubt have challenged it under Article 173 of the Treaty.

[25]   It follows from the foregoing that, in factual and legal circumstances such as those of the main proceedings in this case, the definitive nature of the decision taken by the Commission pursuant to Article 93 of the Treaty vis-à-vis the undertaking in receipt of the aid binds the national court by virtue of the principle of legal certainty.

[26]   The reply to be given to the first question must therefore be that the national court is bound by a Commission decision adopted under Article 93(2) of the Treaty where, in view of the implementation of that decision by the national authorities, the recipient of the aid to which the implementation measures are addressed brings before it an action in which it pleads the unlawfulness of the Commission's decision and where that recipient of aid, although informed in writing by the Member State of the Commission's decision, did not bring an action against that decision under the second paragraph of Article 173 of the Treaty, or did not do so within the period prescribed.

Note
See also the analogy drawn in *TWD Textilwerke Deggendorf GmbH* v *Commission* (Cases T–244/93 and T–486/93) [1995] ECR II-2265, where the Court of First Instance limited access to Article 184 of the EC Treaty (now Article 241 EC) (p. 683) where an available action under Article 173 of the EC Treaty (now, after amendment, Article 230 EC) had not been initiated. In the above ruling the Court is careful to make plain that it does not intend to overturn its pre-existing receptivity to the use of Article 177 of the EC Treaty (now Article 234 EC) as a means of indirect challenge to Community acts.

Rather, it considers that it is dealing with a special situation in which a firm declining to pursue the available routes of the direct action should not subsequently be able to rely on the preliminary reference procedure. By contrast, in *Eurotunnel SA and others* v *SeaFrance* (Case C-408/95) [1997] ECR I-6315, challenge to the validity of Directives 91/680 and 92/12 establishing transitional arrangements for 'duty free' shops failed on the merits, but was treated as permissibly advanced via proceedings at national level involving a preliminary reference under Article 177 of the EC Treaty (now Article 234 EC) even though the applicant had not attempted to employ Article 173 of the EC Treaty (now, after amendment, Article 230 EC), for it was not obvious that the applicant would have had individual concern for the purposes of a direct action and clearly would not have had direct concern. The message is that a firm immediately affected by a Community act must decide its litigation strategy with an eye to the two-month time-limit contained in the final paragraph of Article 230. Read M. Ross (1994) 19 EL Rev 641, A. Arnull (1995) 32 CML Rev 7, J. Usher in A. Campbell and M. Voyatzi (eds), *Legal Reasoning and Judicial Interpretation in European Law* (1996).

Questions
1. *In principle* do you accept the Court's concern in Case C–188/92 that legal certainty would be compromised were a party in the applicant's position permitted to avail itself of national proceedings supplemented by Article 234 in order to contest Community acts?
2. *In practice*, in the light of your examination earlier in this chapter of the twists and turns of the Court's approach to standing under Article 230, do you consider that the Court's reference to the ability *without any doubt* (para. 24 of the ruling in Case C–188/92) of the applicant to make use of Article 230 represents a workable criterion for lawyers who in future must advise clients as to when they should invest time and money in pursuing an Article 230 challenge, in order to preclude the subsequent unpleasant discovery that the Article 234 route is barred?

(ii)   Article 234 and the validity of Community acts
The next case was an important milestone in the Court's development of the preliminary reference procedure as a tool of judicial review of Community legislation. It has already been discussed at p. 157 above, but the core of the judgment bears repetition here.

Foto Frost v *HZA Lubeck Ost (Case 314/85)*
[1987] ECR 4199
Court of Justice of the European Communities

[15]   . . . [T]he main purpose of the powers accorded to the Court by Article 177 [now 234] is to ensure that Community law is applied uniformly by national courts. That requirement of uniformity is particularly imperative when the validity of a

Community act is in question. Divergences between courts in the Member States as to the validity of Community acts would be liable to place in jeopardy the very unity of the Community legal order and detract from the fundamental requirement of legal certainty.

. . .

[17]   Since Article 173 [now 230] gives the Court exclusive jurisdiction to declare void an act of a Community institution, the coherence of the system requires that where the validity of a Community act is challenged before a national court the power to declare the act invalid must also be reserved to the Court of Justice.

. . .

[19]   It should be added that the rule that national courts may not themselves declare Community acts invalid may have to be qualified in certain circumstances in the case of proceedings relating to an application for interim measures; however, that case is not referred to in the national court's question.

[20]   The answer to the first question must therefore be that the national courts have no jurisdiction themselves to declare that acts of Community institutions are invalid.

The Commission Decision was held invalid.

Note

Once this case is placed in the general context of the Community's judicial review procedures, it is perhaps easier to appreciate why the Court was eager to deny the competence of national courts to hold Community legislation unlawful (*cf.* p. 159 above). The proposition that the European Court is indeed properly treated as 'the ultimate umpire of the system' is carefully defended by J. Weiler and U. Haltern in 'The Autonomy of the Community Legal Order – Through the Looking Glass' (1996) 37 Harvard Intl L Jnl 411. This is a matter monitored by the Commission. In 1998 its research revealed that no national court had declared a Community act invalid ((1998) OJ C-354/184–186). As already suggested at p. 159 above, the stance of the *Bundesverfassungsgericht* on judicial competence to fix the outer limits of Community competence has the potential to cause tension in the light of the European Court's perception that its own exclusive jurisdiction is essential to the very unity of the Community legal order.

Zuckerfabrik Suderdithmarschen v *HZA Itzehoe (Case C-143/88);* *Zuckerfabrik Soest* v *HZA Paderborn (Case C-92/89)*
[1991] ECR I-415
Court of Justice of the European Communities

These cases involved two separate disputes between firms and German customs offices concerning demands for the payment of levies. The firms challenged the national administrative measures before German courts; the basis of the challenge was the validity of the Community legislation setting up the structure. The questions referred to the European Court concerned, first, the circumstances in which the national court could grant interim relief against the contested measures, it being clear from *Foto Frost* that the final decision on validity of Community legislation belongs with the European Court; and, secondly, questions about the validity of the challenged Regulation itself.

The Court insisted that in order to ensure that the preliminary reference procedure under Article 177 of the EC Treaty (now Article 234 EC) works effectively, it must be possible for a national court to grant interim relief suspending the operation of a national measure based on impugned Community legislation, pending the Court's final ruling on validity. It pointed out that it had already ruled that interim relief must be available before a national court asked to rule on the compatibility of national law with Community law (*Factortame*, p. 729 below), and added that no different solution should apply where the dispute was about the compatibility of secondary Community law with Community law. The Court then went on to explain the circumstances in which such interim relief should be granted by a national court.

[23]   It must first of all be noted that interim measures suspending enforcement of a contested measure may be adopted only if the factual and legal circumstances relied on by the applicants are such as to persuade the national court that serious doubts exist as to the validity of the Community regulation on which the contested administrative measure is based. Only the possibility of a finding of invalidity, a matter which is reserved to the court, can justify the granting of suspensory measures.

[24]   It should next be pointed out that suspension of enforcement must retain the character of an interim measure. The national court to which the application for interim relief is made may therefore grant a suspension only until such time as the Court has delivered its ruling on the question of validity. Consequently, it is for the national court, should the question not yet have been referred to the Court of Justice, to refer that question itself, setting out the reasons for which it believes that the regulation must be held to be invalid.

[25]   As regards the other conditions concerning the suspension of enforcement of administrative measures, it must be observed that the rules of procedure of the courts are determined by national law and that those conditions differ according to the national law governing them, which may jeopardize the uniform application of Community law.

[26]   Such uniform application is a fundamental requirement of the Community legal order. It therefore follows that the suspension of enforcement of administrative measures based on a Community regulation, whilst it is governed by national procedural law, in particular as regards the making and examination of the application, must in all the Member States be subject, at the very least, to conditions which are uniform so far as the granting of such relief is concerned.

[27]   Since the power of national courts to grant such a suspension corresponds to the jurisdiction reserved to the Court of Justice by Article 185 in the context of actions brought under Article 173, those courts may grant such relief only on the conditions which must be satisfied for the Court of Justice to allow an application to it for interim measures.

[28]   In this regard, the Court has consistently held that measures suspending the operation of a contested act may be granted only in the event of urgency, in other words, if it is necessary for them to be adopted and to take effect before the decision on the substance of a case, in order to avoid serious and irreparable damage to the party seeking them.

[29]   With regard to the question of urgency, it should be pointed out that damage invoked by the applicant must be liable to materialize before the Court of Justice has been able to rule on the validity of the contested Community measure. With regard to the nature of the damage, purely financial damage cannot, as the Court has held on numerous occasions, be regarded in principle as irreparable. However, it is for the national court hearing the application for interim relief to examine the circumstances particular to the case before it. It must in this connection consider whether immediate enforcement of the measure which is the subject of the application for interim relief would be likely to result in irreversible damage to the applicant which could not be made good if the Community act were to be declared invalid.

[30]   It should also be added that a national court called upon to apply, within the limits of its jurisdiction, the provisions of Community law is under an obligation to ensure that full effect is given to Community law and, consequently, where there is doubt as to the validity of Community regulations, to take account of the interest of the Community, namely that such regulations should not be set aside without proper guarantees.

[31]   In order to comply with that obligation, a national court seised of an application for suspension must first examine whether the Community measure in question would be deprived of all effectiveness if not immediately implemented.

[32]   If suspension of enforcement is liable to involve a financial risk for the Community, the national court must also be in a position to require the applicant to provide adequate guarantees, such as the deposit of money or other security.

[33]   It follows from the foregoing that the reply to the second part of the first question put to the Court by the Finanzgericht Hamburg must be that suspension of enforcement of a national measure adopted in implementation of a Community regulation may be granted by a national court only:

(i)   if that court entertains serious doubts as to the validity of the Community measure and, should the question of the validity of the contested measure not already have been brought before the Court, itself refers that question to the Court;

(ii)   if there is urgency and a threat of serious and irreparable damage to the applicant;

(iii)   and if the national court takes due account of the Community's interests.

Note
There is a sure indication that the Court was aware in the *Zuckerfabrik* cases that it was establishing an important principle. The decision is against the applicants; the legislation is held valid. Yet the Court had not dealt with the matter in brief, as it could have done. It took time to explain the applicable principles of law.

In the next case the Court added a further, fourth criterion. There seems little doubt that the addition reflects the Court's concern to sustain uniformity in the application of Community law. Equally there can be little doubt that the Court is aware of potential fracture between its own approach and approaches currently tempting national courts (p. 15 above). The decision is a preliminary ruling on questions referred from a German court, the *Verwaltungsgericht* of Frankfurt-am-Main.

Atlanta Fruchthandelsgesellschaft mbH and others v Bundesamt für Ernährung und Forstwirtschaft (Case C–465/93)
[1995] ECR I-3761
Court of Justice of the European Communities

The challenged act was Council Regulation 404/93 on the common organisation of the market in bananas, establishing a common import regime. The applicants, traditional importers of bananas, found themselves with import quotas which they viewed as insufficient. Among other strategies to challenge the system, they brought proceedings before the German courts to attack measures associated with the implementation of the EC regime. The European Court was asked questions on the national court's power to order interim measures disapplying an EC Regulation pending a preliminary ruling by the Court on its validity. The Court stated that the case afforded it 'an opportunity to clarify' the conditions established in *Zuckerfabrik* (Cases C–143/88, C–92/89), p. 702 above.

[35]   In *Zuckerfabrik* (paragraph 23) the Court held that interim measures may be adopted only if the factual and legal circumstances relied on by the applicants are such as to persuade the national court that serious doubts exist as to the validity of the Community regulation on which the contested administrative measure is based. Only the possibility of a finding of invalidity, a matter which is reserved to the Court, can justify the grant of interim relief.

[36]   That requirement means that the national court cannot restrict itself to referring the question of the validity of the regulation to the Court for a preliminary ruling, but must set out, when making the interim order, the reasons for which it considers that the Court should find the regulation to be invalid.

[37]   The national court must take into account here the extent of the discretion which, having regard to the Court's case-law, the Community institutions must be allowed in the sectors concerned.

[38]   The Court further held in *Zuckerfabrik* (paragraph 24) that the grant of relief must retain the character of an interim measure. The national court to which the application for interim relief is made may therefore order interim measures and maintain them only for so long as the Court has not ruled that consideration of the questions referred for a preliminary ruling has disclosed no factor of such a kind as to affect the validity of the regulation in question.

[39]   Since the power of national courts to order interim relief corresponds to the jurisdiction reserved to the Court of Justice by Article 186 in the context of actions brought under Article 173 of the Treaty, those national courts may grant such relief only on the same conditions as apply when the Court of Justice is dealing with an application for interim measures (*Zuckerfabrik*, paragraph 27).

[40] In that respect the Court held in *Zuckerfabrik* (paragraph 28), on the basis of settled case-law, that interim measures may be ordered only where they are urgent, that is to say, where it is necessary for them to be adopted and take effect before the decision on the substance of the case, in order to avoid serious and irreparable damage to the party seeking them.

[41] As to urgency, the damage relied on by the applicant must be such as to materialise before the Court of Justice has been able to rule on the validity of the contested Community act. As to the nature of the damage, purely financial damage cannot, as the Court has held on numerous occasions, be regarded in principle as irreparable. However, it is for the national court hearing the application for interim relief to examine the circumstances particular to the case before it. It must in this connection consider whether immediate enforcement of the measure with respect to which the application for interim relief is made would be likely to result in irreversible damage to the applicant which could not be made good if the Community act were to be declared invalid (*Zuckerfabrik*, paragraph 29).

[42] Furthermore, a national court called upon to apply, within the limits of its jurisdiction, the provisions of Community law is under an obligation to ensure that full effect is given to Community law and, consequently, where there is doubt as to the validity of Community regulations, to take account of the interest of the Community, namely that such regulations should not be set aside without proper guarantees (*Zuckerfabrik*, paragraph 30).

[43] In order to comply with that obligation, the national court to which an application for interim relief has been made must first examine whether the Community act in question would be deprived of all effectiveness if not immediately implemented (*Zuckerfabrik*, paragraph 31).

[44] In that respect the national court must take account of the damage which the interim measure may cause the legal regime established by that regulation for the Community as a whole. It must consider, on the one hand, the cumulative effect which would arise if a large number of courts were also to adopt interim measures for similar reasons and, on the other, those special features of the applicant's situation which distinguish him from the other operators concerned.

[45] If the grant of interim relief represents a financial risk for the Community, the national court must also be in a position to require the applicant to provide adequate guarantees, such as the deposit of money or other security (*Zuckerfabrik*, paragraph 32).

[46] When assessing the conditions for the grant of interim relief, the national court is obliged under Article 5 [now 10] of the Treaty to respect what the Community court has decided on the questions at issue before it. Thus if the Court of Justice has dismissed on the merits an action for annulment of the regulation in question or has held, in the context of a reference for a preliminary ruling on validity, that the reference disclosed nothing to affect the validity of that regulation, the national court can no longer order interim measures or must revoke existing measures, unless the grounds of illegality put forward before it differ from the pleas in law or grounds of illegality rejected by the Court in its judgment. The same applies if the Court of First Instance, in a judgment which has become final and binding, has dismissed on the merits an action for annulment of the regulation or a plea of illegality.

[47] In the present case the Court, adjudicating on the same factual situation as that which gave rise to the proceedings before the national court, has held that the Member

States which bring an action for annulment of the regulation, being responsible for the interests, in particular those of an economic and social nature, which are regarded as general interests at national level, are entitled to take judicial proceedings to defend such interests. They may therefore invoke damage affecting a whole sector of their economy, in particular when the contested Community measure may entail unfavourable repercussions on the level of employment and the cost of living (order in *Germany* v *Council*, cited above [Case C–280/93 R) [1993] ECR I–3667], paragraph 27).

[48] The national court, when called upon to protect the rights of individuals, may indeed assess the extent to which refusal to order an interim measure may be liable to have a serious and irreparable effect on important individual interests.

[49] However, if an applicant is unable to show a specific situation which distinguishes him from other operators in the relevant sector, the national court must accept any findings already made by the Court of Justice concerning the serious and irreparable nature of the damage.

[50] The national court's obligation to respect a decision of the Court of Justice applies in particular to the Court's assessment of the Community interest and the balance between that interest and that of the economic sector concerned.

[51] Accordingly, the answer to the second question put to the Court by the Verwaltungsgericht Frankfurt am Main must be that interim relief, with respect to a national administrative measure adopted in implementation of a Community regulation, can be granted by a national court only if:

(1) that court entertains serious doubts as to the validity of the Community act and, if the validity of the contested act is not already in issue before the Court of Justice, itself refers the question to the Court of Justice;
(2) there is urgency, in that the interim relief is necessary to avoid serious and irreparable damage being caused to the party seeking the relief;
(3) the court takes due account of the Community interest; and
(4) in its assessment of all those conditions, it respects any decisions of the Court of Justice or the Court of First Instance ruling on the lawfulness of the regulation or on an application for interim measures seeking similar interim relief at Community level.

Note
On the very same day the Court answered questions relating to the validity of the same Regulation, 404/93, referred to it by the same court in litigation between the same parties: *Atlanta Fruchthandelsgesellschaft mbH and others* v *Bundesamt für Ernährung und Forstwirtschaft* (Case C–466/93) [1995] ECR I–3799. The Court observed that an action for annulment of the Regulation brought by Germany under Article 173 of the EC Treaty (now, after amendment, Article 230 EC), based on comparable pleas to those covered by the questions referred, had already been dismissed as unfounded (*Germany* v *Council* (Case C–280/93) [1994] ECR I–4973). The European Court had there found no violation of Community law principles including that of undistorted competition, nor of fundamental rights including the right to property; neither had the Court in Case C–280/93 been prepared to test the

Regulation against the standards of the GATT which it viewed as too 'flexible' to be apt for application in the context of a direct action for annulment (the Court has subsequently transplanted this reluctance to the incorporation of the Standards of the WTO, which has replaced the GATT: Case C-149/96 *Portugal* v *Council* judgment of 23 November 1999). Nothing new had been advanced in the preliminary reference to alter the Court's findings in Case C-280/93, excepting only a submission based on lack of reasons within the meaning of Article 190 of the EC Treaty (now Article 235 EC) (p. 58 above) which the Court did not accept. The Court therefore found no basis to impugn the validity of the Regulation. Subsequently, a claim for damages was unsuccessful; Case T-521/93 *Atlanta AG and others* v *Council and Commission* [1996] ECR II-1707, from which an appeal failed in substance in Case C-104/97P *Atlanta AG and Others* v *Council and Commission*, judgment of 14 October 1999. (On some of the background tensions in the 'banana cases', see N. Reich (1996) 7 EJIL 103; S. Peers (1999) 4 *Euro Foreign Affairs Rev* 195.)

Whereas *Atlanta* (Case C-465/93) explores the criteria according to which the application of national measures adopted pursuant to a Community act may exceptionally be suspended in national proceedings in which the validity of the Community act is impugned, the next case in this saga, also involving the Community's disputed bananas regime founded on Regulation 404/93, saw the Court unwilling further to extend the powers of national courts.

T. Port GmbH v *Bundesanstalt fur Landwirtschaft und Ernahrung* (*Case C-68/95*)
[1996] ECR I-6065, [1997] 1 CMLR 1
Court of Justice of the European Communities

The applicant company's aim was to secure an increased quota of bananas. Proceedings were initiated before a German court, which made a preliminary reference asking for guidance on the powers of a national court to grant interim relief to traders pending a Commission determination on a request for an increased quota; specifically, could the national court make an interim order granting an increase? This goes beyond that which the Court accepted was within the competence of a national court in *Zuckerfabrik* and *Atlanta*, and in *T. Port* the Court, having referred to those cases, was not prepared to make that extension. Traders must seek judicial protection before the Community judicature in such circumstances.

[52] However, the situation now raised by the national court is different from the situation at issue in those cases. The present case is not about granting interim measures in the context of the implementation of a Community regulation whose validity is being contested, in order to ensure interim protection of rights which individuals derive from the Community legal system, but about granting traders interim judicial protection in a situation where, by virtue of a Community regulation, the existence and scope of traders' rights must be established by a Commission measure which the Commission has not yet adopted.

[53]   The Treaty makes no provision for a reference for a preliminary ruling by which a national court asks the Court of Justice to rule that an institution has failed to act. Consequently, national courts have no jurisdiction to order interim measures pending action on the part of the institution. Judicial review of alleged failure to act can be exercised only by the Community judicature.

[54]   In a situation such as that in the present case, only the Court of Justice or the Court of First Instance, as the case may be, can ensure judicial protection for the persons concerned.

[55]   It is to be remembered that, under the procedure provided for in Article 27 of the Regulation, the Commission is to adopt transitional measures following an opinion of the Management Committee before which the matter is brought by a representative of the Commission or of a Member State.

[56]   In circumstances such as those in the main proceedings, it is for the relevant Member State, urged if necessary by the trader concerned, to request initiation of the Management Committee procedure, should this be necessary.

[57]   Having regard to the hardship which the applicant in the main proceedings claims to be suffering, the applicant may also approach the Commission directly and request it to adopt, in accordance with the Article 27 procedure, the specific measures which its situation requires.

[58]   Where the Community institution fails to act, the Member State may bring an action for failure to act before the Court of Justice. Likewise, the trader concerned, who would be the addressee of the measure which the Commission is alleged to have failed to adopt, or at least directly and individually concerned by it, could bring such an action before the Court of First Instance (see Case C-107/91 *ENU* v *Commission* [1993] ECR I-599).

[59]   It is true that the third paragraph of Article 175 of the Treaty entitles legal and natural persons to bring an action for failure to act when an institution has failed to address to them any act other than a recommendation or an opinion. The Court has, however, held that Articles 173 and 175 merely prescribe one and the same method of recourse (Case 15/70 *Chevalley* v *Commission* [1970] ECR 975, paragraph 6). It follows that, just as the fourth paragraph of Article 173 allows individuals to bring an action for annulment against a measure of an institution not addressed to them provided that the measure is of direct and individual concern to them, the third paragraph of Article 175 must be interpreted as also entitling them to bring an action for failure to act against an institution which they claim has failed to adopt a measure which would have concerned them in the same way. The possibility for individuals to assert their rights should not depend upon whether the institution concerned has acted or failed to act.

Note

Notice in these cases the Court's concern to build through analogies between Community level and national level. The Treaty provisions governing remedies are singularly incomplete, and the Court here shows itself bent on developing the system. These judgments are important examples of the Court's function of constructing the Community legal order. *Foto Frost* (Case 314/85), *Zuckerfabrik* (Cases C-143/88, C-92/89) and *Atlanta* (Case C-465/93) all appear in the 'Notice for Guidance on References by National Courts for Preliminary Rulings' issued by the Court in 1996. The Notice is set out at p. 160 above.

Notice, too, that the Court develops not only Community law. In doing so, it also contributes to the equalisation of national practice. The cases concern protection against Member States' acts based on Community legislation which is allegedly invalid under Community law. For the comparable situation of protection against Member States' acts in alleged violation of substantive Community law, see the Court's judgment in *Factortame* (Case C-213/89) at p. 731 below. It must there be considered how wide-ranging is the Court's commitment to the development of the Community legal principles governing effective remedies applicable in this area.

(iii)   The effect of an Article 234 ruling

ICC v *Amministrazione delle Finanze (Case 66/80)*
[1981] ECR 1191; [1983] 2 CMLR 593
Court of Justice of the European Communities

The facts are set out at p. 148 above. The Court held:

. . . [A]lthough a judgment of the Court given under Article 177 [now 234] of the Treaty declaring an act of an institution, in particular a Council or Commission Regulation, to be void is directly addressed only to the national court which brought the matter before the Court, it is sufficient reason for any other national court to regard that act as void for the purposes of a judgment which it has to give.

Note
Accordingly, a finding in Article 234 proceedings that Community legislation is invalid should be respected by other national courts. In practice, the effects of an Article 234 ruling of invalidity may not be significantly different from the impact of an Article 230 ruling, which according to Article 231 renders the act 'void'.

The Court has also claimed the power under Article 234 to rule on the validity of Community legislation in a nuanced manner. Validity need not be all or nothing.

Société de Produits de Maïs v Administration des Douanes (Case 112/83)
[1985] ECR 719
Court of Justice of the European Communities

This was a reference under Article 177 of the EC Treaty (now Article 234 EC) from a French court relating to the validity of Commission Regulation 652/76.

[16]   It should in the first place be recalled that the Court has already held in its judgment of 13 May 1981 (Case 66/80 *International Chemical Corporation* [1981] ECR 1191) that although a judgment of the Court given under Article 177 of the Treaty

declaring an act of an institution, in particular a Council or Commission Regulation, to be void is directly addressed only to the national court which brought the matter before the Court, it is sufficient reason for any other national court to regard that act as void for the purposes of a judgment which it has to give.

[17]   Secondly, it must be emphasized that the Court's power to impose temporal limits on the effects of a declaration that a legislative act is invalid, in the context of preliminary rulings under indent (b) of the first paragraph of Article 177, is justified by the interpretation of Article 174 [now 231] of the Treaty having regard to the necessary consistency between the preliminary ruling procedure and the action for annulment provided for in Articles 173, 174 and 176 of the Treaty, which are two mechanisms provided by the Treaty for reviewing the legality of acts of the Community institutions. The possibility of imposing temporal limits on the effects of the invalidity of a Community Regulation, whether under Article 173 or Article 177, is a power conferred on the Court by the Treaty in the interest of the uniform application of Community law throughout the Community. In the particular case of the judgment of 15 October 1980, referred to by the Tribunal [Case 145/79], the use of the possibility provided for in the second paragraph of Article 174 was based on reasons of legal certainty more fully explained in paragraph 52 of that judgment.

[18]   It must be pointed out that where it is justified by overriding considerations the second paragraph of Article 174 [now 231] gives the Court discretion to decide, in each particular case, which specific effects of a Regulation which has been declared void must be maintained. It is therefore for the Court, where it makes use of the possibility of limiting the effect on past events of a declaration in proceedings under Article 177 [now 234] that a measure is void, to decide whether an exception to that temporal limitation of the effect of its judgment may be made in favour of the party which brought the action before the national court or of any other trader which took similar steps before the declaration of invalidity or whether, conversely, a declaration of invalidity applicable only to the future constitutes an adequate remedy even for traders who took action at the appropriate time with a view to protecting their rights.

Note

Cf. the second paragraph of Article 231, at p. 643 above. Notice once again the Court's interest in bringing about coherence between the different routes for challenging Community acts.

The Court's approach in this case to the validity of Community legislation also finds a parallel in its approach to the interpretation of Community law. In *Defrenne* v *SABENA* (Case 43/75), at p. 98 above, it insisted that it alone has the competence to limit the implications of its ruling at national level.

(F) THE INTERRELATION OF THE SEVERAL REMEDIES

It should now be plain that although Article 230 constitutes the major direct means of challenging Community acts before the Court, other avenues of redress may be open to applicants. These include other avenues before the Court, as well as procedures at national level involving the use of the Article 234 preliminary reference procedure.

An extract from para. 23 of '*Les Verts*' (Case 294/83) was set out at p. 683 above to demonstrate how at Community level Article 241 may allow the applicant to circumvent the hurdles of the Article 230 direct action. Here now is the full text of para. 23, which shows how in addition Article 234 may serve that purpose via the action at national level.

Parti Ecologiste 'Les Verts' v Parliament (Case 294/83)
[1986] ECR 1339
Court of Justice of the European Communities

[23] It must first be emphasized in this regard that the European Economic Community is a Community based on the rule of law, inasmuch as neither its Member States nor its institutions can avoid a review of the question whether the measures adopted by them are in conformity with the basic constitutional charter, the Treaty. In particular, in Articles 173 [now 230] and 184 [now 241], on the one hand, and in Article 177 [now 234], on the other, the Treaty established a complete system of legal remedies and procedures designed to permit the Court of Justice to review the legality of measures adopted by the institutions. Natural and legal persons are thus protected against the application to them of general measures which they cannot contest directly before the Court by reason of the special conditions of admissibility laid down in the second paragraph of Article 173 [now the fourth paragraph of Article 230] of the Treaty. Where the Community institutions are responsible for the administrative implementation of such measures, natural or legal persons may bring a direct action before the Court against implementing measures which are addressed to them or which are of direct and individual concern to them and, in support of such an action, plead the illegality of the general measure on which they are based. Where implementation is a matter for the national authorities, such persons may plead the invalidity of general measures before the national courts and cause the latter to request the Court of Justice for a preliminary ruling.

Note
In this chapter there have been many other examples of the Court's concern to draw analogies between different levels of enforcement and remedies in order to ensure the structure displays an internal coherence. See the *Zuckerfabrik* cases at p. 701 above; and read para. 10 of the judgment in *Universität Hamburg* (Case 216/82), at p. 693 above; para. 17, *Foto Frost* (Case 314/85), at p. 700 above; para. 39, *Atlanta* (Case 465/93), at p. 704 above; para. 17, *Société de Produits de Mais* (Case 112/83), at p. 709 above. This is part of the Court's process of 'constitutionalising' the Treaty (p. 79 above).

17 CONTROL OF MEMBER STATES

(A) CONTROL AT COMMUNITY LEVEL

Articles 226 and 227 EC

Article 226

If the Commission considers that a Member State has failed to fulfil an obligation under this Treaty, it shall deliver a reasoned opinion on the matter after giving the State concerned the opportunity to submit its observations.

If the State concerned does not comply with the opinion within the period laid down by the Commission the latter may bring the matter before the Court of Justice.

Article 227

A Member State which considers that another Member State has failed to fulfil an obligation under this Treaty may bring the matter before the Court of Justice.

Before a Member State brings an action against another Member State for an alleged infringement of an obligation under this Treaty, it shall bring the matter before the Commission.

The Commission shall deliver a reasoned opinion after each of the States concerned has been given the opportunity to submit its own case and its observations on the other party's case both orally and in writing.

If the Commission has not delivered an opinion within three months of the date on which the matter was brought before it, the absence of such opinion shall not prevent the matter from being brought before the Court of Justice.

Note

Article 227 is plainly politically sensitive and has been little used (but see *France* v *UK* (Case 141/78) [1979] ECR 2923; and *Belgium* v *Spain* (Case C-388/95) judgment of 16 May 2000).

Articles 226 and 227 EC were Articles 169 and 170 EC pre-Amsterdam, though the text of both was unaffected by the Amsterdam Treaty.

(i)   The nature of Article 226

R. White and A. Dashwood, 'Enforcement Actions under Articles 169 and 170 EEC' [now 226 and 227 EC] (1989) 14 EL Rev 388, at pp. 388–389

(Footnotes omitted; numbering altered to reflect the post-Amsterdam Treaty.)

The nature of Articles 226 and 227 EC

. . . Under both Article [226] and Article [227] the procedure falls into two distinct phases. In a first 'administrative' phase, the Commission receives observations on the allegation of non-compliance from the Member State (or in proceedings under Article [227], the Member States) concerned and defines its own position in a reasoned opinion. An attempt is made to reach a satisfactory settlement without resorting to litigation, and in the great majority of cases this has proved possible. Where it is not, an action is brought by the Commission or by the complaining Member State in the European Court. The aim of the action is to obtain a declaration by the European Court that the defendant Member State has failed in a specified manner to fulfil its obligation under specified provisions of Community law. The Member State will be bound under Article [228] to take the necessary measures to comply with the judgment.

The procedure under Article [226] represents a considerable advance on the rules that normally apply in public international law where a state fails to fulfil its obligations under a treaty. In the first place, a right to prosecute infringements is given to the Commission, an institution specifically charged with protecting and promoting the interests of the Community as a whole. This makes it much more likely that effective action will be taken than if the Decision depended exclusively on Member State's estimation as to what would best serve their particular interests. Secondly, by virtue of their adherence to the EEC Treaty, Member States accept the compulsory jurisdiction of the European Court. No express declaration of acceptance is required; and no reservations or time limit may be imposed. These special features of the procedure are explained by the vital role the Member States are called upon to play in the concrete implementation of Community policies and rules.

However, the procedure does not go so far as to allow an action to be brought in the European Court by individuals or firms whose interests have been harmed by a Member State's failure to fulfil an obligation under the EEC Treaty. Two courses are open to a private party in such circumstances. One would be to lodge a complaint with the Commission, which might lead to the initiation of proceedings under Article [226]. The other would be to bring proceedings in the courts of the Member State concerned, assuming the Community provision in question is a directly effective one, and an appropriate national remedy is available. To help establish the infringement, it may be necessary to ask the national court to make a reference to the European Court under Article [234] for a preliminary ruling on the interpretation of the Community provision.

Note

A State may be liable even for violations committed by bodies which are constitutionally independent.

Commission v Belgium (Case 77/69)
[1970] ECR 237
Court of Justice of the European Communities

The action arose out of a discriminatory tax on wood imposed by Belgium. This was a violation of Article 95 of the EC Treaty (now Article 90 EC) (see Chapter 6).

[11]   The defendant does not dispute the existence of discrimination resulting from the provisions which form the subject-matter of the proceedings.

[12]   Following a series of steps taken by the Commission the first of which dates back to 1963, the Belgian Government has shown its willingness to take the necessary measures with a view to eliminating the discrimination complained of.

[13]   A draft law intended to make possible a revision of the disputed scheme was put before Parliament in 1967 and provisions were later adopted in order to revive this draft law which had lapsed owing to the dissolution of the Belgian Parliament in the meanwhile.

[14]   In these circumstances the Belgian Government considers that the delay in enacting the law amounts as far as it is concerned to a 'case of *force majeure*'.

[15]   The obligations arising from Article 95 of the Treaty devolve upon States as such and the liability of a Member State under Article 169 arises whatever the agency of the State whose action or inaction is the cause of the failure to fulfil its obligations, even in the case of a constitutionally independent institution.

[16]   The objection raised by the defendant cannot therefore be sustained.

[17]   In these circumstances, by applying a duty at the same rate, as laid down by Article 31–14 of the Royal Decree of 3 March 1927 as amended, to home-grown wood transferred standing or felled and to imported wood calculated on its value at the time of the declaration of entry for home use, the Kingdom of Belgium has failed to fulfil its obligations under Article 95 of the Treaty.

Commission v Belgium (Case 1/86)
[1987] ECR 2797
Court of Justice of the European Communities

Belgium had failed to implement in time Directive 80/68, a measure designed to combat water pollution.

[8]   The Belgian Government has explained that the delay in transposing the Directive in respect of the entire country is due to the fact that, as a result of the institutional reforms of 8 August 1980, the national government's powers in regard to the environment have been transferred to the regions, which involved the creation and organization of new institutions, such as the Brussels region, established in 1985. Furthermore, it has pointed out that a draft decree has been approved by the Walloon Executive for the purpose of implementing the Directive in the Walloon region and is shortly to be submitted to the Conseil d'État (State Council) before being submitted to the Conseil régional wallon (Walloon Regional Council), and that for the Brussels region a draft royal decree is in preparation.

[9]   It must be stated that the fact that the procedure for the adoption of implementing measures has been initiated in respect of the Walloon region and the Brussels region does not put an end to the failure to fulfil obligations. Furthermore, according to settled case-law, a Member State may not plead provisions, practices or circumstances existing in its internal legal system in order to justify a failure to comply with obligations resulting from Community Directives.

[10]   Accordingly, it must be held that, by failing to adopt within the prescribed period all the measures necessary to comply with Council Directive 80/68 of 17 December 1979, the Kingdom of Belgium has failed to fulfil its obligations under the EEC Treaty.

Note
Practical difficulties are no excuse for infringement of Treaty obligations.

Commission v *UK (Case 128/78)*
[1979] ECR 419
Court of Justice of the European Communities

The UK failed to introduce legislation requiring the use of recording equipment in road transport – tachographs.

[6]   It is not denied that provision for the installation and use of the recording equipment has been made by the British legislation only on an optional and voluntary basis as regards both vehicles engaged in intra-Community transport and those engaged in national transport. On the other hand, the British legislation has maintained in force the obligations relating to the keeping of an individual control book which were abolished by the said Regulation.

[7]   The defendant claims that this arrangement is sufficient to meet the objectives of promoting road safety, of social progress for workers and of the harmonization of conditions of competition. It maintains that the implementation of Regulation No 1463/70 on its territory is best achieved by the installation and use of the recording equipment on a voluntary basis, though this may be made compulsory at an appropriate time. It adds that implementation of the Regulation involving compulsory measures would meet with active resistance from the sectors concerned, in particular the trade unions, which would result in strikes in the transport sector and would therefore seriously damage the whole economy of the country.

[8]   It contends that since, in the case of the United Kingdom, the objectives of the Community policy in this field can be achieved just as satisfactorily by the maintenance of the system of the individual control book as by the compulsory introduction of recording equipment, the alleged failure to fulfil an obligation is of a purely technical nature and, in view of the difficulties referred to, should not be taken into account. Moreover the installation and use of recording equipment is in practice already guaranteed in respect of intra-Community transport by the fact that the other Member States have made it compulsory.

[9]   Article 189 of the Treaty provides that a Regulation shall be binding 'in its entirety' in the Member States. As the Court has already stated in its judgment of 7 February 1973 (Case 39/72 *Commission* v *Italian Republic* [1973] ECR 101) it cannot

therefore be accepted that a Member State should apply in an incomplete or selective manner provisions of a Community Regulation so as to render abortive certain aspects of Community legislation which it has opposed or which it considers contrary to its national interests. In particular, as regards the putting into effect of a general rule intended to eliminate certain abuses to which workers are subject and which in addition involve a threat to road safety, a Member State which omits to take, within the requisite period and simultaneously with the other Member States, the measures which it ought to take, undermines Community solidarity by imposing, in particular as regards intra-Community transport, on the other Member States the necessity of remedying the effects of its own omissions, while at the same time taking an undue advantage to the detriment of its partners.

[10]   As the Court said in the same judgment, practical difficulties which appear at the stage when a Community measure is put into effect cannot permit a Member State unilaterally to opt out of fulfilling its obligations. The Community institutional system provides the Member State concerned with the necessary means to ensure that its difficulties be given due consideration, subject to compliance with the principles of the common market and the legitimate interests of the other Member States.

[11]   In these circumstances, the possible difficulties of implementation alleged by the defendant cannot be accepted as a justification.

[12]   Further, as the Court said in the case mentioned above, in permitting Member States to profit from the advantages of the Community, the Treaty imposes on them also the obligation to respect its rules. For a State unilaterally to break, according to its own conception of national interest, the equilibrium between the advantages and obligations flowing from its adherence to the Community brings into question the equality of Member States before Community law and creates discrimination at the expense of their nationals. This failure in the duty of solidarity accepted by Member States by the fact of their adherence to the Community strikes at the very root of the Community legal order.

[13]   It appears therefore that, in deliberately refusing to give effect on its territory to the provisions of Regulation No 1463/70, the United Kingdom has markedly failed to fulfil the obligation which it has assumed by virtue of its membership of the European Economic Community.

(ii)   The Commission's discretion
The procedure under Article 226 occupies two phases – the administrative and the judicial. To what extent is the Commission obliged to initiate and see through the administrative phase?

R. White and A. Dashwood, 'Enforcement Actions under Articles 169 and 170 EEC' [now 226 and 227 EC] (1989) 14 EL Rev 388, at pp. 398–400

(Footnotes omitted; numbering altered to reflect the post-Amsterdam Treaty.)

Article [211] places a general duty on the Commission to ensure that the provisions of the . . . Treaty and the measures taken by the institutions pursuant thereto are applied. How is that duty to be discharged within the framework of Article [226]? Is the Commission required to take action wherever it encounters a possible infringement of Community law by a Member State and, if it cannot achieve a settlement, to follow each stage of the proceedings through to judgment in the European Court?

The first paragraph of Article [226] appears to create an obligation by using the words 'it *shall* deliver a reasoned opinion,' but this is conditional on a discretionary judgment made clear by the earlier words 'if the Commission *considers* . . .' The language of the second paragraph makes it clear that, if the Member State fails to comply with the reasoned opinion within the stipulated time, the Commission has a discretion as to whether an application should be made to the European Court. In a case brought under the corresponding provision of the Euratom Treaty [Case 7/71], Advocate General Roemer expressed the view that any automatic application of the procedure or compulsion to initiate it must be ruled out; and the European Court said:

> '. . . by reason of its nature and its purpose, this procedure involves a power on the part of the Commission to consider the most appropriate means and time limits for the purposes of putting an end to any contravention of the Treaty.'

The answer therefore seems to be that, while the Commission is bound to work actively for the removal of infringements, it has discretion to decide what steps should be taken for this purpose, and when they should be taken.

In his Opinion in the *Euratom* case, Advocate General Roemer went on to give some examples of factors that might militate against a Decision by the Commission to initiate proceedings formally against a Member State [Case 7/71]. One such factor was the possibility that an amicable settlement might be reached and another the relative unimportance of the effects produced by the conduct in question. The Advocate General also alluded to the fact that the alleged infringements of the *Euratom* Treaty had overlapped with the political crisis of 1965 and 1966 in the Community; if they had been taken up then, it might have been even harder to resolve the crisis. Finally, he suggested, it might be relevant that a change in the law was expected in the near future.

An analysis of the actual practice of the Commission over the years in exercising its discretion under Article [226] would exceed the scope of the present paper, but certain broad trends and principles may be identified.

In the first place, a Decision was evidently taken by the Commission that came to power in 1977 under the Presidency of Roy Jenkins to prosecute infringements much more vigorously than in the past, a policy continued by the Commissions headed by Gaston Thorne and Jacques Delors. One aspect of this change of policy has been that proceedings are now invariably brought against Member States that fail to transpose directives into national law.

Secondly, a clear preference is shown for reaching a friendly settlement, if at all possible. This is considered by the Commission to be a quicker and surer remedy than a fight to the finish in the European Court.

Thirdly, there are certain classes of case in which the Commission regards action under Article [226] as inappropriate. One such class consists of infringements caused by national courts or otherwise putting in issue the constitutional arrangements of Member States. Another is where political developments have resulted in a shift in the basic consensus underlying the Community, such as over majority voting on the Council. The criterion is a treacherous one since, it has been pointed out, the consensus between the Member States in certain areas is questionable, and strict application of the law can help to sustain it. It has also been suggested that the Commission will not take action on isolated acts of national authorities, where the legislation and administrative practice of the Member State are in conformity with Community requirements.

In Case 415/85 Ireland challenged the jurisdiction of the European Court on the ground that there was a political motive behind the Commission's application and hence an improper exercise of the discretion. The European Court speedily and firmly rejected this argument, referring to its established case law and affirming that the bringing of an Article [226] action is objective in nature and is a matter for the Commission in its entire discretion.

Note

See also A. Evans, 'The Enforcement Procedure of Article 169 EEC: Commission Discretion' (1979) 4 EL Rev 442; R. Rawlings, 'Engaged Elites: Citizen Action and Institutional Attitudes in Commission Enforcement' (2000) 6 ELJ 4.

The Commission's discretion was confirmed by the Court in *Star Fruit Co.* v *Commission* (Case 247/87) (see the extract at p. 682 above).

On the legal nature of the reasoned opinion, see *Commission* v *Germany* (Case C-191/95) [1998] ECR I-5449.

(iii)   The effectiveness of Article 226

R. White and A. Dashwood, 'Enforcement Actions under Articles 169 and 170 EEC' [now 226 and 227 EC] (1989) 14 EL Rev 388, at pp. 411–412

(Footnotes omitted; numbering altered to reflect the post-Amsterdam Treaty.)

The effectiveness of infringement proceedings

Studies have shown that at each formal stage in proceedings under Article [226] a high proportion of cases is settled before it becomes necessary to proceed to the next stage. Audretsch notes that, roughly speaking, 14 per cent. of all presumed infringements reach the stage of recorded infringements, that is, an Article [226] letter is sent to a Member State in respect of them. Six out of every 10 such cases are resolved before a reasoned opinion is issued. Seven out of every 10 of cases reaching this stage are settled without the need to advance to the judicial stage. Only six out of every hundred recorded infringements reaches the stage of a judgment by the European Court. This is a considerable achievement for a procedure concerned with the behaviour of states and is a clear indication that the proceedings exert effective pressure on Member States to remedy infringements. The ultimate fate of having their failure to fulfil an obligation under the EEC Treaty formally established by the European Court is one the Member States are evidently anxious to avoid.

. . .

Though the data is inexact, it appears that more than half of the enforcement proceedings taken to the European Court relate to the failure of Member States to implement directives, either wholly or in part. The remaining cases are split across a wide range of areas of Community law, though the application of the rules of the internal market accounts for about a fifth of all infringements. These are, of course, qualitatively of considerable importance because they imply infringements of basic principles of the EEC Treaty. It appears that such cases are accorded some priority by the Commission.

In the small minority of cases that have run their full course the Member State concerned has almost always taken the steps necessary to comply with the judgment, although sometimes after a considerable delay. Ireland, for example, took three years to amend the legislation on origin marking that gave rise to the *Irish Souvenirs* case [Case 113/80]; while it was only in 1986 that France complied with judgments of 1980 and 1982 relating to discriminatory legislation on alcohol advertising [Cases 152/78, 83/82]. In the *Mutton and Lamb* case [Case 232/78] an eventual solution was found through political negotiations.

These cases suggest that the EEC system might benefit from the conferment on the European Court of a power to impose financial sanctions, as an incentive to timely compliance and to discourage opportunism. However, the ultimate guarantee of the effectiveness of infringement proceedings is Member States' recognition that respect for the rule of law in the Community is a condition for its survival. A Member State that adopted a policy of ignoring adverse judgments of the European Court would not be able to remain a member of the Community for very long.

. . .

Note

The suggestion in the final paragraph of this extract that a power to impose financial sanctions would improve compliance with EC law is pertinent. The Maastricht Treaty added such a procedure, which is now found in Article 228 EC.

Article 228 EC

1. If the Court of Justice finds that a Member State has failed to fulfil an obligation under this Treaty, the State shall be required to take the necessary measures to comply with the judgment of the Court of Justice.

2. If the Commission considers that the Member State concerned has not taken such measures it shall, after giving that state the opportunity to submit its observations, issue a reasoned opinion specifying the points on which the Member State concerned has not complied with the judgment of the Court of Justice.

If the Member State concerned fails to take the necessary measures to comply with the Court's judgment within the time-limit laid down by the Commission, the latter may bring the case before the Court of Justice. In so doing it shall specify the amount of the lump sum or penalty payment to be paid by the Member State concerned which it considers appropriate in the circumstances.

If the Court of Justice finds that the Member State concerned has not complied with its judgment it may impose a lump sum or penalty payment on it.

This procedure shall be without prejudice to Article 227.

Note

The Commission has publicised the criteria on which it will base its assessment of the amount to be paid by a defaulting Member State pursuant to Article 228(2); (1996) OJ C242/6, (1997) OJ C63/2.

In assessing the likely impact of Article 228(2) on the incidence of default by Member States, you should also take account of the Court's ruling in *Francovich* (Cases C-6/90 and C-9/90, p. 128 above) that Member States may be liable to individuals in damages before national courts, elaborated in the package of rulings of March 1996 including '*Factortame III*' (Case C-48/93), p. 737 below. Remember 'dual vigilance' at p. 93 above.

The next extract provides a statistical flavour of Commission practice. The reference in the first paragraph to the 'action plan for the internal market' invites reference back to Chapter 5 where the Plan is discussed at p. 204. Practice under Article 226 which shows a preference for informal resolution of disputes shares with the current emphasis on administrative coordination in the management of the internal market a strong desire on the part of the Commission for cost-effective, non-litigious rule enforcement. This is a pre-Amsterdam document (p. 29 above), so be aware that references to Article 169 should now be treated as references to Article 226.

The Commission's Sixteenth Annual Report on monitoring the application of Community law, 1998
(1999) OJ C354, p. 5

1. INTRODUCTION

The Commission has placed the proper application of Community law by the Member States high among its objectives, to enable Community citizens to enjoy the full benefit of European integration. As can be seen from this report, the sixteenth since the resolution passed by the European Parliament on 9 February 1983, it has provided itself with the practical means of attaining this objective, both through the unprecedented enhancement of the facilities for use of the infringement procedures provided for by Article 169 of the Treaty and by greater use of administrative cooperation, notably via the action plan for the internal market.

1.1 Statistics for 1998

More than ever in the past, the Commission was active in its role as guardian of the Treaties in 1998, as can be seen from the figures below.

— the number of reasoned opinions issued in the course of the year reached an all-time high at 675; this is 102% upon the figure of 334 for 1997, and it is the result of far stricter and far quicker action by the Commission following the internal reforms made since 1996 and strengthened in 1998,
— the number of Article 169 letters is down from 1,461 in 1997 to 1,101 in 1998, simply because the number of proceedings for failure to transpose directives fell; Article 169 letters for failure of legislation to comply with Community law or for incorrect application of Community law rose from 432 in 1997 to 486 in 1998, an increase of 12% (and 42% upon 1996),
— the number of cases referred to the Court of Justice, at 123, was stable; compared with the number of Article 169 letters and reasoned opinions, this makes it quite clear that the bulk of infringement cases are solved before there is any need to go to the Court,
— in 1998 Commission departments were very active in detecting cases of non-conformity and incorrect application of Community law, since the number of cases detected by them rose by 52% from 261 in 1997 to 396 in 1998 (this figure includes cases opened as a result of parliamentary questions or petitions),
— the number of complaints received by the Commission continued the upward course started in 1997, rising by 18% from 957 in 1997 to 1,128 in 1998 (and

by 38% from the 1996 level); the figure would be even higher if the 4,000 or so identical complaints about the new Swedish legislation on controls on shipments and parcels containing spirits and tobacco and the hundreds of complaints about the taxes applied by certain Belgian local authorities on satellite dishes were added (given the number of complaints on the latter subject, a standard-form acknowledgement of receipt was published in the 'C' series of the Official Journal and on the Community institutions' website),
— termination decisions fell by 7%, from 2,112 in 1997 to 1,961 in 1998, which is evidence of the large number of cases solved in relation to the application of Community law,
— the speed with which cases were dealt with also rose: 25% of Article 169 letters sent in 1997 concerned infringement proceedings opened in the course of the year, but the figure rose to 48% in 1998; there was an even sharper rise in the corresponding figure for reasoned opinions, as 19% of those issued in 1998 concerned proceedings commenced in 1998, as against 1% in 1997,
— as for transparency, the number of cases on which a press release was issued rose from 248 in 1997 to 334 in 1998.

Note

An important element in furthering the effectiveness of Article 226 is the Court's ability to make interim orders against defaulting States. The power is conferred by Article 243, which states: 'The Court of Justice may in any cases before it prescribe any necessary interim measures.'

This is a flexible provision, but the Court has imposed relatively strict conditions on its own capacity to make interim orders. This runs parallel to its attitude to the grant of interim relief against acts of the Community institutions discussed in the previous chapter, at p. 677 above.

Commission v UK (Case C-246/89R)
[1989] ECR 3125
Court of Justice of the European Communities

The Commission's action related to the UK's Merchant Shipping Act 1988. The Commission took the view that the Act violated Community rules forbidding discrimination on grounds of nationality. Under the arrangements governing the accession of Spain to the Community, the volume of catches which Spanish fishing vessels could make in Community waters was regulated. Many Spanish fishing vessels were re-registered by their owners as British and fished under the British flag, thereby taking advantage of enhanced access to Community waters, but continued to land catches in Spain and to earn profits for Spanish nationals. At the start of January 1986, the UK introduced new licensing requirements for British fishing vessels. These were supplemented by the Merchant Shipping Act 1988. The thrust of the requirements was the demand that a genuine economic link with the UK be shown beyond the mere fact of registration. British ownership and management was required. In challenging the 1988

Act, the Commission argued that its provisions contravened the Treaty rules prohibiting discrimination on grounds of nationality contained in Articles 7, 52 and 221 of the EC Treaty (now, after amendment, Articles 12, 43 and 294 EC). It initiated an action under Article 169 of the EC Treaty (now Article 226 EC), but it also asked the Court to make an interim order against the UK under Article 186 of the EEC Treaty (now Article 243 EC).

[20]   Under Article 186 of the EEC Treaty the Court may in any cases before it prescribe any necessary interim measures.

[21]   Under Article 83(2) of the Rules of Procedure, interim measures such as those requested may not be ordered unless there are circumstances giving rise to urgency and factual and legal grounds establishing a prima-facie case for the measures applied for.

[22]   It must be considered whether these conditions are satisfied in this case.

[23]   As regards first of all the condition of existence of a prima-facie case, the Commission points out that it is contesting solely the nationality requirements laid down by section 14 of the Merchant Shipping Act 1988. These requirements prohibit nationals of the other Member States from acquiring, through a company, a British fishing vessel and from managing a company operating such a vessel under the same conditions as British nationals. This constitutes direct discrimination, in flagrant breach of the prohibition of discrimination on grounds of nationality, which cannot be justified either by the Community rules on fishing quotas or by the United Kingdom's obligations under international law.

[24]   For its part, the United Kingdom considers that the national provisions contested by the Commission do not infringe Community law. Any Member State is at liberty to lay down the conditions for registration of ships and for flying its flag. International law requires the United Kingdom to lay down these conditions in such a way that the ship has a genuine link with the United Kingdom, enabling that country to exercise effectively its jurisdiction and control over the ship. The conditions contained in the Merchant Shipping Act 1988 correspond to those imposed by other Member States for flying their flag.

[25]   The United Kingdom further considers that the nationality requirements introduced by the 1988 Act are justified by the present Community legislation on fisheries; that legislation, although it establishes a common system, is based on a principle of nationality for the purposes of the distribution of fishing quotas. Under Article 5(2) of Council Regulation 170/83 it is for the Member States to determine the detailed rules for the utilization of the quotas allocated to them and thus to lay down the conditions which the vessels authorized to fish from these quotas must satisfy.

[26]   It must be observed that the system of national quotas established by Council Regulation 170/83 constitutes, as the United Kingdom contends, a derogation from the principle of equal access for Community fishermen to fishing grounds and to the exploitation thereof in waters coming within the jurisdiction of the Member States, which is itself a specific expression of the principle of non-discrimination laid down in Article 40(3) of the EEC Treaty.

[27]   That derogation is justified, according to the recitals in the preamble to Regulation No 170/83, by the need, in a situation where there is a dearth of fishery resources, to ensure a relative stability in regard to fishing activities in order to safeguard the particular needs of regions where local populations are especially dependent on fisheries and related industries.

[28]   The possibility cannot therefore be excluded that in their legislation concerning in particular the registration of fishing vessels and access to fishing activities the Member States may be led to introduce requirements whose compatibility with Community law can be justified only by the necessity to attain the objectives of the Community system of fishing quotas. As the Commission itself has admitted in these proceedings, such requirements may be necessary in order to ensure that there is a genuine link with the fishing industry of the Member State against whose quota the vessel may fish.

[29]   However there is nothing which would prima facie warrant the conclusion that such requirements may derogate from the prohibition of discrimination on grounds of nationality contained in Articles 52 and 221 of the EEC Treaty regarding, respectively, the right of establishment and the right to participate in the capital of companies or firms within the meaning of Article 58.

[30]   The rights deriving from the abovementioned provisions of the Treaty include not only the rights of establishment and of participation in the capital of companies or firms but also the right to pursue an economic activity, as the case may be through a company, under the conditions laid down by the legislation of the country of establishment for its own nationals.

[31]   These rights prima facie also include the right to incorporate and manage a company whose object is to operate a fishing vessel registered in the State of establishment under the same conditions as a company controlled by nationals of that State.

[32]   As regards the United Kingdom's first submission based on its obligations under international law, it is sufficient to note, at this stage, that in this respect nothing has been put forward which at first sight could necessitate any derogation from the abovementioned rights under Community law in order to ensure the effective exercise of British jurisdiction and control over the vessels in question.

[33]   It must therefore be held that, at the stage of these proceedings for the grant of interim relief, the application in the main proceedings does not appear to be without foundation and that the requirement of a prima-facie case is thus satisfied.

[34]   As regards, next, the condition relating to urgency, it should be borne in mind that the urgency of an application for interim measures must be assessed in relation to the necessity for an order granting interim relief in order to prevent serious and irreparable damage.

[35]   The Commission makes the observation that the establishment of the new register of British fishing vessels has had the effect of forcing the entire 'Anglo-Spanish' fleet to remain idle. According to its information the registration in that register of a number of those vessels is precluded solely by reason of the nationality requirements at issue, since the vessels in question could satisfy the other requirements under section 14 of the Merchant Shipping Act 1988, in particular that relating to management and control from the United Kingdom. The owners of the vessels in

question are suffering heavy losses as a result of the vessels' remaining idle and will in the short term be forced to sell them under very adverse conditions. Under British civil law these losses cannot later be recovered by means of actions brought against the British authorities.

[36] The United Kingdom contends that the interim measures applied for would in practice be ineffectual. Leaving aside the nationality requirements, the United Kingdom denies that the vessels forced to remain idle would be able to satisfy the requirements for registration, in particular those relating to residence in the United Kingdom and the management of the vessel from the United Kingdom. The suspension of the application of the nationality requirements, requested by the Commission, could not, therefore, prevent the damage alleged and there is accordingly no urgency. The United Kingdom stresses moreover that the interest which the Commission may have in obtaining these interim measures must be weighed against the United Kingdom's interest in achieving a lasting settlement of the problems caused by the 'Anglo-Spanish' vessels for the British fishing industry. The measures adopted to that end by the British authorities in 1983 and 1986 remained ineffective and only the introduction of requirements that are clear and easy to administer makes it possible to resolve these problems.

[37] It must be held in the first place that for fishing vessels which until 31 March 1989 were flying the British flag and fishing under a British fishing licence the loss of the flag and the cessation of their activities entail serious damage. There is no ground for believing that, pending delivery of the judgment in the main proceedings, these vessels can be operated in the pursuit of alternative fishing activities. The aforesaid damage must also, should the application in the main proceedings be granted, be regarded as irreparable.

[38] It is true that, for there to be urgency, it is necessary that the interim measures requested should be of a nature to prevent the alleged damage. At the present stage of the proceedings the possibility cannot however be excluded that a number of the vessels in question may, as the Commission maintains, satisfy the registration requirements if the application of the nationality requirement is suspended.

[39] Finally, as regards the balance of interests, it is not established that the interim measures applied for may jeopardize the objective pursued by the British legislation at issue, namely to ensure the existence of a genuine link between the vessels fishing against the British quotas and the British fishing industry.

[40] It appears prima facie that the registration requirements laid down by the new legislation, other than those relating to nationality, and the measures adopted by the United Kingdom authorities in 1983 and 1986 would be sufficient to ensure the existence of such a link. The United Kingdom itself considers that the 'Anglo-Spanish' vessels, which do not have that link with the United Kingdom, will not be able to satisfy the aforesaid requirements.

[41] It is true that the nationality requirements would be easier to administer than the requirements relating to the actual operation of a vessel. A Member State may not however plead administrative difficulties in order not to comply with the obligations laid on it by Community law.

[42] It follows that the condition relating to urgency is also satisfied. The interim measures applied for must therefore be ordered.

On those grounds, THE PRESIDENT hereby orders:

(1)   Pending delivery of the judgment in the main proceedings, the United Kingdom shall suspend the application of the nationality requirements laid down in section 14(1)(a) and (c) of the Merchant Shipping Act 1988, read in conjunction with paragraphs (2) and (7) of that section, as regards the nationals of other Member States and in respect of fishing vessels which, until 31 March 1989, were pursuing a fishing activity under the British flag and under a British fishing licence.

(2)   The costs, including those relating to the intervention, are reserved.

Note
Read generally, Gray, C., 'Interim Measures of Protection in the European Court' (1979) 4 EL Rev 80. In October 1991, the full Court ruled that the UK was indeed in breach of its Treaty obligations ([1991] ECR I-4585). The substance of this case will be readdressed below, for challenge to the Act was also initiated before the English courts.

Note
The fact that a State puts an end to its violation before the Court has the opportunity to rule on the matter does not automatically lead to the proceedings being dropped by the Commission.

Commission v *Greece (Case 240/86)*
[1988] ECR 1835
Court of Justice of the European Communities

The Commission's action related to obstacles to cereal imports which it considered incompatible with, *inter alia*, Article 30 of the EC Treaty (now, after amendment, Article 28 EC). When the matter reached the stage of a hearing before the Court, the Greek Government contested the case's admissibility.

[12]   The Greek Government considers that since the barriers to cereal imports were lifted before the action was commenced it is devoid of purpose.

[13]   At the hearing the Commission acknowledged that the failure to fulfil obligations had been remedied but nevertheless asserted that it had an interest in obtaining a ruling in respect of measures adopted by the Hellenic Republic in the past.

[14]   As the Court has consistently held (see most recently the judgment of 5 June 1986 in Case 103/84 *Commission* v *Italian Republic* [1986] ECR 1759), the subject-matter of an action brought under Article 169 [now 226] is established by the Commission's reasoned opinion and even where the default has been remedied after the period laid down pursuant to the second paragraph of that article has elapsed, an interest still subsists in pursuing the action. That interest may consist in establishing the basis for a liability which a Member State may incur, by reason of its failure to fulfil its obligations, towards those to whom rights accrue as a result of that failure.

[15]   Since the Hellenic Republic did not comply with the reasoned opinon of 25 November 1985 within the period stipulated by the Commission the action is admissible in so far as it concerns the subject-matter of the dispute as defined by that opinion.

(B) CONTROL AT NATIONAL LEVEL

The Court's ruling in *Commission* v *Greece* (Case 240/86) above, leads logically into the next stage of the discussion; control at national level. The Court mentions the possibility of liability arising out of the State's violation of Community law obligations. A State in violation of Community law may be challenged before its own national courts. The principles of direct effect, supremacy and the Article 234 preliminary reference procedure all come into play.

Many of the cases considered in Part One of this book now deserve attention from this perspective. Re-examine the following cases as illustrations of the ability of private parties to control States in the context of proceedings at national level:

- *Van Gend en Loos* (Case 26/62), at p. 91 above;
- *Costa* v *ENEL* (Case 6/64), at p. 82 above;
- *Pubblico Ministero* v *Ratti* (Case 148/78), at p. 103 above;
- *Broeckmeulen* v *Huisarts Registratie Commissie* (Case 246/80), at p. 150 above.

Of course, the structure also permits private parties to challenge at national level acts of other private parties in violation of Community law. This is illustrated by many of the cases connected with the competition rules, the enforcement of which was examined separately in Chapter 13, and, for example, by *Defrenne* v *SABENA* (Case 43/75), at p. 95 above.

Question
Consider the application in *Star Fruit Co.* v *Commission* (Case 247/87), at p. 682 above. How else might the challenge to the French practices have been framed?

Note
Community law establishes substantive rights. It also establishes the constitutional principles which allow a private individual to rely on those rights at national level to defeat conflicting national law – direct effect, plus supremacy, plus the preliminary reference under Article 234. However, Community law has long had little impact on the national law of remedies. A variety of *national* remedies were sought for violation of Community law rights in the cases listed above. The Court explained the division of function between Community law and national law in the next case.

Comet v *Produktschap (Case 45/76)*
[1976] ECR 2043
Court of Justice of the European Communities

Comet argued before Dutch courts that it had paid sums to Produktschap on the export of plants and bulbs which were incompatible with (what was then) Article 16 (Chapter 6; Article 16 was a transitional provision deleted by the Treaty of Amsterdam). It sought reimbursement. The defendant argued that the claim could not succeed because it had been lodged after the expiry of the limitation period for such actions under Dutch law. A Community right; but national procedures. The issue was referred to the European Court. In the following extract, the Court first explains the nature of Comet's argument designed to defeat Dutch procedural law, and then disposes of the case.

[9]   The applicant in the main action contends, on the other hand, that the primacy of Community law means that it overrules any decision which constitutes an infringement of it and that, before the national courts, which are bound to protect the rights conferred on it by Article 16, it possesses, in consequence, an independent right of action which is unaffected by limitations provided for under national law which are liable to weaken the impact of the direct effect of that article in the legal order of the Member States.

[10]   Thus, the question referred seeks to establish whether the procedural rules for proceedings designed to ensure the protection of the rights which individuals acquire as a result of the direct effect of a Community provision, in the present case Article 16 of the Treaty and Article 10 of Regulation No 234/68, especially the rules concerning the period within which an action must be brought are governed by the national law of the Member State where the action is brought or whether, on the other hand, they are independent and fall to be determined only by Community law itself.

[11]   The prohibition laid down in Article 16 of the Treaty and that contained in Article 10 of Regulation No 234/68 have direct effect and confer on individuals rights which the national courts must protect.

[12]   Thus, in application of the principle of cooperation laid down in Article 5 [now 10] of the Treaty, the national courts are entrusted with ensuring the legal protection conferred on individuals by the direct effect of the provisions of Community law.

[13]   Consequently, in the absence of any relevant Community rules, it is for the national legal order of each Member State to designate the competent courts and to lay down the procedural rules for proceedings designed to ensure the protection of the rights which individuals acquire through the direct effect of Community law, provided that such rules are not less favourable than those governing the same right of action on an internal matter.

[14]   Articles 100 to 102 [now 95 to 97] and 235 [now 308] of the Treaty enable the appropriate steps to be taken as necessary, to eliminate differences between the provisions laid down in such matters by law, regulation or administrative action in Member States if these differences are found to be such as to cause distortion or to affect the functioning of the common market.

[15]   In default of such harmonization measures, the rights conferred by Community law must be exercised before the national courts in accordance with the rules of procedure laid down by national law.

[16]   The position would be different only if those rules and time-limits made it impossible in practice to exercise rights which the national courts have a duty to protect.

[17]   This does not apply to the fixing of a reasonable period of limitation within which an action must be brought.

[18]   The fixing, as regards fiscal proceedings, of such a period is in fact an application of a fundamental principle of legal certainty which protects both the authority concerned and the party from whom payment is claimed.

[19]   The answer must therefore be that, in the case of a litigant who is challenging before the national courts a decision of a national body for incompatibility with Community law, that law, in its present state, does not prevent the expiry of the period within which proceedings must be brought under national law from being raised against him, provided that the procedural rules applicable to his case are not less favourable than those governing the same right of action on an internal matter.

Note

At this stage, then, the applicant able to show a violation of Community law is dependent on existing national procedures, which may thwart the claim. Procedural law varies from State to State, with the result that in practice the means of enforcement of Community law are not uniform State by State. (See J. Bridge, 'Procedural Aspects of the Enforcement of EC Law through the Legal Systems of the Member States' (1984) 9 EL Rev 28.) Paragraph 14 of *Comet* (Case 45/76) hints at the way to resolve such disunity, but little progress has been made (except in the special case of public procurement).

However, the judgment in *Comet* (Case 45/76) does not confer absolute autonomy on the national system. In the concluding words of para. 13, and in para. 16, it offers two Community law qualifications to the approach which a national court may adopt in providing remedies for a litigant which has suffered loss as a result of violation of Community law. It may be difficult for national law, responding to these two qualifications, to apply the requirements of Community law to the existing framework of the national law of remedies.

Garden Cottage Foods v *Milk Marketing Board* (p. 539 above), which involved private parties, deserves attention from this perspective.

It has become apparent that the requirement that the national system offer effective remedies in support of Community law (a modern rewriting of para. 16 of the judgment in *Comet* (Case 45/76)) has potency before national courts. The European Court has been increasingly prepared to make specific the nature of the obligation cast on national judges by Article 10 EC effectively to protect Community law rights. There is now a significant Community input into national remedies law.

Consider *Commission* v *UK* (Case C-246/89R), at p. 721 above. Re-read the summary of the facts. While the Commission was pursuing the UK at Community level, private parties were acting before English courts to protect their interests. Factortame was one of several Spanish fishing undertakings holding a British registration which alleged that it had been discriminated against on grounds of nationality contrary to Community law. It saw the imminent prospect of severe curtailment of its fishing operations. Factortame wished to challenge the UK's Merchant Shipping Act 1988, which it did by an application for judicial review of the decision of the Secretary of State for Transport which brought particular provisions of the Act into force. This raises fundamental issues of constitutional law in the UK relating to Parliamentary Sovereignty. The *Factortame* litigation provides an extremely important indication of modern British judicial thinking about the constitutional implications of membership of the Community. However, in the present context the tale deserves attention for the European Court's view of the impact of Community law on national remedies and procedures.

R v Secretary of State for Transport, ex parte Factortame *(Case C-213/89)*
[1990] ECR I-2433; [1990] 3 WLR 852
Court of Justice of the European Communities

Factortame's claim that the Act violated Community rules prohibiting discrimination was initially treated in straightforward fashion; a reference was made by the High Court to the European Court requesting assistance in the interpretation of relevant points of Community law ([1989] 2 CMLR 353, Case C-221/89 – eventually, in July 1991, the Court ruled in terms favourable to Factortame – [1991] ECR I-3905.) But what should happen pending that ruling? Should the Act apply, or should it be suspended? The House of Lords ruled that as a matter of English law it had no power to make the award of interim relief against the application of the statute which Factortame had sought (*Factortame* v *Secretary of State for Transport (No. 1)* [1989] 3 CMLR 1, [1990] 2 AC 85, [1989] 2 All ER 692). However the House of Lords referred to the European Court the following questions relating to the impact of Community law on available remedies:

1. Where:

(i)   a party before the national court claims to be entitled to rights under Community law having direct effect in national law ('the rights claimed'),

(ii)   a national measure in clear terms will, if applied, automatically deprive that party of the rights claimed,

(iii)   there are serious arguments both for and against the existence of the rights claimed and the national court has sought a preliminary ruling under Article 177 [now 234] as to whether or not the rights claimed exist,

(iv)   the national law presumes the national measure in question to be compatible with Community law unless and until it is declared incompatible,

(v)   the national court has no power to give interim protection to the rights claimed by suspending the application of the national measure pending the preliminary ruling,

(vi)   if the preliminary ruling is in the event in favour of the rights claimed, the party entitled to those rights is likely to have suffered irremediable damage unless given such interim protection, does Community law either

    (a)   oblige the national court to grant such interim protection of the rights claimed; or

    (b)   give the Court power to grant such interim protection of the rights claimed?

    2.   If Question 1(a) is answered in the negative and Question 1(b) in the affirmative, what are the criteria to be applied in deciding whether or not to grant such interim protection of the rights claimed?

The European Court ruled within 13 months in June 1990.

[17]   It is clear from the information before the Court, and in particular from the judgment making the reference and, as described above, the course taken by the proceedings in the national courts before which the case came at first and second instance, that the preliminary question raised by the House of Lords seeks essentially to ascertain whether a national court which, in a case before it concerning Community law, considers that the sole obstacle which precludes it from granting interim relief is a rule of national law, must disapply that rule.

[18]   For the purpose of replying to that question, it is necessary to point out that in its judgment of 9 March 1978 in Case 106/77 (*Amministrazione delle Finanze dello Stato* v *Simmenthal SpA* [1978] ECR 629) the Court held that directly applicable rules of Community law 'must be fully and uniformly applied in all the Member States from the date of their entry into force and for so long as they continue in force' (paragraph 14) and that 'in accordance with the principle of the precedence of Community law, the relationship between provisions of the Treaty and directly applicable measures of the institutions on the one hand and the national law of the Member States on the other is such that those provisions and measures . . . by their entry into force render automatically inapplicable any conflicting provision of . . . national law' (paragraph 17).

[19]   In accordance with the case-law of the Court, it is for the national courts, in application of the principle of co-operation laid down in Article 5 of the EEC Treaty [now Article 10 EC], to ensure the legal protection which persons derive from the direct effect of provisions of Community law (see, most recently, the judgments of 10 July 1980 in Case 811/79 *Ariete SpA* v *Amministrazione delle Finanze dello Stato* [1980] ECR 2545 and *MIRECO SaS* v *Amministrazione delle Finanze dello Stato* [1980] ECR 2559).

[20]   The Court has also held that any provision of a national legal system and any legislative, administrative or judicial practice which might impair the effectiveness of Community law by withholding from the national court having jurisdiction to apply such law the power to do everything necessary at the moment of its application to set aside national legislative provisions which might prevent, even temporarily, Community rules from having full force and effect are incompatible with those requirements, which are the very essence of Community law (judgment of 9 March 1978 in *Simmenthal* judgment, cited above, at paragraphs 22 and 23).

[21]   It must be added that the full effectiveness of Community law would be just as much impaired if a rule of national law could prevent a court seised of a dispute governed by Community law from granting interim relief in order to ensure the full effectiveness of the judgment to be given on the existence of the rights claimed under

Community law. It follows that a court which in those circumstances would grant interim relief, if it were not for a rule of national law, is obliged to set aside that rule.

[22] That interpretation is reinforced by the system established by Article 177 of the EEC Treaty whose effectiveness would be impaired if a national court, having stayed proceedings pending the reply by the Court of Justice to the question referred to it for a preliminary ruling, were not able to grant interim relief until it delivered its judgment following the reply given by the Court of Justice.

[23] Consequently, the reply to the question raised should be that Community law must be interpreted as meaning that a national court which, in a case before it concerning Community law, considers that the sole obstacle which precludes it from granting interim relief is a rule of national law must set aside that rule.

Note

The Court's brisk reformulation of the question causes it to be rather dismissive of the view advanced by the UK that *Simmenthal* (Case 106/77, p. 83 above) was not directly in point because the rights under Community law in that case had been firmly established and were not, as in *Factortame*, merely claimed. Advocate-General Tesauro was rather fuller in his treatment of the role of interim protection in a system of effective remedies.

R v Secretary of State for Transport, ex parte Factortame
(Case C-213/89)
[1990] ECR I-2433; [1990] 3 WLR 852
Court of Justice of the European Communities

(Footnotes omitted.)

ADVOCATE-GENERAL TESAURO: . . . Sometimes the right's existence is established too late for the right claimed to be fully and usefully exercised, which is the more likely to be the case the more structured and complex, and the more probably rich in safeguards, is the procedure culminating in the definitive establishment of the right. The result is that in such a case the utility as well as the effectiveness of judicial protection may be lost and there could be a betrayal of the principle, long established in jurisprudence, according to which the need to have recourse to legal proceedings to enforce a right should not occasion damage to the party in the right.

Interim protection has precisely that objective purpose, namely to ensure that the time needed to establish the existence of the right does not in the end have the effect of irremediably depriving the right of substance, by eliminating any possibility of exercising it; in brief, the purpose of interim protection is to achieve that fundamental objective of every legal system, the effectiveness of judicial protection. Interim protection is intended to prevent so far as possible the damage occasioned by the fact that the establishment and the existence of the right are not fully contemporaneous from prejudicing the effectiveness and the very purpose of establishing the right, which was also specifically affirmed by the Court when it linked interim protection to a requirement that, when delivered, the judgment will be fully effective; or to the need to 'preserve the existing position pending a decision on the substance of the case'.

Now that the function of interim protection has been brought into focus, such protection can be seen to be a fundamental and indispensable instrument of any judicial system, which seeks to achieve, in the particular case and always in an effective manner, the objective of determining the existence of a right and more generally of giving effect to the relevant legal provision, whenever the duration of the proceedings is likely to prejudice the attainment of this objective and therefore to nullify the effectiveness of the judgment.

The requirement for interim protection, moreover, as has already been noted, arises in the same terms, both where the establishment of the right's existence involves the facts and, consequently, the determination of the correct provision to be applied, that is to say where the uncertainty as to the outcome of the application involves – although the expression is not perhaps a happy one – 'the facts', and where it is a question of choosing between two or more provisions which may be applicable (for example, a classification problem), irrespective of whether both are presumed to be valid or whether one is presumed to be incompatible with the other, which is of a higher order or in any event has precedence.

In particular, where, as in the case now before the Court, the determination as to the existence of the right not only involves a choice between two or more provisions which may be applicable but also involves a prior review of the validity or compatibility of one provision *vis-à-vis* another of a higher order or in any event having precedence, the difference is merely one of appearance, particularly when that review is entrusted to a court on which special jurisdiction has been conferred for the purpose. This situation, too, is fully covered by the typical function of judicial proceedings, which seek to establish the existence of and hence to give effect to the right, so that the requirement that the individual's position be protected on a provisional basis remains the same, inasmuch as it is a question of determining, interpreting and applying to the case in question the relevant (and valid) legal rules.

It follows that what is commonly called the presumption of validity, which attaches to laws or administrative acts no less than it does to Community acts, until such time as it is established by judicial determination that the measure in question is incompatible with a rule of law of a higher order or in any event having precedence, *to the extent that such a procedure is provided for*, does not constitute a formal obstacle to the interim protection of enforceable legal rights. In fact, precisely because what is concerned is a presumption, which as such may be rebutted by the final determination, it remains necessary to provide a remedy to compensate for the fact that the final ruling establishing the existence of the right may come too late and therefore be of no use to the successful party.

In fact, it is certain and undeniable that a provision, whether it is contained in an Act of Parliament or a Community act, or in an administrative act, must be presumed to be valid. But that cannot and must not mean that the courts are precluded from temporarily paralysing its effects with regard to the concrete case before them where, pending a final determination on its validity *vis-à-vis* or compatibility with a provision of a higher order or having precedence, one or other of the legal rights in question is likely to be irremediably impaired and there is a suspicion (the degree of which must be established) that the final determination may entail a finding that the statute or administrative act in question is invalid.

In brief, the presumption that a law or an administrative act is valid may not and must not mean that the very possibility of interim protection is precluded *where the measure in question may form the subject of a final judicial review of its validity*.

Far from running counter to the principle of the validity of laws or administrative acts, which finds expression in a presumption that may always be rebutted by a final determination, interim protection in fact removes the risk that that presumption may lead to the perverse result, certainly not desired by any legal system, negating the function of judicial review and, in particular, of the review of the validity of laws. To take a different view would amount to radically denying the possibility of interim protection, not only in relation to laws, but absolutely, given that any act of a public authority, whether it is a rule-making instrument properly so-called or an individual decision, is presumed to be valid until the outcome of the judicial review of its validity.

Note
It was then for the House of Lords, equipped with the ruling that it possessed the power to grant interim relief, to decide whether to exercise that power on the facts of the case before it. Their Lordships considered the case appropriate for the grant of relief in favour of Factortame, pending the final ruling ([1991] 1 All ER 70, [1990] 3 CMLR 375). Lord Bridge was moved by some well-publicised denunciations of the European Court's alleged intrusion on the sovereignty of the UK (see especially Hansard, HC Debs, vol. 174, 20 June 1990) to remark that

> there is nothing in any way novel in according supremacy to rules of Community law in those areas to which they apply and to insist that, in the protection of rights under Community law, national courts must not be inhibited by rules of national law from granting interim relief in appropriate cases is no more than a logical recognition of that supremacy.

What is particularly interesting in this area is the extent to which the European Court is presiding over the development of a coherent legal order governing remedies. Interim relief at Community level has been examined; at p. 677 in relation to Community acts, at p. 721 in relation to Member State practices. Interim relief at national level from Community acts was examined at p. 701 (consider *Foto Frost* (Case 314/85), the *Zuckerfabrik* cases (Cases C-92/89 and C-143/88) and *Atlanta* (Case C-465/93)). Here now is the missing link; interim relief at national level from Member State practices allegedly incompatible with Community law. It is interesting and important to assess the extent to which the Court is bringing all these procedures into line. The process is far from complete, and naturally lacks the comprehensive coverage of legislation, but the Court appears gradually to be building the Community legal order through jurisprudence in linked but not identical areas.

Further reading
The following articles cover aspects of *Factortame* prior to the European Court ruling in Case C-213/89:

Barav, A., 'Enforcement of Community Rights in the National Courts: the Case for Jurisdiction to Grant an Interim Relief' (1989) 26 CML Rev 369.
Gravells, N., 'Disapplying an Act of Parliament pending a Preliminary Ruling: Constitutional Enormity or Community Law Right?' [1989] *Public Law* 568.

The following consider the situation after the European Court ruling:

Barav, A., 'Omnipotent Courts' in Curtin, D. and Heukels, T., (eds), *Institutional Dynamics of European Integration* (1994).

Donaldson MR, Lord, 'Can the Judiciary control Acts of Parliament?' (1991) 25 *The Law Teacher* 4.

Gravells, N., 'Effective Protection of Community Law Rights: Temporary Disapplication of an Act of Parliament' [1991] *Public Law* 180.

Oliver, P., 'Interim Measures: Some Recent Developments' (1992) 29 CML Rev 7.

Pappadias, A., 'Interim Protection under Community Law before the National Courts' [1994/2] LIEI 153.

Note

The Court's concern with *effective protection* of Community law rights seems to underlie the *Factortame* ruling. Article 10 EC, which was Article 5 EC pre-Amsterdam, requires national authorities, including the judiciary, actively to support EC law and if necessary to adjust their 'normal' approach under domestic law. 'Effectiveness' also underlies the obligations which the European Court has imposed on national courts to give effect to unimplemented Directives (Chapter 3). The landmark ruling in *Francovich* (Cases C-6/90 and C-9/90, p. 128 above) is inspired by Article 10 and effective protection of Community law rights. *Francovich*, like *Factortame*, demands that national courts adjust their domestic law of remedies where this is required in order to provide effective protection to EC law rights. *Francovich*, like *Factortame*, envisages a minimum level of protection which must be available to the Community law litigant in the national system. *Francovich* demonstrates the operation of the principle of effectiveness beyond the limits of direct effect.

English courts have responded. In *Garden Cottage Foods* v *Milk Marketing Board* (p. 539 above) the House of Lords was prepared to award damages in the event of the violation of EC competition law by a private party. By contrast, the Court of Appeal in *Bourgoin* v *MAFF* [1986] QB 716, [1985] 3 WLR 1027, refused to consider the award of damages against public authorities in the absence of an abuse of power even where it had been established that a violation of Article 30 of the EC Treaty (now, after amendment, Article 28 EC) had occurred. Judicial review was the appropriate path for an English law litigant and the Court of Appeal considered that the Community law litigant should follow that same path. The theme of requiring adjustment of traditional national techniques which underpins the European Court's Article 10 jurisprudence on *effective protection* forced reconsideration of *Bourgoin*. Lord Goff in *Kirklees BC* v *Wickes Ltd* ([1992] 3 All ER 717, 734) commented, albeit *obiter*, that 'since the decision of the European Court in *Francovich* . . . there must now be doubt whether the *Bourgoin* case was correctly decided'. The Community law rules applicable to the liability of national authorities must now be examined in light of the package of cases decided by the European Court in March 1996, including '*Factortame III*' (Case C-48/93). See p. 737 below.

The next extract locates these rulings in the context of a process of the judicial harmonisation of national remedies and invites consideration of the wider role played by the Court in the Community system.

F. Snyder, 'The Effectiveness of European Community Law: Institutions, Processes, Tools and Techniques'(1993) 56 MLR 19, 45-7

In *Francovich*, the Court of Justice recalled that, in the absence of Community provisions, it was for national legal systems to lay down the procedural steps for legal action to ensure the full protection of Community rights.[156] These 'conditions of substance and form' were not to be less favourable than those governing national remedies, and they were not to make the enforcement of Community rights impossible.[157] While thus recognising that Community rights are to be enforced primarily in national courts,[158] the Court's jurisprudence has nonetheless impinged increasingly on national legal remedies. At the same time as national administrative law is being influenced considerably by general principles of Community law, such as proportionality,[159] the Court of Justice is beginning to contribute to the restructuring of national procedural systems.[160]

In the celebrated *Factortame*[161] case, the Court of Justice set aside the rule of English constitutional law that an injunction cannot be granted against the Crown, at least where the rule prevents the enforcement of a right conferred by Community law. In *Emmott* it declared that, where an individual wishes to rely as against a Member State on rights contained in a directly effective directive, time does not begin to run, and therefore the individual cannot be time-barred even under the normal domestic rules on limitations on actions, until such time as the directive has been properly transposed into national law.[162] More recently, in *Zuckerfabrik*,[163] the Court held that interim measures should be available when the legality of Community law was being questioned before a national court, and a national court has a duty to consider granting such relief if requested by a party to do so.[164] These steps towards the gradual

---

[156] [Joined cases C–6/90 and C–9/90 *Francovich and Bonifaci* v *Italy*, para. 42 of the judgment].

[157] See Case 45/76, *Comet* v *Produktschap voor Siergewassen* [1976] ECR 2043.

[158] See Green and Barav, 'Damages in the National Courts for Breach of Community Law' (1986) 6 YEL 55; Oliver, 'Enforcing Community Rights in English Courts' (1987) 50 MLR 881; Steiner, 'How to Make the Action Suit the Case: Domestic Remedies for Breach of EEC Law' (1987) 12 EL Rev 102; Ward, 'Government Liability in the United Kingdom for Breach of Individual Rights in European Community Law' (1990) 19 *Anglo-American Law Review* 1.

[159] See Schwarze, *European Administrative Law* (London: Sweet and Maxwell, 1992).

[160] See Duffy, [(1992) 17 EL Rev 133], pp. 137-138.

[161] Case C221/89, *R* v *Secretary of State for Transport, ex p Factortame Ltd and Others* [1990] ECR I-2433.

[162] Including where the directive has been implemented but in terms which vary from the directive such that the implementing measure does not fully represent the rights contained in the directive: Case C208/90, *Emmott* v *Minister for Social Welfare* [1991] 3 CMLR 894, 916 (para. 23). [But see p. 131 above on the current status of *Emmott*.]

[163] Joined Cases C-143/88 and C-92/89, *Zuckerfabrik Suderdithmaschen et Zuckerfabrick Soest* v *Hauptzollamt Itzehoe* [1991] *Recueil* I-415, nyr in English, noted Schermers (1992) 29 CML Rev 133.

[164] In addition, the conditions for suspending community acts could not vary from one Member State to another. See further Oliver, 'Interim Measures: Some Recent Developments' (1992) 27 CML Rev 7, 24-25; Barav, 'Enforcement of Community Rights in the National Courts: The Case for Jurisdiction to Grant Interim Relief' (1989) 26 CML Rev 369.

reshaping of national remedies can be viewed as a fourth element in the Community judicial liability system.

The four elements in this system need to be appreciated as a whole from two different perspectives. Seen from the bottom up, they help to provide judicial protection for the individual. Seen from the top down, they perform an essentially political function of social control.[165] These two perspectives are complementary, one representing the view of individual actors or organisations, and the other representing a conception of the Community legal system as a whole. Both perspectives are essential in order to understand the contribution and the limits of the judicial liability system in ensuring the effectiveness of Community law.

Seen from the second perspective, the judicial liability system embodies a type of structural reform, not by administrative negotiation but by adjudication. In the United States, constitutional lawyers have focused on the Supreme Court. In the late 1970s, they identified a new kind of public law litigation, 'institutional litigation', which

> typically requires the courts to scrutinize the operation of large public institutions. The suits are generally brought by persons subject to the control of the institutions who seek as relief some relatively elaborate rearrangement of the institution's mode of operation.[166]

Views have differed as to the novelty of institutional litigation.[167] All agree, however, that in institutional litigation, '[l]itigation inevitably becomes an explicitly political forum and the court a visible arm of the political process'.[168]

It is tempting to apply these observations to the Court of Justice. After all, in the Community, as in the United States, the institutional vacuum resulting from executive and legislative inaction led to an increased role for the judiciary. In both systems, the appropriateness of such a judicial response has been the subject of intense controversy.[169]

It is suggested, however, that the precise analogy is misplaced. First, the Court of Justice is activated by individuals and organisations who, in contrast to plaintiffs in American institutional litigation, are not inmates of institutions in any specific sense. Second, the judicial liability system in the Community has been developed by the

---

[165] This point is argued forcefully with regard to appeal courts in general: Shapiro, 'Appeal' (1980) 14 *Law and Society Review* 629. Note that a similar dual role in the Community legal order is played by the concept of institutional balance: see the Opinion by Advocate-General Van Gerven in Case 70/88, *European Parliament* v *Council* [1990] ECR I-2041. Whether such a duality of function is characteristic of other basic concepts of Community constitutional and administrative law remains to be seen.

[166] Eisenberg and Yeazell, 'The Ordinary and the Extraordinary in Institutional Litigation' (1980) 93 *Harvard Law Review* 465, 467-468. See also, e.g., Chayes, 'The Role of the Judge in Public Law Litigation' (1976) 89 *Harvard Law Review* 1281; Cox, 'The New Dimensions of Constitutional Litigation' (1976) 51 *Washington Law Review* 791; Diver, 'The Judge as Political Powerbroker: Superintending Structural Change in Public Institutions' (1979) 65 *Virginia Law Review* 43.

[167] Chayes and Cox argue that its procedures and remedies depart significantly from the model of traditional litigation: see Chayes, *op cit* n 166; Cox, *op cit* n 166. In contrast, Eisenberg and Yeazell, *op cit* n 166, suggest that the only new features are its substance, especially new rights, and its power.

[168] Chayes, *op cit* n 166, p 1304; Diver, [(1979) 65 *Virginia Law Review* 43], p. 65.

[169] With regard to the Community, see Pescatore, 'La carence du législateur et le devoir du juge' in *Rechtsverglechung, Europarecht und Staateninegration, Gedachtnisschrift für L.-J. Constantinesco* (Saarbrucken: Europa Institute, 1983) and Rasmussen, *On Law and Policy in the European Court of Justice* (Dordrecht: Martinus Nijhoff, 1986).

Court of Justice mainly through the Article 177 [now 234] procedure: the reach of the Court into the operation of national public institutions, including administrations, is restricted by the fact that its jurisdiction is limited in principle to interpreting (or ruling on the validity of) Community law. Third, and consequently, Community litigation does not involve the negotiation by the Court of Justice with defendant institutional parties of detailed rules regarding the internal organisation of national institutions.

In the United States, it has been argued that:

The demands of structural reform have magnified the explicitly political dimensions of litigation. Parties have used litigation less as a method for authoritative resolution of conflict than as a means of reallocation of power. Rather than an isolated, self-contained transaction, the lawsuit becomes a component of the continuous political bargaining process that determines the shape and content of public policy. This transformation in the character of litigation necessarily transforms the judge's role as well.[170]

In the Community, it is suggested, the role of 'political powerbroker'[171] in this strong sense has been resisted thus far by the Court of Justice. Nonetheless, there are common features and this brief comparison with the United States Supreme Court is instructive. It enables us to begin to situate Community law litigation in the political process, at both the Community and the national levels, and it illuminates the political dimension of the Community judicial liability system. By elaborating the elements of this system, rather than by institutional litigation in the American sense, the Court of Justice has played a central role in organising and reshaping relations among Community institutions and between the Community and the Member States.

Note

With these comments about the Court's actual and potential role in mind, this chapter concludes with the major decisions of the Court delivered in March 1996. These rulings are of fundamental significance in the development of Community law in general and in the control of violations by the Member States in particular. It was the Court's first major attempt to provide some clarification to its interpretation of the role of Article 5 of the EC Treaty (now Article 10 EC) in *Francovich* (Cases C–6/90 and C–9/90), p. 128 above (contrast its reticence in *H Banks & Co. Ltd* v *British Coal Corporation* (Case C–128/92) [1994] ECR I–1209, p. 544 above).

Brasserie du Pêcheur SA v *Germany* and *R* v *Secretary of State for Transport, ex parte Factortame Ltd and others* (Joined Cases C–46/93 and C–48/93)
[1996] ECR I–1029, [1996] 1 CMLR 889
Court of Justice of the European Communities

Factortame was not content with its success in establishing the availability of interim protection against a domestic statute (p. 729 above), or with the final ruling that the UK had acted in violation of its Treaty obligations

---

[170] Diver, [(1979) 65 *Virginia Law Review* 43], p. 45.
[171] *ibid.*

(p. 729 above.) Factortame sought compensation for loss suffered as a result of action in 1989 by the UK authorities that had been shown to be unlawful under EC law. This raised questions about the application of *Francovich* liability to violations of primary Treaty provisions, rather than in the specific instance of failure to implement a Directive. Questions of the culpability required to ground liability, which (as R. Caranta observes in the extract at p. 132 above) had not been addressed in *Francovich*, were also raised. A preliminary reference was made by the High Court in the UK. This was joined to a reference made by the *Bundesgerichtshof*, the German Federal Court of Justice, which arose out of a complaint by a French company based in Alsace which claimed that it had suffered loss as a result of German restrictions on trade in beer which had been shown to be incompatible with Article 30 of the EC Treaty (now, after amendment, Article 28 EC): see the 'Beer Purity' case, *Commission* v *Germany* (Case 178/84, p. 297 above). Here too the national court was in search of elaboration of the scope of State liability in damages for loss caused by violation of Community law.

The Court first traced the nature and scope of the principle of State liability for acts and omissions of the national legislature contrary to Community law:

[16] By their first questions, each of the two national courts essentially seeks to establish whether the principle that Member States are obliged to make good damage caused to individuals by breaches of Community law attributable to the State is applicable where the national legislature was responsible for the infringement in question.

[17] In joined Cases C–6/90 and C–9/90 *Francovich and Others* [1991] ECR I–5357, paragraph 37, the Court held that it is a principle of Community law that Member States are obliged to make good loss and damage caused to individuals by breaches of Community law for which they can be held responsible.

[18] The German, Irish and Netherlands Governments contend that Member States are required to make good loss or damage caused to individuals only where the provisions breached are not directly effective: in *Francovich and Others* the Court simply sought to fill a lacuna in the system for safeguarding rights of individuals. In so far as national law affords individuals a right of action enabling them to assert their rights under directly effective provisions of Community law, it is unnecessary, where such provisions are breached, also to grant them a right to reparation founded directly on Community law.

[19] That argument cannot be accepted.

[20] The Court has consistently held that the right of individuals to rely on the directly effective provisions of the Treaty before national courts is only a minimum guarantee and is not sufficient in itself to ensure the full and complete implementation of the Treaty (see, in particular, Case 168/85 *Commission* v *Italy* [1986] ECR 2945, paragraph 11, Case C–120/88 *Commission* v *Italy* [1991] ECR I–621, paragraph 10, and C–119/89 *Commission* v *Spain* [1991] ECR I–641, paragraph 9). The purpose of that right is to ensure that provisions of Community law prevail over national provisions. It cannot, in every case, secure for individuals the benefit of the rights

conferred on them by Community law and, in particular, avoid their sustaining damage as a result of a breach of Community law attributable to a Member State. As appears from paragraph 33 of the judgment in *Francovich and Others*, the full effectiveness of Community law would be impaired if individuals were unable to obtain redress when their rights were infringed by a breach of Community law.

[21]   This will be so where an individual who is a victim of the non-transposition of a directive and is precluded from relying on certain of its provisions directly before the national court because they are insufficiently precise and unconditional, brings an action for damages against the defaulting Member State for breach of the third paragraph of Article 189 [now 249] of the Treaty. In such circumstances, which obtained in the case of *Francovich and Others*, the purpose of reparation is to redress the injurious consequences of a Member State's failure to transpose a directive as far as beneficiaries of that directive are concerned.

[22]   It is all the more so in the event of infringement of a right directly conferred by a Community provision upon which individuals are entitled to rely before the national courts. In that event, the right to reparation is the necessary corollary of the direct effect of the Community provision whose breach caused the damage sustained.

[23]   In this case, it is undisputed that the Community provisions at issue, namely Article 30 [now 28] of the Treaty in Case C–46/93 and Article 52 [now 43] in Case C–48/93, have direct effect in the sense that they confer on individuals right upon which they are entitled to rely directly before the national courts. Breach of such provisions may give rise to reparation.

[24]   The German Government further submits that a general right to reparation for individuals could be created only by legislation and that for such a right to be recognised by judicial decision would be incompatible with the allocation of powers as between the Community institutions and the Member States and with the institutional balance established by the Treaty.

[25]   It must, however, be stressed that the existence and extent of State liability for damage ensuing as a result of a breach of obligations incumbent on the State by virtue of Community law are questions of Treaty interpretation which fall within the jurisdiction of the Court.

[26]   In this case, as in *Francovich and Others*, those questions of interpretation have been referred to the Court by national courts pursuant to Article 177 [now 234] of the Treaty.

[27]   Since the Treaty contains no provision expressly and specifically governing the consequences of breaches of Community law by Member States, it is for the Court, in pursuance of the task conferred on it by Article 164 [now 220] of the Treaty of ensuring that in the interpretation and application of the Treaty the law is observed, to rule on such a question in accordance with generally accepted methods of interpretation, in particular by reference to the fundamental principles of the Community legal system and, where necessary, general principles common to the legal systems of the Member States.

[28]   Indeed, it is to the general principles common to the laws of the Member States that the second paragraph of Article 215 [now 288] of the Treaty refers as the basis of the non-contractual liability of the Community for damage caused by its institutions or by its servants in the performance of their duties.

[29] The principle of the non-contractual liability of the Community expressly laid down in Article 215 [now 288] of the Treaty is simply an expression of the general principle familiar to the legal systems of the Member States that an unlawful act or omission gives rise to an obligation to make good the damage caused. That provision also reflects the obligation on public authorities to make good damage caused in the performance of their duties.

[30] In any event, in many national legal systems the essentials of the legal rules governing State liability have been developed by the courts.

[31] In view of the foregoing considerations, the Court held in *Francovich and Others*, at paragraph 35, that the principle of State liability for loss and damage caused to individuals as a result of breaches of Community law for which it can be held responsible is inherent in the system of the Treaty.

[32] It follows that that principle holds good for any case in which a Member State breaches Community law, whatever be the organ of the State whose act or omission was responsible for the breach.

[33] In addition, in view of the fundamental requirement of the Community legal order that Community law be uniformly applied (see, in particular, Joined Cases C–143/88 and C–92/89 *Zuckerfabrik Süderdithmarschen and Zuckerfabrik Soest* [1991] ECR I–415, paragraph 26), the obligation to make good damage caused to individuals by breaches of Community law cannot depend on domestic rules as to the division of powers between constitutional authorities.

[34] As the Advocate General points out in paragraph 38 of his Opinion, in international law a State whose liability for breach of an international commitment is in issue will be viewed as a single entity, irrespective of whether the breach which gave rise to the damage is attributable to the legislature, the judiciary or the executive. This must apply a *fortiori* in the Community legal order since all State authorities, including the legislature, are bound in performing their tasks to comply with the rules laid down by Community law directly governing the situation of individuals.

[35] The fact that, according to national rules, the breach complained of is attributable to the legislature cannot affect the requirements inherent in the protection of the rights of individuals who rely on Community law and, in this instance, the right to obtain redress in the national courts for damage caused by that breach.

[36] Consequently, the reply to the national courts must be that the principle that Member States are obliged to make good damage caused to individuals by breaches of Community law attributable to the State is applicable where the national legislature was responsible for the breach in question.

The Court then turned to the conditions under which the State may incur liability:

[37] By these questions, the national courts ask the Court to specify the conditions under which a right to reparation of loss or damage caused to individuals by breaches of Community law attributable to a Member State is, in the particular circumstances, guaranteed by Community law.

[38] Although Community law imposes State liability, the conditions under which that liability gives rise to a right to reparation depend on the nature of the breach of

Community law giving rise to the loss and damage (*Francovich and Others*, paragraph 38.)

[39]   In order to determine those conditions, account should first be taken of the principles inherent in the Community legal order which form the basis for State liability, namely, first, the full effectiveness of Community rules and the effective protection of the rights which they confer and, second, the obligation to cooperate imposed on Member States by Article 5 [now 10] of the Treaty (*Francovich and Others*, paragraphs 31 to 36).

[40]   In addition, as the Commission and the several governments which submitted observations have emphasised, it is pertinent to refer to the Court's case-law on non-contractual liability on the part of the Community.

[41]   First, the second paragraph of Article 215 [now 288] of the Treaty refers, as regards the non-contractual liability of the Community, to the general principles common to the laws of the Member States, from which, in the absence of written rules, the Court also draws inspiration in other areas of Community law.

[42]   Second, the conditions under which the State may incur liability for damage caused to individuals by a breach of Community law cannot, in the absence of particular justification, differ from those governing the liability of the Community in like circumstances. The protection of the rights which individuals derive from Community law cannot vary depending on whether a national authority or a Community authority is responsible for the damage.

[43]   The system of rules which the Court has worked out with regard to Article 215 [now 288] of the Treaty, particularly in relation to liability for legislative measures, takes into account, *inter alia*, the complexity of the situations to be regulated, difficulties in the application or interpretation of the texts and, more particularly, the margin of discretion available to the author of the act in question.

[44]   Thus, in developing its case-law on the non-contractual liability of the Community, in particular as regards legislative measures involving choices of economic policy, the Court has had regard to the wide discretion available to the institutions in implementing Community policies.

[45]   The strict approach taken towards the liability of the Community in the exercise of its legislative activities is due to two considerations. First, even where the legality of measures is subject to judicial review, exercise of the legislative function must not be hindered by the prospect of actions for damages whenever the general interest of the Community requires legislative measures to be adopted which may adversely affect individual interests. Second, in a legislative context characterised by the exercise of a wide discretion, which is essential for implementing a Community policy, the Community cannot incur liability unless the institution concerned has manifestly and gravely disregarded the limits on the exercise of its powers (Joined Cases 83/76, 94/76, 4/77 and 40/77, 15/77 *HNL and Others* v *Council and Commission* [1978] ECR 1209, paragraphs 5 and 6).

[46]   That said, the national legislature – like the Community institutions – does not systematically have a wide discretion when it acts in a field governed by Community law. Community law may impose upon it obligations to achieve a particular result or obligations to act or refrain from acting which reduce its margin of discretion, sometimes to a considerable degree. This is so, for instance, where, as in the

circumstances to which the judgment in *Francovich and Others* relates, Article 189 [now 249] of the Treaty places the Member State under an obligation to take, within a given period, all the measures needed in order to achieve the result required by a directive. In such a case, the fact that it is for the national legislature to take the necessary measures has no bearing on the Member State's liability for failing to transpose the directive.

[47]   In contrast, where a Member State acts in a field where it has a wide discretion, comparable to that of the Community institutions in implementing Community policies, the conditions under which it may incur liability must, in principle, be the same as those under which the Community institutions incur liability in a comparable situation.

[48]   In the case which gave rise to the reference in Case C–46/93, the German legislature had legislated in the field of foodstuffs, specifically beer. In the absence of Community harmonisation, the national legislature had a wide discretion in that sphere in laying down rules on the quality of beer put on the market.

[49]   As regards the facts of Case C–48/93, the United Kingdom legislature also had a wide discretion. The legislation at issue was concerned, first, with the registration of vessels, a field which, in view of the state of development of Community law, falls within the jurisdiction of the Member States and, secondly, with regulating fishing, a sector in which implementation of the common fisheries policy leaves a margin of discretion to the Member States.

[50]   Consequently, in each case the German and United Kingdom legislatures were faced with situations involving choices comparable to those made by the Community institutions when they adopt legislative measures pursuant to a Community policy.

[51]   In such circumstances, Community law confers a right to reparation where three conditions are met: the rule of law infringed must be intended to confer rights on individuals; the breach must be sufficiently serious; and there must be a direct causal link between the breach of the obligation resting on the State and the damage sustained by the injured parties.

[52]   Firstly, those conditions satisfy the requirements of the full effectiveness of the rules of Community law and of the effective protection of the rights which those rules confer.

[53]   Secondly, those conditions correspond in substance to those defined by the Court in relation to Article 215 [now 288] in its case-law on liability of the Community for damage caused to individuals by unlawful legislative measures adopted by its institutions.

[54]   The first condition is manifestly satisfied in the case of Article 30 [now 28] of the Treaty, the relevant provision in Case C–46/93, and in the case of Article 52 [now 43], the relevant provision in Case C–48/93. Whilst Article 30 imposes a prohibition on Member States, it nevertheless gives rise to rights for individuals which the national courts must protect (Case 74/76 *Iannelli & Volpi* v *Meroni* [1977] ECR 557, paragraph 13). Likewise, the essence of Article 52 is to confer rights on individuals (Case 2/74 *Reyners* [1974] ECR 631, paragraph 25).

[55]   As to the second condition, as regards both Community liability under Article 215 [now 288] and Member State liability for breaches of Community law, the decisive test for finding that a breach of Community law is sufficiently serious is

whether the Member State or the Community institution concerned manifestly and gravely disregarded the limits on its discretion.

[56]   The factors which the competent court may take into consideration include the clarity and precision of the rule breached, the measure of discretion left by that rule to the national or Community authorities, whether the infringement and the damage caused was intentional or involuntary, whether any error of law was excusable or inexcusable, the fact that the position taken by a Community institution may have contributed towards the omission, and the adoption or retention of national measures or practices contrary to Community law.

[57]   On any view, a breach of Community law will clearly be sufficiently serious if it has persisted despite a judgment finding the infringement in question to be established, or a preliminary ruling or settled case-law of the Court on the matter from which it is clear that the conduct in question constituted an infringement.

[58]   While, in the present cases, the Court cannot substitute its assessment for that of the national courts, which have sole jurisdiction to find the facts in the main proceedings and decide how to characterise the breaches of Community law at issue, it will be helpful to indicate a number of circumstances which the national courts might take into account.

[59]   In Case C–46/93 a distinction should be drawn between the question of the German legislature's having maintained in force provisions of the Biersteuergesetz concerning the purity of beer prohibiting the marketing under the designation 'Bier' of beers imported from other Member States which were lawfully produced in conformity with different rules, and the question of the retention of the provisions of that same law prohibiting the import of beers containing additives. As regards the provisions of the German legislation relating to the designation of the product marketed, it would be difficult to regard the breach of Article 30 by that legislation as an excusable error, since the incompatibility of such rules with Article 30 was manifest in the light of earlier decisions of the Court, in particular Case 120/78 *Rewe-Zentral* [1979] ECR 649 ('Cassis de Dijon') and Case 193/80 *Commission* v *Italy* [1981] ECR 3019 ('vinegar'). In contrast, having regard to the relevant case-law, the criteria available to the national legislature to determine whether the prohibition of the use of additives was contrary to Community law were significantly less conclusive until the Court's judgment of 12 March 1987 in *Commission* v *Germany*, cited above, in which the Court held that prohibition to be incompatible with Article 30.

[60]   A number of observations may likewise be made about the national legislation at issue in Case C–48/93.

[61]   The decision of the United Kingdom legislature to introduce in the Merchant Shipping Act 1988 provisions relating to the conditions for the registration of fishing vessels has to be assessed differently in the case of the provisions making registration subject to a nationality condition, which constitute direct discrimination manifestly contrary to Community law, and in the case of the provisions laying down residence and domicile conditions for vessel owners and operators.

[62]   The latter conditions are prima facie incompatible with Article 52 of the Treaty in particular, but the United Kingdom sought to justify them in terms of the objectives of the common fisheries policy. In the judgment in *Factortame II*, cited above, the Court rejected that justification.

[63]   In order to determine whether the breach of Article 52 thus committed by the United Kingdom was sufficiently serious, the national court might take into account, *inter alia*, the legal disputes relating to particular features of the common fisheries policy, the attitude of the Commission, which made its position known to the United Kingdom in good time, and the assessments as to the state of certainty of Community law made by the national courts in the interim proceedings brought by individuals affected by the Merchant Shipping Act.

[64]   Lastly, consideration should be given to the assertion made by Rawlings (Trawling) Ltd, the 37th claimant in Case C–48/93, that the United Kingdom failed to adopt immediately the measures needed to comply with the Order of the President of the Court of 10 October 1989 in *Commission* v *United Kingdom*, cited above, and that this needlessly increased the loss it sustained. If this allegation – which was certainly contested by the United Kingdom at the hearing – should prove correct, it should be regarded by the national court as constituting in itself a manifest and, therefore, sufficiently serious breach of Community law.

[65]   As for the third condition, it is for the national courts to determine whether there is a direct causal link between the breach of the obligation borne by the State and the damage sustained by the injured parties.

[66]   The aforementioned three conditions are necessary and sufficient to found a right in individuals to obtain redress, although this does not mean that the State cannot incur liability under less strict conditions on the basis of national law.

[67]   As appears from paragraphs 41, 42 and 43 of *Francovich and Others*, cited above, subject to the right to reparation which flows directly from Community law where the conditions referred to in the preceding paragraph are satisfied, the State must make reparation for the consequences of the loss and damage caused in accordance with the domestic rules on liability, provided that the conditions for reparation of loss and damage laid down by national law must not be less favourable than those relating to similar domestic claims and must not be such as in practice to make it impossible or excessively difficult to obtain reparation (see also Case 199/82 *Amministrazione delle Finanze dello Stato* v *San Giorgio* [1983] ECR 3595).

[68]   In that regard, restrictions that exist in domestic legal systems as to the non-contractual liability of the State in the exercise of its legislative function may be such as to make it impossible in practice or excessively difficult for individuals to exercise their right to reparation, as guaranteed by Community law, of loss or damage resulting from the breach of Community law.

[69]   In Case C–46/93 the national court asks in particular whether national law may subject any right to compensation to the same restrictions as apply where a law is in breach of higher-ranking national provisions, for instance, where an ordinary Federal law infringes the Grundgesetz of the Federal Republic of Germany.

[70]   While the imposition of such restrictions may be consistent with the requirement that the conditions laid down should not be less favourable than those relating to similar domestic claims, it is still to be considered whether such restrictions are not such as in practice to make it impossible or excessively difficult to obtain reparation.

[71]   The condition imposed by German law where a law is in breach of higher-ranking national provisions, which makes reparation dependent upon the legislature's act or omission being referable to an individual situation, would in practice make it

impossible or extremely difficult to obtain effective reparation for loss or damage resulting from a breach of Community law, since the tasks falling to the national legislature relate, in principle, to the public at large and not to identifiable persons or classes of person.

[72]   Since such a condition stands in the way of the obligation on national courts to ensure the full effectiveness of Community law by guaranteeing effective protection for the rights of individuals, it must be set aside where an infringement of Community law is attributable to the national legislature.

[73]   Likewise, any condition that may be imposed by English law on State liability requiring proof of misfeasance in public office, such an abuse of power being inconceivable in the case of the legislature, is also such as in practice to make it impossible or extremely difficult to obtain effective reparation for loss or damage resulting from a breach of Community law where the breach is attributable to the national legislature.

[74]   Accordingly, the reply to the questions from the national courts must be that, where a breach of Community law by a Member State is attributable to the national legislature acting in a field in which it has a wide discretion to make legislative choices, individuals suffering loss or injury thereby are entitled to reparation where the rule of Community law breached is intended to confer rights upon them, the breach is sufficiently serious and there is a direct causal link between the breach and the damage sustained by the individuals. Subject to that reservation, the State must make good the consequences of the loss or damage caused by the breach of Community law attributable to it, in accordance with its national law on liability. However, the conditions laid down by the applicable national laws must not be less favourable than those relating to similar domestic claims or framed in such a way as in practice to make it impossible or excessively difficult to obtain reparation.

The Court proceeded to deal with three further, related questions, and provided the following answers to the questions referred to:

1.   The principle that Member States are obliged to make good damage caused to individuals by breaches of Community law attributable to the State is applicable where the national legislature was responsible for the breach in question.
2.   Where a breach of Community law by a Member State is attributable to the national legislature acting in a field in which it has a wide discretion to make legislative choices, individuals suffering loss or injury thereby are entitled to reparation where the rule of Community law breached is intended to confer rights upon them, the breach is sufficiently serious and there is a direct causal link between the breach and the damage sustained by the individuals. Subject to that reservation, the State must make good the consequences of the loss or damage caused by the breach of Community law attributable to it, in accordance with its national law on liability. However, the conditions laid down by the applicable national laws must not be less favourable than those relating to similar domestic claims or framed in such a way as in practice to make it impossible or excessively difficult to obtain reparation.
3.   Pursuant to the national legislation which it applies, reparation of loss or damage cannot be made conditional upon fault (intentional or negligent) on the part of the organ of the State responsible for the breach, going beyond that of a sufficiently serious breach of Community law.

4. Reparation by Member States of loss or damage which they have caused to individuals as a result of breaches of Community law must be commensurate with the loss or damage sustained. In the absence of relevant Community provisions, it is for the domestic legal system of each Member State to set the criteria for determining the extent of reparation. However, those criteria must not be less favourable than those applying to similar claims or actions based on domestic law and must not be such as in practice to make it impossible or excessively difficult to obtain reparation. National legislation which generally limits the damage for which reparation may be granted to damage done to certain, specifically protected individual interests not including loss of profit by individuals is not compatible with Community law. Moreover, it must be possible to award specific damages, such as the exemplary damages provided for by English law, pursuant to claims or actions founded on Community law, if such damages may be awarded pursuant to similar claims or actions founded on domestic law.

5. The obligation for Member States to make good loss or damage caused to individuals by breaches of Community law attributable to the State cannot be limited to damage sustained after the delivery of a judgment of the Court finding the infringement in question.

Note

The Court has clearly taken the scope of *Francovich* liability beyond the specific issue of non-implementation of Directives and it has established an approach which places emphasis on the context of particular infractions. As para. 46 of the ruling indicates, the issue of non-implementation of Directives itself could lead to liability in circumstances as clear-cut as those prevailing in *Francovich* itself, but not in others. This was made plain in a ruling delivered just three weeks later.

R v H.M. Treasury, ex parte British Telecommunications (Case C–392/93)
[1996] ECR I-1631
Court of Justice of the European Communities

The litigation arose out of the UK's implementation of Article 8(1) of Directive 90/531, in the field of public procurement. The Court ruled that the UK had not implemented the Directive correctly. It was asked to consider the scope of State liability in a case of incorrect implementation.

[40] . . . A restrictive approach to State liability is justified in such a situation, for the reasons already given by the Court to justify the strict approach to non-contractual liability of Community institutions or Member States when exercising legislative functions in areas covered by Community law where the institution or State has a wide discretion – in particular, the concern to ensure that the exercise of legislative functions is not hindered by the prospect of actions for damages whenever the general interest requires the institutions or Member States to adopt measures which may adversely affect individual interests (see, in particular, the judgments in Joined Cases 83/76, 94/76, 4/77, 15/77 and 40/77 *HNL and Others v Council and Commission* [1978] ECR 1209, paragraphs 5 and 6, and in *Brasserie du Pêcheur and Factortame*, paragraph 45.)

[41] Whilst it is in principle for the national courts to verify whether or not the conditions governing State liability for a breach of Community law are fulfilled, in the

present case the Court has all the necessary information to assess whether the facts amount to a sufficiently serious breach of Community law.

[42] According to the case-law of the Court, a breach is sufficiently serious where, in the exercise of its legislative powers, an institution or a Member State has manifestly and gravely disregarded the limits on the exercise of its powers (judgments in *HNL and Others* v *Council and Commission*, cited above, paragraph 6, and in *Brasserie du Pêcheur and Factortame*, paragraph 55). Factors which the competent court may take into consideration include the clarity and precision of the rule breached (judgment in *Brasserie du Pêcheur and Factortame*, paragraph 56).

[43] In the present case, Article 8(1) is imprecisely worded and was reasonably capable of bearing, as well as the construction applied to it by the Court in this judgment, the interpretation given to it by the United Kingdom in good faith and on the basis of arguments which are not entirely devoid of substance (see paragraphs 20 to 22 above). That interpretation, which was also shared by other Member States, was not manifestly contrary to the wording of the directive or to the objective pursued by it.

[44] Moreover, no guidance was available to the United Kingdom from case-law of the Court as to the interpretation of the provision at issue, nor did the Commission raise the matter when the 1992 Regulations were adopted.

[45] In those circumstances, the fact that a Member State, when transposing the directive into national law, thought it necessary itself to determine which services were to be excluded from its scope in implementation of Article 8, albeit in breach of that provision, cannot be regarded as a sufficiently serious breach of Community law of the kind intended by the Court in its judgment in *Brasserie du Pêcheur and Factortame*.

Note

In relation to all breaches of Community law, not simply those arising out of the process of implementation of Directives, it appears that an assessment of the gravity of the breach is required in determining the availability of compensation. This is a condition the fulfilment of which seems hard to predict in advance. For further examples involving exploration of the seriousness of the breach for these purposes, see *R* v *Ministry of Agriculture, Fisheries and Food, ex parte Hedley Lomas (Ireland) Ltd* (Case C-5/94) [1996] ECR I-2553; *Dillenkofer* v *Germany* (Joined Cases C-178 *et al*/94) [1996] ECR I-4845 *R* v *Secretary of State for Social Security, ex parte Sutton* (Case C-66/95) [1997] ECR I-2163; *Klaus Konle* v *Austria* (Case C-302/97), judgment of 1 June 1999. For the application of the ruling in Joined Cases C-46/93 and C-48/93 in claims for compensation before domestic courts see, for the UK, *R* v *Secretary of State, ex parte Factortame* [1999] 4 All ER 906 (House of Lords; see in particular the speech of Lord Slynn for a survey of the facts and the evolution and application of EC law) and, for Germany, *Brasserie du Pêcheur* [1997] 1 CMLR 971 (noted by Deards (1997) 22 EL Rev 620). The Commission has begun to track application at national level of the rulings in *Francovich* and *Brasserie du Pêcheur/Factortame* see, e.g., the 16th Annual report on monitoring the application of Community law, covering 1998 ((1999) OJ C354 at p. 191). This reflects the significance of these legal

principles in improving the policing of State compliance with Community
law.

Further reading
(See also p. 137 above)
Barav, A., 'State Liability in Damages for Breach of Community Law in the
   National Courts' (1996) 16 YEL 87.
Caranta, R., 'Learning from Neighbours: Public Law Remedies Homogeniz-
   ation from Bottom up' (1997) 4 Maastricht Jnl Euro & Comp Law 220.
Craig, P., 'Once More unto the Breach: the Community, the State and
   Damages Liability' (1997) 113 LQR 67.
Craufurd Smith, R., 'Remedies for Breaches of EC Law in National Courts:
   Legal Variation and Selection', in P. Craig and G. de Búrca, *The Evolution
   of EU Law* (Oxford, OUP, 1999).
Himsworth, C., 'Things Fall Apart: the Harmonisation of Community
   Judicial Procedural Protection Revisited' (1997) 22 EL Rev 291.
Oliver, P., 'Annotation' (1997) 34 CML Rev 635.
Prechal S., 'EC Requirements for an Effective Remedy' in J. Lonbay and A.
   Biondi (eds), *Remedies for Breach of EC Law* (Chichester, Wiley, 1997).
Smith, F., and Woods, L., 'Causation in *Francovich*: the neglected problem'
   (1997) 46 ICLQ 925.
Steiner, J., 'The Limits of State Liability for Breach of EC Law' (1998) 4
   Euro Public Law 69.
Van Gerven, W., 'Bridging the Unbridgeable: Community and National Tort
   Laws after Francovich and Brasserie' (1996) 45 ICLQ 507.

Questions
1.   To what extent are public authorities entitled to expect protection under
the law where an honest but mistaken attempt to meet legal obligations may
result in liability to an indeterminate class for an indeterminate time and in
an indeterminate amount? To what extent has the European Court responded
to such concerns?
2.   To what extent has the Court in these decisions brought its case law on
the liability of *national* authorities acting in violation of EC law into alignment
with its case law on the liability of *Community* authorities acting in breach of
EC law (Article 288 EC, p. 685 above)? Is such alignment desirable?
3.   To what extent do the Court's recent judgments in this area display a
willingness to perform a task of harmonisation of Community and national
rules relating to interim protection and liability in damages which ought to
be the preserve of the legislature, not the courts?

FINAL QUESTIONS

1. 'EC law represents, more evidently perhaps than most other academic subjects, an intricate web of politics, economics and law. It virtually calls out to be understood by means of a political economy of law or from an interdisciplinary, contextual or critical approach. Nevertheless, it has often been regarded . . . simply as a highly technical set of rules, a dense doctrinal thicket where only the ignorant or the foolish would jump in and scratch out their eyes . . .' (F. Snyder, *New Directions in European Community Law*, p. 9) Discuss.

2. '. . . [T]here are two vital differences between the formal structure of traditional international law and that of European Community law. These differences represent a particularly strong limitation upon State sovereignty and justify the common description of the Community as "supranational" rather than an international entity. First, even viewed from the limited perspective of the traditional subjects of international law – the sovereign Member States – the formal structure of European Community law displays those features that characterize a well-developed legal system as opposed to a simple set of primary rules. Second, Community law and the Community legal system penetrate deeply and pervasively into the Member States. This penetration is manifested in particular by the direct and indirect modification of the legal position of individuals – the traditional subjects of municipal law.' (M. Jones, 'The Legal Nature of the European Community: A Jurisprudential Analysis using H.L.A. Hart's Model of Law and a Legal System', (1984) 17 *Cornell International Law Journal* 1, at pp. 15–16.) Discuss.

3. 'There is no motivation for European unification that is surpassed by the desire for peace.' Discuss.

SELECTED BIBLIOGRAPHY

This bibliography is by no means exhaustive. However, in it the student should find enough sources to assist in deeper exploration of Community law.

Concentrating on substantive law

Chalmers, D., and Szyszczak, E., *European Union Law Two: Towards a European Policy?* (Aldershot: Ashgate, 1998)

Oliver, P., *Free Movement of Goods in the EC*, 3rd ed. (London: ELC, 1995)

Concentrating on institutional and constitutional law and practice

Andenas, M. Hadjiemanuill, C., Gormley, L., and Harden, I (eds), *European Economic and Monetary Union: The Institutional Framework* (Dordrecht: Kluwer, 1997)

Chalmers D., and Szyszczak E., *European Union Law One: Law and EU Government* (Aldershot: Ashgate, 1998)

Hartley, T., *The Foundations of EC Law*, 4th ed. (Oxford: OUP, 1998)

Hix, S., *The Political System of the European Union* (Basingstoke: Macmillan, 1999)

Lenaerts, K., and Arts, D., *Procedural Law of the European Union* (ed. Bray) (London: Sweet & Maxwell, 1999)

Lenaerts, K., and Van Nuffel, P., *Constitutional Law of the European Union* (ed. Bray) (London: Sweet & Maxwell, 1999)

Neville Brown, L. and Kennedy, T., *The Court of Justice of the European Communities*, 4th ed. (London: Sweet & Maxwell, 1994)

Nicol, W. and Salmon, T., *Understanding the New European Community* (London: Harvester Wheatsheaf, 1994)

Weiler, J.H.H., *The Constitution of Europe: Do the new clothes have an emperor?* (Cambridge: CUP, 1999)

Concentrating on competition law

Bellamy, C. and Child, G., *Common Market Law of Competition*, 4th ed. (London: Sweet & Maxwell, 1993)
Furse, M., *Competition Law of the UK and EC* (London: Blackstone Press, 1999)
Goyder, D., *EC Competition Law*, 3rd ed. (Oxford: Clarendon Press, 1998)
Kerse, C.S., *EC Antitrust Procedure*, 4th Ed. (London: Sweet & Maxwell, 1998)
Korah, V., *An Introductory Guide to EC Competition Law and Practice*, 6th ed. (Oxford: Hart Publishing, 1997)
Whish, R., *Competition Law*, 3rd ed. (London: Butterworths, 1993)

Covering all or most aspects of the Community legal order

Arnull, A., *The European Union and its Court of Justice* (Oxford: OUP, 1999)
Craig, P., and De Búrca, G., *The Evolution of EU Law* (Oxford: OUP, 1999)
Craig, P., and De Búrca, G., *EU Law*, 2nd ed. (Oxford: OUP, 1998)
Kapteyn, P. and Verloren van Themaat, P., *Introduction to the Law of the European Communities*, 3rd ed. (ed. Gormley) (London: Kluwer, Deventer/ Graham and Trotman, 1998)
Mathijsen, P., *A Guide to European Union Law*, 7th ed. (London: Sweet & Maxwell, 1999)
Shaw, J., *European Community Law*, 2nd ed. (Basingstoke: Macmillan, 1996)
Steiner, J. and Woods, L., *Textbook on EC Law*, 6th ed. (London: Blackstone Press, 1998)
Weatherill, S., and Beaumont, P., *EU Law*, 3rd ed. (London: Penguin, 1999)
Wyatt, D., and Dashwood, A., *European Community Law*, 3rd ed. (London: Sweet & Maxwell, 1993)

Covering development of aspects of the Community legal order

Dehousse, R., *The European Court of Justice* (Basingstoke: Macmillan, 1998)
Heukels, T., Blokker, N., and Brus, M., *The European Union after Amsterdam: A Legal Analysis* (The Hague: Kluwer, 1998)
Krämer, L., Micklitz H.-W., and Tonner, K., *Law and Diffuse Interests in the European Legal Order* (Baden-Baden: Nomos, 1997)
Nielsen, R., and Szyszczak, E., *The Social Dimension of the European Union*, 3rd ed. (Copenhagen: Handelshøjskolens Forlag, 1997)
O'Keeffe D., and Twomey P., *Legal Issues of the Amsterdam Treaty* (Oxford: Hart Publishing, 1999)

O'Keeffe, D. and Twomey, P. (eds), *Legal Issues of the Maastricht Treaty* (Chichester: Chancery, 1994)

Rasmussen, H., *On Law and Policy in the European Court of Justice* (Dordrecht: Martinus Nijhoff, 1986)

Rasmussen, H., *European Court of Justice* (Copenhagen: Gadjura, 1998)

Shaw, J., and More, G., *New Legal Dynamics of European Union* (Oxford: OUP, 1995)

Snyder, F., *New Directions in European Community Law* (London: Weidenfeld and Nicolson, 1990)

Tridimas, T., *The General Principles of EC Law* (Oxford: OUP, 1999)

Weatherill, S., *Law and Integration in the European Union* (Oxford: OUP, Clarendon Law Series, 1995)

INDEX